HOW TO WRITE AND SPEAK BETTER

How to Write and Speak Better

Reader's Digest

PUBLISHED BY
THE READER'S DIGEST ASSOCIATION LIMITED
London · New York · Montreal · Sydney · Cape Town

READER'S DIGEST
HOW TO WRITE AND SPEAK BETTER

Compiled, edited, and designed
for The Reader's Digest Association Limited, London
by Toucan Books Limited
in association with
WordCraft Editing and Writing Limited

Printed in Great Britain

ISBN 0 276 42030 6

Contributors

EDITOR
John Ellison Kahn, DPhil

ASSOCIATE EDITOR
Andrew Kerr-Jarrett, MA

Sylvia Chalker, MA
Alan Cohen, BA, ALAM
Philippa Davies, BA, ADVS
Nicholas Jones, MA, MIL
Owen Kahn, PhD
Patricia Morris, PhD
David Scott-Macnab, PhD
Rudolph Spurling, MA
Nuala Swords-Isherwood, DPhil
Louise Sylvester, MA

CARTOONS BY
Larry

Contents

Introduction   7

Style and Structure   13
The Art of Writing   14
The Elements of Prose   23
Aspects of Effective Style   59
Patterning Your Text   91
Editing Your Own Writing   103
The Mechanics of Writing   105

The Building Blocks of Good English   111
The Words We Use   112
Improve Your Vocabulary   139
Mastering Grammar   165
The Secrets of Punctuation   212
Dictionaries and How to Use Them   258

Writing at Work, Home, and College   269
Writing Letters at Work   270
How to Write Reports   314
Writing for Meetings   324
Job Applications   331
Writing Letters from Home   344
Invitations and Announcements   386
Modes of Address   404
Coping with Exams   423
Studying Techniques   434
Essay Writing and Research   444

The Skills of Good Speaking   461
Improving Your Voice and Speech   462
The Art of Conversation   481
Public Speaking   495
Using Visual Aids   509
Being Interviewed by the Media   513
Job Interviews   522
Dealing with the Boss   532
Dealing with Subordinates   540
How to Run a Meeting   547
Negotiating and Selling   554

Ready-Reference Word Guide   559

Quiz Answers   633

Index   649

Acknowledgments   655

Introduction

YOU CAN HEAR the fashionable phrase *good communication skills* widely bandied about these days. The phrase amounts to little more than 'writing well and speaking well', a fairly modest-sounding acquirement. The skills themselves, however, are anything but modest in their practical effects – without them, you cannot function efficiently, whether as housewife or businessman, office secretary or club secretary, employee or employer, information hunter or bargain hunter, colleague or student or friend.

A MATTER OF SKILL

The greater your skills in speaking and writing, the greater your chances of success in many aspects of life, from friendships to business dealings. To build up a successful relationship with someone – a new acquaintance, a son or daughter, a boss, a client, a salesman – you must maintain or hone the skills that help you to say what you mean and to understand what others are saying to you.

Note the repetition of the word *skills* in the previous paragraphs: *skills* rather than *gifts*. Being skills, they can be learnt. This book will help you to learn them – or rather, will help you to *improve* the skills you already have, show you How to Write and Speak Better.

CUTTING OUT THE STATIC

Writing and speaking are sometimes compared to another form of communication – broadcasting. A radio transmission, for example, has three elements: a transmitter, a signal or message, and a receiver. But perfect communication is far from guaranteed. A crackling sound sometimes comes over the airwaves – static, or interference, caused by a loose wire perhaps, or a thundery sky.

Speaking and writing also have the three elements – transmitter, signal, and receiver – and also often suffer from 'interference'. What is it that distorts the message between transmitter (you) and receiver (your reader or listener)? It might be an obvious culprit such as an inadequate vocabulary or nervous twitchings or a noisy street. Or it might be some subtler factor such as lack of consideration for your audience or lack of confidence in yourself. This book identifies and diagnoses these and various other types of 'interference', and explains how to eliminate them – to the point where your reader or listener can 'tune in' effortlessly to what you are saying.

Just as few people will stay tuned to a crackly, or boring,

or sloppily presented broadcast, so a slapdash letter or poorly constructed speech will usually fail to get through. Whenever you have something to say, it pays to think how you can say it more clearly, more elegantly, more effectively.

The book offers a range of techniques, for a range of occasions: from office reports and college essays to letters of complaint and wedding speeches; from the broadest of strategies (remember your audience, say) to detailed tips (try to position the verb near the beginning of the sentence; look the interviewer in the eye, and so on).

If you want to read methodically through the book, the text will help you step by step to develop your skills in speaking and writing. If you want to concentrate on particular aspects – job interviews, say, or vocabulary building, or business letters – each section is more or less self-contained to enable you to do so.

Either way, your journey should prove not just informative but interesting and enjoyable too. The editors and writers have aimed to make it a pleasure cruise as well as a voyage of discovery. The book is packed with anecdotes to drive a point home, and with real-life examples to illustrate the most inept as well as the most effective ways of speaking and writing. There are dozens of quizzes and test-yourself panels too: do try your hand at them – active participation makes for more effective learning.

The book is divided into five main sections (colour-coded on the edge of each page, for easy reference). A brief comment on each:

Style and Structure deals with the general ABCs of good prose – accuracy, brightness, clarity, and so on – and the mechanics of writing: how to set about it in a businesslike way, breaking through 'writer's block', doing background research, avoiding illogical arguments, arranging your ideas in the best possible order, and so on.

This section also alerts you to the pitfalls facing the speaker or writer: the lure of clichés and vogue words (*meaningful dialogue*), or the quicksands of ambiguity (*We heated up the cocoa because it was cold*), or the mixed-metaphor trap (*an oasis of democracy in a sea of communism*). Above all, it dispels the most widespread myths about writing, for example:

☐ that you need to plan everything perfectly before setting pen to paper

☐ that complex or very delicate ideas have to be expressed through difficult words or convoluted grammar

☐ that grandiose writing, involving long sentences and high-falutin phrases and abstract nouns, reads more impressively than straightforward, simple writing

Even the most experienced and confident of report-writers could benefit from some of the advice in this part of the book.

The next section, **The Building Blocks of Good English,** serves as a modern schoolroom, where you can revise (in a livelier way than that of the traditional schoolroom) the elements of English – the principles of grammar and punctuation. Here you can also learn methods of improving your vocabulary. The chapter on mastering grammar covers such topics as:

☐ defining the parts of speech – nouns, verbs, adjectives, prepositions, and so on – and their various forms and characteristics: collective and proper nouns, transitive and intransitive verbs, comparative and absolute adjectives, personal, demonstrative, and relative pronouns, and the like

☐ problem verbs and troublesome plurals – should you write *cargoes* or *cargos?* Should it be *The media was informed* or *The media were informed? The hen has lain in the sun all day* or *The hen has laid in the sun all day?*

☐ various tricky grammatical choices:
I'd stop that if I was/were you
I like those kind of cars/those kinds of car
Bacon and eggs is/are among my favourite foods
Everyone must arrange his/their own transport
Between you and I/me, he's failed
Who/Whom do you think caused the accident?

☐ traditional disputes over expressions and phrasing:
split infinitives (*to boldly go*)
gerunds (*I hope you don't mind me/my asking*)
misrelated or dangling participles (*On arriving at the hospital, the door was opened by a cheerful nurse*).

The third main division, **Writing at Work, Home, and College,** narrows the focus further, to concentrate on specific types of writing – from the job application to the agenda for an Annual General Meeting; from wedding invitations to letters of condolence; from book-review essays to footnotes in a thesis. It also discusses in great detail the best tactics to adopt in the exam hall, as well as the long run-up to exams – from taking lecture notes to tips on last-minute revision.

The Skills of Good Speaking covers general aspects of speech – improving your voice control, overcoming nervousness – as well as particular problems, from conducting an everyday social conversation to being interviewed on the radio, from running a meeting to making a sales presentation to asking for a rise or complaining to the boss.

The final section, the **Ready-Reference Word Guide,** is a detailed catalogue of the most common worries and snares in English spelling, pronunciation, vocabulary, grammar, and usage.

It includes succinct discussions or reminders of such topics as:

☐ controversial pronunciations – for instance, *contro**ver**sy* rather than ***contro**versy*

☐ tricky spellings – *all right* (rather than *alright*), *vaccinate* (contrast *vacillate*)

☐ contentious meanings and uses – *hopefully* in the sense 'I hope' (as in *Hopefully she'll be forgiven*), or *data* as a singular noun (as in *The data is unreliable*)

☐ 'confusibles' – pairs of words whose meanings are carelessly switched, as with *flaunt* and *flout,* or *prone* and *supine*

☐ 'false friends' – words easily misused through their similarity to other, more familiar, words: for instance, *enormity* (which does not mean 'enormousness') and *scarify* (which does not mean 'scare')

MAKING WORDS WORK FOR YOU

No matter how you approach this book – whether as a systematic course book, or as a reassuring reference work, or simply as an entertaining browse – it should sharpen your ability to express your thoughts and feelings, and reduce progressively the frustrations (and dangers) of failing to 'get through'.

The spiral effect is remarkable. Communicate clearly, and you actually start to *think* more clearly, and this in turn improves your communication skills still further. Similarly, as your powers of self-expression increase, so does your confidence, and vice versa.

The upward spiral should continue to the point where words, spoken or written, come fully under your command. Their role in your daily life will transform itself – from a source of worry to a source of support, always doing your bidding promptly, elegantly, and effectively.

Pronunciations are printed between slash marks or diagonal lines: the pronunciation of *genuine*, for instance, is represented as / **jen**new-in /.

Note how stress is marked in words of more than one syllable: the stressed syllable is printed in **bold type** to distinguish it from unstressed syllables.

Where alternative pronunciations are given, these are sometimes represented simply by the syllables that vary: the pronunciation of *adversary*, for instance, would be printed / **ad**vər-səri, -sri /.

Where a foreign sound cannot be perfectly expressed by any of the symbols listed below, an approximation to it is given wherever this is possible.

a, **a**	as in *trap* /trap/, *backhand* /**bak**-hand/
aa, **aa**	as in *calm* /kaam/, *father* /**faa**thər/
air, **air**	as in *scarce* /skairss/, *parent* /**pair**-ənt/
ar, **ar**	as in *cart* /kart/, *party* /**par**ti/
aar, **aar**	as in *carnation* /kaar-**naysh**'n/, *sari* /**saar**i/
aw, **aw**	as in *thought* /thawt/, *daughter* /**daw**tər/
awr, **awr**	as in *swarm* /swawrm/, *warden* /**wawr**d'n/
ay, **ay**	as in *face* /fayss/, *native* /**nay**tiv/
b, bb	as in *stab* /stab/, *rubber* /**rub**bər/
ch	as in *church* /church/, *nature* /**nay**chər/
ck	SEE k
d, dd	as in *dead* /ded/, *ladder* /**lad**dər/
e, **e**	as in *ten* /ten/, *ready* /**red**di/
ee, **ee**	as in *meat* /meet/, *machine* /mə-**sheen**/
eer, **eer**	as in *fierce* /feerss/, *serious* /**seer**-i-əss/
er, **er**	as in *term* /term/, *defer* /di-**fer**/
ew, **ew**	as in *few* /few/, *music* /**mew**zik/
ewr, **ewr**	as in *pure* /pewr/, *curious* /**kewr**-i-əss/
ə	as in *about* /ə-**bowt**/, *cannon* /**kan**nən/
ər	as in *persist* /pər-**sist**/, *celery* /**sel**ləri/
f, ff	as in *sofa* /**sō**fə/, *suffer* /**suf**fər/
g, gg	as in *stag* /stag/, *giggle* /**gig**g'l/
h	as in *hat* /hat/, *ahead* /ə-**hed**/
i, **i**	as in *grid* /grid/, *ticket* /**tick**it/
ī, **ī**	as in *price* /prīss/, *mighty* /**mī**ti/
īr, **īr**	as in *fire* /fīr/, *tyrant* /**fīr**-ənt/
j	as in *judge* /juj/, *age* /ayj/
k, ck	as in *kick* /kik/, *pocket* /**pock**it/, *six* /siks/, *quite* /kwīt/

l, ll	as in *fill* /fil/, *colour* /**kull**ər/
'l	as in *needle* /**need**'l/, *channel* /**chann**'l/
m, mm	as in *man* /man/, *summer* /**summ**ər/
'm	as in *rhythm* /**rith**'m/, *blossom* /**bloss**'m/
n, nn	as in *fan* /fan/, *honour* /**on**nər/
'n	as in *sudden* /**sudd**'n/, *cotton* /**kott**'n/
ng	as in *tank* /tangk/, *finger* /**fing**-gər/
o, **o**	as in *rod* /rod/, *stockpot* /**stok**-pot/
ō, **ō**	as in *goat* /gōt/, *dodo* /**dō**-dō/
ŏŏ, **ŏŏ**	as in *would* /wŏŏd/, *pusher* /**pŏŏsh**ər/
o͞o, **o͞o**	as in *shoe* /sho͞o/, *prudent* /**pro͞od**'nt/
oor, **oor**	as in *poor* /poor/, *surely* /**shoor**li/
or, **or**	as in *north* /north/, *portion* /**por**-sh'n/
ow, **ow**	as in *stout* /stowt/, *powder* /**pow**dər/
owr, **owr**	as in *sour* /sowr/, *dowry* /**dowr**-i/
oy, **oy**	as in *boy* /boy/, *poison* /**poyz**'n/
p, pp	as in *crop* /krop/, *pepper* /**pep**pər/
r, rr	as in *red* /red/, *terror* /**terr**ər/
s, ss	as in *list* /list/, *box* /boks/, *sauce* /sawss/, *fussy* /**fuss**i/
sh	as in *ship* /ship/, *pressure* /**presh**ər/
t, tt	as in *state* /stayt/, *totter* /**tott**ər/
th	as in *thick* /thik/, *author* /**aw**thər/
th	as in *this* /thiss/, *mother* /**muth**ər/
u, **u**	as in *cut* /kut/, *money* /**mun**ni/
v, vv	as in *valve* /valv/, *cover* /**kuv**vər/
w	as in *wet* /wet/, *away* /ə-**way**/
y	as in *yes* /yess/, *beyond* /bi-**yond**/
z, zz	as in *zoo* /zo͞o/, *scissors* /**siz**zərz/
zh	as in *vision* /**vizh**'n/, *pleasure* /**plezh**ər/

FOREIGN PRONUNCIATIONS

kh	as in Scottish *loch* /lokh/, Arabic *Khalid* /**khaa**-lid/, or German *Achtung* /**akh**-tŏŏng/
AN, ON	as in French *Saint-Saëns* /saN-soNss/ – the N indicates that the preceding vowel is nasalised.

KEY TO COLOURED SYMBOLS

? **doubtful or informal usage** – think twice before using this word or construction

?? **inappropriate or non-standard usage** – avoid if possible in formal contexts

X **incorrect usage** – avoid at all times

Bear in mind that a mistake attributed to an author or
journalist may not really be of his or her making:
in newspapers in particular, a writer's words
might have been hurriedly recast by a sub-editor,
or mis-set by the typesetter.
And note too that the extracts quoted are usually
printed in the standard spelling and
punctuation used in this book even
if the original text used different conventions.

Style
and
Structure

The Art of Writing

MOST WRITING is a private activity but a public service. You may dash off a protest letter in the solitude of your study, or compile a report in the office after everyone has gone home for the night, or scribble a few secret paragraphs of your romantic novel at the kitchen table while the baby is sleeping, but in each case your intention is the same – that eventually your writing will become the reading matter of someone else, that your private words will 'go public'.

Writing, in other words, is above all for communication – for conveying ideas and feelings from your mind to another mind. Apart from a few oddities – filling out a crossword puzzle, or writing 'LS loves JM' in the sand at low tide – this is true of all writing tasks. Even with such activities as taking lecture notes, or recording a funny incident in your secret diary, you are still writing to communicate . . . to communicate with your future self.

The hallmarks of good writing, then, are the hallmarks of all good communication. The ABCs of both are these:

accuracy, appropriateness, attentiveness to your audience, avoidance of ambiguity

brevity or conciseness, brightness or buoyancy

correctness (of usage and grammar), clarity, consistency, concreteness

All of these hallmarks will be discussed at various points in the first section of this book. In the meantime, to see the results of ignoring them, take a sobering look at the following passages, and ask yourself this question: why do educated people, with English as their mother tongue, write so badly?

?? As Britains largest Estate Agents, you may note with interest that Prudential Property Services, have opened in Hampstead Village with a vengeance, eager to help you with your property requirements.

I am sure that you must receive numerous letters from other agents but with this office linking our Highgate and Little Venice offices with support of 33 other central London offices, Prudential Property Services offers a client and customer care second to none.

– estate agent's advertising circular

?? I take grave exception to the article . . . It breaks the basic code of proper journalism because whilst purporting to be an interview it is, in fact, using a bastion of the middle ground as a cheap clothes-peg on which to hang a lot of boring preconceptions written, or stored in the mind of the writer, long before she ever saw my editor, plus a whole load of unrinsed, indeed unwashed, inaccuracies. Upon meeting him, if she were of any freedom of mind, most must have seemed to be untrue.

It is not very pleasant to have ones life work dismissed as 'soft', a really sexist statement if ever I read one. It was Mr Rees-Mogg's conviction in, and support of, my novel handling of the fashion page which sought to prove that dress has major social implications, that we are busy killing off an industry, which incidentally is the largest employer of female labour, which in educational terms has been more than any country in the world and which in retail terms is incompetent. His allowance to me to print these views I think undermine the remarks of your interviewer. I was free to photograph punks in the garage or to prognosticate talent around the globe. Mr Rees-Mogg regarded dress as a hard a subject as detente.

– a *Times* journalist, letter to *The Guardian*

?? It is one of the major conclusions and recommendations of this paper that the importance of the work of the accountancy profession and the challenges of the impact of change are both such as to require, firstly, in the public interest, that it is clear to members of the public (who use, or who have to rely on, or who are dependent on the quality of the services of the profession) who it is who are the members of the profession, who are subject to regulation, supervision and discipline and of whom certain standards of skill, competence, experience and integrity can be expected, and, secondly, in both the professional and the public interest, that the challenges of the impact of change are faced as a single profession acting in unison.

– university professor,
report on the accountancy profession

In each case, the writer seems to be violating two very broad and very obvious principles of good writing – being mindful of the reader, and being logical in one's thinking.

REMEMBER YOUR READERS

Since writing is primarily for communication, you have to keep your reader constantly in mind as you write. This is not always so easy to do. Faced with an intense or convoluted writing task, you may often become very inward-looking, struggling to put your thoughts into words and get the words down on paper. You will then need to force yourself continually to emerge from this self-absorption.

> You must keep your eyes forever on your Reader. That alone constitutes Technique.
> – Ford Madox Ford, *The English Novel*

That means more than just typing neatly, or avoiding a personal shorthand that only you can follow. It means taking trouble – ordering your thoughts in the most methodical and logical sequence, and wording them in the most lucid language. If you fail to take that trouble in clarifying your ideas, you will put the reader to a great deal of trouble in deciphering them.

> You write with ease to show your breeding,
> But easy writing's curst hard reading.
> – Richard Brinsley Sheridan, *Clio's Protest*

As it happens, it is not so difficult to think yourself into the mind of another person: you probably do it every day, whenever you speak to anyone.

Think how carefully you pitch the level of your voice and speech according to circumstances. If you are speaking to someone hard of hearing, you tend to speak louder than usual. If you are speaking to a child or to a foreigner, you tend to use simpler words and shorter sentences than usual, and to talk at a slower pace. If you are speaking to the bishop, you probably adopt a more formal and respectful tone than you use with your workmates.

In fact, an inappropriate level of speaking often provokes laughter or ridicule – the precocious child who speaks (or tries to speak) like an adult; the professor who talks to his family over the dinner table as though he were addressing students in the lecture hall; the drag artist who mimics the voice and speech patterns of someone of the opposite sex. (For three pointed examples of inappropriate levels of speaking, see the panel overleaf.)

Most well-adjusted adults, however, are finely tuned to the needs of the listener. They unconsciously decide on a likely level of difficulty, and then adjust it if necessary with chameleon-like sensitivity to changing conditions. To the listener's frown of puzzlement they respond by slowing down the pace, or repeating the point in different words, or emphasising different features. To the listener's sigh of impatience they respond by speeding up, or shifting direction.

With writing, things are not so easy: you get less guidance from your 'audience', and they get less from you. Listeners derive information not just from the speaker's words but also from his tone of voice, his pauses, his facial expressions, his gestures, his 'body language', and so on. Readers, by contrast, have only the words to guide them (together with a few crude typographical aids, such as italics and exclamation marks). Similarly, most speakers with a live audience enjoy immediate 'feedback', and can modulate their level instantly to ensure that the message is getting across. Writers, by contrast, usually get their readers' feedback only after the act of writing is finished.

When writing a letter or report, then, keep thinking of the readers' likely response to the contents, the style, and the tone. As for contents: don't, for example, burst into detailed technical explanations if your readers are all laymen. But if your readers are all experts, then do use some technical jargon, for brevity's sake, and avoid long-winded non-technical explanations. (If the readers include experts and laymen, you will have a tricky balance to strike: you will probably want to lean more towards catering for the laymen.)

As for style: if some of your readers are fairly unsophisticated, take care not to use language that goes over their heads. If all your prospective readers are highly educated and well-read, on the other hand, don't patronise them by writing in a grossly simplified, plodding style (though you should not resort to a high-falutin style either, in some

THE WRONG LEVEL OF LANGUAGE

In all three passages below, the gentle humour derives from the speaker's uncharacteristic or inappropriate use of language.

First, an extract from a famous short story by Saki (the writer H.H. Munro – 1870-1916).

> Somehow there seemed an element of embarrassment in addressing on equal terms a domestic cat . . .
>
> 'What do you think of human intelligence?' asked Mavis Pellington lamely.
>
> 'Of whose intelligence in particular?' asked Tobermory coldly.
>
> 'Oh, well, mine for instance,' said Mavis, with a feeble laugh.
>
> 'You put me in an embarrassing position,' said Tobermory, whose tone and attitude certainly did not suggest a shred of embarrassment. 'When your inclusion in this house-party was suggested Sir Wilfrid protested that you were the most brainless woman of his acquaintance, and that there was a wide distinction between hospitality and the care of the feeble-minded. Lady Blemley replied that your lack of brainpower was the precise quality which had earned you your invitation, as you were the only person she could think of who might be idiotic enough to buy their old car. You know, the one they call "The Envy of Sisyphus", because it goes quite nicely up-hill if you push it.'
>
> – Saki, 'Tobermory'

Next, an anecdote from Edith Wharton (1862-1937), the American novelist.

During her motoring holidays in England, she sometimes took Henry James, the writer, with her. On one trip the chauffeur brought them in to Windsor after dark, but did not know the way to the King's Road, their destination.

> While I was hesitating and peering out into the darkness James spied an ancient doddering man who had stopped in the rain to gaze at us. 'Wait a moment, my dear – I'll ask him where we are'; and leaning out he signalled to the spectator.

> 'My good man, if you'll be good enough to come here, please; a little nearer – so,' and as the old man came up: 'My friend, to put it to you in two words, this lady and I have just arrived here from *Slough*; that is to say, to be more strictly accurate, we have recently *passed through* Slough on our way here, having actually motored to Windsor from Rye, which was our point of departure; and the darkness having overtaken us, we should be much obliged if you would tell us where we now are in relation, say, to the High Street, which, as you of course know, leads to the Castle, after leaving on the left hand the turn down to the railway station.'
>
> I was not surprised to have this extraordinary appeal met by silence, and a dazed expression on the old wrinkled face at the window; nor to have James go on: 'In short' (his invariable prelude to a fresh series of explanatory ramifications), 'in short, my good man, what I want to put to you in a word is this: supposing we have already (as I have reason to think we have) driven past the turn down to the railway station (which in that case, by the way, would probably not have been on our left hand, but on our right) where are we now in relation to . . .'
>
> 'Oh, please,' I interrupted, feeling myself utterly unable to sit through another parenthesis, 'do ask him where the King's Road *is*.'
>
> 'Ah – ? The King's Road? Just so! Quite right! Can you, as a matter of fact, my good man, tell us where, in relation to our present position, the King's Road exactly is?'
>
> 'Ye're in it,' said the aged face at the window.
>
> – Edith Wharton, *A Backward Glance*

Finally, an amusing extract from one of Dickens's finest novels.

The scene is a dinner party. Mr Podsnap, a very self-satisfied businessman, is holding the party, and engages one of the guests, 'a foreign gentleman', in conversation.

> 'How Do You Like London?' Mr Podsnap now inquired from his station of host, as if he were administering something in the

nature of a powder or potion to [a] deaf child; 'London, Londres, London?'

The foreign gentleman admired it.

'You find it Very Large?' said Mr Podsnap, spaciously.

The foreign gentleman found it very large.

'And Very Rich?'

The foreign gentleman found it, without doubt, enormément riche.

'Enormously Rich, We Say,' returned Mr Podsnap, in a condescending manner . . .

'Reetch,' remarked the foreign gentleman.

'And Do You Find, Sir,' pursued Mr Podsnap, with dignity, 'Many Evidences . . . of our British Constitution . . . ?

The foreign gentleman . . . did not altogether understand.

'The Constitution Britannique,' Mr Podsnap explained, as if he were teaching in an infant school . . . 'I Was Inquiring . . . Whether You Have Observed in our Streets as We should say, Upon our Pavvy as You would say, any Tokens –'

The foreign gentleman with patient courtesy entreated pardon; 'But what was tokenz?'

'Marks,' said Mr Podsnap; 'Signs, you know, Appearances – Traces.'

'Ah! Of a Orse?' inquired the foreign gentleman.

'We call it Horse,' said Mr Podsnap, with forbearance. 'In England, Angleterre, England, We Aspirate the "H", and We Say "Horse". Only our Lower Classes Say "Orse"!'

'Pardon,' said the foreign gentleman; 'I am alwiz wrong!'

'Our Language,' said Mr Podsnap, with a gracious consciousness of being always right, 'is Difficult. Ours is a Copious Language, and Trying to Strangers. I will not Pursue my Question.'

– Charles Dickens, *Our Mutual Friend*

misguided attempt to impress them). The constant watchword is: appropriateness. Write simply – bearing in mind that simple writing varies according to the reader's level of sophistication.

As for tone finally: pitching it correctly is rather like dressing correctly. A lounge suit may be appropriate for a job interview, but it would be inappropriate for the Lord Mayor's banquet on the one hand, and for the school picnic on the other. Similarly, Queen Victoria would shudder at any hint of overfamiliarity from a subject, but equally she disliked Mr Gladstone's habit, she said, of speaking to her as if she were a public meeting. So too in your 'tone of voice' when writing: pitch the tone too high, and you will come across as pompous; pitch it too low, and you will come across as impudent or discourteous. If all your readers are friendly colleagues of yours, say, use a reasonably familiar or informal tone. If your readers are bureaucrats or managing directors, on the other hand, use an appropriately respectful and formal tone (not a toadying or self-abasing tone, however). Don't confuse *formal* with *stiff*. A formal tone still attracts and involves the reader; a stiff tone distances and alienates the reader.

The obvious problem remains: what to do when you do not know who your readers will be? The best policy is to err on the side of caution – assume that they have high status but little technical expertise.

The result should be a fairly formal tone, a fairly non-technical and lucid vocabulary, and a fairly methodical analysis and explanation of the contents – as in this book, and in most non-fiction aimed at the general public.

Above all, remember that *someone* has to do the work if communication is to take place successfully. An inverse proportion operates: the more work you as writer do to get it right, the less work the reader has to do. And vice versa. If you slack, it will be the reader who does the bulk of the work – or perhaps not: he may simply view the whole thing as a discourtesy, and give it up as a bad job.

BE ATTENTIVE AND LOGICAL

Many of the commonest faults in everyday writing – faults of grammar, usage, or style – can be put down to simple lack of concentration. The writer, when challenged, readily recognises and corrects the mistake, and usually explains it away by saying 'I just wasn't thinking'.

LOGIC IN GRAMMAR AND USAGE

The sentences below are all guilty of breaking some rule of grammar or usage.

For some practice in honing your logical and grammatical skills, why not try to pinpoint the error in each case, and give it a name if you can. And then write a correct version (you might find it helpful to turn to the chapter on grammar, pages 165-211, and the final section of this book, the *Ready-Reference Word Guide*). The answers and explanations appear below.

The more you learn about good usage, the more you realise how unjust its bad reputation is. Far from being a dull and bookish subject, it opens up many fascinating pathways into what is perhaps the defining characteristic of human-ness – our use of language.

Here now are the incorrect sentences. You might find similar examples every day in company reports or business letters.

1. ✘ The result of all these lengthy legal actions, counterclaims, and appeals, stretching over several months, were simply huge bills from the lawyers and nothing else.

2. ✘ The result of all these lengthy legal actions, counterclaims, and appeals simply produced huge bills from the lawyers and nothing else.

3. ✘ Having brought these legal actions and counterclaims and appeals without success, the huge bills dealt the Company a further blow.

4. ✘ The Board was united in their support of the Company's legal actions and appeals.

5. ✘ The Board expressed its interest and concern over the outcome of the Company's legal actions and appeals.

6. ✘ The Company brought legal actions, counterclaims, and lodged an appeal.

7. ✘ Not only did the Company bring legal actions but also counterclaims.

Some of the sentences can have two or even three correct versions. These all appear below, together with a description or an explanation of the original mistake in each case:

1. The result of all these lengthy legal actions, counterclaims, and appeals, stretching over several months, was simply huge bills from the lawyers and nothing else.

The subject of the sentence remains singular – *The result* – despite all the other plural nouns that follow it: *actions, months,* and the rest. It was these that lured the writer into using the plural verb *were*. By the time he came to write the verb, he had lost track of the singular subject, and so fell into the common trap – 'failure of agreement' or 'concord failure', you could call it. What he wrote, in effect, was ✘ *The result were huge bills.*

2a. All these lengthy legal actions, counterclaims, and appeals simply produced huge bills from the lawyers and nothing else.

2b. The result of all these lengthy legal actions, counterclaims, and appeals was simply huge bills from the lawyers and nothing else.

The writer had fused two different patterns into a single sentence here: *A produced B* and *The result of A was B.* Since *produced* here means 'resulted in', the sentence in effect was saying ✘ *The result of A resulted in B.*

You can analyse this error in either of two ways – as simple tautology, or as 'anacoluthon' – that is, shifting inconsistently from one grammatical construction to another.

3. Having brought all these legal actions and counterclaims and appeals without success, the Company was dealt a further blow by the huge bills.

The structure of the original sentence suggests that it was the huge bills, rather than the Company, that brought all the legal actions. For the correct sense to emerge smoothly out of the syntax, the phrase *the Company* should take the prominent position in the sentence, immediately following the comma. The error in the original sentence was a 'misrelated participle', often loosely called a 'dangling participle'. (A participle, very roughly, is an incomplete verb ending in *-ed* or *-ing*.)

Here are a few more examples of such misconstructed sentences:

✗ Cone-shaped and rising two feet from base to top, the magician placed his wizard's hat carefully on his head.

✗ Wrapped in a sheet of newspaper, Auntie munched her fish and chips cheerfully until the bus arrived.

4a. The Board was united in its support of the Company's legal actions and appeals.

4b. The Board were united in their support of the Company's legal actions and appeals.

British English allows a 'group noun', such as *Board*, *jury*, or *team*, to take either a singular or a plural verb in most contexts. (Perhaps it slightly favours the plural nowadays, while Australian English and especially American English favour the singular.) Either way, consistency is essential. The original sentence, by using the singular verb *was*, had chosen to treat *Board* as singular – only to treat it as plural a few words later by using the plural form *their*. No: either *was* with *its*, or *were* with *their*. But not a mix.

5. The Board expressed its interest in and concern over the outcome of the Company's legal actions and appeals.

Try the test of omitting a phrase – in this case *and concern*. What remains is ✗ *The Board expressed its interest over the outcome*. The noun *interest* takes the preposition *in*, not *over*. Had the passage read *distress and concern over the outcome*, that would have been perfectly acceptable: *distress* like *concern* does take the preposition *over*, and can omit it by treating it as 'understood' here, since it pops up a few words later.

Omitting a word or phrase by treating it as 'understood' is known as 'ellipsis'. The mistake in the original sentence consists of a 'faulty ellipsis' – that is, omitting a word or phrase without grammatical justification.

6a. The Company brought legal actions, counterclaims, and an appeal.

6b. The Company brought legal actions, pursued counterclaims, and lodged an appeal.

6c. The Company brought legal actions and counterclaims, and lodged an appeal.

The pattern *A, B, and C* holds good only if all three items enjoy the same grammatical status. In sentence 6a. above, the three items are all objects of *brought*. And in 6b., they are all clauses: *brought legal actions* and *pursued counterclaims* and *lodged an appeal*.

In the original sentence 6, however, the three items were not all of equal status: the second item, *counterclaims*, is an object of *brought*, while the third, *lodged an appeal*, is a full clause (verb plus object). The error here might be called 'false symmetry'.

Sentence 6c. above restores the symmetry by absorbing the second element of the original sentence 6 into the first element, thereby reducing the number of elements from three to two. The pattern is now simply *A and B*. The two elements, properly symmetrical elements, are both full clauses: *brought legal actions and counterclaims and lodged an appeal*.

7a. Not only did the Company bring legal actions but it also brought counterclaims.

7b. The Company brought not only legal actions but also counterclaims.

Not only and *but also* are 'correlative conjunctions', just as *neither* and *nor* are, or *both* and *and*. Correlative conjunctions serve to introduce parallel constructions – which naturally have to be parallel; that is, of the same pattern or structure or status. In the original sentence 7, they are anything but that: the construction following *Not only* is a long clause, *did the Company bring legal actions*; the construction following *but also* is a mere noun: *counterclaims*. The mistake was, once again, one of 'false symmetry' or 'faulty parallels'.

The corrected versions restore the symmetry: 7a. by turning both constructions into clauses; 7b. by turning both into objects of *brought*.

How can you avoid or correct all of the errors discussed here? You do not need any deep and detailed knowledge of English grammar and syntax; all you need is – attentiveness and logic: attentiveness for identifying risky phrases, and logic for testing them.

Even the experienced writer, to whom all the tricks and pitfalls are second nature, loses concentration at his peril. For the inexperienced writer, all the more so. The slightest lapse of attention will probably result in a lapse of logic, or some grammatical error or stylistic flaw. Constant vigilance is the key.

Vigilance, rather than expertise. No matter how few of the traditional grammar and usage rules you claim to know, you can avoid most of the common errors by simply keeping your wits about you as you write. Just as you would use your common sense and experience to test each sentence for ambiguity or tautology, for clichés or awkwardness, so you can usually use common logic to test for grammatical or stylistic correctness.

Would it be acceptable to write *They have invited my daughter and I to the wedding*? Test the sentence by reordering the crucial phrase *my daughter and I*. Could you write *They have invited I and my daughter to the wedding*?

Similarly, would it be acceptable to write *The new components will cost the same or even less than the previous ones*? Test the sentence by leaving out the second option *or even less*. Could you write *The new components will cost the same than the previous ones*?

The panel on pages 18 and 19 lists samples of many other common errors of usage. Try your hand at identifying and correcting the error in each case.

LOGICAL LAPSES

The importance of logic for writers does not stop with grammar and usage. It serves as a yardstick for the contents, too – the soundness of the ideas expressed, the order in which they are presented, the validity of the links between them.

False contrasts and logical leaps. Take the simple words *but*, *however*, and *although*. They are extremely useful and extremely common linking words; perhaps for that very reason the careless writer all too often scatters them needlessly or even incorrectly across the page.

In their usual meanings, they all signal an opposition of some kind – a contradiction or limitation of a neighbouring idea: *I tried hard but failed; Although she eats almost nothing, she keeps putting on weight.* The careless text deviates from this requirement in one of two ways. Either the

neighbouring idea turns out to be a 'false contrast' – not really an opposing idea at all, but a perfectly compatible idea. Or the neighbouring idea remains unstated altogether: the text makes a 'logical leap' over it, leaving the poor reader to work out what it is. Here are examples of each:

?? He defrauded his employers ingeniously over the years, but they never found out.

?? The red team won in the end, but the blue team came second.

The first of those sentences serves up a false contrast. The two ideas linked by the word *but* turn out, on close inspection, to be in harmony rather than in conflict. Since the fraud was ingenious, it is hardly surprising that the employers never found out about it. The conjunction *and* or *so* would make better sense than *but*. If the adverb read *glaringly* rather than *ingeniously*, a true opposition between the ideas would indeed exist, and *but* would then earn its keep.

In the second of the sample sentences, the word *but* comes across not really as wrong but rather as puzzling. What is it doing there?, the reader wonders. It must have some purpose. But there is a missing link. Presumably that link is a comment on the blue team's abilities or expectations. The entire complex thought was perhaps something along these lines:

> The blue team fared much better than anyone dared hope. It didn't quite manage to win, true enough: the red team won in the end, but the blue team came second – a magnificent effort.

The original sentence had made a logical leap over the vital piece of background information, and the reader was left floundering to make sense of it all.

Not that all logical leaps are unacceptable. In fact, most everyday reasoning uses logical leaps to speed through to its conclusion – all in the interests of economy, so long as the logical gaps are so visible and narrow that the reader or listener can hop across them without effort. All the following sentences involve logical leaps, but none of them is difficult to follow:

> I'm sorry I'm late: there was a traffic jam near Hyde Park.

> No wine for me thanks – I'm on antibiotics.

> Well, Mr Jackson says *recommend* has only one *c*, and he's a teacher.

Suppose the sentences had read rather differently – as follows:

?? I'm sorry I'm late: it's St Patrick's Day.

?? No wine for me thanks – I'm off to Burma next week.

?? Well, Mr Jackson says *recommend* has only one *c*, and he's left-handed.

The logical gaps here are far too wide for the reader or listener to cross unaided. The speaker or writer has left out some crucial logical links between the first and second halves of the sentence each time. As it happens, the full and proper expansion of the three cryptic remarks could be as follows:

> I'm sorry I'm late. I was held up by a traffic jam near Hyde Park, caused by a big parade there. I hadn't realised that it's St Patrick's Day today, and that almost every Irish person in London would be flocking to the park to join the march.

> No wine for me thanks. I had a couple of inoculations this afternoon in preparation for my trip to Burma next week. The jabs can make you feel a bit woozy as it is, and the doctor warned me that any alcohol on top of them would really knock me out.

> Well, Mr Jackson says *recommend* has only one *c*, and he ought to know: he's left-handed, and left-handers are very good at spelling and other language skills because of the different way their brain works.

Convincing or not, at least these explanations are now clear. The several linking ideas have emerged, and the logical gaps have been bridged accordingly.

Logical flaws and fallacies. In some forms of writing, reason plays a very minor role: a letter of condolence, for instance, obviously relies on emotional expression rather than logical presentation to be effective. A charity appeal may direct itself to the reader's sympathies rather than to his reasoning faculty. An advertisement or election manifesto may seek to flatter (or frighten) rather than reason the reader into submission.

But for most everyday writing – letters of complaint, office reports, job applications, and so on – a well-reasoned argument is all-important. The effectiveness of the writing hinges on its logical rigour. You weaken your case each time you draw a false conclusion from your data, or offer a woolly explanation, or try to rationalise away an inconvenient truth, or quote an irrelevant authority in support of your view (ten thousand Frenchmen *can* be wrong).

Here are some samples of dubious reasoning – deliberate or accidental – of a kind you might come across every day in writing or speaking:

?? Those who are truly patriotic will join me in the boycott.

?? Consult your conscience and decide for yourselves whether to kowtow to this decree.

?? New-fangled gadgets like this just make life more difficult.

Choosing emotion-laden words is to argue by *rhetoric* rather than reason. The argument is won before it has properly started. A *new-fangled gadget* is almost by definition something undesirable. Give a dog a bad name, and it is as good as dead. Give firmness the name of *intolerance*, or freedom the name of *licentiousness*, or schooling the name of *brainwashing*, and logic no longer has any place in the debate.

That holds true of favourable naming too, of course – euphemisms, that is: *initiative* for cheating, *prudence* for cowardice, and the like. (For more on euphemisms, see pages 88 and 89.)

?? We can disregard your views on import duties: you work for a local car factory, so naturally you want imported goods to be taxed.

?? Do you really think he's the right person to act as Treasurer? You know he left his wife recently.

Personal remarks do not make sound counter-arguments: they are irrelevant to the validity of the person's opinion.

X You must try Harrison's Herbal Hangover Cure. I took a teaspoonful at breakfast this morning, and by midday I was feeling as right as rain.

Just because one event follows another in time, that is no proof that they are related as cause and effect.

X Badger-baiting is not the cruel sport that people would have you believe, since the badgers actually enjoy a good scrap.

X She can't be trusted – she never looks you in the eye when you talk to her.

These are examples of 'begging the question'; that is, basing a conclusion on a dubious premise – one that itself first needs to be proved.

✗ The stage is a finer vehicle for art than the cinema, as most objective critics agree. By objective critics, I mean those critics who have not been dazzled by the surface glitter of the film medium.

A 'circular argument' here, a special form of begging the question. What the claim really amounts to is this: Plays are more artistic than films, for those who regard plays as more artistic than films. In other words, the premise is really identical to the conclusion, however well-disguised their sameness may be in the original passage.

✗ You've always liked cars, yet now you want to restrict their access to the village.

This fallacy is a 'blanket generalisation'. You cannot assume that a preference, trend, regulation, motto, or the like is meant to hold good in all circumstances. Most rules allow for certain qualifications or even exceptions.

✗ You would shoot a mad dog, wouldn't you? – then you must favour capital punishment for crazed murderers such as the 'Norwich Knifeman'.

The reasoning here takes a very risky 'logical jump'. The premise that it jumps over is a dubious one: 'Crazed murderers deserve equivalent punishment to mad dogs' or even 'The way you treat human beings corresponds to the way you treat animals'. Whether or not such a premise is accurate, it should at least appear openly, so that the reader or listener can inspect it and if necessary reject it.

✗ Members of the jury, kidnapping is a monstrous crime. I trust that you will show your horror of it by finding the accused guilty as charged.

This reasoning goes beyond a mere logical jump – it represents a complete 'logical break'. The premise is quite irrelevant to the conclusion. Kidnapping is a monstrous crime, but that has nothing to do with the guilt or innocence of someone charged with it.

✗ Are you still beating your wife?

✗ I suppose you're one of those fanatical feminists.

✗ It was either through stupidity or through carelessness that you lost the package – either way, you deserve to get the sack.

Each sentence contains a hidden claim – possibly justified, but not necessarily so.

If it is not justified, it puts the reader or listener in a difficult position, unable to supply a simple response. Instead he or she has either to unravel the original question or statement, or to take issue with its wording.

The complex responses might turn out to be these:

'I never have beaten my wife.'

'I am a feminist, yes, but not fanatical.'

'It was neither stupidity nor carelessness – it was an accident, and I certainly don't deserve the sack for that.'

The remaining chapters in this section of the book deal first with the building blocks of writing (words, sentences, and paragraphs), then with its general architecture (structure), then with some details of design and decor (conciseness, puns and metaphors, slang, euphemisms, jargon, and so on), and finally with the mechanics of the process (collecting the material, and – for many people, the most difficult part – actually getting down to doing the writing).

The Elements of Prose

THE STANDARD units of prose texts in English – from the humblest office memo to the longest novel – are words, sentences, and paragraphs.

There are larger units – chapters, for example – and smaller units as well: 'morphemes', or the atoms of language, such as the word-forming elements *en-* and *-ing* and the root *dur*, all going to make the word *enduring*. But such units have little bearing on good style, which is the subject of this section of the book.

This chapter will deal successively with the three elements, then – the word, the sentence, and the paragraph – each with its own individual set of problems . . . and opportunities.

Words – an Embarrassment of Riches

English has an enormously rich vocabulary, larger and more varied than that of any other language. This has great advantages – and a few dangers.

THE VAST VOCABULARY OF ENGLISH

The main advantages are: variety and precision. The corresponding dangers are needless variation and high-falutin wording.

Variety. The variety of synonyms gives writers and speakers great scope for effective expression.

Suppose you are dealing with the idea of happiness, and have used the word *happy* several times already. You can turn perhaps to *cheerful, gratified, blithe*, or *buoyant* instead. Or if happy seems too tame, you have a number of more intense adjectives to choose from: *exuberant, elated, rapturous, ecstatic*, and so on. Or if you want something a little more slangy, you might try *jaunty* or *cock-a-hoop*.

The variety of synonyms also enables writers and speakers to avoid ambiguity. (The English vocabulary is particularly susceptible to ambiguity precisely because of its richness – another kind of richness this time: richness of meaning.) So many English words have multiple senses. The word *revolting*, to take a simple example, can mean either 'rebelling' or 'disgusting' according to the context. And if the context fails to make clear which meaning is intended, ambiguity results: hence the old joke, **?** *The peasants are revolting*. Replace *revolting* with either of its synonyms, *rebelling* or *disgusting*, and

the ambiguity disappears at once. For a more detailed discussion of ambiguous words and phrases, see the panel overleaf.

Precision. The other great benefit bestowed by the verbal treasure house of English is precision. If you want to capture the idea of a serene and saintly kind of happiness, the word *beatific* is available; of a dangerously exaggerated or unstable kind of happiness, *euphoric*; of a triumphant and celebrating kind of happiness, *exultant* or *jubilant*. A similar precision and variety can be found among the synonyms for *old*, as the following engaging extract makes clear. It was written by the editor of *The Sunday Telegraph*, who objected to being described as an 'ageing dandy':

> Nobody would describe an old building in good repair as 'ageing'. Only a disused and crumbling dump with cracked paint and peeling plaster gets described as 'ageing'. For future reference let all authors know that just as the preferred appellation for furniture of a certain age is *antique*, and for monuments, *ancient*, and for wine, *vintage*, and for soldiers, *veteran*, and for clergymen, *venerable*, that for hacks is, for want of a better word, *seasoned*.
>
> – Peregrine Worsthorne, *The Spectator*

A good thesaurus, synonym dictionary, or reverse dictionary provides hundreds of equally striking examples of the flexibility and wealth of the English vocabulary. (See the chapter on vocabulary-building, pages 141-164, for a detailed discussion

AMBIGUOUS WORDS AND PHRASES

The 'famous last words' of Lord Palmerston were reportedly these:

> Die, my dear doctor? – that's the last thing I shall do.

A pharmacist apparently used the following dubious boast as an advertising slogan:

? We dispense with accuracy.

Behind clever puns on the one hand and embarrassing blunders on the other lies verbal ambiguity – the openness of a word or phrase to more than one interpretation.

Newspaper headlines provide a constant stream of amusing ambiguities: **?** *Cyprus fighting mushrooms*, **?** *Health Minister appeals to nurses*, **?** *Icelandic fish talks* – that kind of thing. Here is a recent example from a leading British newspaper:

? Dog attacks prompt calls for registration scheme
> *– The Independent*

Such headlines are ambiguous only in theory. No informed reader would really misunderstand them. The following headline is genuinely ambiguous, however:

? Envoy critical after shooting.
> *– The Guardian*

Does *critical* mean 'disapproving' here – the envoy was critical of the lax security arrangements, perhaps – or does it have the modern sense of 'critically ill'? (The article eventually revealed that the second of these meanings was the one intended.)

A further example from the British press now – from a news story rather than a headline:

? The Oxford United coach was held up in a traffic jam and arrived with only three minutes to spare.
> *– The Times*

(It emerged later in the article that *coach* referred not to the man in charge of training the team, but to the bus carrying the team to its match.) Here is a final selection of sentences whose ambiguity is due to the uncertain meaning of a word or a phrase within them:

? He played Hamlet as well as Macbeth.
? The country had no capital at the time.
? The doctor prescribed a certain remedy.
? She was driven from her home by her husband
? There are two outstanding results.
? I don't discuss my wife's affairs with my friends.
? The editor wants more humorous stories.

Once again, the context will often indicate the preferred meaning. Even then, however, it is usually worth making the meaning of a sentence clear and unambiguous in its own terms. The richness of the English vocabulary, coupled with the versatility of English sentence structure, offers enormous scope for rewording or rephrasing a text until it is free of all unwanted ambiguity.

---

of the subject.) But do beware: thesauruses and synonym dictionaries list near-synonyms mostly, rather than exact synonyms. You cannot simply substitute one 'synonym' for another.

So much for the benefits of a rich vocabulary.

Now for the dangers.

High-falutin. An old anecdote relates how a tipsy man (Dr Johnson, according to one version) refused the offer of a friendly arm to lean on. 'I'm not so drunk that I can't walk without your help,' he said. And then, after pausing to think for a moment, rephrased his refusal: 'I'm not so inebriated as to be incapable of unassisted perambulation.'

Hardly an improvement in clarity, though it might have raised a laugh.

The truth is, the best word for 'drunk', in most contexts, is *drunk*.

The Victorian statesman Disraeli, in a speech in 1878, delivered a famous put-down of his great rival Gladstone. Ironically mimicking the very fault he was complaining of, he described Gladstone as 'a sophistical rhetorician, inebriated with the exuberance of his own verbosity'.

If you have a good vocabulary (and sometimes, worse still, if you have not), the temptation is to spurn the obvious word in favour of a high-falutin synonym. So *edifice* displaces *building*, for example, and *to insinuate* displaces *to suggest*. This habit is fine in moderation, and in the right company. But it soon begins to smack of showing off.

In everyday speaking and writing, you are hardly likely to refer to a well-dressed barber, say, as a *tonsorial artist in full sartorial splendour* (except in jest). But the chances are that you do occasionally succumb to the temptation of a 'fancy' synonym – saying *apropos* when you just mean *about*, or using an archaism such as *erstwhile* or *whence*, or writing *expedite* in a business letter, instead of *speed up* or *help*.

Very broadly speaking, the plain term tends to be good old native English (Anglo-Saxon) in origin, and the fancy or high-falutin term tends to be Latin (often via French) or Greek in origin. But this is not to suggest that you should shun Latinate words: sometimes there is simply no native English equivalent. And even when there is one, it could well have an unacceptably quaint or old-fashioned ring to it. Compare the following three terms: *polychromatic*, *multi-coloured*, and *many-hued* – respectively Greek, Latin, and native English in origin. In some technical contexts, *polychromatic* may be appropriate; in some literary contexts, *many-hued* may be appropriate. But most often, the appropriate adjective is *multi-coloured* – the Latinate rather than the native English term.

Here now is a list of some of the commonest 'fancy' terms used in business letters (or commercial correspondence, to use the fancy term). When you next use any of them, at least pause to ask yourself whether it really is contributing anything to your writing, apart from an artificial and possibly *un*impressive glitter:

affluent	rich, well off
alternative	other, different
anticipate	expect, await
append	add
assist	help
commence	begin, start
consequential	resulting, touching
contiguous	near, touching
designate	name, label
desire	want
desist	stop
differential	difference
dispatch	send
endeavour	try
feasible	possible
inaugurate	open, set up, start
initiate	begin, start
inquire	ask
manifest	clear, obvious
modification	change
pertaining to	about, regarding, relating to
peruse	read
proceed	go, walk, drive
propitious	favourable
proportion	part
purchase	buy
remittance	payment
terminate	end
transpire	happen
utilise	use
whilst	while, whereas

Sometimes the pompous synonym takes the form of a fine-sounding phrase rather than a single fancy word. Such phrases (listed in the left-hand column below) may well improve the rhythm of a sentence occasionally, or add some welcome variety. But for the most part they fail to add anything (apart from length) to the clarity and incisiveness of the simple words (in the right-hand column).

afford an opportunity	let, enable
at the present time	now
come to an agreement	agree
for the purpose of	for
give consideration to	consider, think about
in an efficient manner	efficiently
in order to	to
in respect of	about, of, with, in
in spite of the fact that	although, even though
in the amount of	for
in the event that	if
in the majority of cases	usually
make a recommendation that	recommend that
owing to the fact that	because
provide a contribution to	contribute to, help
there can be no doubt that	clearly, no doubt
there is a possibility that	possibly, perhaps
with regard to	about, of, with, in
with the exception of	except

RECOGNISE THE RHYMES?

Here are the openings of three nursery rhymes rewritten in such a high-falutin vocabulary as to be almost unrecognisable. Almost, but not quite: can you recognise them? The answers, and the plainly worded original versions, appear on pages 633-648.

Behold repeatedly the precipitate progress of that triad of sightless rodents; unanimously they coursed apace on the heels of the agriculturalist's matrimonial consociate, who summarily excised their caudal appendages.

Coruscate, scintillate, asteroid,
Your constitution exercises my cogitations.

It transpired that a superannuated adult female was domiciled in an item of footwear.

The use of a high-falutin word carries within it a further risk – that of getting the word or its sense wrong. Very slightly wrong perhaps, but no less embarrassingly for that.

The word *edifice*, for instance, nowadays distinctly suggests an impressively large or imposing building; describe your little holiday cottage as **??** *a pretty 200-year-old edifice* and you will only amuse, rather than impress, your reader or listener. And to replace *suggests* in the previous sentence with the more 'impressive' verb *insinuates* would be not just inappropriate but wrong. (Only one sense of *to suggest* matches *to insinuate* in meaning, and that is not the sense used in the sentence above.)

The risk in choosing a high-falutin word such as *insinuate* does not stop there. Two further pitfalls lie in wait – malapropism and false tone.

The following sentence uses *insinuated* in the correct sense but with quite the wrong tone: **??** *The boss insinuated that I'm to get promoted very soon.* The trouble is, *to insinuate* should convey an unfavourable or slightly sneaky tone, not the favourable tone that it conveys here.

And as for malapropism: even if you intend *insinuated* in the correct sense and with the appropriate tone, you may get your tongue or pen in a twist, and say or write *incinerated* instead.

(See the panel *Malapropism* opposite.)

Elegant variation. The second major danger of a rich vocabulary, affecting many insecure writers and speakers, is the danger of variety for variety's sake, or 'elegant variation' as the usage expert H.W. Fowler called it. This consists in needlessly choosing a different word from one used earlier, often simply for the sake of avoiding repetition.

Suppose, for example, the opening sentence of this paragraph had mentioned *the peril of variety for variety's sake*: would that mark an improvement? Surely not. The change certainly does eliminate the repetition of the word *danger* – but it introduces a very old-fashioned and inappropriate term instead. If you wanted to eliminate the repetition of *danger*, you could find better ways of doing so – you could change the phrase *the danger of* to *that of*, or you could simply delete it altogether.

Here are some other typical examples of elegant variation:

? The hats on view at Ascot today are remarkably similar to the headwear I used to see here 30 years ago.

? You have been giving information to the Press that not even the chairman is permitted to divulge.

? If you think that Simon is conscientious about his tennis training, you should see how diligent he is when revising for exams.

? Gooch took nearly three hours to score his fifty, whereas Greenidge reached his half-century in a mere 45 minutes.

The switch from *hats* to *headwear* or from *fifty* to *half-century* not only comes across as showy or pretentious; it actually weakens the effect of the communication, by blurring the link or contrast between the two elements in each case. Far better to repeat the words *hats, fifty,* and so on each time.

This weakness is neatly illustrated in the following quotation:

? Judging the success or failure of a film, Roland Joffé believes, should be a matter of measuring the distance between end results and a director's original intention.

In Hollywood on the other hand success or failure is often assessed simply by subtracting the cost of a film's production from total box-office receipts.

– Simon Banner, *The Times*

MALAPROPISM

If you use an impressive-sounding word, make sure that you use it correctly! Remember, the higher a high-falutin writer rises, the further he or she has to fall.

Writers and speakers can misuse a word in several ways.

☐ They can get the sense slightly wrong, as in **✗** *a fine, dark red, fulsome wine* (the adjective needed is *full-bodied* perhaps).

☐ They can get the tone slightly wrong, as in **??** *relishing the fulsome reviews of my novel* (the adjective *laudatory*, or *flattering*, or even *adulatory* perhaps, is as far as one should go: *fulsome* nowadays has a tone suggesting excessive or insincerely extravagant praise).

☐ They can get the form of the word wrong, in spelling or pronunciation, through confusion with some other word or words: for example, **✗** *foolsome*, **✗** *falsesome*.

To write **✗** *foolsome* instead of *fulsome* is to make the kind of mistake known as a malapropism, so called after *Mrs Malaprop*, a comic character in the play *The Rivals* (1775) by the Irish playwright Richard Brinsley Sheridan. Mrs Malaprop's name is based on the word *malapropos*, / **mal-ap**prə-**pō** /, meaning 'inappropriate or out of place', from French.

Not that Mrs Malaprop was the first literary character to commit malapropisms. Two of Shakespeare's comic characters were particularly fine exponents: Dogberry the constable in *Much Ado About Nothing* and Bottom the weaver (and amateur actor) in *A Midsummer Night's Dream*. Here are some of their finest specimens (with the correct words in brackets each time). First, Dogberry:

> Comparisons are odorous (odious)
> Our watch, sir, have, indeed, comprehended two auspicious persons (apprehended, suspicious).

Next, some of Bottom's malapropisms:

> He himself must speak through, saying thus, or to the same defect – Ladies . . . (effect)

Thisby, the flowers [have] odious savours sweet (odorous).

Mrs Malaprop's own malapropisms include:

> A progeny of learning (prodigy)
> He is the very pine-apple of politeness (pinnacle).

Malapropism has a curious half-brother, sometimes called Malentendu (the French word for 'misunderstanding' or 'misunderstood') – a close friend of Propaganda and Saucy Innuendo. This time it is the reader or listener, rather than the writer or speaker, who gets the sense of a word wrong. What the writer or speaker gets wrong – often deliberately, as in music-hall jokes or old seaside postcards – is the tone of the word, and he thereby encourages misunderstanding even though he uses the word in its correct sense.

A particularly notorious example took place in 1950, during the Senate elections in the United States. The late Claude Pepper, who was to become a famous and long-serving senator for the state of Florida, was the victim of a smear campaign. His opponent apparently used to deliver the following speech to unsophisticated voters in rural areas:

> Are you aware that Claude Pepper is known all over Washington as a shameless *extrovert*? Not only that, but this man is reliably reported to practise *nepotism* with his sister-in-law, and he has a sister who was once a *thespian* in wicked New York. Worst of all, it is an established fact that Mr Pepper before his marriage habitually practised *celibacy*.
>
> – quoted in *Time* magazine

Difficult though it is to believe, a handful of innocent but misunderstood nouns such as *extrovert* and *nepotism* really did contribute to the election result, according to political observers. Pepper lost overwhelmingly. A testament to the power of words, if nothing else – or to the abuse of that power.

If you ever feel that you need protection against abuse of this kind, you know what to arm yourself with – a good dictionary.

ELEGANT RHYMES

Here are three nursery rhymes 'improved' by elegant variation. The dull and repetitive original versions are printed on pages 633-634.

Deedle deedle dumpling, my son John
Went to bed with his stockings on,
One shoe off, and a single item of footwear
  unremoved,
Deedle deedle dumpling, my firstborn.

Bye, baby bunting,
Daddy's gone a-hunting,
Mummy's set out a-milking,
Sister's sallied forth a-silking,
Brother's departed to buy a skin
To wrap the infant bunting in.

There was a crooked man, and he walked a
  meandering mile;
He found a misshapen sixpence upon a
  gnarled stile;
He bought a contorted cat, which caught a
  deformed mouse,
And they all lived together in an asymmetric
  little house.

A clever contrast is lurking in this passage, and would come over very pointedly if only the two paragraphs were worded in parallel throughout.

But the writer allows the explicit parallel to emerge only once – in the phrase *success or failure*. Twice he indulges in elegant variation instead – from *judging* to *is assessed by*, and from *measuring the distance between* to *subtracting . . . from* – leaving the poor reader to make the translation each time in order to appreciate the contrast.

How much punchier the passage would be if the second paragraph, repeating unashamedly the crucial words of the first paragraph, read as follows:

In Hollywood they believe otherwise. Judging the success or failure of a film there is simply a matter of measuring the distance between production costs and total box-office receipts.

REPETITION

Underlying most 'elegant variation' lies a widespread fear among inexperienced writers – the fear of repeating a word. And underlying this fear in turn is probably some old schoolroom rule: 'Never use

the same prominent word twice in a sentence, or even in two successive sentences'. Such a rule has its uses, true enough, but only within limits. It certainly does not hold good in all circumstances.

Bad repetition. Repeating a word or a phrase (or sometimes even a syllable) is undesirable in two specific cases; first, where it would sound awkward; secondly, where a simple substitute – a verb such as *does* or a pronoun such as *them* – would do the job just as efficiently.

To deal with this latter case first. Consider these two sentences:

?? Chromium-enriched steel oxidises and corrodes very slowly, whereas pig-iron oxidises and corrodes alarmingly fast.

?? Children easily get bored during the vacation, so we have developed our Summersaver Ticket especially for children.

The stilted or overfussy effect here derives entirely from the needless repetition. For a natural idiomatic wording, substitute the phrase *does so* near the end of the first sentence, and the word *them* at the end of the second.

Chromium-enriched steel oxidises and corrodes very slowly, whereas pig-iron does so alarmingly fast.

Children easily get bored during the vacation, so we have developed a Summersaver Ticket especially for them.

But beware: you cannot always automatically make such simple substitutions. One ever-present danger for the unwary writer, from pronouns in particular, is that of slipping into ambiguity:

?? Children easily get bored during the holidays, so we have developed a Summersaver Ticket especially for them.

Does the pronoun *them* perhaps refer to *holidays* now rather than to *children*?

(For a more detailed discussion of the dangers lurking within pronouns, see page 34.)

The other undesirable kind of repetition is that which produces a 'jingle' – an awkward duplication or clashing of sounds, a jarring rhyme, or the like.

Jingles come in three main varieties.

The most prominent variety occurs when the writer just, carelessly and boringly, repeats the word without realising it, often in a different sense or a different idiom or a slightly different form.

In the following extract, the word *find* appears twice in the first sentence, and the sequence *opening-open-openings* appears in the second.

?? Following our successful launch last year we have continued our expansion programme and on the back page you will find full details of where to find your local store and how to get there.

During the course of this year we will be opening even more stores so keep your eyes open for details of more openings in your area.

            – gift store catalogue

To start with, the repetition of *find* in the first paragraph: *on the back page you will find more details of where to find your local store* . . . There are any number of ways of improving the sentence. Here are just two:

On the back page are full details of where to find your local store . . .

On the back page you will find the address of your nearest store . . .

Next the sequence *opening-open-openings* in the second paragraph. The idiom *keep your eyes open* is easy to replace, first of all: *keep your eyes peeled, keep your eyes skinned, be on the lookout, watch out.* As copywriter, you would then go on to change one of the two remaining words as well. Simplest would be to delete the final phrase altogether, and get rid of *openings* in that way. Failing that, you could find a substitute for the earlier term, *opening* – what about *establishing, setting up,* or *starting up*?

Here are three more examples of unthinking, pointless, and jarring repetition of a word:

? Now that our lawyer has served notice on the landlords, they should start taking notice of our grievances at last.

? If you cannot see how serious a mistake that is, I'd seriously suggest you look for another job.

? It is sufficient to point out that without sufficient funds we are obviously simply unable to proceed.

The second variety of jingle occurs when the writer heedlessly repeats a prominent syllable or sound, thereby producing an ugly rhyme or half-rhyme or alliteration. The last example above illustrates this

type of jingle too. The repetition of the syllable *-ly*, in *obviously simply*, grates on the ear, and so too does the crude repetition of the /owt/ sound in *point out that without*.

Here are some more examples – rhymes, half-rhymes, and unintended alliterations:

? The prisoner confessed that he had been feeling depressed for some time.

? We await clarification on your solution to the confrontation.

? Apparently he is currently virtually completely bankrupt.

? Slit the strap into three thin thongs, and thread these through the ring.

For some quotations containing similar jingles, see the panel *Sounding good* overleaf.

The third variety of jingle occurs when the writer repeats overfrequently a non-prominent word – a conjunction such as *but* or *though*, for example, or a preposition such as *from* or *of*. The resulting jingle is a very subtle one, true enough, but sensitive readers will detect it – and dislike it – each time you commit it in your writing.

? From Coleridge's point of view, the man from Porlock was far from immune from criticism.

? The report of the loss of such a large number of files of secret data is of concern to all of us.

Once again, a thorough restructuring of the sentence is the best solution:

For Coleridge, the man from Porlock was certainly subject to criticism.

We are all concerned about the reported loss of so many files of secret data.

Good repetition. Repeating a word or phrase, then, in most circumstances, is something you should try to avoid. In most circumstances, not in all. Sometimes it turns out to be a virtue rather than a failing. It can help the writer to emphasise or focus an important idea (as by using the phrase *in most circumstances* in the first two sentences of this paragraph). And it can help to tighten the link between two related ideas. These are positive virtues, increasing the power of the language.

But the primary virtue of repeating a word or phrase is a more negative one – it helps the writer to avoid confusion or ambiguity.

SOUNDING GOOD

Good written English differs markedly from typical spoken English in several respects. Unrehearsed everyday speech is usually very loosely structured and repetitive, and often ungrammatical. Try transcribing a tape-recording of a meeting or phone conversation, for instance, and you will probably be appalled at how awkwardly and meanderingly your transcript reads.

The following published passage – a single sentence – was presumably dictated to a secretary or into a tape recorder – and it shows.

?? For professional footballers the past four days since their last game has been an important period because, as I am sure you can appreciate, the heat that we played in against Watford and the humidity against Everton is a situation where the players do sweat – at least I hope they do! – and their preparation for today's game would have been of a professional idealogy [sic] because as a Manager I must make sure that their recovery period makes them as fit as possible as they go out to face Oxford today and that they have no lethargic apprehensions either mentally or physically because they are at the end of the day – believe it or believe it not – they are only human beings, but also professionals and Don Howe and myself would have made sure that the preparation for today's match is one that nobody can turn round and say the preparation for this game is not right.
    – Bobby Gould, introduction to
    a football-match programme

But in one particular respect, written English should imitate spoken English. Good writing should *sound* good.

Even when reading quickly and silently, almost all readers sound the words out in their head to a certain extent. So if the rhythm goes wrong – too monotonous on the one hand, or too jerky on the other – the reader's concentration will waver. And if the sound pattern of the words goes wrong – an unintended rhyme or jarring jingle, such as *extremely unseemly* – the reader's inner ear will baulk.

On the other hand, the pointed repetition of a word (*good writing should sound good*, for example) will strike most readers as impressively emphatic.

And a deliberate item of word-play or alliteration (*jarring jingle*) refreshes their interest and prolongs their attention span.

In the following extracts, the jingles are on *place* and *fireplace*, and on *muted* and *transmuted* respectively:

? The original Rosebud sledge from Citizen Kane, which he bought at an auction for £30,000, hangs in pride of place above the fireplace.
    – John Hiscock, *The Daily Telegraph*

? The bounds of Pymdom . . . are narrow; the love affairs of its inhabitants are muted, unrequited love is transmuted by time from rapture to the cosiness of woollen combinations . . .
    – Shena Mackay, *The Sunday Times*

Take a look at the passage on pidgin languages, quoted on pages 55-56. The word *pidgin* occurs, in one form or another, in six of the twelve sentences. In the second paragraph, the word *language* appears, in one form or another, in four successive sentences; and the word *creole*, in one form or another, in three successive sentences. And the reader feels grateful for such repetition, rather than irritated by it. If the author had used the pronoun *it* or *them* instead of actually repeating the noun so often, the reader might easily have become confused: what exactly does *it* or *them* refer to?, he or she would keep asking.

In the following passage, the author's needless fear of repetition has resulted in an incomprehensible presentation of the scene:

As he was abreast of Roschmann, the SS officer grabbed his arm, swung him round and slapped the army man across the face with his gloved hand.
    – Frederick Forsyth, *The Odessa File*

How many men does this scene feature? A careful study of the context reveals that only two were involved – an SS officer called Roschmann, and an 'army man'.

Suppose the writer had been bold enough to repeat the name *Roschmann* instead of resorting to the 'elegant variation' of *the SS officer*, and to repeat the word *him* instead of switching to *the army man*. The passage would then have made proper sense (though hardly graceful and efficient prose – for that, only a drastic restructuring would do). See the panel *Effective repetition* below for other aspects of this problem.

SPECIAL RISKS

Threats to good style can come from the most innocent-sounding words or grammatical constructions. Here are some of the special risks associated with the various parts of speech.

Prepositions and conjunctions. Being such familiar and unassertive words, prepositions and conjunctions often lure the careless writer into excessive repetition. Note the overuse of *of* in the following passage:

? She lamented the disappointing findings of her own monitoring of the use students made of lists of reserved books which she posted at the appropriate shelves.

         – Civil Service research report

(For further examples, see page 29 above.)

Verbs. Verbs present the inattentive writer with two general temptations: to overuse the passive voice, and to overuse the verb *to be*. See pages 47-52 for a full discussion of these dangers. Here are a few examples as a foretaste. First the overused passive:

? The meeting was attended by three bidders, who were invited by the treasurer only after he had been bribed by the chairman.

Then, the overuse of the verb *to be*:

EFFECTIVE REPETITION

Repeating a word or phrase can have positive advantages, alongside the negative virtue of averting confusion. It can serve to emphasise ideas and drive a point home, and to link two separate ideas by signposting their similarity or contrast. And it can produce a number of rhetorical effects as well – such as humour, persuasiveness, or a sense of nostalgia. Many sentences derive their force from skilful repetition of a key word, such as *special* in the following example:

> The special effects are stunning, but they are the only thing special about the film.

In the following extract, from an article on the fate of soccer in the U.S., the writer uses repetition very effectively to convey his amused frustration and mock-urgency – note specifically the repetition of *well-mannered* and the chant-like refrain of *We need* ...

> The American players, for example, were described in the press as well-mannered. How can you get the ink necessary for success in sports by being well-mannered?

> We need heated arguments on the field between participants and officials, like in baseball ...

> We need blood, like in hockey ...

> We need bruising collisions, like in [American] football, and a proper amount of concussions per game.
>   – Ira Berkow (U.S.), *The New York Times*

Finally, two passages – one from fiction, one from non-fiction – in which the writer chooses each time to repeat a person's name rather than always using the expected pronouns *he* and *him*.

> Mr Kelada was chatty. He talked of New York and of San Francisco ... Mr Kelada was familiar. I do not wish to put on airs, but I cannot help feeling that it is seemly in a total stranger to put mister before my name when he addresses me. Mr Kelada, doubtless to set me at my ease, used no such formality. I did not like Mr Kelada.
>   – Somerset Maugham, 'Mr Know-All'

> In April 1982, Greek-born Dimitris Sgouros walked on to the platform of Carnegie Hall, New York and made his American debut playing Rachmaninoff's awesome 3rd Piano Concerto, a massive work which stands at the peak of the romantic virtuoso tradition. Sgouros totally dominated its technical demands. Sgouros was twelve years old.
>   – Robin Ray, 'Infant Prodigies',
>   theatre programme note

? It's likely that he is eager to be of help.

? It is worth noting that there were more debts than it was possible to predict.

More specific dangers in the use of verbs include the following:

☐ omitting the object. Some verbs that traditionally require an object (that is, transitive or reflexive verbs) today often seem to shed that object: *Enjoy yourself!* might become **?** *Enjoy!* and *Let's discuss this* is often reduced to **?** *Let's discuss*. Whether prompted by a need for streamlining or simply by laziness, this trend has little to recommend it.

☐ omitting the preposition. North American English sometimes streamlines various phrases by dropping the usual preposition after the verb: *to approximate the truth, to provide him an excuse, to protest the war*. Such uses remain unacceptable in British English, however common they are becoming. The standard British idiom remains *to approximate to the truth, to provide him with an excuse, to protest against the war*.

☐ adding prepositions or adverbs. Here is another North American tendency that is increasingly being imitated in British English. The simple *We consulted him* becomes 'smartened' into **?** *We consulted with him; to miss the start* becomes **?** *to miss out on the start; to win* and *to rest* become **?** *to win out* and **?** *to rest up*. Always pause to consider whether the adverb or preposition really does change the sense of the verb and thereby earn its keep. If not, leave it out.

☐ using inelegant 'converted' verbs. Over the centuries, many English nouns have, through 'conversion', come to be used as verbs: *to question a suspect, to knife a victim, to service a car*, even *to lunch a guest* and *to blue-pencil a report*. But such conversions are not automatically justifiable. Think twice before using the most inelegant of trendy verbs – such as: **?** *to author a report*, **?** *to critique a report*, **?** *to round-table a report*.

☐ using, unacceptably, verbs developed from nouns by 'back-formation'. The verb *to televise*, to take an obvious example, grew out of the noun *television*. Less obviously, *to edit* (1791) derives from *editor* (1649). Similarly, *to scavenge, to extradite, to legislate, to manipulate, to automate*, and *to diagnose*. Once again, however,

don't assume that every verb formed in this way is bound to be acceptable. Many careful speakers disapprove of *to liaise* (from *liaison*), *to self-destruct* (from *self-destruction*), and **?** *to enthuse*, for instance, at least in formal speech and writing.

☐ using unacceptable *-ise* or *-ize* verbs. Another long-established means of forming verbs is by adding *-ise* or *-ize* to a noun or adjective: *to magnetise* from *magnet*, *to legalise* from *legal*, and so on. Some modern formations of this kind have not gained full acceptance in Standard English: **?** *to politicise*, **?** *to prioritise*, **?** *to comprehensivise*, **?** *to accessorise*, **?** *to routinise*, and so on. Some careful speakers and writers still avoid even *to finalise, to decriminalise*, and *to hospitalise*.

Adverbs and adjectives. The risk hidden in these two parts of speech is that of over-egging your writing with them. Too much of a good thing is usually, when it comes to writing or speaking style, worse than too little.

For a start, thoughtless adjectives and adverbs are often the main culprits in clichés and tautologies: clichés such as **?** *a fond farewell*, **?** *swingeing cuts*, **?** *under active consideration*, **?** *a silvery moon*, and **?** *a crucial role*, and tautologies such as **?** *the actual facts*, **?** *free gifts*, **?** *an arid desert*, **?** *grateful thanks*, and **?** *future prospects*. (For a more detailed discussion of such clichés and tautologies, see pages 61 and 83.)

Then, constant use of adjectives and adverbs betrays an immature style. School compositions, for instance, are often embarrassingly ornate, with almost every noun and verb clutching its own decorative adjective or adverb: **??** *The fiery stars twinkled brightly in the pitch-black sky as the utterly exhausted ploughman walked painfully back from the parched field to his modest cottage* – that kind of thing.

Then, heavily adjectival prose tends to create a hectoring tone, as if bullying or pleading with the reader. It suggests a lack of confidence on the writer's part that he makes up for by over-emphasising or overdecorating his arguments.

If every crisis is an **?** *acute crisis*, if every emergency is a **?** *dire emergency*, if every problem is a **?** *serious problem*, then the whole idea of a crisis, an emergency, or a problem becomes devalued. And the reader loses faith in your powers of discrimination. The adjective has been called the enemy of the noun. If you think about it for a moment, you will probably agree that the stark announcement *We're in trouble* has a more chilling or nerve-racking ring to it than **?** *We're in real trouble.*

Similarly, the simple *I'm certain* has a quiet confidence about it that conveys *greater* certainty than the shrill **?** *I'm absolutely certain.* And again, the adverb in **?** *That is entirely beside the point* or **?** *Your duty is perfectly clear* simply weakens the force of the assertion in each case. Such emphases only illustrate the old rule: 'More means worse'.

Adjectives and adverbs do earn their keep when they *define* and *refine* rather than simply *emphasise.* In the sentence *We're in financial trouble*, the adjective *financial* has a truly informative function. A phrase such as *a widely publicised crisis* or *a medical crisis* tells the reader much more than the phrase **?** *an acute crisis.*

But even then, adjectives and adverbs are 'light' parts of speech, when weighed alongside verbs and nouns. For a more vigorous style, try to replace some of your most heavily adjectival or adverbial phrases with colourful nouns or verbs. More vivid than **?** *She walked unsteadily towards the penniless man's filthy hut* is *She tottered towards the pauper's hovel.* A *rattletrap* sounds more interesting and vivid than a **?** *noisy, worn-out old car.*

Nouns. Concrete nouns, such as *rattletrap* or *hovel*, often conjure up a vivid picture in the reader's mind, and so make for lively and effective writing. Abstract nouns, such as *accommodation* or *mobility*, are another matter.

For the most part, they are less vigorous than concrete nouns: *aristocracy* as against *lords and ladies*, for instance, or *the highest reaches of management* as against *the top managers.*

And they tend to be less vigorous than their corresponding verbs as well. If you are tempted to use an abstract noun derived from a verb – *implication, diminution,* or *advocacy,* say – consider redrafting the sentence slightly, to allow in a verb instead to carry the meaning: *imply, diminish,* or *advocate* here, though an unrelated verb will often work just as well.

? What are the implications of this setback for our sales figures?

sounds considerably more pointed and direct when recast as:

What does this setback imply/mean for our sales figures?

Or, more streamlined still:

How will this setback affect our sales figures?

Similarly:

?? The diminution in the frequency of resignations among senior management should afford some reassurance to the directorate

comes across as far less affected and flabby if rewritten as:

Now that fewer senior managers are resigning, the directors should feel somewhat reassured.

And:

?? If there really is a pattern of incompatibility and an incapacity for resolution of differences, then reconciliation is simply not an option

reads more elegantly when rephrased as:

If you really are incompatible and cannot resolve your differences, you simply cannot live together again.

Among the most notorious abstract nouns are *basis, situation, process, problem*, and so on. You can usually get rid of them – to the advantage of the text. Here are examples of the unattractive use of these abstract nouns, together with simpler alternatives:

employment on a part time basis	part-time work
the negotiating process	negotiations
weather conditions	the weather
celebrations of a festive character	festivities
has an alcohol problem	drinks too much

(For the further hazards of abstract nouns and of abstraction in general, see pages 75-78.)

A second special risk associated with nouns is that of overusing them in their role as adjectives. Within limits, this role is a very valuable one. Concise phrases such as *an unemployment crisis* and *a book reviewer* rely on the nouns *unemployment* and *book* (known technically as 'attributive nouns' when used in this way) instead of conventional adjectives. English idiom welcomes such phrases, and works more economically and efficiently through having them.

But as with so many blessings, this flexibility invites overuse. Long strings of nouns, inspired perhaps by newspaper headlines such as *Germ war secrets leak row* (from the *Daily Mail*) or *City corruption scandal enquiry verdict*, now appear increasingly in the main text of official documents, business reports, and everyday writing.

They may help to make the sentence shorter, and take the writer less time to write, but they have a clogging effect and so take the reader longer to unravel and understand. A phrase such as **?** *the budget deficit conference delegates* reads far more awkwardly than *the delegates to the conference on the budget deficit* (or even *the deficit in the budget*).

Similarly, you could redraft the sentence

? The lead-poisoning epidemic investigation team has questioned several Midland restaurant equipment manufacturers

to something far less convoluted like

> The team investigating the epidemic of lead poisoning has questioned several manufacturers of restaurant equipment in the Midlands.

Pronouns. Being a form of shorthand, pronouns sometimes encourage brevity at the expense of clarity. Writers fail to make quite clear what the pronoun refers to, and ambiguity results.

Certainly pronouns are a great help in reducing repetition. For instance, the awkward sentence

? If the babies dislike fresh milk, try boiling the milk

recovers immediately if you end with the simple pronoun *it*:

> If the babies dislike fresh milk, try boiling it.

But suppose the original sentence had used the singular *baby* rather than the plural *babies*. The 'improved' version would then emerge as this famous traditional ambiguous sentence:

?? If the baby dislikes fresh milk, try boiling it.

The following extract is similarly open to a comic misinterpretation:

? On the way back, the guide showed us a piece of baleen, the special filter mechanism certain whale species have in their mouths which acts as a sieve and from which they used to make corset bones.

– Sue Arnold, The Observer

The bizarre image of a group of whales sitting in a workshop and stitching corsets comes irresistibly into the mind.

Such sentences are only theoretically ambiguous. No sensible reader would really mistake their meaning. In the following examples, however, needless use of pronouns could cause the reader real uncertainty:

?? We heated up the cocoa because it was cold.

Was the cocoa cold, or the weather?

?? Just before her father died, her mother reclaimed her and took her to live in Italy, where she was set up with an Italian lover called Alessandro.

– Auberon Waugh, The Independent

Does *she* refer to mother or daughter? Similarly,

?? Irene mentioned the invoice to her mother before she left for work.

?? The players told the fans that they were ashamed of their behaviour.

?? David asked Noel if he could help him assemble his new bookcase.

One traditional short-cut method for dispelling such ambiguity is repeating the noun or name immediately after the puzzling pronoun:

> Irene mentioned the invoice to her mother before she, Irene, left for work.

This seems acceptable enough, perhaps; but it betrays a very poor style: the sentence no longer flows smoothly. And in complicated sentences, the repetition becomes laughable and the jerky rhythm becomes almost intolerable:

?? The players told the fans that they, the players, were ashamed of their, the fans', behaviour.

?? David asked Noel if he, David, could help him, Noel, assemble his, Noel's, new bookcase.

You might as well just leave the pronouns out altogether. (When P.G. Wodehouse produced such ungainly constructions, it was for deliberate comic effect.) The appropriate solution, as so often, is to recast the sentence drastically:

> The players were ashamed of the fans' behaviour, and told them so.

> David asked Noel: 'Can I help you to assemble your new bookcase?'

Sentences – Length and Structure

The careful crafting of sentences is perhaps the most important step of all in creating an easily understandable piece of writing.

The two major faults in sentence construction are *overloading* – that is cramming too much in, and thereby producing an ungainly, straggly, overlong sentence – and *misarranging*: that is, positioning the words poorly, and thereby producing ambiguity or confusions.

POSITIONING OF WORDS

To choose the right words is not enough. You have to position them correctly as well. A slight mispositioning of a single word, and your sentence may convey quite the wrong sense. The following rueful apology illustrates the danger strikingly:

> Our front page report yesterday on microwave cooking mistakenly stated that in tests of 83 cook-chill and ready-cooked products, Sainsbury's found the instructions on 10 products always failed to ensure the foods were fully heated to 70° C. The story should have said the instructions failed always to ensure the foods were fully heated to 70° C – that is, they sometimes failed to ensure this.
>
> *– The Guardian*

The rule of thumb for positioning is this: a word or phrase should stand as close as possible to any other word or phrase related to it in meaning or grammar. The main risk in defying this very simple rule is – ambiguity.

Consider these careless sentences:

✗ Write down your ideas about gardening on a postcard.

✗ I leaned back in my chair contentedly, watching the baby playing and puffing away at my cigar.

✗ Now that you've watched me at target practice, try shooting yourself.

✗ To advance her career, she needs to do a solo recital badly.

✗ He went out to face the lion after taking farewell of his wife armed with only a light rifle.

In each case, the final word or phrase should appear earlier in the sentence, closer to the word or phrase it relates to. For instance, *Write down on a postcard your ideas about gardening* and . . . *she badly needs to do a solo recital.* (Such 'logical' word order does usually eliminate ambiguity, but it may sound stilted in some cases. So sometimes the wisest course is to recast the sentence altogether.)

The examples listed above are ambiguous only in theory. Sometimes, however, the two rival meanings really do seem equally likely:

? The committee made recommendations for tax reforms in 1989.

What does *1989* relate to? The committee's discussions, or the tax reforms? Probably *tax reforms*, since that is positioned closer to *in 1989* than *committee* or *recommendations* is. But a nagging uncertainty persists. A careful writer would redraft the sentence to read as follows, depending on the sense intended:

> In 1989, the committee made recommendations for tax reforms.

> The committee recommended tax reforms due to come into effect in 1989.

Here are some other genuinely ambiguous statements. Try to work out in each case how to reposition the dubiously placed word or phrase, or how to recast the sentence if necessary:

? You won't catch butterflies resting on your bed.

? The women are trying to get the project started again.

? I did not protest because I lost the election.

? The machine only seems to go wrong when Sam is operating it.

(For details of two other types of careless ambiguity within sentences, see the panel overleaf.) The moral is: keep your wits about you when composing a sentence, or ambiguity may creep in.

LENGTH OF SENTENCE

An English sentence can in theory grow infinitely long and complex:

> . . . this is the dog that chased the cat that killed the rat that ate the malt that lay in the house that Jack built.

TWO TYPES OF AMBIGUITY

Among the many types of ambiguity discussed at various points in this book, two of the subtlest and most easily committed are *uncertain range* and *thoughtless brevity*.

Uncertain range. According to its position in a sentence, a word can apply to a varying range of elements within the sentence.

? The moths have attacked all my fine imported hats.

Does this mean that all my hats are damaged, or only some of them? Similarly:

? She went travelling with her three scholarly friends.
? He had only two rotting teeth.
? Perhaps the sentence has a different ironic interpretation.

Various strategies are available to remove the ambiguity from such sentences. Some take the form of very minor adjustments. You could adjust the last two examples to read as follows (assuming that the change does in fact produce the meaning you intend):

> He had only two (rotting) teeth.
> Perhaps the sentence has a different and ironic interpretation.

To convey the rival meaning in each case, however, you would probably have to restructure each sentence quite drastically:

> Most of his teeth were perfectly healthy – only two of them were rotting.
> That is not the only ironic interpretation that the sentence has; there is another.

Although the word *and* proved useful above in resolving an ambiguity, it is far more often responsible for producing ambiguity. Its presence in the middle of a sentence tends to generate doubts about the range of a word's reference: does the adjective in the first noun phrase apply to a second noun as well?

? We offer iced lemonade and tea to drink, and chocolate eclairs and biscuits to eat.

Are the biscuits all chocolate biscuits? And is the tea iced tea? If so the adjectives *iced* and *chocolate* should perhaps have been repeated,

to make the meaning quite clear. If not, each pair of nouns should have been reversed, to make the sentence unambiguous:

> We offer tea and iced lemonade to drink, and biscuits and chocolate eclairs to eat.

Similarly:

? She is inclined to refuse to cooperate and to report on her colleagues' behaviour.

(Does she tend to report on her colleagues' behaviour, or does she usually refuse to report on her colleagues' behaviour?)

The word *to*, as the above example shows, is another fertile source of confusion.

? It is easy to imagine the chaos that would ensue if a member of these forces refused to obey the orders of his commanding officer if his union told him not to.
> – G.C. Hampson, letter to *The Times*

(If his union told him not to – what? Not to obey? Or not to refuse to obey?)

Finally the scope of negative words – *not, never, hardly*, and so on – is notoriously difficult to control.

? You were not paying attention the whole time.
? He was hardly happy and eager to get rid of me.

(A comma after *happy* would resolve the ambiguity in one way. To resolve it the other way, you could change the *and* to an *or*; or you could insert an extra *hardly* before *eager.*)

Thoughtless brevity. The lazy omission of words on the one hand, and the overzealous attempt to pack too much meaning into too little space on the other – these two tendencies are responsible for many an ambiguity. As the Roman poet Horace put it, 'I toil to be brief, and become obscure'. One traditional example of such reckless brevity is:

? He likes me more than you.

The context might indicate which of the two possible meanings is intended here. If not, the ambiguity must be eliminated by the addition of a word or phrase. On the one hand,

He likes me more than he likes you.

On the other,

He likes me more than you do.

Here is a similar example:

? I've just read in Options magazine that a young woman called Luella from Plymouth has won a tycoon-of-the-year award for her meteoric success in the window business. I wish Luella had come to me instead of Sid.
– Sue Arnold, *The Observer*

(Does this mean 'I wish Luella rather than Sid had come to me' or does it mean 'I wish Luella had come to me instead of going to Sid'?)

Another traditional example is illustrated by such phrases as **?** *old ladies' clothing* or **?** *an American history teacher*. If the context is unhelpful, this last phrase would have to be reworded either as *a teacher of American history* or as *an American teacher of history*.

Finally, three rather more complicated examples of ambiguity that result from the omission of a word or phrase:

? The little boy walked amiably towards the man intending to kidnap him.

(Add *who was* after the *man*.)

?? Very few inmates bothered to protest at this abuse, and just took the new indignity with silent submissiveness.

This reads *Very few inmates . . . took the new indignity with silent submissiveness*, which is clearly not the intended meaning. Add *most of them* after *and*, and the correct meaning now comes across unambiguously.

?? The total vocabulary of English is immense and runs to about half a million items. None of us as individuals, of course, knows more than a fairly limited number of these, and uses even less.
– Sir Randolph Quirk, *The Use of English*

This reads *none of us . . . uses even less*. What the writer means was *each of us uses even less* (or more correctly, *even fewer*) or *we use even less*, and that is what he should have written.

That particular sentence is easy enough to understand, of course, since the structure varies so little from one clause to the next. But in general – many studies into readability have shown this – the longer and more complex a sentence becomes, the more difficult it is for the reader to understand it. Children's stories, accordingly, tend to have short and simple sentences. At the other extreme, academic philosophical treatises might still contain very long and convoluted sentences in dauntingly high proportions.

But increasingly nowadays, professional writers favour (because readers demand) a fairly simple 'unliterary' style even for complex subject matter. Most of the news reports in *The Times*, for instance, are now, in the late 20th century, far less complex (in syntax, not in content) than those of the early 20th century. You have only to compare the two *Times* extracts in the panel overleaf.

Not that all good writers avoid lengthy sentences. Good writing, by good writers, can accommodate very long sentences, where appropriate. Long sentences, but not straggly sentences. Here are three accomplished examples.

This work is not about evil, but about good, and just as we know that the killers we see on the stage really existed, and really killed, and also that the tormented Gens and his kind really existed, and were really tormented, and know in addition that the real Weiskopfs did truly sell death for a profit, and the real Herman Kruk did spend much of his time splitting political hairs (though much more of it trying to save the volumes that would preserve the knowledge of Jewish culture) – just as we know all these things, and face them with pity, anger, incredulity, we know one more thing, and that the most remarkable of all.
– Bernard Levin, *The Times*

We were sitting that evening in an office at WOCN-Union Radio on Flagler Street, and outside in the reception room there was an armed security guard who would later walk Agustin Tamargo to his car, Miami being a city in which people who express their opinions on the radio every night tend, particularly since 1976, when a commentator named Emilio Milian got his legs blown off in the WQBA-*La Cubanísima* parking lot, to put a little thought into the walk to the car.
– Joan Didion (U.S.), *Miami*

LENGTH OF SENTENCE – CHANGING WITH THE TIMES

Here are extracts from two editorial articles in *The Times* of London. They appeared on the same day – 82 years apart. Note how the style of writing has changed. The language of *The Times* in the late 20th century certainly remains fairly formal and sophisticated by modern standards, and the sentences are fairly long, averaging about 20 words in the 1989 extract here. But the writing is still far simpler and less stilted than that of *The Times* in the early years of the century. The sentences in the 1907 extract average nearly 40 words in length. And more to the point, their syntax is vastly more convoluted.

He has also discovered, however, that when Molotov put his hasty signature to the agreement with Ribbentrop, he and Stalin started the clock of a sizeable time bomb. Its tick is heard louder by the day, especially in the Baltic Republics and what is now Soviet Moldavia.

Reform at home has dictated that foreign policy be recast. Tippex has been applied to the script from which the late Mr Gromyko read so glumly and for so long. 'No' has given way to 'maybe' and even occasionally to 'why not?' It is in West Germany that Mr Gorbachov's charm offensive has made the deepest inroads. The Soviet leader's siren song about a common European home has beguiled large numbers of West Germans, and for many in the Federal Republic reunification is ceasing to be a repressed dream. The relationship between Germany and the Soviet Union is once again of major importance in Europe.

– *The Times*, 23 August 1989

It is highly characteristic of our English way of doing business that, while many days are often spent by the House of Commons in wrangling about controversial trifles, a couple of hours at the fag-end of the Session suffices for the introduction and acceptance of a measure of high Imperial interest.

Such is the happy fate of the Northern Nigerian railway, disposed of yesterday in a couple of clauses of the Public Works Loans Bill. Mr Runciman, the Secretary of the Treasury, introduced the Bill, and Mr Churchill explained the proposal at some length, repeating in greater detail the facts which he had briefly indicated a little more than a fortnight ago. While, of course, repudiating the hint of the other side, that the Bill savoured of protection, Mr Churchill claimed that it was part of 'the policy of improving the communications by sea and land across the surface of the British Empire'.

– *The Times*, 23 August 1907

In all, I made about a dozen automobile tours of the country, as well as innumerable regional jaunts, and in one long and lonely drive through the late winter, spring, and summer of 1942, as an accredited 'war' correspondent reporting from the American grandstand to an audience of embattled Britons, I found myself rediscovering – on retread tires at the compulsory thirty-five miles an hour – the whole American landscape, region by region, county by county.

– Alistair Cooke, *America*

But before imitating such sentences, consider:

☐ For all their length and complexity, these sentences still yield up their meaning with beautiful efficiency.

☐ The writers quoted are all widely and deservedly renowned. They have earned their popularity – both as thinkers and as 'stylists' – and are entitled to the occasional flourish or indulgence.

Do you feel quite sure that you too have earned this right? And even if you do, are you sure that your readers will recognise that right, and invest the extra effort needed?

☐ Each of the passages quoted is striving not just to communicate information but also to create some added effect – a forceful insistence, a feeling of nostalgia, a sense of irony or drama. If it were just a matter of conveying a simple idea (as so much everyday writing is: letters, business memos, and so on), each of the writers would resort to correspondingly short and simple sentences.

Short sentences, on the whole, produce clearer and more easily digestible writing than long sentences do. This is not to say that you should shun all long sentences, or that you should set yourself a limit of 20 or 15 or 12 words per sentence. In fact, a succession of very short sentences tends to grate on the ear. It may be appropriate for a recipe, or an instruction manual, or a short story by Ernest Hemingway, but in most everyday writing – such as letters, office memos, and reports – the staccato effect would be unpleasant and distracting.

Most good everyday writing combines fairly short and reasonably long sentences into a smooth-flowing sequence that draws no attention to itself but serves purely as a vehicle for meaning. The best style, for everyday purposes, is the most inconspicuous style.

Unfortunately, this is not the *natural* style of a great many everyday writers. What comes naturally to them is to write very long and straggly sentences time after time. To them a full stop (or colon or semicolon or other punctuation mark that signals a clear break) is just a kind of pause for breath rather than an aid to clarity.

To avoid writing such gangly sentences, or to catch and correct them later if you do write them, try the following tests and techniques:

Check the frequency of full stops. When rereading or editing a piece of writing, cast your eye down the page to see how often full stops appear.

Include question marks and exclamation marks in your search – they usually signal the end of the sentence. And you can include semicolons and colons as well, since they indicate distinct breaks in thought or meaning.

If you notice a series of three or more wide lines (five or six narrow-column lines) without a full stop or any of the other punctuation marks mentioned, sound the alarm bells. Inspect the sentence thoroughly and test its structure with a view to subdividing it. Is it really working efficiently as a single sentence? Does it unravel its meaning in a logical order? Is it not perhaps saying two or three different things that could better be said in two or three different sentences?

Check the frequency of linking words. Just when a sentence should be drawing to a close, the

Using various simple techniques, you can easily check if your sentences are too long.

inexperienced or hurried writer often prolongs it artificially by scribbling the word *and* or *because* or *which*, and developing a new line of thought.

If you spot even a single *because* in the middle of a lengthy sentence, try the following little trick and see if it works. Replace *because* with a colon. Here is an ungainly sentence from an early draft of a chapter of this book:

? Had the passage read *distress and concern over the outcome*, that would have been perfectly acceptable, because *distress* like *concern* does take the preposition *over*, and can omit it by treating it as 'understood' here, since it pops up a few words later.

The sentence becomes tighter and more incisive if divided into two clear-cut statements by means of a colon, rather than shackled into a seemingly single statement by means of the linking word *because*:

Had the passage read *distress and concern over the outcome*, that would have been perfectly acceptable: *distress* like *concern* does take the preposition *over*, and can omit it by treating it as 'understood' here, since it pops up a few words later.

The conjunction *and* is less conspicuous than *because*, and for that reason is an even more frequent culprit. In fact, using *and* to yoke two distinct statements needlessly together is probably the most common cause of overlong sentences:

?? Your policy is due for renewal and you can continue your insurance by paying the single premium due by the renewal date shown above.
— insurance company's renewal notice

?? During this period share prices may alter and it should be remembered that share prices can go down as well as up.
— building society's information leaflet for a share issue

?? Our key elements of product presentation and information are all backed by the highest standards of customer service and remember our stores are always fun to shop in.
— gift store catalogue

Not that inexperienced writers have a monopoly on this quirk. Here is a telling sample from a professional journalist:

? The investigation is being hampered by the fact that only small quantities of wreckage have been found, and a naval vessel with sensitive sonar equipment is still trying to locate the remains of the aircraft in the sea off Cromer.
— Rodney Cowton, *The Times*

The *and* here serves little purpose. A full stop, or at least a colon, should follow *found* to give proper prominence to the two distinct ideas.

A quick check should eliminate this flaw in your writing. If you spot the word *and* embedded in the middle of a very long sentence, inspect it to see if it really is doing any proper work there. If not, delete it and put a full stop or semicolon in its place (but not a comma – see the next section).

Another group of linking words frequently responsible for overlong sentences is the set of relative pronouns *who*, *which*, and *that*. Overusing them generates a needlessly complex sequence of subordinate clauses:

?? Neil Simon, who is, without doubt, America's leading comedy writer, started his career when only sixteen years old, writing with his brother Daniel, scripts for radio. With the advent of television he progressed to shows like *The Ed Sullivan* programme and, in particular, two and a half years with the highly successful *Bilko* series which is still showing throughout the world. His first play for Broadway was *Come Blow Your Horn*, which had a limited success and encouraged him to write his first real smash Broadway hit, *Barefoot in the Park*. In fact,

during the 1966-67 season in New York, theatregoers could have seen *Barefoot in the Park; The Odd Couple; Sweet Charity* and *The Star-Spangled Girl*, which were all running simultaneously.
— West End theatre programme

Each of the five lengthy sentences here contains a relative pronoun – the first has *who*, the next four have *which*. Almost all of the sentences could benefit from subdividing.

Look out for the 'comma splice'. Sometimes two distinct statements, clumsily jammed into a single sentence, are linked not even by the conjunction *and* but by a simple comma. The result is a 'comma splice' or 'run-on sentence' – a much criticised error of style or usage.

X But I was not content with that life, something was lacking . . . This last puzzled me, the idea of Miss Cooke being her own pupil was beyond my grasp.
— Emlyn Williams, *George: An Early Autobiography*

X The book is *not* an autobiography, its intention is narrower and is stated in the title and text, it is no more than an investigation of the relationship between my father and myself.
— J.R. Ackerley, *My Father and Myself*

In each case, the comma is quite inadequate. A full stop, colon, or semicolon is needed to reflect the independence of the various ideas.

In certain special cases, the comma can be used appropriately to link independent ideas – when their wordings are symmetrical in structure, for instance: *I came, I saw, I conquered*; or *Swords for two, coffee for one*. (See also page 216.) But in general, the comma splice is unacceptable: however short the sentence, it is too long if it has two independent clauses linked by a mere comma.

Look out for long or dubious parentheses. All too often in complex writing, a sentence will contain within itself an extremely long and independent phrase, or even another entire sentence, that could appear just as happily in a sentence of its own. Or *should* appear in a sentence of its own, since often it is not just very long but also largely irrelevant to the sentence containing it.

? The tiny island of Saramit (in the winter at any rate: I wouldn't know about the summer, since I never like to travel too far from my Cotswold home during the summer months) still boasts a very uncrowded and unspoilt beach.

If all the material within the brackets were shifted to the end and made into a separate sentence, the passage would flow far more elegantly, and the sense would unfold far more smoothly.

An intrusive phrase or sentence of this kind is known as a parenthesis, pronounced / pə-**ren**-thə-sis /. It functions rather like a long detour off the main road during a journey – the advantage of extra scenery is usually more than offset by the extra time and effort needed. A long parenthesis usually lies within brackets (known as *parentheses*, to confuse matters), but not always. Dashes, or even – as this very sentence demonstrates – mere commas, can also serve to enclose a parenthesis. And as that previous sentence also demonstrates, you can have parentheses within parentheses. But as a rule, it is best to have nothing of the sort, particularly when the sentence is overlong or overcomplicated as it stands. As in the following quotation:

? The background to this paper has been a recognition and concern that, while in many respects the accountancy profession in the UK was constantly changing and developing to meet new situations and new requirements – in professional standards of accounting and auditing, in ethical standards, in education, in European involvement, in international involvement, in government relationships, in range of services and so on – the volume of current and urgent issues and the rate and extent of change in matters which affected the profession left most members of the profession insufficient time and energy to stand back and review the position as a whole as a basis for considering on a longer term basis the role and function of the accountancy profession, including the services to be offered, and the organisation necessary to enable it to meet its responsibilities.

– university professor,
report on the accountancy profession

To convert an opening sentence such as that into a properly simple and inviting message, you would have to do more, true enough, than just remove and transfer the double parenthesis (stretching from the first comma to the second dash). But that would at least represent a good first step. When editing or redrafting your own texts, do make sure to take that step if you ever notice a parenthesis of comparable length or intrusiveness.

Above all, say one thing at a time. An old schoolroom rule runs: One idea per sentence. This is far too simple and restrictive, and would make for very dull and jerky reading. But the underlying message remains sound: Take care not to overload a sentence; try to keep separate ideas separated, by a comma at least if not by a full stop; unravel the sentence if the first draft is too tightly packed.

Consider the following convoluted passage. It comes from a source where you might least expect to find it – the opening of a news story.

? The disclosure yesterday by Sheffield Forgemasters that the eight steel tubes seized by Customs and Excise on their way to Iraq because they 'could be used as the barrel of a large artillery gun' were actually part of a much larger consignment of 52 tubes, compounds the unanswered questions surrounding this extraordinary affair.

– David Fairhall, *The Guardian*

This sentence contains wheels within wheels within wheels, with only a single comma (and that one unjustified by the syntax) to mark them off. As the opening paragraph of a news story, it really does call for a clearer and more inviting wording. Many alternative versions come to mind (though several of them would shift the focus unacceptably). Here are two possible recastings; note how each of them dispenses the information bit by bit rather than in a single spurt:

Sheffield Forgemasters, at the centre of the Iraqi Supergun affair, yesterday succeeded only in compounding the puzzle. They disclosed that the full consignment was in fact for 52 steel tubes. The number seized by Customs and Excise (on the grounds that they 'could be used as the barrel of a large artillery gun') had been a mere eight.

When Customs and Excise seized the eight steel tubes bound for Iraq, on the grounds that they 'could be used as the barrel of a large artillery gun', several pressing questions arose. Far from answering them, Sheffield Forgemasters have only compounded the puzzle by their disclosure yesterday – that the eight impounded tubes were actually part of a much larger consignment of 52.

The next extract, unlike the last one, has plenty of commas to break up the text. Perhaps that is part of the problem: the writer felt no need for a full stop halfway through, since he knew he was strewing punctuation marks about quite generously already:

? Concern about nitrates has risen over recent years because, in some parts of the country, there has been an increase in nitrate levels in tap water mainly caused, it is thought, by more intensive farming methods with greater use of nitrogen fertilisers.

– Dr Barry Lynch, *Radio Times*

But the passage clearly does need a full stop halfway through, or at least a semicolon. The purpose of the passage is to offer the reader two *reasons* – but they are reasons for quite different phenomena in each case, and therefore deserve separate treatment in separate sentences. The first is the reason for the rise in public concern; the second is the reason for the increased nitrate levels in tap water. Properly distributed across two sentences (at least) the information would come across more clearly and more elegantly:

> Concern about nitrates has risen over recent years, because, in some parts of the country, there has been an increase in nitrate levels in tap water. This increase is mainly caused, experts believe, by more intensive farming methods with greater use of nitrogen fertilisers.

That is a start, at any rate. Perhaps you feel that each of the new sentences still suffers from overloading, and would benefit from further unpacking in turn.

Now for two particular species of overloaded sentence that deserve individual treatment.

TWO SPECIES OF OVERLOADED SENTENCE

To reduce or disentangle an overlong or over-complex sentence, it is helpful to analyse it to find the basis of its awkwardness.

Two subtle but common failings are discussed below. Spot either of them in your own writing, and you are halfway to remedying the problem.

The buried complication. What creates the complexity in the following sentence?

? However, it would appear from your letter that those items of software for incorporation within the hardware/software package are imported into the UK not by HWW, but by the customer (e.g. BritChem Islip), who will pay any VAT due on the importation . . .

– accountant's letter

Overloaded sentences just weigh the reader down.

The overloading here is not really the fault of the syntax (the sentence structure) – that is fairly straightforward. The main difficulty lies in the complicated noun phrase *those items of software for incorporation within the hardware/software package*. The poor reader first has to grasp this intricate concept; only then can he go on to follow its fortunes. The writer has failed to see the need for a two-step procedure here, and instead has shot all the information out needlessly in a single blast. The trick is to establish the concept quite clearly in an introductory sentence – to put the concept on display rather than burying it. The full stop gives the reader breathing space – he can test his comprehension by rereading the sentence until he has really mastered the concept. Once he is confident of having done this, he can join the writer in taking the next step. And the next. And so on.

> However, it would appear from your letter that there is a problem with a certain class of items – namely, those items of software for incorporation within the hardware/software package. They are imported into the UK not by HWW, but by the customer (e.g. BritChem Islip). So it is the customer who will have to pay any VAT due on the importation . . .

(Note the second full stop here, just before *So*. It is not quite so important as the first, but it does mark a

AN UNACCEPTABLY LONG SENTENCE

Consider the following overloaded sentence from a newspaper. Professional journalists, no matter how hurried, really should do better than this: it would have taken only a minute or two more to unravel the various ideas within the story and assign them to separate sentences or at least independent clauses.

?? Ernest Saunders, the former Guinness chairman and chief executive, has been given leave to apply for a High Court judicial review of his being refused legal aid to appeal to the House of Lords against the Court of Appeal's refusal to stay the action brought against him by Guinness pending the outcome of his criminal trial.

– The Independent

And here are a few nursery rhymes, 'stylishly' rewritten as a single sentence in each case. The original versions, with their several short sentences or easily distinguishable and absorbable clauses, appear on pages 633-634.

Little Bo-peep, having lost her sheep and not knowing where to find them, on being advised to leave them alone and assured that they would come home dragging their tails behind them, fell into a deep sleep, during which she dreamt she heard them bleating and from which she awoke only to find it a joke, for they were still a-fleeting, upon which she took up her little crook and, determined to find them, found them indeed, though it made her heart bleed, for they'd left their tails behind them.

There was a crooked man who walked a crooked mile, in the course of which he found a crooked sixpence upon a crooked stile, later buying a crooked cat which caught a crooked mouse, enabling them all to live together in a crooked little house.

Goosey goosey gander,
Whither shall I wander
But upstairs and downstairs
And in my lady's chamber
Where I met an old man
Who wouldn't say his prayers
And whom I took by the left leg
And threw down the stairs.

slight shift in thinking again, and once more allows the reader a brief pause to collect his thoughts.)

The non sequitur. Sometimes an overloaded sentence not only contains two unrelated ideas, but suggests – through its grammatical form – that they do in fact have some close relation to each other:

X Awarded the MBE in 1965 for her charity work, she has also appeared in a minor film role.

That kind of thing. It is known as a non sequitur, pronounced / **non sek**wi-tər /, originally a Latin phrase meaning 'it does not follow'. Among the most common culprits are photo captions and brief pen-portraits:

?? GIRAUDOUX, Jean (1882-1944):
French playwright
A professional diplomat, Giraudoux had a tremendous stage vogue in France in the 1930s.
– Kenneth McLeish,
The Penguin Companion to the Arts
in the Twentieth Century

?? Meireles, Cecilia ... Orphaned at three, she travelled widely, visiting the Orient which has been a lasting influence on her work.
– Denis Brass,
in The Fontana Dictionary of Modern Thinkers

?? Back on our screens as Taggart's sidekick (ITV, Thursday), James began his career as a hospital lab technician, where he met his wife Jacqui, who was also working there.
– TV Times

Advertisements and brochures are also often guilty of non sequiturs – the rhythm and momentum lure the copywriter into making silly connections:

X Intended as an anti-personnel device, Personal Revenger has an integral key ring and a torch ... Measuring just 5" x 4", the Multi-Sharp is a DIY necessity.
– gift store catalogue

X Situated in one of Highgate's premier roads this three-bedroom 1st floor flat has full gas central heating. Hewn from an imposing Victorian property the flat is in reasonable condition.
– estate agent's brochure

Perhaps the non sequitur arises each time through the writer's attempt to back into the sentence – that is, to reverse the usual structure by placing the main clause at the end rather than at the beginning. This is a risky procedure, and should be used very sparingly in English. When handled properly, however, it can be very effective in conveying information, by building up the reader's interest before revealing the point – so long as the opening phrase or phrases really do relate closely to the main clause. Here is a daring example that carries a successful rhetorical punch:

> *The Heart.* Weighing less than one pound, the size of a fist, having scant resemblance to the simple arrow-pierced emblem carved on trees, pumping the body's entire blood content through its chambers every minute, beating throughout life, growing from less than an ounce at birth, starting work months before and continuing to beat thereafter, the heart is a formidable pump.
>
> – Anthony Smith, *The Body*

PUT THE WEIGHT NEAR THE FRONT

As a rule get to the point as quickly as possible – whether in a report, a paragraph, or a sentence.

There are exceptions, of course: you may want to build up to a dramatic climax, or to surprise the reader . . . in which case, delay getting to the point as long as possible – whether in a joke, a suspense story, or a sentence once again.

In the following quotation, for instance, in the second sentence, the author deliberately, for the sake of rhetorical effect, holds back the main point until the very end:

> But Vic didn't resent her high-flown language. That she used it unselfconsciously in conversation with him, whereas she had spoken normal English to the rest of the family, he took as a kind of compliment.
>
> – David Lodge, *Nice Work*

But in most everyday prose, the sentence should announce its intention early on. Be punctual – first get the point across, and only then fill in the background or add the details.

Look again at the opening sentence of this section. It would surely lose a lot in clarity and impact if it put off the main clause till the end:

? As a rule – whether in a report, a paragraph, or a sentence – get to the point as quickly as possible.

Such 'unpunctuality' is particularly noticeable in sentences containing a list of details or examples. All too often, inexperienced writers set about enumerating all the items on the list before actually explaining what the significance of the list happens to be:

? During the 1960s the relaxation of sterling controls, the opening of the money markets and the expansion in corporate finance activities through a long series of contested mergers and acquisitions, gave rise to a spate of growth and further diversification of activities.

> – draft chapter,
> in a handbook on financial services

The ordering of elements here is quite exasperating. The poor reader has to keep in his mind three financial developments without understanding the reason for grouping them together. Only at the end, once the point is made in the final clause, can he make sense of them. It is rather like handing a guest three hot chestnuts in quick succession, which he has to juggle desperately until you get round to giving him a plate. Far better to offer the plate first, if you have any consideration for your guest. If you have any consideration for your reader, you would rewrite that frustrating sentence above. Here are two ways of doing it:

> The 1960s saw a spate of growth and further diversification of activities, thanks to three main developments:
>
> – the relaxation of sterling controls
> – the opening of the money markets
> – the expansion in corporate finance activities through a long series of contested mergers and acquisitions

This is a simple reversal of the two principal sections of the sentence: the causes and the results. A slightly more complex rewrite involves splitting up one of the sections (the causes) – mention it near the beginning of the sentence, but give the details of it at the end of the sentence. So:

> During the 1960s various factors gave rise to a spate of growth and further diversification of activities. The three principal factors were these:
>
> – the relaxation of sterling controls
> – the opening of the money markets
> – the expansion in corporate finance activities through a long series of contested mergers and acquisitions

One giveaway in the original sentence was the positioning of the main verb – right near the end. This suggests a quick-check test that you can apply

SENTENCES WITHOUT FULL VERBS

The schoolroom rule that 'every sentence must have a full verb, and stand on its own as a complete utterance' may well be a good rule for schoolroom writing. But not for all writing. Effective style resists being shackled in that way. If a short verbless sentence or 'sentence fragment' is best suited to convey the message – as the second sentence of this paragraph is – then that is the sentence to use.

A verbless sentence is fairly common in answer to questions – *Of course not. Fine, thank you* – and sometimes in questions themselves: *What now? How so? The alternative?*

It often serves as a brief, punchy introduction to some important statement: *To business. . . . So much for that proposal . . .*

It can be strikingly effective as a supplement, qualification, or contradiction of a statement:

She looks 90 years old. Perhaps older.

Criticism as a profession is losing, has lost, much of its respectability. Pity, that, and a sad thought for the coming year.
– Frank Delaney, *The Listener*

Professor Terence blithely airs his reactionary views at banquets and conferences alike. A kind of upper-class Alf Garnett.

Many 'sentence fragments' are, in effect, subordinate clauses of a complex sentence, detached from the main clause and presented as a separate unit for greater emphasis:

And so my dear brother is gone. Though not forgotten.
They advised me to sell up and move to Chicago. Which is what I did.

(The last sentence here, or sentence fragment, does have a full verb, but would not ordinarily stand on its own as 'a complete utterance'.)

Finally, verbless sentences and sentence fragments can be used for deliberate dramatic or descriptive purposes:

The light retreats slowly, the wind drops, the birds return to their nests. Twilight and silence. A star quivers into view. Then another, and another. Until the whole night sky is ablaze.

Sentence fragments, including verbless sentences, achieve their effects by means of contrast – contrast with self-sufficient sentences that do have full verbs. If overused, the sentence fragment loses its rarity value and hence its effectiveness. Furthermore, it begins to draw attention to itself and threatens to become an irritating mannerism. If it is used sparingly, however, it can prove very effective in imparting ideas or creating atmosphere; and that is sufficient justification of it, whatever the schoolroom view may be.

to all long, straggly sentences: identify the main verb; if it appears near the end, try to bring it nearer to the beginning. It will surprise you how much more readable the sentence suddenly becomes – it now sounds more like English and less like German. Here, now, is another example of the overdelayed main verb:

? The death of Mrs Enid Sylvester, former president of the National Welfare Institute and a life-long campaigner for the rights of the disabled has been announced.

Newswriters on the BBC are usually very mindful of the problem here. You might hear the newsreader say, in a very brief report:

The death of Mrs Enid Sylvester has been announced.

But in the expanded version, the verb *has been announced* cannot comfortably remain at the end of the sentence. The experienced newswriter would shift it to a position near the beginning of the sentence, and what you would hear is this:

The death has been announced of Mrs Enid Sylvester, former president of the National Welfare Institute and a life-long campaigner for the rights of the disabled.

Even if the main verb appears near the beginning, a sentence might still be guilty of 'unpunctuality' – some other crucial words are loitering at the end. For example:

? We are writing to bring certain matters arising from our inter-departmental meeting of 25 May 1990 to your attention.

SENTENCE TYPES – MANY AND VARIED KINDS OF CONSTRUCTION

Structuring a sentence is something that comes naturally to most good and experienced writers – and to many weak and inexperienced writers too, unfortunately.

A great many factors should go into choosing and ordering the information: for example, the relative importance you attach to each of the elements, the tone and emphasis you want to convey, or the links you want to establish with the sentence that comes before.

Sentences come in various forms according to the way you analyse them.

If classified according to its purpose, a sentence might be: a *statement*, a *question*, an *exclamation*, an *imperative* (command).

(For more details on these and other technical terms, see pages 167-172.)

If classified according to the kinds of clause it contains, a sentence might be:

☐ simple – having only one clause: *They need our help.*

☐ compound – having two or more main clauses: *They need our help, and we can give it, but they won't accept anything from us.*

☐ complex – having one main clause and one or more subordinate clauses: *They need our help, though they don't like to admit it.*

☐ compound-complex – having two or more main clauses and one or more subordinate clauses: *They need our help and will get it when we arrive, though they'll resent it.*

If classified according to the arrangement of its clauses, a sentence may take different names again. A compound sentence, for instance, may also be a *balanced* sentence – its clauses are carefully arranged to support one another in structure and meaning: *I came, I saw, I conquered; They have a shortage and we have a surplus, so two problems have a solution.*

Or it may be an *antithetical* sentence – the clauses balance each other in structure but contrast in meaning: *Man proposes, God disposes; They are too proud to ask for help, but they are too needy to refuse it.*

And a complex sentence subdivides in turn. It will usually have one of two basic structures – *loose* or *periodic*.

In a loose sentence the main clause (or the main point) comes first, with the subordinate clause/s following: *They resented our arrival instead of welcoming us, even though they needed our help.* In a periodic sentence, the main clause or point comes last, with the subordinate clause/s preceding it: *Even though they needed our help, instead of welcoming us they resented our arrival.* (A mixture of these two basic structures produces a mixed sentence, in which the main clause lies in the middle. *Even though they needed our help, they resented our arrival instead of welcoming us.*)

An extended passage of good mature prose will usually contain most of these kinds of sentence, and so it should: variety helps to keep the reader interested.

Weak or inexperienced writers often reveal their inadequacy by getting the mixture wrong. Young children tend to rely exclusively on simple or compound sentences, avoiding the sophistication of complex sentences; business managers and professional people tend to go to the other extreme, churning out dull complex or compound-complex sentences one after another and avoiding the refreshing sharpness and sparkle of simple sentences.

One odd failing of so much business writing is its preference for the periodic sentence over the loose sentence – that is, its tendency to leave the main point till last, to put the 'weight' of the sentence at the end. This is perhaps due to half-remembered school lessons: the periodic sentence enjoyed high status as more 'elegant'. Put the weight at the end, misguided teachers would say, and your writing will then assume an impressively solemn or sophisticated tone.

That may apply – though only occasionally – to school essays, and to descriptive and narrative writing generally. But for most everyday writing, the modern advice is quite the reverse: Put the weight near the front.

Transfer the final phrase to an earlier position, and the reader will be able to comprehend the sentence much more quickly and easily:

> We are writing to bring to your attention certain matters arising from our interdepartmental meeting of 25 May 1990.

Similarly:

? The police are treating the death of Mrs Enid Sylvester, former president of the National Welfare Institute and a life-long campaigner for the rights of the disabled, as suspicious.

The phrase *as suspicious* should move from the end to an earlier position:

> The police are treating as suspicious the death of Mrs Enid Sylvester, former president of the National Welfare Institute and a life-long campaigner for the rights of the disabled.

The writer of the following note got it right, positioning the phrase *before 9.00 pm* in mid-sentence rather than its 'natural' position at the end of the sentence:

> The BBC does not broadcast before 9.00 pm programmes that it believes to be unsuitable for children.
>
> – note in *Radio Times*

Sometimes, unfortunately, the unpunctual sentence does not quite lend itself to such a straightforward adjustment. In the following two examples, you cannot simply take the delayed phrase and move it to an earlier position:

? Wasn't the pie in which four-and-twenty blackbirds were baked and which on being opened prompted the birds to sing a dainty dish to set before the king?

? The governor of Alaska declared Prince William Sound and the nearby port of Valdez, the southern terminal of the trans-Alaska oil pipeline, a disaster area.

> – James Bone and Andrew Morgan, *The Times*

The best way of dealing with the first of these sentences is to recast it quite drastically – along the lines of Mother Goose's original version, perhaps (see pages 633 and 634).

In the second sentence, you could try a subtle trick similar to one mentioned earlier – breaking up a complex noun phrase into two, and inserting the overdelayed end-phrase into the middle:

> The governor of Alaska declared Prince William Sound a disaster area, together with the nearby port of Valdez, the southern terminal of the trans-Alaska oil pipeline.

Here is the best strategy, then, when faced with unpunctual sentences. The first step is to try shuffling the elements: take the overdelayed end-phrase and try slotting it in at various points earlier in the sentence. If that works, well and good. If not, move on to the second step: recast the sentence.

THE 'UNPUNCTUAL' SENTENCE

Try this short exercise in rewriting 'unpunctual' sentences. Redraft each of the three passages below. You may have to vary your technique from one to the next: the last of them, for instance, needs a thorough restructuring. Suggested answers appear in the quiz answers section, pages 633-648.

1. **?** Owing to a lack of communication between departments, key management issues of utilisation, matching property to service needs, the reduction of running costs, and indirectly owned property are not being addressed by the corporation.

   – management consultant's report

2. **?** The Prime Minister's decision to refuse funding for a survey of sexual behaviour to further research about the spread of Aids, and a new way of counting people in the poorest category of the population which reduced the number by one million, caused controversy.

   – Rosie Waterhouse, *The Independent*

3. **?** Just how the secret of Andrew Young's July 26 meeting with Zehdi Labib Terzi, the leader of the permanent UN observer mission of the PLO, got out is [itself] still a secret.

   – *San Francisco Chronicle*

THE PASSIVE

The following two sentences are virtually identical in meaning, but not in impact. Which of them has the greater force?

> If a particular idea can be expressed adequately in both the active and the passive voice, it is recommended that the active voice usually be used, so long as that can be done without the meaning or emphasis being impaired.

If you can express a particular idea adequately in both the active and the passive voice, you should usually use the active voice, so long as you can do so without impairing the meaning or emphasis.

The second, surely. It conveys the advice far more directly and forcefully. This is thanks largely to its *active* verbs. That is, the subject of each clause (*you*) is acting out the verb – actually *doing* the impairing, the using, the expressing, and so on.

The first of the sample sentences is feeble and mealy-mouthed by comparison. It reads perhaps like a hesitant suggestion rather than a piece of forthright advice. It is strangely impersonal – as if addressed to a computer rather than to human beings. And this effect is largely due to all the passive verbs. That is, the subject of each clause (*idea, voice, emphasis,* and so on) is on the receiving end of the action of the verb – the impairing, for example, is here done to the subject (*emphasis*), whereas in the other sample sentence the impairing is done by the subject (*you*).

To put it another way: with an active verb, the subject is *doing something*; with a passive verb, the subject is *having something done to it*. Or more technically, in the active voice the grammatical subject is also the logical subject (actor, doer, agent) of the verb, whereas in the passive voice the grammatical subject is the logical *object* (sufferer, victim, receiver) of the verb. (For further details of active and passive, see page 168.)

Active verbs also differ from passive verbs in the effect they tend to produce. As the very word suggests, an *active* verb typically creates a strong and vigorous impression. And a *passive* verb, as the very word suggests, seems to convey a docile and timid impression. Compare this next overdelicate and passive piece of advice – from a manual for writers, of all places – with the more active version that follows it:

? In their own interests writers and others are strongly advised to make preliminary enquiries before submitting MSS., and to ascertain terms of work. Commission varies. The details given in the following entries should be noted carefully in respect of syndication.

– Writers' and Artists' Year Book

We strongly advise writers and others, in their own interests, to make preliminary enquiries before submitting MSS., and to ascertain terms of

work. Commission varies. When it comes to syndication, note carefully the details in the following entries.

This is not to urge that you should banish passive verbs altogether from your writing. They certainly have their uses, for example:

☐ when the doer of the action is unknown, uncertain, or irrelevant: *If magnesium is exposed to oxygen, it ignites immediately*

☐ in many standard phrases or idioms: *The game was abandoned; not to be sneezed at; someone to be reckoned with.* (But some passive phrases are just silly: **?** *A good time was had by all*)

☐ when the focus is already on the object of the action: *Those gravestones seem to invite bad luck – last night they were desecrated once again by a vandal*

☐ when it would add some variety to the prose, or improve the rhythm, or help to sharpen a joke, or produce some other useful stylistic effect

But on the whole, try to use the active voice rather than the passive. It not only engages the reader's attention more firmly; it also makes things easier for the reader to understand.

When editing your writing, you can usually correct needless passive verbs to active verbs quite easily. Just switch the positions of the two key words or phrases, and adjust the verb.

So: *Our car was then tested by your workman* becomes *Your workman then tested our car.*

And: *The police were immediately informed* (the words *by us* being left unstated here) becomes *We immediately informed the police.*

Sometimes you can fiddle more freely with a clumsy passive construction. Consider this quotation:

It is important for audit purposes that reconciliations are reviewed by management and that this review is verified.

– auditor's report

Get rid of the two passives, certainly, but why not streamline the whole sentence at the same time?

For audit purposes, the managers should review reconciliations and also verify this review.

Some passive sentences are 'defective' in that the doer-element is missing: there is no *by*-phrase, either explicit or unstated. Here are three examples:

A crisis was precipitated when the chairman walked out.

When food intake is reduced, the metabolism is regulated immediately.

Fuel costs are included in the Sundry column.

Clearly you cannot convert such sentences to the active form – what would you use for the subject of the sentence? But if you do want to tighten them up slightly, you can always use a different verb – an intransitive verb (roughly, a verb that does not take an object: see page 169). So:

A crisis arose when the chairman resigned.

When food intake declines, the metabolism compensates immediately.

Fuel costs appear in the Sundry column.

Though passive verbs have their uses, as outlined above, all too often writers resort to the passive for very dubious reasons:

☐ it supposedly sounds impressive: **?** *Two oddities were noted by our inspectors, and duly reported to the assessor* (actually, only bureaucratic minds are impressed by such language)

☐ it supposedly sounds more courteous or dignified: **?** *Your cooperation is greatly appreciated;* **?** *The inconvenience caused is deeply regretted* (more formal and impersonal, certainly, than *We greatly appreciate your cooperation* and *I deeply regret the inconvenience*)

☐ it supposedly sounds less forward, since it can avoid personal pronouns such as *I, we,* and *you*: **?** *Steps should be taken* . . . **?** *Scrupulous records should be kept* . . . (why assume that your readers are so touchy when it comes to receiving advice?)

☐ it relieves the writer of personal responsibility: **?** *It is recommended that* . . . (but would such wording really let you off the hook more readily than if you had written *I recommend that* . . . ?)

☐ it supposedly conveys a tone of scientific objectivity: **?** *Some signs of subsidence were observed* . . . (pseudo-scientific, maybe – which intelligent readers will find *un*impressive)

Of those suffering from passivitis of this kind, one group stands out: report writers, of all kinds.

? A blow was inflicted to the right temple some hours earlier, and severe concussion must have been sustained.

? The damp course was inspected thoroughly, and various inadequacies detected. Damp patches were clearly observed on two of the cellar walls.

? Since late orders are processed manually, extra risks are incurred. The program should be modified to enable late orders to be dealt with through the computerised stock control system instead.

Here is an extended analysis and recommendation from a report on the efficiency of a business:

? Purchases are made using numbered order forms, copies of which are retained. On delivery of the goods, the order is checked and the supplier's delivery note is usually, but not always, retained. There is no other documentary record of goods received from suppliers having been checked on receipt.

On receipt of purchase invoices, the details are logged and the invoices passed to the relevant head of department to check the details . . .

We recommend that a formal system of checking and recording goods received be introduced. We further recommend that all purchase invoices be checked against order forms and records of goods received prior to authorisation.

– management consultant's report

At least the writer says *We recommend that* rather than *It is recommended that*. A small mercy, but why did the writer not use active verbs and plain wording throughout?

Whenever your buyers make a purchase, they use a numbered order form, and retain a copy of it. On delivery of the goods, your warehouse attendant will check the order and usually, though not always, retain the supplier's delivery note . . .

We recommend that you introduce a formal system of checking and recording goods . . .

And so on. Perhaps he felt that the client would find such plain wording unimpressively blunt or even amateurish. 'Paying a high fee, the client expects high style too, not just good advice; he wants his money's worth in prose as well as in expertise.'

Or so the writer is assuming. But it is only an assumption – have the consultants of the world ever put it to the test? If you happen to write reports of this kind – whether for a client or for the boss –

PASSIVE OR IMPERATIVE

Here is another piece of ponderous prose that relies heavily on the passive voice:

SUBMITTING MANUSCRIPTS

? Care should be taken when submitting manuscripts to book publishers. A suitable publisher should be chosen, by a study of his list of publications or an examination in the bookshops of the type of books in which he specialises. It is a waste of time and money to send the typescript of a novel to a publisher who publishes no fiction, or poetry to one who publishes no verse, though all too often this is done. A preliminary letter is appreciated by most publishers, and this should outline the nature and extent of the typescript and enquire whether the publisher would be prepared to read it (writers have been known to send out such letters of enquiry in duplicated form, an approach not calculated to stimulate a publisher's interest). It is desirable to enclose the cost of return postage when submitting the typescript and finally it must be understood that although every reasonable care is taken of material in the Publishers' possession, responsibility cannot be accepted for any loss or damage thereto.

Authors are strongly advised not to pay for the publication of their work. If a MS. is worth publishing, a reputable publisher will undertake its publication at his own expense, except possibly for works of an academic nature. In this connection attention is called to the paragraphs on *Self-publishing* and *Vanity publishing*, at the end of this section.

–Writers' and Artists' Year Book

This extract is essentially a piece of extended advice. But why does it not use simple imperatives to express the advice, as most advisers do? *Take care when submitting manuscripts ... Choose a suitable publisher ...*

Presumably the writer of these paragraphs, oversensitive to the reader's supposed sense of dignity, felt that such forthright imperative wording would seem rather coarse or familiar.

Hence the use of statements rather than imperatives or instructions – statements couched in the passive, and sounding fussy as a result: *Care should be taken...A suitable publisher should be chosen ...* and so on.

Note two other off-putting features recurring throughout the passage:

☐ the grandiose vocabulary: *enquire* (= *ask*), *desirable*, and *thereto*, for instance

☐ the use of abstract nouns: for instance,... *works of an academic nature ...; ...by a study of his publications or an examination ... of the type of books ...* (how much more vividly it reads when phrased as *studying his list of publications or examining... the type of book ...*)

Try now to identify all the uses of the passive in the text. Then rewrite the passage in a more forceful form, eliminating the passives wherever possible, simplifying the vocabulary, and reducing the number of abstract nouns. For the answers, see pages 633-648.

Here now are two nursery rhymes recast, in the genteel or bureaucratic style, to include the passive in preference to the active wherever it is possible. The original versions, for the purpose of comparison, appear in the quiz answers section, pages 633 and 634.

Cross patch,
The latch should be drawn.
It is further recommended that sitting by
   the fire take place and that spinning be
   attempted.
A cup should be taken,
And drunk up.
It is advised that the neighbours then be
   called in.

A little pony named Dapple Grey
Was owned by me.
He was sent to a lady
To be ridden a mile away.
He was whipped by her, he was slashed by
   her,
He was ridden through the mire:
My pony will now not be lent by me
For any lady's hire.

why not try using simple active verbs wherever possible, and watching the reader's response? The chances are that he or she will find it refreshingly forthright and lucid, and welcome the opportunity of taking in your comments and advice without having to decode them first.

One useful tip – a rough test for passivitis that you can conduct quickly and easily. Cast your eye down the page looking for all of these 'dangerous' words: *is, are, was, were*, and *be, been, being*, especially in conjunction with the *-ed* ending of another verb (as in **were** *punish***ed**, or *have* **been** *notifi***ed**).

In an over-passive text they will show up in abundance, dotted about all over the page. Not that every *is* or *are* indicates a passive verb, but a surfeit of them certainly suggests a surfeit of passives, and alerts you to the need to redraft the passage into a more active – and hence more engaging, more accessible – style.

To sum up (using the active-voice version of the advice at the start of this section):

If you can express a particular idea adequately in both the active and the passive voice, you should usually use the active voice, so long as you can do so without impairing the meaning or emphasis.

THE VERB TO BE

Passive verbs are not the only 'inactive' verbs. A number of verbs also display very little liveliness in their own right: the verb *to be* in particular (*is, are, was, has been*, and so on) and the related verbs *become* and *seem*.

These verbs rank among the most common and useful in the language, and the last thing you should do is shun them.

But do notice, and remember, that they tend to be very bland: as with rice or tofu, such flavour as they have is absorbed from their surroundings.

Try, accordingly, to replace them from time to time. Precisely because they are so useful, inexperienced writers tend to rely on them excessively, even when obvious substitutes put in a claim.

Instead of the tired old phrasing, such as *The debts are still a source of anxiety*, try a slightly sharper version such as *The debts remain a source of anxiety*, or a snappier, more personal version such as *We continue to worry about the debts*. Instead of the bland wording *Method A is much better than*

TO BE OR – SOME OTHER VERB

As an exercise, write new versions of the following sentences, eliminating the verb *to be* each time – either by introducing a 'fuller' and more vivid verb in its place, or by rephrasing things quite drastically. A set of possible answers appears on pages 633-648.

It is vital that you bring the documents with you.

There are far too many items on the agenda.

There is no shortage of ideas.

It would be a great help to us if you withdrew your objection.

It would be pointless to carry on taking those pills.

Menu C is the commonest choice among diners.

A hybrid word is a combination of word-elements from two or more languages.

Hybrid words used to be the object of pedants' ridicule.

There are several types of hybrid word.

Punishing a child disproportionately is a sure way of causing resentment rather than cooperation.

Life is still hard for the ethnic Germans, of whom there are still about two million within Soviet borders.

Method B, try using a more active verb: *Method A surpasses/outshines/eclipses Method B*.

Two particularly overworked formulas are *there is* (or *there are*) and *It is*.

First, *there is/are*:

There are no copies left.
There are twelve applicants for the one job.
There's a question you're going to answer.
There have been no subsequent violations.

What about these punchier variations?

No copies remain.
Twelve people have applied for the one job.
You're going to answer a question.
No subsequent violations took place.

As for the phrase *it is*:

> *It is necessary to point out that* payment falls due on Monday.
>
> *It is important to remember that* the original deadline has already passed.
>
> *It is a well-attested fact that* church attendance actually increased last year.
>
> *It should be clear by now that* methane fully deserves the title 'greenhouse gas'.

Any number of tighter and more effective opening phrases come to mind:

> *I have to point out that* payment falls due on Monday.
>
> *Remember that* the deadline is fast approaching.
>
> *Surveys have shown that* church attendance actually increased last year.
>
> *Clearly then*, methane deserves the title 'greenhouse gas'.

In fact, in most contexts all four of the *it is* formulas listed above could quite happily stand down in favour of the single phrase *Note that* – as in *Note that church attendance actually increased last year* – or it could even disappear without any replacement whatsoever.

After all, can the extended sentence *It is necessary to point out that payment falls due on Monday* really claim any greater force or effectiveness than a very short and pointed sentence such as *Payment falls due on Monday*?

OUT OF COURT AT WIMBLEDON

Here is the text printed on the back of a ticket for a centre court seat at Wimbledon during the 1987 tennis tournament. Some legalese is perhaps unavoidable, since the ticket is a legal document. But in general, the wording is needlessly pompous, bureaucratic, and curt, rude in tone, and poor in grammar and style. Identify as many flaws as you can in clause (i). Then write a 'plain English' version of the entire text, conveying the same information in a way that is both less objectionable and easier to follow. Answers on pages 633-648.

?? CONDITIONS OF SALE

(i) In the event of any curtailment or abandonment of play due to any cause whatsoever, it is regretted that no refund can be made to the holder hereof.

(ii) The holder of this ticket is expressly warned that it is NOT available for any day except that printed on the face thereof.

(iii) The AELTC regrets that it is not able to exchange tickets.

(iv) The Committee reserves the right to refuse admission.

(v) Flashlight photography is forbidden.

Paragraphs – One Topic at a Time

Glance quickly at the two upper pages reproduced in the panel opposite, and decide which of them looks more inviting to read.

If you prefer the second, as most people do, this is largely because it simply contains more paragraph breaks. On appearance alone, with its short chunky paragraphs, it seems to promise the reader a more interesting time than the first page does.

That first page looks very old-fashioned and very discouraging, with its single paragraph break near the top and its wall of unbroken print after that. (In the book from which it comes, several paragraphs run to nearly three pages each.)

The prospect of reading such a page is rather like that of wading through a marsh without the benefit of stepping-stones.

Paragraphs, then, divide up a piece of writing in an appealing and hospitable way. Whether indented from the margin or – as in this book – set off by an extra line of space above and below, they offer resting places for the reader's eye and mind.

But they have a more important function than that: hinting at the structure and development of the whole text. Each paragraph break tells the reader, in effect, that he has finished with one topic or theme and is now embarking on a new one.

The traditional rule is: one theme or topic per paragraph.

> Just as the sentence contains one idea in all its fullness, so the paragraph should embrace a distinct episode.
>
> – Winston Churchill, *My Early Life*

LONG PARAGRAPHS VS SHORT PARAGRAPHS

32   ETHICS SINCE 1900

could actually *consist in* its being consistent with other statements, though this might be a test of its truth.

Metaphysical philosophers, then, stand convicted of the naturalistic fallacy. So far are they from reinstating ethics, after the ravages upon it of the utilitarians, that they actually make matters worse, for the non-naturalism of their version of the fallacy might deceive people into thinking that no fallacy had been committed. Moore's treatment of the metaphysical moral philosophers is a particularly good example of the extreme and marvellous literalness of his mind. He represents metaphysicians as just asserting that a number of extraordinary objects, such as the true self, or the real will, exist; and as simply asserting that goodness is to be analysed in terms of such objects. Of course they do assert these things, but not perhaps quite in the manner which Moore suggests. If anyone started to expound a metaphysical system in Moore's language, or Moore's tone of voice, he would not, it is true, win much acceptance for his theory. But what Moore in no way allows for, and it may be thought rightly, is the very different tone of voice of these philosophers themselves. Moore makes no concessions to the satisfaction which is to be gained from the contemplation of a highly general theory, from which truths about human conduct are to be deduced, as a mere part of the whole. This is the kind of satisfaction which is to be got from reading Spinoza, in whose system human passions and human behaviour are fitted into the general scheme, and propositions about them are supposedly deduced with the rigour of Euclid from propositions about the nature of substance. It would be useless, as a means of giving this particular kind of pleasure, to invent a system, the point of which was exclusively to account for human obligations and which, in order to do this, considered nothing but human nature. The metaphysical pleasure precisely consists in *not* being the centre of the universe, but in seeing familiar problems, such as the problem of how it is right to behave, somehow reduced, and also answered, by being shown to be part of a

56   REASON IN ETHICS

of philosophical ethics is largely a record of attempts to identify evaluation with some form of inductive or deductive inference.)

All the same, past practice does not justify present neglect. We are all familiar with the idea of 'giving reasons' in contexts other than logical, mathematical and factual. The most that can be said for the advocate of the imperative doctrine is that this wider use of 'reason' and 'valid' is an everyday and colloquial, rather than an esoteric and technical one. But this does not justify him in declaring that ethical judgements have *no* validity: all that it does is to help to explain the logical temptation to which he gives way.

Furthermore, past practice, conditioning present preoccupations, can hardly be the only reason for the plausibility of the imperative doctrine. It would be surprising if no deeper, 'paralogistic' source could be found—and I think it can.

Historically, as I pointed out, the imperative approach is a reaction against the objective and subjective approaches. Like so many reactions, it goes a little too far, and in doing so makes the same mistake as its opponents.

'When two people are in ethical disagreement,' said the first philosopher, 'they contradict one another. If they are to do this, there must be something in the object they are discussing for them to contradict one another about. Therefore, goodness must be a property of the object.'

'Nonsense!' replied the second philosopher. 'Goodness is no property of the object. All they are doing is expressing divergent reactions to the object: the contradiction is only apparent. It is in their attitudes towards the object, not about any property of it, that they disagree.'

'A plague on both your houses!' retorts our third philosopher. 'You're both overlooking the rhetorical force of ethical judgements. People who have ethical disagreements are not talking about their own attitudes, and they are not talking about any property of the object either. The truth of the matter is that they

The page above, with its slab of almost unbroken print, looks very daunting to read.

This page – from a different book – has many short paragraphs, and looks fairly inviting.

– 39 –

weight of insights can grow so great that the only feasible vehicle for it is the capacious novel-sequence.

Empiricism then, long discredited, was on the retreat, not just in the field of psychology, but on other fronts too. In physical science, Einstein and Heisenberg were bringing the old notions of physical reality into question. In philosophy, an early existential thrust routed all avowedly systematic ontologies, and showed them to be inadequate as a basis for fiction. "Felt life" in the novel, the Jamesian "illusion of life", was alone true to the new philosophical agnosticism. Even in the American heyday of naturalism, a concerted avante garde was always snapping at its heels, and proposing alternative technical mechanisms – mechanisms of planned derangement, devised to crack open reality and release its energies: symbol, myth, temporal dislocations, and so on. Bergsonian views of time pervaded the intellectual atmosphere, and were absorbed by writers such as Proust and Thomas Wolfe. Theories of psychoanalysis precipitated an outbreak of minutely detailed self-scrutiny, manifesting itself in so many novels and in all those autobiographical sequences already enumerated. Sholem Asch's Three Cities trilogy was written explicitly with Freud's theories in mind. Abnormal psychology was humanised and made comprehensible. And the emphases in speculative normal psychology encouraged the proliferation in fiction of detailed accounts of childhood, the unravelling of memories, and records of dreams. New techniques developed to deal with this subject-matter – conjuring with the time-sequence, random association of ideas, and stream-of-consciousness – all demanding great concentration and collaboration of the reader. And this in turn required an exhaustive spelling out of the cues if decipherment was to be at all accurate.

Analogously, an intensifying and destabilising secularisation meant that novelists could no longer leave unsaid their background of assumptions, and that they had to agonise over and justify at length any opinions which they did hold. This absence of old certainties made the writer diffident even with regard to his analyses of his own characters. It has been suggested that Romain Rolland was so bad ("neurotic" might better describe it) that he could not rest content unless each point-of-view were represented in depicting a personality or an incident. Much the same

'Urgent' moves on new nuclear link to cancer

By ANDREW LOUDON

THE Government last night promised 'urgent consideration' of a new study linking the nuclear industry to child leukaemia.

Researchers said the reproductive systems of men working at British Nuclear Fuels' Cumbria reprocessing plant could have been damaged by radiation before they became fathers.

They said it could have caused genetic mutations in sperm and their children might then have been born with a higher than normal risk of developing leukaemia.

Junior Health Minister Roger Freeman, whose department commissioned the research to look at a 'cluster' of leukaemia cases near the plant, said the Government noted the results of the study 'with concern' and had referred them to the Committee on Medical Aspects of Radiation in the Environment (COMARE).

Health Secretary Kenneth Clarke, speaking later on BBC television, said: 'When you look at acceptable costs in the industry, leukaemia is not an acceptable cost.

'The nuclear industry gets exposed to more scrutiny and higher safety standards than any other. So long as we can make it really safe there are great advantages in nuclear power.

'The management of British Nuclear Fuels now need to address themselves urgently to make sure exposure to individuals working at Sellafield does not give rise to risks of this kind.'

BNF said the report's main conclusion was unexpected.

A spokesman said: 'We expect that there will be concern because of the implications of the report. We are offering medical counselling for anyone who wants it.'

FULL STORY: PAGE 17

An academic thesis or research report will tend to have extremely long paragraphs.

In many newspaper articles, the typical paragraph consists of just a single sentence.

(The question remains, of course – how to define a theme or topic or episode? The best rule of thumb is: narrowly. The tighter the limits, the safer you are.)

In a complicated research report or academic study, say, a single paragraph might extend over a page or more. In advertising and light journalism, by contrast, every sentence often begins a new paragraph. (See the lower two pages reproduced in the panel on page 53.)

Studies have shown that short paragraphs greatly improve the 'readability' of any extended passage of writing. Readers find the short paragraph less daunting, and their concentration and comprehension benefit markedly. Accordingly, editors and publishers nowadays frown on the very lengthy paragraph, and insist on subdividing it into two or more smaller paragraphs even if this means splitting up a single 'theme'.

The converse does not hold good, however. Two distinct topics need two distinct paragraphs, no matter how short these paragraphs may be. In the following passage, for instance, each of the current paragraphs cries out for subdividing.

? All the harbour restaurants serve good food. I recommend Halil's, Set (for fish), Rihtim and Marti. A stroll after lunch in the old town will reveal fragments of Venetian wall while the castle, apart from its intrinsic interest, now houses the oldest vessel ever to have been raised from the sea bed: parts of the hull of a Greek trader of circa 300BC, brought up a half a mile offshore in 1969, still with amphorae, oil flasks, plates and even jars of almonds preserved within it.

Girne's shops are well-stocked now. Among local products, the pottery, sheepskin and glasswork are good. I like to have a haircut when I'm abroad: the barbers are generally cheaper and always more attentive. The signs to look for here are *berber* or *kuafur*. An expatriate brigadier gave me good advice: 'Ask for "Army Short but not Turkish Army Short".'

– Richard Snailham, *The Observer*

In each paragraph the break should come between the second and third sentences. This redistributes the information into four tidy paragraphs altogether, each dealing appropriately with its own topic or theme. (The second of the four paragraphs would now benefit in turn from subdividing into two or three separate sentences.)

ORDERING OF SENTENCES

Just as the words within a sentence should appear in the best possible order, so the sentences within a paragraph should be ordered appropriately – no leaps of logic, no intrusions between two crucially connected steps in your argument. An obvious requirement, perhaps – but not so easy to fulfil.

To bring the point home, consider the following jumble of sentences from a modern novel. In their original order they formed a single full paragraph. (In the paragraph preceding it, the heroine had heard the bell ring, and set off to open the front door.) Try to rearrange the sentences to restore them to their proper well-structured sequence.

1. He seemed to be hunched up in a funny way, which must have been why she had not known him at once.

2. Then Tim's voice asked if he could come in.

3. At first she failed to recognise the person standing outside.

4. When she could see his face properly it was quite a shock.

5. The light was patchy and the general shape of whoever it was told her nothing.

The correct sequence, as followed in the actual novel, runs 3, 5, 2, 1, 4.

In other words:

At first she failed to recognise the person standing outside. The light was patchy and the general shape of whoever it was told her nothing. Then Tim's voice asked if he could come in. He seemed to be hunched up in a funny way, which must have been why she had not known him at once. When she could see his face properly it was quite a shock.

– Kingsley Amis, *Difficulties with Girls*

(For a similar exercise, try the quiz opposite.)

MAKING CONNECTIONS

When creating the sentences of a paragraph, the skilled writer arranges them – often unconsciously – in the most effective order possible. The basis for such ordering is usually either *chronological* or *logical*: chronological when the sentences depict a series of events, typically in the order in which they occurred; logical when the sentences build up an argument or develop a theme, each sentence explaining or qualifying or somehow expanding on the one before or after.

A paragraph needs more, however, than just well-written sentences in a well-arranged sequence.

To reinforce the links between the sentences, and to help the reader to appreciate their ordering, the considerate writer draws on a repertoire of special words (or phrases) – such as *then, finally, therefore,*

JIGSAW PARAGRAPH PUZZLE

Rearrange the following seven sentences into the well-structured paragraph they originally formed. (Just to establish the context: in the book from which the paragraph is taken, the preceding paragraph had been discussing some of the differences between American and British pronunciation of vowel sounds.)

As cues, attend not just to the sense of each sentence, but to the 'signposts' as well – the linking words such as *however* or *for example*, and the pronoun *it*. The answer appears on pages 633-648.

1. As a result, southeastern English on the whole moves faster than American English, since there are fewer stresses.

2. Northern English speech, however, is closer to American in movement than southeastern English is.

3. In general, southeastern English uses more violent stress contrasts and a wider range of pitch than American does.

4. This is the case, for example, with words ending in -ary, like *military* and *temporary*, where the American has a secondary stress on the third syllable.

5. There are also differences between British and American English in stress and intonation.

6. Where the Englishman gives a word one heavy stress and several very weak ones, the American often gives it a secondary stress on one of the weak syllables.

7. And it tends to have more reduced vowels than American English (as in the third syllable of *military*).

---

or *however*. These may be called 'link words' or 'signpost words' according to their function.

Grammatical signposting. Link words or signpost words, to put it another way, serve two extremely useful purposes.

First, as link words, they stitch the phrases and sentences delicately together, unifying them into well-formed paragraphs and often linking paragraphs to one another in turn. The passage by Churchill, quoted above, continues with this further comparison:

> And as sentences should follow one another in harmonious sequence, so paragraphs must fit on to one another like the automatic couplings of railway carriages.
> – Winston Churchill, *My Early Life*

Secondly, as signpost words, they guide the reader along the path of the writer's intended meaning.

In the cause of this second function, you have to be particularly alert and considerate when writing. Leave out one major signpost, and the reader will lose his bearings. Mislabel a signpost – writing *but* instead of *and*, for example – and the reader will head off in quite the wrong direction.

For the skilful use of signpost terms, examine the following extract. (It forms part of a discussion of pidgin languages – specifically, the expansion of a pidgin into a widely used common language.)

> Of course, when a pidgin becomes widely used, its form changes dramatically. To begin with, pidgins are very limited forms of communication with few words, a few simple constructions (mainly commands), helped along by gestures and miming. Tarzan's style is not very far from reality, in such cases. But when a pidgin expands, its vocabulary increases greatly, it develops its own rules of grammatical construction, and it becomes used for all the functions of everyday life.

A very significant development can then take place. People begin to use the pidgin at home. As children are born into these families, the pidgin language becomes their mother tongue. When this happens, the status of the language fundamentally alters, and it comes to be used in a more flexible and creative way. Instead of being seen as subordinate to other languages in an area, it starts to compete with them. In such cases linguists no longer talk about pidgin languages, but about *creoles*. Creolised varieties of English are very important throughout the Caribbean, and in the countries to which Caribbean people have emigrated – notably Britain. Black English in the United States is also creole in origin.

– Professor David Crystal, *The English Language*

Almost every sentence contains a signpost word or phrase: the most conspicuous ones are *of course, to begin with, but, then, when this happens, in such cases*, and *also*.

These signposts fall into various classes:

☐ straight ahead: *and, in addition, furthermore, also, moreover* . . .

☐ straight ahead, road clears: *so, therefore, in such cases, thus, on the contrary* . . .

☐ straight ahead, road narrows: *for example, for instance, in fact, alternatively, specifically, in some cases, ideally, above all, in conclusion* . . .

☐ detour: *by the way, incidentally, curiously, perhaps, note that* . . .

☐ caution, slow down: *actually, not that, naturally, oddly enough, of course, mind you* . . .

☐ stop and go back: *but, however, by contrast, on the other hand, though* . . .

Take care to keep the reader confident of his whereabouts by planting signposts wherever necessary. And take particular care not to misdirect him by miswording them. Consider the following pairs of sentences – what a difference in emphasis results from the switch of a single signpost:

I understand your feelings, and I'm going to proceed with the experiment.
I understand your feelings, but I'm going to proceed with the experiment.

In such cases you are entitled to give chase.
In some cases you are entitled to give chase.

Note that the lenses can remain in place overnight.
Not that the lenses can remain in place overnight.

In addition, sample A lasts longer than sample B.
On the other hand, sample A lasts longer than sample B.

Karpov countered by castling, of course.
Karpov countered by castling, oddly enough.

TOPIC SENTENCES

Since a paragraph deals with a given topic, it often mentions that topic, directly or indirectly, in one particular sentence.

The *topic sentence*, as it is called, usually appears at or very near the start of the paragraph. In that position, it serves as a particularly useful cue for the reader. He now has a rough idea, at the outset, of what lies in wait for him as he explores the paragraph's contents.

Sometimes, however, the writer wants to build up to a climax. Or to spring a surprise. Or to pose a problem and only later reveal the answer. In such cases, he positions the topic sentence at or near the end of the paragraph.

(Look again at the previous two paragraphs. Each of them exemplifies the type of structure it describes. In the first of them, the topic sentence stands at the very beginning of the paragraph. In the second, the topic sentence comes at the very end.)

The only firm rule for the positioning of the topic sentence is, as always, appropriateness. In everyday writing – business reports, personal letters, and so on – the appropriate position for the topic sentence in most paragraphs is near the start. In dramatic narrative writing – adventure stories, for instance – topic sentences more often occur appropriately at the end of paragraphs.

Very seldom is it appropriate to position the topic sentence in the middle of the paragraph. If, when editing your own writing, you do come across a topic sentence in a middle position, try to justify it to yourself. If you cannot, shift it. Or break the paragraph immediately before or after the topic sentence, thereby automatically reassigning it to a start- or end-position. And if you come across two topic sentences within a single paragraph (as in this one), perform the simple editorial task of splitting it into two separate paragraphs. Remember, only one topic per paragraph.

TRANSITIONS

And now for something completely different.

That catch phrase from *Monty Python's Flying Circus* directs its satirical thrust at continuity announcers or 'linkmen'. On radio or television, it is they who have the task of devising or explaining the bridge between one programme and the next.

TRANSITIONS IN BROADCASTING – THE CONTINUITY ANNOUNCEMENT

Here is a clever transition or 'bridge' between two items on a weekly magazine programme on the radio. Following an extract of serious modern music, the presenter repeats the composer's name and identifies the composition, and then introduces a further musical item – a comic take-off of Verdi's opera *La Traviata*, this time:

> Berio, in 'The Labyrinth' on Radio 3.
> Cantabile presented an opera with a pretty labyrinthine plot, on Radio 2: 'La Triviata' . . .
> – Margaret Howard, 'Pick of the Week',
> BBC Radio 4

The presenter has actually forged a double link here – *the labyrinthine plot* of the second item puns on the title of the first item, *The Labyrinth*. And the phrase *Radio 2* harks back contrastingly to the phrase *Radio 3*.

Continuity links are not always as smooth as that. All too often they sound extremely strained. Various producers or announcers appear in fact to run a secret competition for the silliest or most far-fetched or most complicated links or bridging announcements.

Exposing the absurdity of such artificial continuity, two comic musicians provided the following satiric link between two numbers they were performing on a radio programme:

> That first piece was the overture to *Tancredi*, by Rossini. The opera is set at the time of the Crusaders.
> The Crusaders fought the heathen Saladin.
> Wooden bowls is what you find salad in.
> Bowls was the favourite game of Sir Francis Drake.
> He fought and defeated the Armada.
> The Armada came from Spain.
> Which leads us neatly to Bizet's opera *Carmen*, which is also set in Spain, from which we'd like to play the seguidilla – from *Carmen*.
> – 'The Classic Buskers', BBC Radio 2

Here are the views of another satirist:

> Radio 4 has invented a kind of English not found anywhere else in the media: the radio link. This consists of taking two topics which have absolutely nothing in common and then finding a link between them, and the more tortuous the better.

> One example comes from a presenter who was linking a murder thriller to a programme about cheese-making: 'And from something blood-curdling to something rather more milk-curdling . . .' She might equally well have said: 'And so from the gruesome to the Gruyère . . .'

> What's amazing is that this sort of contorted thinking has not spread. It seems a natural way of doing the Radio 4 news headlines:

> 'New controls were announced today by President Mubarak to bring tourism back to Egypt. And talking of pyramid selling, that's just one of the many financial devices that Mrs Thatcher promised this afternoon to examine more closely, as she spoke in the Mother of Parliaments. But it was the Mother of Russian dissident Yuri Orlov who made the headlines in Moscow today with a brave declaration of liberty. A brave declaration of another kind was made by David Gower in Jamaica, where England are only 356 behind the West Indies and their steaming attack, though steaming is hardly the word to apply to the weather which will continue cold and frosty . . .
> – Miles Kington, *The Times*

Sometimes, when two consecutive programmes or items appear to have nothing in common at all, the only possible 'bridge' is a desperate admission that no bridge exists. Hence, 'And now for something completely different.' (See the panel above, for a further discussion of continuity in broadcasting.)

In writing, sentences are often directly linked to one another, subtly by means of pronouns such as *it*, or boldly by means of 'signpost' terms such as *furthermore* or *on the other hand* (see page 55). The same words and phrases can also serve to link paragraphs and even larger sections.

When two ideas or items have no direct connection, however, what can the writer do? The obvious answer is: restructure the text, placing one or both of them in a different position, next to other ideas or items that do have a direct connection with them. But if the two unconnected ideas have to remain side by side, the writer can fall back on two standard – and generally effective – techniques:

- the continuity announcer's trick of delving very deeply for some common factor that will serve as the 'bridge'

- giving up altogether the pretence of a connection, and relying instead on the physical appearance of the page – different typefaces, subheadings, and so on – to pattern the material and help the reader to keep his bearings

To illustrate the two techniques, here are some extracts from various book reviews.

In a long review of two novels – by Margaret Drabble and David Lodge – the reviewer reaches the midpoint of her article and has to shift her attention from the one book to the other:

> Margaret Drabble will go on asking questions about the world, but it seems beyond her scope as a novelist to suggest the answers.
>
> In Drabble's book, Alix's husband gives a series of talks on the Victorian novel; in David Lodge's *Nice Work*, Robyn Penrose is an expert on that group of Victorian novels which Raymond Williams called 'industrial novels'.
> – Hilary Mantel, *The New York Review of Books*

Almost by sleight-of-hand, the reviewer has switched books.

Similar cunning transitions occur a dozen times in the review extracted below. Here are just a few of them, beginning with the switchover from a biography of Ian Fleming:

> And yet for all his shortcomings as a man, Fleming had few equals in the business of getting people to turn the page. An even more spellbinding entertainer was the late lamented Lord Olivier, whose obituaries will have whetted people's appetites for Anthony Holden's respectfully received tome, **Olivier** (*Sphere* £5.99). If not the definitive work (what a meal Ken Tynan would have made of *that*!), it is streets ahead of the great mummer's ill-advised *Memoirs*.
>
> One of the things about Olivier was that he knew when to ham it up. So did Winston Churchill, whose props included a wardrobe full of distinctive hats and an inexhaustible supply of

cigars. Churchill's greatest role, as wartime Prime Minister, is covered by the latest two volumes of Martin Gilbert's colossal Life: **Finest Hour 1939-1941** and **Road to Victory** (*Minerva £7.50 each*).

Churchill once compared Soviet foreign policy to 'a riddle wrapped in a mystery inside an enigma'. As with its foreign policy, so with its first leader. So what was Lenin really like? This is the question Ronald W. Clark set himself to answer in **Lenin: The Man Behind the Mask** (*Faber £7.99*). What he reveals is a man who embodied two contrasting qualities, ruthless single-mindedness allied to a gift for brilliant administration.

Single-mindedness was also the hallmark of Truman Capote, as we learn from Gerald Clarke's beguiling biography **Capote** (*Cardinal £6.99*). Capote's goal was fame – literary fame to begin with, and then when he'd achieved that, social fame . . .
– Michael Barber, *Books* magazine

In contrast, many book reviewers treat each book quite independently. The reviewer forges no links – smooth or strained – from one to the other. Layout alone establishes whatever unity the text can boast:

- **The Cardinal of the Kremlin** by Tom Clancy (Fontana, £4.50) – Perestroika is in operation but neither superpower trusts the other . . . all told in short bursts which disorientate the reader by transporting him across the world in successive paragraphs. Exciting, but confusing.

- **Out of Chingford: Round the North Circular and Up the Orinoco** by Tanis and Martin Jordan (Coronet, £3.50) – One thinks of explorers as being rather aristocratic; not so Tanis (a hairdresser) and Martin (a painter) Jordan. With few resources they indulge their passion for travel . . . they enjoy every moment. And so do their flabbergasted readers . . .

- **Theatrical Anecdotes** chosen by Peter Hay (Oxford, £5.95) – There are millions to choose from and Mr Hay has made a fair selection, though perhaps too American-biased for British tastes. My favourite: after a disastrous performance, Ralph Richardson is seen outside his dressing-room stopping passers-by to ask: 'Has anyone seen my talent? It was always small, but it used to be shining.'
– David Holloway, *The Sunday Telegraph*

Aspects of Effective Style

THE BEST style is *clear* style, and clear style is for the most part plain style. This does not mean dull style: plain style allows a great deal of variety, a fair amount of wordplay and metaphor, and even the occasional ironic jibe or dramatic flourish. But the background remains fairly simple, as it always must do if the adornments are to stand out as effectively and distinctively as possible.

Plain and Unpretentious Style

The best style is one that seems effortless rather than laboured – though it often takes a great effort to produce that effect.

> A good style should show no sign of effort. What is written should seem a happy accident.
> – Somerset Maugham, *The Summing Up*

It is a style that focuses squarely on the contents, and serves the cause of clear communication, rather than drawing attention to itself.

> Effectiveness of assertion is the alpha and omega of style.
> – George Bernard Shaw, *Man and Superman*

> Have something to say, and say it as clearly as you can. That is the only secret of style.
> –Matthew Arnold, quoted in G.W.E. Russell, *Collections and Recollections*

> The language should be so pellucid that the meaning should be rendered without an effort to the reader . . .

> The language used should be as ready and as efficient a conductor of the mind of the writer to the mind of the reader as is the electric spark which passes from battery to battery.
> – Anthony Trollope, *An Autobiography*

What plain style stands opposed to is a relentlessly 'high style' – the 'fine writing' of the show-off writer, the self-conscious 'purple patch' that carries on and on until it ceases to be a patch and becomes the main fabric of the text, the grand rhetoric that hides rather than illuminates the writer's thoughts:

> The florid style is the reverse of the familiar. The last is employed as an unvarnished medium to convey ideas; the first is resorted to as a spangled veil to conceal the want of them.
> – William Hazlitt, 'Of Familiar Style'

Take care not to slip into such florid style – especially in everyday letters or reports. If you do have a tendency to indulge in 'stylish' style, edit your first draft rigorously to tone it down.

An old tutor of a college said to one of his pupils:

> Read over your compositions, and wherever you meet with a passage which you think is particularly fine, strike it out.
> – Dr Johnson,
> quoted in *Boswell's Life of Dr Johnson*

If you write to *impress* the reader, you will precisely fail to impress him. If you write to *express* yourself and your ideas, clearly and sincerely, then you very probably will impress the reader. 'Trying to be clever,' in other words, or 'trying too hard', only increases the risk of appearing foolish. Pretentiousness will impress only the shallow and gullible.

Consider just two examples of clever writing – *clever* in the bad sense:

> Allan MacEachen, Hecate-like, whispers a beguiling exorcism into the trembling ears of the Liberal Party's platform committee on the weekend, 48 hours before two by-election votes, neither of which the party has a hope of winning. No need to be spooked by Brian Mulroney, the Deputy Prime Minister incants. Right. Not until Birnam wood comes to Dunsinane hill. Besides, the Prime Minister's office has moved to a political war-footing.
> – Michael Valpy, *The Toronto Globe and Mail*

The chameleon qualities of Volpone and Mosca are imitative of the ideologues of society, and also represent a strategy for resistance. Jonson's characters strive to be relentlessly self-inventive, like Howard Barker's protagonists who compulsively destabilise truth in their artistic and artful insistence on preserving the coarseness which remains essential to human interaction; and like David Rudkin's Promethean heroes who reach after some form of new mythology which might embrace, rather than demonize, the urgings of their instinctive selves.

When the promises of conventional social morality prove hollow, Jonson's character go to be animals and demons in a time of animals and demons. Volpone delights in his ability to be a Protean shapeshifter, until he is doomed to stay forever in the shape he has assumed, like Satan the serpent; Mosca glories in his own sense that he could skip out of his skin 'like a subtle snake' and 'change a visor swifter than a thought'. Their exhilaration, in which the audience share, is that of self-animalising quicksilver wraiths . . ., their felon forms rippling with lithe beauty, mercurials who triumph over their entropic landscapes through sheer imagination.
– David Ian Rabey, London theatre programme

Why can't they just say what they mean?

Brevity and Conciseness

Brevity is not quite the same thing as conciseness. The difference is one of quantity vs quality of material – volume vs concentration.

Brevity, however desirable, is not always possible. A complicated letter or report cannot always hope to be brief. If it has to cover a lot of ground, it will necessarily cover a lot of paper as well (though if it is structured and laid out considerately, its length need not put the reader off too badly).

But what is always possible is conciseness – succinctness, concentrated efficiency. That is, conveying *each point* as briefly as possible, even though there are too many points for the text as a whole to be brief.

So, a long text may still be admirably concise; and a brief text may be needlessly wordy and diffuse.

The virtues of conciseness are most obvious in the case of poetry – 'an ocean within a tear'.

> He that uses many words for the explaining any subject, doth, like the cuttle fish, hide himself for the most part in his own ink.
> – John Ray, *On the Creation*

> Words are like leaves; and where they most abound,
> Much fruit of sense beneath is rarely found.
> – Alexander Pope, *Essay on Criticism*

> In composing, as a general rule, run your pen through every other word you have written; you have no idea what vigour it will give your style.
> – Sydney Smith,
> quoted in Lady Holland's *Memoir*

That is, a wealth of meaning or feeling is packed into relatively few words. In other forms of creative writing, such as plays and novels, conciseness may seem less important.

In a thriller, for instance, the story needs considerable spinning out for the tension to build up and for the climax to work effectively. True: but what keeps the story going should be *action* – the twists and turns of the plot – rather than wordy descriptions of any one incident. No matter how long the narrative grows, it can still remain tight. For a simple comparison of a tight narrative with a flabby narrative, see the panel opposite.

In everyday writing tasks too, conciseness makes for effectiveness. Waffling in an essay, overexplaining in a letter of complaint, redundancy in an office memo – these serve only to reduce the impact of your message. The more long-winded a piece of writing, the greater the risk of losing your reader – either because his mind wanders or because his patience snaps. To write concisely, on the other hand, is to do the reader a courtesy. Simply, it saves him or her a great deal of time.

But remember that, as always, an inverse proportion operates: to ensure that the reader spends less time reading, you the writer have to put in more time writing. You have to structure your ideas systematically (see pages 91-102) so that you avoid saying the same thing at two or three different points in the text. And you have to edit your early drafts ruthlessly – cutting all redundant words and phrases (see below), deleting uneconomical frills such as flowery adjectives (see page 32 above),

TIGHT WRITING VS FLABBY WRITING

Consider the following two versions of a text – the conclusion of a short story written for a training course. The narrator recalls an incident from his childhood. He and his twin brother, aged ten at the time, are waiting in the local barber's shop to have their hair cut. The barber, preparing to shave another customer, is stropping his razor and grinning at the two boys. A voice on the radio is meanwhile reporting a local murder case – an elderly woman had had her throat cut while eating dinner in bed.

First version

The police broke into the house the next afternoon. They searched the kitchen and hall, but found nothing out of the ordinary. They then rushed upstairs. Even though they knew what to expect, they were shocked at what they saw. Entering the bedroom, they saw the corpse staring back at them from the bed. She was still sitting upright, but the napkin at her throat now had a dark reddish-brown stain on it.

The barber put down the leather strap. He tested the razor with his thumb. Then he waved it in the air for a moment, and brought it gently down to rest just below the customer's ear.

This was too much for my brother and me. We looked at each other, and the tension broke. We launched into action. Without a word we jumped up, clutching our hats, and raced out of the shop.

Edited version

The police broke into the house the next afternoon. They searched the kitchen and hall: nothing.

They rushed upstairs to the bedroom. And saw the corpse staring back at them from the bed. Still sitting upright – but the napkin at her throat now had a dark stain.

The barber put down the leather strap. He tested the razor with his thumb. Then he waved it in the air for a moment. Then he brought it gently down to rest, just below the customer's ear.

I looked at my brother. My brother looked at me.

Without a word, clutching our hats, we raced out of the shop.

What makes the edited version so much tighter and more effective and more dramatic? Above all, the simple deletion of various inefficient words, phrases, or sentences. Inefficient because unnecessary for the purpose of the story. The word *reddish-brown* is unnecessary: a *dark stain*, in this context, needs no further explaining. Similarly, the sentence *We launched into action* adds nothing, except wordiness, to the account of the scene.

reducing clichés and flabby phrases to tight single words (such as *at the present moment in time* to *now* – see page 25), trimming digressions and any other points of doubtful relevance, fusing two oversubtle ideas into a single broad idea, and so on.

Paradoxically then, it takes more time and effort to write something concisely than to write it long-windedly and repetitively:

> I have made this letter longer than usual, only because I have not had the time to make it shorter.
>
> – Blaise Pascal, *Lettres Provinciales*

The final version will take longer to emerge, but it will gain considerably in impact.

REDUNDANCY – TAUTOLOGY AND PLEONASM

One common form of long-windedness is 'redundancy' – in effect, saying the same thing twice, the needless repetition of a single item of information (as in this sentence).

It is like killing a fly twice over.

Two technical terms referring to redundancy in language are *tautology* and *pleonasm*. In logic, a *tautology* is a statement that is true no matter what happens: *Either it will rain tomorrow or it will not rain tomorrow*. In language, *tautology* is the repetition of an idea in different words: **✗** *Pair off in twos*; **✗** *7.30 p.m. in the evening*.

Pleonasm is rather broader. It does not necessarily entail the repetition of an idea. It is just the overelaboration of the idea through using more words than necessary. To speak of **?** *meeting up with a friend* is usually pleonastic, since *meeting a friend* conveys the meaning quite adequately.

Many tautologies or pleonasms are built into the natural idiom of English, and it is quite pointless trying to drive them out: *silly fool, young lad, old crone*, and *over and done with*, for instance. Legal jargon and religious language are full of redundancies: *lift up, rise up, join together, null and void, last will and testament*, and so on.

Many other common redundant phrases are distinctly dubious, however. In varying degrees, they do obstruct streamlined communication:

> past history
> future prospects
> grateful thanks
> usual habits
> free gifts
> new innovations
> advance warning
> a downward plunge
> an indirect allusion
> an essential prerequisite
> no other alternative
> the actual facts

the general consensus
the consensus of opinion
to mix things together
to circle round something
to divide it up
to rest up
more preferable
unjustly persecuted
the reason is because
a new addition to the family
when it was first founded
to set a new world record
to repeat again
an audible click
a relic of the past
a minimum of at least four weeks
the chief protagonist of the play
Everybody voted unanimously in favour.
Entrance is restricted to ticket holders only.
Two further points must be added.
There were other consequences apart from bankruptcy and distress.
Zappo kills flies dead.
There is no need for undue alarm.
From time immemorial it has always been the custom.
For the 20th time the OAU convenes again.
The envelopes are available in a range of different colours.
It is time you modernised these outmoded procedures.
So I enclose a photocopy of the document herewith.
We need to know by Monday whether you are agreeable or not.

Consistency

If you write of the 'staff Training Unit' at one point, don't write 'Staff Training unit' elsewhere. If you refer to the newspaper as 'the *Times*' in paragraph 1, don't call it '*The Times*' in paragraph 5.

Many an inattentive reader, while failing to observe simple errors in a piece of writing, will nevertheless pounce on any internal inconsistencies such as those, and react indignantly to them. 'If the writer is careless in small matters,' the reasoning goes, 'how can I trust him in large matters?'

The writer's air of authority, so important for winning the reader round, tends to disperse increasingly with each inconsistency that the reader notices. Hence the use of 'house style' by newspapers and publishers – the set of preferences for one usage or spelling over another. The policy in this book is to use the following conventions:

☐ the spelling *-ise* rather than *-ize* in words such as *realise* or *materialise*

☐ single quotation marks rather than double

☐ the pattern *23 September 1991* for dates, rather than *23/9/91* or *September 23 1991* or *23rd September 1991*

☐ the spelling *biased* or *focused* in preference to *biassed* and *focussed*

You might favour the opposite convention in each case. Fine – so long as you use it consistently.

Consistency applies to more than just spelling and punctuation. It applies to more complicated matters as well, such as layout, and choice of grammatical construction.

CONSISTENCY OF LAYOUT AND GRAMMAR

Equal treatment for equal items.

If two sections of a report, say, have equal status, make sure that the two headings enjoy an identical degree of prominence – both in bold italics perhaps, both in the centre of the line rather than against the margin, and so on.

If you are inconsistent in these matters, and allow a larger typeface for one heading than the other, for example, the reader will misread your intentions, and assume that the one section has greater importance than the other.

Similarly, use parallel constructions for parallel items. If you present a list of five rules, for instance, make sure that they all have the same basic grammatical structure. Avoid inconsistent wording, as in this example:

X Accordingly, before allowing access, please make sure in future that you:
1. stop all visitors or clients as they arrive at the door.
2. ask them to state which staff member they will be seeing.
3. you must then get clearance by phone from the staff member named.
4. please make sure that the visitor then signs the visitors' book and receives a visitor's lapel badge.

5. they must wear this badge at all times while in the building.

Rules 1 and 2, which are worded as imperatives or commands, follow on correctly from the introductory words.

Rule 3, although imperative in intention, is worded as a statement: delete the words *you must then* to make it imperative in form as well.

Rule 4 is worded as an imperative, but it wrongly begins with *please*. Not only is this inconsistent or 'unparallel' with the previous items, but it also ignores the introductory words, which already contain the word *please*.

Rule 5 has a quite different pattern from the other items. To get it into line, turn it into an imperative too, as by adding the words *explain to them that* at the start.

Here is one further example of an asymmetrical list:

X If you're thinking of buying more shares, or of selling your shares you can do so through the Abbey National Sharelink service – this allows you to:

- buy shares by phone
- sell shares by post
- and there are phone numbers for you to ring if you need help.

– building society's Share Issue information leaflet

With a bit of thought, the copywriter could have reworded the last of the three items to parallel the other two – something like this, perhaps:

- ring for help or advice, on any of our phone numbers.

Brightness

Try to instil as much liveliness or bounce into your writing as appropriate.

Many everyday writing projects cry out for a light and lively touch: letters of congratulations, for example, or articles in the parish magazine. Readers of these would welcome some teasing gossip or bouncy wordplay. In fact, they may even demand it: they will abandon after the first paragraph your lengthy report on the progress of the church roof restoration fund, however accurate and worthy it is, unless you have managed to make it witty and

entertaining and *interesting* as well – both in content and in style.

The phrase *as appropriate*, in the opening sentence above, marks an important qualification. If you try to make your office memos or your letters to the borough council as bright and lively as a James Bond novel or a *Yes Minister* script, you will fail to produce a successful piece of writing. Such business documents have a precise and serious purpose, and require correspondingly precise and serious wording.

Yet even here, you can do much to keep up the reader's level of interest. 'Precise and serious wording' does not have to be dull.

Consider the following bland observation:

? Interviewees need not dress inappropriately smartly.

It is so abstract and general that an inattentive reader might simply fail to take it in. It needs replacing, or supplementing, by a more graphic and concrete statement – something creating a picture in the reader's mind:

> Nobody expects a student attending his first job interview to dress in a pinstripe suit.

Concrete imagery, as in the example just quoted, is only one of many ingredients that go in to making a lively style. (For a more detailed discussion on concreteness, see pages 75-78 below.) Among the other ingredients are: variety of phrasing, figures of speech, and wordplay. The virtues – and sometimes the dangers – of each of these ingredients are discussed below.

VARIETY OF PHRASING

Even the most conscientious of readers find that their level of attention tends to sink occasionally. It is the writer's task to keep topping it up, before it falls below the danger line. And with the inexhaustible reservoir of the English language to draw on, the writer has no excuse for failing in that task.

To dispel or prevent monotony, you need to inject variety into your writing – variety not just of vocabulary (see pages 23-31), but of phrasing as well, the patterning of sentences.

(Not that you should use variety for variety's sake, or strain to avoid repeating a word or phrase. Such 'elegant variation' only draws attention to itself. Proper variety is functional: as well as reviving the reader's interest, it often produces subtle distinctions of meaning or emphasis.)

One of the simplest ways of introducing variety into your prose is by varying the length of your sentences. Within limits. Don't allow straggly sentences into your text, even in the cause of variety. Think of the permitted range within which you should vary as being between short and longish rather than between short and long. (For a full discussion of the widespread vice of overlong sentences, see pages 42-44 above.)

Varying the length of your sentences often entails varying the complexity of your sentences as well – simple, compound, and complex sentences; balanced and periodic sentences, and so on. (For a description of these various types, see page 46.) Perhaps it is more a matter of *checking* that your text contains a reasonable variety than a matter of deliberately introducing a variety into the text while compiling it.

TURNS OF PHRASE

For more sophisticated variations, you may need to employ a more deliberate strategy – to keep a conscious lookout for opportunities of using specific stylistic tricks and turns of phrase: of using *say* instead of *for example* sometimes, say; or of using *in place of* sometimes in place of *instead of*, or *to be in a position to bid* instead of *to be able to bid* or *can bid*, or *something along the lines of this* instead of *something like this*.

No exhaustive list of such devices is available; the selection below should serve as little more than a stimulus for your own powers of varied phrasing.

conventional	varied
But that does not mean that you should use variety for variety's sake.	Not that you should use variety for variety's sake.
These notes will be invaluable in your preparation for future interviews.	These notes will be invaluable when it comes to preparing for future interviews.
I have said quite enough about the Ashby incident, and shall now discuss the similar problems arising out of the related incident at Banville.	Enough of the Ashby incident. The related incident at Banville raises corresponding problems: ...
Let us now turn to the question of compensation.	To turn now to the question of compensation.
If you strain or overwork your voice, it will rebel and wear out.	Strain or overwork your voice, and it will rebel and wear out.
That then is the general problem, but we	So much for the general problem;

still need to discuss your specific role in it.

If you speak more effectively, people will listen more attentively.

Another useful exercise for the neck is as follows: drop your head forward and stretch the rear neck muscles.

Your facial muscles will then become more expressive. As a result, you will communicate more effectively still.

now for your specific role in it.

The more effectively you speak, the more attentively people will listen.

Another useful exercise for the neck: drop your head forward and stretch the rear neck muscles.

Your facial muscles will then become more expressive. Result: you will communicate more effectively still.

INVERTED WORD ORDER

One of the subtlest ways of varying your sentence patterns is by means of 'inverted word order'.

The typical word order of the English sentence is so familiar that the reader does not usually notice it:

Several new books appear on this week's list.
The scythe was a favourite weapon for many new recruits.

It is only when this normal word order changes that the sentence becomes 'marked':

Appearing on this week's list are several new books.
For many new recruits a favourite weapon was the scythe.

The usual word order – precisely because it is usual – becomes monotonous if followed dutifully sentence after sentence. 'Invert' the pattern from time to time, and you will retain the reader's attention for that much longer. (But only where it comes naturally: otherwise you will produce a sense of strain.) The context often allows, or even invites, an inverted ordering. Note how, in the following passage, the second sentence seems quite natural in its unusual word order:

Chapter 5 makes several unusual proposals, including one that is highly controversial. About that proposal the author says a great deal more in chapter 8.

The reason it seems so natural is twofold: first, it links elegantly on to the first sentence; secondly, it

is in keeping with the sensible English tendency to begin a sentence with known or 'given' information, and to place 'new' information at the end.

Inverted word order does more than ward off monotony, however. It can also help to create a number of literary effects – dramatic, ironic, emotional, and so on:

Suddenly the door flew open.
Handsome he's not.
Came the dawn.

Never in the field of human conflict was so much owed by so many to so few.

– Winston Churchill,
speech in the House of Commons

FIGURES OF SPEECH

Contributing hugely to the liveliness of talk and writing is the use of figures of speech – those colourful expressions in which words deviate from their literal sense in order to create a dramatic image or a forceful impression in the mind of the reader or listener.

Here is a list of the better-known figures of speech and rhetorical devices. It carries an implicit warning: Overuse can damage the health of your writing. By all means try to incorporate some of them (if appropriate) into anything you write: this should help to engage the reader's interest, and even to win the reader's acceptance of your views. But use them only in moderation. Figurative speech is like seasoning or sugar: too much of it, and it stops giving pleasure and starts to cloy.

alliteration	use of words starting with or containing the same letter or sound: *The furrow followed free*
antithesis	an expression in which contrasting ideas are carefully balanced: *More haste, less speed*
apostrophe	an old-fashioned direct address to an absent or dead person or a thing: *O Freedom! hear our cry!*
assonance	repetition of vowel sounds, producing a half-rhyme effect: *slow progress over the cold plateau*

asyndeton	omission of conjunctions: *I came, I saw, I conquered*	paradox	an apparently absurd or self-contradictory statement that may nevertheless be true or wise: *Her gentleness was too hurtful to bear*
ellipsis (also known as *aposiopesis*)	omission of words, or sudden breaking off in mid-sentence, for dramatic effect: *The door opened, and . . .*	pathetic fallacy	the assigning of human feelings or characteristics to natural or inanimate objects: *The trees groaned*
euphemism	an inoffensive expression used in place of a sharper or more explicit one, such as *to pass away* for *to die*	personification (also known as *prosopopoeia*)	the representation of an object or idea as human: *the jovial Moon smiling benignly down at us*
hyperbole	exaggeration or over-statement for emphasis: *I could eat a horse*	polysyndeton	repetition of conjunctions for rhetorical effect: *went to Florence and Venice and Rome and Naples*
innuendo	an indirect or subtle suggestion, often intended as a veiled accusation: *Not everyone would be able to believe that*	rhetorical question (also known as *erotema*)	a question asked for effect or to convey information rather than to elicit an answer: *Isn't it a lovely day? How could anyone support such a useless project?*
irony	use of a word or words to convey something markedly different from the literal meaning: *It's a secret, so only half of London knows about it*; a common component of sarcasm, though not necessarily so cutting	simile	comparison of two unlike ideas or objects, typically using the word *like* or *as*: *lips like rosebuds, and kisses like wine*
litotes (also known as *meiosis*)	understatement in which an idea is tellingly conveyed, typically by contradicting its opposite: *He's not exactly sober*	syllepsis	use of single word to apply to two others, in different ways: *He held his tongue and my hand* (see *zeugma*)
metaphor	description of one thing in terms of another that is related to it by analogy: *She sailed across the room*	synecdoche	use of the name of a part to refer to the whole, or vice versa, such as *forty sail* to refer to forty ships
metonymy	use of a concrete term to refer to some wider idea that it characterises, such as *the Crown* for the monarchy	transferred epithet (also known as *hypallage*)	deliberate misapplication of an adjective to a noun: *his sleepless pillow; the condemned cell*
onomatopoeia	use of words whose sound suggests their meaning: for example, *sizzle, splash, crack, buzz, zap*	zeugma	use of a single word to apply to two others, especially when it is appropriate to only one; a faulty syllepsis: *He held his tongue and his promise* (see *syllepsis*)
oxymoron	a phrase linking incongruous or contradictory terms: *a wise fool*		

Here, now, is a handful of quotations illustrating a few of these figures of speech. First, an almost poetic description, from the sports pages of a daily newspaper, of a veteran Australian rowing champion, famous in his time not just for his victories but for his outrageous techniques and cheeky personality. The passage relies heavily on *alliteration* and *assonance* for its effectiveness.

> Sam Mackenzie is back from Australia to stir up the Thames for the first time in a quarter of a century . . . He won the Diamonds for six successive years from 1957. Nobody could get near him.
>
> The rough diamond indeed. He was a farmer's boy from Parramatta, ockerish and cocky with a larrikin's Just William cock-a-snook sneer. But a back-bending brute in a boat. It's been good to sit at his feet this week.
>
> – Frank Keating, *The Guardian*

Next, an *ellipsis*, the equivalent of a pointed silence in speech full of mischievous meaning or unspoken hints. The passage comes from the daily diary column in *The Times*:

> Blunkett's office, showing a commendable sense of humour, collapsed in fits of giggles when I pointed out the error. At least, I trust it *is* an error . . .
>
> – Nigel Williamson, *The Times*

Next, two examples of *syllepsis* – the first being a brief description from the listings of the week's radio programmes:

> But poor widowed Marjorie, coaxed along for an evening's distraction from her recent bereavement, can scarcely raise her gin and lemon, let alone a smile.
>
> – Madeleine Kingsley, *Radio Times*

The second example is probably the most famous syllepsis of all:

> When they left off at ten minutes past eleven, Miss Bolo rose from the table considerably agitated, and went straight home, in a flood of tears and a sedan chair.
>
> – Charles Dickens, *The Pickwick Papers*

Then, from a more recent novel, a passage that culminates in an extremely vivid *metaphor*. What makes the metaphor all the more impressive is that it develops out of the very unpromising and half-dead metaphor *carpet of snow*:

> Robyn got out of the car and looked through railings across the car park to a brick office block and a tall windowless building behind it, a

prospect almost as depressing as the prison she had seen that morning. Only the carpet of snow relieved its drabness, and that was being rolled up by a man driving a small tractor with a scoop on the front.

> – David Lodge, *Nice Work*

Next, a few similes, from three of the modern masters of prose writing. Here are some samples of their art:

> Outside the bay the reefs seethed and bubbled as though hot swords were cooling in water.
>
> – Laurie Lee, *I Can't Stay Long*
>
> Then, as the sun went down it seemed to drag the whole sky with it like shreds of a burning curtain . . .
>
> The children crowded the doorway, watching me expectantly as though I was a firework just about to go off.
>
> – Laurie Lee,
> *As I Walked Out One Midsummer's Morning*
>
> I turned to Aunt Agatha, whose demeanour was now rather like that of one who, picking daisies on the railway, has just caught the down express in the small of the back . . .
>
> I'm not lugged into Family Rows. On the occasions when Aunt is calling to Aunt like mastodons bellowing across primeval swamps . . . , the clan has a tendency to ignore me.
>
> – P.G. Wodehouse, *The Inimitable Jeeves*
>
> The Right Hon was a tubby little chap who looked as if he had been poured into his clothes and had forgotten to say 'When!'
>
> – P.G. Wodehouse, *Very Good, Jeeves!*
>
> By the end of lunch in the full humid heat of the day I would take a siesta, my sleep disturbed by the heavy movement of the vultures on the iron roof above my head (I have seen as many as six perched up there, like old broken umbrellas).
>
> – Graham Greene,
> introduction to *The Ministry of Fear*

Finally, for good measure, a *hyperbole* from another work of Wodehouse's:

> He was in the sort of overwrought state when a fly treading a little too heavily on the carpet is enough to make a man think he's one of the extras in *All Quiet On The Western Front*.
>
> – P.G. Wodehouse,
> *Tales From the Drones Club*

That far-fetched yet deadpan description of a hangover raises two other important points about style, incidentally. One, you can, with a bit of imagination, almost always find something fresh and arresting to say about anything, even about a subject as hackneyed and unpromising as a hangover. Two, if a stylistic trick works, it works: even outrageous exaggeration, in defiance of the 'rules', comes off if handled deftly enough – in this case, by means of the deadpan tone and the throwaway-line casualness of the rhythm. It helps, of course, if you happen to be P.G. Wodehouse.

METAPHOR AND ITS DANGERS

Of all these figures of speech, metaphor and simile are probably the best known, the commonest, and the riskiest.

They not only adorn and enliven writing and speech. They are often essential to communication: conveying a complex idea from one mind to another is sometimes virtually impossible without the aid of some comparison or image. Hence all the 'dead metaphors' – dead but indispensable – in our language: *the legs of a table, a fiery speech, a sparkling personality*; and the half-dead metaphors too: *eagle-eyed, blowing one's own trumpet, a flood of protest*. Texts vary in the amount of imagery they can bear. A symbolic poem may need an image in every line. A financial analysis of projected sales figures would read oddly if it contained more than two or three metaphors a page.

A masterly author can indulge in a very heavy dosage of very inventive metaphors without losing control. A rich but palatable mixture results, as in the following quotation. It comes from a novel, as it happens, but could just as well come from a personal letter or an article in a leisure magazine. The subject is the 'dreadful tropical energy' affecting everything in the East – it invaded even the smart colonial suburbs of Singapore before the war.

> Foliage sprang up on every hand with a determination unknown to our own polite European vegetation. Dark, glistening green was smeared over everything as if with a palette knife, while in the gloom (the jungle tends to be gloomy) something sinister which had been making a noise a little while ago was now holding its breath.
>
> If you left your bungalow unattended for a few months while you went home on leave, very likely you would come back to find that green lariats had been thrown over every projecting part and were wrestling it to the ground, that powerful ferns were drilling their way between its bricks, or that voracious house-eating insects, which were really nothing more than sharp jaws mounted on legs, had been making meals of the woodwork. Moreover, the mosquitoes in this particular suburb were only distant cousins of the mild insects which irritate us on an English summer evening: in Tanglin you had to face the dreaded anopheles variety, each a tiny flying hypodermic syringe containing a deadly dose of malaria. And if, by good fortune, you managed to avoid malaria there was still another mosquito waiting in the wings, this one clad in striped football socks, ready to inject you with dengue fever.
>
> – J.G. Farrell, *The Singapore Grip*

Despite the dazzling variety of comparisons here – *palette knife, lariats, wrestling, drilling, hypodermic syringes* – there is no sense of excess or 'mixed metaphors', only an appropriate sense of lushness that matches beautifully the lushness of nature that the author is describing.

But it remains a risky game to play. The following passage, also by an accomplished novelist, tries too hard. The various similes and metaphors are slightly strained: they draw attention to themselves rather than to the subjects they are meant to be illuminating. The language is too richly spiced – it begins to cloy. And being overemphatic in this way, as well as very varied, the images clash – farmyard vs crossroads vs battlefield – and produce the rather head-spinning feeling that mixed metaphors always do.

> **??** Resembling a cockerel unexpectedly reprieved from the poultryman's hand, returning ruffled but unrepentant and rampant to his familiar midden, Miss Prosser had seated herself at the big desk in the assembly hall. Behind it she became a much more formidable character than a younger sister . . . All the classrooms were grouped about this rostrum – it lay at her school's crossroads – and through the glass partitions she presided over everything that went on, a conductor detecting the faintest false note in the din of learning.
>
> First she unlocked, opened and closed a battery of drawers in a salvo of officious bangs.
>
> – J.L. Carr, *A Day in Summer*

The mixed metaphor is all too easy to produce.

(For more on mixed metaphors, see the panel overleaf.)

Cloying imagery of this kind does not necessarily involve mixed metaphors. Even a single metaphor can tempt the writer into overindulgence. The language becomes too rich – often at the expense of the meaning: all sauce and no meat. The following extract is verging on the contrived and 'clever':

? Japan's big five carmakers – Toyota, Nissan, Honda, Mitsubishi Motors and Mazda – are heading for some nasty potholes. During the first ten months of this year, Japanese carmakers sold nearly 4.6m cars and vans at home . . . but in a market that is expected to turn down. The brakes have already been slammed on in America, while Europe may soon go slow, too.
– *The Economist*

Loosen the restraints any further, and you risk producing this kind of overrich concoction:

?? The fire of life burnt very low now. His consciousness dimmed and brightened, as a dying flame might surge and subside. The wick was all but burnt out, yet the vital fire clung to it and would not quit. It was not a calm death: he blazed and writhed and sputtered. It was painful to watch. Yet the doctor stayed his hand: who would wish to snuff that valiant taper rather than let it burn itself out?

In reaction to such overdosing, writers sometimes go too far in the opposite direction – they undernourish the text by feeding it only impoverished metaphors and similes. These may be simple clichés – **?** *as bright as a button*, **?** *turning up like a bad penny*, **?** *a different kettle of fish*, **?** *having eyes in the back of your head* – which provoke a yawn in the reader rather evoking a striking image in his mind. Or they may be overtimid, half-hearted, uncommitted metaphors – **??** *ending a gulf* rather than *bridging/narrowing a gulf*, or **??** *passing a target*, **??** *reducing a bottleneck*, and so on.

Finally, beware of the bewitching power of metaphor. Just as poetry thrives on figures of speech, so too, unfortunately, does propaganda: to speak of *rivers of blood* is far more stirring and scaring than to speak merely of *civil unrest*. Don't abuse metaphoric language in this way, or be manipulated by it. To *compare* a reality to something quite different is not to *convert* it into that reality. To give a dog a bad name (or to call a man a *mad dog*) is not in itself reason enough to hang him.

WORDPLAY

Deliberate wordplay serves as a stimulant to the reader – so long as it fits into the context and does not sound strained. You may venture a rhyme – from time to time. Or launch into a little light alliteration. And the occasional pun or paradox may occasion some light relief.

Here are a few witty paradoxes, epigrams, and inverted popular sayings of the kind that may spice up your writing if used sparingly and aptly:

He who goes against the fashion is himself its slave. (Logan Pearsall Smith)

A woman can forgive a man for the harm he does her, but she can never forgive him for the sacrifices he makes on her account. (Somerset Maugham)

He is now fast rising from affluence to poverty. (Mark Twain)

Self-denial is indulgence of a propensity to forego. (Ambrose Bierce)

He has occasional flashes of silence that make his conversation perfectly delightful. (Sydney Smith)

Work is the curse of the drinking classes. (Oscar Wilde)

THE MIXED METAPHOR AND ITS RELATIVES

A succession of metaphors or similes drawn from different fields of comparison sometimes produces a laughably clashing effect – even when they are dead or half-dead metaphors. There are many celebrated examples that make the point without need of comment:

✗ We stand on the abyss – let us march forward together.

✗ You are sitting on the fence and burying your head in the sand.

Mr Ian Smith, when Prime Minister of Rhodesia, reportedly said: ✗ *Are we going to sit back and take this lying down?* And Sam Goldwyn the film producer apparently once complained that ✗ *Every director bites the hand that lays the golden egg.* Similarly:

✗ West Berlin is an oasis of democracy in a sea of communism.
– John Hosken, *The Listener*

✗ So let me look at the roots of a few sacred cows.
– Sir John Donaldson, *New Law Journal*

✗ That's an invitation to cock my leg over a wild goose and go off into a mare's nest.
– Lord Bancroft, BBC Radio 4

Perhaps the most famous example of bizarrely mixed metaphors is that attributed to an 18th-century Irish politician:

✗ Mr Speaker, I smell a rat; I see him forming in the air and darkening the sky; but I'll nip him in the bud.
– attributed to Sir Boyle Roche, quoted in *The Oxford Book of Quotations*

In a series of letters to *The Times* in 1989, readers listed favourite mixed metaphors that they had come across over the years.

An American participant at an Oxford seminar, for instance, earnestly declared that 'Chaucer stands with one foot in the Middle Ages, while with the other he salutes the rising dawn of the English Renaissance.'

The magazine *Community Care* recently described the Department of Social Security as a 'backwater clogged with hot potatoes'.

At a scientific meeting, one scientist accused another of 'trying to bolster up the scaffolding of a collapsing hypothesis with a red herring'.

The Mixed Metaphor has two well-known cousins, both discussed elsewhere – Malapropism (see page 27) and the Unintended Pun (see page 72). It also has three rather more obscure cousins – the Dubious Metaphor, the Inappropriate Metaphor, and the Mixed Idiom (or Mixed Cliché) – which deserve a brief mention here.

The *Dubious Metaphor* is one that does not quite work; for example, **?** *defusing tension.* You can *ease* or *reduce* tension, or perhaps defuse a *tense situation*, but hardly **?** *defuse tension* – the two ideas, like oil and water, simply refuse to mix properly. That example is taken from a BBC radio programme, as are all these other dubious combinations:

?? unravelling highlights
?? chalking up a landmark
?? sabotaging the atmosphere
?? a last-ditch summit
?? ironing out teething troubles

The *Inappropriate Metaphor*, next: like the Dubious Metaphor, it usually contains dead or half-dead metaphors. The clash this time is between the metaphor and the context:

? There has been a spate of droughts in recent years.
? That man in the wheelchair is always jumping to conclusions.
?? He goes around stirring up apathy.
? Your insurance claim is proceeding like a house on fire.

Here is an 18-century example, from a judge, later to be Lord Chief Justice of England; convicting a butler of stealing wine, the judge apparently said:

✗ You burst through all restraints of religion and morality, and have for years been feathering your nest with your master's bottles.
– Lord Kenyon, quoted in George A. Morton and D.M. Malloch, *Law and Laughter*

The *Mixed Idiom*, finally, is just as common, and just as subtle – easy to commit and difficult to detect. The phrase **??** *pays the consequences* blends 'pays the price' and 'takes the consequences'. Similarly, **??** *by far and away the best* ('by far' + 'far and away'). Note, however, that if used deliberately, the Mixed Idiom (especially in the guise of the Mixed Cliché) can be very striking in its grotesque way:

✗ green behind the ears
✗ throwing a sponge in the works
✗ deaf as a dodo
✗ A nudge is as good as a wink to a blind bat
✗ You're not as young as you should be
✗ This food is bone cold
✗ She didn't bat a hair
✗ If the boss finds out, I'll be in hot soup
✗ It's enough to drive you out of your bend
✗ You could have knocked me down with a ton of bricks

Comedians use clashing imagery as part of their stock-in-trade. And good writers sometimes playfully mix their metaphors or idioms to witty effect:

> Earlier in the year the Justice Department had more or less dropped the case, saying that an FBI inquiry had uncovered 'no credible evidence of wrongdoing'. Now the House sub-committee has poured oil on these smouldering embers by strongly challenging that finding.
>
> – Harold Jackson, *The Guardian*

> When we Woosters put our hands to the plough, we do not readily sheathe the sword.
>
> – P.G. Wodehouse, *Right Ho, Jeeves*

But unless you are very confident of bringing it off, don't risk such mischievous juggling with language when it comes to your own writing or speaking. As a rule, ensure that your idioms and figures of speech within any sentence are all consistent with one another.

Within any sentence. Once a new sentence or (to be quite safe) a new idea has begun, you certainly can draw on a new image without committing 'mixed metaphor'. Though as always, beware of overspicing.

> She ran the whole gamut of the emotions from A to B. (Dorothy Parker)

> Never do today what you can put off till tomorrow. (*Punch*)

> If a thing is worth doing it is worth doing badly. (G.K. Chesterton)

And here are a few puns, of a kind to make the reader sit up and take notice:

> We must all hang together, or assuredly we shall all hang separately. (Benjamin Franklin)

> His sins were scarlet, but his books were read. (Hilaire Belloc)

> Mrs Forbes is a secretary who won't be dictated to. (*Radio Times*)

> You can always tell a Balliol man, but you can't tell him very much.

> The neighbours were arguing from different premises.

> For a man with a moustache, drinking soup can be quite a strain.

> It's all just mind over matter – never mind, it doesn't matter.

> The cat ate some cheese, then waited for the mouse with baited breath.

> Is life worth living? It depends on the liver.

> Old professors never die – they just lose their faculties.

There are double puns too, as in the strip-tease theatre called 'The Steeple' (where the belles peel).

And even triple puns, as in the ranch, inherited by three brothers, called 'Focus' (where the sons raise meat/sun's rays meet).

Too much of that kind of thing, however, and the reader quickly rebels:

?? Hans-Joachim, the young hero, lands himself 'a plum job' as head of the soft fruits department. But when he arrives in Brussels, trailing clouds of glory, he finds himself in a bit of a jam. The reason? A mountain of rotting plums proves a sticky problem.

> – Debbie Lawson, preview of
> *The Gravy Train* on Oracle teletext

Overuse is an obvious danger, then, but it is not the only one. Equally distracting and distressing is

THE UNINTENDED PUN

The unintended or inappropriate pun is familiar to most writers:

?? A titanic struggle is underway for ownership of the Tashioko shipping company.

?? Most of the salesmen are out of the office attending the manager's funeral: we're operating on a skeleton staff today.

?? The word *aeromobile* never really got off the ground.

?? She's forever carping about the canteen food, especially the fish-pie.

?? Those two newsreaders don't work well as a team – they're not really on the same wavelength.

?? The Football Association *must* tackle the problem of the professional foul.

?? To all trainee pilots! Our new crash course will qualify you for your flying licence within two months.

?? Why do you bring up the subject of seasickness whenever we go sailing?

?? He had the misguided idea of admitting girls into the Boy Scouts.

And so on.

Psychologists have attempted to explain this common phenomenon: it seems that most people have a kind of mental thesaurus, and tend to flip through it in a flash when deciding which words to use in any given context.

If your mind is set to a particular topic (the takeover struggle for a shipping company, say), and you need an intensifying adjective to describe it, your mental thesaurus will highlight any word that falls within the same frame of reference (*titanic* rather than *gigantic*, say). Most writers and speakers remain quite unconscious of this process, and therefore fail to notice how inappropriate the chosen word happens to be.

Here are a few more examples – fairly obscure sometimes, but some reader or other did observe them ... and was distracted from the text as a result.

A police spokesman reportedly said:

?? A hole has appeared in the road. Fife police are looking into it.
> – quoted in Fritz Spiegl,
> *Keep Taking the Tabloids!*

?? The executive's first thoughts were naturally of suicide ... Still the executive dithered ... He found it impossible, in the absence of some trigger, to come to any clear decision.
> – Thomas Pynchon (U.S.),
> *The Crying of Lot 49*

?? For Sale. Two leather sofas. £800. Will split.
> – small ads, *Swindon Messenger*

Here are two unintended puns with a musical theme. (To make matters worse, the first quotation begins with a misrelated participle – see pages 195-199).

?? Heard in stores and shopping centres throughout the country, many retailers – though by no means all – clearly regard piped music as a sound selling device.
> – *Which?* magazine

?? ... one of Pakistan's finest Qawwali (Islamic devotional music) duos. Since 1953, they have been instrumental in popularising Qawwali throughout the world.
> – *Radio Times*

Finally, a few very subtle examples.

Here are the clues, in case the puns elude you: *clamping, coffee beans*, and *pause*.

? As from this weekend, police will be clamping down on motorists in an effort to stamp out the problem of double- and even treble-parking in Golders Green Road.
> – *Jewish Chronicle*

? A housekeeper serves coffee from a silver coffee pot. Lord Bauer is full of beans; slim, neatly dressed, gregarious.
> – Michael Davie, *The Observer*

? Would-be pet lovers should pause for thought before rushing out to acquire a feline friend.
> – Teresa Hunter, *Moneycare* magazine

wordplay that falls flat: a bad pun is far worse than no pun at all, and your readers' groans will weaken the force of your arguments:

? The Channel Tunnel project is having trouble making ends meet.

A still subtler danger lies in wait, and you will have to keep very alert to detect it – 'accidental wordplay'. The unintended rhyme or half-rhyme grates on the reader's ear (see page 29). And the unintended pun draws the reader up short, either in puzzlement or in disrespectful laughter:

?? You should have taken steps to get the staircase repaired.

?? You're going to buy that leaky old boat of his! – I wouldn't touch it with a bargepole.

When rereading and editing any piece of writing of yours, do keep a lookout for dangers of that kind. For a more detailed discussion of this common pitfall, see the panel *The unintended pun* opposite.

THE STRIKING OPENING

'Hook' the reader firmly at the outset, or else – like a fish – he will escape. If he can, he will stop reading your unpromising text altogether, and pass on to something more interesting. And if he has to read it, he will do so inattentively or grudgingly or both.

Take the opening two paragraphs of the chapter *The Art of Writing* (page 14). How would you have reacted if they had read as follows?

> Although a piece of writing is typically done in private, the intention is almost always that it should be read by some other person or people.

> Writing, in other words, is above all for communication. With a few exceptions, all writing tasks are undertaken for the purpose of conveying ideas and feelings from the writer to someone else, even if that someone else is the writer himself at some later date.

Hardly an encouragement to read on. The wording is clear and accurate maybe, but certainly dull.

An arresting opening, by contrast, seizes the reader's attention and ensures continued reading. Look at the selection of openings in the panel on page 75, for instance. If you picked up a book and read a first sentence or paragraph like those, it would take enormous will-power to put the book down without reading any further.

GIVE EXAMPLES

The theme or message of a piece of writing usually has to nestle within a rather dull or abstract statement, or a generalised warning or command:

> Alan Ayckbourn has marvellous insight into the embarrassment caused by everyday domestic mishaps.

> Exhaust emissions from lead-free petrol engines still present health hazards.

> Don't use the passive voice repeatedly in your sentences.

To convey such generalities, however, the skilled writer precisely avoids generalities as far as possible. He lists *specific cases* rather than just general findings. He uses *concrete examples* rather than abstract declarations to make his point. It is these case histories and examples that give colour or drama to the writing, and prevent the reader's attention from straying.

Show, don't tell. In descriptive or narrative writing – as in an autobiography or a novel – one standby formula is 'Show, don't tell'.

Fiction writers have two broad strategies at their disposal:

☐ to tell the reader what to think; that is, to explain and clarify the plot and characters, as in *Mary was envious of her sister's new dress*.

☐ to *show* everything to the reader; that is, to present the plot and characters in action – in small dramatised scenes, one after the other: *Mary's eyes narrowed as her sister approached, wearing a dress that Mary had never seen before*.

Modern novelists and critics tend to favour the *showing* strategy, sometimes to the point of banishing or condemning the *telling* strategy absolutely. In fact, most good fiction, old and new, subtly blends the two modes. The writer should not spoonfeed (and bore) the reader by too much telling; but he or she is surely entitled now and then to small nudges of telling as a means of guiding the reader's understanding or sympathies.

Literary critics champion *showing* on the ground of its greater artistry. For everyday writing, however, the question is not of artistry but of effectiveness. Simply, what is the best way of getting your point across to the reader? The answer, in most contexts, is going to be: tell and show. Make the point explicitly, and then give the evidence for it. State your generalisation, and then list several examples to back it up.

(Or, if you want to approach it from the other direction: show and tell. First reveal all your data, and then state your conclusion. Relate the fable, and then draw the moral.)

Here is an engaging example of the tell-and-show technique. It comes from a chapter of memoirs – either literary writing or everyday writing, whichever you prefer to view it as:

> My father had later another Aberdeen terrier, answering to the pleasant name of Scrubbins . . . a dog of considerable character and a most faithful friend to my father. Once or twice my father took him to the University Library, left him outside and forgot him. Scrubbins quite unperturbed went to the nearest cab-stand, where he was well known, and took a hansom home. One little scene in which he figured comes back to me. My sister was being married in the forbidding precincts of the Cambridge Registry Office and Scrubbins had been left at the door. We were all ranged in due order before the table and the proceedings had begun, when a deliberate pit-a-pat was heard in the passage. Somebody got up to shut the door but the Registrar hastily interposed; the marriage, it appeared, would not be legal unless it were open to all comers to attend. So Scrubbins pattered in and behaved with perfect discretion and decorum. He added a cheerful note to the rather grim ceremony, and if there had been a vestry we were all satisfied that he would have signed his name in it.
>
> – Bernard Darwin, *Pack Clouds Away*

Putting things into focus. Consider the following passage, from a magazine article on the new edition of the *Oxford English Dictionary*.

Note how smoothly and unobtrusively the writer puts things into focus in each paragraph by citing precise examples.

> On 30 March this year the second edition of the *Oxford English Dictionary*, prepared by John Simpson and myself, was published. This combines the contents of the *Supplement* with the first edition. Up till now, people wishing to explore the full range of meanings of the most important words have had to investigate both the first edition and the *Supplement*. So, for the word 'satellite', there were five senses in the first edition, the root meaning being 'an attendant', the second 'a secondary planet', and so on. The *Supplement* added not only the recent (1936) usage, 'a man-made orbiting object', but also a further eight meanings including a large number of phrases ('satellite television') and scientific uses . . .
>
> . . . The text has increased by 34 per cent: the new edition appears in twenty volumes (21,728 pages). It has been further enhanced by the addition of about 5,000 words and meanings which were neither in the first edition nor in the *Supplement*, covering a broad spectrum of usage, for example: axion, born-again, cold-call, compact disc, factionalize, junk food, keypad, mini-series, nuclear winter, screen editor, throw a wobbly.
>
> – Dr Edmund Weiner, 'Newspeak',
> *Oxford Today*

For readers struggling to comprehend the rather complex general message in each case, the examples suddenly crystallise the meaning, and everything becomes clear.

Here is another helpful passage, from a book of travel writing:

> 'Room with bed for two,' said the proprietor, flinging open a door at the extreme end. He contrived to invest it with an air of extreme indelicacy, which in no way prepared us for the reality.
>
> It was a nightmare room, the room of a drug fiend or a miscreant or perhaps both. It was illuminated by a forty-watt bulb and looked out on a black wall with something slimy growing on it. The bed was a fearful thing, almost perfectly concave. Underneath it was a pair of old cloth-topped boots. The sheets were almost clean but on them there was the unmistakable impress of a human form and they were still warm. In the corner there was a washbasin with one long red hair in it and a tap which leaked. Somewhere nearby a fun-fair was testing its loud-hailing apparatus, warming up for a night of revelry. The smell of the room was the same as the corridor outside with some indefinable additions.
>
> – Eric Newby, *A Short Walk in the Hindu Kush*

Imagine if the passage had ended after the phrase *nightmare room*. The reader would hardly have

ARRESTING OPENINGS

Here are a few captivating opening paragraphs or sentences from various novels. Non-fiction too reads all the better for an interesting opening – it lures the reader in. On a smaller scale, even the humblest business report would benefit from an incisive start. It might stimulate the prejudiced reader into paying more attention.

> I was singing the hired assassin in *Rigoletto* the time I was propositioned to become one myself.
>
> – Angus Hall, *The Rigoletto Murder*

> Nobody could sleep. When morning came, assault craft would be lowered and a first wave of troops would ride through the surf and charge ashore on the beach of Anopopei. All over the ship, all through the convoy, there was a knowledge that in a few hours some of them were going to be dead.
>
> – Norman Mailer (U.S.), *The Naked and the Dead*

> When a day that you happen to know is Wednesday starts off by sounding like Sunday, there is something seriously wrong somewhere.
>
> – John Wyndham, *The Day of the Triffids*

> The scent and smoke and sweat of a casino are nauseating at three in the morning. Then the soul-erosion produced by high gambling – a compost of greed and fear and nervous tension – becomes unbearable and the senses awake and revolt from it.
>
> – Ian Fleming, *Casino Royale*

> Hale knew, before he had been in Brighton three hours, that they meant to murder him.
>
> – Graham Greene, *Brighton Rock*

> It was a bright cold day in April, and the clocks were striking thirteen. Winston Smith, his chin nuzzled into his breast in an effort to escape the vile wind, slipped quickly through the glass doors of Victory Mansions, though not quickly enough to prevent a swirl of gritty dust from entering along with him.
>
> – George Orwell, *Nineteen Eighty-Four*

> I am going to pack my two shirts with my other socks and my best suit in the little blue cloth my mother used to tie round her hair when she did the house, and I am going from the Valley.
>
> – Richard Llewellyn, *How Green Was My Valley*

> By ten-forty-five it was all over. The town was occupied, the defenders defeated, and the war finished.
>
> – John Steinbeck (U.S.), *The Moon is Down*

come away with a vivid impression of the scene. In the event, the author develops the phrase by adding example after example to it, each of them reflecting his acute observation of concrete detail.

Note how the examples cover four of the five physical senses – sight, touch, hearing, and smell – and how they vary from the lethally precise (*forty-watt bulb, one long red hair*) to the menacingly uncertain (*some indefinable additions*).

ABSTRACT VS CONCRETE

Here is a famous rallying cry of Churchill's:

> Implementation of these plans will necessitate a significant proportion of sacrifice on our side, as well as considerable input of commitment and a high expenditure of energy and resources.

Not quite. The actual words that Churchill used, on more than one occasion, but most famously in a speech to the House of Commons on 13 May 1940, were these:

> I have nothing to offer but blood, toil, tears, and sweat.

(For two similar parodies, see the panel *The lure of abstraction* overleaf.)

Business writing is notoriously prone to abstract language – clinical, formal, unemotional:

? A copy of our new Smoking Policy is attached for your information... To provide us all with the opportunity to prepare for and adapt to the requirements of this new policy, the implementation will not be effected until 1 January 1990...

THE LURE OF ABSTRACTION

Show-off writers choose high-falutin abstract words in preference to simple or concrete words and images. To unsophisticated or insecure readers, this may well come over as vastly learned and impressive, but experienced and sceptical readers treat it for what it is – insipid, pompous, and boring.

In his famous essay 'Politics and the English Language', George Orwell offers an extreme example of abstractitis – a modern rewrite of a famous biblical passage. Can you work out which verse he is 'improving' here?

??Objective consideration of contemporary phenomena compels the conclusion that success or failure in competitive activities exhibits no tendency to be commensurate with innate capacity, but that a considerable element of the unpredictable must invariably be taken into account.

The biblical passage undergoing this indignity is *Ecclesiastes* 9:11.

> I returned, and saw under the sun, that the race is not to the swift, nor the battle to the strong, neither yet bread to the wise, nor yet riches to men of understanding, nor yet favour to men of skill; but time and chance happeneth to them all.

And in the following extract, an Oxford professor, in mimicking the 'house style' and copy-editors of an American publisher, has rewritten a few famous lines of Shakespeare's.

Can you recognise them?

??Humans are of the type of material that constitutes dreams, and their relatively brief existences terminate, as well as taking their inception, in a state of unconsciousness.

> – Richard Gombrich,
> letter to *The New York Review of Books*

The lines he is parodying here are those spoken by Prospero:

> We are such stuff
> As dreams are made on, and our little life
> Is rounded with a sleep.
> – *The Tempest*, IV, i

Your understanding and cooperation in the introduction of this policy will be most appreciated.

> – office memo

Note all the abstract nouns in addition to *policy*: *information, opportunity, requirements, implementation, understanding, cooperation,* and *introduction*. Businesslike, certainly; courteous and inoffensive, yes; but not exactly warm and friendly, and not exactly gripping. (For a more detailed discussion of abstract nouns, see page 33).

A more personal, informal, and inviting memo would run more along these lines:

> Please read the attached copy of our new Smoking Policy . . .

> To enable us all to prepare for and adapt to the new policy, we are pausing for a few months – until 1 January 1990 – before launching it officially. . . .

> Introducing a new policy such as this is never easy. Thank you for helping us to do it as smoothly and painlessly as possible.

Professional writers too, who ought to be immunised, succumb surprisingly often to 'abstractitis'. Here is the first paragraph of a magazine article, on the subject of doing office-work from home. Hardly the most riveting opening, especially in a general-interest magazine for the non-specialist reader:

? Massive strides forward in the flexibility of information-technology and the resultant availability of affordable and sophisticated equipment is making working from home a real possibility for hundreds of thousands of people.

> – William Golden, 'On the Home Front', *West End Connexions* (British Telecom)

There are many things wrong with this passage: the use of *is* instead of *are* after the plural subject; the jingle in the phrase *making working*; and the clichés (*massive strides forward, a real possibility*). But the feature to concentrate on here is the use of the unexciting abstract nouns *flexibility, availability,* and *possibility,* and the non-specific noun phrase *affordable and sophisticated equipment*. None of these terms produces any image in the reader's mind; none has power to seize the attention; none packs any punch. A more effective opening would list some concrete nouns – *fax machine, phone-linked computers,* and the like.

ABSTRACTION AND DULLNESS

Here is a two-part test on the pitfalls of abstract and dull language.

First, a quiz. Below are a few nursery rhymes – as if written by an old-style office manager, civil servant, or sociologist. Can you identify the original nursery rhyme in each case?

The answers are on pages 633-648.

> A man who arrogantly takes liberties when alone with women will tend, at the approach of any other men, to withdraw hastily from the situation.

> Catastrophe resulting from needless risk-taking is often irredeemable, no matter how extensive any subsequent attempts at damage-limitation might be.

> Among those most likely to suffer from malnutrition, physical abuse, and other manifestations of child neglect are the offspring of the single mother who is inadequately housed and overwhelmed by the burden of domestic responsibilities.

> A mutually exclusive though equitable distribution of consumables between marriage partners according to their differing tastes tends to ensure an economical and harmonious domestic relationship.

Next, a rewriting exercise.

The vague and abstraction-ridden sentences below might pass muster if they appeared at the end of a detailed paragraph. Here, however, they read almost like parodies of bad writing. As an exercise try rewriting them.

Think up any background details that you care to, and work them into your version.

The first passage might change to this:

> Of the 420 listeners who completed our questionnaire, 83% responded that *Night-beat* is now either 'more interesting' or 'much more interesting' than before, following the start of the nightly half-hour phone-in on 12 September 1990.

Your turn now. For possible redraftings of the other examples below, see pages 633-648.

> There was widespread agreement that the programme had recently shown an increase in quality.

> 1. This latest development will have a significant impact on price stability.

> 2. Several of the promised features are missing.

> 3. Market research suggests a more favourable outlook for the product's long-term profitability than previous assessments had indicated.

> 4. The vehicle's performance is quite unsatisfactory.

> 5. A different approach is advisable, drawing on outside expertise as well as internal management experience.

And who is under discussion in the passage? Not you or the boss or anyone else you can identify with or relate to or form a mental picture of; instead, a vague faceless uncountable mass, *hundreds of thousands of people*.

Finally, note the form of the passage: a generalised statement. Such generalisations are far easier to absorb if preceded by specific examples – as in the following suggested rewrite of the paragraph:

> You have just finished compiling that financial report, and are checking it on your computer screen. It looks fine. You lift the handset of your phone and place it into the rubber socket alongside. You dial the boss's number and tap a couple of keys on the keyboard. Half an hour later your fax machine spurts into life, printing out the boss's comments and his suggested revisions. What have you been doing during that half-hour? Taking a bath perhaps, preparing lunch, or feeding the cats.

> For you, and hundreds of thousands of office workers like you, working from home is now a realistic option – thanks to flexible modern information-technology and sophisticated yet low-cost office machines.

The new features in the first paragraph all contribute to the task of inviting the reader in. The very first word, *You*, is probably the most attention-grabbing word in the language; and it encourages the reader to take a personal interest in the contents, to relate it to his own life.

The nouns are mostly concrete, referring to physical objects that the reader easily 'sees' in his mind: *computer screen, phone, cats*, and so on.

The form of the paragraph is that of a short real-life scene – something that the reader can play through like a film clip in his own imagination.

Reinforcing this dramatic presentation are the verbs – mostly active and vivid: *list, dial, spurts, feeding*. Finally, a clever twist in the dramatic scene – a shift of perspective, from an office to your own home – rounds the paragraph out.

By the time the second paragraph arrives, the battle is over: the reader's resistance has crumbled, and he reads on eagerly. The second paragraph can safely proceed now to draw the moral. The reader has his bearings, and no longer finds it either difficult or boring to follow the more abstract wording and the more generalised message.

In the panel *Abstraction and dullness* on page 77, you can read some other typical vague and abstract sentences – the kind of sentence that turns up again and again in business reports, summaries of meetings, or letters of complaint. Examine them closely, to establish exactly why they are so bland; and then try adding some seasoning of your own.

The trick is to ask yourself constantly as you write, *What? Where? Who? How? When? Why?* If an answer does emerge at any point, decide if it is relevant. If so, work it into the sentence that gave rise to it.

True enough, you do sometimes need to be vague. The relevant details might be confidential, and you have to conceal them for that reason. Or you may want to draw your reader out – to encourage him to come up with some answers for himself. Remember, however, that it is the writer who should do the spadework as a rule, not the reader. The more trouble you take in communicating your thoughts and information clearly, the faster and more accurately your reader will absorb it all, and the happier he will be with you.

High-Risk Types of Wording

Many traps and temptations lie in wait for the unwary writer – clichés, jargon, and the like.

Not that all such modes of writing are subject to a blanket ban. The occasional cliché or slang term may prove very effective in the right context; euphemisms and jargon terms certainly are appropriate in certain circumstances. But do at least be mindful of all these high-risk types of wording.

JARGON

If the following quotations were written for experts, their wording would be perfectly 'appropriate':

?? The fusion of conflicting tendencies in the figure of the monster in horror films has the dream process of condensation as its approximate psychic prototype.
　　　　– Noel Carrol (U.S.), *Film Quarterly*

?? The investigation of aesthetic ideologies is a first step in a much larger project of developing a theory of decentred cultures predicated on the conflictive heterogeneity of cultural production.
　　　　– Jim Collins, *Uncommon Cultures*

?? Every living cell is a special, Frölich-style, quantum sub-class within Prigogine self-organising dissipative systems.
　　　　– Danah Zohar (U.S.), *The Quantum Self*

The trouble is: the books and article in question are intended not for nuclear physicists, professional psychotherapists, and sociology professors, but for laymen – educated laymen, true enough, but non-specialists all the same.

How is the author in each case meant to be serving the interests of these readers by writing such unintelligibly technical sentences?

The word *jargon* has both a neutral and a negative sense today. In its neutral sense, *jargon* is the professional language of a specialised group, its technical vocabulary that allows for efficient and accurate communication. Physicists, for instance, talk of *quarks* and *leptons*; if they had to use layman's language to spell out their ideas each time, they would be able to exchange hardly any ideas at all. Similarly, philosophy lecturers might use the jargon terms *sensibilia* and *meta-representation* as shorthand counters when conducting a debate.

Note that such jargon terms are not always obscure words: physicists also speak of *black holes*; computer programmers of *gates*; financiers of *dawn raids* and *white knights*; wine experts of *breed* and *elegance*, and so on. It is the *concepts*, rather than the words themselves, that baffle the layman. (Here lies the main difference between jargon and slang: slang tends to consist of words for very familiar and unbaffling concepts – such as *smashed*, *high*, and *busted* for 'drunk', 'drugged', and 'arrested'.)

If only jargon kept to its proper function as a professional shorthand, the word *jargon* could shake off its other, negative sense. But jargon strays beyond its rightful limits in several ways.

'Insiders' use jargon not just for the purpose of efficient communication, but with ulterior motives too – as a kind of secret code or badge to reinforce its group identity and exclude outsiders from the magic circle; as a weapon to impress, browbeat, or bamboozle those outsiders into awe or submission; and as a screen to blur their meaning in order to shirk commitment or responsibility.

To look at each of these abuses in turn.

Elitist jargon. Laymen or 'outsiders' have long railed against the elitist and self-congratulatory overuse of jargon between insiders. Increasingly nowadays, some insiders themselves – 'professional traitors' – are questioning the amount of jargon used by their colleagues. Do we literary critics, some critics now ask, really need terms such as *engagé* or *textuality* to convey our ideas? Aren't we really just showing off, perhaps?

In a famous déflation of his fellow-professors' writings (specifically their 'grand theories' rather than just their use of high-flown language), an American sociologist 'translated' a few particularly jargon-ridden passages, such as the one in which *sociology* is defined as dealing with

?? that aspect of the theory of social systems which is concerned with the phenomena of the institutionalisation of patterns of value-orientation in the social system, with the conditions of that institutionalisation; and of changes in the patterns, with conditions of conformity with and deviance from a set of such patterns, and with motivational processes in so far as they are involved in all of these.
– Talcott Parsons (U.S.), *The Social System*

The plain-worded rewriting of this passage reads:

Sociologists of my sort would like to study what people want and cherish. We would also like to find out why there is a variety of such values and why they change. When we do find a more or less unitary set of values, we would like to find out why some people do and others do not conform to them. (end of translation)
– C. Wright Mills (U.S.), *The Sociological Imagination*

Here is (part of) another passage that is badly in need of translating:

?? A 'value-orientation' aspect . . . concerns, not the meaning of the expected state of affairs to the actor in terms of his gratification-deprivation balance but the contents of the selective standards themselves.

The concept of value-orientations in this sense is thus the logical device for formulating one central aspect of the articulation of cultural traditions into the action system.

. . . Expectations then, in combination with the 'double contingency' of the process of interaction as it has been called, create a crucially imperative problem of order. Two aspects of this problem of order may in turn be distinguished, order in the symbolic systems which make communication possible, and order in the mutuality of motivational orientation to the normative aspect of expectations, the 'Hobbesian' problem of order.

The problem of order, and thus of the nature of the integration of stable systems of interaction, that is, of social structure, thus focuses on the integration of the motivation of actors with the normative cultural standards which integrate the action system, in our context interpersonally.
– Talcott Parsons (U.S.), *The Social System*

The laconic translation reads as follows:

People often share standards and expect one another to stick to them. In so far as they do, their society may be orderly.
– C. Wright Mills (U.S.), *The Sociological Imagination*

Thank goodness that at least some 'insiders' refuse to preserve intact the cosy masonic character of unintelligible jargon. They struggle to make their own writing as lucid and jargon-free as possible, to make it act as a Welcome sign to all readers rather than as a sign warning that 'Trespassers will be prosecuted'.

Jargon to manipulate. Now for the second abuse of jargon – its use by insiders to manipulate rather than just exclude outsiders: that is a charge traditionally levelled against consultants – doctors and lawyers in particular. Doctors allegedly blind their patients with science, 'explaining' an oily skin as *chronic epidermal seborrhoea*, for instance. And lawyers allegedly blind their clients with verbiage – their *ex parte applications* and *garnishment orders* and *hereinafters*, and so on.

The lawyers' traditional excuse is that only 'legalese' can establish exact definitions and close all legal loopholes. Yet increasingly, lawyers are finding that simpler wording is possible after all. Some large American law firms now employ editors to revise the wording in letters sent to clients, and even to advise on the wording of contracts. And in New York and some other U.S. cities, local by-laws now require landlords, estate agents, building societies, and the like to word their loan agreements, leases, and other contracts in language that the layman can understand.

In Britain a few years ago, the City Council in Bradford boldly – and successfully – rewrote its rule books in 'plain English', retaining a group of 'non-experts' – a journalist, a librarian, teachers, and so on – to redraft the regulations in consultation with a lawyer.

The results were fascinating. Not only did the revised version appear to keep all sealed loopholes sealed; it also, people claimed at the time, succeeded in sealing some loopholes that in the original version had been left open.

Here is an example of the changes made – taken from the Council's 'Standing Orders for Contracts'. First, the original passage in 'legalese':

?? After expiration of the period specified in the public notice, invitations to tender for the contract shall be sent to not less than four of the persons who apply for permission to tender, selected in the manner determined by the appropriate Committee, Special Sub-Committee, College Governing Body or an Officer referred to in 3(1) above generally or in relation to a particular contract or category of contracts or, if fewer than four persons have applied and are considered suitable, to all such persons.

Here now is the passage after it had been redrafted into 'plain English':

After the closing date, at least four contractors, chosen by the appropriate Committee, Special Sub-Committee, College Governing Body or appropriate Officer, must be asked to tender. If there are fewer than four, all those considered suitable must be asked to tender.

Not only is this new version much easier to understand, but it also alerted the Council to a weakness in the standing orders; namely, that the 'appropriate . . . Officer' might, acting on his own, use improper criteria in deciding which contractors are 'suitable' – that the original rules were not tight enough to guard against corruption. (Whether this loophole has really closed is open to doubt.)

The wider moral here is surely this: that even in specialised contexts, jargon should be kept to a minimum if outsiders are likely to encounter it. *The Journal of Plasma Physics* is one thing: few non-scientists will ever have to grapple with its contents. But Bradford City Council's 'Standing Orders for Contracts' is another: it is precisely intended not just for lawyers but for builders, plumbers, and other contractors as well.

What happened in Bradford is also now happening in the country as a whole.

In the wake of a government report in 1981, most official forms – including the tax return – have become far simpler to understand than they used to be. The Civil Service College now runs courses on drafting simple, jargon-free reports, forms, and other documents. So too banks, insurance companies, county councils, and the like.

The everyday writer can no longer cite these institutions as models to justify his own use of bureaucratic jargon or gobbledygook. If you are on the receiving end of a document written in incomprehensible officialese, send it back with a request for a clear explanation in plain English. If you are responsible for writing such a document . . .

Jargon that obscures meaning. The third and worst abuse of jargon now: its use to blur or obscure meaning. Instead of refining or clarifying or streamlining one's meaning – as 'good' jargon does – bad jargon is valued precisely for its lack of precision. Without officialese, bureaucrats might have to express their thoughts plainly and thereby give offence. With officialese, however, they can be as bland and inoffensive as anyone, can avoid committing themselves to definite decisions, and can avoid responsibility when things go wrong.

That celebrated American jargon-monger and language-mangler Alexander Haig, for instance, during his time as U.S. Secretary of State, was quoted as saying: **??** 'Because of the fluctuational predisposition of your position's productive capacity as juxtaposed to government standards, it would be momentarily injudicious to advocate an increment.' Haig was simply – simply? – turning down an application for a pay increase.

'Officialese' is characterised by such evasive qualities as the passive voice (*Orders were given for two loads to be delivered* instead of *I ordered two loads*), abstractions and impersonal statements (*a review of the available facts by the department concerned has determined that . . .*), and above all, a jargon-ridden vogue vocabulary (*inadvisable, feedback, interface, input, prioritise*, and so on).

Politicians, civil servants, military spokesmen, and other bureaucrats remain adept, when pressed to explain their policies or defend their actions, at sending up a smoke screen of new jargon terms or euphemisms, sometimes specially invented for the occasion. Some of the finest moments in the BBC situation comedy *Yes, Minister* are those in which bureaucratic jargon is satirised. The following is a fine example:

(Sir Humphrey Appleby): ' . . . We've just heard from the Special Branch that your protection is being withdrawn . . . The police have suffered an acute personnel-establishment shortfall.'

(The Rt. Hon. James Hacker, MP): 'What?'

'They're short-staffed . . . They overheard a conversation . . . to the effect that in view of the somewhat nebulous and inexplicit nature of your remit, and the arguably marginal and peripheral nature of your influence on the central deliberations and decisions within the political process, there could be a case for restructuring their action-priorities in such a way as to eliminate your liquidation from their immediate agenda.'

. . . 'Well, what does it mean in English?'

'Well, Minister, it means – that you're not really important enough for it to be worth assassinating you.'

In real life, the most celebrated examples of such verbiage seem to come out of the United States. In the early 1970s, for instance, a White House aide announced that an earlier statement issued by the

PSYCHOBABBLE AND SOCIOLOGESE

Sociologese permeates journalism and fashionable conversation to such an extent today that many speakers have virtually ceased to notice it. One amazing reminder of its prevalence is the 'buzz-phrase generator' – a set of three columns (or discs) of sociological vogue words that can combine into a huge number of meaningless but impressive-sounding jargon phrases. The first and second columns list adjectives; the third column lists nouns. Here is a very abbreviated version:

column 1	column 2	column 3
divergent	compensatory	dysfunction
elitist	diagnostic	polarisation
operational	empirical	quotient
supportive	socio-economic	synthesis
viable	unstructured	validation
integrated	digital	mobility
responsive	logistical	contingency

By combining these items in different ways, the user can produce such euphonious phrases as *elitist compensatory validation* and *operational diagnostic dysfunction*.

Psychobabble too, originally a North American disease, is beginning to infect British English.

(The term *psychobabble* was coined by the American writer R.D. Rosen in 1977, but the phenomenon goes back much further than that.) Beginning with the Freudian terms *complex, repression, sublimation, projection*, and so on, laymen have been adopting psychological terminology into their own self-analyses – invariably debasing the words in the process. Later examples include *paranoid* for 'suspicious or worried', and *schizoid* or *ambivalent* for 'undecided'.

The next development, in about the mid-1960s, was that American laymen began inventing their own pseudo-psychological terms – *uptight, hang-ups, laid-back, personal space*, and so on. These eventually found their way into the vocabulary of some professional psychotherapists, bringing the wheel of jargon full circle.

administration should now be considered 'no longer operative'. Translation: it had been wrong – or untruthful.

The jargon of the American military establishment is particularly notorious: *anticipatory retaliation* = a surprise attack, for instance. In 1983, Admiral Wesley L. McDonald, reluctantly admitting the navy's ignorance of events in Grenada just before the American landing on the island, phrased it in this way: **??** 'We were not micromanaging Grenada intelligence-wise until about that time frame.'

Bureaucratic language has infected our language widely, then. Fortunately, official awareness of it is increasing – and official discouragement of it too.

Moreover, the lay public is clamouring for reform.

Newspapers and magazines have taken to publicising the more outrageous specimens of officialese, and unofficial organisations have sprung up on both sides of the Atlantic to monitor and combat the blight of jargon – the Plain English Campaign in Britain, and in the U.S. The Committee on Public Doublespeak (a committee of the U.S. National Council of Teachers of English).

Both of these organisations award annual prizes – either for the best-written and most jargon-free documents of the year, or for the worst-written and most jargon-ridden documents of the year. In 1983, for example, the American organisation's third (booby) prize went to a firm of accountants which in its inventory of a client's building had listed the fire alarms as *combustion enunciators*. And in 1987 the British organisation gave a Golden Bull Award and 'first prize' for poor writing to the Automobile Association, for the following opening sentence in an insurance services leaflet:

?? Whereas a written application and declaration has been made and accepted such application and declaration shall, the fee having been paid, form the basis of the Contract and we the undersigned accordingly confirm that under the terms of a master policy issued by certain BIA insurance companies and a separate master policy issued by certain Underwriters at Lloyds, such Companies and Underwriters being Underwriters of the Contract (together 'the insurers') in each case to Automobile Association Insurance Services Limited on behalf of and for the exclusive benefit of members of the Automobile Association, the Owner shall be indemnified against loss occurring during the Period of Cover in accordance with the terms of the said master policies a summary of which is contained herein for Mechanical or Electrical Breakdown arising in connection with the Vehicle Covered without recourse to contribution from the Owner except where specifically stated.

The temptation of jargon. In your own speaking and writing – whether for everyday purposes or in the course of official work – jargon lurks as an ever-present temptation. Critics lampoon it constantly: the pseudo-intellectual slipping on a linguistic banana-skin of his own making, the office boy trying to impress his employers with a few of their own favourite phrases, ever so slightly misused . . . But to no avail. The allure of jargon remains as powerful for laymen as it does for bureaucrats and specialists. (Two of the most glaring types of layman's jargon are psychobabble and sociologese. For some details on them, see the panel on page 81.)

How can you defend yourself against the siren-call of jargon in your own writing? The best defence, as always, is to be mindful of the danger. Keep alert.

And keep reminding yourself of the following obvious truths and tactics:

☐ If jargon has 'always' been used in a particular context, that does not justify its continuing use there. Even if business letters have traditionally contained such formulas as *inst, prox, ult, re, please send same*, and *your esteemed favour*, that is no reason for you to use such 'commercialese' in business letters today.

☐ Even if a text is drafted by 'experts', it might still be worded more simply and intelligibly without loss of accuracy.

☐ If a text sounds 'impressive', this is no guarantee that it is any more reliable than a straightforward, more modest version would be.

When confronted by a jargon word or phrase, you can test its acceptability by asking these common-sense questions: Does it really convey a meaning? Would I use it in conversation? Could it be replaced by a simpler synonym or paraphrase? Is it being used for any purposes other than clear communication, and if so, are these purposes legitimate?

If everyone were to apply these simple tests to their choice of words, a great deal of the needless jargon now current would disappear overnight.

TECHNICAL RHYMES

Here are some familiar nursery rhymes rewritten for 'technical experts'. Try to cut your way through the thicket of jargon and identify them. For the answers and the original versions, see pages 633-648.

Report. Subject advanced towards repository to procure osteal specimen for *Canis familiaris*. Result: no specimen found. Conclusion: intended or prospective beneficiary deprived.

Proceeding on my routine patrol about the two-tier premises, I encountered in the boudoir a gentleman of advanced years, conducting himself in a most improper manner. I was obliged to employ a certain degree of force in order to subdue and apprehend him.

A domestic pet openly admitted, under repeated questioning, to having gone to the capital expressly intent upon a social encounter with the ruler, and while there, to having instilled fear in a diminutive rodent beneath an article of furniture.

In direct consequence of my castanea sapling with its precious albeit extremely low yield, a royal Iberian delegate was despatched to conduct negotiations.

Reports are coming in of an outbreak of mysterious behaviour by i.) two culinary utensils and ii.) one domesticated mammal. The factors underlying this phenomenon appear to be a.) an uncharacteristic partnership between a second domesticated mammal and a stringed instrument, and b.) the journey through space on the part of a third domesticated mammal.

CLICHÉS

The old joke, 'Avoid clichés like the plague', takes the principle slightly too far. Clichés have their uses. They serve as a kind of shorthand in informal letters or hasty memos. To describe a family row as *a storm in a teacup* or *making a mountain out of a molehill* is to communicate a simple thought in a fairly efficient way. It saves the writer time and effort looking for a fresh metaphor (such as *Tweedledum and Tweedledee fighting over a rattle*) or devising a lengthy and complicated explanation (such as *an overexcited airing of our differences, quite disproportionate to the trifling matter that caused them*). And it saves the reader time and effort trying to decode such a rewording.

In less casual writing, however, the objections to clichés hold good. Since language mirrors thought, the tired and unimaginative language of clichés suggests tired and unimaginative thinking. Readers or listeners often cannot help regarding the opinions of a cliché-user as second-hand. If he cannot take the trouble to *express* his thoughts in a fresh or careful way, people feel, then he has probably been too lazy to *consider* his thoughts in a fresh and careful way. Fairly or unfairly, he is often regarded as slightly insensitive – rather like the bore who is always telling stale jokes.

The word *cliché* comes from the French. Its literal meaning there is 'stereotype' or 'stereotyped' – a stereotype being, originally, a metal printing plate cast from a mould. (The French verb referring to this process, *clicher*, developed in imitation of the sound made when the matrix, or mould of type, was dropped into the molten metal to make a stereotype plate.) From this image of a printing plate, turning out the same page again and again, came the sense of 'a phrase, idea, or situation that has been used too often – a trite, hackneyed expression', a cliché.

Clichés come in many shapes and sizes (to use a cliché). Here is a suggested inventory of the varieties of cliché, with a few examples of each. There is naturally some overlap among them.

Homilies, platitudes, and stale proverbial sentiments. Well-intentioned though these no doubt are, as advice or consolation, they often succeed only in irritating the hearer:

> He who pays the piper calls the tune.
> It's no good crying over spilt milk.
> It takes all kinds to make a world.
> Slow and steady wins the race.

The overused idiom. These set expressions or phrases have long since lost their impact:

> conspicuous by his absence
> to add insult to injury
> a tower of strength
> at the drop of a hat

A particularly common kind of clichéd idiom is the 'duet' or the 'trio' – a pair or threesome of words that seems to be an inseparable combination, to go together like '... a horse and carriage':

> part and parcel
> by leaps and bounds
> without rhyme or reason
> cool, calm, and collected
> hook, line, and sinker
> every Tom, Dick, and Harry

Tarnished images and faded similes. Various metaphors, which might have been sparkling when they first appeared, have become dulled through overuse and lost their original metaphorical point.

> Silence reigned supreme
> to keep your nose to the grindstone
> to beat about the bush
> down memory lane

A close relative of the dead metaphor is the faded simile:

> as bold as brass
> to sell like hot cakes
> like a bat out of hell
> to turn up like a bad penny

Dead quotations and pointless allusions. These most often come from Shakespeare or the Bible, and are often misquoted. This type of cliché is particularly appealing to the show-off:

> more sinned against than sinning
> the writing on the wall
> to turn the other cheek
> Lead on, Macduff (or, to quote Shakespeare
>   correctly, 'Lay on, Macduff')

The inevitable adjective. Many writers and speakers seem unable to use a noun without using its traditional accompanying adjective as well:

> *cherished* beliefs
> a *concerted* effort
> *blissful* ignorance
> *sweeping* changes

Adverbs too are sometimes tightly linked to a particular verb or adjective – *inextricably* linked, you might say:

> *hermetically* sealed
> *deadly* serious
> *hopelessly* lost

Nicknames, titles, or sobriquets. Again, the showing-off side of people prompts them to avoid calling a person, place, or thing by its ordinary name, and to choose instead some 'different' title – facetious or solemn – that is in fact no different from the title used by millions of others:

> your better half
> the Antipodes
> yours truly
> the Bard of Avon

Professional slogans. Politicians, lawyers, 'celebrities', and public officials tend to have a repertoire of formulas 'suitable for all occasions':

> No comment
> a man who needs no introduction
> last but not least
> agree to differ

Needless foreign phrases. Foreign languages are another favourite hunting-ground for show-off chiché-mongers:

> la dolce vita
> terra firma
> c'est la vie

Finally some clichéd phrases of recent coining, as evidence that the cliché-industry is (to adapt a cliché) alive and well and living in our midst.

Three types can be identified here. First, those irritating counters used unthinkingly in informal everyday exchanges:

> over the moon
> the best thing since sliced bread
> No way
> the name of the game

Secondly, some modern journalistic clichés:

> political wilderness
> a legal minefield
> informed sources
> If X didn't exist, we'd have to invent him.
> a thought-provoking portrayal (in book reviews)
> primitive plumbing (in travel articles)

Thirdly, those clichés used in business and bureaucratic language – a combination of cliché and jargon:

> at the end of the day
> a proven track record
> the bottom line
> meaningful dialogue
> first bite of the cherry
> I hear what you're saying (= I understand you
>   but disagree)

CLICHÉS AND CLASSICS

The Prince of Wales, lamenting recently the poor use of English by many British people, gave an interesting example of the kind of language he was objecting to. He 'rewrote' some of Shakespeare's most famous lines using a few of the clichés, vogue words, and generally sloppy phrases that now characterise so much speaking and writing.

Here first is Shakespeare's own version:

> To be, or not to be: that is the question:
> Whether 'tis nobler in the mind to suffer
> The slings and arrows of outrageous
>   fortune,
> Or to take arms against a sea of troubles,
> And by opposing end them? To die: to sleep;
> No more; and, by a sleep to say we end
> The heartache and the thousand natural
>   shocks
> That flesh is heir to, 'tis a consummation
> Devoutly to be wish'd. To die: to sleep;
> To sleep: perchance to dream: ay, there's
>   the rub;
> For in that sleep of death what dreams may
>   come
> When we have shuffled off this mortal coil,
> Must give us pause.
>   – Hamlet, in *Hamlet*, III, i

The Prince of Wales's parody of the passage went as follows:

?? Well, frankly, the problem as I see it at this moment in time is whether I should just lie down under all this hassle and let them walk all over me, or whether I should just say OK, I get the message, and do myself in.

I mean, let's face it, I'm in a no-win situation, and quite honestly, I'm so stuffed up to here with the whole stupid mess that I can tell you I've just got a good mind to take the easy way out. That's the bottom line. The only problem is, what happens if I find, when I've bumped myself off, there's some kind of ... ah, you know, all that mystical stuff about when you die, you might find you're still – know what I mean?

Here now are two nursery rhymes rewritten almost entirely in clichés. Can you recognise which nursery rhymes they are? For the answers and the original, unclichéd, versions, turn to pages 633-648.

> Ride like the clappers on your stately
>   mount to Timbuctoo:
> A blonde bombshell there, on a noble steed,
>   is a sight for sore eyes.
> Dripping jewellery and dressed to the
>   nines,
> She'll make enough noise to wake the dead.

> If you feel sick as a parrot,
> Go into purdah within your own four walls.
> Toast your tootsies and twiddle your
>   thumbs.
> Lift the old elbow
> And permit yourself a wee dram.
> Then extend a hearty welcome to your
>   nearest and dearest.

VOGUE WORDS

Vogue words are those terms that come suddenly – and sometimes very briefly – into vogue.

They clutter fashionable conversation and pretentious journalism alike: *parameter, quantum leap, flavour of the month, osmosis* (in the sense of 'any gradual absorption'), and so on.

Vogue words have characteristics of both jargon and clichés – on the one hand, like jargon, supposedly impressive-sounding and conferring 'insider' status; on the other, like clichés, often thoughtless, stale, and imprecise as a vehicle for conveying ideas.

? The handsome 34-year-old world No 6 has emerged from a lazy coaching summer to be savaged in the Premier League by hungry young Englishmen ... David Lloyd, of Edgbaston Priory, Gawain Briars of Nottingham, and, this week, Geoff Williams of Manchester Northern.

As if to illustrate that the syndrome is one of age differential, rather than national complex, he also fell in the World Masters championship to the new 20-year-old world No 2, Chris Dittmar.
            – Colin McQuillan, *The Times*

Note the three clear-cut vogue words here –*syndrome, differential*, and *complex* – and a further three contenders: *savaged, hungry*, and *fell*. So far from sounding truly impressive, such writing comes across as strained and sometimes merely silly.

Here is another quotation heavily weighed down with vogue words: *escalation* is again an 'impressive' vogue word; *realistically, genuine*, and perhaps *scale* are 'imprecise' vogue words:

? To date Alfonsin has shown no sign of coping realistically with the very genuine possibility of an escalation into hyper-inflation on a Weimar scale, and if this happened, as it might very well, Argentina might become another Lebanon.
– Peregrine Worsthorne, *The Sunday Telegraph*

Note that vogue words are typically not newly coined terms. They tend to be long-established terms that, suddenly and mysteriously, are on everyone's lips, perhaps with a slightly changed meaning – the verb *to share*, for instance, as in *I'd like to share a few thoughts with you*. Or consider the verb *to relate* – a venerable and indispensable term that suddenly, in the 1960s, caught the imagination of trendy Americans (probably through its specialised use by psychologists and sociologists) and became one of the hallmarks of the decade: *I really relate to Castaneda's ideas; How do you relate to a low-sodium diet?*

Note too an important qualification: many new terms or meanings that come into widespread use are in fact genuine and worthy additions to the language. They fill gaps in the English vocabulary, and do not deserve to be branded as vogue words or shunned as mindlessly conformist. The word *monetarism*, for example, became particularly fashionable in the 1980s because the *concept* of monetarism became particularly fashionable. Or take the popular terms *low profile* and *scenario*, as in *She should keep a low profile until the scandal blows over* and *One worrying scenario is that the Old Guard will seize power once again*. How else could a writer express economically the complicated concepts represented here by the two terms?

So too, perhaps with the terms *antisocial, counterproductive, spin-off, upmarket*, and *status symbol*. Used in their proper places, such popular terms are extremely helpful to speakers and writers. But even then, use such fashionable words sparingly. And when you do venture a fashionable word, stop to think whether it is not perhaps just a vogue word. And if it is, whether you really want to use it at all.

For a list of the various types of vogue word, see the panel alongside.

VOGUE WORDS – A ROLL OF INFAMY

Here is a brief classification and list of vogue words, with several clear-cut examples:

☐ words that have broken out from some specialised sphere of discourse – legal, political, scientific, psychological, or the like – into general use (often distorting the original meaning, not just extending it). The phrase *quantum leap*, for instance, leapt from the domain of nuclear physics.

What about the following?

adrenalin	logistics
ambivalent	masochism
born-again	overkill
catalyst	paranoid
chain reaction	personal equation
charisma	psychological moment
clone	repression
dichotomy	state-of-the-art
double bind	symbiosis
feedback	syndrome
fellow traveller	synergy
fixation	trauma
progression	viable
interface	workshop

☐ words that have a wide range of senses and can be used again and again, like a versatile overcoat, in quite different contexts. The user is spared having to tailor his or her vocabulary to any particular occasion. Why struggle to find a sharp specialised word to dress your idea in, when a lazy vogue word is available that more or less passes as suitable? (This is not to say that these words should never be used – only to warn against using them where sharper, more precise words are available.)

authentic	major
backlash	marginal
basic	massive
constructive	meaningful
contemporary	operative
credible	perspective
dimension	phenomenal
dynamic	realistic
environment	relevant
facility	significant
factor	situation

These 'vague words' are sometimes used not as an easy substitute for a sharper word, but as a needless piece of verbal padding. Such lean, efficient wording as *experts in nuclear physics* might be fattened up into *experts in the field of nuclear physics*. Plain old *wet weather* supposedly sounds more impressive as *wet weather conditions*. A simple *from me* is inflated to *from these quarters* or *from this direction*.

☐ high-falutin or up-to-date equivalents, adopted by speakers in order to sound impressive or expert:

ambience = surroundings
archetypal = typical
compassionate = understanding
concept = a rough plan
conceptualise = to imagine
deploy = to use or place
dialogue = discussions
embattled = worried, hard-pressed
ersatz = artificial
escalate = to rise or increase
fiefdom = power base, territory controlled
finalise = to finish
global = worldwide
implement = to carry out or achieve
literature = printed information
manipulate = to control or sway
meaningful = important
mentality = mind, attitude
meticulous = careful
minimal = small
motivate = to encourage
objective = unbiased or fair
ongoing = current, continuing
optimal = ideal, best
optimistic = hopeful
palpable = obvious
pedigree = record, experience
perception = an opinion or view
personnel = staff or workers
pragmatic = practical
rationale = reasons
repercussions = results
sabotage = to spoil or wreck
subjective = personal or biased
synthesise = to combine or combine into
utilise = to use
venue = a place or setting

☐ silly overstatements, no longer just the monopoly of teenagers:

amazing
awfully
bloodbath
crisis
dire
epoch-making
fabulous
fantastic
inconceivably
infinitely

magic
revolution (*a revolution in headwear*)
sensational
tragic
ultimate
unique
unbelievable
unreal
unthinkable

☐ slangy synonyms, typically from journalism or the various modern urban subcultures.

These words are adopted in order to sound tough or 'with it':

bid = an attempt
crusade = campaign
curbs = restrictions
deliver = to accomplish, achieve
enjoy! = enjoy it, or enjoy yourself
flak = criticism
gag = to censor
in = fashionable
must = a necessity
nous = common sense, intelligence
probe = an investigation
relax! = calm down
slam = to criticise
smear = an insulting or libellous allegation
supremo = a person having full authority

☐ pretentious or threadbare metaphors, again mostly from tabloid newspapers

bombshell = a surprise
breakthrough = an advance or success
facelift = an improvement
front-runner = a leading contender
knee-jerk = unthinking, automatic
marathon = going on for a long time
massage = to falsify or distort slightly
mileage = advantage
orchestrate = to organise deliberately
overtones = hints
strongman = a political despot, a dictator
target = to strive for, intend
thaw = an improvement in relations
traumatised = distressed
whitewash = to gloss over mistakes

EUPHEMISM

To tell an employee *I am letting you go* is more sensitive than to tell him *You're fired*. To speak of *a social disease* instead of *a sexually transmitted disease* is needlessly coy and cautious.

Euphemism – the use of an inoffensive word or phrase in the place of a harshly explicit one – has these two sides to it: delicacy on the one hand, overdelicacy on the other. The line between them is a thin one, and varies from context to context. To use the words *died* and *dead* when consoling bereaved relatives might be risky: a euphemism such as *passed away* would suit the purpose. But in other settings, it would be ludicrously inappropriate: **??** *The police burst in with guns blazing: three members of the gang passed away instantly, and the remaining two were seriously wounded.*

As always, keep alert to your audience and to the context: from them you can take your cue for using a euphemism or avoiding one.

And be mindful of the dangers:

☐ Euphemism, like slang and jargon, often becomes quickly outmoded. The frontiers keep advancing, since the euphemistic word in due course becomes standard, and so calls for another euphemism in turn. The word *undertaker*, for instance, probably began life as a euphemism (perhaps for *undertaker of burials*), but has acquired a taint of its own, and is losing ground to the new euphemisms *funeral director* and *mortician*. Or consider this chain of euphemisms, one succeeding another as it fell from favour: *living in sin, living as man and wife, cohabiting, living together, shacking up*. Make sure, when avoiding a taboo term, that your favoured euphemism is up to date and has not itself acquired embarrassing overtones.

☐ Euphemism is often imprecise, and potentially misleading. What does the euphemism *sexual assault* refer to exactly – *rape* or *attempted rape*? The context may make it clear, but it may not. So too with various replacement euphemisms for the words *lavatory* and *toilet* (which were themselves euphemisms originally), such as *cloakroom* in British English, and *bathroom* or *restroom* in American English: these words still retain their original sense, after all.

☐ Euphemism is open to misuse and manipulation. Politicians, advertisers, economists, and bullies of all kinds exploit euphemisms to gloss over ugly truths without actually lying. The panel below lists some salient examples – sometimes amusing, sometimes sinister.

ABUSING EUPHEMISMS

For many people who 'live by the word' – public officials, PR spokesmen, advertisers, campaigners, and the like – euphemism is a favourite weapon. Advertising copywriters, for instance, scared of alarming potential customers, temper the harsh reality: an *economy-size* or *standard* carton (small), a *budget* ticket (cheap), dresses for the *full-figure* woman (fat), *adult* films (pornographic).

Sociologists and psychologists indulge wholesale in 'sentimental' (left-wing) or 'cosmetic' (right-wing) euphemisms: *disadvantaged, lower-income levels, adjustment problems, slow learner, underachieving, shrinkage* (losses through shoplifting), and so on.

Journalists reputedly draw on a 'secret' code of euphemisms that skirts the libel laws without for a moment puzzling regular readers: *convivial* (drunk), *ruddy-faced* (drunken), *steadfast* (obstinate), *irreverent* (rude), *outspoken* (insulting or threatening), *pert* (small and plain), *creative accounting* (fraudulent tampering with the figures), *The project is in abeyance* (it is suspended because disastrous).

The estate agent's copywriter used to be the butt, fairly or unfairly, of jokes by housebuyers, amused or unamused. Among his alleged euphemisms were: *conveniently located for local transport facilities* (overlooking noisy railway lines), *sun-drenched* (too hot in summer), *a renovator's dream* (very tatty), *would benefit from some minor structural improvements* (condemned as unsafe, about to collapse).

Most notorious of all are political and military spokesmen. Their dubious contributions to the language include the following typical items: *pacification* (battering into submission), *logistical strikes* (bombing raids), *border realignment* (seizure of territory), *frank discussions* (a slanging match), *revenue enhancements* (tax increases), *containment* (concealing information from the public).

In general, the appropriate name to call a spade by is *a spade*. Don't feel that you have to show how forthright and plain-spoken you are by calling it *a bloody shovel*. But equally, don't go to the other extreme – and draw just as much embarrassed attention – by calling it *a manual earth-mover*.

SLANG

Almost by definition, formal writing should generally avoid slang and other informal language. Generally, but not invariably. Slang has several virtues that make it worth including occasionally in most everyday types of writing.

It is forthright and unpretentious – *batty, keep your hair on* – yet often deliberately sensitive: the slangy phrase *No can do*, for instance (perhaps borrowed from pidgin English), probably acquired its popularity through being a relatively soft and apologetic way of refusing a request. Above all, slang is lively and inventive, in its onomatopoeic zest – *pizzazz, slob, to zap* – and its snappy use of metaphor:

> Keats never put into a sonnet so many remote metaphors as a coster puts into a curse.
> – G.K. Chesterton, 'A Defence of Slang'

The slangy term *loanshark*, for instance, might well convey your idea – not just your feelings – far more effectively than *moneylender*, and far more economically than *harsh and unrelenting moneylender*. The easily visualised image of a shark, and the associated ideas of cruelty and inescapability, make for a powerful and effective act of communication. Similarly, to call someone *a gasbag* is to characterise him no less unambiguously – and far more strikingly – than to call him *a talkative bore*.

This powerful shock effect of slang can help greatly to combat the tedium of formal prose. What dispels monotony is precisely a change of tone. A well-placed slang term will often startle the flagging reader back into attentiveness just as a sudden joke or a dramatic flourish would.

> I have occasionally suspected that HM Treasury flipped its departmental lid when it gave its blessing three short years ago to Section 30 of the Wildlife and Countryside Act.
> – Lord Bruce-Gardyne, *The Sunday Telegraph*

Two obvious cautions. First, remember that the shock effect of slang depends on its positioning, its relevance, and above all its rarity. To dot slang terms liberally about a text is to reduce rather than increase their forcefulness. And to use a slang term at the very start of a text is to squander its effect by miscuing the reader. If you begin a letter of complaint with the sentence *No more fudging – just tell me where the hell my order has got to*, the reader will probably lean back defiantly in reaction to your aggressive and bloody-minded tone. If you use the same sentence at the very end of an otherwise courteous and very formal complaint, the reader might well sit up and react very placatingly and cooperatively in response to your understandably insistent and no-nonsense tone.

Secondly, remember that the border between formal and informal is a shifting one, not just historically (18th-century writers railed against 'slang' terms such as *banter, mob, coax, gamble, bored*, and *touchy!*) but socially too. A phrase that hits just the right note of formality for a young advertising director – *clinch the deal, swings and roundabouts* – might strike your old head-teacher as insufferably flippant. Be sure of your ground before interspersing any colloquialism or informality – let alone a full-blooded vulgarism – into a formal piece of writing.

SEXIST LANGUAGE

Whatever your feelings about feminism, you should be alert to the sexist overtones of much traditional English wording – and reduce them as much as the text allows and the reader expects.

Some choices are very simple. In most contexts refer to women as *women* rather than *ladies* (which can sound patronising or overdeferential) or *girls* (which almost always sounds belittling). Address a woman as *Ms Brown* rather than *Miss Brown* or *Mrs Brown*, if you know that that is her preference.

Where possible, avoid old-fashioned words that convey a distinctly demeaning attitude towards women, especially where the counterpart male term either does not exist or has no correspondingly negative tone: *spinster* (contrast *bachelor*), *usherette* (contrast *usher*), *mistress* (no male equivalent), *old maid* (no male equivalent), and so on.

Many *-ess* endings are now frowned on, and can simply be dropped. Use the neutral (or 'male') *author* rather than the 'marked' *authoress*; similarly, use the neutral term each time rather than *instructress, manageress, proprietress, editress, sculptress*, and *poetess*. (On the other hand, *waitress* and perhaps *hostess* remain unavoidable, and *actress* is actually preferable, since the sex difference here is obviously relevant.)

Sometimes the only possible neutral form is a quite different word. Instead of *charwoman* or *charlady*, many people now favour *cleaner*. For *steward/stewardess*, the common term now is *flight attendant*; for *barman/barmaid*, you could substitute, for instance, *bartender*.

Where the traditional form clearly favours a *-man* ending, you could still use a neutral term: *spaceman* suggests *astronaut; newsman – reporter; foreman – supervisor; fireman –fire fighter;* and *manned by – staffed by*. (Even though *man* can still have a neutral sense – *Laughter is what distinguishes man from the lower animals* – its male overtones persist. Best avoid such words as *spacemen* and *foremen* then, if you include women within your range of reference.)

What about *chairman/chairwoman*? You could once again use an unrelated neutral term, such as *convenor* or *presiding officer*. The usual neutral form nowadays is *chair* or *chairperson*. Neither is entirely satisfactory – **??** *Mr Chairperson;* **?** *Madam Chair;* **?** *What does the chair think?*

A similar prissy or overearnest tone affects *layperson, salesperson, spokesperson,* **?** *businessperson,* and **?** *sportsperson.* And what is the plural – *spokespersons* or *spokespeople*? Again, neither is quite satisfactory. Perhaps the best compromise in such cases – offending neither the feminist nor the traditionalist – is to use a long-winded phrase where necessary: *No spokesman or spokeswoman attended; Various spokesmen and spokeswomen issued bulletins*. That is what you have to do anyway with nouns where the *-person* form is not a serious option: *All the aldermen and alderwomen attended; Write to your congressman or congresswoman.*

Some other attempts to 'neutralise' sexist terms tend to arouse controversy too: *mankind* sometimes gives way to *humankind*; and *man-hours* to *person-hours*. Take your pick: the chances are that you will affront some reader whichever choice you make. As for words such as *snowman* and *manhole*, the proposed alternatives **?** *snow sculpture* and **?** *utility tunnel* are probably too confusing or too strained to be worth risking.

And some other long-established and very useful terms seem to have an ineradicable sexists bias – *mastery, masterful, masterpiece, kingdom*, and so on. They cannot be adapted (except in jest, as in *mistress-piece*); and to boycott them would simply be to impoverish the language.

The most vexing problem concerns *he, him*, and *his*. As with *man*, these terms are often used neutrally – *If anyone here wants to upgrade his computer, he should remember what Mrs Murray told him* – yet their persistent male overtones are undeniable. In this particular example, you could easily devise a non-sexist phrasing by applying one of two standard techniques. Either you could use the second-person forms *you* and *your*: *If you want to upgrade your computer, you should remember . . .* Or you could recast the sentence into the plural: *Those who want to upgrade their computers should remember . . .* But it will not always work. You will often tie yourself up in knots trying to find a suitable rewording.

The other suggested strategies are no more reliable. The traditional approach – using *he* or *she, his* or *her* – results more often than not in awkward twists: **?** *If anyone here wants to upgrade his or her computer, he or she should remember . . .* Using *she, her, hers* instead of *he, him, his* (or alternating the two sets) tends to look very contrived; so too does *one* and *one's*; and all the more so does the use of new terms such as *herm* ('her or him') or *s/he* ('she or he'). And to use *they, their, them* after *anyone, each*, or the like is to fly in the face of strict grammar: **??** *If anyone here wants to upgrade their computer, they should remember . . .*

If you cannot find a natural rewording (by using plural forms, or *you* and *yours*), you will have to choose between a strained wording (by using *he or she*, or *one* and *one's*) and the original 'sexist' wording (using *he, him, his*) – if possible, with an apologetic explanation. Base your decision, as always, on the likely response of your readers: will the protests of the purists outweigh those of the feminists, or vice versa? Though you cannot please everybody in this matter, you can try to calculate which course of action will keep people's objections to a minimum.

Patterning Your Text

To COMMUNICATE effectively, a message or document needs effective structuring. Even a very simple text such as a joke relies heavily on its structure – the sequencing of its elements – to make a proper impact. (See the panel below.)

Simple ideas translate fairly simply onto the page. It is when your ideas are particularly complex that you struggle to put them into writing. 'Information overload' is an exasperating condition: the data or ideas spinning around in your head are too intertwined to unravel and classify. You try ordering them on paper – you experiment with various approaches, but each just seems more of a tangle than the one before. Eventually you scribble down all the ideas in an almost random order and decide that this version contains the gist of what you want to say: you know it does not really work, but maybe the reader will not notice.

Usually the reader will notice. And he or she will come to one of two possible conclusions: either that you yourself do not know what you are trying to say, do not understand the information you are pretending to communicate; or that you cannot be bothered to explain the information properly.

THE STRUCTURE OF A JOKE

The good comedian builds a joke up carefully: all the necessary details appear one by one (and sometimes some unnecessary details too, partly to distract the listeners from predicting the ending); the events move forward towards a climax; and everything falls suddenly into place when the point of the joke finally emerges, like a revelation, in the punch line.

How *not* to structure a joke is the subject of the following parody. The teller, in her impatience to raise a laugh, delivers the punch line at the beginning rather than the end:

Anyway, there's this old Jewish man who is trying to get into the synagogue during the Yom Kippur service, and the usher finally says to him, 'All right, go ahead in, but don't let me catch you praying.' (PAUSE) Oh, did I mention that the old man just wants to go in and give a message to someone in the synagogue? He doesn't actually want to go into the synagogue and *pray*, you see.

(PAUSE. FROWN) Wait a minute. I don't know if I mentioned that the old man doesn't have a ticket for the service. You know how crowded it always is on Yom Kippur, and the old man doesn't have a ticket, and he explains to the usher that he has to go into the synagogue and tell somebody something, but the usher isn't going to let him in without a ticket. So the old man explains to him that it's a matter of life and death, so then the usher thinks it over and he says to the old man, 'All right, go ahead in, but don't let me catch you praying.' (PAUSE. FROWN. STAND AND BEGIN EMPTYING ASHTRAYS) Ach, I don't think I told it right, Al, *you* tell it.

    – the mother, in Dan Greenburg (U.S.),
    How to Be a Jewish Mother

Crucial though the joke's structure is for the effectiveness of the joke, it is in fact a rather unusual structure. Like suspense stories, jokes are designed to keep the reader or listener guessing. The structure serves to *conceal* the point of the text ... until the last minute, that is. In most texts, however – from telephone messages to Annual Reports – the point needs to be *revealed* at every stage. Constant clarity, rather than obscurity, is the aim. The object is to keep the reader *informed*, not to keep him guessing. He wants the punch line right away, as it were: only then will he begin to take a proper interest in the details, the explanation, and the background.

Either way, the reader is likely to come away feeling distinctly unimpressed.

> What is written without effort is in general read without pleasure.
> – Dr Johnson, quoted in
> *Johnsonian Miscellanies*, edited by Birkbeck Hill

Remember the inverse proportion: the more effort you make in writing the text, the less effort the reader will have to make in order to understand and appreciate it.

The trick lies in not losing patience. Keep wrestling with the problem, and eventually everything will fall into place, rather like a Chinese puzzle. The solution suddenly seems obvious, and you can write down the information, in all its complexity, as clearly and methodically as if you were giving instructions for running a bath.

In fact, it is less a matter of *the* solution than of *a* solution. Often, any of several structures could impose a logical and coherent order on the whirl of material. All you have to do is remain patient long enough to find just one of them.

CLASSIFYING OR STRUCTURING

A complex set of ideas or information may well lend itself to several good systems of grouping or ordering. These would vary from writer to writer, or from purpose to purpose. Take a random group of 15 people: depending on the setting, they might be divided into *old vs young* (by an opinion pollster), *successful vs unsuccessful* (by an employer), *guilty vs not guilty* (by a jury), *forwards vs backs* (by a rugby coach), *men vs women and children* (by the captain of a sinking ship), and so on.

The writer of the following newsletter report knows exactly what she wants to say, but she has not thought sufficiently about the best way of saying it – in other words, she has not structured her information properly. The passage hops from one idea to another, rather than taking the reader systematically through all the phases.

> The committee is still arguing the merits of the two rival suggestions for this year's theatre outing. There is a strong case for London's West End, because the coach ride would as usual be relatively quick and cheap. On the other hand, Stratford-upon-Avon provides a more pleasant and relaxing setting for a day trip, and it should also be more interesting since we have never

been there before, though if the weather is bad during the afternoon London certainly has more to offer.

A simple 'tree diagram' (or thought-pyramid or organisation chart) would have helped the writer to structure the paragraph properly:

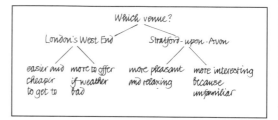

The central idea, at the top of the diagram, is that of choosing a venue. This then branches out into the rival options – London's West End and Stratford-upon-Avon. And each of these divides in turn into two sub-branches – the two arguments in favour of the venue in question.

You can now rewrite the paragraph by virtually transposing the diagram into linear prose. The process is almost effortless, and the product – the new version of the paragraph – is clear, schematic, and forceful:

> The committee is still arguing the merits of the two rival suggestions for this year's theatre outing. The two proposed venues are: London's West End and Stratford-upon-Avon.
>
> Arguing in favour of London are the following two considerations:
>
> * the coach ride would as usual be relatively quick and cheap
> * if the weather is bad in the afternoon, there is still a great deal to do and enjoy
>
> Arguing in favour of Stratford, on the other hand, are two counter-considerations:
>
> * it provides a more pleasant and relaxing setting for a day trip
> * it should also be more interesting, since we have never gone there before on our theatre outing

Note the rhetorical 'signposts' here (see page 99). First, the early naming of the competing suggestions in the sentence *The two proposed venues are: London's West End and Stratford-upon-Avon.* Before launching into the arguments, the paragraph pauses to identify the two rival claimants. The reader gets his bearings right away.

Secondly, the repeated phrase *Arguing in favour of...* This spells out the structure of the paragraph, and again directs the reader's expectations, alerting him to the symmetry between the two sections.

Thirdly, the phrases *on the other hand* and *two counter-considerations*, reinforcing the idea of an opposing set of arguments.

For some other comparable small-scale examples of poor structuring, see the nursery rhymes in the panel below.

THE STRUCTURE OF NURSERY RHYMES

Here are some familiar nursery rhymes in an unfamiliar guise – as if composed by a poet who lacked the patience to structure his ideas properly before committing them to paper. Silly, of course. Yet so much everyday writing betrays a similar thoughtlessness.

For the original, well-structured versions of the nursery rhymes, see pages 633-648.

All the king's horses and all the king's men couldn't put Humpty Dumpty together again, following his fall. He had been sitting on a wall prior to falling.

There was a crooked man who found a crooked sixpence upon a crooked stile. This was while he was walking a crooked mile. He lived together in a little crooked house with a crooked cat and a crooked mouse which the crooked cat had caught. The crooked man had bought the crooked cat with the sixpence, you see.

Hey diddle diddle!
The little dog laughed
To see the fun –
i.e. the cow's jumping over the Moon.
Another effect was that the dish ran away
    with the spoon.
Maybe the cat and the fiddle also had
    something to do with it all.

Some birds began to sing
When a pie was opened.
Wasn't that a dainty dish
To set before the king?
There were four-and-twenty of them –
    birds, I mean.
Blackbirds actually. Did I mention
They'd been baked in the pie?
No? Well you can't be expected to
    remember everything
If all they pay you for your song is sixpence
And a pocketful of rye.

As a contrasting exercise – contrasting in scale and skill – try to work out the structure of a long magazine article or broadcast. Take notes as you proceed, and then draw up a diagram or summary revealing the bones and ligaments of the structure.

Here, for instance, is a brief description of a typical edition of *Newsdesk* in mid-1990 – a half-hour news programme on the BBC World Service, beginning at midnight GMT.

Five main features go to make up the programme, though they are hardly evenly weighted. In reverse order: the last three – the Press Review, Financial News, and Sports News – take only about two minutes each. The feature before that – News about Britain – takes roughly six minutes. The opening feature – World News – dominates the programme, taking up 15 or 16 minutes.

The World News is itself divided into three sections, in a particularly helpful way:

First come four or five 'news headlines' covering the main stories (about 30 seconds). Then more detailed versions of each of those stories, and a few others (totalling about five minutes). Then 'our correspondents' reports' – consisting of in-depth coverage of the main stories, and some other topical stories, in the form of recorded reports by the BBC journalists based in the various countries involved (totalling about 12 minutes).

Especially helpful to the listener is the constant 'signposting' by the presenters – repeatedly mentioning the programme, the station, the time, and so on. In the 'correspondents' reports' phase, for instance, the co-presenter begins with an outline of the story each time, and identifies the journalist and the city – typically repeating these markers at the end of each report.

Planning the Structure

For some lucky creative writers, planning apparently takes place subconsciously. The poem or play or story seems to present itself fully formed to the writer's mind, in a dream or flash of inspiration perhaps, though no doubt the planning process has been ticking over for some time somewhere deep in the brain. One well-known example is Coleridge's drug-induced daydream, in which he developed the complete wording of 'Kubla Khan'. On waking, he started writing the poem down from memory . . . until interrupted by a worldly intrusion – a visit from a 'person on business from Porlock'.

Or a creative writer may have such a disciplined mind that, in consciously devising plans, he can work out and rearrange the most complex details without having to write anything down. Anthony Trollope would work out in his head, often when walking in the woods, the detailed actions and thoughts and even conversations of his various characters, and these would eventually find their way almost unchanged into the pages of his novels.

Some everyday writers manage to develop a similar skill in their specific subject. An experienced lawyer, for instance, might simply dictate to his secretary, word-perfect, an extremely complex letter of advice to a client.

Few everyday writers, however, can plan their writings so fast and fluently. For most people, it takes pencil and paper and a lot of painful mental effort, rather than just some spontaneous reflection and a good memory, to formulate plans for whatever it is that they are writing.

The standard method of arriving at a fully-fledged plan is by drawing up a schematic outline, though some people prefer to use a modern technique of plunging straight into a rough draft.

PLANNING BY SCHEMATIC OUTLINES

A writer's plan or outline is in some ways like a traveller's itinerary. Follow the instructions, and you will produce a well-ordered document, just as the traveller will catch his trains. But the writer's outline is not really as strict as a travel plan. It is a set of guidelines rather than a set of rules. It enables you as writer to convert your thoughts fairly smoothly into words, but at the same time it allows you the freedom to make tactical adjustments as you go along. An outline, like the text itself, can go through several drafts.

The first step is just to note down on a sheet of paper every relevant point you can think of. So much mental energy gets wasted by the struggle merely to retain in your memory all those ideas buzzing across your consciousness. Once you have jotted them all down, your mind will be free to concentrate on organising them effectively.

The case study below traces the various steps in compiling the plan of a fairly straightforward piece of writing – an office report. For more complicated pieces of writing – such as a college research project, say, or a detailed proposal for a charity drive – arriving at a well-developed plan might take a great deal more time and tinkering. But the principles remain the same:

- ☐ Jot down all the points that occur to you, in random order if necessary. (At this early stage, you may have not even the vaguest pattern in mind; once you do begin to detect one, you can rearrange all the points when writing them down a second time.)

- ☐ Read them through: this in turn will generate further ideas.

- ☐ Edit them: underline the most important ideas; write a question mark against the dubious ideas; cross out the trivial or irrelevant ideas; link related ideas by means of an arrow.

- ☐ Study them: further connections will become apparent between various distant ideas; common themes will emerge, each embracing several individual points; finally, a provisional structure will occur to you that will organise all the ideas into a single coherent whole.

- ☐ Redraft your plan to represent this possible structure: a tree diagram usually works best, revealing clearly the relative importance of the various ideas, and the ways in which they relate to one another.

- ☐ Test the structure: Is it neat enough, or are there straggly strings of unintegrated items? Does it give equal prominence to items of equal importance? Is it perhaps too neat, forcing some item on to a branch of the structure simply because it does not seem to fit anywhere else? If so, try reassembling a few branches using a different arrangement of items.

PLANNING BY ROUGH DRAFTS

Some writers lose patience with methodical planning. Either they cannot generate enough ideas in the first place, or else they simply cannot find any pattern among the ideas they have, and so cannot draw up a structural outline.

Either way, they find that the breakthrough comes only when they actually begin writing the text. Or rather, writing a draft version of the text: the final version will probably differ unrecognisably from this preliminary effort.

It does not matter where you begin. Just pick on any promising idea, and take it for a walk, so to speak. The act of writing itself focuses the mind: one idea sparks off another, connections begin to form, and eventually an all-embracing structure might suggest itself. Quite what the psychological mechanism is remains unclear, but the trick is well-established in folk-wisdom: 'How do I know what I think till I hear what I say?' the legendary chatterbox replies when accused of aimless prattling.

The technique of 'written prattling' works best if conducted according to a few basic rules:

☐ Write as quickly as you can. Don't worry about a polished style, or even about finishing a sentence or paragraph. If a new idea occurs to you as a good follow-up, start writing it up directly even if the previous idea remains only halfwritten. The point is to develop a *structure*, not to develop a tidy text.

☐ Keep jotting down new ideas – or new patterns of ideas – on a separate sheet of paper as they occur to you. In this way you might discover surprisingly quickly that you can stop writing your rough draft, since enough material has emerged to form the basis of a satisfactory outline plan after all.

☐ Once you have nothing more to write, put the draft to one side and try drawing up an outline plan from scratch. Perhaps the intense act of writing has churned up and fermented your ideas in a very productive way, enabling you to discern their proper pattern at last. Only if you still fail to see a clear structure should you return to your draft and read it through for clues. And if nothing satisfactory comes of that either, try the

whole exercise all over again, using a different starting-point this time.

☐ Above all, remain uncommitted. Your draft version is not meant to be the basis for your final version. Take it for what it is: a catalyst, or a form of therapy – a means to jolt you into the correct reaction or perception, but not itself the object of the exercise. Its purpose is to bring clarity: once it has done that, put it away and start your writing project in earnest – compiling a plan, writing a proper draft, and editing and refining that into a final version.

The case study that follows demonstrates the more traditional technique of schematic outlines. Being a fairly straightforward assignment, it lends itself to that approach. But you could just as easily – and as quickly – get the same result by using the rough-drafting technique. And for more complicated writing tasks, you might find the new technique far more efficient than the traditional one.

A CASE STUDY

Suppose you land yourself with the following delicate writing assignment. Your boss has made an unwise decision, about new office equipment. You disagree with most of it, and tell him so. Impatient and headstrong man that he is, he will not listen to your arguments. You decide to put your protest in writing – perhaps he will see reason if he sees it in black and white.

With all your objections buzzing round in your brain, you set to work jotting them down on a sheet of scrap paper. Here is the way your thoughts run (together with your jotted notes summarising them each time):

Here we go again – the boss is off riding one of his hobby-horses as usual. He only has to clap eyes on a new machine and he must have one for himself, however inappropriate. He's like a child in a toy shop. (Note: NEW *technology is fine – but only if it's* APPROPRIATE *technology*.)

What brought it on this time, I wonder? Must have been that visit he made on Tuesday to the Accounts Department, with all that fancy new machinery they've just installed.

Can't he see how different our requirements are from theirs? (*Accounts Dept has different needs from ours – false comparison*.) They need word processors: they send out dozens of long and nearly identical letters to different clients. But we use standardised forms – and that's what our clients like. (*Word processors? – unlike Accounts Dept, we use standardised forms.*)

And so on, through all your grumbles (and occasional enthusiasms) about each item of equipment that the boss has fallen for. Your last idea is this: many of the office responsibilities are currently handled by the Stationery Room, and to change that would reduce rather than increase efficiency in your department.

What emerges from this exercise finally is a set of notes something like this (see right) – though probably far less tidy.

Now that you have all your ideas down on paper, you can take a cool hard look at them. Try shuffling them about into different patterns, to find the most effective structure.

One feature you might notice right away – that there is a certain amount of repetition in the notes. Various terms, such as *Prefer, No space available*, and *Expensive*, appear more than once. This duplication should alert you to the possibility of restructuring your plan in various ways.

At the moment your notes appear to be divided into key points (those on the left) and sub-points (those on the right).

And once you have done that, you can delete lines 6 and 7 (and, as an afterthought, line 5 as well), and lines 12 and 13.

Looking once more at your plan, you might notice that your final key point – *Stationery Room* – is out on a limb. It should be grouped with your other general considerations – at the beginning rather than the end. So shift lines 19-21 (by drawing an arrow) up to near the top – in effect positioning them to follow line 2.

1		NEW technology is fine - but only if it's APPROPRIATE technology.
2		Accounts Dept has different needs from ours - false comparison.
3	Word-processors ?	- unlike Accounts Dept, we use standardised forms
4		- prefer to take on an office typist + buy one word-processor, for her
5		- training for all the clerks - time-consuming + pricey
6		- expensive ! — 14 word-processors !
7		- no space available on desks
8	memory-phones	- useful only for outgoing calls
9		- Accounts Dept need them - we don't
10		- 3 memory-phones OK - but not 14 !
11	Giant photocopier	- pointlessly sophisticated for our modest needs
12		- VERY expensive
13		- very bulky - no space available
14		- prefer to buy 2 additional mini-copiers
15	Fax machine	- faster than using the Stationery Room's fax-service
16		- space available in recess
17	Dictating machine	- very efficient, any time and any place
18		- buy 2 additional mini-recorders
19	Stationery Room	- it's their responsibility to handle tricky orders
20		- always been very dependable
21		- they're the experts ➝ greater efficiency

But duplicated sub-points are probably quite important, and perhaps rate promotion. Test them to see. If they are suitable, make the necessary adjustments to your plan. Between lines 2 and 3, for instance, you could now insert two new lines:

No space available – for word processors, giant photocopier

Expensive – word processors (+ training), giant photocopier

A further inspection of your plan reveals another hidden theme to you: line 4 (*Prefer to take on an office typist . . .*), line 10 (*Three memory-phones, OK*), and line 14 (*Prefer to buy two additional mini-copiers*) have something in common. They represent your favoured alternatives. They are the positives (among all the negatives) to add to your unqualified support for the fax machine and the dictating machine. Why not jot each of them down once again, together in a group this time – at the end perhaps? In that way, you can conclude with a positive set of proposals, having spent most of the report discouraging the boss's proposals with a series of negative arguments.

As a final adjustment to your plan, you can divide the key points off into sections. Lines 1 and 2 and 19-21, for instance, form a distinct introductory group: you can head it *General considerations*. And lines 15-18 form a separate group too, which you can label *Approved proposals*. These sections are clearly differentiated from the main group of lines 2a-14, to which you can give the contrasting title, *Specific objections*.

This main grouping is further subdivided in turn. There are two problems common to some of the proposed machines (*No space available* and *Expensive*), and there are the problems unique to each type of machine (*word processor, memory-phone, giant photocopier*). These subsections can also take contrasting headings: *Common problems* and *Individual problems*.

Finally, the recently added lines 21a-21d form your own set of proposals. You can give them the heading *An alternative scheme*.

Your revised outline will look like this (see right).

Or you could, to make the structure even clearer, draw up a fresh outline, using some hierarchy or other graphic layout that helps you to grasp the structure as a whole. A 'tree' diagram might work best of all here – rather like the one on page 92, though far more complex this time. You would have three main branches this time – *Boss's ideas: valid, Boss's ideas: invalid, My own proposals* – each branch with its own sub-branches and sub-sub-branches in turn.

Whichever outline you devise, use it as the basis for writing up your text. Don't be hidebound by it, how-

ever: you may well find, while you are doing the writing, that new ideas occur to you from time to time, or that old ideas seem to need rearranging into a different sequence. You may also find that your write-up fails to satisfy you, and that you have to do a lot of rethinking and rewriting before you feel you have reached a definitive version.

The panel *A well-presented document* overleaf reproduces the final draft of the report. No need to read it through: just note the appearance of the pages, and how helpfully they reflect the structure of the text itself. Whether or not it succeeds in persuading the boss to admit his mistakes and adjust his proposals, it will at least impress him with its clear and methodical construction.

Different types of document – an invitation to a party, or a notice-board announcement – would benefit from even more adventurous designing: a variety of colours, an eye-catching slogan, a picture or pattern, and so on.

GENERAL CONSIDERATIONS
1   NEW technology is fine - but only if it's APPROPRIATE technology.
2   Accounts Dept has different needs from ours - false comparison.

SPECIFIC OBJECTIONS
2a Common problems   No space available for word-processors, giant photocopier.
2b   Expensive - word-processors (+ training), giant photocopier
    Individual problems

3   Word-processors ?   - unlike Accounts Dept, we use standardised forms
4   - prefer to take on an office typist + buy one word-processor, for her
5   - training for all the clerks time-consuming + pricey
6   - expensive! - 14 word-processors!
7   - no space available on desks

8   memory-phones   - useful only for outgoing calls
9   - Accounts Dept need them - we don't
10   - 3 memory-phones OK - but not 14!

11 Giant photocopier   - pointlessly sophisticated for our modest needs
12   - VERY expensive
13   - very bulky - no space available
14   - prefer to buy 2 additional mini-copiers

APPROVED PROPOSALS
15 Fax machine   - faster than using the Stationery Room's fax-service
16   - space available in recess

17 Dictating machine   - very efficient, any time and any place
18   - buy 2 additional mini-recorders

19 Stationery Room   - it's their responsibility to handle tricky orders
20   - always been very dependable
21   - they're the experts → greater efficiency

AN ALTERNATIVE SCHEME
21a   Favoured alternatives - three memory-phones
21b   - buy 2 additional mini-copiers
21c   - office typist! + one word-processor
21d   plus the fax-machine and dictating-machine/s, as proposed.

A WELL-PRESENTED DOCUMENT

Reproduced here are the four pages of the office report in its final version. Notice the physical appearance of the document – its methodical layout, revealing the text's structure by means of careful spacing, subheadings, typefaces, indenting, numbering, and so on.

M E M O

To: JNH
From: DL

19 October 1990   4 pages

The proposed purchase of new office equipment

Your idea of updating and re-equipping the office is very welcome. But I remain worried that the precise proposals put forward are not the best and most cost-effective way of achieving your aims. An alternative scheme, detailed on pages 3-4, would prove both more efficient and less expensive.

General considerations

1. New technology can be a great help, and some of the items of equipment you listed would be invaluable for our department. But others would not be appropriate for our purposes, I believe.

2. Our department's needs are far lower than other departments' when it comes to modern office machines. The Accounts Department, for example, needs very sophisticated equipment to process all its complicated correspondence. But our department is not really comparable, since most of our paperwork consists of standard forms and letters.

3. The Stationery Room is there to serve us as always, and we should continue to draw all the benefit from them that we can. Without any cost to ourselves, they can take many of the routine office duties off our shoulders. In particular, they have a giant photocopier of their own, which they are experts at operating, and it's in the interests of efficiency that we continue to use them for our mass-photocopying.

Specific objections to some of the proposals

Common problems

Office space. The office is fairly cramped, as we all know: the clerks have recently been complaining about lack of elbow-room. And to make matters worse, we may have to add a new member of staff soon (see my proposals below). The various crannies that are free could accommodate a small Fax-machine and a new Mini-copier or two (see my proposal 2 below), but there is simply nowhere to put a bulky Giant Photocopier without sqeezing the clerks even more tightly together. And to impose Word-processors on them would make their desks intolerably cramped.

2

Expense. The machinery you want amounts in total to some £35,000 basic. Added to this initial capital expenditure are the hidden costs:

- service contracts on all the equipment (≈£1,000 per annum);

- a new phone line for the Fax-machine;

- training the 11 clerks to use the Word-processors: a full three-day training course costs £500 per head (total £5,500), plus 33 lost man-days (notional cost: a further £8,250).

So, if we follow the current proposals exactly, the immediate cost to the department would be almost £50,000. (This consumes our entire office-equipment budget for the next four years. How would we explain this to the MD?) New equipment may well lead to savings through increased efficiency, but the savings would obviously come nowhere near £50,000, even over a period of 10 years.

Specific problems

Word-processors. Our department would gain little from a string of Word-processors. The chief value of a Word-processor is for producing corrected copies of lengthy documents, or for producing a series of near-identical letters to various addresses. Other departments, such as Accounts, generate such documents and letters constantly, and therefore benefit hugely from Word-processors. Our department very rarely generates such texts – nine-tenths of our paperwork is on pre-printed standardised forms. (These are popular with our clerks and our clients alike, as the 1989 survey showed. The forms are easy to follow and easy to fill in.) The covering letter is seldom more than two or three lines long. To dash it off on one of our typewriters takes a clerk no longer than it would take him to set up and then personalise a template-letter on the Word-processor.
True enough, the occasional lengthy document does slow the typical clerk down. But the best solution to this problem is not to give him a Word-processor of his own, but rather to give him access to a typist with a Word-processor. (For details, see my proposal 2 below.)

Memory-phones. Again, our department differs from other departments, such as Accounts, in that nine-tenths of our phone-calls are incoming calls. The advantage of Memory-phones is in making outgoing calls, as you rightly pointed out.
The only people in the department who have to make frequent outside phone-calls are you, me, and Marjorie. So it would be a very good idea to order three Memory-phones. But 14 would be far beyond what is necessary.

3

Giant Photocopier. Our current volume of photocopying is nowhere near the recommended level for one of these machines: my estimate is that our total number of copies per month is 1,800 (less than six per cent of the Accounts Department's, for example). And most of our photocopying jobs are simply one-off copies of one-page documents. Our Mini-copier is the right machine for such a low workload.
The occasional larger jobs that we have go to the Stationery Room, who are competent if slightly slow. Not that our own photocopying set-up is perfectly efficient. There are improvements to be made (see proposal 2 below for my solution), but a Giant Photocopier is not the way to achieve them.

Support for various proposals

Fax-machine. Your proposal to install a Fax-machine in the office is a very good one. Although the Stationery Room has always handled our needs very proficiently, a machine of our own would certainly reduce the turn-around time. A compact model would fit very conveniently in the recess between your door and Marjorie's.

Dictating machine. Another good idea. May I suggest that we add a further two mini-recorders to the basic package (mini-recorder, playback machine, pedal control, headphones) – Marjorie and I both feel we would benefit from the flexibility they offer.

An alternative scheme

Balancing cost and improved efficiency, I propose the following scheme as the most practicable one for re-equipping the department.

1. Memory phones: we should buy and install three of these - one for you, one for me, one for Marjorie.

2. Short documents.

    a. Faxing: a small Fax-machine, installed in the recess outside your door, will service both incoming and outgoing fax messages very efficiently.

    b. Photocopying: the present arrangement is inadequate, I agree. A queue sometimes forms at the Mini-copier. And for some of us there's a long walk to get to it - it's about 35 yards away from my desk, for instance. So one sometimes has to endure a double waste of time.

4

The solution is to buy two additional Mini-copiers, and to position them well apart - one next to the vending machine, and the other in the alcove by the fire-escape. (Each Mini-copier costs only one-twentieth the amount that the Giant Photocopier costs.)

3. Long documents. The chief drain on our efficiency is our occasional handling of long documents - dictating them, typing them, and photo-copying them.

    a. Dictating: the purchase of three mini-recorders, together with one playback machine with accessories, will enable you, me, and Marjorie to dictate long letters and reports very efficiently at any time or place convenient to us.

    b. Typing: it's time we took on an office typist to help the clerks - mornings only, to start with.
    She alone will have a Word-processor. Whenever the clerks have a long document to type, they can simply give it to her. Their clerical work (which they're good at) can then progress with fewer diversions for typing (which they're mostly bad at), and their productivity should increase accordingly.

    c. Photocopying: the new typist will supervise this as well. (She will have various responsibilities other than typing. I see her becoming a progress-chaser in due course, and general 'facilitator' in the day-to-day running of the office, to relive me of part of those responsibilities.) One of her extra duties will be to take care of the big photocopying jobs. She can carry them to and from the Stationery Room directly, instead of waiting for the post-boy to deliver them, and she can chivvy the Stationery clerk to hurry up.

Two obvious reservations:

- the cost: an extra half-salary is certainly a burden on our budget, but I calculate that the expense will be more than offset by increased productivity;

- the space: the new typist will make things even more crowded, but we shall cope. Initially it will be mornings only. And the clerks themselves have indicated that they would gladly put up with the further crowding if that means they can have a typist at their disposal.

I'd be more than happy to discuss all these matters further with you if you remain unconvinced one way or the other. If not, do let me know your decision, and I can set about arranging things at once.

Structural Signposting

Here is some folk wisdom for writers and speakers: First I tells 'em what I'm going to tell 'em, then I tells 'em, then I tells 'em what I've tellt 'em.

For much everyday writing, that serves as an excellent motto. In particular, it harks back to the golden rule: Remember the reader. Every time the poor reader opens a letter or report written by you, he feels as though he is entering a strange town for the first time, with no idea how to find his way about. What he needs is some bold signposts.

COMMON TYPES OF SIGNPOST

Here are some typical forms of signpost for use in everyday writing. They help to keep the reader continually conscious of his whereabouts.

The heading. This is the basic welcome to the reader. He knows at once, very roughly, where he is.

In a business letter, the heading is less conspicuous than in a report: it comes after the salutation (preferably not prefaced by the stilted word *re*):

Dear Mrs Braithwaite,

Your claim for a refund on
your Zadok pressure cooker

Thank you for your letter of 19 October 1990, in which you . . .

Reference or identification. This might take the form of an account number (if dealing with a bank), for example, or a date (of a letter to which you are now replying), or a commission number: *Market Research report no. 167.*

Table of contents. In a longish report, research paper, academic thesis, or the like, a table of contents provides the reader with a panoramic survey. His reading should be faster, better focused, and more efficient now, as a result of knowing what lies ahead.

Subheadings and sub-subheadings. Like street names, these serve as constant reminders to the reader of his whereabouts. This very page (with its three distinct levels of heading) illustrates the point.

Advance warnings. These are the small 'traffic signs' within the running text – letting the reader know in good time what he is about to encounter. Suppose you are listing three reasons in favour of a

particular course of action. Preface them, as a help to the reader, with the simple traffic sign: 'There are three reasons for this suggested course of action.' If you have to digress from your main line of argument, let the reader know – 'A brief digression here, to explain the background to the scheme' – or else he will think he is still on the main road, only to realise suddenly that he is lost.

Milestones. These small cues complement the advance warnings within the text. They inform the reader how far he has progressed along a certain road or line of thought. Suppose that each of the three reasons that you have to list is very long and detailed. You might intersperse reminders every so often just to reassure the reader of his bearings: 'That is the primary reason for the course of action I propose. A second reason is as follows' or 'The last of the three reasons is this . . .' Similarly, when you come to the end of a digression, inform the reader so that he knows his whereabouts again: 'So much for the background to the scheme. To return now to the details of its budget and schedule . . .'

Summaries. In lengthy documents, don't limit yourself to a single summary at the very end. Pause to take stock – to summarise or repeat – whenever the weight of information risks overloading the reader's powers of concentration or memory.

One of the most important places for a full summary is the very beginning of the document – an 'executive summary' or 'abstract', it is sometimes called. Lazy or hurried readers, if they read nothing else, can at least get the gist of your report in that way. Another old rule of friendly report-writing: Don't wait till the conclusion before stating your conclusions. You can state them – or at least hint at them – very near the start.

LAYOUT AND TYPOGRAPHY

The mere physical positioning and appearance of the text on the page can help the reader enormously in keeping his or her bearings.

If you have to identify six short items, say, list each of them on a separate line, prefaced by a dash or asterisk. (Limit such lists to six or seven items. If you have more than that, try to subdivide them into two or more groups, and introduce each group separately by identifying its theme.) If you have main headings,

EXERCISE IN REWRITING

The extract below is extremely difficult to follow, partly because of its high-flown style, and partly because of its unhelpful structure.

Read it carefully – it eventually yields up its meaning – and then rewrite it in plain and well-structured English. (Make use of any relevant strategies suggested in this chapter and in the earlier chapters on style.)

About 450 words should do it – half the length of the original. One version appears in the quiz answers section, pages 633-648.

It is frequently said by top managers that, were they ever inclined to ask themselves if there might be problems or opportunities deserving their attention other than those continuously arising from the daily round, they would at once send for some reputable firm of business consultants – company doctors, management professors, experts from Boston, confidential advisors, and so forth. The idea that what might be lacking is something personal to the top managers themselves, something, moreover, that they alone might one day be able to put right, would strike them as very strange. It would be even stranger to them to suggest that, not only were they themselves alone in being able to put things right, but that only they, too, could discover the avenues to successful amendment. But since there can be no learning without action and no action without learning, if change is to be brought about by the purchased services of outsiders, independently of any involvement at a personal level of the top managers who commission those outsiders, then there can be no learning – that is, no preparation among those at present in charge to meet the recurrent challenges of the future. The enterprise will therefore become dependent upon its external advisors until it can no longer afford to meet their fees and expenses – a condition now frequently encountered. Nor is this all. The external consultant generally claims expertise in such-and-such a field, and, on this account, will diagnose the affliction (or interpret the hope) of his client management in terms of it; for a month or more everything will go as he predicts, the pattern uncovered will fit the forecast already made, and the plan of action will build upon the personal enthusiasms of members of the host management. The outside consultants who have prepared the plan – not seldom by piecing together fragments of their past prescriptions to other clients – will gradually 'phase themselves out', leaving those on the spot to implement what still needs to be done. With their wide connections across a fast professional culture, the itinerant experts are able quickly to find the super-specialist needed (it might seem) to advise upon some highly technical obstruction to success . . .

The assignment of a visiting fellow from another enterprise also anxious to do something about its more obstinate and ill-structured embarrassments has little in common with the engagement of professional experts. Were the fellows of the Inter-University Programme to carry visiting cards to widen their possibilities of future employment, they would endorse them in red capitals: *'Our strength, just like your own, lies in our ignorance of your troubles.'* For, while the expert may *pretend* that his first desire is to see the problem as it is seen by the management that needs to do something about it, he is in his particular business for quite a different reason; the visiting fellow, on the other hand, is clearly another manager in fact, anxious to interpret the trouble as a manager among managers, and to learn from his hosts as much as they are to learn from him. He does not seek to prolong his engagement with his hosts, nor to withhold unpleasant advice that may prejudice the willingness of his clients to meet their financial obligations – since there are none. He is not hoping, as are many consultants, that he may be offered an appointment in the firm he is setting out to help, so that his advice will not be coloured by quite adventitious possibilities having nothing to do with the original reasons for his being in the action learning programme at all. Faced with a temporary check, the visiting fellow has no headquarters office he may ring for instant support from another itinerant expert; he will need to open up some fresh line of questioning with his hosts. Unlike the professional consultant, he will not be spending a lot of his time trying to find out what the most powerful person in the receiving organisation believes the problem to be in order to present to him a solution based upon that interpretation; the visiting fellow will, laboriously and with little thanks, be trying to reconcile the myriad views and experiences of large numbers of his new colleagues in such a manner that these now start to suggest to him what might be going on and how it may be improved upon. While *in practice* the expert consultant is desperately striving to use every interview he conducts as a means of assembling every shred of an idea from others into what he will claim as his own solution, he must be very cautious about creating the impression that he is circulating as the thirstiest of learners: his official status is a teller of others, an instructor of babes, a guide to the foolish, an enlightener dispelling the darkness, a leader of the blind, and so forth. He must be extremely cautious about giving an impression that there is anything he has to learn. The visiting fellow, on the other hand, gets his authority to help his new colleagues from his own eagerness to learn by recording the explanations of what they themselves imagine to be wrong; as the supreme non-expert, he is, at least at the outset, in no position to question what they say, nor to stem their desire to say it – and hence to learn from what they are trying to tell him about that which, they feel, seems to pass their own understanding. As Saint Paul reminded us all: 'Let no man deceive himself. If any man among you seemeth to be wise in this world, let him become a fool that he may be wise.' It is one of the texts upon which action learning is founded, but rarely seen on the Christmas cards from experts.

– Reg Revans, *ABC of Action Learning*

subheadings, and sub-subheadings, be sure to distinguish them clearly – use different type-sizes or typefaces if you can. If not, at least try to position them differently:

☐ main heading in the centre of the page

☐ subheading next to the margin but on a separate line

☐ sub-subheading next to the margin, and followed on the same line by the text.

And make generous use of line spaces. A double space between subsections; a triple space perhaps between main sections.

Make sure to operate all these markers consistently, giving equal treatment to equal-status items (see page 63). Such tricks all help in their small way to show the reader the structure of the document as a whole.

For a good example of a clear and helpful layout, glance once again at the panel *A well-presented document* on page 98.

Certain types of document, as mentioned earlier, cry out for a still more eye-catching layout and design: posters, information leaflets, informal invitations, and the like. Look, for example, at the imaginative invitation, reproduced on page 398, to the annual rugby-club dance.

And suppose you were put in charge of remedying the bus company's information notice, discussed in the panel *Passenger information* overleaf.

Once you had restructured the actual information, and reworded the text along the lines suggested, you would start thinking about the *look* of the notice: first, the simple layout – headings, spacing – and then the broader design, including such devices as:

☐ large bold lettering in the headline

☐ a variety of colours, both to grab the attention and to help the reader to classify all the information quickly

☐ a slogan or two, humorous if possible

☐ an exclamation mark, perhaps, or the dot-dot-dot of an ellipsis

☐ a picture or pattern – perhaps a big red bus in this case, or an ornamental border (but *not* one consisting of an endless queue of passengers waiting at a bus stop!)

PASSENGER INFORMATION

Here is a notice that appeared on various London buses in early 1988. The information it tries to convey will not go into a single, simple message. It has many aspects and complexities, which obviously overwhelmed the person writing it.

Try to restructure the notice and present it in a way that passengers can understand rather more easily.

Two possible solutions are suggested below, but do write a version of your own before looking at them.

BUS FARES FROM JANUARY 10 1988
Buses 216, 237 and 290 in Surrey

Return fares will be introduced for journeys outside Greater London on Bus 290, and these tickets will be inter-available for return journeys on route 216 between Staines and Sunbury.

Some single fares will be increased by up to 20p, but on Route 237 only fares for journeys crossing the Greater London boundary will be increased, and local fares within Surrey will be unchanged.

Here now are the two possible versions of a more readable notice.

Buses 216, 237, and 290 in Surrey

New arrangements, starting 10 January 1988.

NEW FARES: Single fares will rise by up to 20p. On the 237 route, the fare increase applies only to journeys into or out of Greater London; fares within Surrey remain the same.

NEW TICKETS: Buses 216 and 290 will both sell return tickets which can be used on either route. The tickets will be available only for journeys outside Greater London.

YOUR LOCAL SURREY BUS

Starting soon . . .

Bus 216 ● local Surrey fares unchanged
　　　　● other fares rising by up to 20p
　　　　● return tickets available if purchased on bus 290

Bus 237 ● fares into and out of Greater London rising by up to 20p
　　　　● other fares unchanged

Bus 290 ● local Surrey fares unchanged
　　　　● other fares rising by up to 20p
　　　　● return fares available outside Greater London – these can also be used on route 216 between Staines and Sunbury

Effective from 10 January 1988

LOCAL FARES UNCHANGED

Note how the two versions structure the material differently, using a distinctive basic division of the material in each case.

The first version divides the subject into two main sections, *New Fares* and *New Tickets*. In fact, the headings could just as well be *Single Fares* and *Return Fares*.

The second version uses a three-part classification, taking each of the three buses in turn.

The main difficulty seems to be this: there is just too much complex information to make a single snappy, eye-catching notice. The bus company should have compiled three different notices, one for each route. (After all, the passengers on bus 237 do not really need the details of route 216.) The second version above would make a good basis: simply break up the information into three parts, and incorporate each part into a separate notice.

Remember, a good notice needs more than just good wording. It needs a thoughtful layout too, and an eye-catching design – here perhaps including a witty slogan with a brightly coloured picture or appropriate diagram.

Editing Your Own Writing

OCCASIONALLY the first draft of a piece of writing has to serve as the final draft as well: an urgent telegram or fax message, for instance, or an exam essay written against the clock. Most writing tasks, however, allow you the opportunity of making extensive revisions – an opportunity that you should always take advantage of, no matter how pleased you may feel after writing the last word of the original draft.

If time allows, put the rough draft away for a few days. When you return to it, you can read it with fresh eyes, and more easily spot its weaknesses.

Here is a checklist of questions to ask yourself and things to do when revising your own drafts.

To start with, try to put yourself in the position of the first-time reader. How would he or she react to this letter or report? Ask yourself the following three broad questions:

What *kind* of document are you reading? – a letter of complaint, a letter of inquiry, an agenda for next week's committee meeting, a sales report? The structure and layout should supply that information almost immediately. If not, make the necessary adjustments to them.

What is the *purpose* or theme of the document? Again, this is something that you should be able to discover almost at once. If the document is a sales report, for example, what exactly is it reporting on – is it sales of unleaded petrol, say, or of any petrol, or of petrol plus diesel?

What is the *message* of the document? Whatever the document contains – vital findings, warnings, threats, recommendations – these components should be crisply and unambiguously defined, so that no possibility of misunderstanding arises.

Then come the more specific inquiries into the clarity and effectiveness of the writing:

The *layout* – that is, the headings and subheadings, the positioning of paragraphs, and so on. Does it contribute as much as it could to communicating your ideas to the reader? Consider improvements such as numbering the various sections.

The *structure* – that is, the ordering of the various points made within any section, and of the various sections within the document as a whole. Is it as logical and methodical as it could be? Try out any promising changes that occur to you: switching two paragraphs, for instance, might suddenly make it much easier for the reader to follow a particular line of reasoning.

Above all, check that you have done enough 'signposting' – announcing your intentions well in advance, indicating clearly what lies ahead, and occasionally summarising what has gone before.

The *contents* – are they accurate? Have you checked and rechecked your figures? Are all your quotations word-perfect? Are you representing your opponents' views fairly? And your reasoning – is it in keeping with logic and fair play?

The *tone* of the writing – is it suitably respectful and courteous without being fawning or overformal, and suitably friendly without being overfamiliar?

The *style* – is it pitched at an appropriate level of difficulty for the intended reader? Not too technical on the one hand, or oversimplified and patronising on the other? Is it interesting and varied without being clever-clever? Does it sound good when read out loud – no jerky rhythms or unintended jarring rhymes, for instance?

Then a more detailed look at the wording:

Is it *consistent*? If you spell *realise* with an *s* on one page, are you sure that you have not spelt it *realize* by mistake on another page?

Is it *correct* – in its spelling and grammar and usage? And the choice of words – is *enormity*, for instance, really the correct noun to use to express the idea of enormousness? Test any suspicions you might have by consulting the ready-reference section at the end of this book, or any good dictionary or usage guide.

Is it *bright* and incisive? When making general points, have you backed them up with lots of concrete examples? Do you use interesting turns of phrase occasionally rather than a constant level of bureaucratic prose? Do you allow the occasional light touch – an ironic simile, for example (*He's as reliable as a weather forecast*)?

Then a close inspection of the individual words, sentences, and paragraphs:

The *words* you have chosen – are they varied enough, and precise enough? Does the adjective *unhappy* really convey your intention, or would *downcast* or *demoralised* or *mortified* not express it more accurately? Or is your vocabulary perhaps, on the contrary, too high-falutin – have you written *sartorial splendour*, for instance, instead of simply *smart clothes*?

Check the adjectives and adverbs. Are they really the most effective words to use? Can you not simply cut them? – to write *the facts* instead of **?** *the actual facts*, or *a crisis* instead of **?** *an acute crisis*?

Can you not choose colourful nouns or verbs in preference to phrases containing adjectives or adverbs? – *trounce* for *defeat overwhelmingly*, or *chatterbox* for *very talkative person*?

Check the nouns. If they tend to be abstract rather than concrete nouns, try to reverse the proportions, and create more images in the reader's mind. Change *housing* to *flats and houses*, if appropriate.

Check the verbs. If the verb *to be* seems to predominate, try to introduce more colourful verbs occasionally. Change *There is a disagreement between them* to *They disagree*.

The *sentences* next: check them for length and complexity, especially if the writing is difficult to follow at times. Whenever your inspection reveals a convoluted sentence structure, containing a high level of words such as *though* or *whereas*, for instance, try to unravel the syntax somewhat. Aim at saying just one thing at a time. In that way you can break the long sentences down into smaller and more digestible units. Check the main verb in any long or troublesome sentence. If it appears near the end, consider shifting it to an earlier position; and if it is in the passive, try turning it into an active verb instead.

And the *paragraphs*. If they look uninvitingly long, try to shorten them. And check that no paragraph contains more than one major idea.

Check that the ideas flow smoothly from sentence to sentence and paragraph to paragraph. If not, consider adding more 'signpost' words to stitch the sentences together – words such as *but*, *therefore*, *first of all*, and *on the other hand*.

In addition, careful revising means keeping an eye out for various risks and pitfalls in your draft. Is the text loose and flabby rather than tight and concise? Are you sure there is no irrelevant detail, and no distracting digressions? No saying the same thing two or three times over in different words?

Check for ambiguity, as caused, for example, by pronouns such as *it* and *he* – **??** *Simon borrowed a fiver from his brother before he left the house* – or by poor positioning of words within any sentence: **??** *They predicted riots in December*.

If you have used any *jargon* or lazy officialese, does it have a genuine function, or is it just showing off? And are you sure that all the readers will understand it properly?

Look out for:

- *mixed metaphors*, such as **✗** *She really knocked us out with her razor-like wit*, and mixed idioms, such as **✗** *By no figment of the imagination can he succeed*

- *clichés*, such as **??** *in the pipeline* or **??** *last but not least*

- *vogue words*, such as **?** *parameters* or **?** *interface* or **?** *incredible*

- *sexist language*, such as **??** *female chairman* or **?** *authoress*

And if you have used any *slang* (such as *He's a brainbox*) or coy *euphemisms* (such as *He hasn't got very much upstairs*), can you confidently claim that it always suits the context?

After revising the draft as thoroughly as time allows, ask yourself one final question. Have you as writer done all the work that you can to communicate your thoughts clearly and efficiently to the readers?

If your answer is No, remember that the readers will then have to put in more work than necessary – and they may choose not to.

But if you can honestly answer Yes to the question, move on to the next stage: typing the document up and dispatching it to the readers – and then going on, with renewed confidence, to your next piece of writing.

The Mechanics of Writing

PICK AT RANDOM several successful full-time writers, and the chances are that they will all differ widely in their working methods and attitudes.

To some of them writing is a humdrum craft, to others a high calling. To some it is a deep mysterious art, to others a painful affliction. For some the pages flow fast and confidently from the typewriter; others chew tormentedly at their pencils and agonise over each word they inscribe. Some plan everything in meticulous detail before setting pen to paper; others just jump in heedlessly, leaving the polishing till later (if at all). Some write to make a living; others write to wage a passionate campaign. Some write from experience, some from imagination, some only after painstaking research.

Professional writers, then, provide no consistent model when it comes to techniques or working practices. But this does not mean that all writing is a haphazard or purely personal skill, and that any one approach is as good as any other. Certainly professional writers vary; but professional writing – whether fiction or drama or journalism – is not really the concern of this book. The everyday kind of writing that most literate people have to do – from job applications to letters of complaint, from exam essays to office memos to wedding invitations – is what the book deals with, and this kind of writing certainly can benefit from a standard approach – a businesslike approach, rather than the romantic or 'inspired' approach that poets and other creative authors are traditionally supposed to follow.

GETTING DOWN TO IT

Even the most experienced professional writers suffer occasionally from 'writer's block'. Either their inspiration dries up, and they find themselves unable to conjure up a single idea or scene worth putting on paper; or they cannot settle down to the task, cannot 'find a way in' to the chapter or article or scene, despite an abundance of ideas. To put it another way, the problem is either what to write or how to write it.

Everyday writers also run up against 'writer's block' of their own. Obliged to write a letter of condolence or a college essay, they cannot think of a thing to say. Required to write up a business report or to draft a letter of complaint, they know exactly what they want to say but fail to get down to it. Instead, they might distract themselves with irrelevant tasks such as tidying up the desk or making tea or phoning a friend. Or they might work themselves up into an unproductive state of anxiety or panic, and chew agitatedly at a pencil instead of writing with it.

COLLECTING THE SUBJECT MATTER

As for what to write – three basic techniques are available to generate ideas: reflection, discussion, and research.

Reflection. Obvious though it sounds, the first stage is all too often ignored: Stop and think. That letter of condolence you have to write – forget the trite sentiments and traditional phrases for a moment, and question yourself about everything and everyone involved.

How well did you know the person who has died? Was the death sudden or long expected? What about the person you are writing to? What tone should you adopt with him or her? – formal? familiar? Would it give comfort, or merely add to the distress, if you mentioned all of the late person's virtues? Would it be appropriate to include some personal reminiscences? If so, which ones and how many? Would it be helpful, or patronising, if you offered advice on coping?

Jot down all the points as they occur to you. You can then rearrange them into an outline, and use that in turn as the basis for the actual letter you write.

Discussion. Why is it that two heads are better than one? Not necessarily because your discussion partner has any new ideas to add. Often it is simply a matter of stimulating more ideas of your own, or refining previous ideas by forcing yourself to explain them clearly to someone else. That report

LESSONS FROM THE MASTERS

If you want to learn the secret of successful writing, who better to look to than famous authors? The trouble is, their lives and methods suggest that the secret has more to do with the habit of working than with working habits. About the only thing that the great writers have in common is their talent. Their working methods, by contrast, are almost as varied as their subject matter and styles.

Some authors seem to need, as George Eliot did, a specially creative mood, or even inspiration, to write effectively, and tend to dry up for days at a time between frenzied bouts of 'inspired' productivity.

Others are extremely *un*romantic about the 'business of writing' as they would call it. They work away regularly and unhurriedly in the study five days a week, as though creating works of art were no different from drafting legal contracts or assessing insurance claims.

Nicholas Monsarrat, author of *The Cruel Sea*, apparently used to work a regular nine-hour day in his study, starting at 6 a.m. The Italian novelist Alberto Moravia would spend a brief but regular three hours at his writing desk each day, between 7.30 and 10.30 a.m.

Businesslike though such writers may be, they are not always without their foibles or superstitions. Melvyn Bragg apparently insists on waiting for a Monday before writing the first word of a new novel. The 19th-century French novelist Honoré de Balzac insisted on having an unripe apple on his desk, and his compatriot Alexandre Dumas the elder, creator of *The Three Musketeers*, would always wear bedsocks when writing. The British novelist and poet Muriel Spark writes exclusively on pale blue jotters, whereas Roald Dahl favours large yellow notepads.

Some authors need absolute privacy and silence in order to concentrate properly. (The French novelist Marcel Proust had to seclude himself in a cork-lined room before he could settle into a creative working mood.) Others seem to need the hustle and bustle of daily life to release their creative juices, and might do their best writing at a table in a boulevard café.

Some authors write, partly at least, in order to cope with or drive away feelings of depression – Anthony Burgess and the late Georges Simenon, among them. Some writers actually seem to thrive on unhappiness – Franz Kafka remains the most famous example, perhaps.

But others write best when they are most at peace with themselves and the world: 'You write better with your problems resolved' is the view of one recent winner of the Nobel Prize for Literature.

> You write better in good health. You write better without [unhappy] preoccupations. You write better when you have love in your life. There is a romantic idea that suffering and adversity are very useful to the writer. I don't agree at all.
>
> – Gabriel García Márquez, quoted in the *Telegraph Sunday Magazine*

Some authors write extremely quickly and fluently. Dr Johnson completed his short novel *Rasselas* in the space of a single week. Balzac could write 200 pages a week when the need arose; so too could the French novelist Stendhal. Others write with excruciating slowness: another great 19th-century novelist, Gustave Flaubert, often managed no more than two pages in a week – sometimes only a single page. His classic novel *Madame Bovary* took him five years of painful full-time writing.

Some authors, such as Anthony Burgess or the late A.J.P. Taylor, happily draft original material directly on a typewriter or word processor. Others, such as Roald Dahl and Fay Weldon, Iris Murdoch and Athol Fugard, seem to need the feel of a pencil or pen in the hand, as if there were some mystical connection between the moving hand and the creative mind.

Some authors dictate their work to a secretary rather than writing it up themselves – Sir Walter Scott, Anthony Trollope, and Joseph Conrad all started doing this towards the end of their careers. Ernest Hemingway did a great deal of his writing while standing up – resting the paper on top of a filing cabinet, for instance. The English author A.N. Wilson types away while sitting up in bed.

If the authors themselves differ so widely in their working methods, what guidance can the everyday writer derive from them?

Perhaps just this: to take writing very seriously, and to work intensely at getting it right – that is, at expressing your thoughts as accurately and clearly as possible.

And one more thing: in the great divide between businesslike 'craftsman' authors and moody 'artistic' authors, between perspiration and inspiration, the everyday writer should come down firmly on the side of the business-like approach. The arty or romantic approach may produce greater poetry or deeper novels, but for everyday writing it falls flat.

Of all businesslike authors, Anthony Trollope's daily routine remains the best-known and perhaps the most impressive. His *Autobiography* records his amazing application and efficiency. For most of his writing life, he had a full-time job as a civil servant with the Post Office, so much of his enormous output (over 60 books, many of them three-volume novels) was the product of his leisure hours.

Hardly leisurely – alongside his Post Office duties and a busy social life, he still found 15 to 20 spare hours a week for his writing. Day after day, year after year, he would sit at his desk between 5.30 and 8.30 in the morning, writing 1000 words an hour. (He planned each novel thoroughly before writing it up – an outline layout on paper, a fully developed scenario in his head. And he kept detailed progress charts to ensure that he stayed on schedule.)

The *Autobiography* outraged many critics and authors of the day. Its no-nonsense view of novel-writing took all the glamour and mystique out of the art – or the craft, as Trollope preferred to call it. He argued that the writer's life should follow much the same pattern as a shoemaker's or upholsterer's or undertaker's, and should be 'bound by rules of labour similar to those which an artisan or a mechanic is forced to obey'. No resting on laurels, no giving in to occasional moods or indolence. Just getting on with the job, and getting it right.

That serves as a fine motto for anyone engaged in any writing task.

you are writing for the boss, say, or that letter of complaint to the council: the chances are that it will turn out both sharper and deeper if you develop and test your views beforehand in a conversation with a friend or colleague – even if he or she knows very little about the subject. A participant in a discussion can serve merely as a sounding board, in other words – but that is a very valuable function in its way.

But if your discussion partner is well-informed on the subject, or has a new angle on it, or simply has a good critical mind, he probably will have some new ideas to contribute, and so much the better. If possible, discuss your views with a friend who has recently written a similar letter or report himself. Or speak to an acquaintance who has some relevant experience or technical expertise or inside knowledge, and who might have some valuable tips to offer – for example, the name of a specific councillor to address the complaint to.

Research. When you do not have the information to write up, go and find it. At an information centre or in a library, by letter or over the phone, in a book or through an interview.

People tend to think of research as something to conduct among books, newspapers, old letters and reports, and so on, and therefore tend to overlook an equally valuable source – other people. Talk to the experts: even if they cannot answer your every question, they might at least point you directly to the particular book or document that you need, and save you a great deal of time in that way.

Suppose you have to compile a report for the Sports Club committee on buying a video-editing machine for the office. A thorough research programme would probably include the following steps:

☐ phone or visit the largest local electronic goods store and ask a senior salesman for some preliminary advice

☐ speak to anyone you know, on similar committees or in business, who may recently have made a similar purchase – and perhaps have researched it all thoroughly already

☐ visit your local library: the librarian should be able to direct you to consumer reports comparing the various models available

☐ phone or write to the manufacturers mentioned there, asking for the brochures, technical specifications, price lists, and so on

WRITING UP

If the only cause of 'writer's block' were lack of information, you could cure the condition quickly by means of the three remedies just described – reflection, discussion, and research.

Unfortunately, there is that second cause of writer's block – lack of application, the simple failure to settle down and get on with the writing – and it is rather more complicated to overcome.

This failure takes two forms. They are: *work avoidance* and *paralysis*.

Work avoidance. The delaying tactics of work avoiders are legion. Almost any distraction will serve: a cup of tea, a radio programme, an untidy desk, noisy neighbours, washing your socks, further research.

The treatment for this condition has a number of ingredients. Decide for yourself which ones correspond to your particular symptoms and needs. And then take the maximum dosage.

The first step is to own up. Confess that you are seeking the distractions rather than simply 'being afflicted' by them. Admit that the remedy is within your own power rather than somewhere 'out there'. Acknowledge that it is up to you yourself to eradicate your delaying tactics.

You might want to look into the psychological reasons for your avoiding of the work. Finding the cause of a problem may be halfway to solving it.

Perhaps it is fear of failure that makes you workshy: if you do the writing, it may turn out below standard. And if that happens, others may pass adverse judgment on you, or you may pass a harsh judgment on yourself. (To reduce the risk of that, you might sidestep the challenge continually – hence your stalling tactics. If you finally do scribble down a hasty and botched text as the deadline looms, you at least have an excuse for its inadequacy: you wrote it in a rush. If only you had had more time, you reassure yourself, you could have done it properly.)

Various other reasons might be at work too – an unconscious wish to spite yourself; or to thwart those who are relying on you. Whether you succeed in learning your own motives, or even try to discover them, you still have to overcome them. And that involves action, not just self-analysis. It means *doing* more, not simply *knowing* more.

In taking the necessary action, be strict with yourself. Impose a harsh regimen (or else you will simply lapse right away – the workshy personality shows great ingenuity in finding loopholes and excuses). If you feel unable to trust your own self-discipline, ask a friend or colleague to check up on you from time to time – even to the point of demanding progress reports if you show any signs of slacking.

For short, one-off writing tasks – such as a single thank-you note – the best advice is simply: Just do it! Decide in advance on a suitable time for the chore – directly after lunch, say, at 2.15 exactly – and treat that appointment as sacred. If necessary, take the phone off the hook to avoid distractions. Sit down at your desk or at the kitchen table, and get writing . . . and don't get up until the chore is completed. In addition to setting yourself a starting time, set yourself a deadline too – 2.45, say. It does not matter if you overrun it; its purpose is to give you a sense of urgency, and focus your attention on the task confronting you.

For longer and more complex writing tasks – such as a research thesis or a lengthy office report or a series of job applications – try the following systematic set of guidelines. They should help to keep you on course.

☐ Make a rough list of all the tasks and activities for the day – writing tasks and leisure activities alike. Then draw up a neat list of all the items in order of priority – top of the list, for example, is to write and send off that urgent reminder to the spare-parts supplier; somewhere in the middle of the list is to check a reference in the library in preparation for that committee report you have to start drafting; near the bottom of the list is to buy a new pencil sharpener and reply to Mary's wedding invitation and iron your shirts and listen to your new Placido Domingo cassette. And so on.

☐ On the basis of this ordered list of tasks, draw up a clear timetable for the day. It need not be absolutely rigid – allow some leeway perhaps for a genuine distraction such as an unexpected visitor – but equally should not allow very much flexibility. So: at your desk by 9.30. No tea break until you have written that letter of complaint to the warehouse and compiled the first draft of that report for the finance department. Delay lunch if the final version of the report still needs the finishing touches.

☐ Make your working environment as favourable and inviting as possible. A good light, a reasonably clear desk, well-stocked drawers of stationery, and so on. Try to get everything fully prepared for an unbroken session of work – a glass of water within reach, a jumper in case you get cold – or else you will be getting up from your desk time and again and breaking your concentration in doing so. Depending on your circumstances, you might also be able to organise some extra helpful features: a radio for quiet background music (if that really improves rather than spoils your concentration), perhaps a telephone answering machine to screen out non-urgent calls, and so on.

☐ At the end of each working session, especially at the end of each day, tidy your desk in preparation for the next session. Lay out a blank sheet of paper as an invitation to get writing as soon as you sit down. If you will be starting a new piece of work, lay out the information or research material as well, ready for immediate consulting. If you will be continuing a previous piece of work, lay out the last page or two, ready for rereading at the start and thereby re-establishing the momentum.

☐ Try to discover the working pattern that best suits your particular mind and body rhythms. People's attention spans vary, and even an individual person's attention span varies according to time of day, degree of familiarity with the task, and so on. Once you have established your own best working pattern, design your timetable to take it into account.

A typical pattern for many people is this: the mind is sharpest in the morning, so the trickiest writing tasks should be undertaken then. After 45 minutes or so, concentration begins to decline; a few moments' break is enough to restore it. (How to spend the break? Close your eyes to rest them, and stretch your arms and shrug your shoulders to relieve muscular tension. Alternatively, a brief change of task – make a phone call, glance at the newspaper, or something similar. But don't get sidetracked: after five minutes at most, return to your writing project until a formal break, such as your scheduled lunch break, comes around.)

Mid-afternoon is usually the mind's slackest time during the working day – the four o'clock flag sets in. New writing would fare poorly if attempted now. The time is better spent on more mechanical tasks – tidying up, making lists, proofreading a previous piece of writing, light editing of a current piece of writing. (For more details on spending an efficient day at your desk, see the chapter on study methods below, especially pages 437 and 441.)

Writer's paralysis. Unfortunately, arranging a clear desk and an undisturbed half hour for yourself is no guarantee that you will get your writing done. The second form of failure lies in wait to induce writer's block in you – *paralysis*. You can overcome all your work avoidance and delaying tactics, only to run into a new obstacle as you gaze down at the work surface of your desk.

Your mind goes as blank as the sheet of paper in front of you – all your ideas vanish. Or else quite the reverse: they all attack you simultaneously, jostling about in your mind and refusing to fall into line.

Or the words just will not come. You write half a sentence and then cross it out. Then you rewrite it. Then you decide on a better form of wording, and write that instead. Then you decide that it is no better after all. After half an hour and half a page of crossings out, you realise that you have not even worded the first sentence! How are you ever going to get the whole text written?

Again, several remedies are available – choose whichever ones sound promising to you, and try them out at once.

☐ Jot down in point form all the relevant ideas that occur to you. Once they are safely down on the page, they will stop buzzing about distractingly in your head. You can then try supplementing and arranging these points into a proper structure, which will form the basis of your first draft. (For details and ways of arranging ideas into a proper structure, see pages 91-102.) This elementary step has the added benefit of breaking down a large – perhaps paralysingly large – project into small manageable sections, which you can now tackle with far greater peace of mind one by one.

☐ If you cannot get all the items organised into a proper structure, never mind – just start writing anyway. You need not begin with the first point on your list – why not begin with the easiest point? That will at least get you going, and once you have some momentum, you should find you can attempt some of the trickier points fairly comfortably as well. You can put them into the proper sequence later.

☐ Don't worry at this early stage about elegant phrasing or methodical ordering of your sentences. Press onwards, rather than going back to refine any earlier point. Just get your thoughts down on paper – as many as possible – no matter how rough and ready. Time enough to tidy them up when it comes to the revising or rewriting stage. In fact, rough writing of this kind often actually helps to churn up your ideas and thereby eventually to clarify your thinking.

☐ Remind yourself constantly that what you are scribbling represents no more than a first draft. You are not committing yourself to anything – in the way that you are in a spoken interview, for instance. (The one big exception is exam essays, where your first draft usually has to serve as your final version as well. For the special techniques of approaching exam essays, see the chapter on exams, especially pages 424-428.)

☐ Think of the wastepaper basket or the fireplace as one of your most important tools in any writing task. Since you can always throw away a page, why bother about getting it right first time? As the Roman poet Ovid put it: 'I have written much, but whatever I thought defective I revised by giving to the flames.' To grasp and accept this rather obvious insight produces in many people an exciting feeling of liberation – as if kicking aside the writer's block instead of slowly wearing it away.

☐ Warm up by writing something quite unrelated to the particular task: write an account of your last weekend or of a dream you had recently, or the recipe for your favourite dish, or the reasons for your inability to start working. Anything, so long as it flows quickly. That should break the cycle of anxiety and inactivity – once the 'paralysis' breaks in this way, your mind and hand should re-engage like gears, and you should be able to move forward.

☐ Try *speaking* your thoughts before putting them down on paper. This too can break the logjam.

Ask your spouse, or a friend or colleague, to listen to you as you deliver an oral summary of the report or essay. Or dictate a rough version into your tape recorder. Once you say your piece out loud, you should find it a good deal easier to 'say' it on paper.

☐ Try to cultivate an extremely casual attitude towards the first draft in order to remove any feelings of tension you may have about it. Pretend, for instance, that it is just a practice exercise rather than the basis of a real document, and that no one else will ever read it. Or make-believe that you are setting a test for candidate sub-editors, and that you deliberately want to compile a very hasty and awkward piece of work that they will then have to redraft as a test piece.

☐ If your shilly-shallying arises from lack of pressure, try imposing some artificial pressure on yourself. Bring your deadline forward – tell yourself that a crisis has arisen and the boss needs your report tomorrow rather than next week. This might give you the impetus to dash off a rough draft at a record pace, leaving you plenty of time to polish it.

☐ If the document you have to write is extremely important, and you are frozen by the awesome responsibility, begin your first draft by writing the words 'Dear Mum' or 'Dear diary', and continue writing up your thoughts in the form of a letter or diary entry. Just as actors overcome stage fright by imagining an audience made up entirely of friends and family, so writers can overcome a paralysing panic reaction by pitching their words at a well-disposed reader (such as a loved one) rather than the actual reader (such as a demanding boss or nitpicking client).

☐ Offer yourself a small reward for each writing project you complete, or even for each page you write. Whatever reward you choose – a chocolate, a five-minute break – it should act as an inducement to you to get started.

The
Building
Blocks
of
Good
English

The Words We Use

ENGLISH is a piratical language, with a long history of plundering other tongues and making off with their words. The richness and vigour of the English vocabulary arise directly from this ability to absorb words from places as far apart as the fjords of Scandinavia, the plains of India, and the islands of the Caribbean.

If English as a language has expanded its bounds wider still and wider, so have the people who speak it – with the result that what began as the language of a group of wandering German tribes has become the mother tongue of more than 350 million people around the globe. And about the same number again have at least a working knowledge of English.

The Roots of English

There has been a language called 'English' for at least 1300 years. It descends from a form of Germanic brought to Britain by the Anglo-Saxons, whose homelands lay along the eastern shores of the North Sea. The Romans settled some of these fierce, fair-haired warriors in Britain as mercenaries, and more came as invaders as the Roman Empire began to collapse and the legions were withdrawn to protect Rome itself.

THE INDO-EUROPEAN HERITAGE

English and the Germanic languages as a whole are part of a much larger family of languages, including most of those of modern Europe and southwest Asia. The common ancestor of this family was the language known to scholars as Proto-Indo-European. Of modern European tongues only a handful – notably Hungarian, Finnish, and Basque – have a different ancestry.

Family likenesses can be traced in many of the words these languages use today. The Hindi word *maharajah*, for instance, derives from the Indo-European root *reg-*, meaning 'to put straight' and, from that, 'to rule'. This same root turns up in Latin in words like *rex*, *regis* (a king) and *rego*, *rectum* (to rule). From these were formed the English words *regal*, *rector*, *correct*, and *direct*. Also from Latin, but this time changed by centuries in early French, come *royal* and *adroit*.

The Germanic form of the same Indo-European root has given English *right* and *rich* (which originally meant 'powerful', and owes its form to French influence). There is also the German *Reich* (originally 'a kingdom'), as well as the Romany (Gypsy) term for a man of authority, *rye*. The Gypsies carried their language from their original homelands in northern India on their journeys west.

Language experts have pieced together a reasonably clear picture of the vocabulary of Proto-Indo-European – which, in turn, reveals much about the people who spoke it, as well as about where and how they lived.

For example, the Indo-Europeans seem to have had words for winter and snow, but not for sea. This suggests that they lived not too far to the south, but away from oceans. They had words for oak, beech, pine, bear, wolf, and deer, but none for donkey, chicken, bamboo, palm, camel, lion, or monkey. Their homeland would thus seem to have been a region of temperate woodland with cold winters.

The Indo-Europeans also had words for pig, horse, cow, dog, and plough, and so must have known something about agriculture.

The commonest theory among scholars is that the original Indo-Europeans lived, at least at times, in settled villages somewhere in eastern Europe or the steppes of western Asia, and that their period as a fairly unified group was probably around 5000-3000 BC. After that they spread out over much of Europe and Asia, leaving as their heritage a bond of shared word roots among the languages of what became widely diverging cultures.

THE LANGUAGES OF EARLY BRITAIN

At the time of the Anglo-Saxon invasions of Britain, the Germanic branch of the Indo-European family had developed into three large groups:

☐ Eastern, represented by ancient Gothic, and now completely extinct

☐ Northern, which became Norse, the language of the Vikings, and ancestor of modern Danish, Swedish, Norwegian, and Icelandic – the last is the language that preserves the most ancient Germanic features

☐ Western, the group that included Anglo-Saxon, and whose descendants include as well as English, modern German, Dutch, Frisian, Yiddish, and Afrikaans

Frisian, the foreign language closest to English is spoken in the north of the Netherlands and as a dying language along the coast of Germany. It is said that a Yorkshireman who concentrates hard can understand much modern spoken Frisian.

ENGLAND, THE ENGLISH, AND THE SAXONS

Until the Anglo-Saxons arrived, the native language of Britain had been Celtic. Celtic-speaking peoples had been settling in Britain throughout the thousand years before the Roman invasion. But very few Celtic words from this period have survived into modern English – *brock* (the badger) is a possible example. Clearly, relations between invaders and native population were far from friendly. The Anglo-Saxons soon pushed the Celts and their tongue back to the fringes and more mountainous parts of the British Isles.

When the Anglo-Saxons evolved a sense of national identity they called their language *Englisc*, and used the word *Angelcynn* ('the kin of the Angles') or *Angelfolc* for themselves as a group or nation. The word *Englaland* first appears around AD 1000.

Of all the Anglo-Saxon kingdoms, the one to achieve greatest prominence was Wessex, the kingdom of the West Saxons. Alfred the Great, who ruled Wessex from 871-899 AD, was remarkable both as a soldier and as a scholar. He managed to beat back Viking invaders and established English as a written language, himself translating a number of Latin works into his native tongue. For the remainder of the Anglo-Saxon period, the West Saxon dialect remained the literary standard.

English established itself as a written language.

What does Old English – or Anglo-Saxon – look like? Here is a specimen from the time of Alfred from a translation into Anglo-Saxon of the *Ecclesiastical History of the English Nation* – originally written in Latin about AD 730 by the north English monk, the Venerable Bede. This extract – slightly shortened and standardised – tells the story of how an angel appeared to the cowherd Caedmon.

> 'Cædmon, sing mē hwæthwugu.'
> Þā andswarode hē and cwæð, 'Ne can ic nōht singan, and ic for þon of þissum gebēorscipe ūt ēode and hider gewāt.'
> 'Hwæðre þū mē āht singan.'
> Þā cwæð hē, 'Hwæt sceal ic singan?'
> Cwæð hē, 'Sing mē frumsceaft.'
> Þā ongan hē sōna singan in herenesse Godes Scyppendes þā fers and þā word þe hē næfre gehȳrde.

'Caedmon, sing me something.'
Then answered he and said, 'I cannot sing (at all), and I for that (reason) from this beer-drinking went out and came hither.'
'Even so, you must sing to me.'
Then said he, 'What shall I sing?'
Said he, 'Sing me the Creation.'
Then proceeded he at once to sing in praise of God the Creator those verses and those lines that he (had) never heard (before).

Plainly, Old English looks very different from the modern language. It has to be learned almost as a foreign language.

The first striking thing about it is the use of various symbols absent from Modern English. Old English borrowed its alphabet from Latin. But it had certain sounds that Latin lacked entirely and so had to find special letters of its own. From the old German alphabet, for instance, it took the þ (for / th /), which survived until at least the 14th century. Later readers mistook this symbol for a *y*, and so, in modern times, people wanting to give their writing a pseudo-archaic look wrote *ye* for *the*. From this came sillinesses such as *Ye Olde Teashoppe*. In fact, *ye* here has nothing at all to do with the old second person plural pronoun found in *Ye holy angels bright*, which is the direct descendant of the Old English plural *you*, *gē*.

Another striking feature of Old English is its use of 'inflections', the endings of words that show their relationships with other words. It had a host of inflections that indicated classifications such as those we now call nominative, genitive, masculine, feminine, and neuter. Around AD 850, for instance, the word for day had six different forms: *dæg*, 'day'; *dæges*, 'of day'; *dæge*, 'in or on a day'; *dagas*, 'days'; *daga*, 'of days'; *dagum*, 'in or on days'. Changes in the language have cut these down to four: *day*, *day's*, *days*, and *days'*.

Old English and the modern language also differ greatly in their vocabularies. Many of the words in the Caedmon passage have fallen out of the language entirely – *hwæthwugu* and *herenesse*, for instance. Some are still familiar but sound archaic, such as *cwæð* ('quoth') and *hider* ('hither'). Others have changed their meanings. The ancestor of the modern *soon* appears in the passage as *sōna*, but in Old English it meant 'straightaway'.

Nevertheless, if you examine the passage carefully, you will see how the core of Modern English vocabulary comes from Old English. The passage contains the origins of *sing*, *me*, *he*, *and*, *can*, *I*, *for*, *out*, and many others. Old English supplied most of Modern English's pronouns, such as *you*, *we*, and *it*; its interrogative words, such as *what*, *when*, and *why*; its prepositions, such as *by*, *in*, and *to*; its common verbs, such as *know*, *drink*, *go*, *work*, and *like*; its auxiliary verbs, such as *shall*, *will*, and *may*; its basic nouns, such as *child*, *book*, *home*, *house*, *name*, and *day*; and its commonest adjectives, such as *good*, *red*, and *small*.

This is what is meant by saying that English is a Germanic language. The vocabulary has been overlaid by words of Latin and French origin, but the heart of the language remains true to the Germanic tongue spoken by the Anglo-Saxons.

LATIN INFLUENCES ON OLD ENGLISH

From the Anglo-Saxon period down to the 17th and 18th centuries, Latin, as well as being the language of church services, was the international language of culture and religion, and it was Latin-learned clerics who taught the English to write.

There appear to have been two distinct periods of Latin influence on Old English. The first corresponds with the 200 years after the arrival of Christianity in Britain in the 7th century. Most of the words it provided in this period were fairly practical. Germanic had already taken in Latin-based words like *church* and *bishop*, but now came many new words related to the new religion and its organisation: *abbot*, *alms*, *candle*, *martyr*, *mass*, *noon*, *offer*, *priest*, *rule*, and *temple*.

Some words dealing with education and culture also date from this period: for example, *school*, *master*, *grammar*, *note*, and *verse* (which appears in the Caedmon passage).

Latin influence waned with the turmoil of the Viking invasions during the later Anglo-Saxon period. But just before AD 1000 there started a new wave of scholarly activity in the English monasteries. From this period come new Christian words (some going back further, to Greek) such as *cell*, *collect*, *demon*, *idol*, and *prime* and new words to do with learning, such as *accent*, *history*, *paper*, and *title*.

THE VIKINGS ARRIVE

From about AD 800 the Vikings, or Northmen, from Scandinavia began their invasions. At first they came to raid and trade, but soon their ships started transporting families of settlers, mainly to the north and east of Britain. Place names ending *-by*, *-kirk*, *-thorp*, and *-toft* are evidence of Viking settlement.

Unlike Latin, with its glimpse of a higher culture, Old Norse had little in the way of novelties to give the Anglo-Saxons. But in the regions where Vikings became dominant many of their words passed into the local dialect, and from there some spread into general English usage. From the Vikings, English gets many of its commonest words – *take*, *get*, *sky*, egg, *husband*, and even *law*. Other loans show just how deep the Norse influence on English was to become. The nouns *band*, *birth*, *bull*, *dirt*, and *skill*, and the verbs *call*, *crawl*, *die*, *lift*, and *scare* are all from Old Norse.

Norse brought new words – and also changed the forms of many existing English words. The Old English words for *grass* and *run* were *gærs* and *yrnan*; the modern forms are from the Norse versions of these words. The 'hard' *g-* in words like *give* is evidence of Norse influence; in Old English a *g-* before a vowel at the beginning of a word was pronounced /y/, as in *yellow*.

Just as place names with Scandinavian elements are commonest in the north and east, dialect words from these areas tend to be of Norse origin. Scots forms like *gang* (go), *kirk* (church), and *waur* (worse) were introduced by the Vikings. People in the northeast of England still call a flea a *lop* – the modern Danish word for a flea is *loppe*. The northern dialect verb *to laik*, meaning 'to play', goes back to the Old Norse verb *leika*. Its form in modern Danish is *lege*. When the Dane, Ole Christiansen, invented new toy building blocks, he used this word as a basis for the name, *Lego*.

Scandinavian influence reaches right into the heart of English. Take the third-person plural personal pronouns, *they*, *them*, and *their*. The Old English word for *they* was *hīe*. In many dialects this started to sound like the singular *he*, which was clearly unsatisfactory. Gradually the northern forms, based on the Old Norse, spread south.

THE NORMAN CONQUEST

The Normans, too, were of Viking stock, but they had been settled in Normandy for over a century when Duke William led his invasion of England in 1066. By then they had become completely 'Frenchified' in customs, culture, and language.

Just as the Norman knights conquered England, so their language, at least for a time, conquered that of the defeated Anglo-Saxons. The new aristocracy in England spoke French, and writing in English on official, cultural, religious, or literary matters all but ceased – though some records, such as the Anglo-Saxon Chronicle kept at the Abbey of Peterborough, were still being made in English until the 1150s. Now the languages in use became Latin, for church and intellectual writing, and the Anglo-Norman form of French for law and literary works. English,

Much basic English vocabulary arose from the Viking invasion.

however, survived among the ordinary people to re-emerge as the common language of England in the 14th century.

Anglo-Norman differed from standard French in several respects, and English would borrow words from each dialect. From Anglo-Norman would come *hostel*, *reward*, and *warranty*; the related words *hotel*, *regard*, and *guarantee* came from standard French a little later.

English people of recent times have given the Anglo-Normans little credit for their achievements. During the 12th century, in particular, a great deal of the finest literature in Europe was produced in this country, but in French. For instance, the oldest surviving version of the story of Tristan and Iseult is the poem (written in Norman French) by Thomas d'Angleterre – Thomas of England.

Comparing words originating from English and French (and thus ultimately Latin) gives an interesting insight into the social divisions of the Middle Ages in England. For example:

from English	from French
pig	pork
sheep, lamb	mutton
cow, bull	beef

Clearly there was one group of people tending the animals and another group that was eating them.

ENGLISH IN THE MIDDLE AGES

English was like a river that suddenly vanishes underground and seems to be lost for ever – until, with a great roar, its waters burst out of the ground in some far-off place.

Even in the early days of the Norman domination, the ordinary people of England had stuck doggedly to the language of their fathers, making little attempt to speak like their masters. Rievaulx Abbey, in North Yorkshire, was founded by Cistercian monks in 1131, and is usually pronounced today in the French fashion / **ree**vo /. But there are still local people who insist that the proper pronunciation is the one their ancestors used: / **riv**vərs /.

Then, in the latter half of the 14th century, English came into its own once more. The now Anglicised aristocracy started using English in preference to French on all occasions, and English again became the all-purpose language – though in the courts Norman French persisted for longer. Modern legal English retains such expressions as *feme sole* (an unmarried woman).

The newly invigorated language found its greatest exponent in the poet Chaucer, writing an English that was exuberant, vigorous, as full of colour as a stained-glass window. But Chaucer's English had changed almost beyond recognition from Old English. Most of the Old English symbols had gone, and the vocabulary had changed even more. French and Latin influence was all-pervasive – Chaucer's writings teem with words borrowed or adapted from French or Latin sources.

English between about 1150 and 1450 is called Middle English. Here is a passage from Chaucer's *Canterbury Tales*. It describes a parson unspoilt by the clerical abuses of his day.

> A good man was ther of religioun,
> And was a povre persoun of a toun,
> But riche he was of hooly thoght and werk.
> He was also a lerned man, a clerk,
> That Cristes gospel trewely wolde preche;
> His parisshens devoutly wolde he teche.
> Benygne he was, and wonder diligent,
> And in adversitee ful pacient.

This looks fairly straightforward to the modern reader. But there are some qualifications.

First, the pronunciation has changed considerably since Chaucer's time, though in fact his spelling is closer to his way of speaking than modern spelling is to modern pronunciation. When Chaucer writes *night* it ought to be read in the Scottish manner, / ni<u>k</u>ht /, as if in a Burns poem. Where he has *line* you ought to pronounce it rather like *leaner*. *Wolde* in the passage rhymes with the modern English *solder* rather than with *good*.

Secondly, some of the words may look familiar but their meaning has changed in the last 600 years. One obvious example here is *clerk*, which in Chaucerian English still has its original meaning of a 'cleric'. Another of Chaucer's characters was a *verray parfit gentil knight* – this does not mean that he was 'very perfect and gentle', but 'truly perfect and well-born'.

Bear in mind that Chaucer, writing in cosmopolitan London, was using the most up-to-date dialect of his age, and the one from which modern Standard English descends.

LATIN OR FRENCH?

It is often difficult to tell whether a particular word has come into English directly from Latin or by way of French. Sometimes the form of the word helps. *Fable*, for example, is from French, while *fabulous* has come a shorter route from the Latin *fabula*. The French, too, were busy borrowing words from Latin during this period, which complicates the picture. Words like *obscure* turn up in French and English at much the same time.

There is often a difference in the kinds of word that came from the two languages. Latin, being the language of the church and higher education, gave English most of the technical borrowings of this, and later, periods. Such words as *benediction*, *opposition*, and *astronomy* are probably direct from Latin. More everyday words, such as *fork*, *beauty*, and *repair* are from French. There are exceptions, however – *ordinary*, for example, is in fact from Latin, and *mutation* from French.

Words from French cover all areas of the English vocabulary but are particularly noticeable in certain fields. Administrative terms are often French: *government*, *parliament*, *crown*, *state*, *oppress*, *court*, and *council*, for example. Legal terms that have passed into the general vocabulary from French include *justice*, *crime*, *judge*, *seize*, *arson*, *heir*, and *innocent*. The military has inherited a large part of its terminology from French: words such as *war*, *peace*, *enemy*, *arms*, *battle*, *defend*, *attack*, *campaign*, and *spy*.

Not surprisingly, many of our words for the aristocracy and their way of life are of French origin: *baron*, *marquis*, *duke*, *noble*, *servant*, *feast*, and *minstrel*, though *earl* is Germanic. The manners and customs introduced by the French-speaking court have given *fashion*, *dress*, *robe*, *collar*, *glove*, and *fur*, and even *blue*, *brown*, *purple*, and some other names of colours. *Curtains*, *chairs*, *cushions*, *blankets*, *towels*, and *basins* are all French.

There are often groups of words with much the same meaning of which one word is native, one French (perhaps a little more formal), and one Latin (decidedly formal). Try to feel the differences in these sets:

from English	from French	from Latin
spell	enchantment	mystery
do	perform	perpetrate
go	depart	vacate
like	enjoy	appreciate, luxuriate
take	seize	confiscate
ask	question	interrogate
fear	terror	trepidation
holy	sacred	consecrated
time	age	era
way	manner	procedure

THE WORLD CONTRACTS

The late 15th to 17th centuries – the English Renaissance – saw more and more borrowings. The introduction of printing by William Caxton in 1476 helped to spread new words. The voyages of exploration and the widening of European trade brought new products to England, each of which needed a name. So did the technical and scientific discoveries of the age. Above all, the spirit of enquiry and the spread of writing and reading for education and pleasure encouraged the adoption of large numbers of new words.

Just about any Latin verb could be turned into an English abstract noun by substituting *-ion* for the *-um* ending of the past participle. So *tractum* (from the verb *trahere*, to drag) gives *traction*; *monstratum* (from *monstrare*, to show) gives *demonstration*; *probatum* (from *probare*, to make or find good) gives *probation*, and so on. The present participles of Latin verbs provided the basis for English adjectives ending in *-ent* or *-ant*, such as *permanent* (from *manens*, present participle of *manere*, to remain), *tolerant*, and *constant*.

Other languages too were beginning to leave their mark on English. Greek had been studied up to a point in the medieval universities, but new access to the philosophical and scientific works of ancient Greece opened the path to a new technical stratum of English vocabulary.

Words such as *anachronism*, *atmosphere*, *antithesis*, *chaos*, *climax*, *crisis*, *emphasis*, *enthusiasm*, *parasite*, *parenthesis*, *pneumonia*, *scheme*, *system*, and *tactics* came into English from Greek by way of Latin. Direct borrowings include *anonymous*, *catastrophe*, *criterion*, *idiosyncrasy*, *lexicon*, *misanthrope*, *orthodox*, *thermometer*, and *tonic*.

There were loans from Arabic too. During the Middle Ages the Arabs were in the forefront of scientific and medical research. English gained terms like *alcohol*, *algebra*, *algorithm* (recently repopularised by computer programmers), *arsenal*, and *syrup*. Some words for Arabic luxuries and customs that had been brought back to Europe by the Crusaders also made their way into English: *artichoke*, *carafe*, *jar*, *cotton*, and *sofa*.

Another language whose influence became ever more important as trade increased was Dutch (or Flemish). Not surprisingly, the area of shipping owes much of its vocabulary to Dutch – *deck*, *dock*, *skipper*, *boom*, and *yacht*, for example. The skill of Dutch artists is reflected in loans such as *easel*, *landscape*, *sketch*, and *etch*.

For much of the Renaissance, Europe looked to Italy for inspiration. The obvious culinary terms (*spaghetti*, *espresso*, and so on) and musical terms (*allegro*, *cello*, *sonata*) are mostly later borrowings. But the Italian culture of the Renaissance and since has also given *arcade*, *balcony*, *brigand*, *bronze*, *caress*, *colonel*, *dilettante*, *fiasco*, *graffiti*, *influenza*, *replica*, *scenario*, *sonnet*, *studio*, and *umbrella*.

The great early colonial powers, Spain and Portugal, provided English with further new words. Spanish loans into English, from then and later, include *anchovy*, *armada*, *bonanza*, *bravado*, *cafeteria*, *cask*, *cigar*, *guerrilla*, *lasso*, *patio*, *ranch*, *siesta*, *stampede*,

The Building Blocks Of Good English

117

and *tornado*. Portuguese has given English *albatross*, *albino*, *brocade*, *cobra*, *creole*, *palaver*, *rusk*, and the wine *port*.

EXPERIMENT AND REACTION

The flowering of English literature during the late 16th and early 17th centuries owes much to the newly discovered resources of the language.

The vocabularies of the leading writers of the age – Shakespeare, Spenser, Jonson, and others – are large and varied, and reveal their delight and interest in words. At the same time, less gifted writers, then as now, grasped at big words to impress their readers or audience. The horrors of some official writing nowadays can be matched by this passage drawn from a letter written by a church minister of the time seeking a benefice:

> I obtestate your clemencie, to invigilate thus much for me, according to my confidence, and as you knowe my condigne merites for such a compendious living.

At the end of the 16th century, John Lyly published two novellas with a central character called Euphues. His ornate style, larded with artificial turns of phrase, became known as *euphuism*. This word can be used nowadays to describe any form of overblown and pretentious prose.

A lively debate raged for much of this period (and since) over the status of loans and neologisms (new words) based on Latin and Greek. Some writers culled obscure terms from the classical languages – known as 'inkhorn terms'. The image is of a dusty scholar poring over ancient manuscripts, his pen at the ready, in search of words with the flavour of the classroom or library.

Most notable among them was the physician and writer Sir Thomas Browne. Many of Browne's coinings seem outlandish to modern ears – *manuduct* (to lead by the hand), *commensality* (the people who share a table), and *paralogy* (unreasonable doubt). But among other words Browne is believed to have introduced into English are *antediluvian*, *hallucination*, *incontrovertible*, *precarious*, and *retrogression*, to say nothing of *electricity*, *medical*, and *literary*.

Other people, such as Queen Elizabeth I's tutor Roger Ascham, urged that English should be kept pure and fixed. Among them was the poet Spenser, who revived words from older forms of English and

its dialects, such as *astound, belt, chirrup, delve, doom, glance, blatant,* and *surly*.

As a rule, however, the poets, playwrights, and ordinary speakers of the language at this period took the pragmatic course – what was pleasant or useful from the classical languages they accepted. What was not they ignored. In the hands of great writers wonderful effects were produced by playing off more common English words against impressive-sounding loans. It is the sudden introduction of a Latin-based word – *liquefaction* – that gives these lines from the 17th-century poet Robert Herrick their force:

> Whenas in silks my Julia goes,
> Then, then (methinks) how sweetly flows
> That liquefaction of her clothes.

THE ENLIGHTENMENT

The tendencies established during the Renaissance continued throughout the 18th century – the period of the 'Enlightenment'. The works of writers like Dr Samuel Johnson and Edward Gibbon are packed with Latin- and Greek-based words that bear witness to their classical educations. And as Britain became a world power in the 18th and 19th centuries, there was a new confidence in the qualities of English. The feeling gained currency that the language had now reached a state of unparalleled elegance and perfection, and that any change could only be for the worse.

There were two important consequences of this new-found confidence. First, the desire to 'fix' English – which lay behind the pioneering work of Dr Johnson and others in dictionary-making and the study of English grammar. Dr Johnson's dictionary, published in 1755, was the first dictionary that seriously attempted a complete coverage of the English vocabulary.

The other result was the formulation of rules of usage – the 'this-is-right-and-you-are-wrong' attitude. Several 'rules' still peddled today come from this period, with little or no basis in the language as it is or ever has been used. There is the 'rule', for instance, that prepositions should not be used to end clauses with. Most of these prejudices were based on attempts to impose Latin grammar upon English. *Preposition*, for example, means literally 'placed in front', hence 'something placed in front of something', and so, said the lawgivers, prepositions could not go at the end.

WORDS FROM EVERYWHERE

Over the last 400 years, as British influence has spread around the world, through trade and the acquiring of a vast overseas empire in the 18th and 19th centuries, English has taken in words from just about every language it has come into contact with. Some of these words have been adopted directly; others have come into English via one of the other European languages. Here are some of the words borrowed at various times. It will give you an idea of the extraordinary variety that English has to offer.

LANGUAGES OF THE BRITISH ISLES

Scots and Irish Gaelic: *banshee, bard, blarney, bog, brat, cadge, galore, plaid, slogan, smithereens, spree, Tory, trousers, whisky*

Welsh: *coracle, corgi, flannel, flummery*

OTHER EUROPEAN LANGUAGES

Modern French: *ballet, brochure, camouflage, chic, cliché, elite, etiquette, garage, gourmet, liaison, menu, naive, pâté, police, prestige, rendezvous, ricochet, suede, verve.*

In addition, English uses many French words and phrases with little attempt at integrating them into English speech patterns: *à la carte, bête noire, coup d'état, cul de sac, fait accompli, hors d'oeuvre, nouveau riche.*

Spanish: *canyon, cockroach, macho, rodeo*

Portuguese: *albino, corral, marmalade, rusk*

Dutch: *boss, brandy, coleslaw, cruise, drill, gin, groove, hoist, kit, loiter, luck, poppycock, skate, sledge, splinter, split, waffle, wagon*

Afrikaans: *aardvark, apartheid, boer, commandeer, commando, trek, veld*

German: *blitz, delicatessen, dollar, kindergarten, kitsch, lager, nickel, rucksack, snorkel, spanner, swindle, waltz, zinc*

Yiddish: *chutzpah, nosh, schlep, schmaltz*

Scandinavian languages: *fjord, geyser, mink, ombudsman, rug, saga, ski, walrus*

Czech: *howitzer, pistol, robot*

Hungarian: *coach, goulash, hussar, sabre*

Russian: *balalaika, commissar, glasnost, knout, mammoth, perestroika, pogrom, samovar*

EASTERN LANGUAGES

Turkish: *bosh, caviar, coffee, horde, kebab, kiosk, yoghurt*

Arabic: *admiral, cipher, crimson, ghoul, harem, hazard, lute, magazine, masquerade, racket, saffron, sash, sherbet, tariff, zero*

Persian: *bazaar, candy, caravan, check, divan, jackal, jasmine, lemon, lilac, magic, orange, paradise, shawl, spinach, talc, tulip, turban*

Hindi: *bangle, bungalow, chintz, chit, cot, cushy, dinghy, jungle, loot, pyjamas, shampoo, thug, toddy, verandah*

South Indian languages: *mongoose, mulligatawny, pariah*

Malay: *(run) amok, bamboo, (tea) caddy, gingham, gong, (motor) launch, paddy, sago*

Chinese: *ketchup, kowtow, kung fu, silk* (a very ancient loan), *soya, tea, typhoon, wok*

Japanese: *bonsai, futon, judo, kamikaze, karate, kimono, origami, rickshaw, tycoon*

Australian aboriginal languages: *boomerang, budgerigar, dingo, kangaroo, wallaby*

Polynesian and other Pacific languages: *kiwi, mana, taboo, tattoo* (on the skin), *ukulele*

AFRICAN LANGUAGES

banana, banjo, chimpanzee, cola, guinea, okra, raffia, voodoo, yam, zombie

AMERICAN LANGUAGES

Inuit (Eskimo): *anorak, igloo, kayak, parka*

North American Indian languages: *chipmunk, hickory, moccasin, moose, powwow, raccoon, skunk, toboggan, tomahawk, totem*

Aztec: *avocado, cocoa, chilli, chocolate, coyote, tomato*

Caribbean languages: *barbecue, cannibal, hammock, hurricane, maize, tobacco*

South American languages: *alpaca, cashew, cocaine, condor, guano, jaguar, toucan*

The Last Hundred Years

The great changes in the world over the last century or so have brought a further flood of new words into English. Many of these are associated with new fields of human activity and knowledge. Here are some lists of recent words, together with some older ones that have taken on new meanings associated with special fields.

Science. A large proportion of scientific coinings are based on Greek word elements.

☐ Medicine and Life Sciences: *allergy, anaemia, anaesthetic, antitoxin, appendicitis, aspirin, bronchitis, carbohydrate, cholesterol, clinic, DNA, endocrine, enzyme, homeopathy, hormone, immunology, insulin, metabolism, natural selection, orthodontist, penicillin, protein, sclerosis, stethoscope, tonsilitis*

☐ Psychology: *egocentric, extrovert, inhibition, introvert, psychoanalysis*

☐ Physics and Electronics: *alternating current, arc light, atomic energy, calorie, dynamo, electron, ion, quantum, radioactive, relativity, ultraviolet*

☐ Chemistry: *benzine, biochemistry, creosote, cyanide, nitroglycerine, ozone, radium*

☐ Space Science: *astronaut, cosmonaut, countdown, launch pad, lunar module, moon shot, space shuttle, spacecraft, stratosphere*

New industries. Here the preference has been for extending the meaning of existing words.

☐ Motor Industry: *automobile, choke, clutch, coach, differential, knock, motor car, motorway, park (a car), petrol, radiator, saloon, spark plug, stall, transmission, truck, tune (an engine)*

☐ Media: *3-D, aerial, AM/FM/VHF, antenna, broadcast, cartoon, cassette, cinema, close-up, fadeout, film, gramophone, loudspeaker, microphone, motion picture, movie, phonograph, projector, radio, reception, reel-to-reel, scenario, stereophonic, Technicolor, teleprompt, television, transmitter, video*

War and politics. The new vocabulary associated with war, the military, and politics, or arising during the wars in this century, has mixed origins. Some is scientific, and therefore mainly compounded of Greek or Latin elements; some is loaned from other languages; much is old, but with new senses reflecting the changing technology of war; and some is slang, of obscure origin:

> air raid, antiaircraft, appease, beach-head, blackout, blimp, blitz, blockbuster, bulldozer, camouflage, cold war, decontamination, dud, dugout, evacuation (of people), flak, foxhole, freedom fighter, intifada, iron curtain, jeep, machine gun, mop up, no man's land, parachute, periscope, police state, resistance, semtex, slacker, spearhead, tank, trench foot, unilateralism, urban guerrilla.

Changing social attitudes have also had an effect on the language. The feminist movement, for example, has given rise to at least one completely new usage – the form *Ms* (pronounced / miz /) as an addition to, if not a replacement of, the traditional forms *Miss* and *Mrs*. And old words have been adapted to remove their sexist connotations – words such as *mankind*, *man-hours*, and *chairman*, which are increasingly being replaced by genderless terms such as *humankind*, *worker-hours*, and *chairperson* or just plain *chair*.

THE SOURCES OF NEW WORDS

Completely new words are very rare – though from time to time some do arise. One example of a word made entirely by artificial processes is the trade name *Kodak*, a 'designer' word consciously using the rare letter *k* to make it stand out. Another earlier example of a consciously created word is *gas*. The Flemish chemist J.B. van Helmont coined it in the 17th century, possibly by analogy with the Greek *chaos*. More recently – in 1907 – the American humorist Gelett Burgess coined the word *blurb*.

But most new words and senses to emerge in the last century or so have done so by other, more established, methods.

Loaning, for example, continues from an ever-increasing variety of languages. Often you can tell approximately how long a loan has existed in English by its form. As a rule, the more English a word looks and sounds the longer it has been in the language. *Warden* is older than *guardian* in English; *line* than *machine*. More recent loans from French, within the last 200 years, include *nouveau riche* and *avant-garde*, though *hors d'oeuvre* entered English as early as 1714.

THE LURE OF THE EAST

Throughout history, Europeans have been fascinated by the mystery and beauty of the East. They have traded in its goods, and later brought much of its territory within their colonial empires. The English language reflects these centuries of close contacts. Even a word as everyday as *tank*, for example, comes from Hindi. The words *orange* and *spinach* both go back, through Old French, to Arabic, and then to Persian.

☐ Choose the words or phrase that is closest in meaning to each of the following words from the East. Turn to pages 633-648 for the answers.

alcove
A: a cloak
B: a recess
C: a courtyard
D: an alcoholic fruit drink

anti-macassar
A: a rare metal
B: a thick sock
C: a chair-covering
D: a guerrilla group

arsenal
A: a medicine
B: a toolbox
C: a stock of weapons
D: a scientific laboratory

attar
A: a head-dress
B: a perfume
C: a weapon
D: the ruler of a state

azure
A: blue
B: confident
C: dark
D: poisonous

calico
A: a cotton fabric
B: a hiding place
C: a type of bean
D: cruelty

cipher
A: a jug
B: a numeral
C: a fir tree
D: a spice

drub
A: to beat with a stick
B: to launder
C: to let some-one down
D: to polish

garble
A: to walk unsteadily
B: to swallow greedily
C: to laugh
D: to confuse

gingham
A: an edible root
B: a kind of pinafore
C: a card game
D: a cotton fabric

hookah
A: a pipe
B: a bird
C: a market
D: a narrow window

kedgeree
A: a stringed instrument
B: a lowly servant
C: a dish of fish and rice
D: a velvety fabric

kowtow
A: to run awkwardly
B: to spring back
C: to be over-respectful
D: to meditate

nabob
A: a wealthy and important man
B: an item of furniture
C: a gold coin
D: a turban

pagoda
A: a writing implement
B: a high-ranking nobleman
C: a temple
D: a lavish tapestry

pariah
A: a priest
B: a social outcast
C: a large fan
D: a plant

pundit
A: a basket
B: a flat-bottomed boat
C: an expert
D: a bear-like animal

purdah
A: a buffet meal
B: a legal document
C: the seclusion of women
D: a meeting of community leaders

shanghai
A: to chatter
B: to kidnap
C: to give charity to
D: to grumble

New compound words also emerge. Recent additions to the English vocabulary include:

> baby-sitter, body language, fingerprint, fire extinguisher, jet engine, know-how, lifestyle, lipstick, mobile home, skydiving, software, spin-off, steamroller, streamline, think tank, trouser suit, zebra crossing.

Many of these words show signs of being new: they are written as separate words or with hyphens, and they often retain stress on both elements. Compare the recent compounds *jet lag* and *death trap* with older ones like *teapot* and *songbird*.

For compounding purposes, new prefixes and suffixes (see pages 139-164) have been adopted and older ones revived. For example, the old prefix *de-* is now added to many newly coined verbs: *deregulate*, *decode*, *defrost*, and many more. The Old English suffix *-dom* has also been given a new lease of life in words like *stardom*, *officialdom*, *beggardom*, *fandom*, and even *hippiedom*.

There are various other less common means of word formation. The coining of acronyms – words formed from the initial parts of a name – is a relatively new phenomenon. In some cases the connection between the acronym and the unabbreviated form is maintained. Most people know that NATO is the 'North Atlantic Treaty Organisation' and that *Comecon* – 'Council for Mutual Economic Assistance' – is something to do with Communist countries and economic blocs. But very often people forget the unabbreviated form, and are surprised to find out that a familiar word is in fact an acronym. *Radar*, for example, came into being from 'radio detection and ranging'; *scuba* is 'self-contained underwater breathing apparatus'; a *laser* is 'light amplification by stimulated emission of radiation'.

Another trend has been the adoption of trade names as ordinary words. It is important to tread carefully here – such names can be protected trade marks, which should be acknowledged and spelt with a capital letter. Among these words are *Ansaphone*, *Biro*, *Dictaphone*, *Hoover*, *Kleenex*, *Linotype*, and *Xerox*.

Portmanteau words (or blends) are usually conscious coinings. The term comes from Lewis Carroll's *Through the Looking-Glass*, which contains such examples as *chortle* (chuckle + snort) and *galumph* (gallop + triumph). *Brunch* and *motel* are two more recent examples.

There is one other interesting source of 'new' words – revival. The verb to *witter* – as in *Stop wittering!* and *He wittered on about all his ailments* – has appeared in dictionaries only from about 1980 onwards. It seems to be a new word that was popularised in the 1970s.

But is it? The *New Oxford English Dictionary* has various forms with similar meanings – 'to whistle or chatter', used of birds – but says that they are mainly Scottish and were last recorded in the 16th century. So *witter* is probably a very old word that went out of fashion, in written language at least, but carried on in dialect and spoken language before resurfacing in recent years.

HOW WORDS CHANGE MEANING

Words constantly change their meanings. You need only consider the word *green* in this sentence: *I was very green when I first came to London*. Twenty years ago this would have referred to my naivety or inexperience. Now it might still mean that – equally, however, it may say something about my attitude towards the environment.

Sometimes the new meaning of a word replaces the old one entirely – you would no longer refer to a horse-drawn vehicle as a *car*. But more often nowadays the old and new senses coexist, at least for a while. You still plant *bulbs* even though you also screw them into lamps to give light.

All the fields of technology that affect everyday life have taken on existing words to complete their terminology. Aeroplanes have *wings* and *take off*. Cars are *driven* and have a *clutch*. Computers have *bugs*. When you use the telephone, you *ring* people or *call them up*. People buy *records*, which does not usually mean they are spending their money on archives. You probably see many more *cranes* on building sites than flying over your house.

Very often there is a figurative element. The basic meaning of *to broadcast* is 'to scatter something such as seeds far and wide'. From that it came to refer to spreading news, and from that to sending out programmes by radio or television. Each step takes you a little further from the 'literal' meaning, though the line of connection remains clear.

Here are some of the common ways in which words change meaning:

By generalisation. Here a word originally with a restricted sense comes to be used more extendedly.

The verb *to arrive*, for example, comes from the Latin *ad ripam* (to the shore or riverbank) but is no longer restricted to water transport.

By specialisation. This is the opposite process. A *hound* was originally any kind of dog, but when the word *dog* was adopted in the Middle Ages the word *hound* came to be used only of larger types of hunting dog.

By degeneration. Words produced by this process include *amazingly, terribly, wonderfully,* and *desperately* in their commonest senses. Here the core of meaning has been removed from specific words, leaving only some vague idea behind.

By deterioration. Here a word comes to have a less favourable meaning than its original one. *Silly* is from an Old English word that meant 'blessed' or 'happy'. Later it came to mean 'humble', before taking on its modern sense. *Lewd* once meant 'ignorant', originally used of someone who was not a member of the clergy.

By euphemism. Here a word is given a new sense and introduced as a euphemism to replace a word that has taken on negative connotations. For example, the myriad words for a lavatory – *toilet, little boy's room, powder room, cloakroom, restroom*, and so on.

By amelioration. This is the opposite of deterioration. Here a word loses pejorative connotations. *Nice* comes from a Latin word meaning 'ignorant'. *Shrewd* once meant 'wicked, mischievous, dangerous'. *Sturdy* in the 18th century meant 'harsh, rough, difficult to deal with'. The word *prestige* originally meant 'an illusion, deception' – and so *prestigious* meant 'deceitful'.

By regeneration. This is the process by which a word considered slang or vulgar becomes part of the standard vocabulary. The following words all came in for criticism during the 18th century as vulgarisms, but they are all now firmly within Standard English:

> budge, coax, joke, mob, nonplus, pig-headed, row (an argument), shabby, sham, snob, stingy, strenuous, tiff, touchy.

Interestingly, many words manage to keep their tone of slang or informality for centuries. As food, *grub* is first recorded in the 18th century. Shakespeare uses *Beat it!* in the sense 'Go away!' And *booze* was an informal word for alcoholic drink as long ago as the 13th century.

When words switch meaning. Another interesting case is the pair of words *disinterested* and *uninterested*. Usage notes in modern dictionaries carefully explain that the word *disinterested* means 'impartial', and *uninterested* means 'not interested'. In Shakespeare's day and after, however, it was the other way round.

ORPHAN WORDS

Look in your dictionary for the derivations of some very ordinary-looking words and all you get is 'Origin obscure', or something like 'Middle English *putten*' (for *put*).

Some of these parentless words in English started as made-up slang expressions, and happened to catch on. Words like *gibberish, hoity-toity,* and *jump* seem to come into this category – *gibberish*, for example, was probably made up to imitate the unintelligible sounds of gibberish.

There remains a list of common words for which no satisfactory etymology has been put forward – words that just appeared at various times in English, ousted the existing term, and live on to this day. The list includes:

> banter, big, boy, crease, gimmick, hijack, job, (put the) kibosh (on), lad, lass, put, slum.

The Spread of English

The various dialects of English differ from the standard language in rough proportion to how long they have had a separate identity. Languages need time to develop in their own directions and take on their own features. For this reason Scottish and northern English are generally more different from standard Southern British English than, say, Australian and New Zealand English are.

Over the last 400 years English has spread to all continents and in each country it has taken on its own peculiarities, creating new words to describe indigenous features of landscape, wildlife, and plantlife, and absorbing words from the local languages. Nevertheless, the vast majority of words in the various dialects are common to all forms. They belong to what is known as 'World English'.

Scottish English developed along its own lines.

SCOTTISH ENGLISH

The special vocabulary of modern Scottish English has a number of sources. In southern Scotland English has been spoken for roughly as long as it has south of Hadrian's Wall, and it has retained differences that existed from its beginnings.

It has also taken in words from Scots Gaelic – best pronounced / **gay**lik / – a Celtic language introduced into Scotland from Ireland at about the same time that English arrived, and which is still spoken in parts of the Highlands and Western Isles. Scottish English, like northern English dialects, also has more Old Norse forms and loans than Standard English. And it has French loans that have passed other dialects by, a legacy of the long political association between Scotland and France known as 'the Auld Alliance'. Even the word *haggis*, for example, is probably of French origin – it is believed to come from *hachis*, minced meat.

Scottish English developed very much along its own lines up to the end of the 16th century. Then in 1603 James VI of Scotland became James I of England, leading in due course to the union of the two countries. After 1603 English came to influence Scots more and more, and Scots lost some of its distinctive features. The dialect that finally developed is called *Lallans* (literally, Lowlands – from the name for the southern plains of Scotland).

Some words peculiar to Scots are familiar to all English speakers as being especially Scottish. In this class come *ay* or *aye* (yes; always, ever), *bairn* (child), *canny* (thrifty; shrewd), *gloaming* (twilight), and *wee* (small) – all of Germanic origin. Another is *bonny* (pretty), possibly from the French *bon* (good).

There are also several common Scottish place-name elements. Of Germanic origin are *burn* (a stream), *brae* (a hill side), and *firth* (an estuary). Of Gaelic origin are *ard-* (high, as in *Ardrossan*), *blair* (a plain, as in *Blair Atholl*), *glen* (a valley), *inver-* (an estuary, as in *Inverness*), *loch* (a lake or inlet of the sea), and *strath-* (a valley, as in *Strathclyde*).

Several originally Scottish words have passed into Standard English. *Bog*, *slogan*, and perhaps *spree* and *trousers* are from Gaelic. *Gruesome* has its origin in Old Norse; while *kerfuffle* and *rampage* are probably modern Scots innovations.

Some Scottish words are familiar in non-British forms of English, but less so in English English. Examples are *folks* (relatives), *janitor*, *infirmary*, and *pinkie* (the little finger), variously used in North America and South Africa as well as Scotland.

There are also particularly Scottish expressions and idioms: *to go for the messages* (to go shopping); *Where do you stay?* (Where do you live?); *It's mines* (It's mine); *the back of eight o'clock* (after eight o'clock); *to give someone a row* (to tell someone off); *to dree one's weird* (to suffer one's fate, to come to a sticky end); *Dinnae fash yersel* (Don't get upset); *Haud yer wheesht* (Hold your tongue); and of course *auld lang syne* (literally 'old long since', and so 'the good old days').

Many Scottish institutions differ from those in England and use their own terminology. This is especially true of the law and education. The *procurator fiscal* is the public prosecutor and coroner; a barrister is called an *advocate*, as he is in South Africa; and the *provost* of a town is its mayor or chief magistrate. Scottish universities are usually presided over by a *rector* rather than a vice-chancellor; *dominies* are schoolmasters, and they used to keep order with a *tawse* or leather belt in an *academy* or fee-paying day school.

Other words referring to particularly Scottish customs, objects, and institutions include: *kirk* and *laird* (from the Standard English forms *church* and *lord*), *plaid*, *whisky*, *clan*, *ceilidh* (pronounced / **kay**-li / – a social gathering), and *Hogmanay* (New Year's celebrations).

IRISH ENGLISH

The native language of Ireland was Irish Gaelic or Erse a form of Celtic similar to that spoken in Scotland. English did not arrive in Ireland until after the Norman Conquest. The first Germanic language spoken in Ireland was in fact Old Norse, in colonies set up by the Vikings from the 9th century onwards.

In many respects the Irish dialects of English are similar to Scots, the influences on them being much the same. But the history of English in Ireland is complicated by episodes such as the settling of Protestants, especially in Ulster in the 17th century. Most of these came from Scotland and the North of England, and they developed their own dialect with many features of Scots English.

There are at least four identifiable types of English used in Ireland. Standard English is used in schools, broadcasting, publishing, and the churches. Anglo-Irish is spoken by Protestants in the Republic of Ireland; while their co-religionists in Ulster speak Ulster Scots. The form that people outside Ireland think of as being typically Irish is that of most Catholic people in the Republic of Ireland, called Hiberno-English.

The three native Irish types overlap. For instance, they all share the pronunciation feature of *rhoticity*. That is, the letter *r* is pronounced after as well as before vowels, as in *far* and *church*, just as it is in American, Scots, and West Country English. Also as in American and Scots, all native varieties of Irish pronounce words like *while* and *whale* with a clear *hw-* sound lost in Standard English.

In vocabulary, Irish English retains several words in their 17th-century meanings. *To annoy* can mean 'to make anxious; to worry'. A *bold* child is a naughty or unruly one. *To cog* means 'to cheat' and *to doubt* can mean 'to believe or suspect'. Like American, Irish retains some old verb forms: *I clum* for *I climbed*, *he digged* for *he dug*.

Hiberno-English is used by about 70 per cent of the population of Ireland. As the language of the oldest stratum of population, it has received the greatest influence from Gaelic. Gaelic, for example, has no words for *yes* and *no*. This is why the typical Irish answer to a question like *Do you come from Dublin?* would be *I do not*.

Some Irish Gaelic words have passed into Standard English, such as *banshee* (originally meaning 'a woman from the fairy mounds'), *bard, blarney* (from the place name), *brat, brogue* (originally from Old Norse), *galore, shamrock*, and *smithereens*. The slang use of *to twig*, meaning 'to catch on or understand' is of Irish Gaelic origin. A *Tory* was originally a 17th-century Irish bandit, a name given to the Anglo-Catholic party in England by their opponents. (The Tories took their revenge by calling their rivals *Whigs*; the original Whigs were an equally disreputable band of Scottish insurgents.)

Many of the idioms too, that grace Irish English are loans from Gaelic. For instance, if you are full to bursting with food you might be *as full as a trout*; if you are *as fat in the forehead as a hen*, you are particularly dense and unintelligent.

In many ways, the Irish have been fortunate in the type of English they have developed. Not only was their native Gaelic a rich and racy language, full of proverbs and witty idioms, but the English they adopted was that of the 16th and 17th centuries – a particularly adventurous period in the language.

Irish English has also had a powerful effect on the forms of English adopted outside Britain. Perhaps half of the population emigrated to America in the 19th century – it is no coincidence that Irish shares with New York Bronx (and, to some extent, Liverpool) the use of a *t* sound for *th* – as in *nuttin'* for *nothing*. In addition, the Catholic Church has often used Irish priests and nuns in its mission schools and hospitals around the world. In many countries, especially in Africa, schoolchildren learning English have done so with a decided Irish turn of phrase.

WELSH ENGLISH

Welsh English differs less from Standard English than Scots or Irish. Until this century the Celtic Welsh language was dominant through most of the principality. Words from Celtic that have survived in Welsh English include *bach* (little one; man, as in *Rees bach*), *del* (pretty one), and *tollut* (a hayloft).

Welsh English has also given fewer words than the Scots or Irish varieties to the standard vocabulary. Of words not especially associated with Welsh culture (*eisteddfod*, for example), only *flannel* and the pudding *flummery* are at all common. Both of these words can also mean 'insincere flattery, waffle'. If you also consider the verb *to welsh* (meaning, 'to avoid paying a debt'), you can see that the Welsh have suffered from decided linguistic discrimination at the hands of the English.

NORTH AMERICAN ENGLISH

The dialects within North America – and their vocabularies – vary much less than those in Britain. There are forms and usages that are restricted to certain areas, such as Canada, but in general North American dialects vary according to social class and race rather than region. The most marked dialects are those of groups outside mainstream society, such as Hispanics and poor rural blacks in the United States.

The dialect of the old South of the United States, especially away from urban centres, also has its own distinctive features. Some are due to the influence of Black English. Others link it to British English rather than to what is known as the 'Standard American' dialect of the United States spoken with a 'General American' accent. The Southern dialect shares this British connection with the dialects of New England, ranging from the speech of the upper classes of Boston to the working-class speech of New York City.

Canadian English comes mainly from the speech of Americans who stayed loyal to the British crown and fled north during and after the American Revolution (1775-83). This dialect was well established by the time of mass immigration from Britain to Canada in the 19th century – and so was relatively little affected by the dialects of the new arrivals. However, many of the immigrants, especially in the Maritime Provinces, were from Scotland – in the language of these parts of Canada there is some Scots influence.

Standard American. Oscar Wilde described Britain and the United States as 'two great countries divided by a common language' – and the divergencies between British and American English have long been a source of good-natured chaffing at best, and annoyance at worst, between British and American speakers of English.

American English and British English may, in fact, be viewed as 'superdialects'. You can class the English of Canada and the Philippines with American English, and that of Australia, New Zealand, and South Africa with the various British dialects. Standard American and Standard British have therefore a special importance. They are, as their names suggest, standards. If you were teaching a foreigner to speak English, you would choose one or other of these two dialects as your basis for doing so.

Standard American descends from the 17th- and 18th-century English spoken by the first settlers. Many of the words and usages now thought of as being typically American are, in fact, relics of these older forms of English that have since disappeared from British English. They include:

> *baggage* – luggage; *cute*; *dove* – dived; *fall* – autumn; *garbage* – rubbish; *gotten* – the past participle of *to get*; *handy* – near; *I guess* – I suppose; *invite* – as a noun meaning 'invitation'; *to loan* – to lend; *mad* – angry; *to meet with* – to suffer, have (*I met with an accident*); *moonshine* – (illicit) liquor; *mugging*; *-wise* – to form adverbs from nouns, as in *electionwise*

But from the first the English-speaking settlers in America were also coining new words and usages, chiefly, as with other New World dialects, to describe unfamiliar features of landscape, wildlife, food, and the like. They created new compounds – *backwoods*, *bullfrog* – and assigned new meanings to existing words. *Corn* (in British English, any cereal plant such as wheat or oats) came to refer only to a particular local cereal – what in Britain is called *maize*. *Lumber*, which originally meant (and still does in British English) odds and ends of stored furniture or anything that is useless or cumbersome, came in American English to mean what the British call *timber*.

The English used in America was influenced too by the other languages it encountered there. From local Indian languages came *hickory* and *persimmon* (both trees), *raccoon* and *possum* (animals), *pecan* (nut), and of course *wigwam*, *tomahawk*, and *squaw*. From Dutch settlers in the region of modern New York (originally New Amsterdam), English speakers borrowed words such as *scow* (a kind of barge) and *sleigh*, and from the French they took *chowder* (soup made from the clams and other seafood that abounded in the creeks and estuaries of the eastern seaboard) and *prairie*.

Then came the 19th century and a vast new flood of immigrants which continued into the early years of this century. The result was an explosion of new words and usages emerging from the native languages of the arrivals – especially Irish English, German, and Yiddish. German and Yiddish expressions such as *Gesundheit* (Bless you!), *schmuck* (idiot, oaf), and *chutzpah* (nerve, gall) are now widely used by Americans in general, just as Central European food, such as *sauerkraut* and *bagels*, is better appreciated in America than in Britain.

Contact with Spanish-speaking American countries, meanwhile – and in the 20th century immigration from these countries, as well as from Italy – further enriched the American vocabulary. Words from these sources, some of which have passed into World English, include *gringo, rodeo, canyon, burro* from Spanish, and *pizza* from Italian.

At the same time, American English has continued to be a fertile source of new words and usages, and the growing importance of the United States in world affairs has been paralleled by an increasing flow of expressive American neologisms into British and World English. The English language would be a lot poorer without such punchy Americanisms as *cheapskate, canoodle, dumb-bell, go-getter*, and *the whole caboodle*.

Other American coinings, many reflecting the changing patterns of life in the 20th century, are now part of World English:

> baby-sitter (and from that *to babysit*), categorise, commuter, gimmick, hospitalise, know-how, snarl-up, stunt, tailback, teenager.

Others include 'buzz' words and expressions such as *a blueprint for success* and *lifestyle*, and slang and informal usages: *laid-back, palimony, to rip off* and *a rip-off*, and *together* (as an adjective describing a person, meaning 'organised').

The Americans also evolved their own forms of spelling. Many of these were promoted by the great lexicographer Noah Webster (with his spelling manual in 1783 and his dictionary in 1828), and they were adopted as badges of linguistic nationalism by the young American republic. Webster argued that his spellings were simpler, more logical, and etymologically sounder than those that prevailed in Britain. Words ending in, for example, *-our* became *-or* in American – *color, armor, behavior, neighbor*. British *-re* became *-er*: *center, specter, miter*. The British double *l* in words such as *travelling* was rationalised to a single *l* – *traveling* – while, in contrast, the British *skilful* became *skillful*: again more logical given that the word derives from *skill*.

Other spelling differences developed, such as *check* against *cheque, tire* against *tyre, pajamas* against *pyjamas*. Of course, not all these spellings were American in origin. In Shakespeare's day *color* and *colour* coexisted, as did *center* and *centre*. But the fact that Americans plumped for *color* and *center* helped to ensure that people in Britain would decide that they preferred *colour* and *centre*.

The vocabulary of industry and technology gives an interesting picture of how the contrasts and similarities between the British and American dialects developed. For ships and sailing, the vocabularies of British and American English are almost identical; the terminology was established before the dialects split, and Americans simply took on the existing words – *keel, halyard, sheet*.

But turn to the railways (also *railroads* in America), and the motor car (or *automobile*) and telephone industries, and the picture is different. These industries developed in the 19th and early 20th centuries when the dialects were most separate, and thus use very different terminologies.

American cars have *hoods* and *trunks*, as opposed to *bonnets* and *boots*. They run on *gas* rather than *petrol*, and drive along *freeways* instead of *trunk roads*. American trains have *cars* as against *carriages*, and run across *grade* rather than *level crossings*. Americans *call collect* instead of *reversing the charges*. American skyscrapers, the earliest of which date from this period, have *elevators* rather than *lifts*.

Then come the aircraft and computing industries. Here the vocabularies are again almost identical in both dialects. The reason is that the advances took place in the age of international communications. The pioneers were mostly Americans, and by this time the British had got into the habit of adopting American terms. So a computer has a *program* rather than a *programme*.

But the flow of words across the Atlantic in the late 20th century has not been exclusively in an easterly direction. The words in the following list all originated in Britain, some in the last 20 years, but passed swiftly into Standard American:

> *Big Brother* (in its sinister sense, coined by George Orwell); *brain drain; breathalyser; central heating; the corridors of power* (coined by the novelist C.P. Snow); *the Establishment; gamesmanship* (coined by the humorist Stephen Potter); *gentrify; hovercraft; iron curtain* (popularised by Winston Churchill); *kiss of life; mandarin* (a high-ranking and influential civil servant); *miniskirt; opposite number* (one's counterpart at work)

Even British slang and informal usages have at times taken root in American English: *gay, mod, perks, posh, spoof, swanky*, and now perhaps even *bonkers, trendy*, and *wally*.

The Building Blocks Of Good English

127

SUSPENDERS OR BRACES – BRITISH VS AMERICAN

Everyone knows some of the differences between American and British vocabulary – *trunk* as opposed to *boot*, *thumbtack* instead of *drawing pin*, *aluminum* as opposed to *aluminium*, *baby carriage* instead of *pram*, and so on. Sometimes, you have to make a choice between them. You might be writing a report, say, for a multinational company, which will be read by both Americans and Britons, and you have to refer to what in British English is called a *current account* and in American English a *checking account*. Which should you choose?

Here are some considerations to bear in mind.

1. Is the word or the thing different?

When an American says *suspenders* where a Briton would use *braces*, there is a real difference in vocabulary – but both people are talking about the same thing. Here the choice is fairly simple. If you are a speaker of British English writing for British readers, you would normally use the word *braces*. If you are writing for American readers who will understand the British word, it is probably best to do the same thing – to use the word that comes most naturally to you.

But does the same rule apply to words such as *expressway* and *motorway*? Are they really identical? *Expressways* tend to be across or into cities, whereas *motorways* are usually trunk roads between towns or regions. If you were a British speaker writing or speaking of an American highway, it would probably be better to use the American word.

Things can get more complicated. It is often hard to decide whether the difference is one of vocabulary or reality. An American *bar* is not quite the same as a British *pub*; the New York *subway* is not really identical to the London *underground*. So what should a British person in New York say or write? Would you choose *underground* or *subway*? If you are talking about underground railway systems in general, you might prefer to use the word you are most familiar with – *underground*. If you are talking about the New York system in particular, it would probably be more appropriate to talk about the *subway*.

2. Is the word or sense different?

Some words that exist in both dialects do not always mean the same thing – words like *faggot* (American: a homosexual; British: a bundle of sticks) and *vest* (American: waistcoat; British: undershirt). Similarly, if you take someone *for a ride* in Britain you are stringing him along in order to deceive him. In America, you are liquidating him or bumping him off. With words or expressions like these an explanation is even more in order. Using them without one could lead to serious – and embarrassing – misunderstandings.

Another, parallel, complication arises with words such as *lift* and *elevator*. It is not really true to say that a *lift* in British is an *elevator* in American. You would be nearer the truth if you said that one of the meanings of *lift* in British corresponds to one of the meanings of *elevator* in America. In America you can still give a hitchhiker *a lift*; in Britain grain might be unloaded using an *elevator*.

Again be careful if your readers or listeners include people from the other side of the Atlantic. Explain your meaning of the word – or use an alternative, unambiguous one.

3. Please can you translate?

Every language has certain words and expressions that defy simple translation in other languages. So have dialects. English has no satisfactory term for the American *Indian giver* (someone who takes back a present he has given) or *to shoot the breeze* (to pass the time in informal chat).

Conversely, you will have to explain to an American what you mean when you talk about being *bowled over*. Once again, be sure to explain – or avoid – such expressions if they are likely to cause confusion.

A final word. In an informal document (a letter to a friend, say), nobody will mind if you dodge around between British and American usages. But for a longer, more formal one (an official report, for instance), the key rule is: Be consistent. Decide which 'superdialect' you are going to use and stick to it.

Canadian English. Canadians like to maintain their identity in the face of their powerful neighbour to the south. American English is, of course, the greatest single influence on modern Canadian, but in some matters Canadians prefer British forms. This is especially true of spelling: though *tire* is favoured over *tyre*, words like *skilful* and *colour* tend to be written as in Britain.

Where, however, Britons and Americans differ in their choice of words, rather than in spelling, Canadians tend to follow the Americans. They talk of *airplanes* (instead of *aeroplanes*), *aluminum* (instead of *aluminium*), *cookies* (instead of *biscuits*), *elevators*, *freeways* and *gas*. But this trend is not unvarying. Like the British, Canadians wash their hands in *basins* (instead of *sinks*), eat *porridge* (instead of *oatmeal*), use *taps* (rather than *faucets*), and refer to the letter *zed* rather than *zee*.

Sometimes usage is mixed. The tendency is to travel with *luggage*, but to put it in the *baggage-car* of a train, labelled with a *baggage-check*. Some Canadians take *holidays* (British); others, however, take *vacations* (American).

Some of the differences are regional. In a survey, it came to light that 81 per cent of people in Ontario used the British word *braces*, but of English speakers in Montreal 58 per cent spoke of *suspenders* (American). Perhaps to emphasise their nationality, it seems that Canadians living close to the U.S. border use more British forms than other Canadians – *asphalt* rather than *blacktop*, *verandah* as opposed to *porch*. The British use of *Eh?* for *Pardon?* is also widespread in Canada.

In the field of politics, Canadian usage is very close to British. The constitution and political system in Canada are much closer to the British than to the American ones. Canada has a *Prime Minister* in a *House of Commons* full of *Members of Parliament*.

Certain words and word meanings are specific to Canada. Some refer to local phenomena, such as the *Mounties* and the *Acadians* (inhabitants of the French-influenced parts of the Maritime Provinces).

Interestingly, French influence is scarcely more evident in Canadian English than in other forms of the language, even though French has been spoken longer in Canada than English. French influence tends to be confined to the names of a few items originally specific to French Canadian culture such as *bateau* (a flat-bottomed boat), *lacrosse*, and more recently *Anglophone* and *Francophone*.

Canadian English has also been one of the main routes through which American Indian words passed into English. Some are now known throughout the English-speaking world, such as *toboggan*, *hooch*, and *totem*. From Inuit, the language of the Eskimos, come *anorak*, *igloo*, *kayak*, and others. Some words of Indian and Eskimo origin show signs of having been current in French Canadian before passing into English, for example *babiche* (a leather thong) and *caribou*.

SOUTHERN HEMISPHERE ENGLISH

English changed considerably between the times of the first British settlements in North America, almost 400 years ago, and those in the southern hemisphere, starting just over 200 years ago. These changes are reflected in the differences between Standard American English, and English in Australia, New Zealand, and South Africa. All these later varieties have much in common, often features shared with southeastern dialects of British English, especially those of London.

Australian English. The first British settlement in Australia took place in 1788. Most of the settlers were transported convicts, from many parts of Britain but mostly from the cities and the southeast.

A distinctive dialect seems to have formed rapidly, based on working-class London speech. Even though later immigrants arrived from all parts of Britain, and from Ireland, they came to adopt the established dialect.

Australia has no noticeable regional dialects. But it does have social dialects. The tendency is for older and upper-class Australians to use more Standard British forms ('Conservative Australian'), and for 'Broad Australian' to be associated with rural areas and the working class. There are many varieties in between, including what the British recognise as being typically Australian speech – 'General Australian'. With the growing cultural confidence of the country, the Australian dialect seems to be diverging ever more rapidly from British English.

The development of a distinctive Australian vocabulary followed the typical pattern of 'transplanted' languages. In the first stage words were borrowed from local languages to describe new animals, plants, features of the landscape, and the like – such as *kangaroo*, *kookaburra*, *boomerang*, and *billabong*. They also borrowed the shrill cry *cooee* used by the Aboriginals to attract attention.

ANGLO-AMERICAN DIFFERENCES

Word lists of British and American differences should be treated with care. Sometimes a difference is absolute; sometimes it is a mere tendency. Words pass between the dialects freely and rapidly, and very often speakers of either dialect have a range of expressions to choose from. In some people's ears the use of *I guess* for *I suppose* is an Americanism; to others it is now World English.

The charts below give only a few samples. For instance, they ignore most slang expressions and new coinings. The charts have three columns: the first gives the British preference and the second the usual form in American. The last column shows the equivalent in World English; this is either a form that may be used in both dialects or, where there is no real equivalent, a definition or explanation. A dash here means that no single form can be used appropriately in both dialects.

British	American	World
aerial	antenna	aerial
aeroplane	airplane	aircraft
aluminium	aluminum	–
anticlockwise	counter-clockwise	–
aubergine	eggplant	eggplant
autumn	fall	autumn
bank holiday	legal or public holiday	legal or public holiday
beetroot	beet	–
biscuit (sweet-tasting)	cookie	–
biscuit (savoury)	cracker	–
bonnet (of car)	hood	–
boot (of car)	trunk	–
bowler (hat)	derby	bowler
burgle	burglarize	burgle

British	American	World
call box	telephone booth	telephone booth
candy floss	cotton candy	–
caravan	trailer, mobile home	–
chemist	druggist	pharmacist
chest of drawers	bureau	chest of drawers
chips	French fries	French fries
Christian name, first name, forename	given name	Christian name, first name, forename
crisps	potato chips	–
cooker	stove	stove
courgettes	zucchini	–
crotchet	quarter note	–
cutlery	silverware	cutlery
current account	checking account	–
dinner jacket	tuxedo	–
doll's house	dollhouse	doll's house
drawing pin	thumbtack	–
dustbin	garbage can, trashcan	–
engaged (telephone)	busy	busy
estate agent	real-estate agent, realtor	–
flat (housing)	apartment	apartment
fortnight	'two weeks'	'two weeks'
frying pan	skillet	frying pan
(back) garden	(back) yard	garden
gents	men's room	men's toilet
to grill	to broil	–

British	American	World
guard's van	caboose	–
handbag	purse	handbag
interval (in a performance)	intermission	–
jeans	blue jeans	jeans
jewellery	jewelry	–
jug	pitcher	–
ladies	women's room	women's toilet
launderette	laundromat	–
lavatory	washroom	toilet
'lavatory in a public building'	restroom	toilet
to lay the table	to set the table	to set the table
level crossing	grade crossing	–
lift	elevator	–
lorry	truck	truck
maths	math	–
mileometer	odometer	–
minim	half note	–
motorway	expressway, freeway	–
mudguard	fender	–
mum(my)	mom(my)	–
nappy	diaper	–
noughts and crosses	tick-tack-toe	–
paraffin	kerosene	–
pavement	sidewalk	–
pernickety	persnickety	pernickety
petrol	gas, gasoline	–
pillar box, postbox	mailbox	–
postcode	zip code	–

British	American	World
pram	baby carriage	–
quaver	eighth note	–
railway	railroad	railway
reverse-charge	collect (call)	–
roundabout	traffic circle, rotary	–
rowing boat	rowboat	–
rowlock	oarlock	–
saloon (car)	sedan	–
sandpit	sandpile	–
serviette	napkin	napkin
shop assistant	sales clerk	–
silencer	muffler	–
single (ticket)	one-way	–
swede (vegetable)	rutabaga	–
sweets	(hard) candy	–
tap	faucet	tap
tie	necktie	tie
timber	lumber	timber
tin (of food)	can	can
torch	flashlight	–
traffic light	stoplight	traffic light
tram	streetcar, trolley (car)	–
undertaker	mortician	undertaker
unit trust	mutual fund	–
wastepaper basket	wastebasket	wastepaper basket
white (coffee)	'with milk'	'with milk'
windscreen	windshield	–
wing (of car)	fender	–
zed	zee	–
zip	zipper	–

The Building Blocks Of Good English

131

Then a distinctive dialect emerged when the settlers started coining new words based on English roots to meet their new living conditions. Words such as *outback* and *bush* (inland or uncultivated country), *back country* (remote areas), *bushranger* (a fugitive), *stockman* (a livestock farmer), and *swagman* (an itinerant worker) mark speakers off as being Australian.

At the same time, some words brought from the mother country were given new senses to adapt them to the new environment. *Oak, broom*, and *cedar*, for instance, usually refer to different plants in Australia from those that bear these names in Britain. *Station*, a word originally meaning nothing more than a place where something 'stands', has taken on new meanings in British English – a *railway station, a police station, a polling station*, and the like. In Australia the word is also used to mean 'a ranch', in compounds such as *sheep station* and *cattle station*. Similarly, *field* has changed its meaning, now being restricted to sports arenas and the like. A *theatre* can also mean a cinema.

Australia soon developed distinctive slang and informal usage. Some Australian slang consists of imported terms that have fallen into disuse in Britain. Some words are old British dialect terms; others derive from 18th- and 19th-century prison jargon. Examples of early imports include *bodger* (useless), *cobber* (a friend), *dinkum* (good, genuine), and *to fossick* (to rummage for).

And of course Australians soon started coining informal words of their own – *to chunder* (to be sick), *to nick off* (to decamp), *bonzer* (excellent), *wowser* (a prude), *sheila* (a woman), *bludger* (a sponger), and *lolly* (a boiled sweet), for instance. The most famous of all, *pommy* or *pom*, as a derogatory term for a British person, goes back almost to the beginning of settlement in Australia. Its origins, like those of much slang, are obscure. Some etymologists link it with possible acronyms such as *POHM* (Prisoner of His/Her Majesty).

As well as coining new words, informal Australian also uses certain old words in novel ways. *Good day!* is a much more informal greeting in Australia than elsewhere in the English-speaking world. *Hooray* can mean 'Goodbye'. *Crook* can mean 'unwell' or 'out of order', and *maggoty* 'angry' or 'irritated'. *Cockatoo* (a loan from Malay by way of Dutch) has wider meanings in Australia than elsewhere; as well as referring to a kind of parrot, it can refer to a small farmer and to a lookout or watchman.

The success of Australian comedians and media personalities in Britain over the last 20 years has introduced much Australian slang and informal usage to audiences outside its country of origin. In some cases it can hardly even be considered particularly informal these days. The use of *to rubbish* in the sense of 'to criticise contemptuously' is of Australian origin.

Like other varieties of Southern Hemisphere English, modern Australian now takes some of its new words from American. To an Australian, *chips* can be potato *crisps*, a *freeway* is a *motorway*, and *tights* are called *pantihose*.

In common with South African English, Australian English has a tendency in colloquial speech to abbreviate words and add the suffix *-ie* or *-o*. This results in forms like *wharfie* (a dock labourer), *arvo* (afternoon), *galvo* (galvanised iron), *garbo* (a dustman), and *nasho* (national service).

New Zealand English. Much of what has been said of Australia applies also to New Zealand. Like the accents, the dialects of the two countries are similar. (To distinguish the accents, listen for the pronunciation of words like *big* and *widow*. Australians pronounce the vowel as a short version of the vowel sound in *keep*; New Zealanders use a short ə-sound more akin to that in *hut*).

The strongest influence on the English of New Zealand has been that of Australia, which is where many of the earliest settlers came from. New Zealand shares with Australia usages that differ from those in Standard English, such as *station* and *theatre*. It also shares much of its colloquial vocabulary: *bludger, crook, lolly*, and *to rubbish*. But *cobber* and *fair dinkum* would sound like deliberate Australianisms in New Zealand.

A number of Maori and Polynesian words have come into Standard English through New Zealand. *Maori* itself comes from a word meaning 'ordinary'. The word *pakeha* (pronounced / **paa**ki-haa /), used for the white population, appears to be of Maori origin. Maori loans include the names of local birds (*kiwi, moa, takahe*) and plants (*kauri, rata, tutu*).

The word *mana* was used in Melanesian, Polynesian, and Maori, and meant the mysterious power inherent in any god or sacred object. It was adopted by historians of religion to describe this kind of aura wherever it occurs. People now use it more generally to mean any kind of authority, charisma, prestige, or influence.

South African English. English in South Africa dates from the founding of the Cape Colony in 1820. In its written form, South African English is almost identical to Standard British English.

Standard British English also remains the spoken norm for the South African upper classes of British extraction, as it does for similar groups in the Commonwealth countries of eastern and southern Africa, such as Zimbabwe and Kenya. It is possible, in fact, to speak of 'White African English'.

In broader dialects, the English of the region has been influenced by other languages, most importantly Afrikaans, but also the native African languages and the languages of Asians settled in South Africa by the British. There are also some relics of older forms of English brought by early settlers. The broadest dialects are those of people who speak English as a second language – Afrikaans English, Cape Coloured English, and varieties spoken by South African Asians and the indigenous groups.

Some words from early Afrikaans have passed into World English, such as *commandeer, commando*, and *trek*. Others, though known throughout the English-speaking world, retain their connections with their country of origin – *apartheid, boer, laager*, and *spoor*. The names of many of the animals of southern Africa come from Afrikaans, such as *wildebeest* and *springbok*, and *aardvark* (literally 'earth pig').

From Afrikaans too come some internationally used topological terms (such as *veld*) and other terms less likely to be known outside the region; for instance *dorp* (a village or country town), *kloof* (a ravine), *koppie* (a small hill), *stoep* (a verandah), and *vlei* (a marsh or lake).

The local Bantu languages, such as Sotho, Xhosa, and Zulu, have given South African terms such as *bonsella* (a small gift), *donga* (an eroded gully), and *indaba* (a conference or discussion). Probably from Malay come the words *babotie* (a dish of curried mincemeat), *sosatie* (a skewer of spiced meat), and *sjambok* (a kind of whip).

Indian languages have given *biriani* (a spicy rice dish), *masala* (a mixture of dried herbs and spices), and *samosa* (a fried savoury pastry). And from Portuguese – the language of the other great colonisers of the region – come *bredie* (a stew), *mealie* (corn on the cob), and *piccanin* (a small black child), used in Australia and elsewhere too, and in many pidgin languages.

Several English words have special senses in South Africa, some of them obsolete in other forms of English, others developed within the country. Older terms persist in *bioscope* (cinema) and *wireless*. Other special uses include *butchery* (a butcher's shop), *cookie* (a fairy cake or cupcake), *granadilla* (passion fruit), and *traffic circle* (a roundabout). Other special South African senses include *coloured* (of mixed race), *just now* (soon), *location* (a township for a specified racial group), *pass book* and *reference book* (identity papers), *rather* (instead), and *robot* (traffic lights).

Some usages can cause real confusion to foreigners. *Man* is used in informal speech even to address women. *Shame* tends to be used to express sympathy or even admiration:

'The cat's just died.' 'Ag, shame.'
'What a beautiful baby. Shame.'

And the use of *no* can be most peculiar, as in these examples:

'How are you feeling?' 'No, I'm fine, thank you.'
'Haven't you been ill?' 'No, I'm much better now, thanks.'

ENGLISH IN THE COMMONWEALTH

In large parts of the former British Empire, English has retained great significance even where very few of the population speak it as a mother tongue. In Africa it is rivalled as a lingua franca only by Swahili in Tanzania and one or two other regions of the east, and by Hausa in Nigeria. Being the language of no particular group, it enjoys the same kind of advantage and status as Latin did in medieval Europe. Even in some former French colonies – Senegal, for instance – English is widely used for communication.

Similarly, in South Asian and some southeast Asian countries such as India, Pakistan, Bangladesh, Sri Lanka, Nepal, and Burma, English is probably the most lasting legacy from colonial times. Attempts have been made, for instance in India, to replace English as the language of government, the courts, and higher education. They have so far failed. The openings that English provides for international commerce and its freedom from regional rivalries have made it indispensable.

South Asian English. The form of English used in South Asia is mainly British, though as elsewhere American is beginning to make itself felt. There are, in fact, many different varieties of English in use in South Asia. The educated classes speak and write Standard English, while further down the social and educational scale forms are influenced by any of the many indigenous languages. At the end of the range there are English-based pidgins.

Standard English has taken in many words from languages in India and other parts of South Asia. Well-known examples include *bangle, bungalow, curry, gymkhana, jungle, pyjamas, thug*, and *verandah*. (Another interesting example of such a word is *ayah*, a nurse, which arrived in English from Hindi, but comes originally from the Latin *avia*, a grandmother, having reached India through early Portuguese traders.)

Within South Asia a large number of local words are used by Standard English speakers, especially to refer to local phenomena – foods, such as the lentils *urad* and *moong*, and articles of clothing, such as *choli, dhoti*, and *sari*. Other examples are:

charpoy – a string bed; *chowkidar* – a nightwatchman; *dacoit* – a robber; *dhobi, dhobi walla* – a laundryman; *gherao* – a protest demonstration, usually involving the siege of an office or building; *goonda* – a hooligan or irresponsible person, also used as an adjective of general insult; *jhuggi* – a squatter settlement; *-ji* – a suffix used to indicate respect, as in *Mamaji, Daddaji, Gandhiji; maidan* – a parade ground or promenade; *mali* – a gardener; *mela* – a fair.

Like other varieties, South Asian English retains some words that have fallen out of fashion in Britain. Asian English sometimes sounds formal because its speakers have learnt it from books. Common examples of this apparent formality are the use of terms such as *demise* (death), *to felicitate* (congratulate), *to do the needful, miscreant*, and *How is your good self?* Standard English compounds are sometimes shortened, such as *keybunch* (a bunch of keys), *pindrop silence*, and *age-barred* (barred by age).

South Asian English has also coined its own words based on English elements to fill local needs. Many of these are unknown to speakers of other varieties. They include:

airdash – to fly from place to place; *co-brother* – one's wife's sister's husband; *cooling glasses* – sunglasses; *duck's egg* – nought; *jack* – support, influence (*You can get nowhere if you have no jack*); *wheat complexion* – a fair complexion.

African English. The English used in black Africa varies widely from place to place, and often has features of the local languages. As English is often taught first as a written language, the spoken language, as in South Asia, is often somewhat archaic and florid. It is also often marked by pronunciations that stick more carefully than is normal elsewhere to the spelling of words, such as the habit of sounding the *l* in words like *walk* and *calm* and the *b* in *climb* and *comb*.

Where necessary, African English has borrowed from local languages words for local phenomena. In West Africa *oga* means 'a boss or superior' and *fon* a 'chief'. *Kente* is the colourful cloth used to make robes in Ghana. Certain local words taken into English are known outside Africa. *Bwana* (boss) and *uhuru* (freedom) are from Swahili, though both probably originate in Arabic. Others have passed into Standard English: they include words such as *safari* (also from Arabic via Swahili), *banana, banjo, chimpanzee, cola, voodoo, yam*, and *zombie* from various West African languages.

Many dialects include direct translations into English of local expressions. *To enstool* in Ghana means to choose and invest as chief; if you have *long legs* you have power or influence; *outdooring* is a traditional name-giving ceremony; if you are *a native of* something in East Africa you do or eat it often. In parts of Africa speakers have also created new expressions in English. A *go-slow* can be a traffic jam; *senior brother* is used for elder brother; and a *been-to* is someone who has been abroad, usually to study.

Pidgins and creoles. English has also been the basis for a number of distinctive pidgin or creole languages, particularly in West Africa, the Caribbean region, and in the former Pacific colonies. A pidgin is a simplified language (usually based on that of a trading nation – in this case English) which arises from the need for people with no languages in common to communicate. The word itself may come from a Chinese pronunciation of *business*. Creoles are pidgins that have been adopted as the mother language of a community. Perhaps 60 million people around the world use pidgins or creoles for everyday purposes.

An English-based pidgin or creole lies at the very limits of what you might call English. Though founded on English, it includes admixtures from local languages, such as the names of products, foods, plants, and animals. Grammatical compli-

SHORT WORDS, TRICKY MEANINGS

'There are so many long words', people sometimes complain, 'that I can't understand it.' And as a rule it is true that the shorter a word is, the easier it is to understand. But not all short words are as simple as *cat* and *mat*, and some that are – or seem – familiar have other, less familiar, meanings.

☐ In the following list of three- and four-letter words, choose the word or phrase you believe is nearest in meaning to the key word. You will find the answers on pages 633-648.

ague   A: a fever
B: a rash
C: a chill
D: a cough

aver   A: to declare positively
B: to keep changing one's mind
C: to deny vigorously
D: to refuse point-blank

awl   A: a tool to make holes
B: a type of knot
C: the mouth of a river
D: syrup from plants

bock   A: a kind of sausage
B: beef
C: beer
D: cider

brig   A: a ship
B: a man's suit
C: an umbrella
D: a dance

cleg   A: a wooden shoe
B: a container for liquid
C: a horsefly
D: a maggot

coy   A: happy
B: silly
C: shy
D: flirtatious

guy   A: to hate
B: to ridicule
C: to comfort
D: to despise

hie   A: to jump
B: to hurry
C: to wish
D: to attack

holt   A: a copse
B: a place of refuge
C: a moor
D: a dip

ire   A: anger
B: determination
C: molten metal
D: a steeple

jape   A: a joke
B: a kick
C: a grin
D: a hopping movement

keen   A: to be eager
B: to wail
C: to prostrate oneself
D: to promote

laud   A: to deserve
B: to cleanse
C: to hold up
D: to praise

lea   A: a mast
B: a meadow
C: a part-song
D: a lord

limn   A: to draw
B: to define the boundaries of
C: to throw light on
D: to evacuate

maw   A: an ogre
B: a jelly
C: a mouth
D: high society

ogle   A: to haunt
B: to frighten
C: to stare at
D: to pray to

rife   A: stolen
B: borrowed
C: widespread
D: rare

rill   A: a musical scale
B: an edge
C: a ledge
D: a stream

roué   A: a chocolate dessert
B: beaten silver
C: a refined lady
D: an immoral man

sot   A: a clod of earth
B: a hound
C: ash
D: a drunkard

wan   A: fat
B: small
C: lined
D: pale

cations in English are also ironed out; for instance, a single form *go* might also be used for *goes*, *going*, *gone*, and *went*. Pronunciation too is altered, to fit into local patterns. For example, Melanesian does not use clusters of consonants, and the English *clear* becomes / ku-**li**-a/ in the local pidgin. Foreign speech sounds are usually avoided; *thing* sounds like *ting* and *the* like *de* or *ze*.

Typically, speakers of pidgins use a variety of gestures and stress and tone patterns to add to the flexibility of the language. Sentences tend to be short and follow simplified patterns: questions, for instance, may be formed solely by a special intonation of a simple statement. Repetition or reduplication is common. It is used:

☐ for emphasis – *bikbik*, for example, is 'very big' in some pidgins

☐ for word building – *tingk-tingk* means 'a thought or opinion', and *benben*, literally 'bent-bent', can mean 'crooked'

☐ to distinguish words that sound the same – *sansan* for 'sand' but *san* for 'sun'

☐ for grammatical purposes – in order to show, for instance, a plural

'Restricted pidgins' are very limited and used for basic communication. *You want? That nice. Me buy? Me give? Okay?* You can hear this kind of pidgin English at any resort that caters for English-speaking holidaymakers.

'Elaborated pidgins' are greatly expanded and far more flexible. The Bible has been translated into various elaborated pidgins; stories are told and proverbs made. And creoles tend to even greater linguistic sophistication. Typically, they arise amongst communities of slaves from mixed linguistic backgrounds. The main purpose is no longer just limited communication with outsiders. So the language no longer has to be 'stripped down'.

There are two main groups of English-based pidgins and creoles. The 'Atlantic group' is found both in West Africa and all round the Caribbean, in Guyana, in parts of Nicaragua and Belize, and in some of the southern states of the USA. *Krio* – the name is derived from *creole* – is one of the main languages of Sierra Leone and the Gambia. Black American English shares features of Atlantic pidgins, such as the elision of the verb *to be* when unstressed: *John sick* is a normal statement; *John is sick* contradicts something someone else has said.

The 'Pacific group' is perhaps related to China Coast Pidgin English, once used widely in trade in the Far East. Various types are found in Australia, in Papua New Guinea and the Solomon Islands, and in Vanuatu, and also to some extent in Samoa and Fiji.

The two groups have much in common – unsurprisingly, since both are based on English. They differ of course in their native elements: *mboma* (a snake) is used only in Atlantic varieties and *kapul* (a tree kangaroo) only in the pidgins of the Pacific region.

In regions where English-based pidgins and creoles are used, there is usually a range of possibilities running from full-blown pidgin to Standard English. Speakers with more education tend to be able to speak something closer to the standard language as well as the local pidgin.

The following examples from Cameroon Pidgin (one of the Atlantic group) illustrate this 'post-creole continuum'. The first sentence is in fully fledged pidgin, the last in Standard English, and the middle two represent stages in between.

> Di tu man pikin kam wan taim.
> Di tu boy dem kam wan taim.
> Di tu boys dem come at once.
> The two boys came at once.

Pidgins and creoles should not be thought of as corrupt forms of English. They are languages or dialects in their own right. In some cases, notably Black American English, they are retreating before the spread of Standard English. In other cases, such as in the West Indies, they continue to coexist with the standard language.

Here and there the usefulness of pidgins and creoles as a lingua franca has given them official status, as in Papua New Guinea. They are now the vehicle for literature, theatre, journalism, and all other purposes that language can be put to. Atlantic creoles are used as the language both of West Indian song and of West African political satire and novel writing.

West Indian English. Caribbean English originates in the pidgins used by West Africans to speak to English-speaking traders and, as slaves in the colonies, to communicate amongst themselves and with plantation overseers. Within a generation these pidgins developed into creoles.

The West Indies, like Britain, has both class and regional dialects. As elsewhere, the educated elite

---

PIDGIN SHAKESPEARE

Elaborated pidgins are increasingly sophisticated languages in their own right. You can use them not only to speak about the ordinary, everyday business of life but to express the deepest human feelings. Do you recognise this well-known piece of Shakespeare written in the pidgin of Cameroon in West Africa?

> Foh di foh dis graun oh foh no bi sehf – dat
> na di ting wei i di bring plenti hambag.
> Wehda na sohm behta sehns sei mek man i
> tai hat
> Foh di shap ston an shap stik dehm foh bad
> lohk wei dehm di wohri man foh dis graun,
> Oh foh kari wowo ting foh fait dis trohbul
> wei i big laik sohlwata so?
>
> – translated by R. Awa

Or this extract from a biblical parable?

> Bot di papa bin tok sei: Ma pikin, you dei wit
> mi ol taim an ol ting wei a getam na yu on.
> Bot i gud med wi glad foseka dis yu broda
> bin don dai an i don wikop fo dai agen.

They come from Hamlet's famous speech:

> To be, or not to be: that is the question:
> Whether 'tis nobler in the mind to suffer
> The slings and arrows of outrageous
> fortune,
> Or to take arms against a sea of troubles,
> And by opposing end them?
>
> – Hamlet, III.i.56-60

And from the parable of the prodigal son:

> But the father said: My son, you are with me
> always and everything that I have is yours.
> But it is good for us to rejoice because your
> brother was dead and he is alive again.
>
> – Luke 15:31,32

---

speak Standard English, with more or less of a local accent. There are also differences between the dialects of different islands and countries, but perhaps not as great as might be expected. For example, the sentence *We plant yams where there is a lot of water* might be in Jamaica *Wi plaan yam we nof waata de*, but in Guyana *We doz plaan yam we plenti waata de*.

West Indian English also has words from Spanish and French, especially in Trinidad and St Lucia; for example *crapaud* (a frog or toad) and *pannier* (a basket), both from French.

The indigenous Carib languages, now extinct, also left their mark: *jiga* or *jigger* (an insect), *kayman* (a crocodile), and *macca* (anything sharp, a thorn). West African languages have contributed words, especially Hausa and Yoruba: *akara* (a beancake), *bosi* (proud, a show-off), *bukra* (white man or woman), *duppy* or *jumby* (a ghost), *fufu* (pounded food), *nyam* or *ninyam* (food, to eat), *pinder* (a peanut), *omi* (water), *tuku-tuku* (short, squat), and *unu* (you, plural), for instance.

West Indian dialect also retains some obsolete English words, such as *box* (to hit, as in *to box someone's ears*), *beforetime*, *beknown*, *glean*, *glebe land*, and *proven*.

There are also words that were taken from British dialects: for example *bubby* (a breast), *buss* (a kiss), *fig* (a segment of an orange), *labrish* (gossip, chitter-chatter, from the dialect word *lab*, to blab, reveal secrets), and *tinnen* (made of tin).

American English too has provided some established terms – *blues*, *bluetail* (a kind of lizard), *bread* (money) – and this element of the vocabulary is growing rapidly.

The cult of Rastafarianism has introduced a host of new terms into Jamaican creole. *Babylon* refers to England, or western society in general, especially the elements opposed to Rastafarianism, such as the police. *Rude boys* are fellow Rastafarians. *I and I* is used for 'we', but stresses group consciousness and solidarity. *Overstand* means 'understand'. The popularity of reggae music has introduced some of these terms to white English speakers as well. *Dreadlocks* has followed earlier West Indian terms such as *calypso* and *ska* into Standard English.

ENGLISH AS A WORLD LANGUAGE

The position of English on the international scene now seems unassailable. The political and economic power of Britain in the last century and of the USA in this makes English a necessity for people looking beyond their immediate environment.

Although such estimates are always open to dispute, it is reckoned that at least 700 million people have a fair degree of proficiency in English, about half of whom have it as their mother tongue. There are perhaps another 300 million who can get by in English. Only the official dialect of Chinese,

Guoyu, rivals English for its number of speakers, but it is limited geographically.

How English is used. Like Latin before it, English has become, in the 20th century, the usual means of communication between people with no other language in common.

English is, for example, the chief language of science and technology. It is estimated that nowadays some two-thirds of scientific papers are written in English, often of a highly formulaic kind. By an agreement made after the Second World War, aircraft pilots and ships' captains on international routes have to have proficiency in radio English. Again, this tends to be fairly formulaic in character. Even within their own countries pilots often use English expressions, such as *Roger, Negative*, and *How do you read?*

Despite the efforts of the French to maintain the status of their language, English has become the language of international diplomacy. It has official status in more countries than any other. It is the official language of the Commonwealth and of the International Olympic Committee. English is one of the six official languages of the United Nations and one of the organisation's two working languages, French being the other.

English is also the language of popular youth culture. Many young people – in Finland, Japan, Peru, or almost any part of the globe – seem to learn as much English from records as from their teachers. Pop musicians in many countries often sing in English, and even put together their own lyrics from a mixture of classroom English and phrases picked up elsewhere.

Attempts have been made to produce a form of 'Basic English', with a simplified spelling, vocabulary, and grammar. But since the real type is so influential and accessible, Basic English is unlikely to get further than Esperanto, Volapuk, and other artificial languages.

The international variety of English has certain tendencies. The number of vowel contrasts is often reduced – there is little lost in having *pull* rhyme with *fool*. Features that foreigners find tricky are simplified. All tag questions (*doesn't she? aren't there?*) are often reduced to *isn't it?* Phrasal verbs (such as *to make off with, to make out*) are used less than in native English (*tolerate* in preference to *put up with*), or changed in form (*to cope up with*), or simplified in grammar (*Your radio, please turn off it*).

English's rich variety of idiomatic phrases is of little use in 'international English'.

Most languages now take in more loans from English than from any other language, often through the medium of pop music, advertising, films, and American culture in general. Over 2000 English expressions have been recorded in French alone. In some countries this trend is resented.

Some, such as France and Iceland, have passed laws banning English words. French people talk of *fast food* and *jumbo jet*, but in official documents these are replaced by *prêt-à-manger* and *gros-porteur*. In Iceland English personal names are banned; and committees put together lists of native-based equivalents for words in the fields of medicine, computing, physics, and the like. Most of them, however, are never used.

Here are some exports from British or American English to other languages:

☐ French: *le best seller, le parking, le sandwich, le smoking* (a dinner jacket), *le weekend*

☐ German: *das Auto, das Baby, der Babysitter, der Bestseller, der Cocktail, der Computer, der Gangster, der Pullover, der Teenager*

☐ Italian: *la pop art, il popcorn, la spray, il supermarket*

☐ Spanish: *béisbol* (baseball), *boxeo* (boxing), *fútbol* (football), *suéter* (sweater)

Some English words turn up over and over again around the world, either as loans or as fully understood foreign terms. Many might have come originally from French, but their popularity is largely due to their being thought of as English (or, more often, American). Examples are:

airport, babysit, bank, bar, bus, camera, cigarette, cocktail, cola, football, goal, golf, hotel, jeans, OK, passport, post, program, salad, soda, sport, steak, stop, taxi, telephone, television, tennis, weekend, whisky.

It is hardly sensible to call some of these words 'English' any more. They are international. The same applies to the international scientific vocabulary. Most languages nowadays use the same stock of Greek and Latin word elements combined according to the same rules. Words like *cardiograph, polyvinyl*, and *telespectroscope* might as easily have been coined in the Soviet Union, Germany, or Italy as in Britain or North America.

Improve Your Vocabulary

SUPPOSE YOU are on a train, with nothing to do except observe your fellow travellers. A couple of professional-looking people are talking earnestly. You hear the words, 'These allergic reactions would seem to contraindicate the use of penicillin.'

Allergic, *penicillin* – these must be medical people. But what was that other word, *contraindicate*? It is not a word you have ever heard before. Why not have a go at working out its meaning?

Allergic reactions are doing something to the use of penicillin. So, *contraindicate* is a verb. Allergic reactions are not desirable. They sometimes follow the use of various drugs. You know that. So the sentence probably means something like: 'Allergic reactions rule out using penicillin or make it impossible or undesirable to use it.' Perhaps

contraindicate is a specialist medical word meaning something along these lines.

Now how about approaching the problem from a different angle? *Contraindicate*? It is a word made up of two parts. The *indicate* part is straightforward. It means: 'demonstrate, suggest, or show'.

What about *contra-*? There are a number of common words that begin with *contra-*: *contradict*, *contraception*, *contravene*. All these words suggest being against something – against what someone else has said, against pregnancy, against a rule or law. So the chances are that *contraindicate* means something like 'suggest against'. The whole sentence would appear to mean that 'Allergic reactions seem to show that penicillin should *not* be used.' Which is precisely what it does mean.

How to Learn New Words

Improving your vocabulary involves a series of steps that are seldom more difficult than this exercise. Throughout your life, from infancy onwards, you have been hearing or reading new words. Very often you hardly recognise them as new. Simply seeing them in context, you deduce their meaning. Either that, or you look at the way they are made up and rapidly put their meaning together bit by bit.

If you know what *counter-* generally indicates at the beginning of a word ('against') and what, say, *revolution* and *productive* mean, it does not take long to work out the meaning of *counterrevolution* (a revolution coming after another one and countering its effects) and *counterproductive* (acting against the productiveness of something) – especially if you see the words in context. Learn how to carry out exercises like this more consciously when faced with a new word, and you are well on the way to a greatly enriched vocabulary.

But there is a difference between 'understanding' and 'knowing'. You may understand – roughly at least – what a word means: it does not necessarily

follow that you know how to use it correctly. People know, or can recognise, more words than they use. How often do you hear or use the words *nefarious*, *parturition*, *superconductivity*, or *enfilade*? Probably not often, though you may have an idea what they mean.

Increasing your word power comes in two stages – which correspond to these two aspects, of understanding and knowing a word. First, there is the 'passive' stage, improving your ability to recognise and interpret words you have not come across before. Then there is the second stage, when you consign to your memory those words you reckon will prove useful. You make these part of your 'active' vocabulary.

This chapter tells you how to go about learning new words. It gives tips on how to make them part of both your passive and active vocabulary, and shows you some of the pitfalls to avoid when using them for the first time. Then come charts of the building blocks of words: the most common word elements – roots, prefixes, suffixes, and the like.

THE POINT OF WORD POWER

Why bother to go to all this trouble to learn new words? Certain British newspapers are said to operate with a vocabulary of around 3000 words. A vocabulary of this size, according to education-alists, requires a reading age of eight. Tests show that foreigners learning English have to master only about 2000 words to be able to say more or less anything they want. If you can get by on 2000-3000 words, why more?

There are a number of reasons. First, a good knowledge of words and how they are formed helps you to handle ideas. It is possible to think without words – in terms of visual images, for example – but ideas visualised in this way are hard to develop or control. The more skilled you become in the precise use of words, the clearer and more precise your thinking will become.

With a larger vocabulary, you will be able to express yourself better. And people who can express themselves well are treated with respect. Articulate applicants do well at job interviews. Students with a good grasp of language and confidence in expressing themselves get higher marks.

And words are fun. Learning how to express yourself more flexibly and precisely, using a greater range of words, is supremely satisfying. Even trivial facts about words can be amusing. Did you realise that *chintz* and *biopsy* are the longest words in English with all their letters occurring in alphabeti-cal order? Or that *abstemious* and *facetious* contain all five vowels in the correct sequence?

But a word of warning, too. Increasing your word power is not just a matter of padding out your conversation with long words. No one likes a show-off. People who use long words to appear superior are not usually well liked. Someone who uses obscure words where everyday ones are adequate becomes a bore. 'Desist from this ver-bosity!' is fine for 'Shut up!' once in a while, but the joke soon wears thin. *Patella* may be fine for your doctor, but it is *kneecap* to your friends.

OPPOSITES AND SYNONYMS

Perspicacious or *perspicuous*? *Complacent* or *complaisant*? In each pair, the words look and sound similar – but they mean very different things. Look up all four words in a dictionary, if necessary, and then have a go at the following questions to check that you have fully under-stood their meanings and usage. For the answers, turn to the quiz answers section on pages 633-648.

A. Which might be used as the *opposites* of these words?

    1. abstruse   2. self-critical
    3. obstructive   4. obtuse

B. Which might be used as *synonyms* for these words?

    1. smug   2. unambiguous
    3. clear-headed   4. obliging

Even worse, people insist on using long or technical words, only to use them incorrectly. Unless you are absolutely sure of a word's meaning, stylistic appropriateness, pronunciation, and grammar, avoid using it.

Most of us make mistakes from time to time, confusing *cassock* and *hassock*, *abstruse* and *obtuse*, *odious* and *onerous*, or *mitigate* and *militate*. But getting caught out is still extremely embarrassing. All the more so when you would have avoided the mistake had you not been trying so hard.

Try also to avoid 'buzz words'. These are words and phrases that people adopt to suggest that they are up to date in some specialist subject, but which are really little more than clichés. People throw words such as *parameters*, *cognitive*, and *coordinates* about in all kinds of field where they have no rightful place to be. They may sound impressive at first, but to a knowledgeable ear such words usually suggest that the speaker does not really know what he or she is talking about.

Intelligent Learning

Now some do's and don'ts for actually learning and using new words. A *don't* to start with: don't try to memorise lists of new words. Before school exams, you may have sat up half the night trying to get into your head expressions like *clints* and *grykes*, *capitalisation* and *exponential*. You probably forgot them the next day. Words learnt parrot-fashion simply will not stay in your head. Only words that you learn in context and that you make real use of in speech and writing are likely to become part of your active vocabulary.

There are three stages. First, use what you know of other words and of the context to make an informed guess – as in the example given at the beginning of this chapter.

Secondly, check your guess in a dictionary. If you come across the word in speech, for example, you will have to find out how to spell it. Does your boss *witter* on or *whitter on*? (In this case, both are correct but the former is more common.) If the word came from your reading, how do you pronounce it? Does *cadre* rhyme with *larder* or *ladder* or what? (The first is better.) How many syllables are there in *interstice*? (Three – the last is pronounced / stiss /; and the stress is on the second.)

Finally, practise the new word. Make up sentences containing the word and helping to spell out its meaning. Write the sentences down if possible. Suppose your new word is *ebullient*. You could write *The captain was ebullient after the team's third victory on the trot*. Try to think of times during the day when you might have used *ebullient*, and say aloud to yourself the sentence you might have used on that occasion.

As you practise the word, try to construct a picture in your mind – this will help you to remember it. Make the picture vivid and colourful. It need not be realistic. Memory works better on pictures than on abstraction – and the more exaggerated the picture, the better. With *ebullient* you might visualise the captain of the winning team laughing, leaping in the air, and shaking everyone's hand – in a word, being ebullient. For a more active memory image, picture a *bull* gambolling in a field.

Any unlikely association will help to fix the word in your mind. To remember that a document which qualifies or alters a will is called a *codicil*, try picturing an old man in bed signing not a piece of paper but a large fish – a *cod*! This should be enough to get you started when you need to recover the word from your memory.

Then, when you are sure you have got the word right, be on the lookout for opportunities to use it in conversation. Feel justifiably proud when you use a word for the first time. Not because it shows you are clever, but because at last you have managed to express precisely or interestingly what you wanted to say. Or just because it is fun to do something new.

One further warning. Don't, in your enthusiasm for new words, correct someone else who uses them! For one thing, it is not polite. For another, your correction may miss its mark. Perhaps he or she is using the word in a quite different sense, or in an extended modern or metaphorical way. Or perhaps you yourself are mistaken, having misunderstood the dictionary definition in the first place.

HOW FOREIGNERS LEARN WORDS

Teaching English to foreigners is big business. Experts have put a great deal of research into finding out how it can be done most effectively. Some of this research is relevant to native speakers of English as well.

Time is short for the teacher of English as a foreign language, and grammar and pronunciation take up the bulk of the lessons. The teaching of vocabulary becomes something of a problem, then.

The best solution, research has shown, is to get students to read. Listening can be useful, but the flow of speech is usually too rapid for them to think about the words that they do not understand. So, if foreigners are serious about learning English, they have to read.

But not just anything. Suppose you were faced with this sentence. It is taken from a translation of a French book about religions:

> In our opinion, it is justifiable to read in this depreciation of history (that is, of events without transhistorical models), and in this rejection of profane, continuous time, a certain metaphysical 'valorisation' of human existence.
> — Mircea Eliade, *The Myth of the Eternal Return*

Imagine yourself as a foreign student of English confronted with this passage. If you looked up every word you did not understand, you would get bored very quickly. Worse still, by the time you had reached the end of a sentence you would have forgotten what the beginning meant.

Tests have shown that if the number of unfamiliar words in a passage exceeds about one in twenty, the reader will lose track. If the proportion is lower, however, the reader can skip over the unfamiliar words and grasp, if not everything, at least the general meaning. This procedure reinforces words that the reader 'half knows'. And then he or she can look up those new words that seem most interesting or important.

The Building Blocks Of Good English

Read constantly to improve your vocabulary.

The lessons for you are as follows: read constantly to improve your vocabulary, but read appropriately. You will not gain much by reading material that has too many unfamiliar words. Take on a challenge, but not an insurmountable one.

Find something you are interested in, such as a novel, a textbook, or a newspaper or magazine with some 'meat' in it. If the material appeals to you, you will put in more effort and the new words you meet are more likely to be of use to you. Authors you might try with rich but clear vocabularies include Graham Greene, Evelyn Waugh, Edna O'Brien, Anthony Burgess, P.G. Wodehouse, and James Thurber. Be conscientious about looking up new words. Words that once left you flummoxed will soon become familiar friends.

Apply this approach to your listening as well. Whether it is to conversations, speeches, the radio, or television, pay full attention. Choose your viewing and listening not simply for relaxation. Listen carefully to news broadcasts, current-affairs programmes, documentaries, serious round-table discussions, and the like.

In particular, listen carefully to people who in your opinion speak good English – since you yourself feel the force of their words. Try to work out what it is that makes their language effective. Rather than blocking out the words that you do not recognise,

concentrate on them. Work out from the context what they could mean. If it is on television that you encounter them, use the pictures to provide clues. And write down new words in a notebook or on a piece of paper. When you next get the chance, check them in the dictionary.

I KNOW THAT WORD

It is not enough simply to learn what a word means. To master a word you have to know when and how to use it. This requires knowing what fields or contexts it occurs in, what its overtones are, what words it 'keeps company' with, and what things it may be used to refer to. Only when you know all these elements can you really claim to 'know' the word and be confident of using it correctly.

Consider the word *manageress*. If a foreigner asked you what it meant, you might at first be tempted to answer 'It's a woman manager'. But is this the whole story? Is a *manageress* simply a manager who happens to be a woman.

Here are some sentences using the word *manager*.

> Dilip's the manager of the best Indian restaurant in town.
> We need a manager for our new hairdressing salon.
> Dr Robbins was finally made manager of the research department.
> The manager of the British hockey team was unavailable for comment.

Try substituting *manageress* for *manager* in the sentences. The first two are fine. But what about the second pair? Using the word *manageress* in these sentences sounds odd. The word *manager* sounds better even though it refers to a woman.

So a *manageress* is not just a manager who is a woman. It is more likely to be a female manager of a shop, hotel, laundry, or the like. Generally speaking, the managers of companies or company divisions, large public institutions and sports teams, remain *managers* regardless of gender.

CONTEXT AND USAGE LIMITS

Consider these two sentences, each describing a different painting:

> The painting shows her face shining with joy.
> The painting shows her face shining with beatitude.

The expressions depicted in the two paintings may be very similar, and both sentences *might* be used to describe the same painting. After all, *beatitude* does mean 'joy'. The problem is that it refers to a special kind of joy. It does not mean the kind of joy you feel on winning a competition, on getting a letter from an old friend, or on gaining promotion at work. *Beatitude* is specifically religious joy, the kind of joy that comes from a sudden understanding of God's beauty and goodness.

So the first sentence could be used of either a religious or a secular painting; the second only of a religious painting. Before you can use the word *beatitude*, you must know that it is normally confined to religious contexts. If you use it elsewhere, you may be using it incorrectly.

Or consider the difference between *oppressing* and *bullying*, and the contexts in which they occur. Someone might *oppress* a section of society or even a country, but a person would *bully* only individuals or small groups. Tyrants and political systems *oppress*. The verb to *bully* is more appropriate for the streets and the school playground.

Words, then, that on the face of it are synonymous can be used correctly only in certain quite distinct contexts or situations. Most good dictionaries indicate what these restrictions are – see *Dictionaries and How to Use Them*, pages 258-268.

Sometimes you may choose between a word with few restrictions on its usage and others with much tighter ones. Consider the sentences *John Wilkes Booth assassinated Abraham Lincoln* and *The hold-up gang killed the guard*. The word *killed* could easily replace *assassinated* in the first sentence, but the reverse does not work in the second: you can hardly say that the gang *assassinated* the guard. Only important public figures can be assassinated, and usually for political reasons.

Be wary too of usage restrictions when trying out synonyms given in dictionaries and thesauruses. The synonyms given may have roughly the same meaning as the word you originally looked up, but the contexts in which they can be correctly used may be quite different. People, as well as ideas, books, and other products of their minds, can be *abstruse*. But you cannot really say that a person is *recondite*, *arcane*, or *esoteric*, though all of these words may be given as synonyms.

Even the experts sometimes disagree about whether a word is appropriate in its context. Can a woman be an *actor* or a *crook*? Can a man be *no spring chicken*? With such terms it is best to play safe. Try to stick to the kind of context in which you first heard or read the word.

On the other hand, don't be too cowed by restrictions. You may, if you wish, deliberately flout them. This often forces the listener to interpret the word in a special way – as when you talk about a *handsome woman* or a *pretty boy*, or about *murdering a sandwich*. Talking of a *cantankerous motor car* conjures up a far more vivid picture – of a car with a distinctive personality – than the words *an unreliable car*.

THE RIGHT WORD IN THE RIGHT PLACE

Hitting the right 'register' – the appropriate level of language for a particular situation – is also important. You might complain to your friends about the *fuzz* or *Old Bill*, but if you come up before the magistrate for speeding, you would be wise to refer to these people as *police officers*.

Information about register is often indicated in dictionaries, by means of the labels *formal*, *informal*, *slang*, *old-fashioned*, *obsolete*. Also included are regional labels (*U.S.*, *Aust.*) and usage labels (*literary*, *poetic*, *humorous*).

It is not that one word is simply better than another. It is more a matter of picking the one that suits the occasion. You do not put on climbing boots to go dancing. Few people, if any, speak to their boss, their drinking companions, their wife, and their children in exactly the same way – and there is no reason why they should.

Mixing registers will produce curious-sounding results. How incongruous it would sound if the boss told a subordinate at work: 'Kindly endeavour to get cracking.' Not that incongruity necessary means that a construction is wrong. You can achieve humorous and satirical effects by such means.

But if you are not in control of the effects you are trying to create, the attempt may well backfire on you.

Think before choosing a word. Ask yourself: 'Is this the right time and place?' If it is not, choose a different word.

CONNOTATIONS

Be careful with connotations. Take this sentence:
?? *That community has been impecunious since the*

shoe factory closed down. One dictionary defines *impecunious* as 'lacking money, penniless'. If that were the whole story, there would be nothing peculiar about the sentence. But there is. *Impecunious* does indeed mean 'poor', but it also has special connotations – extra layers of meaning.

In the first place, it suggests a temporary poverty. Grinding, long-term lack of money is not impecuniousness. Moreover, *impecunious* is better used to describe an individual than a class or group of people. You can use it of a group when each member is viewed as a single individual, but hardly of the group as a whole. So *impecunious students* sounds acceptable, while an **??** *impecunious community* does not.

But, above all, an *impecunious* person tends to be poor in a rather romantic, respectable, almost voluntary way, with hopes of better things. Students, artists, musicians, and the like can be *impecunious*. Sweatshop labourers and the unemployed cannot. People who have no say or little say over their lack of money are *poor*, *impoverished*, or *destitute*. A good dictionary should make all these connotations clear, often in short 'synonym essays' comparing near-synonyms.

The connotations of the words you use will convey a great deal to your reader or listener about your attitude towards a subject. So it is vital to choose words with the right connotations. By choosing a word with the wrong ones, you may very possibly give a strictly accurate description and yet convey a completely wrong impression.

English has many sets of words that 'mean' the same thing but in quite different ways – some in an appreciative way, others in a pejorative (negative) way. You may describe an acquaintance as *plump*; an unkinder observer may describe him as *fat* or, worse, *obese*. You may call a female friend *homely*; others may refer to her as *plain* or downright *ugly*.

A supporter may find a particular politician *suave*; an opponent may find him *unctuous*. *Resolution* and *determination* are virtues; *intransigence* and *pig-headedness* are vices. A person may say of himself that he likes 'to drink socially'. One friend may say of him that 'he likes a drop', another that 'he's a soak'. These expressions all 'mean' that the person likes his drink, but they give very different impressions of the extent of his imbibing.

Some words have different connotations according to the other words you use them with. A *plausible*

theory is one put forward in good faith, with the frank admission that it is only guesswork. A *plausible villain* is one who is the more dangerous for being believable.

Be aware too of regional or national differences. To most people in Britain, *liberal* has positive connotations to do with generosity and open-mindedness. In some right-wing quarters in the United States, however, *liberal* is used as a term of political abuse, like *pinko*, suggesting either extreme left-wing views or woolly left-wing views.

GRAMMAR

Some words are restricted to very particular uses. If you have learnt a word in one grammatical context, don't automatically assume that you can use it in another context.

Suppose you come across a sentence like this: *Michelangelo was a consummate draughtsman*. You look up *consummate*. Your dictionary tells you it means 'supremely accomplished or skilled'. This is true enough, as far as it goes.

A few days later, when the right opportunity presents itself, you glibly announce that **??** *Michelangelo's draughtsmanship was consummate*. Unfortunately you have overstepped the grammatical limitations on the word. *Consummate* is not, as the dictionary seems to suggest, an adjective like *accomplished* and *skilful* that can be used either before or after the noun it refers to. It can be used only in certain positions in the sentence. Consider these two sentences: *He's an utter idiot*; **X** *This idiot is utter*. The second is clearly wrong. *Utter* can be used only *before* the noun it qualifies. So too with *consummate* above.

To avoid such confusions, try to keep your first attempts at using a new word close to the way it was used when you made its acquaintance. As you come to hear or read it more often, so you will come to be increasingly confident of its grammar.

THE COMPANY IT KEEPS . . .

The *collocations* of a word are the typical phrases or contexts it occurs in. Nothing can be *varicose* except a *vein*. *Delinquents* tend to be *juvenile*. Your county, borough, or district has a *council* rather than a *government*. And your political party or trade union has an *executive* rather than a *board* or *committee*. If you want to avoid being noticed, you might *play possum* or *lie doggo* – but you cannot *lie possum* or *play doggo*.

Here are a few more curious examples of English collocations:

☐ Butter goes *rancid* but milk goes *sour*.

☐ *Damp* and *moist* mean the same when used to describe a cleaning rag, but are not interchangeable when applied to, for example, English summers or tearful eyes.

☐ *Orders* are normally *given* and *decrees* are *issued*. But you can do either with a *command*.

Some dictionaries are better than others at showing typical collocations. Always look carefully at the examples given after a definition. They are chosen to show how the word is typically used.

Unfortunately, all too many collocations are now clichés: *to deny categorically, spiralling inflation*, and so on. Try to avoid them. It is always possible to deny something *utterly, entirely*, or *strenuously*, rather than *categorically*. Inflation can *go up, increase*, and do many things other than *spiral*. Political discussions and wage negotiations need not always be *frank and serious*.

THE SYNONYM GAME

Test your knowledge of English synonyms. Play the *I am plump; you are fat; he is obese* game with the following ideas.

Write down various adjectives corresponding to each concept listed below, ordering them according to their tone or intensity – from mild, favourable, or sympathetic, through neutral, to extreme, unfavourable, or hostile. Some suggested answers appear in the quiz answers section, pages 633-648.

1. thinness

2. poverty

3. stupidity

4. carefulness

5. meanness

6. modesty

7. friendliness

8. politeness

Word Elements

Reducing words to their basic components is a crucial aid to guessing their meaning – but sometimes you will have to look hard to identify these components. A word element – root, prefix, or the like – is called a *morpheme* or *morph*. The word comes from the Greek for 'form'. The trouble is that some morphs change their form and meaning in particular words. You will need to learn the intricacies of these possible variations to sharpen your ability to recognise new words and to hazard a guess at their meanings.

The most stable morphs are combining forms (forms such as *Franco-* or *pseudo-*) and Greek roots. This is because most have been borrowed recently and consciously. Modern words with Greek elements are like office blocks – clearly thought out and functional.

Rather different are words that go back to Old English, or to Latin words that passed into early French before coming into English. The longer a word exists in a language, the more time it has to go its own way, take on new meanings, and change its sounds. Older words are like rambling old houses with hidden corners that you do not expect.

Take, for example, the Latin prefix *in-* (related to the English *un-*). It changes its shape considerably according to the word it is prefixed to: *inelegant* is straightforward, but what about *impossible, illegal*, and *irrelevant*?

As for the difficulty caused by changed meaning: it is easy to accept that *repel* and *repulse* come from the same Latin word *repellere*, 'to drive back'. Both have the idea of pushing away. It is harder to see the connection between *revolution* and *involve*. In fact, the *-volu-* in *revolution* and the *-volv-* in *involve* both come from the Latin *volvere*, 'to turn or roll'. A *revolution* is clearly a turning around. But where is the idea of turning in *involve*? The answer is that the original meaning of *involve* was 'to tangle, entrap' – this sense is still clear in the phrase: *a long and involved argument*. Only by extension has *involve* arrived at its more common modern meaning of 'to bring about as a consequence, or be bound up with'.

A further complication is that words often come from different parts of the same (usually Latin) word. *Refer* and *relate*, for example, are derived from exactly the same Latin verb *ferre*, 'to carry', whose past participle was *latum*. For a parallel, think of the different forms of the English verb *go* – I *go*, you *went*, she has *gone*.

The charts that follow in this chapter list many common elements used in English word-building. They show the most frequent variations on these elements, and indicate some of the shades of meaning they have acquired. A few of the most important roots, combining forms, and affixes are discussed in the main text below.

ROOTS: VARIATIONS ON A THEME

Words evolve in curious and different ways. The chart beginning opposite gives only an overview of various roots used in English and how different words have developed from them. Here are case studies of a few selected roots.

Words from *ac, acr, acu*. *Acid* is from the Latin adjective *acidus*, meaning 'sharp, sour'. It has the same root as *acer* – keen, sharp. Even in Latin *acid(us)* had both modern meanings: 'sour -tasting' and 'sour in temperament, disagreeable'. From *acid* come words such as *acidify* and *acidity*.

Acrid also uses the Latin suffix *-id* , meaning 'with a particular quality'. *Acrid* is used mainly to describe smells and tastes: *acrid smoke*.

Acerbic comments are harsh, bitter, and cutting. They might be made during an *acrimonious* dispute – one full of bitterness and *acrimony*.

Acute comes from a Latin word meaning 'sharpened' or 'coming to a sharp point'. So an *acute* angle is one that is less than 90 degrees. Hence the word came to mean 'reaching a crisis, critical' and also 'intense, to the point'. We speak of a problem as becoming *acute*; of a toothache as giving us *acute* pain; or of a person as having an *acute* mind or being *acutely* aware of something.

Acuity is sharpness of mind and quickness of understanding. *Acumen* too, though it is usually a long-term quality, like shrewdness.

Acupuncture is the sharp puncturing of the skin with needles.

Words from *cad, cas, cid*. From the basic meaning, 'to fall', found in *cadence*, the fall or

intonation of speech or music, this root often has the secondary meaning of 'to befall' or 'to happen'.

A *casual* meeting happens by chance. *Casual* work is work that you happen just to 'fall into'. A *casualty* is someone who 'falls' in a battle or accident.

Decadent means literally 'falling down', but in a moral or cultural sense. The Roman Empire became *decadent*. In fact, it *decayed* – another word using the same root.

An *accident* is something that happens by chance. So too, very often, is an *incident*. *Incidental* details are secondary ones, happening along with a main event. The *incidence* of something is how often it happens – you may hope for a low *incidence* of crime in your neighbourhood.

Occasion originally meant a 'falling down or towards', using the prefix *ob-*. An opportunity might 'fall towards' you. *Occasional* now 'means happening now and then'. So you might take the *occasional* day off work.

Occident also means a 'falling towards'. Here it is the sun that is doing the falling, and what it is falling towards is the west. So Europe, being in the west, is an *occidental* continent.

Words from *ced, cede, ceed, cess*. The basic meanings – 'go, yield, give way' – are clear in *cede*. One country may *cede*, or yield or give up, land to another after a defeat in a war.

Ante- in *antecedent* means 'before'. *Antecedents* are therefore things or people that went before (or *preceded*) something. Stephenson's Rocket was the *antecedent* of today's railway locomotives.

The *con-* in *concede* means 'thoroughly, utterly'. So *conceding* to an opponent means yielding or giving up completely. You can also *concede* defeat. To *concede* also means 'to grant, admit, acknowledge as being true'. You will surely *concede* that this is so. It is only a small *concession*.

Ex- means 'beyond', so something that *exceeds* your expectations 'goes beyond' them or surpasses them. Something that is *exceedingly* good is good beyond what you expect – that is, very good. The noun from *exceed* is *excess* – an immoderate amount, a surplus. You should always avoid *excess* in all things. *Excess* fat is too much fat, as when you are overweight.

If you *proceed*, you 'go forward'. This might be down the road, or it might mean that you begin to

ROOTS: THE HEARTS OF WORDS

The root is the basic part of a word. It usually shows the general area of meaning. As you study the following chart, you will notice that the Latin or Greek root word is often very simple and straightforward in meaning – *mitto*, I send, for example, or *venio*, I come.

Yet English words using, say, *-mit-* or *-miss-*, *-ven-* or *-vent-*, often have a technical or abstract meaning, or sound more formal than their synonyms. Consider *transmit*, *circumvent*, *convene*. How did this come about?

Simply, for centuries French and Latin were the languages of learning and sophistication, while English was a vulgar language for everyday uses – see *The Words We Use*, pages 112-140. Even after English had become the standard language at all levels of society, Latin-based words tended to remain more formal or technical than those derived from Old English.

Roots marked with an asterisk (*) are discussed in more detail in the main text.

Root	Language of Origin	Word in original language	Meaning in original language	English examples
*ac, acr, acu	Latin	acer, acris	keen, sharp	acid, acerbic, acrid, acute, acupuncture
am, amat	Latin	amo, amatum	love	amateur, amicable, amorous, enamoured
annu, enni	Latin	annus	year	annals, annual, annuity, perennial
anthrop	Greek	anthropos	human being	anthropology, misanthrope, philanthropist
aud, audi, audit	Latin	audio, auditum	hear, examine	audible, audience, audition, auditorium
bel, belli	Latin	bellum	war	belligerent, rebel
*cad, cas, cid	Latin	cado, casum	fall	accident, casual, decadent, occasion
cap, capt, cip, cept, ceit, ceiv	Latin	capio, captum	take, seize	capable, capture, concept, deceit, except, receive, recipient
carn	Latin	carno, carnis	flesh	carnal, carnival, carnage, carnation
*ced, cede, ceed, cess	Latin	cedo, cessum	go, yield, give way	antecedent, concede, exceed, process
celer	Latin	celer	fast, rapid	celerity, accelerate
cogn	Latin	cognosco, cognitum	know	cognisant, cognition, recognise, incognito
cord	Latin	cor, cordis	heart, mind	cordial, accord, discord, record
corp, corpor	Latin	corpus, corporis	body	corps, corpse, corpulent, corporation

→

Root	Language of Origin	Word in original language	Meaning in original language	English examples
cred	Latin	credo, creditum	believe, trust	credit, creed, credible, credentials, credulous, accredit, discredit
cur, curs, cours	Latin	curro, cursum	run, go	current, cursor, concur, discourse, occur, precursor
dent	Latin	dens, dentis	tooth	dental, dentist, indent
derm, dermat	Greek	derma	skin	dermatitis, epidermis, hypodermic
dict	Latin	dico, dictum	say, speak	dictate, diction, addict, contradict, edict
duc, duct	Latin	duco, ductum	lead	ductile, conduct, conducive, produce
*fac, fact, fect, fict	Latin	facio, factum	do, make	fact, factory, facile, fiction, affect, effect, efficient, perfect
fer, lat, late	Latin	fero, latum	bear, carry	confer, differ, offer, prefer, refer, suffer, transfer, collate, relate
flect, flex	Latin	flecto, flexum	bend	flexible, deflect, inflection, reflex, reflection
flu, flux	Latin	fluo, fluxum	flow	fluid, fluent, fluctuate, flux, effluent, influence
frang, frag, fract, fring	Latin	frango, fractum	break	fraction, fracture, fragile, fragment, infringe, refract
gam	Greek	gamos	marriage	gamete, monogamy, bigamy, polygamous
*gen, gener, geni, genit	Latin	geno, genitum; genius; genus, generis; gens, gentis	give birth to, produce; guardian spirit; kind, type; race, people	gender, gene, general, genealogy, generate, generous, genesis, genial, genius, genital, genre, gentle, gentry, genuine, engine, ingenuity, ingenuous, oxygen
grad, gress	Latin	gradior, gressus	to step, go	gradual, graduate, aggression, centigrade, digression, progress
*grav	Latin	gravis	heavy, serious	grave, gravity, aggravate

Root	Language of Origin	Word in original language	Meaning in original language	English examples
greg	Latin	grex, gregis	crowd, herd	gregarious, congregate, egregious, segregate
gyn	Greek	gune	woman	gynaecology, misogynist
hom, homin	Latin	homo, hominis	human	homicide, hominoid, homage, bonhomie
jac, ject	Latin	iaceo/iacio, iactum	throw; lie; stick out	abject, adjacent, conjecture, eject, inject, object, project, reject
lat, late		see *fer*		
leg, lig, lect	Latin	lego, lectum	choose; read	elect, eligible, intelligent, lecture, legible
leg	Latin	lex, legis	law	legal, legislate
lig	Latin	ligo, ligatum	bind	ligament, religion
log, logi	Greek	logos	word; reason	logical, analogy, epilogue, prologue
loqu, locut	Latin	loquor, locutum	speak	loquacious, colloquial, elocution, eloquent, interlocutor
man, mani, manu	Latin	manus	hand	manual, manicure, manifest, manuscript
mater, matr	Latin	mater, matris	mother	maternal, matrimony, matrix, matron
mit, miss	Latin	mitto, missum	send, let go	mission, missile, admit, commit, dismiss, omit
mon, monit	Latin	moneo, monitum	warn, advise, remind	monitor, monument, admonish, premonition
mov, mot, mob	Latin	moveo, motum	move	move, motion, motor, mobile, emotion, promote, remove, mob
nom, nomen, nomin	Latin	nomen, nominis	name	nominate, nominal, cognomen, misnomer
nov	Latin	novus	new	novelty, novice, renovate
pater, patr	Latin	pater, patris; patria	father; own country	paternal, paternity, patriotic, repatriate
ped	Latin	pes, pedis	foot	pedal, pedestrian

→

Root	Language of Origin	Word in original language	Meaning in original language	English examples
pel, puls	Latin	pello, pulsum	drive, push	pulsate, compel, expulsion, repulsive
*pend, pens	Latin	pendo, pensum	hang; weigh; pay	pendulum, compensate, depend, dispense, suspend, pensive
phil, philo	Greek	philos	loving	philosophy, philanthropy, francophile
pon, pound, pose, posit	Latin	pono, positum	put, place	position, positive, compose, component, deposit, expound
port	Latin	porto, portatum	carry	portable, porter, export, report, support
put, putat	Latin	puto, putatum	think, reckon	putative, compute, dispute, reputation
quir, quest, quisit	Latin	quaero, quaesitum	seek, ask	question, acquire, conquest, inquisitive, require, requisite
rupt	Latin	rumpo, ruptum	break	rupture, corrupt, disrupt, eruption
scrib, script	Latin	scribo, scriptum	write	conscript, describe, inscription, postscript
sect	Latin	seco, sectum	cut	section, intersect, sector, vasectomy
secut, sequ	Latin	sequor, secutum	follow	sequel, consecutive, consequence, execute
*sed, sede, sid, sess	Latin	sedeo, sessum	sit, settle, be situated	sedate, sedentary, sediment, session, obsess, resident, preside, supersede
soph	Greek	sophia	wisdom	sophistry, sophisticated, philosophy
spec, spic, spect	Latin	specio, spectum	look, look at	spectator, spectacles, conspicuous, expect
tact, tang, ting	Latin	tango, tactum	touch	tact, tactile, tangent, tangible, contact, contingent
temp, tempor	Latin	tempus, temporis	time	temporary, temporise, contemporary, extempore
*ten, tin, tent, tain	Latin	teneo, tentum	hold, keep	tenacious, contain, contents, continent

Root	Language of Origin	Word in original language	Meaning in original language	English examples
terr, ter	Latin	terra	land	territory, terrace, terrestrial, interred
theo	Greek	theos	god	theology, theocracy, apotheosis, pantheon
*tract	Latin	traho, tractum	drag, draw, pull	traction, tractor, attract, contract, extract, subtract
ven, vent	Latin	venio, ventum	come, move towards	adventure, convene, event, invention
ver, verac	Latin	verus	true	veracious, verily, very, aver, verdict
*vers, vert	Latin	verto, versum	turn, change	advertise, convert, diversion, invert, reverse, subversive
vict, vinc	Latin	vinco, victum	defeat, win	victory, convict, convince, province
vid, vis	Latin	video, visum	see	video, vision, visit, advise, evident, provide, television
vir	Latin	vir	man, male	virile, virago, triumvirate
vit, viv	Latin	vita; vivo, victum	life; live	vital, vitamin, vivid, vivacious, convivial, revive
voc, vok	Latin	voco; vox, vocis	call; voice	vocabulary, vocal, vocation, advocate, evoke, provoke
*volt, volv, volut	Latin	volvo, volutum	roll, turn	convolvulus, evolve, involve, revolt

do something, or simply that you do something next: *Having insulted me he then proceeded to kick me*. From *proceed* come words like *proceedings* and *proceeds* ('the returns or yield of some action', as in *the proceeds from the sale of their flat*).

A *process*, the way you *proceed* to do something, is a method, or course of action. A *process* can also be a 'going forward' in time. 'Going forward' is part of *procession* and *processional* too. (Don't confuse *proceed*, which means 'go forward, progress', with *precede*, which means 'go before'.)

On the other hand, if your hairline is *receding* it is going backwards. A *recess* is 'a going backwards', especially a hole or cavity in a wall, or the time taken while you withdraw from something for a break. Courts of law and Parliament, for instance, go into *recess* when they adjourn.

Compare this root with *sed, sede, sid, sess* overleaf. They are easily confused. If you can think etymologically, you will avoid spelling *supersede* with a -c- or *intercede* with an -s- .

Words from *fac, fact, fect, fict*. Most of the many words using this root still have a clear idea of doing or making. A *fact* is something done, or made true. A *factory* is where things are made. The *manu-* in *manufacture* is Latin for 'by hand', as in *manuscript*.

151

Fiction is something made up in your head – whether a story or a lie.

Facile means, literally, 'able to be done'. It has come to mean 'easy to do, requiring little thought or skill'. So a *facile* answer or person is a shallow or unconvincingly glib one. *Facility* is easy skill as in *speaking Chinese with facility*. A *facility* makes your life or work easier – it might be a building, room, or piece of equipment.

To *affect* a person or thing is to do something to (*ad*-) it. What has been done to it, that is, the result or consequence of an action, is an *effect*, literally 'done from' (*ex*-). You can also *effect* a change, an arrest, or a cure, that is, do it or bring it about. An *efficient* method or machine does or performs its function with little wasted effort.

Something *infected* is literally 'done in'. Something has got into it and is affecting it for the worse. Wounds may get *infected* by bacteria. Your mind might be *infected* by doubt.

The prefix *per*- means 'through' or else 'thoroughly'. A *perfect* piece of work is one that has been gone through or done completely.

Other words using the *fac* root and its variants include *affection, defect, deficient, factor*, and *proficient*. Even the suffix *-ify* is related. To *beautify, unify*, or *petrify* something means to make it more beautiful, make it one, or turn it into stone.

Words from *gen, gener, geni, genit*. A book could be written on this root – meaning 'mind, spirit, give birth to, produce' – especially if you took into consideration the distantly related English word *kind*. There are obvious connections between, on the one hand, *kind* and *gentle*, and on the other *kind* and *genus: generic, gender, homogeneous* (of a single kind) and *genre* (a kind of literature, such as novel or poem).

The root has varied meanings since it was shared by Latin and Greek. And in each language it produced a wide range of derived words, many of which have passed into English, or into French and from there into English.

The most basic meaning appears to reside in the word *genius*. This was originally a personal or guardian spirit, as in Aladdin's *genie* of the lamp. And people still speak of the *genius* of a place – that is, its special spirit or atmosphere. From here it is easy to see how the root came to have the idea of 'type, sort'.

As personal spirits were believed to pass on to the individual at birth, the root came to be associated with childbirth (*genital, progeny*), and then to the general idea of producing (*generate*), and to the idea of tribes and peoples (*gentile*). Your natural spirit was connected with your mind or intelligence (*genius, ingenious*), and with natural human qualities (*genuine, ingenuous*), including kindness and good humour (*generous, genial*). The words *gene, genetic, genesis*, and *genealogy* also fit into the pattern clearly, but what about *engine*? Originally, an engine was any clever device, trick, or plan, not just a machine or motor. So it is based on the idea of intelligence.

And *general*? That meant originally 'belonging to a whole species or kind', as in *a general election*. The army general has *general* power over a whole group of soldiers.

And where do *oxygen* and *hydrogen* fit in? Both were made up from Greek roots at the end of the 18th century. *Oxygen* is literally 'acid maker', which describes one of its chemical properties. And *hydrogen* is 'water maker'. The *hydro*- in *hydrogen* is the same as in *hydraulic, hydrofoil*, and *hydroelectricity*, that is 'water'. If you burn *hydrogen*, you produce water.

Words from *grav*. The basic meanings of this root are 'heavy, serious'. If you look *grave*, you have a serious expression. (The word has nothing to do with the *grave* in which people are buried. That word comes from a Germanic root meaning 'to dig'.) Seriousness is therefore *gravity*. This word also refers to the heavy pull of the Earth. Hence *to gravitate*, 'to be pulled or attracted towards'.

Aggravate is made up of *ad*- , to, + *grav* + -*ate*, to make. So *aggravating* something means adding to its heaviness or seriousness. You might *aggravate* a cold by going out in the rain. From this meaning comes the more common modern sense of 'to annoy, provoke'.

Words from *pend, pens*. The meaning of 'hanging down' is clear in the *pendulum* of a clock or a *pendulous* necklace. *Suspend, suspension*, and *suspense* also originally implied hanging down. Think of a *suspension* bridge. These words have now taken on many more meanings – *suspended* without pay, a film full of *suspense*.

Depend also originally meant 'to hang down or from'. You can say in English that *Our success hangs on your cooperation*.

Don't confuse the words *dependence* and *dependency*. Either can mean 'the state of being dependent on something', as in *dependence on drugs*. But only *dependency* can refer to the colony or country that *depends* on another, such as *the Falkland Islands dependency*.

Hanging things in a balance has always been the best-known method of weighing them. This is what a *dispensing* chemist did – he weighed out prescriptions. He also *dispensed* with them. That is, he gave them out or got rid of them after weighing. This is the meaning behind expressions like *Can you dispense with my help today?* From here you get to *indispensable* and other related words.

Balances were also used to weigh out bullion for payment. So the Latin root came to have the extra meaning of 'to pay'. To *expend* means 'to pay out'. You may *expend* your energy on a project. Something you can do without is *expendable*. The idea of payment is even more apparent in *expense*, *expenses*, *expensive*, and *expenditure*.

The word *spend* itself was brought into English at an early stage, and lost its prefix. It appears to come both from *expend* and from *dispend*, a lost word from Old French that used to mean 'to squander' or 'to waste'.

From *weighing* things in a balance it is not so far to the idea of *weighing things up in the mind*, that is 'thinking about them'. The Latin verb *penso* was derived from *pendo*, and meant 'to weigh again and again' and so 'to think'. From this, by way of French, English gets the word *pensive*, meaning 'thoughtful, deep in thought'.

Other words using the *pend*, *pens* root include: *append*, *appendage*, *appendix*, *compensate*, *impending* and *pendant*.

Words from *sed*, *sede*, *sid*, *sess*. The Latin verbs *sedeo*, *sedo*, and *sido* are distantly related to our native English verbs *sit* and *set*. Latin also had related words with the stem *sit*. From these come many words relating to position, such as a building *site* or a *situation*.

The potential confusion between this root and the root *ced*, *cede* makes it worth while trying to learn which words use which root. If you do, it will help your spelling.

The idea of 'sitting' is often prominent in words derived from *sedeo*. A *sedentary* job involves a lot of sitting. A *session* is a 'sitting', as of a court, and so a single meeting of any organised group. The chairman might *preside* at this meeting, which means that he 'sits in front' of it. From this come words like *president* and *presidential*.

From 'sitting' it is a short way to the idea of 'settling' and from there to 'relaxation'. A *sediment* is a deposit of solids that has settled at the bottom of a liquid. Someone who is *sedate* is easy-going and unruffled. This state can be achieved artificially by taking *sedatives*.

The place where you are settled is your *residence*. You *reside* there. Hence *resident* and *residential*. The word *reside* can also be used figuratively – the highest judicial power in Britain *resides* in the House of Lords.

Obsess, *obsession*, and *obsessive*, have the prefix *ob-*, meaning 'in front of'. The original Latin word meant to 'ambush' or 'besiege'. It is easy to see how an *obsession* might be thought of as something that 'besieges' someone.

Words from *ten*, *tin*, *tent*, *tain*. The idea of 'holding' or 'keeping' is clear enough in the basic meanings of words like *contain*, *contents*, *detain*, *detention*, and *retain*. The base form turns up in the words *tenacious* and its stronger form *pertinacious*. Both imply 'holding on' stubbornly. You might keep a *tenacious* grip on your possessions. The derived nouns are *tenacity* and *pertinacity*.

Some words using the root are more difficult to relate to the original meaning. A *continent* is a mass of land that 'holds together'. A *lieutenant* (straight from French) is someone who 'holds a place or position' in lieu, or in place, of another – that is, a deputy. *Maintain* and *maintenance* have the idea of 'keeping by hand', that is 'looking after'.

With *pertain* and *appertain* the connection with the root has been masked by the words' later development. Both imply 'holding through or throughout', but their modern meaning is little more than 'to affect' or to 'be connected with'. *Pertinent* means 'apposite, relevant' and *impertinent* once meant only the opposite. But making irrelevant comments is rude and if you do so today you are now guilty of *impertinence*.

Related words include: *tenable*, *tenancy*, *tenant*, *tenure*, *abstain*, *abstention*, *continue*, *entertain*, *obtain*, *sustain*, and *sustenance*.

Words from *tract*. The Latin word *traho*, *tractum* is cognate with (has the same distant origins as) the

English words *drag*, *draw*, and *draught*, as in *draught horses*. It shares the same area of meaning. A *tractor* is a machine for pulling. If you break your leg, it may have to be put in *traction*. Something you find *attractive* draws you to it. When a dentist *extracts* a tooth he pulls it out. Yeast *extract* is 'drawn' or refined out of yeast. In *subtraction* you 'drag' one number away 'from under' another.

Many of these words have more figurative meanings. Both *detract* and *distract* are 'to draw away'. So flu can *detract* from your enjoyment of your holiday. A *detractor* is given to fault-finding or slander. Noise might be *distracting* when you are trying to concentrate – that is, it draws your mind away from your work. It might drive you to *distraction*. If you are *distraught*, you are confused by fear or anxiety.

Retracting a statement is the same as 'withdrawing' it. And your cat may play with its claws *retracted*, 'drawn back'.

In all its many meanings *contract*, together with its derivatives, comes from the idea of 'drawing together'. If a bridge in cold weather or a business in bad times *contracts*, it shrinks. 'Drawing together' or 'pulling in' leads to the idea of 'taking in' or 'taking on'. You might *contract* an illness, or a debt. Or *contract* to do a job, which means 'to promise'.

Words from vers, vert. The basic sense of 'turning' is clear in words such as *reverse*, *obverse*, and *invert*. The purpose of an *advertisement* is to turn you to it, or to the product it displays. The *a-* in *avert* comes from *ab-*, 'away'. So you might *avert* your gaze from something, or try to *avert an accident* by taking precautions. If you have *an aversion* to something, it 'turns you off'.

Divert and its derivative *diversion* both contain the idea of 'turning away'. You can *divert* someone's attention from something. Traffic might have to turn off the main road, because of roadworks, and use a *diversion*. These words can also have the sense of 'distraction, entertainment'; a hobby is a *diversion*, something that turns your attention away from your everyday work, for instance. Related to these words are the adjective *diverse*, meaning 'varied', and its noun *diversity*.

This leads to the idea of 'change'. A *version* of something is that thing with some changes made to it. Most of the meanings of *convert* and *convertible* have the idea of change. A *convert* is someone who has changed to a new religion or set of beliefs. You

can *convert* your pounds into francs at a bank. If two people exchange ideas or small talk, they *converse* or have *a conversation*.

Other common words using this root are: *controversy, conversant, incontrovertible, inverse, irreversible, subversive, traverse*.

Words from volt, volv, volut. The basic meanings here are 'roll, turn'. The bindweed plant gets its other name, *convolvulus*, from its winding and twisted growth.

The 'rolling' or 'turning back' in words such as *revolve*, *revolt*, and *revolution* can be of different sorts. With the first it is usually physical – records *revolve* on a turntable. But it can be figurative: *The story revolves around two characters*. *Revolt* and *revolution* often have the idea of political or social turnarounds. The verb *revolt* and its derivatives have the extra sense of 'turning away in disgust': *Soggy cornflakes are revolting*.

PREFIXES: SELECTED CASE STUDIES

It is usually easy to identify prefixes. But as you will notice in the chart beginning opposite, their final consonant often 'adjusts itself' to be more like the sound that comes after it. Prefixes ending in *-d* and *-n* are the most susceptible to variation.

Here are a few detailed case studies of prefixes and the words that use them.

Words with ad-. The *ad-* prefix is primarily a Latin preposition meaning 'to, near, at'; it is distantly related to the English word *at*. Even in Latin it was much used as a prefix.

Its oldest meaning remains clear in some words. *Adjacent* means 'lying by or near'. *Adhere* means 'to stick to', whether it is a stamp sticking to an envelope or people sticking to their principles.

If you *adapt* yourself to prevailing conditions you 'adjust to' them. Not long ago in English *admire* meant only 'to wonder at, be surprised at'. (The root *mir* occurs in words like *miracle*.) Now *admire* usually means 'to have great esteem for'.

Two things that are in *accord* are the same 'at heart'. So the noun *accord* has come to mean 'agreement, harmony', and the verb means 'to agree or be in harmony with'. It has gained the secondary meaning of 'to treat in agreement with what is right and proper'. You can, for instance, *accord* someone a fine welcome.

PREFIXES: ELEMENTS THAT GO IN FRONT

The word *prefix* itself provides a good example of a prefix and how prefixes work. *Prefix* is made up of the prefix *pre-*, meaning 'before', and the root *fix*, 'to join or fix'. So a prefix is a word element joined on or fixed at the beginning of a word. Prefixes fall into a number of distinct groups:

☐ Latin (and occasionally Greek) prepositions: *ad*jacent, *extra*ordinary, *meta*bolism.

☐ Negative prefixes: *un*bending, *in*escapable, *mal*function, *non*committal, *mis*begotten.

☐ Prefixes that indicate number, degree, or amount: *ambi*dextrous (using *both* hands), *bi*centenary (*two*-hundredth anniversary), *semi*circle (*half*-circle).

☐ Ordinary English words, of whatever origin, whose meanings remain unchanged in compound words: *extra*-special, *over*weight, *under*water, *back*stroke.

Prefixes marked * in the following chart are explained in more detail in the main text opposite and on pages 158 and 159.

Prefix	Language of Origin	Meaning in English	Examples
a-	Greek	not, without	amoral, ahistorical, asexual
ab-, abs-, a-	Latin	off, away, from	abdicate, abduct, abhor, abnormal, abort, absent, absolve, abstain, abuse
*ad-	Latin	to, near, at	adapt, adjacent, admire, adopt, abbreviate, accord, affair, aggravate, alleviate, annex, appear, arrive, associate, attend
ambi-	Latin	both, around	ambiguous, ambitious, ambivalent
an-	Greek	not, lacking	anaesthetic, anaemic, anaerobic
ante-	Latin	before	antecedent, antedate, antenatal, anteroom
anti-	Greek	against, opposed to	antibiotic, anticlimax, anticlockwise, antidote, antipathy, antiseptic
bi-	Latin	twice, double	bicycle, bigamy, bilateral, bilingual, binoculars
cata-	Greek	down, off, away	cataract, catacombs, cataclysm, catarrh
circum-	Latin	around, on all sides	circumnavigate, circumlocution, circumspect, circumstance, circumvent
cis-	Latin	on this side	cislunar, cisalpine
*com-	Latin	with, together, thoroughly	combat, combine, compatriot, concede, coexist, cohere, colleague, collide, confide, congregate, correspond
contra-, counter-	Latin	against, opposite	contraband, contradict, contravene, counterattack, counterfeit
*de-	Latin	away, off, less	debar, debase, declare, defend, dehumidify, decipher, decline, demote, descend
deca-, dec-	Greek	ten	decade, decagon, Decalogue, decennial
deci-	Latin	a tenth	decibel, decimal, decimate

→

Prefix	Language of Origin	Meaning in English	Examples
demi-	Latin	a half	demigod, demilune, demitasse
di-	Greek	two, twice	dioxide, diphthong
dia-, di-	Greek	through, across, apart	diachronic, diagonal, dialysis, diaphragm, dialogue
dis-, dif-, di-	Latin	not, down, less, away	disable, discount, disarm, dissolve, dishonest, dissuade, different, diffuse, digress
epi-	Greek	on, over	epicentre, epidermis, epiglottis, epigram
ex-, e-, ef-	Latin	out of, from, former	exclude, exhume, exit, exhale, extort, effervescent, emit, evade, ex-president
extra-	Latin	more, outside	extraordinary, extracurricular, extraterrestrial
for-	Old English	completely, prohibited	forlorn, forspent, forswear, forbid
fore-	Old English	front, before	forehead, foreground, forecast, foresight
hecto-, hect-	Greek	hundred	hectare, hectogram
hepta-, hept-	Greek	seven	heptagon, heptameter
hexa-, hex-	Greek	six	hexapod, hexagram
*hyper-	Greek	over, too much	hyperactive, hypercorrect, hypersensitive
*hypo-, hyp-	Greek	under, less than, too little	hypodermic, hypochondria, hypothermia, hypothetical, hypotenuse
in-, en-, em-	Latin	in, into, inside	incarnate, income, embrace, enclose
in-, il-, im-, ir-	Latin	not	inactive, illiterate, impossible, irresistible
inter-	Latin	among, between, with each other	interbreed, interfere, interject, interlude, intercept, international
intra-, intro-	Latin	inside, within, inwards	intravenous, intramural, introduce, introverted
kilo-	Greek	thousand	kilometre, kilogram
mega-	Greek	large, a million	megaphone, megalith, megawatt, megahertz
meta-, met-	Greek	behind, after, changing	metacarpal, metazoan, metabolism, metamorphosis, metonymy
milli-	Latin	thousand	millibar, millisecond
mis-	Latin	badly, wrong	misrepresent, misspell, mistake, misanthrope
mono-	Latin	one	monomania, monocle, monochrome, monorail, monotonous, monopoly
multi-	Latin	many, much	multifarious, multiple, multifaceted
non-	Latin	not	nonchalant, nonconformist, nonentity, nonsense, non-toxic

Prefix	Language of Origin	Meaning in English	Examples
*ob-, oc-, of-, op-	Latin	towards, over, against, utterly	obese, object, obtrude, obtuse, occupy, offend, oppress, opportunity
octo-, oct-	Latin	eight	octopus, octane, octet, octuple
penta-, pent-	Greek	five	pentacle, pentagon, Pentateuch
*per-	Latin	through, by, by means of, utterly, badly	perambulator, percolate, perennial, pervade, percussion, perfect, persist, perjure, perfidious, pernicious, perdition
poly-	Greek	much, many	polygamy, polytechnic, polygon, polythene
post-	Latin	after, behind	postwar, post meridiem (p.m.), postpone
pre-	Latin	before	preface, precaution, prefabricated, precept
pro-	Latin	for, in place of, before, forwards	proceed, progress, pronoun, produce, profane, profess, provide, procure, project
quadri-, quadr-	Latin	four	quadrilateral, quadrangle, quadrant, quadrille
quasi-	Latin	like, as if	quasi-intellectual
re-	Latin	back, again, utterly	recall, refresh, rebuff, rebel, refrigerate, revise, reinforce, remind, revile
retro-	Latin	backwards	retrograde, retrospection
se-	Latin	aside, apart, away, without	separate, select, secure, secede, seduce, sedition, segregate
semi-	Latin	half	semiconductor, semidetached, semitone
septi-, sept-	Latin	seven	septuagenarian, Septuagint
sex-	Latin	six	sextant, sextile, sextuple
*sub-, suc-, suf-, sug-, sum-	Latin	under, almost, secondary	submarine, submit, subordinate, succumb, suffer, suggest, summon, support, surrogate, suspect, sustain
super-, sur-	Latin	above, on, beyond, too much	superhuman, supernatural, superficial, supercilious, surcharge, surcoat, surtax
tetra-, tetr-	Greek	four	tetrachloride, tetrahedron, tetrameter
trans-	Latin	across, beyond	translate, transform, transgress, transparent
tri-	Greek	three	trio, triad, triangle, triplicate
ultra-	Latin	beyond, too much	ultraconservative, ultraviolet
*un-	Old English	not, back	unhappy, uncouth, unbend, untie
under-	Old English	beneath; too little	underwear, underwater, underpay, underrepresented, underweight
uni-, un-	Latin	one, single	unicycle, unanimous, universe, unity

The Building Blocks Of Good English

If you *associate* with someone you 'join yourself to' that person. Or you can *associate* things mentally, such as Easter and daffodils. Business *associates* are joined together by common interests.

Words with com-. This prefix has two distinct meanings. First, it can mean 'with' or 'together', as in *combine, compatriot, coexist*, and *cohere*. But it was also used as an 'intensifier' to give the idea of 'very, thoroughly'.

Using the meaning 'with' or 'together' are: *collaborate*, to work with; *combat*, literally, to strike with or against; *compact*, pressed together; *compassion*, that is, fellow feeling; *compose*, to put together or arrange; *congregate*, literally, to form a crowd together; and *correspond*, literally, to answer to, as when two stories *correspond*.

The intensifier use turns up in: *compel*, to push thoroughly, and so to force someone to do something; *complete*, totally full; *commotion*, extreme movement or intense uproar; and *consume*, literally, to take up completely.

Words with de-. Like others, the prefix *de-* has several different meanings. Its most basic sense is 'away, off'. You can see this meaning in the words *debar*, to shut out or away; *defend*, to ward off danger or attack; and *defer*, to put off or delay.

It can also mean 'less' or 'down', as in *decline*, to bend or sink downwards, both literally, as of one's head, and of things like health; *demote*, to move down, especially in status; and of course *descend* and *decrease*.

The other common function of *de-* is to show the reverse of an action, that is, the opposite or undoing of the action. Hence, *depreciate*, the opposite of *appreciate; decipher*, literally, to take out of code; *deform*, to spoil the shape of; *dehumidify*, to take the humidity out of; and *depopulated*, used to describe a region when part of the population has moved away.

Words with hyper- and hypo-. The basic meaning of this pair are: *hyper-*, too much; *hypo-*, under.

They are perhaps the most confusing pair of prefixes in English. For example, *hyperthermia* is an unusually high temperature or fever, while *hypothermia* means quite the opposite – an abnormally low body temperature, usually as a result of exposure to cold. Unless you make a special effort to pronounce the latter with a clear / ō /, the two words sound the same!

Hyper- means 'too much, excessively': *hyperactive, hypercorrect* (used, for instance, of a person who pronounces the *-k-* in *asked*), and *hyperbole*, an exaggeration used for rhetorical effect.

The meanings of *hypo-* are more difficult to define. It often suggests 'under' or 'beneath', as in *hypodermic*, 'under the skin': *a hypodermic injection*. But the commonest words using *hypo-* have moved a long way from this meaning. The *hypotenuse* of a right-angled triangle is the line 'under' or opposite the right angle. *Hypochondria*, morbid anxiety about one's health, comes from the belief that the seat of fear in the body was under the breastbone. A *hypothesis* is a belief that 'underlies' a line of thought, that is, a reasoned guess.

Words with ob-, oc-, of-, op-. It is often difficult to recognise *ob-* as a prefix because of its variants and its lack of consistent meaning.

The 'towards' or 'against' meaning can be seen in words such as *obtrude*, literally, to thrust towards, and so to force an opinion 'upon others'. *Object* contains the idea of throwing against. From this comes the meaning 'to criticise, oppose', as when you *object* to someone's behaviour or to a statement. An *object*, a thing, was originally something thrown in the way and thus something tangible, or a goal or purpose.

An easier etymology is that for *opportunity*. An *opportune* wind was one that blew you towards the port, and thus a favourable one.

Ob- can also act as an intensifier. This comes out in *obnoxious*, 'thoroughly poisonous'; *oppress*, 'to press or lie heavily upon'; *obtain*, 'to take (firm) hold of'; and *obdurate*, 'thoroughly hardened', and so 'hardened against persuasion, unyielding; hardhearted or pig-headed'.

Words with per-. The basic meaning of *per-* is 'through'. If you *perambulate* the grounds of a stately home, you walk around or through them. The root here is *ambul*, from which English gets *amble* and *ambulance*. A *perambulator* will help you when walking around with your baby.

Other 'through' words using *per-* include *percolate, persist, pervade*, and *persevere*.

There are also many words using *per-* with the sense of 'badly'. In some a sense of 'completely' and 'badly' often blend. If you *perjure* yourself, you 'swear wrongly'. If someone's influence is *pernicious*, it is thoroughly destructive and harmful. If you are *perfidious* – as Albion (England) is reputed to be by certain other nations – no one can trust you because of your bad faith. Sin leads to *perdition* or eternal damnation.

Words with *sub-*, *suc-*, *suf-*, *sug-*, *sum-*. The 'under' meaning of *sub-* is most obvious in words such as *submarine*, which can be both an adjective and a noun; *subcutaneous*, 'situated or applied beneath the skin'; and *subterranean*, underground.

More figuratively, it turns up in *subconscious*, 'below the level of normal conscious thought'; *support*, 'to carry from beneath, to hold up or give strength to'; and *subsidy*, money that 'sits under' something, and so a grant to support it.

If you *submit* to something, you 'send yourself under' it; in other words, you allow it to have power over you. Something that *substantiates* what you say 'stands under' it and backs it up. If you *suffer* from something, you 'undergo' it.

Sub- can also indicate that something is 'secondary', or 'subordinate'. *Subordinate* itself means 'below in rank or order' and so 'less important'. Something that is *substandard* is not up to scratch.

A *sub-four-minute mile* is run in 'under' or 'less than' four minutes. A person who is *subhuman* is 'less than' or no better than an animal.

Words with *un-*. People tend to think that *un-* is solely a negative prefix. It is, of course, often used as such. And unlike most of the other negative prefixes it can be added to just about any adjective. If you want to make up a word to say that a picture is 'not pretty', the word has to be *unpretty*. *Impretty* or *mispretty* simply will not do.

There are, however, plenty of *un-* adjectives that have no matching positive form. You can have fun making up words like *kempt* and *couth*. Is a greatly praised person a *sung* hero?

Before verbs, on the other hand, *un-* generally conveys the idea of reversing the action of the verb. In this it resembles the *de-* prefix. To *unbend* is not 'not to bend' but 'to straighten up after being bent'. Other words of this type are *untie* and *unwrap*.

SOME COMMON COMBINING FORMS

Most words using combining forms were coined deliberately and consciously, with a view to being 'transparent' in meaning – at least to those with a classical education and the right technical back-ground. Here are some details of various combining forms, with a discussion of the words made with them. (See also the chart, pages 160-162.)

Words using *bene-*, *benign-*. Like its opposite *male-* (bad), *bene-* (good, well) is simply a Latin adverb used to modify the meanings of words. A *benediction* is a 'good speaking', particularly a blessing in church. A *benefactor* is a 'do-gooder', though without negative connotations; it is most often used to mean a 'patron'. The person who receives the *benevolence* of a benefactor is a *beneficiary*. People who inherit are *beneficiaries* of a will. *Beneficial* means 'doing good', in the way that fresh air *benefits* your health.

A related form, *benign-*, meant originally 'well-born' or 'noble'. It now turns up in words meaning 'kind, friendly', such as *benign* and *benignant*. You can compare the change in meaning of the word *gentle*, which also started off meaning 'noble', as in *gentleman* and *of gentle birth*.

Words using *-logy*, *-ology*. The common combining form *-logy* (meaning 'study, knowledge') and its derivatives, *-loger* and *-logist*, are ultimately from a Greek word *logos*, 'word, speech'. A related form turns up as the root in words such as *monologue* and *prologue*. An *apology* is a speech in defence.

Knowledge and 'word' are closely related in the Bible. Saint John's Gospel begins as follows: 'In the beginning was the Word'. This is the Greek *logos*, but in Greek philosophical terms it meant 'reason' or 'intelligence'.

Not all *-logy* words mean 'the study of something'. Most do – *palaeontology*, *zoology*, *anthropology* – but others suggest 'speech' or 'expression'. *Phraseology* is a good example.

Words using *omni-*. An all-powerful ruler is *omnipotent*. An all-knowing god is *omniscient*. An animal that eats both meat and plant foods is said to be *omnivorous*.

The modern word *bus* is a contraction of *omnibus*, which in Latin means 'for all, for everybody'. That is, a *bus* is not a private vehicle: everyone may use it.

Words using *pan-*. The Greek equivalent of *omni-* is *pan-* (all, everywhere). It usually occurs in more technical words than its Latin counterpart. A *panacea* is a 'cure-all', a medicine or policy that will solve all problems. A *pandemic* is an extremely wide-ranging epidemic. *Pantheism* is the belief that God can be found everywhere and in everything.

COMBINING FORMS: BUILDING BLOCKS OF NEW WORDS

Combining forms are word elements that can be used to form new words by combining them with words that already exist, other combining forms, or various affixes – elements such as *pseudo-* in *pseudonym*, *hypno-* in *hypnosis*, or *-logy* in *zoology*.

Unlike many roots and affixes, combining forms usually have a single form and a clear, consistent meaning. This is because most are fairly recent in the language, and many are technical and therefore less susceptible to change in day-to-day use.

Most combining forms come from Greek or Latin – in some cases, from Greek via Latin. Many combining forms turn up also as roots, and some might be viewed as prefixes or suffixes. (Most forms expressing number or amount are listed in the chart of prefixes.) Once again, entries marked * are discussed in greater detail in the main text.

Combining form	Language of Origin	Meaning in English	Examples
aer-, aero-	Latin	air, atmosphere	aerobic, aerodynamic, aerofoil, aerial
agro-, agr-	Latin	field, farmer	agriculture, agrarian, agrochemical
-algia, -alg-	Greek	pain	neuralgia, analgesic
Anglo-	Latin	England	Anglo-French, Anglo-Saxon, anglophile
archae-	Greek	ancient	archaeology, archaeopteryx
arch-, archi-	Greek	first, main	archangel, archbishop, archetype, architect
-arch; -archy	Greek	ruler; form of government	matriarchy, monarch, oligarchy, patriarch
astro-	Latin	star	astronaut, astronomy, astrology
aut-, auto-	Greek	self	autocrat, autograph, automatic, automobile
*bene-; benign-	Latin	well, good; kind	benediction, benefactor, beneficial, benefit, benevolent, benign
biblio-	Greek	book	bibliography, bibliophile, Bible
bio-	Greek	life	biography, biology
calc-, calci-	Latin	chalk, pebble	calcite, calciferous, calculus, calculate
cent-	Latin	a hundred	centipede, century, centimetre
centr-	Latin	middle	centrifuge, centrobaric, centralise
chrom-	Greek	colour	chrome, chromatic, chromosome
chron-, chrono-	Greek	time, age	chronic, chronology, chronometer, synchronic, synchronise
-cide	Latin	kill, killer	suicide, regicide, insecticide, genocide
cosmo-	Greek	world, universe	cosmology, cosmopolitan, cosmic
-crat; -cracy	Greek	ruler; form of government	democrat, autocrat; bureaucracy, technocracy

Combining form	Language of Origin	Meaning in English	Examples
crypto-	Greek	hidden, secret	cryptogram, cryptic, crypto-fascist
dys-	Greek	bad	dysentery, dyslexia, dyspeptic
ecto-	Greek	external	ectoderm, ectoplasm
ego-	Latin	I, self	egotism, egocentric, ego-trip
endo-	Greek	inside	endogamy, endocrine, endodermis
equ-, equi-	Latin	equal	equable, equator, equilibrium, equivocal
ethno-	Greek	race, people	ethnology, ethnocentric, ethnic
eu-	Greek	good	euphonium, euphemism, eugenics
ferro-	Latin	iron	ferroconcrete, ferromagnetic
geo-	Greek	the Earth	geocentric, geography, geometry
-gram	Latin	writing	diagram, telegram
-graph-	Greek	draw, write	biography, graphic, graphite
gyro-	Greek	circle	gyroscope, gyrocompass
helio-	Greek	sun	heliotrope, heliocentric
hetero-	Greek	different	heterogeneous, heterosexual
haem-, hem-	Greek	blood	haemoglobin, haematite, haemorrhoids, haemophilia, haemorrhage
homo-	Latin	same, equal	homogeneous, homosexuality
hydro-	Greek	water	hydroelectric, hydrofoil, hydraulic, dehydrate
hypno-, hypn-	Greek	sleep	hypnosis, hypnotic, hypnotherapy
-itis	Greek	inflammation	appendicitis, meningitis
iso-	Greek	equal, alike	isobar, isotherm, isomer
lacto-, lact-	Latin	milk	lactoprotein, lactose, lactic
lign-	Latin	wood	lignite, lignocellulose, ligneous
litho-	Greek	stone	lithograph, lithosphere, monolith
*-logy, -ology	Greek	study, science, knowledge	zoology, phonology, phraseology
macro-, macr-	Greek	large, long	macrocosm, macrobiotic, macroscopic
mal-, male-	Latin	bad, badly	maladroit, maladministration, malignant, malediction, malevolent
meso-	Greek	middle	mesomorphic, Mesopotamia, Mesozoic
meteor-	Greek	weather, atmosphere	meteorology, meteorite, meteoric

The Building Blocks Of Good English

→

Combining form	Language of Origin	Meaning in English	Examples
-meter	Greek	measuring device	barometer, metre, metricate
micro-	Greek	small	microscope, micrometer, microdot
mid-	Old English	middle	midnight, midriff, midwinter
-monger	Old English	seller, dealer	fishmonger, gossipmonger, costermonger
-morph	Greek	shape	morphology, amorphous
neo-	Greek	new	neologism, neo-Nazi, Neolithic
neuro-, neur-	Greek	nerve	neurosurgeon, neuralgia, neuron
*omni-	Latin	all, utterly	omnipotent, omnivorous, omnibus
ortho-	Greek	straight, correct	orthopaedics, orthography, orthodox
-osis	Greek	process; disease	metamorphosis, osmosis; tuberculosis, neurosis
palaeo-, paleo-	Greek	old, ancient	palaeontology, palaeography, palaeolithic
*pan-	Greek	all, everywhere	panacea, pantheism, Pan-African
-pathy, -path	Greek	disease, feeling	antipathy, psychopath, sympathy, pathological, pathology
petro-, petr-	Latin	stone	petrify, petroleum, petrology
-phobia, -phobe, -phobic	Greek	fear, aversion	claustrophobic, agoraphobe, xenophobia
phon-, phono-	Greek	sound	phonograph, phonetics, telephone, stereophonic, anglophone
photo-	Greek	light	photograph, photoelectric
pseudo-, pseud-	Greek	false	pseudonym, pseudo-intellectual
-stat	Greek	regulator	thermostat, rheostat
stereo-	Greek	solid, 3D	stereobate, stereophonic, stereoscopic
*syn-, sym-, syl-	Greek	together, same	synchronise, synagogue, syndicate, syllable, sympathy, symphony, system
tele-, tel-	Greek	far, long-distance	telephone, telepathy, telecommunications
thermo-	Greek	heat	thermometer, thermodynamics
topo-	Greek	place	topography, toponym
-trope, -tropic	Greek	direction, version, change	heliotrope, phototropic, tropic, troposphere
zoo-	Greek	animal	zoological, zoomorphic

Like many combining forms, *pan-* can be used almost at will to create new words in the right conditions. It is now generally used with a geographical sense, as in *the Pan-African Congress* and *the Pan-American Games*.

Words using *syn-*. The Greek *syn-*, like the Latin *com-*, means 'together'. Like many initial combining forms and prefixes, it may change slightly in form depending on what letter follows it.

As *syn-* it appears in *synchronise*, 'to make-together-time'; *synonym*, a 'together-name'; *synthesis*, a 'bringing together of parts to make a whole'; and *synagogue*, the place where Jews come together to worship. A *syndrome* is a 'running-together'. The word refers to a set of symptoms or effects that usually occur together and are characteristic of a disease or condition.

Before an *-l* the form changes to *syl-*. A *syllable* is a sound 'taken together'. Before a *-p* or *-m* the form becomes *sym-*. A *symposium* was originally a 'drinking together' or 'party'. Socrates, according to Plato, used one such party to collect, and criticise, his colleagues' ideas about love. Hence any serious round-table discussion is called a *symposium*. In a *symphony* the sounds should match 'together'. If you show *sympathy* for people you 'feel together' with them, or share their feelings.

Other *syn-* words include: *syntax, syndicate, synod, synopsis, synthetic, syllogism*, and *symmetrical*.

SUFFIXES: INCONSPICUOUS ENDINGS

Suffixes are of various types: they may create diminutives (such as *-let* in *booklet*), nouns (such as *-ism* in *communism*, or *-ist* in *communist*), verbs (such as *-ise* or *-ize* as in *hospitalise*, or *-ify* as in *electrify*), or adjectives and adverbs (*-ful* in *peaceful*, or *-ly* in *gladly*).

Suffixes are probably the simplest and least problematic of word elements. They feel so natural that people often fail to recognise them as separate components. Consider these inconspicuous and extremely common suffixes:

-al as in *burial*	*-ism* as in *heroism*
-ant as in *deodorant*	*-ist* as in *pianist*
-en as in *brighten*	*-less* as in *countless*
-er as in *baker*	*-ly* as in *friendly*
-ful as in *sinful*	*-ment* as in *excitement*
-hood as in *childhood*	*-ness* as in *kindness*
-ic, -ical as in *ironic/al*	*-ous* as in *joyous*
-ion as in *action*	*-ship* as in *friendship*
-ish as in *boyish*	*-ty* as in *novelty*
-ise as in *harmonise*	*-y* as in *risky*

A chart of the more unusual and interesting suffixes appears overleaf.

Suffixes are not particularly versatile: the suffixes in *fretful* and *feckless*, for example, cannot be switched. Only in jest could you speak of *a fretless and feckful young man*.

The Building Blocks Of Good English

DIMINUTIVES IN DISGUISE

Not all diminutives are obvious. The word *molecule*, for example, is a diminutive, derived ultimately from the Latin *moles*, mass, bulk, with the suffix *-cule*, indicating smallness.

☐ To fill the gap in each sentence below, choose a word with a diminutive suffix – such as *-ule*, *-et*, *-kin*, and *-let*. It may take a moment's thought to recognise the suffix and identify the correct answer. Check your findings by turning to pages 633-648.

1. Sprinkle a few . . . . . . of sugar on to each biscuit.

2. The fans wore scarves and . . . . . . in team colours.

3. We had to practise with a . . . . . . at our life-drawing classes.

4. A knight whose title passes on to his eldest son is called a . . . . . .

5. From the expensive . . . . . . on her lap, Lady Windermere drew the fateful letter.

6. The newcomers treated the locals as a lot of ignorant . . . . . .

7. My last manager ordered her second-in-command about like a menial . . . . . .

8. The dancer's . . . . . . flashed and jangled on her wrists.

9. This tough old hen was sold to us as a 'tender, young . . . . . .'!

10. Oxygen is carried around the body by the red blood . . . . . .

SUFFIXES: ENDINGS THAT MODIFY MEANING

Suffixes are often 'piled up', one after the other. Take the word *realistically*. You have to go back to Latin for the root *re-*, which meant 'a thing' (as opposed to an idea). Latin also had the word *realis*, meaning 'real' or 'actual'. The same *-al* suffix, making an adjective from a noun, turns up in words such as *national* and *comical*. Further suffixes have then been added:

☐ *-ist*, denoting a person connected with something, as in *communist*

☐ *-ic*, turning a noun into an adjective meaning 'typical of someone or something', as in *Gaelic* or *tragic*

☐ *-al*, again; with little added meaning, as with *problematic* and *problematical*

☐ *-ly*, turning an adjective into an adverb, as in *happily* or *possibly*

Many long words in English are little more than simple words with suffixes tacked on.

Suffix	Language of Origin	Part of Speech	Meaning	Examples
-able, -ible	Latin	adjective	indicates that something is capable of, inclined to, or causing	audible, uncountable, terrible, peaceable
-acity	Latin	noun	indicates a quality or state of being	audacity, capacity
-cle, -cule, -ule	Latin	noun	indicates small size	particle, molecule
-ee	Latin	noun	indicates the recipient of an action, or someone in a particular state	licensee, addressee, escapee, employee
-ess	Greek	noun	indicates a female	hostess, lioness
-et, -ette, -let	Old French	noun	indicates smallness or lesser status	islet, cigarette, maisonette, booklet
-fy, -ify	Latin	verb	indicates making or becoming	electrify, gratify, pacify, falsify
-kin	Old English	noun	indicates small size	bodkin, catkin, lambkin
-ling	Old English	noun	indicates smallness or lesser status	darling, duckling, fledgling, seedling, hireling
-most	Old English	adjective	indicates the superlative degree	uppermost, hindmost
-oid	Greek	adjective	indicates resemblance	ovoid, humanoid
-some	Old English	adjective	indicates a tendency	meddlesome, awesome
-trix	Latin	noun	indicates a female	aviatrix, executrix
-tude	Latin	noun	indicates a condition or state of being	exactitude, longitude
-wise	Old English	adverb	indicates manner or direction, or reference to	clockwise, taxwise
-y, -ie, -ee	Latin	noun	indicates smallness	Mummy, Johnnie

Mastering Grammar

*Before the serjeant begins to teach young soldiers
their exercise of the musket, he explains to them
the different parts of it; the butt, the stock, the
barrel, the loops, the swivels, and so on; because,
unless they know these by their names, they cannot
know how to obey his instructions ... This species
of preliminary knowledge is absolutely necessary
in all ... callings of life; but not more necessary
than it is for you to learn ... how to know the sorts
of words one from another.*
–William Cobbett, in a letter to his son, 1823

WHAT WAS true in Cobbett's day remains true now. Engineering students are expected to know their arithmetic, music students to have practised their scales. No one can write good letters, memorandums, or reports, or master word processing, let alone literary composition, without having first learned the basics of grammar. 'Today,' according to the columnist Simon Jenkins, now editor of *The Times*, 'not to understand the structure of a sentence is an overwhelming obstacle in the way of most gainful employment ...'

Many people find grammar a bore, because it reminds them of the schoolroom. But understanding grammar will in some ways free you from its grip, making you the master of words rather than keeping you as their slave.

The grammar of words is the way they change (*one dog, two dogs*) or order themselves (*the big house*, **X** *the house big*) when used together. Obviously learning to speak or write would be very difficult if every word had its own ways of behaving. Fortunately, there are general patterns, called 'rules' of grammar. These can be *descriptive*, describing what happens in fact, and based on how people actually speak and write; and *prescriptive*, setting out how, in the opinion of experts and authorities, people ought to speak or write. So: it is a descriptive rule of general English grammar that the past tense of *hangs* is *hung* – that is the way most people use the word; it is a prescriptive rule that *hung* should be *hanged* when the verb means 'to kill by hanging

by the neck'. Purist grammarians make this distinction; many educated users of Standard English do not.

There are two major problems in learning grammar. One is the problem of the 'phoney' rules of many purists. These rules include some of the best-known 'rules' of English grammar – rules like 'Don't end a sentence with a preposition' (in fact, it is often perfectly acceptable to do so – see page 209), or 'Say *It is I*, not *It is me*' (see page 183).

The other is the problem of ever-changing rules. Grammar rules are not laid down once and for all. They evolve. You no longer use *thee* and *ye* in everyday language. You no longer say *thou art* or *mine eyes* or *it raineth*. If language did not develop, people in Britain might still be speaking the Middle English of Chaucer, or something even older.

Perhaps you worry about some usages that you often hear or read. What about *my husband and I*? Or *Come quick*? Or *Everybody must bring their own sandwiches*? Or *There were less people than I expected*? Are these perhaps examples of genuine new trends? Or are they careless and ungrammatical? And what about problems such as when to use *who* and when to use *whom*?

This chapter gives advice on these and other problem areas in current English usage. But first a section defining the key terms and concepts of grammar – the different parts of speech and the structure of the English sentence.

165

GRAMMAR – A PRELIMINARY QUIZ

As an 'aptitude test' for English grammar, this quiz appears at the start of the chapter rather than at the end. Why not try your hand at it at once? (If you feel uneasy about it, you can return to it later instead, once you have read the chapter through.)

☐ Which is the preferable form in each sentence below? For the answers, turn to the quiz answers section at the back of the book, pages 633-648.

1. There were fewer/less spectators than expected.

2. The results of this complicated lawsuit remain/remains to be seen.

3. The city of Dresden, which/that was virtually burnt to the ground during the war, now flourishes again.

4. I don't suppose that either of them care/cares one way or another.

5. That is one of those setbacks that really is/are unavoidable.

6. The chairman, together with his two young daughters, have/has accepted our invitation.

7. The Cabinet has/have all been sworn to secrecy.

8. All those/Everyone present should pay their subscriptions on the way out.

9. Every man, woman, and child were/was rescued.

10. Neither fire nor flood is/are ever likely to deter him.

11. They had a dreadful row, and between you and me/I, his wife has now walked out on him.

12. The audience gave my wife and I/me a standing ovation.

13. Pierre challenged the directors, who/whom he regarded as incompetent to run the company.

14. Please would you allow Joe and I/me to escort you home.

15. Who/Whom do you think is going to win?

16. Who/Whom do you consider most likely to win?

17. They pleaded with whomever/whoever was within hailing distance.

18. I hope you don't mind my/me dropping in like this.

19. It's unfair to expect us/we public figures to know all the answers.

20. Isn't that the same man as/that she was dancing with last night?

21. Ruth Ellis was the last woman hanged/hung in Britain.

22. Workmen lay/laid the tarpaulin down on the grass.

23. She shrunk/shrank back in horror.

24. Nobody dare/dares stand up to her.

25. I shall/will find an answer, if it's the last thing I do.

26. I would/should go and pick a fight with a karate expert!

27. If I were/was younger, I'd be happy to take the risk.

28. Glamorgan may/might have won the match had they not gone and dropped three catches.

29. They asked if I was/were prepared to reconsider.

30. He will likely/probably call again on Thursday.

31. The water in the basin has frozen solidly/solid during the night.

32. It's one of the most unusual/unique game parks in Africa.

33. You can phone direct/directly to Moscow.

34. Regrettably/Regretfully, your application has been refused.

Grammar: The Rudiments

Words are classified according to their 'parts of speech' – that is, the part they play in a sentence. Most modern grammarians list nine different parts of speech. They are:

nouns – *horse, milk, damnation, Monday, Jack*
verbs – *go, contemplate, be, must*
adjectives – *happy, enthusiastic, awake*
adverbs – *sadly, soon, very, however*
pronouns – *I, she, everyone, yourself*
determiners – *a, the, my, every, any*
prepositions – *in, of, opposite, regarding*
conjunctions – *and, or, while, if, that*
interjections – *Oh!, Well!, Alas!*

WHAT IS A NOUN?

The most typical nouns are the names of people, things, and substances, such as *Peter, house, girl*, and *milk*. Sometimes, the thing described has no solidity, shape, or dimensions: words such as *existence, thought, happiness*, and even *sake*, as in *for my sake*, refer to abstract qualities, and so are called 'abstract' nouns.

Typically, nouns:

☐ can be used with *the* in front of them: *the house, the lightning, the absence*. Other similar words, known as 'determiners', also turn up only before nouns: for example *a, my, every* – see page 170.

☐ have different forms for the singular and plural – *a boy/two boys, the teaching/the teachings, goose/geese*.

☐ can be made possessive – *the dog's dinner, my children's teacher, grass's usefulness*.

☐ can serve as subjects of verbs (The *milk* came straight from the cow), as objects of verbs (I drank the *milk*), as complements of verbs (That seems to be *milk*), as complements of prepositions (There's a fly in the *milk*). See the panel, *Subject – verb – object*, alongside.

There are some exceptions:

Proper names. These are words like *John, London, Hinduism*, and *Telecom*, which do not normally take *the*. In most other respects they function like nouns, however – for example, as subjects of verbs (*John is silly*) – and can often be turned into common nouns when needed: *It's not like the Telecom that I used to work for*. Proper nouns are usually written with a capital, as are many common nouns, such as *Tuesday* and *June: We'll see him on Tuesday; It happened two Junes ago*.

Uncountable nouns. These are nouns that have no plural form: **X** *lightnings*, **X** *informations*. They are often called 'mass' nouns, because they tend to name quantities of something rather than naming

---

SUBJECT – VERB – OBJECT

Most sentences in English start with the pattern Subject – Verb: *The cat sat . . . , I ate . . .*, and so on. The other constituents that can appear in sentences are:

Objects. The object is typically the person or thing that the verb 'acts' upon – *Dog bites man; I ate an ice cream*. The objects here are *man* and *ice cream*. Some verbs can have two objects, as in *They cooked me a dinner* and *You've saved me £5*. Traditionally, the object that could be introduced by *to* or *for* is called the indirect object; other objects are called direct objects. In the first example, the indirect object is *me*, since you can say *They cooked a dinner for me*. Indirect objects can also usually be dropped. So in the second example, *me* is again the indirect object, which can be left out without overdistorting the sentence: *You've saved £5*.

Complements. These complete or give further information about either the subject or the object. In both sets of examples below, the complements are *confused* and *king of England*. Subject complements are in a sense 'equal' to the subject, as in *Henry is confused* and *William became king of England*. Object complements are in a sense 'equal' to the object, as in *We got Henry confused* and *The barons made William king of England*.

Adverbials. These add further information, often showing how or where or when the verb 'happens', in the same way that an adverb does. For example, the phrases *with gusto, on Tuesday*, and *in Paris* in the following sentences: *He did it with gusto; I went there on Tuesday; Mary saw that picture in Paris*.

things that are regarded as units – compare the countable noun *facts* with the uncountable or mass noun *information*, for example. Countable and uncountable nouns differ in grammar: *I want a house*; *I want food*. Sometimes the grammar is necessary to show what the noun means: *I can see wood/a wood*. Uncountable *wood* is a substance obtained from trees and used to make furniture; countable *wood* is a group of trees.

When nouns are used like adjectives. Sometimes nouns are used to describe other nouns – rather like adjectives (see opposite). In the phrase *the Yorkshire child labour inquiry report scandal* all the words except *the* are nouns – *Yorkshire, child, labour, inquiry*, and *report* are used to describe *scandal*. (Not that you should use such inelegant strings of nouns freely: see page 32).

Similarly, in the phrases *Easter egg, love affair, and history book*, the first word is a noun each time. So adjectives and nouns share the property of being able to appear in the 'attributive' position before nouns: compare *fast car* (*fast* is an adjective) and *sports car* (*sports* is a noun).

WHAT IS A VERB?

Verbs are sometimes defined as 'doing' words – words that indicate what is being done in a sentence. But this is not always helpful. In the sentence *This is hard work*, presumably what is being done is work. But *work* here is a noun, whereas the verb is *is*.

Without doubt, the best test for a verb is this: does it have forms that indicate whether the action takes place now or at some time in the past? – *work/worked; take/took*. (But note that some do not actually change their form; for example, *spread/spread, hit/hit*.)

Most verbs fall into one of three categories. The first two types can exist on their own, and are called 'main' or 'lexical' verbs.

☐ 'doing' verbs (in a very wide sense), such as *approach, do, go, like*, and *want*. The verb tells you something about the activities of its subject: *Fred approached the fierce lion.*

☐ 'being' and 'becoming' verbs, which make some kind of equation between the subject and the complement that follows them. In a sense *John became manager* says 'John = manager'; *You sound bored* says 'You = bored'. 'Being' verbs

USEFUL TERMS THAT GO WITH VERBS

Verbs are the most complex and varied part of speech. Here are a few useful terms describing different types and parts of verbs and their various functions:

Finite/non-finite. A *finite* verb is one used in the normal way, usually with a subject and a tense – for example, *write* and *writes* in *I write, She writes*. When a verb lacks tense, it is *non-finite*. The non-finite forms are the *-ing* form (*sinking*), the past participle (*sunk*), and the infinitive (*sink*, in *It will sink*, or *to sink*, in *It seems to sink*).

Impersonal verbs. These are verbs that do not take true subjects, as in *It rained*. Many verbs can be used both personally and impersonally, such as *seems* in *Jack seems to be here* and *It seems Jack's here*.

The -ing form. This can be used like an adjective (*writing paper*) and in progressive tenses (*She was writing*): in both of these cases it is called the 'present participle'. It can also carry out noun-like functions (*Writing is fun*), in which case it is called a 'gerund'.

Passive/active voices. Generally, a verb or sentence in the *passive* voice is one in which the action of the verb is done to the subject: *The man was arrested; They were introduced yesterday*. A verb or sentence in the (more common) *active* voice is one in which the subject does the action: *Inspector Jones arrested the man; The priest introduced them yesterday*. Note that your style will be more vigorous if you keep mainly to the active voice; *Lineker scored a scorcher* is livelier and more immediate than *A scorcher was scored by Lineker* (see also page 47).

The past participle. This is the part of a verb, such as *written* or *arrived*, used to make perfect tenses – as in *I have written but the*

include *be, sound, seem*, and *represent* (as in *That represents a step in the right direction*); 'becoming' verbs include *get* (*bigger*), *grow* (*weary*), and *turn* (*nasty*).

☐ 'auxiliary' verbs, which do not exist on their own but as part of a verb phrase, as in *were* (*coming*), *has* (*said*), *do* (*know*), *might have been* (*killed*).

letter hasn't arrived – and in passives, as in *It was written in blood*.

Perfect forms. These are the verb forms consisting of *have* plus the past participle: *They've gone shopping* (present perfect); *I had already written to my MP* (past perfect or pluperfect). Note the difference between the present and past here: *They have mended the fence, and it looks better than ever* (the effect is still present and relevant); *They had mended the fence, but it fell down again* (the effect is no longer present or relevant).

Phrasal verbs. These are 'verbs' made up of a true verb plus one or more small words that change the meaning considerably. Just consider the difference between *He told me* and *He told me off; to tell off* is a phrasal verb.

Progressive forms. These are the verb forms consisting of *be* plus the *-ing* form – *He's sleeping, Joan was walking to work*, and so on. They indicate that something is happening over a limited stretch of time.

Reflexive verbs. These are verbs whose object and subject are the same thing or person, and so have *myself, itself*, or the like as an element. Some verbs are always reflexive: we may *pride ourselves on* something, but we cannot *pride* anything else. Other verbs may or may not be used reflexively: we can *enjoy ourselves* or *enjoy the concert*. The pronouns *myself, ourselves*, and so on used with reflexive verbs are duly known as reflexive pronouns.

Strong/weak verbs. *Weak* verbs make their past tense and past participle by adding *-(e)d* to the basic form, as in *I turn, I turned, I have turned*. By contrast, *strong* verbs change their inner form, as in *I draw, I drew, I have drawn*.

Subjunctive/indicative moods. Many languages, including French, have two parallel sets of tenses – distinguished as the *indicative*

and *subjunctive* moods. The indicative is used for discussing events, states, and facts. The subjunctive is used in certain grammatical patterns to discuss non-factual situations.

In English only a few distinct subjunctive forms survive:

☐ Present subjunctive. This uses the infinitive (minus *to*). It can appear in very formal contexts after words expressing some sort of proposal or command (*It is imperative that doctors be aware of this condition; He suggested that Cripps take the next flight home*), and in certain fixed phrases such as *God save the Queen* and *Far be it from me*.

☐ Past subjunctive. In spite of its name, this is generally used to talk about something hypothetical in the present or future. Its best-known use is the form *were* in, for example, *If I were you, I wish I were older*.

(For more on the subjunctive, see page 194.)

Transitive/intransitive. *Transitive* verbs take direct objects, or occur in the passive – *She hit me; I was hit* – whereas intransitive verbs take no direct object: *She vanished without trace*. Some verbs are fully transitive. You cannot just say **✗** *He scrutinised* or **✗** *He used* – one has to *scrutinise* or *use* something. But many verbs can be used transitively or intransitively. Compare *She always argues with me* (intransitive) and *She always argues her cases very clearly* (transitive).

(Note that American and British English often differ over the transitive and intransitive use of certain verbs. In both varieties, you can *write a letter* (transitive), but whereas in American English you can *write your Congressman* (direct object – transitive) to *protest a tax* (transitive), in British English you would *write to your MP* (indirect object – intransitive) to *protest against a tax* (intransitive).

WHAT IS AN ADJECTIVE?

Adjectives go with or 'qualify' or 'modify' nouns, and sometimes pronouns. They are often used to describe the thing that the noun refers to.

Adjectives tend to turn up in one of two places:

☐ before nouns in noun phrases, as in *elegant*

handwriting, lumpy gravy, and *the very idea*. This is the 'attributive' position.

☐ after 'being' verbs, as in *Clive's stupid, You became happy*, and *It sounds unlikely*. This is called the 'predicative' position. Here the adjective refers back to the subject – *stupid* describes *Clive, happy* describes *you, unlikely* describes *it*.

Most adjectives are 'gradable' – they can be 'more' or 'less'. You can, for instance, put *very* and similar words in front of many of them: *very funny, fairly interesting*. (Some adjectives are not really gradable – **??** *more unique* – or not gradable at all: **✗** *more atomic*. See page 202.)

Gradable adjectives have three levels of comparison: the basic adjective, the comparative, and the superlative. So, in *quiet, quieter, quietest* or *sympathetic, more sympathetic, most sympathetic*, the *-er* or *more* form is the comparative, and the *-est* or *most* form is the superlative. The comparative is used to compare two things: *Wendy's bigger than her sister*. The superlative is used for three or more – *Wendy's the biggest girl in the school*.

WHAT IS AN ADVERB?

Just as an adjective describes, or qualifies or modifies, a noun, so an adverb typically modifies a verb. It tells how, when, where, why, or how often an action takes place: *He plays well; Jane left sulkily; They arrived late; Don't sit there*. Adverbs share many of the features of adjectives, such as comparison – *tiredly, more tiredly, most tiredly*.

The most typical kind of adverb is derived from an adjective by adding *-ly*: *tiredly, sulkily*. But beware – many words ending in *-ly* are in fact adjectives: *friendly, lonely*, sometimes even *kindly*, as in *She is a kindly old soul*.

Adverbs are the ragbag of grammar: *only, so, even, quite, soon, here, specially, prettily, probably*, and *however* are adverbs, but grammatically they do not have a lot in common.

Adverbs can also modify adjectives and other adverbs, as in *a very unusual colour, only four men*, and *They came extremely quickly*. Sometimes, they appear 'outside' the normal structure of sentences, telling you something about the speaker's attitude towards the event reported: *Regrettably, we can't come; Perhaps they'll agree*. They can also be used when making a transition from one sentence to another: *Jane liked him a lot. I, however, know better – he's an absolute rotter*.

WHAT IS A PRONOUN?

Pronouns are nouns in disguise, and have almost exactly the same uses as nouns. For instance, you can replace the subject of the sentence *His girlfriend's called Julie* with the pronoun *she* – *She's called Julie*. But unlike nouns, pronouns almost always turn up on their own: they cannot usually have *the, a, all*, and the like in front of them.

There are several groups of pronouns, including:

☐ indefinite pronouns, ones that stand in place of an undefined person or thing: *anybody, something, no one*, and so on.

☐ reflexive pronouns, ones that reflect back on the noun or pronoun – such as *themselves* in *Only idiots talk to themselves*.

☐ demonstrative pronouns, ones that identify or point out the person/s or thing/s referred to – specially the words *this, that, these*, and *those* (when used independently rather than before a noun): *Of the colours available, I like these best, but my wife prefers those*.

☐ relative pronouns, ones that relate one part of a sentence to another – *who, whom, whose, which*, and so on: *Here is the chauffeur whom you hired yesterday*.

☐ personal pronouns, ones that indicate the speaker, the person/s spoken to, or the person or thing spoken about: *I, you, him, mine*.

Personal pronouns – the most important pronouns – retain the last vestiges of 'case' in English. Case governs the way in which the form of a word changes according to its function in a sentence.

Consider these two sentences:

Jim likes Anne.
Anne likes Jim.

Here it is the word order alone that enables you to know who is doing the liking and who is being liked. But if the names are replaced by personal pronouns you get:

He likes her.
She likes him.

Here it is not just the order but the form of the words that supplies the information. The form of the word as a subject (*he, she*) is called the subjective or nominative case; as an object (*him, her*) it is called the objective case. There is a third, possessive case (*mine, hers, ours*).

WHAT IS A DETERMINER?

Determiners are small words used before nouns to tell you which one, or how many, or whose, and so on. For example: *the* man; *a* schoolgirl; *all* people; *every* chance; *no* peace; *some* buttons; *any* information; *both* tigers; *your* friends; *their* money. What are now known as *determiners* were formerly sometimes (confusingly) included among adjectives since they turn up in front of nouns. But that is almost all they have in common with adjectives.

Many determiners look like pronouns. The word *that* in *That idea's daft* is a determiner because it comes before the noun, but in *That's daft* it is a pronoun because it is on its own as the subject of the sentence.

The two commonest determiners *the* and *a/an* are called 'articles'. *The* is the definite article; it refers to a defined thing or person *Bring me the chair* (the one definite or specific or only chair). *A/an* is the indefinite article; the object or person it refers to is not defined – *Bring me a chair* (any chair will do).

WHAT IS A PREPOSITION?

Prepositions are again mostly little words. They typically come in front of noun phrases and pronouns, and tell you something about place, time, reason, and so on. Examples are *on* the bus; *at* home; *opposite* the table; *until* Tuesday; *after* Christmas; *at* the weekend; *of* butter; *by* looking. Phrases of this sort are called prepositional phrases.

Some prepositions ('compound prepositions') are made up of more than one word: *in front of, because of, apart from, according to*. American English has a tendency to use such compound prepositions more than British English – *in back of* as well as *behind*, for instance.

WHAT IS A CONJUNCTION?

Conjunctions (*and, but, or, because, when, if*) are joining words. They can be of various kinds:

☐ 'coordinating' conjunctions, which join two things that are grammatically equal in the sentence: John *and* Jane, sink *or* swim, He came *but* he didn't stay.

☐ 'subordinating' conjunctions, which usually link clauses and show that one is grammatically more important than the other: He laughed *when* I told him; You're tired *because* you went to bed late; I'll do it only *if* you pay me.

☐ 'correlative' conjunctions, which indicate a parallel or mutual relationship between two

---

PREPOSITION OR ADVERB?

Prepositions are sometimes confused with adverbs. The word *in* is a preposition in *I was in the house*; it comes in front of the noun phrase *the house*. But *in* is an adverb in *I was in*; here, it modifies the verb.

The words *up* and *down* can similarly be used as prepositions and adverbs: *The ball rolled down* (adverb); *The ball rolled down the hill* (preposition).

Note that it is not correct in Standard English to fuse these two functions, and use *up* and *down* to mean 'to' or 'at':

??I'm going down the pub.
??She lives up that end of town.

These should read *down to the pub* and *up at that end of town*.

---

parts of a sentence: *both ... and ...; neither ... nor ...* (See also page 204.)

WHAT IS AN INTERJECTION?

Interjections are words like *Oh, Well, Hello*, and *Alas*. They live on their own, outside the structure of the rest of the sentence, as in *Well, I'm blowed*.

WHAT IS A SENTENCE?

So much, then, for the individual parts of speech. In isolation they mean little. Only when words form part of a *phrase* or *sentence* do they begin to serve a proper communicative purpose.

The best way to think of a sentence is as a word or string of words that makes sense on its own – that is, as a complete grammatical unit. So *Hello*, and *Well I never!*, and *Easy come, easy go*, and *Bother it!* are sentences. So too is *I can*, in response to the question *Who can speak French?* However, these are hardly typical sentences.

A 'normal' sentence consists of one or more clauses. These are like mini-sentences, mostly with a main verb plus all the other constituents attached to it.

Take this sentence:

When I'd got back from work and was having a shower, my wife said that she'd seen just the curtains that we'd been looking for.

USEFUL TERMS THAT GO WITH CLAUSES

English has three main types of subordinate clause. They are:

Relative clauses. These usually follow nouns and affect their meaning in an adjective-like way. They are introduced by relative pronouns such as *who* or *which*. For example:

> The girl *that came* is called Sally.
> The people *who we saw* are French.
> The man *whose house we bought* has died.

Relative clauses can also refer to the whole of what has gone before, as in

> He arrived late, *which upset the crowd*.

Adverbial clauses. These, like adverbs, affect the way you view the verb in the main clause.

They are typically introduced by conjunctions such as *until, as if, where*:

> Don't do it *until I arrive*.
> She screamed *as if she were mad*.
> I found it *where I'd put it*.
> *If you say that again*, I'll scream.
> I'll help you, *although you don't deserve it*.

Clauses without verbs. Some clauses exist without full finite verbs.

> *While waiting for the bus*, we were drenched by a downpour.
> There was John, *sitting at his desk and overcome with mirth*.

In both of these sentences the italicised parts look like ordinary clauses that have had parts changed or deleted – *While (we were) waiting for the bus, (who was) sitting at his desk, and (who was) overcome with mirth*. They are known as 'non-finite' or 'verbless clauses'.

The verbs are *'d got, was having, said, 'd seen, 'd been*. So there are five clauses:

1. (When) I'd got back from work – *adverbial clause*

2. (and when I) was having a shower – *adverbial clause*

3. my wife said – *main clause*

4. (that) she'd seen just the curtains – *noun clause*

5. that we'd been looking for – *relative clause*

The main clause is the point of the sentence, and can stand alone. The sentence here can be summed up as *My wife said (something)*. All the other clauses are what are known as 'subordinate' clauses.

When discussing style, grammarians speak of three types of sentence:

Simple sentences. These contain a single clause, as in *My little brother has been playing football in the mud*.

Compound sentences. These contain two or more 'coordinate' main clauses but no subordinate clauses, as in *My little brother has been playing football in the mud and (he has) come home filthy from head to foot*.

Complex sentences. These contain subordinate clauses, as in *My little brother has been playing football in the mud, although he was told not to*.

(For a more detailed discussion, see page 46.)

WHAT IS A PHRASE?

The word 'phrase' is often used loosely to mean any group of words that form a unit. In grammar, it means a word or group of words that has a single function within a clause or another phrase.

Take the sentence *The boy patted the dog*. Although there are five words, there are three distinct parts – *the boy, patted*, and *the dog*. So *the boy* is a phrase, in this case a 'noun phrase' acting as the subject; *patted* is the verb; and *the dog* is another noun phrase, here the object of the verb.

Now take a sentence that is clearly ambiguous: *She attacked the man with the knife*. The pronoun *she* is the subject phrase, and *attacked* is the verb. But what about the rest?

There are two ways of analysing the sentence. In one (where the man has the knife), *the man with the knife* is one constituent part – a noun phrase, acting as the object of *attacked*. It can be broken down further into a noun phrase *the man*, plus a subordinate prepositional phrase *with the knife*.

In the other meaning (where she uses a knife when attacking the man), the full object is now simply *the man*. You could reword the sentence as *With a knife she attacked the man* or *She attacked the man viciously*. The phase *with the knife* is therefore an adverbial phase – it acts like an adverb.

THAT OR WHICH?

Consider these two sentences:

The town that/which has beautiful buildings will always attract tourists.

The town, which is a popular tourist centre, is famous for its beautiful buildings.

In the first sentence, either *that* or *which* is suitable. The relative clause here is a 'restrictive' clause – that is, it defines the noun *town*, specifying the kind of town in question. The clause usually has no commas before or after.

In the second of the specimen sentences, only *which* is suitable. The relative clause is here a 'non-restrictive' clause – it simply gives some incidental information about the noun *town*. It is usually cordoned off by commas.

In restrictive clauses *which* and *that* are both freely and widely used nowadays (though some usage experts still urge *that* wherever possible, in order to keep a neat distinction between restrictive and non-restrictive clauses). But if there is already a *which* in the sentence, then *that* tends to be preferred: *Which is the horse that won last time?* And vice versa: *Is that the horse which won last time?*

And there does seem to be a slight preference for *that* in three important constructions:

☐ in clauses relating to the pronouns *anything, everything, nothing,* and *something: Can you think of anything that has to be finished before the weekend?*

☐ in clauses following a superlative: *the most versatile computer that has ever been produced in a British factory*.

☐ in relative clauses following *it is* constructions: *It was the dog that died, not the man*.

(For further details, see page 217.)

The Building Blocks Of Good English

Singular or Plural

The rules for making the plurals of nouns (one *sheep*, two *sheep*; one *vertebra*, two *vertebrae*) can be found in the next section. This section deals with questions like 'Should one talk about *fewer* police or *less* police?'

SUBJECT-VERB AGREEMENT

Problems can arise when the subject of a sentence is a long phrase or stands at some distance from its verb. Which verb form should you use in the following sentences?

The smell of garlic and onions was/were overpowering.
The glamour of money and success has/have gone to her head.
Everything except the flowers is/are ready.
The results of all this delay was/were unforeseen.
The result of all these delays, even though they were due to factors beyond our control, was/were several claims for damages.

If you are not sure how to decide, prune down the sentence leaving only the main subject noun and its verb. It is then easy to see what the correct verb form should be:

The smell . . . was . . .
The glamour . . . has . . .
Everything . . . is . . .
The results . . . were . . .
The result . . . was . . .

ONE OF . . .

One common error is to use a singular verb after phrases like *one of the men who* . . . :

✗ He's one of those people who never listens to reason.
✗ That's one of the few regulations that really works.

Here the subjects of the verbs *listen* and *work* are *who* and *that*. These relative pronouns refer not to *one* but to *those people* and *few regulations*.

He's one [example] of those *people who never listen to reason*.
That's one [example] of the few *regulations that really work*.

Contrast the examples above with sentences like *One of those plugs is broken* (that is, *One is broken*) and *That's the only one of all these plans that really works* (that is, *That's the only one that really works*).

MULTIPLE SUBJECTS – MARY, AS WELL AS ANNE

Two singular subjects joined by *and* normally form a plural: *Marcia and Edwin were there*. But this works only for *and*. Other words or phrases added to a singular subject do not make it plural:

> The President, together with his aides, was/ **X** were there.
> The President, as well as the Secretary for State, is/**X** are in China.
> Smith, in addition to Brown and Jones, was/ **X** were sent off.

WE WAS ROBBED

X Well, I likes that.
X He just don't know what to do.
X We was robbed.
X I were here first.
X Remember, you ain't seen a thing.

These sentences, though acceptable in some regional dialects, are not correct in Standard British English unless used in a deliberately jocular way. True, modern English verbs change relatively little when applied alternately to *I, you, he, she, we* and *they* – compare the rich variety in Latin: *amo* (I love), *amas, amat, amamus, amatis, amant* and so on – but they do change slightly. In the examples above, the speaker in each case has used the wrong form.

In Standard English, the first four sentences should be *I like that, He just doesn't know what to do, We were robbed*, and *I was here first*. The informal word *ain't* is often used to mean 'am not', 'are not', 'is not', 'have not', or 'has not'; but speakers of Standard English choose it only for deliberate effect or as a joke. Here the standard form would be *You haven't seen a thing*.

There is one common complication in this whole area – the contracted form *Aren't I?* Here Standard English breaks the rules to avoid the clumsiness of the strictly logical contraction **X** *Amn't I?* (See page 252 for a more detailed discussion.)

The test is this. Can you move the phrase without difficulty? If you can – *The President was there, together with his aides* – the extra phrase is not part of the subject.

The same rule applies when a singular subject is followed by a phrase beginning *and not* or *but not*. For instance: *A junior minister, but not his superiors, is to attend*. The same test works once again: *A junior minister is to attend, but not his superiors*. By contrast, you might have a double (plural) subject even though there seems to be only one singular noun, such as the word *Town* in the following example:

> Both the Old and the New Town in Edinburgh are worth visiting.

This is short for *Both the Old Town and the New Town* and thus is plural. Compare *This green and pleasant land is being ruined by tasteless development*. Here there is just the one land that is both green and pleasant.

X WAS OR WERE Y?

You often face a similar choice when a sentence has two noun phrases either of which could serve as subject or complement. For example:

> Your best bet is/are free tickets – Free tickets is/are your best bet.
> Trains were/was his obsession – His obsession was/were trains.

Generally, you should make the verb agree with the subject (*Your best bet is free tickets*); or better still, rephrase the sentence to avoid the problem:

> Your best bet is to get free tickets.
> Trains had become his obsession.

In sentences beginning with *there* the verb usually agrees with the following noun or pronoun, as in *There's nothing there except tower blocks; There are so many things I have to do; There are lots of people coming*.

A singular verb is always used when *it's, it is*, or *it was* are used to focus on something: *It's the elms that died, not the beeches; It was the Joneses I was afraid of*.

CLAUSES AS SUBJECTS

Clauses can act as subjects of verbs. They usually take a singular verb:

That such things should occur is surprising.
To treat 18-year-olds as children is patronising.
Caring for all aspects of home and family takes a lot of time.

What-clauses are different, however. Here agreement depends on whether the clause refers to a thing or to several things:

What was their garden is now a car park.
What seemed good reasons at the time now look unconvincing. (That is, the reasons now look unconvincing.)

Sometimes you can choose, especially when the complement of the main verb is plural, though the singular form remains slightly preferable:

What we need is/are donations – Donations are what we need.
What I saw was/were two enormous balloons – Two enormous balloons were what I saw.

COLLECTIVE NOUNS – ENGLAND ARE WINNING

Collective nouns are singular nouns that refer to a group of people or things; for example, *audience, committee, class, family, the government*, and *team*.

In American and Australian English these words are generally treated as singulars – that is, they take singular verbs, and are referred to as *it*. British English, however, is more flexible:

The audience was/were more enthusiastic than it/they expected to be.
Scotland has/have won the Cup.

The difference often lies in how you view the subject. If it is regarded as a single unit, you are likely to use a singular verb; if it is regarded as a group of individuals, a plural verb is more likely.

The company has outperformed itself this year.
The Cabinet is united on this.
The Cabinet have long been fighting among themselves.
The jury have/**??** has been told not to discuss the case.

Words like *majority* and *minority*, *pair* and *couple*, are best treated in the same way. Use the singular verb form if you are thinking of a quantity or a single unit; use the plural verb form if you are thinking of a group of individuals:

Only a minority of the public is in favour.
The majority of my friends agree with me.

A pair of those shoes costs at least £100.
The pair were sitting together in the corner.

Whatever you do, be consistent. Mixing singular and plural is unacceptable: **X** *Parliament is back in business after their summer recess*.

A BATCH OF PAPERS HAS/HAVE ARRIVED

Generally, a subject consisting of a singular noun plus an *of*-phrase takes a singular verb: *A flock of sheep was seen in the distance*. But there are some exceptions:

A vast quantity of fakes were released onto the market.

The 'notional' meaning here (see the chart, *Notional agreement*, below) is clearly 'many fakes' – hence the plural verb form.

Sometimes the choice of verb can affect the meaning. *A vast quantity of fakes was released onto the market* suggests that they all came from one source; using *were* avoids this suggestion.

KIND OF . . . ; SORT OF . . .

Constructions such as *this kind of*, *that sort of*, and *this type of* are in common use: *That kind of car is expensive to run*.

NOTIONAL AGREEMENT – BACON AND EGGS IS MY FAVOURITE BREAKFAST

A double subject joined by *and* typically takes a plural verb: *Bacon and eggs are both expensive*.

But when two nouns – even plural ones – go together to refer to a single person, thing, or idea, a singular verb is needed. 'Notional' agreement, as this is known (in contrast to strict grammatical agreement), is very common in English. For example:

Bacon and eggs is my favourite breakfast. (The dish bacon and eggs . . .)
My sister and best friend is here. (My sister, who is also my best friend . . .)
Sons and Lovers is by D.H. Lawrence. (The novel *Sons and Lovers* . . .)
The Five Bells sells real ale. (The Five Bells pub . . .)
Six weeks is a long time in politics. (A period of six weeks . . .)

But making these constructions plural can be a problem. Suppose you are discussing several makes of car. The possibilities seem to be:

? Those kind of cars are expensive to run.
✗ That kind of cars is/are expensive to run.
? Those kinds of cars are expensive to run.
Those kinds of car are expensive to run.

Purists point out that *kind* and *sort* are singular, and condemn **?** *those kind of* and **?** *these sort of*, widespread though they are.

The two standard options are the 'all-plural' *those sorts of things*; and the mixed *those sorts of thing*. The first often feels more natural, but the second is probably preferred by purists.

EVERYONE AND THEIR DOG?

Which is the correct usage – singular or plural – after indefinite pronouns such as *anybody*, *someone*, *no one*, and *everybody*? And after singular nouns referring to people but not specific as to sex, such as *teacher* and *child*?

In very simple sentences, the answer is correspondingly simple – such words are singular and as a result take singular verbs:

Everybody knows the earth is round.
Anyone who thinks otherwise is daft.
Someone is knocking on the door.

But how would you fill in these?

If anybody calls, tell . . . I'm not at home.
Nobody wants to be ill, ... ?
Would everybody please take all . . . things with . . . .
A teenager should have learnt how to look after . . . things.

Traditionalists, if pressed, would have to insist on singular forms throughout, including singular masculine pronouns:

If anybody calls, tell him I'm not at home.
Nobody wants to be ill, does he?
Would everybody please take all his things with him.
A teenager should have learnt how to look after his things.

This formal approach is hardly satisfactory nowadays in contexts that include women. And yet to use *he or she*, *him or her*, and so on sounds pedantic and is often clumsy or impossible:

??We trust that everybody will enjoy himself or herself and, at the end of the show, take his or her things with him or her.

One widespread solution to this problem is to use *they* and *them*:

? If anybody calls, tell them I'm not at home.
? Nobody wants to be ill, do they?
? A teenager should have learnt how to look after their things.
? Would everybody please take all their things with them.

Purists object to this approach, though the usage is long established:

Now leaden slumber with life's strength doth fight,
And every one to rest themselves betake . . .
– Shakespeare, *The Rape of Lucrece*

If you feel uneasy about using *they* and *them* in this way, try to avoid the problem by rewording such sentences whenever possible:

If anybody calls, say I'm not at home.
Nobody wants to be ill, surely?
Would you all please take your things with you.
Teenagers should have learnt how to look after their things.

(For more details on avoiding 'sexist' pronouns, see pages 89-90.)

EACH, EVERY

These words are singular, and so the verb they go with should be singular as well – even when the subject includes *and*:

Every item is numbered.
Each man, woman, and child was given £10.
Each of the members has accepted responsibility for this decision.
Every chair and table in the place was smashed.

However, when *each* comes after a plural subject and verb it does not affect the verb:

The people were each given £10.
The members have each accepted responsibility for this decision.

EITHER, NEITHER

Again, these words are singular, and strictly speaking require a singular verb:

Neither candidate was satisfactory.
Neither of them pays any attention.
Neither works.
Either Fred or William is going to do the job.

In practice, however, plural agreement occurs very frequently, especially after *neither*, when its 'notional' meaning combines *both* and *not*.

So you can just about get away with:

? Neither of the candidates were satisfactory (that is: Both the candidates were not satisfactory)
? Neither Fred nor William are going to do the job.
? I don't think either of them know about it.

When two plural subjects are joined by *either... or...* or *neither... nor...*, the verb obviously has to be plural:

Neither the Dutch nor the Belgians were pleased by this announcement.
Neither the Smiths nor the Joneses were at all well-disposed towards the new neighbours.

The problems start when different parts of the subject would normally require different verb forms. Which should it be?

Either the children or my husband cook/cooks the breakfast.
Neither you nor she has/have to tell him.
Either she or I is/am/are going to win.
Either the shop steward or the managers is/are going to have to back down.

There is no straightforward answer here.

One practice is to match the verb to the nearest noun: *Either the children or my husband cooks the breakfast*; *Neither you nor she has to tell him*. But the third example sounds rather awkward: **?** *Either she or I am going to win*.

As so often, the best policy is to avoid the problem by rewording:

Either the children cook the breakfast, or my husband does.
Neither you nor she must tell him.
If she doesn't win, I shall.
One side or the other is going to have to back down – either the shop steward or the managers.

Similarly, don't spend time worrying whether to say *One or both of them is/are lying*. Say rather *One of them is lying, or perhaps both are* or *One or both of them must be lying*.

Remember that *neither* and *either* (like *between* and *both*) should be used when only two items are under consideration. Avoid such common erors as:
?? *Neither Adam nor Bill nor Carol was prepared to help us in our hour of need.*

FEWER, MORE THAN, LESS

A common mistake is to say or write: **X** *Less people came to the concert than I expected*. The constructions *Many a*, *more than one*, and *none* can also cause problems.

Fewer, less. In strict grammar *fewer*, like *few* and *fewest*, goes with plural nouns; and *less*, like *little* and *least*, with mass or uncountable nouns (usually singular in form). So it should be *fewer people* but *less information*. Even so, many people use *less* even before plural nouns:

?? I noticed markedly less people and vehicles on the road than usual.
?? The much-wanted criminal was sighted in no less than 15 countries.

Avoid it! Careful users dislike this usage intensely.

An exception or two: some uncountable plural nouns can take *less* except in very formal contexts: **?** *wearing less clothes*; and *less* is correct when used in measurements: *cost less than 25 pence*; *finished in less than six months*.

Many a, more than one. These constructions are usually treated as singular:

Many a good driver finds skidding an alarming experience.
More than one accident here has happened in the fog.
?? More than one accident here have happened in the fog.

None. *None* is usually considered the equivalent of 'not one', and so takes a singular verb:

None of us is going to do the deed.
None of the riders was wearing a crash helmet.
? None of the riders were wearing crash helmets.

However, *none* can sometimes be understood as 'not any' or 'no people', and so takes a plural verb and pronouns:

There are none so blind as those who will not see.
I'd like some eggs to eat, but there are none in the fridge.

Putting Nouns into the Plural

The plurals of most nouns in English are formed, of course, by adding -s or -es. This section deals with the exceptions to this simple rule – some of them English words with problem plurals, others foreign words borrowed by English but retaining their foreign plurals.

The text here does not pretend to give an exhaustive list of irregular plurals. All it can do is indicate the danger areas, with some examples in each. If you are ever in doubt about the plural of a rare word not mentioned here, check it in a good dictionary.

WORDS ENDING IN -F OR -FE

Some of these words change their ending to -ves in the plural, but some end simply in -s. A few allow a choice. Here are some examples:

☐ ending -s: *beliefs, carafes, chiefs, cliffs, cuffs, handkerchiefs, oafs, proofs, roofs, safes*

☐ changing to -ves: *calves, elves, halves, knives, leaves, loaves, scarves, shelves, sheaves, wives, wolves*

☐ taking either plural: *dwarfs/dwarves, hoofs/hooves, wharfs/wharves*.

Note *one life, two lives* – but two paintings of bowls of fruit are *two still lifes*.

WORDS ENDING IN -Y

Words ending in a consonant plus -y – such as *lady, baby,* and *Gypsy* – change -y to -ies in the plural: *ladies, babies, Gypsies*. The only important exception to this rule is proper nouns, which can form a plural by adding -s: for example, *both Sallys, all the MacNallys*.

Note that there is no apostrophe in any of these plural forms. If the word is both plural and possessive, the apostrophe goes at the end of the word, as in *ladies' room* (see pages 228-229).

Most words ending in a vowel plus -y simply add -s. So: *bays, jockeys, decoys, guys, buoys,* and so on. (British English therefore has a useful contrast between *storey/storeys* and *story/stories*.) Exceptions to this rule are:

☐ words ending -quy. These change -y to -ies: *soliloquies, obloquies,* and *colloquies*.

☐ the word *money*. This has the specialised plural *monies – He was sued for the return of all monies paid into the company –* as well as a regular plural *moneys*.

Elsewhere, when the plural -ies appears to be formed from any -ey word, it can be explained as the plural of a variant singular without the -e: so *flunkies* is the plural of *flunky* rather than of *flunkey*: similarly, *fogies, bogies,* and *phonies*.

WORDS ENDING IN -O

Most simply add -s – including:

☐ words where the -o is preceded by a vowel: *cameos, cuckoos, embryos, radios, portfolios, studios, tattoos, zoos*

☐ shortened words: *hippos, photos, rhinos, typos, videos*

☐ many 'exotic', un-English words: *albinos, armadillos, dittos, Eskimos, Filipinos, infernos, quangos, stilettos*

Some, however (including many quite everyday words), take -es: *cargoes, dominoes, echoes, heroes, potatoes, tomatoes*.

Others use either ending, though with a preference for the one shown here: *buffaloes, commandos, frescoes, ghettos, halos, mangoes, mottoes, porticoes, tobaccos, volcanoes, zeros*.

(See also the section *Problem plurals with foreign words*, opposite page.)

WORDS ENDING IN -S

A noun ending in -s presents a number of problems. Can it be put into the plural at all? If so, how? If not, does it take a singular or plural verb?

Many native English or fully established nouns ending in -s make their plurals in the normal way: *bus/buses, kiss/kisses*. But with others the rules are more complicated.

Uncountable nouns. Words like *news* and *billiards* are singular uncountable: *This news is worrying; Billiards is becoming more popular*.

More problematic are words ending -ics, denoting fields of study or activity. Some are also uncountable: *athletics, gymnastics*. Others are singular or plural according to meaning:

> Ethics is a difficult subject.
> The ethics of their behaviour are distinctly dubious.

Others give rise to uncertainty:

? Metaphysics is/are not my cup of tea.

Diseases are usually regarded as uncountable nouns – *Rabies is terrifying* – but some allow for variation: *Measles is/are nasty. Have you had it/them?*

Plural-only nouns. Some plural nouns have no singular form: *bellows, belongings, clothes, congratulations, odds, proceeds, proceedings, remains, riches, thanks*.

Others do have a related word without *-s*, but with a different meaning: libel *damages*/storm *damage*, tinted *spectacles*/a *spectacle* worth seeing, *customs* at the airport/a *custom* of the tribe.

Plural-only words usually take a plural verb – *These trousers are dirty* – but are not usually countable: **X** *six clothes*, **??** *three trousers*. Some that have two equal parts (*jeans, pliers, scissors, tights, trousers*) are usually counted by using the word *pair*: *one pair of scissors, two pairs of trousers*.

Note that some singular forms do exist in set phrases: a *scissor* movement, a *trouser* press.

Versatile nouns. Some *-s* words can be used as both singular and plural: one *crossroads*/two *crossroads*, *gasworks, gallows, headquarters*.

Proper names with -s. Most place names ending in *-s* are singular: *Naples/Paris/the Thames/Wales is beautiful*. Even the names of countries with a plural feel normally take singular verbs: *The Netherlands is partly below sea level*. (A plural verb may, however, be used when the name denotes the country's sports team or the like: *The Netherlands/ Philippines/United States have won 16 gold medals* – see page 175.)

Mountain ranges and groups of islands, when not also the name of a country, are normally plural: *The Himalayas/The Hebrides are far away*. But you cannot speak of **X** *a Himalaya*, **X** *a Hebride*, or **X** *an Alp*, except as a joke.

Note the spelling of the plural of proper names: keeping up with the *Joneses* – no apostrophe usually, unless in the possessive.

PLURALS WITHOUT -S

There are four main types of English plural without the characteristic *-s* ending:

Words with Old English plurals. *Children, brethren, men, women, feet, geese, teeth, mice, lice*, and *pence* rarely cause problems. But remember that the possessive is written *children's, women's*, and so on – not **X** *childrens'*.

Plural-only nouns without -s. These include *cattle, people, police*. Their nearest singular equivalents are usually *cow, person*, and *policeman/ policewoman*. *People* can, of course, be singular when it refers to a race or nation, as in *This people subsists on yam and manioc*.

'Zero' plurals. Here the singular and plural forms are the same, as in *one sheep/two sheep*. Measurement nouns often have zero plurals: *He weighs 12 stone; She's over six foot tall; Give me two dozen*. Note also *four aircraft* and *all her offspring*.

Problems arise with animal words. Animals that you hunt or catch often have zero plurals: *deer, grouse, plaice, salmon*. Some animal words – *duck* and *herring*, for example – usually have a zero plural when they are being shot or caught, but tend to have normal plurals when regarded as individual specimens. So you might say *They went to the marsh to shoot duck at sunrise* but *We went to the park to feed the ducks at tea-time*.

The plural *fishes* is used in technical writing, usually to emphasise individual fish or species of fish: *Salmon and trout are both food fishes*. Otherwise, use *fish*: *I don't eat fish; He brought home three fish*.

Nationalities. Nationality nouns ending in a 'hissing' sound (a *sibilant*) have zero plurals: *five Japanese/Chinese*. Those with *-man* change to *-men*: *Frenchmen, Scotsmen*. Others make regular plurals with *-s*: *Americans, Bangladeshis, Germans, Scots*. Some nationality adjectives can be used as plural nouns in a general sense: *the French, the Dutch, the Spanish*.

PROBLEM PLURALS WITH FOREIGN WORDS

The main guideline for making the plurals of foreign words in English is this: you are speaking English, not Latin, Greek, or French. What the plural is in the language of origin is irrelevant, unless custom has made it the plural in English as well. Custom says

The Building Blocks Of Good English

PLURALS – A QUIZ

Which of the plural forms is preferable in each of the following sentences? For the answers, turn to pages 633-648.

1. Which of the Mollys/Mollies are you talking about?
2. He has learnt Hamlet's soliloquys/soliloquies off by heart.
3. They object to all experiments on animal embryos/embryoes.
4. How many storeys/stories/storys is that office going to have?
5. Please buy two trout/trouts at the fishmonger.
6. My husband and I both had to have our appendixes/appendices removed last year.
7. The country has had only three or four censuses/censi this century.
8. The stigmas/stigmata of tiger lilies have certain unique characteristics.
9. Field guides seldom explain which fungi/funguses are edible.
10. What are the criterias/criteria/criterions for membership?
11. The doctors put forward conflicting diagnoses/diagnosises.
12. What a treat – the world's two leading sopranos/soprani on the same stage.
13. My granddaughters are the sweetest little cherubs/cherubim you've ever seen.
14. She weighs nearly 15 stone/stones.

And which verb form is preferable in these sentences?

15. Those pliers you requested has/have arrived from the warehouse.
16. The media has/have had a field day in covering the scandal.
17. I see that bangers and mash is/are on the menu for lunch.
18. Politics is/are my favourite subject.
19. Six weeks is/are a long time to wait for delivery.
20. The executive have/has been debating the matter among themselves.
21. Neither of them ever pay/pays any attention.
22. To get young children to swallow pills is/are very difficult for most mothers to manage.

that there is one *criterion* but two *criteria*. But people also speak correctly of football *stadiums* and of *forums* for debate. Often, as with *formulas* and *formulae*, both native and foreign plurals exist.

Here are some foreign word-endings to watch out for – some Latin, some Greek, some French, some Italian, and so on – with examples of how they usually form their plurals.

Ending -a. If the word is Latin in origin, the plural ending tends to be *-ae*; if Greek, *-ata*.

First, words of Latin origin:

Words that always take the Latin plural include *larva/larvae*, *alumna/alumnae*, *vertebra/vertebrae*. Others take either Latin or English plurals: *amoebas/amoebae*, *formulas/formulae*, *cicadas/cicadae*, *tibias/tibiae*, *tracheas/tracheae*, *verrucas/verrucae*.

Note that the *-ae* plural is commoner in formal, technical contexts. And that the forms can have different meanings: insects have *antennae*, but radio masts have *antennas*. See also the chart *Singular or plural?*, page 182.

Next, words of Greek origin:

These generally take the English *-s* plural, but the Greek ending is also possible (though rare): for example, *dogmas/dogmata*, *schemas/schemata*, *traumas/traumata*.

Note the following special cases:

☐ *stigma*. The Greek plural *stigmata* usually refers to marks or sores, corresponding to Jesus's wounds, that appear on the hands and feet, or bodies of some religious people. *Stigmas* usually refers to the central part of a flower that receives the pollen. *Stigma*, meaning 'a token or mark of shame', is usually uncountable, as in: *There is less stigma attached to mental illness than there used to be*.

☐ *criteria*. This is plural, and should not be used in the singular – **X** *a criteria*. Its singular form is *criterion*.

☐ *paraphernalia*. This form is a Greek plural. In English, it is generally an uncountable noun: *All this photographic paraphernalia takes up an awful lot of space*.

Ending -eau, -ou, -ieu. French words ending in these vowel clusters typically take an *-x*, in the plural in their original language – *beau/beaux*, *château/châteaux*, *bijou/bijoux*, *adieu/adieux*. In English such words usually take the -*s* ending, but -*x* can also be used – in which case the plural would probably be pronounced identically to the singular, as in French.

Ending -*es*. Greek words ending -*es* do not change in the plural: *one series/two series, one species/two species* – never **X** *one specie.*

Ending -*is*. Most such words follow the Greek in taking the ending -*es*: *analysis/analyses*, *axis/axes*, *basis/bases*. Similarly, *crises*, *diagnoses*, *hypotheses*, *neuroses*, *oases*, *theses*.

Note that the plural ending is pronounced / seez /. This distinguishes the plurals of *axis* and *basis* from those of *axe* and *base* – pronounced / siz /.

Ending -*ix*, -*ex*. Latin words with these endings can usually take either the English plural -*es* or, less commonly, the Latin -*ices*: *apex/apexes* or *apices*, *matrix/matrixes* or *matrices*, *suffix/suffixes* or *suffices*, *vortex/vortexes* or *vortices*.

Note the following special cases:

□ *codex*. This always takes the Latin plural, *codices*.

□ *appendix*. *Appendixes* are removed by surgery. *Appendices* are additions to a book.

□ *index*. *Indices* are signs or statistical reflections – *the indices of prices and wages* – though *indexes* is acceptable. Alphabetical listings at the backs of books are always *indexes*.

Ending -*o*. Italian words ending -*o* usually take regular English plurals (*solos, sopranos, tempos, virtuosos*), unless they have very strong Italian connections (*mafioso/mafiosi, palazzo/palazzi*).

Ending -*on*. Some Greek words ending -*on* always take the English -*s* ending in the plural: *electrons, lexicons, neutrons, protons, skeletons*. Some take either the English plural or the Greek -*a* plural: *automatons/automata, phenomenons/phenomena*. Some can take only the Greek plural: *criterion/criteria, ephemeron/ephemera*.

Note that *ephemera* is often used uncountably to refer to collectors' items made of paper – such as old playbills and tickets.

Note too the usage with *phenomenon*. The -*s* plural is acceptable when *phenomenon* has its modern sense of 'a marvel or wonder' – *This furniture group has become one of the retailing phenomenons of the*

last decade. The -*a* ending is correct for the philosophical *phenomenon*, referring to something that appears real to the senses whether it actually exists or not: *These phenomena have long puzzled scientists of all nations.*

Ending -*um*. Some words ending -*um* always take the Latin -*a* plural: for example, *addendum/addenda*, *bacterium/bacteria*, *erratum/errata*, *ovum/ova*. Others take either English or Latin plurals: *memorandums/memoranda*, *stratums/strata*, *curriculums/curricula*, *stadiums/stadia*, *forums/fora*, *gymnasiums/gymnasia*. Others again take only the English plural (the -*a* ending sounds either absurd or affected): *albums*, *asylums*, *museums*, *pendulums*, *premiums*.

(See also the chart *Singular or plural?*, page 182.)

Ending -*us*. The Latin plural for most of these is -*i*. Many -*us* words, however, always take the English plural -*uses*: *censuses*, *circuses*, *hiatuses*, *platypuses*, *prospectuses*, *sinuses*, *viruses*. Note that *apparatus* can have an -*es* plural, *apparatuses*, but is more often used as an uncountable noun: *We need this apparatus.*

Other -*us* words take either English or Latin plurals. With some, the Latin -*i* ending is usually preferable: *cacti/cactuses*, *octopi/octopuses*, *hippopotami/hippopotamuses*, *narcissi/narcissuses*, *radii/radiuses*. With others, the English is more usual: *abacuses/abaci*, *focuses/foci*, *crocuses/croci*.

Others take the Latin ending almost exclusively: *alumni*, *bacilli*, *colossi*, *fungi*, *gladioli*, *stimuli*. But even with these the English ending -*uses* is seldom downright wrong.

Note that there is another set of -*us* nouns, which in Latin take a different plural: -*era* or -*ora*. But these too can usually take the -*es* ending: *corpus/corpora* or *corpuses*, *genus/genera* or *genuses*. (See also the chart *Singular or plural?*, page 182.)

Other foreign plurals. Words of French origin ending in -*s* do not change in the plural in writing, though in speech the -*s* is pronounced in the plural: one *corps* (pronounced / kor /) but two *corps* (pronounced / korz /).

Lasagne and *spaghetti* (actually plural in Italian) are treated as uncountable nouns in English: *Some spaghetti is green*. *Graffiti* is also generally treated as uncountable, though some people insist that it should be plural, the singular being *graffito*: *Some graffiti is/are offensive*; **?** *an unpleasant graffito*.

The plural of Hebrew *kibbutz* is *kibbutzim*, though *kibbutzes* may also be used. *Cherub* and *seraph* either take the English *-s* plural or add *-im*: *cherubim* and *seraphim*. When referring to chubby baby angels in art and to innocent children, the word is almost always *cherubs*.

SINGULAR OR PLURAL?

The *-a* ending often indicates a Latin or Greek plural. A common mistake is to take such words as singular forms of English – **X** *a bacteria*, **X** *a strata*, **X** *a phenomena*, **X** *a criteria* – and to give them an *-s* plural. **X** *three stratas*, **X** *various criterias*.

With some *-a* words, the rights and wrongs of usage are not so clear-cut. They have been, or still are, the subject of some controversy.

Propaganda. This word may look like the plural of a Latin *-um* word, but that is not really its origin or its function. It is an uncountable or mass noun in English, and takes a singular verb: *All this propaganda against drugs is proving counterproductive*.

Insignia. The Latin singular *insigne* is now used only in technical contexts in English. You can use *an insignia* as a singular noun, and *insignias* as a plural, but perhaps the best and safest usage is that of *insignia* as plural: *These insignia of office are most impressive*.

Regalia. This is the plural form of the Medieval Latin *regale*, meaning 'a royal right'.

In English, *regalia* is used either as a plural noun or as an uncountable noun: *The regalia are/is beautifully displayed*.

Opera. In origin, *opera* is the plural of the Latin *opus*, 'a work'. But *opera* is now clearly a singular noun in English, with its own plural *operas*; and *opus* usually takes the English plural *opuses* to avoid confusion: *Mozart opuses 25 and 26; two of Mozart's operas*.

Agenda. This word is now clearly accepted as a singular noun, with the plural *agendas*: *These two agendas are almost the same*.

Candelabra. Formal and technical usage sticks to *candelabrum* (singular) and *candelabra* (plural). In less formal usage, however, people often speak of one *candelabra*, two *candelabras/candelabrums*.

Data. This word is commonly used as an uncountable noun: *We haven't much data; several important pieces of data*. This usage is standard in the computer industry, and widely accepted in North America. But purist users of British English dislike it, insisting that *data* must be treated as a plural: *These data are insufficient for our purposes*. The singular *datum* is now rarely used. The forms **X** *a data* or **X** *some datas* are impossible.

Media. This was originally a plural form with the singular *medium*.

The *media*, referring to newspapers, television, and the like, is now often used as a collective or mass noun, with a singular verb: **?** *The media has put its force behind these demands*. But purists insist that *media* must take a plural verb, and would therefore rewrite the example as follows: *The media have put their force behind these demands*.

Like *data*, the word is hardly a true plural, however, and cannot really be counted: **??** *The news was carried in three media*; **??** *One medium that has reacted is radio*. This would normally be *one branch of the media*. A widespread error is to use *media* to refer to a single branch of the media. Never say **X** *a media* or **X** *medias*.

Note that when the word *medium* is used to mean 'a person who conducts seances', the plural is *mediums*.

Pronouns and Case – My Husband and I

X *Don't talk to I like that*. This is normal usage in some regional dialects, but not in Standard English. In Standard English, it should of course be: *Don't talk to me like that*.

People often get confused between 'subjective' forms of pronouns (those used for subjects of sentences – *I am happy*; *Did they come?*) and the forms used for objects of sentences (*The boss told* me; *The boss knows her*) or as the complements or objects of prepositions (*The boss spoke to us*; *The boss lives near them*).

TWO TOGETHER – BETWEEN YOU AND I

The phrase *between you and I* is so widely used nowadays (and is found in writing as far back as Shakespeare) that some careful speakers now accept it as standard usage. However, it is clearly wrong grammatically – this becomes obvious when you reverse the order of the pronouns: **✗** *between I and you*. The preposition *between* requires the object form of pronouns that follow it. The correct wording is *between you and me*.

The probable reason for the popularity of *between you and I* is, paradoxically, the early coaching that many children receive in good grammar. Children have a tendency to use the phrase *you and me* where *you and I* is appropriate – **✗** *You and me* (or *Me and you*) *are going to get our hair cut today* – which concerned parents and schoolteachers are at pains to correct, perhaps too insistently: 'No, not *you and me*; you must say *you and I . . .*'

The responsive child goes too far, and uses *you and I* even when grammar requires the object form *you and me*. This 'hypercorrection' – that is, 'correcting' a construction that is already correct into a form that is incorrect – occurs in many other contexts:

✗ Let you and I pray.
✗ Let Sally and I give you a lift home.
✗ The news came as a great shock to my husband and I.
✗ They must be cursing you and I back at headquarters.

To check on such constructions, simply try the pronoun on its own. Clearly, *Let I pray* is wrong – as is *They must be cursing I*. If the pronoun is wrong on its own, it is wrong in combination.

Some people also get confused when a pronoun is joined directly to a noun:

✗ Us men will have to try a bit harder.
✗ That's quite a problem for we wives and mothers.

The test is the same. You would not say **✗** *Us will have to try . . .* or **✗** *. . . a problem for we*. So the correct forms are:

We men will have to try a bit harder.
That's quite a problem for us wives and mothers.

Note an apparent exception: if the subject contains a phrase like *some of. . .* or *many of. . .* plus a pronoun. Here the pronoun is always the object of *of*, no matter where in the sentence it occurs. So you would not say **✗** *Some of we men will have to try a bit harder*, but rather *Some of us men will have to try a bit harder*.

MYSELF AND OTHER SELVES

The *-self* words have various more or less acceptable uses in English, including these:

☐ as *emphatic* pronouns, as in *Even he himself can't say*; *I myself swim regularly*. (Use such emphasis sparingly: many stylists dislike it.)

☐ to indicate 'on one's own' or 'unaided', as in *I cooked dinner myself*.

☐ as *reflexive* pronouns, as in *He hit himself on the thumb* and *Why do you talk to yourself?*

They are also often used as a kind of personal pronoun, as in **??** *Please read the documents and return them to ourselves* and **?** *The matter will be decided between the Minister and myself*. But this usage is considered to be incorrect – incorrect in that the *-self* words here do not 'reflect' back to previous words in the sentence.

When in doubt about using a *-self* word, prune the sentence down. If the ordinary personal pronoun will do, the *-self* form is inappropriate. If you can say *We shall write to you* (which you can), you cannot say:

?? We are in receipt of your letter of 25 November and, when we have studied its contents, shall make a decision and write back to yourselves.

IT'S ME OR IT'S I?

The most controversial question about pronouns is whether to use the subject or object case after *is*, *was*, and other forms of the verb *to be*.

In earlier times, grammarians trying to model English grammar on Latin argued that the verb *to be* cannot have an object and insisted on using subject pronouns after it, as in *It is I* and *Was that she?* This habit survives in the common American usage when answering the phone: *Can I speak to Maria Higgins? – This is she*.

But what comes after *to be* is not really a subject either. It is a complement. Modern Standard

English remains undecided about what to do here, but the fact is that most people nowadays say *It's me* and *Was that her?* This is acceptable usage for everyone except the most formal and traditional.

As always, you can rephrase things to avoid the problem entirely. In answer to the question *Who's there?*, you do not have to say either *It's I* or *It's me*: you can say, uncontroversially, *I am* instead.

Note that if a *who*-clause follows the personal pronoun, Standard English usually prefers a subject form. For example:

It's I who do the shopping.

Colloquial English, on the other hand, would probably still favour *me* here, together with various other changes:

It's me that does the shopping.

WHO OR WHOM?

Should you write *who* or *whom*? *Whoever* or *whomever*? These forms often cause difficulties.

In questions. In the following sentences, which interrogative pronoun is correct?

Who/Whom do you want to see?
Who/Whom were you speaking to just now?
Do you know who/whom to ask?
Somebody is playing tricks on us, but who/whom?
Who/Whom do you think is the most promising candidate?
Who/Whom do you consider to be the most promising candidate?

In theory, the same rules apply here as to the personal pronouns: use *who* as a subject, *whom* as an object. In practice, *who* is widely used in both roles, especially in speech; *whom* is regarded as rather formal. You do have to use *whom* after prepositions, as in *From whom did you get it?* But this slightly stiff wording is less common than *Who/Whom did you get it from?*

To decide whether *whom* is possible, try to reconstruct the underlying statements. *Who do you want to see?* is related to 'You want to see him/her/them' – object. So, in the first three examples above, *whom* is the correct form according to strict grammar:

Whom do you want to see? (You want to see him/her/them.)

Whom were you speaking to just now? (You were speaking to him/her/them.)
Do you know whom to ask? (You ask him/her/them.)

Contrast:

Somebody is playing tricks on us, but who? (He/she is playing tricks.)
Who do you think is the most promising candidate? (I think he/she is.)

But:

Whom do you consider to be the most promising candidate? (I consider him/her to be.)

In relative clauses. Why are the first two sentences below formally correct and the third wrong?

The people whom I met on holiday in Spain knew my cousin.
An old man whom I was introduced to also knew her.
X She was angry with the managers, whom she felt were underestimating her talents.

Once again, ask yourself whether the pronoun is functioning as subject or object. In the first two sentences the underlying statements are 'I met them on holiday' and 'I was introduced to him'. So the object case *whom* would be formally correct (though *who* nowadays sounds more natural and occurs more often in speech). You could also use *that*, or omit the relative pronoun altogether, as in *The people (that) I met on holiday knew my cousin*.

The third example is trickier. The writer has used *whom* because it seems to be the object of 'she felt'. But it is not. In fact, 'she felt' is, as it were, bracketed off from the main structure of the sentence; the underlying statement is '(She felt that) they were underestimating her talents'.

So the sentence should read:

She was angry with the managers, who she felt were underestimating her talents.

Whom would be correct in the next sentence, however:

She was angry with the managers, whom she felt to be hostile towards her.

Here the underlying statement is 'She felt them to be hostile', not **X** 'She felt they to be hostile'.

As with questions, *whom* is essential after a preposition: *You know the man from whom I bought it*.

But again, a more natural wording would be *You know the man* (*that* / **?** *who* /*whom*) *I bought it from*.

Whoever. The rules that apply to *who* and *whom* also apply to *who*(*so*)*ever* and *whom*(*so*)*ever*.

> Whoever/Whomever you ask, you get the same reply.
> **X** She talked on and on to whomever was prepared to listen.

Strictly speaking, *whomever* is grammatically correct in the first sentence, but it sounds very stiff, and is far less commonly used than the colloquial *whoever*. In the second example, *whomever* is a hypercorrection. The pronoun is the subject of *was prepared*. (It is the whole clause, *whoever was prepared to listen*, that is the object of *to*.) So the sentence should be: *She talked on and on to whoever was prepared to listen*.

BIGGER THAN ME, AS BIG AS ME

Should you use subject or object pronouns after *as* and *than*? There is no problem when you state your meaning in full:

> I'm not as clever as she is.
> She's much luckier than I am.

Here, *as* and *than* are conjunctions introducing clauses of comparison, and the pronouns are subjects followed by verbs. So the subject pronouns *she* and *I* are correct.

The problem arises if you shorten the second clause and leave out the verb. Strict traditionalists argue that *as* and *than* are still conjunctions and so you still need subject pronouns. But most people find this very formal:

> I'm not as clever as she.
> She's much luckier than I.

Many modern grammarians take the view that in these cases *as* and *than* can be regarded as prepositions, and that the object pronouns *her* and *me* are more natural:

> I'm not as clever as her.
> She's much luckier than me.

Beware of ambiguity. Always repeat the verb if there is any danger that your meaning might not be clear:

> The cat loves me more than him.

Theoretically this should mean 'The cat loves me more that it loves him'. But in casual writing it might be intended or taken to mean 'The cat loves me more than he loves me'. To be on the safe side, spell things out:

> The cat loves me more than it loves him.
> The cat loves me more than he does.

BUT ME, OR BUT I?

But is usually a conjunction: *I like the idea but I think it's impractical*. But when it means 'except', is it still a conjunction?

> Nobody but I took the idea seriously.

Or is it a preposition, which takes the object pronoun *me* instead?

> Nobody but me took the idea seriously.

Unlike the *as* and *than* examples, these cannot be expanded into a reasonable sentence by adding an extra verb: **X** *Nobody took the idea seriously, but I did*. So *but* seems to be a preposition, and *but me* to be logically correct. If you remain uneasy, you can always avoid the whole issue by rewording:

> I was the only person who took the idea seriously.

JUST LIKE ME

Traditionally, *like* is a preposition not a conjunction: *My son looks just like me*; **??** *My son walks just like I did at his age*. In this second example, *like* should strictly read *as* or *in the same way as* instead. (For a more detailed discussion of the complexities here, see the *Ready-Reference Word Guide*.)

Since *like* is a preposition, it should take the object form of pronoun. Take care not to use the subject form (an especially tempting error when a distracting *and* precedes the pronoun): **X** *Wendy, like Robert and I, goes to bed very late*.

AMBIGUITY – WHOSE IS HIS?

Consider this sentence:

> **?** A supermarket supervisor has been charged with the attempted murder of his boss at a New Year's Eve party, and with the murder of his wife two days later.

Whose wife was murdered?

Pronouns are a useful way of avoiding tedious repetition. But because they have so many uses they are potentially ambiguous. Whenever a sentence becomes ambiguous, try to rectify it by making matters explicit. Here the obvious ways would be:

> ... the murder of his own wife ...
> ... the murder of the boss's wife ...

Even if the meaning of a pronoun is clear from the context, the effect may be absurd: **?** *If your child dislikes spinach, try steaming it*. Careful speakers would repeat the noun here – ... *try steaming the spinach* – or, better still, invert the order: *Try steaming spinach if your child dislikes it*.

Another dangerous way of treating pronouns is to leave them hanging in mid-air, with no noun to refer to. The following is ungrammatical:

X Even if you dream only occasionally, you should write them down.

Write what down? The sentence would be better as:

> Even if you have dreams only occasionally, you should write them down.

ME DOING, OR MY DOING?

Which of these sentences is correct?

> I hope you don't mind me asking?
> I hope you don't mind my asking?

The same problem occurs with nouns:

> I was amazed at Paul saying that.
> I was amazed at Paul's saying that.

Purists point out that *asking* and *saying* in these sentences are gerunds – that is, they act like nouns (see page 168) – and so should take a possessive, just as in sentences like *I hope you don't mind my question* and *I was amazed at Paul's insolence*.

Nevertheless, idiom often favours *me asking* and *Paul saying that*, especially in informal contexts.

Certainly the possessive form – *my, Paul's* – is more formal, and is clearly preferable at the beginning of a sentence:

> His saying that was very strange.
> **?** Him saying that was very strange.

And it must be used if the *-ing* word is so noun-like that it is followed by *of* plus a noun or pronoun:

> We enjoyed his parodying of the minister.

On the other hand, possessives are awkward or impossible in some contexts:

> You can depend on something/**??** something's turning up.
> She did it without either of us/**X** our knowing.
> She did it without her brother or sister/**??** sister's knowing.
> I caught him/**X** his rifling through the files lying on my desk.

If you are worried in particular cases, avoid the problem altogether by rewording – *I hope you don't mind that I asked; You can depend on it that something will turn up*, and so on.

ONE IS NOT AMUSED

The personal pronouns in English are usually said to be *I, you, he, she, it, we*, and *they*, and their non-subject forms, *me, him*, and so on. But what about *one*?

One as a generalised pronoun meaning *anyone* or *everyone* has its uses – for example, when a confusion might arise between 'general' *you* and second-person *you*.

??You rarely know what to do in these circumstances, but it's been a great help speaking to you, Miss Rowland.

The first *you* would be better changed to *one*. Or the sentence could be rephrased entirely, as in *It's often difficult to know what to do* ... But be careful how you use *one* elsewhere: there is always a risk that it will sound clumsy or pompous. Consider the following examples:

1. One is delighted to hear that you'll be able to attend.
2. You really should listen to one when one is speaking to you.
3. Lawyers have to reserve judgment. One's never sure how to proceed in such cases until the papers arrive giving you full details of the brief.
4. One gets the feeling that there's something fishy, don't you?
5. Back home in Little Compton, one always went to Bob Reynolds, the town's general odd-job man, to have their car fixed or a new pump installed.
6. As the war progressed, it became clear that one would have to tighten one's belt, stop thinking only of oneself, and obey the orders that one's leaders gave one.

Without doubt, *one* is most objectionable when used in place of *I* or *me*. In example 1, for instance, *one* clearly refers to the speaker: why then not simply write *I am delighted* . . . Example 2 compounds the awkwardness by using *one* twice, first as an object pronoun, then as a subject. Far better to say: *You really should listen to people when they are speaking to you.*

A further risk with *one* is that of inconsistency: once you start 'one-ing' in a sentence, you have to keep it up to the end, according to a traditional rule. In American English it is sometimes considered acceptable to say *One has to do a lot of homework and hand it in to his/your teacher the next morning*, but not in standard British English. Examples 3, 4, and 5 break this rule.

Now look at example 6. Here the speaker has indeed 'one-d' consistently, only to find that the *one's* and *oneself's* have piled up and produced a very awkward sentence. Here again, using the neutral *people* or the less formal *you* would represent a great improvement.

Problems with Verbs

✗ He's fell in the water.
✗ Who done that?

No adult speaker of Standard English would say or write such sentences unless quoting or joking. In each case the speaker has confused the past tense of a verb with its past participle. The past tense is the one you use by itself (*fell*, *did*); to make perfect tenses (after *have*, *has*, and *had*), you need to use the past participle (*fallen*, *done*).

So here the sentences should be:

He's (He has) fallen in the water.
Who did that? (past)/Who's done that? (perfect)

This kind of mistake is particularly common with *get, got, got*. Notice that although *have got* ('have' – *I've got an interesting job*) and *have got to* ('must' – *I've got to go to the shops*) are usually present in meaning, their form is a perfect tense. *Got* on its own in these senses is used only as a past tense. So the following two sentences are unacceptable:

✗ What you got in your hand?
✗ I just got to make a telephone call.

The correct forms are *What have you got in your hand?* and *I've just got to make a telephone call.*

Note, however, one common American usage of *got* (now occurring quite often in British English): *I got to go on television*, meaning 'I had the opportunity to' or 'I was able to'. If conveying this sense, the second example above would be acceptable – 'I just managed to make a telephone call.'

IRREGULAR VERBS – I SWAM THE CHANNEL

The problem of deciding between past and perfect does not arise for regular English verbs. The forms are the same: *I talked, I have talked*.

The difficulties arise with irregular verbs, where the past and the past participle forms are different (*go, went, gone*; *bite, bit, bitten*; and so on). Some require special comment.

Drunk, swum, and others. In many dialects the past participle form of verbs like *sing* and *drink* is used for the past tense. For instance, people say **✗** *The ship sunk* and **✗** *We begun yesterday*. This is wrong in Standard English. The following list shows current Standard English usage:

	Past	Past participle
begin	began	begun
come	came	come
drink	drank	drunk/drunken
ring	rang	rung
run	ran	run
sing	sang	sung
sink	sank	sunk/sunken
spring	sprang	sprung
stink	stank	stunk
swim	swam	swum

With some verbs, there are alternative forms for the past and past participle. The verb *spin*, for example, has *spun* and the old-fashioned *span* as past-tense forms: *She spun/❓ span some cotton.* The past participle is *spun*: *She has spun some cotton.*

Shrink has *shrunk* and *shrank* as past-tense forms. Most people use *shrunk* to mean 'got smaller', as in *The pullover shrunk in the wash*, but *shrank* to mean 'recoiled', as in *He shrank back in horror*. The past participle is *shrunk*: *The pullover has shrunk in the wash*. The form *shrunken* is now used only as an adjective: *a shrunken head*.

All the other similar verbs have lost the distinctive past form completely, such as *slink, slunk, slunk* and *wring, wrung, wrung*.

LAY, LIE

Do you *lie in* on Saturday mornings, or *lay in*? Do you *lay* the rug on the floor, or *lie* it? People often use the verb *to lay* for *to lie* (and occasionally *to lie* for *to lay*). But in Standard English the two verbs are quite distinct.

To lay is almost always transitive – that is, it takes a direct object, or occurs in the passive. Its primary meaning is 'to cause (something or someone) to lie down, to place (something or someone) in a stationary or reclining position': *Please lay the fish knives to the right of the butter knives; Please lay the rug down over the tiles; the Board is laying down guidelines for staff to follow in emergencies like this.* Sometimes, *to lay* is used in an extended sense: *to lay the table; to lay a ghost; to lay the blame on someone; Now I lay me down to sleep.* And in two exceptional cases, it can be used intransitively: *The hens won't lay until the storm subsides; The ship is laying aft.*

To lie means primarily 'to recline, to be positioned on a flat surface, or to move into such a position'. It is always intransitive in Standard English – that is, it takes no direct object (see pages 167 and 169).

The chief reason for the confusion between *to lay* and *to lie* is that the past of *to lie* is *lay*: *We lay in the grass all morning; Mountains lay to the north, impenetrable swamps to the south.* But, the other forms of the two verbs are always different: *lie, lay, lain, lying, lies;* and *lay, laid, laid, laying, lays.*

Here are some typical non-standard uses of *lay* and *lay*, together with their correct forms in Standard English:

Non-Standard	Standard
✗ Let it lay	Let it lie
✗ He laid down on the grass	He lay down on the grass
✗ Lie the baby on the bed	Lay the baby on the bed
✗ He was laying on the grass	He was lying on the grass
✗ Your papers have laid there for weeks	Your papers have lain there for weeks
✗ When were the railway lines lain?	When were the railway lines laid?

Defective verbs. A couple of verbs are defective; that is, they lack parts.

Stride has no acceptable past participle: *Did you see that man who's just* **??***strode/* **??***stridden round the corner.* Use *gone striding*, or rephrase the sentence in some other way.

Swell too presents difficulties. The form *swelled* is now acceptable as the past tense – *Where he kicked me, my leg swelled up.* Avoid *swole*: **??***my leg swole up.* The past participle is usually *swollen*, though *swelled* is sometimes used – *The crowd was swelled by curious onlookers* – especially if the increase was deliberate or desirable.

TROUBLE WITH TENSES

Which should you say?

> Margaret said I owe her £100.
> Margaret said I owed her £100.

Sequence of tenses. Traditional grammar, based on Latin, has taught that the second is preferable. The rule for reported speech went like this: if the main verb is past, the verb in the reporting clause must be too.

For English this simply is not correct. Certainly *owed* is fine in the example above, but – supposing I still do owe Margaret the £100 – the form *owe* is perfectly acceptable.

In fact, there is a slight difference of emphasis between the two sample sentences. The first emphasises the fact of owing; the second the fact of saying so. Things that are still considered to be true are likely to be reported by a present tense, and vice versa:

> Copernicus discovered that the Earth went/goes round the Sun.
> Ptolemy believed that the Sun went round the Earth.

Double have. ✗ 'If I'd have known, I'd have told you.' This is a colloquialism often heard today, though rarely seen in written English. The *have* in the *first* clause is superfluous and ungrammatical. Change to:

> If I'd known, I'd have told you. (If I *had* known, I *would have* told you.)

A warning, by the way, about spelling. It is all too easy to write ✗ *I'd of done it if I'd known* and ✗ *You might of told me.* The words *have* and *of* may sometimes sound the same, but they are not the same word.

Double perfects. The so-called double perfect is not always ungrammatical, but it is usually unnecessary, and a single perfect tends to make the meaning clearer.

Take, for example, these sentences:

X He shouldn't have tried to have deceived them.
?? I would have liked to have heard Callas sing.
?? You'd think she'd have been happy to have taken the credit.

The first sentence is clearly wrong. You do not 'try to have deceived' someone; you 'try to deceive' him or her. So the sentence should read: *He shouldn't have tried to deceive them*.

The second example could retain either of the perfect verbs, but each would convey rather different meanings:

I would have liked to hear Callas sing.
I would like to have heard Callas sing.

The first means that on some occasion in the past you wanted to hear Callas sing, but did not. The second expresses your present regret at a missed opportunity.

The third example would be better as:

You'd think she'd have been happy to take the credit.

She took the credit; she presumably did not want to; and this is surprising.

A double perfect may occasionally be justified:

I think Henry VIII would have preferred not to have married Anne of Cleves.

This makes sense because it has a past (*would have preferred*) and a 'before the past' (*to have married*). He did marry her; but later (though still in the past) he regretted it. The sentence with a single perfect verb, *He would have preferred not to marry her*, suggests that he did not want to marry her at the time of the marriage.

Unnecessary perfects. Perfect infinitives – (*to*) *have done* – are sometimes used unnecessarily after a past tense:

? I expected to have met you here at 6 o'clock.

The 'pastness' is already expressed in the word *expected*. So the likely meaning would be conveyed

The so-called double perfect . . .

by *I expected to meet you here at 6 o'clock*. (The problem is that, out of context, such a sentence may be ambiguous. Does it mean that I was here at 6 o'clock waiting for you but you failed to turn up? Or does it mean that we did indeed meet here at 6 o'clock as arranged?)

At times, however, a perfect infinitive is not merely justifiable but even necessary – to convey something that is hypothetical or incorrect. Here are two examples:

I was very worried, because I was hoping to have heard my results by then (but I still hadn't).

I believed the Brazilian to have won (but he didn't).

BAD VOICES – THE DOUBLE PASSIVE

Consider these two sentences:

The service is expected to be resumed shortly.
X The service is hoped to be resumed shortly.

Why is the 'double passive' acceptable in the first, but ungrammatical in the second?

The answer lies in the underlying active sentence in each case – that is, the active sentence from which the 'double passive' is generated:

We expect the service to be resumed shortly.
X We hope the service to be resumed shortly.

(Note: when testing the acceptability of a double passive in this way, you should go back only one step – turning the main verb into the active, but leaving the other verb in the passive still. If you turn both verbs into the active, the distinction disappears: it is just as acceptable to say *We hope to resume the service shortly* as it is to say *We expect to resume the service shortly*).

Here are some further examples of faulty double passives:

X A cheerful atmosphere is endeavoured to be created.
X The mountain was attempted to be climbed.
X The contract is proposed to be withdrawn.

Other verbs that generate such ungrammatical double passives include *try, begin, hope, omit, threaten, promise*, and *undertake*.

Here now are some more examples of acceptable double passives:

Seven people are reported to have been wounded. (From: *They report seven people to have been wounded*.)

The paintings are believed to have been smuggled out of the country. (From: *People believe the paintings to have been smuggled out of the country*.)

The family was assumed to have been rehoused. (From: *Someone assumed the family to have been rehoused*.)

The operation was expected to have been completed by then. (From: *They expected the operation to have been completed by then*.)

Other verbs that you can use in this type of double passive include *consider, find, imagine, judge, presume, reckon*, and *suppose* – though not *want, desire*, or *like*, even though they fit the pattern.

(Some verbs used in this way have no active equivalent. You can say *He's rumoured/said to have been awarded £1 million*, but not **X** *They rumour/say him to have been awarded £1 million*.)

Many verbs, it is true, can quite properly be used in sentences beginning *It is hoped/believed* and the like, followed by a passive *that*-clause. But this would not represent a true double passive – merely passives in two separate clauses of a sentence:

It is proposed that the contract be withdrawn.
It is hoped that the service will be resumed shortly.

I WILL AND I SHALL

When do you say *shall* and when do you say *will*? The choice between these two forms is a complex one. In statements and exclamations, purists continue to insist on the following rules – in the English of England, at least:

☐ After *I* or *we*, use *shall* to indicate future time: *We shall meet at the usual place at 6 o'clock*. But use *will* to indicate determination, intention, a promise, an assurance, and so on: *I will get you out of this mess if it's the last thing I do*.

☐ After the second and third persons, singular and plural (*you, he, she, it, they, Peter, the dog*), it is the other way round. So: *James will pick you up at the station at 7.30* – future time. But: *They shall have the car, whether you like it or not* – determination.

Unfortunately, there are several complications. In Scotland and Ireland, and probably in North America, the distinctions above were never widely acknowledged in the first place, let alone observed. And even in England little attention is now paid to them. Furthermore, *shall* and *will* have other functions and meanings, which cut across the rules above – as in:

The fine shall not exceed £50.
You shall complete payment within three years.
According to section 3, I shall be answerable only to the directors themselves.

In such legal phraseology, *shall* is often used to indicate obligation or compulsion in the first person as well as in the second and third.

And *will*, can often, especially in British English, indicate inference or assumption – *That will be Simon ringing; That will have been Simon* – and repeated or habitual action: *We will sit for hours at a time just staring into space; Boys will be boys*.

Will also tends to be used in indirect commands, especially military commands, rather than the emphatic *shall*: *You will assemble at 1800 hours for embarkation; The fourth brigade will advance ten kilometres to the north*.

So what should you do? As it happens, the need to choose between *shall* and *will* arises fairly seldom.

In the first place, most people use the contraction *'ll* in informal usage – both in spoken and increasingly in written English – and so avoid the issue altogether. And even in formal English, people tend to draw on the many alternative expressions for both future time and determination, intention, and so on – *must, is going to, is determined to, presumably,* and the like. For example:

> We are going to meet at the usual place at 6 o'clock.
> I am determined to get you out of this mess.
> They must have the car, whether you like it or not.

When you cannot avoid a choice, try to follow the rules given above, bearing in mind the exceptions also listed.

SHALL WE/WILL WE/SHOULD WE DANCE?

In questions, the choice between *shall* and *will*, is more complicated, since *should* and *would* come into the equation as well. Which form you use depends on the kind of question.

Questions that seek advice or information, or make a suggestion. The rules here are as follows:

☐ Use *shall* before *I* or *we* – *What shall I/we do? Shall we dance? Shall I open the window?*

☐ Use *should* (or sometimes *shall*) before *he, she, it, you, they, the cat, Mary,* and so on – *Should/Shall Peter cook the meal, instead? Should he put another log on the fire?*

Questions that put forward a request. Use *Will you...?* or *Would you...?* – *Will you lock up when you leave? Would you help me to lift the table, please? Would you move the lamp?*

Questions that seek information about the future. If you are asking for a prediction that does not depend on the speaker or the subject of the sentence, use *will* – *What will I/we need? Will they believe us? Will I pass my exams?*

If, however, you are asking for information about the future that depends at least partly on the speaker or the subject of the sentence, follow these rules:

☐ Use *shall* for *I* and *we* – *When shall we three meet again? What shall I do tomorrow?*

☐ Use *will* for *he, she, it, Harry, the cat, they,* and *you* – *Why will he do that? How will you deal with this situation?*

Again, there are exceptions to the rules. Instead of *Shall I open the window?*, North Americans often use the form *Should I* (rather than *Shall I*), and Scottish and Irish people *Will I open the window?*

HE WOULD, OR HE SHOULD?

The traditional rule (in the English of England) is that *I* and *we* take *should*, and that *he, she, it, they, the newspapers, Fred,* and so on take *would*.

> I thought I should come second or third, but I never expected to win.
> If we persevered, we should meet our quota.
> I thought he would come second or third, but I never expected him to win.
> If you persevered, you would meet your quota.

But as with *shall* and *will*, the rule is not recognised in Scotland, Ireland, or North America; and in England *would* is increasingly displacing *should* with *I* and *we*.

Moreover, both *should* and *would* have several special uses that do not come under the rule. *Should*, for example, can be used to express:

☐ duty, necessity, or strong probability – *You should always check your rear-view mirror; Your parents should have arrived by now.*

☐ anticipation or assumption: *The meeting should end in half an hour, at this rate; Your parents should be here at about 10.30.*

☐ condition or contingency – *Should he so much as move, blow his head off; If you should ever change your mind, come and see me again.*

☐ surprise or indignation – *Who should bump into us at the theatre but your parents!; That he should do such a thing!*

Would can be used to express:

☐ habitual action – *As a child, I would gaze at the stars for hours every night.*

☐ stubbornness (chiefly British English) – *I would go and back the wrong horse, fool that I am! I would discuss politics with the barber!* (Compare: *I should discuss politics with the barber.*)

☐ irony – *So, I would appear to be under arrest again.*

☐ conjecture about the past (chiefly British English): *That would have been John on the phone last night.*

LEARNED OR LEARNT?

Many irregular verbs, like regular ones, have the same form for the past tense and past participle – often ending in *-t* (*met, lent, slept,* and so on) or *-d* (*fed, heard, told,* and so on).

Some verbs have alternative spellings and pronunciations for their past forms – a regular one, such as *learned* or *spoiled,* and an irregular one, such as *learnt* or *spoilt.* Other verbs of this sort are *burn, dwell, kneel, lean, leap, smell, spell,* and *spill.*

British speakers (and writers) tend to use the *-t* form, especially for the past participle, and especially for *burnt, knelt,* and *leapt.* And even if they write *burned* or *learned* or the like, they tend to use the *-t* pronunciation. North Americans tend in the opposite direction, both in spelling and pronunciation, especially for *leaned, learned, spelled, spilled,* and *spoiled.* However, they often speak and write of a *spoilt* child and *spilt* milk, and readily use *dwelt, knelt,* and *leapt.*

A subtle distinction in meaning sometimes seems to differentiate the *-t* form from the *-ed* form. The *-ed* form perhaps emphasises the duration of the action: *We burnt the letters last night* and *I dreamt about her last night* on the one hand; *The fires burned all night* and *I dreamed about her all night* on the other.

None of the alternatives is wrong, in any usage, in any dialect. You should, however, try to be consistent in your spelling.

MAY I? MIGHT I?

In requests, the difference between *may* and *might* is one of tone. If you want to ask permission to do something, *May I . . .?* is the standard formula:

> May I smoke?

The use of *Might I . . .?* is either more tentative, or more firm:

> Might I ask you a favour?
> Might I suggest, my friend, that we look at these figures again?

Can I . . .? is also often used when people are asking about general rules and customs – see below at *May I? Can I?*

Both *may* and *might* can also be used when referring to present or future possibilities. *May* suggests a serious possibility and *might* suggests a remote possibility:

> Oh dear, it looks as if I may miss the last train. Just in case, bring your sleeping-bag – you might miss the last train.

When referring to past possibilities, only *might* should be used after a main verb in the past (like *warned* below):

> The last time we came here, you warned us that we might miss the last train.

It is a common error, especially in British English, to use *may* instead of *might* in such constructions.

When *may have* and *might have* are used to express past possibilities, *may have* suggests that this possibility is still alive, and *might have* suggests that the possibility no longer exists. A common error, especially in British English, is to use *may have* where *might have* is the appropriate form:

> **??** She may have lived if doctors had heeded the warning signs.
> **??** Barnes was perfectly positioned, and may have scored yet again had he not been fouled.

At least the meaning is clear here, though the grammar is faulty. But sometimes the grammatical error can lead to ambiguity or give a quite false impression. Suppose the last of the examples had stopped after the word *again:*

> Barnes was perfectly positioned, and may have scored yet again.

Out of context, this appears to mean that Barnes did perhaps score a goal (but that the referee disallowed it). If the intended sense was that Barnes had a chance of scoring a goal but failed to do so, then *might have* would be the correct wording.

MAY I? CAN I?

Can and *may* provoke some odd ideas in 'popular' grammar. When adults tell children *Don't say, 'Can I leave the table?'; it should be 'May I leave the table?',* the assumption often seems to be that *can* is restricted solely to ability – *Am I able to leave the table?* – and has nothing to do with either permission or compulsion.

In fact, the distinction between the two verbs is far more subtle. *Can* does have a meaning relating to permission – specifically when the permission is general or of unknown origin. You would hardly say **?** *May children under 12 see this film?* or **?** *I may do whatever I want*. You would use *can*.

May is used when you are giving permission yourself (*You may go now*) or when you are asking permission of a specific person: *May I go now?* So *Can I smoke here?* is a question about general rules and customs; *May I smoke here?* is a specific request for permission from someone with the power to grant it.

In many contexts, either *can* or *may* will do. If you have to ask your manager for a day off work you could say *Can I* or *May I have tomorrow off?* There may be a theoretical difference: *Can I . . . ?* – Is there anything against it? *May I . . . ?* – Do you say I can? But in effect it comes down to the same thing.

DARE, NEED, USED TO

The 'modal' verbs *can, may, might, shall, should, will, would, must*, and *ought to* are grammatically distinctive in three respects:

☐ Their third person singular present form has no *-s* ending – *He/she/it can*. Compare: *He/she writes*.

☐ They form questions by simply inverting the subject and verb – *Would you . . . ?* Compare: *Do you write?*

☐ They take the infinitive without *to* – *I must go*. Compare: *I want to go*.

Few native speakers of English (once they have chosen between *can* and *may*, or *shall* and *will*, for instance) have problems in using these verbs. But difficulties can arise with the verbs *dare, used to*, and *need*, which sometimes behave like ordinary verbs such as *move* or *write*, and sometimes like modal verbs such as *can* and *should*.

Dare. This verb behaves like an ordinary verb in sentences such as these:

She dares/dared to contradict her teacher.
Does/did she dare to tell him the truth?
She doesn't/didn't dare to complain.

But it behaves like *can* and *should* in questions, in negative or 'near-negative' sentences, and in certain subordinate clauses:

Who would dare say a thing like that?
How dare you be so rude?

Nobody dare/dared question his authority.
Jenny hardly dare/dared tell you.
Hugh daren't/dared not complain.
I don't believe he dare face me again.

Don't mix the two types. Say either *if she dares to tell him* or *if she dare tell him* – but not **✗** *if she dares tell him*.

Need. This verb behaves as an ordinary verb when it means the following:

☐ 'to lack' or 'to have need of something': *You need treatment; Do you need a torch?*

☐ 'have to' or 'must': *Do you need to keep saying that? He needs to pull his socks up; She doesn't need to tell us twice.*

But it behaves like *can* and *should* in questions and negatives, in the present tense: *Need you keep saying that? He needn't do any work*. Note that *All you need do is smile* is semi-negative; it means the same as *You needn't do anything other than smile*.

Again, don't mix the two types, You can say *Need we go?* or *Do we need to go?* but not **✗** *Do we need go?* You can say *No one need know* or *No one needs to know*, but not **✗** *No one needs know*.

Two further points of interest:

We must leave and *We need to leave* mean much the same thing. But this is not true of their negatives. *We mustn't leave* means the same as *We may not leave* – we are compelled not to leave. *We needn't leave* means that we can choose – we are not compelled to leave.

And note the difference between *I didn't need to write* and *I needn't have written*. Both imply that my writing was not necessary. But the first leaves it open whether I wrote or not, while the second makes it clear that I did.

Used to. This verb too can operate either like *can* and *should* or like an ordinary verb, but with certain reservations.

Purists dislike the question forms **?** *Did/Didn't you use to wear glasses?*, though it is very common, especially in American English. The alternatives, *Used you to wear glasses?*, *Usedn't you to wear glasses?*, and *Used you not to wear glasses?*, are all rather formal – and the last is also ambiguous.

Similarly, some purists regard as non-standard the negative form **?** *I didn't use to like cabbage*. But *I usedn't/used not to like cabbage* strikes others as old-fashioned. The form *I never used to* ... is acceptable in cases where the action could be repeated: *I never used to eat cabbage*. But it is less acceptable to purists when referring to a past state: **?** *I never used to like her*.

One solution is to avoid the structure altogether: *Didn't you wear glasses at one time? I didn't like cabbage, and never ate it*.

SPLIT INFINITIVES – TO BOLDLY GO

Imagine taking your car to the garage for repairs. The mechanic asks you to sit at the wheel while he observes the engine. He instructs you to put your foot on the accelerator and then, when he shouts, to lift it off at once.

You might report his instructions in this way:

> He told me to suddenly stop revving the engine.

A split infinitive. (Or, to be precise, a split 'to-infinitive', since *stop* in *I can stop* is also an infinitive.) According to purists, in American as well as British English, the word *suddenly* is improperly positioned: nothing should come between *to* and *stop*. (This 'rule' has a very flimsy historical basis – certainly not a good logical one.)

Now look at the sentence again:

> (1) He (2) told me (3) to (4) stop (5) revving the engine (6).

The positions 1 to 6 mark the only places that the adverb *suddenly* could go in the sentence. But if it goes into position 1, 2, or 3 it is the telling that is done suddenly; and if it goes into position 5 or 6 it is the revving. Only in position 4, the split infinitive position, is it the stopping that is sudden. To maintain the meaning, you would seem to have no option but to split the infinitive – though you might decide instead to rephrase the sentence drastically.

It is usually adverbs or adverb phrases that split infinitives. As a rule, adverbs of time (*soon, shortly, yesterday*, and so on) and manner (*easily, silently*, and so on) sit uncomfortably within infinitives and should be avoided – **??** *I hope to soon know*; **??** *You'll be able to easily manage it*; **??** *She started to silently hope for his return*. By contrast, some short words, such as focusing adverbs, sound much better – **?** *I refuse to even think about it*; **?** *He told me to only walk and not run*; **?** *I'd like to also play the guitar*; *You need to partly boil the potatoes*; **?** *We were able to really understand her problem*.

Still more nearly acceptable are cases where the infinitive clause serves as a kind of reported speech, echoing the actual words said or thought. It is hard to object to sentences such as *He asked me to kindly open the window* and *I'm old enough to well remember trolley buses*. You might reasonably say **?** *The council's going to compulsorily purchase the land*, because *compulsory purchase* is such a fixed expression. The pronoun *so* sounds idiomatic in the 'splitting position' too: *You have been right to so decide*.

Some apparent cases of split infinitives are deceptive. In *We intend to more than double our profits*, the words *more than double* act as an ordinary transitive verb, as if they formed a single word.

The normal position for most adverbs of time and manner is at the end of the clause. So: **??** *I need to immediately see you* can become *I need to see you immediately*. This position tends to be more natural than putting the adverb in front of the *to*. Compare **?** *They wanted him deliberately to flout the law* and *They wanted him to flout the law deliberately*.

A further disadvantage of the position before the *to* is that it leads more easily to ambiguity. In *They are planning quietly to scrap the law*, is it the planning or the scrapping that is quiet? If the former, putting *quietly* before *planning* makes things clearer; if the latter, the position after *law* serves the purpose.

When the infinitive takes a more complex form, such as *to be writing* or *to have written*, you will rarely have any problem. The obvious way to 'unsplit' sentences like **??** *I prefer to idly be lying in bed* is to put the adverb after the auxiliary verbs ... *to be idly lying* .... This pattern suggests a way out in other cases too: you could change **??** *You don't need to always complain* into *You don't need to be always complaining*.

The best policy, then, is to avoid split infinitives where possible by shifting the adverb (in the direction of the end of the sentence rather than of the start). Failing that, you could always rephrase the sentence to avoid the problem. But if all fails, rather split the infinitive than allow ambiguity.

IF I WAS YOU

Consider these sentences:

? I wouldn't do that again if I was you.
X If that were indeed the case, why didn't they phone and tell us?

X They asked if I were going with them.

X There's some doubt whether he were present at the time.

The *were* subjunctive, or past subjunctive, is used to talk about hypothetical or 'untrue' situations: *If I were you* . . . , *If George were to ask them* . . .

In each case, the event is either 'untrue' (I am not you) or hypothetical (George has not asked them yet). So the commonest place to find *were* subjunctives is in conditional *if*-clauses, where you would otherwise find the 'hypothetical' use of the past tense: *If I knew, I should tell you* (but I don't).

The *were* subjunctive is also found in clauses of comparison:

He acted as if he were mad.

They live in stone-age conditions, as it were.

Many people use the indicative: **?** *If he was to come.* . . , **?** *She looks as if she was frightened*. Such usage is not absolutely wrong, but is best avoided in formal speaking and writing.

The other setting for *were* subjunctives is in the (very formal) type of conditional clause that begins with the verb:

Were he able to join us, he certainly would.

Beware of hypercorrection – using *were* when it should be *was*. Don't use the *were* subjunctive in *if*-clauses referring to actual or likely past events. So the second example at the beginning of this section should read:

If that was indeed the case, why didn't they phone and tell us?

And don't use *were* after *whether*, or where *if* really means *whether*. So the next two examples at the beginning should read:

They asked if I was going with them.

There's some doubt whether he was present at the time.

Finally, a note on the present subjunctive. It can be used, very formally, in *if*-clauses in present tense sentences, but it tends to sound very stiff:

If he be elected, he will bring in sweeping changes.

The following sentences are incorrect; however:

X If he be found guilty and receives a prison sentence, his family will suffer.

X If he be not found at once, we demand that the search be intensified.

The first is wrong because it shifts for no reason between subjunctive *be* and indicative *receives*. The clause should be either *If he be found guilty and receive a prison sentence,* . . . or (preferably) *If he is found guilty and receives a prison sentence,* . . .

The second example has *not* in the wrong place: in present subjunctive *if*-clauses, *not* precedes the verb. So you should correct the clause to read: *If he not be found at once,* . . . This sounds so stiff and formal, however, that it is better to say *If he isn't found at once,* . . . instead.

Dangling Participles and Lack of Symmetry

What is wrong with this sentence, typical of so many guidebooks? *Crossing the bridge, a courtyard lies in front of you*.

The answer is that, according to the strict rules of grammar, it makes no sense. Its literal meaning is this: 'A courtyard crosses the bridge and it lies in front of you.'

MISRELATED CONSTRUCTIONS

Here are some more 'nonsense' sentences:

?? On opening the door, Mary's gaze at once fell on the cradle.

X Wide-brimmed and furry, the prince raised his hat and waved it at the crowd.

X A brilliant but outrageous comedian, Lenny Bruce's sketches both amused and unsettled his audience.

?? When making up prescriptions, some tablets have to be divided into four.

X Born in Turkey, I was amazed that Kemal fits so well into English society.

X As Prime Minister, I should like to ask you a question about your cabinet reshuffle.

X Like most cars with four-wheel drive, I find the new Toyota handles excellently on rough surfaces.

X Having observed the series so far, it is obvious how it continues.

X Being an inveterate smoker, there are always several ashtrays lying about my room.

Modern English grammar requires that the opening phrases of a sentence should – with certain exceptions – relate to the first noun or pronoun or equivalent that follows. Each of the examples just cited displays a conflict between this requirement and the intended meaning. The opening phrase in each case (except the last) is known to grammarians as a 'misrelated modifier' (or 'misrelated adjective/ participle/phrase').

Clearly it was not the courtyard that crossed the bridge, or Mary's gaze that opened the door. No prince is wide-brimmed and furry, sketches are not comedians, and tablets do not make up prescriptions. I was not born in Turkey, nor am I Prime Minister, or a car with four-wheel drive. (Note that an introductory *on* or *when*, as in two of the examples listed above, is sometimes considered to improve the construction slightly.)

The Lenny Bruce example demonstrates 'false apposition'. When two noun phrases that refer to the same thing occur side by side – as in *my friend Bill Wilson* or *the other gas, carbon monoxide* – they are in 'apposition'. The phrase *A brilliant but outrageous comedian* should be in apposition to *Lenny Bruce*, but the sentence puts it alongside *Lenny Bruce's sketches* instead.

In the last two examples, the main clauses consist of an impersonal *it is* construction and a *there are* construction, providing no foothold at all for the opening participle in each case (*Having observed...*, *Being...*). The participle accordingly seems to be 'hanging' or 'dangling' in mid-air; hence the name *hanging participle* or *dangling participle* (or *detached/disconnected/suspended participle*).

Various remedies are possible, according to the structure of the opening phrase in each case. The correct noun or pronoun can be moved nearer to the start of the sentence:

> Like most cars with four-wheel drive, the new Toyota handles excellently on rough surfaces, I find.

If the correct noun or pronoun happens not to appear in the sentence at all, you will have to introduce it:

> A brilliant but outrageous comedian, Lenny Bruce devised sketches that both amused and unsettled his audience.

In doing so, you might have to change the main clause from active to passive or vice versa:

> When making up prescriptions, you will sometimes have to divide tablets into four.

The main clause might have to be altered in various other ways:

> As Prime Minister, could you please answer a question about your cabinet reshuffle?

Sometimes the opening phrase rather than the main clause should be altered in form:

> As Mary opened the door, her gaze at once fell on the cradle. (Here the opening phrase has been expanded into an adverbial clause.)

Or you could move the opening phrase to the middle of the sentence, to a position immediately following the noun or pronoun it relates to:

> The prince raised his hat, wide-brimmed and furry, and waved it at the crowd.

As for the dangling participles, you can remedy them either by introducing the missing subject –

> Having observed the series so far, you can easily see how it continues

– or by expanding the participle phrase into a full clause:

> Since I am an inveterate smoker, there are always several ashtrays lying about my room

Note that a misrelated construction need not occur at the beginning of a sentence. It can occur just as readily at the end or in the middle:

X The museum is very nice, but unlike the art gallery I wouldn't want to visit it again.

ACCEPTABLE DANGLING PARTICIPLES

The prohibition against misrelated and dangling participles allows certain exceptions.

First, old-fashioned 'absolute constructions':

> Mary having opened the door, her gaze at once fell on the cradle.

Secondly, where the participle-like word is functioning as a preposition or conjunction:

> Regarding item 8, this matter should be decided at once.
> There were four of us, not counting the dog.
> Seeing he's here, business can proceed.
> You'll be all right, provided you make sure to keep your head down.

Other forms normally allowable in this way include: *according to, assuming, barring, concerning, considering, depending on, excepting, failing, following, given, granted, including, owing to, providing, supposing*. Two common *-ing* words, *during* and *pending*, are only prepositions and never verbs.

A final exception is participles that, though remaining verbal, help to form phrases that offer some sort of comment on the whole sentence:

> Broadly speaking, there's little to choose between them.
> Talking of holidays, is Trevor back from his yet?
> Put plainly, you're a wimp.

Other phrases used in this way include: *allowing for exceptions, all things considered, strictly speaking, putting two and two together, put simply, taking everything into account, using the term loosely*, and *coming down to details*.

Some participle phrases of this kind are on the borderline still:

? Judging from previous research, this new star cluster is likely to have a high carbon content.
? Referring to your recent inquiry, our price is £10.99.
? Having said that, her performance nevertheless remains an impressive debut.
? Based on information received, the police yesterday raided the house in north London.

To be on the safe side, you could reword each of these examples easily enough: *If previous research is anything to go by . . .* or *To judge from previous research . . .; Regarding your recent inquiry . . .; That said, her performance . . .; Acting on information received . . .*

AMBIGUITIES

It is crucial to get verbless clauses and prepositional phrases in the right place, near the words they belong to. Otherwise, even when they don't 'dangle', they risk being ambiguous or misleading:

? Barbados only just defeated Trinidad, handicapped by a spate of recent injuries.
? I witnessed the girl walk deliberately past the fans shouting abuse.
? I saw you using my new binoculars.

All the sentences have elements that could refer to more than one noun. Was it Barbados or Trinidad that was handicapped? Who was shouting abuse,

the girl or the fans? Did I see you through my binoculars, or were you using them when I saw you? To resolve the ambiguity, you should either change the word order or add some words to clarify the meaning:

> Handicapped by a spate of recent injuries, Barbados only just defeated Trinidad.
> Barbados only just defeated Trinidad, who were handicapped by a spate of recent injuries.

> I witnessed the girl walk deliberately past the fans and shout abuse at them.
> I witnessed the girl walk deliberately past the fans, who were shouting abuse at her.

> I saw you by using my binoculars.
> I saw you while you were using my binoculars.

Now a slightly different problem:

? Following several new leads, the police have made a number of arrests.

Here the ambiguity lies in the word *following*. Is it a participle (*The police have been following several new leads*)? Or is it simply a preposition meaning 'after'? Here are two possible revised versions:

> Having followed several new leads, the police have made a number of arrests.
> The police have made a number of arrests after several new leads.

Now try correcting these examples, each containing ambiguously placed prepositional phrases:

? He was forced to abandon his attempt to sail the Atlantic single-handed on Monday.
? The body of Mr Chopra was cremated yesterday in the compound of the newspapers he edited for security reasons.
? These claims have been dismissed as mere bravado by the police.

In the first example, *on Monday* is closer to *sail* than to *forced*, and suggests a remarkable sailing speed – crossing the Atlantic in a single day! Presumably what is meant is *On Monday he was forced to . . .*

In the second, *for security reasons* probably goes with *cremated*, and again the prepositional phrase would be better at the beginning.

In the last, unless the police are swaggering, the words *by the police* should appear earlier in the sentence, close to *dismissed: These claims have been dismissed by the police as mere bravado.*

AMBIGUITY AND WORD ORDER

Careless word order is perhaps the commonest cause of ambiguity. Sentences need to be thoughtfully structured to ensure the intended relationship between words or phrases, and to avoid any unintended relationship. The rule of thumb is to place related words as near to each other as possible.

Hence the comically ambiguous advertisement ✗ *A piano is being sold by a lady with carved legs* is easily rectified by shifting the last phrase *with carved legs* to a position closer to the noun *piano* that it relates to: *A piano with carved legs is being sold by a lady*.

With truly ambiguous sentences, such an adjustment may resolve the ambiguity in one direction, but not in the other.

Take, for example, this sentence: **?** *The government ordered an inquiry into the unrest last year*. Does *last year* relate to *ordered* or to *unrest*? If to *ordered*, you can shift *last year* to a position alongside it: *The government last year ordered an inquiry into the unrest*.

But if *last year* relates to *unrest*, you will have to add an extra word or phrase to remove the ambiguity: *The government ordered an inquiry into the unrest that occurred last year* (or simply, *the unrest of last year*).

Here now are several more examples of ambiguity – real ambiguity, with a pair of rival meanings, or merely comic and theoretical ambiguity – based on poor word order.

You might try restructuring or rephrasing each sentence to produce the intended meaning or the two possible meanings.

At all events, examine all the examples closely with a view to learning the dangers and avoiding them in your own writing.

> Mary Wiggins wants to play Lady Macbeth very badly.
> My supporters urged me to speak with great fervour.
> The officer testified that Dr Henley had cycled past the protesters hurling insults.
> The mayor shook hands awkwardly with the visitor, inconvenienced by an attack of arthritis.
> Please send us your ideas about planting seedlings on a postcard.
> A volley of gunshot was used to disperse the riot by the police.
> The militia was criticised for firing tear gas into the crowd yesterday without causing serious injury.
> Further north are the hills covered in heather that visitors find so attractive.
> You'll never find a policeman just walking here in the park.
> Children, this fruit is not to be eaten without washing first.

NON-PARALLEL CONSTRUCTIONS

If elements in a sentence are proposed as parallel in kind, they should be presented as parallel in structure. The following sentence fails to meet this simple requirement:

✗ She is stubborn, selfish and has a sharp temper.

The three elements are not symmetrical here, and should not be organised as though they were. Either rearrange the elements so that they no longer pretend to be equally weighted –

> She is stubborn and selfish, and has a sharp temper

– or make them symmetrical in structure:

> She is stubborn, selfish, and quick-tempered.

Such failures of symmetry are particularly common with 'correlative conjunctions' such as *either . . . or . . .* and *not only . . . but also . . .*

✗ Not only is that a very unfair statement, but also quite untrue.

The structures following *not only* and *but (also)* should match each other closely. In this example, however, the *not only* element contains a verb, whereas the *but also* element does not.

The sentence can be reconstructed so that both elements have a verb, or neither element has:

> That statement is not only very unfair, but also quite untrue.

> Not only is that a very unfair statement, but it is also quite untrue.

Next, consider this faulty construction:

✗ The actors were criticised both by their friends and their enemies.

Again, the correlative conjunctions *both* and *and* demand matching constructions. Yet here the *both*-phrase contains the preposition *by*, whereas the *and*-phrase lacks it. The two elements can, theoretically, be brought into parallel in either of two ways:

The actors were criticised both by their friends and by their enemies.

? The actors were criticised by both their friends and their enemies.

The second version here remains unsatisfactory, however, since it introduces an ambiguity into the sentence: the phrase *both their friends* could be taken on its own to suggest that the actors have only two friends.

Adjectives and Adverbs

Is it acceptable to speak of *a very unique experience*? Can you properly say that someone was doing something *sillily*? Should you write *tireder* or *more tired*? Are you standing *firm* or *firmly*? Where do you put *only* in a sentence? This section deals with questions such as these.

ADJECTIVES ENDING IN -LY

Many adverbs are formed by adding *-ly*, sometimes with minor spelling adjustments, to an adjective. Hence all the adjective-adverb pairs such as *careful/carefully* and *terrific/terrifically*. So what is wrong with the following?

✗ He walked leisurely down the street.
? The editor smiled friendlily, as if trying to put me at my ease.
?? They giggled sillily with embarrassment.
? You'll likely have trouble with that machine.

In the first example an adjective is being used incorrectly as an adverb. The *-ly* ending can be tacked onto some nouns to form adjectives, as in *beastly, brotherly, cowardly, friendly, ghostly, heavenly, leisurely, lovely, masterly, motherly, princely, scholarly, sisterly,* and *worldly*. Other adjectives have *-ly* as part of the stem, such as *ghastly, holy, jolly, silly,* and *ugly*.

There is also a group of *-ly* adjectives formed from other adjectives, though often with altered meanings: *dead/deadly, elder/elderly, good/goodly, kind/kindly, lone/lonely, low/lowly, sick/sickly*. (To complicate matters, *dead* can also be an informal adverb: *You're dead right!*)

In the second and third examples above, *-ly* adjectives have been turned into adverbs by the addition of a further *-ly*, but the results are uncomfortable. The only safe way of using such adjectives adverbially is by including them within an adverbial phrase:

He walked in a leisurely fashion . . .
The editor smiled in a friendly manner, . . .
They giggled in a silly way . . .

The last of the examples is distinctive. *Likely* is both an adjective – *That's a likely story! You're likely to have trouble* – and an adverb.

Standard British English idiom demands a qualifying word in front of the adverb: *likely*.

You'll very/quite/most likely have trouble with that machine.

The original sentence here – **?** *You'll likely have trouble . . .* – sounds odd to English ears, though it is perfectly correct in American English, and also in Scottish, Irish, and many other varieties.

Note the word *kindly*. It can be an adverb from *kind*, with two uses:

He treated them kindly.
Would you kindly stay in your seats.

It is also an adjective, as in *a kindly old man*, and in this meaning it would require a phrase when used adverbially: *He smiled at me in a kindly fashion.*

Note too the group of *-ly* words relating to periods of time, where the adjective and adverb have the same form: *hourly, daily, nightly, weekly, fortnightly, monthly, yearly*:

I've just got my yearly pay rise. (adjective)
I get a pay rise yearly. (adverb)

ADJECTIVE OR ADVERB

With *hard, fast, straight* and similar versatile words, usage is very simple: they can be either adjectives or adverbs. With other words, you sometimes may face a tricky choice:

> The ice-cream tastes (delicious/deliciously).
> All my plans have gone (wrong/wrongly).
> Tessa looked (hungry/hungrily).
> The milk had frozen (solid/solidly).

Do you need an adjective or adverb after verbs such as these? Or, to put it another way, are such verbs 'doing' verbs (which require adverbs) or 'being' verbs (which require adjectives)?

The test for 'being' verbs is that the subject in some way equals the complement. All four examples above pass the test: it is fair to say 'the ice-cream = delicious', 'All my plans = wrong', and so on. So in each case the adjective form is the correct one.

Adverbs often show how the activity of a 'doing' verb takes place: *I live frugally*. In the third example above, it would be possible to say *Tessa looked hungrily at the steak*. Here, it is the manner in which she is looking that is described, not Tessa herself. Other pairs of similar sentences are possible:

> The children ran wildly around the garden.
> The children ran wild.

> She pleaded innocently to be let go.
> She pleaded innocent.

> You must stand firmly against such injustice.
> You must stand firm.

Now, what about these?

> Fine furniture does not come (cheap/cheaply).
> Think (positive/positively).
> You guessed (wrong/wrongly).

In all these examples, either the adjective or the adverb is acceptable, according to the way in which you view the sentence.

In the first, for instance, if you think 'Furniture = not cheap', *cheap* is correct; if you think that the getting of the furniture is not cheap, the adverb *cheaply* is correct. It does not matter.

Two special cases, finally:

> I feel (bad/badly) about what happened.
> He phoned (direct/directly).

For most people, *bad* and *badly* in the first example are again equally acceptable options. But for some traditionalists *I feel bad* means only 'I feel unwell' and *I feel badly* means 'I regret', and *badly* is therefore the correct choice. In the second

example, *direct* is not in fact an adjective but an adverb too, meaning 'without going through a telephone operator', whereas *directly* would here mean 'immediately'. So either word could be correct – but not both in the same context. Similarly, *The train went direct/directly to Oxford*.

QUICK OR QUICKLY

Unfortunately, the distinction between 'doing' and 'being' verbs does not tell the whole story. Style too comes into consideration. Which of the following pairs is correct?

> I couldn't get away (quick/quickly) enough.
> Drive (slow/slowly).

SPEAK FREE, SPEAK FREELY

Test your knowledge. Complete the sentences with the correct adverb. For the answers, turn to the quiz answers section, pages 633-648.

1. clean(ly) a. I'm sorry, but it went . . . out of my head.
b. You'll never cut . . . with those blunt scissors.

2. close(ly) a. Guard this secret . . .
b. I don't like people who stand too . . .

3. direct(ly) a. The coach goes . . . to York.
b. The coach is leaving . . .

4. even(ly) a. Try to spread the paint . . . over the wall.
b. You're not . . . trying.

5. free(ly) a. We were afraid to speak . . .
b. Children are allowed in . . .

6. hard(ly) a. I'm working too . . .
b. I . . . have time to think.

7. high(ly) a. I cannot recommend that hotel too . . .
b. I cannot jump as . . . as I used to.

8. just(ly) a. They were dealt with . . .
b. That's . . . what I imagined.

9. late(ly) a. Have you read any good books . . . ?
b. As usual, Tom arrived . . .

10. near(ly) a. Don't be afraid to come . . .
b. He . . . didn't come.

11. pretty/prettily a. I was . . . pleased, actually.
b. She was . . . dressed in pink.

The answer is that both versions are correct in each case, though the one with the adjective is less formal than the one with the adverb. *Quick* and *slow* are at heart adjectives, but like *fast* they often serve as adverbs too. This is especially true of their comparative forms: *Tom got there quicker*; *Please drive slower*.

Some people dislike this usage. In formal speaking and writing, it is usually safer to stick to adverbs: *I could not get away quickly enough*; *Please drive more slowly*.

The adjectives *sure* and *real* are also used as informal adverbs, especially in American English: *She's real pretty*; *Sure I can*. More formally, these should be *She's really pretty* and *I certainly can*.

ONLY

In the use of *only*, natural idiom is often at odds with logical word order. It is quite natural to say *John only gave his sister £5*. But purists would say that *only* relates to *£5*, and so should go directly before it: *John gave his sister only £5*. In the same way, they argue, *I only saw Mary yesterday* strictly means that I saw her but did not, say, speak to her; the sentence should be *I saw only Mary yesterday* (I saw Mary, but not her husband Edward or any of her children) or *I saw Mary only yesterday* (it was only yesterday that I saw her).

In informal usage, however, the most natural place for *only* is usually just before the verb. The context usually helps to make the meaning clear, and in speech the intonation does too: in the previous example, a stress on *Mary* or *yesterday* (or *saw*) would accurately convey the sense intended.

But if ambiguity really does threaten, it is doubly important to position the *only* as close as possible to the word or phrase it modifies. Suppose you received the following note:

? I shall only send you £5 towards the appeal if you write to me again.

Would you write again, or not? A properly helpful and unambiguous message would position the *only* either before *£5* or before *if*, depending on the intended meaning.

OTHER CONTROVERSIAL –LY WORDS

Various other words ending in -*ly* have provoked a certain amount of controversy among thoughtful writers and speakers. The two most notable such words are *firstly* and *hopefully*.

Firstly. Traditionalists dislike the use of *firstly*, and often *lastly* too, to introduce items in a list. They prefer *first* and *last*, even though *secondly*, *thirdly*, *fourthly*, *fifthly*, and so on introduce the items in between. The traditional rule is difficult to justify but risky to ignore.

To temper the inconsistency somewhat, you could use the phrases *first of all* and *last of all* instead.

Hopefully. In the sense of 'in a hopeful way', *hopefully* is a long-established and unobjectionable adverb: *We travelled more hopefully after hearing the news of Nicholas's miraculous release*.

In its more modern sense of 'I hope that' or 'with luck', it has aroused the opposition of purists: **?** *Hopefully the letter will arrive tomorrow*.

Among the objections are: that it is an Americanism; that it is ill-formed (it should perhaps be *hopedly* or *hopeably* instead); that it usurps the older sense of *hopefully*, and could even cause ambiguity (**?** *Hopefully he has paid off the last of his debts*), and that as an adverb it has the grammatical duty to modify a verb, an adjective, or another adverb – but not an entire clause.

This last objection is no more cogent than the others. Modern English has a great many 'sentence' adverbs, widely used to reflect the attitude of the speaker or writer – *Unfortunately, I can't join you* – or the truth or likelihood of the event mentioned: *Probably I'll go straight home*.

Not that all such 'sentence' adverbs escape criticism. Purists dislike the use, or at least the widespread overuse, of *basically*, for instance, at the beginning of sentences: **?** *Basically, the melting of the fuse wire breaks the electrical current*. And three other -*fully* words often attract similar criticism to that of *hopefully*: namely, *mercifully*, *thankfully*, and *regretfully* – often used in place of *regrettably*.

CURIOUSER OR MORE CURIOUS

'Curiouser and curiouser!' cried Alice (she was so much surprised, that for the moment she quite forgot how to speak good English).
– Lewis Carroll,
Alice's Adventures in Wonderland.

The general rules for making comparative and superlative adjectives are these:

☐ Short adjectives usually add *-er* and *-est* (*big, bigger, biggest; wet, wetter, wettest*).

☐ Longer adjectives usually use *more* and *most* (*curious, more curious, most curious; cheerful, more cheerful, most cheerful*).

A couple of exceptions. Some short adjectives take *more* and *most* rather than *-er* and *-est* (**X** *wronger*), especially those derived from verbs (**X** a *spoilter* child; **X** He's *boreder* than her). And three-syllable adjectives made up of *un-* plus a two-syllable adjective that takes *-er* and *-est* will usually do so too (*unhappier, untidiest*). Compounds sometimes have two forms, as with *more kind-hearted* and *kinder-hearted*.

In general, American English tends to prefer the *-er* and *-est* comparison while British English tends to prefer *more* and *most*. When in doubt, use *more* and *most*.

Occasionally tone may come into the picture. Using *-er/-est* with adjectives that normally use *more/most* can sound a little disapproving or sarcastic. Compare the following pair:

His favourite hobby is pure mathematics, the more abstract the better.
His favourite hobby is pure mathematics, the abstracter the better.

ADVERBS WITHOUT -LY

Many adverbs do not end in *-ly*. Examples include *always, soon, today, ever, yet, away, here, so, too*.

One unusual adverb is *hard*, as in *They fought hard*. It contrasts with the 'semi-negative' adverb *hardly*, meaning 'scarcely'. Other cases where the adverb has the same form as the adjective include *fast* (*He drives fast*) and *straight* (*It flew straight at me*). There are no such words as **X** *fastly* and **X** *straightly*, despite the existence of *slowly, quickly, crookedly*, and the like. Notice the adverbial use of *fast, sound*, and *wide* before certain adjectives:

I was fast/sound asleep. (Contrast: *I was sleeping soundly*.)
The baby's wide awake.

Some *-ing* words are used similarly: *spanking new, hopping mad, raving mad*, and *boiling hot*. You cannot speak of a **X** *spankingly new car*.

Adverbs follow rather different rules. Some short ones take *-er* and *-est* – *sooner, soonest* – including many that are identical with adjectives: *earlier, earliest; faster, fastest;* and *later, latest*.

Most adverbs, however, even those of two syllables, take *more* and *most: more fully, most wisely*.

Remember that when only two things are under consideration, the adjective should take the comparative (*-er, more*) form rather than the superlative (*-est, most*): **X** *Of her two novels, the second is surely best*. A few idioms do allow this oddity – *May the best man win* – but avoid it elsewhere.

ABSOLUTE ADJECTIVES

Some adjectives cannot be used in the comparative or superlative. Obviously you cannot say **X** *a more nuclear missile* or **X** *the most medical student*. You cannot even say that the missile is **X** *very nuclear* or the student **X** *nearly medical*. They are nuclear and medical, and that is that.

Some adjectives should not normally be used in the comparative or superlative, since they already imply a complete or final degree. If something is *perfect*, for instance, it cannot be improved on, so **X** *more perfect* and **X** *most perfect* are not usually possible. Neither are **X** *less perfect* and **X** *least perfect*, since once something is less than perfect, it is imperfect.

Strictly speaking, such *absolute* or *ungradable* adjectives should also not be modified by words such as *absolutely, totally, utterly*, and *very*: **?** *an absolutely perfect somersault*. Yet idiom seems to have given its blessing to such constructions, though they are really tautologous.

Absolute adjectives can be modified by *nearly, not quite*, and so on: *an almost perfect somersault; Her performance was well-nigh perfect*.

There are dozens of other absolute adjectives. Here is a sampling: *absolute, complete, contemporary, entire, essential, everlasting, extreme, ideal, indispensable, invaluable, supreme, total, unique:* **??** *the most indispensable book ever published;* **??** *a fairly/very unique film*.

Many apparently absolute adjectives are usually exempted from the restrictions, however. Few people would object to the use of *the purest water; a fuller description; an even more cloudless day; a very thorough search*.

Handling Negatives

Negative sentences are a fertile source of confusion. All too often the sentence structure turns out, on close analysis, to produce a meaning exactly the opposite of the one intended.

The 'double negative', for example, produces a positive sense in modern English (in earlier forms of English, and in some other languages, a double negative simply reinforces the negative sense): *I wouldn't say that he isn't telling the truth*.

Unless both writer/speaker and reader/hearer keep their wits about them, the communicating of complex negative ideas goes awry.

NEAR NEGATIVES

Consider these sentences:

X I barely knew no one at the meeting.
X No judge but the most stony-hearted could deny the ice-dancers anything but full marks.
X No head injury is too trivial to ignore.

Near-negative words such as *hardly*, *barely*, *scarcely*, *rarely*, and *seldom* are usually ungrammatical with fully negative words. So the first sentence should read like this: *I barely knew anyone at the meeting*.

Negative sentences are usually thought of as containing *not, no, none, never, nobody*, and so on. But they can be made in other ways too, as by the use of *un-, without, unless, ignore, deny, fail*, and *miss*. These words can cause real confusion if carelessly combined with the usual negative words.

The second sentence has tied itself in knots with too many negatives – *no, but, deny, but*. It actually says the opposite of what is presumably intended. Far safer to untangle the ideas, and write: *Only a stony-hearted judge could have given the ice-dancers anything less than full marks*.

Try to keep to at most two negatives or negative-like words in a sentence. And take particular care when starting a sentence with a negative. As soon as you have got to *No one can but refuse to* . . . you know you are lost. And if you are not, your reader or listener will be.

Even an apparently simple sentence, such as the third of the examples above, ties itself in knots when it mishandles negatives. Analyse it carefully, and

you will see how misleading it really is. The supposed meaning is properly conveyed by any of the following versions:

> No head injury is too trivial to treat.
> No head injury is trivial enough to ignore.
> No head injury, however trivial, should be ignored.
> All head injuries, however trivial, should be treated.

NEGATIVES AND CLAUSES

You need to take particular care in complex sentences where there are negatives or near-negatives and two verbs.

X Customs officers noticed that the yacht was not flying a yellow flag, indicating it had come from abroad with dutiable goods.

Grammatically, this implies that *not* flying a yellow flag indicates that a ship has come from abroad with dutiable goods. But this can hardly be what is intended. The real meaning comes out much more clearly in this version:

> Customs officers noticed that the yacht was not flying a yellow flag, as it should have been to indicate that it had come from abroad with dutiable goods.

Another problem with complex sentences is the scope of negatives. If, to take a simple example, you say *I didn't meet her*, it is *meet her* that is negated. But if you say *I didn't meet her in Outer Mongolia*, the implication is that you did meet her, and it is only *in Outer Mongolia* that is negated. There are often problems working out exactly which words are negated and just how far the negative extends in a sentence. In the following examples, the negative words either carry over too far in each sentence or do not extend far enough:

X It was not seriously thought that the negotiating team would be presenting any new offers, and that, instead, the talks would have to be adjourned until next year.

X No orders will be given special attention, but will have to wait their turn.

X It will be their home for life if they don't fall behind with the rent and are evicted.

✗ No one would argue that in an ideal world such problems would not exist.

? I wouldn't be surprised if he didn't pay me back.

In the first sentence the *not* in the main clause, *It was not seriously thought*, grammatically covers both *that*-clauses. But logically it should not apply to the second. It would be better to end the sentence after *offers* and begin again: *It was instead expected that the talks would have to be adjourned until next year*.

In the second, *no orders* has to be the subject of both clauses. So: *No orders . . . will have to wait their turn* – which is nonsense. Again it would be better to create two sentences – *No orders will be given special attention. All will have to wait their turn*.

The third example shows the opposite mistake. Stripping out the first of the *if*-clauses you get: *It will be their home for life if they . . . are evicted*. The *don't* does not affect the *if*-clause. Generally, *if . . . not* becomes clearer as *unless*, as here: *It will be their home for life unless they fall behind with the rent and are evicted*.

The fourth is a classic double negative. *No one* and *not* cancel each other out. Negative subjects are often problematical. You could try something like *Everyone would agree . . .* instead.

The last example is a particularly common type of double negative. The sentence is correctly grammatical if it means that I expect him *not* to repay me.

But is this in fact the intended meaning? Many people might take it the other way – I do expect him to pay me. For the sake of clear communication, then, such usages are best avoided. Either say *I wouldn't be surprised if he paid me back* (if you expect him to pay) or (if you think it unlikely) say *I'd be surprised if he paid me back*.

NO QUESTION

No question is a phrase that often gets unwary users into a tangle. What do these sentences mean?

There's no question of a compromise on Britain's central demands.

There can be no question that the viciousness of the attacks took him aback.

? There's no question of Sam's arriving late.

? There's no question that the CEGB can buy 70 million tons of coal at world marginal prices.

There can be no question but that the Crown could have been entitled to an injunction to restrain publication.

Custom has it that if there is no question *of* something (happening), it is 'out of the question'. There is no possibility. So the first sentence should mean the same as: *There can be no compromise*.

On the other hand, if there is no question *that* something happened, it means that it definitely did happen. There is no doubt. So the second sentence means the same as: *The viciousness of the attacks most certainly did take him aback*.

Not surprisingly, the two constructions get confused, and sentences can be taken to mean the opposite of what they say. The third example – using *no question of* as in the first sentence – ought to mean that Sam will definitely turn up on time. But usage is so uncertain that it might mean that he will definitely turn up late. The fourth example ought to mean that the CEGB definitely can buy the coal at these prices. But again, it might be taken to mean that they cannot.

Only the form *no question but* (*that*) is unambiguous. It always means that the thing is certain. In the fifth example the Crown could definitely have secured the injunction. Unfortunately, the form *no question but* (*that*) sounds very old-fashioned. The best solution is to avoid the expression altogether. Use *no possibility* or *no doubt* instead.

CANNOT HELP BUT

In formal English, you should avoid such sentences as **??** *I cannot help but admire her*. It contains in effect a *triple* negative, and so carries a negative sense in grammar, whereas the intended meaning is clearly positive. The construction seems to be a blend of two others: the rather formal *I cannot but admire her* and the recommended *I cannot help admiring her*.

NEITHER . . . NOR . . .

Consider these two sentences:

✗ Keep straight on, swerving neither left or right.
✗ An assistant commissioner said they could neither vouch for the truth nor accuracy of the reports.

What is the matter with each of them? *Neither... nor...* is not *neither...or...* as in the first example. And the *neither...nor...* construction must balance, which it fails to do in the second sentence. The elements that follow *neither* and *nor* should be grammatically symmetrical, generally having the same pattern of parts of speech. So the second sentence should read either *they could neither vouch for the truth nor confirm the accuracy of the reports* or *they could vouch for neither the truth nor the accuracy of the reports*. But as it stands the sentence does not balance.

(For more details on the usage of *neither* and *nor*, see pages 176 and 177.)

NOT...BUT...

Once again the two elements should be grammatically symmetrical:

> We shall fly not the green flag but the blue one.
> We shall not fly the green flag but display the blue one.

In colloquial idiom, these two structures are mixed:

? We shall not fly the green flag but the blue one.

Avoid such imbalance, expecially in formal writing. Take care, however, not to let ambiguity creep in when you balance the construction:

? The new militancy presents a danger to democracy. It is trying not to make a point but to deny a hearing.

The intended meaning here is surely *not trying to make a point* but the actual wording, for the sake of symmetry, has been twisted into *trying not to make a point*. Only a fairly drastic rephrasing will resolve the problem: *It is not trying to make a point – it is trying to deny a hearing*.

(For *not only...but also...*, see the section on 'non-parallel constructions', pages 198 and 199.

NOT...BECAUSE...

In writing especially, *not...because* can give rise to serious ambiguities. Consider these sentences:

> I didn't go because I was ill.
> I didn't go, because I was ill.

The problem seldom occurs in speaking. The first version, without a pause after *go*, suggests that I did go (to the doctor's, for instance), but for some reason other than illness. The second reports that I did not go, and then gives the reason for my not going. The sentences would also probably be distinguished by a rising voice pitch in the first and a falling one in the second.

In writing, the distinction hinges – precariously – on a single comma. Many people leave out the comma in sentences with the second meaning. To be on the safe side, you could rewrite both versions. The first could be something along the lines of *I went not because I was ill, but to get some jabs* or *It wasn't because I was ill that I went*. The second could become *Because I was ill I didn't go*.

Leaving Words Out

Language would be tedious if you had to spell everything out and keep repeating yourself. Fortunately, you can often leave words out, since listeners or readers mentally supply them for themselves. When you do this in a correctly grammatical way, you are using 'ellipsis'.

Ellipsis is very common in casual speech: *Coming? Read any good books lately? Know what I mean? Seen it all before, frankly*. In each case, the sentence has left out the subject and auxiliary verb, since they are obvious in the context.

But these examples are exceptional. The first rule of normal ellipsis is that you may usually omit words only if they are 'recoverable'; that is, if they actually appear somewhere nearby in the text itself. You

cannot usually omit words that people can only guess at.

VERB PHRASES – I CAN AND HAVE SAID SO

Consider this sentence:

?? All future editions will or have been corrected at this point.

You cannot just pick and choose what to omit. If you recover the missing pieces here you get either **✗** *All future editions will been corrected* or **✗** *All future editions will corrected*. Neither of these is English. Rewrite it either as *All future editions will be or have been corrected* or as *All future editions will be corrected or have been* (already).

Here now are some further examples of unacceptable ellipses:

?? No convict has ever or can ever escape.
X My brother refuses to and my sister insists on speaking French.
X We are, and must, work in London.

The mishandling of the *-ing* form of the verb, as in the last two examples, is generally considered to be especially awkward.

By a curious convention, 'faulty' ellipsis is more acceptable if it occurs *after* rather than before the 'recoverable' word has appeared. Compare these two sentences:

?? I shall always and have always loved you.
I have always loved you, and always shall.

Only a pedant would insist on adding the words *love you* at the end of the second sentence. Here are two more examples that most people would accept as standard:

> They went to the shops because they were asked to (go to them).
> I live in London and my brother (lives) in Edinburgh.

There is a particular limitation on ellipsis in passives. Take a sentence like *I had seen him but I hadn't been seen by him*. Although *seen* is shared, it cannot be omitted because in the first clause it is in a perfect construction while in the second it is passive: **X** *I had seen him but hadn't been by him*. Ellipsis only works if the shared forms are both passive or both not:

> We were told but my sister wasn't (told).
> He has told me and I have (told) her.

X He has told me, but my sister wasn't (told).

NOUN PHRASES

You can often leave out parts of noun phrases. The main noun, for example, need not be repeated if the second noun phrase contains numerals, colour adjectives, or superlatives:

> There's your mouse, but where are my two?
> Just behind the green car I can see the white approaching.
> I've had some marvellous holidays, but this was the best ever.

Note that you can usually recover a singular from a plural (*mice* from *mouse*), and vice versa (*holiday*

from *holidays*). What you cannot do is omit a noun after just any adjective.

?? There's the fat mouse, but where's the thin?
?? Behind the fast car I can see the slow approaching.

In each case, an extra word should be added at the end – either the original noun once again (*mouse, car*) or the pronoun *one*, as in *Behind the fast car I can see the slow one approaching*.

And you cannot recover a singular from a plural – or a plural from a singular – if they both occur within the same phrase:

X The avoidance of tax was the sole or one of the main purposes of the transaction.

This should read: *was the sole purpose or one of the main purposes*. As it stands, the sentence reads: **X** *was the sole . . . purposes*.

PREPOSITIONS AND CONSTRUCTIONS

A simple test for many 'parallel constructions' (see page 204) is this; if a part of one element has been omitted as 'understood', try inserting the 'understood' element and see if it really fits; alternatively, leave out the second of the elements and see if the sentence still makes sense.

X She is as talented, if not more talented than, any of the male riders in the team.

The two related components are not properly matched: to match *more talented than*, the earlier phrase should read *as talented as*. To see how the syntax has gone wrong, leave out all the parenthetical words between the two commas. The need for an extra *as* at once becomes apparent.

Similarly:

X The performance of an alcohol-fuelled car is comparable – or slightly better – than that of a petrol car.

For the sake of symmetry, and syntax, a *to* should be added after *comparable*, and the sentence should be repunctuated: *is comparable to – or slightly better than – that of a petrol car*.

One final example of the common error in which a single preposition is applied to both parallel elements where it is in fact appropriate to only one:

X Employers remain ignorant or uninterested in the abilities of polytechnic graduates.

Correct this so that it reads: *Employers remain ignorant of or uninterested in the abilities of polytechnic graduates.*

LISTS – THE GOOD, BAD, AND THE UGLY

Consider these two sentences:

X I need a knife, fork, and a spoon.
X There are buses at 10 a.m., noon, and at 4.30 p.m.

With linked phrases, anything omitted in the second must remain omitted from then on. Either share the article throughout – *I need a knife, fork, and spoon* – or repeat it each time: *I need a knife, a fork, and a spoon.* Similarly, either *There are buses at 10 a.m., noon, and 4.30 p.m.* or *There are buses at 10 a.m., at noon, and at 4.30 p.m.*

OTHER FAULTY ELLIPSES

Your ear will usually alert you to awkward or unacceptable ellipses, even when you cannot really analyse what precisely is at fault.

X He told the meeting of a curate whose car was stoned and had a steel bolt thrown at him.

You cannot recover *who* from *whose* (as here), or vice versa. The sentence as it stands suggests that it was the curate's car that had a steel bolt thrown at 'him'. Rewrite as: *. . . curate whose car was stoned and who had a steel bolt thrown at him.*

X It was because of the especially cold winter and oil prices rose dramatically that there was so much hardship.

You cannot recover *because* from *because of*. Rewrite as: *It was because of the especially cold winter and because oil prices rose dramatically that there was so much hardship.*

ELLIPSIS AND AMBIGUITY

Sometimes the problem is not so much one of grammar as one of uncertain meaning. It may be unclear which words have been omitted, or even whether any words at all have been omitted.

?? He was hardly happy and eager to get rid of me.

Was he hardly eager to get rid of me, or was he rather unhappy and also eager to get rid of me? A comma after *happy* would suggest the latter interpretation. But it would be better to repeat the *was*: *He was hardly happy and was eager to get rid of me.* If the intended sense is, however, that he was hardly eager to get rid of me, it would be better to reword: *He was hardly happy or eager to get rid of me*; or *He was hardly happy, and not at all eager to get rid of me.*

In this next example, the problem is whether any ellipsis is intended. Have any words been omitted?

? We offered them iced lemonade and tea to drink, and chocolate eclairs and biscuits to eat.

Was the tea iced as well, and were the biscuits covered with chocolate? If so, the words *iced* and *chocolate* should be repeated for clarity's sake. If not, the elements should be reversed in each case: *We offered them tea and iced lemonade to drink, and biscuits and chocolate eclairs to eat.*

Problems with Prepositions

English prepositions puzzle foreigners constantly, and often lead unwary mother-tongue speakers of English into error as well. You may, for instance, speak of having **X** *a passionate interest for opera.* This should be *a passionate interest in opera*, but you were perhaps misled by the model of *a passion for opera.*

Or you may speak of feeling **X** *a simultaneous affection and irritation with Henry.* This should be *a simultaneous affection for and irritation with Henry*; here you have allowed the single preposition *with* to do service for both nouns where it is appropriate to only one of them – *irritation.* (See overleaf for some further examples).

WHICH PREPOSITION?

A good many of these errors arise by analogy with a similar phrase. If you are *fond of* children, you have a *fondness for* (not *of*) them. You may show a *dislike of* small dogs, but *take a dislike to* the neighbours. A person acts *in view of* new information but *with a view to* new successes. The police may *charge* someone *with* manslaughter, but the suspect is arrested on a *charge of* manslaughter.

Often there is more than one possible choice. Preparations might be *adequate to* or *for* a party. You might ask a question *apropos* the party or *apropos of* the party. To *conform to* or *with* a custom is to observe it. You might *replace* an old hat *by* or *with* a new hat. A man can either *tyrannise,* or *tyrannise over*, his clerk.

Usually, however, the choice of prepositions is not a free one. The context, or the intended sense, necessitates the use of one preposition rather than another. When a person *admits* or *admits to* something, he or she confesses it: *He admits (to) having stolen the jewels.* When something *admits of* something, it permits it, as in: *The facts admit of only one explanation.*

You connive with a person, but *at* a wrongful action. If something *consists of* something else, it is made up or composed of it: *The United Kingdom consists of Great Britain and Northern Ireland;* if it *consists in* something, it has it as a basis: *The beauty of the city consists in its ancient buildings.*

You may be *disgusted at* an action, *with* a person or action, *by* a person, thing, or action. You may *correspond with* the sales manager in Singapore because your job in London *corresponds to* his.

If you are *possessed of* something, you own it: *possessed of a sharp tongue;* but if you are *possessed with* or *by* something, you are controlled by it: *possessed with sudden rage.*

A person could be very *susceptible to* flattery or disease, but a theory is *susceptible of* an interpretation. You may feel *sympathy* (compassion) *for* a person, but you would be *in sympathy* (agreement) *with* a point of view.

COMPARED WITH, COMPARED TO

One particularly notorious case is that of *compare.* The traditional distinction between *compare with* and *compare to* is now widely neglected, though worth preserving.

To *compare to* means 'to liken to' – to note similarities between dissimilar things: *Shall I compare thee to a summer's day?; She compared my hairstyle to shredded wheat.*

To *compare with* means 'to examine side by side with' – both for similarities and differences: *Compare Britain's trade record in recent years with France's; Why are local trains so tatty compared with inter-city trains?*

Curiously, however, *comparable to* often serves both functions, and *in comparison with* almost always does.

A CLEAR PREFERENCE

In many cases, particularly where usage is changing, one preposition rather than another is to be preferred for serious writing. Here is a brief list:

> an *affinity between/with* (not *to/for*)
> to *brood on/over* something (not *about*)
> *consequent on* something (not *to*)
> to *die of* something (better than *from*)
> to *forbid* someone *to do* something (not *from doing* it)
> to *prevent* someone *from doing* something
> to *prohibit* someone *from doing* something
> *identical to* something (not *with*)
> *oblivious of* something (better than *to*)
> to *prefer* something *to* something else (not *than*)
> *junior/senior/inferior/superior to* someone or something (not *than*)

And *different from* is generally preferred in British English to *different to*, and clearly preferable to *?different than*, though sometimes this form allows for a more streamlined construction.

BELT AND BRACES – ON WHICH WE RELY ON

A common error with prepositions is using too many, or too few.

✗ There are two extremes from which we have to move away from.

✗ She's the girl to whom I was speaking and you sent the letter to.

In these examples the speakers have started off with the formal 'preposition + relative pronoun' construction, and then repeated the pronoun at the end, as if it were the informal construction.

In English, however, this 'belt and braces' approach is not grammatical.

What about this sentence now?

✗ With regard to whom you were speaking, you should have been more discreet.

It displays the opposite mistake. It is a preposition short. The *to* is part of *With regard to*, so it cannot be part of *to whom*. For obvious reasons, **??** *With regard to to whom you were speaking, . . .* is not a sensible option. Neither really is **?** *With regard to whom you were speaking to, . . .* An altogether better solution is to reword in some way; for example: *As for the person to whom you were speaking, you should have been more discreet.*

PREPOSITIONS AT THE END

Prepositions usually occur immediately in front of the noun, pronoun, or other word that they relate to. In Latin they almost always do so; what is more, their name comes from the Latin *pre-* (before) + *position* – so some people believe that sentences should not end with prepositions.

The 'rule' was probably introduced by the poet John Dryden in the 17th century, and encouraged by the historian Edward Gibbon in the 18th. But as actually formulated by Bishop Lowth in the 18th century, the rule did no more than recommend avoiding the end position where possible. And it is not always possible. The following sections give some guidelines that will help you through this problem area.

RELATIVE CLAUSES – THE GIRL I SENT IT TO

Take these two casual sentences:

That's the man we sold it to.
What's that you're looking at?

Sticklers for the preposition rule might turn these into *That's the man to whom we sold it* and *What's that at which you're looking?* The first 'corrected' version is grammatical, but very formal – and using very formal grammar in a less than formal setting represents a lapse of appropriateness if not a lapse of grammar. The second 'corrected' version is so awkward that it scarcely rates acceptance as a Standard English sentence.

Shifting the preposition from the end can be particularly clumsy or confusing when the preposition then becomes widely separated from the word it relates to. Which sentence in the following pair is better? That is, which of the two sentences is more comprehensible?

It's the kind of book that even after months of study one can reach only a very vague understanding of.

It's the kind of book of which even after months of study one can reach only a very vague understanding.

The first, surely.

And if the preposition is part of a fixed phrase or idiom, you simply cannot shift it to an earlier position in the relative clause. You can say *That's the kind of glass through which you cannot see*. But

FLOUTING THE RULE

As generations of ironic schoolchildren have put it, 'Never use a preposition to end a sentence with.'

The traditional ban on ending a sentence with a preposition is one of the most illogical 'rules' of English grammar – and one that has often been flouted by good users of English.

The author of a famous writing guide, for one, clearly felt no impropriety in ending sentences with prepositions:

The peculiarities of legal English are often used as a stick to beat the official with.
– Sir Ernest Gowers,
The Complete Plain Words

And a number of modern writers have been equally happy to flout the traditional rule:

None the less, for all the squalor and gore, felicities of syntax are what the book aspires to be full of.
– Martin Amis, *The Observer*

Geoffrey Robertson, who has been an inquisitor in Granada's hypothetical cases, pressed magistrates and clerks a good deal harder, one was entertained to see, than they are used to or altogether care for.
– Nancy Banks-Smith, *The Guardian*

Finally, an extract that amusingly reinvokes the shadow of the schoolroom:

'So if Raschid has anything to say perhaps he had better say it to me. Not that I think he will. I know Raschid of old and Raschid knows me, and Raschid, though a fool, is not such a fool as to try anything on that he can't get away with.' He thought for a moment and amended this statement. 'With which he can't get away.'
– Anthony Burgess, *Devil of a State*

you cannot say **X** *That's the kind of lie through which you cannot see*; you have no option but to say *That's the kind of lie which you cannot see through*.

QUESTIONS AND EXCLAMATIONS

Questions beginning with *wh*-words – *who, what, why*, and so on – and ending with a preposition can

GRAMMAR QUIZ

Test your grammar. All of the sentences below are incorrect or dubious in one way or another. Try to identify the fault each time, and rewrite the sentence (in more than one way, if necessary) into a fully acceptable form. For the answers, see pages 633-648.

1. A knight's armour could weigh as much or more than the knight himself.

2. I'd hurry up if I was you.

3. The smell of lemons and limes waft me back to childhood.

4. She is one of those women who never lets bureaucracy stand in her way.

5. That book contains less anecdotes than its companion volume.

6. The minister as well as his advisors are shown emerging from the meeting.

7. Everybody should provide their own transport.

8. There's so many things I have to remember.

9. I find these sort of comments most unhelpful.

10. Congress has reassembled after their break for the public holiday.

11. If anyone phones, tell them I'll be back at six o'clock.

12. Neither of them were prepared to help the old woman cross the street.

13. The media was unsparing in its criticism.

14. Either Sam or his wife are going to babysit for us.

15. All the available data suggests that acid rain is the culprit.

16. The standard criteria is a high IQ.

17. That book has two indices – an author index and a general index.

18. My younger son, just between you and I, has been shortlisted for a scholarship to Cambridge.

19. Whom do you think is most likely to succeed?

20. The onlookers suddenly vanished like they had evaporated.

21. Please allow my husband and I to offer our condolences.

22. What a challenge that would be for we women to face.

23. Joel complained to the governors, whom he suspected were misusing the school funds.

24. The assistant murdered his boss and later attempted to murder his wife.

25. Please bear in mind that the argument is between the vicar and myself, and concerns nobody else.

26. However seldom you dream, you should write them down.

27. I simply can't stand him humming like that the whole time.

28. One can always try herbal remedies, can't you?

29. It's the same poem that I recited last week.

30. Your new proposal seems hardly different at all than the one I've just rejected.

31. As a lifelong music buff, there is nothing more delightful than the Salzburg Festival.

32. Entering the gallery, my attention was at once drawn to the large sculpture in the corner.

33. You should have tried to have let me know at once.

34. The day-trippers promenaded leisurely along the broadwalk.

35. She would of agreed readily if only you had asked her.

36. The fortress will be attempted to be stormed at dawn.

37. If they'd have heard about the auction in time, they'd have probably put in a bid for the statue.

38. All former pupils are hoped to be invited to the reunion.

39. I'll be very surprised if she dares tell him.

40. Whatever you may feel about it, I shall press ahead.

41. How can you expect to fully understand my anxieties?

42. The cat seems to like me more than you.

43. He was stark naked except for the blue socks and shoes on his feet.

44. Jack had a row with his father just before he went on holiday.

45. The commission reported on the trade imbalance in 1989.

46. The victim may have recovered if a blood transfusion had arrived in time.

47. She ran about as if she was possessed by a demon.

48. If the verdict be guilty and he goes to prison, the public will rejoice.

49. He lay the rug along the flagstones.

50. Even the best-laid plans sometimes go wrongly.

51. The argument can only be settled between the two leaders themselves.

52. I feel even tireder today than I did yesterday.

53. The Reading train nowadays goes directly to Oxford.

54. A backwater provides the most ideal conditions for pollination.

55. Hopefully, his reign of terror is now over for ever.

56. No new applicants will be considered, but will have to reapply for the post in January next year.

57. Regretfully, profits fell by 20 per cent last year.

also often be reworded. Again many questions of this kind are acceptable, though formal:

> To whom are you referring, may I ask?
> For whom was he looking?

Others, however, sound absurd:

?? About what is your book?

? On what does it depend?

It is more or less impossible to avoid end prepositions after exclamations containing *wh*-words. For example:

?? What an embarrassing thing about which to talk!

?? Into what a fine mess you've got us!

OTHER STRUCTURES TO THINK ABOUT

In many other constructions too, final prepositions are natural or even unavoidable.

For instance, in the passives of prepositional verbs:

> We were well looked after.
> The whole question needs looking into.

Consider also constructions with an adjective plus *to* infinitive –

> She's lovely to look at.
> He's impossible to live with.

– or with an indefinite pronoun plus *to* infinitive:

> That's something to look forward to.
> I've got nobody to talk to.
> Is there anyone to write to?

Only by wholesale rewording could such sentences reasonably avoid the end preposition.

Not that the end preposition is always equally clear, elegant, and acceptable. In formal relative clauses and some questions, in particular, an earlier position may well be preferable:

> Do you know the girl on the deck of whose father's ship Alec stowed away?

?? Do you know the girl whose father's ship Alec stowed away on the deck of?

And longer prepositions such as *during* and *throughout*, and multi-word prepositions such as *with regard to* and *because of*, usually sound very awkward in the end position:

?? Which century did the Renaissance take place during/throughout?

?? That's the scandal he resigned because of.

The Building Blocks Of Good English

The Secrets of Punctuation

THE CHIEF purpose of punctuation is to make the meaning of a written passage clear. Punctuation marks are not just an optional frill: they are essential to the accurate exchange of written information. Punctuate carelessly, and you will communicate inefficiently and probably misleadingly – ambiguity thrives on poor punctuation.

You can look at punctuation in another way: in many cases, it is to the written word what pause and intonation and emphasis are to the spoken word – a means of making ideas and thoughts clearer and easier to grasp by breaking them down into logical units.

DISTINGUISHING MEANINGS

Observe how the apostrophe, or its absence, changes the meaning of these three sentences:

> These are my brothers (= These people are my brothers).
> These are my brother's (= These things belong to my brother).
> These are my brothers' (= These things belong to my brothers).

Sometimes punctuation shows that the writer intends one grammatical structure rather than another – and the difference can be important. Consider the following sentence:

> My aunt, who lives in Scotland, is 93 today.

This implies that I have only one aunt. Take away the commas and the meaning changes:

> My aunt who lives in Scotland is 93 today.

This implies that I have more than one aunt, and am referring to the aunt who lives in Scotland, rather than the one who lives in Wales. (For more details on such sentences, see page 173.)

Punctuation can also show which words in a sentence go together to make a phrase or clause. Note the difference that the placing of a comma makes in the following pair of sentences:

> I told Sarah, and Ruth and Rebecca went straight to the hospital.
> I told Sarah and Ruth, and Rebecca went straight to the hospital.

If the comma were omitted altogether, you could not determine which meaning was intended.

A famous example of the importance of commas is the following apocryphal pair of sentences:

> King Frederick says Voltaire is an ass.
> King Frederick, says Voltaire, is an ass.

In the first sentence, Voltaire is the ass. In the second Frederick is the ass. The simple addition or removal of commas totally transforms the meaning.

Learning to punctuate well has two sides. In the first place, there is the relatively straightforward business of learning the rules, and putting them into practice – this chapter will help you to do that. But, secondly, and equally important, you must learn to put yourself in the position of your readers and anticipate any likely difficulty or misunderstanding of theirs. Take the sentence:

? As Joe Orton Gary Oldman was a great success.

It is not exactly incorrect, but it might well cause readers a moment of puzzlement before understanding dawns. It might seem momentarily to refer to someone called *Joe Orton Gary Oldman* or *Joe Orton Gary*. The author's intention would have been immediately clear, however, if he or she had taken the trouble to insert a single comma:

> As Joe Orton, Gary Oldman was a great success.

Here are two more examples of 'false starts':

? As soon as he discovered that he was lost.
? However much has been said about her.

A comma after *that* and *However* would have saved the reader any momentary disorientation. Here is another, subtler, example:

? The doctor explained that these symptoms do not always disappear and call for further tests.

The subject *these symptoms* is followed by two clauses, or predicates – one negative and one positive. The shift from one to the other would be much easier to follow if an extra comma were introduced to divide them:

> The doctor explained that the symptoms do not always disappear, and call for further tests.

This example suggests another principle: if a sentence is hard to punctuate, you could try reformulating it rather than just repunctuating it:

> The doctor explained that the symptoms do not always disappear, and that they call for further tests.

PUNCTUATION AND STYLE

Punctuation can serve other purposes besides simply distinguishing meanings. It can also produce delicate effects of style. It can alter, for example, the flow of a sentence, bringing certain words into greater prominence.

> The aims of writers and publishers of all sorts are clarity and suitability to the general style. If these two aims are achieved, consistently, the punctuation is good.
> – Harrison Platt, Jr (U.S.), 'Guide to Usage',
> in *The American College Dictionary*

The two commas in the second sentence do not alter its truth one way or the other, but they do produce an interesting change of effect. The word *consistently* has greater prominence with the commas than it would have without them.

PUNCTUATION, HEAVY AND LIGHT

Some aspects of punctuation are rule-governed, and some are matters of judgment and taste. Not that your judgment and taste are always going to hold sway: publishers, newspapers, bosses, and so on tend increasingly to impose 'house styles', and may change much of your punctuation.

There are two broad tendencies in punctuation nowadays – you could call them 'heavy' punctuation and 'light' punctuation. In simple terms, heavy punctuation is the tendency to use as many different marks as possible and as often as possible. Its aim is to make sure that the reader interprets the text exactly as the author intended. It forces the reader's attention on to small units of text, such as phrases or even single words. Light punctuation, by contrast, gives more scope for the reader to sort things out for himself for the sake of a text that flows more quickly.

One characteristic of light punctuation is its use of commas. Light punctuators tend to use commas instead of brackets, dashes, and semicolons, and to use the comma itself as little as possible. They write *leaves, flowers and fruit* rather than *leaves, flowers, and fruit*. On the whole, the drift now is towards lighter punctuation, and even the heaviest of punctuation today seems light by comparison with that of past centuries.

In general, heavy punctuation is appropriate for the serious discussion of complex ideas – but it can seem ponderous. Light punctuation is appropriate for journalism and fast-moving fiction – but it can lead to misunderstanding, and sometimes actually slows the reader's progress by forcing him or her to reread a confusing passage.

The aim in this book is to follow a middle course suitable for most writers in most circumstances.

This chapter discusses each of the standard punctuation marks in turn, as well as related topics such as italics and abbreviations.

The Building Blocks Of Good English

The Full Stop

X At last they decided it was lunch-time the picnic was at home on the kitchen table.

This string of words clearly needs some kind of break between *lunch-time* and *the*. You could use a semicolon (a comma would not be enough), perhaps adding an appropriate connecting word: *... it was lunch-time; however, the picnic ...* You could also – most simply – make it into two sentences with a full stop in between:

At last they decided it was lunch-time. The picnic was at home on the kitchen table.

The chief use of the full stop (or *stop*, or *point*, or in American English, *period*) is to end an 'assertion' – typically a declarative sentence (one that is not a question or an exclamation) such as:

Swallows fly south for the winter.

Such a sentence may consist of several parts:

AMBIGUOUS MESSAGES

Telegrams – unavoidably, since they cannot reproduce punctuation marks – bear out the truth that careless punctuation leads to ambiguity. One joke has it that Stalin received a telegram from his hated rival Trotsky, which Stalin read as an apology:

> You were right. I should apologise.

What Trotsky had in fact meant was:

> *You* were right? I should *apologise*?!

Another example – true this time – is the telegram that triggered off the infamous 'Jameson Raid' in 1895. This was a raid by British forces under Dr Leander Starr Jameson against the independent Transvaal republic in southern Africa. The telegram was sent to Jameson by allies of his within the Transvaal. The text, without punctuation, read as follows:

> It is under these circumstances that we feel constrained to call upon you to come to our aid should a disturbance arise here the circumstances are so extreme that we cannot but believe that you and the men under you will not fail to come to the rescue of people who are so situated.

Where was the first full stop intended to go? Those who sent the telegram probably meant it to come after *should a disturbance arise here* – thereby simply putting Jameson on the alert, in case his help should be needed.

But when the text was wired to *The Times* in London, the full stop was placed after *come to our aid* instead – thus creating the impression of a firm and urgent invitation.

A literary example of confused meaning through punctuation occurs in Shakespeare's *A Midsummer Night's Dream*, when Quince the carpenter reads the prologue to the 'Pyramus and Thisby' play that he and his fellow rustics are putting on:

> Consider then we come but in despite.
> We do not come as minding to content you,
> Our true intent is. All for your delight
> We are not here. That you should here
> repent you,
> The actors are at hand . . .

A more correct reading would be:

> Consider then, we come (but in despite
> We do not come) as minding to content you.
> Our true intent is all for your delight.
> We are not here that you should here
> repent you.
> The actors are at hand . . .

In other cases, poor punctuation produces a pair of rival meanings:

? For all the members know the chairman will resign.

(To distinguish the two meanings, insert either a comma or the word *that* after *know*.)

? Once I learnt that I could no longer rely on him.

(Insert a comma either after *once* or after *that*.)

? Very little was known when Miss Hill was writing about the life of Flora Mayor, and her three novels for some reason . . . failed to interest those who have written critical histories of the novel.
> – David Holloway, *The Daily Telegraph*

Does the *about* here relate to *known* or to *writing*? If to *known*, then commas should be inserted either side of the clause *when Miss Hill was writing*; if to *writing*, then a single comma could be placed before *when*, or else a small rephrasing could be made, such as *Very little was known when Miss Hill was studying the life of Flora Mayor* . . .

To finish, here are a few lighter-hearted uncertainties. Consider these newspaper phrases, and think how a well-placed hyphen (and sometimes comma) might resolve the ambiguity. First two headlines:

✗ Man eating wolf
✗ Scarlet coated woman in club scandal.

Next, two captions under photographs:

✗ The long sought after dachshund safely back home.

✗ Mr and Mrs Staple, celebrating their ruby wedding, surrounded by their eight children and twenty odd grandchildren.

Swallows fly south for the winter, if I'm not mistaken, and fly north for the summer.

It may even include an indirect question:

I want to know whether swallows really do fly south for the winter.

(Don't be tempted to use a question mark here in the place of the full stop – see *The Question Mark*, pages 235-237.)

Note that when an assertion serves as a title (as of a book or pop group), it does not take a full stop: *You Can't Go Home Again* (novel by Thomas Wolfe), *Frankie Goes to Hollywood* (pop group).

ABBREVIATIONS, LISTS, NUMBERS

Full stops are also widely used after abbreviations – *e.g., M.A., a.m., etc.* – and after numbers and letters listing points, as in an outline or list of contents:

I. The French Revolution
  I.a. Its causes
  I.b. Its results
II. The Napoleonic Period

The full stop is often used after capital Roman numerals. Small Roman numerals, Arabic numerals, and letters may take brackets: (ii) (a) (1) or ii) a) 1).

In British style, addresses sometimes end with a full stop and have a comma at the end of each line:

The Reader's Digest Association Limited,
Pegasus House,
Blagrove,
SWINDON,
Wiltshire,
SN5 8YY.

SPECIAL USES OF THE FULL STOP

A useful stylistic device is to treat as separate sentences (and so to end with full stops) groups of words not ordinarily considered as sentences:

Three o'clock. Half past three. Four o'clock. Sisters Ursula and Jane, Solomon, Gulab and the cart had not come in. Mother Morag had been up since midnight.
    – Rumer Godden, *The Dark Horse*

'Who's going to think that?'
'Well exactly, love. The answer is other publishers. Are going to think that. Impressing *them*, that is the object of the entire exercise.'
    – Kingsley Amis, *Difficulties with Girls*

In the second example, the 'ungrammatical' full stop after *publishers* conveys how the speaker timed his answer. It is often used in this way in dialogue to indicate natural pauses.

Emphatic interjections. The terms *full stop* and *period* may themselves be used in informal speech as emphatic interjections. The effect is to discourage all further discussion, either by rejecting any modification of a preceding statement or by reinforcing that statement:

He's not just the best composer working in musicals today – he's the best composer working today, period.

I'm sorry, but from now on that's how it's going to be. Full stop.

No, we don't stock silk – in fact we don't stock material full stop.

(See also pages 234 and 235, and 239 and 240.)

The Building Blocks Of Good English

The Comma

Within sentences, the comma is easily the most important punctuation mark. Its most typical use is to separate main clauses linked by conjunctions such as *and, but, or, for,* and *nor*:

The cottage was almost in ruins, but the garden was lovely.

Commas are also used to separate off non-essential (or 'parenthetical') elements from the rest of a sentence (*Tell him, if you see him, that he's won*) and to indicate words left out (*Queen Victoria was related to the Kaiser; the Kaiser, to the Emperor*).

COMMAS AND CLAUSES

The comma is most likely to be used between clauses when the clauses are long, contrasted, and complete. The following compound sentences may, but need not, have commas:

The cottage was old(,) but the garden was new.
The cottage was almost in ruins(,) and the garden was a mess.

And the following compound sentence would probably not have a comma:

Mary mixed the dough and baked the bread.

(Here, the subject of the second clause, *Mary*, has been omitted, since it is identical to the subject of the first).

When such clauses are not linked by a conjunction, try using a semicolon:

The cottage was almost in ruins; the garden looked lovely.

Note the different treatments of *nor* and *neither*:

The cottage was not exactly modern, nor was the garden.

The cottage was not exactly modern; neither was the garden.

Nor is considered a conjunction, but *neither* is considered a linking adverb.

You can use a semicolon instead of a comma before a conjunction such as *but* if you want to emphasise the contrast:

The cottage was in ruins; but the garden was a sheer delight.

The higher the price. Sometimes you can separate main clauses by commas even though they have no conjunctions:

The higher the price (is), the worse the quality (is).

Such 'proportional' expressions take commas, unless very short: *the more the merrier*.

Tags and comments. A different example, now:

He's a lovely baby, isn't he?

Isn't he? is a 'tag question' (others are *aren't you? didn't he? wasn't it?*); before such tags the comma is almost obligatory. Similarly:

I was just visiting, you see
You're wrong, you know.

Before short 'comment clauses' such as *you know*, the comma is again almost always used.

I came, I saw, I conquered. Where you have very short main clauses, and more than two of them, you can use a comma (or a semicolon or colon):

I came, I saw, I conquered.

Similarly:

The office is his wife, music is his mistress.
I don't make them, I just sell them.

THE COMMA SPLICE

Using commas between main clauses not linked by conjunctions can give rise to the 'comma splice' or 'run-on sentence'. This error is common in British English, particularly among inexperienced writers, as the following mimicking example recognises:

✗ I wanted to impress Pandora with my multi talents, I think she is getting a bit bored with my conversation about great literature and the Norwegian leather industry.
– Adrian, in Sue Townsend's
The Secret Diary of Adrian Mole Aged 13¾

The author's hero would be marked down in an exam for writing this sentence with a comma rather than with a colon, semicolon, or full stop.

As this next example shows, however, it is not only young writers (or impersonators of them) who are guilty of the comma splice. The author was for many years the literary editor of *The Listener*:

✗ His scanty grey hair had been doctored, obviously by himself, no barber could have made such a mess of it.
– J.R. Ackerley, *My Father and Myself*

These are just acceptable. Although unrelated grammatically, the two main clauses in each case are related structurally. When a balanced contrast is being made, and the two ideas are constructed symmetrically, a comma is permissible, though a semicolon or colon would be appropriate too.

(For the positioning of commas alongside quotation marks, see pages 234 and 235.)

WORDS LEFT OUT

Ellipsis is the omission of certain words. In the following example, what is omitted is an element given in an earlier clause:

Antony loved Cleopatra; Romeo, Juliet.

The comma between *Romeo* and *Juliet* stands for the missing word *loved*. In fact, you could probably get away without the comma here, because Romeo and Juliet are so well known. But in the next example, where the second pair of lovers is less well known, you should definitely use the comma – or people might think there is someone who is called 'Thisbe Pyramus'.

> Cleopatra loved Antony; Thisbe, Pyramus.

Here is another, more complex example. The comma after *wet* is in effect shorthand for the words *she wore*:

> Miss Crane had become used to ignoring the weather. In the dry she wore wide-brimmed hats, cotton or woollen dresses and sensible shoes; in the wet, blouses and gaberdine skirts, gumboots when necessary, with a lightweight burberry cape and an oilskin-covered solar topee.
>
> – Paul Scott, *The Jewel in the Crown*

COMMAS RESEMBLING BRACKETS

Here are some examples of commas used, in pairs (rather like brackets), to separate parenthetical elements in a sentence:

> Tell him, however, that I still need his help.
> Tell him, Margaret, that I still need his help.
> Tell him, above all, that I still need his help.
> Tell him, please, that I still need his help.

Among the elements that can be separated in this way are the following:

☐ elements in contrast with the core of the sentence: *Tell him, not his brother, that he must get here in time*.

☐ elements that supplement the core of the sentence: *She told me that some, if not all, of the women had suffered beatings at some time*.

☐ non-restrictive relative clauses – that is, those that describe rather than identify or define (see page 173): *The novel, which is not so well written, is more interesting than the biography*.

☐ elements 'presenting' or giving the source of direct quotations: *'I know,' he replied, 'that she still needs my help.'*

☐ 'appositional' material – that is, a noun or noun phrase that follows another and explains or describes it: *Sue Townsend, the author of the book, impersonates a teenager*. Commas are not always wanted in appositional material, however: *James Caan the actor views things very differently*. In this second example, the words *the actor* is a 'defining' or 'restrictive' phrase. In

the first example, *the author of the book* describes rather than defines: it is a 'non-restrictive' phrase, and therefore one that demands commas.

Make sure in constructions like these to use both commas, not just one or the other – and that they are in their correct places. It is all too easy to position the second comma wrongly:

✗ She told me that some, if not all of, the women had suffered beatings at some time.

✗ Goldwyn was an important influence on, perhaps the founder, of the studio system.

In the first sentence, the second comma should come after *all*; in the second, after *of*.

If you can remove the words between the commas, leaving a sentence that still makes sense (*She told me that some of the women . . .*), the commas are in the right places.

I love her, Patrick. Sometimes commas are used to set off single words – *Ah* and *Patrick* here:

> Ah, I still love her, Patrick.

At other times, they are used to set off longer expressions. Generally, the longer the expression, the more important the comma:

> On Thursday the 26th of September, rumours began circulating in Fleet Street.
> In 1964(,) rumours began circulating in Fleet Street.

> When I'm tired after a hard day's work, I sit down.
> When I'm tired(,) I sit down.

And commas are more important if the subordinate expression is at the beginning or in the middle of a sentence than if it is at the end:

> If you see him, don't hesitate to call the police.
> Don't hesitate, if you see him, to call the police.
> Don't hesitate to call the police(,) if you see him.

Read each sentence aloud, and you will hear why the comma is less necessary in the last.

Tell her, if you see her, . . . If possible, avoid using a comma between two elements that are essential to the sentence. It is quite correct to write:

> Tell him, if you see him, that I still need his help.

But it is nowadays incorrect to write:

✗ Tell him, that I still need his help.

The phrase *that I still need his help* functions here as object of the verb *tell*, and should not be separated from it by a comma.

Parenthetical, or not parenthetical. Note that there is considerable leeway in deciding what is essential and what is additional or parenthetical information. You could write, perfectly correctly:

Sir John Moore died gloriously at Corunna.

But you could also put:

Sir John Moore died gloriously, at Corunna.

Here you mean: 'Sir John Moore died gloriously, and it happened at Corunna'. Similarly:

Sir John Moore died, gloriously, at Corunna.

Here you mean: 'Sir John Moore died at Corunna, and his death was glorious'.

COMMAS IN LISTS

Commas are used between items in lists of more than two, but are nowadays considered optional before *and* and *or*:

I came, saw(,) and conquered.
shoes, ships(,) and sealing wax
a happy, alert(,) and intelligent child
in, on(,) or under the home

. . . strong in will
To strive, to seek, to find, and not to yield.
– Tennyson, 'Ulysses' (1842)

In British usage, it is common nowadays to omit the final comma.

But for fine distinctions – as in this book – the final comma is retained to ensure that the last two items on the list are clearly distinguished.

The final comma is also sometimes necessary to avoid ambiguity:

In their sandwiches they like peanut butter, egg and cress, and cheese and tomato.

Here the final comma makes it clear that *egg and cress* is one unit and that *cheese and tomato* is another, separate, unit.

Hard work and good luck. When the series consists of only two items connected by a conjunction, commas are not usual:

Hard work and good luck are essential to success.

Sometimes, in fact, commas are impossible, as when the linked items interact:

Hard work and good luck are sometimes interdependent.

But sometimes commas are useful in giving greater emphasis to an item, or in drawing attention to its unlikely presence in the sentence:

Hard work, and good luck, are essential to success.

Here, the meaning is perhaps 'Hard work is essential to success – but don't forget good luck.'

You could use brackets or dashes instead:

Hard work – and good luck – are essential to success.

Lists of adjectives. These present a number of special problems when they do not include *and, or,* or *but.* In the first place, some types of adjective have relatively fixed positions in relation to one another: adjectives of shape, for example, generally come before adjectives of colour. With sequences of such adjectives you can leave out commas:

a round silver casket.

When such adjectives occur out of sequence, however, commas are more likely:

a silver, round casket.

With sequences of other adjectives, commas are possible, but no longer obligatory:

a happy(,) alert(,) intelligent child
an intelligent(,) alert(,) happy child

However, ungradable adjectives (those that do not take *more, most, -er,* or *-est*) are hardly ever preceded by commas:

a silver filigree casket
a happy Russian child.

The 'head' (usually a simple noun) of a sequence of adjectives is not normally preceded by a comma. Obviously it would be wrong to write: **✗** *a silver, casket.* Similarly, the second comma in **?** *a round, silver, casket* should be omitted – unless you want to give some special emphasis.

When the head is a compound noun, problems arise. Compare *important white papers* (= white papers that are important) and *stiff white paper* (= paper that is white and stiff). In the first example, the head is not simply *papers* – it is *white papers.*

There is therefore no comma after *important*. In the second example, the head is the single word *paper*, and *white* is simply an adjective in the same way as *stiff* is. You could place a comma before *white* this time: *stiff, white paper*.

COMMAS IN NUMBERS

Commas are used to separate large whole numbers into units of three, as for thousands and millions:

153,601   3,561,245

For most simple four-figure numbers, commas are optional:

4635 or 4,635

Commas are not used in four-figure years, page numbers, house numbers, or room numbers:

AD 2001   page 1525   2647 Durham Drive

Sometimes, a half-space is used instead of a comma – especially in calculations made in the metric system. The Reader's Digest *Universal Dictionary* says of the African volcano Kilimanjaro:

It has two peaks, Mount Kibo (5 895 metres; 19,340 feet), Africa's highest peak, and Mount Mawenzi (5 354 metres; 17,564 feet).

The reason for using a space rather than a comma is this: in European countries and South Africa, a comma is used (instead of a full-stop 'decimal point') to separate whole numbers from decimal fractions – so that *2.8* is written *2,8*. To retain the commas in large whole numbers could, therefore, easily invite trouble.

Where British usage probably favours *33,426.525* litres, continental and South African conventions require *33 426,525* litres. Imagine the confusion if that half-space were still a comma.

NAMES, TITLES, AND ADDRESSES

In lists of names arranged by surname, the comma comes after the surname:

Cooper, Gary . . .
Cooper, James Fenimore . . .

This procedure is also followed with certain titles and the official names of some countries:

Domingo, Placido . . .
Dominic, Saint . . .
Dominica, Commonwealth of . . .

THE COMMA AND MEANING

A comma can change meaning drastically:

To the pure by nature, all things are pure.
To the pure, by nature all things are pure.

For numbers of four figures only, commas are optional.
For numbers of four figures, only commas are optional.

Sometimes the presence of a comma, although not strictly required by the syntax or the sense of the sentence, can save the reader from a false start. Think how confusing the following sentence might seem initially, if the first comma had been left out:

In writing, the battered simile and the forgotten metaphor may well be ludicrous or inept or repellent.
– Eric Partridge, *A Charm of Words*

And think how much less confusing (and amusing) this next example would have been had a comma been inserted before the *and*:

Juliane Koepcke, a 17-year-old German girl, survived a 10,000 foot fall when her aeroplane broke up and then walked for ten days through the Peruvian jungle.
– *The Times*

The comma is also used:

☐ between a name and a following title or honour: *Arabella Smith, BA, MA, PhD; T.S. Eliot, OM; George Bush, President of the United States.*

☐ between the name of a street and the name of a town: *76 Ramillies Drive, Leeds*. Note that when an address is reproduced on separate lines, as on an envelope, the commas are often left out. It used to be common in British usage to find a comma between a house number and a street name: *76, Ramillies Drive*. This practice is no longer so common.

☐ between the name of a town and the name of a state, county, or country (*Paris, Texas* and *Paris, France*). Note that this last is the usual American practice, even in ordinary text. In British usage, however, people usually limit this form to the address on an envelope or at the head of a letter. In ordinary text, it is usual to write *Paris in Texas*.

☐ in dates to separate day, month, and year: *Sunday, July 29th, 1990*. In the following pattern, however, the comma is optional nowadays: *29 July(,) 1990*. If only the month and year are specified, the comma is even more likely to be omitted: *July(,) 1990*.

Note that short dates do not have to be followed by a comma when used in a continuous text: *In November 1989 the Chancellor resigned*. How-ever, if a comma is used before the year, you have to use one after the year as well: *In November, 1989, the Chancellor resigned*.

☐ in letters, after the 'salutation' and the 'com-plimentary close': *My darling, . . . Dear Bill, . . . Dear Mr Sammler, . . . With all my love, . . . Yours sincerely, . . .* In American English, however, the salutation of a business letter takes a colon: *Dear Mr Sammler: . . .*

The Hyphen

The hyphen (-) looks like a short dash, but hyphen and dash are used very differently. Basically, the dash separates whereas the hyphen unites.

Knowing when to use a hyphen, and when not to, is a common problem even for experienced writers. Should you write *a middle-aged man*, *a middleaged man*, or *a middle aged man*? (In fact, the hyphenated form is best here. A compound adjective preceding a noun is usually hyphenated or fused, but the fused form here looks odd.)

One trouble with hyphens is that their use varies from British to American English, and from author to author and from publisher to publisher.

No complete and satisfactory set of rules seems possible. So the following discussion is concerned with what is generally true, and offers recom-mendations rather than rules.

MARKING OFF WORD-ELEMENTS

The hyphen can be used between a word and a prefix, suffix, or combining form – such as *pseudo-* or *counter-*. Its main function is to prevent ambiguity and awkward combinations of letters.

Before a suffix. The use of the hyphen before a suffix is fairly rare nowadays, but the hyphen is still needed sometimes to prevent unattractive sequen-ces of more than two identical letters: *bull-like*, as opposed to *workmanlike*.

After a prefix or other word-element. The hyphen is most often used:

☐ when the main part of a word begins with a capital letter: *un-American, non-European*.

☐ when the main part of a word begins with the letter that ends the prefix or combining form: *pre-emptive, counter-revolutionary*.

☐ when the prefix is repeated: *anti-anticommu-nism, sub-subcommittee*.

☐ when the hyphen helps to prevent confusion between a new formation and a conventional one with the same prefix: *re-creation* (not *recreation*) or *re-formed* (not *reformed*): *The crowd re-formed and headed for the presidential palace*. In speech, the prefix of such formations often has a stronger stress and fuller vowel sound than the unhyphenated form.

Note that some prefixes and combining forms are particularly likely to take hyphens. These include *ex-* (*ex-wife, ex-directory*) and *non-* (particularly when joined to a word beginning with a vowel: *non-interference*).

COMPOUND WORDS

The hyphen is used to unite separate words into compound forms that function as a single unit. But many compound forms can also be written with spaces between their components, or even 'set solid' – that is, as a single word with neither spaces nor hyphens.

head waiter	tax payer
head-waiter	tax-payer
headwaiter	taxpayer

American English probably uses the hyphen less often than British English does, and British English uses it less often nowadays than it used to. In the past, the word *tomorrow*, for example, was written *to-morrow*.

Your own reading has probably produced an unconscious set of guidelines about how to hyphenate compounds, and you can trust your intuition – up to a point. Here, however, are some tips to help you if your confidence falters.

Compound adjectives. Some of these, such as *coffee-flavoured*, *high-falutin*, and probably *well-read*, take hyphens in all circumstances.

Others, such as *up-to-date* and probably *well-received*, tend to have hyphens only when used attributively (roughly, in front of the noun). If used predicatively (roughly, after the noun), they tend to appear as a set of separate words:

> Here is a report that is up to date.
> Here is an up-to-date report.
> Her novels are always well received.
> Her well-received novels include . . .

Some compound adjectives, however, resist the hyphen even in front of the noun.

> freshly frozen fish
> a dark green shirt
> *in vitro* fertilisation

Here are some further guidelines:

☐ If the compound adjective has a noun as its first word, it tends to take a hyphen in any position: *a coffee-flavoured liqueur, a liqueur that is coffee-flavoured, community-orientated research, two carbon-based acids, a women-only meeting*.

☐ If the compound adjective has a noun as its second word, it typically takes a hyphen too: *a high-fibre diet, several double-density discs, an all-male choir*. Note that such adjectives (really noun phrases) usually appear before the noun rather than after it.

☐ If, however, the noun phrase is a very common one, widely used in its own right, it tends not to take a hyphen when used adjectivally: *her patent leather shoes, many word processor applications, new Labour Party policies, sports car racing, the market research department*.

☐ If the compound adjective begins with a short, single adverb such as *fast, well*, or *soon*, it tends to take a hyphen when positioned before the noun (though not necessarily when positioned after the noun): *her soon-forgotten setbacks, a well-acted play*. If the adverb is long, such as *brilliantly* or *instantly*, the compound adjective tends to do without the hyphen: *a brilliantly acted play, her instantly forgotten setbacks*.

If none of the above conditions quite applies, try looking the compound adjective up in a good dictionary. If you fail to find it there, the chances are that it remains two separate words at all times.

Other compounds. Noun compounds consisting of two words are increasingly fused into a single word (often in spite of very awkward consonant sequences such as *rdr* or *stgr*): *boardroom, boatrace, jawbone, postgraduate, standby, takeover, weekend, wellbeing, yachtswoman*.

If the compound consists of more than two words or elements, however, it is most unlikely to be fused into a single, solid compound. It retains its traditional hyphens (*will-o'-the-wisp, mother-in-law, jack-of-all-trades*) or spaces (*son of a gun*).

Hyphens are also common when the compound contains an apostrophe and has developed a figurative sense: *cat's-eye, crow's-nest*.

Hyphens are commonly used when, say, a compound verb (verb and adverb) gives rise to adjectives and nouns. Thus *to run down*, with various meanings, yields the adjective *run-down* and a noun written *run-down* or *rundown*. Conversely, a compound noun such as *cold shoulder* can give rise to the hyphenated verb *to cold-shoulder*. This change in function and spelling has a corresponding change, in speech, of stress or intonation.

Hyphens are also frequent in compounds whose elements are coordinated, so that neither element is less important than or subordinate to the other. For example: *a fighter-bomber, the secretary-treasurer, a psychological-sociological approach*.

Ambiguity and shared elements. Use the hyphen if it helps to avoid ambiguity:

> a Turkish-bath attendant/a Turkish bath-attendant
> a German-history teacher/a German history-teacher
> After finishing-school in Geneva, she went home to Luton/After finishing school in Geneva, she went home to Luton.

Here is an example of a possible misreading caused by the omission of a hyphen:

✗ He said there had been clear evidence of sheep rustling on the mountainside

> – quoted in Fritz Spiegl's
> *Keep Taking The Tabloids*

This would have been clearer had it read *evidence of sheep-rustling*.

When several hyphenated compounds share an element, that element need not be repeated, but the hyphens should be. So: *German-speaking and*

Spanish-speaking or *German-* and *Spanish-speaking;* a *three-course meal* or a *four-course meal* or a *three-* or *four-course meal*.

A hyphen is also sometimes used to represent the omitted part of a solid compound – that is, a compound intended as one word rather than as hyphenated: *both micro-* and *macroeconomics, inter-* and *intranational.* And the hyphen can stand in for the first part of the compound, not just the second: *a three-wheeled and -doored vehicle, many craftsmen and -women.*

As these examples show, it is occasionally possible for a hyphen to be followed or preceded by a space, odd though the idea might seem.

USING HYPHENS IN NUMBERS

Compound numbers between 21 and 99, if they are spelt out, are written with hyphens. So: *seven hundred and forty-five* (745); *forty-five thousand and fifty-three* (45,053).

The same holds true for fractions whose numerators and denominators are between one and 20; *three-quarters* (¾), *seven-sixteenths* (⁷⁄₁₆).

For fractions whose numerators or denominators are between 21 and 91 each part is treated separately, with whatever hyphens are appropriate, and there are no hyphens between numerator and denominator: *seven sixty-firsts* (⁷⁄₆₁), *thirty-five ninety-eighths* (³⁵⁄₉₈).

Fractions whose numerators or denominators are larger than 99 should be written as numbers rather than words wherever possible, which avoids the problem of hyphenation. Note, however, that *hundredth/s, thousandth/s, millionth/s,* and so on, can be preceded by a hyphen when they are part of the denominator of a fraction: *three six-hundredths of a second* (³⁄₆₀₀).

HESITATION AND LINKS

When speech is represented in writing, dashes or ellipses ('three dots') are used to show hesitation between words; but hyphens are used to show the repetition of individual sounds in a word, as in stuttering or stammering:

D-D-Damme, I don't know what you are d-d-driving at, or what you mean, but you had getter g-g-go where you belong!
– Billy, in Herman Melville's *Billy Budd*

The hyphen is also sometimes used to link the beginning and ending points of a series:

pages 34-36   the Paris-Dakar route

Here it means 'to', or 'up to and including'. It can also mean 'versus': *the Spurs-Chelsea match.*

In such constructions the dash is often preferred to the hyphen. In printing, a special 'en-dash' is often used, intermediate in length between a hyphen and a proper dash. In writing and typing, however, a hyphen serves to represent the en-dash.

WORD BREAKS

A hyphen is used when a word has to be broken at the end of a line of print:

He had become extremely anti-social, according to that busybody who lived next door.

When a word is broken in this way you cannot always tell whether its hyphen would be there if the word were all on one line: *anti-social*, in the example above, might have been intended as a single, unbroken word.

There are few simple hard-and-fast rules about end-of-line hyphenation. But most publishers agree on the following guidelines. (Remember, if in doubt about a word, that many good dictionaries indicate the syllable-breaks within words.)

☐ Never break single-syllable words at the end of a line: **✗** *wid-ths*, **✗** *match-ed.*

☐ Generally, if there are two successive, independently sounded vowels or two successive independently sounded consonants, break the word between them: *con-tiguity, devi-ation.*

☐ When a single vowel forms a full syllable in the middle of a word, break after rather than before it: *sepa-rate* rather than **✗** *sep-arate.*

☐ Avoid breaking a word after the first letter or before the last letter or the last two letters: **✗** *a-thwart*, **✗** *pati-o*, **?** *happi-ly.*

☐ If a compound is already hyphenated, break it at the hyphen – *un-American* – rather than elsewhere: **✗** *un-Ameri-can*

☐ If a compound is fused into a single word, break it between the elements: *tender-hearted* not **??** *ten-derhearted; play-group* not **✗** *playg-roup, mountain-side* not **??** *moun-tainside.*

SUSPENDED SENTENCES

Typesetting is frequently computer-controlled nowadays. Computers are programmed with instructions on hyphenation, and the word-breaks are made automatically.

But the hyphenation programmes are not perfect, and many doubtful word-breaks creep in. The following letter appeared in a Californian newspaper:

- I was recently surprised to learn from the News that a man in our community pre-ached in his spare time. After I read on, I realized the man didn't pre-ache, he preached.

Upon polite enquiry to the editor of this newspaper, I learned that the typesetting computers have been programmed to divide words after the first vowel that follows a consonant.

I both pre-ache and preach for the day soon that the print computers will somehow be reprogrammed...and that typesetters will be more careful with end-of-line hyphenations.

Until those wonderful events occur, newspaper readers will continue to be startled or saddened by actual printed lines such as the following:

An old man in his dot-age saw spots before his eyes. Her mother was a rat-her formidable obstacle to his marriage. She gave him a 'come hit-her' look when he came home late. Crowds watched the old bat-her leaving the surf. He wore a habit, but hat-red showed through the disguise. The vet used a big cat-heter to relieve the sick tiger. She said he drank like a fish, and often came home so-used to the gills.

– John Cartan, quoted in *Reader's Digest*

- [ ] If possible, avoid breaking a word if it produces a distracting unrelated word or an odd-looking syllable either side: **X** *ath-wart*, **X** *bed-raggled*, **X** *ex-tractor*, **X** *leg-end*, **X** *the-rapist*.

- [ ] If possible, avoid breaking numbers, dates, abbreviations, and names.

There is perhaps a surviving difference in practice between British and American publishers. Americans tend to divide syllables simply according to the pronunciation: the British often divide syllables according to the history and structure of the word. The word *structure*, in fact, might be divided differently: always *struc-ture* in America, sometimes *struct-ure* in Britain (the elements of the word being the stem *-struct-* and the suffix *-ure*).

The interplay of all these various conventions can produce some odd results: **?** *unself-conscious*; **?** *pre-First World War*; **?** *ex-Justice of the Peace*; **?** *the Old Bailey-Oxford Circus bus*.

If the effect is intolerably odd, either hyphenate all the elements or reword the phrase altogether. So: **?** *a pre-First World War ambulance* might become **?** *a pre-First-World-War ambulance* or *an ambulance from before the First World War*.

The Semicolon

The most characteristic use of the semicolon is to separate clauses that might have been two different sentences, but are closely connected in thought or meaning. For example:

The house was dark; the woman was extremely frightened.
(= The house was dark and the woman was extremely frightened.)

Musicians have been threatening to take over Shakespearean productions for some time now; here they do it, with encouraging results.

– Robert Cushman, *The Observer*

(Note that the semicolon is not followed by a capital letter.) The use of the semicolon between two independent clauses serves to emphasise or add weight to the second clause:

He says so; but how can I trust him? (The choice of semicolon rather than comma here emphasises the tone of mistrust.)

This use of the semicolon can be especially handy when the clauses that it links contain commas:

The sun, a bright yellow ball, shone; the children, happy as always, played.

Note that when two parallel clauses are joined by a semicolon, a comma can be used to represent a missing element in the second of them:

Anthony loved Cleopatra; Pyramus, Thisbe.

ALTERNATIVES TO THE SEMICOLON

The preceding principle is a description, not a rule: the clauses linked by a semicolon can often be punctuated in other ways. They can be separate sentences:

The house was dark. The woman was extremely frightened.

If you feel that there is a logical relation between the clauses, or if they have similar structures, a colon can be used:

The house was dark: the woman was extremely frightened.

If the clauses are as short as these, they may be linked by a comma only:

? The house was dark, the woman was extremely frightened.

Many people, however, still object to such a 'weak' form of punctuation.

Semicolon and conjunction are not mutually exclusive. Both can be present in formal style:

The house was dark; and the woman was extremely frightened.

But here a comma, or no punctuation at all, would be more likely:

The house was dark(,) and the woman was extremely frightened.

SEMICOLONS WITH ADVERBS

Although the conjunctions *and*, *but*, and *or* are preceded by a semicolon only in certain circumstances, some adverbial expressions very similar to them – such as *none the less* or *however* – tend to

take a semicolon (if not a full stop) in front of the clause they appear in:

He fought hard; however, he lost./
He fought hard; he lost, however.
He fought hard; nevertheless, he lost./
He fought hard; he lost nevertheless.
He fought hard; all the same, he lost./
He fought hard; he lost all the same.

Contrast this general use of the semicolon with the options available before *but*:

He fought hard but he lost.
He fought hard, but he lost.
He fought hard; but he lost. (very deliberate)

The semicolon is also used before adverbial elements that cannot move so freely within a sentence, and that introduce explanations or examples:

He fought hard; that is, he continued to fight after he had been wounded.
He fought hard; for example, he continued to fight after we thought it was all over.

If the introductory element is omitted, the semicolon should be replaced by a colon:

He fought hard: he continued to fight after he had been wounded.
He fought hard: he continued to fight after we thought it was all over.

THE SEMICOLON IN LISTS

Semicolons are very helpful when it comes to linking clauses that already contain commas:

The group consisted of Edward North, BA, MA; William Robinson, MA, Ph.D.; and Mary Ellen Martin, MD, Ph.D.

In the wardrobe there were dresses and coats; hats, scarves, and gloves; and hundreds of shoes.

This hardly fits in with Nicolson's view of the English character. The English national characteristics are, according to him: good humour, tolerance, ready sympathy, compassion; an affection for nature, animals, children; a fund of common sense; . . . a respect for individual character rather than for individual intelligence; a dislike of extremes, of overemphasis and boastfulness; a love of games; diffidence; shyness; laziness; optimism.

– George Mikes, *English Humour For Beginners*

The Colon

The colon (:) is a tricky and insufficiently understood form of punctuation. Its correct use is to introduce material that explains, amplifies, or interprets what precedes it:

> They didn't sleep last night: they must be tired.
> They are tired: they didn't sleep last night.
> They are tired: let them go and lie down.

Note that what precedes a colon need not be a complete sentence:

> Another Monday morning: it was pouring with rain.

What follows the colon need not be a sentence either, in which case the colon functions rather like such expressions as *namely* or *that is*:

> It is high time we considered Mozart's predecessor: Haydn.

Note that a sentence or phrase that follows a colon should not start with a capital letter, except in special cases (mentioned below) or when you want to give special emphasis.

COLONS AND LISTS

What precedes the colon should typically be able to stand on its own. So it would be incorrect to write the following:

✗ Another composer worth listening to is: Haydn.
✗ There are other composers worth listening to, including: Haydn.

Omit the colon in each case.

But the colon is acceptable if you use it to introduce a number of items listed separately:

> Dyson at once rushed after him, pelting him with the old beer cans and whatever else came to hand, which included: Tetley's tea-bags, ex-U.S. Air Force sparking plugs, overdue library books, rubber reducing garments, and genuine reproductions of Old Masters.
> — Michael Frayn,
> *Towards The End Of The Morning*

When the listed items are indented, you can supplement the colon with a dash or a hyphen:

> The missiles included:–
> (a) Tetley's tea-bags

> (b) sparking plugs
> (c) overdue library books
> (d) reducing garments
> (e) reproductions of Old Masters

This double punctuation mark is now, however, quite rare.

PARALLELS AND CONTRASTS

A colon may also be used between expressions of parallel (or contrasting) structure or meaning:

> Man proposes: God disposes.
> To the left, a whirlpool: to the right, a desert.

It is possible to have more than two parallel constructions of this kind:

> Man proposes: God disposes: posterity benefits.

Nowadays, however, a semicolon would be likely to replace the colon:

> Man proposes; God disposes; posterity benefits.

Nevertheless, the parallel or balancing colon is graceful, and perhaps deserves a revival.

QUOTATIONS AND SALUTATIONS

The colon is used, after the identification of the speaker or writer, to introduce a quotation – for example, in the text of a play:

> Apemantus: Beast!
> Timon: Slave!
> Apemantus: Toad!
> — Shakespeare, *Timon of Athens* IV iii

(Note that quotation marks are not used here.) The colon is also used in published accounts of official proceedings, speeches, and so on, to introduce a long passage in direct speech:

> Opening the meeting, the Mayor said: . . . [Then comes a word-for-word report of the speech]

Similarly, it is used when introducing a long quotation, especially when it is not heralded directly by *said*, *remarked*, or the like:

> Questioned about her approach to the subjects of her films, Dineen responds with a typical lack of pretension: 'I'm not sure that I have a technique as such. I mean, either you get on with

them or you don't. And I'm a nice enough sort of girl, so you strike up "a friendship".'
– Sean French, The Observer

Note that a long quotation need not have quotation marks: it can be indented (as throughout this book). If the quotation is indented, the first letter of the first word after the colon is usually capitalised.

Mottoes, adages, and slogans, when introduced by a colon often have the first word capitalised:

> My best friend has a favourite saying: Do it now.

Salutations. The colon may also be used after a formal salutation preceding a message:

> Ladies and gentlemen: It gives me great pleasure to introduce ...
> My fellow Americans: Let me say at the outset ...
> To whom it may concern: Regarding the rule ...

Instead of a colon, you could use a comma after salutations like the first two, particularly if the following message is short. When the colon is used, a capital letter tends to follow.

In American English, a colon is used in the salutation of a business letter, whereas a comma is used in the salutation of a friendly letter:

> Dear Sirs: Dear George and Dick,

But in British English a comma is used everywhere:

> Dear Sirs,   Dear George and Dick,

HEADINGS AND REFERENCES

The colon is used after various headings in correspondence:

> To: Subject: Reference:

Similarly, it can be used to introduce subtitles (note that the subtitle usually begins with a capital letter):

> *Scars Upon My Heart: Women's Poetry and Verse of the First World War*

In bibliographical references the colon may be used after the place of publication:

> London: 1986
> London: Academica Press

The colon may also be used after the volume number of a serial publication to introduce issue numbers or page numbers:

> *The London Review* IV:3
> *Journal of Ceramic Science* 29:368-72

The colon may also be used between the act number and the scene number of a play:

> *The Merchant of Venice* IV:iii

In biblical references, the colon comes between chapter and verse:

> Isaiah 16:23-27

In American English, the colon is used in expressions of time: *9:30 am*. In British English, this would normally be: *9.30 a.m.*

Both British and American English allow the colon in abbreviated dates: *1:3:91*. This style is much rarer than *1/3/91* or *1.3.91*. Remember, too, that in the USA these formulas would refer to 3 January 1991 whereas in Britain they refer to 1 March 1991.

In mathematics and in general contexts, a colon indicates a proportion or ratio:

> The ratio of successes to failures was 1:5.
> Mix the powders in the proportions 3:7:8.

The Dash

The principal use of the dash (–) is to surround, as commas and brackets do, any material that is included in a sentence without being structurally essential to it:

> I met Anthea – she's the girl who lives next door – and we went to the cinema together.

IN PARENTHESIS

Compare the use of the commas, brackets, and dashes in these three sentences:

> The postman, a good friend of mine, denied the charge.
> The postman (a good friend of mine) denied the charge.
> The postman – a good friend of mine – denied the charge.

Of the three marks of punctuation, the dash is the most striking. Its sheer visibility is what makes it so appropriate when setting off the parenthetical material from its surroundings. This separating off of part of the sentence is either for the sake of emphasising it, or because it is very long or markedly different in tone or structure. The following series of sentences illustrates more sharply the likely choice of punctuation:

> The postman, a good friend of mine, denied the charge.
> The postman (a good friend of mine, incidentally) denied the charge.
> The postman – and he claims to be a good friend of mine! – denied the charge.

As the last example shows, material set off by dashes can be followed by an exclamation mark (or a question mark), though not by a full stop.

As a rule nowadays, neither of the dashes enclosing a piece of text is preceded by a comma, and the second dash is no longer followed by one (in the way that the second bracket can be), even when the grammar seems to demand such a comma. So it is not only wrong now to write:

X The postman, – he claims to be a friend of mine, – denied the charge.

It is probably also now considered quite wrong, however logical, to write:

?? Although he is a friend of mine – or so he claims –, I have to admit he looks guilty.

Dashes (like commas) are not usually put next to full stops or semicolons or colons either. So if the parenthetical material comes at the end of a sentence (or before a colon or semicolon), it would have only the one dash or comma placed in front of it, as here:

> The postman denied the charge – and he claims to be a friend of mine.

> Many of the subtleties reveal themselves only on second reading – a backhanded compliment, probably, in a fiction-crammed, hurried world.
> – Joy Grant, *The Times Literary Supplement*

Afterthoughts, and changes of direction. Often, as in the last example, the parenthetical material introduced by the single dash might be called an afterthought. Here is another example:

> The guest of honour was supposed to make a speech but did not seem to consider it necessary – not a very nice way to treat his many admirers who had struggled to get there that night.

Another item typically introduced by the single dash is the change of direction in a train of thought:

> The incident took place in 1987, the year of my marriage as it happens – but I digress.

(Note that the dash here could appropriately be replaced by a full stop.)

The single dash also introduces an elaboration of a word, which is first repeated:

> You could call it a compliment – a compliment of a very backhanded kind, of course, but a compliment nevertheless.

Another way you can use the single dash is to introduce a punch line, a climax, or even a deliberate anticlimax, after a careful build-up:

> The footsteps came nearer and nearer, up the gravel pathway, step by step onto the porch, and along the groaning boards to the front door. The handle turned, the door slowly creaked open – and in walked my wife.

SUMMARISING, EXPLAINING, INTERRUPTING

The single dash may also be used before or after a clause that summarises a series of words or phrases. There is a relatively sharp transition between the two halves of such sentences as:

> Talent, hard work, good luck – these are the ingredients of success.
> Success has three ingredients – talent, hard work, good luck.

In the second sentence, a colon would nowadays be preferred to the dash:

> Success has three ingredients: talent, hard work, good luck.

Related to this use of the dash is its use to 'explain' preceding material:

> + – plus
> × – times
> = – equals

Here the dash may be read out as 'means'.

Like the colon, the dash can also be used in place of such expressions as *namely* or *that is*:

> Whoever wins that election will have within his grasp the greatest prize of the country's post-war era – the Chancellorship of a united Germany.
> – John Eisenhammer, *The Independent*

The single dash may come at the end of a sentence, if the sentence is incomplete or interrupted:

Josephine and Constantia got up too.

'I should like it to be quite simple,' said Josephine firmly, 'and not too expensive. At the same time I should like –'

'A good one that will last,' thought dreamy Constantia, as if Josephine were buying a nightgown.

– Katherine Mansfield,
'The Daughters of the Late Colonel'

Instead of the dash here, the writer could have used the dot-dot-dot of the ellipsis (*I should like . . .*) though that would suggest a gradual trailing off rather than a sudden interruption.

OMISSIONS AND HESITATIONS

The single dash is also used to indicate the omission of all or part of a taboo word:

The b– door's stuck!
B– off!

(The expression *Dash it!*, as a softened version of *Damn it!*, derives from this practice. In former times, when the exclamation *Damn it!* was considered unfit for print, the printed form used instead was *– it!*, which was read out as *Dash it!*)

The dash also indicates the omission of all or part of a name that the author must not or will not reveal:

The Marquis de B– rode at dead of night back into the town of D–

Dashes are also used to indicate hesitant speech.

Going – going – gone!
I – um – er – well – that is – I love you.

Discover – nonsense – too much shaken up by the breakdown – besides – extreme caution – gave up the post-chaise – walked on – took a hackney coach – came to the Borough – last place in the world that he'd look in – ha! ha! – capital notion that – very.

– Mr Jingle, in Dickens's *Pickwick Papers*

Here, the 'en-dash' may be used – shorter than an ordinary dash (an 'em-dash') but longer than a hyphen. (The dot-dot-dot may also be used here.)

Note, however, that for the stammering of sounds or syllables, hyphens are used rather than dashes:

I l-l-l-love you.

LINKS AND REFERENCES

The single dash is also used between the first and last points in space or time:

Newhaven – Dieppe
Monday – Friday

This dash can be read out as 'to'. Once again, it is often printed as the shorter 'en-dash'.

You may in fact use several such dashes, especially when listing the points on an itinerary:

London – Newhaven – Dieppe – Paris

The single dash is also the traditional way of indicating the source of a quotation:

– *TLS*, 22 June 1984
– George Eliot, *Middlemarch*

The dash combines with the colon to form another symbol (:–) – see page 225 above. And note, finally, that ordinary typewriters and word processors do not feature the dash. It can be represented either by two successive hyphens, or by a single hyphen with a space either side. The difference between an en-dash and an em-dash cannot really be represented except by a typesetter.

The Apostrophe

Apostrophes have two chief purposes: to indicate possession and other kinds of relationship (*Robert's pen, the government's decree, for pity's sake*), and in contractions (*isn't* for *is not, can't* for *cannot, o'er* for *over*).

POSSESSIVES

The basic rules for possessives are fairly straightforward. They are as follows:

☐ The apostrophe comes before the *s* if the noun is singular: *one judge's opinion, Mary's daft notion, Mike's wristwatch.*

☐ The apostrophe comes after the *s* if that *s* serves to make the noun plural: *the judges' opinions, the girls' varied notions, the Joneses' new house.*

☐ The apostrophe comes before the *s* if the noun is already plural without the *s*: *the people's palace, the women's varied notions.*

However, there are complications – with certain pronouns, and with nouns ending in *s*.

Pronouns. Possessive personal pronouns ending in *s* take no apostrophe: *its*, *ours*, *whose*, *theirs*, and so on. Indefinite pronouns (except for *each*) do take an apostrophe: *anyone's*, *either's*.

Nouns ending in *s*. For these, as well as for nouns ending in *-x, -z, -nce, -ese*, and so on, things are not at all straightforward. The ear is as good a guide as any: whatever sounds best will usually be best.

So: the cottage where Keats lived is *Keats's cottage*; similarly *Marx's study*. The house where Dickens lived is probably *Dickens's house*, though formerly it might have been *Dickens' house*; similarly the *Chinese's office*. (North American English is slightly more conservative perhaps: *Keats' cottage* and *Dickens' house* and similar constructions are often used by Americans and Canadians.)

The modern tendency is to add *-'s* to all singular nouns ending in *s*, though the longer the word, the likelier it is that a simple apostrophe, without the *s*, will be acceptable: *Zeus's thunder* but *Euripides' plays; Brahms's trio* but *Berlioz' Requiem*.

I'M, WON'T, SHAN'T

The apostrophe is used to form contractions with some verbs: *isn't* (= is not), *I'm* (= I am), *where's* (= where is), *wouldn't* (= would not), *can't* (= cannot), *don't* (= do not). Such contractions are very common in speech and much informal writing. They tend to fuse the words into one, and the apostrophe takes the place of the missing letter or letters (see also page 252). Note that for very formal writing these contractions are usually not considered appropriate.

The apostrophe is also found in the contracted ('clipped') forms of some single words.

☐ Some of these survive chiefly in older poetry. Very often it is *v* that is omitted, as in these contractions: *e'en* (even), *e'er* (ever), and *o'er* (over). Note that these contractions are literary, and so very formal rather than informal.

☐ Similarly, the word *of* is sometimes contracted to *o'*, especially in certain set phrases: *Jack-o'-lantern*, *will-o'-the-wisp*, *six o'clock*.

☐ English has a number of contracted words that are in current use, and are marked as contractions by the presence of the apostrophe: *ass'n*

(used in writing to represent *association*), *ma'am*, *fo'c's'le*, and so on. The modern tendency is to drop the apostrophes if possible: *bus*, *phone*, *plane*, *flu*, *bosun*.

☐ The apostrophe can also be used to indicate the omission of part of a number: *musicals of the '30s; the winter of '79*. The modern tendency is again to omit the apostrophes here.

Note that the contraction of a single word is sometimes called elision. The loss of a letter, if at the end of a word is called *apocope* (*goin'* for *going*); if at the beginning, *aphesis* (*'ware* for *beware*); and if in the middle, *syncope* (*e'en* for *even*).

O'Connor and M'Quillan. The form *O'* is found in many surnames, typically of Celtic origin: *O'Connor*, *O'Reilley*, *O'Herlihy*. The *O* is derived from the Irish *o*, 'a grandson or descendant'; the apostrophe is inserted to link this element to the rest of the name. It is not always present, however. The two elements might occasionally be fused – *Oherlihy* – or left quite open: *O Herlihy*.

The form *M'* is occasionally found in Celtic surnames too: *M'Quillan*. Here the apostrophe marks a contraction, of *Mac-* or *Mc-*. The Gaelic *Mac-* means 'son of'.

PLURALS WITH APOSTROPHES

The apostrophe is used to indicate certain plural forms. It is used:

☐ to indicate the plural when a word is referred to as a word, without regard to its meaning:

There are three *but*'s in the sentence.

But use the regular plural, without an apostrophe, if the word has a separate meaning:

No ifs or buts, young man.

☐ to form the plurals of letters, numerals, and symbols:

Mind your p's and q's.
There are three 5's in 555.
There were $'s in his eyes.

The apostrophe is also sometimes used to form the plurals of abbreviations and of expressions that use numerals: *many DJ's, several MP's, the 1950's*.

However, the apostrophe is often omitted in these cases, and with reason: a plural can easily be confused with a possessive.

ABBREVIATIONS

Another major use of the apostrophe is to accompany an abbreviation that functions as a verb:

> He KO'd the champion.
> She has OD'd on heroin.

THE DISAPPEARING APOSTROPHE

In proper nouns, the apostrophe seems to be in decline. The official names are now *Barclays Bank, Pears Cyclopaedia, Beechams Products, Boots* (chemists), *Citizens Advice Bureau*, and so on.

Note too that many place-names where you might expect -'s end in fact with a simple s: *St Albans* (Hertfordshire, England), *St Andrews* (Fife, Scotland), *Regents Park, St Pancras Station*. On the other hand, *St David's* (Dyfed, Wales), *St James's Park*, and so on. Two adjacent stops on the Piccadilly line of the London underground are *Barons Court* and *Earl's Court*! Always check in a good atlas or road map to ensure that you are spelling a place-name correctly.

On the whole, however, the apostrophe is very resilient, and resists pressures to disappear. Nothing came of George Bernard Shaw's project to streamline written English by banishing or reducing apostrophes. Their value in clarifying meaning far outweighs their nuisance value.

Quotation Marks

The main purpose of quotation marks – also called, informally, *quote marks* or *quotes* and *inverted commas* – is to enclose material that is brought into a text from outside it, such as quotations from books, or words used by other people.

> As Polonius said, 'Neither a borrower nor a lender be.'

> 'You've really got to get your act together,' I told him sternly.

In both handwriting and printing, a clear distinction is made between quotation marks at the beginning of quoted material (',") and those at the end (',"). On a typewriter keyboard no such distinction is possible: single quotation marks are represented by an apostrophe (') and double quotation marks by a special symbol equivalent to a double apostrophe ("). The same is often true of word processors.

In handwriting, typing and word processing, and American printing, double quotation marks are normal (single quotation marks being used to enclose quotations within quotations).

In British printing, single quotation marks are nowadays more common. There is perhaps a gain in elegance and economy in this, but it does have one disadvantage – the closing quotation mark is identical to an apostrophe, and the reader might therefore momentarily think that he or she has reached the end of a quoted passage when in fact it is only an apostrophe:

> Stacy always spoke bitterly of 'that damn' high-falutin' ship's steward O'Reilly', who had first laughed at his rustic manners and then cheated at cards.

For better or worse, however, single quotation marks are dominant in British printing; they are used in this book, for example, and the following discussion will be about single quotation marks unless otherwise stated.

Where single quotation marks are standard, the role of the double quotation marks is to enclose quotations within quotations. So:

> She asked, 'Did he say "hearing" or "earring"?'

If there are ever quotations within quotations within quotations, you simply go on alternating between single and double quotation marks:

> She asked, 'Did he say, "The word 'earring' needs a hyphen"?'

Many other languages, notably French and German, have different conventions from those described here. Indeed, English itself has not always had these conventions: the King James Bible, for instance, does not use quotation marks at all. And many modern authors – James Joyce and Alan Paton, to name two very different kinds of novelist – dispense with quotation marks in various works, commonly using a dash instead to introduce direct speech.

DIRECT AND INDIRECT SPEECH

Quotation marks are used to enclose direct quotation, by contrast with indirect quotation – that is, quotation paraphrased by the author:

> She said, 'What did you say?' (direct speech)
> She asked what he had said. (indirect speech)

It is a common blunder – or a common act of dishonesty – to blend these two conventions:

> **X** She admitted she 'might have been wrong, but she had thought she was doing her duty'.

Surely the words actually spoken by her would have been ' . . . I thought I was doing my duty'. The writer should either have used the exact wording, or else have closed the quotation after *wrong*.

The words *yes* and *no* are not usually put in quotation marks unless they are part of a direct quotation:

> The management has said No to our pay claim.
> She said, 'No, you cannot.'

'I said,' said she. The words that introduce, present, or comment on direct quotation may come before, after, or in the middle of the quoted words. This 'presentational material' is usually set off from the direct quotation by commas:

> She wrote, 'No you cannot'.
> 'No,' she wrote, 'you cannot.'
> 'No, you cannot,' she wrote.

The most common presentation verbs are ones such as *say* and *write*. But there is a problem with them – overfrequent repetition of these verbs can become tedious. Note, however, that far more verbs can assume the presentational role after the quotation than before it:

> She said, 'Get you gone, foul fiend.'
> 'Get you gone, foul fiend,' she said/ordered/ bellowed/cried/shrieked.

Turning the order around like this can be a useful way of avoiding repetition.

Note also that the presentational material itself is sometimes 'inverted' – that is, the verb comes before the subject:

> 'No, I will not,' said Mrs Thatcher.

Paragraphs in quotations If the quoted passage has more than one paragraph, the normal convention is to put opening quotation marks at the beginning of each paragraph (as if to refresh the reader's memory), but to put closing quotation marks only where they would naturally occur – at the end of the quoted material:

> I asked her how she began in films.
> 'I went to the London College of Printing 12 or 13 years ago, doing photography and film . . . I made a degree film and it showed at the ICA during their Rock Week.
> 'I got a job with a video company on the grounds of that – I can't quite think why. . . I applied to the National Film School, because my boyfriend was there at the time. I think I got in because it was the year of the girl. They have these occasional waves when they take minorities.'
>
> – Sean French, quoting
> Molly Dineen, *The Observer*

ACCURATE WORDING

The wording within quotation marks should, as far as possible, be identical to the wording of the original text. In the sentence, *'No,' she wrote, 'you cannot'*, the *you* has a small *y* rather than a capital, accurately reflecting the original quotation.

And if the original text had consisted of two sentences – *No, you cannot. It's impossible* – this too would be apparent in the punctuation:

'No, you cannot,' she wrote. 'It's impossible.'

The capital *I* of *It's* is retained in the quoted version.

The punctuation of the quoted version, however, cannot always be identical to that of the original.

Full stop, semicolon, question mark. The full stop of the original is replaced by a comma if the presentational material follows it:

'No, you cannot,' she wrote.

But suppose the original text had been punctuated with a semicolon rather than a comma in the middle – *No, you cannot; it's impossible.*

If given as direct quotation, with the presentational material coming in the middle, you would put a comma after *cannot*, and switch the semicolon to the end of the presentational material – like this:

'No, you cannot,' she wrote; 'it's impossible.'

The same applies to a colon or full stop:

'No, you cannot,' she wrote: 'it's impossible.'
'No, you cannot,' she wrote. 'It's impossible.'

But the question mark and exclamation mark are different – they remain true to the original text by appearing within the quotation marks:

'Well, you cannot!' she wrote. 'It's outrageous.'

The dash is more versatile: it can appear outside or inside the quotation marks, and if inside can appear within the first set or the second set. The likeliest location for it is inside the second set:

'You simply cannot,' she wrote, ' – it's not on.'

Contraction and expansion. If you want to quote only part of the original wording, omitting some words in the middle, replace the omitted words with an ellipsis – the 'dot-dot-dot'.

'No, . . . impossible,' she wrote.

Suppose, conversely, that you wanted to quote more than the original – to add an explanation, for instance. You can do this by enclosing the added material within square brackets.

'I am going to have a serious crack at the 7.36sec world record [held by Greg Foster] next week,' Jackson said.

– *The Times*

In general, avoid the 'dot-dot-dot' and square brackets when you can. If they occur more than once or twice, they clutter the text.

ALTERING THE PUNCTUATION

When quoting from other texts, a writer has the basic duty to reproduce that text accurately. But what he or she can change, as a rule, is the punctuation conventions. If the quoted text, for instance, used double quotation marks, the writer may change them to single quotation marks in line with the surrounding text. (So too perhaps with spelling changes – from *-ize* to *-ise*, for instance.)

What about punctuation changes at the start and end of a quoted passage? Suppose you want to quote just a portion from the middle of a sentence. It is clearly tempting to begin that quoted portion with a capital letter and to end it with a full stop.

Many publishers allow this liberty; others, more pedantic, refuse to allow it, and insist that any such changes must be explicitly acknowledged, typically in the following way:

She noted, in her report: '[T]hese children are clearly unruly, but what we need to find out is whether they are amenable to discipline . . . '

QUOTATIONS MARKS – OR NOT?

Not all direct quotations have to be enclosed in quotation marks.

Allusions. An allusion, even one that accurately quotes the original, no longer takes quotation marks if it has passed into general idiomatic usage:

He had to support four children, his hostages to fortune, and so could not risk losing his job.

The phrase *hostages to fortune* occurred originally in an essay by the philosopher Francis Bacon, in turn echoing the Roman poet Lucan.

Another example:

Ever since Queen Medbh and her Dun Cow, people have enjoyed getting dismal about Ireland. Things fall apart once again in *The Railway Station Man*, not least the heroine's yellowing teeth.

– Jonathan Keates, *The Observer*

The words *Things fall apart* are the opening words of the poem 'The Second Coming' by W.B. Yeats.

Well-known quotations. Even when the author is identified, the quotation might not take quotation marks if it is well known and if it is integrated into the surrounding text:

It is the heart of winter now, but we remain in good spirits. Can spring be far behind? as Shelley rhetorically asked. We are assured of better days, and soon.

Dramatic dialogue. The dialogue of a play dispenses with quotation marks.

Cordelia: Nothing, my lord.
Lear: Nothing?
Cordelia: Nothing.
Lear: Nothing will come of nothing. Speak again.
        – Shakespeare, *King Lear* I i

Published reports. A similar practice is often adopted in the published reports of official proceedings. In fact, any long quotations can generally be introduced by a colon, indented from the surrounding text, and freed of quotation marks (as is the practice in this book):

Simons goes on to say:
    There are seven types of ambiguity, according to some . . .

Direct and indirect quotation. Note that the two types of quotation may be combined for literary effect. When this is done, observe the punctuation conventions of each type:

She thought, 'I shall never get away.' The family would engulf her.

QUOTATION AND AUTHORIAL DISCLAIMER

In all the examples so far, the quotation marks have in effect been saying, 'These words are not my words now: they are other people's words, or my words in other circumstances.'

This use of quotation marks can be extended to serve as a kind of 'authorial disclaimer': to indicate that the words are used in a special way. (Hence the expression 'in inverted commas', as in *After a few drinks, he gets very friendly . . . in inverted commas.* Some people even crook their fingers in the air when they use words that call for quotation marks.) In the first sentence of this paragraph, for example, the words *authorial disclaimer* are in quotation marks to show that they constitute a technical term – or perhaps only to show that the phrase is not ideal, but the best term available. Note that italics or (if the text is typed or handwritten) underlining is sometimes an alternative to such quotation marks.

This use of quotation marks may distance the author in several ways from the words quoted:

A GRAND 'FAIR'

A common and ludicrous error with quotation marks is the attempted use of them simply to give emphasis. You might have seen signs such as these:

✗ A grand 'Fair' will be held in the Village Hall.
✗ 'Fresh' Tomatoes.

The writer of the first sign is presumably trying to make the word *fair* stand out; the writer of the second is probably trying to emphasise that the tomatoes are really fresh. But educated readers could argue that it conveys just the opposite impression: that the fair is really hardly a real fair at all, and that the tomatoes might be considered fresh by some, but are not really so. It is just like saying:

God preserve me from such 'friends'!

Such quotation marks indicate irony; they do not reinforce your message. For emphasis, use italics, underlining, capitalisation, exclamation marks – anything but quotation marks.

☐ God preserve me from such 'friends'! (= the word is inappropriate and is being used in an ironic way).

☐ A certain 'je ne sais quoi' (= the words are foreign: italics would be more usual here).

☐ I went in to have a 'butchers' (= the word belongs to a different level of language from the rest of the text; in this case, cockney slang).

☐ Accused 'tried to bribe judge' (= allegedly: for legal reasons, newspaper headlines use inverted commas to indicate allegations or rumours).

Two warnings: first, take care not to overuse quotation marks when being ironic or when apologising for an inadequate word.

It can be very irritating to the reader to see quotation marks scattered over the page unless they are truly serving the purpose of quotation.

Secondly, it is usually enough to use the quotation marks only once when indicating your authorial disclaimer. Subsequent uses of the word or phrase can do without the quotation marks. The phrase *authorial disclaimer*, for example, has no quotation marks in the previous sentence, since it has already appeared in them once.

The Building Blocks Of Good English

GLOSSES AND TITLES

Single quotation marks have another special use – a rather technical one, but common in books about language. It is the use of quotation marks to enclose a gloss, or interpretation. The expression being glossed will often appear in italics:

The French word *lait* means 'milk'.

Compare:

The French word *lait* is synonymous with *milk*.

The first sentence talks about a word and its meaning. The second sentence talks about two words – *lait* and *milk*.

Note that such glossing is usually made in single quotation marks, even by Americans.

Quotation marks also distinguish certain kinds of title from the surrounding text. Nowadays a fairly clear distinction is made between those titles that are in quotation marks and those that are italicised.

The titles in quotation marks tend to be of relatively short works. They include the titles of articles, chapters or parts of books (except for the Bible), pamphlets, lectures, stories, short poems, short pieces of music, and, in general, single radio and television programmes. Italics are used for the titles of longer works, such as periodicals, books, plays, longer musical works such as operas, and some-

INSIDE OR OUT: PUNCTUATION PROBLEMS WITH QUOTATION MARKS

Which of these is correct?

'No, you cannot,' she wrote.
'No, you cannot', she wrote.

In other words, on which side of the closing quotation mark or marks should the comma be placed?

The comma. In American English, the answer is simple: a comma (or a full stop) never comes directly after the closing quotation marks – it always falls just within them.

In British English, things are more complicated. The comma usually falls within the quotation marks if followed by presentational material such as *he said* or *Alfred replied*:

'I think so,' Alfred replied.

However, when the quoted material is followed by something other than *he said, she wrote*, or the like, then the comma – in British usage – usually comes after the closing mark:

I hate the word 'palimony', and shun it.

(The American usage here would be to place the comma within the quotation marks – double quotation marks this time.)

In British usage, it is possible for the comma to come after the quotation mark even though the quotation is followed by *she wrote*:

Although she said on the phone 'Yes, you can', she wrote 'No, you cannot' in her letter.

The reason for this reversal is that the *she wrote* applies not to the first quoted passage but to the second.

The full stop. The original text might well have a full stop, but this is no guarantee that the quoted version of it will have one:

'No, you cannot,' she said.
She said 'No, you cannot' and she meant it.
Did she really say 'No, you cannot'?
To think that she said 'No, you cannot'!

But when the quotation comes at the end of an ordinary declarative sentence, a full stop is obviously needed. Does it go inside or outside the closing quotation mark or marks?

In American English, the rule is the same as that for the comma: the full stop always falls just within the closing quotation marks. In British usage, however, the full stop will fall within the closing quotation mark only if two conditions are both met:

☐ the quoted words ended with a full stop in the original (or at least can stand on their own as a complete utterance)

☐ the quoted words are preceded by a punctuation mark

So:

Mary Magpie said, 'You should try to be perfect in an imperfect world.'
'Listen to me,' Mary Magpie said. 'Try to be perfect in an imperfect world.'

times radio and television series and serials. The names of paintings are also usually italicised. So you might refer to:

> the article 'New Light on Old Bones' in *New Scientist* (article in periodical)

Tennyson's 'Ulysses', Homer's *Odyssey*, and Joyce's *Ulysses* (short poem, long poem, novel)

the TV show 'M.A.S.H.' based on the film *M.A.S.H.*
Oscar Wilde's short story 'The Happy Prince'
Leonardo da Vinci's *Mona Lisa*

The Question Mark

On the face of it, the use of the question mark is fairly straightforward – it comes at the end of a direct question:

> Would you like a drink?
> Do you want coffee or do you want tea?

It is also used after a quoted question:

> She asked, 'How are you?'
> 'How are you?' she asked.
> I asked, 'Would you like a drink?'
> 'Would you like a drink?' I asked.

This holds good even when the quoted sentence is interrupted by the presentational material:

> 'You should try,' Mary Magpie said, 'to be perfect in an imperfect world.'

Note – in keeping with the rule – that if only half the sentence is directly quoted, then the full stop would fall outside the quotation mark:

> Mary Magpie urges us 'to be perfect in an imperfect world'.

And if the opening quotation mark is not directly preceded by a punctuation mark, then the full stop would again, as a rule, fall outside the closing quotation mark:

> My motto is 'Try to be perfect in an imperfect world'.

Note the difference that a preceding punctuation mark can make. If a colon were inserted after *is*, then the full stop would probably go back inside the closing quotation mark:

> My motto is: 'Try to be perfect in an imperfect world.'

The question mark. With the question mark and exclamation mark, British and American usage are at last in agreement.

If the quotation, considered alone, demands a question mark or exclamation mark, then it gets one – within the closing quotation mark or marks. But if it is the surrounding sentence that demands one, then it is placed outside the quotation marks:

> She said, 'Do you like caviar?'
> Did she say, 'I adore caviar'?

Note, in the two examples just quoted, that a full stop might have been expected at the very end of the first sentence, and directly after the word *caviar* in the second sentence. It is omitted, however, because the 'stronger' question mark (or exclamation mark) in each case makes the full stop unnecessary. A comma also sometimes disappears when a question mark or exclamation mark is in the immediate neighbourhood, as in the following example:

> 'Caviar!' he exclaimed.

But where the surrounding wording is not presentational material, then a comma can exist near a question mark or exclamation mark:

> She said 'Shut up!', but I continued shouting.

A further problem: what if both the quotation and the surrounding sentence require a question mark or exclamation mark?

> Did she say, 'Do you like caviar?'?
> To think that she said 'Shut up!'!

Some authorities would omit the second question mark and second exclamation mark here: certainly they look odd, even though they are justified by logic. It is your choice.

But if you need *both* marks, you must use them:

> Did she really say 'Shut up!'?

But it is not used in an indirect question:

> She asked if I wanted a drink.
> I asked them whether they were now happily settled into their new house.

However, complications exist. 'Tag questions' (such as *aren't you?* in *You're well, aren't you?*) usually take question marks whether said with a rising or falling intonation. But sometimes they take exclamation marks instead:

> She's beautiful, isn't she!

And sometimes a question may not have the usual structure of a question:

> He said what?
> He said *that*?
> He arrived at midnight?
> Surely that's wrong?

In all these cases, the question mark reflects the tone of voice and inflection used when the sentence is spoken.

A tricky problem occurs when questions function as requests. Such requests come in various degrees.

First, a tentative request for permission (spoken with a rising tone at the end, just like a straightforward question):

> Could I have an apple?
> Would you mind very much if I smoked?
> I wonder if I might ask you to open the window?

Here a question mark seems appropriate, even in the last example, which is constructed like a statement rather than a question.

Second, a rather more confident request (spoken without a rising tone), expecting action, rather than a spoken reply, by way of response:

> Could I have an apple, please(?)
> Would you open the window for me(?)
> Would you mind fetching the kettle(?)

Here the suitability and unsuitability of the question mark are evenly balanced.

Next, a 'request' that is spoken in a flat tone, like an instruction, and functions as a piece of advice rather than as a request:

> Could you pass me that apple, please.
> Would everyone wishing to visit the Eiffel Towel please assemble in the lobby.

Here a question mark would be very unlikely.

Finally, a sarcastic sneer, though still with the structure of a request:

> Would you mind not poking me in the eye.
> Would you open the blasted door.

A question mark seems quite inappropriate here. An exclamation mark is far more likely.

HALF-QUESTIONS AND EMBEDDED QUESTIONS

Questions do not have to be in the form of a complete sentence:

> What? Yes? Over there?
> Why not come tonight?
> Coffee? Coffee or tea?

Such questions might take the form of split-off parts of a longer sentence, each part having a capital letter and ending with a question mark:

> Do you want coffee? Or do you want tea?
> What will happen if it rains? If the match is cancelled? If the train is late?

Conversely, a question – or even a series of questions – may be embedded in a larger sentence:

> Who was next for the chop? was the thought in everyone's mind.
> A story that answers the questions What?, Where?, and When? may still leave other important questions unanswered.
> Who knows about editing the book?, proofreading the book?, printing the book?

Although logically correct, these constructions look clumsy. If possible, try to rephrase:

> There was one thought in everyone's mind: who was next for the chop?
> A story that answers certain important questions – What? Where? When? – may still leave other equally important ones unanswered.
> Who knows about editing the book? Or proofreading it? Or printing it?

Alternatively, when the different parts of a series of questions do not begin with a typical question word (such as *what*), the whole series may have only one question mark, at the end:

> Who knows about editing the book, proofreading the book, printing the book?

For positioning the question mark in such questions (or any others) either inside or outside quotation marks, see page 234 for details.

EXPRESSING DOUBT OR EMPHASIS

The question mark can be used to express doubt about a fact:

> Geoffrey Chaucer (1340? – 1400)
> Geoffrey Chaucer (?1340 – 1400)

(In the first example, only the date of birth is considered doubtful; in the second, both dates are put in doubt.)

The question mark can also be used – on its own, doubled, even trebled, or in combination with the exclamation mark – to express doubt, often ironic, about a characterisation:

> With such friends (?), I don't need enemies.
> Can they really have meant that??
> They gave the job to Louise?!

A special punctuation mark called the 'interrabang' or 'interrobang' has also been invented:

> They gave the job to Louise?

– but it is hardly ever used.

Be very sparing with these forms. Keep them for personal letters and other informal writings.

But note that *?*, *??*, *?!*, and *!?* are used in chess notation, indicating a mistake, a blunder, a dubious move, and an exciting but risky move: *RXP??*

The Exclamation Mark

Exclamation mark is the usual name in British English. In American English, the usual name is *exclamation point*.

In general, the exclamation mark is used far less today than it used to be. It is rather like a rich sauce – cloying if used lavishly, and not really needed at all if the dish is already sufficiently spicy. The wording in *You're a right idiot* is explicit enough to make the meaning quite clear, regardless of the punctuation.

An exclamation mark is often used, but not always needed, to express a high degree of emotion, emphasis, or excitement. Its most typical uses are after interjections and similar exclamations:

> Hurrah! Good Heavens!
> For Pete's sake!
> Shh! Encore!

It is used too after words expressing or suggesting loud, sharp noises:

> Crash! Boo! Wham! Zap! Kapow!

And it can come after certain types of exclamatory utterance, the most typical of which begin with *How, What,* or *That,* or have the form of questions (usually negative questions):

> How charming you are!
> What a charming creature you are!
> A charming creature you are!
> Aren't you just charming!
> That such a thing should happen to me!
> Oh for the wings of a dove!
> If only I'd thought of that!

COMMANDS AND REQUESTS

Although the exclamation mark is often used after imperatives or commands, it does not have to be. Strength of feeling is the deciding factor:

> Please do not walk on the grass.
> Shut up!

Furthermore, when a question is used as a request, there is a range of possibilities reflecting increasing urgency and decreasing politeness:

> Would you mind passing the salt?
> Would everyone wishing to visit the Eiffel Tower please assemble in the lobby.
> Would you mind not poking me in the eye with your umbrella!

OTHER TRICKS AND USES

Like the question mark, the exclamation mark may be used to comment on a preceding word or phrase. Such punctuational comments, usually in brackets, are often ironic in tone.

> With such friends(!), I don't need enemies.
> Sh! Shh!! Shhh!!!
> She's won! She's won!! She's won!!!

Once again, use these devices sparingly, or the reader will stop taking you seriously.

An exclamation mark may follow a question mark and thereby reinforce it. It often adds an element of incredulity to the question:

> (Are you telling me) they gave the job to Louise?!

NEW WORDS FROM OLD BOOKS

The stories of the Bible and the myths of ancient Greece and Rome have contributed much to western culture. They have also added to our stock of words. The word *money*, for example, is derived ultimately from the name of a Roman goddess, Juno Moneta, whose temple was used as a mint in ancient Rome.

☐ In the list below, choose the word or phrase you believe is nearest in meaning to the key word. For the answers turn to pages 633-648.

aeolian
A: flavoured with garlic
B: produced by the wind
C: bewitched
D: lightheaded through lack of sleep

bacchanalian
A: riotously drunken
B: mortally ill
C: deeply offended
D: desperately unhappy

chimerical
A: exciting
B: pessimistic
C: lucky
D: imaginary

gorgon
A: an ugly woman
B: a cheese
C: a keyboard instrument
D: a stone figure

iridescent
A: patriotic
B: white-hot
C: rainbow-like
D: aggravating

Janus-faced
A: very ugly
B: extremely beautiful
C: pessimistic
D: hypocritical

jeremiad
A: a complaint
B: a casket
C: a waterfall
D: a miser

jeroboam
A: a large wine-bottle
B: a lockpicker
C: a wartime enemy
D: a venomous snake

jovial
A: religious
B: greedy
C: patient
D: merry

Junoesque
A: of stately beauty
B: possessive
C: exuberant
D: of sober, motherly habits

martial
A: long-suffering
B: sporting
C: warlike
D: extra-terrestrial

matutinal relating to
A: old age
B: ulcers
C: mornings
D: underground

mentor
A: an adviser
B: dishonesty
C: an ancient monument
D: a lover

mercurial having a character that is
A: changeable
B: dull
C: sociable
D: bad-tempered

narcissism
A: drug culture
B: meanness
C: self-love
D: hedge-cutting

nemesis
A: a submarine
B: a type of parasite
C: an avenger
D: a marble statue

odyssey
A: a long journey
B: a dwarf
C: an island group
D: a soft fabric

paean
A: a form of taxation
B: a song of praise
C: a naval rank
D: a castle keep

palladium
A: a fish-tank
B: a safeguard
C: a circus arena
D: a trophy

Philistine
A: a town-dweller
B: an uncultured person
C: a gardener
D: a tone-deaf person

saturnine
A: jolly
B: annoying
C: lustful
D: gloomy

Similar uses occur in chess notation, indicating a good, excellent, dubious, or risky move:

RXP! RXP!! RXP?! RXP!?

For the use of exclamation marks in quotations, see pages 234 and 235.

A final note about typing exclamation marks. Some typewriter keyboards do not include one. It is easy to make one up, however, by using the backspace key to type a full stop and an apostrophe in the same space. The keyboards of most word processors, however, do include an exclamation mark.

Brackets

There are two main kinds of bracket: crescent-shaped ones, ( ), and square ones, [ ] – for square brackets, see below, pages 240 and 241. In British English, words in either kind of brackets are said to be 'in parenthesis'.

The basic function of brackets is to separate the bracketed material clearly from what surrounds it. Typical examples of short bracketed material include dates and references:

Contemporary Verse (1918-1960)
The Decision (Tuesday, Radio 3)

But the use of brackets is more versatile and often more sophisticated than this.

BRACKETS VERSUS COMMAS

In general, material set off by brackets is less closely integrated with its surroundings than material set off by commas:

The principal Catholic service, the Mass, was never broadcast by the BBC (except occasionally in Northern Ireland) until the Second World War.
– John Whale, *The Times Literary Supplement*

Both *the Mass* and (*except occasionally in Northern Ireland*) can in theory be omitted from the sentence. But the omission of the former would seriously impair the sense of the sentence, whereas omission of the latter would not.

If the contrast between the set-off material and the surrounding text is particularly abrupt, writers often use dashes rather than brackets or commas.

And only brackets or dashes, not commas, can enclose a complete sentence, as in this example:

He found the plates and threw me in the two-cell jail with a county delinquent who should have been in the home for the old since he couldn't feed himself (the sheriff's wife fed him) and sat through the day drooling and slobbering.
– Jack Kerouac (U.S.), *On the Road*

BRACKETED SENTENCES

The two examples above are of bracketed material within a sentence. But there are also bracketed sentences within paragraphs:

It was Frederick Ashton who confirmed Seymour's stylistic affinity with Isadora Duncan in a wonderful solo which he devised for her, to five Brahms waltzes, as an evocation of the dances he remembered seeing Duncan perform. (Seymour recently surfaced from 'retirement' once more to take Royal Ballet classes – albeit in sneakers – to prepare for her performance of the Isadora solo at the Met's celebratory gala in New York.) Ashton was also to provide . . . the perfect role for a mature ballerina – Natalya Petrovna.
– Julie Kavanagh,
The Times Literary Supplement

Note that here the bracketed material is an independent sentence, and so begins with a capital letter and ends with a full stop. In the Kerouac quotation above, by contrast, the bracketed material falls within a sentence, and therefore neither begins with a capital letter nor ends with a full stop. The only important exception to this rule is adages, mottoes, quotations, and the like – and even here there is no full stop:

My grandfather's favourite saying (When in doubt, say nowt) is forever etched on my memory.

The Kavanagh example also shows the use of dashes to set off material within material already bracketed: it is usually clearer to use dashes or commas than to have brackets within brackets.

OTHER PUNCTUATION AND BRACKETS

In other respects, punctuation within brackets is straightforward. Full stops after abbreviations are perfectly acceptable, as are question marks and exclamation marks:

Yet (how could you defy her?) everything was eternally new; the old cry of the sea-gulls, the old tingle of the breeze . . .

– Graham Swift, *The Sweet-Shop Owner*

As for the punctuation that surrounds bracketed material, it too is straightforward. In general no mark of punctuation should come immediately before an opening bracket in the middle of a sentence, but it is fine to put punctuation marks before or after a closing bracket:

Yesterday, as the moat around the field rose to unprecedented heights (or should that be depths?), the miracle was that we managed to effect an official BBC linkup.

– David Gower, *The Times*

EMPHASIS, OPTIONS, AND EXPLANATIONS

Some writers put brackets round certain adjectives or phrases that come before nouns:

A number of (unsuitable) candidates offered their services.

The effect, curiously, is to give the bracketed material greater prominence than if the author had simply written:

A number of unsuitable candidates offered their services.

Brackets are also used to enclose material that offers a choice of words or concepts: *the gang(s) of youths who roam our streets*. This means roughly 'the gang or gangs who roam our streets'.

Similarly: *The clinic tests both men and women for (in)fertility*. The bracketed (*in*) serves as a kind of shorthand. In effect, the sentence means roughly:

'The clinic tests both men and women for fertility or infertility, as the case may be.'

Another way of presenting such alternatives is by the use of the solidus or diagonal stroke instead of brackets: *the gang/s of youths*.

Here are some other typical uses of brackets to present supplementary or explanatory material:

at seventy (70) miles per hour
the year 1985 (5745 in the Jewish calendar)
the first man to jump 8 ft (2.4 metres)
British Association of Applied Linguistics (BAAL)
The degree of B.Ed. (Bachelor of Education)

BRACKETS IN LISTS

Brackets can also enclose letters or numbers used to order items in a list:

. . . an author who hadn't actually finished the book when its typescripts went to the printers, and was simultaneously (a) composing two whole episodes while (b) trying to cope with proofs on the margins of which he (c) added some 30 per cent of the final text while (d) intermittently rolling on the floor with pain . . .

– Professor Hugh Kenner,
The Times Literary Supplement

Normally, the brackets are used in pairs. But sometimes it is possible to use the final bracket only, especially when the listed items appear on separate lines:

There are three points to consider here:

1) . . .
2) . . .
3) . . .

Square Brackets

Square brackets, [ ], also called *brackets* in North America, are rather technical marks of punctuation. Many typewriter keyboards do not have them; you can improvise square brackets by combining the solidus or slash (/) with hyphens typed at the top and bottom. Many people simply put in square brackets by hand if required. With word processors this is not generally a problem.

Use square brackets to enclose editorial corrections, comments, or explanations in material written by someone else:

Beethoven's *Eroica* Symphony of 1800 [1801] is perhaps his best-known work.

At times the narrative voice is heard protesting: 'Our Hooste gan to swere as he were wood [mad]'.

It is then, perhaps, worth discussing whether Boccaccio's major work [*The Decameron*] influenced Chaucer's *Canterbury Tales*.

Sic. A typical comment of this kind is the [*sic*] that informs readers that the preceding text is to be taken literally, however odd it may appear:

'In his retiracy [sic] after 1946,' the biographer comments, 'the senator continued to take an active interest in the economic and cultural revival of his home state.'

Here the [*sic*] is used because the usual form is *retirement* rather than *retiracy*. Note, however, that the *sic* is often enclosed in round brackets instead.

Insertions. Square brackets enclose words (or even letters) inserted into a text instead of, or in addition to, the words originally there. Such inserted words are not comments or corrections, but are intended to be read as part of the text, which should as a result be clearer or easier to follow:

> If the main participants are to be believed – risky, this, since according to their amanuensis, Piers Paul Read, 'thieves [are] facile liars' – the robbery and its aftermath also involved widespread corruption by many police officers and prison warders.
>
> – Clancy Segal, *The Listener*

How scrupulous a writer should be in quoting a text is a matter of some debate. Some purists insist on complete fidelity to the original, resulting in such passages as this:

> As Marlowe argues, '[t]hat is special pleading . . . [and] begging the question at one and the same time . . .'

Some writers allow much more elasticity:

> As Marlowe argues, 'that is special pleading [and] begging the question at one and the same time'.

See page 232 for a fuller discussion of these different approaches.

With question marks. Square brackets help to prevent confusion about the source of one sort of 'comment': the question mark inserted into a text to indicate doubt. Compare these sentences:

> Beethoven's Eroica Symphony was composed in 1800 (?).
> 'Beethoven's Eroica Symphony was composed in 1800 [?]'

In the first example, the doubt is in the mind of the author of the original sentence, of which (?) is a part.

In the second example, the doubt is in the mind of the editor or reviewer, who has inserted [?] into a sentence that did not at first contain it.

BRACKETS WITHIN BRACKETS

Square brackets are sometimes used to enclose a parenthesis within a parenthesis:

? My aunt (I never knew what she looked like [she died before I was born]) left the brooch to my mother.

This practice may lead to confusion about whether the material in square brackets is part of the original text or an editorial interpolation. So it is perhaps better to use some other punctuation:

> My aunt (I never knew what she looked like – she died before I was born) left the brooch to my mother.

The Building Blocks Of Good English

Three Dots

The punctuation device known as an *ellipsis* (plural, *ellipses*) is usually represented by three dots in succession (. . .), though sometimes by an indefinite number (. . . . . .). The dots are usually called *ellipsis*, but may also be called *leaders*.

They are typically used three at a time to indicate the omission of words in a quoted passage:

> The dots . . . may also be called leaders.

Ellipsis is also used to indicate the omission of whole sentences. Suppose the original text is:

> The princess pleaded with him. She promised him anything in return. Eventually he agreed.

You could quote the first and last sentence only:

> The princess pleaded with him. . . . Eventually he agreed.

Here there are the same three dots, each surrounded by spaces . . . but this time preceded by a fourth dot – the full stop, at the end of the first sentence, which has no space before it.

> The princess pleaded . . . . She promised him anything in return. Eventually he agreed.

Here, the space before the first dot shows that the first sentence is incomplete. The fourth dot is the full stop this time.

> The princess pleaded . . . Eventually he agreed.

Here, the three evenly spaced dots suggest to the

reader that something has been omitted from the end of the first sentence – and that one or more sentences have been omitted between the first sentence and the last.

This distinction, it is true, is ignored by many writers and publishers: increasingly, the tendency is to follow the pattern of the third example regardless of the type of omission.

Ellipsis can also show the omission of, say, one or more lines of poetry. The convention here is to use as many dots as necessary to fill up one line:

> Tyger, tyger, burning bright
> . . . .
> What immortal hand or eye
> Could frame thy fearful symmetry?

Ellipsis is also used to show hesitation in speech:

> I . . . um . . . er . . . well . . . that is . . . I love you.

Dashes could also be used here, but the effect of ellipsis can be to suggest a trailing off or fading away of the voice rather than sudden breaks.

Yet another use of ellipsis is to convey the idea of 'etc., and so forth', in order to indicate the continuation of something:

> The even numbers are 2,4,6,8(,) . . .

The reader is meant to understand that the sequence continues *10,12,14*, and so on. Note that the final comma is optional.

SURPRISE ANNOUNCEMENTS

You can also use ellipsis for a variety of rhetorical effects – to indicate to the reader a certain reluctance to spell things out, for instance; or to suggest a build-up to a surprise announcement or to the reversal of expectation. (A dash is often used for the same purpose.) An example of this 'rhetorical' ellipsis can be found near the start of this article:

> Here there are the same three dots, each surrounded by spaces . . . but this time preceded by a fourth dot.

In the following example, the ellipsis serves to indicate a thoughtful pause, heralding a slight modification of the idea previously expressed:

> I thought how quickly and easily all the ties of one life could be broken and those of a new one built up . . . it was sad to reflect that the new friends were probably just as transitory, and the

links with them just as fragile.
> – Lynne Reid Banks, *The L-Shaped Room*

Some writers use ellipses at the end of a sentence instead of using a full stop, even though nothing has been omitted at all. This stylistic tic is perhaps intended to suggest that each sentence, though complete, leaves much unsaid. It is a handy device for gossip columnists:

> Well, so the egregious Clive Beauchamp has been seen at yet another disco with yet another sultry blonde 'business acquaintance' . . . Everyone is now asking when Mrs Beauchamp will find out . . .

In a personal letter the effect may be amateurishly touching; in journalism it is merely amateurish. A full stop at the end of a complete sentence may be less suggestive than such ellipsis, but it is more forthright and honest – full stop.

ELLIPSIS IN QUOTATIONS

Suppose you are writing a history essay, and want to quote from the following passage – not the whole of it, just the part that has been italicised here. How do you punctuate your quotation?

> And here we first encounter the tragic paradox that was to bedevil, and decisively influence, *the Russian revolutionary movement* at every stage of its history: it *remained estranged and remote from the Russian people whose cause it had espoused*, but who responded to it with indifference, suspicion and even hostility.
> – Tibor Szamuely, *The Russian Tradition*

The normal procedure nowadays would be to write:

> The Russian revolutionary movement . . . remained estranged and remote from the Russian people whose cause it had espoused.

The original sentence does not end at this point, and begins slightly earlier than the quoted sentence. Purists would insist that the curtailed version therefore both begin and end with three dots, and even that the capital *T* at the beginning should be enclosed in square brackets (see page 232).

Increasingly, however, the tendency is to take small liberties at the beginning and end of a quotation, and to restrict the three dots to the middle of a quotation. Of course, if the quoted version does not make a full sentence in itself, then dots will have to be used before or after (or both).

The Slash

This punctuation mark, represented by a diagonal stroke (/), is also called the *solidus*, pronounced /**sol**li-dəss /; its plural is *solidi*, / **sol**li-dī /.

The solidus may also be called the *slant*, the *oblique* (in British English), the *bar*, the *virgule*, the *diagonal* (in American English), or the *stroke*. The term *stroke* is used especially when you are reading out a written text: the written words *section B/72* might be read out as 'section B stroke seventy-two'.

THE SEPARATING FUNCTION

The solidus is commonly used to separate alternatives:

> Everyone knows that he/she is mortal.

> You need a lot of luck and/or hard work to succeed at anything (this means that you need a lot of luck, or hard work, or both).

> *loth/loath* (this means that the two forms are regarded as acceptable spelling variants of a single word).

> Sarah had a distracted/absent-minded air which intrigued all who knew her (this means that each of these words might be appropriately used in this particular sentence).

> The way, occasionally blocked by unused branches from the annual fellings, at last arrives at the scattered village of Le Petit Celland, where the café/shop/petrol-station provides the first refreshment since Cuves.
> – Adam Nicolson, *Long Walks in France*

In the last example, the slashes mean, of course, that the establishment combines the functions of café, shop, and petrol station.

New formations are possible by the use of the solidus: one product of the move to avoid sexism in language is the formation *s/he*, an even more economical way than *he/she* of expressing the idea 'he or she, as the case may be':

> Everyone knows that s/he is mortal.

The solidus may also come before an optional element: *vowel/s*. It is here the equivalent of a pair of brackets: *vowel(s)*. The meaning in each case is 'either a vowel or vowels'.

In expressions of time, the solidus can separate successive units:

> 1962/1963   May/June

> the weekend of 25/26 November

A dash or hyphen may be used instead, and is usual when the units are not successive.

> 1914 – 1918   May – September

The solidus can also be used in writing dates:

> 18/9/87

When successive lines of poetry are written as a single line, the solidus is used to indicate the line-break of the original:

> No one so much as you/Loves this my clay/Or would lament as you/Its dying day.
> – Edward Thomas, 'No One So Much as You'

The solidus is also frequently used:

☐ in writing fractions – $\frac{1}{2}$, $\frac{3}{4}$, $\frac{7}{8}$

☐ to indicate subsections in legal documents – *section B/72*

☐ to represent or replace the word *per* – *80 km/hr, 33 rev/m*.

(Note that this last expression would be read aloud as 'thirty-three revolutions per minute', not as **X** 'thirty-three revolutions stroke minute'. And note too that the expressions *mpg* and *mph* use *p* rather than the solidus.)

Capital Letters

Various style manuals present conflicting rules for capitalisation. One authority approves of *The Mayor of Hackney*; another prefers *the mayor of Hackney*. One urges you to write *the Board of Governors*; another favours the form *the board of governors*.

At first glance, this kind of disagreement is utterly confusing and even depressing: if the experts disagree, what guidance for the non-expert? At second glance, however, it provides the key to understanding the function of capital letters.

Capital letters give importance, distinction, and emphasis. This explains why every sentence begins with a capital letter – to emphasise that a new thought has begun; why the simple phrase *white house* becomes the *White House* when it signifies the seat of presidential power in the United States; and why a brand of machine is trademarked *Hoover* – to stop it from becoming a generic term for any kind of vacuum cleaner.

Once capital letters are viewed as a means of assigning special significance to words, it becomes obvious why the authorities are bound to disagree.

They tend to assign significance to those things that loom largest in their lives. Thus, government insiders are more likely to write *the Government* and *the Mayor* than those outside; people unconnected with a school are less likely to care about its *board of governors* than those who work for the school or have children who attend it.

The only blanket rule is: Be consistent. If you decide to start a word with a capital letter in one place, make sure that you capitalise it throughout.

Capital letters are often referred to as 'upper-case letters', and small letters are often called 'lower-case letters'. Both terms come from printing. In the days when type was set by hand, all the letters for each typeface were kept in a large tray that was divided into dozens of compartments – one for each letter or punctuation mark. The tray, known as a 'case', was propped on a sloping rack; the capital letters were stored at the top end of the rack, the 'upper case', farther from the printer's darting fingers, because they were used less often. Ordinary letters, which were needed more often, were stored close to hand for speed, in the 'lower case'.

Here are some guidelines on which 'case' to use.

NOUNS – PROPER AND COMMON

The formal or official names of particular persons, places, or things – in short, proper nouns – always take capitals because of the distinction these names deserve: *Jane Austen, Primrose Hill, Rolls-Royce, the Eiffel Tower, Manchester University*. So too with nicknames and other titles: *Vinegar Joe, the Empress of the Blues, the New World, the Lake Poets*.

Capitalise proper adjectives too (forms derived from proper nouns): *Panamanian* (from *Panama*), *Dickensian* (from *Dickens*), *Hamlet-like* from *Hamlet*, *Kafkaesque* (from *Kafka*).

Some common words and expressions (known as 'eponyms') are derived from proper names – *watt*, for instance, the unit of power named after the Scottish inventor, James Watt. Many of these retain their capitals: *an Arcadia, an Adonis, a Casanova*. Others have lost their connection with the original name, so they take the lower case:

ampere	jersey
to hebraicise	morocco leather
boycott	to pasteurise
dutch auction	platonic love
sandwich	braille
chinaware	silhouette
guillotine	ohm

The following expressions, however (and others like them), do not command the same measure of general agreement. In such cases, you are free to choose the form you prefer – so long as you then follow that style consistently:

bohemian existence	herculean
irish coffee	pullman car
dutch oven	scotch whisky
french windows	turkish bath

When a lower-case prefix is attached to a proper noun or adjective, the main part of the word usually keeps its capital letter (and is usually preceded by a hyphen): *un-American, anti-British, pro-Nazi, non-Jewish, mid-Atlantic* (but the regular *transatlantic*).

With common nouns the rule is broadly this: give a common noun a capital letter when it forms part of a proper name but not when it is used alone or in place of a proper name. For example: *Aunt Jane, my aunt; Lake Windermere, the lake; the Waldorf-Astoria Hotel, this hotel; the Leeds Piano Competition, this competition*.

FIRST WORDS

Give a capital letter to the first word of a sentence and of any phrase that is used as a sentence:

Can you believe they are getting married?
Not me.
Astonishing!
Here is the news.

And give the same treatment to the first word of a sentence that is quoted:

I overheard her say, 'If this gets out, heads will roll. The first in line for the chop will be you, do you hear?'

The words *yes* and *no* sometimes take a capital letter in the middle of a sentence even when not enclosed in quotation marks:

> If you have lost your savings, write No in the space provided.

Give a capital letter to the first word of an independent question within a sentence:

> The question now is, Will public pressure produce any response from the government?

When several such questions follow a common introduction, capitalise the first word of each:

> Here are the questions we want to put to the management: Do you believe these working conditions are safe? What safety measures have you implemented? When? Have you any plans to introduce a safety code? If not, why not?

After a colon. Use a capital letter for the first word following a colon if:

- the material preceding the colon is a short introductory word like *Remember* or *Note*

- the material following the colon is a quoted sentence or starts with a proper noun, a proper adjective, or the pronoun *I*

The only difficult decision about using a capital after a colon occurs when two independent clauses (in effect, two complete sentences) are brought together within the same sentence with only a colon between them. The decision whether or not to use a capital depends on the importance you attach to the second clause. If the second clause simply explains or illustrates the idea presented in the first clause, don't use a capital at the start of it:

> If they believe your version, it is for only one reason: they want to believe it.

However, if the second clause is presented as a formal rule or if it expresses the main thought (and the first clause just introduces it), then you may safely begin the second clause with a capital:

> The new rules about jewellery at school are these: No girl may wear earrings unless they are plain stud earrings, and no other jewellery is acceptable except a plain cross.

Poetry. The first word of each line of poetry is customarily given a capital letter:

> Round the cape of a sudden came the sea,
> And the sun looked over the mountain's rim:

> And straight was a path of gold for him,
> And the need of a world of men for me.
> — Robert Browning, 'Parting at Morning'

Some poets, however, deviate from this rule – and other rules of punctuation – for special effect:

> as freedom is a breakfastfood
> or truth can live with right or wrong
> or molehills are from mountains made
> – long enough and just so long
> will being pay the rent of seem
> and genius please the talentgang . . .
> — e.e. cummings (U.S.), *Fifty Poems*

PERSONAL NAMES

As a rule, use a capital letter for the first letter of each word in a person's name, as well as any initials used in the name. However, respect individual preferences on this point. The poet quoted above, e.e. cummings, wanted his name treated without capitals at all. And British surnames beginning with *ff* are often written without capitals. The London telephone directory has both *Ffoulkes* and *ffoulkes*, both *Ffytche* and *ffytche*. As it happens, the *ff* used in such surnames originated not as a double *f* at all, but as an old-fashioned form of the capital *F*.

Names with prefixes sometimes pose special problems. In surnames beginning with *O'*, capitalise both the *O* and the first letter following the apostrophe: *O'Brien*, *O'Sullivan*. In surnames beginning with *d'*, *da*, *de*, *del*, *della*, *di*, *du*, *l'*, *la*, *le*, *van*, and *von*, individual preferences can vary quite widely: the London telephone directory includes *Van Den Berg*, *van den Berg*, *Van den Berg*, and *Van Denburgh*. There is similar variation in *Mc* – or *Mac* – surnames: the London telephone directory lists *McNair*, *MacNair*, *Macnair*, and even *Mcnair*.

When a surname begins with an uncapitalised particle and is used on its own in running text, without a title, a first name, or even initials preceding it, it is common practice in English to give the particle a capital letter in order to prevent a misreading: *Mr de la Mare*, *Walter de la Mare*, *W. de la Mare*, but *De la Mare*, and in an index reference *De la Mare, Walter*.

(The French would never do this, however: they would always write *de Gaulle*, for instance, except at the beginning of a sentence.)

When a name like *La Salle* (with a space after the particle) has to be written in capital letters, write

LA SALLE. However, if the name is *LaSalle* (with no space), write *LaSALLE*. Similarly, *McGREGOR*.

Titles with personal names. Give a capital letter to all titles that precede personal names – titles of a personal nature (*Mr, Mrs, Ms, Miss, Lady, Sir*) as well as titles that indicate rank in an organisation or status in a profession (*President, Chairman, Mayor, General, Corporal, Dr, Professor*).

When titles indicating rank follow a personal name or take the place of a personal name, they are not capitalised as a rule: *Mrs Roberts, the director of the steering committee*. Exceptions include:

☐ high-ranking government or opposition officials – *the Prime Minister, the Chancellor of the Exchequer, the President, the Foreign Secretary*

☐ heads of state and other international figures – *the Queen, the Pope, the Dalai Lama, the Polish Ambassador*.

However, when such titles are used with a general rather than specific reference, they are often left without the capital letter: *a Polish ambassador, various heads of state, a 20th-century pope, one of the more tight-fisted chancellors*.

ORGANISATIONS

Give a capital letter to the formal names of all types of organisation – business, political, educational, religious, and social: *Ford Motor Company, Fabian Society, Oxford University, Church of Edward the Confessor*. Note, however, that you do not usually give capitals to articles (*the, a, an*), short prepositions (*of, for*), and short conjunctions (*and, or*).

Sometimes the common-noun element of the name of an organisation is used in place of the full name – in a letter, for example, once you have made it clear that you are writing about the *General Electric Company*, you might afterwards refer to *the company*. This is referred to as a 'short form'. Don't give capitals to short forms except in legal documents or other formal writings where the short form is intended to convey the full force of the complete name. So, in ordinary letters or reports you might write:

> The manager at the Elegant Hands Glove Company said that the company would not raise its prices during the next 12 months.

In a contract or a letter of agreement, however, an Elegant Hands official would probably write:

> For a period of 12 months from the date of this agreement, the Company agrees not to increase the prices shown in the attached catalogue.

Note, however, that when two or more organisations are referred to that share the same short form, that short form is often not capitalised: *London University, Glasgow University*, and *Manchester University*, but: *London, Glasgow*, and *Manchester universities*.

Government organisations. Give capitals to the formal names of all government organisations at national, county, provincial, and local level: *The Scottish Office, Somerset County Council, Brent Housing Office*. The word *administration* is sometimes given a capital: *the Bush Administration, the Administration*. And the names of all international organisations start with capitals: *the United Nations Security Council, the World Bank, the Council of Europe, the Organisation of African Unity*.

It is customary to give a capital to the short forms of key national government organisations: *the House* (of Commons); *the Ministry* (of Agriculture, Defence, and the like). Short forms of local bodies are not usually treated in this way except by insiders.

The term *government* alone (referring to the national government) commonly takes lower case. However, in a context where it has the full force of an official name, it can safely be capitalised: *the Government issued the following statement*.

Political parties take capital letters: *the Labour Party, the Republican Party*. So do the members of political parties: *the Democrats, the Conservatives*. For political views, rather than political parties, use a small letter: *outraged republican opinion; a more conservative policy*. Note too: *the Right, the hard Left, the Centre*, but *right-wing* and *left-wing*.

PLACE NAMES

Give capital letters to names of places, both natural and man-made: *Tower Bridge, the Eiffel Tower, Muswell Hill, the Thames Valley, the Empire State Building, Heathrow Airport, the Bridge of Sighs, Mount Everest, Alderley Edge, the Dead Sea*.

As a rule, however, don't capitalise a short form used in place of the full name: *the mountain, the river, the bay*. In a few special cases, because of longstanding identification of a short form with a specific place, the short form is capitalised. Thus, you might fly out to *the Coast* (referring to the West

Coast of the United States) or cross the *Channel* (English, of course) on your way over to *the Continent* (of Europe).

So too, imaginative or poetic-sounding names clearly identified with a specific place are capitalised: *the Garden of England* (Kent); *the Bay Area* (San Francisco); *the Big Apple* (New York City).

Give *city* a capital only when it is part of the official name or part of a well-established imaginative name: *Mexico City*, *the Eternal City* (Rome), but *the city of Detroit*.

Similarly, give *state* a capital only when it follows the state name or is part of an imaginative name: *the state of Washington*, but *Washington State*; *the Tarheel State* (North Carolina); *the States* (referring to the United States).

OTHER USES OF CAPITALS

Capital letters make an appearance in many other places and many 'special cases'. Here are some of the more common of them:

Academic subjects. The names of recognised subject fields are usually written without capitals, but they tend to be capitalised when the reference is to a course, degree, or examination in the subject: *She studied chemistry* (= the subject chemistry), *She won the Nobel Prize for chemistry* (= the subject chemistry), but *She got a distinction in Chemistry* (= a chemistry exam or course).

North, south, east, west. Give capital letters to *north, south, east*, and *west* (and related words like *northeast*, and *southwest*) when they are part of a proper name – *North Carolina, South America, East Riding* (formerly part of Yorkshire), *Northwest Territories* (Canada), *Northern Territory* (Australia), *Southeast Asia*. Similarly, when they refer to a specific region that is distinctive because of certain social, cultural, or political characteristics: *out West* (in the United States), *out East* (in or to Asia as seen from Britain), *up North, down South*. However, put these words in lower case when they simply indicate location or direction: *northern Australia* (as distinct from *Northern Territory*), *somewhere east of Suez, travelled west of the Rockies*.

Similarly, use capitals with *northern, southern, eastern*, and *western* (and related words) when they refer to social, cultural, or political aspects of a region: *Eastern religions, Western governments* (but a film about cowboys is a *western*). And leave these terms in lower case when they refer simply to the climate, the geography, or the general location of a region: *northerly gales, the northeast face of Everest, the southwestern region of the country*.

Days, months, seasons, events. Use capitals for the names of days and months, but use lower case for the names of seasons except in the rare instances when they are personified: *Wednesday, February, all through the spring and summer*, but *harsh Winter with her bitter winds*.

Use capitals for the names of all holidays and religious days: *New Year's Eve, April Fool's Day, May Day, Ash Wednesday, Holy Week, Passover, Rosh Hashanah, Ramadan, Tet*.

Don't use capitals for the names of decades and centuries except in imaginative references: *before the sixties, during the nineteen-thirties, in the twenty-first century, the early nineteen hundreds*, but *the Roaring Twenties, the Gay Nineties*. (Usually numerals rather than words would be used here.)

Use capitals for the names of events and the names given to historical or cultural periods: *the Renaissance, the Enlightenment, International Year of the Child, the French Revolution, the Second World War, Prohibition, the Age of Reason*.

References to cultural and geological periods usually have capitals: *the Stone Age, the Dark Ages, the Middle Ages, the Elizabethan Age, the Age of Reason, the Neolithic Period, the Jurassic*.

More recent references, such as *the space age* and *the nuclear age*, are usually lower case, unless they appear in the same context with a capitalised reference to an age; then, for the sake of consistency, they are capitalised too – *from the Middle Ages to the Space Age*.

Races and religions. Use capitals for the names of races, nationalities, tribes, languages, and similar terms referring to ethnic groups: *Caucasians, Basques, the Arabs, the Cherokees, Slavonic*. Designations based on colour are customarily in lower case: *a black woman, a white youth of about 17*.

Use capitals for all references to a supreme being: *God, the Father, the Son, the Holy Spirit, the Lord, the Messiah, Allah, the Almighty, the Word, the Supreme Being*. The pronouns *he, his*, and *him* used to be capitalised under all circumstances when referring to a supreme being. Today these pronouns are often put in the lower case when there is a specific reference to God nearby: *Trust in the Lord and honour him* (or *Him*) *always*, but *Pray with your heart and He will hear you.*

Use capitals for all references to people revered as especially holy: *Blessed Virgin, Mother of God, Stella Maris, the Apostles, John the Baptist, Saint Francis, the Prophet, Buddha.*

Give capitals to all references to the Bible and other sacred writings; but don't underline or italicise these references as you would do when referring to other books or writings:

> the Apostles' Creed
> the Authorised Version
> the Bhagavad Gita
> the Book of Mormon
> Genesis
> the Koran

The adjective derived from the word *Bible* is also often given a capital letter still, but the current trend favours lower case: *a fine biblical scholar.*

Capitalise the names of religions, their members, and sometimes their buildings: *Anglican, Orthodox Judaism, Jehovah's Witnesses, Buddhism, Roman Catholicism, the Western Wall, St Paul's Cathedral* (the official name of a specific building), but *the only cathedral in the county* (merely a reference to a specific building).

The word *church*, when it refers to the total institution, may be either upper or lower case – *the Church of England, the Baptist church* – but should be only lower case when two or more churches are referred to together: *the Roman Catholic and Eastern Orthodox churches.*

Capitalise references to important religious events: *the Creation, the Fall, the Flood, the Exodus, the Last Supper, the Crucifixion, the Resurrection, the Second Coming.* However, as a general rule leave in lower case any references to religious rites and services: *to attend a mass* (but *celebrate the Mass*), *a vesper service, a baptism, a christening, a bar mitzvah, a seder.* The names of certain Christian sacraments are capitalised, however: *Eucharist, Holy Communion, Anointing of the Sick.*

Plants and animals. For names of plants and animals, the scientific convention is to use a capital letter for the name of the genus but not the name of the species (even if derived from a proper name): *Arum maculatum* (lords-and-ladies), *Sorbus acuparia* (European mountain ash), *Sus scrofa* (pig), *Monodon monoceros* (narwhal), *Equus caballus*

(horse). When writing the nontechnical names of plants and animals, capitalise only proper nouns and adjectives: *London pride, Michaelmas daisy, Labrador retriever, Exmoor pony.*

Flight 123. Use capitals for words followed by a number or a letter to indicate sequence: *Room 101, Flight 123 now boarding at Gate 15B, in Form 4A.*

Works of art and literature. Use capitals for the first and last words in titles, and all other words except articles (*the, a, an*), short conjunctions (*and, but, or*), and short prepositions (*by, for, to*). Longer conjunctions or prepositions, however, are often given capitals:

> *The Mill on the Floss*
> *Cider with Rosie*
> *The Way of All Flesh*
> *A Tale of Two Cities*
> *The Well of Loneliness*
> *All About Eve*
> *The Man Without a Country*

Authorities disagree on the treatment of hyphenated words in titles. Many give only the first element a capital, but on the whole it is better to treat each element according to the guidelines given above, for the sake of both consistency and appearance:

> *The Four-Gated City*
> *Nineteen Eighty-Four*
> *A Summer Bird-Cage*

AVOIDING AMBIGUITY

Although the trend is to avoid capitals if there is a choice, it is best to use a capital if that would prevent ambiguity. In *The cabinet is collapsing*, it is unclear whether *cabinet* refers to a piece of furniture or the council of government Ministers. In *The Cabinet is collapsing*, this ambiguity has been resolved: so *Cabinet*, referring to the council of Ministers, is still given a capital *C* by many publishers, and *Minister* a capital *M* (to distinguish the government official from a clergyman). So too *the Party, the Opposition, an Act* (of Parliament), *a Bill* (before Parliament), *the Bench, the Bar, the Continent, a Scout* (a Boy Scout).

Two final points. First, if you remain uncertain about any particular word, consult a good dictionary. Apply its recommendations consistently, in order to keep your own usage consistent. And secondly, note that other languages have other rules: German, for example, capitalises all common nouns as well as proper nouns. English too tended to do this in the past, but the practice died out in the 18th and 19th centuries. In French, the title of a book or film or organisation has all initial letters in lower case except those of one or two important words near the beginning. And the language of advertising often bends the rules for the sake of providing eye-catching or fashionable designs.

Italics

Italics acquired its name in a peculiar way. The sloping type was first used in 1501, by the Venetian printing house of Aldus Manutius, in an edition of Virgil that was dedicated to the land of Italy. (The Latin word was *italicus*, from the Greek *italikos*.)

The ordinary typeface is known as *roman*. This sentence for, example, is printed in roman, a typeface derived from the style used in ancient Roman inscriptions and manuscripts.

In handwritten or typewritten text, italics are represented by underlining. Italics and underlining are often used for decoration or to be eye-catching, as in advertisements or chapter-headings. As with all unusual or attention-getting habits in writing, italics should be used sparingly if they are to retain their effect.

ITALICS IN TITLES

Italics are used for the titles of self-contained publications (written works that are separately published, rather than being part of a collection) and of most works of art:

> Jane Austen's *Persuasion* (novel)
> Bizet's *Carmen* (opera)
> *The Listener* (magazine)
> *The Independent* (newspaper)
> Havel's *Temptation* (play)
> Rodin's *The Thinker* (sculpture)
> Woody Allen's *Annie Hall* (film)

A major exception is the Bible, whose name is printed in roman, as are the names of its books (John 16:43) and its major divisions: the Old Testament, the New Testament, the Pentateuch. You may treat other sacred scriptures in this way as well: the Koran, the Torah, and so on.

A distinction is often made between long poems, which might be published on their own, and short poems. Titles of long poems are referred to in italics; titles of short poems go in quotation marks:

> Milton's *Samson Agonistes*
> Keats's 'Ode to Autumn'

A distinction is also made between titles of books and titles of short stories, articles, or chapters:

> Kipling's *Kim* (novel)
> Kipling's 'William the Conquerer' (short story)

The result is that the same title can be referred to in different ways:

> Jerzy Skolimowski's film *The Shout* was based on Robert Graves's short story 'The Shout'.

A distinction is also often made between the names of works of music, which are italicised, and their descriptions, which are often simply in roman:

> Schubert's *Trout Quintet*
> Schubert's Quintet in C

Note that the *-s* suffix in the plurals of such italicised titles is sometimes shown in roman:

> examining three *Newsweek*s.

But this can look clumsy. It is probably better to italicise the whole word: *Newsweeks*.

Italics are also used for the names of vehicles:

> the *Brighton Belle* (train)
> HMS *Ark Royal* (ship)

But they are not used for trade names:

> a Ford Fiesta

Italics are also used to refer to court cases:

> the case of *Regina* v *Smithson*

The *v* of *versus* is usually printed in roman.

What about the word *the* – is it part of the title? Sometimes it is and sometimes it is not. The periodical now known as *New Scientist* was originally *The New Scientist*. Handel's oratorio is *Messiah*, not **X** *The Messiah* as it is often described.

When *The* (or *A*) is part of a title, some people prefer to leave it out when it sounds awkward. Thus you can have either of the following:

> Chaucer's *The Canterbury Tales*
> Chaucer's *Canterbury Tales*

The Building Blocks Of Good English

ITALICISING WORDS AND PHRASES

Italics are used when referring to words, letters, and figures as such:

> The word *euphonious* is beautiful.
> the name *Cleopatra*
> Some people do not pronounce their *h*'s.
> Is that number *113*?

(Note the way the plural, *h*'s, is written.) This use of italics makes it possible to distinguish between such pairs of sentences as:

> *Socrates* has eight letters.
> Socrates was a Greek philosopher.

Use italics for words and phrases from foreign languages:

> As tags go, she is *grande dame* where I am *jeune fille*, and she leads all her life to match it.
> – Margaret Drabble, *A Summer Bird-Cage*

Note that when such expressions are 'glossed' (given a brief definition or translation), the gloss generally appears in single quotation marks or in brackets.

> (French) *coup de maître*, 'masterstroke'
> (German) *Gleitzeit*, 'flexitime'.

Some foreign words and phrases have effectively become part of the English language. It is not always easy to distinguish such expressions from those that still feel essentially foreign:

> Her coup d'etat was a real *coup de maître*.

The phrase 'coup d'etat' here is familiar enough to be printed in roman, but *coup de maître* is not nearly so common in English.

Contrast this treatment of foreign terms with the treatment of variant, dialectal, or deviant English terms – here quotation marks instead are used:

> They all got medals, or what some people would call 'gongs'.
> We got pushed off the pavement in New York – I mean the 'sidewalk'.
> I can't warm to 'hearties' like the Beauchamp twins.

Italics are used too for the technical names of plants and animals – a particular type of scientific Latin:

> The horse (*Equus caballus*) has affected the course of history profoundly.
> The lilac (*Syringa vulgaris*) has medical uses.

DIFFICULTIES WITH ITALICS

The interplay of all the conventions governing the use of italics is bound to produce difficulties: sometimes a word or phrase deserves to be italicised on two or three different counts. The name of a ship or aircraft, for instance, should be in italics; and a film title should be in italics: but what about the name of a ship or aircraft as part of a film title?

As it happens, the films *Raise the Titanic* and *The Flight of the Phoenix* simply ignore the problem – perhaps the best approach.

Nevertheless, it is a pity that the role italics have of setting a word or phrase off from its context cannot really be maintained if that context itself is in italics. With quotation marks, subdivisions are possible, by shifting from single quotation marks to double quotation marks and back again. But to alternate between italics and roman might not work, since the roman part might simply blend into the surrounding roman context:

? Have you read *A Study of Dante's* Inferno by Professor Lowe?

Other solutions are possible, less uncompromising about the rules, but at least less confusing as well:

> Have you read *A Study of Dante's* INFERNO by Professor Lowe?
> Have you read 'A Study of Dante's *Inferno*' by Professor Lowe?
> Have you read *A Study of Dante's 'Inferno'* by Professor Lowe?

and the simplest (and likeliest):

> Have you read *A Study of Dante's Inferno* by Professor Lowe?

A typical technical name of this sort will consist of two parts: the genus (capitalised) and the species. Higher groups are traditionally put in roman:

> *Homo sapiens* belongs to the family Hominidae, the order of Primates, and the class Mammalia.

ITALICS FOR EMPHASIS

In ordinary writing, italics play an important role in showing that a word or phrase demands special emphasis – for the sake of urging the reader to reflect on it, for example, or as indicating a contrast:

> Certainly he can refuse – but *then* what?
> The body was not *in* the shed but *under* it.

Consider this simple example:

> She arrived on *Tuesday*

(as distinct from Wednesday). Such emphasis in writing corresponds to various devices of pronunciation and intonation in speech, and can often clarify an otherwise ambiguous sentence. So, in informal writing, the interpretation of:

> I only saw her on Tuesday

would usually be 'I didn't see her on any other day'. However, if you write:

> I only *saw* her on Tuesday

you are implying that you did not *speak* to her.

Traditionally, this use of 'emphatic' italics (or underlining) has been discouraged by schoolteachers, editors, and purists generally. They consider it the easy way out – and instead prefer to restructure the sentence, as by means of the 'it is' construction:

> It was on Tuesday that she arrived.

But such a technique is not always appropriate.

Sometimes, italics are the least objectionable form of emphasis. It is no improvement to reword

> I only *saw* her on Tuesday

as

> **??**My only contact with her on Tuesday was a visual one.

Paragraphs

A paragraph is a distinct division of a piece of writing. It expresses some thought or point relevant to the whole of the piece, but is to some degree complete in itself. As far as punctuation goes, a paragraph begins on a new line, even where this means leaving most of the previous line empty. It is often marked by being 'indented' from the edge of the page. And in typing, an extra line of space is often used between paragraphs. In the punctuation of dialogue, each new speech or speaker usually means a new paragraph.

Paragraphing provides resting-places for the reader. At the end of each paragraph, he can pause and take stock of what he has read so far. There are no rules on how often these resting-places should occur. In much light journalism and advertising, almost every sentence seems to start a new paragraph. In more serious writing, a paragraph can last for a page or more. Most paragraphs contain at least three sentences, but an occasional one-sentence paragraph is refreshing to the eye.

If a single topic needs room to develop, you can make it more digestible for the reader by breaking it up into more than one paragraph. But the converse is not true: two unrelated topics call for two separate paragraphs, no matter how short such paragraphs may be. (For further advice on the use of paragraphs, see pages 52-58.)

Abbreviations

When writing private letters, you will probably abbreviate words and names in any way you find useful and understandable.

In print and formal writing, however, it is best to observe the well-established rules for the thousands of possible abbreviated forms.

The first rule is: When in doubt, spell it out. In general writing such as formal letters, fiction, history, and magazine articles, only a handful of well-known abbreviations tend to be used: *a.m.*, *MP*, *Mrs*, *St* (= Saint as in *St John*), or *USSR*, but probably

not *e.g.*, *lb*, *Mt*, *St* (= street), *SW*, or *UK*. In technical and business writing, however, abbreviations are heavily used, and provide an invaluable space-saving service.

FULL STOPS IN ABBREVIATIONS

Abbreviations are often identified by full stops: for example, *M.A.* (Master of Arts); *a.m.* (ante meridiem); *G.B. Shaw* (George Bernard Shaw). But this rule is not always followed. The full stop is often left out, for example, in abbreviations that consist entirely of capital letters: *BBC, MA, TLS, NNW*. This tendency is less strong with the abbreviations of people's names: *T S Eliot* is less likely than *T.S. Eliot*.

Note too, that the capital letter takes a full stop only if it stands for a complete word: *TB* (tuberculosis), *TV* (television), and *MS* (manuscript) therefore cannot take a full stop. And full stops tend to be omitted in acronyms such as *UNESCO* or *NATO*.

When an abbreviation ends with the last letter of the abbreviated word, British English often considers it a 'contraction' rather than a true abbreviation, and writes it without a full stop (*Dr, Mr, Jr*). American English is far more likely to use a full stop (*Dr., Mr., Jr.*) – this is still quite acceptable in British English, though less and less common.

The distinction is a controversial one, however. It seems rather odd to find *Dr* (contraction – no stop) and *Prof.* (abbreviation – hence full stop) in a single text or even sentence. For consistency's sake then (or perhaps just through ignorance), the recommended distinction is increasingly disregarded. In British English at least, a blanket omission of the full stop after such abbreviations is now generally favoured.

Note that if an assertion ends with an abbreviation, and that abbreviation ends with a full stop, no more full stops are needed:

> She works for the B.B.C.
> She works for the BBC.

MAKING ABBREVIATIONS PLURAL

A few single-letter abbreviations indicate their plural form by simply doubling the letter: the full stop, if used at all, is placed after the second of these letters. So, the word *page* can be abbreviated as *p.* or *p*, and *pages* accordingly becomes *pp.* (with a stop after the second *p*) or *pp* (without any stop at all). Some other abbreviations undergo fairly drastic changes: *Mr* becomes *Messrs*, from French *Messieurs* (obviously it could not be spelt as *Mrs*).

For the most part, however, a simple *s* is added to the abbreviation: *five backbench MPs/M.P.s*. Don't insert a needless apostrophe here – *M.P.'s* is the possessive, not the plural. Note that if the abbreviation contains more than one full stop, they are unaffected by the addition of the *s* – *five M.P.s, three successive l.b.w.s*. But if there is only a single, final full stop, it shifts its position and follows the *s* – *a message for Capts. Kane and Hilson*.

Scientific terms tend to retain the singular form when the plural sense is intended: *one kg, four kg*, and so on.

The possessive is formed by the simple addition of -'s or -s' – *the PM's latest proposal* (or *P.M.'s*); *the J.P.s' conference*, and so on.

CAN'T, SHAN'T, FLU, AND OTHERS

Several types of construction resemble abbreviations, but have different punctuation rules.

Contractions. *Can't, mustn't, shan't*, and so on take an apostrophe to represent the missing letter or letters. Note, however, that *shan't* has only one apostrophe, whereas it should really have two. Take care to place the apostrophe in the correct position – it corresponds to the missing letter, not to the syllable break: *shouldn't* not **X** *should'nt*.

Clipped forms of words. These include *Tom, flu, phone*, and so on. Few are spelt with an apostrophe nowadays – *fo'c's'le* (for *forecastle*) and *bo's'n* (for *boatswain*) are extreme examples. *Cello* used to be spelt with an apostrophe in front of it, the full form being *violoncello*, but this would seem pedantic today. And to spell *flu* as *'flu* is not only pedantic but inconsistent, since there are missing letters after as well as before the contracted form.

Cello is today quite at home in even the most formal contexts – so too are *bus, chips, cinema, cox, curio, perm, pram, taxi*, and *zoo* – so much so that many people are scarcely aware of the fuller forms (*omnibus, chipped potatoes, cinematograph, coxswain, curiosity, permanent wave, perambulator, taximeter cabriolet*, and *zoological gardens*).

Flu is slightly less formal, but still perfectly suited to most ordinary contexts: similarly *bike, disco, exam, fan* (in the sense of 'enthusiastic supporter' – from *fanatic*), *fridge, gym, phone, photo, pop music* (from *popular music*), *pub, quad, recap* (from *recapitulate*), *vet* (from *veterinary surgeon*), and so on.

Some clipped forms are fairly informal still – *telly* and *ref*, for example; also *ad* (for *advertisement*), *bookie* (*bookmaker*), *deli* (*delicatessen*), *gent, info, mike* (*microphone*), *prelims* (*preliminaries*), *prof, wellies* (*Wellington boots*), and so on.

All varieties – from the most formal to the most slangy – tend to be spelt without any apostrophe.

Acronyms. These are strings of letters or syllables that are pronounced as if they spelt a complete

LONG WORDS ARE EASY

Flex your mental muscles on some long words. Whether or not you have heard or seen any particular word before, you should have a good mental workout by working out the meanings.

Don't let the words frighten you. Take a word like *anthropogenesis*. It looks pretty daunting – but try breaking it up. *Anthropo-*: what is an anthropologist? Someone who studies man, his behaviour, and so on. Presumably, *anthropo-* refers to mankind, then. And *-genesis*? That refers to origins – think of the book of the Bible. You are there: *anthropogenesis* is the study of the origins of man.

☐ Try to give a definition each time of the word in italics. The charts of combining forms, roots, prefixes, and suffixes on pages 147-164 should be a help. For the answers, turn to pages 633-648.

1. Modern methods in *geochronology* have proved that the Earth's magnetic field fluctuates greatly.

2. Kepler built upon Copernicus's new *heliocentric* theory to formalise the laws of planetary motion.

3. In recent years Mexico City has grown from a conurbation into a *megalopolis*.

4. Odysseus and his men were in dire peril after falling into the hands of Polyphemus, the leader of the *anthropophagi*.

5. The religious life of the coastal tribes reveals elements of *ichthyolatry*.

6. The *zoomorphic* designs carved on the long ships suggest adherence to some unknown cult.

7. She seems to forget that one can be a perfectly sincere feminist without being an *androphobe*.

8. You can see an interesting collection of *palaeolithic* remains on display in Room Thirty-Six of the museum.

9. Many disputes in Shakespearean studies would be settled if we possessed even a single *holograph* of his work.

10. But in their mating patterns, the upper classes still lay themselves open to the charge of *endogamy*.

11. During the seventh and eighth centuries the *Heptarchy* maintained a balance of power in England that was finally disrupted by the Vikings.

12. The syndrome is caused by the failure of the body to produce sufficient *haemostatic* agents.

13. My mother's *idiolect* includes a very marked 'telephone manner' and a distinctive way of telling you to do things.

14. The later stage of fermentation with yeast takes place in an *anaerobic* environment.

15. The *iconoclastic* activity of the early Kirk resulted in the loss of many ecclesiastical treasures.

16. Amoebae and other one-celled creatures propel themselves by means of a *pseudopod*.

17. The *hypocaust* in the villa outside Bath must have consumed enormous amounts of timber.

18. Before the Chinese invasion, Tibet was a *theocracy*.

19. This study takes a detailed *synchronic* view rather than making the usual attempt to trace the causes of the problem.

20. The development of the *mammogram* has greatly reduced the danger of cancer to women.

21. Beneath the city ruins the archaeologists found the remains of a vast *necropolis*.

22. The *mesocephalic* appearance of the skull suggests that it originated in China or northwest Europe.

word. *U.N.* or *UN* is an abbreviation, whereas *UNESCO* (/ yōō-**nes**ko /) and *Comintern* (/ **kom**min-tern /) are acronyms – the former from initial letters (*U*nited *N*ations *E*ducational, *S*cientific, and *Cul*tural *Or*ganisation), the latter from the initial syllables of *Com*munist *Intern*ational. Syllable acronyms such as *Comintern* (or *Benelux*) are never written with full stops, and letter acronyms such as *UNESCO* (or *Fiat, NAAFI, NATO, OPEC, Wrens*, and so on) almost never have full stops either nowadays. Acronyms denoting common objects – such as *radar* (*ra*dio *d*etection *a*nd *r*anging) and *scuba* (*s*elf-*c*ontained *u*nderwater *b*reathing *a*pparatus) – are by now fully accepted as common nouns, and of course take no full stops.

Scientific terms. With weights and measures the full stop is seldom used – *kg*, without the stop,

stands for *kilogram* or *kilograms*; *mm* for *millimetre* or *millimetres*; *cwt* for *hundredweight*; *ft* for *foot* or *feet*; *amp* for *ampere/s*; *yd* for *yard*. The standard abbreviation of *yards* should be *yds*, though in fact **?** *yds.* with the full stop seems to be just as frequently used nowadays.

The abbreviation of *miles per hour* seems equally acceptable without and with the full stops – *mph* and *m.p.h.*

Note that *lb* stands for *pound* or *pounds*: the form **?** *lbs* represents an undesirable mix of the English plural-ending *-s* and the Latin *libra* (singular) or *librae* (plural).

Chemical symbols such as *Ca* (calcium), *Fe* (iron – from the Latin *ferrum*), or H_2SO_4 (sulphuric acid) never have full stops.

Numbers

When should a number be expressed in words, and when in figures? Rules vary from publisher to publisher. For your own purposes, consider the different effects of the two forms. Numbers expressed in figures stand out; numbers spelt out in words recede into the middle distance, along with all the other words in a sentence. Figures give the appearance of being precise, accurate, crisp – and sometimes informal. Numbers expressed in words convey an air of approximation – or of formality.

Contrast, for example, an office memo announcing a staff meeting and an engraved invitation to a church wedding. The memo might announce the meeting for *10.30 a.m. on 27/3*. The invitation might announce the wedding ceremony for *half past ten on the twenty-seventh day of July in the year of Our Lord one thousand nine hundred and ninety*. These two forms mark the extreme limits of number style – figure style and word style.

USING FIGURES

This is the style used in business and technical writing and in journalism, since most of the numbers here usually represent important information that should stand out.

Here are some guidelines:

☐ Spell out numbers from one to ten inclusive, but use figures for all numbers above ten: *About 75 people attended the introductory lecture, but*

only 24 registered for the course. (Some publishers place the limit at 9, some at 12).

☐ If a sentence or paragraph contains related numbers and some are above ten and some below, practice varies. Some publishers stick steadfastly to the above: *We need only eight to 13 volunteers*. Other publishers put all the related numbers in figures: *We need only 8 to 13 volunteers to keep the three day-care centres operating during the summer months*. The number *8* is in figures, since it is paired with *13*, but *three* remains spelt out, since it is not related to the number of volunteers.

☐ Large numbers of more than a million can be expressed all in figures, or in a mixed form: *6,800,000* or *6.8 million*.

USING WORDS

This style is used in writing that is formal, literary, or nontechnical; where not many numbers are used; and where figures might look distracting.

Here are the guidelines:

☐ Spell out numbers from one to a hundred.

☐ Spell out higher numbers that can be written in one or two words: *six thousand*. A hyphenated compound like *thirty-eight* is considered one word; so *thirty-eight million* falls within the two-word limit.

☐ Large numbers over a million that would require more than two words if spelt out can be expressed all in figures or in the mixed form again: *6,800,000* or *6.8 million*.

☐ If there is a clash between the preferred styles of related numbers, practice again varies. Some publishers stick to the rules regardless: *a target of three million units, but sold only 1,682,544.* Other publishers would bring these numbers into line, expressing them both in figures: *Despite predictions that we would sell more than 3,000,000 units, we sold only 1,682,544.*

MAKING THE CHOICE

Your choice of style should depend on the effects you are aiming for – and the policy of the publication you are writing for. Is it important that the numbers stand out for emphasis or easy reference? If so, choose the figure style. Are the numbers not especially significant, or is the writing somewhat formal (though not technical)? If so, choose the word style.

More important than the choice itself is the need to be consistent. If you choose the figure style for a particular occasion, then write *15th May* (or *15 May*) rather than *the fifteenth of May*; both forms are 'correct', but the former would be more appropriate in view of your general choice of style.

Some number expressions call for special handling, regardless of which basic style you have chosen. Here are some guidelines to help you when dealing with these expressions.

MOSTLY FIGURES

Even if you are following a word style, certain number expressions almost always require the use of figures. In such cases even the numbers from one to ten are expressed in figures.

With dates. Here, there is a variety of possible styles to choose from:

7 October 1990	(this is now the standard form in British publications and those of several other countries)
October 7 1990	(this is the commonest form in the USA and Canada, and is still used by some British publications)

7/10/90 7.10.90 7-10-90	(these styles of representing 7 October 1990 are common in Britain and other English-speaking countries – even Canada – but not in the USA)
10/7/90	(this is the U.S. style for 7 October 1990)
90.10.7	(this is the style now recommended by the International Organisation for Standardisation. It is being increasingly adopted, in technical, manufacturing and banking contexts, in Europe and South Africa)

In view of the possible confusions over a date written as *7/10/90*, it is perhaps best to avoid it except in informal writing.

In more explicit writing of the date, there are several possible forms: *the 7th of October* (emphatic or informal) or *the seventh of October* (more formal) or *October 7th, 1990* or *7th October 1990* (these last two are not standard in the USA).

With time. Most publications now favour the form *2 o'clock*. Another modern tendency, not yet so widespread, is to omit the full stops in *a.m.* and *p.m*: *3.40 am*. To avoid the danger that the abbreviation will be read as the common verb *am*, some publishers omit the space as well: *3.40am.*

On the Continent, the 24-hour clock is widely used in timetables. The International Organisation for Standardisation recommends the forms *08 00* and *16 30* – to be read as *eight hours* (not *eight hundred hours*) and *sixteen hours thirty* (not *sixteen-thirty hours*). These conventions are common in technical contexts, but not yet in everyday use.

With money. In statistical or informal contexts, use figures to express specific amounts: *£2, £24.50, about £600, £27.5 million, 50 pence worth, 50p worth.* Use words to express indefinite amounts – *millions of pounds* – and isolated references where figures would be too prominent: *not worth two cents, a story called 'Simon and Sara and a fifty-pence piece'.*

In technical contexts. Use figures to express percentages, ratios, measurements, and proportions: *an 8.4 per cent increase, a 60-40 split, a surcharge on packages of more than 10 pounds, 6 parts of gin to 1 part of vermouth.* Similarly, with scores, votes, and the like: *an 88-to-56 victory,* *a majority of only 59 votes, count backwards from 10 to 1, multiply by 3.1, divide by 2.* The same rule applies to pages and chapters: *chapter 3, ch 3, p 6, pp 4-8.*

With ages. There is a tendency to use a number when specifying the age of a young child: *a 6-year-old boy, a child of 3.* The spelt-out forms are still quite acceptable, however.

MOSTLY WORDS

Some types of number expression almost always require the use of words – even if you have chosen to follow a figure style.

At the beginning of a sentence. Spell out any number as the first word of a sentence, and also any related numbers that follow it: *Eight to fifteen per cent of the voters are undecided.* If the spelt-out number requires more than two words or if figures are preferable, try to reword the sentence: *Between 8 and 15 per cent . . .*

With indefinite numbers. For example: *hundreds of men, thousands of women, tens of millions of hungry people.*

With fractions. Spell out straightforward fractions that stand alone; that is, without a whole number preceding them. So: *one-third the usual time, three-quarters of the student body.* But: *less than $2\frac{1}{2}$ inches of rain* (the whole number precedes the fraction); *a $\frac{3}{4}$-inch pipe* (technical measurement); *multiply by $\frac{3}{8}$* (a number used as a number), and *sacrificed $\frac{7}{17}$ of their holdings* (too long and complicated to be spelt out neatly).

In dialogue and direct quotations. For example: *'She earned five thousand pounds in 1955,' he said enviously.* Note, however, that the year date remains in figures.

FINAL POINTS

Here, finally, are a few technical guidelines – when to use commas, how to form plurals, the use of Roman numerals, and so on.

Commas in numbers. When expressing numbers in figures, use commas to set off thousands, hundreds of thousands, and so on, in numbers that run to more than three digits: *1,435,647.* The comma is now often omitted in a four-digit number: *1250.* Never use commas in page numbers (*page 1518*), year numbers (*2001*), or similar expressions.

Instead of the comma, a thin space is now often used in metric measurements – *23 021 km* – and on the Continent, a full stop is sometimes used in expressing sums of money: *38.561.235 Frs.*

Note that in the Continental system too (also in operation in South Africa), the decimal point is replaced by a comma: *220,5m; DM26.381,55.*

When to add noughts. When expressing amounts in whole units of currency (*£56*) or time on the hour (*7am*), don't add noughts – **?** *£56.00,* **?** *7.00 am.* The exception to this rule is when such expressions are displayed together with others that include real sub-units, as in a column of numbers where a consistent appearance is important:

£56.00	7.00pm
£27.25	8.15am

However, a nought before a decimal point can be useful to show that no whole numbers are involved: *0.5.* Remember, too, not to combine *£* with *p,* or *$* with *c,* or the like: it is correct to write *25p, £3,* and *£3.25,* but not **X** *£3.25p.*

Forming plurals. To form the plurals of figures, just add *-s: during the 1980s, the '80s, temperatures in the 20s.* The use of the apostrophe *-'s* – *the 1860's, in the low 20's* – is permissible, but is now used less and less frequently.

To form the plurals of spelt-out numbers, follow the standard rules for adding *-s* or *-es: ones, twos, thirds, sixes, eighths, twenties, hundreds, hundredths, thousands, millions.*

When to use hyphens. When expressing numbers in words, hyphenate all compound numbers between 21 and 99, whether they stand alone (*twenty-five*) or are part of a large number (*twenty-five hundred*). But do not hyphenate other parts of a spelt-out number: *sixty thousand, eighty-five million.* Fractions too are almost always hyphenated: *three-quarters, seven-tenths.*

Fifteen hundred. When saying or spelling out round numbers between 1100 and 1950, people tend to use hundreds only, not thousands and hundreds: *1500 metres/feet/people* is represented as *fifteen hundred;* and *1550* probably as *fifteen hundred and fifty.* But *1567,* say, would tend to be *one thousand five hundred and sixty-seven* (note the absence of commas – this is the most economical style). Of course the year *AD 1567* is referred to by hundreds: *fifteen hundred and sixty-seven* or simply *fifteen sixty-seven.*

Twenty 8-page brochures. In expressions such as *twenty 8-page brochures* or *six 4-room flats*, put one of the numbers in words and the other in figures for the sake of clarity. As a rule, spell the first of the numbers, unless the second number will make a much shorter word: *2000 eight-page brochures; 27 or 28 four-room flats*.

Sequences. In a sequence of numbers (*during the years 1980-1985, on pages 348-356*), a hyphen may be used to replace the word *to*. (Abbreviations of such hyphenated sequences are possible: *1980-85.*) However, if the sequence begins with the word *between*, use *and* rather than a hyphen: *between 1980 and 1985*, not **X** *between 1980-1985*. If the sequence begins with the word *from*, use *to* rather than a hyphen: *from page 348 to page 356*, not **X** *from page 348-page 356* or **X** *from pages 348-356*.

When to use Roman numerals. Upper-case Roman numerals are used after names and titles: *Louis XIV, Tom Vandibs III.*

Lower-case Roman numerals are generally used to number the pages of the introduction to a book: the eighth page of the introduction will typically bear the number *viii* rather than *VIII* or *8*.

Capital Roman numerals may also be used to number the chapters or appendices of a book, the stanzas of a poem, the acts of a play, or other major divisions of a written work, though Arabic numbers sometimes serve these functions too. A typical reference would be *Hamlet III iv 145* – that is Act III, scene iv, line 145.

Some periodicals use Roman numerals for their volumes; others use Arabic numerals. Both of the following forms, for example, are common and quite correct:

New Literary History Volume XV No. 3; Spring 1984

The Historical Journal Volume 27 No. 2; June 1984

A combination of Roman and Arabic numerals is often used for the sections of an outline:

I	Introduction: Genre and Literary History.
II.1	The novel: from Defoe to Dickens.
II.2	The novel: from Dickens to date.
III	Poetry.
IV.1	Drama: Shakespeare and before.
IV.2	Drama: After Shakespeare.
V	Other genres.
VI	Conclusion: The Future of Genre.

MASTERING ROMAN NUMERALS

What do the figures *MCMXC* mean when they flash in tiny characters on your television screen at the end of a programme? They tell you – in unhelpful Roman numerals – the year in which the programme was made: 1990.

Understanding the Roman system of writing numbers can be a little tricky – it is so different from our own (Arabic) system of numerals. In fact, however, the Roman system is perfectly logical, and once its secrets have been mastered becomes easy to decipher – though hardly convenient for everyday use.

In the Roman system I stands for 1, V for 5, X for 10, L for 50, C for 100, D for 500, and M for 1000. Numbers between these are formed by combinations of the basic units. For example:

1 –	I	6 –	VI
2 –	II	7 –	VII
3 –	III	8 –	VIII
4 –	IV	9 –	IX
5 –	V	10 –	X

Note the principles. 1-3 are straightforward – formed simply by totting up the *I*s. Similarly, 6-8 are formed by adding *I, II*, and *III* to the 5 numeral, V. Slightly more complicated are 4 and 9, though here again the thinking is strictly logical. In both cases the initial *I* indicates subtraction – take 1 (*I*) from 5 (V) to get 4.

The same principles apply to higher numerals:

10 –	X	200 –	CC
20 –	XX	300 –	CCC
30 –	XXX	400 –	CD
40 –	XL	500 –	D
50 –	L	600 –	DC
60 –	LX	700 –	DCC
70 –	LXX	800 –	DCCC
80 –	LXXX	900 –	CM
90 –	XC	1000 –	M
100 –	C	2000 –	MM

Numbers between these are formed by piling on the appropriate numerals. So 77 is LXXVII, and 777 is DCCLXXVII. Test your understanding by working out the following Roman numerals: DCLXXVIII, IC, MLXVI, MCMXXXIX, DCCCLXXXVIII. For the answers, turn to the quiz answers section, pages 633-648.

Dictionaries and How to Use Them

SURVEYS HAVE shown that people go to dictionaries, if at all, for little other than meanings and spellings. But there is a great deal more to be found in a good dictionary. It can help you to produce good English, not just understand it. It is your best friend in the quest to increase your command over words.

A quick look in a bookshop will show you that the English-speaker is spoilt for choice in dictionaries. They come in all sizes, and with a variety of special features. Your first task is to find one that is right for you, one that will give you the kind of information you need.

Choosing a Dictionary

Bear in mind, first, that biggest is not necessarily best for you. The largest dictionary of English is the *New Oxford English Dictionary (NOED)*. It fills 20 substantial volumes of tight print, and is a magnificent work of scholarship. It gives over 19 pages on the verb form of the word *set* alone. It will tell you when, where, and by whom a particular word was first used with a certain meaning. It will also tell you a great deal about variant spellings used, say, by 15th-century Scottish poets. If this is the kind of information you need, the *NOED* is for you. But if you want the meaning of *lugubrious* or *eschew*, the *NOED*'s mass of detail can get in the way. It was not designed for everyday use.

So ask yourself what exactly you want your dictionary for. Is it to help you to read, understand, and enjoy the great classics – Shakespeare, Milton, Dr Johnson? In this case, you will want a dictionary that gives the definitions and usage of, for example, archaic words. Or do you intend using it to help you with crosswords, or to arbitrate during games of Scrabble, in which case you will need one with lots of headwords but short definitions.

Remember, you cannot expect a single reference work to tell you everything you want to know, and nothing you do not. But you can see to it that the one you finish up with comes closest to your ideal.

ENCYCLOPAEDIC DICTIONARIES

Would an encyclopaedic dictionary be useful? It can be an invaluable all-purpose reference book. Perhaps you need a list of the twelve apostles or

seven deadly sins. Maybe you want to know how to pronounce *Reykjavik*, the capital of Iceland. What were the dates of the Thirty Years War, and where was it fought? Who wrote *Don Quixote*? What is the Dow-Jones average? When was Charles Dickens born? A good encyclopaedic dictionary will give answers to such questions.

It will also sometimes give you a fuller idea of the meanings of words. Take the expression *a little Hitler*. An ordinary dictionary might define it as 'a person who acts in a high-handed manner'. But this misses a part of the full meaning. Some historical facts are called for, and an encyclopaedic dictionary will provide them. Many encyclopaedic dictionaries also have illustrations. These often give information – about, say, machines, plants, or animals – much more quickly and efficiently than could be achieved by verbal explanations.

UP TO DATE AND BRITISH

The language is changing constantly – according to some estimates, English takes in standard new words at the rate of 1000 a year – and, as a result, dictionaries need to be updated regularly. Make sure that any dictionary you are interested in has been revised at least within the last ten years; look at the back of the title page. And carry out a quick spot check on recently minted words – such as *yuppy*, *bilateralism*, *glasnost*, and *big bang*. An up-to-date dictionary should have them.

If you are British, you should obviously go for a British dictionary rather than an American one.

There are many excellent American dictionaries, but, not surprisingly, they look at language from an American point of view. Often they will not mark a term such as *thumb tack* as being peculiar to American English. Sometimes, they do not even list the British equivalent of such a term – in this case, the corresponding term is *drawing pin*.

British dictionaries are usually much better at distinguishing what is special to British English – *three-line whip*, *grass* (informer), *swede* (vegetable) – and at covering words from the whole range of 'World English': Australian, South African, Caribbean, and Canadian, as well as American English.

CHECK THE DEFINITIONS

Watch out for 'vicious circles'. Look up a word like *condescending*. You might find it defined simply as 'patronising'. You then look up *patronise*, and find 'to treat condescendingly'. This is scarcely helpful. Worse still, it ignores a usage difference: although a *patronising attitude* and a *condescending attitude* are the same, you usually *patronise* a person, but *condescend* to do something. The verbs are by no means interchangeable.

And then there are 'vicious spirals'. You look up one word and are given two or three synonyms, none of which you understand fully. You look them up, and find further incomprehensible terms. By the time you do reach a word you are confident of, you have strayed so far from the original word that you are little the wiser.

Check also on technical definitions. As you browse in the bookshop, look up a few entries like *amoeba*, *cyclotron*, *halogen*, *tort*, and *VHF*. If the definitions leave you scratching your head, and you think you will indeed need to look up these kinds of word, the dictionary is not for you.

HOW COMPLETE IS IT?

Does the dictionary include plenty of idioms? You expect to find *chickenpox*. Do you also find *to chicken out* and *chicken-and-egg* as in *It's a chicken-and-egg situation*? Think of a few such idioms and try to find them.

Often the problem is knowing where to locate idioms. Most dictionaries put the entry under the first reasonably specific word in the idiom. So *to take French leave* would be listed at *French*, and *to fly in the face of something* at *fly* or possibly *face*.

There are many ways of choosing a dictionary.

Good dictionaries also cover some of the more technical sides of language. Does your dictionary include common word elements: prefixes such as *pre-*, *sub-*, *over-*, or combining forms such as *pseudo-* or *macro-*? If these are clearly explained, the entries can help you greatly.

OTHER FORMS AND USAGE

Does a dictionary you are considering give other forms of words – past participles and the like? Does it indicate, where necessary, which is the British and which is the American form – *dived* (British) as opposed to *dove* (optional in US English).

Does it give instructions on how to use particular words? Are there, for instance, labels indicating that a word is slang, obsolete, old-fashioned, or generally restricted to a particular country or region? For example:

> **red·eye** *n.* 1. *U.S. Slang.* Whisky of an inferior grade . . .

Does it explain the difference between, say, *practicable* and *practical*? A *practical* suggestion is one that is useful and based on common sense, but a *practicable* one is one that is capable of being put into practice. Some dictionaries include usage notes on such points.

Does your dictionary give etymologies – the history of each word, which language it derives from, and how its usages have changed over the centuries? Knowing how a word is built from its constituent parts will help you with other words using the same parts. When you have seen enough words beginning with *ex-*, you will come to realise that this often gives a word a meaning of 'out of' or 'from'. So if you come across the word *excogitate* you may not have to look it up to realise that it means 'to think out or through'.

Knowing the origins of a word can help you to spell it correctly. You are unlikely to miss out the first *r* in *berserk* if you know that the word means literally 'bear-shirt' – some Vikings dressed as savage animals to increase their courage in battle.

HOW IS IT ORGANISED?

Does the dictionary look clear and easy to use? Some dictionaries ignore alphabetical order to some extent. *Contentious*, say, might be listed not on its own, but under *contend*. If you do not know that the two words are related, you may have some difficulty in finding *contentious*.

Are the actual entries easy to understand? Some dictionaries simply supply the headword, its pronunciation and part of speech, and then an undifferentiated list of definitions. Others are much clearer: different meanings are separated out into numbered items, starting with the more common or central, and going on to rarer or more limited meanings. Uncommon usages may be illustrated by examples – as, for instance, in this entry from the Reader's Digest *Universal Dictionary*:

> **shy** . . . 1. Easily startled; timid. Said especially of an animal. 2. Nervous in company; unsure of oneself; reserved. 3. Distrustful; wary; cautious.

4. Informal. Not having paid an amount due, as one's ante in poker. *5. Informal.* Short; lacking: *We're still £5 shy.* 6. Reluctant to engage in or associate with a specified thing, activity, or group. Usually used in combination: *work-shy*.

CHECK THE PRONUNCIATIONS

Are the pronunciations clear? There is usually a key at the beginning – browse through that. Are stress patterns shown clearly? This is particularly important in cases where there are nouns or adjectives and verbs with the same spelling, but different stress patterns. Take the words *accent* and *object*. Does the dictionary indicate clearly that in both cases the stress lies on the first syllable when the word is used as a noun, on the second when used as a verb?

Check on words such as *controversy*. Some dictionaries are prescriptive, rather than descriptive – that is, they tell you how they believe people ought to pronounce a word, rather than how people actually do. With *controversy*, for instance, a prescriptive dictionary might insist on the older pronunciation that stresses the first syllable. However, many people nowadays stress the second. The most useful dictionary will probably give both pronunciations, with perhaps a usage note on their frequency and history.

SUPPLEMENTARY MATERIAL

Dictionaries generally give charts of weights and measures, but some give more – for example, proofreaders' marks, mathematical and musical symbols, or military ranks. These charts are usually placed at the back, but they may also be entered at relevant points in the main text. Such information can be very useful.

How to Use a Dictionary

Almost all dictionaries come with a section at the beginning telling you how to use them, generally with detailed, annotated examples. When you get home with your new purchase, or next time you take it down, read its introductory sections. They will tell you a great deal about the kind of information you can get out of your dictionary.

Later, as you use the dictionary to look up words, make a point of checking in the key anything in an entry you do not understand. Soon you will find yourself confident of both meanings and usage.

Here are some general notes – see also *Reading a dictionary entry* opposite.

THE PRELIMINARIES

These are the details that come first in the definition, providing information about the

READING A DICTIONARY ENTRY

An entry is made up of several parts. Different symbols and typefaces draw your attention to key features of the word – its pronunciation,

The dot in the headword shows where you can break it at the end of a line. Then come the word's pronunciation (with regional variations), its part of speech (verb), and the spellings of other forms.

for example, and how to spell its various forms – as well as its definitions. Here is an entry from the Reader's Digest *Universal Dictionary*:

This definition has two parts – first, the verb's transitive (-tr.) meanings, then the intransitive (-intr.) meanings. Note, in the second part, the information on how to use the word, and the example sentence.

> **ex·pound** (ik-spównd, ek- || *West Indies also* -spúngd) *v.* **-pounded, -pounding, -pounds.** —*tr.* **1.** To give a detailed statement of; set forth. **2.** To elucidate or explain; interpret. —*intr.* To make a detailed statement; explain a point of view. Usually used with *on*: *He was expounding on his favourite sport.* —See Synonyms at **explain.** [Middle English *expoun(d)en,* from Old French *espondre,* from Latin *expōnere,* to put forth, expose : *ex*-, out + *pōnere,* place, put.] —**ex· pound·er** *n.*

To save space, dictionaries use 'run-ons' – related words, with different parts of speech. Here there is just one run-on: the noun expounder – that is, someone who expounds.

Here is the etymology, giving the historical development of the word. This one traces it back from the word's first appearance in English, through French, to its origins in Latin.

Cross-references lead you to other entries in the dictionary where you might find further grammatical information, or etymological details, or synonyms, or notes on usage.

different forms of the word, the way it is pronounced, and its part or parts of speech. Don't be tempted to skip this part of an entry – it provides important information.

The headword. Sometimes you will have to think a little when deciding which headword to turn to. For instance, if you come across the words *indices* or *descries,* you may not immediately think to turn to *index* or *descry.*

There are few easy rules to help you here – the English language is full of irregularities. However, as you gain experience of using a dictionary, and grow more familiar with the workings of the language, you will find yourself developing an instinct for where to locate words.

Bear in mind too that the same word – or what appears to be the same word – can be headword for two, or more, quite different entries. Take the word *league* in the book and film title *Twenty Thousand Leagues under the Sea.* Clearly it indicates some kind of measurement of distance, but what distance? You take down your dictionary and look it up. Under *league,* you find something like this:

An association of states, organisations, or individuals formed to promote common interests; an alliance.

The definition goes on in the same vein. This has nothing to do with your sense of *league.*

The problem here is that there are, in fact, two words spelt *league* – each with a quite distinct etymology and set of meanings. The word you looked up is *league* as in *The League of Nations* or a *league competition* in football. This word derives from the Latin *ligare,* to bind. All its senses contain the idea of a group, whether of states or clubs, bound together for some common purpose.

Now turn back to your dictionary, and look further down the page. Immediately below the first entry for *league,* you will find another – giving you what you are looking for:

Formerly, a unit of distance, usually equal to three miles.

In most dictionaries, such 'homonyms' – words that sound and are spelt the same but have different meanings – are given separate entries. A similar group is 'homographs' – words of the same spelling, but different pronunciation, such as *to row* (a boat), and *to row* (with your neighbour). These are also treated separately.

Another problem when trying to find the right headword is abbreviations. Where will you find *R.S.P.C.A.*, for instance? At the beginning of the R section, with other sets of initials starting with R? Or between, say, *rozzer* and *rub*? Or right at the end of the dictionary in a list with other abbreviations? Find out which policy your dictionary adopts.

The pronunciation guide. Each dictionary has its own system for showing pronunciation. Study the introductory section explaining this.

Most dictionaries for native English-speakers still use some kind of 'respelling' system. In such a system, the elements of the word are made to look as much as possible like normal spelling patterns. Take, for example, the entry for *expound* given in the panel on page 261:

(ik-spównd, ek- ‖ *West Indies also* -spúngd)

Here, the *ow* symbol stands for the vowel sound in words like *cow* and *foul* – and *McLeod*. The *ik-* and *ek-* alternatives mean that the first syllable can be pronounced either way, with *ik-* being more usual. The accent over the vowel – *ów* – shows that this syllable is stressed.

All British dictionaries give the pronunciation in RP (Received Pronunciation, roughly 'BBC English'). Some also indicate the general American pronunciation. A few, as in the example above, give other regional variants.

Some dictionaries – particularly those for foreign learners of English, but also an increasing number of those for English-speakers – use the International Phonetic Alphabet (IPA) to show pronunciation. This is a specially devised set of symbols that can be used to show exact pronunciations in all languages. It is certainly the most accurate and flexible system. The only trouble is that it uses several symbols unfamiliar to the general reader, and can take a little time to learn.

One of its symbols, however, is used in just about all dictionaries: the *schwa* – ə. This is the neutral, unstressed vowel in the first and last syllables of *banana*. Any written vowel can turn up, when spoken, as a *schwa* – *a*bout, wait*e*r, sim*i*lar, *o*ccur, citr*u*s. It is also often dropped from words, as when *difference* is reduced to two syllables.

The part of speech. When the same word exists as more than one part of speech, its entry is divided into different sections. For example, *explosive* – which can be both an adjective (as in *an explosive device/temper*) and a noun (*plastic explosives*):

explosive . . . *adj.* 1. Pertaining to or involving an explosion . . .
~ *n.* 1. A substance, especially a prepared chemical, that explodes . . .

Lexicographers decide in such cases which is the most common or the central use of the word, and place it first. You would be surprised if the first usage dealt with at *up* was its verbal use, as in *They've upped their offer*.

Note the part of speech markers carefully – they give vital information about how a word is used. What is special, for example, about each of these words: *banns* (as in *banns of marriage*), *alms*, *forceps*, *sheep*? The answer is that each has peculiarities about its singular and plural forms.

Banns (in this sense) and *alms* are never used in the singular: *These alms were given* . . . , *the banns were read* . . . They might be marked in a dictionary *n.pl.* (plural noun). *Forceps*, on the other hand, has an *s*-ending even in the singular – it might be marked *n.sing. Sheep*, which is the same in the singular and plural, would be marked:

sheep . . . *n., pl.* **sheep** . . . .

How to spell the other forms. Are you *editting* or *editing* a document? It is easy to forget. In a dictionary you should find an entry like this:

edit . . . **-ited, -iting, -its**

Editing, then, is correct.

Or perhaps you are confused between British and American spellings. Might you be guilty of *cavilling* or *caviling* at your workload? Have you *spelt* or *spelled* a word correctly? You cannot remember the British form in each case. A good dictionary should give you the information you need. For example:

cavil . . . **-illed** or *U.S.* **-iled, -illing** or *U.S.* **-iling**
spell . . . **spelt** or *chiefly U.S.* **spelled, spelling, spells**

Sometimes, there will be more than one correct (British) spelling of a word. Usually, the first form given in the dictionary is slightly preferred:

medieval, mediaeval . . .
realise, realize . . .

Whichever spelling you choose, remember to be consistent if you use it again in the same document.

If the two possible spellings of a word are completely different, the dictionary entry for the less common one may consist of no more than a cross-reference to the more common spelling; for example:

gaol ... see **jail**.

Style labels. These indicate regional limitations or particular contexts in which a word tends to be used. For example:

inspan ... *Chiefly South African* ... To harness (a draught animal) as to a wagon ...
hie ... *Poetic*. To go quickly ...
Miocene ... *adj. Geology*. Of, belonging to, or characteristic of the geological time and rock series of the fourth epoch of the Tertiary period.

THE DEFINITIONS

Take once more the sample entry for *expound* given on page 261. Its definitions run as follows:

–tr. **1.** To give a detailed statement of; set forth. **2.** To elucidate or explain; interpret. *–intr.* To make a detailed statement; explain a point of view. Usually used with *on*: *He was expounding on his favourite sport.*

Notice how the meanings are divided into sub-meanings. Because there is more than one sub-meaning for *expound* as a transitive verb (that is, one that takes a direct object – see page 169), these are numbered – the first usually is the most common. Note also the *to* at the beginning of each definition. This is used to stress that the word being defined is a verb.

Make sure to read the definitions carefully, and that you understand exactly what they mean. This sounds obvious, but it is all too easy to read the first few words, and assume that you have got all the information you need. With *expound*, a quick glance at the definitions may suggest that the word means little more than 'to put forward' or 'to suggest'. Look more carefully, however, and you will find it indicates something rather more formal and detailed. When you expound a subject, you do so systematically and probably at some length, in order to explain it fully.

Sometimes the kind of object a verb typically takes will be indicated in the definition:

compound ... *–tr.* ... To settle (a debt, for example) by agreeing on an amount ...

With this meaning of *compound*, you can use only this particular word, *debt*, or one similar in meaning to it. You might compound a debt, claim, or liability, but hardly, say, a shipment.

Many verbs and adjectives tend 'to go with' certain other words; the resulting phrases are known as 'collocations'. Only metals, for example, can *rust*, and only animals are *brindled*. Such associations may be shown like this:

rust ... To become corroded, as a result of oxidation. Used of metals ...
brindled ... (Of an animal.) Tawny or greyish with streaks or spots of a darker colour ...

Grammatical information and examples. Many dictionaries will give you grammatical information about the word you are looking up. Make sure you take it in. The entry for *expound*, for instance, gives this: 'Usually used with *on*'. Since the note is positioned directly after the intransitive definition, the information it gives applies only to this meaning of the verb.

Then comes an example sentence illustrating the use of *on*: *He was expounding on his favourite sport*. Examples – whole sentences as here, or phrases – might illustrate other important points about a word's meaning or usage. Again, don't ignore them. Like a picture, a carefully thought out example can be worth a thousand words when explaining a meaning. Take this example showing a use of the word *prodigal*:

a prodigal waste of his talents.

After reading it, you are unlikely to confuse *prodigal* with superficially similar words, such as *generous*. The example indicates the negative overtones that *prodigal* usually has.

Examples can also indicate collocations:

blaze ... Any bright, conspicuous display: *a blaze of colour; a blaze of publicity* ...
Plural. Slang. Hell. Used euphemistically, especially in the phrase *go to blazes* and as an intensive: *gallop like blazes; What the blazes is going on here?*

Cross-references. These direct you to further information that has some bearing on the word but is placed under some other headword. The *expound* entry gives this:

See Synonyms at **explain**.

If you turn to *explain*, you find these lines:

Synonyms: *explain, elucidate, expound, explicate, interpret.*

If you want to find how these synonyms differ, you could look each up at its own entry.

Run-ons. Once *opulent*, say, has been defined in an entry, there is not much point in giving separate definitions for *opulently* and *opulence*. These 'run-ons' are usually at the end of the entry.

Be careful. *Running* used as a noun may be completely predictable from the meaning of the verb *to run*: *We were impressed by her running in the race* or *His running of the company has come in for criticism*. But the corresponding conversion does not apply to a word like *packaging*: though it can be simply the noun form of the verb *to package*, it can also refer to the materials in which something is packaged. In this case, a dictionary may indicate the first meaning in a run-on under *package*, and give a separate entry, under its own headword, *packaging*, for the second sense of the word.

Usage notes. For words that are commonly misused or confused, some dictionaries give usage notes. Here is an example from the Reader's Digest *Universal Dictionary*, under *distinct*:

Usage: *Distinct* and *distinctive* are seldom interchangeable. *Distinct* has the meaning 'unmistakable' or 'clear' in most of its uses; *distinctive* has the meaning 'distinguishing', 'setting something apart from others'. The contrast can be seen in such phrases as *a distinct smell*, where the smell is pronounced, compared with a *distinctive smell*, where the smell is uniquely identifiable.

The etymology. Etymologies tend to use a great number of abbreviations. Some dictionaries go from the oldest form to the present one; others go from the first form of the word in English back to its origins in other languages. See, for example, the *expound* entry on page 261.

Thesauruses and Other Word-Finders

The word *thesaurus* means 'a treasure-house or treasure' in Latin. And a thesaurus can indeed be an invaluable aid to good writing. But it is a treasure that needs to be handled with care.

The basic point to remember when using a thesaurus is that it is no substitute for a dictionary – it makes no claims to be. It is a word-finder. A word has slipped your memory, you turn to the thesaurus, and it will help you to find it. Or you want to express something more elegantly: you consult your thesaurus and it will lead you to alternative ways of saying what you want to say. But don't expect it to tell you how to use the words or expressions you find. Only a dictionary can do that.

The trouble is that many people forget this when using a thesaurus. They turn to the thesaurus in search of fine words and expressions, unearth a few, are not quite sure how to use them, but use them none the less.

The result can be appalling. In an extreme case, someone might use a thesaurus to turn this:

I've been trying to get in touch with you to ask about tomorrow morning's trip

into this:

I have been endeavouring to achieve communication with you with a view to canvassing your sentiments regarding the antemeridian peregrination determined for the succedent day.

The writer turns to *try* and finds *endeavour*; he turns to the perfectly acceptable expression *to get in touch* and finds the generally less acceptable *to achieve communication*, and so on.

The second sentence is not grammatically incorrect. It is just ludicrously pompous. To use a thesaurus to produce any inappropriately highfalutin sentence is to abuse it.

TWO TYPES OF THESAURUS

There are two kinds of thesaurus: the 'synonym dictionary' and the thesaurus proper. Two prominent synonym dictionaries are the Reader's Digest *Family Word Finder* and the *Longman Synonym Dictionary*. By far the best known thesaurus is *Roget's Thesaurus*, which is also available in a condensed version.

Synonym dictionary. This is outwardly similar in layout to an ordinary dictionary. Each word is listed in its proper alphabetical place, but instead of definitions it lists synonyms or near-synonyms: words that might replace it in various contexts.

Moreover, the synonym dictionary spreads its net unusually wide. You would not expect to turn to *neutral* in a normal dictionary, and find *uncommitted* listed as one of its definitions. But the two words might turn up together in a synonym dictionary, since either might describe, say, the foreign policy of a country such as Switzerland. In other words, synonym dictionaries also provide synonyms for a word's more unusual senses.

In a synonym dictionary, the entry for a 'polysemous' word – one with several distinct senses – is usually split into sub-entries. The division into sub-entries may be based on actual meaning, or what contexts the word is used in, or what words it tends to go with.

Consider the entry for *dramatic* from the *Longman Synonym Dictionary*:

> **dramatic**, *adj*. 1. theatrical, theatric; dramaturgical, dramaturgic; scenic, stagy; operatic; thespian, histrionic, histrionical, Roscian, *Sl*. hammy.
>
> 2. vivid, graphic, expressive, meaningful; moving, touching, affecting, emotive; powerful, potent, forceful; telling, cogent, effective.
>
> 3. striking, impressive, sensational, spectacular; startling, sudden, surprising; thrilling, exciting, stirring, breathtaking, electrifying, nerve-shattering.

As with a thesaurus proper, the synonym dictionary does not generally attempt to define and distinguish the various synonyms offered. You have to look them up in a standard dictionary.

For instance, you might find *dilatory* and *work-shy* listed in the same subsection at *lazy*. And in a sentence like *We found that John tended to be dilatory when asked to do something new*, the two adjectives are indeed more or less interchangeable: using *dilatory* might simply be a polite way of saying that John was *work-shy*. But the two words are not always interchangeable. You might exhibit a *dilatory* attitude, whereas only a person can be described as *work-shy*. And, while both words mean 'lazy' in a way, *dilatory* refers to slowness or unwillingness to get on with a task, while *work-shy* suggests trying to avoid the work altogether. This is an important distinction that an ordinary dictionary would make plain.

The thesaurus developed a long time ago.

Roget's Thesaurus. The true thesaurus is organised on different principles. The man who devised the system was a British doctor, Peter Mark Roget (1779-1869). Wishing to improve his ability to express himself in lectures, he created what he called a 'classed catalogue of words'. His system was complicated. He worked out a series of areas of meaning – words relating to 'Abstract Relations', words of 'Matter', words of the 'Affections', and so on. Each section he then further divided and subdivided, all the time grouping words into more and more precise areas of meaning. Most words appeared more than once, according to their different shades of meaning.

In Roget's original *Thesaurus*, published in 1852, the user had to master the system of categorisation. Suppose you had forgotten the word *inarticulate*. You would have had to turn to the section headed 'Intellect', then the subsection 'Means of Communicating Ideas', and so on down until you reached the grouping that contained your word. In spite of the obvious difficulties, the *Thesaurus* was a massive bestseller, running through 28 editions before Roget died at the age of 90.

Thesauruses are still organised according to Roget's basic principles, but now come with indexes.

How to use a thesaurus. What is the missing word in this sentence describing a cruel murder?

> The robbers opened fire on the bank staff without any show of . . . . .

It is not exactly *pity* – but something rather like it. You are looking for a word that means the kind of pity that stops you doing something wrong, a sort of mixture between *pity* and *conscience*.

Go to *pity* in the index of your thesaurus (you could equally well try *conscience*). You find:

pity
> *leniency* 736 n.
> *be sensitive* 819 vb.
> *lamentation* 836 n.
> *benevolence* 897 n.
> *pity* 905 *n.*, vb.

All of these terms – *leniency, be sensitive,* and so on – refer you to numbered sections of the thesaurus where you might find your target word. Which of them is closest to what you mean? *Leniency*: that is a possibility – make a note of it. *Be sensitive* is less useful. It is a verb, and you are after a noun. *Lamentation*: that is too wide of the mark. So is *benevolence*: it would yield words like *charity* and *alms*, which contain a different sense of pity. And lastly *pity* itself: this could be fruitful. So it looks as if Sections 736 and 905 are your best bets.

Try them. Section 736 duly offers a list of nouns, of which the first is *leniency* itself. Also appearing are *tenderness, indulgence, forbearance, mercy, clemency,* and *compassion* (as well, of course, as *pity*). You may have to look up the obscurer words in your dictionary. You do so, but find nothing to capture the idea you are after.

So you turn to the other section – 905. The beginning of the first paragraph here reads:

> **N.** *pity*, springs of p., ruth; remorse, compunction . . .

Compunction? . . . *The robbers opened fire on the bank staff without any show of compunction.* The very word you need. It is more precise than *mercy* or *pity*, and better than *remorse* – that is what the robbers might feel afterwards, not at the time. *Without . . . compunction* includes exactly the right idea of an absence of any feeling of guilt on the robbers' part for what they were doing.

Note at this point one of the chief virtues of a thesaurus over a synonym dictionary – its flexible handling of different parts of speech. Suppose, for example, an exciting new actor had just made his mark for the first time on the London stage. In an article for a local paper, you want to describe how critics, journalists, and chat-show hosts have been competing with each other to interview the young star. The first sentence that comes to mind is this: *Sidney Walker has received a great deal of attention and congratulations.* Only, it sounds weak. It is the phrase *attention and congratulations* that is wrong.

First, you look up *congratulation* in the index of your thesaurus, and find that the word has its own entry in the book. You are looking for a noun. So you read through the nouns listed: *congratulation, compliments, best wishes, salute, reception,* and more. But nothing seems strong enough. Don't despair. There are also some verbs listed. Run your eye over them. They start off with obvious items like *congratulate* and *pay one's respects,* but a little further down is a group reading: *fête, mob, rush, lionise, celebrate.*

That looks better. Either *fête* or *lionise* seems right. All you have to do is change the sentence about a bit: *Sidney Walker has been fêted in the media* or *Sidney Walker has been lionised by the media.*

Finding new words. In cases like the one just described, you use the thesaurus to jog your memory. You probably know the word you end up with perfectly well – it just did not occur to you immediately. What do you do if you feel that there must exist a word that encapsulates something you are trying to say, but you are not sure that you will recognise it when you see it?

Here, you have to use a thesaurus (or a synonym dictionary) and an ordinary dictionary in tandem to get at the word or phrase you want.

Suppose you are writing to one of your former school teachers. You know him reasonably well – so the tone is fairly informal. It is not as if you were writing to a newspaper, or a prospective employer. On the other hand, it is not exactly as if you were writing to an old friend. You want your style to be reasonably light, but you also want to express yourself clearly and elegantly.

You are describing your problems at work. A new person has joined your company, and he keeps 'sucking up' to the boss. His name is Rudolph. What is more, you do not trust him. You suspect he is on the make, and is capable of being quite ruthless. How can you best describe this person?

Suck up to – that was the first term that occurred to you. But it is not exactly the kind of expression you want to use here. It smacks too much of school-children's slang.

In the index of your thesaurus you find:

suck
. . . .
. . . .
– up to
   be servile 879 vb.
   flatter 925 vb.

Either of these could be useful. (You might have thought of *smarmy* or *snide*, and they would probably have led to the same references.)

Whatever you are looking for, you cannot be sure whether it is to be noun, adjective, or verb. Is it *He's a terrible χ? Or He's an χ nuisance? Or He's always χ-ing the boss?* Keep an open mind.

You go to Section 879, run your eye down the list, and find some promising items. Then you turn to Section 925. This starts with *toady* and includes words like *hypocrite*. You take a careful note of all the likely candidates.

Combining the two sections (and leaving out some entries that obviously do not apply), you come up with a list of words worth considering:

Nouns: toady, timeserver, yes-man, rubber stamp, bootlicker, groveller, crawler, hypocrite, Uriah Heep, flatterer, sycophant, leech, flunkey, minion, tool, cat's-paw

Adjectives: servile, subject, slavish, subservient, submissive, compliant, timeserving, tergiversating, bowed, crawling, obsequious, unctuous, oily, ingratiating

Verbs: stoop to anything, demean oneself, cringe, creep, crawl, grovel, truckle, kowtow, ingratiate oneself, curry favour, worm oneself into favour, butter up, dance attendance on

What a tiresome surplus of words for your purposes – still, you can reject many of them straightaway. Rudolph behaves in the way he does, not because he is afraid of the boss. So you can jettison words like *grovel* and *kowtow*. Neither is it because he is in a position of total powerlessness. So out go words like *flunkey*, *minion*, *subject*, *bowed*, and *slavish*. Again, it is not as if he is being used (it is far more likely that he is using others). So *tool*, *cat's-paw*, and words like these are also inappropriate.

Obsequious? . . . sucking up? . . . BOOTLICKER! . . .

By means such as these you cut down the list:

   bootlicker, butter up, crawling, curry favour, ingratiate oneself, obsequious, oily, sycophant, tergiversating, timeserver, toady, truckle, unctuous, Uriah Heep, worm oneself into favour, yes-man

Now is the time to start devising experimental sentences. Here are a few examples of the process you should go through:

bootlicker. That sounds quite good – and insulting. All smiles and willingness to help.

butter up. This would produce a sentence such as: *Rudolph spends his time buttering up the boss*. Not strong enough.

obsequious. The dictionary says: 'displaying ingratiating servility'. You are not quite sure about this – it seems to conjure up something too cringing. But you like the sound of it and keep it in mind.

sycophant/sycophantic. Not bad if you really want to put Rudolph down – it definitely has an aptly demeaning ring to it. *There's this rather oily little sycophant at work*.

tergiversating. What does that mean? Whatever the answer, you would be unhappy about using it. You would not be sure you were using it correctly.

unctuous. The dictionary says it means: 'characterised by affected, exaggerated, or insincere charm or earnestness'. So it is rather like *oily*, but far more dramatic. You will bear it in mind.

Uriah Heep. This is from Dickens – *David Copperfield*. Heep was always ready to please at work, claimed to be 'very 'umble', and turned out to be a backstabber. It sounds good – and has a bit of colour too.

worm oneself into favour. There are variations on this. *Rudolph's wormed his way into the boss's good books*. True enough. But perhaps lacks punch.

You should now have cut your list down to half a dozen possibilities – for instance, *fawn*, *obsequious*, *pander to*, *sycophantic*, *unctuous*, *Uriah Heep*, and perhaps *bootlicker*. It is time to work out exactly what it is you want to say about Rudolph, what sides of his character you want to stress.

How about this? *There's a rather unctuous type called Rudolph who has just joined our firm*. It brings out his 'oiliness' without resorting to slang. Ultimately, the choice is yours. The dictionary and thesaurus can only supply the ammunition. They cannot write your sentences for you.

Of course, you will not go through this process for every single word in the letter – just the one or two most trenchant ones. And as you get practised at using a thesaurus, you will soon learn to earmark or reject at a glance.

Such exercises provide a very useful training. They get you to compare and contrast words that might be used interchangeably, and to find out exactly when it is best to use each of them.

REVERSE DICTIONARIES

A reverse dictionary can also help you to locate a word you are looking for, and more directly than a thesaurus. It is especially useful in semi-technical fields, for instance. Consider the words that you hear repeatedly in reports of earthquakes but which are liable to slip the mind. What is the word for the point at which the earthquake's intensity is greatest? Or the machine – and the scale – measuring the strength of an earthquake?

Here is part of the entry under *earthquake* in the Reader's Digest *Reverse Dictionary*

– area on the Earth's surface directly above the point of origin of an earthquake EPICENTRE

– instrument for detecting and measuring tremors of the Earth's crust as caused by earthquakes or explosions SEISMOGRAPH
– scale registering the magnitude of an earthquake RICHTER SCALE

Or suppose you cannot remember the name of the place where, according to medieval Christianity, ordinary people or souls went after death to cleanse themselves of their sins before going on to heaven? You look up *heaven*, but do not find what you are searching for. Turn, however, to *hell*, and you will find something like this:

– region or state in the afterlife between heaven and hell, in which venial sinners can atone PURGATORY

This illustrates an important point about all word-finders, including reverse dictionaries – you do not always find what you are looking for at the first place you think of. You may have to use a little imagination trying other possible places.

A reverse dictionary can help too with more everyday words. You want to say that you are *over the moon* about getting a new job, but you do not want to sound like a football manager. Another way of saying this is *very happy*. But you are looking for a more precise or arresting way of saying it. You go to *happy* and find among the various definitions:

– excitedly happy, filled with joy, as after a triumph or success ELATED, EXHILARATED, EXULTANT

Any of these three will do perfectly well for your purpose.

Elsewhere you will find clusters of words that refer to broadly the same thing or action but distinguish subtly different aspects of it. You want to describe the way in which an angry prima donna left the room. Try *walk*. Here you find:

– walk about casually, usually for pleasure, stroll, stretch one's legs AMBLE, DANDER, PERAMBULATE
– walk in a proud or pompously affected way STRUT, SWAGGER
– walk or run awkwardly LOLLOP, WADDLE, GALUMPH

Finally you reach what you feel may be the right answer:

– walk with conspicuous movements to express impatience, anger, or the like FLOUNCE

Writing at Work, Home, and College

Writing Letters at Work

LETTER-WRITING is essential to many business tasks: you may be required to sell a product by mail, answer queries from potential customers, or simply make or accept an offer in clear and binding terms. A well-constructed letter can help you to win new business and to improve and develop your relationship with clients. A skilfully written letter can smooth troubled waters and heal wounded feelings. This chapter gives advice on how to deal with most kinds of business correspondence – from letters answering enquiries or dealing with complaints to sales letters, invoices, and estimates.

First a word of warning. The language of business is the same as that of everyday English. Many people seem to think that a special vocabulary is necessary in business, that readers expect it, or are impressed by it. None of this is true.

Remember that all good writing follows the same basic principles. Certainly, a business letter is different from a letter you write to a friend, or a thank-you note you send to your hostess after a weekend party. The difference, however, is not in *how* you write, but in what you write *about*. In business correspondence, as in all good writing, simplicity and straightforwardness are best.

Consider the manager of a company one of whose salesmen has asked for an increase in salary. In everyday conversation, he or she would probably say something like this: 'Oh Bill, about that rise you wanted. I'm thinking about it and I'll let you know next week.' But many managers, acknowledging the application in writing, would reply like this:

```
Dear Mr Thompson,

We refer to your recent application,
in which you requested a substantial
rise in remuneration. We wish to
advise that the matter is under
consideration.
```

Not only is this letter stilted and pompous, but the person receiving it would probably have to read it more than once to understand its meaning.

How, then, should the manager acknowledge the employee's application? If the company is relatively small, his reply might read like this:

```
Dear Bill

Your application for a salary rise
is before me now. I will make a
decision on it early next week --
when I have had an opportunity to
review sales figures and accounts. I
will let you know what the decision
is as soon as I can.

Yours

John
```

In a larger organisation, where manager and salesman do not know each other well, the answer might be more formal, but still straightforward.

```
Dear Mr Thompson

Application for salary increase

The Board of Management, which
regularly reviews salaries, will be
meeting at the end of this month.
Your application will be considered
then, and I will let you know the
Board's decision as soon as
possible.

Yours sincerely

J.W. Leroux
```

THINK BEFORE YOU WRITE

Before you begin a letter, you must know what you want it to achieve. Here are some hints:

☐ Reread any previous correspondence between you and the person you are writing to. And make sure you have in front of you all items of information – facts, figures, and so on – that you may have to pass on in the letter.

☐ Consider the main purpose of your letter. Is it intended to pacify an angry customer, to quote a price, or to say No to a request? Whatever the reason, have it firmly in your mind before you start to write.

☐ Is there a secondary purpose to your letter? If you quote a price, should you also make a bid for an order? If you turn down a request, should you suggest an alternative course of action? An angry customer has to be won back as well as pacified. Decide how you are going to handle such matters before you write the first word.

☐ Set aside a specific time for dealing with letters – a time when you will not be interrupted. Good planning requires concentration. Some people set aside the first hour in the morning, when telephones ring less frequently and visitors are few. Your thoughts are also sharper then; they have not yet been clouded and muddled by the day's problems.

☐ Make notes as you plan. This will help you to think more clearly, and will also help to avoid unnatural words and phrases when you come to write the letter.

PLAN YOUR LETTER

The main text of most business letters has three parts, and the order of these parts is fixed. Use them to make a plan of your letter.

☐ Your reason for writing. If there is more than one, be explicit.

☐ The facts that you are presenting. Make a list and put the facts in a logical order.

☐ What you want the person receiving the letter to do for you. Again make a list, and put the most important item first.

In some letters, when you are chasing a debt for example, there may be an extra part:

☐ What you intend to do if you do not get satisfaction from your letter.

Suppose, for example, you are responsible for the computer system of a big firm of chartered accountants. You are having problems, and have just heard of a company that specialises in your kind of system. You think they may be able to help you, and are writing to enquire. Your plan might look like this:

Why writing: New system recently installed – UNIX operating system. Problems.

All good writing follows the same basic principles.

Facts: Business software doesn't meet our requirements. Also problems with communications software.

What want them to do: Inspect system and see what can be done. Phone me and arrange date.

MAKING THE FIRST DRAFT

Having made a plan, you are ready to make your first draft. Get straight to the point of your letter. Say what you have to say – and no more. Remember, the best letters give the most important information in the shortest time and most accessible form.

Opening the letter. Identify the subject matter in the first paragraph. It is often a good idea to include a heading so that the person receiving the letter knows at a glance what it refers to.

```
Dear Mr Rackstraw

Integrated business software

We are a company of chartered
accountants dealing mainly with
small businesses and the self-
employed. We have recently had a new
computer system installed using a
UNIX operating system, but we are
running into problems with it.
```

If you have already been in correspondence with the person you are writing to, refer to the last letter.

```
Dear Mrs Robeson

Thank you for your letter of 12
October 1990. Our board has now
reached a decision on the joint
marketing scheme you suggested.
```

The body of the letter. The basic rule is to follow the three parts of business letters listed on page 271 – your reason for writing, the facts you are presenting, what you want the other person to do for you. Very often, you will have a number of facts to present in each section. Find a logical order for presenting these facts – you may, for instance, order them by importance, or chronologically.

Keep your paragraphs short. Aim to describe or explain one idea only in each – single-sentence paragraphs are fine. Most longer paragraphs can simply be split at some relevant place.

Keep your sentences short too. If a sentence starts going over three lines, it is probably too long and you should look for ways to cut it in half.

The letter from the firm of chartered accountants might continue like this:

```
We have found that the business
software that came with the system
does not meet all our requirements.
There have also been problems with
our communications software.

You have been recommended as an
expert in computerised accounting
systems. We should therefore like
you to visit us to inspect our
system and discuss our needs.
```

Sometimes it helps to separate out items and number them. Compare these two examples, and notice how much clearer the second is:

We can offer you a loan of £25,000 on our usual terms and conditions if you agree to a second mortgage on your home, which would have to be valued by an officer of this bank.

We are happy to offer you a loan of £25,000 on the following conditions:
1. Provision of a second mortgage on your home.
2. Valuation of your home by an officer of this bank.
3. Repayment according to our usual terms and conditions.

Watch your language. Aim for maximum clarity of style in your letter. Check for ambiguity. If you write something like *The meeting will be held at a time to be determined later in the year*, stop and think. And – if this is what you mean – rewrite it as *The meeting will be held later in the year but we have not yet decided on the date*. Here are some further points of style to remember:

☐ Favour verbs over nouns, especially when the nouns are abstract or piled up into long phrases. *In the absence of precise instructions regarding the return of goods* could become *Since you have not told us exactly how we should return the goods . . . .*

☐ Avoid clichés and jargon – sentences like this: *We need to achieve conceptual communication criteria with a view to bringing about a dynamic parameters analysis*. Anyone writing this sort of gobbledegook is probably sacrificing accuracy as well as readability. It is hard to see what exactly the writer does mean, but presumably it is something like this: *We need to stay in touch so that we can work out what limits we're going to work within*.

☐ Don't use abbreviations such as *ibid., inst.,* and *ult*. Spell things out instead. On the other hand, it is usually permissible nowadays to use contractions such as *don't, she'll, there's,* and *isn't* – though you should still avoid these in the most formal letters.

☐ Avoid long-winded turns of phrase. Write *Please let me know . . .* – not *I would appreciate your informing me . . .* Say *We have decided to put off the decision until next Wednesday* – not *It has been decided by the company that the issue will be finalised in the near future*.

☐ Use active sentences. If what you mean is *In this case we should wait*, there is little point in writing *Under the circumstances it is considered inadvisable to proceed*. Train yourself to notice limp passives such as: *it should be pointed out that, it was felt necessary, it cannot be denied that,* and *it is recommended that*.

Closing the letter. End the letter on a firm and positive note. Avoid vague closings like:

Thanking you in anticipation.
Hoping to hear from you.
Assuring you of our best attention at all times.

Let your close say what you mean:

Please phone me to discuss terms and arrange a date.

Whatever the answer, I would be grateful for a prompt reply.

Please contact me if I can give you any further help.

EDITING THE DRAFT

Now check your draft. It may go through several stages before it is ready for typing.

In particular, look for places where you could simplify or shorten the letter, and for places where you could improve the style – be it the wording, sentence structure, or paragraphing. Always aim to 'edit down' rather than to 'edit up', though of course you may find that your first draft lacks something important and needs adding to.

At every stage, ask yourself, 'Does that say exactly what I want it to say? In the best possible way? In the fewest and clearest words?' And make sure to check for mistakes of grammar, spelling, and punctuation.

When you have got the letter just right, it is ready to be typed. Then, before you sign the typed version, check the letter carefully once more for typing errors and the like.

One last point. Always keep copies of business letters. How else can you prove that you really did reply to that urgent request for information, or that you offered to do the deal for £5000 not £8000?

CAREFUL PRESENTATION

Careful drafting must be matched by careful presentation. A business letter must be neatly and attractively presented; it should, of course, be typed – though, if you wish, you can add a handwritten postscript to someone you know well.

Stationery. One key to effective presentation is attractive stationery. If your company does not have good office stationery, make sure it gets some – soon. You cannot go wrong with A4-sized headed letter paper, plus matching unheaded sheets for letters that go over one page, and matching envelopes. It is also useful to have A5 (half the size of A4) headed paper for short notes. A good printer will help you to design your stationery, or there may be a designer on your staff.

By law your company letterhead must give, as well as your address, the following information:

☐ the company's trading name – stating also if it is a limited company

☐ the company's registration number, and place of registration

☐ the address of the company's registered office – if this is different from the address of your particular office

☐ the names of the directors (plus sometimes their nationality) – unless the company was formed before 23 November, 1916

☐ the shareholders' liability if the company is exempt from using *Ltd* in its name

If your company has a logo – a picture or symbol used as its emblem – you will probably want to include that in your letterhead as well. You should also include, of course, your telephone number, and any fax numbers and the like.

You can be flexible about presenting this information. You can put the important elements – the company name, address, and telephone number – in the top right-hand corner in the traditional way. Or spread them in one or two long lines across the width of the top of the page. Or arrange them in a column in the centre at the top. Get your designer or printer to show you a number of specimens in different typefaces, and experiment until you find a striking but appropriate format.

Layout. By convention, there are two styles for laying out business letters – blocked and semi-blocked (see the panel on pages 274 and 275). The basic difference between the two is that in blocked letters every line of text begins flush with the left-hand margin, and paragraphs are indicated only by a blank line between them. In semi-blocked letters, the first line of each paragraph is indented. Neither style is 'better' than the other – but, having chosen one, stick to it.

Here is a run-down of the constituent parts of a business letter – for further advice on these matters, see the chapter on writing letters from home (pages 344-385). They are:

☐ your address, plus the information listed above that you are legally obliged to give. If you have office stationery all this will be provided.

☐ the date. This is especially important in business letters – as proof that you did indeed write on a particular date, and so that people replying can indicate which of your various letters they are

BLOCKED AND SEMI-BLOCKED – LAYING OUT YOUR BUSINESS LETTERS

Here are two examples of business letters, one blocked, the other semi-blocked. Note the differences between them.

In the blocked letter (below left), the date goes flush with the left-hand margin, above the references. Very often, with a blocked layout, you use open punctuation for the recipient's address and the conclusion – that is, there are no commas at the ends of lines. Note also that the salutation and conclusion both lie flush with the left-hand margin.

In the semi-blocked letter (below right), the date goes on the right, across from the reference. With semi-blocked layouts it is more common to use closed punctuation for the recipient's address and the conclusion – you put the commas at the ends of most lines, and a full stop at the end of the final line. Here, by contrast with the blocked layout, the conclusion is centred.

Notice also the labels, *p.p.* and *Enclosure*. Occasionally, someone other than the writer of

TOBY OLD & SONS LTD

Mafeking Courtyard
Redhills Street
Colchester
Essex CO1 2AG
Tel: 0206 579519
Fax: 0206 579625

5 June 1990

Our ref: CO/jp/25
Your ref: SM/wk/102

Ms Sandra McEwen
Marketing Director
Easisprung Sofas Ltd
26 Wellstead Road
London   SE15 6JE

Dear Ms McEwen

PROPOSED JOINT MARKETING STRATEGY

We are writing in answer to your letter of 23 April 1990, having given the points you raise our due consideration. You asked that our company set up a joint approach in marketing stategy with yours, and we are now able to tell you what we have decided.

The board has concluded that the scheme you suggest would not justify itself in the medium to long term.

We therefore feel that we cannot for the time being see any way that your proposals could be put profitably into effect, but we shall inform you if at any stage this position changes.

Yours sincerely

Julia Patt

p.p. Cyril Old
Managing Director

Directors: William Old (Chairman), Cyril Old, Peter Young
Registered in England no 983761

the letter may have to sign it – if, for example, the writer is out of the office by the time the letter has been typed. In this case, another person may sign it, and either type or write *p.p.* or *per pro* in front of the name of the writer.

This stands for *per procurationem* (on behalf of), and indicates that the person signing is officially authorised to do so for the writer.

If you send further documents with the letter, such as an invoice, as here, or a report or a cheque, indicate this by typing *Enclosure/s* or *Encl/s* near the bottom left-hand corner of the page. *Encls 4* warns the person receiving the letter that there should be four different enclosures. You might specify the enclosure or enclosures – *Encl: Surveyor's report*.

Notice, finally, that much of the information which businesses are legally required to put in their letterheads (see page 273) has in both these cases been tucked away in small print at the foot of the page.

This allows the important information – the address and telephone and fax numbers – to stand out more clearly at the top of the page.

WILBRAHAMS OF THE STRAND LTD

TEA AND COFFEE MERCHANTS
59 The Strand
London WC2Y 7GH
Tel: 071-251 7890
Fax: 071-251 7823

Ref: TD/ip/2   9th October, 1990

Muffins' Tea House,
8 The High Street,
Chopping Mudbury,
Avon BA9 0KL.

Dear Miss Mapp,

Order no: jy/10896

Thank you for your order for 300 caddies of Earl Grey tea and 250 of Lapsang Suchong.

We are able to deliver the Earl Grey immediately but regret that the Lapsang Suchong will not be available before 14 November.

We regret that we are no longer able to supply goods on credit. Our invoice is enclosed, and we shall send out the available goods as soon as we receive your remittance.

Yours sincerely,

T. Drinkall,
Sales Director.

Enclosure

Directors: Robert Wilbraham Alison Rawdon Thomas Drinkall
Registered in England no 736510

answering. Remember to give the year as well as the day and month. Various forms are possible: *5th June, 1990; 5th June 1990; 5 June 1990; June 5th, 1990; June 5, 1990*. Avoid the form *5/6/90*, which would mean June 5 in Britain, but May 6 in North America.

☐ reference numbers. These make filing easier and allow letters to be traced later. Generally, references consist of two sets of initials with a final number. For example – *Ref: MH/jp/22*. The initials in capitals are those of the writer of the letter – Maria Hartnell. The ones in lower case are those of the typist – Jane Potter. The number indicates where the letter is filed – so *22* directs the searcher to shelf, box, or drawer 22. If you are replying to a letter with a reference, give that as well – label the other person's reference number *Your ref:* and yours *Our ref:* . . .

the name, title, and address of the person you are writing to. This means that anyone finding a copy of your letter in the files at a later date knows whom you were writing to and where.

☐ a salutation. If possible, always address your letter to a named person (for further advice on this, see *Modes of Address*, pages 404–422) – *Dear Mr Blenkinsop, Dear Mrs Hartnell*. Use the form *Dear Sir* (or *Sirs*) or *Dear Madam* only if you really cannot find out a recipient's name. If you know the person reasonably well, and are on first-name terms, use his or her first name (*Dear John*) – but still type out the name and title formally above the salutation.

☐ the text.

☐ a conclusion. In general, if you address the person by name, you conclude *Yours sincerely*. Using the form *Dear Sir* or *Dear Madam*, you conclude *Yours faithfully*. If you have addressed the person by his or her first name a number of forms are common – *Kind regards, Regards, Best wishes*, for example.

☐ your signature, name, and title. Below your signature type your name – signatures are generally pretty illegible, and this helps the person receiving the letter to address you correctly when replying. The typed name is not preceded by *Mr, Mrs*, or any other title. However, a woman may put a title in brackets after her name – *(Mrs), (Ms), (Miss)*. Beneath your name you can specify your position, such as *Managing Director, Personnel Manager*, or *Assistant Editor*.

FAXES, TELEXES, TELEGRAMS

One of the most useful of modern telecommunications inventions is the fax (facsimile) machine. This enables you to send text or even illustrations instantly to anyone within reach of another fax machine anywhere – whether Alice Springs, Los Angeles, or your office.

A fax is no substitute for a letter when it comes to making a formal approach to a potential customer, replying to an enquiry, or the like. Where it is invaluable is in sending someone facts, figures, or even a short report or set of proposals in response to, say, a phone call.

Generally, companies have standard forms which they attach to the information being faxed, with perhaps a hand- or type-written note added.

```
              CHAFFINCH BOOKS LTD
           25 Little Sussex Street
               London EC1Z 9BY

FAX TRANSMISSION
FAX NO 071-251 1692

FOR ATTENTION OF: Rebecca Schloss
COMPANY: Morgan Zimmerman, New York
FROM: Robert Simsville-East
DATE: 20 Nov 1990
TIME MESSAGE SENT: 5 pm
NO OF PAGES: 4
```

Rebecca

Here are the new proposals, revised in the light of our phone conversation this afternoon.

RN

Telexes and telegrams. Since telexes and the like are charged according to length or time of transmission, brevity is at a premium.

```
From: E. Iqbal, Production,
      Lancaster Office
To:   L. Nystrom, Production,
      Odense

Please advise on possible delivery
dates for order 17/GOW, 2000 Type 4
bearing sets. Order sent 15 May, now
urgent.
```

Day-to-Day Trading

This section gives examples of the kinds of letter you will have to write in the course of your everyday business – covering letters, estimates, invoices, letters informing clients of price increases, answering customers' enquiries, and so on.

COVERING LETTERS

When you send samples or documents, there should always be a covering letter. Use the letter to say exactly what you are sending, to give any explanations you think will help, and to ask for an acknowledgment.

Dear Mr and Mrs Campbell

I enclose the Surveyor's Report and various other documents relating to the property 6 Alans Way, Leek, Staffs. The documents are:

1. House-buyer's report.
2. Building Society Valuation Report.
3. Guarantees from Knight & Sons, Builders, relating to repairs to the roof.
4. Guarantees from Squires & Co., Builders, for the damp-proofing work recently completed.
5. Copy of our Land Search report.

Kindly acknowledge safe receipt.

We await your further instructions in this matter.

Yours sincerely

Gordon Greenway

Encls 5

ESTIMATES, QUOTATIONS, AND TENDERS

An estimate or quotation offers specific services or goods to a potential client at a certain price.

The difference between the two is that an estimate may be amended at a later date, whereas a quotation is legally binding if accepted.

Estimates and quotations are usually made on standard forms, though you can produce a one-off form yourself or use ordinary letter paper. Remember to include the following items (as well, of course, as the usual letterhead information – address, telephone number, date, and so on):

- a reference number, plus any reference number that the prospective customer requires

- full details of the goods or services

- the price per unit and, where applicable, the price of the required quantity

- all other fees or charges, including carriage

- your terms and conditions of payment – for example, when the 'nett' payment (in other words, what remains to be paid after deposits and so on have been deducted) is due

- the initials *E & O E*, standing for 'Errors and Omissions Excepted', a safeguard reminding the receiver that the price may be different if something has been overlooked or if a mistake has plainly been made

---

COMPUTER TRAINING LTD.,
54 Wells Street,
Bristol
BS2 5YP.
Telephone 0272 893524.

21 October, 1990
Our ref: QU/45b/90
Your ref: TRP/fs

Mrs Alice Ogden,
General Insurance.

QUOTATION

For ten two-day training courses in secretarial word-processing skills at £240 each:

Course charges	2,400.00
Plus VAT	360.00
TOTAL	2,760.00

Terms: nett payment, 30 days from date of invoice

VAT no. 458 2940 449   E & OE

Tenders. A tender is usually produced in response to an advertisement, and is in competition with tenders from other companies. It is an offer to supply goods or services at a certain rate, but usually needs to be set out in considerably greater detail than an estimate or quotation. Often, the organisation seeking tenders will supply forms.

Tenders require careful detailing of estimated costs. Here is a very simple example of a letter to a liquidator with an offer to buy assets:

Dear Sir

<u>Liquidation of assets of</u>
<u>Peters Furnishings</u>

We submit the following offer to buy assets of Peters Furnishings, now in liquidation:

Unsold stock as per your list of assets	15,500
One delivery van	1,000
Office fittings, items 6-9 on your list of assets	1,500
TOTAL	£18,000

If you agree to this offer, we shall pay you by cheque immediately and make arrangements to collect these goods within four weeks.

Yours faithfully

Laura Winterbottom

INVOICES

An invoice is a demand for payment, sent out either before or after delivery of goods or services.

TIM HARPER
Builder
45 Glen Road, London NW2 5PT
Tel. 081-548 3982

INVOICE

For re-laying garden path:

48 paving slabs @ £2.30 each	110.40
Turf	25.40
Labour, as agreed	95.00
	£230.80
VAT	34.62
TOTAL	£265.42

PRICE INCREASES

No customer will welcome a price increase. When giving the bad news, make sure that you:

☐ write as far in advance as you can

☐ give the date from which the price rise becomes effective

☐ specify exactly what is going up in price, and by how much

☐ explain the reason for the price increase, and pass on your regrets for the inconvenience

---

To:	All sales representatives and agents
From:	Fiona O'Suibne, Sales Manager

PRICE INCREASES

Please note the following price increases with effect from Monday, 2 September, 1991.

All types of cured and preserved pork: 10% on list price.

All types of sausages and pies: 12% on list price.

Except:
Individual-sized chicken and mushroom pies:	10%
70% meat pork sausages:	10%
All pizzas:	15%

All types of Continental Style patés: 14% on list price.

Full details of the new prices are given on the attached Schedule A.

The increases are a result of increased livestock commodity and production costs. These have increased by 15% since the current price list came into effect, but we do not feel that we can increase prices by the full amount at present.

KINDLY WARN CUSTOMERS THAT IF CURRENT CONDITIONS CONTINUE WE SHALL HAVE TO CONSIDER INCREASING PRICES AGAIN WITHIN THE NEXT FIVE MONTHS.

ANSWERING CUSTOMERS' ENQUIRIES

On the face of it, answering enquiries is simple. All you have to do is go through what the customer asked and provide the necessary information.

But there is more to it than that. See your reply as a sales letter as well. There may be no question of selling anything immediately, but try to prepare the ground for future trading. Show yourself in the best light and eager to cooperate.

Dear Mr Dogsworthy,

Axminster carpets

Thank you for your enquiry of 9 November about Axminster carpet, type 34B. I have enclosed our price list and catalogue, and you will find the details on page 12.

There are two further pieces of information you might find helpful:

1. The prices quoted are our normal trade prices. However, on orders of over £5000 we offer an extra discount of 4 per cent. We also offer a discount of 10 per cent to customers contracted to us as sole suppliers.

2. We would draw your attention to pages 13 and 14 of the catalogue. The Axminster-type carpets described here are new to our range, so you may not be aware of them. As you will see, their specifications are very similar to type 34B but they are, in general, up to 15 per cent cheaper than our traditional range.

All the carpets shown in the catalogue are in stock, and we can supply all but very large orders within seven days.

If you need any further details, please do not hesitate to be in touch.

Yours sincerely,

Alphonse Harris.

ACCEPTING AND CONFIRMING PROPOSALS

As always, be clear and keep to the point when accepting and confirming proposals. (For an example of a letter *rejecting* a proposal, see the letter on page 274.) When accepting a proposal, don't forget that by accepting goods you may bind yourself legally to pay for them. The next example covers the company against such implications.

Dear Sir

Supercup coffee-vending machine

I confirm that your Mark III 'Supercup' coffee-vending machine was installed by your fitters on 13 May and is in good working order. So far it has not been tested to the limit of your specifications (250 cups a day without refilling).

I suggest that we keep the machine on approval for the next two weeks. If there is no fault, we shall be happy to sign your leasing agreement and pay for the trial period. However, if the machine fails to meet your specifications, we reserve the right to return it to you, with payment for the trial period only.

Yours faithfully

Robin Inglestone

Confirming. Agreeing or confirming previously discussed matters can be done simply.

Dear Sirs

The Aberdeen Fisheries Exhibition

This is to confirm the points agreed in our recent discussions:

1. We will be taking a display stand at your exhibition for our range of marine lights and lamps.

2. The cost of the stall and display area, measuring 12 feet by 8 feet on the ground floor of the exhibition hall, is £100 a day. Payment is to reach you by 12 August 1990.

We look forward to receiving final details of the location of our stand before 24 June.

Yours faithfully

Birger Persson

Writing at Work, Home, and College

Money Matters

Relations with your bank are among the more nerve-racking aspects of running a business.

And then there are the problems of chasing up debts. Some large companies are notoriously slow in settling accounts and so leave smaller clients with serious cash-flow problems.

YOU AND YOUR BANK

When writing, address the bank manager or departmental head by name if possible.

To speed the letter through to its intended destination, mention the relevant department on the envelope, so that it reads, for instance, *The Manager, Small Businesses Section*.

Mr Alfred Higgins
The Manager
Foreign Department
Bradshaw's Bank

Dear Mr Higgins

Current account no. 22439018

Kindly draw a draft for DM 2,420.00 payable to:

    Gombrich Gmbh
    6920 Bergneustadt
    W. Germany.

The sterling equivalent should be debited to our current account. The draft should be sent direct to me at the address given.

Yours sincerely

Amy Weston

Applying for a loan. This is more complicated. You write by name to the manager or sub-manager in charge of business loans. You will be expected to include a sales forecast, a profit and loss statement, and a cash-flow analysis. In your covering letter, get any bad news out of the way first.

Dear Mr McCarthy

In response to your request I now enclose our cash-flow forecast for 1991. It shows sales, costs, and cash balances on a monthly basis.

Please note the following points.

1. Sales forecast. Our market research suggests that sales will remain fairly static for the first half of the year, but should increase in the second half. We anticipate an increased demand for our furnishings for the Christmas market. Overall we do not expect sales to increase by more than 15 per cent over last year's level; this figure is reflected in the schedule.

2. Costs. The figures given are based on previous years plus inflation for factors such as promotion, production costs, and raw materials. Fixed costs take into account a projected pay rise of 8 per cent in March and the costs of taking on temporary staff during the busy August-to-November period.

3. Profitability. Our profit margins on sales are expected to remain static at around 10 per cent. This takes into account a price rise throughout our range of 8 per cent, though we shall have to look at this more carefully some time in early summer.

4. Cash flow. Our largest outstanding capital loan will be fully repaid in June. For the rest of the year, cash income should exceed outgoings comfortably. The area of doubt remains the first half of the year. The position in part depends on our being able to recover certain large debts from creditors and/or the official receiver. This is the reason we are applying for a bridging loan to cover us until September.

5. Conclusion. We expect our position in 1991 to be very similar to that in 1989 and 1990, for which you have our final and half-yearly interim accounts. While the first half of the year will present certain cash-flow difficulties, we anticipate a healthy balance on all accounts by the end of the year.

I trust you find these comments helpful. If there is any other information you require, please do not hesitate to phone me personally.

I look forward to meeting you to discuss this matter in detail on 24 October.

Yours sincerely

Alexander Knight

Postponing payments on a loan. A letter to your bank manager asking for a 'moratorium' (a temporary suspension of your payments on a loan) might be based on the next example. If you are reasonable, the bank will probably agree to your request. The deal will earn them more interest, and, in any case, they will not want to push you into bankruptcy and then have to try to recover what they can from the official receiver.

Dear Sir

Business Development Loan
Ref. A590234

I am writing about our repayments of the above loan, at present £830 a month.

You will understand that the current high rate of interest on mortgages

---

280

has resulted in a fall-off in demand for garden improvements, and to get new business we have had to reduce our tenders by up to 25 per cent. In addition, we are having problems collecting debts for work completed for householders.

You will also be aware that several local companies in our line of business have recently been forced to close. We are therefore receiving a higher than usual number of enquiries from potential customers, who would like work done when market conditions stabilise. We are unwilling to lay off skilled staff, since we anticipate an upturn in business later this year.

I would therefore ask you to grant us a three-month moratorium in our payments; that is, the final repayment would be deferred from 1 June 1990 to 1 September 1990.

Yours faithfully

Aaron Roberts

CHASING DEBTS

Letters chasing debts are known as 'letters of collection'. Your approach depends on how serious the debt is, how many times you have written before, and what you know about your creditor. Some will pay up only if threatened with drastic action; others respond to a 'softly-softly' approach but grow awkward if they think they are being harassed. At all events, you do not want to throw all your best punches in the first round – there may be many more rounds to come.

Be prepared to make a nuisance of yourself. As a general rule, several niggling 'reminders' work better than the occasional threat. If necessary, simply send out photocopies or reprints of former letters, with a slip to say: *We are still waiting for your reply to our letter of . . .*

Here are some further tips on letters of collection:

☐ Don't use form letters. If you have a word processor, use it to make your letter look as if it is a one-off. And find a name of a recipient. If that person is not responsible, he or she will probably let you know who is.

☐ If the company you are chasing up has a trading account with you, send a copy of its current statement. You can stamp it, possibly in red, with the words *Payment Due* and then fill in the date by hand.

BILLS THAT WILL NOT GO AWAY

If you cannot meet a bill, it is not much good hoping your creditors will not notice. They will. In which case, it is better to get your word in first. Write to say when you will be able to pay. Make it clear that your problems are merely temporary. Try to include a cheque in partial settlement, or suggest a schedule of repayment by instalments. This way you are much more likely to get them to agree to a delay or moratorium.

Letters asking to defer payment are normally sent to the other company's accountant or credit control manager.

Dear Mr Golightly

Your Invoice no. XC/280 for £3250.00

This payment becomes due on November 5, 1990, two weeks from today.

I am writing to request an extension of the period of payment. At present we have temporary cash-flow problems due to non-payment of sums of money owed to us and considerable capital investment in new projects. These projects should start bringing in revenue within the next two months.

I would therefore like to defer the settlement of your account until January 5, 1991. Thereafter we will of course revert to the usual terms of our trading agreement.

I enclose our cheque for £500.00, in partial settlement of the account.

I hope you will be able to agree to our request for this deferment. We do anticipate an increase in orders with you during 1991, as a result of our current expansion programme.

Yours sincerely

S T Mather

☐ In your first letter, cover yourself with something like *As we have not heard otherwise from you, we assume that you are satisfied with the goods supplied*. You might also cover yourself with a sentence to this effect: *If you have already sent your cheque, please disregard this letter*.

☐ If, after a couple of letters, the people who owe you money are still not answering, send a copy of your letter to the company's chief accountant or, after that, its managing director, marked *PRIVATE AND CONFIDENTIAL*.

☐ Try to be tactful. You do not want the company to go to a competitor next time.

☐ Vary your tactics. Don't adopt a regular schedule of, say, four letters of increasing insistence at monthly intervals. People will get wise to this trick and ignore the first three.

☐ Ask yourself how you got into this mess. And vow to be more careful in future.

First reminder. If appropriate, enclose a copy of a statement or invoice with this first letter.

```
Dear Miss Cash

Account no. XJ9 / Invoice no. 23/91

I note from our records that the
above account, dated 24 March 1992,
is now overdue. The amount owing is
£185.00.

We assume you are satisfied with the
work performed, and therefore ask
that you settle this account as soon
as possible.

Yours sincerely

A. Rooker (Mrs)
Credit Controller
```

Second reminder. Note how the tone of this letter is much more abrupt. Don't bother with the 'I'm sure there must be some mistake' approach. It will almost certainly be ignored.

```
Dear Miss Cash

Account no. XJ9 / Invoice no. 23/91

I wrote to you on 4 May about your
company's unpaid account for
£185.00. We have not received a
reply to this letter, and would
appreciate a speedy settlement of
this account.

We wish to remind you that our
credit terms are based on settlement
within 30 days of invoice, and we
supply goods only on the
understanding that these terms are
adhered to.

Kindly let us know if there is any
reason why you cannot settle this
account immediately.

Yours sincerely

A. Rooker (Mrs)
Credit Controller
```

Third reminder. This is where you head for the top; that is, the person you reckon is best equipped to make sure that something is done – the company's chief accountant or managing director.

Before you send a third 'reasonable' reminder, ask yourself whether the company deserves it. If your answer to that question is No, you should go straight to stage four.

```
Dear Mr Sharp

Account no. XJ9 / Invoice no. 23/91

I write to point out that your
company has not settled the above
account for £185.00, despite
reminders sent on 4 May and 26 May,
and so has breached the terms of its
credit agreement with us.

You may be unaware of this. If so,
kindly make sure that this account
is settled immediately. If we have
not received your cheque within the
next two weeks, we shall be forced
to trade on a strictly cash basis in
future.

Yours sincerely

Donald Cameron
Financial Controller
```

Final straws. Here is a selection of final reminders in which various courses of action have been resorted to – from placing the matter in solicitors' hands to instigating legal proceedings in a Small Claims Court.

```
Dear Mr Sharp

FINAL REMINDER

Account no. XJ9 / Invoice no. 23/91

You have not replied to our letters
of 4 May, 26 May, and 15 June.
Unless you settle this account for
£185.00 within the next ten days we
will have no choice but to place
this matter in the hands of our
solicitors.

Yours sincerely

Donald Cameron
Financial Controller
```

In the next letter, the company removes the debtor's credit status, and insists that all bills must be settled 'on a pro forma basis', that is, they must be settled invoice by invoice.

Dear Mr Sharp

Account no. XJ9 / Invoice no. 23/91

Despite our letters of 4 May, 26
May, 15 June, and 30 June, we still
have not received the £185.00 that
you owe us. We have therefore
removed your credit status with our
company and your current orders with
us will be processed on a pro forma
basis.

If this account is not settled by
Tuesday, 28 July 1992, we shall put
a stop on processing all orders from
your company.

Yours sincerely

Roy King
Chief Executive

Dear Mr Sharp

FINAL DEMAND
Account no. XJ9 / Invoice no. 23/91

We note that despite our frequent
letters you have failed to settle
your account with us for £185.00.

Since you have chosen not to
cooperate with us in this matter, or
even acknowledge our letters, we
have instigated proceedings with the
Small Claims Court in Norwich. You
are therefore to regard this letter
as formal notification of the
summons.

Yours sincerely

Roy King
Chief Executive

And along with this last letter there might be a summons to appear in court – for about a fortnight after the date of the letter. Note, however, that the letter itself serves as a notification of the summons.

Chasing debts is never a pleasant business – far from it. However, going about it methodically, as outlined above, should be effective and will help you to keep at least some peace of mind.

When Things Go Wrong

In this section you will see some examples of letters answering complaints and of letters making them. There are also some specimens of letters you might have to write when matters come to a head – how to terminate business relationships, and how to avoid and deal with litigation.

DEALING WITH COMPLAINTS

Needless to say, how you answer a complaint depends entirely on whether you think it is justified or not. If you do not know, play for time.

Dear Mrs Murphy

We have received your letter of 4
October, in which you complain that
the consignment of our office
furniture delivered the previous day
was damaged when it reached you.

We are looking into the matter and
shall write more fully within the
next two weeks. I have asked our
Credit Control department to hold
back your invoice until then.

Yours sincerely

Leslie Weller
Sales Manager

Here are some general principles for handling letters of complaint.

☐ Never open such letters with *Dear Sir* or *Dear Madam*. People who complain should be given special treatment – use their names.

☐ Get someone with an impressive job title to sign such letters. The person complaining is more likely to be mollified if a letter comes from the Office Manager or Sales Director rather than from a junior clerk.

☐ Start your letter by thanking the person complaining for his or her letter – even if you have to grit your teeth to do so.

☐ Never admit responsibility unless you really are to blame. But never say directly that you think the person complaining is to blame, either. There are various forms of words you can use, such as: *I'm sure there must be some mistake*.

☐ Be sympathetic and understanding. The person complaining is less likely to tighten the screws if he or she thinks there is a warm human being at the other end.

☐ Even if it is unclear whose fault it was, be magnanimous. Offer a little free gift, a short deferment on an invoice, or some other crumb of comfort. In most cases a dignified retreat is better in the long run than slogging things out uncompromisingly.

Apologising. Occasionally, a downright apology will be necessary in response to a complaint. There are two ways of accepting responsibility. A letter of apology is just that – you admit that you are in the wrong. Alternatively, you can write a 'letter of correction'. This goes one better: it offers something in compensation for your mistake.

In one way, letters of apology are unlike other business letters. The maxim 'The shorter the better' for once does not apply. People like to think you have gone out of your way to deal with them personally, and a long and detailed catalogue of your efforts will usually gratify them.

The rule is to sound sincere but not to grovel. Admit your mistake, explain how it came about, and say what you will do to improve matters. The challenge is always to pacify the person complaining so thoroughly that he or she has a higher opinion of you after reading your letter than before the incident took place.

Here is an example of a letter apologising for a delay in delivering goods:

```
Dear Mr Williams,

     Thank you for your letter of
4 September 1990.

     You remind us that on 23 August
we delivered only 50 of the 100 C4D
microcircuits due on that date. The
reason for this delay is that
delivery of the capacitors used in
this circuit was delayed by our
suppliers. I am pleased to inform
you that these components have now
arrived and we are giving priority
to completing your order.

     The outstanding 50 circuits will
be finished by 12 September and
should reach you by 14 September.

     I trust that this meets your
requirements, and apologise for the
delay.

                    Yours sincerely,

                    Barry Fairfax.
```

Now an example of a letter of correction – written by a delivery service in answer to a complaint about the late arrival of a parcel containing perishable foodstuffs. Remember that a suitable offer of compensation will speak in your favour not only in the customer's eyes but also if the matter ever comes before a court.

```
Dear Mrs Jones

I am writing in answer to your
letter of 4 October.

First, let me apologise on behalf of
Quicksilver Parcel Services for the
delay in the delivery of your
parcel. It appears that someone put
the parcel among those to go abroad,
which were then sent to another
office for sorting. The mistake
became apparent only four days later
when Customs and Excise queried our
applications for export licences.

As a result of this incident we have
now changed our system for the
initial sorting of parcels.

We note that the contents of the
parcel were insured for £50.00. In
your letter, however, you mention
the extra cost to your restaurant of
having to replace the fish at short
notice. We feel it appropriate to
compensate you for the trouble our
carelessness has caused and
therefore enclose our cheque for
£65.00.

We hope you find this arrangement to
your satisfaction.

Yours sincerely

Miss Anne Fordyce
Customer Relations
```

Rebutting unjustified complaints. What do you do when you feel the complaint made against you is unjustified? What you do *not* do is to write back calling the complainer a cheat or a fraud. However great the provocation, try to stay cool.

Investigate thoroughly, so that you have all the facts at your fingertips. Then be sympathetic, and polite, but firm. Once again, remember that you can smooth ruffled feathers by a gracious retreat, without having to admit you were wrong.

Initial letters can be quite simple.

```
Dear Mr Swan

Order for 50 sacks of grass seed

Thank you for your letter of 22
March stating that you received only
49 sacks of grass seed instead of
the 50 ordered.
```

```
I have checked our carriers' dockets
with our Despatch Department and
these show clearly that 50 sacks did
leave our premises in the
consignment to you. Could I ask you
to recheck and see whether you do
not in fact have 50 sacks?

Yours sincerely

J. Flowers
Transport Manager
```

There are various tactful ways of saying you disagree with a complaint. For example:

I appreciate how busy you are and I am very grateful for the trouble you have taken in writing to me. I do apologise, therefore, for having to query one or two of the points you raised . . .

We have done business together for many years and I have come to value your judgment and accuracy. On this occasion, however, may I suggest that you are mistaken/not in possession of all the facts.

Thank you very much for your letter. I wonder, though, whether you have considered . . .

We have considered your point of view carefully. Now we ask you to consider ours.

Here is an example of a letter tactfully disagreeing with a complaint:

```
Dear Mr Widgerly-Rathbone,

    Thank you for your letter of 12
April, in which you complain that
you and other members of your party
were abused by the manager of Le
Petit Chou and evicted from the
restaurant with unnecessary force.

    I was of course most distressed
to hear that customers had been
treated in this way in one of our
restaurants and immediately
instigated an inquiry. I have spoken
to Mr Grundy, the manager, and two
of his waiters who were working that
night. I have to say that their
account of the events differs
somewhat from yours.

    I am sure that you meant no harm
by your high-spirited behaviour on
the occasion, especially after your
university's victory in the Boat
Race. But you will understand that
most of our customers come to us for
a quiet meal in congenial
surroundings and are perhaps not so
pleased when other customers sing
lustily in the restaurant and dance
on the tables.
```

```
    Mr Grundy assures me that he
applied no more force than was
necessary in persuading you and your
party to leave. He is certain that
neither he nor any of his waiters
was responsible for the bruising on
Miss Chadwyck's eye.

    I therefore regret that I cannot
agree that you were badly treated by
our staff, though I shall of course
be happy to hear anything else you
wish to say on the matter.

        Yours sincerely,

        Jean-Antoine Offenbach.
```

Finally, a letter for when you have come to the end of your tether and are quite sure that the complaint was unfounded.

```
Dear Mrs Drinkwater

Thank you for your letters of 11
August and 22 August, in which you
complain about the quality of
plastering work done in your home.

I have given careful consideration
to all the points you raise, but, as
explained in my earlier letter
enclosing the surveyor's report, I
regret that I am unable to take this
matter any further.

Yours sincerely

Nelly Haines
```

MAKING COMPLAINTS

Your first move when complaining should be to reach for the telephone. Contact the company concerned and find out precisely whom you should direct your complaint to. And if you are going to get very angry, it is best to do so orally – preferably not in front of witnesses. Written outrage is liable to come back and haunt you later.

Then back yourself up with a carefully worded and reasonable letter, in which you make absolutely clear the cause for your complaint, and what you want done about it. Needless to say, you must be extra careful not to write anything factually in-accurate or potentially libellous.

One tactic that very often pays off is writing direct to someone in the senior management of the company. Suggest that this person may not be aware of what is going on among his staff and that you are sure he would do something about it if he were

GIFTS FROM LITERATURE

If someone has *a Jekyll-and-Hyde personality*, he or she tends to undergo sudden and perhaps frightening changes in mood or behaviour. The expression comes from the character in Robert Louis Stevenson's novel of 1886. There are many other words and phrases in English similarly derived from the names of literary characters and places.

☐ In the following list, choose the word or phrase you believe is nearest in meaning to the key word. For the answers turn to pages 633-648.

diddle
A: to question
B: to play cards
C: to cheat
D: to make pancakes

euphuism
A: a substitute for an offensive word
B: an affectedly elegant style
C: beautiful speech
D: rejoicing

Falstaffian
A: fat and jolly
B: timid and helpless
C: slim and glamorous
D: short and ungraceful

gamp
A: an umbrella
B: a naughty child
C: an injured leg
D: a picnic basket

gargantuan
A: terrifying
B: stony
C: toothless
D: enormous

Grundyism
A: cheerful generosity
B: narrow-minded morality
C: gloomy pessimism
D: pretended expertise

Lilliputian
A: an ancient statue or monument
B: a herb garden
C: a small person
D: a Biblical scholar

lotus-eater
A: a person who has no appetite
B: a person who neglects work for the sake of pleasure
C: a person about to be married
D: a person who has survived a catastrophe

malapropism
A: seasickness
B: an evil intention
C: an error in arithmetic
D: a misuse of words

Pecksniffian
A: having an extremely large nose
B: habitually talking about virtue
C: habitually giving long-winded speeches
D: having an unhealthy interest in graveyards

quixotic
A: endlessly questioning oneself
B: dangerously treacherous
C: impractically romantic
D: extremely eccentric

serendipity the faculty of
A: making others feel calm and happy
B: making lucky discoveries by chance
C: making others bow down and worship
D: making the best of a bad situation

utopian
A: interesting and very much worthwhile
B: depressing and hopeless
C: useful but unpleasant
D: ideal but impractical

yahoo
A: a coarse person
B: a triumphant cry
C: a foreigner or recent immigrant
D: a needless fuss

aware. In this way you provide him with a face-saver if he was, in fact, the person who was responsible for the mess in the first place.

Dear Mr Armitage

<u>Our order ref. 45/22</u>
<u>Invoice no. BE/3/4962</u>

The order with the above reference was delivered by your carriers to our shop last Wednesday, May 1, 1991. We wish to point out that:

1. You failed to include any of the records from your Light Classical selection, as requested in our phone call of April 23, and acknowledged by you the next day.

2. The pressing of <u>Songs from the Musicals</u>, of which our delivery contained ten copies, appears to have gone wrong. Three customers have returned their discs to us, complaining of too much background noise, and I have tested two others and come to the same conclusion.

Will you therefore send us immediately ten new copies of <u>Songs from the musicals</u> (XT 1834) and the Light Classical records as ordered, and, if necessary, arrange for the defective copies to be collected.

You must appreciate that customer satisfaction is crucial in the record retail business. This is not the first time that we have had cause to complain about your service. We trust that it will be the last.

Yours sincerely

Ilona Nincic
Manageress

Terminating business relationships. The point may come when you have had enough of unreasonable delays, shoddy workmanship, or bad service. You have written countless letters of complaint – and still no satisfaction.

How you go about terminating an unsatisfactory business relationship depends largely on how you feel. You might feel that you have nothing to lose by letting off some steam. The only rule if you do is to avoid open abuse or anything that might be interpreted as defamatory. Sarcasm is a much better weapon.

Note also two simple ways to be rude: start your letter with *Dear Sir* or *Dear Madam* and omit the *Yours faithfully*.

Countless complaints – and still no satisfaction.

Dear Sir,

I'm sure your business would run more smoothly if you spent as much time and ingenuity in managing it as you do in avoiding paying your creditors.

All business between your company and ours is at an end.

Simon Mander.

LEGAL IMPLICATIONS

Letters that might have serious legal implications are best left to your solicitors. However, there are certain rules you should follow to make it less likely that you will need to have recourse to the law.

☐ Never accept in writing estimates, invoices, complaints, or accusations, unless you are absolutely sure that they are correct.

☐ Never make a commitment to do something unless you know you will be able to deliver.

☐ Never put on paper anything potentially defamatory or any imputation of illegal, dishonest, or incorrect behaviour.

☐ Tell the truth. Anyone who bases a decision on a statement which you have made knowing it to be false has the right to legal redress.

□ Address letters containing sensitive information to the person for whom they are intended, and mark the envelope *Private* or *Confidential*.

□ Send invoices, demands, valuable documents, and the like by registered post. Registering a letter is taken as proof of posting.

Head any letter that might have legal implications *Without prejudice*. This implies that your letter is not necessarily your final or unqualified word.

Dear Sirs,

<u>Without prejudice</u>

Thank you for your letter of 12 May, and your tender for the canteen service for our Watford factory.

We would like to inform you that we are still awaiting certain other tenders and shall not make our final decision until after the announced deadline (31 May). However, we would like to make the following comments:

1. The quality of food and service you propose meets our requirements in all possible ways, and we are thus interested in your tender.

2. The price you quote is 5 per cent above the maximum stated in our letter inviting tenders.

We should like you to reconsider your price and see whether you can reduce it slightly. Under the right conditions we would be willing to go up to 2 per cent over our announced maximum. If you are able to meet this price, your tender would be looked on favourably by our board.

Yours faithfully,

Harry Rubinstein,
Chief Executive.

Threatening legal action. A threat of legal action is normally the last in a long line of increasingly acrimonious letters. Be short – no need to dredge up all the unpleasantness that has gone before.

Dear Sirs,

A letter has come into our possession, addressed to one of our clients, in which you refer to us as 'a load of cheapskate, tight-fisted, shoddy, incompetent cowboys'. In addition, we note that you have had a letter published in the <u>Stornoway</u>

<u>Gazette</u> in which you claim, in more temperate language, that we have defrauded you.

Needless to say, we reject these allegations and regard them as impertinent and defamatory. We require that you:

1. Send to our solicitors, McLeod & McLeod, a written apology for these comments within the next four days.

2. Place, at your own cost if necessary, an entry in next Friday's <u>Stornoway Gazette</u> withdrawing as groundless your previous letter and apologising unconditionally.

Unless you do so, we shall take such steps as are advised by our solicitor to protect the good name of this company and to seek financial compensation.

Yours faithfully,

Iain Inglis.

Dealing with a threat of legal action. If you get a letter like the one above, you have four choices. You can ignore it, and see what happens. You can write back saying effectively 'Sue and be damned'. You can attempt a compromise, however late in the day. Or you can do what they ask.

The last is often the most painless, the simplest, and the cheapest. Turning the other cheek usually pays off in the long run. Even if you win the lawsuit, your name is going to be hauled through the mud. Whatever the circumstances phone your legal adviser at once. Don't do anything until you have heard what he or she has to say.

Dear Sirs,

I have received your letter in which you announce your intention of taking to law the matter of my supposed £5 debt to you.

As stated in my previous letters, I have no intention of paying for defective goods. I have however instructed my solicitor, Robin Walsh of 14 Queen's Street, Bracknell, to act for me in this matter. You, and your solicitor, should therefore address any correspondence on this matter direct to him.

Yours faithfully

Eleanor Aquitaine

Selling Letters

Every business letter is a sales letter. At least, every business letter should be written as if it were a sales letter. After all, your letters – their appearance and the attitude you display in them – reflect on you.

Every answer to an enquiry might be the jumping-off point for future trade. Every letter of apology should be a tacit promise to do better for your clients in the future. Even a 'rote' letter rejecting a job applicant should avoid cold, unsympathetic language that makes its recipient feel hard done by.

Your letters represent an important part of what is called 'corporate image'. Make yours good.

SELLING BY MAIL

If you get an agency to write your advertising material, make sure you go over it carefully before giving it your approval. The agency may be skilled in the use of words and images. But they are unlikely to know much about the hydraulic presses, satellite dishes, computer software, or catering services you are trying to sell.

One hint: selling by mail can be expensive. You do not want to have thousands of leaflets, letters, and envelopes printed without getting results. So, before you start any large campaign, try a dummy run first. Sample shots in limited areas should tell you whether your material is getting through. Then you can decide whether to take things further.

Your first decision is who gets your sales letters. Existing customers are a good place to start. Your firm ought to have customer lists; make sure they are kept up to date – people move and change jobs.

You might also be able to buy or hire customer lists from other companies. And mail shots can be better directed by using computerised data bases, which allow you to select, say, all the married people aged between 30 and 45 in a given set of areas.

Phone books too (especially the *Yellow Pages*) and electoral registers can be useful – as can your local papers. If, for example, you sell goods – kitchen equipment, say – likely to be bought by newly married couples, you might scan the papers' weddings and engagements columns. Try to think of other similar tactics for reaching potential customers – builders, for instance, might want to keep an eye on estate agents' notices outside houses.

Some Chambers of Commerce are ready to provide lists of traders in specific fields in their areas. Specialised market research organisations also often supply useful registers – at a price.

Finally, you might look at some of the special directories that list the names and interests of British and international companies: *Sell's Directory of Products and Services*, *Kelly's Manufacturers' and Merchants' Directory*, *The Times Top 1000*, *The Kompass Register of British Industry and Commerce*, and *The Guide to Key British Industries*.

THE PERSONAL TOUCH

Sales letters should:

> arouse interest
> describe, explain, and convince
> clinch the deal

It is obviously much easier to achieve these objectives in an individual letter targeted at a single potential customer. A well-worded circular, however, can bring your name before thousands, and you can keep your more finely honed letters for those who respond to the circular.

Remember that using modern word-processing 'mail merge' programmes means that individual letters can easily be tailored out of pre-existing paragraphs. Even wide-circulation letters can be 'personalised' with the name of the recipient.

But be very careful when using such short-cuts. Remember the priest who, wanting to produce a service sheet for the marriage of a couple named Mary and Bill, directed his word processor to substitute *Bill* for *Mary* throughout – and finished up at one point in the service with the response *Hail Bill! Mother of Christ*.

All good sales letters are to some extent 'targeted'. Your first task is to imagine the intended recipient as he or she opens your letter. What do you see? Is it a businessman trying to clear his in-tray before rushing off to a meeting? Or is it a skilled technician looking for something to match very precise specifications and willing to move heaven and earth to find it? Or is it a wealthy collector with a house full of antiques that might be in need of repair? Or a young couple sitting at home and wondering how they can afford to carpet their living room?

When you compose your letter, imagine you know the person you are writing to, and write accordingly. Follow the first rule of marketing, which is: 'The more individual the approach, the more likely you are to get a response'. A crusty local solicitor is unlikely to be impressed by a letter written in a tone of back-slapping, hail-fellow-well-met chumminess. Few ordinary couples will choose your vacuum cleaner just because you tell them it has a 1200-watt motor. On the other hand, that is the kind of technical information that might just tip the balance with someone running an office cleaning service. Another key piece of advice for anybody wanting to sell can be given in eight words: 'Put yourself into the mind of the buyer.'

WRITING YOUR SALES LETTER

The format of your letter depends largely on your selling strategy. Are you writing a single letter giving all the necessary details? Or do you have catalogues or leaflets that need a personalised covering letter?

Here are some general rules that apply to all kinds of sales letter:

☐ Pay particular attention to appearance and presentation. Is your stationery good enough? Is it right for the length of your text? Is your layout uncluttered and eye-catching?

☐ Keep your letters short. Few people read everything that drops through their letter box. So your letter has to grab potential customers, and then keep them, and it is less likely to do that if it goes over a page. If you really need to say more, send a separate enclosure.

☐ Keep everything clear and simple. Use short sentences and paragraphs, especially at the beginning and end of your letter.

☐ Keep things bright and interesting. Don't be patronising or overtechnical. And be sparing of superlatives. What product is not *ideal* or *excellent* or *unbeatable value?* If anything, err on the side of understatement rather than overkill. The hard sell comes later, when someone has shown enough interest to reply.

☐ Even in an enclosure, sift out the really important points from the incidentals, and jettison the latter. If there is specialised material that must go in (technical specifications, legal clauses, and the like), tuck it away in footnotes or endnotes, or on a separate sheet of paper.

☐ Make it as easy as possible for your readers to reply. Give them precise instructions about what to do to order your goods or services – if they are left to fend for themselves, they will probably not bother. You might include stamped, addressed reply envelopes or cards.

☐ In one-off letters to individual customers, keep the ball in your court. Finish up with the promise that you will phone personally next Thursday, or whatever. Don't just leave it to the customer to respond – he probably will not.

OPENINGS

By far the most important sentence in any selling letter is the first. It is, after all, often the only one that gets read. Try to make it a paragraph on its own.

In any case, keep your opening paragraph down to five lines at the very most. This is where you tackle the first of your three tasks, arousing interest.

Here are some tried and tested gambits. Note how many of them attempt to flatter without sounding condescending.

The striking statement

Save 25 per cent on your heating bills.

We have cash to give away.

Good news to all our regular customers! From next week, we are . . .

Selling *Supertech* floor-polishers is easy.
Why? Because they're the best you can buy.
I should know. It's my job to sell them.

The startling fact

70 per cent of homes in your area are double-glazed. Is yours?

£50,000 to be won!

The pertinent question

Do you want to earn £50 a week from home?

Are you ready for 1992?

What would your family do if you were laid off?

The anecdote

Recently I visited the Appleford Centre for the Physically Handicapped. Let me tell you about it . . .

This is the story of a man who didn't insure his garage.

An analogy

There's a company in Reading, no larger than yours, that has increased its turnover by 56 per cent in the last year from a £15 investment. And without any special offers.

Some companies are better equipped to face times of economic recession than others.

The offer you cannot refuse

Special Offer to *Gardener's Times* Readers Only!

We'll repaint the front of your house free, if . . .

The gift – a 'bribe for listening'

It will take you less than an hour to read our booklet *Get Ahead in Business*.

Fill out and return our form. It could mean a holiday in Barbados for you and your family.

You are special

As one of our most valued customers, you will want to know about . . .

We deal only with the most go-ahead companies in Matlock. That's why we're writing to you.

You have been selected to view our new range of bathroom furniture.

You fit the bill

If people hadn't told us you were the best music shop in town, we wouldn't be writing to you.

Asking or offering a favour

May I ask a small favour of you? Read this letter, and then see whether you still think the same about roller blinds.

I want to do you a favour. If you'll let me . . .

Nostalgia

Do you remember where you were when you first heard *Be My Baby*? The memories will flood back as you listen to *The Spectre of the Sixties*, fourteen of the best from the genius of Phil Spectre.

You were a child once. And Christmas was a time of hopes and dreams.

THE MEAT OF THE LETTER

This is where you describe, explain, and convince. What can your product do for your reader? How is it better than all the others?

It should not be difficult if you really believe in what you are selling. If you can communicate your own enthusiasm to your reader, you will be nine-tenths of the way there. So be clear in your own mind what the strongest selling points of your product are. Then devote a short paragraph to each.

Again, there are well-tried methods of creating credibility – of proving that your product really is the best. In the first place, bear in mind the old advertising maxim: 'Sell the sizzle, not the steak.' In other words, concentrate on the benefits that the product offers the customer, rather than a nuts-and-bolts description of it. Don't just tell your customer that your product is 'made with 20,000 steel rivets'. Say what the rivets will do for him or her – '20,000 steel rivets mean that it'll stand up to the hardest wear.'

Here are some examples of ways to reinforce the credibility of your offer.

The guarantee

We're so convinced of the quality of our *Anti-Puncture Strip* that if your tyre punctures within six months of fitting, we'll replace both the strip and the tyre free of charge.

The free sample

Don't just take my word for it. See for yourself. I enclose a copy of our *HGV Handbook* for you to keep. Then you can judge our claim for yourself – that it's an essential part of the cab equipment of all international freight lorries and coaches.

Free trial

Our Water Cooler has to be seen to be believed. So we will install one in your workshop, free of charge, for a trial period of 14 days. If you're not satisfied, we'll remove it, at no cost to you.

Testimonials

'I don't think I've ever spent £15 more wisely,' says Mr A. B. of Barry. 'Using your *Tax Savers' Guide* I cut my liability by more than £450 in a year when my profits went up.'

Reputable user or sponsor

Who do you look up to in your area? *Oxford Mills*? *D.S. Franklin & Sons*? *St. Jude's College*? *The Latimer Seminary*? These are just a few of the companies and organisations for which we are sole caterers. Because they can trust us to provide the right lunches at the right prices.

Statistics of acceptance

Over 4000 households in your county will attest to the efficiency and superb quality of our *Decalc* water softeners.

Reference to the reader's experience

Before you opened this letter you probably thought fax machines were too expensive for the self-employed. Now you know better.

Reference to the writer's experience

If I could arrange for you to meet, in person, the Technical Staff of Softply Paper Mills, you'd be as impressed as I was this morning. I have just come from the meeting. I sat there fascinated, watching these men and women enthusiastically discussing the material we had produced for them to solve their particular production problems.

Test results

In a recent survey by the British Tourist Authority, our holiday cottages were ranked:

Excellent for location
Excellent for facilities
Good for upkeep
Good for customer service
OUTSTANDING FOR VALUE

The reason why

Modern production methods and our 'cut out the middleman' marketing strategy allow us to offer you our office furniture at discount prices . . .

Offer of comparison

Our industrial clothing washers may be more expensive than some of our competitors'. But look at the extras you get . . .

The case history

Country Air health farms and sanatoriums have not been advertised for two months now – we simply have no vacancies. Yet we receive up to 15 calls and letters a day from interested people who have been with us before or heard of us from others. Only those who book now can be sure of a vacancy for next spring.

The raw materials

Here are a few facts about the last issue of *Selling Trends*: to produce it our 15 editors consulted 200 companies, interviewed 300 key businessmen, and travelled over 7000 miles.

ENDING YOUR LETTER

Save your clinching point for the very end. If possible, find something personal that sums up the points you have already made. Keep up the gentle pressure. Here are a few endings that have been used with successful results.

Limited-time or limited-quantity offer

Owing to demand, this unique offer must be limited to one per customer – £5 will bring you every feature of our complete service.

Our discount prices, listed in the catalogue, are effective until 31 May. You'll notice that they give you a 7 per cent discount if you order right away.

Urgency

You can't leave stocking up till the last moment. Use the enclosed order form to tell us your needs. Specify your delivery date. We'll do the rest. Send no money until the invoice arrives. You'll be ready for summer, long before your rivals.

The personal appeal

How would you like to be the first household in your area with stone cladding?

Will you be able to sleep soundly until your premises are guarded by our trained dog-handlers?

Making the response easy

We have enclosed a stamped reply card. All you need do is tick the products you're interested in, and one of our representatives will phone you within the week to fix an appointment.

Phone us at any time. Our 24-hour switchboard will be ready to take your orders. And within 15 minutes one of our couriers will be on his way to you with a delicious hot pizza.

Sales services

Call me today for a free demonstration. Arrange a time for one of our skilled sales staff to call.

I hope you won't mind my taking the liberty of phoning you on Tuesday morning next week, when you've had time to consider this one-off offer.

Availability

These electric toothbrushes, and a host of other small household electrical goods at knockdown prices, are available only from Millers, 221 High Street, Chesterton.

We will be demonstrating our fog lamps on Stall 145 at the International Fisheries Exhibition in Aberdeen from 6 to 10 May, 1991. Hope to see you there.

For the convenience of people in your area, we maintain an office at 45 Market Street – tel: 39405. Drop in or phone at any time.

SOME SAMPLE SELLING LETTERS

Here is an example of a one-off sales letter to a potential customer:

```
Dear Mr Huntly,

    The manager of a small business
has better ways to spend his time
than vetting applicants for clerical
jobs. I'm sure you wring your hands
whenever a good secretary leaves you
or takes time off.

    We can help you. Most agencies
give secretaries a short typing test
and leave it at that. We do better.
As well as testing their typing,
shorthand, and other skills
thoroughly, we take the trouble to
chase up their references. We find
out exactly what they can, and
can't, do. We want the best for
them, which means the best for you.

    So the temporary staff we provide
are actually handchosen for the job.
They're not necessarily better. Just
better at the particular task you
need doing.

    No more spending half your day
showing the new secretary how to use
the word processor. No more draft
accounts looking more like junior
school maths exercise books. No more
credit slips sent out as invoices.
Just simple, smooth efficiency.

    Why not try us next time you need
a temp? Please phone Anthea Lively
on 0367 39572 for full details of
our staffing services. You won't be
disappointed.

            Yours sincerely,

            Harry Morely,
            Director.
```

The special touch. You are the Customer Service manager of an airline. One day a letter comes from an elderly lady. She has never flown before in her life but now wants to visit her daughter who lives in Canada. She is nervous about flying, afraid of airsickness and other problems she has heard about, and worried about being strapped into her seat for such a long journey. But she is keen on the idea of this new experience.

Picture her in your mind. You want to reassure her, and encourage her. She is a bit chatty in her letter. So can you be in yours.

```
Dear Mrs Edwards,

    I envy you. There is nothing
quite like a first flight. Least of
all anything like a first flight in
one of our 757 luxury airliners. It
will be the perfect prelude to what
I hope will be a wonderful holiday
in Canada with your daughter.

    I don't think you need worry
about airsickness. Do you feel sick
in cars? Because tests have shown
that fewer people suffer in planes
than in cars or trains. And you
don't need to worry about being
strapped into your seat for an
eight-hour flight. Apart from five
to ten minutes as you take off and
land, you're free to walk about the
passenger cabin as you wish.

    You'll be served with a hot meal
while on your flight, and our
stewardesses will bring you tea,
coffee, and other drinks whenever
you want.

    The worst part of flying is after
take-off and landing. Some people
find that the changes in air
pressure cause some discomfort in
the ears. To help with this, our
stewardesses hand out boiled sweets
to suck on the way up and down. This
usually does the trick.

    Some people suffer from jet lag
-- disorientation because the time
is earlier in Canada than it is
here. Most people find it worse on
the way back than on the way out.
The best way to overcome it is to be
well rested before you fly, and to
try to sleep during the flight. And
generally to take it easy.

    The flight that would suit your
purposes best leaves London Heathrow
at 12:30 p.m. on Tuesday, 2 June and
arrives in Toronto at 2:45 p.m.
local time. These times should make
it easy for you to get to the
airport here, and for your daughter
to be there to meet you at the other
end. The cost is £380 for standard
class or £540 for our special Club
Class. These prices include
everything, such as airport taxes
and the cost of your meal and
drinks.

    Here's what I've done. To make
sure you'll have a seat on that
plane, I've gone ahead and made a
```

```
provisional booking for you, which
we can hold for ten days. Please
call me or my secretary Helen
Sparrow to confirm that this is
right for you, and to sort out the
details of your return flight.

    I hope your flight with us will
be a memorable part of a memorable
trip. I'm sure your daughter, ·and
Canada, will be delighted to see
you.

        Yours sincerely,

        Martin Hendricks.
```

You can hardly expect to have the time to produce replies like this on every occasion. But let it be an ideal to strive towards in your treatment of customers and their individual needs.

A letter for a large-scale mail shot. Here is a letter suitable for sending to several potential customers in one mail shot. Note that the person's name has been included in the salutation.

```
Dear Mr Meek,

This letter is your invitation to a
glass of wine. And perhaps much more
than that.

We met you last year while you were
looking for reliable and fast
hauliers to handle your freighting
needs.

Things have changed since then. Last
year we were just one of many. Now
we're in a class of our own.
Whatever your needs are, we can
handle them. Thanks to our new fleet
of refrigerated trucks we now offer
the widest range of freight carriage
in the whole of Northamptonshire.
And thanks to our flexibility, we
can deliver at 24 hours notice to
all parts of the British Isles.

So whether it's forty tons of raw
plastics or a single highly
sensitive microchip, we can get it
there with the least fuss, in the
least time, and with absolute
security.

And the glass of wine? You'll find
it at our display stand at the
Kettering Trade Fair, 5-8 June.

We look forward to meeting you
again,


Ravi Daryanani
Managing Director
```

Circulars. Circulars are leaflets handed out or delivered through letter boxes. Keep them short. Few people read more than a few lines unless they are seriously interested in what you have to say.

CASCADE SHOWERS

What can be more relaxing than a shower after a hard day at work? Or put more life into you first thing in the morning?

Yes, you say, but they never work. One moment freezing, the next scalding the skin off your back.

You've never tried a CASCADE SHOWER. Cascade Showers have a special mixing unit that minimises temperature variation. So once you've got the temperature right, that's the way it stays.

The advantages you know already – lower heating bills, all-over cleanliness, no time wasted waiting for the bath to fill.

Fill out the coupon with your name, address, and telephone number. One of our skilled installers will phone you back and arrange to visit. He'll be able to advise you on the type that would suit your bathroom best.

But be quick. Our team of experts are in this area only until the end of October.

COVERING LETTERS

Direct mail selling usually involves a leaflet or catalogue, a covering letter, and a coupon or order form for answers.

Here is an example of a covering letter to go out with a glossy brochure.

```
Dear Garden-lover,

    Gardening becomes more
complicated year by year. New
varieties, new fertilisers, new
equipment.

    But just how useful are these
things? And how safe? And where, and
when, should they be used?

    The Garden Lover has the answers
to all these questions. Not the
answers the manufacturers will give
you, but the results of years of
work by independent testers and
experts.

    Read the brochure that comes with
this letter and find out whether
everything in your garden really is
rosy.
```

If you want your garden to be really green, fill out the coupon and send it off in the envelope provided with your cheque for £12.50 payable to Moss Publications.

Yours sincerely,

Pete Moss.

The letter you would use to send out a catalogue or price list is very similar.

A MESSAGE FROM OUR SALES DIRECTOR

Dear Customer

Hello again, and welcome to our new-look 1992 catalogue.

In response to customer comments we've completely rearranged our catalogue to make it easier to find your way around. But that's nothing compared with the new range of books that we have on offer, all at ridiculously low prices.

The first section deals with book sets. We've got encyclopedias, 'Complete Works', and collections to suit every reading taste.

The second section is on illustrated books. Not that many of our books aren't illustrated. But here you'll find art books, travel books, cookery books, and many other large-format, colour-plated books.

Part three is our renowned crime, mystery, and adventure series. As well as old favourites, we have many new editions on subjects that range from murder in Martinique and robbery in Rio to double-crossing in Dulwich. Girls, guns, guts -- stories you can't put down.

Number four is humour. Laugh with Larry and Lorna. Chuckle with Chaplin. Roll in the aisles with Alain Robbe-Grillet.

And lastly, children's books. Again the range is enormous -- it grows every year. Stories, activities, hobbies, and pets. And much more.

And all at bargain-basement prices. Because we buy in bulk, and we hand the savings on to our customers.

Use the enclosed form to order your pick of our choice.

Happy reading.

Herbert Reed

PRESS RELEASES

Press releases inform the world of a new product or service. If you write your release well, newspaper and magazine editors – often hard put to fill their publications – will sometimes publish your article almost word for word. You could hardly hope for better publicity – your own product written up in your own words.

The most important thing of all when composing a press release is to bear in mind that what is news to you and your company is not necessarily of interest to the public at large.

Newspapers sell news, and your story could be up against a lot of competition. Think: what is the news angle on this story? What will make it of interest to the general reader of the newspaper or magazine in question? And then try to make it a story that the editor will be glad to run.

Here are some further tips:

☐ Specify when you want the release to appear. Put in a heading such as *For immediate release* or *Not to be published before May 24*. This is important – you do not want the release (or any article based on it) to appear several weeks, say, before your product is ready for sale.

☐ Type on only one side of the paper. Use double spacing throughout. Leave wide left-hand margins for the editors.

☐ Use follow-on lines at the end of each page, such as *high-resolution video display* . . . Close the last page with: - *end* -.

☐ Use the first paragraph to give the main point. Give more detailed information in the paragraphs that follow.

☐ Write the release with the intended publication in mind. See that your style is appropriate for the readership in, for example, the amount of technical information given. If necessary, find a local slant for the material.

☐ Provide the name and telephone number of someone who can be contacted for further details or confirmation.

☐ Check every word for accuracy. Make doubly sure that all technical information is correct and up to date. You certainly do not want to be caught out in what is supposed, after all, to be your area of expertise.

```
                              SMITH'S CYCLES

PRESS RELEASE                                        Smith's Cycles,
For immediate release                                      Unit 14,
                                        Bridgetown Industrial Estate,
                                                Swansea SA14 2BP.
                                                Tel: 0792 484903.


3 July 1991

                       Local Firm in the Limelight

     In the new clean, green age, with its interest in fitness and fresh
air, cyclo-cross has become one of the fastest growing sports in the
country. Ten years ago cyclo-cross was very much the poor relation of
rallying and scrambling. That's all changed. Cross-country cycling is big
business. And Smith's Cycles, sited in modern premises on the Bridgetown
Industrial Estate, is in the forefront.

Hand-made bicycles

     Bert Smith started producing top-quality mountain and cross-country
bikes in 1983 in his garage at home. By 1985 many leading racers were
coming to him for specialised adjustments and repairs. Two years later
Smith's Cycles entered a works' team in the National Championships,
attracting three of the best talents in the world of cyclo-cross including
Geronwy Thomas, who finished second overall in 1989.

Dedicated staff

     Smith's Cycles has long since outgrown Bert's garage. It moved to its
present modern premises in 1985. These premises look nothing like the
average bicycle repair shop. Nor like a conventional bicycle-manufacturing
plant. The highly skilled works team are more at home with high-tech aides
such as laser cutters and simulation computer programmes. There's even a
small chemical laboratory for analysing lubricants and lightweight alloys.

     In eight years Bert Smith has gone from working on his own to running
a company with twenty-five full-time employees. They range from drivers
and receptionists to the team of highly qualified technicians under Dr
Myfanwy Preece, who oversees the technological development side of the
business. And then of course there are the riders, some of whom are
rapidly becoming household names.

New departures

     Plans are now under way to develop into new areas. The competition
bikes are designed and built for individual riders and can cost anything
up to £5000. But in May this year a new production line was set in motion,
customising bikes produced by brand-leading manufacturers such as Radley
and Peuter. This should put Bert's expertise within the range of a far
greater number of customers who want the very best in mountain and cross-
country bikes.

     Bert tells us: 'There has been a lot of interest from abroad, mostly
from France, Italy, the Low Countries, and Scandinavia, but also from
Japan and America. We're developing contacts in Germany and the expanding
markets in Eastern Europe, where cyclo-cross has long been a major sport.
We have orders for at least the next year for our new range of production-
line bikes, and we'll probably have to take on more staff as business
expands.

     'But we don't want to lose sight of our competitive beginnings. It's
only at the top end that you can really test your machines against the
world's best. Our staff are gaining experience all the time. I don't think
we've seen anything like the "perfect" cross-country bike yet - but we're
confident that our present team can get as close to it as anyone in the
world.'

Sport for all

     Bert went on: 'Of course our bikes are expensive. But we now aim to
use the advances we've made ourselves, rather than license them out to
large-scale manufacturers. Our bikes open up a new world of recreation,
and we want as many people as possible to share it.'
```

If you go up to Aberrwst on Saturday week, look around for the red and green works van. You're likely to see Bert and the team hard at it, making last-minute adjustments before the fifth round of the National Championships.

And as you see one of the red and green bikes churning downhill through the mud at a terrifying speed, think not just of the rider but of the hours of patience and skill that went into producing the bike.

Your dream of owning one of these machines is no longer so remote. They're here in Swansea, and getting cheaper all the time.

- end -

For further information, please contact
Fred Morgan, Office Manager, Smith's Cycles.

FOLLOW-UP LETTERS

Don't assume that once you have made a sale you are home and dry. Keeping customers is if anything more important than finding new ones. You have made the initial contact, so don't spoil the good work by taking your customer's goodwill and continuing interest for granted.

Dear Mr Peterson

Thank you very much for your Order no. 532/P/91 for 600 super-pressure pump gaskets. The order is now being made up and should be with you by the end of next week, as requested.

We like to think that we maintain a personal touch in dealing with our customers. So please do not hesitate to phone me if you have any questions about this and future orders.

I am taking this opportunity of enclosing our current price list and some order forms, so that any future business between us can be conducted speedily.

Yours sincerely

Alfred Watts
Sales Manager

Writing is especially important if for some reason you cannot fulfil an order.

Dear Mrs Antrobus

Thank you very much for your order for a copy of our new publication The Encyclopedia of Dog Care. We are very sorry that owing to an unprecedented and unexpected demand, this book has temporarily sold out. We are having a new run printed at present, and your copy should be on its way to you in about three weeks.

Meanwhile, to compensate you for any disappointment, I have the pleasure of enclosing our book Showing Dogs, which I ask you to keep free of charge.

Yours sincerely

F. Basset

You may also have other services to offer existing customers.

Dear Miss Handford

Congratulations on your new Hiwani 1200cc Super-Racer. You now own probably the best high-performance motor bike in the world. We hope it gives you many hours of happy and fault-free motoring. We have every confidence that it will.

But as I'm sure you realise, things can always go wrong, and you may find that you need adjustments made to some of the controls and specifications of your machine. For our best customers, we offer a comprehensive range of services to help them get the best out of their bikes. This includes engine-tuning, fitting accessories, and a priority repair service, as well as three-monthly service check on all components.

This service costs £120 a year to people, like you, who have bought their motor bikes from us. I enclose a leaflet giving full details, together with an application form.

Happy motorbiking

Jeff Broom
Manager

Letters to Your Staff

In this section you will find some examples of typical letters or other communications that a manager or employer might be called upon to write to a member of staff.

A CHANGE IN JOB CONDITIONS

Occasionally, you may have to reallocate staff. Remember, it is always best to discuss your employees' new duties with them personally first, and then to confirm the details by letter or memo. And in some cases – if a reallocation affects someone's terms or conditions of employment as laid down in his or her contract – such discussion becomes essential. Any change in the terms of someone's contract must, by law, be agreed by both employer and employee.

Dear Ingrid

I would like to confirm the details of our recent discussion and give more precise instructions on private client allocation within the tax department.

We decided to assign some of our clients to Martin Redding, so that these jobs will not take up so much of your time. The ones we agreed to assign to Martin were: Major Carnforth, Sir Inigo and Lady Higgs, and all the Chadwyck family. It occurs to me that Martin might as well take over the Jermyn accounts, too, since the Jermyns are related to Major Carnforth.

This will leave you more time for our business customers, and you will therefore be able to specialise in this area.

There will be no change in your salary for now, but your new responsibilities will be taken into account in the forthcoming pay review.

Yours

K. Todd
Head of the Tax Department

PAY RISES AND PROMOTIONS

Notifications of pay rises should be kept simple. When writing to announce a promotion, combine details of new rates of pay and of new duties.

Dear Anthony

Following our talk yesterday, I am pleased to confirm the details of your new job:

1. From the first of next month you will take over sole responsibility for all our marketing projects in Europe.

2. You will no longer be expected to oversee any projects in North America.

3. Your new job title will be European Marketing Manager.

4. You will now report to me, Susan Warder, Executive Marketing Manager.

5. You will be put on pay scale E5. This represents a rise of £1420 from £24,240 to £25,660 a year.

Many congratulations on this promotion. I am sure you'll make a thoroughly good job of it.

Yours

Susan Warder

REFUSING A PAY RISE

Suppose an employee you want to keep has asked for a pay rise, which has been turned down – perhaps by a higher authority than your own. How do you inform him or her? Be as tactful as possible and give a valid reason.

Dear Mr Jellicoe

The Board has now met and discussed your application for a rise in pay. I regret to inform you that on this occasion it has been turned down.

As you will know, work in the transport business has been slack recently, and our finances are, unfortunately, not able to stretch to pay increases before the annual review in August. The Board has asked me to pass on the message that in better conditions your application might have been looked upon favourably. We are all aware of your efforts on behalf of the company, and emphatically do not want you to feel that you are not appreciated.

I hope you will be able to accept

```
this disappointment for the time
being. Let us hope that August will
bring you better news.

Yours sincerely

Bob Driver
Haulage Manager
```

PRAISE AND REPRIMANDS

A handwritten letter of (deserved) praise can do wonders to inspire your staff.

Dear Cornelius,

It is only a week since I asked you to look into the dreadful muddle in Stock Control. I anticipated that with this on top of your normal duties we would not be able to expect any improvement for some time. However, it is clear that your efforts have already produced significant and reassuring results. We at least have some idea of how much old stock there is, and thus what needs disposing of.

Many congratulations. Keep up the fine work

Yours sincerely

Bill North.

Reprimands. These can be more difficult to handle than praise. At the least you stand the risk of alienating your staff. At worst you could later find yourself before an industrial tribunal held at the request of someone you have fired.

The most important maxim to remember when reprimanding people is: Find something good to say. Most people have something that they do well. If you lead with this, and then tell them that they appear to have slipped from their normal standards, they are likely to respond reasonably to the reprimand – and their work will improve. If you lead with the failure and leave it at that, they will be defensive and resentful, and remember the reprimand as a reprimand only. After all, your object should be to improve the employee's work performance – not to vent your own frustrations.

Most companies and organisations have standard rules and procedures for disciplining people who work for them. Stick to these: they are designed to ensure fairness and consistency.

ASKING FOR A PAY RISE

Composing a request for higher pay is not unlike writing your c.v. – see the chapter on job applications, pages 331-343. You have to 'sell yourself' – show why you should be singled out rather than anyone else. You do not need to go into as much detail as you might in a c.v., but you do need to present good reasons to explain why the company ought to be paying you more than it is.

Present your proposal positively. Suggest that a rise will help you to work better, and show how you have earned it. Appeal to your employer's sense of fairness. But don't make the mistake of comparing your salary with that of one of your colleagues – unless, of course, there is a legal reason for parity. Don't threaten to resign unless you really are prepared to leave.

```
Dear Mr Young,

    As you know, I have been working
in the Planning Section of the
Education Authority for eighteen
months. During this time, two
experienced members of staff have
left, and only one has been
replaced.

    One of those who left was Mrs
Emily Burridge, the head of the
section. Since I had received more
training than the others in the
section, I took over most of Mrs
Burridge's responsibilities,
including training new staff, in
addition to my regular duties. I
have therefore often had to work
late or take work home, for none of
which have I received extra pay.

    I enjoy my work and the new
responsibilities. I have no reason
to think other than that I am coping
with them effectively, and this has
its own satisfaction. The
satisfaction would be all the
greater if it were recognised from
above. I would therefore ask you to
consider moving me from my current
Pay Scale 3 to Pay Scale 4. I have
read the specifications for Scale 4
and it demands no significant duties
that I am not handling already.

    Would you be kind enough to
investigate my position and see
whether or not you agree with me?
Perhaps we could talk about this in
a couple of weeks' time.

        Yours sincerely,

        Katriona Murray.
```

299

APPRAISAL REPORTS

Many companies nowadays have a system of annual appraisals. These involve one-to-one interviews between an employee and one of his or her managers (for advice on these, see page 536), and a written report assessing the employee's progress, and contribution to the company, over the last year. As a manager responsible for writing someone's appraisal report, you are duty-bound to make sure that it is scrupulously fair. After all, that employee's chances of promotion and an increased salary in the coming year depend very substantially on what you write about him or her in the report.

Writing a report for a really good, or a really bad, employee is usually fairly easy. The problems arise when the person in question is competent, average, and unremarkable. If that is the case, say so. Here is an example of a reasonably hard-hitting report on just such an employee, one who has done quite well in some areas, not so well in others.

Note that while the appraiser undoubtedly discussed the contents of this report with the employee, the report itself would probably not have been shown to her. The advantage of this procedure is that it allows the appraiser to be absolutely honest, without fear of upsetting the feelings of the employee. In some companies, however, the report is seen by the employee, who has a chance to make comments on what has been written. This procedure means that the appraiser has to be considerably more tactful in wording any reservations about the employee's performance. On the other hand, it has the advantage of getting the employee more closely involved in the whole process.

DONCASTER ENGINEERING PLC

PERFORMANCE APPRAISAL REPORT   STRICTLY CONFIDENTIAL

Staff member: Isobel Gowdie
Date: 13/2/90
Current job title: Sales representative, Industrial Cleaners
Division: Marketing B3
Last appraisal: 13/2/89
Appraiser/manager: Alison McHeer, Head of Marketing
Date of start of current position: 9/4/88
Job description (delete as appropriate):
   Up to date   In need of revision (specify below)

A1. Refer to last year's appraisal objectives (section A3). In which areas has the employee been successful? What has the employee achieved of note in the last year?

Miss Gowdie has managed to rationalise the combining of Southern and Southwestern Sales Areas with only a 5 per cent loss in sales. This is better than was forecast. She has also mastered the specifications for the new line of floor polishers (TRB/3b) and produced a report for other reps explaining these changes succinctly.

A2. How has this success been achieved?

Miss Gowdie has shown herself willing to put in a reasonable amount of overtime and to work at home to bring herself up to date with changing conditions. She has also improved her personal knowledge of work and accounts procedure, and is showing increased confidence in her ability to handle large and complicated accounts.

A3. What can you do to build on these strengths? How can effective performance be improved, for example, by training, delegation of responsibility, or specialisation?

The proposed major overhaul of our product range will require new specifications for reps. In view of her successful report on last year's minor changes, I think we could assign Miss Gowdie the task of a thorough revision of the manual, with a corresponding reduction in her time on the road.

B1. In which areas has the employee been less successful?

While Miss Gowdie has successfully maintained our market share among large institutional customers, she has not improved our sales to smaller clients. I feel she lacks the confidence to approach possible new customers. She is not good at delegating responsibility, and so places unnecessary strain on herself. Moreover, her thorough approach, though commendable in many ways, has resulted in her spending too much time on minor matters.

B2. Were there any special circumstances that prevented the job holder from performing effectively? Has anybody helped or hindered performance? Did you give direction during the year?

My absence through injury in autumn doubtless contributed to Miss Gowdie's problems in organising her time. She has since received advice, and later a mild warning, on her failure to increase coverage of non-institutional clients. I have also tried to increase her self-confidence, and in this there may have been some success.

B3. What can be done to overcome these difficulties? Does the employee need more or less supervision/training/specialisation? Does the job description need to be changed.

There seem to me to be two possibilities. First, matters could be left as they are, with some further training and supervision in the matters mentioned in B1 and B2; I would have to oversee Miss Gowdie's delegation of responsibilities, at least for the time being. Secondly, her position could be made more 'office-based'. Miss Gowdie plans to marry in the not-too-distant future, and might therefore welcome a change from travel. The task mentioned in A3 could be assigned to her, and she could also see to the rearrangement of travel rosters and area coverage. This would leave me more time for the accounting side and for seeking new custom.

C. Appraiser's overall comment.

While Miss Gowdie is competent and thorough, I am not sure that she is best employed as a sales rep. Her organisational skills are of more use to us than her marketing ability. Her fine grasp of detail would be better employed in junior management.

D. Comment on the employee's relationships with other staff and his/her attitude to work.

Miss Gowdie is well-liked but tends to become wrapped up in her own tasks and problems. There has been some noise among junior staff that she can be quarrelsome at times. As her confidence increases, this irritability of hers may decrease proportionately.

She is active in various Company activities, particularly sporting.

Signed: *Alison McHeer*

E. Comments of appraiser's manager

Ms McHeer's suggestions should be considered at the Advisory Board meeting later in Spring.

Miss Gowdie appears to have made some progress over the last year, though not perhaps as much as we had hoped.

Signed: *Ralph Tinchell*

Director of Sales and Marketing

Here are some further points to bear in mind:

☐ Weigh up every word of your draft letter of reprimand, and be ruthless in deleting words that cannot be thoroughly justified.

☐ Choose the style of letter appropriate to the offence and, more particularly, to the recipient. Should it be *I'm disappointed in you*? Or perhaps *You must change your attitude*, or *You're letting the side down*? Or even *If things don't improve, there'll be changes around here*?

☐ Make sure your letter is absolutely clear and in a logical order, so that the recipient will see precisely what you mean. Use specific language, so that he or she knows exactly what the problem is, what corrective action must be taken, and what improvement you expect.

☐ Ask yourself not just if what you are writing is true but if it is the whole truth, without guesswork, prejudice, or rumour.

☐ Ask yourself, 'Does this letter contain anything that might rebound on me? What are its long- and short-term effects likely to be? Are they worth the potential trouble?'

☐ If you have any doubts, submit your letter to a 'neutral' colleague. And if that colleague has any doubts about the letter, scrap the whole idea. Call in the people concerned, and thrash the matter out face-to-face.

Here is an example of a reprimand addressed to an individual employee.

```
Dear Nicola

We have always valued the work you
do in the department, and been
impressed by your general
efficiency. However, I recently had
cause to look over some accounts
relating to pension contributions. I
must say that I was disappointed by
what I found, and even more so by
what I didn't find. Many of the
ledgers do not appear to have been
brought up to date for some weeks,
and the correspondence files
contained too many letters
complaining of unanswered queries.

I'm sure I don't need to remind you
that it is your responsibility to
keep the pension scheme papers up to
date. I realise that your department
has had difficulties with staff
changes recently, but that is all
the more reason for you to give
these matters extra attention.
```

```
You will understand how unpleasant
it is for me to write in this vein,
and I trust that I shan't have to do
so again. We rely on you, among your
other duties, to oversee this part
of our staff facilities. The general
staff have done very well in meeting
quotas in the last months, and it is
the duty of this company to see that
their interests are given the care
they deserve.

I shall be examining these accounts
again in a fortnight and expect to
find them up to date by then. Please
let me know if there are any special
difficulties with which you may need
help.

Yours sincerely

Gregory Mortimer
Senior Company Accountant
```

Here is a reprimand addressed to the whole staff.

```
INTERNAL MEMO

To:   All employees in the spinning
      mill
From: Factory Supervisor
Date: 4.2.1991

Reports have reached me of a number
of incidents and practices in the
spinning mill that have fallen below
the normally high standards of
behaviour of our staff.

In particular:

1. There have been a number of
thefts, both from personal lockers
and from Stores. I would urge staff
to think carefully before bringing
valuable personal possessions to
work, and to take greater care to
ensure their safety if they do.

It goes without saying that theft of
company or employee's property
constitutes gross misconduct and is
punishable by dismissal.

2. Please ensure that the locker
room and staff tea room are kept
tidy at all times. Please do not
leave waste paper, food, plastic
cups, and so on lying around; use
the bins provided.

3. Some members of staff have been
using the photocopier in the lobby
without authority. Please ensure
that you have a signed slip from
your foreman before using this
machine.

I am sure that you appreciate these
problems, and that you will do your
best to help to resolve them.
```

FORMAL WARNINGS

Other than for 'gross misconduct' – vandalism, theft, and the like – you should not sack people summarily. Prior to dismissal, the employee is usually entitled to a 'formal warning' – in effect, a last chance. Even this should be issued only after a formal investigation into the facts surrounding the alleged offence.

Remember that at every stage of the disciplinary process the accused person should have the opportunity to appeal and to have a colleague present during interviews.

If you do proceed with a formal letter of warning, make sure that it is reasoned and explicit. Let the employee know exactly where he or she stands. If the employee ignores the warning, you can take more drastic action. And remember, warnings are demands, and should be worded as such.

```
Dear Miss Lee

I regret to inform you that your
recent performance has not been up
to the standards demanded of staff.
In particular:

1. Staff handling fresh foods are
expected to maintain the highest
standards of hygiene. On 2 April you
were seen smoking in a prohibited
area, and warned about such action.
Do not do this again.

2. We have received two customer
complaints about short measure. You
have been shown how to fill cartons
on the delicatessen counter, and
should follow the instructions to
the letter.

3. We have also received complaints
that you spend time chatting to
friends who come in as 'customers'.
While you are quite at liberty to
exchange greetings with people you
know, you may not hold up queues in
order to do so. And you may not
allow personal friends to jump the
queue.

I expect to see an immediate and
sustained improvement in your
attitude and behaviour as outlined
above. If you fail to comply, the
company reserves the right to
terminate your contract with the
normal conditions.

Yours sincerely

Jeremiah Copley
Store Manager
```

DISMISSAL

Firing someone demands a cold, formal letter. By law, you normally have to give notice in writing, and give reasons (for further advice on this, see the chapter on dealing with subordinates, especially page 546). Failure to observe these procedures, or inaccuracy in the details of the reasons for the dismissal, could land you in an industrial tribunal. When the employee is in a trades union, speak to the union representative before sending the letter.

Here is a checklist of items to be included:

☐ the date.

☐ the employer's name. If your company does not have special dismissal forms, you can use company notepaper.

☐ the employee's full name, together with his or her job title and department.

☐ the date of termination of employment. Make sure you know what rights of notice the employee has before sending out the letter.

☐ the reasons for dismissal. Remember, these must be specific.

☐ a signature on behalf of the employer.

☐ if necessary, a duplicate copy to be signed by the employee as evidence of receipt.

```
Dear Miss Markan

This letter is to confirm that you
will cease work for the Company with
effect from Friday, 12 October 1990.

This action follows our letters of
warning dated 31 July and 17 August
1990, concerning your carelessness
in performing the work for which you
were employed. Specific instances
were detailed in the letters
mentioned and in our recent
discussions. To these may be added
your recent offensive and insulting
behaviour in the Audit Office.

Yours sincerely

Norbert Frampton
Personnel Manager
```

Letters notifying summary dismissal are similar, but the need to observe the formalities is even greater. Remember that an employee always has the right to appeal against his or her dismissal, usually to the Managing Director, whose decision is final.

```
         NOTIFICATION OF SUMMARY DISMISSAL

Name of employee:  Miss I. H. Markan
Job title:         Assistant
                   Production Manager
Department:        Production
Date:              11 July 1991


Details of offence:

At 5.30 p.m. on Tuesday, 9 July 1991,
you were seen by Mr S. Grass
removing three files relating to
your work and taking them to the
Maintenance Department. There you
were stopped as you were about to
put these files into the furnace of
the Company's heating system. On
being questioned, you admitted that
it had been your intention to
destroy the files, claiming you
found them 'boring'. Mr Grass
accordingly informed you that he
would report your conduct to me.

This matter was discussed at a
disciplinary hearing earlier today
and you were deemed to be guilty of
gross misconduct. You are therefore
dismissed from the company's
employment with immediate effect.

You have the right to appeal if you
consider you have been wrongly or
unfairly dismissed. If you wish to
appeal, you must submit your reasons
in writing within three days to Mrs
V. Rumbold, Managing Director of the
company.

You are asked to sign the duplicate
copy of this letter and give it to
your departmental manager in
acknowledgment of receipt of this
notification of summary dismissal.

Michael Donelly
Michael Donelly
Personnel Manager


I acknowledge receipt of this
notification of dismissal.

Signed: I. H. Markan   Date: 11 July 1991
```

LAYING STAFF OFF

Letters of redundancy are more complicated than letters of dismissal. The terms of redundancy have to be set out in full, and there is even greater need to give satisfactory reasons for the action that you are taking. In the nature of things, redundancy notices are written more in sorrow than in anger. Do everything in your power to make life easier for staff you are forced to lay off.

If you have to lay off a lot of staff at one time, write to each of them individually. You can often reduce the overall distress by calling for 'voluntary redundancies', with offers of more generous compensation for those who put themselves forward.

Remember too that it is your legal responsibility to consult the relevant trade union or staff representative body before announcing redundancies.

Here is an example of a letter sent to each member of a department, requesting volunteers and offering some compensation.

```
Dear Mrs Scrimgeour
As you will be aware, following the
abandonment of the Winter Floodlit
League, demand for luminous cricket
balls has dropped sharply. Your
department has therefore not been
making the profit necessary to
justify its present staff level. The
Company is forced to make savings,
and it is my unpleasant duty to
reduce labour costs by cutting staff
in your department by six as soon as
possible.

The Company regrets the hardship
that this decision will inevitably
cause. In order to limit this
hardship, we intend, in the first
instance, to try to achieve the
necessary reduction through
voluntary redundancies.

To encourage volunteers, we are
offering the following terms:

1.  Statutory redundancy pay, plus 25
    per cent of such pay.

2.  A lump cash sum of £500 for each
    completed year of employment with
    the company.

We are very sorry to be forced to
make this announcement: so many in
the department have given loyal and
valuable service to the Company over
a number of years. But financial
pressure has left us no choice.

Unfortunately, if no volunteers come
forward, individuals will have to be
chosen by the management. We
hope that this can be avoided.

Anyone interested in accepting
redundancy or wishing to have fuller
details can come and discuss this
matter with me in strict confidence.

Yours sincerely

Anthony Ellis
Personnel Manager
```

HANDING IN YOUR NOTICE

All resignations should be given in writing. If you are quitting a temporary job, the letter can be very short. Remember that the usual minimum period for giving notice is one month. And a longer period may be specified in your terms of employment.

Dear Mrs Black

I intend to stop working for Bert Weedon Builders on Friday, 7 August 1991. Kindly have my wages made up to that date and see that my P45 is ready for collection on my last day.

Yours sincerely

Horace Batchelor

Longer-term and more important posts require more detailed letters, to maintain the company's goodwill. Your letter of resignation should be fairly formal, as it will go into company records. Remember to:

☐ give notice of the date on which you will be leaving (subject to the terms and conditions of your contract).

☐ express your appreciation. Mention such things as the opportunities, friendship, and fun you have had.

☐ remind the employer of your achievements in the job, especially if you are going to be needing letters of reference – but don't overdo it.

☐ explain briefly why you are leaving.

☐ suggest how you can be replaced, if you think the company will have problems.

☐ leave the door open for your boss to call you in, beg you not to go, and offer you incentives to stay on.

Here are two further examples of letters of resignation.

The first is fairly straightforward: James Hooke is leaving his company to seek a better-paid job elsewhere.

But the conditions under which someone quits a job are not always amicable – as Paul Mendelson makes clear in the second letter.

Dear Michael,

After serious thought, I have taken the decision to leave the Company on Friday, 21 March 1991. We have spoken of this before, and I'm sure you will understand my present need to find work with higher pay such as a larger organisation would provide.

I have enjoyed my two years at Newton & Leibnitz greatly. The work has been varied and challenging, and I shall miss many of my fellow members of staff. I regret that financial pressure is making this move necessary.

I trust that the optical machine-tools that I designed and supervised the construction of will continue to function as well as they have done so far. I shall be happy to answer specific queries about them after my departure.

I shall of course help in training my replacement when he or she is appointed. I hope that we shall still have some kind of contact after I have left.

Please make up my salary and outstanding holiday pay to the date of my leaving. I shall give Personnel instructions relating to my pension contributions when I have your acknowledgment.

With thanks for everything,

James Hooke

Whatever your reason for resigning, keep your letter calm and dignified. This is not the place for outbursts of anger and recrimination.

Dear Malcolm

I have decided to resign from Marshall Engineering with immediate effect.

As you know, I have voiced strong objections to the Board's decision to start supplying military hardware to Potamia, which the Board has chosen to ignore. This has made my position in the Company intolerable, and I would rather leave now than carry on in an atmosphere of ill will. I'm sure you will appreciate that this is the best way.

For these reasons it would be best if I could leave at once without working out my period of notice. Could you kindly arrange to see me later today to discuss this and other outstanding matters?

Yours

Paul Mendelson

Taking on Staff

Advertisements in newspapers, specifications to employment agencies, and bulletins for the staff notice board all need to describe the job on offer. The length and detail of the description depend on where you are advertising.

You will probably have to think carefully before you decide exactly what you want to go into the advertisement, and what can be left to the letters you will send out to applicants. Start off by making a detailed job description. It should include the purpose, duties, and conditions of the post, and so on. Then you can extract the essential parts when announcing the vacancy.

The subheadings in the following example can be used for just about any job description. In simple cases you might not need to distinguish 'purpose' (a general description of the post), 'duties' (the day-to-day tasks the recruit will have to carry out), and 'responsibilities' (the supervision of personnel, money, and equipment).

```
                    OCEAN HARVEST LTD.
                     Job description

Job title        Assistant Production Manager
Department       Fish Processing
Reporting to     Production Manager, Fish Processing


Purpose          To ensure smooth day-to-day running of the processing
                 and packing departments, and to supervise orders from
                 smaller customers.

Duties           i.   Keeping work rosters up to date on a daily basis.
                 ii.  Taking instructions from Marketing on adjustments
                      to the production line to meet temporary needs, and
                      putting these instructions into effect.
                 iii. General supervision of workforce; allocating staff
                      to specific jobs; training new staff.
                 iv.  General supervision of production plant; giving
                      instructions to technical and maintenance
                      personnel.
                 v.   General supervision of orders from certain of our
                      smaller customers.
                 vi.  Checking that orders are correct when they leave
                      the factory.

Responsibilities i.   Ensuring that plant and machinery is in proper
                      state of repair and cleanliness; ordering
                      replacements from stores.
                 ii.  Making recommendations regarding:
                      a. utilisation of plant
                      b. utilisation of workforce
                      c. processing of orders
                 iii. Directing a workforce consisting of 2
                      engineers, 2 fork-lift truck drivers, 12 male
                      manual staff, and 42 female manual staff and
                      packers.

Relationships    Reporting to the Production Manager or, in his
                 absence, to the Production Executive. The job holder
                 will also have to work with suppliers and technicians
                 from outside.

Conditions       Office facilities are provided in the works office
                 within the processing plant. The duties are mostly
                 situated in the processing plant, though some contact
                 with stores, the technical department, and the offices
                 will be necessary.

                 Hours will be according to our shift rota, alternate
                 weeks 8 a.m. to 4 p.m. and 4 p.m. to midnight. At busy
                 seasons the job holder will be expected to work some
                 weekends as necessary.
```

```
Pay and holidays    Salary range £13,500 - £15,400.
                    Annual holiday 21 days plus public holidays.

Qualifications      The job holder should have a proven record in the
                    processing of fish (or other perishable foodstuffs).
                    He/she would normally have an appropriate degree (in
                    Food Sciences, Engineering, or the like), though other
                    qualifications (such as HND) will be considered.
```

ADVERTISING FOR AN EMPLOYEE

Make sure you get out your advertisements in time. Too many people leave advertising until the last moment and have to rush the whole hiring process. By adopting a consistent format for advertisements you can save yourself a lot of trouble. The advertisement should include the following:

☐ your company logo, if the advertisement is to be fairly large.

☐ your company name. Especially in small advertisements, place this at the bottom rather than the top. People looking for work tend to skim the tops of advertisements looking for the basic job titles, and want to be able to find them quickly.

☐ a brief description of the duties. Cut out the clichés. All workplaces are 'pleasant and congenial' in the eyes of their owners, and they all like to think of their companies as 'go-ahead' or 'progressive'. Stick to items such as pay, fringe benefits, career prospects, the location of the job.

☐ a brief description of the kind of applicant you are looking for, with details of experience demanded and qualifications.

☐ a direct statement of the pay offered. There can always be a bit of bargaining at the interviews.

☐ a clear statement of what kind of reply is required, to whom, where, and before when. Say whether references are requested at this stage. Give any reference numbers.

Secretary/Assistant required in a private Art Gallery. £4500 – £5500. Duties include relief receptionist/telephonist work, for which training will be given if necessary. Good typing (50 wpm) and clerical skills essential. Apply in writing, with full details of previous experience, to **The Curator, Ellis Art Galleries, Augustine Road, Wansford**.

HGV Class 2 driver required by construction company until September 1990. Full- or part-time. Clean licence essential. £5.50 an hour. Immediate start. Please phone Leslie Griffiths 0545 21894.

Assistant Production Manager
Fish Processing

Applications are invited for the post of assistant production manager in a large plant processing and packing seafoods. Experience in processing fish or perishable foodstuffs is essential, together with some knowledge of basic accounts procedure. The chosen applicant will be expected to direct a workforce of about 50, be responsible for the efficient use of plant, and link with other departments to meet production schedules. He or she should hold a degree in food sciences or engineering, though candidates with corresponding qualifications and/or experience will also be considered.

Salary £13,500 – £15,400. 21 days' paid holiday a year.

Full details and application forms can be obtained from *Mrs A. Dixon, Personnel Manager, Ocean Harvest Ltd., Immingham Road, Grimsby*. Please quote reference AD/APM/91/e2. Closing date for applications: 14 June.

EMPLOYMENT AGENCIES

If you are recruiting through an agency you should send basic job descriptions with a covering letter, such as this:

```
Dear Mrs Chambers

Please will you note that we have
the following vacancies:

1. Sales representative. To cover
East Anglia and sell and lease
building products and plant to
retail outlets and small companies.
Age range 25-40. Must have
successful experience in selling,
and be well-spoken and presentable
in appearance. Clean driving licence
essential. Basic salary £12,000 -
£13,500, plus commission. Company
car.
```

2. Trainee credit controller.
Suitable for school-leaver. 5 GCSEs,
including English and Maths. The job
involves both UK and overseas
accounts. Some knowledge of
bookkeeping would be an advantage.
Good references. Salary £5,500 –
£6,200.

Please let us know if you have
anyone suitable on your books.
Kindly do not send any candidates
who fail to meet these requirements.

Yours sincerely

Anthony Ellis

ACKNOWLEDGING APPLICATIONS

It is courteous to acknowledge all applications as they arrive. Many companies send out a rote letter, addressed 'Dear Applicant' – but with modern word-processing systems it is a simple matter to make the letter more personal by inserting the applicant's name.

Dear Miss Lynch

Thank you for your application for
the position of Programmer in our
Basingstoke offices. We are
considering applications at present
and will write to you again within
three weeks.

Yours sincerely

Norbert Frampton

Then, when you have sorted through the applications, it is time to invite those you have short-listed to an interview.

Dear Miss Lynch

We have studied your application with
interest, and would like to see you
for an interview. I have marked you
down for 11 am on Wednesday, 10
October. Please phone Mrs Sandra
Hacker on Ext. 2784 to confirm that
you will be able to attend. If the
time is not suitable, please discuss
an alternative with Mrs Hacker.

We shall be happy to reimburse you
for your travelling expenses.

I look forward to meeting you.

Yours sincerely

Norbert Frampton

CHECKING ON REFERENCES

The simplest way to contact referees named by applicants is by phone, though many companies will expect a letter first. And sometimes phoning is not possible, in which case a simple letter will do.

Dear Mr Aphelion

We are considering Miss Eunice Lynch
for the position of Programmer in
our IT department. The post requires
a general familiarity with data
processing on IBM mainframes and a
good knowledge of COBOL.

Miss Lynch has named you as a
referee. I believe she worked for
you as an IBM Programmer and Analyst
from 1987 to 1989. I would be most
grateful if you would give me your
opinion of Miss Lynch and any
comments you have about her
suitability for the post. I can
assure you that anything you say
will be treated in the strictest
confidence.

Yours sincerely

Norbert Frampton

OFFERING SOMEONE A JOB

The applicant has done well in the interviews and her references were satisfactory. You want to offer her the job.

Dear Miss Pearse

Following our interesting discussion
last Wednesday, I am pleased to
offer you the post of Sales Manager
in our EFL division, starting
Monday, 5 November 1990.

I enclose two copies of our
statement of Terms and Conditions of
Employment for the post. Kindly sign
the bottom copy and return it to us
as soon as possible to confirm
acceptance of this offer. Please do
not hesitate to contact me if you
have any questions. I also enclose a
cheque for £12.50 to cover your
travel expenses to the interview.

I look forward to welcoming you to
the company, and hope that your
career in our EFL division will be
long, pleasant, and rewarding.

Yours sincerely

Norbert Frampton

The next example is slightly different – it is a conditional offer of employment.

Dear Miss Chedwyn

We are glad to offer you the post of Cashier, starting on Monday, 5 August 1991. This offer is subject to receiving good references for you. Please will you therefore give us the names of two people who have known you for at least two years. At least one should be a current or former employer.

The position is also subject to a probationary period of three months. You will undergo training for three weeks, followed by a trial period. If your probationary period is satisfactory, you will be offered the post permanently.

During the probationary period your weekly wage will be £65. Assuming the post is made permanent, you would then be paid monthly, with an annual salary of £6300.

We look forward to seeing you at 9.30 a.m. on 5 August. I shall write again when your references have been received.

Yours sincerely

Augustina Dixon

TURNING DOWN A JOB APPLICANT

How much you say depends on whom you are rejecting and how he or she applied. When you are answering an 'on spec' enquiry you do not need to say more than this:

WRITING A JOB REFERENCE

You may want to supply references over the phone. It gives you the opportunity to find out exactly what the reference is for. And you may find it easier to say exactly what you think about the person – whether it is praise or warning that you have to offer – when you do not have to commit yourself in writing.

If you do give your reference by letter, remember that such letters are, by convention, formal and dull, revealing comparatively little about the person in question. If you have real feelings to express, positive or negative, you will have to go beyond the normal formulas, or speak in code.

Here, first of all, is a neutral, positive reference:

Dear Sir,

   In reply to your letter of 10 August, I am happy to supply a reference for Mr Dar.

   I knew Mr Dar at the time that he worked for this company, between 1987 and 1990. I always found him pleasant to work with, completely trustworthy, and competent in his duties as an electrical technician in our workshop. I am sure he would be an excellent chief technician in your industrial electronic repairs works.

      Yours faithfully,

      Anthony Ellis.

And here is an enthusiastic reference:

Dear Sirs

I am very happy to recommend Miss Lucy Pardew. During her years with us (1986–88), she showed herself to be reliable and hard-working. She showed a capacity for new ideas, many of which were implemented with profitable results, and paid close attention to all aspects of her duties. Her ability to get on with people around her won the respect of her colleagues and subordinates, and was instrumental in producing a congenial and cooperative working environment.

Yours faithfully

Saskia van Zyl

Employers may refuse to comment in writing rather than give a bad reference and so risk a libel action. Here, however, is a carefully worded warning:

Dear Mr Bryant

Orlando Driscoll worked as a sales representative for us from 1988 to 1989. His charm made him popular with clients at the outset, but he was made redundant when we found that sales in his area did not merit a separate representative there.

Yours in confidence,

Michael Donelly

Dear Mr Abbot

Thank you for your letter of May 9, in which you enquired about work openings within this company.

I regret to inform you that at present we have no vacancies, but we shall keep your letter on our files and let you know if anything suitable comes up.

In the meantime, I wish you well in your search for employment.

Yours sincerely

Norbert Frampton

Letters rejecting applicants for an advertised post at the first stage of selection are very similar.

Dear Mrs Bailey

Thank you for your application for the post of Senior Sales Executive with this company.

We have given your application serious consideration but I regret to inform you that we are unable to take your application any further on this occasion.

May I take this opportunity of wishing you well in your search for suitable employment.

Yours sincerely

Norbert Frampton

When someone within your company has applied for a post and been rejected, some sympathy and explanation are required.

Dear Fred,

This is to let you know that your application for promotion to Area Manager has been turned down by the board. I'm sure this will come as a great disappointment to you: I have been asked to pass on the gist of the selection panel's comments.

First, as you know, competition for the position was very strong. The man we have finally accepted has a first-class record in management and I'm sure will be a great asset to the company.

Secondly, the panel felt that you had not yet been in your current position long enough to qualify for

CONTRACTS OF EMPLOYMENT

Companies usually send out a Statement of the Terms and Conditions of Employment with the job offer. This Statement has to conform to legal standards.

It must include, or make reference to:

☐ the names of employer and employee

☐ the date of commencement of employment

☐ the period of any relevant previous employment

☐ the title of the job

☐ the rate of pay and the method by which it is calculated, including overtime rates, bonuses, commission, fringe benefits

☐ when the employee is paid, such as monthly or weekly, and on what date

☐ the hours of work

☐ holiday entitlement

☐ conditions relating to sick leave and sick pay

☐ any entitlement to pensions and pension schemes

☐ the notice that must be given by employer and employee

☐ any disciplinary rules that may affect the employee

☐ the name or job title of the person to whom the employee can apply for review in the event of disciplinary action, and how such applications should be made

☐ the name or job title of the person to whom the employee can apply to seek redress for any grievances against the company, and how such applications should be made

☐ whether the employment is subject to a contracting-out certificate issued under the Social Security Pensions Act 1975

Very often, rather than giving actual details of, say, disciplinary procedure, the contract will simply cross-refer to a Staff Manual or the like – see, for example, clauses 5 and 9 in the specimen contract alongside.

SCOTT-AUSTEN LTD.,
Downlands Way, Coleraine, Northern Ireland.
Telephone 0265 43008

EMPLOYMENT CONTRACT
Full Time

```
Employer:                      Scott-Austen Ltd. ('The Company')
Employee:                      Alison MacCleary
Initial Job Title:             Stock Controller
Date of Commencement
of Employment:                 6 November 1990
Previous service to count:     Nil
```

This contract incorporates the statement of particulars required to be given to you pursuant to the Employment Protection (Consolidation) Act 1978

All changes at any time which affect the contents of this statement, or of any documents mentioned in it, will be either announced to you in writing or issued in the form of a memorandum which will be entered in the Staff Manual. The Staff Manual and any other documents relating to your terms and conditions of employment will be available for your inspection in the Personnel Office.

1. Remuneration

(a) Your salary will be £7700 per annum.

(b) Your salary will be payable monthly in arrears on the 27th day of each month (or on the first subsequent working day).

(c) The Company will review your salary once in each calendar year on 30th September and, at its sole discretion, may decide to award you an increase.

2. Hours of Work

Your working week will be Monday to Friday from 9.00 a.m. to 5.00 p.m. with a one-hour paid lunch-break, usually taken between 1.00 p.m. and 2.00 p.m.

3. Overtime

You may be requested to work overtime by the Company but the allocation of overtime working is solely at the Company's discretion. At the time of your being asked to work extra hours your Manager will agree upon the terms of recompense, in other words, time off or a rate of pay.

4. Holidays

(a) In addition to Public Holidays, you are entitled to 20 working days' paid holiday in each complete period of one year from 1st April to 31st March worked, to be taken at such time as shall be agreed upon between you and the Company.

(b) Your holiday entitlement will be reduced pro rata in the event that you work for a part only of a holiday year, and you will be entitled to be paid in respect of any holiday entitlement due to you at the date of termination of your employment with the Company.

(c) Holiday entitlement accrues at the rate of 1.67 days per month.

(d) You may not take any holiday during the first three months of employment, but your holiday entitlement shall accrue during this period.

(e) Only in very special circumstances may holiday entitlement arising in respect of one holiday year be carried over into the following year. In such a case you must obtain a letter of authority signed by a Director.

5. Illness or Incapacity

(a) At the discretion of the Company you will be paid your basic salary during any absence from your duties hereunder caused by illness or incapacity for a period based upon your length of service with the Company, as set out on page 12 of the Staff Manual.

(b) You must notify your Manager (or if he/she is not available some other senior member of staff) by telephone as soon as it becomes apparent that you will not be able to attend to your duties.

→

←

(c) All other conditions relating to absence due to illness or incapacity are set out on page 12 of the Staff Manual.

6. Pensions

As the Company has a contracting-out certificate in force under the Social Security Act 1975, eligible employees may be invited to contribute to its pension scheme. Details of the Company pension scheme will be given to eligible personnel by the Financial Director.

7. Period of Notice

(a) The period of notice required to be given by you in writing in respect of the termination of your employment is 4 weeks.

(b) The period of notice required to be given by the Company in writing in respect of the termination of your employment is:

If employed for less than 4 years: 4 weeks.
If employed for more than 4 but less than 12 years: 1 week for each complete year of service.
If employed for over 12 years: 12 weeks.

(c) The Company may terminate this Agreement without notice if at any time you:

(i) are found guilty of wilful neglect in discharge of your duties as listed under your job title in Section 2 of the Staff Manual;

(ii) are found guilty of gross misconduct as defined in Section 3 of the Staff Manual;

(iii) become bankrupt or make any composition with your creditors;

(iv) become of unsound mind or if, while you are a patient within the meaning of the Mental Health Act 1959, an order be made in respect of your property under Section 102 of that Act;

(v) are convicted of any criminal offence (other than an offence under the Road Traffic Legislation for which a penalty of imprisonment is not imposed) in the United Kingdom or elsewhere.

(d) The Company reserves the right to pay salary in lieu of notice.

8. Confidentiality

Your work with the Company may give you access to confidential information concerning the trade secrets, organisation, business, finances, transactions, or affairs of the Company, its subsidiaries, clients, agents, or customers. You must not make use of, or reveal to any third party, any such confidential information without the Company's express consent in writing. This applies equally during your employment and after the termination of your employment.

9. Disciplinary Rules & Grievance Procedure

The Company's policy in respect thereof is set out in Section 4 of the Staff Manual.

10. Note

These Terms and Conditions of Employment supersede all previous contracts between the Company and the employee, whether written, oral, or implied.

Any change in these terms and conditions will be notified to you in writing.

I accept and acknowledge receipt of an identical copy of this Employment Contract.

Signed by the employee: *Alison MacCleary*

Signed for and on behalf of the Employer: *Ferdinand Scott-Austen*

Date: *9th November 1990*

the promotion. They were impressed
with all reports on your work, but
feel that you still have to pick up
experience 'in the raw' before being
suitable for upper management.

The board have asked me to say
that if, in a year or two's time, a
comparable position falls vacant,
they would welcome another
application from you. Please do not
think that the company does not
appreciate your outstanding
contribution.

Best wishes,

Belinda Postlethwaite.

WELCOMING A NEW RECRUIT

As manager or employer, you might consider it a
nice touch to have a note of welcome waiting for a
new employee on his or her arrival. Or you can mail
it shortly before the person's employment starts.
The letter also offers you the chance to give a few
helpful and reassuring details about the job.

Dear Miss MacCleary

Thank you for returning our
Statement of the Terms and
Conditions of Employment duly
signed. We look forward to seeing
you on 6 November.

When you arrive, please could you
report to reception at 10 a.m. and
give your name to the receptionist.

You will then be taken to your
manager, Mrs Wilson, who will give
you further instructions and show
you around the offices and works. At
12 a.m. there will be a meeting for
all new staff, at which various
points of company policy will be
explained and you will be able to
ask questions.

During your first few weeks with us
you will be supervised by our Stock
Controller, Sammy Fitzgerald. He
will instruct you in your duties and
our working procedures.

I hope that you will enjoy working
for us and find your time here
rewarding, and that we shall have a
long and profitable relationship.

Welcome to Scott-Austen.

Yours sincerely

Michael Donelly
Personnel Manager

QUILL, WAX, AND POUNCE BOX

In the age of the computer and word processor, it is hard to imagine what offices were
like before the invention of even the typewriter.
All letter-writing and bookkeeping tasks were
done by hand, using feather quills and the
accompanying paraphernalia of pounce box
(to sprinkle sand over the paper to dry the ink),
wafers, sealing wax, and so on. In the following
extract from Charles Dickens's novel *Nicholas
Nickleby*, the hero makes his start as a
bookkeeper in the offices of the benevolent
Cheeryble brothers, under the keen eye of their
head clerk, the meticulous (but engagingly
good-natured) Tim Linkinwater.

Tim Linkinwater turned pale, and, tilting up
his stool on the two legs nearest Nicholas,
looked over his shoulder in breathless
anxiety. Brother Charles and brother Ned
entered the counting-house together; but
Tim Linkinwater, without looking round,
impatiently waved his hand as a caution
that profound silence must be observed,
and followed the nib of the inexperienced
pen with strained and eager eyes.

The brothers looked on with smiling faces,
but Tim Linkinwater smiled not, nor moved
for some minutes. At length, he drew a long
slow breath, and, still maintaining his
position on the tilted stool glanced at
brother Charles, secretly pointed with the
feather of his pen towards Nicholas, and
nodded his head in a grave and resolute
manner, plainly signifying 'He'll do.'

Brother Charles . . . exchanged a laughing
look with brother Ned; but, just then,
Nicholas stopped to refer to some other
page, and Tim Linkinwater, unable to
contain his satisfaction any longer,
descended from his stool, and caught him
rapturously by the hand.

'He has done it!' said Tim, looking round at
his employers and shaking his head
triumphantly. 'His capital *B*'s and *D*'s are
exactly like mine; he dots all his small *i*'s
and crosses every *t* as he writes it. There an't
such a young man as this in all London . . .
not one. Don't tell me! The City can't produce
his equal. I challenge the City to do it!'

How to Write Reports

A REPORT can be anything from a two-line hand-written memo to a bound volume with hundreds of closely typed pages. It may deal with the fate of the national economy and be read by government ministers. Or it may deal with the fête of your local horticultural society and be read by the members of its fund-raising committee.

The key principle of report writing could hardly be simpler. It is a question of identifying the key facts of a particular matter, and then presenting them in the right order as simply and directly as possible.

Writing a report may involve laborious research, and then seemingly endless juggling with words, facts, and figures to present the gathered information in the most effective way. But it is almost always worth the effort. Your report, with its detailed information, its conclusions, and its recommendations, provides the basis for decisions. And decisions make the wheels of the world go round.

The 'terms of reference' of a report direct the writer or writers to cover certain clearly defined topics – to investigate a particular product, say, or an event, company, or proposal. The terms of reference also dictate the kind of report, whether it should be:

☐ an investigation or examination report, in which the writer describes the investigation carried out and its findings – and no more

☐ a recommendatory report, in which the writer suggests courses of action in the light of his or her findings

☐ a progress report, in which the writer investigates the state of play at a particular point in, say, a long-term training programme

A very long and formal report might contain all the following components:

OPENING SECTIONS

☐ Title (title page)

☐ Terms of reference/objectives

☐ Table of contents

☐ List of charts, diagrams, and illustrations

☐ Preface

☐ Acknowledgments

☐ Abstract – or summary of the findings to be detailed in the body of the report

BODY OF THE REPORT

☐ Introduction

☐ Investigation, and its outcome

☐ Conclusions and recommendations

APPENDICES

☐ Endnotes

☐ Bibliography

☐ Supplementary material – such as extra figures and facts

☐ Index

If you are commissioned to write a short report, don't try to cover all the details described in this chapter. The principles certainly remain the same, especially when it comes to writing the body of the report, but only a few of the sections will be applicable to your report.

Preliminary Strategies

Before doing any research or writing, build up a clear picture of who your readers will be. Will they be company directors or technicians, local councillors or national leaders? And how extensive will your readership be – a handful of senior managers or a wide range of company employees? The clearer you are about your readership, the easier it will be to write a successful report.

The make-up of your readership will determine:

☐ how you shape the report as a whole – where you place the emphases

☐ what you can afford to omit, or what you can assume the reader already knows

☐ how to pitch the language, especially when it comes to using technical terms

As you write the report, remind yourself constantly of your typical reader. Bear in mind that he knows far less about the topic than you do: after all, you have now done a great deal of research, and have become something of an expert on the subject. Keep thinking of the questions he might be asking as he reads the report. Ask yourself: 'Have I expressed myself clearly? Now what would the reader like to know next?'

Don't on the other hand, treat your reader as an ignoramus. A patronisingly oversimplified report is just as irritating to the reader as an unintelligible overtechnical report.

Don't intrude your opinions. Your task is to provide facts, not personal views – unless you were asked for them in the terms of reference. Be objective and balanced. Present all sides of a question. The only place where you may legitimately present decided opinions is in the recommendations section.

Be absolutely clear about your terms of reference. If you have any doubts about the range or depth of a listed topic, ask for clarification.

Be clear too about the expected level of commitment. Is the report to be a major work, taking up a great deal of your time and energy? Or is it really just a small matter, not much more than an extended memo? Should you write 100 pages – or two?

Try to find out the context in which the report has been requested. Why do those who commissioned it want it? Perhaps to resolve a disagreement between members of the board or committee. If so, make especially sure to present both sides of the questions scrupulously fairly.

Draw up a systematic timetable. Find out when the report is due, and how much time you will be allowed off work, say, to do it. Break the project down into small tasks, and work out a day-by-day or week-by-week schedule. (Don't forget to budget for emergencies – a rail strike, illness, and so on.)

But don't be hidebound by your timetable. Some tasks will take longer than you expect: new leads will emerge during the research, drawing you along unexpected byways. Some tasks may take less time than you expect. Always be prepared to adapt or deviate from your timetable, but do keep one item sacrosanct – the final deadline.

Research

Your first task is to gather the necessary information. This is a more complex and demanding job than many people realise. For a start there are so many different activities involved. Depending on the kind of report you have to write, your research might involve a number of the following: rummaging in libraries, interviewing people, conducting laboratory experiments, listening to tapes, watching training videos, and so on. Each of these requires a distinctive frame of mind, and each may take you to a quite different location. The specialised books and records you need may be available only in a London library, while the people you have to interview may be in Glasgow.

PLANNING YOUR RESEARCH

Don't be put off by the size of the task that lies ahead. Once again, prepare a plan, breaking up the job into manageable chunks.

First you must identify the main topics to cover. Begin by studying the terms of reference. Then work out how and where you will get the information you need on each topic. Will it involve, say, library work, interviewing people, conducting experiments, phoning round to suppliers of equipment?

Plan this phase of research very thoroughly. Where exactly is the best place to get the information you need? How exactly will you conduct the experiment? Does that library really have the complete set of records you want? Phone them to find out. They may not have the full set, in which case a visit there would have been wasted time. Or they may suggest a library much closer to you that would serve your purpose equally well.

Now work out your schedule. Allow yourself plenty of time. How long do you have for the entire process of preparing and writing the report? You may have to assign half that time or more to the research.

Make a list of the tasks to be done and places to be visited. Work out the best order for tackling them – not necessarily the straightforward topic-by-topic order. A particular library, for instance, may have information relevant to two widely separated topics, and you would obviously deal with both of them there and then, rather than return to the library two or three days later.

MAKING AND STORING NOTES

There are two sides to research – gathering your material, and ordering it. Don't neglect either. As you collect your information, you should be constantly classifying it into clearly labelled groups and subgroups – so that later you can retrieve items as efficiently as possible.

Here are a few useful note-taking schemes for report writing. Choose whichever of them suits you and your working habits, and then stick to it.

Using index cards. Write your notes on these, starting a new card for each new subject. At home or in the office you should have a filing drawer or cabinet (or even a shoe box) organised according to topic. At the end of each research session you slot your cards into it at the appropriate place.

Suppose you have been researching security devices for your residents' association, and are now at last writing up the report. When you come to write the section on burglar alarms, you simply turn to the relevant part of the file and find gathered there all your notes, made at various times, on burglar alarms.

Index cards come in two main sizes. The smaller ones are handier – you can easily fit them into a jacket pocket or handbag – but the larger ones are more practical if you have to take extensive notes.

Using note pads. The principle is the same as for index cards, but the pages go into loose-leaf folders rather than cabinets. They give you more room than index cards, but can be more awkward to use sometimes – when taking notes in shops or on the street, for instance.

Using bound notebooks. The great advantage of these is that you cannot lose vital sheets of notes; the great drawback is lack of flexibility. You cannot move notes from one book to another according to topic. However, an alphabetical division of the notebook, or a careful indexing system, could overcome that problem.

Choose hardback notebooks – so that you can take notes easily when standing up if necessary. Quarto size is generally best, small enough to be handy, large enough to give you room. Ideally the book should have an alphabetical thumb index down the long outer edge of the pages. If not, divide the book up into sections of your own choosing at the outset.

Using word processors. If you have access to a portable 'laptop' word processor, this might suit you best of all when it comes to taking notes. You simply carry it with you to, say, the library, and type your notes straight into it. Later, back home or at the office, you can reorganise and classify the material at your leisure.

A non-portable word processor has its uses too. You may have to take longhand notes initially, but if you type them up afterwards, classifying and clarifying them, this might well save time in the long run.

Using a cassette recorder. This is impractical for confidential notes, and for any workplace where the sound of your voice would disturb others. But for outdoor interviews, say, a small modern cassette recorder with built-in microphone can be ideal. But remember that you will have to make a transcript.

Whichever method you choose, do keep updating and reorganising your notes. And always bear in mind two further rules.

One: never trust your memory. If you have not bothered to take notes, the chances are that you will forget something important.

Two: keep your notebook or file cards on you at all times. You never know when you will come across information that might be useful.

QUESTIONNAIRES

For some kinds of research, you will need to compile questionnaires – when you want to find out public attitudes towards your company's proposed new trademark, for example, or when polling employees' feelings about early retirement.

Compiling questionnaires is far from straightforward. Here are some tips. First, on the wording and content of the questions.

☐ Phrase your questions as simply as possible. *Would you retire...?* rather than **?** *Are you prepared to contemplate retirement...?* Above all, avoid jargon or technical terms if any of the respondents is a non-expert.

□ Phrase your questions in such a way as to invite a very brief answer (such as *yes, no, probably*). Again, *Would you retire...?* rather than **?** *How do you feel about the idea of retiring...?*

□ Be specific: *Would you retire at 62...?* rather than **??** *Would you be prepared to retire earlier than scheduled...?*

□ Be clear, making no assumptions and risking no ambiguity: *Would you retire at 62 if offered right then the full 65-year-old's pension?* rather than **??** *Would you retire at 62 rather than 65?*

□ Arrange the questions in a logical order, revealing a clearly developing train of thought.

□ If you do want to include any trick questions – to check the respondents' consistency or sincerity, say – slip them in skilfully and inconspicuously. If an odd question suddenly appears without any apparent relation to the surrounding questions, it will only succeed in alerting the respondents to the danger.

□ Keep the questionnaire as short as possible. The longer it goes on, the more unreliable the later responses become – either through the respondents' fatigue or resentment.

□ Don't allow your own prejudices to slip into the question. It can bias the answers. Ask: *Do you agree or disagree that we should introduce a 'No smoking' rule? Please give reasons*, rather than *Why do you think we should introduce a 'No smoking' rule?*

Secondly, some tips on how to get the right layout for your questionnaire.

□ Keep the layout simple. Divide the questions into sections, if necessary, and give each section a clear heading.

□ Where the respondent has to give figures in answer to questions, provide clear vertical columns in which he or she can fill them in.

□ Use an easily legible typeface for the printing.

□ Use a tough paper if the conditions demand – if the questionnaire is going to pass through several hands, for instance.

□ Experiment with layouts if time allows. Leave plenty of space for full answers, bearing in mind that some people's handwriting is much larger than other's, but not so much space as to encourage the respondents to waffle.

Arrange the questions in a logical order, revealing a clearly developing train of thought.

KNOWING WHEN TO STOP

The inexperienced researcher faces an unexpected problem: knowing when to stop researching. The trick is to pause every so often, check the original brief, and assess the material you have accumulated. If you notice important gaps, you had better continue researching, if time allows.

But if you feel reasonably in command of all the topics, and have a broad idea how they relate to one another and how the report as a whole might take shape, then call a halt to your research. Overdoing it may just confuse your ideas, and will certainly leave less time for actually writing them up.

To test if you are ready to move on to the next stage, try answering these questions:

□ Do you have a 'feel' for the subject as a whole? Do you feel on top of the individual topics?

□ Are you beginning to see why the report was commissioned in the first place?

□ Do you know, at least hazily, the shape you want the report to take?

□ Have you gathered balanced information? Have you tapped a variety of research sources? If you have interviewed 100 people and not read a single book on the topic, or read 100 books and not spoken to one person, should you not broaden your search slightly before committing yourself to the writing?

☐ Is your material balanced? If you have a mass of notes on one aspect of the report, and scarcely any on another aspect, does that reflect their relative importance, or does it point to inadequate researching?

Drafting

When you begin the drafting stage of report writing, don't make the mistake of starting at the beginning. Leave the opening sections of the report – the title page, terms of reference, table of contents, and introduction – to the very end.

The reason for this contrary ordering is simple. You cannot introduce your report without first knowing what is going into it. Only as you are writing up the investigation and its outcome will your ideas become clear: new ideas, or at least new emphases, will occur to you, and you may even find yourself reaching quite different conclusions from those that seemed to be emerging during the time you were engaged in the research itself. 'Writing up' gives the final shape to your discoveries.

In fact, you will probably need several trial drafts, and will probably experiment with different ways of organising the material. To produce something that reads easily and logically, you will probably have to write your report with considerable difficulty, and in an illogical sequence.

And don't expect perfection. You can gnaw away at a piece so long as time allows, but eventually you have to call a halt. Afterthoughts will plague you. If only I had altered that page, switched those two lines, given that point greater emphasis . . . The awful truth is that the conscientious report writer will never feel that his report is perfect.

Don't, however, make this an excuse for shoddy presentation. At least build into your timetable some spare time at the end for last-minute improvements and polishing.

PLANNING THE STRUCTURE

There are two basic approaches to planning your structure – planning by outlines, and planning by rough drafts. Each approach produces in the end a clear, well-ordered list of points (the basis from which you will write up your first full draft). But the routes to this list are rather different. Here is a summary of them:

To plan by means of a schematic outline. Jot down any ideas that occur to you for inclusion in the report. Read them through: they will probably generate further ideas, which you should jot down too. Study them, noting relationships between them, then start grouping various items under broad headings. Shift these various headings about, until the best sequence emerges.

To plan by means of a rough draft. Just pick on any one idea, and start writing as if you were drafting a full report. Write as quickly as possible, and without direction. Ignore grammar, logical development, and so on.

Each time a new idea occurs to you, start writing it up at once. When new ideas tumble out too fast, jot them down on a separate sheet of paper (grouping them according to themes, if possible).

The very act of writing so intensely should help not only to generate relevant ideas, but also to churn them about productively, and to crystallise them into a coherent pattern. You can now compile a well-structured outline very quickly, and begin writing a proper draft on the basis of that.

The body of the report. Bear in mind, when outlining the body of a report, that you need to cover the following three aspects:

☐ a description of your investigations – the experiments you conducted, for example, the surveys and interviews you carried out, the documents you consulted

☐ an account of the findings that emerged from the investigations – the legal position, say, or the statistics on public attitudes

☐ your interpretations of the findings – the trends you observe, plus possible explanations for them

Most reports cover a number of distinct topics. You will now have to choose between two rival structures – either dealing with each topic in turn (in each of the three aspects), or with each aspect in turn (going through the topics one by one).

Another choice may confront you when it comes to ordering the sections and subsections: whether to proceed from low-priority or known information to high-priority or new information (thus producing a dramatic structure – building up to a climax) or vice versa (on the assumption that readers pay more attention to early sections).

Starting with the new or most important information, is usually safer, but if you suspect a hostile response from your readers, you may decide to try the other approach – easing them gently into your way of thinking to convert them to your views.

Experiment with various structures – shuffling small points between groups, shifting the sequence of large sections – until you settle on an outline that best balances all your competing emphases.

PREPARING FOR WRITING UP

You can now start to put flesh on the bones of your structure, by jotting down notes alongside each item in the outline.

Rely on your memory at first, and see what that throws up. As you make these notes, so your thoughts on the various subjects will clarify. All the time, you will be ordering and assimilating the raw information – and the later task of writing the first draft will be that much easier.

Next return to your notes. Sort them into batches according to the sections of your structure. Then read carefully through them, underlining the phrases and sentences you think most important.

Transfer key facts, insights, and thoughts to your index cards, thus continuing the process of clarifying and refining what you want to say.

Think too at this stage about any illustrations, charts, or diagrams you may want to include. You may have most of them prepared already, if only in sketch form. You need now to spend time making clean copies. You may also want to have some of them photographed, photocopied, or professionally redrawn. Deal with this task now, rather than later, to allow plenty of time for corrections.

WRITING UP

At last you are in a position to start writing up your first draft. Plunge straight in. Don't wait for inspiration. Don't bother about style or grammar at this early stage. Just write.

BIRTH PANGS: THE CREATIVE PROCESS

Getting started – that is always the challenge as you embark on any creative enterprise. You may be a composer seeking inspiration for a symphony, a painter or novelist starting out on a long-planned masterpiece – or a company employee scratching your head as you set about the first draft of a report on recruiting policy for your boss. There is always the same tension – the same glaring emptiness of the white page or canvas – the anxiety about where to make the first mark. Winston Churchill – a keen amateur painter – knew these feelings. In this passage he describes the pangs and joys of beginning a painting.

> ... the next step was to *begin*. But what a step to take! The palette gleamed with beads of colour; fair and white rose the canvas; the empty brush hung poised, heavy with destiny, irresolute in the air. My hand seemed arrested by a silent veto. But after all the sky on this occasion was unquestionably blue, and a pale blue at that. There could be no doubt that blue paint mixed with white should be put on the top of the canvas. One really does not need to have an artist's training to see that. It is a starting-point open to all. So very gingerly I mixed a little blue paint on the palette with a very small brush, and then with infinite precaution made a mark about as big as a pea upon the affronted snow-white shield. It was a challenge, a deliberate challenge; but so subdued, so halting, indeed so cataleptic, that it deserved no response.
>
> *Thoughts and Adventures* (1932)

Remember, deep thought alone never got a report written. The only way to get going is to get going. Time enough, once you have a rough draft, to add and subtract, rethink and re-edit, hone and polish.

The second or revised draft requires a more reflective approach. Test the structure and the links or transitions between sections. And correct the style and grammar this time. Modulate the tone – formal without being dull. As a general rule, lean towards the third person – *her, she, they*. But where appropriate, boldly use the first person – *I, we* – and the second *you*. Don't allow too much of your personality to intrude but don't hide it altogether.

Crisp objectivity then – not cold and clinical objectivity, however – is the hallmark of good report writing, not only of long formal reports, but also of shorter, less formal reports and memos.

Wherever possible express yourself in positive rather than negative terms. Emphasise what was done, rather than what was not. Use sober, factual language, not superlatives or extravagant expressions. Positive but restrained language conveys an impressively authoritative tone.

CONCLUSIONS AND RECOMMENDATIONS

Having completed the body of the report – describing the investigation and its outcome – you now have to add your conclusions and any recommendations, and to draft the introduction.

For your conclusions, first summarise your general findings. Bring together the various results of, say, your laboratory experiments or market research. List some of the points that seem to emerge consistently from these results.

Secondly, indicate what one can deduce from these findings – what the root causes are, for instance, and how changes can be made. So, in explaining poor sales of a particular product, you might highlight the public's dislike of its packaging. You could then show how the sales and design departments have already addressed this problem by making the necessary changes, and how sales have improved as a result.

Finally, list your recommendations – if the terms of reference ask for them. This section might well be the most forceful part of the report: you bring home to your readers the practical implications of your findings – exactly what steps to take to improve security in the new marketing strategy.

Typically and logically, the recommendations section would appear near the end of the report. But not always. Your instructions may be to insert your conclusions and recommendations near the beginning. Or you may simply feel that further action is urgent, and that the recommendations for such action should have far greater prominence in the report than the background details of research procedures. In this case, revise the order of the report drastically. After a brief introduction, state your conclusions and recommendations. You can then omit the abstract (see below), and go on to write the 'body' of the report.

THE INTRODUCTION

The purpose of an introduction is to set the scene. Keep it short. It should take no more than a sentence or two to explain, for example, that what follows is an analysis of current security arrangements in the company. Note that shorter reports, especially those destined for a select group or committee, sometimes begin with the address, the date, and a salutation, as though taking the form of a letter. The salutation might read, for example, 'Dear Sir' or 'Gentlemen'.

Opening and Closing

Once you have completed the first draft of the report, spend as much time as necessary polishing it – rewording awkward sentences, filling in gaps, reordering items to tighten the links between them.

Then it is time to compile and attach the preliminaries. Most of these apply to formal and long or longish reports. On short or informal reports, they would usually look out of place.

THE TITLE PAGE

Choose your title carefully. The shorter the better – anything more than a dozen words begins to look unwieldy, but don't sacrifice clarity. Your choice of words should be so apt and precise that the reader will get his or her bearings immediately.

Position the title about four inches from the top – just above the middle of the title page. Run it across two or three short centred lines. (Choose carefully where you break each line.) Other title-page information follows beneath – specifically, the name of the author or authors, the date, and who commissioned the report (if applicable):

Report on Security Devices
in Mainwaring Court

by

Fred Murray

18 October 1990

For: The Residents' Association, Mainwaring Court, London NW7 6BC

If the report is of a meeting, include the names of those present just after the title. List them in two groups: under the heading *Present*, those who are members of the board or committee; under the heading *In attendance*, those who were present but are not members.

TERMS OF REFERENCE

Next, on a new page, state the terms of reference or objectives you were given. Traditionally, you use the infinitive form of the verb: *to report on*, *to investigate*, or the like. For example:

TERMS OF REFERENCE
In accordance with the instructions of the Joint Committee, to report on the security devices used by residents of Mainwaring Court, especially in comparison with Harrow Hall.

Below this, explain your procedure – that is, give the reader a brief account of how you obtained the information, and what methods you used to process it. For instance:

This report is based on the results of a wide survey, conducted by questionnaire or personal interview, with 85 per cent of the residents of Mainwaring Court and Harrow Hall responding.

If necessary, you can also justify briefly the approach you have taken. If you chose a particular starting point or way of working, in the face of an obvious alternative, now is the time for you to explain your reasons.

TABLE OF CONTENTS

This gives a complete list of the section and subsection headings, with the number of the page on which each begins. In long formal reports, the table of contents is crucial. It not only enables the readers to find a specific section they are looking for, but also gives them an overview, and hence a feel for the report as a whole.

Initially, do no more than pencil in the page numbers. You will probably find yourself making last-minute adjustments, cutting and expanding sections, or changing their order. It only takes one extra paragraph to add a page to the whole report – and to throw your page numbering out of sequence.

Following the table of contents, include if necessary, a list of charts, diagrams, and illustrations, again with page numbers attached.

THE PREFACE

A brief preface or foreword is necessary only for a very long report. It provides you with another opportunity to qualify or justify your approach. You may need to excuse a gap in your research, for example, or to explain why you chose to include a section that seems of doubtful relevance. In a long report, it is also a good idea to give a brief summary of your objectives and conclusions right at the start.

ACKNOWLEDGMENTS

This section gives you the chance to note or thank people and institutions that have helped you in your research – perhaps your research assistant, or a newspaper library, or simply colleagues or friends who gave you moral support.

Most people appreciate seeing their names in print, but often you cannot mention every person involved. It should be enough to write, for instance, 'the Head Librarian, Ms Jones and her members of staff'. Make sure to spell people's names correctly. In the case of financial aid, you should definitely acknowledge the individuals or groups who provided any (though not the amounts provided).

THE ABSTRACT

An abstract, or synopsis, usually takes the form of a single, tightly packed paragraph. It should summarise the aim, results, and recommendations of the report. The reader should be able to tell, from a glance at it, what the outcome of the research was.

Take great care over the abstract; it is one of the trickiest sections to write. To condense a 100-page report into one short paragraph is bound to oversimplify things, but should not distort them. Try to reflect at least the salient points, and to convey the tone and emphasis of the report.

FOOTNOTES, ENDNOTES, AND BIBLIOGRAPHY

In compiling your report, you may refer to a published work, or even quote directly from it. In each case, you need to provide full details of your source. You can do this in any of three ways: in a footnote (a note at the foot of the page); in an endnote (a note at the end of the report, or at the end of the section); or in a bracketed reference (immediately following the quotation or statistic in the running text).

All three forms of reference try to balance two conflicting problems – inconvenience when it comes to checking, and distraction or ugliness. Endnotes are least distracting or ugly, since they are tucked away out of sight at the end; but for that very reason they are most inconvenient to find and check. Bracketed references within the running text are extremely convenient, but can be a distracting eyesore when dotted liberally about the page. Footnotes, providing the best balance perhaps, are unfortunately the most difficult to type (though some word processors can now fit them in automatically on the page).

The style of footnotes and endnotes varies from publisher to publisher, and institution to institution. Find out if the company or institution sponsoring your report has its own 'house style'. If not, you could follow this typical pattern:

> 5 Winston Pie and Wilfred Smyth, *The Nature of Nurture* (New York: Proud Press, 1930), p 111.

If you have a formal bibliography at the end of the report, you would typically enter the same book as follows, using full stops this time to separate the main elements.

> Pie, Winston, and Wilfred Smith. *The Nature of Nurture*. New York: Proud Press, 1930.

Do remember to acknowledge every single quotation you use in your report, and every borrowed idea or phrase (though where possible try to consolidate neighbouring citations into a single reference note, for economy's sake). And don't forget to acknowledge too every illustration, chart, list of figures, and so on that you have borrowed from elsewhere.

SUPPLEMENTARY MATERIAL

Some information may be relevant to the report but not fit easily into the main body: a set of graphs, say, or some background letters and articles. It is less distracting to position them at the end of the report. So too with extra statistical or technical information: if the reader is likely to want to reinterpret it rather than rely on your analysis, provide it in a separate appendix.

Some supplementary material may not lend itself for binding within the report – slides, for instance, or models or samples. For slides, a special transparency pocket is available which can be stuck to the binding. For bulky or three-dimensional items such as samples, try to find a way of binding, boxing, or framing them so that the design and colour harmonise with the report itself. The two parts then obviously 'go together'.

NUMBERING AND LETTERING

Traditionally, each section of a long report has an identifying number or letter. As with the table of contents, this numbering helps the reader to follow the overall structure of the report.

The conventional order for numbering and lettering sections is as follows. If the report has no more than two layers of heading, the main sections take Arabic numerals – 1, 2, 3 – and the subsections take lower-case letters in brackets: (a), (b), (c). In more complex hierarchies, introduce progressively capital letters – A, B, C – and then capital Roman numerals – I, II, III – for higher sections. For the lower sections add bracketed lower-case Roman numerals at the end: (i), (ii), (iii).

A detailed layout might then look like this:

A. FIRST MAJOR SECTION

I. First Subsection of Major Section

1. **Subsidiary matter**
Text . . .
2. **More subsidiary matter**
More text . . .

(a) subsection
(b) another subsection

(i) a sub-subsection of point 2(b)
(ii) and another

An alternative system is becoming increasingly popular, using only Arabic numerals and decimal points. It is sometimes called the Dewey system, after the system of cataloguing library books.

1. NUMBERING

1.1. **The First Subsection Heading**

1.1.1. Each paragraph or section under the above heading would be labelled progressively 1.1.1., 1.1.2., and so on.

1.2. **The Second Subsection Heading**

1.2.1. Similarly, each successive section under the heading reads 1.2.1., 1.2.2., 1.2.3. and so on.

1.2.2. In this way, every heading, subheading, and even paragraph has its identifying number.

1.2.3. The advantage of this system is its relative simplicity: it makes for easy cross-referencing, and enables readers to keep their bearings well.

2. PROBLEMS IN NUMBERING

2.1. **When to start numbering**

2.1.1. If you make any changes within a subsection you will have to go back and change all the numbers after it. So leave the numbering until last, if possible.

THE INDEX

If the report is very long and complicated, you may feel that it needs an index as well as a table of contents. Remember, however, that a good index can be very difficult and time-consuming to compile. Professional indexers will do this job for a fee, but it is unlikely you will receive funding for this.

Think twice before undertaking to compile an index yourself. If time is short, keep your ambitions under restraint. Aim for a very simple, modest index.

Begin indexing only when you have made absolutely the last change to the report. Go through the text, highlighting the key references that merit indexing. Then quickly write each reference on to an index card with its corresponding page number.

Sort the index cards into alphabetical order. Then fuse identical references into a single index entry (with two or more page numbers) and analyse related references into a complex entry:

compatible disks 16-17, 103
compensation
– of employees 26
– of clients 41
– seeking legal advice 25

SIGNING AND DATING

As author you are usually obliged to sign the report and date it. No matter how short it is, the report is your work, and you must take responsibility for it. If the report was written by a team of people, it is usually signed by the chairman or chairwoman.

Writing at Work, Home, and College

THE GREEK WORD FOR 'WORD'

Psychology is the scientific study of the mind, and *musicology* is naturally the study of music. There are more and more 'ologies' these days now that science and knowledge in general have been divided into so many different branches. The useful half-word *-ology* or *-logy* comes, via Latin, from the ancient Greek word *logos*, meaning – 'a word'!

☐ The following columns list various academic or scientific studies and their subjects. Pair them up. Answers are on pages 633-648.

1. cardiology	14. ichthyology	a. insects	n. bones
2. conchology	15. meteorology	b. elections	o. earthquakes
3. cosmology	16. neurology	c. tumours, cancer	p. tissue
4. dermatology	17. oenology	d. shells	q. fossils
5. entomology	18. oncology	e. knowledge	r. the universe
6. epistemology	19. ophthalmology	f. wine	s. weather
7. eschatology	20. ornithology	g. blood	t. nervous system
8. ethology	21. osteology	h. the heart	u. animal behaviour
9. etymology	22. palaeontology	i. the eyes	v. handwriting
10. graphology	23. pharmacology	j. word origins	w. the afterlife
11. haematology	24. psephology	k. birds	x. medical drugs
12. histology	25. seismology	l. fishes	y. China
13. horology	26. sinology	m. clocks	z. the skin

Writing for Meetings

Suppose you agree to help to organise the village fête, and decide to set up a meeting to make plans for it. Or suppose your boss asked you to keep a record of a business meeting. Fairly typical occurrences, surely.

If you belong to any organisation – whether it is a staffing committee at your place of work, a residents' association, or the local bird watchers' society – the chances are that at some time you will have to arrange or officiate at a meeting. And that means doing the paperwork.

There are four main kinds of documentation associated with meetings:

- [ ] the notice of meeting. This is the invitation to members of the group, and informs them where and when the meeting is to take place.

- [ ] the agenda. This is a numbered list of subjects that will be under discussion at the meeting.

- [ ] supplementary material. This would include, for example, a copy of the audited accounts, or the chairman's annual report, circulated before an Annual General Meeting (AGM).

- [ ] the minutes. This is a record of the proceedings of the meeting.

Follow the guidelines and models in this chapter, and you will prove an asset at the meetings you organise or record.

(To streamline the discussion in this chapter, a certain amount of shorthand terminology is necessary. The term *chairman* will be used to apply to any convener, male or female. The word *group* is used of any committee, board, team, or similar body.)

NOTICE OF MEETING

Circulate this at least a week before the meeting. Sometimes the rules or 'standing orders' of a group say that members are entitled to at least 14 days' notice. Failure to inform even one member eligible to attend can make a meeting invalid.

Notices of meeting vary widely, but usually specify:

- [ ] the title of the group that is to meet

- [ ] the kind of meeting it is to be – an Annual General Meeting, say, a regular monthly meeting, or an *ad hoc* meeting that has been called for a special purpose

- [ ] the date and time of the meeting

- [ ] where the meeting is to be held

- [ ] the name of the member calling the meeting

When circulating the notice, you would generally enclose the agenda as well, though if the agenda is not yet ready, you can send it out later.

AGENDAS

Every meeting needs an agenda. Its purpose is to tell the participants where they are going, just as the minutes will tell them where they have been. Even if you send out the agenda later than the notice of the meeting, make sure that it still reaches all the participants well in advance of the meeting itself.

Meetings traditionally follow a clearly defined pattern. (For a detailed discussion, see *How to run a meeting*, pages 547-553.) There are three parts:

- [ ] the preliminaries – short routine items, such as the reading of the previous meeting's minutes

- [ ] the 'Special business' – the heart of the meeting, when major issues are discussed at length

- [ ] 'Any other business' – matters that are not on the agenda, and can be dealt with quickly

The average meeting will cover only a selection of the many possible items that a formal agenda could include. But a very formal and lengthy meeting might list the following items on its agenda:

1. Election of chairman and officers
2. Secretary's reading of notice of meeting
3. Secretary's reading of minutes of last meeting

SPECIMEN NOTICES OF MEETING

ART ORIGINALS LIMITED
50 Short Road
London EC1 1AA

18 December 1990

Our ref: JJ/ls/99

Mr G Grosz
15 Harrow Hall
66 Long Lane
London WC1N 2AX

Dear Mr Grosz

A meeting of the Board of Directors of
Art Originals Limited will be held in
the Blue Boardroom on 15 January 1991
at 5 p.m., following the AGM.

A copy of the Agenda is attached.

Please contact me if you cannot attend.

Yours sincerely

J. Johns (Ms)
Company Secretary

ART ORIGINALS LIMITED
50 Short Road
London EC1 1AA

NOTICE
ANNUAL GENERAL MEETING

Notice is hereby given that the
Fifth General Meeting of the
Shareholders of Art Originals Limited
will be held at the Stanmore Centre
Conference Room 5
on 15 January 1991 at 12 noon
to receive the Report of the Directors
and the Auditors
for the year ending 31 March 1990

Any member unable to attend may, in
terms of the standing orders, appoint a
proxy to attend the meeting and to vote
on his or her behalf. A copy of the
agenda for this meeting is enclosed.
By order of the Board.
Dated this day 18 December 1990

J. Johns (Ms)
Secretary

Here are two examples of notices of meeting. Note that the notice can take the form of a letter (left), or of an announcement (right). It can also be typed at the head of the agenda (overleaf).

4 Matters arising from the last meeting
5 Secretary's reading of correspondence received
6 Chairman's opening remarks
7 Matters adjourned from previous meeting
8 Treasurer's report
9 Report from working parties or subcommittees.
10 Motions – with names of proposers and seconders
11 Any other business
12 Date of next meeting
13 Vote of thanks to the chairman
14 Chairman's reply to vote of thanks
15 Meeting closed or adjourned by chairman

For an Annual General Meeting, the agenda would probably include the following items as well:

Chairman's or Directors' report
Secretary's report
Annual accounts
Auditors' accounts
Appointment of auditors
Subscriptions (if this is the Annual General Meeting of a club or society)
Election of officers and committee members or company directors

Drawing up the agenda. Usually, the chairman and secretary work together to prepare the agenda for a meeting. The first step is to list all possible items. Consult other officers – the treasurer, for example – for matters that they may want raised. Check the minutes of the previous meeting – you may discover some matters adjourned until this meeting, or decisions taken that require some kind of follow-up. Collect any letters or memos that the meeting will need to hear or consider. Ask participants if they have any motions they want to put forward.

Now decide how much ground you want the meeting to cover, and in how much detail. And decide how long it should take – the shorter the meeting, the less chance of participants losing interest or leaving before the end. A good chairman or secretary has a well-judged idea of how much time the members are likely to want to spend on each item of business. If more than three or four major items or debates call for discussion, it may be best to spread them over two or more meetings rather than cramming them all into one.

Then decide on the order of items. Place important and complicated matters at the top of the 'Special business' section – to be discussed while the members' minds are still fresh. Remember, major items are not necessarily mainstream items – some major items are adjourned matters from the previous meeting, or unripe matters that will not be resolved until the next meeting. But they remain major items, nevertheless, and call for discussion in the 'Special business' section. Don't diminish them by assigning them to the 'Matters arising' section or the 'Any other business' section. If necessary, subdivide all the major items into categories under different headings, and enter them all in the 'Special business' section.

Structure each category or section of the agenda to ensure a logical order of development – as far as possible, each item should lead on naturally to the next. An ill-ordered agenda will probably invite objections at the meeting, and a demand for changes to it. Some member will have to propose a motion to adjust the agenda, and a debate and vote will have to follow – a time-consuming and irritating disruption. Avoid it by anticipating likely difficulties and by planning the meeting and agenda very carefully in the first place.

Try to be fairly specific when wording the agenda. Avoid vague phrasing such as 'The financial situation'. If the question is actually 'The allocation of surplus funds' or 'Writing off bad debts', say so. The point of each item should be perfectly clear. Wording the agenda clearly in this way may prevent much of the misunderstanding or confusion that all too frequently occurs at meetings. It will also help the members to think more constructively about the issues, and to formulate relevant and well-prepared arguments beforehand, thereby ensuring more efficient discussion and a more productive meeting generally.

Specimen agenda. Here is an example of an agenda – for a meeting of the Staff Training Unit of a large company. Observe that the notice of meeting precedes it as part of a single document. Note too that it is numbered, and see how the numbering breaks up – items 1-4 are the preliminaries, 5-7 the 'Special business', 8-9 the concluding items.

```
        NOTICE OF MEETING

A meeting of the Staff Training Unit
will be held on 7 June 1990 at 2.30
p.m. in the Committee Room.

            AGENDA

1. Apologies for absence
2. Minutes of meeting held on 4 May
3. Matters arising from the minutes:
       Raffles prizes
       Complaints about heating
       Caretaker's overtime
4. Correspondence
5. Report on Computer Training Session
6. Recruitment of Assistant Training
   Manager (report attached)
7. Need for more secretarial
   assistance
8. Any other business
9. Date, time, and place of next
   meeting
```

Here are some further points to bear in mind.

Correspondence. If the letters or memos to be read out have an important bearing on the business of the group, the agenda should include brief summaries of them.

Take this extract from the agenda for a Management Committee meeting of a small company that sells art materials:

4 *Correspondence*
Letter 201: complaint about glue being sold in paint bottles.
Letter 202: invitation from suppliers Sharpey and Son, addressed to all staff and management, for Christmas Eve party.

Motions. Sometimes specific motions are included in the agenda. Take this extract from the agenda for a meeting of the Residents' Association Committee of a block of flats.

5 *Existing security measures*
Motion: Mr Dix proposes
THAT all residents of Harrow Hall should contribute an equal sum to the cost of repairing the burglar-proofing of the recently vandalised storeroom windows.

6 *New security devices*
Motion: Mrs Lewis proposes and Mr Ray seconds
THAT residents of Mainwaring Court and Harrow Court submit a joint order for mortise locks in order to obtain a better discount from the wholesalers.

Times. You might want to put a time limit on each item to make sure of fitting in all the items during the time available overall for the meeting. If so, you must – out of courtesy – inform the participants beforehand. The simplest way of doing that is to mark on the agenda the allotted time for each item to begin. For example:

Marketing review	– 10 a.m.
Publicity report	– 10.40
Staffing	– 11
Any other business	– 11.15

Enclosures. You may have to circulate other papers with the agenda if members are to be properly prepared for the meeting – such as the report on 'Recruitment of Assistant Training Manager' mentioned in the sample agenda opposite.

These 'agenda papers' may include diagrams, charts, lists of statistics, balance sheets, reports, and letters. When you circulate the agenda for an Annual General Meeting, you will probably enclose the organisation's audited accounts.

If sending out more than one agenda paper, give each document a number – Agenda Paper 1, Agenda Paper 2, and so on – and cross-refer to it on the agenda. Label each illustration or chart to make quite clear what it refers to.

Special agendas. As chairman or secretary, you may find it useful to have a special copy of the agenda with a large right-hand margin. This allows you to jot down notes and reminders to yourself before and during the meeting.

THE MINUTES

Minutes of a meeting are kept for several reasons.

☐ They provide proof that members of a group came together, discussed certain issues, and reached certain decisions. Without such a record, any or all of this could be forgotten, or – in the event of a legal dispute – denied.

☐ They provide a useful reference for anyone unable to attend the meeting. A quick glance will enable him or her to grasp what its highlights were and what decisions were taken.

☐ They help to hold participants to their promises, and to turn their promises into actions – the minutes record all such commitments and oblige the participants to report the outcome back to the group.

Minutes vary in form and content, on the basis of the kind of meeting being recorded, and the degree of formality and detail required by the chairman. The chief executive of a public company, for instance, will probably be more exacting than the chairman of the local folk-dancing club.

No matter how much they differ in detail and tone, their basic purpose is always the same, however – to provide a brief, authoritative account of the meeting and of the decisions reached. Not that minutes should aim to give a blow-by-blow account. They rarely record, for example, the length or intensity of a debate, or bickering between various factions, or the difficulty in achieving a resolution.

Taking minutes. Usually, it is the group's secretary who takes the minutes – that is, takes notes during the meeting of what is said and decided. If there is no secretary, the chairman must assign the task to one of the participants, preferably a volunteer.

On no account should the chairman attempt to take minutes. A chairman who does this will probably do both his jobs badly. However, a good chairman will make sure to control the pace of the discussion so as to allow the secretary to take down notes as accurately as possible.

If the role of secretary falls to you, remember that it is better to have too many notes than too few. Jot down all important points, decisions, and arguments, and who made them. Use language you feel comfortable with. Suppose you are secretary for a management meeting of a manufacturing company. The subject arises of the alleged incompetence of the Chief Purchasing Manager, and feeling runs high among the members of the group. You might note:

> Grosz and Johns (me!) want Smithson OUT. Much song & dance. Vin [V.G. Vincent, Managing Director] won't hear of it.

When you later come to write up these notes into official minutes, what emerges is this:

> Mr Grosz proposed and Mr Johns seconded THAT the Purchasing Department be disbanded.
> The Chairman adjourned discussion of this proposal until the next meeting.

Develop a personal shorthand if you have not got one already. Devise simple abbreviations for people's names and for commonly used words – *equiv* for 'equivalent', *mgr* for 'manager'.

Writing up the minutes. Write up the minutes as soon as possible after a meeting, while events are still fresh in your mind.

Before you start, check on the customary style. Look at copies of past minutes and consult the organisation's standing orders. Perhaps only resolutions are recorded. Or is some account given of the debate that preceded them? Make sure too that you confer with the chairman. Does he have anything specific that he wants you to record, or favour any particular style?

Remember the two vital rules of keeping minutes – be clear and be objective. Don't use technical language or abbreviations that could puzzle any likely reader: the aim of minutes is to clarify, not obscure, the business and outcome of a meeting. And don't embark on your own analysis or interpretation of the business of the meeting. Simply state the facts: the motions put forward, the objections raised, the decisions taken, and the course of action proposed.

Some minutes also feature a column down one side of the page headed *Duties* or *Actions to be taken*. In this column, and opposite relevant minuted items, appear the names of members of the group – those who have agreed to undertake certain tasks before the next meeting. The 'action column' is a discreet reminder to them of their promises.

For a detailed example of minutes see the panel opposite. Note also the following points:

The Heading. This should list the name of the group, the time and date of the meeting, and the place at which it was held.

Record also those present at the meeting. List them as in the example opposite, or divide them into three groups: the chairman or chairwoman; the women present, traditionally prefaced by 'Mesdames'; and the men, prefaced by 'Messrs'.

> Present:
> Ms E Reading (in the Chair)
> Mesdames: Morton, Riley, and
> Oppenheim
> Messrs: Thornton, Summers, and
> Nicholson

Traditionally, company minutes feature people's job titles before or after their names – *Mrs M Gilchrist, Assistant Production Manager*, for example, or *Senior Secretarial Supervisor: Ms Sandra Satajay.*

SPECIMEN MINUTES

Here are the minutes of an imaginary meeting held by a Residents' Association. Note that the minutes are numbered. Some groups' minutes start with number 1 at each meeting. Many others, as here, tend to carry over the numbering from one meeting to the next (until a new calendar or financial year re-sets the numbering to 1 again). Here the final minute of the previous meeting was 71, so this set of minutes begins at 72.

The advantages of this system are these: it reflects the steady progress of the group's policy-making over a period of time, and it makes it easier to cross-refer from one meeting or minute to another (see Minute 74).

Notice also Minute 73 – *Minutes of the previous meeting*. Typically, these have been circulated in advance and are therefore 'taken as read' or formally 'ratified' by a vote. The chairman signs them, thereby indicating that all members present have read and approved them.

Occasionally, however, a member of the meeting wants to correct or alter the minutes. He or she puts this wish before the meeting in the form of a motion. If the motion is carried, the current meeting's minutes will record it, and the necessary adjustments are made to the previous meeting's minutes.

Important letters also demand a mention in the minutes – see Minute 75. Sometimes, the letters are numbered in a similar fashion to the minutes. For example:

> The secretary reported that two letters addressed to the Committee had been received since the last meeting:
>
> Letter 555: Messrs Keys & Stock queried the delay in payment of their invoice for consultancy work in February. The secretary reminded them that the matter was still before the independent arbitrators, whose report is due next week.
>
> Letter 556: LocoCo Toys sent a general invitation to a cocktail party in Miami to launch their new line in dolls, 'Great Villains'. The secretary declined on behalf of all members of the Committee.

RESIDENTS' ASSOCIATION OF MAINWARING COURT

MINUTES
of the meeting of the
Residents' Association of
Mainwaring Court
held on 14 June 1990 at 7 p.m.
in the hired rooms over
the Kilmarnock Arms

Present:
Ms E. Reading (in the Chair)
Mr D. Thornton
Mr R.B. Summers (Secretary)
Miss S. Riley
Miss K. Morton
Ms N. Oppenheim
Mr R. Nicholson

Distribution: Those present, plus Mrs
L. Lead, Mr P. Clay, Dr D. Carter.

72 Apologies for absence

Apologies for absence were received
from Mrs L. Lead, Mr P. Clay and Dr
D. Carter.

73 Minutes of previous meeting

It was resolved
THAT the minutes of the meeting on
12 April 1990, previously circulated
to all members, be ratified and
signed as an accurate record.

74 Matters arising

Minute 65:
Mr Nicholson informed the meeting
that he had, reluctantly, removed
the bright orange sign reading
Noticeboard from above the
noticeboard. He regretted the
decision of the Residents'
Association, which had forced this
artistic climbdown on him.

75 Correspondence

Mr Summers read aloud a letter from
the Residents' Committee of the
nearby flats, Harrow Hall,
requesting a joint meeting to
discuss local security problems.

It was resolved
THAT the secretary should reply to
the Residents' Committee of Harrow
Hall, stating the Association's
interest in the idea and suggesting
a time and place.

Carried unanimously.

76 Charity Collection

Owing to Mrs Lead's departure for a
holiday in Majorca, her motion on
distributing the charity monies was
postponed until the next meeting.

It was resolved
THAT in future charity monies should
be deposited in the Association's
bank account at the earliest
opportunity.

77 Use of noticeboard

77.1 Mr Thornton proposed, and Ms
Oppenheim seconded, the motion, and
it was resolved
THAT the noticeboard in the foyer be
used for Residents' Association
matters only.

Passed by 5 votes to 2. Mr Nicholson
recorded his opposition to the
proposal.

77.2 Ms Oppenheim proposed and Miss
Riley seconded the motion
THAT before any item be displayed on
the noticeboard, a motion be put to
members of the Association to vote
on its suitability.

The motion was not put to the vote.

At Madam Chair's suggestion, the
meeting agreed to an adjournment of
the matter until the next meeting.

78 Date of next meeting

It was agreed that the next meeting
be held on 16 August 1990 at 7 p.m.
in the hired rooms over the
Kilmarnock Arms.

79 There being no further business, the
meeting closed at 9 p.m.

Edith Reading.

E. Reading
Chairperson
14 June 1990

For very large meetings – an Annual General Meeting, for instance – you obviously cannot list everyone present. But you should give the number of people present, if possible, together with the name of the chairman or chairwoman:

> 112 members were present. Ms M. Nisbet was in the Chair

Finally, give a list of those to whom the minutes should be distributed.

Recording resolutions. At their barest, minutes simply record resolutions passed. But 'preambles' are often included, explaining briefly the background or discussion. Some groups even minute summaries of members' arguments in each debate.

Voting too is sometimes recorded – either after the wording of the resolution (as in the specimen minutes on the previous page), or before it:

> It was resolved by ten votes in favour and three votes against with two abstentions
> THAT . . .

Several other possible occurrences in a meeting also require minuting: the adjournment of a motion, a member's request that his or her vote be recorded, and so on.

Several traditional conventions govern the wording, proposing, and debating of motions during a meeting, and many of these conventions carry over into the minutes. Here are some of them:

☐ the use of the word *that* before each motion

> It was resolved
> THAT the Chairman . . .

☐ the use of the subjunctive form of the verb, and the widespread use of passive verbs:

> It was resolved unanimously
> THAT the Chairman be congratulated on standing up to the landlords' ultimatum, and that he be urged to continue his efforts . . .

Note too that each minute has a distinct heading (following the lead of the agenda very often). In keeping with the purpose of minutes to provide easily accessible information about a meeting, headings serve to guide the reader's eye to the item he or she is looking for.

An alternative format for minutes bases itself on the words *Noted* and *Resolved*. For example:

75 JOINT SECURITY MEASURES

75.1 *Noted* that the Residents' Committee of the nearby block of flats, Harrow Hall, has requested a joint meeting to discuss local security problems.

75.2 *Resolved* that the secretary should reply to the Residents' Committee of Harrow Hall, stating the Association's interest in the idea and suggesting a time and place.

76 CHARITY COLLECTION

76.1 *Noted* that Mrs Lead left unexpectedly for a holiday in Majorca. Her motion on distributing the charity monies was accordingly postponed until the next meeting.

76.2 *Resolved* that in future all charity monies should be deposited in the Association's bank account at the earliest opportunity.

Distribution. Once you have typed up your official version of the minutes, show it to the chairman for his approval, and then run off a number of copies. Circulate these to all members who attended the meeting, to members who should have been there but were not, and to any other people you think should know what happened and was decided.

Keep one copy for the 'minutes book'. Formerly this was a bound volume into which the minutes were laboriously transcribed by hand, to prevent anyone from removing or altering pages. Nowadays, minutes are more often pasted onto numbered pages in a bound volume, or stored in files.

Job Applications

IMAGINE yourself as a busy personnel manager. You are looking for a new clerk for your firm's accounts department. That is all you want. What you get is a flood of applications. To draw up a reasonable short list, you have to do a lot of sifting, and it is likely to be very coarse sifting in the early stages.

You turn your tired eyes to application number 37. It is handwritten, on a sheet of paper torn from a wire-bound notebook. The applicant has misspelt your name. His qualifications and work experience seem suitable enough, but he has also included a lot of information not requested in the advertisement and irrelevant to the job. This information has a slightly facetious tone about it into the bargain. And his punctuation is appalling.

Does number 37 get on to the short-list? The chances are that you place his letter, without a second glance, into the rejects pile, and that two days later he receives a rote rejection letter.

What are the qualities that you want in an applicant? Competence, confidence, enthusiasm, and courtesy. What in an application would suggest that he or she has these qualities? Clarity of thought and layout, relevance and conciseness, brightness of tone without informality. Just the qualities you expect in business letters that the person you finally appoint will one day have to write for your firm.

OPENING MOVES

Now put yourself on the other side of the picture – in the position of the applicant for a job. Your application is your first contact with the prospective employer. It is your opportunity to create the right impression from the outset. Whether you are applying for the post of apprentice electrician, senior salesman, or tax inspector, you can increase the chances of a favourable response to your application by wording and setting it out carefully.

The first rule is: follow the instructions given in the advertisement. Supply all the information and papers requested. At this stage don't go any further.

Quote the source of the advertisement ('job pages of *The Sunday Times*', 'jobcentre noticeboard'). If the employer is interested and wants further information, such as the name of a referee, he or she will ask you for it later.

In most cases, your initial application will consist of two elements: a covering letter, in which you state why you are writing, and a c.v. (*curriculum vitae*, sometimes called a *résumé*), giving details of your education, training, and relevant work experience.

Keep the covering letter short and completely to the point. You can afford to be more expansive in the c.v. The c.v. is the place to strengthen your application by mentioning details that do not relate directly to the job, such as sporting achievements or charity work. But be careful. Don't give undue emphasis to these outside interests. And don't list anything trivial or off-putting.

Make a draft beforehand of what you want to put into your application. Keep two things constantly in mind: what kind of person the company is looking for, and what you have to offer that corresponds to this. Find out as much as possible about the work involved and also about the company you are applying to. This will ensure that you present yourself in a way that matches the requirements of the job.

Suppose it is a clothing manufacturer that has advertised the vacancy. Find out what it specialises in: fashion garments? industrial clothing? Try to identify something in your own past experience to link you with that particular company. If you have ever done business with them before, say so in your application. Show that you know what they do. Show that you are interested.

WHAT TO SAY

You have to sell yourself when applying for a job. You must not stretch the truth, but you should certainly emphasise your strong points: your achievements, abilities, and potential, your interest

Writing at Work, Home, and College

in and suitability for the job. Play down as far as possible any failings, deficiencies, and dark secrets. Unless specifically asked, why confess that you are simultaneously applying for a job with a rival company? Such an admission will only count against you in the selection process.

On the other hand, don't try to conceal any obvious shortcomings, such as lack of experience or qualifications. These would emerge soon enough, at the interview stage probably, or if you get past that, in the office or on the shop floor. Either way, the employers will not thank you for wasting their time. Own up to these disadvantages, but counter-balance them by stressing your adaptability and eagerness to learn. All new jobs have to be learned to some extent.

But 'own up' even more boldly to the advantages you can claim. If you are applying for a job that will involve working at a computer terminal, don't fail to explain that you can type and operate a computer. Make sure to mention your knowledge of French when applying to a company with European or African interests. Remember to list your more general acquirements, things that any employer might want to know about – a clean driving licence, for instance, or a competence in first aid.

PRESENTATION

Always type your c.v., or get it done for you by a typist or a typing bureau. It should look welcoming to the reader – clear and neatly laid out. Show the firm right away that you are up to their standards. And of course make sure the spelling, grammar, and punctuation are correct.

If you write the covering letter by hand, make it legible and tidy, and use good unlined paper. Blue ink is perhaps preferable to black, and a fountain-pen to a ball-point.

Remember, the person processing your application at this stage knows nothing about you except what he or she can see in your letter and c.v.

Think about the personality of the company you are applying to. A local government department would expect a conventional application. But an advertising agency, for example, may welcome something more original – perhaps in the form of an advertisement, with the c.v. (on coloured paper maybe) 'selling' you as the product.

Always keep copies of your old c.v.s and letters of application; these will save you a great deal of time and effort when you next apply for a job.

Writing your Curriculum Vitae

The chances are that you are applying for more than one job. So it is worth having a standard c.v. prepared. You might want to make a capsule version as well, for those times when the advertisement asks for no more than 'brief details of past experience' or the like.

But don't send your standard c.v. out unthinkingly with every application. Very often it is better to produce a one-off version, tailor-made to the requirements of the job advertised. If you own a word processor you can adjust the standard pattern with little trouble to fit the specifications each time. It is far easier to adapt an existing c.v. than to devise one from scratch.

A c.v. should follow a fairly standard layout. Look through all the examples given here and work out the form best suited to you and your present application. No two people have the same history and background. You may have to combine features from several of the examples before producing a c.v. that is just right.

A c.v. should be as long as, and no longer than, you need to tell prospective employers what they want to know. If possible, keep it down to one side unless you have a great deal of relevant experience. And, once again, make sure to set it out clearly and neatly. Send it off only when you are satisfied with its clean, fresh appearance. If it is badly dog-eared, or poorly photocopied, it will look like a hand-me-down from a previous (unsuccessful) application. This is not the impression you want to create.

DESCRIBING YOUR WORK EXPERIENCE

Put yourself in the shoes of the personnel manager reading a c.v. once more. What is the most important thing you are looking for in your potential recruits? Unless you have advertised specifically for school or college leavers, it is undoubtedly work experience that counts for most. It follows that the most important part of the c.v. will be the section describing previous jobs and the skills acquired there.

There are two ways of going about this. The first, and more traditional, is to present a set of 'job descriptions': you list the jobs you have held and describe briefly what each job entailed – for an example, see the panel overleaf. The second way, increasingly popular nowadays, is to present a 'skills profile'. Here the emphasis is less on a job-by-job account of your working life, and more on the set of skills you have acquired.

Job-description c.v. You do not have to describe in detail all the duties of all your previous jobs. Give just enough to create interest and suggest competence. Make sure you mention anything special that will count in your favour, such as:

☐ rapid promotions or increases in salary

☐ special responsibilities or recognition from your previous employers

☐ how you may have helped your previous employers by increasing their turnover, profits, or productivity, or by cutting their costs

So, a bare-boned listing such as *1982-85 Dodo Publishing* is not really satisfactory. Far better to provide some meat – something along these lines:

Jan 1982 – July 1986. Accounts assistant at Dodo Publishing, Long Lane, Milton, Essex.
Entry in ledgers; computerised accounts; preparing drafts for senior accountants. Assisted in computerisation of accounts system, such as preparing and entering entries from old ledgers. The system set up has proved effective and the company's accounting costs were cut by more than 20 per cent.

But make sure it really is meat rather than fat. Don't stray into unfocused and generalised remarks about your work. Consider these three entries.

Sept 1985 – March 1988. Sales representative. Marine Paints Ltd.

Sept 1985 – March 1988. Sales representative. Marine Paints Ltd, Billsly Trading Estate, Billsly, Boston, Lincs.
Responsible for selling in the Humberside area to small boat owners. Thanks to a new product range the firm's sales increased in my area by 18 per cent during this period. Left for better paid job and increased responsibility.

Sept 1985 – March 1988. Sales representative. Marine Paints Ltd, Billsly Trading Estate, Billsly, Boston, Lincs.

My work was to travel all over Humberside, selling paint to small boat owners. This often involved working outside normal office hours. I had to adjust to changes in our product range but was able to increase the firm's sales by a considerable amount.

The first tells you almost nothing. The last is wordy, self-congratulatory, and imprecise, and it suggests that the writer felt himself hard done by while carrying out his normal job. The second hits the right note of self-promotion while appearing to be modest, and it drops a hint about a position of special responsibility.

What other details should you include? It is a good idea – again following the lead of the second example above – to mention why you left your previous jobs, especially if you did not hold them for long. You should also mention why you are looking for a new job now. It will not help your cause, however, to mention that you have been fired. And avoid references also to 'personality clashes' and the like. In such cases, if you think hard enough, you can usually find some way of putting a better light on events. (For some hints on how to deal with these matters, see the section *Special situations*, page 337.)

Similarly, don't go into detail about any family problems or hard-luck stories. A brief mention is sufficient. After all, if you lost your job because the company you were working for went bankrupt, you need hardly give a lengthy defence of yourself. Employers will understand the problem – unless, of course, you were the person to blame for the firm's going bankrupt.

Should you mention your previous or current salaries? If you decide to, the information should go between the job descriptions and the reasons for leaving. For example:

May 1987 – June 1989. Trainee copywriter and full copywriter. Joshua McGrath & Associates advertising agency.
Dealt with large local accounts (especially in engineering and travel). Duties included copywriting, media planning, client conferences, liaison with designers and artists. Salary: £18,000 per annum.
Left before birth of first child.

And if you ever received a special pay rise, mention that as well. Potential employers might well view a substantial pay rise in a previous job as evidence of

SPECIMEN JOB-DESCRIPTION C.V.

Note how the c.v. is clearly divided into different sections. Note also the style of the job descriptions. You do not *have* to use this abbreviated form of wording but it does make the descriptions easier to write, and to read. If you use whole sentences, most of them will start with *I*, and will sound rather egotistical. Abbreviated style also makes the document shorter and, in addition, it helps the main points to stand out better.

Follow the example of this c.v. in the ordering of the items, giving most emphasis to your latest work. The employer will be more interested in what you have been doing recently than in what you were doing ten years ago. That is why the c.v. starts with the most recent position and works backwards in time.

Give details of your education in reverse order too. Your most recent qualifications are likely to be the most relevant to your work. Give the name and location of your schools, colleges, and so on. No need to go into great detail however, unless you have only recently finished full-time education.

```
Thomas A. Waters
34 Heath Road
London N17 2PK
Tel. 081-627 9804

28 August 1990

                    CURRICULUM VITAE

Sept 1983 to present. London Regional Sales Manager: ABC Electronics Ltd,
38 North Way, London N9 4JU.
                Supervising sales force of 15, selling radio and TV components.
                Responsible for recruitment, training, and the setting and
                fulfilment of sales goals. During this period regional sales
                rose on average 25 per cent annually.
                Family ownership of the firm prevents my further promotion in
                the foreseeable future.

Aug 1979 - June 1983. Sales representative: Camden Hardware, 24 Queen's St,
Camden, Northants.
                Sold hardware to shops and supermarkets in the E. Midland area.
                Opened up new outlets and increased company's market share in
                the area from 8 per cent to 11 per cent.
                Company went into liquidation. Took up work in London.

Nov 1977 - July 1979. Watson Engineering, Unit 12, Shiply Trading Estate,
Shiply, Northants.
                Designed machine tools for small electronics manufacturer.
                Promoted to deputy foreman after ten months.
                Left to become full-time salesman on increased pay.

References available on request.

                        Education

Nene College, Northampton 1974-77. HND electronic engineering.
Hills Road Comprehensive, Northampton. 1966-73. A-levels: Mathematics (C),
Physics (D). 6 O-levels.

                        Other points

Clean driving licence.
Certificate in Business Accounts (evening classes)

                        Personal

Age: 34
Nationality: British
Married, two children (ages 7 and 4)
Good health
Personal interests: soccer referee; carpentry; films.
```

outstanding work there. (Express this pay rise as a percentage – this puts a clear statistical value on your performance.)

But a word of warning. Don't at this stage mention the kind of salary you are now looking for. If you name too low a figure, you may be selling yourself short; if you suggest too high a figure, you may be putting yourself out of the reckoning at the first hurdle. If you are good enough and potential employers want you enough, they may be willing to find extra money to pay you. At all events, this is a matter for the interview, or even for negotiation after a firm offer of employment.

Skills profile. Here the approach is different – for an example, see page 336. You first give a deliberately bare-boned listing of your jobs so far; then you list the various skills you have learned in these jobs – particularly, of course, those most relevant to your present application. There is a minimum of prose.

Suppose you have been working for a publishing company for a number of years. You have gained wide experience in special aspects of the business: commissioning of authors, copy-editing, indexing, basic page design, blurb writing and proofreading. List all these skills. You also have a certain amount of experience of, say, market research, writing press releases, and picture research. List these too. The relevant section in your c.v. would look something like this:

Chaffinch Books, London   1985-88

- commissioning of authors
- copy-editing, proofreading, indexing
- basic layout and design; picture research
- writing blurbs and press releases
- market research

The chief advantage of this approach is that your skills stand out at a glance. The prospective employer just runs his eye down the page and takes in immediately the range of your experience – no need for him to dig around. When he has dozens of c.v.s on his desk, he will thank you for that.

PERSONAL AND OTHER DETAILS

Your c.v. should also give brief details of your education: degrees, certificates of further education, A-levels, and the like, as well as the places where you were educated, and the dates between which you attended them. (For examples, see the specimen c.v.s on pages 334 and 336.)

List too any other relevant skills, qualifications, and experience – under a heading such as *Other details* or *Additional information*. You must decide what is relevant to your application, but be sure to mention these items at least:

☐ knowledge of any languages – all too few job applicants do know any foreign languages and as business becomes more and more international an aptitude for languages is something that employers are increasingly looking for

☐ industrial or office skills – if you know how to type, for example, you might mention that, even though you are not going for a job as a typist; your knowledge of typing may be a useful qualification if the job you are applying for involves using computers, say

☐ educational qualifications gained outside the normal educational system – perhaps a business qualification you have gained through attending evening classes

☐ publications

People often include hobbies and outside interests here as well. Employers generally like this as it gives them a feel for the personality of the applicant.

As for other personal details, you do not have to mention whether you are married or have children or anything about your personal life at all. But do specify your age or date of birth. And to spare yourself any later embarrassment, do mention any serious health problems.

CAPSULE C.V.s

In addition to a full c.v., you should keep a capsule version prepared. When a company expects a large response to a 'Situations Vacant' advertisement it often asks for 'brief details of your career'. This is a warning to stick to the central issues.

Choose from your c.v. what you think the employer will be most interested in. To some extent this will depend on the type of work being offered. Pick the points that relate most closely to the advertised job, and leave out all those that have no bearing on it.

Suppose that Thomas Waters (see page 336 and opposite) has seen an advertisement for a post as marketing executive with a large computer company. He has experience of marketing in electronics, but not specifically in computers. He might then adapt his c.v. in the following way:

SPECIMEN SKILLS PROFILE

Now here is the Thomas Waters c.v. organised as a skills profile. Notice the differences. In the first place, the name and address are now placed centrally at the top of the page with a rule underneath. This helps to give your c.v. a crisper and more stylish appearance. Then comes the leading 'career aim'. This is where you make clear the kind of job you have set your sights on. Give the field of employment you are interested in (here, sales) and the level. Use words such as *build, develop*, and *cultivate* to suggest that the job you are aiming for will be a natural progression from what you have done before.

THOMAS A. WATERS
34 Heath Road, London N17 2PK
081-627 9804

CAREER AIM	Family ownership of my present company means that promotion is unlikely in the foreseeable future. I am therefore looking for a new position, one that will build on my skills and experience in sales and management, and allow me scope for upward movement.

EMPLOYMENT	ABC Electronics Ltd,	1983–present
	38 North Way, London N9 4JU	
	Camden Hardware	1979–1983
	24 Queen's Street, Camden, Northants	
	Watson Engineering	1977–1979
	Unit 12, Shiply Trading Estate, Shipley, Northants	

EXPERIENCE Managerial	. Supervising (as London Regional Sales Manager, ABC Electronics) a sales force of 15, selling radio and TV components
	. Setting sales goals and ensuring their fulfilment – 25 per cent average annual rise in regional sales during my time at ABC Electronics
	. Recruiting and training sales personnel
Sales and Manufacture	. Selling hardware to shops and supermarkets in E. Midlands Manufacture area (for Camden Hardware)
	. Opening up new markets in E. Midlands – leading to increase in company's market share in area from 8 per cent to 11 per cent
	. Designing electronics machine tools (for Watson Engineering)

EDUCATION	Nene College, Northampton HND in electronic engineering	1974–1977
	Hills Road Comprehensive, Northampton A-levels: Mathematics (C), Physics (D) 6 O-levels	1966–1973

ADDITIONAL	. Full clean driving licence
	. Certificate in Business Accounts (by evening classes)
PERSONAL	Age 34 Nationality: British Married, two children (ages 7 and 4) Good health
INTERESTS	Soccer referee; carpentry; cinema

Sept 1983 to present. London Regional Sales Manager. ABC Electronics Ltd, 38 North Way, London N9 4JU.
Supervising sales force of 15 selling radio and TV components; recruitment, training, and sales projections. Regional sales have risen on average 25 per cent annually.

Aug 1979 – June 1983. Sales representative. Camden Hardware, 24 Queen's St, Camden, Northants.
Selling hardware. Increased company's market share in East Midlands from 8 per cent to 11 per cent.

HND in electronic engineering
Certificate in Business Accounts

Age: 34

SPECIAL SITUATIONS

Not everybody has sailed through life from one long-term job to the next. What if you have been unemployed? What if you have gone bankrupt? Or been fired? Or withdrawn from the labour market for several years to raise a family?

If you have had a long period off work, give a reason in your c.v., and try to show that you have used the time constructively. You do not need to worry about the odd month between jobs. But you can probably find a good reason to account for longer periods when you were not working.

Feb 1984 – Sept 1985. Not working, owing to need to look after sick mother.

May 1988 – Oct 1988. Travelling in Europe – temporary jobs, such as grape-picking.

It would be a very unsympathetic employer who found fault with someone fresh from education who chose to spend a little time seeing the world. In fact, many employers might view your doing so as a positive advantage.

Or you might simply write something like this:

Dec 1987 – Sept 1988 Unemployed. Time spent looking for work and attending courses on motor mechanics at Ramsey Technical College, Ramsey, Hampshire.

Employers understand about unemployment. If you can show them that your time out of work was not wasted in idleness, they will be predisposed in your favour.

An applicant may have taken on freelance work or a consultancy during a period of unemployment:

1988 – present. Freelance book editor.

1986 – 1988. Independent consultant. Experience showed that I was better suited to working within a company structure than as an independent entrepreneur.

Don't, however, exaggerate the extent of this work. Remember that you are going to have to back up your claims if you get called to interviews.

Suppose that you tried to set up your own business and got your fingers burned. It happens to a lot of people. You have nothing to be ashamed of, so don't hide what happened. Word your job description carefully to suggest a sensible appreciation of what went wrong and that you have learned from your mistakes. Hint that you now think it is time to settle down. But by all means mention the positive sides of this period of your life.

March 1982 – July 1984. Operated own car-repair business. Found that the business side of self-employment is not my strong point and not to my liking, and that I work better when concentrating on the technical side.

Whatever your reason for going bankrupt, being unemployed, or suffering any other setback, don't apologise. Anyone can make mistakes. As long as your mistakes have harmed no one but yourself and you have learned from them, no one will hold them against you. Be prepared, however, to discuss them fully – interviewers are sure to be curious.

One last case. What do you do if you were fired from your previous job for incompetence? Or if you did not get on with your boss there? A vague account is all you need to give in your c.v. None of the following would be stretching the truth too far:

Left because job required skills I did not have.

Felt that I was unsuited to this kind of work.

Work proved to be other than I had expected.

Company reorganisation eliminated position.

Whatever you decide to say, your position will be much stronger if some senior person in your old firm will put in a good word on your behalf. The chances are that prospective employers will be in contact with your previous places of work for references. Make sure you prepare for this by clearing the ground beforehand.

Writing at Work, Home, and College

C.V.s FOR A FIRST JOB

Suppose you are applying for your first job after leaving school or college. The employer cannot expect much in the way of work experience – he or she will look for ability, enthusiasm, and readiness to learn. Your c.v. will clearly therefore concentrate on your education, but you should also make the most of any previous part-time work that you have done. Potential employers will be more impressed if you have shown initiative.

Think too about any extra-curricular activities you have engaged in while in full-time education. Perhaps you were involved in a school or college theatrical group. It may not seem to have much relevance to your application for a job in the Ministry of Agriculture. But think again. That ability to act implies an ability to project yourself – a very useful quality in, say, important meetings. Potential employers may note that detail with interest.

Below is the c.v. of someone who has just finished at school and is looking for a first full-time job. Note that Mary Jackson has named her former headmistress on her c.v. This implies that Mary has secured the headmistress's promise to provide a reference if requested.

Many people new to the job market will be sending out a general c.v. to several companies in their area. If you are in this position, try to be specific about the kind of work you want to do; Mary Jackson at least gives the impression of knowing what she is looking for. And direct your applications to companies that you know might offer the kind of work you want. There is no harm in varying the c.v. a little according to the company you write to. You could, for instance, express an interest in being trained for specific kinds of work, when you write to companies that operate such programmes.

```
Name:            Mary Elizabeth Jackson
Address:         57 Shakespeare Avenue, Ripon, Yorks. Tel. 629454
Personal:        Single
Age:             17

Education:       Batley Lane Comprehensive, Batley Lane, Ripon.
                 (Head: Mrs S.L.Watson) 1984-1989.
                 O-levels - English (C); Mathematics (D);
                 History (D); Economics (E).
                 CSEs - four.
                 Form prize for improvement, 1988.
                 Acting Form Captain, 1988.

Other details:   Office skills - Certificate for 1-year course at
                 Ripon College of Further Education.
                 Typing - 60 wpm.

Employment:      Royal Mail - Christmas post delivery assistant,
                 1987-88.
                 Working at weekends at Budgens (checkout assistant).
                 Temporary typist for Goodlife Employment Agency,
                 summer 1989.

                 References available.

I have greatly enjoyed the office work that I have been doing on a
temporary basis since leaving school. I am looking for suitable permanent
employment which uses my secretarial skills and gives me the opportunity of
developing them, as in bookkeeping or sales promotion.

Interests:       Jazz ballet; acting (have performed in productions
                 of Walworth Amateur Dramatic Society).

Date:            27 September 1990
```

The Covering Letter

The covering letter, introducing your c.v., is the first thing of yours that the personnel manager will see – and one of the most important letters you will ever write. So, it is important to make sure you start off on the right foot.

There are two basic kinds of application letter: a specific reply to an advertisement, and a general 'on spec' letter to a firm. Certain points are common to both. Make sure you spell the firm's name correctly. And also the name of the person you are directing the letter to – don't write to *Mrs Stevenson* unless you are sure that the Liz Stevenson whose name appeared in the advertisement is indeed a married woman. Before the letter goes into the envelope, proofread it to see if there are any mistakes. Pay attention to detail.

Of course, if you know people in positions of authority in the company you are applying to, name them. If appropriate, you might send the letter direct to a person you know, with the request to pass it on.

To start with, a good example of how *not* to write a covering letter:

```
Dear Sir,

I wish to apply for the position of
Technical Officer advertised last
week.

I was a trainee with Telecom and did
the telecommunication course, I have
had experience in sound recording on
tape and also in cutting records,
and have installed public address
systems, I have experience in
operating film equipment, I am 32.

Yours faithfully,

Joe Smith.
```

Whether or not Mr Smith is the best man for the job, he is unlikely to get it. Quite apart from his errors in punctuation and failure to organise his material into any coherent order, the letter is simply too imprecise. What is this 'telecommunication course' that he attended? Where did he obtain his work experience? If his letter is as slipshod as this, will his work as an employee be any more reliable?

Mr Brown will probably do better.

```
Your ref: 45C/89/mk

Dear Sir/Madam,

            Technical Officer

    I was very interested to see your
advertisement for a technical
officer in today's Evening Mail, and
would like to be considered for the
post.

    As you will see from the enclosed
c.v., I was trained by Telecom and
have completed their in-house
diploma course in telecommunications
(two years, part-time). Since then I
have gained fairly wide experience
in sound engineering, both in full-
time employment and as a freelance
-- in particular as a recording
engineer and in setting up public
address systems. I gained valuable
recording experience, too, in the
film industry. I would very much
welcome the new opportunities that
working for a large organisation
such as yours would bring.

    I can supply references if you
need them, and can arrange for an
interview at any time, but would
need to have a little warning
beforehand.

    I hope to hear from you.

            Yours faithfully,

            Stephen Brown.
```

Joe Smith may be better suited to the job than Stephen Brown. But there is little doubt which of them will get further in the selection process.

Your covering letter will have four key elements:

1. The position you are applying for. Give the reference, if there is one. Mention where you saw the job advertised (newspaper and date). If you heard about it in some other way, give the details.

> My friend, Jill Banks, who works in your design department, has brought to my attention the vacancy for a stock controller in your company.

> I am writing about the post as a plumber which I saw advertised at the Oakington Jobcentre.

2. An indication of your interest in the job and keenness to get it. Show enthusiasm.

The position sounds very interesting.

This sounds like just the kind of work I have been looking for.

3. The reasons why you think you are suitable for the job. In particular, give a very brief summary of the most important details from your c.v. And be sure you make some reference to the attached c.v., or else the reader might overlook it.

Here you have to decide which points from your c.v. are most impressive and concentrate on them. Is it your experience? Your potential? Or your fast rise within your present company? Remember, the advertiser may be swamped with replies. It is your task to work out what he or she is looking for and to show, in the snappiest way possible, how you match up to it. Don't apologise for any apparent lack of modesty.

4. A statement of your availability for interview and willingness to provide references.

REPLYING TO AN ADVERTISEMENT

Read the advertisement carefully. Perhaps it stresses the employer's need for someone with a good general background and with supervisory experience. The following example is deliberately pitched to respond to the specifications.

Dear Sir/Madam,

Your advertisement for a production manager in the May 12 Journal caught my attention since your requirements closely parallel my working experience. I should like to be considered for the post, which sounds interesting and challenging.

As the enclosed c.v. indicates, I have more than ten years' experience in all phases of plastic production. For the past five years I have supervised a workforce of 15 people.

I should be very happy to discuss this in more detail with you. You can reach me at either of the above phone numbers, and I would be available for interview any afternoon.

Yours faithfully,

Celia Nichols.

There are times when a more jaunty tone may be appropriate. If the advertisement asks for 'commu-

nicative abilities' or 'self-confidence', this is virtually an invitation to you to be a little pushy. But don't overdo it.

Dear Mrs Henryson

The sales position with your company advertised in yesterday's Post sounds just the kind of thing I have been looking for. I hope that my c.v. will convince you that I am well cut out for such a position.

You ask for someone with initiative. I think my current employers would agree that increasing sales by 35 per cent in three years shows some initiative! And I know I could go further still in a larger company with a more varied range of products and wider markets.

I am quite happy in my present work, but find it a little limiting. From what I know of your company, this would not be a problem working for you. I should be happy to discuss this at an interview, but I will need a bit of notice to arrange time off from work.

May I ask you not to contact my current employer, at least for the time being. You will appreciate that it would create difficulties for me if he felt that I was dissatisfied with what I am doing at present.

Yours sincerely

William Jones

Suppose you want to apply for a job but suspect that your qualifications are inadequate. Don't apologise. Instead list your other qualities to counterbalance what you lack. Stress your interest and zeal, and your willingness to learn.

Dear Mr Thomas

I am applying for the post of senior packaging inspector with your company, advertised in the Globe on Wednesday 24 March.

You state that you are looking for a fast learner. I believe that I may be a good man for the job. The job itself sounds highly motivating, especially after my three years' experience in freight delivery management. For some time now I have wanted to move up from my present position, which has started to become routine. The job at your company sounds just the right step upwards: I am sure I could come to

---

grips with it right away, and master the details quickly.

You will find enclosed a summary of my qualifications and working experience.

Yours sincerely

Geoffrey Halford

GENERAL COVERING LETTERS

With general 'on spec' applications, things are rather different. You are plunging into the unknown. You do not know if the company you are applying to is recruiting at all, or what qualities it might be looking for.

First, do your research. Find out what areas the company specialises in, what it is well-known for. Tailor your letter accordingly. Suggest that you are especially interested in that company, and that with your background you are particularly suitable for it. You must mark yourself out from the crowd if you are going to whet the company's interest. If possible, find the name of the personnel manager, if there is one, or someone else within the company to address your letter to – as senior as possible.

Dear Mr Haydon

I have recently completed an HNC in textile manufacture, and am currently looking for suitable long-term employment. My main interest at college was in dyes and fabric treatment. While at college I held exhibitions of my work, which received favourable comments from staff and the local press.

I have only recently moved to this area. Your company was brought to my attention by one of my teachers at Blendon Technical College, who said that you were involved in progressive work in dyes, and suggested that I should contact you. While I realise that I have much to learn in this field, I am very keen to start with a company known for its forward-looking policies.

If you think you have any suitable vacancies for me, could you please let me know. I would be grateful to speak to you at any time.

Yours sincerely

Nigel Smart

GETTING BACK INTO THE WORK-FORCE

As a final case study, take this common and troublesome situation: you are a woman who has been away from work for some years while raising a family. As a result, you are worried about being accepted back into the work-force at the level where you left off.

Some of the things you might stress in your covering letter are: the stamina, economic expertise, management skills, and creative imagination you have needed during the years in which you have been running your home, raising your children, and so on. And you should mention any voluntary or temporary work you have done, or any continuing contact with a previous employer.

Here is a letter, in response to an advertised post, from a fairly well-qualified woman who for the last nine years has not been in full-time employment – though she has done some part-time work.

Dear Mrs Warren

COPYWRITER

I am writing to apply for the post advertised in today's Evening Post.

As you will see from the enclosed career details, I have wide experience of copywriting. During the six years I worked for Joshua McGrath & Associates in the 1970s, I handled some large local accounts, including those of Greystone Engineering and Small World Travel. Since leaving full-time employment in order to start a family, I have advised Joshua McGrath on a number of campaigns, and taken on freelance copywriting for the agency.

I have also undertaken voluntary activities, including teaching English in the homes of non-native speakers. This has increased my awareness of the needs and tastes – their television-watching habits, for instance, and shopping preferences – of an increasingly important audience for advertisers: people from non-British backgrounds.

I enclose several samples of copy I have written in recent years.

I look forward to hearing from you.

Yours sincerely

Katherine Turnbull

References and Back-up Letters

Almost everyone needs a reference at some time or other, so it is sensible policy to cultivate people who might act as referees when the need arises. If possible, they should be people of solid social standing – headteachers, doctors, managers in reputable companies, and so on.

Not that you necessarily want them to draw up a reference for you right away. Just put them on standby. Employers rarely ask for references to accompany initial applications.

How do you indicate on your application that you can supply references if required? One effective method is this: when compiling the job descriptions in your c.v., give the names of your supervisors or superiors at your previous and current places of work. And if possible, list phone numbers at which they can be contacted. (You should warn them, if you can, to expect such a call, and confirm that they are in fact willing to put in a good word for you.) Another, simpler, method is just to write, either in your c.v. or in your covering letter, *References are available on request*.

In the covering letter, you can always request the firm not to contact your current employers, as any such approach would compromise your position with them – unless, that is, the new firm is really serious about offering you a job. Such requests are standard practice. (See the example on page 340 for a discreetly worded request of this kind.) But if your current employers already know of your wish to leave, and if they are willing to lend you their support, by all means name them as referees.

If you succeed in getting the job of your choice, you will of course write to your referees to let them know and to thank them for their help. But bear in mind that most referees are on long-term standby – you might want to call on their services once again, or perhaps several times even, when you apply for further jobs in years to come.

Such long-standing referees need occasional 'topping up' – either to sustain their goodwill, or simply to remind them who you are. So drop them a note from time to time to let them know what you are doing, or to alert them that you might soon be needing their help again.

The level of formality you should use in these letters is something for you to decide for yourself – it varies according to your relationship with the referee in question. Here is a fairly informal example.

> Dear Sue
>
> As you see, I'm back on the job hunt. Sometimes I wonder whether I did the right thing in leaving your department, but the prospects sounded promising in that new post. I'm sorry to have to bother you again, but it really is time for me to move, and I hope you'll be willing to give me as good a reference as you did last time. Please let me know.
>
> I hope that all is well with you. Please send my best wishes to anyone left from my days with the company, and especially to your husband.
>
> All the best
>
> Bob Lofthouse

WHAT COMES NEXT?

The employer has been impressed by your application: you receive a telephone call or letter inviting you for interview. If it is a letter, you must acknowledge receipt, both out of courtesy and as a confirmation of the arrangements. You can do this with a phone call, or a letter – or perhaps best, both.

A beneficial side effect of sending a letter is that it will impress the reader as evidence of your serious interest in the job; it will also show that you pay attention to detail.

> Your ref. rt/8945/2
>
> Dear Mrs Thompson
>
> Thank you very much for your letter of 12 May. As I stated on the telephone, I shall be happy to come for the interview on 26 May at 2.00 pm, and shall arrange to have my references sent on to you direct as requested.
>
> I look forward to meeting you.
>
> Yours sincerely
>
> Hilary Cummings

If you are invited to an interview and are, for any reason, unable to make the time or date mentioned, you must, of course, contact the employer as soon as possible – preferably by phone – to ask for a new appointment. Again, though, it will almost certainly go down well if you send a letter confirming the details. This is good practice in business – and you want to show yourself as businesslike.

```
Your ref. rt/8934/2

Dear Mrs Thompson

Thank you for your letter of 12 May.
As I said on the telephone, I am
very sorry that I cannot attend the
interview for the post of technician
on 26 May, as I have to go to a
family funeral. But I will be able
to come at 11 pm on the 28th May.
Thank you for arranging that.

I apologise for any inconvenience
-- I do hope you understand.

Yours sincerely

Richard Plane
```

WHEN THE OFFER ARRIVES

Your interview went well, and a letter arrives formally offering you the post. A prompt reply is called for. A phone call followed by a confirming letter is once again best.

```
Your ref. 3418/nj/jb

Dear Mr Burns

Thank you for your letter of 5 June
offering me the post of Sales Clerk
in your company.

As I stated on the telephone, I am
delighted to accept the position,
and look forward to starting work
with you on 1 July.

Yours sincerely

Brian Bull
```

If for some reason you decide not to take the job, common courtesy obliges you to write back and state your reasons.

```
Dear Mr Burns

Thank you very much for your letter
of 5 June offering me the post of
Sales Clerk with your company.
```

```
I am afraid that after careful
consideration I have decided that I
cannot accept the position. My
current employer, on hearing that I
was intending to leave, has shown
his confidence in me by offering to
fund me on a sandwich course in .
business administration at our local
College of Further Education. This
would clearly improve my career
prospects, as well as providing a
welcome change in my working
conditions.

I do apologise for such a late
withdrawal, and hope that it does
not inconvenience you too much.  I
know you will understand the reasons
for my decision. I would like to
thank you for your confidence in my
abilities.

Yours sincerely

Brian Bull
```

APPLICATIONS – A CHECKLIST

Before you seal the envelope containing your application, and post it, give your material one final, very careful, check through. Do this, preferably, the day after you have composed the application, when your mind is fresh.

☐ Check that you have enclosed all necessary components of your application: the c.v., the covering letter – and any extras that may have been requested. Advertisements often ask, for instance, for specimens of your previous work.

☐ Double-check all names and titles. Have another look at the advertisement. Are you sure it is *Mrs*, not *Miss* or *Ms*, MacAndrew you should send the application to? And is it *MacAndrew*, rather than *McAndrew*? Is she the *Personnel* (or *Human Resources*) *Manager*, or the *Personnel Officer*?

☐ Double-check in a dictionary all spellings, and check other details, such as dates. A tiny slip of the typewriter could make your date of birth 1983 rather than 1963.

☐ Check the look of things. Is your covering letter neatly centred in the page? If not, retype it. Check the envelope too. Is it the right size? Your application must emerge crisp and clean; it will not if you have crunched it all into a tiny envelope.

Writing at Work, Home, and College

Writing Letters from Home

LETTERS ARE THINGS that many people like to put off. A letter arrives from the building society, full of awkward questions about a request to extend your mortgage, about the state of the drains, about whether your endowment policy should be cashed in, and about countless other tricky matters. Where do you find the information they need, and then how do you go about expressing it all in a letter back? And it is not just official letters that can leave people scratching their heads. How, for example, do you go about thanking those dull relatives in Grantham who sent you £25 for your birthday? Other than 'thank you' you do not have much to say to them. Or, on another occasion, is 'Congratulations on the new baby' all you can think of? It does not sound very congratulatory.

This chapter is designed to provide you with the tools for making letter-writing less of a chore, whatever the situation. You will find suggestions on how to deal with most of the kinds of letter you will have to write.

TWO EXAMPLES

Compare the following two letters written to the editor of a local newspaper. Which do you think the editor was more likely to use?

```
                    Donald William James,
                     42, Highway Avenue,
                           Trumpton.

Dear Sir,

    It really is disgusting. I've
been taking your paper for six years
now, ever since I moved to this
town, and I don't think I've ever
read such biased nonsense in all
that time. I've noticed your
standards going downhill for some
time now but you seem to have
reached rock bottom, and if things
don't improve I'll cancel my
subscription.

    The article in your last issue
about amenities must have been
```

```
written by someone with no
experience of living in this town,
as is shown by his approval of the
council's plans, which seem to
ignore the general opinion of
residents. Some of what it said
appears to have been lifted straight
from council propaganda and I think
your journalists ought to learn to
get out and look for facts for
themselves, which is what a
journalist is supposed to do. The
article was wrong about the number
of tennis courts and provision for
elderly and handicapped people.
You've published other articles that
make the same mistakes. I've written
to my councillor but as she's on the
committee I can't expect much from
her. The open-air pool was shut for
most of last summer for what they
said were essential repairs at the
time of the year when most people
might want to use it, which was
something you didn't mention.
Everyone I speak to is fed up with
second best. You don't seem to care.

    Yours,

    Donald William James.
```

```
                    Mrs Megan Jenkins
                    Flat 5, Walton House
                         Town Hill Road
                              Trumpton

                    17 September 1990

The Editor
The Trumpton News and Journal
High Street
Trumpton
Dear Sir

Recreational Amenities in Trumpton

I read with some incredulity the
article on page 4 of the last issue
of The Trumpton News and Journal
(Friday, 14 September), titled
'Trumpton -- the Town with
Everything'. The situation described
by your reporter bore little
resemblance to the town that I live
in, and I am sure that I am not alone
in wishing to put the other side of
the case.
```

Amenities in the town have not
improved over the last two years.
It's true that the plans for a youth
centre in Market Street have been
agreed, though the council continue
to veto the start of the building
work, claiming lack of funds.

Against this should be set:

1. The closure of the public outdoor
swimming pool in Shrewsbury Road for
most of last summer.

2. The closure of the Pensioners
Centre -- due, it is said, to
persistent vandalism. (Are the
vandals the OAPs themselves?)

3. The cancellation of plans to
build a centre for handicapped
people.

4. The scrapping of plans for a
playground on the Berwyn Estate.

5. The failure to improve the pitted
surfaces on the town's only four
public tennis courts (in Mostyn
Park).

We've all heard or read the honeyed
tones of Mayor Steven and the
councillors on the Amenities
Subcommittee. Our mayor has a fine
baritone to match his dashing good
looks, and the committee accompany
him with the tunefulness of a Welsh
male-voice choir. He certainly seems
to have sung himself into the heart
of your reporter.

I for one, as the mother of three
teenagers in the town, have grown
rather weary of our mayor's
blandishments. And I hope that other
readers who share my opinion will
write both to you and to their
councillors. It's not the money that
this town's lacking; it's a little
will and enterprise from those who
have charge of it.

Yours faithfully

Megan Jenkins

The only conceivable positive effect of Mr James's letter is to persuade the editor to publish Mrs Jenkins's. Both letters express much the same opinion. But Mr James's is unusable as it stands.

What faults does it commit?

☐ It lacks a date, and any heading or reference in the first paragraph to direct the editor to the subject. It fails to specify which article has annoyed Mr James so badly. It also mentions 'other articles' without saying which.

☐ It is insulting to the public officials and (even worse if Mr James wants his letter published) it is insulting to the editor of the paper and his journalists. Outraged bluster is no substitute for reasoned criticism.

☐ It is vague and short on facts.

☐ It makes impotent threats against the newspaper, and unsupported claims about public opinion. It is also full of irrelevant material, such as how long Mr James has been living in the town and his dealings with his councillor.

☐ Most of the letter is a single 'paragraph', making it a challenge for any reader. The material in that paragraph is disorganised, wandering off the subject and back onto it without any apparent reason. The sentences are too long.

Compare Mrs Jenkins's approach. Mrs Jenkins has obviously planned her letter. She has chosen what she wants to say and spent some time putting it into a logical order. She has made an effort to get the editor on her side; at most there is gentle and good-humoured chiding. She attempts to use humour when dealing with her political opponents, which is a good deal more effective (and publishable) than insults.

Mrs Jenkins, in other words, reveals most of the virtues of a good correspondent.

☐ She makes clear precisely what she is going to write about both in the heading and in the exact reference in the first sentence. She is polite in her request to be allowed to express her opinion. She admits also that there are two points of view.

☐ She states her main points clearly, and in a logical order. She is also positive in her attitude. She has practical suggestions for those who share her opinion. And, best of all from the editor's point of view, she encourages others to write to his paper, which is what he wants.

☐ She says just the right amount about her personal situation to show why the matter affects her. She presents herself successfully as 'Everywoman'.

In short, she comes across as a rational and reasonable human being – just the kind of reader the editor values.

If Mrs Jenkins can write letters like this to a newspaper, the chances are that she can also write clear, coherent, and considerate letters of all kinds –

to companies, public institutions, friends, and family. Whether she is enquiring about travel arrangements or expressing her thanks for a friendly favour, she will get her message across. She sets methodically about the task of writing.

WHAT MAKES A GOOD LETTER-WRITER?

There is nothing magical about learning the skill of letter-writing. It is just like any other skill – the first and paramount requirement is to practise. The second is to take your time.

Peace and quiet are important too. You cannot expect to put together a decent letter with one ear listening to television, or while being jolted around on the bus, or in the five frantic minutes before you rush off to work.

Before you write, think about what you are going to say – not in a vague general sense but in detail. Make notes and a plan. Then, as you write, stop frequently to consider how the letter is going, and how you are going to tackle the next section.

Better still, write a rough draft first; then carefully edit and revise it into a final, fully polished form. (For various useful techniques, see pages 103-104, and 109-110.)

Taking time will help you with another key principle: take care. Keep your full concentration on what you are doing. Planning beforehand will help. If you have got the subject matter sorted out before you start, you will be able to keep your mind on how best to put it into words.

Taking care is also a question of the 'little things'. Don't scribble down a word if you are not sure that it means exactly what you want to say or that you are spelling it properly. Before you write it is the time to look it up in a dictionary.

Pay attention also to your layout, to your handwriting or typing, and to your paragraphing. Bear in mind the impression your letter will make. (For further advice on presentation, see pages 273-276.)

THE ABC OF GOOD LETTER-WRITING

What you are aiming for in any letter you have to write can be summed up in three words – accuracy, brevity, and clarity. They are, in fact, the ABC of all good writing. The best thing you can do for your reader, whoever he or she might be, is to give the most and best information in the least time.

Accuracy. This requires precision – not just of facts but of expression and thought. Your official letters should give an impression of calm efficiency, the sort of efficiency you expect of whoever is going to have to deal with them. Your personal mail, however complicated the ideas you may want to express, should show your reader exactly what happened and what you think about it.

Accuracy requires attention to detail. You could seriously annoy your best friend if you kept spelling the name of his new girlfriend *Catherine* when he has just sent you a letter telling you all about *Catharine*. And you might annoy your son's class teacher if you assume that she is called *Mrs* Russell when in fact she is unmarried.

Before you start writing, make sure you have got all the relevant facts. In official letters, always quote references, names, dates, and the like. You can greatly help the busy person who will have to sort out your enquiry if you make clear in a heading or the first sentence what you are writing about.

If your letter has two purposes, say so at the outset before treating the first in full.

A strong, clear start to your letter will help both you and your reader to direct your minds to the matter in hand. Compare the following as openings to letters to an MP urging him to take an interest in educational cuts in your area.

> I am writing to urge you, as our MP, to put what pressure you can on the Northamptonshire Local Education Authority to stop them selling the playing fields attached to King's Street Primary School for housing development.

> Educational facilities in this area have been going downhill of late and soon even the most basic will be lacking. When I was at school education meant something in this country.

The first opening makes everything plain; the second is a platitude.

How much detail do you need to give to make your letter accurate? The answer is, enough to say exactly what you need to say without ambiguity, and no more. Don't expect your reader to be familiar with you and your problems, or the intricacies of the subject you are writing about. In your personal mail, don't write to friends you have not seen for years, expecting them to know all about your personal circumstances. If there is any chance your reader will not know who you are talking about, there is no harm in saying *Keith (that's our younger son) will be starting at Bristol University in autumn* or *Shelley, who's five now, is an interesting and affectionate child.*

This filling in of details is even more important in official letters. Your bank manager sees dozens of letters every week and you cannot expect him to remember the one you wrote three weeks ago. You can always start: *I wrote to you on 25 April and am still waiting for a reply to two of the points raised.* Then you should go on to repeat the points.

Brevity. At first sight, this might seem incompatible with accuracy. How can you be brief when you have to give full and accurate details?

The secret is, of course, to give all the details your reader requires and no more. Sifting the essential from the non-essential facts can be time-consuming. The 17th-century French philosopher Blaise Pascal once wrote to a friend: 'I have made this letter longer than usual, only because I have not had the time to make it shorter.' And it certainly does take more time and effort to write a short letter than a long one. But time spent in refining your letter will be time saved in getting a satisfactory response to it.

Official letters, especially, should be no longer than needed. If all you have to say is *Please, where can I get information about train times and prices within the Soviet Union?*, that is all you need to write. *I'm sorry Mildred wasn't in school on Thursday and Friday; she had a cold* will be enough to satisfy your daughter's teacher that she was not playing truant on the days in question.

Remember that most people you write official letters to are as busy as you are. It is in your interest not to annoy them by rambling on with irrelevant information. So decide before you start what the essential facts are that you need to present – and cut out anything else. Even if you can think of ten good reasons why a proposed road scheme should be scrapped, choose only the three or four that seem strongest when you come to write to the commission of inquiry.

But don't be so brief as to be cryptic. As you write, both expand and cut. If you find something unclear, try adding a couple of words to sort out the ambiguity. And wherever you find something redundant, be it an unnecessary word, phrase, sentence, or paragraph, strike it out ruthlessly. Make your letters lean and fit, with plenty of meat and no fat.

A strong, clear start will help your reader.

In personal letters you can be more expansive. Most people enjoy taking their time when reading letters from friends, and often a mere two paragraphs will seem curt and impolite. But even in personal letters, don't ramble. Talk about what your reader is likely to be interested in – don't get bogged down in the trivia of your everyday life.

Clarity. This is largely a matter of style and organisation, and you will find several suggestions on how to make your writing clearer later in this chapter. Accuracy and brevity will help you to be clear. If you have got your ideas in order before you start, you will be much more likely to set them down coherently. And if you keep your letters fairly short, you will stand less chance of losing the thread along the way.

Think of your reader as you write. Put yourself into his or her place. Would you find what you are writing easy to understand? Or are you getting lost even as you write?

One useful tip to help to improve the clarity of a letter that has to present a number of facts or reasons is to put each item on a new line or in a separate paragraph. Number your points if this will help, especially if you are going to have to refer to them individually later in your letter. The following letter to a newspaper may not be very exciting, but there is no faulting it on the grounds of clarity.

```
Sir

I believe that traffic lights should
be installed at the crossing over
French Street into Unwin Park. There
are three reasons for this:

1. Children from the Conston Estate
need to cross the road to play in
the park.

2. French Street has become very
busy since Queen's Road was closed
to traffic.

3. The street lighting at this part
of the road is inadequate.

Yours

Hilda Grange (Mrs)
```

PROMPTNESS

Promptness of reply is the fourth key virtue of letter-writing. It is important for two reasons. The longer a letter hangs over you, the more difficult it is to get started. This does not mean that as soon as you have ripped a letter from its envelope you ought to dash off the reply. Your reply to something complicated and official will probably gain from being allowed to mature in your mind for a day or so. By then, you may have found a better way of answering than you might otherwise have done. Your ideas will probably have come into sharper focus and your needs and intentions will be clearer.

But a longer delay can be construed as rudeness or inefficiency. Being prompt in your business letters is a matter of self-interest. Promptness is even more crucial in the most important letters of all: the personal ones in which you show real consideration for someone – thank-you notes, letters of congratulations and best wishes, 'get well soon' cards, letters of condolence, and so on. These kinds of letter warrant no delay. The moment your conscience tells you a letter of this sort is due is the moment you ought to set about writing it.

The Tools of the Trade

One of the best investments you can make as a letter-writer is in a typewriter or word processor. You are going to have to write letters for the rest of your life. Why not make sure that people can read them? Learning to type is not difficult. There are courses to take, or you could learn from a book.

Typing has two great advantages over handwriting. It is always legible (and so does not distract from what you have to say), and it makes it much easier to lay your letters out neatly – which is especially important with business letters.

Typewriters do not have to be expensive. Perfectly serviceable manual or electronic ones can be picked up cheaply through newspaper advertisements or from second-hand dealers. Then at the top end of the scale there are word processors. Even these can cost under £500, and you do not have to be a technical wizard to be able to master them.

Word processors have a number of advantages. You can juggle your text and layout around at will before you print the letter out, and you always have copies of your letters instantly available. Some also cut out many of the chores of letter-writing. At the touch of a button your name and address and the date can be inserted in your chosen standard format at the top of the letter.

A word of warning about the quality of print with word processors. Many come with dot-matrix printers – ones that form letters with a series of dots. With these, make sure to use the option generally called Near Letter Quality – printing out using this option takes longer, but the quality of the print using the faster Draft Quality option is not good enough for letters.

With daisy wheel printers – the same as those on electronic typewriters – there is no problem. Best of all are laser printers which produce book-quality print-outs, but these are expensive.

Some people still insist that typewriters and word processors belong in the office and are unsuitable for personal correspondence. This idea is dying out. The general view now is that the advantages of typing outweigh its impersonality. In more personal letters, as to friends and members of the family, you can always type the main text – the news, any enquiries, and so on – and then handwrite special notes at the bottom.

However, there do remain some occasions when writing is preferable to typing. These are the occasions when the personal touch is most important: invitations (when these are not printed) and replies to them; letters of congratulation and thanks; letters of condolence. Most people would find that typing such letters showed a lack of respect or decorum. (When writing them, do make sure that your handwriting is neat and legible.)

PAPER, ENVELOPES, AND INK

For all normal purposes, the rule about stationery is this: err on the side of sobriety. Avoid anything that could distract from the contents of your letter. For typing, the best thing to use is plain white A4-size typing paper.

Consider investing in some headed notepaper. It will enhance all your correspondence, whether business letters to company chairmen or personal thank-you letters. Really impressive notepaper can also be a wonderful boost to your confidence when settling down to write a letter – it need not be expensive; your local printer can give you a quote. Remember that printing the heading is considerably cheaper than engraving it, and a printed heading can look just as good. There are different styles for laying out the heading (see overleaf) – your printer will show you samples.

When ordering headed paper, do it in bulk. It saves both money and the trouble of frequent reordering. It is a good idea to order two sizes – full sheet A4, and half-size A5 for shorter notes. Order matching envelopes at the same time.

Even if you do not have headed notepaper, keep a good stock of stationery ready. The choice is immense. Larger-sized plain white paper is always safe. Off-white, cream, grey, light blue, or light brown are also acceptable. Slightly more adventurous colours are common, but usually in pastel shades. Designs and bright colours are not a good idea – it is then the paper that grabs the reader's attention, not what you have to say.

If you have to write abroad frequently, keep a stock of light 'airmail' paper and envelopes. If you use airmail or other very thin paper, write on one side only. It is annoying for the reader to have to sort out the text on one side of the paper from that on the other showing through.

Younger people may prefer more florid designs. But they ought to realise that green ink on mauve paper embossed with emblems and pictures will give their

INDEPENDENT ADJECTIVES

What adjective do you use when referring to a hand? *Handy* will not do, of course. You have to use a quite different word – *manual*. And, generally speaking, you use the word *dental* (not *toothy*!) as an adjective when referring to teeth. Similarly, *canine* for things to do with a dog, and *lunar* for things to do with the Moon.

☐ Here are two lists, one of adjectives, the other of the nouns they serve. Try to match the appropriate noun to the adjective in each case. For the answers turn to pages 633-648.

adipose	ocular	equine	blood	goat	clothes
arboreal	olfactory	farinaceous	horse	cat	bird
avian	paschal	feline	wolf	brother	heart
avuncular	pulmonary	ferric	letter	lungs	twilight
bovine	renal	fraternal	star	liver	iron
caprine	sartorial	gastric	kidneys	fox	Ireland
cardiac	simian	haemal	stomach	monkey	Greece
cranial	solar	Hellenic	day	lips	eye
crepuscular	stellar	hepatic	ox or cow	skull	bear
diurnal	ursine	Hibernian	Easter	tree	worm
episcopal	vermicular	labial	sun	fat	flour
epistolary	vulpine	lupine	uncle	sense of smell	bishop

age away and tell unknown readers more about them than perhaps they wish to tell. If your teenage daughter announces that she has to write to a training college with her application or to a newspaper with an enquiry for a school project, offer her a piece of your own stationery.

For the very young, anything is permissible if it will encourage them to write letters – animal or toy designs, swirls of colour all over the page, whatever they like. Take them with you to the shop when you go to choose. If they think the paper really is theirs, they are more likely to use it.

Of course, personal letters do not have to be written on notepaper. You can use postcards, greeting cards, folded paper with designs and matching envelopes. The only rule here is not to use this kind of stationery for business correspondence and for serious personal letters, such as letters of condolence. For letters like these, the plainer the stationery you use the better.

Finally, a word on ink. When you write by hand you ought to use a pen. Pencil is too faint. Some ball-point pens produce a reasonably pleasing script, but don't use them if they are scratchy. A fibre-tip pen or fountain pen (as long as the paper is not too absorbent) usually produces better results.

Avoid red ink. It strains the eyes. Blue or black ink is always acceptable, especially on white paper. On light blue paper, dark blue ink is perhaps preferable to black. You should try out a few possible combinations of paper and ink and see which appeals to you.

Setting Your Letters Out

The main thing to be said about layout is this: Keep it tidy. Here are some further general and specific hints that will help:

☐ If you have only a short note to write and are using large paper, work out about how long the text will be and try to centre it between the top and the bottom of the page.

☐ Make sure your margins are wide enough – say an inch all around, but less if the paper is smaller than A4.

☐ Before you insert paper into a typewriter, pencil in a little mark just over an inch from the bottom of the page to show you when to stop typing and change sheet. You should rub out all pencil marks afterwards. (This problem does not arise with word processors, which make the page breaks for you.)

Every letter should contain these elements:

☐ your address

☐ the date the letter was written

☐ a salutation

☐ the text

☐ a conclusion and your signature

Certain types of letter, especially official letters, can have other elements, such as references and the address of the recipient. For advice on these, see the relevant sections opposite and on page 352.

YOUR ADDRESS

If you have headed notepaper, your address is, of course, already there. If not, you will have to type or write it in. A common custom with official letters is to include your name as the first line of the address. You must decide what you want to be called – *Mrs Keith Walker*, *Mrs Rose Walker*, or *Rose Walker*. If your headed notepaper does not include your name, you can always type it in neatly directly above the heading:

Sarah Middleton,
Flat 15,
Wansdyke House, . . .

Personal handwritten letters are different. Here it is usual not to put in your name until you sign it at the end, though by all means do so if the letter is more than one page and is going to someone who will not recognise your handwriting.

There are three ways to set out the address. Most popular for personal correspondence is the indented form. In this format each line of the address is set in a space or two from the one above:

Coniston House,
Wintermore Lane,
Sonning Common,
Reading RD4 5PQ,
Berks.
Tel. 0734 245267.
Sunday, October 7th.

Many people, however, prefer the block form for official letters. Here each line of the address starts directly below the one above. You may find it simpler to lay out the address by this method.

> Mrs Julie Yenches,
> 14B Northwold Road,
> London SW8 2LR.
> Tel. 081 986 4528.

The third way is to centre your name and address at the top of the sheet. For headed notepaper, you might want to have your name in bold or large print. To save space when using this layout, it is quite common to combine elements of the address on a single line under the name, as here:

> Mr & Mrs Arthur Galway,
> 'The Dower House',
> Fifield Lane, Dorney Wood,
> Berkshire SL4 2HP.
> Tel. 0753 62454.

Don't forget your postcode. It can go after the town or county name, or on a line on its own.

The commas or full stops at the end of the lines are no longer considered important. Leave them out if you prefer a more streamlined look.

If you own a fax machine, you could simply enter the number between your phone number and the date. (But the fax number then looks just like a phone number, and the reader might try dialling it when phoning you. If you enclosed it in brackets, that ought to alert the reader to the danger.)

In notes it is quite common to start with the salutation, and to have the return address at the bottom, usually to the left – this is also the general practice on invitations (see pages 386-403). So a note of condolence might end:

> With fondest regards,
>
> Alan Mitchell

'Tall Trees'
Brampton Road
Horsted Keynes
W. Sussex RH14 8UT
Tel. 0245 932471

When you are away from home. You do not usually need to give an address in letters or postcards written on holiday. But you ought to give some indication of where you are writing from:

> Milan, Tuesday.

If, however, you do need to include your home address in a letter written while on the move – perhaps on business – use this format:

> As from: 70 Willowbrook Avenue,
> London SW13 8AD.

If you are staying with someone, and want your correspondent to write back to you at your temporary address, use the formula *c/o* ('care of') with the name of the person you are staying with:

> c/o Mrs Wilfred White,
> 'The Red House',
> Pangworth,
> Somerset BAT 9JO.

If you are staying with a married couple, it is usual to give the name of the wife – your hostess.

THE DATE

All business letters should show day, month, and year. In personal letters it is usual to give the day and month – the year is less important.

Avoid the *5/7/89* or *14.2.91* style. People do not generally think of months in terms of numbers. There is a greater danger, too. The format differs from country to country, and this can cause real confusion. In particular, to an American *8.4.90* means 'August the fourth, 1990'. In most of the rest of the world it would be 'April the eighth'.

So the best way to show the date in an official letter is *5 June, 1990*. The comma is optional. You could also use *5th June, 1990*. Either of these is fine in personal correspondence too, or you might give the day of the week and the date without the year – *Tuesday, 5 June*.

By far the most usual place to date your letter is at the very end of the address. If you use headed notepaper, type or write the date in at the appropriate place.

As with the positioning of your address, in personal notes you can use the old style of putting the date at the end. A note should not go over one side, so the date will never be hard to find. If you use this method, put the date to the left, either alone or under your address.

THE RECIPIENT'S ADDRESS

Here the ways divide. It is normal practice in official letters to include the name and address of the person you are writing to. In personal letters this would be considered off-puttingly formal.

In official letters, give the name and address of the recipient flush against the left margin, starting a couple of lines below the date. A name or job title is always included, even if it is only *The Editor* or *H.M. Inspector of Taxes*.

If you are in doubt about whom to address your letter to, look at the chart in the chapter on modes of address, page 404. The address should be given precisely as it appears on any correspondence you have from the person you are writing to.

REFERENCES

Once again, these are only given in official letters. Leave a line below the recipient's address – it is simplest to keep all references flush against the left margin. Enter *Your ref.*, leave a couple of spaces, and copy the reference exactly as on correspondence from the company or organisation you are writing to. For *Your ref.* you might of course have to substitute something such as *Your order no.* or *Passport no.* or whatever is required.

If there are two or more references, give them all, with a new line for each. Only then can you be sure that you have done everything in your power to enable the recipient to handle you letter with the maximum of efficiency.

You can take a line to write *Enclosure* or *Encl.* when you are enclosing something with the letter. You can also say what the enclosures are, as in: *Encl. – Driving licence no. 616373 NJ8YX*. If more than one enclosure has to be detailed, it is usually better to put them in a list after your typed name at the very end of the letter.

If you want to give a reference of your own, leave a line after *Your ref.* and write *My / Our ref., Our job no.*, or whatever is appropriate.

DEAR FRED

The salutation is again set flush against the left margin, at least two lines below the last written line before it.

If you really do not know the name of the person you are writing to, use *Dear Sir* or *Dear Madam*. But this formula does sound rather old-fashioned, and it is better to try to find out the recipient's name and to use that instead.

In personal letters you can vary the salutation as you wish. You could have anything from *Dear Mother and Father* or *My dearest Angelica* to *Hello, Jim, my old mate* or *Oy, there, Bill, you idle scoundrel*. It would depend entirely on your relationship with the recipient and your mood at the time of writing.

A good rule in all cases of doubt is to salute the reader with the name you know him or her by. It would be bad form to salute an old friend with *Dear Mrs Evans* if you normally called her *Mary*. If your accountant is a personal friend but you are writing on business, the layout should be as for an official letter, but the salutation might be *Dear Tom*.

Americans have slightly different customs from the British. They prefer, especially in very formal letters, the salutation *My dear Sir*. They also use *Gentlemen* when writing to an organisation. There is one other difference between British and American usage: in Britain you follow the salutation with a comma; in North America a colon is more usual.

THE SUBJECT HEADING

In an official letter, you can help the recipient by listing the main subject in a 'subject heading' – often underlined, and no more than two lines long.

Position it two lines below the salutation, and leave another blank line before starting the text.

So you might, if writing to a newspaper editor, use the heading *Street lighting in Newark*. And to help the bank deal with your request, you might write *Changes to Standing orders; Account no. 25379340*.

```
                    Mrs Elizabeth Pritchard
                         24 Whitney Road
                        Oxford OX2 6RF
                        Tel: 0865 251727

Miss Roberta Frank
Sales Department
Wilson & Co
Carfax
Oxford OX1 2LP

Your ref: OX34194/PL/rf
Invoice no: 345 - 2

My job no: 128b

Dear Miss Frank

Tailoring adjustments

I write in answer to your letter of
7 January.
```

In a personal letter, a subject heading would strike quite the wrong note – unless intended as a joke. But the opening words might still contain a reference to a previous letter, as a helpful cue to the reader:

> 2 Highridge Cottages
> Turnfield Lane
> Moresby
> York Y6 4HF
>
> 16th August
>
> Dearest Madge,
> What a pleasure to get your note today. Many congratulations!

THE TEXT

Set out your text clearly, above all in typed official letters. Keep your paragraphs short and leave a clear line between each. Traditionally, each new paragraph was indented at the beginning. Nowadays, however, it is common not to indent – so be especially sure to leave a clear line between paragraphs. This makes the text less monolithic on the page and helps to break up the contents into manageable sections – for more details of the two kinds of layout, see pages 274 and 275.

If you are writing by hand and need to spell out some word unequivocally – a name, for example – write it in block capitals.

Write on only one side of the paper in official letters. In personal letters you can use both sides, but not if the writing shows through from the other side. In longer letters, number each page except the first.

If you find that you are coming to the end of a page and still have a fair amount to write, don't squeeze your writing up. And don't be tempted to write in the margins. It can be frustrating when you have almost no space left to write just *Yours sincerely, Joan Wright*; do nevertheless start a new sheet rather than spoil the appearance of the current one.

Before you put the finished letter into its envelope, arrange the sheets in order. Fold the sheets in such a way that the top of the first page shows. If there is just a single fold, it is customary to insert the letter so that the crease is at the top of the envelope, but this is hardly crucial.

THE CONCLUSION

Leave at least one clear line after the end of the text before putting in the conclusion. With typing, it looks neater if you leave two. The conclusion may be indented or flush with the left margin.

The traditional rule is that a letter starting *Dear Sir* or *Dear Madam* ends with *Yours faithfully*. *Yours truly* may be used as an alternative but it is a little old-fashioned. If you start with *Dear Miss Patel* or *Dear Sir George*, end with *Yours sincerely*. When you are writing to thank someone for a favour, you might use *Gratefully* or *Yours in gratitude*, though your thanks are better included in the main text than in the closing.

Respectfully is used only by tradesmen to a customer or by an employee to the boss, and even then sounds rather sycophantic. And except on very specific formal occasions, such as in open letters to royalty and certain government officials, never use closings like *I have the honour to remain . . .* and *Your obedient servant*.

In personal letters the choice is much wider and you have the chance to use your imagination. How you end your letter will depend on your relationship with the recipient and the tone and purpose of the letter. Fairly safe, all-purpose closings include *Yours, As ever, Best wishes, All the best*, and *(Kind) Regards. With thanks, Good luck!, See you soon*, and the like are fine when appropriate. *Keep smiling!, Be good, How's it going?, Hoping to hear from you*, and so on make cheerful endings to light letters between friends. *Affectionately, (With) Love*, and the like are for your dearest friends and family. In family letters people often sign off with a mention of their relationship to the reader, such as *Your loving son/father/mother* or *Best wishes from your uncle, aunt, and cousins*.

The closing can be a whole sentence and part of the last paragraph of the text:

> Looking forward to seeing you at Christmas. Until then, all the best and love to you all,
>
> Tina Allen

YOUR SIGNATURE

Leave a three or four-line gap before entering your signature. That way your name will stand out clearly. If you have typed the letter, use blue or black ink for signing.

Sign your name clearly and with pride.

You may want to give a little thought to your signature. If over the years it has degenerated into a meaningless squiggle, think about overhauling it. Instead of using your worst and quickest hand for your name, sign it clearly and with pride. Make sure it can be read.

Women should consider whether they want to include their marital status in their signature. It might help people who have to write back to you if you include *Mrs, Miss,* or *Ms* – in brackets after the surname. Of course, if you put your name plus any appropriate title at the top of the letter, this is unnecessary.

Don't include honorific, military, professional, and academic titles and the like in your signature.

Never sign an official letter for someone else, other than in clearly defined situations at work – see page 274. This applies even to a married couple writing a letter to a newspaper, say. If more than one person needs to sign a letter they should do so individually. It looks tidiest if each signs on a separate line. The person who actually wrote or composed the letter should sign first.

In personal letters, the situation is different. It is common practice for a wife to sign *Clive and Eileen* when writing to friends, or to sign *Mum and Dad* to her children.

THE ENVELOPE

Most letters look best in matching envelopes. You can get A4 sized envelopes to take A4 typing paper. Most special notepaper and greetings cards come with their own envelopes.

Whatever happens, try to find an envelope that suits your paper. A small note looks silly in a large business envelope; large notepaper will have to be folded over and over to fit into small envelopes.

Any correspondence that is too thick to send by normal post should be sent as a parcel. You should register your mail at the Post Office if it contains anything valuable, or if you might need proof of sending – so as to avoid any possible threat of legal action if you do not settle an account.

Don't be careless about addressing your mail. A court in Britain once sent out a summons to a man whose address was given on the envelope as *No fixed abode*! You want your letter to reach its destination, and the best way to see that it does so is by observing sensible rules about addresses.

Write as clearly as you can. If necessary, print in block capitals. It is customary to write or type the town and post code in this way. Do *not* forget the postcode if you know it.

Whenever possible, give a name. Even if this is not the name of the person who will be dealing with the matter you raise in your letter, he or she can pass it on to the person who will.

Some business addresses can be very long, especially when you have to include the job title and department. You can combine elements on one line as long as this causes no confusion. Give the name of the recipient on its own line and make sure all important elements stand out.

> Miss Sandra Bryant,
> Assistant Manager, Personnel Department,
> Watson's Engineering, Watson House,
> Unit 12, Friary Way,
> Home Trading Estate,
> Morton, SCUNTHORPE,
> Humberside
> GR12 7PM.

When writing a personal letter to a friend at work, you might put *Personal, Private and Confidential*, or the like. The usual places are the top or bottom left corners of the envelope. These are also the places to write *Please forward* if you know that the person you are writing to no longer lives at the address you have for him or her.

Occasionally in official letters, it can be helpful to include a heading on the envelope. It might be *Passport Application* or *Invoice 238* or the like. Write this in either the top or bottom left corners. Make sure it does not confuse the address in any way; the address should always stand clear and alone as the central item on the envelope.

The thing that is most often forgotten on envelopes is the return address. You want your letter to get through. But if it does not, for whatever reason, you want to know that it has not. If it contains anything important or valuable you want to get it back. So, make sure your address is clearly visible.

There are two places where you can enter your return address – in the top left corner, or on the back flap. Make sure it cannot be mistaken for the destination. One way to do this is to write it in continuous form:

> N. Hammond; 14, Queensway Road; Bradford; W. Yorks BD12 0PV.

Personal Letters

Sir Philip Sidney, the Elizabethan soldier and poet, was composing the first of his sonnets. He racked his brain in search of ways to express his love. He considered the range of well-established poetic images and turns of phrase for 'improving' his poetry. Somehow they all rang false. Finally, a voice within him whispered the solution: 'Fool, said my Muse to me, look in thy heart and write.'

Look in your heart, as you sit down to write your letter to a friend, and you too should find ample subject matter. Pause and think deeply about your friend. Reread his or her last letter to you, and forget about fine words and fancy phrases. A letter in which sincere feelings are expressed with sincerity is a good letter.

As a rule, knowing what to write should not be difficult. There is often some special reason for writing – to thank an aunt for a gift, to condole with a friend who has lost his wife. You need only think of what you would like to say if you were there in person, or what you hope people would say to you if the tables were turned. As ever, it pays to give a little thought to content beforehand, and to arrange it into some kind of order. But then take up your pen and get your message down on paper. Quickly, preferably at a single sitting. This is your chance to let your full personality come across.

PERSONAL LETTERS ARE PERSONAL

Another 'rule' for successful personal letters is this: however much you talk about yourself in the bulk of the letter, it should start and end with the person you are writing to. The simplest way to do this is to see that the word *you* (or *your*) occurs in the first and last sentences.

Even in the main body of the letter, don't write too much about yourself. In a long letter, come back to the recipient from time to time: *You know the kind of thing I mean . . . Don't you remember, we did the same thing when we were young . . . I can tell you this, but I'd be terribly embarrassed to tell some people . . . You like her books, don't you?* And even if you have a lot of news to give, split it up with paragraphs on other subjects. Try to avoid strings of sentences beginning with *I* – they will make you seem very self-centred.

Remember too, when you are answering a letter, to pay attention to what it had to say. This will show that you take the person you are writing to seriously. Ask about points that the letter did not make clear. Comment on the various pieces of news it contained. Make sure to answer all the questions it asked.

Finally, remember that writing gives a permanence to matters that would otherwise be soon forgotten. It is very tempting to open your heart and let the words flow out. But avoid writing letters that would embarrass you if they appeared for general consumption with your name beneath them. If you sense you have been a bit overemotional or demanding, put the letter to one side overnight. If you still want to send it in the morning, go ahead; if not, the wastepaper bin is a better place for it than the post box.

THANK YOU VERY MUCH

Many people find thank-you letters difficult. And yet to thank people in writing for hospitality or other favours is nowadays considered a basic common courtesy.

One problem with thank-you letters is only imaginary. You may feel that *Thank you for the teapot; it was lovely* is a bit brusque. But it is better than saying nothing. Remember, thank-you letters do not have to be long. Sincerity of tone will more than make up for brevity.

Another problem is more complex. Remembering to write thank-you notes for presents and special favours like hospitality is simple. But it is easy to forget to thank people who have given you their time over long periods – former teachers, helpful colleagues, social workers, policemen, church ministers, and such people. These people deserve your thanks too, and the thanks will touch them even more when unexpected.

Imagine how much it might mean to a retired teacher who has worked away at a generally thankless profession for 30 years, when a former pupil bothers to write this:

> Dear Mrs Harrison,
>   I realise that we sometimes used to give you hell in class. Sorry about that. But I look back upon your lessons as a time that awoke new ideas and interests in me, and I'm sure I'm not the only one of your former students to do so. What I learnt from you has stuck with me, and still proves useful.
>   I trust you are well and enjoying your retirement.
>   Best wishes,
>   Gillian Philpott (formerly Edwards, left school in 1984).

What to say. There are several easy variations on the theme of 'thank you'. As appropriate, you could try these as openings:

> We are very grateful to you for your hospitality / kind thoughts / time . . .
> We cannot thank you enough for . . . ·
> We did enjoy the party / present / trip very much. What a lovely idea!
> It's not stretching the truth to say that, thanks mainly to you, the journey / fair / sale was the best yet . . .
> You have done us a very good turn. We hope we can repay this debt before long . . .
> It's really a delight to . . .

Very often little more need be said. But you may like to fill out a letter of thanks to friends or relatives with a few pieces of personal news.

Thank-you letters to people you know socially, rather than through business, ought to be handwritten. It makes them more personal.

> Dear Sally,
>   I can't tell you how much your visit cheered me up. Life gets dreadfully boring here in hospital, despite the best efforts of the nurses, so it was a wonderful surprise to see you coming in through the door with the bunch of irises and the magazines. It's always good to see you, but all the more so at the moment.
>   I'm feeling much better now and they say I'll be out after a fortnight. If you're in town again it would be great to see you, but maybe it would be better to wait until I'm home and can extend a little hospitality.
>   Once again, many thanks for thinking of me,
>   Judy

Thank you for the present. Thank-you letters for presents should be written within a couple of days of receiving them. For Christmas presents, try to get the letter off before the New Year. The letter need not be long. All it has to contain is your thank you, naming the particular present; a word or two about how much the gift is appreciated (even if it is not really very exciting); and a few words of news.

> Dear Aunt Joan and Uncle Tony,
>   I had a wonderful birthday, made even better by the cheque you sent with your card. Despite your fears, I didn't blow all the money on the day. I think it will go towards my summer holiday — we're planning to take a car round the north of Norway.
>   Before that, I've got exams. You might be surprised to hear that I'm working quite hard for them, but of course I'd love to see you if you're passing through this way.
>   Give my love to the children.
>   Many thanks from your loving niece,
>   Charlotte.

Young children should be encouraged, cajoled, nagged, and if all else fails, forced to write thank-you notes. Little matter, in this instance, if the spelling and punctuation break down in places.

> Dear aunty Shirley, uncle John & Carl
>
> Thank you very much for the £5 you sent me that help me get up to £45. I also got lots of other presents as well.
>
> lots of love
> Ben xxx
>
> P.S Down West ham, up Aston Villa.

After big occasions, such as weddings, sending out thank-yous for presents can take a little longer. If possible, write as soon as the present arrives, but it might be necessary to wait until after the wedding and honeymoon. However large the wedding, and however many gifts there are, they should all be acknowledged within two months.

Generally, wedding presents are sent to the bride, and she is the one who writes the letter back. But she should include her husband in the thanks. Address the letter to the mistress of the house of the senders, though again thanks to the husband should be included. But where the present is from good friends of both bride and groom, both can sign, and the letter can be sent to the whole family.

So a formal letter of thanks might read:

> Dear Mrs Howard,
>
> It was most thoughtful of you and Mr Howard to send us the beautiful glass wine decanter. It matches a set of goblets that John's cousins gave us, and now stands in pride of place on the living-room dresser.
>
> It was sad that you were unable to come to the wedding, but I hope you'll be able to visit us soon and enjoy some wine from your gift.
>
> We hope that all is well with you and Mr Howard.
>
> John sends his thanks and greetings. And so do I.
> Yours sincerely,
> Harriet Adams.

Here is a letter of thanks to close friends:

> Dear Tessa and Pete,
>
> Many, many thanks for the rug. We might have known that you'd find something that was both attractive and useful, but it was a wonderful surprise. As we sit in our new home with our feet up in front of the fire, there it will be to remind us of you constantly. We hope you come and admire it for yourselves as soon as possible.
>
> All well here - hope it is with you.
> With love from
> Polly and Andy

Thanks for your hospitality. As soon as you get home after staying a night or more in someone's house, you ought to write with thanks to the hostess. 'Bread-and-butter letters', as they are known, can be problematical because often you do not know the people well. Make your note short, but adopt an informal tone.

> Dear Mrs O'Connell,
>
> Thank you very much for having me to stay during my trip to Cork. I'm very grateful for your hospitality and enjoyed meeting you and Mr O'Connell very much. I felt thoroughly spoiled by your wonderful cooking, and after our conversations I now know much more about your delightful part of the country.
>
> If you are ever in this area, please get in touch and I would love to return your favour.
> Yours sincerely,
> Hilary Marsden.

Remember, however, to be sincere. Your hostess will be quick to think you are being sarcastic if you compliment her on her cooking when cooking is not her strong point, or if you refer to her rambling draughty mansion as 'warm and cosy'.

Above all, take special care with your letter of thanks after your first stay with people who are going to figure large in your life – your girlfriend's parents, for example.

Dear Mr & Mrs Daly,
You can imagine that I was very apprehensive when Vanessa told me that it was time I met her parents, and that I would be visiting you. Parents aren't always thrilled to see the kinds of people their children bring home.

I needn't have worried. The nerves that got worse and worse as we drove into Ampthill disappeared as soon as we arrived at the house and I saw how happy you were to see Vanessa again, and when you extended the same goodwill to me. It was a wonderful weekend, and I hope we have the chance to get to know each other better in the near future.

Thank you very much for making me feel so welcome in your home.

Yours sincerely
John Almonds

do not have to be long, but they should go off as soon as the good news reaches you. The essential element in such notes is a sincere appreciation of the achievement, whether it is a birth of a child, an engagement, a promotion, passing an exam or driving test, or a graduation.

Congratulations on births are usually very short – but a bunch of flowers or an article of baby clothing will more than make up. Notes are normally written by hand. You might use a card, perhaps an amusing one – though you should avoid some of the more garish or tasteless ones that are on sale.

Dear Mary and George,
Many congratulations on the birth of your little girl. Please let us know when you've chosen a name for her. And we'd love to pay you a visit to admire her when you feel up to it.
Meanwhile, here's a romper suit for her. Not very exciting, but you can never have enough of them.
Sleep and relax all you can now. It'll be the last chance you get for the next few years.
Love,
Steve

A little humour is fine in letters of congratulation, but don't try too hard – or your humour may end up pompous or heavy-handed.

Sometimes you cannot accept an offer of hospitality. Even so, you should include thanks in your letter crying off. You have been invited, say, to visit relatives in Coalville. You do not really want to go, and pressure of work happily makes it impossible.

Dear Cousin Maureen,
It was lovely to get your letter. Thanks for the news. I'm so glad to hear you're all keeping well and that David has thrown off his flu. I'm sorry that we can't make it for the gathering next Saturday. Debbie's taking a class to the hockey international at Wembley and I'm left at home looking after the children. But it was very kind of you to think of us, and please pass on our greetings to the assembled party. I'm sure you'll have a great time!
Best wishes,
Tom

Dear Owen,
I always knew the company would see sense and learn to value you. If you handle your other clients as you've always handled me, the firm has a bright future indeed ahead of it. Well done on your partnership!
Or should I assume the company was afraid of losing its best darts player and ace goalkeeper?
Best wishes,
Dora Watney.

CONGRATULATIONS AND GOOD LUCK

Sharing in the good fortune of others is always a pleasure. And one of the pleasures of success is receiving messages of congratulations. These notes

Letters and cards carrying good wishes are very similar. Keep them short, but show that your hopes for the reader are genuine. And be sure to offer encouragement.

> Dear Lucy,
> Just a note to wish you every success in
> your exams. We've watched you do well
> through school and have every confidence
> that you'll breeze through the next stage
> in your career. Your attitude towards those
> things is right, and you've got nothing to
> worry about.
> Now back to your books!
> Aunt Mabel and Uncle Harry

Get well soon. One of the worst things about being ill is that it cuts you off from normal life. It can be a great consolation knowing that people are thinking about you and wishing you well. Other people suffer similar problems – for example people in the forces abroad or with lonely jobs in isolated places.

When someone first goes into hospital, or if the person is in for only a brief stay, an attractive 'Get Well Soon' card, with perhaps some flowers, is usually the best thing to send. But when your friend is recuperating, he or she will appreciate something more substantial.

The process of writing letters to sick or lonely people is rather different from that of writing normal letters. In the first place, if you know them well, you ought to write regularly, so that they have a date to look forward to. And, almost uniquely among letters, the advice to keep things brief does not apply here. The more the better. If the letter is too long to read at one session it can always be put aside for the next day. Make your letter to an invalid easy to read; use large handwriting.

Try to keep things light and cheerful. Tell jokes and bits of news from the world outside that you think will amuse your reader. Avoid comments on the person's illness, unless you are sure it is not too bad. You might also bulk up your letter with newspaper or magazine clippings and other suitable light reading material.

LETTERS OF CONDOLENCE

Letters of condolence should always be written by hand and sent as soon as the news reaches you. Offer sympathy and what comfort you can. Keep your letter brief and simple – the recipient will be too preoccupied to want to plod through pages and pages. Don't pour out floods of emotion – it will ring

Sharing the good fortune of others . . .

false. And avoid all mawkishness, and euphemism – *the grim reaper . . . Life goes on . . . gone to a happier place . . .* Don't quote chunks from the Bible, unless you are writing to someone you know has deep religious convictions.

Your job in your letter is to help the bereaved person to face up to his or her loss. If you can, mention some future event or propose a meeting to turn the survivor's thoughts away from the past and onto the future.

The best tone to adopt is a personal and natural one. Think hard of the person who has died, and of the survivor. Find ways of praising the dead person without sounding pompous. Perhaps best of all is to recount some incident from that person's life that will keep his or her memory warm in your mind – some act of special kindness or consideration, or even something funny.

Never mention the manner of the person's death. The survivor will not want to be reminded. And don't compare 'this' death with any others, unless you are a very close friend and have suffered a similar loss yourself.

Deaths create a lot of legal bureaucracy and changes in routine, which those affected are often in no state to deal with. Offer to do what you can to assist in these practical matters. Here, for instance, is a letter to someone whose sister has died.

Dear Jack,

We were terribly shocked to hear of Mabel's death. Everyone who knew her will miss her very much. It will be strange going into the Post Office and not seeing her behind the counter, peering over her glasses. Our village has lost someone who can never be replaced.

You are in our thoughts and if there's anything we can do to help you at this difficult time, please let us know.

With deepest sympathy,
Heather and Simon Reid.

It often happens that you do not know the person you are writing to. You knew the person who died but not the family. Introduce yourself in the fewest words possible before offering your tribute.

Dear Mrs Hawkins

I was very sorry to read of the death of your husband in the Society's Magazine. It came as a great and sad shock.

You won't know me. Your husband was my manager at the Gloucester branch when I started working for the Society, but I was moved to my current branch eight years ago.

Like everyone else, I shall always remember John for his kindness and understanding. But I have special reasons to feel very grateful to him.

The first months in any job are difficult, and coming straight from school into a building society can be unnerving. But John was always ready with his help and encouragement, and I cannot tell you how much easier his confidence in me made my early days at work.

In particular, there was an occasion when I had misdirected a batch of invoices. Rather than the display of anger I expected, John simply told me to be more careful in future and stayed with me late into the evening helping to sort out the mess I had

created. Then he took me to the pub and told me stories of far more serious catastrophes that he'd seen during his working life.

Now I have people working under me, and I hope that I show the same kind of good-natured tolerance to them as he did to me. If I do, it is largely due to his example.

If there is anything I can do to help you in what must be a very difficult time, please let me know.

Yours sincerely
Walter Parshall

Your letter will be a little different when the death came after long suffering or illness.

Dear Gerry,

What can we say? Beatrice had suffered for so long that death must have come as a mercy to her. She was always in our thoughts, and we remember her with much affection.

But it must have still come as a great blow to you. Is there anything we can do to help you? Please phone us if there is.

It occurs to me that you might appreciate some help with the legal miseries of settling her estate. As you know, Linda has a great deal of experience in these matters and would be pleased to do what she can.

We both send our fondest sympathies, and hope to see you soon.

Yours sincerely,
Linda and Ian

Commiseration. Letters of commiseration are like letters of condolence. Don't dwell on the misfortune. Instead, offer practical help, and suggest that things will improve. When things go wrong, it is after all good to know that someone cares and has confidence in you.

Dear Phil,

The news that you and Rebecca had separated came as a shock, though not as a complete surprise. I can hardly say it is for the best, and I imagine that you are pretty confused yourself at present.

Things will, of course, sort themselves out eventually. The future may seem like an impenetrable wall for now, but you'll find a way through.

Mother told me that you were terribly upset about the children. I know how much they mean to you, and whatever may have happened between you and Rebecca, you have always been a wonderful father to them. I know that they're very fond of you and will be missing you.

I hope Rebecca will be reasonable about you and the children, but if you have to resort to the courts you know you'll have the whole family behind you. If it's all too painful, I'd be quite willing to do what I can. For instance, would it be helpful if I wrote to Rebecca?

Maybe the best thing you could do is to come and stay with me for a few days. It might help to have someone around. I'll do my best to make things cheerful.

Let me know. Try to look after yourself.

Your loving brother
Andy.

LETTERS OF APOLOGY AND ANGER

The art of graceful apology is well worth mastering. For one thing, a show of reasonableness when you have done something wrong can save you from losing friends. It can even, in extreme cases, save you from heavy legal costs.

Apologies should be made sincerely, but with dignity. Don't crawl and grovel, even if you have set fire to a friend's house while staying there. Instead, offer to do all you can to repair any damage or pain you have caused.

Letters of apology should be short and to the point, and normally written by hand. Come straight out with your apology, put forward (humbly) any mitigating circumstances, and then offer your token of peace.

But be warned. If it is a matter concerning money, be careful how you word your letter. By all means say you are sorry for what has happened, but don't admit blame – at least, not without a go-ahead from your lawyer. You might find yourself presented with a substantial bill, without any way of contesting it.

Dear Mr and Mrs Vincent,

The children have just come in and told me that our dog has broken out and uprooted all your dahlias. I know it won't compensate you for all the work you've put in, but I shall be going to the garden centre for some new ones this afternoon. I hope you'll accept them.

I've locked the dog in the house. He's looking very crestfallen. And he won't be out in the garden untied until we've done something about the fence. I assure you it won't happen again.

Yours sincerely,
Amy Lightfoot

A piece of your mind. From time to time you may feel yourself called upon to let someone know that you find his or her behaviour unacceptable. Someone you always thought of as a friend goes angling after your job or spreading malicious gossip. Or your son writes back from college saying he has failed his exams, squandered his grant, and picked up a fine for rowdy behaviour. You have reached the end of your tether.

Obviously, the best thing to do is to thrash things out face to face. But this is not always possible, and you may have to write. If relations have come to such a pass that you never want to see the person again, you may feel that putting it down in writing sets a firmer seal on matters.

Consider carefully before you write a letter with rebukes or accusations. You must decide exactly what effect you want to produce, and choose your words accordingly. Then leave your letter to 'mature' and reread it before sending it off. Taking that precaution might possibly save a great deal of hard feelings.

Even if your intention is to find fault, you should still try to be tactful. You do not want to make a permanent enemy of the person you are writing to. So tone down your criticism:

I find it hard to believe that you, of all people, would say such things of me . . .

It would be such a shame if we fell out over a trivial matter like this . . .

Normally, I find your ideas sound. But on this occasion I must disagree with you . . .

I fear you are mistaken . . .

Presumably you have not been fully informed . . .

You must have misunderstood . . .

Formulas such as these reduce the harshness by stressing that the reader, usually, is a decent sort of person and that what he or she has done to upset you is out of character. The reader will lose no face by apologising.

Whatever you do, avoid open rudeness and accusations. They will only lead to aggravation, if not litigation. In addition, weapons like wit, reasonableness, coolness, and restraint are far more effective than open hostility and abuse. Even breaking off relations completely is much better done with cold precision than flaming ire: *Dear George, I have had enough of your comments. Our friendship is now at an end.*

Suppose a friend owes you some money and is stalling on repaying it. The warnings in this letter are fairly clear, but they are expressed without threats and recriminations, and are thus more likely to produce the desired result.

Dear Rob,

I'm sorry that I need to write this letter, but I have somehow to make you realise how pressing this matter is. I've asked you on three occasions now if you could give me back the £250 I lent you, and I must repeat that I really need the money. You will remember that, at the time, you promised to repay it within the month, and that was four months ago. I'm still waiting to hear from you.

We have been friends for several years, and I've always found you good company and thought of you as a man of integrity. It would be a shame if one little disagreement were to come between us, and I can only imagine that you don't realise how important this matter is to me. Or perhaps there is some special reason why you can't let me have the money; in which case I think you ought to tell me.

Please write,

Graham

LOVE LETTERS

Many romances have been thrown into jeopardy by off-handedness, a too casual or forced approach, or a faked attempt at cleverness in a hastily written letter, or by a cloying sentimentality. The first letter from someone you have hitherto found attractive may give you a nasty shock. It sounds distant or unlike the person you thought you knew, or it seems childish and silly, and you start having second thoughts.

You hardly need to be told to think of the person you are writing to. But think too of the impression your letter will make. Maybe it is quite innocent, the way your letter from holiday refers to 'nice people I met by the pool' or 'candle-lit meals June and I have enjoyed together'. But think what you would feel if you received such a letter. Would not jealousy raise its head?

By all means be funny. But remember that you will not be there to smooth out any misunderstandings if, for instance, your girlfriend thinks you are being funny at her expense.

Of course, extol the virtues of the person you are writing to. But four or five pages of unremitting compliments is likely to become a bore. Better to spread them around among lively incidents and little personal jokes that you know will amuse.

Like all very personal letters, love letters should be written by hand.

You should see the harbour here, Susan. It's beautiful at night, like the harbour at home when we were there at Easter, though warmer. You wander up and down the waterfront in shirt sleeves and listen to the fishermen arguing and the seabirds squawking.

There's a funny little restaurant that I've taken to eating in. Patrice is very proud of his bouillabaisse, and I'm rather fond of his wine. He's from the north, where he left his girlfriend, and we spend long evenings boring each other silly with stories about the girls we've left behind. He says if I can get you down here he'll put on something really sumptuous. And I'm sure he would, especially for you, my dearest.

Everything's fine. But it could be better, and you know why. I'd gladly send you money for the ticket if you could get away. Then I'd probably see less of the fishermen and seabirds as we walk along the jetty, but I can live without them.

POSTCARDS FROM HOLIDAY

There are two ways of dealing with the duty of writing postcards home from holidays. You can attempt to write a 'mini-letter', in which case good manners demand that you ought to say a few words about the people you are writing to. Or you can find some witty, short comment to scrawl across the card and leave it at that. *Why didn't you tell me there were sharks at Skegness? . . . Greetings from Crete, suburb of Dusseldorf . . . Sun, sea, cheap wine. Just like Swindon.*

Note that in postcards you can omit the salutation (*Dear Bob and Nina*) and the final *With love . . . Best wishes . . .* or whatever.

Thanks for making the journey to the airport so easy. I hope you managed to get back through all the traffic on the M25. All's well here. The hotel is fine — ten minutes from the sea. The children are enjoying the beach, and we're enjoying the rest. Say hello to the gang at work. I do miss it all so much!
Perry.

LETTERS OF INTRODUCTION

Don't give letters of introduction lightly. A letter of introduction is a special favour that should be granted only to good friends, who you feel sure will get on well with the people you are introducing them to. And don't forget the responsibility you are imposing upon the recipient of the letter to meet and entertain the people you are introducing.

Don't, as a rule, ask for a letter of introduction. Leave it to your friends to decide whether or not they want to introduce you to other friends.

When writing a letter of introduction, you may want to leave the person being introduced in the dark. Suppose your cousin Pete is going to a conference in Aberdeen, and you have old friends, the

A witty, short comment to scrawl across the card.

MacIntyres, who live there. You write them a letter telling them when and where Pete will be staying, and ask them to contact him.

But don't tell Pete that you have written. This leaves the MacIntyres free to ignore your request if – for whatever reason – they want to.

Another important point. In your letter to the MacIntyres, tell them something about Pete, and why you think they might get on well with him.

That is the usual modern way of doing things – the old-fashioned method is different. The procedure here is to write two letters, one to send by mail to the hosts to warn them of the visitor's arrival, the other the actual letter of introduction which you give to the visitor. This is a short note addressed to the hosts and introducing the visitor, which he presents on arrival. The visitor would normally make contact with the hosts, rather than vice versa.

The drawback with this method is that it denies the hosts the option of not offering hospitality. In certain circumstances, however – with older people, say – you might still want to use this method. Here is an example of a letter you might give to a friend to present to the hosts.

> Dear Ruth,
> I'm giving this note to Steven Price, an old friend of mine, who's visiting Rochester for a few days on business. He's excellent company and a fund of amusing stories, and would be able to fill you in with all kinds of news about events in your old home town.
> I'm sure it would be a pleasure for you to meet him, and hope you'll be able to get together.
> Best wishes,
> Nell.

Note that, as with all other letters you give to people to deliver by hand, you should leave the envelope unsealed. This is a fine old-fashioned courtesy, enabling the bearer to read the letter to see what you have said about him or her.

HOW TO SAY PLEASE

Asking favours for another is much easier than asking them for yourself. A 'begging letter' requires considerable tact.

Get your request over near the start of the letter, and make sure to present a good reason for needing the money or whatever. Don't be coy. Talk about *money* rather than *financial assistance* or *your help*. Say exactly how much you need, with a breakdown if necessary of particular amounts you need for particular debts – and be honest about the likelihood and date of repayment.

Try to think of other news to include in the letter, so that it will not appear totally mercenary.

Don't dwell excessively on the awful consequences that penury will bring upon you or your family – or people will think their arm is being twisted – but make it clear that your position is very serious. A certain amount of humour, at your own expense, will not come amiss.

> Dear Aunt Gwen,
> I'm sorry I haven't written for a while, and even sorrier that the occasion of this letter isn't entirely altruistic. The fact is that I've been engaged in a time-consuming and, I fear, losing battle to keep my head above water financially. Business in the construction industry has been very slack and my debts have now got out of hand. I'm afraid also I've been a bit naive about certain contracts, a mistake I shan't be making again.
> I'm now at the stage where unless I can find £2,000 quickly the loan company will repossess our plant and I will be declared bankrupt. We have managed to keep up to date with the mortgage payments so far, but it hasn't been easy.
> I don't like coming to you asking for money, but I see no other way out. If you feel you could lend me something I should be very grateful. As I said, the immediate problem is £2,000, but any extra would be more than welcome. I hope that business will pick up in spring, and shall of course pay back any loans as soon as it is humanly possible.
> I can imagine you shaking your head and saying 'Tut, tut, I knew the lad would come to no good.' And of course you're right. But believe me that it's not for want of trying that I find myself without two pennies to rub together.
> Please write and let me know how you feel about this.
> Yours affectionately,
> Elliot Nevin

Business Letters from Home

Even in the age of telephones, a letter is often the best way of doing business. A well-written and calmly thought-out letter can persuade where an argument over the phone, for instance, would fail. A letter can bring you the exact information you are looking for, and it can improve the chances of your request being dealt with swiftly and satisfactorily. It can even spare you embarrassment if you have been at fault or are unable to pay a bill.

When you write, state your specific business simply and firmly. Don't make gratuitous remarks about the failings of the people you are writing to. Just let the reader know precisely what you expect done, and that you expect it to be done quickly and thoroughly, and that you expect to be kept informed about what is going on. And remember always to keep copies of your letters, and any other relevant documents.

WHOM TO WRITE TO

If you are in doubt about whom to write to, go for the top. When you do not know who the person at the top is, phone up and find out. There is only one approach better than this. And that is if you know someone influential in the company or organisation. If it is a close friend, write your letter in the normal, formal way of official letters, addressing it to whoever you think is responsible. But send it personally to your friend, with a note asking him or her to pass the letter on.

If you do not know the person so well, write a single official letter to that person, but after the heading explain who you are. Then get straight on to the matter in hand.

Dear Mr Jameson,

Postal deliveries

You may remember me. I was a colleague of your son Frank when he worked at Trent Engineering, and visited your house on a number of occasions.

I need some information about proposed changes to delivery times in this area, and hope that you will be able to find someone who can supply this.

Writing and phoning. Decide first whether a letter or the phone will better help you to achieve what you want. Phone up organisations that do not reply to letters, and quietly insist on service. Phone if it is just a simple enquiry that you are sure can be answered with the minimum of fuss.

But remember: the advantage of a letter is that you can take your time composing it, making sure you have got everything exactly right. A letter also gives the recipient something tangible to deal with. You can present complicated facts and opinions better in writing than on the phone. And a letter serves as proof of your communication. An unhelpful organisation may deny that you ever phoned.

Getting what you want. There are four principal types of letter to companies – enquiries and requests, replies, complaints, and excuses for non-payment. Some letters serve multiple purposes. You may, for instance, be both supplying some requested information and asking something yourself. If you do, make sure that each part is separate – for instance, in separate paragraphs.

Dear Mrs Sedgwick

Installation of gas central heating

I acknowledge receipt of your letter of 14 March with your estimate of the cost of installing central heating in this house.

In reply to your three queries, please note the following:

1. The Gas Board has confirmed that the mains supply to the house is in order. A copy of their letter is enclosed.
2. We do not require insulation in the loft, since this work has already been done.
3. When the price is agreed we want the work to be started as soon as possible.

We require some more details before a final agreement can be made.

1. What are the heat output figures for the radiators that you propose to install?
2. What are the approximate running costs per year?
3. What is the capacity of the hot water tank? What does that mean in terms of, say, bathfuls?
4. Can you send details of your guarantee?
5. Can you provide written confirmation that your company is affiliated with the Confederation for the Registration of Gas Installers or equivalent trade association?
6. When would you be able to start the work? And about how long would it take?

If any of these matters affects your quotation, please let us know.

Subject to suitable replies on these matters, we hope that a final figure can be settled. We would then be able to give you a definite answer as to whether the proposed work should go ahead.

I look forward to receiving your reply.

Yours sincerely

Simon Carling

ENQUIRIES AND REQUESTS

Companies and public organisations are usually happy to supply all sorts of information – it is, after all, good publicity for them. Here are five rules to follow in all letters of enquiry:

Writing at Work, Home, and College

- [ ] For each item of information you want, use a separate line or paragraph.

- [ ] Unless you are asking for confidential information and want to justify your request, do not bother to say why you need the information. Few companies care, and if they do they can always ask you.

- [ ] State in the opening sentence what the subject of your enquiry is.

- [ ] Be neither demanding nor ingratiating. Phrases such as *I'm sorry to take up your valuable time* are asking for your letter to be ignored. If the information you are looking for is unavailable or confidential, they can write and tell you so.

THE ART OF THE PUT-DOWN

On occasion, giving people a piece of your mind may involve putting them in their place. In the art of the put-down you can take as no better example this letter – at the same time, supremely dignified and supremely crushing – which the 18th-century lexicographer Dr Samuel Johnson sent to the nobleman, and self-styled patron of the arts, Lord Chesterfield. Johnson wrote it at the time of the publication of his famous *Dictionary of the English Language*. Chesterfield, who had declined to help Johnson when the dictionary was beginning, proceeded to give it his blessing once it was on the verge of success.

TO THE RIGHT HONOURABLE THE EARL OF CHESTERFIELD.

February 1755

My Lord.

I have been lately informed by the proprietor of the *World* [a journal] that two papers in which my Dictionary is recommended to the public were written by your Lordship. To be so distinguished is an honour which, being very little accustomed to favours from the Great, I know not well how to receive, or in what terms to acknowledge.

When upon some slight encouragement I first visited your Lordship I was overpowered like the rest of Mankind by the enchantment of your address, and could not forbear to wish that I might boast myself *Le Vainqueur du Vainqueur de la Terre* [the conqueror of the conqueror of the Earth], that I might obtain that regard for which I saw the World contending, but I found my attendance so little encouraged, that neither pride nor modesty would suffer me to continue it. When I had once addressed your Lordship in public, I had exhausted all the art of pleasing which a retired and uncourtly Scholar can possess. I had done all that I could, and no man is well pleased to have his all neglected . . .

Seven years, my lord, have now past since I waited in your outward rooms or was repulsed from your door, during which time I have been pushing on my work through difficulties of which it is useless to complain, and have brought it at last to the verge of publication without one act of assistance, one word of encouragement, or one smile of favour. Such treatment I did not expect, for I never had a Patron before . . .

Is not a Patron, My Lord, one who looks with unconcern on a man struggling for life in the water and when he has reached ground encumbers him with help. The notice which you have been pleased to take of my labours, had it been early, had been kind; but it has been delayed till I am indifferent and cannot enjoy it, till I am solitary and cannot impart it, till I am known and do not want it.

I hope it is no very cynical asperity not to confess obligation where no benefit has been received, or to be unwilling that the Public should consider me as owing that to a Patron, which Providence has enabled me to do for myself.

Having carried on my work thus far with so little obligation to any Favourer of Learning I shall not be disappointed though I should conclude it, if less be possible, with less, for I have been long wakened from that dream of hope, in which I once boasted myself with so much exultation.

> My Lord,
> Your Lordship's Most humble
> Most obedient servant
>
> S.J.

☐ Thank them in advance and, if you have asked for something unusual and get what you want, write back to acknowledge receipt with thanks.

A polite request. Here is a letter designed to win the cooperation of a manufacturer when something has gone wrong with one of his products.

Dear Mr Thomas,

Request for spare parts

Your company is well-known for the quality and reliability of its goods and services, so I have no hesitation in writing to you now.

For Christmas three years ago we gave our two sons, aged eight and ten, your Electronic Soccer Game. It has been in frequent use since. The other day a welded joint snapped, rendering the game useless. This joint connects a leg to the casing of the game. The boys play the game energetically, and it won't stand up to this kind of use any more.

Is it possible to return the game to you for rewelding? The boys, and their parents, would be very grateful if it could be repaired.

Yours sincerely,

Howard Simpson.

Writing to the authorities. You need to be polite when writing to the authorities – but you should try to be very concise as well. Consider this letter to the Vehicle Licensing Office:

Dear Sir/Madam,

Loss of Road Fund Disc

My car, a green Ford Escort, registration C 707 JGH, was recently broken into. Among the things stolen were papers relating to the car, including the Road Fund Disc. This was valid until June 1990.

Please send a copy of the disc.

Yours faithfully,

Angelo Zanone.

Technical enquiries. Even quite complicated enquiries can be dealt with easily if you organise your material beforehand. In this letter there is a lot of technical detail, but it is explained simply, and the writer's needs are specified precisely.

Audrey Balfour
Technical Support
Arrow Computers

Dear Audrey Balfour

Display/ROM for Arrow PC

I need some information about screen display of characters for my Arrow L14 personal computer.

As a translator of Danish I wish to be able to display special characters outside the ASCII 32-255 range. Computers in Denmark ascribe ASCII numbers to the symbols concerned. On my Arrow, the corresponding keys display the normal ASCII symbols (| and \).

On your advice, I bought and fitted a Samson Graphics Card Plus with RAM Font. This enabled me to change the display of the necessary characters in ASCII files. However, for unknown reasons this method does not work in WordWrite 2. When I enter WordWrite, the RAM fonts are lost and replaced with special display fonts, which are essentially the same as ASCII. As this is the word processor I use and my use for these symbols is restricted to word processing work, your solution proved ineffective.

Computers sold in Scandinavia do not have this problem. They display the correct Danish symbols under all circumstances. I don't know whether Arrow PCs are imported into Denmark, but certainly other IBM clones are.

What I would like to know is therefore this:

1. What is fitted into Danish computers to enable display of special Danish characters? I imagine it is a different ROM, but am not an expert in these matters.
2. If this is the case, do you have any information about the use of different ROMs in the Arrow computer?
3. If I could get a Danish ROM (or whatever) from a supplier there, would it work in the Arrow? If this depends on other factors, could you say what they are?

I should be very grateful if you could supply this information. I can be contacted at home by telephone at most times.

Yours sincerely

John C. Andrews

The enquiring student. Many school and college projects require students to collect information from companies and other organisations. Here, it is a good idea to say why you want the information. Companies are much more likely to give you semi-confidential details if you show, briefly, that you are putting them to useful purposes. You should also give an idea of your age; it will help the person dealing with your query to decide what is appropriate to your level.

Here is a good example:

Dear Mr Roberts,

I would greatly appreciate your help in preparing an article about the marketing policies of large companies. It is to be published in the students' yearbook of the Manchester School of Business Studies, at which I am a second-year student.

The article will discuss shifts in advertising strategy over the past ten years -- for instance how firms have adapted to changes in consumer attitudes and buying power and to fluctuations in the state of the economy. If the information is available, I would be interested to hear how your advertising strategy -- targeting, image presentation, media mix, and so on -- has changed over the last ten years, and the reasons for these changes.

I intend to illustrate the article and it would be helpful if you could send copies of advertisements and promotional material you have used over this period.

Any information you can give me would be gratefully received. Any material I use will be acknowledged in the article. I will of course send you a copy of the yearbook once it has come out.

With thanks,

Rosemary Arkwright.

REPLIES

People are constantly receiving enquiries through the post – enquiries about their financial standing, their work and interests, requests for information touching some piece of business, or enquiries from the bank on some matter related to a loan.

When you reply to such queries, make sure you do so promptly, accurately, and politely. It is usually in

your interests to keep things moving quickly and smoothly. Impress the other people with your efficiency, and – with any luck – they will respond with comparable efficiency in their turn.

Replies are simpler to write than enquiries. All you have to do is take the questions one by one and answer each in turn, preferably on separate lines. You can number them, but if so make sure that your numbers correspond to those of the questions you are answering. Unless you have a second reason for writing, don't bother to say anything else.

Confirmations and acknowledgments. Most replies can be very short. Typical replies include acknowledgment of receipt:

Dear Mrs Watkinson

I acknowledge receipt of your letter of 12 March. I shall answer the questions you raise when I have heard from my bank.

Yours sincerely

Alan Bryant

Similarly straightforward are letters confirming details. If everything was correct, you need do no more than announce your confirmation. Sometimes a point may need more comment.

Dear Miss Pierce

Your ref. BK124it7

Thank you for your letter of 23 February regarding the booking of our holiday in Italy.

I confirm that the answers to your queries 1-3 and 5-6 are all yes.

Concerning point 4, please note that we would prefer not to travel by night. But this is all right if it is the only option for June 23.

Please will you now go ahead with the final bookings and confirm as soon as possible that these have been made.

Yours sincerely

David W. Willis

Forms and stupid questions. Some replies are more difficult. Replies – to credit card companies, say – sometimes involve filling in forms, and these are notoriously difficult to deal with. (For some good examples of how *not* to answer questions on forms, see the panel overleaf.) In particular, you may find yourself being asked things that plainly do not apply in your case. *What is your telephone number?*, when you are not on the phone. *Where were you living in 1986?*, a year you spent travelling in central Africa. *When did you start your current employment?*, when you have been a self-employed musician since you left school.

If you are asked an awkward question, deal with it firmly but politely. On forms, state clearly that the question is *Not applicable* – though if the form is an application for a place at college or a job, it might be sensible to give an explanation: *I spent the year travelling in central Africa*. If you are writing a letter, answer the questions you can, then deal with those you cannot.

Here, for example, is an answer to an enquiry from a mortgage company.

Deal promptly and efficiently with enquiries.

> Dear Mr Parker
>
> I reply to your letter of October 25.
>
> In answer to your questions:
>
> 1. My children are aged 6 and 4.
> 3. I work as a freelance book editor. If you need confirmation of my income you may contact my accountant, whose name I have already given you.
> 4. I am not in receipt of Income Supplement or any benefit other than child allowance.
>
> In answer to point 2, I am also unable to give you the name of my husband, since I am unmarried.
>
> In answer to point 5, I regret that I am unable to give you the name of my solicitor, since I do not have a solicitor.
>
> Yours sincerely
>
> Jenny Jones

People sometimes have problems dealing with forms that do not give enough space for all that they have to say. What if Section 4 tells you to list your children, and gives you only four lines to name all six? Or if your list of qualifications to go into Section 6B is particularly long and impressive? The best approach is to write across the section *See attached sheet*. Then take a clean sheet of paper, and put your name and any references at the top. Write clearly *Information for Section 4*, and set out all the details using the same layout as on the original form. You should staple the sheet to the form or fix it on with a paper clip.

Saying No. Sometimes it is hard to say No, but if you have to, do it with a polite apology and a good excuse. In this letter a local sportsman has to decline an invitation to open a charity bazaar. At times like these a prompt reply is essential, so that other arrangements can be made. All the better if you take the trouble to write the letter by hand.

> Dear Mrs Wright,
> Thank you very much for your invitation to open the bazaar. I would very much like to help you but I'm afraid that I shall have to refuse, as I'm competing in a race in Winchester on the Saturday in question.
> I'm very sorry about this. In any case, I hope the event goes off well and perhaps I'll be able to help you on some future occasion.
> Yours sincerely
> John Ellison

INSURANCE HOWLERS – HOW NOT TO FILL IN A FORM

If motorists had to pass a test in writing skills as well as driving skills, there would be fewer licensed drivers on the road.

The following statements have all appeared, over the years, on insurance claims forms, in the section calling for a summary of the details of the accident.

To avoid the collision I ran into a lorry.

My car was legally parked as it backed into the other vehicle.

An invisible car came out of nowhere, struck my car, and vanished.

The indirect cause of the accident was a little guy in a small car with a big mouth.

I was thrown from my car as it left the road. I was later found in a ditch by some stray cows.

As I approached the intersection a sign suddenly appeared in a place where no stop sign had ever appeared before. I was unable to stop in time to avoid the accident.

To avoid hitting the bumper of the car in front I struck the pedestrian.

The guy was all over the road. I had to swerve a number of times before I hit him.

I pulled away from the side of the road, glanced at my mother-in-law, and headed over the embankment.

In an attempt to kill a fly, I drove into a telephone pole.

The telephone pole was approaching. I was attempting to swerve out of the way when I struck the front end.

I had been shopping for plants all day and was on my way home. As I reached an intersection a hedge sprang up obscuring my vision and I did not see the other car.

I had been driving for 40 years when I fell asleep at the wheel and had an accident.

I knocked the man over. He admitted it was his fault as he had been knocked over before.

Coming home I drove into the wrong house and collided with a tree I don't have.

The other car collided with mine without giving warning of its intention.

A truck backed through my windshield into my wife's face.

A pedestrian hit me and went under my car.

I thought my window was down, but I found it was up when I put my hand through.

I collided with a stationary truck coming the other way.

I consider neither vehicle to blame, but if either was to blame it was the other one.

The pedestrian had no idea which direction to run, so I ran over him.

I saw a slow-moving, sad-faced old man as he bounced off the roof of my car.

I told the police that I was not injured, but on removing my hat found that I had a fractured skull.

I was sure the old fellow would never make it to the other side of the road when I struck him.

A stationary tree collided with me.

COMPLAINING

At some time in their lives most people find themselves with a defective car, or a stereo system that comes with some essential component missing, or some other similar problem.

Don't feel shy or embarrassed about complaining. Good shops, providers of services (such as travel agents), and manufacturers welcome feedback from customers and will do their best to help. They want to know about defects in their goods. And if the dealers are bad, it is your duty to yourself and to others to see that they do not get away with it.

```
The Manager,
Northern Allied Bank,
Pickering.

Dear Sir,

        Account no. 45093591

    Today I received a two-monthly
statement of my account held with
your branch. It included a debit for
```

```
£8.50, described as 'Fees and bank
commission'.

    I have always kept my account
with you in credit of at least £50
and often much more. These fees
appear to have arisen at the time my
account was moved to your branch
from the Penrith branch, and a large
debit was mistakenly charged against
it. I am therefore not responsible
for these fees.

    Kindly see that my account is
credited with the sum of £8.50.

        Yours faithfully,


        Sandra Heighton (Miss).
```

Don't forget, if your complaint receives satisfactory treatment, to write back to the company with a short note of thanks.

Whom should you complain to? If your new sofa collapses the moment you sit on it, the first thing to do is look at the labels or papers that came with it, particularly the guarantee. The papers will often give you precise details of what to do if you are dissatisfied with the product.

If things are not clear, complain to the shop, retailers, agent, or distributor you bought the article from. (By law, the transaction of selling goods involves a contract between the seller and buyer. So if you buy faulty goods you have rights against the seller.) Sometimes, however, it is best to go to the manufacturer, as when you buy something with inadequate instructions, or when you need a replacement part for an article that the retailer no longer stocks.

If it is a service that you want to complain about, go to the provider of the service – the telephone company, say, travel agent, airline or tour operator. If you get no satisfactory response from these, complain in this order, to:

☐ an advice bureau, such as the Citizens' Advice Bureau, the Department of Trading Standards, the Office of Fair Trading in London, or the recognised trade association or regulatory authority (a Citizen's Advice Bureau will give you details of these)

☐ the local press, or the relevant technical or trade press – or even a radio or television consumer programme

☐ your solicitor or MP

The tone of your letter. When complaining, you must get your tone and approach right. Remember that even the best run businesses are not infallible. Good companies accept and admit this, and have provision for dealing with unsatisfied customers. Your letter is more likely to work if you sound hurt rather than outraged, if you assume that it is all an oversight rather than bloody-minded inefficiency. If you do not get satisfaction you can always change your tack later.

Consider these two versions of the same complaint written to the telephone company. Which of the two do you think is the more likely to be heeded and acted upon?

```
Dear Sir or Madam

You really are incompetent. But what
more can we expect? You obviously
don't care in the slightest about
your customers. Have you any idea
how much time, trouble and money you
cost me by your inefficiency?

Not content with giving my number
incorrectly (23415) you ignore my
express instructions regarding how I
want my name entered. We pay extra
in this household to have two
separate entries, for my wife and
myself, and so you would think that
you could allow us to be entered
with the names we choose. Anyway, an
entry like B. Jenkins is absolutely
useless. Look for yourselves and see
just how many people there are in
this area with that name. I wanted
my forename included for obvious
reasons but you simply ignore my
request. Make sure that these
mistakes are put right immediately
or I shall have to deduct a sum from
the rental part of my bills in
future.

Yours faithfully

Bruno Jenkins
```

```
Dear Sir or Madam

Mistakes in Phone Book

Please note these two mistakes in
the new (1991) edition of the
Cardiff Phone Book.

My number is given as Radyr 23415.
It should be Radyr 23451.

My name is given as B. Jenkins.
There are several B. Jenkins's in
Cardiff. I specially requested, and
paid, to be entered as Bruno
```

```
Jenkins. You will appreciate that
there are not quite so many who bear
this name.

Kindly do something immediately
about the former mistake, so that my
calls may be directed to me.

Yours faithfully

Bruno Jenkins
```

If you do not receive satisfaction...

Obviously the second is better. In this version, Mr Jenkins presents the facts about his telephone number in an orderly fashion and makes clear exactly what he wants done.

What to put in your letter. A letter of complaint should include the following:

☐ any reference number that the company has given you.

☐ a detailed description of the product: brand, model, serial or identification number, size, colour, price, and the like.

☐ place of purchase, together with the name and address of the retailer.

☐ date of purchase.

☐ copies of relevant documents. Note that they should be copies. Keep the originals yourself.

☐ a short description of the problem, sifting the main points from incidental details.

☐ details of any steps you have already taken, including copies of any relevant letters.

☐ a clear statement of what you expect the company to do for you – to refund the purchase cost, for example, to compensate you for your trouble, to provide free servicing, or to replace the defective article.

☐ if necessary, a description of what you might do if you do not receive satisfaction, such as contacting regulatory bodies or writing to the press. Sound as if you would rather not have to go to such extremes, but leave no doubt that you will if forced to.

Here is a sample letter to a car dealer.

```
Dear Mr Atherton

Demand for services: your ref 435/rd

In March this year I bought from you
a used red Ultra van, year of
manufacture 1987, licence number
D 425 OVR, motor number A45693B,
price £6,000.

Since then, every time I have driven
the vehicle another fault has come
to light. I enclose a copy of a
report made by my garage, John Brook
and Sons, which lists 23 major
faults. You will note that they also
suspect that the mileometer has been
tampered with.

I have discussed this matter with
you over the telephone and at your
showrooms on several occasions. You
will have letters that I wrote to
you on 4 April, 14 April, and 29
May, none of which I have received
replies to. You took the vehicle
back for repairs between 18 April
and 8 May, but the faults continue
to become apparent.

I have now been in contact with Mrs
Chowdry of the Dewsbury Trading
Standards Office. She assures me
that it is your legal duty to
correct the faults listed and that
her office will support my claim for
redress. This would include an
element to compensate me for loss of
business while the vehicle has been
out of service.

I am very dissatisfied with the
vehicle and your after-sales
service. I expect your reply to this
letter before 18 July, either:

1. Offering to correct ALL the
   listed faults, or
```

2. Refunding the full purchase
   price.

Enclosed you will find copies of:

    the report made by John Brook
    and Sons
    your sales certificate
    your receipt for the purchase
    of the vehicle
    the registration documents
    your guarantee

I look forward to receiving your
reply. Failure to respond to this
letter will result in my going back
to the Trading Standards Office with
a view to initiating steps to recoup
my losses.

Yours faithfully

Robert West

Complaint about bad services. You can use the same tack when you have to complain about services – a ruined holiday, for instance.

Dear Mr Ripley

My family returned on 13 August from
your Supertan Greek Holiday,
reference GR 841. We wish to
register our dissatisfaction with
the treatment we have received.

The holiday was booked through
Flyaway Travel, 65 The Square,
Livingstone, Scotland on 4 March and
fully paid at the time. The holiday
ran from 29 July to 12 August. We
asked especially to be booked at the
Hotel Athena in Rhodes, since we
preferred a small hotel in the town
to a larger one along the coast. We
requested one double room and two
singles. The price of the holiday
was to include half pension.

All these details were confirmed in
your letter of 23 March.

On arriving at the Hotel Athena the
manager, Mr S. Pottakis, told us
that you had booked only the double
room and one single, for one week
only, and that the evening meal at
the hotel was not included. For the
first week Mr Pottakis was able to
find us an extra single room, though
three floors below our other rooms,
and small and cramped and facing a
breaker's yard. He kindly accepted
your confirmation of booking as
proof that he could recoup from you,
but insisted that we pay for any
meals we took at the hotel.

Despite trying for five days to
contact your agent on Rhodes, Mr V.
Alexandrou, we were unable to speak
to him. Either there was no one at
his office or we were told that he
was away on business.

At the end of the first week we had
to move from the Hotel Athena to the
Hotel Pasiphae, which is three miles
out of town. This is a large, modern
hotel, quite unlike what we had
wanted. Again, it was only thanks to
the kindness of Mr Pottakis and the
manager of the Hotel Pasiphae, Mr P.
Karavias, that we did not find
ourselves on the streets. Mr
Karavias accepted payment by
Eurocheque (£540) for our rooms and
food and kindly offered to defer
cashing the cheque until August 20.

Your mistakes in booking, of which
we had no warning, have not only
ruined our holiday but cost us
dearly.

We therefore require from you:

1. A letter of apology and
   explanation.
2. Repayment of our meals at the
   Hotel Athena.
3. That you pay Mr Pottakis for the
   single room at the Hotel Athena.
   He has, I believe, now been in
   contact with your agent.
3. That you pay Mr Karavias the sum
   of £540 without delay.
4. A token payment in respect of
   the trouble you have caused us.
   I suggest £200.
5. That you write to Mr Pottakis
   and Mr Karavias, apologising for
   your negligence, and to your
   agent on Rhodes enquiring into
   his absence when needed.

I enclose copies of our certificate
and confirmation of booking, of our
bills for food at the Hotel Athena,
and of our invoice from the Hotel
Pasiphae.

I look forward to a reply confirming
that you have paid Mr Karavias
within the next week, and to the
other matters before 10 September.

I write this letter on the advice
of the Association of British Travel
Agents, of which you are a member.
They have told me to contact them
again if you fail to reply
satisfactorily.

Yours sincerely

Jane MacAndrew

Writing to a consumers' organisation. Your first contact with a Citizens' Advice Bureau or other such organisation would normally be by phone or by visiting. But the people there will usually ask you to put your complaint in writing. When you do write to them, say what you have already done to get redress and send copies of the most important documents – above all, be sure to send copies of any letters that have passed between you and the firm you are complaining about.

Consider the nightmare tale of woe in this letter to a consumers' organisation.

The Consumer Organisation,
High Street, Brechin.

Dear Miss Caws,

Following our conversation on the phone yesterday, here is an account of the problems that our washing machine developed while still under warranty. It contains the same details as a letter I sent on 30 October 1990 to the Alpa Co, the manufacturers and guarantors of the machine.

24 Sep 1989	Machine delivered and installed.
27 Sep 1989	Machine siphoned water out while it was filling. Serviceman called on 1 Oct and said he did not know what was wrong, but fitted a new gear casing.
11 Oct 1989	Machine started spraying out water again. This time the man who had originally installed the machine called, on 13 Oct 1989, and repaired it. For a while it worked properly.
23 Nov 1989	Machine started leaking, at first only small amounts. This got worse over the ensuing month, and seemed to occur on the second rinse.
5 Jan 1990	I wrote to Mr Smelt of Alpa and asked for a qualified person to rectify the fault.
10 Jan 1990	I phoned Mr Smelt and asked why no one had called. Mr Smelt promised to look into the matter.
17 Jan 1990	Serviceman called and said the machine needed a new part that he did not have in his van. He taped up the inlet pipe and said he would call back the next day.
19 Jan 1990	I phoned Mr Smelt and said the serviceman had not called back. He said he would see to the matter.
5 March 1990	Serviceman called and replaced the pipe again and made other adjustments.
24 March– 18 May 1990	The machine was not used since we were abroad.
31 May 1990	Machine ground to a halt, during the spin after the first rinse, with some smoke.
6 June 1990	A new motor was installed.
27 June 1990	The machine started leaking again. I phoned Mr Smelt but he said that owing to illnesses, holidays, and so on, there would be no serviceman available before late July.
8 Aug 1990	Serviceman called and was unable to find what was wrong.
14 Aug 1990	Serviceman called and took the machine away, promising to return it within a week.
30 Aug 1990	Machine returned. It worked properly until 1 Oct 1990, when it started spraying water again. I phoned Mr Smelt, but he said that as the one year's guarantee had now expired I would have to pay for future repairs.

It seems clear that something inside the machine has been cutting the plastic inlet hose, and that no real effort was made to correct this fault.

I enclose copies of various items of correspondence that have passed between me and the company during the period of guarantee and since. I also enclose copies of the receipt for purchase, of the guarantee, and of the technical report when the machine returned from the company's workshop.

I feel that the company has treated me badly. As you will see, they continue to insist that the period of cover is finished and refuse to offer any compensation for the trouble I have suffered.

```
    At this stage I would prefer the
company to refund the original
purchase price. However, I would
also be satisfied if the machine
could be put into working order and
the period of its guarantee
extended.

    Please advise me what I should
do next in this matter.

        Yours sincerely,

        Gladys Unwin (Mrs).
```

CASH-FLOW PROBLEMS

Inability to meet financial commitments can be extremely embarrassing. If your finances have deteriorated beyond the point of no return, there is not a lot you can do other than apply for Legal Aid and put your affairs in the hands of the Official Receiver. But more often it is a case of temporary insolvency after an unexpected mishap – time off work through illness, say.

Creditors are not interested in getting involved in lengthy and costly litigation. If they are satisfied that they will get their money back in the end, they will usually be happy with the extra interest.

The essential things to do are:

- ☐ write to your creditor and explain your circumstances. Apologise sincerely. But don't cringe.

- ☐ offer to pay off your debt in regular instalments, and enclose the first payment. For accounting purposes, credit managers prefer this method to repayment in dribs and drabs. Once your cheque is cashed, you can claim that your creditor has acceded to your suggestions for repayment.

Don't, however, let your creditor get you to sign a form binding yourself to regular payments – not unless your legal adviser, such as the Citizens' Advice Bureau, assures you this is all right. You have nothing to gain – and plenty to lose – from a written undertaking of this sort.

Inability to meet financial commitments can be extremely embarrassing.

```
Dear Mrs Keston,

    As noted in your letter of 15
November, I am in arrears with my
daughter's school fees for this
term.

    I apologise for this failure. My
brother in Zambia died recently and
I have been involved in considerable
expense, with time off work, going
out there to settle his affairs.

    I am now in a position to start
settling this debt, which you say
amounts to £2300. I propose to send
you £300 a month until the debt is
cleared, and enclose a cheque for
this sum as the first payment.

    I trust you are able to agree to
this proposal.

        Yours sincerely,

        Sidney Spender.
```

Writing to Officials and Representatives

As with other business letters, letters to public officials and elected representatives should explain your problem briefly and clearly, but forcefully and forthrightly, and should state exactly what you want done. Once again, try to keep your tone light and friendly. Remember that most officials, councillors, and MPs are flooded with letters, many from people who were angry or distressed when they wrote. These letters are not always very articulate. Try to make yours stand out.

ADVERTISING IN THE NEWSPAPER

The Classified Advertisements sections of newspapers and magazines are popular reading. If you are looking for fellow phillumenists (matchbox collectors) in your area, if you have been given a new stereo system and want a few pounds for your old one, if you are looking for a flat, you can place an advertisement and people will see it. When you send in your advertisement (whether by letter or phone), don't forget to state clearly which section of the columns it is for. You will not have much joy if your advertisement to sell a unwanted sofa goes in the *Situations Vacant* column.

Writing advertisements is the ultimate test of your ability to say the most in the fewest words. Usually there is a minimum charge that allows a certain number of words: if you go over the limit you will have to pay more.

There are well-known and perfectly allowable tricks to shorten your prose, like those used by editors writing headlines. Miss out words like *a* and *the* and *is* – as long as the message remains clear. And use lots of full stops, dotting them about between key words and simple phrases rather than complete sentences. Instead of the sentence *There will be a meeting of the Leeds panel of football referees on Tuesday, 17 August* for example, you might write this: *Leeds panel of football referees. Meeting. Tuesday 17 August*.

Look at the way advertisements similar to the one you want to place are worded. Base your style on the ones you find most effective.

> Kittens, 3 months, seek good homes. Non-pedigree. Phone Bath 39872.

A word of warning. When shortening your advertisements, make sure that you do not introduce ambiguities, perhaps unintentionally funny ones:

> Student seeks room. Must have bath. Urgent.

> Holiday bungalow to let. 10 mins from sea. 3 bdrms, lounge, ktch. Outside toilet, 2 miles Orford.

> Reg King Photographic Studio. Have your children shot for Christmas.

LETTERS TO OFFICIALS

A common mistake is writing to the wrong official. Make sure to distinguish clearly between local and national matters, and between civil servants and elected representatives.

The provision of most services and amenities comes under local government – so direct your letters on such matters to the local authorities.

But which authority? You may have to do some research. Decide which area of public life your point comes under. It is generally the county that is responsible for roads, education, planning, registration of births, deaths, and marriages, and the like. It is the city, town, borough, or district authority that deals with amenities (such as rubbish collection), housing, and social and emergency services. Health matters are separate and come under the local health authority; your local Community Health Council is there to give advice if you have a complaint about local health services.

Remember that most local councils have telephone information services, which should help you to track down the best person to write to. If you can, find the official's name and then address your letter directly to him or her.

If the matter you wish to raise comes under the national government, or if you are not getting anywhere with the local authorities, write to the relevant ministry or official body – such as the Passport Office or Vehicle Licensing Office. Again, phone to find out the best person to write to.

Here is a letter that could be sent either to The Clerk to the County Council or to The Director for Roads and Transport. Note the heading. It will help the letter to reach the appropriate person promptly.

```
Dear Sir/Madam,

     Road Safety and Improvements
     Bishops Road, Kidderminster

     Is there any chance of getting a
couple of 'sleeping policemen' on
Bishops Road (off Victoria Road),
Kidderminster? One on the narrow
section near Victoria Road; the
other nearer St Peter's School.
```

```
      This road is, in places,
extremely narrow. There is a primary
school at its end. Some vehicles
drive very fast up and down it, and
ought to be slowed down.

      I notice with pleasure that you
are putting humps on the nearby
Thorn Avenue. Couldn't you do the
same on Bishops Road?

              Yours faithfully,

              Carl Meek.
```

Confirming conclusions. Sometimes you will prefer to arrange an interview with an official, so that you can deal with your problem face to face rather than by correspondence. Even so, it is a good idea after the interview to write back, confirming what was said when you met.

```
Dear Miss Cummings,

      Thank you for giving your time
today. It was useful to talk to you
about the continued stubble-burning
in the Melford area. You have PC
Foot's report on the various
incidents.

      You agreed to bring the matter
up with the Environment Committee of
the county council, and to let me
know what can be done to enforce the
regulations.

              Yours sincerely,

              Hilary Cousins.
```

WRITING TO ELECTED REPRESENTATIVES

If you need to break a log jam with permanent officials, turn to elected representatives. For local matters write to a local councillor. For national ones – or as a last resort for local matters – you should write to your MP.

Find out the name of your councillor from the clerk of the council, and write to him or her care of the council. If you do not know the name of your MP, contact your local Electoral Registration Office. Write to MPs either care of the constituency office of the local party or at The House of Commons, London SW1. A number of politicians, both local and national, also hold regular 'surgeries' where you can raise matters with them in person.

As with all kinds of letters, be quietly reasonable. You may loathe the politics of your representative,

but don't say so – unless, of course, your letter is a specific attack on his or her party's policies. And try not to sound like an official document or set speech at a committee meeting. Avoid expressions such as *assisting parents/guardians in their decision-making processes* and *approaching executive members of the board with a view to hastening provisional adjustments in non-indexed contributions*. The simpler and clearer the letter, the better the chance that your representative will pay attention to it.

Here is an example of a letter, opposing plans to widen a road, written to a local councillor:

```
Cllr. Mary Sandford
c/o Somerset City Council

Dear Councillor Sandford

I want to urge you to oppose the
plans for widening North End Road,
Yeovil.

There are two main grounds why I
think you should do this:

1. There is already too much traffic
in the town and too few parking
places. The money would be better
spent putting up car parks on the
edge of town and introducing bus
connections from them into the
centre. This kind of 'Park and Ride'
system worked excellently where I
used to live in Plymouth.

2. The plans mean using part of the
playground of St. Mark's School for
widening the road. The school
already has little enough space for
play. And the extra traffic, within
40 yards of the main school
buildings, would create a pollution
hazard for the children.

I hope you will use your influence
on the council's transport sub-
committee to see that the proposal
is not accepted, or at least that it
is modified to spare St. Mark's
School.

Yours sincerely

Edith Parker (Mrs)
```

Writing to MPs. Writing to your Member of Parliament is a last resort. Make sure before you use this tactic that you have already tried all the normal channels. Your MP will not be best pleased – and therefore not very helpful – if he or she discovers that before writing you did not even go to the police about your next-door neighbours' rowdiness.

Remember too that there is a limit to what an MP can do. MPs who are not government ministers – in other words, most of them – have no power to make or change decisions made by, say, government departments. On the other hand, they do have considerable influence. They can put you onto the best people to deal with your business – the Countryside Commission, Race Relations Board, and so forth.

And very often they will write to these bodies themselves, enclosing a copy of your letter. You also will probably have to write to the body, but the fact that an MP has shown an interest in you will ensure that officials give your case their full attention.

Bear in mind also that many peers too are happy to help people with official matters. If you know one, or know of one who may be interested in your point, write to him or her care of The House of Lords, London SW1. But unlike elected representatives, peers are not bound to take up your case – so be especially polite.

Dear Lord Membury,

    I know you take an interest in matters of animal protection. I thought you might want to know about the following sad case. Is there any way that this problem could be rectified?

Whoever you write to, don't suppose that one letter will solve all your ills. In the end it is up to you to see that things are done. Follow any advice you receive. Read carefully all leaflets, forms, and official documents you are sent as a result of your query. And act upon them.

An MP's mailbag. Politicians receive a lot of mail. Here are some tips, mostly gathered from questionnaires sent out to them, on how to make politicians take notice of a letter:

☐ Keep it short and neat. The maximum should be two pages – but the shorter the better. As always, state clearly what you are writing about at the beginning of your letter – use a heading. Write legibly. Lay the letter out properly. Take care over spelling, especially, of course, the spelling of your MP's name.

☐ Get your facts right. Present them clearly. Distinguish rigorously between fact and opinion. Don't make unfounded assertions about people in general. Aim to tell your MP something

he or she did not know before. Draw your MP's attention to any important details you think he or she may have missed.

☐ Spell things out. If you are against a proposal in a Bill before Parliament, say, specify the Bill's full name and, if possible, the clause you are referring to. An opening like *I think you should oppose Clause 16 of the Financial Services Bill* is far better than *I have just read in the paper that the government is considering reducing tax relief on certain annuities*, and leaving the MP to work out exactly which proposal you are referring to.

☐ If you have a special interest in the subject you are writing about, say so clearly. If you are the secretary of your local anglers' club, then mention this when writing to your MP about river pollution. If you are against some proposals in an Education Act, your MP will certainly take your comments more seriously if you happen to be a teacher.

☐ Give your reasons. Don't just register your disgust at cuts in funding for part-time staff in schools. Point out the effect this will have on the availability of minority subjects such as music and languages. Giving your reasons will help your MP when he or she writes back to you or elsewhere on your behalf.

☐ Don't just criticise. Come up with specific proposals for how the problem could be improved or dealt with differently. Don't just say that you cannot get any peace because you live under the flight path of a new airport. Let your MP know that if the planes took off in the opposite direction they would be disturbing nothing more than a few seagulls. Say in plain words what you think your representative should do in the matter.

☐ Include essential documents. Don't overdo this, sending your MP an entire file on your battles with the local council. But do send the one or two key documents, articles, or whatever that will put the case in context.

☐ Most important of all, give your letter a personal slant. Say how the issue will affect you. Say how it will affect others in your community. Make your letter a vivid contrast to your MP's usual, boring reading. When you write to urge tighter controls on air pollution, say a few words about the state of your washing when it comes in off the line.

Tell your MP about the distress your neighbour suffered when her son was injured by a drunken driver, if you are pressing for freer use of breath tests on motorists.

Here are some examples of letters to MPs. The first is written by someone who has exhausted all the normal channels and needs some support from her MP. The second is on a specific Bill before Parliament. The third is a general plea for action.

Dear Mr Bentley,

I would be grateful for your help with a housing problem.

I am a widow with two teenage children. I applied to the Housing Department of Ealing Borough for rehousing three years ago, but am still in my present one-bedroom flat. There has been a great amount of correspondence between me and the Housing Department and I have filled in numerous forms and been to several consultations. They promised to do what they can, but I have not heard from them for six months.

Please would you ask them to give my case special attention, or at least let me know what my chances are of being rehoused.

Yours sincerely,

Martha Weston.

Dear Sir

I strongly urge you to assist in having Clause 24 of the Finance Bill passed in its current form.

It would be a considerable help to physically handicapped people like me to have the proposed extra £350 tax allowance. Handicapped people have enough problems finding well-paid work. We do our best, and this proposal would give us a little benefit for our efforts.

Respectfully

Harry Masters

Dear Sir Leonard,

Please would you do what you can to make the police enforce the laws on selling alcohol to people under 18.

We live beside an off-licence that regularly flouts this law and often have to put up with youngsters making a racket outside, and worse. As parents of growing children we do not want them to grow up with daily scenes of young drunkenness.

We've contacted the police on several occasions but they do not seem to treat the matter seriously. They usually arrive too late to find any proof or are reluctant to act.

New laws are unnecessary. We only want the enforcement of existing ones. It would need an initiative from above to persuade the police to change what appears to be their current attitude. Perhaps a question to the Home Secretary in the House might bring this matter to wider attention.

Yours sincerely,

Paul and Nina Schofield.

Sometimes, humour (though never sarcasm) can be effective, as in this example:

Dear Mr Quain

Public transport in Upper Rillsdale

I'm sure this is not the first letter you've had about the public transport facilities in your constituency, and it won't be the last.

A month or so ago I was returning home from a trip to Manchester. Owing to a hold-up (points failure?), the train from Manchester missed the connection with the branch line at Silsby, and I spent a tedious hour and a half waiting for the next train to Upthorp. Arriving at Upthorp, I found that the last bus to Highfell Village had left ten minutes before. The bus company, when I enquired why the bus went before the train arrived, told me it was to do with overtime rates for drivers.

Finally, I found a bus going to Addlebury, which dropped me at the Grey Tarn crossroads. From there, in pitch darkness and steadily driving rain, I walked the two miles to Highfell. I was not in a good mood when I got home -- my wife claims that I swore at her and kicked the dog. I think it was that way round. I also caught a cold.

We're very fortunate living in this beautiful and exclusive area -- so exclusive that it appears at times to be impossible to get into and out of it. We should be welcoming travellers rather than hiding our light so firmly under a bushel.

The cuts in transport are regrettably understandable. But what I don't understand is why such transport as exists should be so badly coordinated. Since my dark night on the mountains I've discovered that there are other examples of buses and trains leaving before 'connections' arrive. And the last bus on Saturdays to Bogthwaite leaves Silsby from right outside the cinema; only it goes ten minutes before films usually finish.

Surely it's not beyond the powers of the railway and bus companies to settle their differences and work hand in hand. Or for both of them to work out which times would be most likely to attract potential customers.

Wouldn't it be possible to set up some kind of coordinating committee for local transport in Silsby, Upthorp, and the upper valleys? A system like this would need its impetus from you -- the three district councils appear to be no longer on speaking terms.

Yours sincerely

Aaron Kaplan

CAMPAIGNING AND LOBBYING

Sometimes you might want to become involved in a larger-scale campaign on a particular issue – a campaign that involves lobbying MPs to persuade them to bring their influence to bear on behalf of your cause. This might be to oppose a particular Bill before Parliament or, say, to drum up support for a group of dissidents in a totalitarian country. At times like this a flood of mail can be very effective in changing politicians' thinking, by making them realise the strength of feeling among their voters on the issue.

Often a pressure group will send supporters mass-produced letters for them to copy and post to their MPs. But simply putting your name to a mass-produced letter and sending it off is too easy, and the MP will interpret it as a reflex response rather than an act of personal conviction.

Instead, take the mass-produced letter, and 'personalise' it. Give your own examples based on

personal experience. Once again, tell your MP how the measure will affect you. Give your reasons for opposing the measure and suggest, if appropriate, alternative measures that occur to you.

Here is an example. There is a Bill before Parliament that would prevent people from walking their dogs across any land on which livestock is grazing. The writer of the letter is urging his MP to oppose the measure in Parliament.

Dear Mrs Charlton,

Clause 13 of the Countryside Bill

While I can appreciate the problem farmers have with some dogs, I can't see that this is such an important matter that it means that ordinary people's access to the countryside should be limited even further. So I'm writing to urge you to persuade the government to drop or amend Clause 13 of the Countryside Bill.

You should remember that footpaths are rights of way. So surely it's the duty of farmers to keep livestock out of fields where they might be subject to disturbance. Or at least to fence it off from the path.

Most dog owners are responsible people. I keep my dog on her lead when going across paths on which livestock is grazing. If farmers are worried about disturbance to their animals, why doesn't the government force all dog-walkers to do the same? This is surely less objectionable than banning them altogether.

The matter certainly needs clarification. Last year I was sworn at and threatened by a local farmer who claimed that my dog was disturbing his sheep. It's true that the dog was barking at them but, as I have said, she was on her lead at the time and so can hardly be said to have been worrying the sheep. This unpleasant incident would not have occurred if the farmer had known that while my dog was on her lead he could have no reason to complain.

Please give this matter your careful consideration and use your influence to see that Clause 13 doesn't reach the statute books, at least in its present form.

Yours sincerely

Selwyn Grabowski

A GAME FOR ALL THE FAMILY

English has many words derived from the names of members of the family, or from words meaning *man, woman, child*, and so on, in other languages, usually Latin.

A *matriarchy* is a society where women are dominant. The word comes from *mater*, the Latin for 'mother', plus the combining form *-archy*, meaning 'form of government' (from Greek *arkhein*, to rule). *Filial* duties and respect are duties and respect due to parents from their offspring, from the Latin *filius*, a son.

You can find several more examples in the list of roots on pages 147-164.

☐ In the exercise below, choose the 'family' word that fits best into the sentence each time. Find the answers on pages 633-648.

1. The Supreme Soviet of the USSR sends ...... greetings to the people of the United States of America.

A: axiomatic B: connubial C: fraternal
D: perfunctory

2. The prodigal son wasted his ...... on wine, women, and gambling.

A: alimony B: hegemony C: inherency
D: patrimony

3. He was quite besotted with her, but his parents considered her no better than a brazen ....

A: consort B: hussy C: janitor D: nymph

4. While at Vassar College she was admitted to the most exclusive ...... in the university.

A: faculty B: fraternity C: sorcery
D: sorority

5. Terry Wogan will not be ...... at the Eurovision Song Contest this year.

A: compatriot B: compere C: proprietor
D: avatar

6. The colonial governor's policy of ...... towards the islanders was well-intentioned but short-sighted.

A: autism B: infantilism C: paternalism
D: structuralism

7. Just because Liz knows her own mind there's no need to brand her a shrew or ....

A: cormorant B: sylph C: clairvoyant
D: virago

8. After the fall of Hitler, the ...... of Roosevelt, Stalin, and Churchill met at Yalta to decide the future of Europe.

A: conclave B: triplicate C: tertiary
D: triumvirate

9. After the war ended, the persecution began of people who had chosen to ...... with the enemy.

A: affiance B: edify C: fraternise
D: subsidise

10. The drag queen minced across the stage in an ...... way.

A: febrile B: effeminate C: ephemeral
D: ineffable

11. While Fred came to ignore his wife completely, his brother grew more and more ....

A: feministic B: misanthropic
C: matrilinear D: uxorious

12. The national scandal of ...... was typified by the appointment of the President's half-witted son as professor.

A: substantiation B: nepotism
C: partisanship D: simony

13. I find his ideas quite shallow and ....

A: adjacent B: synthetic C: puerile
D: venial

14. The leaders of the coup claimed they were only carrying out their ...... duty.

A: grandiose B: federal C: parsimonious
D: patriotic

Letters to the Media

If you feel strongly about a particular issue, it is always worth writing to the media with your opinions. Even if your letter does not get published, the editor concerned will take note of your views – and if there are enough letters expressing similar sentiments, they can influence the coverage or prominence that newspapers or radio or television stations give to events.

Where to write. Choose your paper, magazine, or programme with care. If you are writing in with an enquiry – about, say, the sound-properties of different stereo systems or for tips on how to breed budgerigars – go for a magazine or programme specialising in that subject.

For matters of local importance, write to local newspapers or radio stations. But if you want to draw public attention to the unforeseen consequences of a Bill before Parliament or bemoan the inaccuracy of weather forecasting, you should consider writing to the national media.

Remember that the tabloids are unlikely to be interested in your observations on international corporate finance, while the more serious newspapers will hardly be riveted by your memories of schooldays with a famous actress.

Remember too that the national broadsheet papers have weekly supplements on subjects such as the arts, education, the media, finance, technology, and computing. These publish readers' letters in their fields. Women's magazines also cover a wide range of topics from travel to education to fashion – and welcome letters in all these areas.

Occasionally, you may wish to make comments (praising or otherwise) on the content of particular articles, programmes, or advertisements, or on matters such as programme scheduling. Clearly, you should write to the people who published the article or advertisement you are commenting on, or to the station that broadcast the programme. But take care. It is not uncommon for the BBC to get letters about programmes that appeared on ITV, and vice versa.

Whom to write to. Generally, letters written to papers or magazines should be sent to *The Editor* and open *Sir* or *Dear Sir* (or *Madam*). At times you can be more specific, and write to, for example, *The Features Editor* or *The Advertising Editor*.

With broadcasting companies the options are wider. You can write to *The Producer* of a particular programme, especially if you wish to make comments on the programme itself or, in the case of some current affairs programmes, if you want to raise points on wider issues.

Remember too that some networks run special programmes devoted to listeners' opinions.

You can also write to the Director General of the BBC or his equivalent at other networks, or the Controller of a particular channel, such as BBC Radio 2 – phone up beforehand to find out the name and correct title of the person. These letters would not be considered for broadcasting, but may be effective if you want a programme taken off the air or continued or moved to another time.

CATCHING THE EDITOR'S EYE

This section deals mostly with letters to your local newspaper. But most of the comments apply equally to letters to other papers and to magazines and radio and television stations.

The editorial offices of newspapers receive a lot of mail. So you will have to make your letter stand out if you are going to see it in print. Here are some useful tips to bear in mind.

SOME DON'TS

☐ Don't touch taboo subjects. Exactly what these are varies from paper to paper, but many refuse to publish letters espousing religious causes or ones that they consider unpatriotic. For obvious reasons a letter that may be libellous or illegal, such as an incitement to violence, will be rejected. Personal attack is also out. With politicians and public figures, you can say what you like about their public lives but not cross the bounds into their private affairs.

☐ Don't make blanket comments on great political events. They are usually too complex to be dealt with in a short letter. Confine yourself rather to particular aspects of an issue. For example, don't say *The budget is awful because it favours the rich*. Say *The proposal to reduce the upper rates of taxation but not National Insurance is appalling because it favours the rich*.

☐ Don't accuse the paper of political bias. By all means say that a particular article presented a partial view, but don't extend your criticism to the paper as a whole.

SOME DO'S

☐ Do, as always, pay attention to layout and neatness. Give your address and make sure your name can be read. No matter how well-reasoned your arguments in the letter, scruffy presentation will immediately raise doubts about you in the editor's mind – and editors are reluctant to publish material from dubious sources.

☐ Do be quick off the mark. Write to monthlies at least two weeks before publication date. To a weekly, get your letter in three or more days before it goes to press. Write to dailies as soon as possible. If you have access to a fax machine, use that to send in your letter.

☐ Do choose a paper that is generally sympathetic to the views you are expressing. Say one of your local papers is publishing a lot of articles about local amenities. That is the one to write to if you are lobbying for a new sports centre.

☐ Do say at the outset why you are writing. The simplest method is to state what you think in the first sentence and why you think it in the second. *Pamela George's interview with the Chancellor on Tuesday's* Newsnight *was utterly spineless. She gave him an unquestioning opportunity to present government propaganda and failed to ask any of the questions that ordinary viewers wanted answered.*

☐ Do back your opinions with hard evidence. And state your credentials. Your letter on violence on the football pitch is much more likely to appear if you are a player or referee.

☐ State your interests. If you are writing against higher taxes on alcohol, and are the manager of a public relations company serving several large brewers, you should 'own up' to your position. Stating your interests often makes it more likely that your letter will be printed – if only to provoke a response.

☐ Do be brief. Specify your complaint, argument, or other comment crisply and clearly. Name only your most important points and arguments. If there are ten good reasons for a plan, choose the best five. *More children get killed on the roads in*

Make your letter stand out.

Britain than anywhere else in Europe. Isn't it time we built more cycle-paths and blocked off roads outside schools to motor vehicles? That says it all. No more is needed. Succinctness is even more important when you write to radio or television stations. The broadcasting media rarely read out more than a couple of sentences from listeners' letters. So try, somewhere in your letter, to sum up the thrust of your argument in the most condensed form. *Many thanks for Peter Selby's documentary on working-class life in Oldham during the Depression. Apart from giving us a vivid picture of the hardships, it left the reader feeling an optimism that such a rich cultural life and caring community could survive in such times.*

☐ Do, above all, make your letter interesting, readable, and lively. Try to maintain the light touch even when discussing serious subjects. If you are criticising something, bear in mind that satire usually convinces better than impassioned invective. And certainly better than offensiveness. Present yourself as calm, rational, decent, and tolerant. Give your own examples and include the odd personal detail. Say how an issue will affect you. Come across as a human being rather than a pundit.

☐ Do, when you have written your letter, go over it carefully. Look for places where you could make it clearer or livelier, where there is a more interesting way of putting your point. And strike out any unnecessary words or sentences. The shorter it is, the more chance it has of being considered for publication.

☐ Do remember, finally, that editors often extract from, rearrange, or reword letters. For instance, to save space when publishing several letters in response to a single article, they will knock out openings like *Zoë Potter's piece on badger-baiting in your June 15 issue revived distressing memories*. But they must not distort what you say. You should complain if they publish a letter with your name that expresses views you disagree with.

SOME SAMPLE LETTERS TO THE MEDIA

```
Dear Sir

Building on Wilson's Fields, Ramsey

Over the last twenty years we've
seen our small country town being
sucked into suburban sprawl and
former local beauty spots
disappearing under concrete.

Now we have only the meadows and
spinneys of what used to be Wilson's
Farm left as havens for picnickers,
play, and wildlife. If the proposal
before the council (reported in your
April 18 issue) to turn the Fields
into an industrial estate goes
ahead, even that will be lost.

Why are the council so taken with
this plan? This town has room enough
for building: on the old coal-yard
at the station, for instance, or
along the Westbury Road. But
Wilson's Fields are unique.

So I beg the council: Save our
countryside for local residents, for
their children, and for generations
still to come.

Yours faithfully

Andrew Kerr
```

If your letter is not intended for publication – you might, say, be writing to the media to urge them to investigate something – you can afford to be more expansive. But still you should not waste words.

The next example is fairly long, but it deals with a complicated subject.

```
Sir

A recent police report blames
failures to secure convictions on
the unwillingness of good barristers
to work at Crown Prosecution Service
rates.

Recently on jury service I had to
try a youth accused of attempting to
stab a policeman. We jurors were
agreed that we did not want people
going around who were liable to
stick knives into others. Yet we
found it very hard to convict.

The attack took place at night and
the defence rested upon a question
of identity. During the trial it
came to light that the police:

1. had failed to fingerprint the
weapon, which had been thrown to the
ground in the fight

2. had failed to hold an identity
parade when the suspect was brought
in for questioning

3. had failed to contact or call
witnesses to the attack, though
there had been several.

The fault lay not with the
barristers but with the shoddy way
the police had handled the evidence.
If the police cannot do better when
one of their own has been attacked,
what can ordinary members of the
public expect?

This case turned out not to be
unique. Time and again during my two
weeks we had to acquit defendants
not because we thought they were
innocent but because the police had
failed to provide prosecuting
counsel with the evidence on which
we could convict.

Surely, rather than complain about
lack of expertise in their lawyers,
the police should be more thorough
in their part in prosecutions. And
if they do not have the facilities
to carry out their duties properly,
these should be provided, with extra
funds if necessary.

Yours faithfully

Adam Nicolson
```

Though political comment makes up the majority of letters to the press and broadcasting networks, they welcome the leaven that letters on other subjects bring – especially if these are likely to persuade other readers to write in. You might want to offer praise or thanks, recall striking events from 'the good old days', contact people with shared interests and concerns, or make an appeal on behalf of a charity.

Here is a light letter of this kind that could easily be slipped into the corner of the letters column of a national or local newspaper.

Dear Madam,

My eight-year-old daughter is doing a school history project. The other day she came home and asked me what life was like in the Middle Ages. She didn't seem convinced by my protestations of ignorance.

But it set me thinking, and I wonder if any reader could help.

1. What's the point of teaching history to kids too young to have any understanding of the time-spans involved?

2. When did people start calling the period between the Romans and the Renaissance 'The Middle Ages'? I bet William the Conqueror and the leaders of the Peasants' Revolt didn't see themselves as being in the 'middle' of anything. In their times, no doubt, they were bang up to date.

3. We call all sorts of things 'modern' nowadays -- modern ideas, modern medicine, modern art, and so on. Won't that seem a bit laughable in a hundred years' time? Or will English have to find a new word and reserve 'modern' to mean 'late twentieth century'?

Yours faithfully,

Jessica Caws.

Some sample letters about the media. The media welcome feedback on their performance. But they like to get more than just complaints. You might like to offer them the occasional word of praise, or make constructive comments on their work.

First, an example of a complaint to the producer of a television play. The letter is written in a reasonable tone and has a serious point to make on an issue that many people feel strongly about – violence on the screen.

Dear Sir,

I'm sure I'm not alone in being offended by your play last Wednesday, The Killing Jar.

It wasn't the language -- people do talk like that and modern drama ought to reflect the way people speak.

It wasn't the sex scenes -- I've got nothing against sex on the television at 11 p.m.

It wasn't even the attitudes expressed by the main character, Fred, towards women and the Irish. Fred was a pretty despicable character and only an already hardened bigot would concur with his views.

What really got me was the violence: the lingering shots of bleeding bodies, the graphic sequence of Fred beating up his girlfriend, the way that the play seemed to justify the police's shooting of bystanders as long as they got the villain.

This kind of thing is liable to affect, even encourage, people with violent streaks in their nature. It's also very ugly. There's plenty of violence in the world and I doubt that presenting it gratuitously on television will help get rid of it.

Yours faithfully,

David Reed.

By contrast, letters of congratulation are usually much shorter.

Dear Sir,

Many congratulations on your new comedy series Mother's Pride. At last, comedy that is neither mindlessly childish nor mindlessly anarchic, and that avoids the temptation of playing for cheap laughs. At times it was difficult to tell whether the lump in my throat was from tears or laughter.

I hope the series maintains the standards of the first episode. I could do with more entertainment of this quality.

Yours faithfully,

Janet Goss.

Writing at Work, Home, and College

Invitations and Announcements

The Reader's Digest Association Limited
WordCraft Editing Limited
and Toucan Books Limited
request the pleasure of your company
at a luncheon to
celebrate the publication of
How to Write and Speak Better
at the Offices of The Reader's Digest
Berkeley Square House
Berkeley Square, London W1X 6AB
on Wednesday, 2 January 1991
at 12.45 for 1.00 p.m.

Lounge suit   *R.S.V.P.*
                        The Secretary to
                            the Chairman

THERE WAS a time, not so long ago, when sending out and replying to invitations and announcements seemed quite straightforward. You just followed the prescribed formulas. If you did everything correctly, all was well. If you did not, society would make its disapproval plain.

Nowadays things are neither so simple nor so risky. People are liable to look on old rules as ridiculous, or even impolite. What girl would take seriously a boy who asked her for 'the honour of the next dance'? At best, she would laugh. At worst, she would rail at him for making fun of her. Few modern girls would put up with mothers who insisted that they should be back by 10 o'clock on an evening out – or that they be chaperoned to a dance.

So too with many of the old 'rules' applying to invitations and announcements – they now seem so impersonal as to be downright rude. Suppose you had to refuse an invitation to an old friend's wedding – because you are working abroad, say. Which of the following replies do you think shows greater consideration for the bride's parents?

Mr Jeremy Russell
regrets that he is unable to accept
the kind invitation of
Mr and Mrs Paul Davies
to the marriage of their daughter
Emily Jane
to
Mr Harold Bennett
at the Church of the Holy Trinity, Englefield
on Saturday, 14 May
or to their home afterwards

Dear Mr & Mrs Davies,
Thank you very much for your invitation to Emily and Harry's wedding. I am very sorry that I shall not be able to be there. As you see, I am at present living in Indonesia.

I shall be writing to the couple soon with my best

386

wishes, and shall be thinking of them when the time comes.

I hope you all have a wonderful time on the day. I imagine you're thrilled and looking forward to the occasion immensely. Knowing Emily and Harry as I do, I am sure that the wedding and reception will both show real style!

Once again, many thanks.

Best Wishes,

Jeremy Russell.

Marking the occasion with a bang . . .

The first reply could have been written by a machine. The second has a quality of warmth and sincerity, without becoming overpersonal towards people the writer does not know. And it gives a genuine reason for turning down the invitation.

Even so, there are still certain rules of etiquette that apply to invitations and announcements on various special occasions.

Special occasions. Throughout the world people feel a need to mark occasions such as marriages, births, engagements, and deaths with some show of formality. In many un-Westernised societies, such 'rites of passage' are accompanied by extremely elaborate rituals. We no longer go as far as they do. But we do still tend to dress up, or to have music and dancing of certain kinds, or to eat and drink expensively. We like to make the day special.

Some modern-minded people object to ceremonies that seem stuffy or artificial. It is not always easy to strike the right balance between the solemn or formal side of the occasion and the personal joy or sorrow behind it.

As a rule, it is for the people most closely involved in organising a ceremony to decide exactly what course to take. Therefore, the bride-to-be and her family make the wedding plans, while a funeral is arranged by the deceased person's closest surviving relatives. The trouble is, these people often have their minds too full of other things to think up their own rules for invitations or announcements.

Hence the need for certain formulas to act as guides. This chapter deals with these 'approved' methods for sending announcements and invitations. Most are simple to follow, and have valid reasons underlying them. So, even if you want to do things your own way, it is a good idea to be familiar

with these standards. At least you can then be aware of how far you may be 'breaking the rules'.

Remember: what may be socially acceptable to your closest friends and immediate family may not meet with the approval of your strait-laced maiden aunt, crusty grandfather, or old-fashioned boss. And if you want the event to go off without giving offence to anybody, you may have to do more things 'by the book' than you otherwise would.

Of the various volumes explaining the details of doing things 'by the book' on formal occasions, the most useful and complete are *Debrett's Correct Form* (edited by Patrick Montague-Smith), and *Debrett's Etiquette and Modern Manners* (edited by Elsie Burch Donald). These should be available in the reference section of your local library. For a balanced, all-purpose, modern approach, however, read this chapter, which gives you the information you will need for most common situations.

Sending and answering. There is another reason for following prescribed patterns, particularly when it comes to sending out formal invitations: following the patterns is convenient.

Inviting people to a wedding, a party, or a funeral requires organisation. You have to let guests know far enough in advance, and you have to establish how many will be coming. Before any large function, you will hardly want to find the time to write personally to all the guests. The best procedure is this: draw up your list of guests (you might get a few trusted friends to advise or remind you of everyone who ought to be invited). Send the guests standard printed invitations and tick their names off the list when the replies start coming in. You can then tell the caterers the exact number of people they will have to provide for.

Not that you need to avoid handwritten letters. But you might as well reserve them for the most special of the guests. And do enclose the formal card as well, if only to serve as a memento.

Now for the other side: any invitations you receive should be answered promptly – within two or three days. Failure to reply is extremely bad manners.

When people have gone to the trouble of offering you hospitality, you must let them know whether you are able to accept, and the sooner the better. Even a curt 'Sorry, can't come' is better than silence.

So too when you receive announcements – of a birth, death, change of address, or the like. It is a courtesy to acknowledge receipt and to offer congratulations or commiserations if appropriate. The sender will at least know that his or her message has arrived, and been noted.

FORMAL INVITATIONS AND ANNOUNCEMENTS

Formal invitations are sent for formal occasions, such as weddings, major receptions, and funerals. It is not necessary to send formal invitations to family and close friends for dinner parties, social gatherings, and the like.

The time-honoured method for sending a formal invitation is by printed or, more expensively, engraved card. A local printer or stationer should be able to show you a range of possible styles, and help you to decide what is appropriate. But your options will be fairly restricted. The exact details of card and script will depend only partly on your own wishes: the occasion itself imposes some restrictions. For instance, while copperplate script is favoured by many brides for their wedding invitations, something less florid is necessary for death notices.

As a general policy of good taste, keep things plain and simple. Avoid gaudiness. A quick look at the commercial cards available for announcing the birth of a baby will provide you with some glaring examples of what to avoid: distracting colours, silly designs, irrelevant details, and a general tone of sentimentality. Enthusiasm of this sort, like profuse expressions of sorrow or sympathy to a bereaved spouse, is best left to a personal letter.

Try to avoid typed invitations or announcements, or typed replies to them. Typing is fine for business, or even for some personal letters. But for formal invitations or announcements it strikes the wrong note – on these occasions, handwriting is best.

Rules for all formal notices. These are the accepted rules for all types of formal invitation.

☐ Use plain white, cream, or ivory card. Certain kinds of decoration are sometimes permissible on the edging, such as gilding or a raised 'platemark', but keep decoration simple. For announcements of deaths and invitations to funerals, a black band around the margins is standard. The size of the card is a matter of personal preference, though conventionally the proportions are about four units by three.

☐ For handwritten invitations, use good-quality plain writing paper – again, white or off-white. You can also use your own headed notepaper. For some 'semi-formal' occasions, general-purpose cards are appropriate. See pages 399 and 400.

☐ The printing on all formal invitations is usually black. Gold can look gaudy. Use black ink if you are writing cards or letters by hand.

☐ Write in the third person (he, she, they rather than I, you, we). Dr and Mrs Watson request the pleasure of Professor John Brain's company . . .

☐ Don't use abbreviations such as Sat., Berks., Capt., or The Hon. Write the words out in full: Saturday, The Honourable, and so on. However, the hosts may abbreviate their own titles if they wish, as in Dr and Mrs Watson. There is no reason not to give dates and times in the form Saturday, 26 January 1991 at 6 p.m., though some people prefer to write out even these more or less in full: Saturday, the Twenty-Sixth of January 1991 at six o'clock.

☐ Centre the lines of text. The only parts that need not be centred are the name of the addressee, which may be written in by hand at the top left; the return address; where relevant, the reason for the function; the reply instructions, such as R.S.V.P. or Regrets only; and any dress instructions. The last three are usually set at the bottom and may be placed either to the left or to the right, whichever seems preferable.

☐ Don't use any punctuation at the ends of lines. There should be punctuation only when words have to be separated within a line and in abbreviations, such as *R.S.V.P.* (or *R.s.v.p.*, which is equally correct).

Contents of all formal notices. The following information should be included in all invitations:

☐ the name/s of the host/s

☐ the name/s of the recipient/s

☐ the nature of the function and, usually, the occasion for it

☐ the address where the function is to take place

☐ the date and time of the function, usually in that order

☐ the address for replies, if this differs from the address of the function

Names and titles. When sending or replying to formal invitations, always use full names where appropriate, including first names. Traditionally, a wife's first name is omitted if she is grouped together with her husband: hence *Mr and Mrs Ivor Stanton*. Children under the age of 15 are usually identified by their forenames alone when they are listed together with their parents.

The commonest formal invitation is to a wedding and wedding reception. A typical example will look something like this:

> *Mr and Mrs Ivor Stanton*
> *request the pleasure of*
> **Miss Patricia Thompson's**
> *company at the marriage of their daughter*
> *Wendy Harriet*
> *to*
> *George Jonathan Randall*
> *at the Methodist Chapel*
> *43 Queen's Street, Newport*
> *on Saturday, 27 January 1990*
> *at 11 a.m.*
> *and afterwards at their home*
>
> *R.S.V.P.*
> *30 Windward Lane*
> *Newport*

Note how the names are given. The hosts and the person invited are given their usual courtesy titles and forenames. The groom is given his full name, while the bride, by custom, is simply referred to by her forenames. Neither groom nor bride is given a courtesy title. For less formal invitations, you may omit the courtesy titles if the guests are close friends or relatives.

Traditionally, when you send an invitation to a married couple or a family, you put the name of the wife alone on the envelope. But on the card you specify exactly who is invited – for example, *Mr and Mrs Clive Norris* or *Mr and Mrs Clive Norris, Andrew, Shirley, and Paul.*

The custom used to be to refer to a married, widowed, or even divorced woman by her (former) husband's first name. No longer – or at least not very often. For obvious reasons, a woman who has divorced Thomas Everett may object to being styled *Mrs Thomas Everett.*

When replying to an invitation, use the name or names given on the card.

MARRIAGE

Tradition and custom are still very strong when it comes to events and announcements related to marriage, but they have modified somewhat over the years. The aim nowadays is to hit the right note of relaxed formality.

Engagements. There are three ways of formally announcing an engagement: by note, at an engagement party, and through the newspapers. The immediate family and closest friends will have heard the news beforehand, usually face to face or over the phone.

You can use any combination of the above three methods. If you hold an engagement party, it is customary to pretend to spring the news upon the guests at the event itself. So an invitation to an engagement party will make no mention of the reason for the occasion. In reality, of course, the 'surprise' will usually surprise no one.

Your more distant family members and friends will hear of the engagement through a handwritten letter from one of you. The letter need not be long or complicated or original. The chances are that you will be writing several such letters, and it is very difficult to say the same thing in new words over and over again. Here is an example:

Dear Aunt Mary and Uncle Jack,

Good news! You've been asking how long I was intending to keep up my bachelor existence. The answer is, not long.

I've just got engaged to a girl I met eight months ago at a company party. Her name is Eleanor (usually called Elly) and she works as a designer at our head office in Stevenage. Her family live near Reading but come originally from Trinidad.

Needless to say, I think she's wonderful. Mum and Dad seem quite taken by her too. I hope you get the chance to make up your own minds soon.

No date fixed as yet for the wedding, but we're both keen to have it fairly soon. September perhaps.

I trust all the family are keeping well. We both look forward to seeing you in the near future.

Best wishes to you and cousins Kate and Michael,

Roger.

If you decide to hold a formal engagement party, the invitation can be any type of formal notice. (Note that in the following two examples it is the parents of the bride-to-be who are giving the party. The couple may, however, decide to host the party themselves, in which case, of course, the invitation would come from them.)

Mr & Mrs Robert Lavelle
request the pleasure of the company of
MR STEVEN WRIGHT
at a party for their daughter
Penelope
at
The Country Suite
The Bear Hotel, Waltham
on Saturday, 10 June 1989
at 8 p.m.

Lounge Suit

R.S.V.P.
17 Streatham Gardens
Waltham

If the engagement has already been announced, the invitation may look like this:

Miss Sarah Goodall

Mr & Mrs Ralph Archer
request the pleasure of your company
at a party to celebrate the engagement
of their daughter
Sarah Linda
to
Derek Broadbent
to be held at
22 Green Walk, Earlingham
on Saturday, 18 March 1990
at 8 p.m.

R.S.V.P.
Dress informal

The differences between the two examples illustrate some of the variations that are permissible in a formal invitation. Note, for instance, that the name of the addressee can either be written at the top left or form part of the text of the card itself. Note too that the return address is assumed to be the same as the address of the function, unless stated otherwise on the invitation.

Engagement notices in newspapers. If you want to announce an engagement in a newspaper, the editorial staff will advise you on the wording. You should, of course, let close friends and family hear the news before it appears in the press. The notice is usually inserted by the bride-to-be's family. If the man comes from a different part of the country, his family may put a notice in a paper in their own area.

Which paper you choose is your decision. No point printing the announcement in the 'Forthcoming Marriages' column on the court and social pages of *The Times* if all your friends and colleagues read *The Guardian* or *The Scotsman*, say. Don't forget your local evening paper as a possible destination. The announcement should be signed by one of the couple, or a parent, and sent in writing to the social editor of the newspaper you have chosen.

In the announcement you should include the names of the couple, and of their parents. You may also add their addresses, and advance notice of the date of the wedding if this is available. Here are two examples. Notice that newspaper announcements have formulas and a style of their own.

Mr L.R. Walker and Miss F.W.P. Booth

The engagement is announced between Leonard, eldest son of Captain and Mrs L.P. Walker of 23 Redhill Road, Aldershot, and Florence, only daughter of Mrs W.I. Booth of 16 Weston Terrace, Bracknell, Berks, and the late Mr Booth. A May wedding is planned.

Mr J.K. George and Dr B.L. Blakey

The forthcoming marriage is announced between Jack, son of Sir Peter George of Little Rampton and Mrs S.M. Weston of Aylesbury, and Bridget, second daughter of Dr and Dr T.O. Blakey of Rotherham.

The same formulas are used for a person who has been widowed or divorced for some time. By custom, however, people awaiting a divorce do not announce their engagement formally.

The following is an example of a widow's engagement announcement:

Capt. H.C. Chambers and Mrs E.P. Anstey

The engagement is announced between Hugh, third son of Major I.C. Chambers of The Red House, Blandford, Staffs, and the late Mrs Chambers, and Elizabeth Penelope, only daughter of Mr and Mrs K.I. Russell of 12 Spring Street, London W4, and widow of Mr Simon Anstey of Settle. Wedding plans to be announced.

Unless you are putting notices in the society journals, you do not need to give more biographical information about the couple. Some magazines, notably *Country Life*, allow fuller engagement announcements, including photographs. Submit the details and photograph to the social editor.

When friends of yours get engaged, it goes without saying that you should write with your congratulations as soon as the news reaches you. The usual procedure is to write to either the woman or the man, but not to both in the same letter. But this is no hard-and-fast rule: it would, for instance, be unnatural to write to only one party if the couple were living together.

These letters call for a reply in turn. One of the couple should answer them with thanks, and give any information about the marriage.

The wedding. To give your guests plenty of time to reply, and to give yourself plenty of time to make accurate catering arrangements, you should send out wedding invitations about eight weeks before the event.

Bride and groom-to-be may have different views.

By tradition, the bride chooses the style of lettering on the invitations, and the hosts (usually her parents) order and pay for the cards. They also draw up the list of guests, though it is customary to offer half the places to the groom's family for suggestions. The cards are sent from the home of the bride's parents or sponsors (an aunt and uncle, say, if her parents are dead), and their address should be given for replies.

As a traditional formality, invitation cards should also be sent to the groom's close relatives and to the presiding minister, even though more personal arrangements are obviously involved as well.

Wedding invitations are traditionally printed on one side of a sheet of stiff paper or card. The other side is left blank. The card may be as large as 7 inches (about 18 cm) in height, and $5\frac{1}{2}$ inches (14 cm) in width. This kind of card will need folding, with the printed side outwards, to fit into the envelope. A somewhat smaller card, about 5 inches (13 cm) high, is probably handier. It will fit unfolded into the special envelopes provided by your printer.

It used to be the custom for very large and lavish weddings, to use two envelopes. An inner ungummed envelope, bearing the guests' names, held the invitation and other enclosures. It was slipped into an outer envelope, which was addressed for posting. Very few people nowadays take things as far as that.

In the blank space on the invitation, write the guest's name in black ink. Address the envelope in the same way. If you are inviting a whole family, you can address the envelope in one of two ways: either to the female head of the household, if there is one, or to the parents 'and Family'. So the envelope might read either: *Mrs Victor L. Borrow* or to *Mr and Mrs Victor L. Borrow and Family*. Strictly, children over about 16, should be sent their own invitations.

Names, titles, and special cases. If the bride's mother or father is giving the wedding alone, for whatever reason, the normal wording is as follows:

> *Dr Richard Pearson*
> *requests the pleasure of the company of*
> Dr. Jack Munro
> *at the marriage of his daughter*
> *Frances*

(and so on).

When the bride's father is no longer alive, and her mother has remarried, the bride's surname may be given in the invitation.

> **Mr and Mrs John Anthony Pearce**
> **request the pleasure of your company**
> **at the marriage of her daughter**
> **Jane Valerie Ingrams**

(and so on).

When the bride's parents are divorced, the invitation is sent out in the name of the parent who acts as host and pays for the reception. If the divorced parents share the responsibilities, both names should appear – the mother's at the top – with the names of the new spouses as well, if appropriate. Here again, specify the bride's surname:

> *Mr and Mrs Brian Nichols*
> *and*
> *Wing Commander and Mrs Kenneth Vintner*
> *request the pleasure of your company*
> *at the marriage of*
> *Elizabeth Clare Vintner*

(and so on).

If the bride is related to the hosts, but is not their daughter, the relationship is usually stated. The bride is free to decide whether she uses her surname or not; she would be well-advised to do so if it is not the same as her sponsors':

> *Mr and Mrs Melvin Ivans*
> *request the pleasure of your company*
> *at the marriage of their niece*
> *Judith Abrahamson*

(and so on).

Invitations to the marriage of a young widow or divorcée are worded as if this were her first marriage, except that the bride may choose to use her married name:

> *Mr and Mrs Stephen Young*
> *request the pleasure of the company of*
> Mr Roderic Glossop
> *at the marriage of their daughter*
> *Evelyn Williams*

(and so on).

Couples may send out their own invitations. This may happen in the following cases: when the partners are older and well-established, and are paying for the reception themselves; when both partners are divorced or widowed; when they have been living together for some time.

The invitations would go out in the name of both parties. For example:

> Nicola Mary Scott and Richard Perkis
> request the pleasure of your company
> at their marriage
> on Wednesday, 14 October 1989

The marital status of the groom does not affect the way he is named.

Be careful how you refer to a groom who is a member of the armed forces. Traditionally, Army captains and higher-ranking officers (and their equivalents in the other forces – lieutenants in the Navy, flight lieutenants in the RAF, and those above), have their titles placed before their names. Their branch of the forces – regiment, squadron, and so on – should be noted below their names in smaller letters. For those of lower rank, their designation usually appears in smaller letters, below their names – as in the following two examples:

> *to*
> *Squadron Leader Henry Owens*
> *54 Squadron*

> *to*
> *Robert William Mercer*
> *Staff Sergeant, Essex Fusiliers*

These customs also apply to the police force, and to brides from the armed forces or police force.

The wording of wedding invitations. As you can see from the many examples above, there is very little variation in the wording of wedding invitations. The custom used to be to request 'the honour of your presence' at the ceremony, and 'the pleasure of your company' at the reception, but this distinction has largely fallen into disuse. Generally the same card is used to invite guests to both the ceremony and the reception.

Don't invite guests 'to a reception at . . .' The usual wording is 'and afterwards at . . . ' See the example on page 389.

If many people are expected, you may allocate special seating for favoured guests and write the details at the top of the invitation card: for example, *Pew no. 8*. Other enclosures may be necessary, especially if the wedding is taking place out of town. You might have a special sheet printed with maps, train timetables, information on parking arrangements, and so on.

The couple may also wish to enclose an *At Home* card with the invitations, giving their new address and the date from which they will be living there. Ideally, an *At Home* card should be smaller than the invitation or announcement, but should be of the same type of paper and use the same typeface.

> **At home**
> **after the sixth of September**
> **47 Longford Drive**
> **London W6E 6NA**

Limited invitations. What if you are having a large ceremony, but only a small private reception or wedding breakfast? Or if the ceremony is to be small and private, but followed by a larger reception? You may need to have special cards printed to invite guests to just one of the events.

> *Mr and Mrs Peter Sedley*
> *request the pleasure of your company*
> *at the marriage of their daughter*
> *Roberta*
> *to*
> *Group Captain Wilfred George Dunstan*
> *at St Mary's Church, Woking*
> *on Saturday, the twenty-first of March, 1990*
> *at three o'clock*
>
> *R.S.V.P*
> *23 Grange Avenue*
> *Woking, Surrey*

> *Rabbi and Mrs Daniel Black*
> *request the pleasure of your company*
> *at a reception*
> *to celebrate the marriage of their daughter*
> *Rebecca*
> *to*
> *Mr Ian Silver*
> *at home*
> *45 Downside Way, London N16*
> *on Sunday 14 May, 1989*
> *at 5 p.m.*
>
> *R.S.V.P.*

Wedding announcements. There are many reasons why you might not be able to invite everyone you would like to a wedding or reception. The ceremony might be taking place abroad; the couple might prefer to do things on a small scale; or the groom's parents may have a huge extended family that they are unwilling to impose on the bride's parents. In such cases, the thing to send is a wedding announcement rather than a wedding invitation. If you receive an announcement of this kind, you are not expected to send a present, but do at least, as a common courtesy, write back to the sender of the card offering your congratulations. This is how an announcement card might look:

*Professor and Mrs Martin Cooper
have great pleasure in announcing
the marriage of their daughter
Yvonne Beatrice
to
Mr Norman Greenfield
at the Tenth Avenue Episcopal Church
Newark, New Jersey, U.S.A.
on Saturday the fifth of August, 1989*

Press announcements and reports. Newspapers that publish engagement announcements also publish wedding announcements.

Announcements of forthcoming marriages state the time and place of the service. Newspapers usually have their own standard wording for this, and will advise you on the procedure when you phone or visit to place the announcement.

To place an advance announcement or to ensure that the wedding itself will be reported, ring the paper at least two weeks before the wedding. The newspaper staff may ask for details, and whether they might send a reporter and photographer. Or they may simply send you a form to be filled in and returned with a photograph after the wedding.

The typical entry in a national paper is worded along these lines:

Young – Marchant: On September 15th, 1990, at the Friends Meeting House, Cirencester, Neil Young to Natalie Marchant.

Like local newspapers and some magazines, the court and social pages of *The Times* and *The Daily Telegraph* describe some weddings in greater detail. The bride's father should submit an account of the wedding to the social editor of his chosen newspaper or magazine, and pay the costs.

A typical description of the wedding reads like this:

Mr N.P. Stevenson and Miss J.K. Wilson

The marriage took place on Saturday, 14th October, at Portsmouth Cathedral between Lieutenant Norman Stevenson, third son of the late Captain Thomas Stevenson and of Mrs T. Stevenson, of Mill House, Petersfield, Hampshire, and Miss Jennifer Kirsty Wilson, daughter of Dr and Mrs Antony Wilson, of 26 High Street, Fareham, Hampshire. The Right Reverend the Bishop of Portsmouth officiated.

The bride, who was given in marriage by her father, wore a gown of plain white silk. She carried a bouquet of white roses. She was attended by Susan Wilson, Sarah Greene, and Irene Mitchell. Lieutenant Alex Copeland was best man. A reception was held at Old Grange, the home of Mrs Gavin Ellis, the bride's aunt. The honeymoon is being spent in Ireland.

Wedding presents. Presents may be sent before the wedding, or taken to the reception. They are usually marked with a small card:

With all good wishes from Uncle Len and Aunt Penny

With much love and best wishes for your happiness. From the Grangers.

The bride should make a list of the gifts, and acknowledge them with a thank-you letter, before or after the wedding. (For advice on the thank-you letters, see pages 355-358 in the chapter on writing letters at home.)

Change of plans. You must let the guests know as soon as possible if the wedding has to be postponed or brought forward.

If the invitations have been printed but not yet been sent, you can include a small card bearing a printed or handwritten message.

The extra card should give reasons for the change of plans, and the new wedding date if this is available. Here is an example:

*Owing to Major Richard Inglis
being called on active service abroad
the date of the wedding has been changed
from 16 March
to
Saturday, 9 March*

A similar card may be sent if the invitations have already gone out.

**Owing to the sudden death of
Mrs Wilbur Evans
the marriage of her daughter
Gloria Jasmine
to
Mr Barry Robertson
has been postponed**

Complete cancellations are more serious. It is the woman's right to announce the breaking off of an engagement, and it is her mother's duty to withdraw the invitations. A card or letter, briefly announcing the cancellation, should be sent to everyone who has received an invitation:

> **Mr and Mrs Anthony Hardcastle**
> announce that the marriage
> of their daughter
> Belinda
> to
> **Mr Brendan Higgins**
> will not take place

If the engagement has been announced in the press, the bride's family may insert an appropriate notice. The notice, normally signed by both parties to the engagement, must be submitted in writing to the newspapers' society editors.

> The marriage arranged between Mr Michael Bradley and Miss Elspeth Linda Edwards will not take place.

If there is no time to send notices, you should of course use the telephone to inform guests of any change of plans. If you have received any presents, return them immediately with a note of thanks.

OTHER FAMILY OCCASIONS

For anniversaries and most other family or personal occasions, the formalities are much less rigorous. A general announcement or invitation card, with wording of your own choosing, usually fits the bill.

But one other major personal occasion does require specially printed cards – namely a bereavement.

Deaths. Except perhaps for memorial services, you will not have time to make elaborate arrangements after a death in the family. Still, some planning has to be done, and many people find that attending to this can help to stop them from brooding over their personal sorrow.

After a bereavement, you will want to have your closest family and friends around you. They will give you advice and assistance on the public side of bereavement, as well as on its personal side. You may take charge of arrangements, or you may delegate this responsibility to a friend or relative.

The exact course of action depends on the relationship between you and the deceased. But in all cases, you should notify close friends and family as soon as possible, usually by telephone.

After this, you should notify the press, usually by telephone, and they will tell you what their standard procedure and wording for death notices are. Alternatively, the undertaker will make these arrangements for you. Most local newspapers publish death notices, as do the main large-format national dailies.

You should also inform appropriate professional journals, and similar publications.

A death notice usually includes the date and place of death, the names of the immediate family, the place and time of the funeral and, frequently, a request that instead of flowers, a contribution should be sent to a charity. Here are two examples of death notices:

> EVANS – Guy Nicholas, on 18 September 1989, at the County Hospital, Worcester. Beloved husband of Elsie Evans and father of Reginald Evans and Georgina Hatton. Funeral Thursday, 11 a.m, at the Baptist Chapel, Smith Road, Worcester. In lieu of flowers, please send donations to the Save the Children Fund.

> THOMAS – On 12 July 1990, while on holiday in Scotland, Derek Longwood Thomas of 12 Georgian Mews, London WC2. Dearly loved husband of Martha. Funeral service at St Winifred's Church, Sandbach on Wednesday, 18 July at 3 p.m. No flowers. Memorial service to be announced later.

If you send flowers to the funeral, or send a contribution to charity, attach a note bearing your own name as well as that of the deceased. Something like this:

> In loving memory of Guy Nicholas Evans of April Cottage, Newton.
> From Simon Jones, 62 Larkspur Close, Chingford.

The charity will send a list of donors to the person who placed the notice, who will then arrange – or personally write – thank-you letters to the donors.

If you send flowers to the bereaved at home rather than to the funeral, the wording on the card should be more personal: 'With deepest sympathy'.

The death notice in the press may include the words 'Funeral private'. If so, you should not attend unless specifically invited. But do still send a letter of condolence to the bereaved family (see page 359.)

More distant family and friends can be informed of the death in one of two ways: by personal letter, or by a simple printed card with a black border and, if desired, a cross or appropriate religious symbol centred at the top. The card may include details of the funeral, and thereby serve as an invitation to that ceremony. It should use a plain typeface.

> Mrs Jennifer Blake
> on the thirteenth of October, 1990
> peacefully at home

> The Reverend Alan Mackenzie
> 3 March 1909 - 12 December 1990
> at the Gordon Bradshaw Nursing Home
> Penrith
> Funeral service
> at All Saints' Church, Penrith
> Tuesday, 19th December at 11 a.m.
>
> R.S.V.P.
> Mr Gordon Mackenzie
> 11 Lancaster Road
> Morecambe, Lancs

You may find it helpful to ask the undertakers to take some of this work off your hands. They can often arrange the printing and sending of funeral invitations or death announcements. To draw up an address list, a relative or solicitor or executor should go through the deceased's address book and mark all those people who seem likely to need to know. Closer friends will be able to write back with personal letters of condolence. Business associates will acknowledge more formally.

If you are the widow or widower or closest surviving relative you should answer all letters of condolence personally. If this is likely to take some time, you can place an interim notice in the personal or court pages of the newspapers, along these lines:

> Mr Alexander Stewart of Alloa wishes to thank all those who have sent letters of sympathy on the death of his wife, Jean. He hopes to write personally to all in the near future.

Or you could have a similar message printed on cards and sent to everyone you intend writing to when you have more time.

Parents should spread the news.

Births. A birth in the family is usually a happy but confused time. It is therefore not bound by the same formality as a marriage or death.

The baby's parents and grandparents should spread the news amongst family and close friends by telephone. Letters or cards (these are available from most stationers) can be sent out to other people likely to be interested.

Be aware that cards announcing births are often among the most tasteless and garish you can buy. Avoid, if you can, cards with babyish designs. As with all invitation and announcement cards, the simpler the better.

You can also insert an announcement in the Births column of national and local newspapers, either by letter or phone. Your notice should look something like the following:

> **Stevens** On July 10th, at the Queen Mary Hospital, Birmingham, to Celia, the wife of Gerald Stevens – a son, Colin Terence.

> **Marriott** On 25 November 1990, at home, 24 Quebec Road, Leeds, to Angela (née Simms) and
>
> Nathan – a daughter, sister to Patrick.

Most newspapers nowadays are quite happy to publish birth announcements for children born out of wedlock:

> **Hughes** On 7 April, at the Knaresborough Hospital, Knaresborough, Yorks, to Katharine Jane – twins, a boy and girl.

The quality national newspapers announce births in their personal columns. Supplementary to these, *The Times* and *The Daily Telegraph* also publish some notices in their court and social pages.

Mrs Henry Arthur Willis gave birth to a son in Roxburgh on September 3.

No matter how you receive the news of a birth, you should make your contribution to the celebrations of family and friends. Letters, cards, and flowers can be sent to the mother at the hospital. British Telecom also have standard telegrams that can be ordered over the telephone.

Anniversaries. There are four special wedding anniversaries: silver (25 years), ruby (40 years), golden (50 years), and diamond (60 years). At these landmarks, many couples like to hold large parties.

An invitation to a major anniversary party follows the model of all formal invitations:

> Mr and Mrs Colin B. Phelps
> request the pleasure of
> Miss Lilian White's
> company at a party
> to celebrate their silver wedding anniversary
> at four p. m.
> on Saturday, 12 June 1990
> in the Bristol Rooms
> at the Westgate Hotel, Buxton
>
> R. S. V. P.   8 Longwood Way
>   Buxton

The corresponding newspaper announcement has the appearance of a wedding notice, and gives the date of the wedding itself:

Phelps – Updike On 10 June 1965 at St Luke's Church, Norwich, Colin Bruce Phelps to Mary Updike. Present address: 8 Longwood Way, Buxton, Derby.

PARTIES AND RECEPTIONS

By now you should be familiar with the layout and wording of formal notices. The examples on pages 389, 390, and 393 can serve as models for printed invitations to other private parties and functions. But what if these are organised or hosted by several people? If you are hosting a formal dance, dinner, or reception at the home of someone else, include both the address of the event and your own address for replies:

> Mr and Mrs Lionel Hawkins
> request the pleasure of your company
> at a buffet supper
> to celebrate the graduation of their son
> Leonard
> at the home of
> Mr and Mrs Stephen R. Wilkinson
> 15 Manchester Road, Stalybridge
> on Thursday, 6 July 1989
> at 7 p. m.
>   R. S. V. P.
>   12 Turnham Gardens
>   Stalybridge

Very often, several people get together to put on a large function. In this case, the first name on the card is that of the person at whose home the function is to take place. If there are no other instructions, this is where replies should be sent.

If the venue is to be outside the home of any of the hosts, and they are each inviting their own guests, the hosts are listed according to seniority.

Invitations to a large coming-out ball, for example, might be set out as follows:

> Mrs Martin Anderson
> Lady Elizabeth Wentworth
> Mrs Ian Pritchard
> request the pleasure of your company
> at a dance for their daughters
> Emily, Dorinda, and Doreen
> at the Old Ballroom
> Windsor Hotel, SW1
> on Friday, the fourth of April
> at 9 p.m.
>
> R.s.v.p.
> 22 Hills Mews   Westbury Hall   'Stockley Croft'
> London W1   Westbury Magna   Stockley
>   Wiltshire   Hertfordshire

Here the order of the hostesses (by seniority) corresponds to the order of the addresses given at the bottom.

Several hosts may, however, find it more convenient to give only one address for replies. Invitations to a reception at the home of Miss Amy White to celebrate the publication of a book produced by her and Mrs Robert Fisher may read this way:

Miss Amy White
and
Mrs Robert Fisher
request the pleasure of your company
at a reception
to celebrate the publication of
The Book of Modern Dance
Thursday, 10 October
at 6.30 p.m.
at 47 Highway Road, London NW3 6RI

R.S.V.P.
Miss Amy White

Imaginative invitations. Preparing the invitations for a less formal function gives you an opportunity to use your imagination. An attractive or amusing invitation, like an original theme for a party, will create interest and anticipation among the guests.

An imaginative invitation does not need to be complicated. But it may take you several attempts to get it right. Before preparing the final version, make sure that you have the wording sorted out, and practise the kind of designs you want. Draft the invitation in pencil first, so that you can make corrections. Then go over it in ink.

For private parties or functions, it often is not worth having the invitations printed. The commonest way of preparing them is to do a single version by hand, and photocopy it for each of the guests.

Here is an example of an invitation to a garden party; it is enlivened by artwork designed to convey some of the spirit and idea of a garden.

Make the most of your handwriting, especially if you have mastered a fine style such as copperplate. If the party has a theme, try to find ways of reflecting this in the invitation. Most important, make the invitation express something about yourself, your ideas, your designs, and your party.

Note that the above example still follows the style and layout of formal invitations – standard wording, centred lines, and so on. You could, of course, break free of these conventions as well. You might try using varied colours, say (using crayons or highlighters if you do not have access to a colour photocopier) or photographs or designs clipped from magazines. For example, invitations to a tasting of this year's *Beaujolais nouveau* would look striking on a tricolour background, or you may want to use a photograph of your new home on invitations to a housewarming party. Magazine advertisements provide a rich source of ideas – and pictures – for such invitations.

The size and shape of the invitation do not matter. You may have reasons for wanting to produce something immense, or something tiny, or something triangular. Your local rugby club might produce for its annual dance invitations shaped like a rugby ball.

The wording will often reflect the special nature of the event: its theme, its guests, or its location. If you can manage a decent piece of verse, so much the better. A party invitation is a golden opportunity for puns and 'in' jokes. The geology department of a British university once sent out invitations to its students in traditional formal style, except that the party was to take place

> in the Senior Refectory
> on Thursday, 10th of June
> at 8 p.m.
> give or take 25,000,000 years

Here are a couple of examples of imaginative invitation cards. The trick is to find something of your own.

> POPE JOHN PAUL II
> THE DUKE AND DUCHESS OF YORK
> IAN BOTHAM
> TOM CRUISE
> MADONNA
> THE DAGENHAM GIRL PIPERS
> MELVYN BRAGG
> are just some of the people
> who have NOT been invited to
> a very select gathering
> at May and Andy's
> 9 Benson Road, Lincoln
> on Saturday, the 12th of October
> at 8 p.m.
> but YOU have been
>
> Confirm by phone
> Dress – optional
> We'll see to food
> You bring a bottle

> I Graham Arthur Wilkinson of 25 Juniper Lane in the city of York (hereinafter called the house) being of sound mind herby declare that
>
> Whereas the tenth day of August (hereinafter called the birthday) is the anniversary of my birth
>
> And whereas I shall shortly therefore graduate formally and finally as a Bachelor of Laws from the University
>
> And whereas it is my desire and intention to provide on that day the bearer of this document (hereinafter referred to as you) with victuals provender music and such other entertainments as to me do seem appropriate
>
> And subject to the conditions laid down in paragraphs 1 to 5 below being satisfied by you with respect to me
>
> 1 that you bring or cause those in your charge to bring to the house on the birthday bottles barrels pipkins flasks buckets or other containers holding alcoholic beverages such as may reasonably be expected to conduce to the spirit of festivity appropriate to such a gathering

> 2 that you and those in your charge shall be present at the house on the birthday not before eight in the evening and not remain in the house after two on the following morning other than by particular permission of me and
>
> 3 that you if you are male and those in your charge whosoever of them may be male shall be attired or otherwise accoutred in such appurtenances or apparel that you or they may be mistaken for a member of the clergy or other religious order or
>
> 4 that you if you are female and those in your charge whosoever of them may be female shall be attired or otherwise accoutred in such appurtenances or apparel that you or they may be mistaken for a member of the order of ladies of the night and
>
> 5 that you shall on or before the third day of August inform me by telephonic, epistolary, or other means of communication of your intentions regarding the abovementioned stipulations I wish it to be known that on the birthday at the house between the times stated in the second condition above I desire you to be present together with such other persons that you may deem fit to have in your charge up to a maximum number of two

All-purpose cards. If you entertain a great deal, you may find it worth your while having general invitation cards printed. These can be used for all but the most formal and informal occasions. You may, for instance, use them for dinner, lunch, and dance invitations. These cards follow the style of all cards for formal occasions, but have blanks left for the hostess to fill in as appropriate. Enquire at your local printer or stationer. An all-purpose invitation card may look like this:

> Dr Ivan Jones & Professor Elise Jones
> request the pleasure of
> .... company
> on ....
> at ...... o'clock
>
> RSVP
> The Residence
> 201 Sandwich Terrace
> London SW1 3MT

In this case, the blanks should be filled in with the name of the guest, the nature of the function, the date, and the time. Other details, such as dress instructions, can be written in at the bottom, on the left or right.

'At Home' cards. For rather less formal occasions, a busy hostess might find it useful to have 'At Home' invitation cards printed. By tradition, it is only a woman, as 'keeper of the household', who uses 'At Home' cards.

In keeping with a confusing but long-standing tradition, the words 'At Home' simply mean that you are inviting the recipient of the card to a function. They do not necessarily mean that the function is to take place at your home. The occasion can be anything from an intimate afternoon tea or garden party (which probably would be at your home) to a full-scale ball or reception (probably given in hired rooms).

'At Homes' are engraved or printed on heavy white, or cream, card. Those intended for special occasions are usually about 4 inches high by $6\frac{1}{2}$ inches wide (10 cm by 16.5 cm). All-purpose 'At Homes' are generally smaller (about $3\frac{1}{2}$ by $4\frac{1}{2}$ inches – 9 by 11.5 cm). Both types of 'At Home' card will have your name, title, and, in most cases, your address printed on them.

'At Homes' can either be printed specifically for a special event or ordered in bulk. In the former case, the details of time, place, type of function, dress instructions, and so on can be included in the printing. Cards ordered in bulk are more versatile, and will bear only the name and address of the hostess, the words 'At Home', and possibly the reply instructions. The hostess fills out the other details by hand.

Here are two examples of 'At Home' cards. The first is a card specially printed for a particular event, and the second is a general-purpose card, completed for the occasion.

'At Home' cards are also useful for confirming invitations that you have extended over the telephone. In this case you can cross out the 'R.S.V.P.' and write in either 'To remind' or 'P.M.' *(Pour Memoire)*.

OFFICIAL FUNCTIONS

If you work in the public relations department of a company you may find yourself having to send out invitations to public functions. The format of these invitations is the same as that of weddings. The invitations are usually engraved or printed on white card in script or roman type.

Official functions vary greatly, and mark many more types of occasion than private functions do. Your invitations might be 'For the Opening of . . .' or 'To mark the two hundredth Anniversary of . . .' or 'For the Presentation of Awards by . . .' You therefore need to be able to apply the principles of invitations to a variety of possible circumstances.

Invitations to official functions often give two times – the time of the function and the time by which guests are supposed to have arrived. A luncheon, for example, might be 'at 12.45 for 1.00 p.m.' For an inauguration ceremony, you might need to add at the end of the main text, something to this effect: 'Guests are requested to be seated by 2.30 p.m.'

At the head of the invitation, name any guests of honour. If the Queen or Queen Mother is attending, the formula is: 'In the gracious presence of Her Majesty The Queen/Her Majesty Queen Elizabeth The Queen Mother'. The term 'gracious' is not used for other members of the royal family. They would be referred to in this way: 'In the presence of Her Royal Highness the Princess Royal'.

Note that it is 'the Princess' (with a small *t*), but 'The Queen' (with a capital *T*). Also, it is only the children of the reigning sovereign who are denoted *'the Prince/Princess'*.

Non-royal guests of honour can be designated in this way: 'To meet / In honour of / In the presence of the Right Reverend and Right Honourable the Lord Bishop of London'.

Here are two examples of how a formal invitation to an official function might look:

The President, Lord Appleton, and Council of
The British Sinological Society
request the pleasure of the company of

Sir Mulberry Hawk

at a dinner to celebrate
the 50th Anniversary of the Society
followed by the presentation of awards
for contributions to Sinological research
to be held in the Maudsley Room
Cardigan College, Oxford
on Thursday, the 24th of February, 1991
at 7.30 for 8.00 p.m.

Dinner Jacket   *R.S.V.P.*
or Evening Dress   *The Secretary,*
        The School of Oriental Studies,
          Bedford Way,
           London W2.

In the presence of
The Vice President of the United States
The President and Board of
Branch Engineering Incorporated
request the honour of the presence of

Mr Ralph Nickleby

at the Official Opening of their U.K. showrooms
at 45 The Strand, London W1
on Wednesday, the fourth of June, 1990
at 3.00 p.m.

Guests should   *R.S.V.P.*
arrive by 2.30 p.m.   *The Company Secretary,*
        Branch Engineering Inc.,
         11-15 Hubert Way,
         London EC2 7MD.

To prevent gatecrashers, you might add the words 'Please bring this card with you' at the bottom. Alternatively, a separate admission card can be enclosed, or sent on receipt of an acceptance. Admission cards should be small enough to fit into a pocket – that is, no larger than $4\frac{1}{2}$ by $3\frac{1}{2}$ inches (11.5 by 9 cm) and printed in roman type.

Admission cards can also be used to allocate seats. If so, each guest will need his or her own admission card. Therefore, you should send separate cards to a husband and wife, even though they may both have been included on the same invitation card.

Seat no. ....

Please admit

....

to the Main Hall, Guildford
for the Mayor's Reception
on Saturday 25 April, 1990
from 8.00 to 11.00 p.m.

To be handed in
at the door

INFORMAL INVITATIONS

For less formal occasions, an invitation by means of a short handwritten note or telephone call is usually good enough. In an informal letter of invitation, use the first and second persons (*I*, *we*, *you*) rather than the third person (*he*, *she*, *they*).

Some hostesses find it useful to have small, folded 'informal' cards for invitations or personal messages. They are usually white or cream. These cards may have your name printed on them.

You can also send informal invitations on a so-called correspondence card. Correspondence cards are usually about the size and shape of a postcard, and unlike informal cards are not folded. Printed along the long top edge are the address and telephone number, and usually the name, of the sender. They differ from 'At Home' cards in that their uses are not restricted to invitations. For this reason, they do not end with the letters *R.S.V.P.* Postcard-size correspondence cards are enclosed in envelopes before posting.

Here are three examples of informal invitations. The first is a short, handwritten note; the second is an informal card; the third is a correspondence card.

---

2 November.

Dear Mr & Mrs Finlay,
 Would you like to come to our place with the children on the fifth at 7 p.m.? We are having a fireworks party with a barbecue and drinks. Please let us know by phone.
 We hope very much to see you then.
   Yours,
   Vivian Smith.

Professor and Mrs Charles S. Turner

Dinner, Friday 23rd October

Please confirm by phone   *8 p.m.*

Mr and Mrs Aubrey Wilson, Oak Tree Cottage, Wendham Lane, Islip OX3 2AP (0865) 435892

Russell & Leslie Morgan

Drinks, Thursday 24th May
7 – 10 p.m.

Regrets only.

REPLIES

How you accept or decline an invitation depends on the type of invitation you have received. All replies should be written by hand, preferably on good quality white or cream writing paper. Cards may be used for less formal occasions.

As a general rule, the formality of a reply should match the formality of the invitation. The wording of the reply usually reflects that of the invitation, so replying is usually a very simple matter. You can even follow the layout of a formal invitation, with short centred lines, though you may, and often should, write in ordinary prose. If your reply is a formal one, don't sign it. When accepting, confirm the details of date and time, but not necessarily the venue. If you have to decline the invitation, give a reason if possible.

An acceptance of a wedding invitation might look like this:

Mr and Mrs Thomas Wright
have much pleasure in accepting
the invitation of
The Right Reverend Henry and Mrs Jenkins
to the marriage of their daughter
Sally Anne
to
Mr Patrick Lucas
On Saturday, the 24th of March, 1990

If possible, give a reason for declining.

A partial acceptance might look like this (note the ordinary layout):

35 Waterford Street,
Usk.

Mrs. George Keith has great pleasure in accepting the kind invitation of the Right Reverend Henry and Mrs Jenkins to the marriage of their daughter Sally Anne to Mr Patrick Lucas on Saturday, the 24th of March, 1990, but regrets that Mr. Keith has a prior engagement and will be unable to attend.

Some formal invitations you can answer in a fairly informal manner. In some cases it is in fact best to be informal, since it gives you an opportunity to say a few words from the heart. For an example of this, see the very beginning of this chapter (page 386). A rigid, formal reply here would have seemed colder and less appropriate. It is up to you to gauge the most appropriate tone for your reply in each case.

If the function is being staged by more than one host, your reply should list the names of all the hosts. So should the envelope, even if only one of the hosts lives at the reply address. So, for the invitation to the ball on page 397, an appropriate reply would read:

> Clock House,
> Little Farnham,
> Buckinghamshire
>
> *Miss Frances Westbrook thanks Mrs Martin Anderson, Lady Elizabeth Wentworth, and Mrs Ian Pritchard for their most kind invitation to the dance for their daughters, Emily, Dorinda and Doreen, on Friday, the fourth of April, and has great pleasure in accepting.*

Certain traditional rules still govern formal replies to invitations to official functions. It is normal to have the 'honour' rather than 'pleasure' of accepting. Here is an example of a reply to an invitation to an official function:

> 14 Wyndham Way,
> Uppington.
>
> *Justice Alexander Rhodes is honoured by the invitation of His Excellency, the Sultan of Oman to a reception at the Embassy of Oman on Wednesday 16 May, at 8 p.m., but regrets that he will be unable to attend since he will be on circuit at the time.*

It was once the custom to treat invitations from royalty as royal commands, to be refused at one's (social) peril. So, if you were forced to refuse, the formula was to accept the invitation officially, and then to add a paragraph asking to be excused.

> *Dr and Mrs Paul English have the honour to accept the kind invitation of His Excellency, the Sultan of Oman to a reception at the Embassy of Oman on Wednesday, 16 May at eight p.m.*
>
> *Since they will be out of the country at the time, they beg to be excused from being present on that occasion.*

For obvious reasons people seldom adhere to this curious practice these days.

Informal invitations usually state whether a reply is needed and, if so, whether by note or telephone.

Written replies should take the form of a short personal letter or card.

A letter accepting an invitation to a cocktail party from a friend might read this way:

> 15 Batley Way,
> Pudsey.
>
> *Dear Margery and Bill,*
> *Many thanks for the invitation to the party next Friday. Of course we'll be delighted to come. Do you think we could bring John's brother, who will be staying with us at the time? We'll assume that you can find room for him, but if there's a snag please give us a call.*
> *Many thanks for thinking of us.*
> *Yours,*
> *Gillian Viney*

If you are unable to attend the occasion you have been invited to, your hosts will be less disappointed if you add a little charm to your letter:

> *Dear Julia,*
> *What a shame! As you can imagine, we'd love to come to the reading. Unfortunately, it's open day at Bill's school, and as governors we really must attend. I do hope it all goes well and that the critics cover you with praise.*
> *Best wishes,*
> *Susan Strong.*

You can use a correspondence card, informal card, or even a tasteful postcard for sending acceptances or regrets. The following example is of a correspondence card reply:

> Christopher and Betty Wordsworth, 105a High Street, Chesterton, Cambridge
>
> *Ingrid and Charlie*
> *Very sorry we can't make it to lunch on Sunday.*
> *Prior engagement with the in-laws.*
> *Chris.*

Modes of Address

How SHOULD you begin a letter to a bishop or a baronet? How should you speak to a member of the Royal Family at an official function? What is the customary way of addressing a business letter to a high-ranking officer in the armed forces? Or to a commission of inquiry? For most people, such problems are unlikely to arise – though it is always worth knowing how to deal with them if they do. But at a more everyday level, modes of address often do cause trouble. If your local vicar happens to be an old friend, you obviously address him in speech by his first name. But if you have to write to him in his capacity as a vicar, what then? You want to get it right. In the following pages you will find ways of opening letters, addressing envelopes, and the like, applicable to most social situations. For further information on writing business and personal letters, see pages 270-312 and 344-385.

Writing to Organisations

If you are writing to an organisation, try first to find out the name of the person who will deal with your letter. See whether you have any correspondence from the organisation – perhaps the writer signed *Dr* or *Ms* or added the title *Finance Director*. Address the envelope accordingly. For instance:

> Ms Stephanie Bristow,
> The Secretary,
> Acme Insurance Company . . .

Alternatively, phone the organisation and ask for the name of the person you should write to, together with how he or she likes to be addressed.

Even if you lack the time or opportunity to find out all this information, don't just send the letter to the organisation in general. There is usually an appropriate office-holder to whom you can address it. If writing to a court, for example, address your letter to The Clerk of the Court – he generally deals with correspondence. Or if you have a complaint to make to a police authority, write to the Chief Constable. Here is a list of such organisations, with the appropriate person to write to in each case.

Armed forces unit – The Officer-in-Charge
Association – The Secretary
Bank – The Manager
Births, deaths, marriages – The Registrar (for Births, Deaths, and Marriages)
Board – The Secretary
Building Society – The Manager

Bureau – The Director
Centre – The Director
Chamber of Commerce – The President/The Secretary
Club – The Secretary
College – The Principal/The Master/The Warden (If possible check the appropriate term.)
Company/Corporation – The Secretary
Commission – The Commissioner/The Secretary
Committee – The Secretary
Community charge – The Registration Officer
Confederation – The Secretary
Council – The Secretary
Court – The Clerk (of the Court)
Department (of a college, say) – The Director/The Commissioner/The Secretary. (If possible, check the appropriate term.)
Electoral roll – The Registration Officer
Federation – The Director/The Director General/The Secretary
Foundation – The President/The Director
Fund – The Secretary
Guild – The Secretary
Institute/Institution – The Secretary
League – The Secretary
Local authority – The Director (for Education, Finance, or whatever)
Local council – The Town Clerk/The District Clerk/The Clerk to the Council
Ministry – The Minister for Transport/The Secretary of State for Education

Museum/gallery – The Director
Newspaper/magazine – The Editor
Office – The (Finance, Sales) Officer/The Director
Organisation – The Director
Police authority – The Chief Constable
(for Cumbria, Merseyside)
Police station – The Superintendent/
The Station Sergeant
Registry – The Registrar
Royal Commission – The Secretary
School – The Head/The Headmaster/
The Headmistress/The Secretary
Society – The Secretary/The Manager
Tax office – H.M. Inspector of Taxes
Tribunal – The Secretary/The Registrar
Trust – The Secretary
Union – The President/The Secretary
University – The Registrar/The Vice-Chancellor/
The Rector (in Scotland)

In a few cases, however, such as estate agents or firms of accountants or solicitors, the custom is to address the group by its name: simply *Walker & Son*, *Samson & Wyatt*, or the like.

The normal way to begin any letter to an organisation is *Dear Sir* or *Dear Madam*. But if you have the name of the relevant person, use that: *Dear Mr Rogers*. If, in the case of a woman, you do not know whether she is *Dr*, *Mrs*, *Miss*, or *Ms*, use her full name on the envelope and for her address at the top of the page but start the letter *Dear Madam*.

When signing off a formal business letter, many people still favour *Yours faithfully* or the older *Yours truly*, particularly if you started *Dear Sir* or *Dear Madam*. *Yours sincerely* is fairly widespread now, but if you want to be absolutely safe, use it only when you have at least a passing acquaintance with the person you are writing to, such as your solicitor.

Speaking and Writing to Individuals

Many people have strong preferences about how they are referred to. Respect these preferences of theirs. Some, for example, like to dispense with titles on political or religious grounds, and to be known simply as *Paul Brown* or *Sarah Graham* – rather than *Sir Paul Brown, Bt.*, or *Lady Sarah Graham*. Be particularly careful with the question of *Mrs*, *Miss*, *Ms* when addressing a woman – for a detailed discussion of this, see page 414. As with organisations, if you have correspondence from the person you are writing to or going to meet, see what style he or she prefers – and use that.

The list that follows gives details of how to address letters and how to begin them, and when face to face how to introduce people to others and address them directly. Unless an alternative formula is listed – as when writing to the Pope – end letters in the normal way: *Yours sincerely*, *Yours faithfully*. Words in square brackets are optional, or alternatives. Where there are two or more possibilities, the more formal is given first.

Note that people are much less formal in their approach nowadays than they used to be. Traditionally, you would open a letter to the Archbishop of Canterbury, for instance, with the words: *My Lord Archbishop*. Today's usage is simply to write: *Dear Archbishop*. Traditionally, you would close a letter to a member of the House of Lords with the somewhat ponderous formula:

I have the honour to remain,
Your Lordship's obedient servant . . .

Nowadays, however, such formality sounds dangerously close to ludicrous – and therefore positively disrespectful. So this chapter gives only the normal usage of today.

Similarly, when addressing people face to face. In the past you would have addressed a duke as 'Your Grace'; nowadays, it is more normal to speak to one as 'Duke'. The exception to this rule of increased casualness is the forms of address for the Royal Family: here a good deal of formality still prevails.

The following sections deal with:

The Royal Family
The clergy (including dignitaries of the Islamic, Hindu, and Sikh religions)
The peerage and non-hereditary titles
Women's titles
Scottish and Irish titles
Untitled people
Government and parliament
Governors and diplomats
The law
The armed forces
Local government
Professional people
The police
Academics

The Royal Family

Unless you know a member of the Royal Family personally, direct your letter to his or her Private Secretary, Equerry, or Lady in Waiting – address it for example, to *The Private Secretary to Her Majesty the Queen*. Ask that the contents of the letter be brought to the attention of Her Majesty (or His or Her Royal Highness).

The Queen

Writing to members of the Royal Family.

Introduced as:	'Her Majesty the Queen'
Addressed as:	A ruling monarch would always address you first. When replying, first use '[May it please] Your Majesty', and thereafter 'Ma'am', pronounced / mam /.

The Duke of Edinburgh

Introduced as:	'His Royal Highness, Prince Philip, The Duke of Edinburgh'
Addressed as:	'[May it please] Your Royal Highness' at first, and there-after 'Sir'

The Queen Mother

Introduced as:	'Her Majesty, Queen Elizabeth, The Queen Mother'
Addressed as:	'[May it please] Your Majesty' at first, and thereafter 'Ma'am'

The Prince of Wales

Introduced as:	'His Royal Highness, Prince Charles, The Prince of Wales'
Addressed as:	'[May it please] Your Royal Highness' at first, and there-after 'Sir'

Other Royal Princes

Introduced as:	'His Royal Highness, The Prince Edward'
	'His Royal Highness, Prince Michael of Kent'

Note that only the children of monarchs are *The* Prince, *The* Princess.

Addressed as:	'[May it please] Your Royal Highness' at first, and there-after 'Sir'

A Royal Princess

Introduced as:	'Her Royal Highess, The Princess of Wales'
	'Her Royal Highness, The Princess Margaret, The Countess of Snowdon'
Addressed as:	'[May it please] Your Royal Highness' at first, and there-after 'Ma'am'

A Royal Duke

Introduced as:	'His Royal Highness, The Duke of Kent'
Addressed as:	'[May it please] Your Royal Highness' at first, and there-after 'Sir'.

A Royal Duchess

Introduced as:	'Her Royal Highness, The Duchess of York'
Addressed as:	'[May it please] Your Royal Highness' first, and there-after 'Ma'am'

The Clergy

THE CHURCH OF ENGLAND

Archbishop

Envelopes:	The Most Revd and Rt. Hon. the Lord Archbishop of Canterbury (or York)
Opening of letter:	Dear Archbishop
Introduced as:	'[His Grace,] The Archbishop of . . .'
Addressed as:	'Your Grace', or 'Archbishop'

Bishop

Envelopes:	The Rt. Revd the Lord Bishop of Oxford
Opening of letter:	Dear Bishop
Introduced as:	'[His Lordship,] The Bishop of Oxford'
Addressed as:	'My Lord', or 'Bishop'

Note that the Bishop of London is *The Rt. Revd and Rt. Hon. the Lord Bishop of London.*

Former bishops and archbishops are referred to by surname, as in *Archbishop Temple*. Never use this style for those in office, however.

Dean

Envelopes:	The Very Revd the Dean of Highfield
Opening of Letter:	Dear Mr Dean, or Dear Dean
Introduced as:	'The Dean of Highfield'
Addressed as:	'Mr Dean', or 'Dean'

Vicar or Rector

Envelopes:	The Revd Nicholas Jones
Opening of letter:	Dear Vicar (or Rector), or Dear Mr Jones
Introduced as:	'Mr Jones'
Addressed as:	'Mr Jones', or 'Vicar' (or 'Rector')

If the clergyman's wife is included, the letters would go to *The Revd Nicholas and Mrs Jones.*

Note that it is always *The Revd Nicholas Jones* – never *The Revd Jones*. Some Anglo-Catholic clergy prefer to be known as *Father – Father Jones*.

Other clergy

Envelopes:	The Very Revd the Provost of Winchester
	The Venerable the Archdeacon of Reading
	The Revd Canon Archibald Roberts
Opening of letter:	Dear Provost/Dear Archdeacon/Dear Canon
Introduced as:	'The Provost of Winchester'
	'The Archdeacon of Reading'
	'Canon Roberts'
Addressed as:	'Provost', 'Archdeacon', 'Canon'

Wives of the clergy do not have special titles. You would address a letter to *The Rt. Revd the Lord Bishop of Durham and Mrs Thomas*, or introduce your local dean and his wife to friends as *The Dean of Highfield and Mrs White*. When the wife has a title of her own, use that – *The Archdeacon of Reading and Lady Margaret Franklin.*

THE CHURCH OF SCOTLAND

Lord High Commissioner to the General Assembly

Envelopes and introductions:	His Grace the Lord High Commissioner
Opening of letter:	Your Grace
Addressed as:	'Your Grace'

Moderator of the Assembly

Envelopes:	The Rt. Revd Professor Adam Nicolson, CBE, The Moderator of the General Assembly of the Church of Scotland
Opening of letter:	Right Reverend Sir, or Dear Moderator, or Dear Professor Nicolson (or other title)
Introduced and addressed as:	'Professor Nicolson' (or appropriate title)

The Clergy

Envelopes:	The Revd Donald Inglis
	The Revd Marcia Inglis

Opening of letter:	Dear Mr Inglis, or Dear Mrs/Miss/Ms Inglis
Introduced and addressed as:	'Mr Inglis', or 'Mrs/Miss/Ms Inglis'

THE ROMAN CATHOLIC CHURCH

The Pope

Envelopes and introductions:	His Holiness Pope John Paul II, or His Holiness the Pope
Opening of letter:	Most Holy Father, or Your Holiness
Addressed as:	'Your Holiness'

The usual way to end a letter to the Pope is:

[I have the honour to remain,] Your Holiness's most humble [or obedient] child.

Non-Catholics should substitute *servant* for *child*.

Cardinal

Envelopes:	His Eminence the Cardinal Archbishop of Westminster, or His Eminence Cardinal Smith
Opening of letter:	Your Eminence, or Dear Cardinal Smith
Introduced as:	'His Eminence Cardinal Smith', or 'Cardinal Smith'
Addressed as:	'Your Eminence', or 'Cardinal Smith'

Apostolic Delegate

Envelopes:	His Excellency Most Revd Thomas Schmidt, or His Excellency the Apostolic Delegate
Opening of letter and addressed as:	Your Excellency
Introduced as:	'His Excellency [Thomas Schmidt], the Apostolic Delegate'

Archbishop

Envelopes:	His Grace the Archbishop of Liverpool, or The Most Revd William Pritchett, Archbishop of Liverpool
Opening of letter:	Your Grace, or Dear Archbishop Pritchett
Introduced as:	'His Grace the Archbishop of Liverpool', or 'Archbishop Pritchett'
Addressed as:	'Your Grace', or 'Archbishop Pritchett'

Bishop

Envelopes:	His Lordship the Bishop of Newtown, or The Rt. Revd Ian Gill, Bishop of Newtown
Opening of letter:	My Lord [Bishop], or Dear Bishop [Gill]
Introduced as:	'His Lordship Bishop Gill of Newtown', or 'Bishop Gill of Newtown'
Addressed as:	'My Lord', or 'Bishop Gill'

Retired archbishops and bishops are addressed by name, as in *The Most Revd Archbishop O'Connor*.

Monsignor

Envelopes:	The Revd Monsignor John Ellison, or The Revd John Ellison
Opening of letter:	Dear Monsignor Ellison
Introduced or addressed as:	'Monsignor Ellison'

Abbot

Envelopes:	The Rt Revd the Abbot of Westbury
Opening of letter:	Right Reverend Father, or Dear Father Jarrett
Introduced as:	'Abbot Jarrett'
Addressed as:	'Abbot [Jarrett]'

Priests of other ranks

Envelopes:	The Revd Patrick O'Callaghan
Opening of letter:	Dear Father O'Callaghan
Introduced as:	'Father O'Callaghan'
Addressed as:	'Father O'Callaghan', or 'Father'

ORTHODOX CHURCH

The different branches of the Eastern Orthodox Church use a variety of titles and forms of address for their higher dignitaries.

Patriarch

Envelopes and introductions:	His Holiness the Patriarch

Opening of letter and addressed as:	Your Holiness

Metropolitan

Envelopes and introductions:	[His Beatitude] The Most Revd Metropolitan Gregory of Sourozh
Opening of letter:	Your Beatitude, or Dear Metropolitan Gregory
Addressed as:	'Your Beatitude', or 'Metropolitan Gregory'

Archbishop

Envelopes and introductions	[His Eminence] The Most Revd Archbishop Michael of Thyateira and Great Britain
Opening of letter:	Your Eminence, or Dear Archbishop Michael
Addressed as:	'Your Eminence', or 'Archbishop Michael'

JEWISH

The Chief Rabbi

Envelopes:	[The Very Revd] The Chief Rabbi Dr Joshua Stein
Opening of letter:	Dear Chief Rabbi
Introduced as:	'The Chief Rabbi'
Addressed as:	'Chief Rabbi', or 'Dr Stein'

Rabbi

Envelopes:	Rabbi Peter Waldmann, or Rabbi Dr Peter Waldmann (if appropriate)
Opening of letter:	Dear Rabbi Waldmann, or Dear Dr Waldmann
Introduced as:	'Rabbi Peter Waldmann', or 'Dr Peter Waldmann'
Addressed as:	'Rabbi Waldmann', or 'Dr Waldmann'

Minister

Envelopes:	The Revd Philip Samuels, or The Revd Dr Philip Samuels (if appropriate)
Opening of letter:	Dear Mr Samuels, or Dear Dr Samuels (as appropriate)
Introduced as:	'Mr Philip Samuels', or 'Dr Philip Samuels'
Addressed as:	'Mr Samuels', or 'Dr Samuels'

MUSLIMS

How you address the *Imam*, or 'prayer-leader', of a mosque depends on whether he is a member of the Sunni or Shiah sects.

Sunni

Sunni tradition uses the term *Sheikh*.

Envelopes and introductions:	Sheikh Muhammed Haleem
Opening of letter:	Dear Sheikh Haleem
Addressed as:	'Sheikh Haleem'

Shiah

Envelopes and introductions:	The Most Revd Imam of the Mosque of Central Bradford
Opening of letter:	Dear Imam Faqih, Dear Hadji Faqih, or Dear Mr Faqih
Addressed as:	'Imam Faqih', 'Hadji Faqih', or 'Mr Faqih'

The term *Hadji* is a title used by any Muslim who has made the pilgrimage to Mecca.

HINDUS

Two of the more common Hindu titles are *Swami* (used by religious teachers) and *Pandit* (a title assumed by some Brahmins – members of the highest, priestly caste). Note the use of the suffix *-ji*, added as a sign of respect.

Envelopes:	Swami/Pandit Muktananda Saraswati
Opening of letter:	Dear Swami/Panditji
Introduced and addressed as:	Swami/Panditji

SIKHS

Every Sikh temple has a *granthi* (reader), who is addressed by the title *Bhai* (brother). Note the use of *-ji* or *Saheb*, as a sign of respect.

Envelopes and introductions:	Bhai Santokh Singh
Opening of letter:	Dear Bhai Santokh Singh, or Dear Bhaiji, or Dear Bhai Saheb
Addressed as:	Bhaiji, or Bhai Saheb

The Peerage and Non-Hereditary Titles

Duke

Envelopes and introductions:	[His Grace,] The Duke of Omnium
Opening of letter:	Dear Duke of Omnium, or Dear Duke
Addressed as:	'Duke'

Duchess

Envelopes and introductions:	[Her Grace,] The Duchess of Omnium
Opening of letter:	Dear Duchess of Omnium, or Dear Duchess
Addressed as:	'Duchess'

Widow of a duke (dowager duchess)

Envelopes:	[Her Grace,] The Dowager Duchess of Omnium, or [Her Grace,] Mabel, Duchess of Omnium (as she prefers)
Opening of letter:	Dear Duchess of Omnium, or Dear Duchess
Introduced as:	'The Duchess of Omnium'
Addressed as:	'Duchess'

For other dowagers, see the section on women's titles below.

The eldest son of a duke is usually a marquess, taking the second title of his father as 'a courtesy title'. See under marquess.

Younger son of a duke

Envelopes and introductions:	Lord George Pangbourne
Opening of letter:	Dear Lord George [Pangbourne]
Addressed as:	'Lord George'

Wife of the younger son of a duke

Envelopes and introductions:	Lady George Pangbourne
Opening of letter:	Dear Lady George [Pangbourne]
Addressed as:	'Lady George'

Daughter of a duke

Envelopes and introductions:	Lady Gladys Pangbourne
Opening of letter:	Dear Lady Gladys [Pangbourne]
Addressed as:	'Lady Gladys'

Marquess

Envelopes:	'[The Most Hon.,] The Marquess of Taunton'
Opening of letter:	Dear Lord Taunton
Introduced as:	'The Marquess of Taunton', or 'Lord Taunton'
Addressed as:	'Lord Taunton'

Marquess can also be spelt *Marquis*.

Marchioness

Envelopes:	[The Most Hon.,] The Marchioness of Taunton
Opening of letter:	Dear Lady Taunton
Introduced and addressed as:	'The Marchioness of Taunton', or 'Lady Taunton'

The eldest son of a marquess is usually an earl. The younger sons and daughters of a marquess are treated as the sons and daughters of dukes.

Earl

Envelopes:	[The Rt Hon.,] The Earl of Brancastle
Opening of letter:	Dear Lord Brancastle
Introduced as:	'The Earl of Brancastle', or 'Lord Brancastle'
Addressed as:	'Lord Brancastle'

Countess (the wife or widow of an earl)

Envelopes:	[The Rt Hon.,] The Countess of Brancastle
Opening of letter:	Dear Lady Brancastle
Introduced and addressed as:	'The Countess of Brancastle', or 'Lady Brancastle'

The eldest son of an earl is usually a viscount.

Younger son of an earl

Envelopes:	The Hon. David Westbury
Opening of letter:	Dear Mr Westbury
Introduced as:	'Mr David Westbury'
Addressed as:	'Mr Westbury'

Wife of the younger son of an earl

Envelopes:	The Hon. Mrs David Westbury
Opening of letter:	Dear Mrs Westbury
Introduced as:	'Mrs David Westbury'
Addressed as:	'Mrs Westbury'

Daughter of an earl

Envelopes and introductions:	Lady Shirley Westbury
Opening of letter:	Dear Lady Shirley [Westbury]
Addressed as:	'Lady Shirley'

Viscount

Envelopes:	[The Rt Hon.,] The Viscount Warburton
Opening of letter:	Dear Lord Warburton
Introduced as:	'The Viscount Warburton', or 'Lord Warburton'
Addressed as:	'Lord Warburton'

Viscountess

Envelopes:	[The Rt Hon.,] The Viscountess Warburton
Opening of letter:	Dear Lady Warburton
Introduced as:	'The Viscountess Warburton', or 'Lady Warburton'
Addressed as:	'Lady Warburton'

Son of a viscount

Envelopes:	The Hon. Owen Wright
Opening of letter:	Dear Mr Wright
Introduced as:	'Mr Owen Wright'
Addressed as:	'Mr Wright'

The eldest son of a viscount has no special title.

Wife of the son of a viscount

Envelopes:	The Hon. Mrs Owen Wright
Opening of letter:	Dear Mrs Wright
Introduced as:	'Mrs Owen Wright'
Addressed as:	'Mrs Wright'

Daughter of a viscount

Envelopes:	The Hon. Lucinda Wright
Opening of letter:	Dear Miss Wright
Introduced as:	'Miss Lucinda Wright'
Addressed as:	'Miss Wright'

Baron

Envelopes:	[The Rt Hon.,] The Lord Thomas
Opening of letter:	Dear Lord Thomas
Introduced as:	'[The] Lord Thomas'
Addressed as:	'Lord Thomas'

Wife of a baron

Envelopes:	[The Rt Hon.,] The Lady Thomas
Opening of letter:	Dear Lady Thomas
Introduced and addressed as:	'[The] Lady Thomas'

The daughters and sons of a baron are treated as the daughters and sons of a viscount.

LIFE PEERS, BARONETS, AND KNIGHTS

Life peer

Envelopes:	The Lord Goss
Opening of letter:	Dear Lord Goss
Introduced and addressed as:	'[The] Lord Goss'

Wife of life peer

Envelopes:	The Lady Goss
Opening of letter:	Dear Lady Goss
Introduced and addressed as:	'[The] Lady Goss'

Children of a life peer

Envelopes:	The Hon. Peter/Wendy Davies
Opening of letter:	Dear Mr/Miss Davies
Introduced and addressed as:	'Mr Davies', 'Miss Davies'

Baronet

Envelopes:	Sir Jasper Jenkins, Bt.
Opening of letter:	Dear Sir Jasper
Introduced as:	'Sir Jasper Jenkins'
Addressed as:	'Sir Jasper'

The abbreviation *Bt.* is nowadays usually preferred to the more old-fashioned *Bart*.

Wife of a baronet

Envelope and introductions:	Lady Jenkins

Opening of letter:	Dear Lady Jenkins	Introduced as:	'Sir Brian Bailey'
Addressed as:	'Lady Jenkins'	Addressed as:	'Sir Brian'

The children of a baronet have no special titles.

Knight (non-hereditary)

Envelopes:	Sir Brian Bailey, KBE (or other decoration)
Opening of letter:	Dear Sir Brian

Wife of a knight

Envelopes and introductions:	Lady Bailey
Addressed as:	'Lady Bailey'
Opening of letter:	Dear Lady Bailey

Women's Titles

Most hereditary peerages pass only to male heirs. If an earl, for example, has daughters but no son, his title usually passes on his death to his brother or a male cousin, rather than to his eldest daughter. There are some special exceptions, however. Scottish peerages, in particular, can usually pass down in the female line. If a Scottish earl dies with no male heir, then his earldom passes to his eldest daughter, who becomes a peeress in her own right – the Countess of Ochterlony or whatever.

Note that an untitled husband of a peeress remains *Mr – Mr Anthony Brown and The Viscountess Eastbourne*. The children of a peeress in her own right take the same titles as those of a male peer of her rank.

If a woman with a 'courtesy' title – a title she bears as the daughter of a peer – marries an untitled man or one with a lesser title than her own, she keeps her title. For instance, if Lady Gladys Pangbourne, the daughter of a marquess, married Sir Jasper Jenkins, Bt., she would be *Lady Gladys Jenkins* rather than *Lady Jenkins*.

A woman bearing the title *The Hon.* who marries a peer's younger son is styled, for instance, *The Hon. Mrs Richards* rather than *The Hon. Mrs Arthur Richards*. If she married a baronet or knight she would be *The Hon. Lady Jenkins*.

Hereditary peeress in her own right

Envelopes:	The Countess of Ochterlony
Opening of letter:	Dear Lady Ochterlony
Introduced as:	'The Countess of Ochterlony', or 'Lady Ochterlony'
Addressed as:	'Lady Ochterlony'

Widow of a hereditary peer

Envelopes:	The Dowager Countess of Brancastle, or Henrietta, Countess of Brancastle (as she prefers)
Opening of letter:	Dear Lady Brancastle
Introduced and addressed as:	'Lady Brancastle'

Life peeress

Envelopes:	Baroness Hawley
Opening of letter:	Dear Lady Hawley
Introduced and addressed as:	'[The] Lady Hawley'

Dame

Envelopes and introductions:	Dame Imogen Proudfoot
Opening of letter:	Dear Dame Imogen Proudfoot, or Dear Dame Imogen
Addressed as:	'Dame Imogen'

A dame is the female equivalent of a non-hereditary knight.

Widow of a baronet

Envelopes:	The Dowager Lady Jenkins, or Belinda, Lady Jenkins
Opening of letter:	Dear Lady Jenkins
Introduced and addressed as:	'[The] Lady Jenkins'

Divorcée

In all cases, from an ex-duchess to the divorced wife of a baronet, the forename precedes the title on envelopes. For example:

Envelopes:	Sarah, Marchioness of Worsted
Opening of letter:	Dear Lady Worsted
Introduced and addressed as:	'[The] Lady Worsted'

Scottish and Irish Titles

The usage for Scottish and Irish titles is distinctive in certain cases.

Eldest son of a Scottish peer or peeress

Envelopes and introductions:	The Master of Lochalsh
Opening of letter:	Dear Master of Lochalsh
Addressed as:	'Master'

The Master's wife is styled *Mrs* unless she (or her husband) has the right to some other title.

Scottish chief or chieftain

Envelopes and introductions:	The MacDonald of MacDonald
Opening of letter:	Dear MacDonald. (If you are a member of the clan, you should open *Dear Chief*)
Addressed as:	'MacDonald'

When talking to a chief, use his clan or territorial name, not his surname. Thus Major Malcolm Munro of Inveratholl, for instance, should be addressed as *Inveratholl*.

Female chief in her own right

Envelopes:	Madam MacKeith of MacKeith
Opening of letter:	Dear Madam MacKeith of MacKeith
Introduced and addressed as:	'Madam MacKeith'

Wife of a Scottish chief or chieftain

Envelopes:	Madam MacDonald of MacDonald. (In some families *Mrs* is preferred to *Madam*)
Opening of letter:	Dear Madam MacDonald, or Dear Mrs MacDonald
Introduced and addressed as:	'Madam MacDonald', or 'Mrs MacDonald'

Eldest son of a Scottish chief

Envelopes:	Hamish MacDonald of MacDonald, yr. (*Yr.* means 'younger'.)
Opening of letter:	Dear Mr MacDonald
Introduced and addressed as:	'Mr MacDonald'

The wife of the eldest son of a Scottish chief would be styled *Mrs MacDonald of MacDonald, yr.* on an envelope, but would otherwise be addressed as *Mrs MacDonald*.

The usage for some Scottish titles is distinctive.

Irish Chieftain

Envelopes and introductions:	The McGillycuddy of the Reeks
Opening of letter:	Dear McGillycuddy
Addressed as:	'McGillycuddy'

The only Irish chieftain not using *The* is O'Conor Don.

Wife of an Irish chieftain

Envelopes and introductions:	Madam McGillycuddy of the Reeks
Opening of letter:	Dear Madam McGillycuddy
Addressed as:	'Madam McGillycuddy'

Irish Hereditary Knight

Envelopes and introductions:	The Knight of Glin
Opening of letter:	Dear Knight [of Glin]
Addressed as:	'Knight', or 'Sir'

Untitled People

Men

Envelopes:	Christopher Long, Esq. (,MBE, BA, if appropriate), or Mr Christopher Long (,MBE, BA) or Christopher Long (,MBE, BA)
Opening of letter:	Dear Sir, or Dear Mr Long
Introduced as:	'Mr Christopher Long', or 'Christopher Long'
Addressed as:	'Mr Long'

The use of *Esq.* is declining. It was originally limited to specific people, such as professional men and the holders of degrees from Oxford or Cambridge.

Never use *Esq.* together with *Mr* or *Dr* or the like. And never use *Esq.* after a woman's name.

Wife or widow

Envelopes:	Mrs Christopher Long, Mrs Frances Long, Ms Frances Long, Frances Long, Ms Frances Short (maiden name), or Frances Short (as she prefers)
Opening of letter:	Dear Madam, Dear Mrs/Ms Long, or Dear Ms Short
Introduced and addressed as:	'Mrs Christopher Long', 'Mrs Frances Long', 'Frances Long', 'Frances Short', 'Mrs Long; 'Ms Long', or 'Ms Short

The whole question of how to address an untitled married woman has become increasingly complicated in recent years. Traditionally, it was all very simple. When you addressed a married woman, you used both her husband's fore- and surnames – as in *Mrs Christopher Long*. For women over 60, it is still probably safe to use this form. But for younger married women, possible alternative forms are available and usually preferable.

First, there is the whole problem of *Ms* (pronounced / miz /) vs *Mrs*. A married woman can use either title. If possible, find out her preference before addressing her. Likewise, which names she uses. Does she prefer it when people address her by her husband's or her own forename? Most younger women prefer the latter – *Mrs Frances Long*. And which surname does she use? Many women nowadays like to keep their maiden name – particularly for professional purposes. Some adopt the continental policy of using a double-barrelled name – *Frances Short-Long*. A woman who keeps her maiden name will probably prefer the *Ms* title – *Ms Frances Short*.

Another problem: how to address a married couple on, say, an envelope? Which is it?

> Mr and Mrs Christopher Long
> Mr Christopher and Mrs Frances Long
> Mr Christopher and Ms Frances Long
> Christopher and Frances Long
> Frances Short and Christopher Long

Again, find out, if you can, which form the couple prefers. Failing that, use your discretion. Probably the safest form is *Christopher and Frances Long*.

Boys of about 14 or under

Envelopes and introductions:	Master Robert Long, or Robert Long
Opening of letter:	Dear Master Long, or Dear Robert
Addressed as:	'Master Long', 'Robert'

Master is old-fashioned and may seem patronising. The safest policy is to use the forename alone.

Unmarried women and girls

Envelopes:	Miss/Ms Valerie Long, or Valerie Long
Opening of letter:	Dear Miss/Ms Long
Introduced and addressed as:	'Miss/Ms Long', or 'Valerie Long'

Traditionally, an eldest daughter is styled *Miss Long*, her younger sisters *Miss Monica Long*, *Miss Jennifer Long*, and so on.

Divorcées

Envelopes:	Mrs/Ms Sheila Long, or Mrs/Ms Sheila Short (maiden name)
Opening of letter:	Dear Mrs/Ms Long, or Dear Mrs/Ms Short
Introduced and addressed as:	'Mrs Long' or 'Mrs Short'

A divorcée may revert to her maiden name or continue to use her former husband's surname.

Government and Parliament

Outside official and parliamentary occasions, politicians should be addressed by their own names and personal titles, if any. On envelopes Members of Parliament are styled *Mrs Georgina West, MP, Sir Edward Briggs, MP*, or the like.

Privy Councillors – that is, all current and former cabinet ministers and some others – are known as *The Rt Hon*. When writing to any of them, use the style: *The Rt Hon. Hugh Grant, MP*. If a Privy Councillor has another title, the style is: *Colonel The Rt Hon. Sir Albert Smith*.

The Prime Minister

Envelopes:	The Rt Hon. James Cecil, MP (for personal mail), or The Prime Minister (for official mail)
Opening of letter:	Dear Prime Minister
Introduced as:	'The Prime Minister', or 'Mr James Cecil'
Addressed as:	'Prime Minister', or 'Mr Cecil'

Lord Privy Seal

Envelopes:	The Rt Hon., The Lord Williams (personal), or The Lord Privy Seal (official)
Opening of letter:	Dear Lord Privy Seal
Introduced as:	'The Lord Williams, The Lord Privy Seal' or 'The Lord Privy Seal'
Addressed as:	'Lord Privy Seal', or 'Lord Williams'

The Chancellor of the Exchequer

Envelopes:	The Rt Hon. Julius Ward, MP (personal), or The Chancellor of the Exchequer (official)
Opening of letter:	Dear Chancellor [of the Exchequer]
Introduced as:	'The Chancellor [of the Exchequer]', or 'Mr Julius Ward'
Addressed as:	'Chancellor', or 'Mr Ward'

The Chancellor of the Duchy of Lancaster is treated in the same way, except that this title replaces *The Chancellor of the Exchequer*.

Secretary of State

Envelopes:	The Rt Hon. Frederick Lanston, MP (personal), or The Foreign Secretary, The Home Secretary, or the like (official)
Opening of letter:	Dear Secretary of State, or Dear Foreign Secretary
Introduced as:	'The Foreign Secretary', or 'Mr Frederick Lanston'
Addressed as:	'Foreign Secretary', or 'Mr Lanston'

You need to use a particular approach when writing to senior politicians.

Minister

Envelopes:	Mr William Perceval, MP (personal) or The Minister for Housing, or the like (official)
Opening of letter:	Dear Minister
Introduced as:	'Mr Perceval'
Addressed as:	'Minister', or 'Mr Perceval'

Lord President of the Council

Envelopes:	The Rt Hon., The Earl of Wycombe (personal) or The Lord President of the Council (official)
Opening of letter:	Dear Lord President

Introduced as:	'The Lord President of the Council', or 'The Earl of Wycombe'
Addressed as:	'Lord President', or 'Lord Wycombe'

The Speaker of the House of Commons

Envelopes and introductions:	[The Rt Hon. Mr Albert Peters,] The Speaker of the House of Commons

Opening of letter:	[Dear] Sir, or [Dear] Mr Speaker
Addressed as:	'Mr Speaker' (in the House), or 'Mr Peters'

Back-bencher

Envelopes:	Mr Steven Price, MP
Opening of letter:	Dear Mr Price
Introduced and addressed as:	'Mr Price'

Governors and Diplomats

Governor-General or Governor

Envelopes:	His Excellency Sir John Selby, Governor-General of Australia
Opening of letter:	Your Excellency, or Dear Sir
Introduced as:	'His Excellency Sir John Selby'
Addressed as:	'Your Excellency'

Ambassador

Envelopes:	His Excellency [Monsieur Claude Blanc, (plus decorations)], The Ambassador of France
	His Excellency [Signor Umberto Varvesi, (plus decorations)], The Ambassador of Italy
Opening of letter:	Your Excellency, or Dear Ambassador, or Dear Sir
Introduced as:	'[His Excellency] [Monsieur Claude Blanc,] The Ambassador of France'
	'[His Excellency] [Signor Umberto Varvesi,] The Ambassador of Italy'
Addressed as:	'Your Excellency', or 'Sir'

A woman ambassador is styled *Her Excellency*.

Social correspondence should be sent to:

His Excellency [Claude Blanc,] The Ambassador of France and Madame Blanc
His Excellency [Umberto Varvesi,] The Ambassador of Italy and Signora Varvesi

High Commissioners of Commonwealth countries are styled in the same way, except that *High Commissioner* is substituted for *Ambassador*.

Envoys-extraordinary, chargés d'affaires, and the like are treated as ambassadors, except that the title *Your Excellency* is not used.

Letters to consuls would be addressed:

Mr Geoffrey Brain, HM Consul

The terms *Agent*, *Consul-General*, or *Vice-Consul* should be substituted where appropriate.

The Law

The titles and forms of address given below should be used only on business or official occasions. For social occasions, you would write to the Lord Chancellor, for example, as to a peer.

High Court judges are usually called *My Lord* or *Your Lordship*. So too are circuit judges when sitting at the Central Criminal Court; in other courts, they are called *Your Honour*. Justices of the Peace and magistrates on the Bench should be addressed as *Your Worship*.

Out of court, circuit judges and retired High Court judges are usually called simply *Judge*.

The Lord Chancellor

Envelopes:	The Rt Hon., The Earl of Worcester, The Lord Chancellor, or The Lord Chancellor
Opening of letter:	My Lord, or Dear Lord Chancellor
Introduced as:	'The Lord Chancellor'

Addressed as:	'Lord Chancellor'

The Lord Chief Justice

Envelopes:	The Rt Hon., The Lord Chief Justice of England
Opening of letter:	My Lord, or Dear Lord Chief Justice
Introduced as:	'The Lord Chief Justice'
Addressed as:	'Lord Chief Justice'

The Lord Chief Justice of Northern Ireland

Envelopes:	The [Rt Hon. Sir George Miller,] Lord Chief Justice of Northern Ireland
Opening of letter:	My Lord, or Dear Lord Chief Justice
Introduced as:	'The Lord Chief Justice'
Addressed as:	'Lord Chief Justice'

The President of the Family Division

Envelopes:	The President of the Family Division
Opening of letter:	Dear President, or Dear Sir Peter
Introduced and addressed as:	'Sir Peter Fairfoul'

Lord of Appeal

Envelopes:	The Rt Hon. The Lord Prichard
Opening of letter:	Dear Lord Prichard
Introduced and addressed as:	'Lord Prichard'

Court of Appeal Judge

Envelopes:	The Rt Hon. Lord Justice Sweet
Opening of letter:	My Lord, or Dear Lord Justice
Introduced as:	'Lord Justice Sweet'
Addressed as:	'Lord Justice'

High Court Judge

Envelopes:	The Hon. Mr Justice Peterson, The Hon. Mrs Justice Caws
Opening of letter:	Dear Judge, [Dear] Madam
Introduced as:	'Mr Justice Peterson', or 'Sir Barry Peterson'

	'Mrs Justice Caws', or 'Dame Jessica Caws'
Addressed as:	'Sir Barry', 'Dame Jessica'

Note that High Court judges are knights (or dames) and are addressed in speech accordingly.

Circuit Court Judges

Envelopes:	His Honour Judge Beaumont, QC
Opening of letter:	[Dear] Sir, or Dear Judge [Beaumont]
Introduced and addressed as:	'Judge Beaumont', or 'Mr John Beaumont'

Queen's Counsel

Envelopes:	Mr Ian Gordon, QC
Opening of letter:	Dear Mr Gordon
Introduced as:	'Mr Ian Gordon'
Addressed as:	'Mr Gordon'

Justices of the Peace

When writing to a Justice of the Peace on official business, use the style *Mr Ernest Pring, JP*.

THE LAW (SCOTLAND)

Lord Justice-General

Envelopes:	The Rt Hon. The Lord Justice-General
Opening of letter:	My Lord, or Dear Lord Justice-General
Introduced as:	'The Lord Justice-General'
Addressed as:	'Lord Justice-General'

Lord Justice-Clerk

Envelopes:	The Rt Hon. The Lord Justice-Clerk
Opening of letter:	My Lord, or Dear Lord Justice-Clerk
Introduced as:	'The Lord Justice-Clerk'
Addressed as:	'Lord Justice-Clerk'

Lord of Session

Envelopes	The Hon. Lord MacAndrew
Opening of letter:	My Lord, or Dear Lord MacAndrew
Introduced and addressed as:	'Lord MacAndrew'

The Armed Forces

When writing to an officer, you should give his service rank and decorations on the envelope: the rank comes before a title, as in *Air Chief Marshal Sir Simon Watts*, followed by the decorations (and the divisional designation in the case of the Army). If an officer has a title, use that when addressing or writing to him, rather than his rank – *Dear Sir Nigel*, not *Dear Admiral Hall*. Note also that an admiral, colonel, or the like, without a title, is addressed in speech as, say, *Admiral Richmond* or *Colonel Paulson*, even though he is, in fact, Rear-Admiral Richmond or Lieutenant-Colonel Paulson.

'Dear' Mr Ogden . . .

THE ROYAL NAVY

Officers from Admiral of the Fleet to Lieutenant

Envelopes:	Admiral of the Fleet Viscount Wood, GCB, KBE
	Admiral Nigel Hall, GCB
	Commodore Charles Bright, MBE, RN
Opening of letter:	Dear Lord Wood
	Dear Admiral Hall, or Dear Sir Nigel (if a knight)
	Dear Commodore Bright

Introduced as:	'Lord Wood'
	'Admiral Hall', or 'Sir Nigel'
	'Commodore Bright'
Addressed as:	'Lord Wood'
	'Admiral Hall', or 'Sir Nigel'
	'Commodore'

Captains, Commanders, and Lieutenants are treated in the same way as Commodores, except that the appropriate title should be used.

Add *Royal Navy*, or more commonly *RN*, after the names and decorations of officers of the rank of commodore or below.

Sub-Lieutenant and below

Envelopes:	Midshipman John Kendall, RN
Opening of letter:	Dear Mr Kendall
Introduced as:	'Mr John Kendall'
Addressed as:	'Mr Kendall'

THE ARMY AND ROYAL MARINES

Officers from Field Marshal to Captain

The form for Army Officers is the same as for higher ranks in the Navy, but with the appropriate titles.

Address members of the Royal Marines in the same style as members of the Army. For lieutenant-colonels and those of lower rank, add *Royal Marines* or *RM* after their names and decorations.

Lieutenant and below

Envelopes:	Corporal Christian McDavid, (or relevant rank), 1st Suffolk Light Infantry
Opening of letter:	Dear Mr McDavid
Introduced as:	'Mr Christian McDavid'
Addressed as:	'Mr McDavid'

ROYAL AIR FORCE

Once again, show the full rank and any personal titles and decorations on the envelope. You may write *Royal Air Force* or *RAF* after this.

NAMING NAMES – A 'SCROOGE' AND AN 'EINSTEIN'

Call somebody a *Scrooge*, and you are telling him that he is mean or stingy. A *Judas* is, of course, a traitor, and an *Einstein* is a genius. Many such names from literature or history or the Bible have found their way into the general English vocabulary.

☐ Choose the word or phrase that you associate most closely with the following names. You will find the answers on pages 633-648.

Adonis
A: a very generous person
B: a tyrant
C: a beautiful youth
D: a bore

Caliban
A: a brutish person
B: a clumsy person
C: a sly person
D: an invalid

Casanova
A: a cheat
B: a pessimist
C: a bachelor
D: a playboy

Cassandra
A: a jolly person
B: a prophet of doom
C: an exceptionally tall woman
D: an accident-prone person

Galahad
A: an argumentative person
B: an embittered person
C: a physically powerful man
D: a gallant man

Jezebel
A: an immoral woman
B: a joker
C: a jealous woman
D: a mother-in-law

Martha
A: a worrier
B: a saintly woman
C: a woman who complains a lot
D: a long-suffering person

Mata Hari
A: a saintly woman
B: a flirt
C: a female spy
D: a spoilt only child

Micawber
A: an optimist
B: an absent-minded person
C: a grumbler
D: a person with a speech impediment

Midas
A: a cruel man
B: a man of great dignity
C: someone with the gift of making money
D: a fool

Baron Münch-hausen
A: an extremely stingy person
B: a teller of tall stories
C: a very rich man
D: a person with many children

quisling
A: a traitor
B: an orphan
C: a fat person
D: a clever child

Rasputin
A: a rascal
B: a faith healer
C: a reckless person
D: a very fat man

Robespierre
A: a jolly person
B: an unprincipled person
C: an effeminate man
D: a fanatic

Svengali
A: a person with powers over others
B: a person with very bad manners
C: a flatterer
D: a physically supple person

Tartuffe
A: a person with a sweet tooth
B: a religious hypocrite
C: an over-dressed woman
D: a person who talks too much

Walter Mitty
A: a card trickster
B: a daydreamer
C: a person paid by his family to stay away from home
D: a well-dressed person

Local Government

Lord Mayor or Lady Mayor

Envelopes:	The Rt Hon. the Lord Mayor of London / York / Belfast / Cardiff
	The Right Worshipful the Lord Mayor of (any of various other cities)
Opening of letter:	My Lord Mayor (formal), or Dear Lord Mayor (social)
Introduced as:	'The Lord Mayor of Cardiff', or 'The Lord Mayor of Cardiff, Sir Frederick Penn'
Addressed as:	'My Lord Mayor', or 'Lord Mayor'

With appropriate adjustments, the same styles apply to Lady Mayors, or female (Lord) Mayors.

Lady Mayoress (the wife of a Lord Mayor)

Envelopes:	The Lady Mayoress of Norwich
Opening of letter:	My Lady Mayoress (formal), or Dear Lady Mayoress (social)
Introduced as:	'The Lady Mayoress of Norwich, Mrs Ellen Staines'
Addressed as:	'My Lady Mayoress', or 'Lady Mayoress'

The husband of a female (Lord) Mayor is called the *(Lord) Mayor's Consort*, but he should be addressed by his own name and title.

Mayors

Envelopes:	The Right Worshipful the Mayor of Reading (or any of various other cities)
	The Worshipful Mayor of (any other town)
Opening of letter:	Mr Mayor (formal), or Dear Mr Mayor (social)
Introduced as:	'The Mayor of Reading', or 'Mr Robert West, The Mayor of Reading'
Addressed as:	'Mr Mayor', or 'Your Worships' (if a group of mayors is being addressed)

Female mayors are still sometimes actually addressed as *Mr Mayor*! But it is far more appropriate nowadays to use *Madam Mayor*.

Councillor

Envelopes and introductions:	Councillor John Young
Opening of letter:	Dear Councillor [Young], or Dear Sir or Dear Madam
Addressed as:	'Councillor', or 'Councillor Young', or 'Councillor Miss Williams', 'Councillor Sir James Frost'

For social correspondence, use the everyday names and titles of the councillor.

Lord Lieutenant

Envelopes and introductions:	Rear-Admiral John Meek, CB, H.M. Lord-Lieutenant of Dorset
Opening of letter:	Dear Sir
Addressed as:	'My Lord Lieutenant'

Sheriff or High Sheriff

Envelopes and introductions:	Mr Henry Queen, High Sheriff of Cheshire
Opening of letter:	Dear Sir
Addressed as:	'High Sheriff', or 'Sheriff', or 'Mr Sheriff'

Professional

MEDICAL

If the person has a personal title, use it in preference to the medical title – *Sir James Wood, MD*, rather than *Dr James Wood, MD*.

Medical Practitioners

Envelopes:	Dr Philip Harty, MD, FRCP, or Philip Harty, Esq., MD, FRCP
	Dr Ann Scott, MD, FRCP, or Miss Ann Scott, MD, FRCP

Opening of letter: Dear Dr Harty

Introduced as: 'Dr Philip Harty', or 'Mr Philip Harty'

Addressed as: 'Dr Harty', or 'Mr Harty'

When writing to medical practitioners without a doctorate, list their relevant academic awards, such as MB, or LRCP. Address them in speech and letters as *Doctor*.

Surgeons

Envelopes: Mr Godfrey Wilson, MS, FRCS

Opening of letter: Dear Mr Wilson

Introduced as: 'Mr Godfrey Wilson'

Addressed as: 'Mr Wilson'

Note that surgeons (and gynaecologists) are usually known as *Mr* or *Mrs* rather than *Doctor*.

Address dentists in the same style as surgeons – the qualifications will obviously be different. You may also call a dentist *Doctor* if he holds a medical degree or has a doctorate in addition to dental qualifications.

CIVIL SERVICE

Address members of the Civil Service by name rather than by position. However, members of the same department may use the appropriate rank or position when introducing or addressing each other *Under Secretary*, for example, rather than *Sir Philip Jones*.

Police

Police Commissioner (Metropolitan and City of London Police)

Envelopes and introductions: [Sir Anthony Pierce (plus decorations)], The Commissioner of Police of the Metropolis

Opening of letter: [Dear] Sir, or Dear Commissioner, or Dear Sir Anthony

Addressed as: 'Commissioner', or 'Sir Anthony'

Chief Constable (other forces)

Envelopes: [Mr Albert North (plus decorations)], The Chief Constable, Merseyside Constabulary

Opening of letter: [Dear] Sir, or Dear Chief Constable, or Dear Mr North

Introduced as: 'The Chief Constable for Merseyside', or 'Mr Albert North'

Addressed as: 'Chief Constable', or 'Mr North'

Address Deputy or Assistant Commissioners or Chief Constables in the same way, substituting the relevant rank.

Other police officers

Envelopes: Commander Paul Saunders, Metropolitan Police (plus decorations), or Mr Paul Saunders (plus decorations), Commander, Metropolitan Police (or whatever the appropriate rank and force are)

Opening of letter: [Dear] Sir, Dear Commander [Saunders], or Dear Mr Saunders

Introduced as: 'Commander Paul Saunders', or 'Mr Paul Saunders'

Addressed as: 'Commander Saunders', or 'Mr Saunders'

The titles *Police Sergeant* and *Police Constable* are usually abbreviated to – *PS*, *PC*. For members of the CID, the term *Detective* precedes the rank, as in *Detective Constable Little, Metropolitan Police*.

Policewomen have *W*. set before their rank, as in *W. Chief Inspector Waters* or *WDC Langley* (Woman Detective Constable).

Academics

University Chancellor

Envelopes and introductions: The [Rt Hon. The Earl of Weston,] Chancellor of the University of Newcastle

Opening of letter: My Lord, or [Dear] Sir (or term appropriate to the Chancellor's social rank), or Dear [Mr] Chancellor

Addressed as: 'Chancellor', or appropriate personal title

For most Vice-Chancellors, use the same styles, substituting *Vice-Chancellor* for *Chancellor*.

Head of a College

Heads of colleges are known as *Masters, Mistresses, Presidents, Principals, Provosts, Rectors*, or *Wardens*, depending on the particular college. Address them in the following styles, substituting the title where appropriate.

Envelopes: The Master of St Simon's College, Oxford

Opening of letter: [Dear] Sir/Madam, or Dear Master of St Simon's College

Introduced as: 'Sir William Bland, Master of St Simon's College'

Addressed as: 'Sir' or 'Madam', or 'Sir William', 'Lady Frederica', 'Dr Fitzpatrick'

Deans, bursars, and those holding other positions within colleges should be addressed according to social rank.

Professor

Envelopes and introductions: Professor John Carrol

Opening of letter: Dear Sir, or Dear Madam, or Dear Professor Carrol

Addressed as: 'Professor'

Use degrees and academic titles, such as MA or PhD, only on official correspondence and letters dealing with academic matters.

Dealing with Further Problems

The whole subject of modes of address – together with the allied field of precedence – has almost endless complications. As these stiff old social traditions continue to loosen up, however, people increasingly relax their observance of the formalities. Ignorance of the proper forms is seldom a major offence nowadays, so long as it is softened by courtesy and goodwill. Far better to be incorrect and courteous than formally correct and insolent.

That said, it obviously remains preferable to get it right. A little effort and research should ensure that.

If you confront an obscure problem that is not covered in this chapter, remember that there are entire books devoted to the intricacies of the subject. One or other of them is bound to yield the answer. Try your local library – it will probably have copies of at least some of the following books:

Burke's Peerage and Baronetage
Montague-Smith, Patrick. *Debrett's Correct Form*
Titles and Forms of Address: published by A. & C. Black
Webster, Jennifer. *Forms of Address for Correspondence and Conversation*
Whitaker's Almanack

RAMIFICATIONS OF ADDRESS

When people have a right to more than one kind of title, the ramifications can be appalling. The following enquiry was addressed to the 'Genuflex' column of *The Daily Telegraph* by Mr Mostyn Sheep-Harris:

> My elder brother Eric, who is in holy orders and also holds medical and dental degrees, joined the police force some 10 years ago and has just been promoted Detective Sergeant. Soon afterwards, through the death of a cousin, he succeeded to the baronetcy.

> When writing, how should I address him, as he is a stickler in such matters?

'Genuflex' replied:

> 'The Revd Det-Sgt Dr Sir Eric Sheep-Harris, Bt, DD, MD, LDS' is the correct form. Should your brother be appointed a Privy Councillor, join the Navy, Army or Air Force, or make a pilgrimage to Mecca, please write to me again.

Coping with Exams

EXAMS TAKE many forms: written or spoken, practical or theoretical. This chapter gives advice on how to make sure you do yourself justice in exams – notably essay-type and multiple-choice ones. But a word of caution. When the day of the exam arrives, the exam is in a sense already nine-tenths over. The result is largely determined by what you have done so far; it is on this that your performance hinges. That crucial run-up – the months of swotting, and the entire year of classwork, lecture notes, and reading – is the subject of the next chapter, *Studying Techniques* (pages 434-443).

General Strategies for Exams

No matter what kind of exam you are about to take, there are certain general points you should remember – the need to relax, for instance, and to think out your answers before you give them, and the importance of careful presentation. The following hints apply to most exams.

TRY TO RELAX

A certain rise in your adrenalin level during an exam is perhaps useful to keep you alert, and probably unavoidable. But panicking is obviously extremely unhelpful. If the symptoms of panic or overanxiety set in – a racing pulse, a mind gone blank – try various relaxation techniques.

Sit still and close your eyes. (If it is an interview-type exam, apologise to the examiners, and ask them to give you a few moments' grace before the exam continues.) Now concentrate on your breathing. Breathe in and out slowly and evenly. Count mentally from one to seven as you breathe in, again as you hold your breath, and again as you breathe out. This helps to stabilise the panic reactions in the body, and helps to damp down the churning turmoil in the mind. Far better to take personal control of yourself than to swallow a sedative.

Once your composure is reasonably restored, you might still have trouble collecting your thoughts. Answers to simple questions may elude you. If so, take things slowly. Don't rummage frantically about in your memory, trying to picture the exact page in the textbook. Instead, go back to first principles and try to arrive at the answer from that direction.

Suppose, for example, a crucial equation just will not come to mind during a chemistry exam. Try to reassemble it by building it from the individual chemical formulae – going back even to the periodic table and valency charts if necessary.

Once you have solved a puzzle or two in this way, your confidence will return and you should calm down. If any question threatens to revive your anxiety, put it to one side and go on to the next one. You can return to the unnerving question later.

THINKING AND PRESENTATION

Think before you leap. Even in an oral exam, you can do some quick planning before beginning your answer. Whether the question calls for a short objective answer (as in multiple-choice tests) or a long thoughtful discussion (as in essay-type exams), resist the temptation to blurt out or scrawl down the response that first comes to your mind.

Pause, and take stock. It may be a trick question, or it may have unexpected depths and angles.

Answer the question. The examiners are interested not just in the raw undigested knowledge of the subject that you may have acquired, but in your ability to apply or manipulate it.

If you are questioned about the results of the Battle of Waterloo, for instance, and you respond with a brilliant account of the events of the battle, what is the examiner likely to think? Not that you are a brilliant student . . . but rather that you are too dim to understand a simple question.

Pace yourself properly. Suppose one of the set pieces in the practical piano exam is the *Minute Waltz* – to be played in one minute. The student, once started on it, had better get cracking. No lingering lovingly over the opening theme . . . or else the ending is going to be somewhat rushed. So too, in a written exam, you had better keep an eye on the clock. There is no point in answering questions 100 per cent accurately if you answer only 49 per cent of the required number.

Neatness helps, and diplomacy too. Naturally it is the content of your answers that largely determines your results. But outward presentation can make a difference too – such as that small difference between a Pass and a Fail.

Examiners are only human: the sight of a dirty T-shirt on a candidate in an oral exam may provoke just enough prejudice on the examiner's part to sink the student's chances of success. A bleary-eyed moderator will hardly feel favourably disposed towards a smudged and cramped exam script that needs an extra effort to decipher.

Similarly, don't provoke examiners unnecessarily by doing or saying things likely to annoy them. If you know, or suspect, that the examiner is a stickler for detail, try to be correspondingly precise in your answers. Not that you should tailor your answers specifically to pander to anyone's prejudices – just that you should avoid needless treading on the examiner's sensibilities.

Handling Essay Questions

Seldom will you have the time, in the heat and dust of a gruelling exam, to hone the prose or even the structure of your answer scripts to the sharpness you are capable of. A three-hour exam does not, as a rule, allow for rewriting of early drafts. In exams, your first draft usually is your final version.

READ THE INSTRUCTIONS

Most essay-type question papers allow you a choice – perhaps you have to answer four questions out of the seven or eight on offer.

But the choice may not be quite so straightforward. You might be faced with instructions such as these.

> Answer question 1, and any three of the other questions on the paper.

> Answer four questions altogether, at least one from each section.

If you ignore or misread the instruction here – neglecting to answer the compulsory question 1, say, or answering four questions from one section and none from the other – you are well on your way to failing the exam.

Look out too for any further complexities in the instructions. Suppose you read:

> Use separate exam-books for each section – don't write section B answers in the same book as section A answers.

You had better make sure to allocate your essays correctly in each case.

One useful technique for avoiding mispositioning an answer is this: make a policy of beginning each essay answer on a fresh right-hand page of the exam book; and make a habit of always slotting your second exam book just behind the page on which you are writing. Each time you move on to a new right-hand page, you will have to shift the second exam book out of the way. If you are starting a new essay, this will cue you to make a decision: should I begin my new essay in the current book, or should I go on to the new book?

Here is another complexity you might come across:

> Question 1 is worth 40 per cent of the total marks for the exam. The other questions are worth 20 per cent each.

This should alert you to two things: first, it is a reminder that question 1 is compulsory; secondly, it suggests that you spend rather more time and trouble over it than over any of the other three questions you will be answering. In a three-hour exam, the ideal proportions would now be:

☐ 15 minutes for settling in, reading the paper, choosing your questions, and jotting down a few preliminary notes

☐ a full hour for question 1

☐ about 30 or 35 minutes for each of the other three questions

☐ if possible, a few leftover minutes at the end for a final read-through or at least a quick check of what you have written.

424

Take your pick. Read through all the questions, quickly but carefully, giving each a 'desirability-grading'. You might, for example, place a tick against question 1 on the question paper (especially if it is a compulsory question!), a question mark against question 2 (indicating your doubts about answering it), a double cross against question 3 (to be avoided at all costs), and so on.

With this grading as a guide, you can then – by a process of elimination – decide on the exact four questions you will be answering: say, questions 1, 4, 6, and 7. Now give these a 'priority grading'.

☐ Perhaps question 6 is your favourite, so code that 1st. (As a rule, you will attempt to answer it first as well – to give you a running start. But if you are feeling nervous, it may be a good idea to delay it for a while and tackle it as your second essay.)

☐ Question 1 comes next, say, so code that 2nd.

☐ Question 7 is next in line: code it 3rd.

☐ Question 4 is the one you are least confident about, so it is best left till last: code it 4th. As the end of the exam approaches, you may find yourself rushing your final question. Better to botch your weakest answer.

Once you have decided finally on the questions you will attempt, reread the instructions to double-check that your choice conforms with them.

High-risk questions. When choosing questions, bear in mind the matter of risk. The more complex a question is, the greater your chances of botching it are – but also your chances of shining. In a paper on Shakespeare, for instance, you might attempt a creative question on Shakespearean comedy in general, in preference to a safe, dull question on a specific comedy such as *Love's Labour's Lost*.

Much like a high-risk investment, a high-risk question might pay good dividends. The examiner will give credit for your courage in tackling it, and will probably make allowances for any occasional mistakes on your part.

Of course, if you are really not confident, it is best to avoid the tricky question and to take the low-risk route, on the principle of Better Safe Than Sorry.

If you do opt to try a high-risk question, you could budget a bit of extra time for it, especially for the planning stage. But only a bit: don't let yourself get carried away by your enthusiasm, or drown in the complexities – or the other questions will suffer.

Check the question. As stated earlier, make sure you answer the question asked. Even a minor misreading can tilt your essay into producing quite the wrong emphases and result in a lower mark than you are capable of. Suppose, for example, the question reads:

'The German electoral system is no more truly representative than the British.' Discuss

... and you read (misread) it as:

'The German electoral system is more truly representative than the British.' Discuss

Your answer, however well-informed, would come over as puzzlingly misdirected.

A useful way of avoiding such misreadings is to underline or circle each key word of the question on the question paper. In the hypothetical example above, the act of circling or underlining individually the three words *no more* and *representative* would probably have ensured a correct approach.

Check the form of the question. Another way of misreading the question is ignoring its form. Is it in the form of a question?

Do you agree with the widespread view that poetry is ... ?

Was it by good luck or good politicking that Attlee managed to ... ?

Or does it take the form of an invitation or a command?

'Poetry is the spontaneous overflow of powerful feeling.' Discuss

Evaluate the role of 'good luck' in Attlee's electoral victory of 1945.

If the question is worded as a question, you must provide an answer, sooner or later. It need not be, indeed should not be, a one-sided cut-and-dried answer: the appropriate response is usually along the lines of 'On the whole, no' or 'Up to a point, yes' rather than 'Absolutely not' or 'No, full stop'. But it should be a clear answer. The examiner must understand which side you are on.

PLAN YOUR ESSAY THOROUGHLY

There is no time in an exam for the common writing procedure for school and college essays – the quick draft, the rethink, the rewrite. In an exam (or any other writing task where time permits only one version), the structure of your text will have to be based on a careful prethink, on planning rather than on drafting and rewriting.

A well laid-out plan is helpful in several ways:

☐ It gives you an overview – which in turn might persuade you to change the structure somewhat, adjust the balance, add new details, shed irrelevances, shift your emphases, and so on.

☐ It helps you to keep to the point – if you do have to digress from your line of argument, your plan will guide you safely back onto the main track.

☐ It helps you to pace your writing sensibly – you can make a rough allocation of the time to spend on each point, and thus monitor your progress.

Here is a brief guide to drawing up a plan.

First, reread the question, and underline or circle the key words. Then, pause and think how to answer the question. Let your response be a genuine one, rather than one contrived to impress.

Usually, there is something to be said on both sides of an issue, so as a rule you will not agree slavishly with the view implied by the question, nor reject it utterly in a spirit of contrariness.

Then, jot down in point form all responses or ideas that occur to you. You can do this on the question paper, or on a sheet of scrap paper, or in the answer book itself. The answer book is in one respect the best place: it gives the examiner an extra glimpse of your knowledge and insight. If time runs out before you have finished your essay, a generous examiner might drag you across the borderline on the basis of your intended answer – as revealed in your plan.

Among these points that you jot down should be:

☐ any comments on the wording of the question – if, say, the question contains a hidden assumption that you disagree with, jot down your objections in point form (but don't overdo this quibbling in your essay)

☐ your specific reply to the question, if it happens to be a question-type question

☐ the general arguments – make sure to include those on both sides of the question

☐ specific examples or evidence to support these general arguments

A list of randomly jotted items is the raw material for an essay, but hardly a well-planned basis for it. To create a plan, you could now read quickly through your list, rearrange the items in your head, and then number them according to their rank or relevance. Or, more efficiently, you could jot down your points in a properly arranged layout in the first place.

Using this system, instead of jotting down all the items one after the other, you position each one at an appropriate spot on the page, where it seems likely to find its final place in the structure that is developing in your mind. Any mispositionings can be rectified by deleting and repositioning the item, or simply by drawing an arrow to transfer it to its appropriate position (see the panel, opposite).

One last tip. As you write up your essay, you will be constantly referring to your outline to guide you. Each time you deal with an item on the outline, cross it out. This serves several purposes: it guides your eye to the next item each time; it helps you to monitor your progress; and – if time runs out – it directs the thoughtful examiner to the remaining points that your essay would have covered had you been able to finish it. So much for the planning. Now for the actual writing of the essay.

WRITING THE ESSAY

Remember your handwriting – to keep it legible. The exam script, unlike your lecture notes or revision notes, is to be read by someone else. It is not enough that you should be able to decipher it: the examiner has to read it too.

Mind your grammar and spelling. Not always easy to do, of course, in the rush. Try to leave five or ten minutes over at the end of the exam to glance through your essay again and spot the clangers.

Watch your style. Take pity once more on the poor examiner, and try to phrase your thoughts clearly. Keep your sentences and paragraphs reasonably short. Keep jargon to a minimum – so far from being impressed by jargon, examiners tend to baulk, and will mark you down unless your essay really justifies the use of it.

As for tone, you can be chirpy and even amusing, but don't be facetious. And don't be pretentious either – if you use a grandiose word without being absolutely sure of the spelling or meaning, you are risking a malapropism.

Make sure that the answer is *your* answer, not the answer of some famous professor or obscure academic article. By all means cite authorities such

ESSAY-PLANNING IN PRACTICE

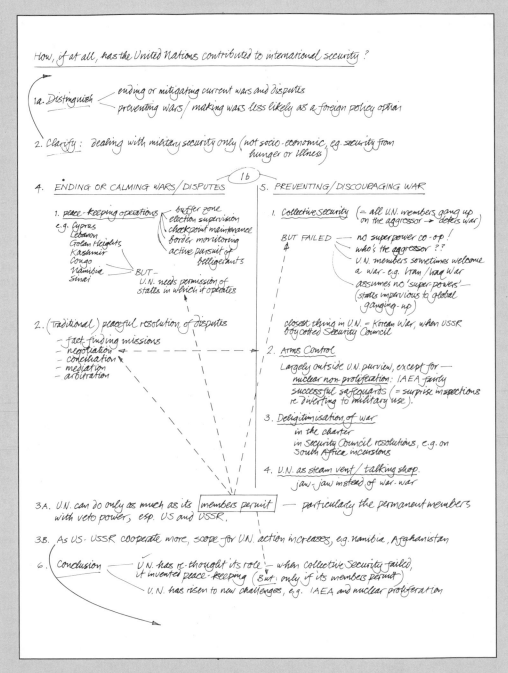

How, if at all, has the United Nations contributed to international security?

1a. Distinguish — ending or mitigating current wars and disputes
— preventing wars / making wars less likely as a foreign policy option

2. Clarify: dealing with military security only (not socio-economic, e.g. security from hunger or illness)

1b

4. ENDING OR CALMING WARS/DISPUTES

1. peace-keeping operations — buffer zone, election supervision, checkpoint maintenance, border monitoring, active pursuit of belligerants
e.g. Cyprus, Lebanon, Golan Heights, Kashmir, Congo, Namibia, Sinai — BUT — U.N. needs permission of states in which it operates

2. (Traditional) peaceful resolution of disputes
— fact-finding missions
— negotiation
— conciliation
— mediation
— arbitration

5. PREVENTING/DISCOURAGING WAR

1. Collective security (= all U.N. members gang up on the aggressor → deters war)
BUT FAILED — no superpower co-op! who's the aggressor?? U.N. members sometimes welcome a war - e.g. Iran/Iraq War assumes no 'super-powers' (states impervious to global ganging-up)
closest thing in U.N. = Korean War, when USSR boycotted Security Council

2. Arms Control
Largely outside U.N. purview, except for — nuclear non-proliferation: IAEA fairly successful safeguards (= surprise inspections re diverting to military use).

3. Delegitimisation of war
in the charter
in Security Council resolutions, e.g. on South Africa incursions

4. U.N. as steam vent / talking shop.
jaw-jaw instead of war-war

3A. U.N. can do only as much as its members permit — particularly the permanent members with veto power, esp. US and USSR.

3B. As US-USSR cooperate more, scope for U.N. action increases, e.g. Namibia, Afghanistan

6. Conclusion — U.N. has re-thought its role — when collective security failed, it invented peace-keeping (But: only if its members permit)
— U.N. has risen to new challenges, e.g. IAEA and nuclear proliferation

The plan above is for an essay on the United Nations, written before the Gulf Crisis of 1990. In the heat of an exam you would be unlikely to write as neatly as this – but aim for a tidy layout. The clearer your plan, the easier it will be to follow – your essay will benefit as a result. Note the arrows linking related points, and reordering the argument.

as these, but don't base your entire essay on a parrot-like restatement of their arguments.

And don't get carried away by your enthusiasm. An exam essay is not a pulpit or a political platform or an editorial column: you may have passionate views on Northern Ireland, or fox-hunting, or abortion, but you should air them only to the extent that they are relevant to the question. The examiners of your Russian History paper simply do not want to know every last detail of your novel theory that *glasnost* is really all a KGB plot.

Begin by writing in the margin (accurately!) the number of the question. (Never write anything else in the margin: examiners consider the margin to be their territory, and are very jealous of their rights.) Don't waste time writing out the question itself. The examiners, who have already waded through dozens of answer sheets, hardly need you to remind them what the questions are.

Get to the heart of your answer promptly. A brief overture is sometimes in order – concisely clarifying some ambiguity in the wording of the question, for instance, or sketching in some background to show your grasp of the general subject area and to help you to define your terms. But only a paragraph or two. Don't spend half the essay setting the scene in this way. Remember, the exam essay is an answer to a question or a response to an order – no need for too many literary fireworks.

The exam essay is not a joke or suspense story either, so don't hold back the key information for the sake of a supposed climax or punchline. You must announce very soon your broad answer or attitude to the question. Don't keep the poor examiner in suspense.

Follow your plan step by step. State your first theme or argument; marshal the examples or facts in support of it; discuss any opposing arguments; and then move on to the next theme or argument. End with a broad assessment of the arguments and counterarguments (but don't waste time summarising the various points all over again in detail), and thence with a clear restatement or refinement of your opening response to the question.

Keep your essay balanced. Keep things in balance, in two respects. First, allocate an appropriate (not necessarily equal) amount of time to each of the arguments you present. Secondly, when discussing the counterarguments each time, do try to assess them fairly: don't automatically dismiss or

diminish them simply because they happen to oppose the view that you have decided to favour in your essay.

Another point. The facts and examples that you cite in support of each argument – keep a tight rein on them, again in two respects. First, remember they have a subordinate or supportive role only, and do not in themselves move your arguments along: so mention them with a minimum of elaboration. (Any irresistible sidelight or digression should be consigned to brackets, or even to a footnote, so as not to interrupt the flow.) Secondly, be selective: it is unnecessary to give an exhaustive list of 'relevant cases'. A short and thoughtful selection is usually more efficient: it saves you time, it impresses the examiner as more incisive, and it reduces the risk of citing irrelevant cases.

Don't waffle. Examiners want quality not quantity. You can say the same thing in three different ways, but the stony-hearted examiners, unimpressed by all this elegant repetition, will give you just the one mark, not three. And anchor all your abstract statements and broad generalisations with specific pointed examples. Take a blandly worded statement of a general idea, such as this:

> The speculations of modern medical science threaten so much of the received wisdom of orthodox history.

How much more powerfully you could convey this idea if you followed it up with a well-chosen example or two:

> The impassioned evidence given by the adolescent girls at the Witches of Salem trial, for instance, is today often ascribed to poisoning (brought about by using flour made from wheat that had been infected by the fungus *ergot*) rather than to mass hysteria or deliberate malice. And the lack of interest shown by Elizabeth I in getting married was probably, it turns out, due to a malformation of the pelvis. So much for the noble myth of the self-sacrificing Virgin Queen.

Don't fuss. Say what you mean. State your views boldly. There is no need, and no time, to qualify every remark with 'in my opinion' or 'it seems to me that . . .' Most exam essays, like most newspaper articles or business reports for that matter, are openly and unashamedly full of personal opinions. No sensible reader thinks otherwise, so there is no need to spell it out every time.

Multiple-Choice Questions

In multiple-choice tests, the task is to pick the correct or appropriate answer from a set of possible answers offered on the question paper. Quiz shows on the radio, 'personality tests' in magazines, market-research questionnaires on street corners, aptitude tests, public-opinion polls, linguistic surveys – all of these rely very often on the familiar multiple-choice procedure. This kind of thing:

> Which of the following tennis stars never won the Wimbledon men's singles title – Jack Kramer, Lew Hoad, Ken Rosewall, Rod Laver?

> How do you tend to pronounce the word *vase*?
> a. vaaz
> b. vawz
> c. vawss
> d. vayz
> e. vayss

> Would you say that you suffer from insomnia . . . never, seldom, from time to time, often, or constantly?

Most people are familiar with multiple-choice tests in educational settings as well – vocabulary tests, IQ tests, 'objective tests' in mathematics or economics or politics, and so on. Such tests have various advantages over essay-type exams.

For a start, they are 'objective': the answer you choose is either right or wrong, so there is little leeway when it comes to marking. Both examiner and student often welcome this limitation – it means that personal preferences and prejudices do not enter into the marking system.

Secondly, multiple-choice tests are very quick to mark. In fact, the marking of these tests is often done by computer.

Thirdly, multiple-choice tests can cover a lot more ground than essay-type exams. They can probe into every corner of the syllabus, thereby testing the breadth of the student's knowledge. Essay-type exams, while far better at testing depth of knowledge, often allow the student to get away with giant gaps in his or her reading.

Multiple-choice tests would seem, then, to reflect fairly accurately the true extent of the student's knowledge or ability. Even so, there are certain techniques for improving your performance in this kind of exam.

HOW TO DEAL WITH MULTIPLE-CHOICE TESTS

Find out in advance as much as you can about the test. Don't arrive 'cold' in the exam hall. The questions themselves will contain enough surprises and puzzles.

Try to get hold of old test papers – both to have a practice run and to familiarise yourself with the general procedure. And ask a lot of advance questions – of your tutor, of past students, or even of some official at the examining board – to establish the rules of engagement beforehand.

Here are some of the details to find out:

☐ What equipment you can or should bring with you. A calculator? A dictionary? A soft pencil?

☐ The role of rough work. Are you permitted to jot down calculations on rough paper? If so, is such paper provided, or must you bring your own? And must you hand it in afterwards, along with your answer sheet?

☐ How the timing of the test works. Is it a test of speed as well as a test of knowledge or accuracy? Do most students actually manage to answer all the questions within the time limits? Is the test divided into various sections, with a time limit on each section and no going back?

☐ How the test is structured. Are all the questions pitched at roughly the same level of difficulty? Or is there a build-up, with the questions getting harder and harder as you work your way through the test? Does it ever happen that there can be two correct answers? Does the examiner have a liking for trick questions?

☐ How the test is marked. If the later questions are more difficult, do they also contribute more marks towards your final score? And – very important – do wrong answers invoke a penalty in the form of marks subtracted? Is there an absolute pass mark (say, 50 per cent) or a relative pass mark (the mark achieved by the top 30 per cent of candidates, say).

Study thoroughly before the test. Remember that multiple-choice tests tend to cover all aspects of the subject. Your preparation should therefore be wide-ranging rather than selective. In fact, you should concentrate on your weaker areas.

Pace yourself properly during the test. Suppose your inquiries have established the following:

☐ that the test is extremely long and almost impossible to complete in the time available

☐ that the later questions are more difficult than the earlier ones, but do not carry a greater proportion of marks

☐ that each question offers you five possible answers, from which you have to select the correct one

☐ that you are penalised for incorrect answers by having a quarter of a mark docked each time

A sensible strategy based on these factors would be:

☐ Work very quickly through the questions, without pausing to double-check the accuracy of the answer each time: the penalty for wrong answers is relatively small, so it is worth risking the occasional miscalculation here for the sake of quick progress.

☐ Leave to one side any question, early or late, that looks unusually time-consuming.

☐ Monitor your reduction in speed as you get to the later and more difficult questions. At some point, it may be more cost-effective to abandon the later questions and return to those earlier questions that you shelved temporarily.

☐ As the final minutes approach, increase the risk-level: commit yourself to an answer if you have even a slight preference for it – the odds remain in your favour, since the penalty for wrong answers is so slight.

☐ Don't, however, blindly fill in any old answer to unexamined questions as the final seconds tick away, since the odds swing against you if you make entirely random guesses.

In all cases, keep your wits about you. The typical multiple-choice test offers four or five possible answers to choose from. The three or four incorrect or irrelevant answers in each case are known as distractors. They are often very plausible.

Examiners like to trap you into choosing the wrong answer by devising tempting distractors.

MULTIPLE-CHOICE CASE STUDIES

Here are some typical multiple-choice questions, drawn from a range of academic and selection tests in school or college. The answers, together with relevant tips, are given as well.

1. The phrase *All that glitters is not gold* is best explained as:
a. Things outwardly attractive are of dubious value
b. An attractive appearance is not a reliable guide to true worth
c. Truly valuable things don't look valuable
d. Unworthy things or people often masquerade as extremely virtuous or appealing

2. The word *parsimonious* means
a. one-sided
b. stingy
c. pious
d. cowardly

These questions both offer tempting distractors, though in different ways. Question 1 provides distractors that are (or seem) confusingly close in meaning or wording to the correct answer.

The distractors in question 2 are cunning in that each represents the correct answer to a slightly different question.

In question 2 *parsimonious* in fact means 'stingy', but a weaker student, hearing subconsciously an echo of *partisan,* would opt for 'one-sided'. Other students, by confusing *parsimonious* with *sanctimonious* or *parsonish,* would choose 'pious' as their answer; or by a faulty association with *pusillanimous* would choose 'cowardly'.

3. The formula for the volume of a hemisphere is:
a. $2\pi r$
b. πr^2
c. $^4/_3 \pi r^3$
d. $^2/_3 \pi r^3$
e. $2\pi r^2$

4. If it takes three violinists 30 minutes to play a concerto, how long would it take six violinists to play a concerto?
a. 15 minutes
b. 30 minutes
c. an hour
d. 2 hours

These two questions add a refinement – they are, in different degrees, trick questions. In answer to question 3, the knowledgeable but careless student might choose option c, reasoning along these lines: 'The question is seeking a formula for volume. The compiler is trying to lead me into temptation by offering some very familiar formulae – $2\pi r$ and πr^2, notably. But he can't fool me: I know that $2\pi r$ represents a one-dimensional value, the circumference of a circle; and πr^2 represents a two-dimensional value, the area of a circle. For the volume of a sphere – a three-dimensional value – the formula is $^4/_3\,\pi r^3$. So I'll fill in answer c.'

All very well thought through . . . only the question deals with the volume not of a sphere but of a hemisphere. The correct answer is therefore d: $^2/_3\,\pi r^3$. The tiny trick in the question may seem unfair, but it is the examiner's prerogative to insert it.

It is unfair too that the sensible though incorrect answer $^4/_3\,\pi r^3$ should not earn even half marks, but be banded together in the no-marks category with such misconceived answers as $2\pi r$ or $2\pi r^2$.

But very few multiple-choice tests provide for a sophisticated marking system that distinguishes between degrees of wrongness.

The answer is either right or wrong. So watch out.

Question 4 is a trick question and nothing else. It masquerades as a test of ratio-manipulation, along the lines of 'If it takes three farmworkers 30 hours to harvest an orchard, how long would it take six farmworkers?' But of course . . . well, if you chose answer a (let alone c or d!), think again.

5. The shape ⟋⟍⟋ is:
a. a quadrilateral
b. a rhomboid
c. a parallelogram
d. all of the above
e. none of the above

6. The 'Star Wars' defence system:
a. was designed to deter terrorist attacks
b. was designed to destroy enemy missiles in flight
c. enjoyed wholehearted support in the U.S. scientific community
d. both a. and c. above
e. both b. and c. above
f. none of the above

These questions provide a new twist. The various answers on offer are not always of the same rank: among them are various combination answers, including *all of the above* and *none of the above*. Of the five answers proposed for question 5, four are in fact correct. The convention in such cases is this: the only appropriate answer is the one that is wholly correct – namely, d: *all of the above*.

But take care: there is a temptation to assume that if you are offered the option of combination answers such as *both a. and c. above* or *all of the above* or *none of the above,* then one of them is going to be the correct answer. This may be so more often than not, but it is not necessarily so. A cunning examiner knows how good these are as distractors, and will occasionally try to beguile you into committing yourself inappropriately to one or other of them.

This is what happens in question 6: 'Star Wars' had nothing directly to do with terrorist attacks, and its support among U.S. scientists was limited and lukewarm; but it was designed to destroy enemy missiles in flight, so answer b. is correct.

7. The value of 5 factorial is:
a. 120
b. 625
c. 25
d. 15
e. 125

8. Which of the following is not considered a 'strategic mineral' by political economists?
a. chromium
b. titanium
c. petroleum
d. cobalt
e. cement

These are fairly straightforward tests of the student's basic knowledge of the subject. Note the small refinement in each case, however. Question 7 requires, in addition to a knowledge of the term *factorial*, a small calculation on the basis of it. (Answer a is correct: 5 x 4 x 3 x 2 x 1 = 120.) Question 8 is an 'odd-man-out' type of question. The correct answer is e – *cement*.

9. Which is the odd-man-out?
a. Molière
b. Machiavelli
c. Rousseau
d. Montesquieu

This is explicitly of the 'odd-man-out' type – with complications. It is here as an example of a bad question, a truly unfair question. The correct answer is probably answer a – *Molière* – since he is remembered as a playwright whereas the other three are best known as writers of political philosophy. But there are two other conspicuous variables as well, which would lead to different answers. Children would probably opt for answer c, *Rousseau*, since his name is the only one that does

Complete the sequence...

not begin with the letter *M*. Or what of the nationality or language variable? In the light of that, the correct answer would be b – *Machiavelli* – all the other three were French and wrote in French; Machiavelli alone was Italian and wrote in Italian.

If you do ever come across a glaringly unfair question such as this, you could try to cover yourself by writing a note to the examiner – either on the answer sheet or on a separate sheet of paper – explaining your objection to it.

10. Complete the sequence: 0 1 3 6 10 ...
a. 15
b. 20
c. 16
d. 18

11. Complete the sequence: 1 2 9 64 625 ...
a. 46656
b. 3125
c. 7776
d. 1296

These questions are familiar tests in mathematical deduction. You have to work out the underlying principle of the sequence, and then make a simple calculation to establish the answer. Question 10 is easy enough: the principle is 'The step increases by 1 each time'. Since the last step in the stated sequence (from 6 to 10) is 4, the next step will have to be 5, resulting in answer a – *15*.

Question 11 is more complicated. It might take some time and puzzlement before you tumble to the underlying principle: the listed numbers correspond to the sequence $1^0, 2^1, 3^2, 4^3, 5^4$ ... The next number should therefore be 6^5. A quick calculation produces 7776 – answer c. This is the kind of complex and time-consuming question that you might well put to one side during the early stages of the test.

12. Complete the sequence: 2 4 7 11 16 ...
a. 21
b. 19
c. 24
d. 32

This, finally, is of the sneaky type deliberately designed to perplex you by sending you down the wrong path. Such questions seldom occur in proficiency tests, being limited typically to the later reaches of graded IQ or resourcefulness tests.

On the face of it, it looks simple enough. Surely it works on the same principle as question 10 above – 'The step increases by 1 each time'? So the number needed to complete the sequence is 22: what is the problem? The problem is that 22 is not among the answers on offer. An entirely different principle underlies the sequence, as it happens: write each of the numbers out as words, and then count the letters – *two, four, seven, eleven, sixteen* ... totalling 3, 4, 5, 6, and 7 letters respectively. The next number in the sequence should therefore have 8 letters in its spelling. Of those on offer, only number 19 fits the bill: *nineteen*, with its 8 letters.

13. Complete the sequence: T T T F F S S E ...
a. N
b. E
c. T
d. M
e. S

This works in more or less the opposite way to question 12: what appears to be a sequence of letters is in fact based on a sequence of numbers. Each letter is the initial letter of a spelt-out number – *ten, twenty, thirty, forty* ... the correct answer is therefore answer a – *N* for ninety. Be grateful that such overingenious questions do not pretend to test anything other than a person's overingenuity, and that you are therefore unlikely to encounter them in the course of ordinary proficiency tests.

EXTRACT FROM A PRE-EXAM TIMETABLE

Week 3	9.30 - 11	11.30 - 1	2 - 2.30	4 - 5.30	7.30 - 9
Monday	Gov't systems - UK III (civil service, local gov't)	Gov't systems - UK IV (judiciary)	H & P of Science - Popper, Kuhn	Brit. Phil. - Hume II	Brit. Phil Utilitarianism I - Mill & Bentham
Tuesday	Gov't systems - France	Gov't systems - USA I (federal gov't)	H & P of Science - final overview I	Brit. Phil. Utilitarianism - modern views & critiques	Brenda's birthday party
Wednesday	Gov't systems - USA II (state gov't)	Gov't systems - USA III (constitution & supreme court)	Brit. Phil. contemp. Ryle & Austin (OMIT?)	Brit. Phil. Wittgenstein's Tractatus	Brit. Phil. - late Wittgenstein I
Thursday	Int'l. Ecs. Int'l Finance I (bal. of payments)	Int'l. Ecs. Int'l Finance II (exchange rates)	(2.30) revision seminar on econometrics - Dr Davis's room	Brit. Phil. - late Wittgenstein II	brainstorming on econometrics - Gerald's digs
Friday	Int'l. Ecs. - Int'l Trade I (free trade & comparative advantage)	Int'l. Ecs. - Int'l Trade II (protectionism I: tariffs/quotas)	(2 - 5) mock exam on econometrics Seminar room		[? post-mortem on mock exam - Gerald's digs]
Saturday	Int'l. Ecs. - Int'l Trade III (protectionism II: non-tariff barriers.)	Int'l. Ecs. - Aid. (Marshall Plan & modern Int'l Aid Orgs.)	shopping & laundry	—	—
Sunday	Catch up: if time, go on to - Int'l. Ecs. - Regional Integration (EC)		—	—	—

Writing at Work, Home, and College

As the exam season approaches, a certain nervousness (if not downright panic) inevitably sets in – no matter how conscientious you have been about your studies during the past year or years. There is so much revision to do, and so little time to do it all. Where should you start? What should you concentrate on? There is just one key rule here: Be organised. Work out a systematic revision timetable for the weeks that remain before the exams begin – and then keep to it. Above is an extract from just such a timetable. Note how thoroughly the candidate has organised his life for each day. Note also that it is not all a question of work. He has wisely allowed himself time to relax (to enjoy a party on Tuesday evening, for example) and to carry out chores – on Saturday afternoon. He has also allowed a suitable amount of leeway in his timetable – on Sunday morning – to allow him to catch up on problem areas, if this proves necessary. (For more on pre-exam timetables, see page 442.)

Studying Techniques

IF ONLY all teachers taught properly. If only they taught not just history, maths, literature, or whatever, but also how to study history, maths, literature... But they so often seem to take that side of things for granted, as if it were simply a matter of common sense.

Here are some of these 'common-sense' studying strategies that students all too rarely put into practice. Later in this chapter, similar strategies are suggested for taking notes and revising.

GENERAL STUDYING STRATEGIES

Reconnoitre is the first key word. Any good general, before advancing into a new zone, is first going to find out as much about it as possible. By any available means, he will gather and analyse all possible information on the terrain, the weather outlook, enemy positions, and so on.

As a student embarking on a course of study, you should make similar researches beforehand:

☐ Speak to other students who have already taken the course, and find out from them the material it covers, the quality of the teachers, the problem areas, and the most useful textbooks.

☐ Shop around if your college or place of learning offers an array of courses. Attend the first class or lecture of several – more than you actually plan to register for – and then make your selection. A good teacher may encourage you to sign up for what seemed at first sight an unpromising course, and a poor teacher may put you off a course that otherwise looks tempting.

☐ Try to get an official copy of the full syllabus for each course beforehand. It will guide you and help to pace you through the course.

☐ Find out about marking systems as well: does class-participation count towards your final result? What proportion of marks do the final exams command? And what proportion the various term tests, research projects, and so on?

☐ Read, before the course starts, some broad introduction to the subject, such as a general textbook. This will give you an overview of the subject, enabling you to appreciate faster and better the details of the subject as you acquire them in lectures and in subsequent reading.

Cultivate the right attitude. The object of study is (or should be) knowledge, not just qualifications. Approach your course with the intention of learning the subject and improving your mind, rather than merely of passing the exam at the end of it. You will not only derive greater enjoyment and benefit from the course, but will amost certainly score better results as well. Those who undertake a course of study purely in the spirit of passing the exam at the end are those most in danger of failing.

Even if the course is a compulsory one, and not to your liking, you will get a great deal more out of it by engaging it aggressively than by simply enduring it. Take up the challenge; be affirmative. In other words, take your studies seriously. Your student years are not just a period of preparation for the 'real business of life' – work and adulthood. They are valuable in themselves. Don't treat them as a time of quarantine.

Keep a balance. The opposite danger is that of taking your studies too seriously. Remember the 'Law of Diminishing Returns' – after a certain point, you actually produce or absorb less if you put in more work. The student, like the doctor or the dockworker, can actually get more work done in an eight-hour day than in a twelve-hour day. An overlong working day produces greater boredom, fatigue, and resentment, and reduces the level of concentration and commitment.

Of course, the threshold varies from person to person, and you will have to discover for yourself what your own optimum is. You should in due course settle down into a relaxed and highly efficient rhythm, combining sessions of intense study with sessions of extracurricular activity: going to the theatre, socialising in the pub, helping with charity work, doing the laundry, playing tennis, sightseeing, debating . . . all the cultural pleasures that enrich your education, together with the routine chores of daily life, should fit comfortably into your weekly timetable without seriously reducing the overall quality of your studies.

Take a businesslike approach. To live your student life to the full in this way, you will have to live it efficiently.

Try to develop a routine. If your mind is sharpest in the morning, for instance, try to organise your day so as to do an hour's reading, writing, or ordering of your notes before breakfast.

As with time, so with place: find out which working environment suits you best, and try to maintain it. The library, or your own room? (Not the canteen or the park.) In solitude, or with a study partner? Background music? (It can be distracting, but it can equally well help to block out distractions.) A well-lighted room, or just a pool of lamplight at your desk? And so on.

Whatever you decide in such matters, make sure you stick to it: the mind will come to associate certain regular places and patterns with intense study, and you will find yourself concentrating better when sticking to these.

Keep ahead of the game. Don't let big backlogs build up – whether of essay assignments or unpaid bills, background reading or unanswered letters. You need to keep a tidy desk – literally and metaphorically. If you feel oppressed by that huge pile of clothes that needs ironing, or by those reams of notes that need filing, these worries will only serve to distract you during lectures or to reduce your concentration in the library or laboratory.

Remember, if you ever fall behind in your work, you are at a great disadvantage. Each succeeding lecture or assignment will be that much more difficult, since it assumes some prior knowledge.

Keeping ahead of the lecturer or demonstrator, by contrast, will provide for richer lecture notes, and will enable you to memorise the subject matter more easily. Always try to do some preparatory work before teaching sessions. Set aside, for example, Friday evening or Sunday afternoon to read ahead in the textbook or to try some advanced theorems for the next week's classes.

Get your fellow-students involved in advance study. If, for example, your lecturer runs a seminar that meets once a week, why not organise a parallel seminar the night before with some classmates to go over the next day's material? You will get much more out of the 'official' seminar if you do, and will feel more confident when taking part in it.

TAKING NOTES

Students can compile two kinds of notes – records and study notes. The trouble is that most students confuse the two: what they compile is records alone, but they treat these as study notes.

Records are essentially a summary – of a lecture, an interview, an article, a chapter, or the like. The form of such notes is dictated by the originator of the text – the lecturer, interviewee, or author.

With study notes, on the other hand, it is the student who decides the form. Their purpose is to sum up the subject, not to sum up someone else's views of the subject.

Suppose you are taking a history course that covers the Peterloo Massacre. You attend a lecture and a seminar on the topic, and read one library book and three articles devoted to it. If you dutifully take notes each time, you will have six distinct sets of notes by the end – six records. A useful basis for a research paper, maybe . . . but overwhelmingly long and repetitive when it comes to studying for exams. What you want is a single unified set of study notes, combining the six records into one well-ordered account, quick to read and easy to absorb.

To look in more detail at the two types of notes:

Records. In science subjects, a lecturer or textbook may well supply a full and accurate account of a topic – the chemical properties of tungsten, say. Every known detail of the subject is made available to you: record them all in your notes, and once you have studied these and memorised them, you can truly claim to be master of the subject.

In the arts and humanities things are more fluid. Political philosophy or literary theory, say, can never really offer 'the last word'. Such subjects are open-ended – you can never hope to give exhaustive, cut and dried answers to such questions as 'the true meaning of Democracy' or 'the role of the Fool in *King Lear*'. No point, then, in recording slavishly everything you hear or read on such subjects. Where there is no gospel truth, you are perfectly entitled to pick and choose. Let your notes reflect this freedom: record only what seems valid or enlightening. Even then, as you will see, these notes will probably prove needlessly cumbersome, and will be replaced by more streamlined study notes. In the meantime, here are a few obvious pointers:

☐ Use standard paper for all your notes – either a notebook or a file pad, but no tatty envelopes, book jackets, or the like. And make sure to file these notes systematically.

☐ Write neatly – you will be grateful later on.

☐ Leave lots of space for additions. Lectures and textbooks alike often structure their information poorly, looping back to add afterthoughts or corollaries. Make allowance for this. You might, for instance, use only left-hand pages for your main notes, leaving the opposite page free in each case for extra details.

☐ Use abbreviations or any other shorthand devices of your own choosing, so long as the notes remain easy to read. Politics students, for instance, may find themselves writing the phrase 'economic development' as *ec dev*. Philosophy students will represent 'knowledge' as *k*, and Aristotle as *Aris*. And so on. One particularly common phrase is 'on the other hand': you will be doing yourself a favour if you devise right away a shorthand symbol for it – what about a horseshoe-shaped symbol Ω, for example, with its suggestion of reversal?

☐ Make clear whose views you are noting – the lecturer's, Aristotle's, or your own? You may get into a scrape later if you misattribute a particular opinion or insight . . . especially if you claim someone else's insight as your own. And make sure, when noting down a quoted passage, that you have got the wording quite accurate.

☐ For books or articles, start making your notes only once you have finished the reading. Unlike a lecture, where you have to take notes as you go along, books and articles allow you to go back and check for the noteworthy points. You will waste a great deal of time and effort if you insist on taking notes on each paragraph as you read it – quite possibly the article or chapter will conclude with a summary anyway. When you want to mark an important point, just draw a light pencil line next to it in the margin (unless it is an old and precious library book). Once you have finished marking the chapter or article in this way, go through it again quickly, incorporating the marked points into your notes, and then go through it all once more gently rubbing out the pencil lines with an eraser.

Study notes. Here is a typical procedure for compiling a really useful set of study notes.

Begin by adopting a proper attitude towards study notes, in three respects.

First, accept that making notes is a central, rather than incidental, part of studying. Set time aside for updating and upgrading your notes. Rereading your notes intermittently during the course is naturally a very good thing; rewriting them is in many ways even better.

Secondly, accept that study notes are quite different from the record-type notes discussed above. Study notes need not be – should not be – written in elegant lines of consecutive prose. They are for studying, not for reciting on stage. The yardstick is one of easy reading.

Thirdly, approach your note-taking (and the course itself) as a two-fold task: grasping the general and the particular, mastering the big picture and the detail, seeing the wood and the trees. So, as well as compiling a set of notes on each topic within the subject, make a point of maintaining an ever-expanding outline of the subject as a whole.

Try to draw up an outline of the whole subject at the very beginning of the course – reflect on your pre-reading or introductory lectures, and formulate a provisional structure or 'mental map' of the subject. You can adjust or supplement this continually in the light of new insights that you acquire as the course proceeds. Each additional feature can then slot into this outline. Keeping in touch with the overview in this way will provide you with a better understanding and recall of each topic.

Similarly, rework regularly your study notes on specific topics. Integrate those six records of the Peterloo Massacre into a single account. Or, far more efficiently, avoid compiling six separate records in the first place; instead, compile one well-structured pattern, and supplement it each time you attend a new lecture or read a new text.

Don't put off this rewriting for long, or you will find your notes getting cumbersome and disorganised. With practice, you can do the rewriting very quickly – rough notes from a 50-minute lecture can typically be reworked (or filtered into your existing notes) in a matter of six or seven minutes. (For more on note-taking, see the panel on pages 438 and 439.)

READING

Don't treat textbooks and articles as written lectures. In a lecture, as in a concert or film, you receive the flow of information passively, bit by bit, in keeping with a strict sequence of disclosure. You the listener have no control over the sequence or the emphases (though you certainly can restructure the information when making notes).

Reading is quite different: it is like visiting an art exhibition rather than listening to a concert or watching a film. You the reader are now very much in control. You no longer have to begin at the beginning and go on at a steady, unvarying pace to the end.

Now you have access to any part of the information at any stage. You can read the conclusion at the very outset (often a sensible policy, though perhaps not in the case of detective novels). You can skim unimportant chapters very quickly, or skip them altogether. You can double back to reread crucial or tricky chapters in the light of later understanding.

An aggressive reading strategy along these lines is far more efficient, as educational studies have proved, than the traditional word-by-word consumption of the printed page. Details of this new strategy follow. But first, three useful guidelines:

☐ Make yourself comfortable. Not too comfortable, of course. A reasonably comfortable but firm chair, a cool atmosphere, a clear desk, a bookrest, lamplight directed from the side or from behind (to avoid glare), a soft pencil to make marks in the margins – these are the ideal paraphernalia for an efficient session of reading.

☐ Limit the length of each session. Between 20 and 40 minutes is the optimum time for a session of intense reading or studying. Take a distinct break after each such session, lasting at least two minutes. Without such a break, your concentration will soon decline steeply. Get up from your desk and stretch you legs. Shrug your shoulders several times to ease the strain on your neck and back. Rest your eyes by closing them for several moments – you could take the opportunity of running through in your mind the essentials of the text you have just been reading.

☐ Define the task. Set yourself a specific amount of material to cover, and a specific time in which to cover it. Two chapters in a 40-minute session, for example. Monitor your progress from time to time, to make sure you are more or less on target. By defining a limited quantity of reading in this way, you will avoid feeling overwhelmed by the vast amount of reading required. And by setting yourself a time limit, you will have the impetus to drive through without deviating.

Here now is a five-point strategy for efficient reading, based on recent psychological research.

1. Prepare yourself mentally by jotting down, very quickly, rough notes of all the things you know or ideas you have about the subject. And jot down too the things you do not know but hope to learn – the questions that you want the text to answer. These two small tasks will give you a 'mental set', and your reading of the text will be much more focused and efficient as a result.

2. Preview the text. Approach a new book in the spirit of a scout: read the blurb on the back cover; look through the table of contents, trying to get into the author's way of thinking; flick through all the pages, glancing at any charts or graphs, and so on; skim the first and last chapters. When preparing to read just a chapter or an article, conduct a comparable preview. Read the first and last paragraphs. Identify all the subsections in order to grasp the structure of the author's argument. Inspect all the captions and footnotes so that you are not sidetracked by them later.

3. Before a thorough reading of the text, limber up by running your eye very quickly down a few dozen pages of print – just three or four seconds per page. Use your forefinger or pencil to guide your eye down each page in a zigzag route. Don't expect to take much in during this helter-skelter survey. The point is to set your speed-gauge very high so that when you do finally begin a detailed read-through of the text, you will move through it at a smart pace.

The effect is very similar to that of leaving a motorway: having driven for some time at 70 mph, you slow down on the off-ramp to what feels like 30 mph . . . only to find that the speedometer is reading 50 mph. Your entire sense of speed has been shifted up a few notches.

4. For the detailed read-through, speed is very helpful. Not only will you get more reading done: you will actually achieve a better understanding of the text. Instead of wrestling with each detail individually as it arises, you will trace the links between the details, and take in the whole sweep of the argument or narrative.

Writing at Work, Home, and College

NOTE-TAKING IN PRACTICE

Be adventurous in the layouts for your notes – you should think of them as diagrams rather than manuscripts.

Opposite is an example of an outline drawn up by a student of International Relations attending a course on Nationalism – it is accompanied by supplementary notes. Note the ways in which the student has chosen to present the information: a minimum of prose – instead, an emphasis on accessibility. The time for prose comes later when the student extracts relevant facts and figures from his notes in order to write his essays.

Such patterned or diagrammatic layouts have several advantages:

☐ They give you an overview of the topic: once familiar with your layout, you can take in the subject matter more or less at a glance.

☐ They show at a glance numerous vital connections between various points. These serve to knit the topic into a coherent whole, and also provide a source of new insights. And the three-dimensional effect of such multiple interconnections and cross-references reflects your actual patterns of thinking far more closely than two-dimensional linear notes do.

☐ They are easily adjusted and added to, allowing you to insert new points or to 'reposition' existing points (by means of connecting arrows – see opposite) without recourse to scissors and paste as in conventional linear notes.

☐ They are very flexible, allowing you to view the subject from several different angles. As a basis for an essay or exam answer, they offer you a variety of different starting points or emphases.

☐ They help you to memorise the various elements. The vivid appearance of the notes brings into play your visual memory to supplement your general powers of recall. And the use of key words focuses your memory on the highlights, rather than diffusing it across all the distracting verbiage of conventional prose records.

1. Social mobilisation suggests the freeing of people from traditional / older social patterns, for attachment to new ones in a larger, vicarious society.

2. Prophets of nationalism include
   1. Rousseau
   2. Mazzini
   3. Sun Yat Sen, Marcus Garvey
   4. Lenin, Stalin, Trotsky
   5. Hitler, Kita Ikki

3. c.f. Renan's definition of a nation, roughly, a spiritual principle produced by a rich heritage and a desire to continue to live together – a daily plebiscite.

4. Growth in number of nation-states:

5. The political map of the world does not say very much about the world's nations. Multi-national states include Yugoslavia, USSR, Sri Lanka, and India.
   NB How unstable these multi-national states are as political units. All four are facing serious secessional movements: eg. Baltic States, Kashmir, Slovenia.

6. Consider Israel's archaeology fervour (witness Moshe Dayan) – intensifies sense of national identity – and its use of biblical interpretation, to bolster border claims based on ancestral homeland.

7. In South Africa, Afrikaner nationalism – has regarded its mission in history as survival of the white (just Afrikaner?) race (previously, also as national liberation from British imperialism). Hence apartheid – imposition of national identities and statehood (but not self-sufficiency) on to other groups.

8. After 1945, colonies became 'new states' – and loci for wars. Since '45, almost all wars (except the anti-colonial wars themselves) have been between 'new states'.

9. Biafra crisis in late 1960s – Ibo secessionism from Nigeria failed. East Pakistan crisis in early '70s – Bangladeshi secessionism from Pakistan succeeded (with help from India).

10. Obverse of multi-national states (see 5.) are multi-state nations (East + West Germany; various Arab countries – all part of 'Arab nation'?)

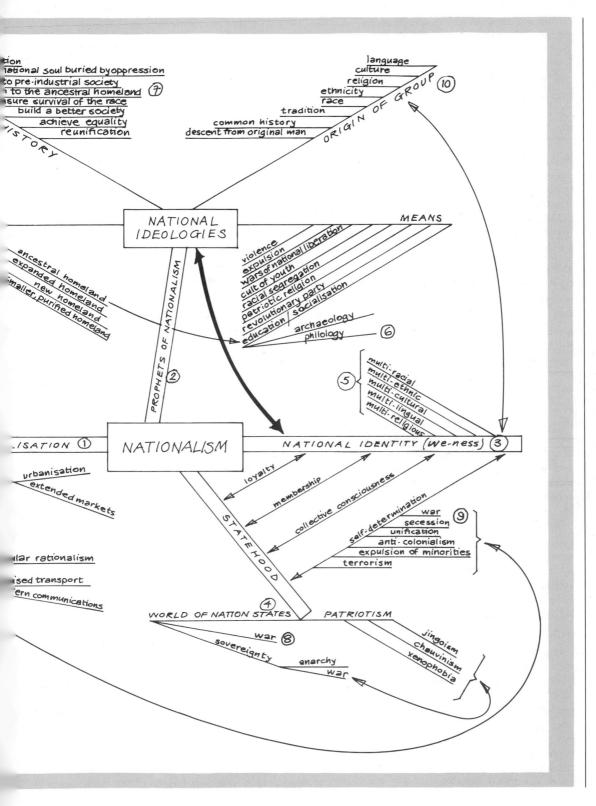

...tion
...ational soul buried by oppression
...to pre-industrial society
...n to the ancestral homeland ⑦
...sure survival of the race
build a better society
achieve equality
reunification

language
culture
religion
ethnicity
race
tradition
common history
descent from original man

ORIGIN OF GROUP ⑩

...HISTORY

NATIONAL IDEOLOGIES

MEANS

violence
expulsion
wars of national liberation
cult of youth
racial segregation
patriotic religion
revolutionary party
education / socialisation

archaeology
philology ⑥

ancestral homeland
expanded homeland
new homeland
...maller, purified homeland

PROPHETS OF NATIONALISM ②

⑤ multi-racial
multi-ethnic
multi-cultural
multi-lingual
multi-religious

...ISATION ①   NATIONALISM   NATIONAL IDENTITY (We-ness) ③

urbanisation
extended markets

loyalty
membership
collective consciousness

STATEHOOD

...lar rationalism
...ised transport
...ern communications

self-determination
war ⑨
secession
unification
anti-colonialism
expulsion of minorities
terrorism

WORLD OF NATION STATES ④   PATRIOTISM

war ⑧
sovereignty
anarchy
war

jingoism
chauvinism
xenophobia

Writing at Work, Home, and College

So your read-through should proceed with a dashing momentum. The only deviation you should allow yourself is to draw the occasional pencil-line in the margin to mark key points. You may vary the pace from time to time, but as a rule only to go faster than your base rate, not to go slower. Across easy passages, or those you have already grasped fully during the preview stage, you should move very speedily.

And across very difficult passages, curiously enough, you should speed up as well: you are likely to come back to them, after all, and the chances are that the difficulties will be resolved anyway by some clarification later on. It is a common mistake to pull up short at obstacles and attempt to dismantle them. Try just jumping right over them instead.

5. Finally, the review and note-taking. Once you have reached the end of the reading task you assigned yourself, take a few moments to go over it in your head, trying to recapitulate the central points or the thrust of the argument. Then return to the beginning of the text, and run your eye down every page once again, to check and reinforce your understanding of the contents. And then quickly compile your notes.

This multi-phase procedure may strike you as far more complicated and time-consuming than a simple old-fashioned plodding word-by-word read of the passage. Put it to the test, and see for yourself. You will find, with very little practice, that the modern technique guides you with far greater speed and comprehension through the complexities of the text.

MEMORISING

If you study consistently throughout the course, you will enter the exam hall with a confident spring in your step, and with your knowledge of the subject stored away in your long-term memory.

If you 'cram' for your exams, your knowledge of the subject resides (if you are lucky) in your short-term memory – a notoriously shallow and unreliable reservoir. True enough, if you time things right, you might just get away with it – you can reproduce your superficial knowledge during the exam, and pass quite adequately. But you will forget almost everything you have learnt very soon after the exam is over. Why throw away something you have taken pains to acquire, when with a slight redirection of effort you can keep it forever?

Long-term memory draws on three basic sources:

☐ clear understanding of the material

☐ repeated familiarisation with the material

☐ anchoring or hooking of the material onto existing knowledge

These three elements are very closely linked, and usually work in conjunction, but you can think of them independently.

Understanding the material. This is crucial. Think how much easier it is to memorise a line of English poetry than a line of poetry in an unfamiliar foreign language. It is not enough, therefore, to be able to reproduce by rote a theorem in geometry or a chemical equation or 'the causes of the First World War'. Unless you really understand the underlying forces, you will sooner or later lose the ability to recall the surface formulation.

Familiarisation with the material. This comes from repeated exposure to it. Rereading the novel, mentally repeating the main points of a history topic, working several times through the theorem step by step, glancing every so often at your study notes – these are the ways of etching the memory traces more deeply into your brain.

Anchoring the material. To attach the material to your existing knowledge, you can forge strong and lasting anchor-cables by deliberately devising a few mental associations. When studying economics or sociology or modern history, for example, try to relate the material to your own life and surroundings rather than thinking of it as an abstract self-contained body of knowledge. When studying electricity, try to relate the theories to familiar everyday things such as light bulbs.

For less systematic material – long lists, for example, of the cranial nerves, or the planets, or the colours of the rainbow – you will need more fanciful associations. The art of *mnemonics* (memory tricks) is based on just such whimsical associations – the colours of the rainbow (red, orange, yellow, green, blue, indigo, violet) come back to mind when prompted by the name *ROY G. BIV*. The nine planets (Mercury, Venus, Earth, Mars, Jupiter, Saturn, Uranus, Neptune, Pluto) lock firmly into the memory when clamped in by the whimsical sentence *Most Volcanoes Expel Mulberry Jam Sandwiches Under Normal Pressure*. (To remember this sentence in turn, exploit to the full one other forceful mnemonic device – visualisation. Picture in your mind's eye, as vividly as you can, a small floating planet surmounted by a huge volcano spewing out sandwiches.)

The daily regimen. A regular and conscientious programme of study will produce good long-term memorisation by drawing on all three of the sources mentioned, but most of all on familiarisation.

The basis is this: just as your memory of a lesson is about to fade, you can revive it by a brief revision. Instead of the usual memory graph – a brief peak followed by a steep decline – your memory graph will now trace a consistent high plateau.

In detail: your memory of a lecture, chapter, or the like begins to fade about ten minutes after its completion. Stem the decline by revising the lesson quickly there and then. A ten-minute revision for an hour-long lesson is about right – go over the key points in your mind, reread the notes you made, and rewrite them in a more systematic way. Then reread these rewritten notes.

A day later your memory will again begin to fade, so restore it once more – just three or four minutes will be enough this time.

One week later, a further three-minute run-through. And a month after that, the same again. From that point on, the lesson should go into the long-term memory, and all you have to do is to top it up by a last read-through a few days before the exam.

To follow this scheme dutifully could hardly be easier. Just keep a detailed diary of each day's work. Then, set aside a revision hour every afternoon or evening, and quickly go through the following:

>   all the study notes compiled yesterday
>   all those compiled one week ago exactly
>   all those compiled one month ago exactly

This programmed system of study should forestall the traditional nervous crisis around exam time: no longer will swotting for exams be synonymous with a nail-biting ordeal. And it should boost your exam performance considerably. What is more you will be taking command of the subject not just for the duration of the exams – but for life.

SWOTTING

One of the commonest afflictions suffered by students is exam-time panic. The symptoms are all too familiar – snappishness, overconsumption of black coffee, red eyes, and a long face. For most students, even the most conscientious, exam time really is a time of stress. This is nothing to be ashamed of: learn to recognise the signs of it in yourself, and take steps to deal with it.

First, look after your physical health.

☐ Watch your diet: take a vitamin supplement if that is necessary.

☐ Take some exercise every day.

☐ Try to get your full quota of sleep.

Then, look after your psychological health.

☐ Try to find time for some leisure activity each day to disperse any tendency towards obsessiveness in your swotting.

☐ Try to dissipate the tension by natural techniques rather than by medication. Yoga, breathing exercises, meditation, listening to records – these are preferable to tranquillisers.

☐ Seek reassurance from your friends and family, and advice from your tutors. Don't become a hermit: during times of stress, social contact is more important than ever.

Here now is a recommended strategy, moving from the general to the particular, for surviving or even flourishing during those weeks of swotting.

Be positive. Swotting can actually be very enjoyable, giving you the chance to bring together all the fragments of knowledge you have acquired during the course, and to see the subject whole at last. It is a marvellously rewarding feeling when it happens, the true 'learning experience' that educationists talk about.

Don't be scared of the approaching exam, or you will only distract yourself from your swotting: the shadow of the exam room is hardly the shadow of the gallows. Nightmares are really not called for.

Don't be cynical about the exam. If you do this, you will stop taking your swotting seriously. Examiners are not usually monsters: they are out to test you, not to trap you. Marking is not a lottery, as your more cynical classmates might insist. Even in the most 'subjective' of subjects – literary criticism or political philosophy, say – examiners do bring objective standards to bear in assessing your exam answers. And your script will in any case often come under the scrutiny of a second or external examiner – a common safety net to ensure consistent and fair marking.

Writing at Work, Home, and College

441

Make time. First, clear your in-tray very quickly. Any classwork outstanding – term essays, belated laboratory reports, or whatever – should be dispatched as quickly as possible, even if this means sacrificing the quality somewhat. Why take an extra week over a minor research paper to score an A rather than a B, when you could use that week to top up your revision for the major exam and thereby score an A rather than a B on that?

Similarly, discharge all extramural responsibilities right away. Pay that visit now to your aunt in hospital; send in those application forms today. If you leave any of these chores hanging over your head, the thought of them will distract you every now and then and reduce your concentration.

Accept that the weeks of swotting will require some sacrifices on your part. You will probably have to cut down on your social and leisure activities. It is all too easy to start feeling sorry for yourself as a result, and to compensate by indulging in little treats – a shopping trip here, an hour in front of the TV set there . . . until you actually end up spending less time at your desk than usual.

Work-avoidance of this kind can have deep psychological roots. The most common of these is fear of failure. Since failing an exam strikes a blow at one's self-esteem, insecure students often subconsciously prepare their excuses beforehand. If they can attribute their failure to a lack of revision rather than a lack of ability, they can salvage their fragile self-esteem. And so they set about compulsively avoiding serious swotting.

If you recognise such temptations in yourself, guard against them as best you can. Resolve to give your swotting priority over everything else. Treat it as an office job: no sneaking off during office hours. You will just have to arrange your shopping or visiting to fit in with your work schedule.

Prepare a pre-exam timetable. And keep to it religiously. Establish the amount of work you have to get through, and analyse it into small sections. Then, calculate how much time you have, and assign a certain proportion of this time to each section of the material. (For an example, see the panel on page 433.)

No exact formula will serve: you may want to give more than their fair share of time to those sections you feel least confident about, and also to any sections that seem most likely to generate exam questions. ('Spotting' questions in this way is quite

acceptable – it is just a matter of emphasising some sections slightly more than others. But the cruder kind of 'spotting' is inadvisable – concentrating exclusively on a few selected sections, and neglecting almost entirely all the other sections. The risks are obvious.)

Make sure to include a lot of cushioning in the timetable – leave free one study hour a day, and one day a week, and three successive days immediately before exams start. These gaps will allow you to catch up if you fall behind, and to enjoy some bonus relaxation if you manage to stay on schedule.

Plan each swotting session in detail. Your timetable will dictate the topic for revision: the finer details will be decided during the first few minutes of each session. Glance through the set of study notes to get some idea of the pace you will have to maintain to get through them all. Then jot down very quickly some rough notes outlining your knowledge of the subject – this will put you in the right frame of mind to read the study notes themselves.

Engage these study notes aggressively: focus your mind sharply to ask constant questions of the notes, and to jump ahead of your reading and predict what the notes will be saying. Remember, you learn and memorise far more effectively when you actively explore the material in this way than when you just absorb it by passive reading.

A full swotting session might last an hour-and-a-half or two hours. Break it up into at least three subsessions, taking a distinct two- or three-minute break each time. This will refresh you and prevent a decline in concentration. End each full session with a rather fuller review of the material – this time, jot down the main points very quickly once again rather than just going over them in your head. Finally, tidy your study notes away, and set out the study notes on the next topic in preparation for the following session.

Supplement your swotting with practice answers. To know your subject matter through and through is one thing: to communicate that knowledge effectively during the exam is another. You must get some practice at writing exams. If your tutor does not require you to take a mock exam, then ask him or her to set you one and mark it. Or get hold of last year's paper and have a go at that.

This exercise will benefit you considerably: it will help you to sharpen or rearrange your thoughts on various topics; it will help you to express your ideas succinctly and coherently; it will help you to pace yourself properly so that you do not overwrite and run out of time in the actual exam.

Try to involve your tutor or classmates in other study exercises as well. You could arrange a late revision seminar with your tutor, for instance, or invite some classmates to a group brainstorming session, focusing on various problem areas.

THE FINAL RUN-UP TO EXAMS

If you keep to your study timetable, you should be able to wind down the swotting in the last few days. Some teachers actually recommend a three-day holiday before the first day of exams. You may consider this an overcasual and overconfident approach in your own case. But for most people it is sensible to try at least to reduce the intensity of their studying and to get some thorough relaxation as the countdown begins. They may find themselves slightly less intellectually prepared, but they will be much better emotionally and physically prepared for the rigours of the exam ordeal, no point cramming in extra facts if you are too jaded or tense to put them to good use when the time comes.

Above all, get a good night's sleep before each exam. If necessary, let your neighbours know your exam timetable, and remind them on the day before to be especially quiet. (While you are about it, ask them to make sure you are up in time the next morning – you do not want to risk oversleeping.)

Pack your bag the night before so as to avoid a rush in the morning. Make sure you take along all necessary equipment – such as a calculator or dictionary if permitted, your identity card or a note of your exam number if applicable, reserve pens or pencils, any necessary geometrical instruments, some high-energy snacks, and so on.

On the exam day itself, make all the necessary common-sense preparations. Dress appropriately: make sure you have an extra jumper, in case the exam hall is unheated. Eat sensibly beforehand – a good breakfast before a morning exam, a moderate but not heavy lunch (and no alcohol!) before an afternoon exam.

Arrive in good time. If there is any danger of train delays, traffic jams, parking problems, or the like, take this into account. In the few minutes before entering the exam hall, take the opportunity of using the toilet so that you are not caught short midway through the exam itself.

On the wisdom of last-minute revision and discussion, opinion is divided. A final quick scanning of your condensed notes over breakfast can provide a useful refreshing of your memory. But remember that you need an alert mind in the exam, not just a well-stocked one. So avoid, if you can, waking up especially early to do extra swotting. And, if you are at all susceptible to panic, avoid discussing the forthcoming exam with your classmates as you mill about outside the exam hall waiting to enter. Likewise, avoid discussing the paper immediately after an exam, if you have another exam coming up soon afterwards. Don't engage in 'post-mortems' with your classmates or even with yourself – such discussions tend to be demoralising rather than reassuring, and serve only to distract you from preparing for the exam ahead.

Writing at Work, Home, and College

Essay Writing and Research

WRITTEN COMPOSITION remains at the heart of the education system. Despite the increasing emphasis on 'classroom participation', practical exams, and oral exams, the written exam and the written assignment still carry most weight in assessing and grading most students.

Written work tests so many attributes – not just the knowledge acquired through studying, but also more general background knowledge, reasoning ability, research skills, observation and insight, and power of expression.

Compositions in school or college range from the one-paragraph report on a nature ramble to the 300-page doctoral dissertation on the international diamond trade. This chapter will deal with the standard and most common types of composition: the essay, the précis, the book review, the science report, and the research assignment.

The Essay

All writing is a venture into communication. It may aim to communicate information (as in a newspaper story) or ideas (as in a magazine article) or advice (as in an advertisement) or beliefs (as in a political pamphlet) or emotions (as in a poem).

What does the essay aim to communicate? The answer to that question is in fact the one common thread that runs through all the various kinds of essay – the essay aims to communicate a personal view of a particular subject. That remains the common driving force of essays as diverse as 'The countryside in winter', 'My last holiday', 'The life story of a pair of shoes', 'The death penalty is a justifiable form of punishment', 'The imagery in *Macbeth*', and 'The causes and effects of the Thirty Years' War'.

Even if all your information – as in the last example – comes directly from textbooks or teachers, the essay should still reflect your own opinions. The way that you sift, select, and order the information is the point of the exercise. If you merely summarised objectively the various scholarly authorities, that might make a good report or article, but not really an essay.

The essay titles just listed cover most of the range of the education system – primary and secondary schools, undergraduate and graduate levels. They also span the range of essay types – descriptive, narrative, analytical. And they embrace the various activities and mental faculties that essay writers rely on – observation, memory, vocabulary, imagination, research, reasoning, and reflection.

No matter what level the essay – primary school or postgraduate – and no matter what type of essay, two very broad principles apply.

Know your own strengths and limitations. For those at school, or attending writing courses – if you have a very unsentimental and down-to-earth imagination, try to avoid the lighter or more whimsical topics such as 'Brown Eggs' (the subject of an essay by G.K. Chesterton) or 'All Fools' Day' (the title of one of Charles Lamb's famous *Essays of Elia*). Opt instead, if you have the choice, for a more serious and reflective topic, something on Truth or Beauty perhaps (the subjects of two of Francis Bacon's classic essays), or for a topic requiring some factual research and careful analysis, such as the relationship between language and politics.

Again, if you have the choice, pick a subject that you have genuine opinions or strong feelings about. Why pretend to feel spontaneous or sincere on some topic remote from your sympathies when you can write on a topic that you really do care about? You may feel a bit of a stick-in-the-mud choosing the title 'The problem of litter' in preference to 'The fate of Tibet', but if you feel strongly about litter and have few opinions or feelings about Tibet, you will write a more interesting essay on litter than on Tibet.

Generally speaking, it is much more difficult to write interesting and impressive essays on whimsical themes and abstract topics. For such essays to come off properly, the writer needs *literary* talent – a commodity in very short supply. Essays on concrete or well-defined topics – the Third Crusade, violence on TV, returning the Elgin Marbles to Greece – require only *writing* talent ... something that most intelligent people have, however undeveloped it may be.

Aim to be interesting. It is more important to be interesting than authoritative. When you present factual information, it should naturally be accurate. But not everything in an essay has to be factual information. Indeed, a surfeit of facts is one of the commonest causes of dullness in an essay. In a good essay, information has to be balanced by illustration and speculation; accuracy by originality; authority by personality; *what* you say by *how* you say it.

Keep in mind the poor teacher or marker – wading through dozens of 'worthy' essays, all disgorging a core of identical information, and many in a nearly identical style. Oh for something different, he or she shrieks silently, and reads with relief and delight any essay that deviates in the least from the tedious standard approach. No matter even if the core of information remains the same, so long as the essay views it from an original perspective – interpreting it in a novel or even heretical way, perhaps, garnishing it with anecdotes, or couching it in an unusual style: ironic, passionate, slightly whimsical ... above all lively and individual.

One useful way of arriving at new insights into a topic is to bombard it with questions. Kipling's verse remains a valuable standby:

> I keep six honest serving-men
> (They taught me all I knew);
> Their names are What and Why and When
> And How and Where and Who.
> – 'The Elephant's Child'

Such 'brainstorming' will seldom be enough, however. You will usually want to supplement it with research of one kind or another. But even then you can stay on the lookout for interesting angles.

As for a 'lively and individual' style, one word of caution: a lively and individual style is something very different from an inappropriate style. Never allow yourself to be carried away into adopting a style or approach that jars with the contents of the

Writing an essay often needs preparation.

essay. No matter how fun-loving and imaginative your usual line of attack may be, you must curb your comic muse when engaging a serious essay topic such as 'Boxing should be banned' or 'The Arms Race in the age of Glasnost'. Flippancy is fine in light-hearted contexts; in serious contexts, it descends into inappropriate facetiousness.

Finally, since the essay does present a personal view, you are almost always entitled to use that most interesting word *I*. The frequency would vary, of course: in the essay 'My last holiday', *I* would probably be the most commonly used word of all; in a more objective essay such as 'The imagery in *Macbeth*', it would be inappropriate to use it more than once or twice.

CONSTRUCTING AN ANALYTICAL ESSAY

Of the various kinds of essay, descriptive ('The countryside in winter') and narrative ('The life story of a corner shop') are now rare outside junior schools, adult literacy classes, creative writing courses, and professional journalism. The typical essay in secondary and higher education is the analytical or expository essay ('The causes and effects of the Thirty Years' War').

The principles of writing the analytical essay are discussed in detail in the chapter on exams, especially pages 424-428. Do reread that section, for a reminder of such requirements as *relevance* (answer the question explicitly, if the title is in the form of a question), *balance* (don't ride your personal hobbyhorse), *concreteness* and *conciseness* (do back up any generalisation with specific examples or quotations – but only a selected few), and so on.

The analytical essay subdivides into the discursive essay ('The imagery in *Macbeth*') and the polemical essay (that is, examining and usually taking sides in an argument – 'The imagery in *Macbeth* is overdone' or 'The death penalty is a justifiable form of punishment'). It is the polemical essay that presents the greatest challenge – and problem – to the writer. You not only have to supply all the information, and organise it into a coherent structure; you also have to modulate it carefully in order to win the reader round to your view. You have to give greater weight to some arguments than to others, adjust your tone and emphasis subtly to increase your persuasiveness, and give a 'fair hearing' to opposing ideas without letting them actually prevail over the ideas that you favour.

Here is a suggested strategy for writing a polemical essay, using as illustration the topic 'Private cars should be banned from city centres'.

First, applying the techniques described elsewhere, draw up your plan – assemble all your ideas on the subject, and arrange them into a coherent structure to use as the basis of your first full draft (see pages 91-102). The bulk of this plan will almost certainly consist of two columns, listing the arguments (and counterargument each time) on both sides of the question. See the panel alongside.

Once you have 'written up' those two columns, you will have the body of your essay.

But, in the meantime, you also need to plan an introduction and a conclusion for your essay. Both of them should be short – no more than two paragraphs as a rule. The reader is impatient both to start and to finish. Don't keep him waiting long for the first argument, and don't delay him for long after you have stated the last argument.

The introduction should not simply be a summary of the arguments to come. And it should typically reveal your own thesis or preference after a brief overture rather than in the very opening sentence. It can be a broad and direct introduction to the subject – a defining of terms (such as *private* or

THE POLEMICAL ESSAY – SAMPLE OUTLINE

An essay on banning private cars from city centres will almost certainly take the form of a debate. You could even write it in the form of a dialogue – putting words into the mouths of two (or more) imaginary debaters. Usually, however, the debate is conducted in a less stark and schematic way than that. The outline below (much fuller and tidier than it would be if you had simply drafted it as a basis for your full version of the essay) offers just one possible approach. Note that it is the case For that has the initiative at first, and then the flow of the argument switches with a number of points being raised Against, to be answered by the case For each time.

TOPIC: PRIVATE CARS SHOULD BE BANNED FROM CITY CENTRES

FOR	AGAINST
1. Car ownership has risen dramatically, and many city centres are being clogged by private cars. The average peak-hour speed of a vehicle moving through central London is now only about 8 mph.	**1.** City centres are public places, and the public should have the right to enter and travel in a city however they please. Even moving at 8 mph, a car is often the easiest means of getting about.
2. Everyone suffers as a result of selfishness. Cars not only produce chemical and noise pollution within cities: they are even contributing to the destruction of the Earth's atmosphere.	**2.** Private cars are not the only polluters of the environment, and should not receive a disproportionate amount of blame.
3. Apart from special groups, such as the handicapped, no one really needs to take a private vehicle into a city in which both taxis and fast, reliable public transport operate.	**3.** Travelling by public transport is often less convenient and cost-effective than by private car. At night, public transport can be dangerous.

AGAINST

4. Many people rely on their cars precisely because public transport is generally poor – expensive, uncomfortable, and unreliable. Driving to work may be slow and frustrating, but no more so than commuting by bus or train.

5. What is needed is more roads, or at least wider roads, and a system of underpasses and flyovers for drivers wishing to bypass the city centre.

6. Alternatively, a system for restricting car use rather than imposing a blanket ban: a toll on single-occupant cars to encourage car-sharing; or an electronic monitoring system to raise funds to subsidise new roads; or a licence-plate check allowing certain cars free access on some days, and others access on other days.

7. Basic freedoms are at issue here too – freedom of movement, and freedom of choice. The very word *banned* raises the

FOR

4. Public transport is hampered by the volume of private traffic. If fewer cars crowded the road, buses and taxis would operate more quickly. And a greater demand for bus and rail services would stimulate them to greater efficiency.

5. The history of traffic control throughout the world clearly shows that increased road capacity often just increases congestion. More roads simply encourage more people to use their own cars.

6. Such systems have been tried in cities as varied as Los Angeles, Lagos, Athens, and Hong Kong. Any early improvements have quickly disappeared. The schemes are not only unsuccessful, but unfair: they discriminate in favour of the rich, who are happy to pay the extra tolls, or even to buy a second car, with a different licence plate.

7. This is a very naive view of liberty. Unrestricted freedom is impossible in a complex society: *your* 'freedom' to be a nuisance may be a

AGAINST

spectre of the suppression of individual liberty.

8. The side effects of a full ban are imponderable. One likely side effect, however, is that heavy commercial traffic would expand to make greater use of roads cleared of cars. So traffic levels would not drop greatly, and the roads would remain just as troublesome for pedestrians and commuters.

FOR

denial of *my* freedom to enjoy a healthy and pleasant life.

8. No, the side effects would instead be an additional ban – on delivery vehicles during the rush hours. That would ensure the smoother flow of public transport. Other side effects, not at all imponderable, would be very beneficial: parking garages could be turned to better use; some streets could be converted into pedestrian-only precincts; noise and pollution would decrease, and city centres would become more congenial places.

The structure here has a simple underlying drama that should serve the goal of persuasion very effectively. 'Act I' (the first three points) lays out the case For, with the corresponding arguments Against each time. 'Act II' (the next three points) works in the other direction: first, an argument Against, with suggested alternatives; then a very telling counterargument For. Finally 'Act III' (points 7 and 8) – two desperate arguments Against, with very dramatic and emotional replies in each case arguing For.

A good writer would confidently draft a similar outline taking just the opposite view. In the outline above, the writer is clearly in favour of banning cars from city centres, and his ordering of the debate cunningly helps to reinforce his case – first stating his own case boldly, then giving his imaginary opponent a fair hearing though without making any concessions to it, and then slowly turning up the emotional and intellectual heat with his own compelling counterarguments.

Writing at Work, Home, and College

banned), say, or an account of the urgency or topicality of the subject (perhaps Parliament is about to debate the subject.)

Or it can be a specific and indirect introduction – a graphic description of a commuter's frustrated efforts to drive to work, say, or the statistics of increasing car ownership and decreasing mobility in town.

Or it could be a combination of the specific and the broad – something along these lines.

> In 1989, the main roads of towns and cities carried a third of all traffic in Britain, while motorways carried a mere 14 per cent. Private car ownership continues to rise, and every year more and more commuters choose to drive themselves to work rather than take public transport. This increasingly inefficient use of road space means that commuter and commercial traffic is slowly grinding to a halt. According to latest estimates, urban traffic jams alone now cost the UK economy more than £3000 million every year.

> The picture is already grim enough; but if the predictions of some traffic analysts come true – doubling of traffic by the turn of the century – the state of our city streets will be little short of chaotic. Drastic action is needed to prevent what has been called 'urban transport Doomsday'.

The conclusion is normally a wrapping-up or clinching of your arguments in a fresh way. If you actually summarise your arguments, do so very briefly. If you can, without any straining, make some allusion to a point in the introduction – perhaps by finally answering a question you posed there, or by repeating an image – that would round out the essay elegantly, and lend it an added feel of unity.

Here is a possible way of concluding your essay on the banning of cars from city centres:

> The British love affair with the private car is rapidly turning sour. What was once a fast, convenient, and liberating form of transport is now all too often slow, frustrating, and dangerous. Certainly the public has every right to own and use private cars; what is clearly not right is that mile-long queues of private vehicles bearing only one or two passengers should hold up for hours fully laden buses.

> New roads are not the answer: they simply encourage further car ownership. The only solution is to use existing road space more efficiently, and this can be achieved only by banning private cars from town and city centres. Park-and-ride schemes, and increased bus services, would be introduced alongside the ban, and mitigate the initial discontent that diehard motorists may feel. And after a very short time the benefits would heavily outweigh the inconvenience – far smoother and faster mobility (on public transport) around town; a network of pedestrian precincts; a generally quieter and cleaner city centre to work in or visit.

Once you have written your first full draft, take a break if possible – the longer the better, when it comes to reading the essay with a fresh eye – and then get down to editing and polishing the text into its final form (see also pages 103 and 104).

Check the contents first – do they cover the ground? Have they included all your main ideas, and all the main findings gleaned from your reading? Have you given enough space to the opposition view, or perhaps made too many concessions to it? Do some ideas simply raise questions without answering them? Do they start new lines of thought that you really ought to pursue?

Then check your analysis of the contents – is it well researched? Have you made any jumps of logic, or committed any logical fallacies? Have you given too much prominence to a marginal idea, and underemphasised one of your key arguments?

Check the structure next – does the essay hold together? Is the ordering of items right? Not jumping about a bit too much? No anticlimax perhaps, that you could eliminate by switching the last two paragraphs? Have you signposted your route adequately, so that the reader knows your intentions constantly, and never loses his bearings?

And check the language – no needlessly highfalutin' words, no overlong sentences or paragraphs? What about the grammar and spelling – no blunders? What about clichés, and jargon, and possible sexism in your choice of examples? And the general sound of the language: can you detect any jarring jingles? Do the sentences flow effortlessly from one to the next?

Finally, check the presentation, the physical appearance of the essay on the page. If you have scored out half a dozen lines on any page, or drawn arrows to reposition paragraphs, you had better rewrite or retype that page.

The Précis

A *précis* (pronounced / **pray**-see /) is a condensation, in your own words, of a piece of writing – capturing the essence of its ideas. It is as much an exercise in comprehension as in writing: without understanding the original text thoroughly, you cannot hope to distil its contents with any accuracy in a précis.

A précis should be about one-third the length of the original. What you need to concentrate on is the general drift or message of the text. Omit most of the embroidery – specific examples, details, and digressions. And you may well have to change the structure drastically, reordering and repacking the ideas into a new logical, flowing narrative.

So a précis differs from a mere *summary*, which simply abridges the original passage, often using the same wording. And it differs too from a *paraphrase*, which is a simplified rewording of a difficult piece of writing (such as an old poem), and does not need to be shorter than the original.

The standard procedure for writing a précis should be as follows:

☐ Start by reading the original passage very carefully, two or three times if necessary, to grasp its message fully. Use a dictionary to look up any word you have doubts about.

☐ Note the main points, rearranging their order if that serves the cause of a more logical development of ideas.

☐ Write a first draft. Use your own words; any direct speech, for instance, you will have to redraft as indirect speech.

☐ Revise or edit the text, concentrating on tightening the structure and reducing the number of words. Delete any needless elaborations such as unhelpful examples or underemployed adjectives. Reduce clauses to phrases where possible, and then reduce phrases to words. For example, the flabby sentence:

When we eventually reached the top of the mountain, we enjoyed a well-deserved lunch with the friends who had accompanied us.

could now read, far more economically,

At the summit, we had a good lunch with our companions.

Here is an example of a précis exercise. Why not try your own hand at it before studying the version attempted below?

First the original piece – the opening paragraph of Chapter 10 of Samuel Butler's famous satire *Erewhon* (roughly, 'Nowhere' spelt backwards) published in 1872.

> This is what I gathered. That in that country if a man falls into ill health, or catches any disorder, or fails bodily in any way before he is seventy years old, he is tried before a jury of his countrymen, and if convicted is held up to public scorn and sentenced more or less severely as the case may be. There are subdivisions of illness into crimes and misdemeanours as with offences amongst ourselves – a man being punished very heavily for serious illness, while failure of eyes or hearing in one over sixty-five, who has had good health hitherto, is dealt with by fine only, or imprisonment in default of payment. But if a man forges a cheque, or sets his house on fire, or robs with violence from the person, or does any other such things as are criminal in our own country, he is either taken to a hospital and most carefully tended at the public expense, or if he is in good circumstances, he lets it be known to all his friends that he is suffering from a severe fit of immorality, just as we do when we are ill, and they come and visit him with great solicitude, and inquire with interest how it all came about, what symptoms first showed themselves, and so forth – questions which he will answer with perfect unreserve; for bad conduct, though considered no less deplorable than illness with ourselves, and as unquestionably indicating something seriously wrong with the individual who misbehaves, is nevertheless held to be the result of either pre-natal or post-natal misfortune.

Here now is an attempt at a précis of the passage:

> If a person falls ill in Erewhon, or becomes bodily incapacitated before turning seventy, he has to undergo a trial by jury as a criminal offender. Serious illness is a serious crime, and is punished severely, whereas loss of sight or hearing after sixty-five is just a misdemeanour, and results only in a fine. By contrast, any act

that we consider a serious crime – forgery, arson, robbery with violence, and so on – though indicating something seriously wrong with the perpetrator, is regarded as arising from some personal misfortune just before or after birth.

Such an attack of 'immorality' results in free and devoted hospital care; or for the wealthy, bed-rest at home – the friends of the perpetrator (or 'sufferer') come to visit and sympathise, and he tells them how it happened.

The Book Review

Evaluating a book is an exercise in comprehension, background knowledge, judgment, and writing skills. Your task is to produce a well-written account of your reaction to the book – to comment on its merits and demerits. To describe or summarise the contents of the book may be helpful, or it may be quite irrelevant; it is certainly not enough.

The first step is obviously to read the book – not a summary of the book, or a set of study notes, or the blurb on the dust jacket, or a classmate's review of it . . . but the book itself. (Some useful reading techniques are described on pages 437 and 440.)

Read actively rather than passively – that is, think constantly about what you are reading, argue with it, challenge it, predict the next turn in the plot or argument, and so on. And jot down notes on your responses while reading. Once you have finished reading, make notes on your overall impression – a feeling of satisfaction? indifference? letdown? But do treat such impressions as provisional only. You should, if you have the time, spend a while thinking about the book: you may well revise your early opinions when you come to draft your review a day or two later.

If necessary, you may want to do some further reading – another novel by the same author, for instance, or a book giving the historical background to the novel, or a critical essay on the novel (though don't simply write your review in the form of a summary of that essay).

Above all, be fair and sincere. Don't praise a work simply because other readers, even experts, have done so. Don't criticise it, on the other hand, just to be clever. Don't condemn a book simply because you disagree with it, or even because you dislike the type of work it is – a romantic novel, say, rather than a war novel. Always ask yourself whether the book is successful on its own terms. If it is a very old book, try to read it not just with a modern eye, but with the eye of a reader living at the time it was written – you cannot fairly judge an old book by today's standards, any more than you can a historical event.

And try also to look at it from the perspective of the author's intention – has the book fulfilled it adequately? – though you certainly may point out that the intention is an unworthy or futile one.

The types of book you are most likely to write a review of are biographies, books of history or current affairs, and above all novels. To consider just the last of these: here are some guidelines, mainly in the form of questions to ask yourself, when writing a review of a novel.

Plot. Try to define and characterise the plot – a straight adventure yarn, a science-fiction fantasy, a grimly realistic account of the interwoven lives of two families over four generations, or whatever. It is essential to say what the book is about, but don't summarise the plot – that takes little skill or insight, and spoils the story for the reader. Remember, your task is evaluation, not description.

In evaluating the plot, address these questions: how unusual or original is the story? Are the incidents believable or far-fetched? If there are controversial contents – scenes of sex and violence, for example – are they serving a useful purpose, helping to advance the reader's understanding of theme and character; or are they 'gratuitous', serving simply to shock? Is the plot perfectly intelligible, or occasionally impossible to follow? Do the incidents follow one another in strict chronological order, or does the author jump to and fro in time? (And, if so, to good or bad effect?) Has the author paced the story well? – no boring patches in the middle perhaps, or an overhurried ending? Is the reader inspired to keep turning the pages? Suspense – does the author attempt to create any, and if so, how successful is it?

Character and dialogue. Are the characters 'real people' – convincingly rounded and combining good and bad qualities? Do you care about what happens to them, or are they cardboard figures, with no light and shade to their personalities, perhaps crudely embodying some single trait such as innocence or greed?

As for dialogue, does it seem appropriate to the speakers each time, and to the situations in which they find themselves? And does it actually add anything to our understanding of the characters? And does it help to advance the plot, or is it just dutiful padding?

Setting and description. Is the descriptive material interesting and convincing? Does it really evoke in the reader's mind a vivid picture of a place or person? Does the historical setting come alive for you and encourage you to 'suspend your disbelief' and enter the world that the novel creates? Are the descriptive passages properly integrated into the story, or are they just 'purple patches' crudely pasted in, as if as an afterthought?

Theme. Can you identify a single dominant theme, or themes? It may be a simple theme such as guilt, courage, or hypocrisy; or a combination of such themes; or a complex theme such as the conflict between love and duty.

An interesting theme is no guarantee of a successful novel. The test is always: has the theme been convincingly illustrated by the plot and characters?

The author and other novels. How 'autobiographical' is the novel – and if it does reflect the author's own life closely, is this to the book's benefit or detriment? And how does this novel fit in with the author's other novels? Does it share themes with them; does it reveal anything about his development as a writer? And how does this novel compare with similar novels you may have read by other writers?

Style, tone, and point of view. Is the novel charming, sentimental, patronising? Is it gloomy or witty, satirical or humourless, irreverent or overearnest, openly farcical? Or perhaps ironic – the most difficult tone to bring off successfully. Does the language cunningly echo the theme or incidents – sensuous or harsh rhythms, for instance, to convey love scenes or scenes of violence?

If the novel is written in the third person, perhaps all the incidents are nevertheless described from the point of view of a single character. Or is there an unrestricted and 'omniscient' narrator, and does this freedom make for a richer or just a looser narrative? If the novel is written in the first person, should the reader take everything on trust, or suspect an 'unreliable narrator'.

In *Gulliver's Travels*, for instance, Gulliver is the 'I' of the novel, but the 'eye' of the novel is Jonathan Swift's satirical eye – very different from that of the solemn Gulliver. But what about Robinson Crusoe – is he Defoe's reliable mouthpiece, or is he too, like Gulliver, an object and vehicle of the author's satire? What about the famous passage where Crusoe, fossicking in the wrecked ship, contemplates a rich find of coins – something quite useless to him, marooned as he is on a desert island?

> I smiled to myself at the sight of this money. 'Oh drug!' said I aloud, 'what art thou good for? . . .' However, upon second thoughts, I took it away, and, wrapping all this in a piece of canvas, I began to think of making another raft.

Is Defoe here admiring Crusoe's practicality and prudence, or is he mocking him gently for his pointless money-mindedness?

In writing a book review, you do not have to come down on one side or the other on such questions, but you should at least mention that the questions do come insistently into the reader's mind, and quote the occasional key passage to give a flavour of the book's tone.

The Science Report

Writing up a science project has two benefits. First, the prospect of writing a report encourages you to plan and conduct the project properly. Secondly, the process of planning and writing the report leads you to understand the project better.

You need an orderly procedure in compiling your report, just as you do in conducting the project itself. The following guidelines apply specifically to the modest research report based on a typical small-scale laboratory project. With minor adjustments, however, they would apply equally to more ambitious writing tasks, such as conference papers or academic theses.

Title. It should reveal the subject-matter clearly, rather than aim to be 'catchy'. Appropriate titles might be 'The life cycle of the silkworm' and 'The optimum temperature for infusing tea'. Inappropriate titles would be 'From ugliness comes silky beauty' or 'The worm turns', and 'Care for a cuppa?' or 'The best T for the best tea'.

Abstract. Next comes a one-paragraph summary of the report – typically 100 to 150 words. It should state the purpose of the project, the methods or procedures followed, the principal findings, and the conclusions. The reader would get enough information in the abstract to decide whether to read the whole report; and if he decides against, he still comes away with a good idea of its contents.

Background information. This is often called the 'Introduction'. This section would give an account of the history and importance of the problem; any previous findings by researchers on this or some related problem; and your reasons for undertaking the project.

The problem. If the project is based on the study of a specific problem, you would now have to define that problem. State whether you are searching for or testing a hypothesis (that is, an assumption or conjecture to be investigated), putting forward a theory, or simply reporting observations made under specified conditions.

Procedures. Your experiments or observations ought to be open to repetition by anyone, so you must describe in detail the equipment and any relevant conditions, such as temperature, pressure, or humidity. Do mention procedures that failed to work, so that they are not repeated. Use photographs, drawings, graphs, and the like if you have any that are useful. Any statistics or numerical data should appear listed in tables.

Report simply and clearly all your observations, such as the behaviour of animals or changes in the appearance of plant life.

Analysis and interpretation of data. To discover the patterns and relationships in your findings, you usually have to order all your data carefully and apply statistical methods to them. With luck, your analysis will support or confirm your hypothesis. Use graphs, diagrams, and any other organised depiction of your data to convey your analysis.

Conclusions. Announce your rejection of any hypotheses not supported by the research, and your provisional acceptance of those that are supported by it (provisional because you will seldom collect enough evidence to support a hypothesis unreservedly).

If appropriate, you might venture to discuss the wider meaning of your research – its potential impact on related research, say.

Mention too, if possible, any problems, revisions to hypotheses, or interesting lines of research suggested by your study.

Summary. Conclude with a summary of the main findings and results of your investigation.

Throughout the piece, remember that a science report, as much as an essay or any other piece of writing, demands a clear and consistent style.

Observe the conventions where there are any: for instance, the use of a small initial letter for the species word and a capital letter for the genus word in technical names, such as *Salix babylonica*, the weeping willow.

Make a point too, in keeping with the scientific tone of the report, to be very precise and specific in your references and explanations. A sloppy cross-reference reading **?** *as described elsewhere in this report* could so easily read *as described in section 3.2 below* if you took a moment's trouble. Similarly, a heedless and unhelpful comment such as **?** *Figure 4 summarises the temperatures and times with respect to the tea samples* would have far greater explanatory power if worded instead as *Figure 4 shows the effects of different temperatures and different durations on the tannin levels*.

Once you have finished your first draft, edit it thoroughly as always, drawing on all the techniques summarised on pages 103 and 104. As always, put yourself in the position of the first-time reader, and test every sentence for clarity.

The Research Assignment

The research assignment – term paper, thesis, or dissertation – is more ambitious than the essay or the small-scale science report.

Typically it takes longer to do and is longer – four years and 100,000 words, perhaps, in the case of a postgraduate history dissertation.

The research assignment is essentially the detailed presentation of an idea or ideas, using external sources to explain or substantiate. It is not simply a rehash of those sources.

The components of the research paper or thesis are straightforward enough: a title, capturing succinctly the problem or field researched; an introduction; several sections or chapters of research findings and analysis; conclusion; bibliography or list of sources consulted. Other common features are the preface (including acknowledgments) and a review of existing studies (or the current state of research) on the same topic.

None of this poses any particular problem: the structure and presentation of your report are often determined by the rule book of your college, and even by the process of your investigation and your actual research findings. What is rather more problematic to the novice thesis-writer is the techniques of conducting research, and the technicalities of citing the research material – footnotes, bibliography, and so on.

RESEARCH TECHNIQUES

The following notes apply not just to large research projects, but also to classroom essays, science reports, seminar papers, and so on.

An old academic joke: if you take your material – data and ideas – from one source, you commit plagiarism; if you take it from 20 sources, you conduct research. More to the point, the teacher or examiner may well catch you out if you limit your investigation of a topic to a single book or article. But even if you do draw on a variety of sources, your responsibility as a researcher is not over.

You have to *absorb* and *adapt* the material, and so contribute something of your own – a new perspective on the material or a new structuring of it, if not actual fresh ideas.

Research begins with your own knowledge and ideas – write down in point form every relevant fact or thought you may have on the subject.

Next, if appropriate, discussion with others, or interviews. Confer with relatives or fellow-students – not just for their ideas, but as a stimulus for further ideas of your own. Talk to the retired colonel down the road for anecdotes about life in India before Independence. Phone the information office at the art gallery to check on the date or authenticity of the sculpture you are describing.

Next, your own books and notes – primary texts if possible, such as the play or novel you intend writing about; then secondary sources, such as your lecture notes or a textbook. The temptation, if you are pressed for time or lacking in confidence, is

Research assignments can be painfully slow.

to ignore your own ideas and simply adopt or adapt those of the 'experts'. Many is the student who has written an essay on *King Lear* or *Liberty* without reading Shakespeare or John Stuart Mill – reading only commentators on them instead. Don't chance it. For one thing, an astute or experienced marker will see through your ruse, and mark your essay down accordingly. For another, even if you carry off the deception, you are only harming yourself and undermining your education in the long run. You will never learn to think independently and judge a topic critically if you always rely solely on other people's opinions.

Next, a library. Begin with your reading list, if your teacher or lecturer has assigned one. If the books you need are inaccessible – as they well might be if others are researching the same topic – you have a number of choices.

You could ask the library assistant to 'recall' the books, or to order extra copies (perhaps on inter-library loan), or to give you the name and address of the current borrower: you could then ask him to share the books with you, or to pass them on to you one by one as he finishes with them.

You could buy the most important of the titles. If you buy them second-hand, and sell them again once you have finished with them, it should not be too expensive an exercise, though it might prove unacceptably time-consuming.

You could try another library nearby. Even libraries outside the public library system, such as university libraries, are often amenable to a personal approach: you might secure a day pass to the reading room, for instance, where you can consult the relevant books or articles.

Above all, you could – and should – look for alternative books and articles. Even if you have ready access to all the items on the reading list, you should not be restricted by it. The teacher or marker will welcome any evidence of extra reading on your part. Not only does it indicate your scholarly initiative, but it will probably produce a more interesting essay or report, containing information new to even the teacher himself.

HOW TO FIND RESEARCH MATERIAL IN A LIBRARY

You probably know the ropes when it comes to libraries in general. The typical library has a catalogue (or catalogues) listing all its holdings – books, magazines, and records alike. Older catalogues come in the form of large ledgers or files, or drawers of file cards. A more recent catalogue would tend to be on microfilm or microfiche. The most up-to-date catalogue would be on computer, and can be consulted at any number of terminals dotted about the library, or even at other libraries within the same system. There will usually be instructions on how to use the system.

The basic catalogue will list books alphabetically according to the authors' surnames. (Note: foreign surnames consisting of two or more words will often present a problem. The name *Laurens van der Post* will probably be listed under *V*; the name *Wernher von Braun* under *B*; the name *Ludwig Mies van der Rohe* under *M*; and *José Ortega y Gasset* under *O*. If you fail to find the reference first time, try looking elsewhere.)

A second alphabetical listing, according to the books' titles, usually exists alongside, either filed separately or interspersed with it. (Note: for the purposes of alphabetising, the words *A, An, The*, and sometimes *On, In*, and the like are disregarded if found at the start of the title.)

A more sophisticated catalogue lists the library's holdings according to topics or themes. You might turn to *E* for books or articles on *ecology*, say, or even to *G* for material on the *greenhouse effect*. Such thematic catalogues cannot really hope to be fully comprehensive. If you fail to find any listing under your chosen topic, try looking under alternative headings – *conservation*, say, or even *biology*. The catalogue item, once you have found it, supplies you with a reference or shelf number – the 'call number' – which in turn indicates the whereabouts of the volume within the library. You should find a map or layout of the shelving system very near the catalogue, enabling you to home in very quickly on the volume and to get your hands on it at last.

Large libraries tend to list their books according to the Dewey decimal system, which classifies them into ten main categories, then into subcategories, and so on, each identified by a set of numbers.

The catalogue is not your only resource in the search for relevant books and articles. One extremely useful, and much-neglected, port of call is the librarian: he or she is probably trained in tracking down source materials both within the library and outside.

Another major resource is the subject bibliography, or specialist reading list. This might simply take the form of an appendix in a recent book on the subject. Or it might consist of an entire book in its own right.

THE DEWEY DECIMAL SYSTEM

This classification system divides library books (except works of fiction and biography) into ten classes with identifying numbers.

000-099—general works (reference books, encyclopedias, bound periodicals)
100-199—philosophy, psychology, conduct
200-299—religion, mythology
300-399—social sciences, economics, government, law
400-499—language (including some dictionaries and grammars)
500-599—natural sciences (mathematics, biology, and so on)
600-699—useful arts (agriculture, engineering, and so on)
700-799—fine arts (sculpture, painting, music . . .)
800-899—literature (including poetry, plays, and essays)
900-999—history (including geography and travel)

Each of these classes has subdivisions and often sub-subdivisions.

In large or specialised libraries, you may find a computerised database to help you in your search – in effect, a sophisticated thematic catalogue.

Once you have tracked down a suitable book or article, you may well find that it refers you in turn to other relevant items. It is often heartening to discover how easily you can keep up the momentum of your research, as one reference leads on to another.

TAKING NOTES

Reading the books or articles is just the first stage. You need to make notes on any information you read that has a bearing on your essay, thesis, or report. And you need to work that information into your own writing eventually.

The general arts of focused reading and note-taking are explained in detail in the chapter on study techniques, on pages 434-443. But do keep this in mind: if you are inspecting a book or article as part of a research project, rather than as part of the study syllabus or exam course, you should be even more sparing and selective when doing your reading and taking your notes. First, examine the contents page and index, and skim through the text to get a feel for what is relevant and what is not. Concentrate on those chapters or sections that bear most closely on the specific topic you are researching. And sift that material very finely in turn when taking notes on its

FILE CARDS FOR RESEARCHERS

Each card typically carries a heading in the top left-hand corner. This might consist of a theme or subtopic; or the name of the author being quoted (such as *Bergson, H:*); or the word *Biblio* (for *Bibliography*).

Cards headed *Biblio* (sometimes of a different colour, and filed separately) bear the full

publishing details of the book or article that is being consulted.

This not only gives the researcher a ready-made bibliography to add at the end of the report: it also serves as a quick source when compiling footnotes or when giving the reference for a quotation.

Social divide in Victorian era

Trevelyan questions Disraeli's 'two nations' dictum.
– yes, Ind. Rev. had polarised v. rich + v. poor,
+ led to urban segregation.
But: increased the middle class, and
    improved life for the (skilled) working-class
    wage-earners.

So – far more than two nations within mid-
    Victorian England.

(Trevelyan vol 4, p.159)

Trevelyan, G. M.   (quote – Vic. marriage)
(on change from social to romantic basis of marriage
in Vic. era at last)

"... the slow and long contested evolution towards the
English love match goes on throughout our social
history until in the age of Jane Austen + the Victorians
free choice in love is accepted as the basis of marriage,
even in the best society, + any more mercenary arrangement is regarded as exceptional + suspect. The
lawless + pagan 'God of love', whose altar the
medieval poets had erected, has been baptized, // and
has settled down as a married man in the England
of Alfred Tennyson and Mr + Mrs Robert Browning."
        (Trevelyan, vol 1. pp 138-142)

Biblio

Trevelyan, G. M.

Illustrated English Social History.

4 volumes. Harmondsworth: Penguin 1949-52
(text 1942, 1944).
1964 reprint in Pelican Books.

Biblio

Rousseau, Jean-Jacques

The Social Contract.

Translated and with an Introduction by
G. D. H. Cole.
London: Dent. Everyman's Edition. 1913.

1966 reprint.

---

contents. Nothing is more discouraging, when you come to write up your report or essay, than a huge pile of undigested and semi-relevant notes: just when you thought your research was over, you have to start researching all over again – this time through your own research material.

One note-taking trick favoured by academic researchers is the use of file cards – ideally, recording only a single item of information or a single quotation on each card. The panel on page 455 illustrates various kinds of file card entry.

Once you have finished all your reading and assembled your full collection of cards, you can use them in one of two ways.

Either as a simple reference file when writing up your report or essay: if you reach a point where you need to quote word-for-word a favourite passage from a book, you just flick through your file cards and retrieve the relevant note.

Or, more creatively, as a help in constructing the essay or report: by careful reordering of the cards, you can virtually compose a draft version of the report or essay without putting pen to paper. The next move would be simply to refine that draft by transcribing the words from each card in turn – modifying them where necessary, and adding linking passages or transitions.

BIBLIOGRAPHY

Different colleges or teachers might expect different amounts of detail in the bibliography at the end of your report, essay, or research paper. Do check with fellow students, teachers, or rule books to find out just what is expected. Here, in the meantime, is a list of possible elements:

☐ the surname of the author/s or editor/s, followed by first names or initials

☐ the complete title, including any subtitle

☐ the place of publication

☐ the name of the publisher

☐ the year of publication

For example:

Else, Gerald F. *Aristotle's Poetics: The Argument*. Cambridge, Mass, 1957.

Foot, Philippa, ed. *Theories of Ethics*. Oxford, 1967.

And here is a list of possible elements in the citation of an article, essay, or chapter:

☐ the names of author/s

☐ the full title (in quotation marks)

☐ the title of the book or journal containing the work cited – plus editor's name if appropriate, place, company, and year of publication (if a book); volume number, date, page numbers of the article (if a journal)

For example:

Thompson, M. 'On Aristotle's Square of Opposition', in *Aristotle: A Collection of Critical Essays*, ed. J. Moravcsik. London, 1968. pp 51-72.

Trilling, Lionel. 'The world of power and groups'. TLS, 23 Oct 1970. pp 1223-24.

The bibliography is usually a single list in alphabetical order according to the author's name. (If the author is unknown, use the title for determining alphabetical position.) But the reader may sometimes find it helpful if you subdivide the bibliography into separate sections, such as *Primary Sources* and *Secondary Sources*.

If you are anxious to do things 'by the book', you can consult a specialist manual. But since no single system has established itself as a universally accepted authority yet, you might as well devise your own conventions.

FOOTNOTES AND OTHER REFERENCES

When you refer to an authority in your writing – whether quoting the actual words of the person or book or simply paraphrasing an idea – you must, if possible, give chapter and verse. There are three standard methods: footnotes, endnotes, and bracketed references within the text.

Footnotes. This method is the most formal and the trickiest. It is commonly used in academic dissertations. (See the panel on page 459.)

The reference differs in style from that in the bibliography. The first reference to any work typically differs in the following ways:

☐ the author's name is in the usual order: forename/s or initial/s and then surname

☐ the place and date of publication are enclosed in brackets, and the reference is generally divided up by commas rather than full stops

DESCRIBING PEOPLE

English is particularly rich in words to describe people's characters. Think, for example, of all the different words and expressions there are to describe someone who is stupid: *gormless, obtuse, moronic, crass, addle-brained, imbecilic, dunderheaded, doltish, inane, fatuous, asinine, foolhardy*, to give but a few of them.

☐ From the following lists, try to match the adjective to the description. The answers are on pages 633-648.

affable	fastidious	magnanimous	redoubtable
callow	gregarious	malleable	sagacious
complacent	gullible	ostentatious	supercilious
contrite	irascible	querulous	sycophantic
effervescent	laconic	quixotic	taciturn
enigmatic	lugubrious	recalcitrant	truculent

1. Alex – poor chap – falls for any kind of unlikely story. He is . . . . . .

2. Ben's for ever dwelling on his miseries and misfortunes. He is . . . . . .

3. Charlie's shameless, always sucking up to the boss. He is . . . . . .

4. Deidre goes around with her nose in the air, and makes you feel you're not good enough for her. She is . . . . . .

5. Eric's always whining and finding fault with things. He is . . . . . .

6. Fred – you can twist him round your little finger. He is . . . . . .

7. Gary has a deep understanding of people and events – if you ever need advice, you should go to him. He is . . . . . .

8. Harry loses his temper very easily – it can be quite alarming. He is . . . . . .

9. Ian's a real old romantic – he's always making large but really quite unrealistic gestures. He is . . . . . .

10. Joan's a woman of few words, but what she does say is pithy and often a touch sarcastic. She is . . . . . .

11. Kate apologised profusely for what she'd done – it was obvious that she felt genuinely bad about it. She is . . . . . .

12. Larry's thoroughly awkward, and seems constantly to be on the look-out for some kind of fight. He is . . . . . .

13. Molly remains generous towards those she's got the better of – not only that, she's also well-disposed towards those who've got the better of her. She is . . . . . .

14. Nell's young and inexperienced, and really doesn't know how to behave amongst grown-ups. She is . . . . . .

15. Oscar keeps his own counsel – I can never get an answer out of him. He is . . . . . .

16. Pauline bubbles with enthusiasm and joie-de-vivre. She is . . . . . .

17. Quentin's a difficult chap to work out, I find – you're never quite know what it is that makes him tick. He is . . . . . .

18. Ruth's impossible to control – thoroughly disobedient. She is . . . . . .

19. Sally's always flashing her wealth about: smart clothes, new jewellery – what a show-off. She is . . . . . .

20. Terry has a pleasant word for everyone one he meets. He is . . . . . .

21. Ulric's so fussy – things are rarely quite good enough for him. He is . . . . . .

22. Veronica . . . I wouldn't like to get on the wrong side of her. She is . . . . . .

23. Wilfred's never so happy as when he's surrounded by other people. He is . . . . . .

24. Xanthea's thoroughly pleased with herself. She is . . . . . .

Writing at Work, Home, and College

☐ a specific page reference appears at the end

☐ the first line, rather than any later line/s, is indented

Later references to the same work no longer need to supply all the details; a shorthand reference serves the purpose this time.

The best form is simply the author's surname. But if you have already cited, or intend to cite, another work by the same author, you would obviously have to repeat the title of the work as well.

Formerly, the shorthand used in later references commonly contained some strange Latin word or abbreviation. For example:

Durkheim op. cit. p. 256 – from the Latin *opere citato*, 'in the work quoted'

Durkheim loc. cit. – from the Latin *loco citato*, 'in the place cited'

ibid. p. 256 – from the Latin *ibidem*, 'in the same work and place' (used to refer to a book or article mentioned in the footnote that immediately precedes this one)

idem – Latin, 'the same, or as mentioned before' (used to refer to the identical source – work and page – mentioned in the immediately preceding footnote)

Although some publishers and editors still favour these conventions, few teachers and markers do. Far better to repeat the author's name each time, and even to repeat the page number, than to send the reader scurrying to his dictionary.

Endnotes. For shorter and more modest research assignments, such as class projects or term essays, footnotes are perhaps an unnecessary extravagance. Instead of entering each reference at the end of the relevant page, you can group all the references together in a single section at the end of the text as a whole. The style of citation remains exactly the same.

Bracketed references. Many modern books and journals, anxious to reduce the number of distracting footnotes and endnotes, adopt a system of including source references within the main text. The reference, in an ingenious shorthand form, simply appears in brackets immediately after the quotation or idea cited.

This system is based first of all on a bibliography (compiled in a slightly different style). All bracketed references implicitly cue the reader to consult the bibliography for further details of the source.

The bibliography this time gives far greater prominence to the year of publication. This item now appears as the second element each time, following the author's (reversed) name:

Foot, Philippa (ed.). 1967. *Theories of Ethics*. Oxford: OUP.

Mitty, W. Garth. 1976. *The Curve of Political History*. Baltimore: Headland Press.

—————1978. 'The Concept of Unity in Modern Historiography'. *Historia Moderna* 5: 275-92.

The reference can now be extremely streamlined. It consists simply of the author's name, the date, and the page number/s. The author's name appears inside or outside the brackets. So:

Likewise early literature. As W. Garth Mitty (1976: 170) puts it, 'the early literary embodiments of mythology mimic its unity in turn'.

PRESENTATION AND LAYOUT

Observe all the other conventions of presentation. To represent italics, for instance, you should underline the relevant words (if you are writing by hand or using a typewriter, that is – many word processors can print italics). To represent a gap in a quotation, write or type three full stops. And so on.

The chapter on punctuation (pages 212-257) should help you with most other tricky decisions.

Here is a quick list of guidelines for friendly presentation and layout of a typescript:

☐ Type neatly, on one side of the page only. Leave wide margins. Use double spacing, or at least one-and-a-half spacing. Use good A4 paper.

☐ Number the pages.

☐ Include on the first page the following elements, neatly set off by generous spacing: your name and address; the name of the marker, teacher, or lecturer, or the title of the course; the date; the title of the report or thesis.

☐ Position any tables and figures (graphs, charts, and the like) as near as possible to the relevant piece of text. Within the text, make an explicit reference to the illustration, assigning it a name or number. Repeat that name or number in the title or caption of the illustration.

FOOTNOTES IN A RESEARCH PAPER OR THESIS

Here are fragments of two consecutive pages of an academic thesis. In particular, note the difference between the detailed form of the first citation of a book and the streamlined form of its later citations. And note too how a lengthy footnote is carried over from one page to the next. Two further points. First, footnotes 2 and 3 on the first of the pages are not really straightforward references to an idea or quotation in the main text. They are 'explicatory' or 'elaborating' footnotes rather than 'authenticating' footnotes. They supply details or comments that may interest the reader but

would clog the main text if added there. Think twice before allowing such footnotes through each time. If the point really is important, you should try to accommodate it in the main body of text on the page. Secondly, footnote 3 on the first page is too long to fit unbroken on that page. You cannot move it all, however, to the second page, since the footnote indicator would still appear on the first page. And you cannot cut back on the main text of the first page to make room for the whole footnote on that page, since the footnote indicator would then move over to the second page.

---

the way that primitive world-views develop is by extrapolation from the observed power of the <u>social</u> environment – the tribal community.[1]

Whichever interpretation is correct, at least both schools agree in imputing this unifying impulse to the primitive society. But that society itself might in turn be subjected to a unified structural interpretation – by modern social anthropologists.[2] Indeed, any social community, primitive or modern, can stand (as its name implies) as an exemplar of the concept of unity.[3]

[1] Emile Durkheim, <u>The Elementary Forms of the Religious Life</u> (1912), trans. Joseph Ward Swain, second ed. (London, 1976), pp 71-86.

[2] And social anthropologists are not alone in this. Historians, epic poets, and novelists all indulge in the same presumption: see W. Garth Mitty, <u>The Curve of Political History</u> (Baltimore, 1976), p 153.

[3] Durkheim, pp 440-42, suggests that the basic mental categories of 'totality', 'unity', and 'coherence' actually derive from an impression,

---

the Homeric cycles. As W. Garth Mitty puts it, 'the early literary embodiments of mythology mimic its unity in turn.'[2]

The same hold true for early historiography: it retained much of the character of mythology, attributing social conditions or upheavals to Fortune or God or the Great Chain of Being.[3] And the Enlightenment preference for empirical explanations still characterised history as a paradigm of unity, an uninterrupted sequence of causal relationships and their manifestations.[4] Like mythology too, history tended to cast up

---

within the primitive mind, of the cohesiveness of the tribal group. Needless to say, I am citing Durkheim's speculations for their explanatory value rather than for any supposed scientific validity.

[1] Durkheim, p 249.

[2] Mitty, <u>The Curve of Political History</u>, p 170.

[3] Durkheim, p 256.

[4] Durkheim, p 259.

☐ Present the finished piece, unless it is extremely long, either in a folder – a transparent plastic folder is best – or simply fastened with a paper clip. Don't staple the pages together. A very long thesis usually calls for professional binding into the form of a large hardback book.

CHECKLIST

During a final read-through of your essay, book review, report, or other composition, make sure to ask yourself the following questions:

☐ Is the subject or purpose of the paper clearly defined for the reader?

☐ Does the paper really engage that subject or purpose? – and in a way that reflects my own views rather than just summarising or quoting the views of others?

☐ Have I backed up my views adequately with well-reasoned arguments, and have I substantiated my general statements with specific evidence and examples?

☐ What about the structure? – is the information well organised and proportioned? have I written a clear, and brief, introduction and conclusion?

In the body of the paper, does the argument jump about too much? Does it leave any loose ends or raise any unanswered questions? Are the links between arguments properly forged, and the transitions from paragraph to paragraph properly signposted?

☐ Are all the contents relevant? Perhaps some paragraphs are just digressions, and interrupt rather than aid the flow of argument?

☐ Is the wording tight and economical? – not a surplus of examples, no over-subtle distinctions, no waffle or redundancy?

☐ Is the language appropriate? No overlong sentences? Not too slangy or too high-falutin'?

☐ Is everything accurate and consistent? – the quotations, and the footnotes and bibliography references? the spelling and grammar? the spacing and style of the subheadings?

☐ Is the presentation right? Neatly written or typed? Have I remembered to write my name on the paper and to number the pages?

If you can answer all these questions to your satisfaction, the composition is ready to submit. If not, revise as best you can in the time available.

OPENING WITH A PUNCH

Start on a striking note – that is a key rule for all writing, and especially for the essay, among the most compact of forms. Seize your reader's attention with a clever image, a surprising statement, or a vivid word-picture, and he will follow you gladly into what lies beyond.

Here are three examples of striking openings from masters of the essay-writing craft.

First, a clever image. It is the start of an essay by Virginia Woolf, 'The Art of Fiction':

That fiction is lady, and a lady who has somehow got herself into trouble, is a thought that must have often struck her admirers. Many gallant gentlemen have ridden to her rescue... But [they], one felt, had a great deal of knowledge about her, but not much intimacy with her. Now comes Mr Forster...

Next, an opening that surprises the reader with a deliberately irreverent view of its subject. It

comes from 'The Two Races of Men', by the 19th-century essayist Charles Lamb:

The human species, according to the best theory I can form of it, is composed of two distinct races, *the men who borrow*, and *the men who lend*. To these two original diversities may be reduced all those impertinent classifications of Gothic and Celtic tribes, white men, black men...

Finally, a word-picture – C.P. Snow on Ernest Rutherford, discoverer of the atomic nucleus:

In 1923, at the meeting of the British Association for the Advancement of Science in Liverpool, Rutherford announced, at the top of his enormous voice: 'We are living in the heroic age of physics.' He went on saying the same thing, loudly and exuberantly, until he died, 14 years later.

The curious thing was, all he said was absolutely true...

The
Skills
of
Good
Speaking

Improving Your Voice and Speech

Mend your speech a little
Lest you may mar your fortunes.
– Shakespeare, *King Lear* (I.ii.96-97)

SPEAKING WELL can have a dramatic effect on your professional and private life. You may not realise how important the sound of your voice is, or how much you yourself judge other people by the way they sound. Yet experts maintain that the impression you make on others often owes much more to *how* you speak – the pitch and expressiveness and clarity of your voice, for example – than to *what* you actually say.

From the quality of your voice and your manner of saying things, people will deduce a great deal about your personality in general and your feelings at the moment of speaking – whether you are feeling confident, say, frightened, excited, or depressed, whether you are charming, aggressive, or friendly. They will glean information about:

☐ your age and sex – if you are speaking on the telephone and they cannot see you.

☐ your physical and psychological condition – poor health often reveals itself in the voice, as does stress.

☐ your personality – if you always speak very quickly, for example, you may give the impression of lacking confidence. If, on the other hand, you drawl your words, you will tend to sound bored or supercilious.

☐ your geographical and social origins, above all from your accent.

☐ your mood – a liltingly 'buoyant' voice, full of expressive changes of pitch and pace, suggests a buoyant mood, whereas a 'tired' or 'flat' voice suggests a more reflective, subdued mood or even depression.

☐ your intelligence or expertise – clear, confident articulation usually indicates a firm and astute grasp of a subject. Stumbling or hesitant speech often indicates confusion or uncertainty.

Such judgments are surprisingly accurate – though not invariably so. Sometimes the impression you create by the way you speak will be unfair, negative, or misleading. You may be a world expert on aviation, for instance, but if you mumble nervously when giving a lecture, you will probably come across as far less knowledgeable than you really are.

A politician may have a harsh, strident voice, or perhaps a jerky, halting style of speaking: either way, this is likely to irritate audiences, and so affect the speaker's prospects of success.

No one, however, needs to be a slave to poor speaking habits. These habits can be broken – and breaking them will certainly be worth the effort. Improve your speech, and you boost your confidence, sharpen the impression you make on others, and communicate more effectively, at work, in public, and in your private life.

Not that, in learning to speak better, you should ever speak in a way that is unnatural to you. Your voice is unique to you, just as your fingerprints are, and to distort it – as by aping a supposedly 'correct' accent – is to distort your true personality and emotional range when speaking.

Modern speech training therefore no longer aims at some standardised ideal. It focuses instead on the unique qualities of every individual voice. The process is one of exploring the natural potential of each voice and freeing it from tension; and also developing the muscularity and responsiveness of the speech organs.

In keeping with this trend, this chapter will help you to identify aspects of your voice and speech that need improvement. It will explain why you tend to sound as you do in these areas, and give exercises that will enable you to work on your voice and speech until you reach the highest level you are capable of when speaking.

What are Voice and Speech?

The first step in acquiring good speech habits is understanding why you sound as you do, and learning how to increase the power, versatility, and control of your voice and speech.

Note, first of all, that voice and speech are not the same thing. Voice is the raw sound produced when the breath vibrates the vocal cords in the throat. Speech is the more specific process of shaping into words the sound of the voice and the energy of the breath, by means of the speech organs in the head.

Voice can exist without speech, but speech cannot exist without voice. Often when you say that you like the way a man speaks, what you really mean is that you like his rich, deep voice.

The process by which voice and speech are produced is as follows:

1. The brain sends signals to the body to prepare breath for making sound.

2. The breath then travels up through the windpipe, where it meets the vocal cords. These are fleshy flexible folds, rather like elastic bands on either side of the voice box; they can open and close, and can be made tighter or looser, thicker or thinner. As the breath forces itself through the glottis (the space between the cords), the cords vibrate, producing sound.

3. These sound vibrations are in turn amplified by the resonating cavities in the body – the chest, the pharynx (the tract between mouth and gullet), the nose and sinuses, and the mouth.

4. Finally, the speech organs in the mouth – the tongue, lips, and so on – shape the sounds into recognisable speech.

The whole process is fairly similar to the workings of a violin or cello. The player's bow (the stream of breath) is drawn across the strings (the vocal cords), which vibrate to produce sound. The sound then resonates through the body of the violin or cello (the chest, pharynx, and head), and is amplified.

THE QUALITIES OF VOICE

So much for the general process by which voice and speech are produced. It is now time to analyse your own voice and speech, and the distinctive qualities that make the way you speak unique to you. These are qualities of tone, pitch, volume, and clarity. As you read this section, think about these qualities, and how you could improve them.

And try to listen to yourself critically in the course of your daily round. Invite your friends to do so too, and to give you their honest opinions.

Of course, some aspects of speech you cannot control. You cannot change, for example, the size and shape of the organs that produce voice and speech. But you can increase the muscularity and tension of your speech organs, your posture, and so on. Improving your speech lies largely within your own power.

Tone. Take an empty wine bottle and blow across its neck to produce a note. Then half-fill the bottle and blow again. You will hear two different tones. But notice that the tone produced by the empty bottle has more resonance and 'body'.

The same principle applies to your voice. Its characteristic tone is produced by the resonating cavities of your body – and the way you use them.

These cavities – the chest, pharynx, and so on, as described above – amplify your voice, but if you use them wrongly they will give your voice an unattractive tone. You need to treat them in a balanced way: if you constrict some cavities – by standing or sitting badly, say – and emphasise others excessively, you will create a 'resonance imbalance', producing a voice that might be described as nasal, metallic, or plummy.

Pitch. The pitch of your voice is determined by the length and thickness of your vocal cords. As these are stretched, they vibrate with a higher frequency, and your voice sounds shriller. As they contract, they vibrate with a lower frequency, and your voice goes deeper. Think of the cello once again: when the player tightens or loosens the strings, this raises or lowers their pitch.

There is a certain pitch at which your speaking voice operates most comfortably. By keeping to this pitch, you can avoid straining your voice.

Volume or loudness. Pitch depends on the frequency at which your vocal cords vibrate; volume depends on the strength of that vibration. You vary the volume of your voice by varying the pressure of your breath on the vocal cords; the greater the

HOW CHILDREN LEARN TO SPEAK

People have had some curious ideas, over the centuries, about children and how they learn language. One 12th-century chronicler records, for example, how the Holy Roman Emperor Frederick II 'made linguistic experiments on the vile bodies of hapless infants, bidding foster mothers and nurses to suckle and bathe and wash the children, but in no wise to prattle or speak with them.' The Emperor wanted to learn whether the babies brought up in this way 'would speak the Hebrew language (which had been the first), or Greek, or Latin, or Arabic, or perchance the tongue of their parents of whom they had been born.'

In the event, his experiments yielded no conclusive results – for, as the chronicler sadly notes, 'the children could not live without clappings of the hands, and gestures, and gladness of countenance, and blandishments.'

The evidence bears this out: children who grow up isolated from normal human contact have no knowledge or understanding of speech. There have been several well-attested cases of children brought up by animals such as wolves, leopards, pigs, and gazelles. None, when discovered, could speak.

The truth is that speech is no sudden miracle or accident. It is a result of a fascinating process of exposure and absorption, experiment and modification.

All normal babies are born with the same speech potential. They possess most of the physical mechanisms that are necessary for speech – though teeth come later – and these are versatile enough to generate the sounds of all languages equally well. From the wide repertoire of sounds at their command, however, children quite naturally begin to specialise in producing those they hear around them.

In the early months, these speech sounds represent language only in a rudimentary sense. They are a means of expressing sensations of comfort, joy, or pain. But even at this stage, children begin to identify and use particular sounds. Some of these – such as / s /, / r /, and / l / – prove more difficult than others. Such sounds may be run together, left

out, or transposed. Who has not heard words like *spway* (for spray), *'nana* (banana), and *'mato* (tomato)?

An exciting time in children's language development begins with their apparent discovery of vocabulary, then of grammar. Gradually they sort out the specific meaning or meanings of words. A little later, they pick up, if not always perfectly, the different endings that indicate plurals, past tense, and so on.

By following these newly discovered patterns too rigorously, children start using logical but incorrect forms such as *goed*, *hitted*, and *mouses*. Eventually they learn 'irregular' forms, and adapt to *went*, *hit*, and *mice*.

The environment in which children are raised is very important, though experts differ in their interpretation of the evidence. Some, for example, believe that a child with older brothers and sisters has an advantage in learning language skills; others suggest that a first-born child has the advantage. Neither view is wholly correct. If parents accept too many errors in the speech of their first-born children, for instance, they impede their command of language, while first-born children may benefit from receiving fuller attention and help.

How can you build up your child's confidence with words? Here are some suggestions:

☐ Always be ready to stimulate and assist when the child is in the mood. Don't turn speaking into a lesson, obligation, or test.

☐ Once your children have started using words rather than gestures or whimpers, encourage all their attempts to express themselves through speech. Respond more readily to a spoken request than to crying or babbling, and they will be motivated to use words all the more.

☐ Satisfy the need for conversation. Children love to talk and listen, even when they understand little about syntax. They develop their skills gradually from simple to complex patterns; and they absorb and store much good language rather than using it right away.

pressure, the stronger the vibration – and the louder the sound. You increase pressure of the breath by one or both of the following actions: breathing out with more force, and contracting your glottis – that is, narrowing the space between the vocal cords.

Draw in a deep breath, and brace yourself as if to shout – you should feel your glottis tighten sharply. By narrowing it in this way, you restrict the space through which the breath passes and so increase the pressure. By contrast, try whispering – your glottis is now completely open. You can still vary the volume of a whisper, however – not by adjusting the glottis this time, but simply by breathing out with greater or lesser force.

Clarity. The clarity of your speech is determined by the speech organs in your mouth – your tongue, lips, palate, teeth, and jaw. For clear speech, these organs need to form a number of different sounds very rapidly. They cannot do their work properly if they are either tense or lazy – all that they produce in each of these cases is indistinct mumbling.

To counter such tension or laziness, and so enunciate more clearly, you can learn to relax or to exercise the muscles of your speech organs. And as you refine the use of your facial muscles, they in turn will become more accurately expressive.

Result: you communicate more effectively – not just in speech but also through facial expression.

MAKING CHANGES

You should now be able to draw up a list: which of these four aspects of your voice and speech need attention? The chances are – to a greater or lesser extent – all of them. The next step is to do something about it. Study first the following sections on posture and breathing. They contain basic advice and exercises that everyone should follow. Then decide which of the succeeding sections apply to you. Follow their advice, and do the recommended exercises.

As you work your way through this chapter, monitor your progress if you can by means of a tape recorder. But make sure that it is a good one: poor-quality equipment tends to emphasise high frequencies, and so distorts the voice's tone. This may mislead or demoralise you.

In addition, if you are not particularly secretive about it, let a colleague, friend, or relative know what you are up to, and that you intend to change certain speech habits. Get him or her to help you by commenting on your progress and offering constructive criticism from time to time.

You may worry that if you start to adjust your speech habits you will sound artificial, and then become self-conscious about speaking. Certainly you will become more aware of your speech at first, but any sense of awkwardness will soon pass. Like dieting, giving up smoking, or learning any new skill, your conscious behaviour will in time become unconscious. The more you practise your new speaking habits, the more natural they will become, the more positive their effect on others will be, and the more you will be reinforced in them. All trace of self-consciousness will vanish in due course.

Don't forget that speaking is essentially a physical process. You will not simply be developing a greater awareness of yourself and your speaking habits: you will also be training muscles, much as an athlete does, exercising your body so that you produce a better speaking voice.

Posture and the Power of the Voice

If your posture is poor, you will present a poor image of yourself. More to the point of this chapter, you will also restrict the power of your voice. If you habitually crane your neck and thrust your chin forward, for instance, you will create tension in your throat and restrict the space in which your voice can resonate. If your shoulders slump forward, you will constrict your rib cage, and lose considerable control over your breathing. So too if you let your spine curve into an unnatural S-shape and your stomach push forward.

Contrast the voice production of a typical adult with that of a baby. How is it that a baby can yell for hours on end without any apparent damage? And that an adult attempting to shout or scream would soon end up with a sore throat and croaky voice? The difference lies in posture: the baby has not had time to develop bad postural habits that inhibit the full natural use of its body. It is as if the baby's entire body is the voice-producing instrument; the adult, by contrast, has compartmentalised his body and reduced the sources of voice production.

Tension travels very quickly through the body.

WHAT IS GOOD POSTURE?

Good posture is the natural alignment of the body. When sitting you should be able to draw a straight line from the ear to the shoulder to the hip bone, and if you are standing, from the hip down to the knee. There should be no tension at the back of the neck, or at the shoulders, elbows, wrists, pelvis, knees, or ankles. The spine takes a natural curve at the neck and at the small of the back, but in each case the curve is slight – anything more marked, and the body's natural alignment has gone wrong.

The relationship between head and neck is most important for a balanced posture. If you hold your head awkwardly, you will put a strain on your neck and shoulders. This in turn will lead you to develop further bad positioning lower down in your body to compensate for the strain in your neck, thereby extending the tension and strain throughout the body. An extreme example of poor posture is that of a sergeant major, who pulls his head right back, then pulls his shoulders back, puffs out his chest, curves his lower back, and locks his knees. Stuck in this dramatic but unnatural pose, his body becomes a mass of stresses and strains.

Tension travels very quickly through the body. If you clench your fist, for instance, and then press your forearm and even your shoulder, you will feel some transferred tension. If you continue to clench your fist and start to speak, you will sense that your jaw is tensing, and that you are literally talking through clenched teeth.

If the mere act of clenching your fist can stifle your voice somewhat, think of the damage you can do by tensing your neck or throat in the very act of speaking. If you always tilt your head downwards or thrust your chin forward when you speak, the tension produces not just a stiff neck and repeated sore throats but a habitually enfeebled and distorted voice as well.

EXERCISES WITH POSTURE

The following exercises should benefit your general posture whether sitting or standing.

☐ Lie on the floor, with a book under your head supporting it at a comfortable level. Bend your legs so that your knees point skywards, and place your feet a comfortable distance away from your body – not so close as to cause your spine to curve. Position your arms along the sides of your body – elbows bent and palms facing skywards. Let your back stretch as flat on the floor as it can. Relax in this position, letting the floor support your whole weight. Your body should maintain its position without any tensing in any part of it. Gently roll your head from side to side to check that your neck is free of tension.

☐ Stand with your back to a wall, with your heels, buttocks, shoulders, and head all touching the wall, and try to think of yourself as spreading upwards along the wall, increasing your height. Start speaking, and notice if you feel an impulse to adjust your posture in any way. If so, resist it. Repeat this exercise regularly until you learn to feel quite comfortable talking in this position.

☐ To relax your head, neck, and spine: stand upright in a clear space and lift your arms above your head. Stretch upwards, and then gently flop forwards, by bending at the waist and knees. Maintaining this position, swing your head, neck, and shoulders gently from side to side. Then, raise yourself up, slowly straightening the spine, vertebra by vertebra. Bring your head up last, taking care to ease back those important vertebrae in your neck.

FALSE FRIENDS – DECEIVING FAMILIARITY

A particular nightmare for people learning a foreign language is the 'false friend' – a word that looks familiar, but really means something quite different from what you might expect. The French word meaning 'to attend' is not *attendre* (that means 'to wait') but *assister!* False friends lurk even within English itself. The word *indifferent* looks as if it ought to mean 'similar' or, in other words, 'not different'. In fact, it means 'uninterested' or 'uncaring'.

☐ In the list below, choose the word or phrase that you believe is nearest in meaning to the key word. Answers are on pages 633-648.

disin-terested	A: bored B: unbiased C: dug up D: delayed
enervate	A: to weaken B: to strengthen C: to excite D: to frighten
enormity	A: a wide space B: great wickedness C: swelling of the joints D: tiredness
friable	A: trapped B: crumbly C: single-minded D: steamy
ingenious	A: shining B: clever C: made without skill D: stupid
insufferable	A: painful B: comfortable C: unbearable D: old enough to vote
libertine	A person who A: is immoral B: loves freedom C: gives generously D: loves books

limpid	A: awkward B: weak in character C: very clear D: clinging
lurid	A: glittering B: shocking C: dangerously attractive D: dark
munificent	A: wordly-wise B: generous C: explosive D: well-dressed
noisome	A: riotous B: irritating C: bloody D: disgusting
officious	A: overhelpful B: boringly routine C: hard-working D: totally miraculous
protestation	A: a supportive suggestion B: boastful behaviour C: a religious objection D: a firm declaration
remonstrate	A: to climb aboard B: to try again C: to exaggerate D: to protest

solicitous	A: argumen-tative B: attractive C: concerned D: wanting to be alone
stricture	A: brainwave B: punishment C: virtue D: criticism
temerity	A: recklessness B: drunkenness C: embarrass-ment D: piety
tortuous	A: reptilian B: high C: twisting D: painful
unsparingly	A: untidily B: abundantly C: wastefully D: inconsid-erately
unstudied	A: lazy B: rare C: natural D: little-known
vicarious	A: by means of a substitute B: pretending to be religious C: having many different parts D: extremely wicked or cruel

☐ Another useful exercise for relaxing the neck: stretch the back of your neck by dropping your head forward. Link your hands together behind your head. Tilt your head gently from side to side, then raise and lower it, then move it in small circles. Imagine all the while that your back and neck are spreading outwards, growing larger and wider. Keep your face forward all the time to ensure that the muscles in your neck are gently eased rather than twisted.

☐ Nod very gently while you talk: this breaks the habit of holding the neck and head in an unnaturally rigid position.

☐ To relax your shoulders, roll them gently backwards and forwards. Lift them up to your ears in small stages, and then allow them to drop down suddenly. Curl them forward, and then thrust them backwards. The more responsive your muscles become to specific instructions, the easier it will be for you to control them if they become tense.

And here, now, are a few further tips:

☐ Getting someone to massage you can be very effective in ridding the neck and shoulders of unwanted tensions.

☐ To master a balanced yet relaxed standing position, imagine yourself as being held up by a rope fixed at the top of your head: the rope eases you upwards. Distribute the weight of your body so that two-thirds of it falls on the balls of your feet and a third on your heels.

Keep your knees slightly bent, as if you were readying yourself for a small jump. Shake your arms and hands gently to loosen and relax your elbows, wrists, and fingers. Then let them hang loosely at the sides of your body, but taking care not to tense up your back and shoulders. Nod your head and roll your shoulders gently.

☐ When sitting, make sure that the back of your chair supports your weight. Sit well back in your chair, so that your posture is upright yet relaxed.

How to Control Your Breathing

Breath is the energy source of voice and speech. To speak well, you need economical and well-controlled breathing. Think once again of the baby: within his tiny body, the breathing apparatus works to full potential, helping to produce that amazingly powerful voice.

To breathe well, you need to use three sets of muscles – your diaphragm (the dome-shaped sheet of muscle below your lungs), your abdomen muscles, and the muscles around your ribs.

If you habitually misuse any of these, or have allowed them to become lazy, you are probably breathing less efficiently than you could be.

Breathing, or respiration, is an unconscious process. That is, you do not have to make a deliberate effort to draw in or expel your breath. But this is not to say that you cannot take conscious control of your breathing: you can, and in doing so, you can develop the muscles that govern it.

These muscles work in the following way. For inhaling, they flatten the diaphragm and let the ribs swing upwards and sideways. This creates space in the lungs, and draws in air automatically. For exhaling, the same muscles cause the diaphragm to rise, and the ribs to drop downwards and inwards.

The lungs are compressed and breath is expelled. This entire process becomes easier and more efficient if you use the lower half of your chest for breathing. The reason for this is twofold: first, your lungs are pear-shaped, and are therefore more spacious in their lower halves. Secondly, your rib cage is more flexible and less enclosed at its lower edge: the upper section is more rigid, being attached at the front to your breast bone.

This efficient breathing from the lower half of your chest is 'abdominal breathing', so named because your abdomen rises and falls with the pressure of your diaphragm. If you observe the way a baby breathes, you will see that his tummy rises when he inhales and flattens as he exhales. He is using abdominal breathing, the easiest, most natural, and most efficient form of breathing.

BREATH AND THE VOICE

Since it is your breath that powers your voice, it follows that your voice will suffer if your breathing is inadequate. Here are some dangers to avoid:

☐ A traditional piece of advice – to take a deep breath before making any sort of effort – is usually bad advice for a speaker. If you take a deep breath when physically tense, your instinct will be to hold your breath, as if bracing yourself for something bad to happen. If you then start to speak, your breath will rush out under great pressure, producing either a strangulated voice (if your vocal cords are tense) or an excessively breathy voice (if the vocal cords are not fully closed). So avoid taking in large gulps of breath if you are about to speak.

☐ The opposite danger is of drawing too little breath before speaking – as a result of poor posture, for instance. A voice underpowered in this way would tend to come across as excessively quiet. But a speaker may try to compensate for this by straining his or her voice. Invariably, the effect of such straining is a harsh, discordant quality in the voice.

☐ Uncontrolled breathing can affect your ability to communicate in another way too. If your breathing is audible when you speak, your listeners are likely to be distracted by it. They will attend to your manner of speaking rather than to the substance, and your message will pale beside the jerky style of your delivery.

BREATH AND STRESS

Unfortunately, few adults breathe in the easy, natural way that a baby does. Most people develop different breathing patterns for different activities.

The worst habits are those developed to cope with stress. A typical stress reaction involves tensing of the shoulders, chest, and neck, followed by a rapid snatching of breath into the upper part of the chest. The function of this instinctual response is to produce a sharp intake of extra oxygen, in preparation for launching an attack or running away from danger. However, such physical activity is hardly likely to occur in most stress situations today – speaking in public, for instance, or sitting in a traffic jam – and the surge in oxygen has no useful effect at all. This 'clavicular breathing' as it is known (after the 'clavicle' or shoulder bone), consists of short, sharp, audible gulps of breath, with clearly visible effort and movement in the chest and shoulders. Wasted effort, for the most part.

And sometimes, actually detrimental effort. By gasping in quick doses of oxygen, you risk overoxygenating your bloodstream and hence your brain. In technical terms, you are 'hyperventilating'. This can make you light-headed and panicky.

The surge in oxygen has no useful effect at all.

Conversely, well-controlled breathing can bring stress under control. If you get into a panic state, you can restore calm by modulating your out-breath, sighing out smoothly and slowly.

Breathing exercises can help you to control stress and at the same time to develop your voice control.

EXERCISES WITH BREATHING

The following exercises are designed to improve your habits of breathing out – after all, you are breathing out rather than in when you talk. Accordingly, don't adjust your usual way of breathing in.

Try not to tense your body anywhere when you do these exercises. Keep checking that your neck, shoulders, and face are relaxed. And don't create tension by trying desperately to get each exercise 'right' straight away. The exercises are for gradual development, not immediate achievement.

Floorwork. Lie on the floor with a book supporting your head at a comfortable level. Bend your legs so that your knees point skywards, and place your feet a comfortable distance away from your body. Relax your back so that it feels as if it is lengthening and widening along the floor. Place your hands on your abdomen, and pant gently, noting the movement of your diaphragm. Then breathe in easily, feeling your stomach rise as you inhale, and lowering as you exhale. This is to help you to learn the movement of the diaphragm and abdomen. Here, now, are some refinements on this exercise.

☐ Breathe in gently – feel your breath dropping into your body comfortably and naturally – and then breathe out on a count of 1. Breathe in again, but this time let your breath out on a count of 2. Follow this procedure up to a count of 6 or 7. This teaches you conscious control over the rate at which you breathe out.

☐ Continuing to keep your hand on your abdomen, breathe out slowly and give a long sigh as you do so, vibrating your vocal cords gently. This teaches you how little effort is needed to produce sound.

☐ Take a breath, then start to breathe out slowly; after a couple of seconds, count aloud from 1 to 5. Keep your hand on your abdomen, and resist the urge to snatch in your breath again as soon as you begin speaking. Resist too the urge to speak as soon as your lungs are full of air. This exercise will help you to control and pace your speech in relation to your breathing.

Repeat these exercises while touching either side of your lower ribs, and feel how their movement is involved in voice production. It should become increasingly clear to you just how much space there is for breath in the middle or 'centre' of your body. A 'centred' person, one who knows how to control breathing for maximum benefit, usually appears relaxed, confident, and alert.

Sitting and standing. Now check your posture again, and then your breathing, when in sitting and standing positions. Use a mirror to ensure that your body is well aligned, and that your shoulders and chest do not rise as you breathe.

☐ Repeat the second exercise from the above section, once while sitting and once while standing. Check regularly that you have not become tense or stiff.

☐ Seat yourself at a table, and read out loud from a book or newspaper placed in front of you. Keep a hand on your stomach; whenever you inhale, you should feel your stomach pushing out as you draw breath low into your lungs. Tape-record yourself while reading, and check that your intake of breath is audible. If you hear a gasping sound, this indicates continued tension in your body.

Pace, Pause, and Rhythm

The way you breathe affects the rhythm and pace of your speech – adversely, in the case of clavicular breathing. By snatching short, sharp breaths in the upper chest, you force yourself to breathe too often to sustain your voice. Your speech will be punctuated by unnatural pauses and gasps.

Abdominal breathing, on the other hand, allows you to sustain your voice for longer periods of time.

By drawing larger amounts of oxygen into the lower half of your lungs, you will not need to pause for breath so often. Your speech will sound more natural, since you can pause to breathe at natural breaks in your sentences: where the commas and full stops would be in written prose.

Pausing at these natural breaks provides a further benefit: it gives you a moment to think about what you are going to say next, and so control the content of your speech. All the more so because relaxed, abdominal breathing regulates the oxygen supply to the brain and so aids clear thinking.

PACE AND PAUSE

The rapid speaker, more than anyone, needs to concentrate on correct breathing and pausing. Speaking rapidly is not necessarily a bad thing. But the rapid speaker has to meet several conditions to be easily understood. First, his articulation must be clear; secondly, he must breathe well; thirdly, he must use pauses effectively. Pausing allows the speaker time to recharge and it gives the listener a chance to absorb what has been said.

If you speak quickly, ask yourself why you do so. Perhaps you are nervous. Or perhaps you feel uncomfortable with silence, and therefore chatter to maintain a continuous flow of sound. More positively, you may be very enthusiastic about a subject, or overflowing with ideas and in a rush to express them. Whatever the reason, do force yourself to pause. If you do not, you may become muddled – you may also irritate or confuse those listening to you.

A slow, ponderous speaker can be just as irritating – and will bore the audience. If you ever notice your listeners' attention wandering, try to speed up your pace. But don't cut back on the pauses.

EXERCISES WITH PACE AND PAUSE

You can teach yourself to pause by concentrating on your breathing pattern. Here are some exercises to teach you how to do that.

☐ Read aloud from a newspaper or book. Just before you run out of breath, say aloud, 'I pause and I breathe.' Take time to inhale, and let your breath drop low, as if into your stomach. Then continue reading on the outbreath. Every time you need to breathe, say the words, 'I pause and I breathe.' Continue the exercise until you feel comfortable using the phrase, and are breathing deeply and regularly. Using a tape recorder can help to monitor this. Then continue reading aloud, but this time say the phrase 'I pause and I breathe' silently in your mind.

☐ With the help of a friend, try the same exercise in ordinary conversation. Choose a simple subject – perhaps what you have done so far that day. Your friend will check that you are pausing and breathing regularly.

☐ If you tend to be overeager, and to rush your speech, ask a friend to fire questions at you. Wait until the end of each question before breathing in. Concentrate on the feeling of your breath dropping into your lungs. Then start to breathe out, and answer in your own time.

RHYTHM

The rhythm of your speech is also closely linked to your breathing habits. It is your breathing that dictates how much energy is available for the flow of speech, and where the breaks come.

Unrhythmical speech grates on the ear. If your speaking rhythm is halting and jerky, broken by frequent gasps for breath, try some of the exercises on relaxation and breath control opposite.

Or try this useful tip: set up a smooth, flowing movement in your body, such as gently nodding your head or swinging a hand from side to side, before you start to speak. Keep this movement going while you speak, and your speech should adopt the smooth rhythm of your physical movement. Practise this regularly, until you become fully familiar with the sensation. In due course, the new speech rhythm will replace the old one, and you can discontinue the accompanying body movements.

Pitch and Intonation

Don't confuse pitch and tone. The pitch of your voice is determined by the length and thickness of your vocal cords, as explained on page 463. You alter it by stretching or relaxing the cords. Tone, on the other hand, is determined by how you use the resonating spaces in your body. If these are restricted because of tension in the body or poor posture, your voice will sound less 'full' and 'rich' than it otherwise might – it will tend to sound reedy and strained.

Poor use of pitch can spoil a good speaking voice. Some speakers tend to stretch their voice beyond its natural limits – resulting in a forced and unattractive sound. Others do not stretch their voices enough – and so tend to sound monotonous when they are speaking.

Here are a number of the ways in which people commonly use pitch poorly, together with some exercises and suggestions to help you to improve your own use of pitch.

SPEAKING TOO HIGH OR TOO LOW

Every voice has a natural middle note. Some speakers habitually pitch their voices too high, especially when under stress – when beginning an important speech for instance. The cause is tension in the throat muscles: the remedy is repeated practising of the neck exercises outlined on pages 466 and 468. The opposite fault is pitching the voice too low – often in an attempt to sound confident. Pushed down beyond its natural limit in this way, the voice can again sound forced and unnatural.

Learn to identify and adapt your middle note. You will sound most natural if you speak around this pitch. Here are two ways of finding it.

☐ Use a piano to help you. Speak at the lowest note that feels comfortable, and then find the note on the piano that corresponds to this. Now move four or five notes up the scale. This should be your middle note.

☐ Try intoning, as if taking part in a cathedral or church service. This should take you automatically to your middle note. Listen to yourself intone, then start to speak on the same note.

CORRECTING YOUR PITCH RANGE

A moderate lilt makes for an interesting voice. Not that you should attempt sharp fluctuations in pitch when speaking, but you must vary the pitch somewhat, and avoid droning in a monotone – or your listeners' attention will start to stray. If your range of pitch is too narrow, you need to tone up the muscles that affect speech. Here are some exercises for doing this:

☐ Practise changing pitch. Say out loud the sentence 'I can make my voice go higher and higher', and make it actually go higher at the same time. Then say, 'I can make my voice go lower and lower', while doing precisely that.

If you find you are not changing pitch smoothly, try conducting yourself, by using your arm as a baton. Raise your arm when you want your pitch to rise, and lower your arm when you want your pitch to fall. Make sure that it is just the pitch that changes, and not the volume. A tape recorder will help you to check this.

☐ Practise changing pitch up and down within the space of a few words. Take the statement 'I can do that', and say it in four different ways:

I can do that

I can do that

I can do that

I can do that

☐ Read aloud from a newspaper. As you start a new point, or a new paragraph, consciously change pitch so that your voice emphasises the change in the content.

☐ Sing and hum as much as you can. This will increase your awareness of the many possible uses of pitch.

☐ Practise using pitch to reflect the emotional content of your speech. Practise saying each of the following statements twice in succession: first, as flatly as you can; then as emotionally as you can, using pitch to express the emotion.

Congratulations! A new job!
Please don't kick the cat.
I won't go. Never. Don't ever ask me again.
That's an interesting thought . . .

☐ Listen carefully to yourself, and then draw a line above each statement showing how your pitch changes (as in the examples above).

The opposite fault is overcolouring your speech by using too many pitch changes. This gives the voice an artificial, insincere quality – more like singing than talking, and with the pitch changes out of step with the meaning of the words.

If you speak in this way, try the last exercise above, drawing lines to correspond to your pitch changes. You will probably find that you raise your pitch markedly on nouns. Try deliberately dropping your pitch a fraction on these words.

USING A REPETITIVE INFLECTION PATTERN

Inflection is the 'tune' of your speech – the pattern of your pitch changes. Even if you colour each sentence by changing pitch appropriately each time, you might still have a dull voice and limited range of expression – unless you vary the 'tune' from sentence to sentence.

One common mannerism is to raise the pitch at the end of every phrase or sentence – to 'inflect upwards'. This is the natural intonation for questions, but if you use it for statements as well (as many Australians do), you will sound hesitant, as though seeking a response from your listeners. Compare these two examples:

Let's go and see Martin. If we find him there,

we can go out for tea. Shall we?

Let's go and see Martin. If we find him there,

we can go out for tea. Shall we?

Sound out these pitch patterns, and you will hear that the speaker in the second example sounds far more controlled and decisive. The first speaker, by contrast, sounds timid and uncommitted.

The opposite fault is to 'inflect downwards' habitually – to use a falling pitch all the time. The effect of such a 'tune' is one of finality – as if everything has already been decided. This uninviting tone discourages free discussion.

To change a repetitive pitch pattern, try 'conducting your speech'. Once again – use your arm as a baton. When you find yourself inflecting upwards, pull your arm downwards to counteract the impulse. If you tend to drop your pitch at the end of each phrase, keep raising your arm to raise your pitch. As usual, a tape recorder will help to regulate the changes. Or a progress report from a friend, even on the basis of five minutes' listening a day, will help you to change a bad habit.

Emphasis and Resonance

As you experiment with your pitch and intonation, consider also your use of emphasis when speaking. Changes in emphasis – the amount of stress put on a syllable – often accompany changes in pitch. The placing of the emphasis (usually on a noun or pronoun) often affects the meaning of a sentence. Compare the following requests:

Would you put that on the *table*, please?
(rather than on the window sill)

Would *you* put that on the table, please?
(everyone else is busy)

Would you put *that* on the table, please?
(not *this* object which has to remain
on the floor)

Would you put that *on* the table, please?
(instead of *under* it, as you did last time)

Clearly then, emphasis is vital to meaning. But a speaker who uses too much emphasis will sound hectoring, like a teacher talking to small children:

X *Would* you *put that* on the *table, please*?

Some people, public speakers and television reporters in particular, use far too much emphasis. They have a message to get across, and they try to drive it home by emphasising it repeatedly. Ironically, this often just alienates listeners, rather than convincing them.

To check on any overemphasising of your own, listen once again to a tape-recording of yourself. If you do emphasise too many words when you speak, make a conscious effort to reduce the number of stresses – only one or two per sentence. Again, use your hand as a baton to conduct yourself: hold your hand in front of your body, and bring it down only on words that need emphasising.

RESONANCE

The voice vibrates in different parts of the body, producing its characteristic resonance. To observe this in action, try the following experiments.

☐ Place a hand on your chest, and sound a low, continuous / hō /. You should feel vibrations in your rib cage. Tap your chest as you make the sound, and notice how this affects your voice.

☐ Try humming the sound / mmm /, and you will feel vibrations on your lips. Make the nasal sounds / ning /,/ nong /,/ nang /: if you then touch the sides of your nose, you should feel vibrations.

The voice works best when all the resonating spaces in the body are fully open and all the vibrating surfaces are free. Don't slump and curve your chest; don't tense and constrict your neck, throat, or tongue; don't clench your jaw.

The neck and throat. To hear the changeable resonance in these areas, sound a low, continuous / hō / again, changing the position of your head as you do so – first tilting it backwards, then restoring it to its normal position, then dropping it forwards onto your chest.

In the first position, with your head tilted backwards and your neck and throat muscles tensed as a result, your voice would have sounded thin and half-strangulated. If you think your voice often sounds like this, try these two exercises.

☐ Breathe in properly, as if dropping your breath low into your body, and then sigh gently as you breathe out. Make it sound like a sigh of relief, as if something is over and done with. Check that your head and neck are well aligned and free of tension. If necessary, rid your neck of tension by nodding your head gently.

☐ Open your mouth wide and breathe in fairly fast, as if yawning. Feel the air on the back of your throat, and then release it by opening your throat as wide as you can. Yawning provides good relaxation for the voice. Now try talking out loud and, as you do so, pronounce all your vowels by again opening your throat as wide as possible. Stretch out each vowel and think of it as pressing your throat outwards.

The soft palate. This lies at the back of the mouth, and is a common site of tension. To locate this area, pronounce the syllable / kə / and then / gə /, sharply emphasising the consonant each time. Then say these sounds in a more relaxed way, and end with a yawning / aa /. The first / kə / and / gə / should identify the position of your soft palate for you. Sounding the final / aa / will have the effect of opening and relaxing your throat.

The tongue. If the muscles of your tongue are too slack or the back of your tongue too tense, this will reduce the space in your mouth for resonance. As a result, the tone of your voice will be muffled and unclear. Here are some remedies.

☐ Loosen up your tongue by darting it in and out of your mouth. Each time you poke it out, stretch it down towards your chin.

☐ Relax your tongue, then poke it out and swing it gently from side to side.

☐ Sound out the syllable / hō / slowly, while positioning your tongue low in your mouth, with its tip touching your lower front teeth. Then start talking out loud, as in the yawning exercise, and stretching out your vowels. Feel how your tongue now returns to the floor of your mouth with its tip near your bottom teeth.

The jaw. A clenched jaw prevents a rich and open tone of voice. It tends to produce an aggressive tone. The tension is often visible with the jaw muscles bulging and twitching just in front of the ears. Here are some exercises to overcome this problem.

☐ To relax your jaw, stroke it gently downwards with your hands until it opens. Don't move your jaw from side to side – this is an unnecessary and unnatural movement.

☐ Hold your chin in one hand and rest your elbow on a table. Keeping your jaw cupped in your hand, tilt your head backward. Now open your mouth and feel your upper teeth and head lift away, while your lower jaw remains where it is.

☐ Take your chin in your hand, and relax the muscles in your jaw. Then gently jiggle your jaw up and down with your hand. Your jaw should be completely relaxed, so that your hand is doing all the work.

The nose. To make certain sounds, called 'nasal sounds', you have to release breath through your nose. Try making the sounds / mm /, / nn /, / ng /; then pinch your nose and try making these sounds again. It cannot be done. (Hence the changes in some consonants when you have a cold: the name *Manning*, for instance, sounds like *Badding*.)

A clear voice therefore requires a clear nose, for breath to pass through. But it is also possible to release too much breath through your nose. If you allow air to escape through your nose while pronouncing vowels, for instance, you will produce a nasal twang. Try pinching your nose while making the vowel sounds. These should not alter: if they do, you are using too much nasal resonance.

Here are some ways of dealing with this problem.

☐ Turn back to the final exercise in the section on the neck and throat (page 473). This will improve your awareness and control of your soft palate, which regulates the release of air into the nose.

☐ Make the following sounds in sequence: / ng /, / kə /, / gaa /. Note how the / ng / is made in the nose, while the vowel sounds of / kə / and / gaa / are made by means of the soft palate and the mouth respectively.

Articulation – Turning Voice into Speech

What turns voice into speech is the action of the speech organs of the head. These are:

☐ the tongue – both the tip and the back of the tongue are used to produce different sounds

☐ the lips

☐ the soft palate – this is movable; it lies at the back of the roof of the mouth

☐ the hard palate – this is immovable; it lies in front of the soft palate at the top of the mouth

☐ the dental ridge – this is just behind the upper front teeth

☐ the jaw

The speech organs form vowels and consonants, and thereby produce words. Vowels are created by the free movement of breath through the mouth. They derive their distinctive qualities by the arrangement of the speech organs in the mouth. Consonants are created when the speech organs form an obstruction to the stream of breath.

VOWELS

Vowels are formed by the movement of the tongue and lips. These organs change the resonating shape of the mouth, and so alter the sound of the air stream travelling through that space.

For maximum distinctness, your vowels should have an 'open' tone. Here are ways of ensuring it.

☐ Relax your jaw and the back of your tongue.

☐ Raise your soft palate.

☐ Make as much space in your mouth as you can.

☐ Position the tip of your tongue as often as possible behind your lower front teeth (see the exercise opposite).

There are three sorts of vowels: pure vowels, diphthongs, and triphthongs.

Pure vowels. These travel from the back, the middle, and the front of the mouth. The following sounds travel from near the back of the mouth: / ōo / (hoot), / ŏŏ / (hook), / aw / (hawk), / o / (hot).

These travel from the middle of the mouth: / er / (heard), / ə / (as in the first syllable of *ahead*), / u / (hut), / aa / (hard).

And these travel from the front of the mouth: / ee / (heed), / i / (hid), / a / (had).

Diphthongs. These are vowels that glide. That is, the tongue and lips shift position as they form the vowel, and create two sounds that glide together.

Diphthongs in English are / ō / (hoe), / ow / (how), / oy / (ahoy), which are formed by the lips; and / ay / (hay), / ī / (high), / air / (hair), / eer / (here), which are formed by the tongue.

Triphthongs. There are two common triphthongs, or three-part glides, in English: / īr / (hire), and / owr / (hour).

EXERCISES WITH VOWELS

To improve the quality of your vowels, practise speaking out loud a vowel sequence, such as the ones following. Take your time, forming each sound accurately but without tension.

> hoot, hook, hawk, hot, heard, hut, hard, heel, hid, head, hand

> hoe, how, ahoy, hay, high, hair, here, hire, hour, shower

If you want to check that your vowels emerge without a nasal twang, repeat the exercise while pinching your nose. Listen (on a tape recorder if possible) for any tell-tale change in the quality of the vowel sound. You can make the exercise more difficult by using a nasal sound in front of the vowels and then performing the nose-pinching test:

> moot, mook, mawk, mot, murder, mud, mart, meal, mid, mead, man, men

> mow, meow, moy, may, my, mare, mere, mire, mour

CONSONANTS

There are two main sorts of consonant: known as plosives and continuants.

Plosives. These are sounds formed through the obstruction of the breath stream by the tongue or lips (the word is related to *explosive*). These organs first stop the breath, then release it with a distinctive sound. The plosive sounds are: / p /, / b /, / k /, / g /, / t /, / d /, / ch /, / j /. Sound them out while watching your face in a mirror, and observe how they are formed.

Continuant consonants. These are formed by a partial blockage of the breath stream. The sounds are: / ng /, / m /, / n /, / l /, / r /, / s /, / z /, / f /, / v /, / th /(as in *thin*), / th / (as in <u>th</u>ose). Try making these sounds, and you will find that, unlike the plosives, they continue as long as your breath lasts.

Both plosives and continuants are further subdivided into 'voiced' and 'voiceless' (or 'unvoiced') consonants. As these names suggest, voiced consonants are made by vibrating your vocal cords, while unvoiced consonants require no assistance from the vocal cords. The sound / p /, for example, is voiceless, whereas / b / is voiced: you cannot produce a *b*-sound without letting your vocal cords vibrate. Try making the following sounds, and decide which one in each pair is voiced, and which voiceless: / k / and / g /; / s / and / z /; / f / and / v /.

The consonants, then, are formed as your speech organs move to restrict, block, redirect, and release your breath. To articulate your speech well, you need to form each consonant clearly. And that means positioning your speech organs carefully and correctly for each sound. Your speech organs need to be agile and energetic to do this; if they are lazy, your speech will sound sloppy and imprecise – as in the Cockney *tha's my favouri' stree'*.

The Skills of Good Speaking

Accordingly, you need to tone up the muscles of your speech organs. For a start, make a conscious effort to hit the final consonants of words – especially *t*'s and *d*'s. For a more long-term remedy, try the exercises described below.

Remember, while doing them, to check that your breathing is regular and your body relaxed. In particular, avoid tensing your neck and shoulders and your jaw. Warm up your facial muscles by first chewing an imaginary sweet.

EXERCISES WITH CONSONANTS

Form each consonant very precisely, using plenty of movement and energy to make the different sounds. Go slowly at first, concentrating on each sound as you form it. Repeat each exercise four or five times, speeding up as you go.

Note that most consonants are grouped in pairs: two sounds formed in exactly the same way in the mouth, but differing in that one is voiced and the other unvoiced.

/ **p** /, / **b** / The lips, after first closing to stop the breath, then part quickly to release the breath with a crisp, popping sound.

> Plant the pretty pink pansies in the pots.
> Practice promotes perfect pronunciation.
> Poor Peter panics when poodles are present.
> Banish the booming blast of that bassoon.
> Boring books belong below, in the basement.
> The big black bull bellowed as Belinda blundered into the bath.

/ **t** /, / **d** / The tongue tip, after touching the dental ridge to stop the breath, drops rapidly to release the sound of the consonant.

> Take those tiny terrors to the teacher.
> Tennis is too tiring and tough to tolerate.
> Tell Tom to tidy this terrible tip.
> Don't dare describe the dreadful defeat.
> David showed daring, dedication, and some decisiveness in doing the deed.

/ **k** /, / **g** / The back of the tongue rises to meet the soft palate and stop the breath before releasing it by dropping quickly.

> Can you count the currency of this country?
> Cream cakes require careful cooking.
> The grey goat grazed greedily.
> Gordon gave the gardener a gift of glorious green galoshes.

/ **ch** /, / **j** / The tip of the tongue, placed against the dental ridge to stop the breath, withdraws slowly, releasing the sound as the breath rushes past.

> The chancellor chose to check the church.
> Choose the cherries and the cheese.
> Chuck chewed the chocolate cheerily.
> January, June, and July are generally jolly.
> The judge joked jovially.
> The budgie jumped onto John's jumper.

/ **m** / The lips close to block the breath; the soft palate descends and the breath escapes through the nose.

> Make mine a martini, Martin.
> Move those massive mounds of mud.
> Many men have mournful memories of the magnificent Major.
> Martha and Mildred made merry in the moonlight.

/ **ng** / The back of the tongue rises and the soft palate descends to block the breath at the back of the mouth; once again, the breath escapes through the nose.

> The singing and shouting were ringing out.
> Bring those things off the wings into the hangar.
> The king tied the ring on with string.

/ **l** / There are two sorts of *l*-sound in spoken English, the 'clear *l*' and the 'dark *l*'. Clear *l*'s occur at the beginning of words (*loud*), and dark *l*'s at the end (*call*). Both types of *l* are made in much the same way: the tip of the tongue is placed on the dental ridge, and the breath is forced around the sides of the tongue. However, for dark *l*'s, the front of the tongue (not the tip) is slightly lower, and the back of the tongue raised higher. Follow the movements of your tongue as you say the word *little*, which starts with a clear *l* and ends with a dark *l*.

> Little lambs are leaping lightly.
> Laughing Larry likes lollipops.
> Pull the full pail from the well.
> Light the lamp with the long spill.

/ **r** / The tongue tip rises to touch the hard palate, just behind the dental ridge. In this position, the tongue causes vibrations in the steady stream of breath. In some English accents and foreign languages, the tongue tip itself vibrates or rolls on the dental ridge. This is known as 'tapping' one's *r*'s. In French, the back of the tongue rolls on the lowered soft palate to produce the distinctive 'throaty' *r*.

Some speakers do not raise their tongues enough, and so produce a sound rather like / w / instead of / r /: *We wan out of the way of the wunaway wailway twain.* In some cases, people simply cannot pronounce their *r*'s – they are what is known as 'short-tongued': see the section on impediments, page 478. Other speakers introduce *r*-sounds where they have no right to be: *The minister for law rand order went back to the drawring board.*

Roderick Random ruefully rang the robber.
The red robot was ready when Robert rang.
Roger, Richard, and Rodney recklessly raced Ralph and Rupert.
Remember that ruthless writer who ran rings round her rivals.

/ **s** /, / **z** /, / **sh** / The tongue tip presses against the ridge of the upper front teeth for / s / and / z /, allowing the breath to escape through a channel along the top of the tongue. The jaw is almost closed, but should not be tense. If the tongue tip is placed too far forward, the sound will approach / th /, producing a lisp. If the tongue tip is too loose on the roof of the mouth, too much air escapes around the sides of the tongue, and the sound will resemble / c /, a 'lateral *s*'. If the tongue tip is placed too tightly against the roof of the mouth, the sound is an overharsh hiss. Try to get the correct position and pressure if you produce faulty *s*-sounds.

For / sh /, the tongue is more curled than when sounding / s /, and the tongue tip positioned against the roof of the mouth rather than the dental ridge. (The voiced version of / sh /, rare in spoken English, is / zh /, as in *pleasure*.)

Six sailors saw the ship sailing out to sea.
'That's so silly,' said Sarah to Samantha.
Miss Marples risked assassination when solving the case of the silver spur.
The zebra zigzagged lazily through the zoo.
Surely syrup, sweets, and sherbet cause spots.

/ **f** /, / **v** / The bottom lip presses against the top front teeth, allowing the breath to escape through the available gaps.

Frank fought to free his friend.
You'll find the fresh food in the fridge.
Follow the frantic fat fellow through the forest foliage.
The vain vicar is verbose, but his vespers are very vivid.
Five frightened victims fled the vile vampire.
He took an evil, vicious, and violent revenge.

/ **th** /, / **th** / The tongue tip touches the back of the top front teeth (further forward than for / s /), or rests between the top and bottom front teeth.

The / th / in *thin* is voiceless and takes greater breath pressure than the / th / in *those*, which is voiced. (In some dialects, / th / and / th / sound more like / f / and / v /, and in others they sound like / t / and / d /.)

Thirty thousand thrilled fans thronged the theatre.
Throw those things onto the path, or they will think you a thief.
Those theological theories are enthralling.

/ **y** / To form this 'semivowel' (functioning as a consonant, but gliding into a vowel sound) the middle part of the tongue rises to the hard palate and then withdraws, releasing the sound, and gliding into a vowel.

He yearned to sail the yellow yacht.
Yolanda yielded her yoghurt to the yokel.
The Yankee youngster yelled for a yard of yarn.
Yes, you have to use the yolks with the yams.

/ **w** / To form this semivowel, the lips are rounded and stretched forward as if to make the vowel / oo / (as in *poor*). Practising this sound can benefit your speech generally – helping to improve resonance and volume control. If you really stretch your lips forward in doing these exercises, you will rapidly tone up the muscles of your lips. (In some dialects, words spelt *wh*- are pronounced / hw /, with a distinct breathing sound at the start.)

Use the words *when, what, why,* and *where* when asking questions.
The wily, white wolf was wandering in the wild woods.
You will wash my wet woollen windcheater willingly, won't you?

/ **h** / The vocal cords remain open, and the breath-stream rushes over them to produce vibration and sound. In some words, the initial *h* is silent, of course: *honest, heir, hour.* But don't drop your *h*'s elsewhere, as in *I 'ope 'arry 'elps us.*

Hard hats are handy headgear when handling heavy loads.
Henry, Harold, and Hilary heartlessly harangued the horrible horseman.
You just have to hope for happiness.
He helped her hunt for her book of a hundred household hints.

Pronunciation – Impediments and Speech Habits

Some people have great difficulty in making certain speech sounds.

There are two possible reasons for this: a physical impediment; and an acquired habit or accent.

IMPEDIMENTS

These vary in seriousness: some are fairly easy to overcome, others very difficult or impossible. Take the relatively minor physical impediment of being what is commonly known as 'short-tongued', but which, in fact, is a result of a short 'fraenum' (the flap that connects the underside of the tongue to the floor of the mouth). This restricts the speaker's freedom to stretch his or her tongue upwards and forwards, and may cause difficulties when it comes to pronouncing *r*'s. A professional speech therapist may well help the speaker to learn techniques for counteracting the effects of the impediment.

HABITS AND ACCENTS

Faulty pronunciation stems more commonly from bad habits of the speech organs rather than malformation or malfunctioning. These habits include, for instance, tension and laziness (discussed above).

A person's accent, really a whole set of speaking habits, often marks him out as a 'faulty' speaker, as with a Cockney who habitually substitutes / f / for / th /: *I fink I'll frow a party on Fursday.*

If the speech organs function properly and are capable of making the correct sound, they simply need re-educating in order to acquire new habits.

Such re-educating is the function of the exercises throughout this chapter. But practice on one's own cannot guarantee a cure. Speakers whose difficulties persist should consider turning to a speech therapist for help.

Accent is a sensitive subject. It touches on questions of social class and cultural identity. Some speakers, accordingly, proudly preserve their accents, while others strive to change them.

The 'standard' British accent is known as 'Received Pronunciation' or RP – the pronunciation of well-educated middle- or upper-class people, typically from southeastern England. 'Standard' does not mean 'correct'. In fact, the very idea of a correct accent is questionable. Far better to think of a good accent as being appropriate and clear. In any case, RP no longer enjoys unrivalled status as the most appropriate accent. The BBC now happily accepts regional accents among its broadcasters – so long as they are clear; that is, so long as listeners understand them as easily as any other.

A heavy regional accent is another matter: a Geordie would do well to adjust his accent if trying to make his mark in a City firm in London. And a heavy social accent would also be inappropriate if used outside its normal social context: a plummy upper-class accent, as much as a broad Cockney accent, might well adversely affect the speaker's personal and professional life.

Changing accent can be a tricky business. Three factors come into play: your consciousness of the need to adapt, your confidence, and your 'ear' – how well you can detect change.

Set modest aims for yourself in altering your accent. Try too hard, and you will only strain or spoil other aspects of your voice, resulting in an unsatisfactory artificial sound overall.

However, you can usefully identify some of the most telltale sounds in your accent, and work on these. Reread the descriptions and exercises in the preceding sections, and practise the exercises.

The pronunciation of individual words in English often presents problems regardless of regional or social accent. How do you pronounce *again*? Is it / ə**gayn** / or / ə-**gen** /? And *controversy* – is it / **kon**trə-versi / or / kən**trov**vərsi /?

These and many other words have two or more acceptable pronunciations. Some people suffer a crisis of confidence when faced with the choice, and instead switch to a different word entirely – often a far less precise or appropriate one. True enough, a blatant mispronunciation can be a source of embarrassment – for the listener as well as the speaker. But that is no need to avoid any particular word forever – consult a good dictionary for guidance or reassurance, and you can use the word confidently next time. Alternatively, you could first try looking the word up in the final section of this book, the *Ready-Reference Word Guide* (pages 559-632).

Projecting Your Voice

The 'power' of a voice comes from projection rather than mere volume, and projection depends on three things: the force of your breath, the clarity of your consonants, and the muscular energy with which you form your words. A good actor can project a whisper from the stage to the back of a large theatre simply through power of breath, and clear and energetic enunciation.

As well as these physical factors, psychological factors play a part. Some people have under-powered voices because of lack of confidence or commitment – they may, for example, feel that they have no real right to be heard, or they may not like the sound of their own voices. Sometimes poor projection derives from nervousness or inatten-tiveness – if you do not actually look at your audience or monitor their reaction, whether you are in a small office or a large public hall, you cannot possibly know how much or how far you should project your voice.

To improve your voice projection, you need first of all to develop your breath control and articulation. Practise the exercises described in previous sections. But take care not to fall into new habits that themselves have a negative effect. One of the most common of these is the tendency to push up the pitch of your voice when you want to increase its volume. Here are some suggested remedies to counteract this habit.

Exercises. Count aloud from one to ten, starting at a low volume, and getting progressively louder. Listen carefully to your pitch – it should stay at a constant level. (As before, it is a good idea to use a tape recorder to check, if possible.)

If the pitch rises, repeat the exercise, using an arm as a conductor's baton once again. But move it from side to side this time, rather than up and down as in previous exercises, to remind you to keep your pitch even and unchanging.

☐ Count again from one to ten, and back, but this time alter the pitch rather than the volume. Speaking quietly, begin at high pitch, and then descend the scale before ascending it on the reverse count.

☐ Then try the opposite approach. Speaking loudly, begin at low pitch, and then ascend and descend the scale.

☐ Repeat the counting exercise, this time trying to alter both pitch and volume at the same time – first in the same direction (start at low pitch and low volume; raise both together as you count from one to ten; lower both together as you count backwards from ten to one), and then in opposite directions (start at low pitch and high volume).

☐ Repeat all three exercises using full sentences rather than numbers.

☐ Throughout all these exercises, check from time to time that you are breathing correctly, and moving your speech organs energetically, and keeping your neck, shoulders, and throat free from tension.

These exercises will help you to master the difference between pitch and volume.

GLOTTAL ATTACK

Good speakers can vary volume and projection fairly effortlessly. Poor speakers, on the other hand, insist on tensing the throat and generating a lot of strain and effort overall. One common habit is that of snapping the vocal cords together repeatedly to provide greater resistance to the stream of breath, on the mistaken assumption that this will increase the volume. The effect is known as 'glottal attack' (the glottis is the space between the vocal cords) – a grating, strangled kind of sound.

To observe how this works, try saying *and* in a sharp, tense tone, as if very angry, and then say *hand* in the same way. You should feel your vocal cords snapping together just before you sound the / a / in *and*. The glottal attack will be less marked, however, when you say *hand*. This is because your vocal cords need to be open to produce the / h /.

Habitual use of glottal attack puts a strain on the voice. It often causes a sore throat, and can eventually damage the vocal cords.

To cure this habit, keep practising the breathing exercises outlined earlier (page 469), to ensure that your breathing is adequately supporting your voice. Learn to relax your throat through yawning and sighing exercises, and check that you put enough energy into articulation. Try the following sup-plementary exercises as well.

The Skills of Good Speaking

Tensing the throat can bring on glottal attacks.

☐ Imagine a series of listeners positioned at various distances from you. Call to them, one by one, using the sounds / hō /,/ haa /,/ hay /,/ hī /. To make this imaginative leap easier, try this procedure: start by focusing your eyes a couple of feet ahead, and project your voice to that point – fixing on a specific object will help. Keep increasing the distance you are focusing on, until you are projecting your voice to a point on the horizon out of the window. Keep checking that your shoulders, neck, throat, and jaw are free of tension, and that your breath is sustaining the volume right until the end of each call. Don't, in other words, allow your voice to fade away as the call progresses.

☐ If you do find the sound dies away, try adding some physical action, such as throwing an imaginary ball. Send the sound out together with the 'ball' to the point you have focused on. Let the energy of your action sustain your call at full volume to the end.

☐ Now try projecting sentences instead of simple sounds. Try these, for example: 'Hello, glad to be here today'; 'I don't want to do that'; 'Are you getting my message?'

Care of the Voice

Misuse your voice and deprive it of rest and it will become worn and tired. Here are some suggestions to help you to keep your voice in peak condition:

☐ Make sure to give your voice regular opportunities to rest. That may not always be possible: if you do have to speak for several hours without a break, at least try to keep up your vocal energy by means of careful breath control and extra movement in articulation. Above all, avoid tension in the throat.

☐ Try to keep clear of smoke and alcohol. One of their effects is to coat vocal cords with mucus and make the voice sound husky – not necessarily an unattractive sound in itself, but you often need to clear it repeatedly, which is unattractive, and eventually painful as well.

☐ Avoid dairy products – milk, butter, cheese, and so on – before an important speaking occasion, if you find, as many actors and public speakers do, that these also increase the production of mucus and thereby roughen the voice.

☐ Avoid eating a heavy meal late at night before going to bed. Acid from your stomach can lie on the vocal cords all night, affecting the way you sound in the morning.

☐ Avoid hot, dry rooms if you can. A dry atmosphere will dry out the throat before long. If necessary, you can improvise a humidifier by placing a damp towel or bowl of water on top of a central-heating radiator, for instance.

☐ Warm up your voice before embarking on a lengthy speech; and your speaking organs too. Practise a few of the articulation exercises in a quiet voice. As usual, check that your posture, breathing and speech organs are free of tension. Pause every now and then to take a sip of water – both to lubricate and to rest your throat.

☐ Practise a few quiet exercises after a long speech as well – the way actors do after a demanding stage performance. Articulation, breathing, and stretching exercises – these will help to prepare the various muscles for rest and restoration.

A single conversation across the table with a
wise man is worth a month's study of books.
– Chinese proverb

THE AIM of this chapter is to help you to become a good conversationalist – and considering that talking is something most people do every day, there are surprisingly few of these. This is partly because a good talker is only halfway there: conversation is an affair of give and take, and a good conversationalist is a good listener too. Good conversation requires concentration, sensitivity, and skill.

Getting Started

Getting launched is often the most difficult part of a conversation. It is easier at work, because at work there is usually a point to get to, and people get to it fairly rapidly. But even there you will need some mastery of one of the mainstays of conversation – the art of 'small talk'.

Other areas that require skill are how to introduce people and at the same time launch them into conversation, how to join someone else's conversation when you yourself have no one to talk to, and, at the other end of proceedings, how to disengage yourself politely from a conversation.

SMALL TALK

For many people making small talk is a nightmare.

They will converse happily about the weighty matters of the day (what is happening in Moscow and Washington and the state of the economy) but small talk (discussing with a stranger such matters as, classically, the weather) is beyond them! As a result they often feel ill at ease when meeting someone new.

Conversation is not just words – it is a complex interplay between people, involving many other signals, seen and implied. Small talk is a key part of this interplay. It is the stage in a conversation when you and the other person seek common ground and establish a relationship. If small talk works, the rewards can be great – it may well lead to a long and fascinating discussion of important matters.

To launch into small talk you need an opening gambit. Talking about the weather has become something of a joke, and many people feel embarrassed to try that old ploy. But there are plenty of other good openers. They do not have to be startlingly original – indeed, the more mundane they are, the more likely the other person is to feel confident and able to respond.

Here are some well-tested and effective openers to get small talk started:

☐ Comments or questions on the surroundings or the event. For example: 'This is a lovely house, don't you think?' Or 'The food looks magnificent'. Perhaps 'It's getting quite crowded'. Or 'I'm afraid I don't know many people here'.

  And then go on to introduce yourself and find out about the other person.

☐ Comments or questions on how you or the other person arrived. 'I thought I'd be late. The train was delayed.' 'Did you find the place easily?' 'Have you come far?' 'The traffic was terrible. I've never known it so bad. How was your journey?' 'Did you have to park miles away?'

☐ Comments or questions on people who are central to the event. For example: 'John's 40th birthday – I can't believe it. Have you known him long?' 'I'm a new client of Helen's. Have you been dealing with her for long?' 'Do you know if Muriel is running many of these product launches?' 'How do you know Veronica and John?'

☐ Comments on current news stories, or recent films, books, or television programmes: 'Have you seen the latest Meryl Streep film? That person rather reminds me of her leading man.' Most people have some interest and knowledge in these areas and like to talk about them.

The first move made, you have the ball in your court, and must keep the rally going. Ask plenty of questions. Make some personal disclosures – venture opinions or information about yourself to help to establish trust. Keep a balance between the two. Don't let small talk become an interrogation. But remember also that disclosing too much about yourself too soon can make the other person uncomfortable. And, to avoid the risk of conflict before the conversation has got properly started, steer clear of controversial topics, such as religion or politics.

Watch how the other person responds. Everyone has his or her own distinctive conversational style. Some people readily ask questions; others find it more natural to make statements about themselves and their opinions. Test other people to find out which they prefer.

If you have made several disclosures and seem to get no response, try an open question – one that requires more than a yes/no answer, such as 'How did you get here?' The more even the balance between question and disclosure on both sides, the better the chance that the small talk will lead to an interesting conversation.

Observe your partner in other ways. Notice details like clothing, grooming, skin colour, apparent age, and accent. You will not necessarily make direct comments on these – that would be too personal. But they will help you to place the other person, and might throw up topics for small talk. From a person's accent, for example, you might discover a fellow Scot. You know your small talk has been effective when you discover that you both have things in common, and can exclaim on what a 'small world' it is.

Here is a conversation that could be overheard at many social occasions. Note the balance of question and disclosure.

A:	Phew! It's quite warm in here.	[Opening comment]
B:	Yes, I wish I'd worn something lighter.	[Disclosure]
	Have you been here before?	[Question]
A:	Yes, I came last year, to the same event.	[Disclosure]
	Were you at that?	[Question]
B:	No, I wasn't in the country at the time. I was living in France. I didn't even know of the company.	[Disclosure]
	Have you been dealing with them for a long time?	[Question]
A:	About five years. Before that I ran my own business.	[Disclosure]
	What were you doing in France?	[Open question]

And they are off . . . In this short exchange, A and B have sown the seeds for a long and interesting conversation. And notice where they started: a mundane comment on the heat.

Two last points. First, remember the importance of a well-stocked mind. To equip yourself with topics for small talk – and for deeper conversations – read the papers, follow sport, watch television documentaries, go to concerts, keep an eye on fashion and social change, look for amusing little stories as you go through each day. Remember that curiosity is the best attribute you can have if you want to be good at conversation.

Secondly, don't believe everything people tell you in small talk – 'Come and stay again soon . . . What a lovely surprise! Just what I've always wanted . . . Why don't you call me?' Very often people making such exclamations and invitations mean no such thing. They are simply using a handy formula to end a conversation, or perhaps to glide over some tricky situation that has arisen.

Taking small talk too literally can, in fact, lead to awkwardness. If your hostess suggests that you 'stay as long as you like', use your common sense. She is unlikely to mean that you can go on staying in her home for the next six months or more. Remember that in conversation even the sincerest of people rarely say precisely what they mean.

INTRODUCING PEOPLE

When presenting people to one another, you help them to start up conversation if, as well as announcing each person's name, you add a snippet of information. For example: 'This is John. He's recently qualified as a doctor.' Or 'This is Helen. She's just back from America.'

When entertaining, try to let people know beforehand if one of your guests has, say, recently suffered a bereavement, had a divorce, or lost a job. This helps the others to avoid potentially embarrassing topics of conversation.

JOINING IN A CONVERSATION

Going alone to social events can be harrowing. Often, you know few people, and find yourself with no one to talk to. In this situation, be bold. Go up to a group of people and join in. But again, use your common sense. Clearly, if two people are huddled together talking intensely, they will not welcome your intrusion. Look for signs that a group is ready for a change – space between people, random exchanges with gaps between comments, people looking around the room. Then approach boldly.

Make steady eye contact with the person who looks least involved, smile and ask something like: 'Do you mind if I join you?'

LEAVING A CONVERSATION

If you want to end a conversation, do so quickly and decisively. This is far more polite than to go on exchanging listless comments with a person, while your eyes travel the room looking for someone else. At an appropriate moment, make a statement such as: 'It's been interesting talking to you', or 'I'd better go and mingle.' Alternatively, make an excuse – to go to get some food or a glass of wine, perhaps, or to find the toilet. If you are sitting, you can indicate that you wish the conversation to end by standing up, telling the other person at the same time how much you have enjoyed his or her company.

Keeping it Flowing

Some conversations refuse to flow – very often this is a result of a clash of the conversational styles of the two people.

A: Do you live in London?
B: Er, yes . . .
A: I've lived in London all my life. Born and bred here. Where were you brought up?
B: Wales.
A: Oh, I adore Wales. Marvellous place. You must have been sad to leave it. I should have been, I'm sure.
B: Well, no, not really . . .

A is all enthusiasm and sympathy. B's style is quieter and more private. A, ever anxious for a close involvement with those she is talking to, plunges in with comments and questions about B. She is almost too interested in B, who finds her interrogation intrusive and rather overwhelming. As a result, he backs off.

The opposite problem is when someone is not interested enough in the other person.

A: Do you live in London?
B: Yes, I do now. I was born and bred in Wales, and left there ten years ago . . .
A: Oh, I adore Wales . . .
B: That was when I joined the army. I couldn't wait to get out of Wales. Travelled the world . . . Middle East, Europe. Marvellous time. Um . . . Have you travelled?

A: Not a great deal . . .
B: Then I came to London and got this job I'm doing in the City. Get back to Wales very little.
A: Oh.

In the first example, A led – her conversational style was dominant. In the second, B is dominant.

Conversation is best when the role of leader passes from one person to the other.

IMPROVING YOUR STYLE

Good conversation requires delicacy and tact, give and take. Learn to recognise and avoid the following all too common conversation-killers.

☐ Talking too much. This is where B offends in the second example above. He never lets the other person have her say, and the conversation becomes a tedious monologue. Ironically, many people talk too much because they are keen to please and feel uncomfortable with pauses. To others, however, their constant flow of chatter seems inconsiderate.

☐ Talking too little. Some people like to assume the role of 'observer' in conversations. They say little and often seem judgmental. Others like to appear 'strong silent types', and intimidate people in this way. All of which can be as off-putting – and selfish – as talking too much.

Trying to be funny can exhaust others.

You risk nothing from conversation if you say nothing. Equally, you gain very little. If you suffer from a feeling of being tongue-tied, try to forget yourself. Focus instead on others. Ask questions. As other people respond, your confidence will grow, and you will find yourself able to take a more active, and enjoyable, part in conversation.

☐ Interrupting. People who are very enthusiastic, or who like to air their views, tend to interrupt a great deal, thereby intruding on the right of others to be heard. If you are like this, learn to restrain your enthusiasm. If, on the other hand, someone is constantly interrupting you, be firm. Use this person's name and ask him straight out to be allowed to continue – 'John, please may I finish what I was saying.'

☐ Too much personal disclosure. Remember, many people have been brought up not to talk about themselves, and can be unnerved if others do so. You may embarrass others if you tell them too much too soon about yourself.

☐ Going into too much detail. Speakers who go into minute details about their hobbies, or who when telling an anecdote describe every tiny thing that happened to them, soon lose listeners. Edit your content when you speak. Give only the important and entertaining information. Allow the conversation to develop as others ask you questions about what you have said.

☐ Constantly bringing the conversation back to yourself. The conversation of some people is all 'I' and 'me'. Don't fall into this trap. If you have a limited conversational range, extend it by asking others for information. If someone appears to be an expert on a topic, ask him or her about it. Most people enjoy airing their knowledge – and through it you can increase your own, and acquire new topics for future conversations.

☐ Trying to be funny the whole time. Few people tell jokes well, and someone who is always trying to be funny can exhaust others. Avoid this trap. Most humour arises spontaneously, and is a shared pleasure in conversation.

☐ Imitating the other person's accent. Some people identify so strongly with others in conversation that they pick up aspects of the other person's accent. They do not do this consciously, but the other person can still feel patronised – or even mocked. If you have a tendency to do this, make a conscious effort to stick to your own accent.

BEING TOO CRITICAL

Some people are hopeless perfectionists. The standards they demand of life are impossibly high – and, as a result, most things fall short of their standards. Being critical is a way of life for them. Whatever the topic – their job, the weather, the people they work with, the state of affairs in the country at large – nothing is good enough for them. Watch out for this tendency – it too can be a most effective conversation-killer.

Remember, if you launch into criticism in the early stages of a conversation, you may well prevent the other person from expressing differing views. Or you may provoke a strong reaction, which results in conflict. There is little to be gained from being critical unless:

☐ you are criticising something that can actually be changed

☐ you offer an alternative to the thing you are criticising

☐ you are specific and clear about what you are criticising, and why

☐ you let others know that what you are saying is only your opinion

☐ you balance your criticism with praise

Remember that people can sense criticism even where it is not intended. Some people, for example, can perceive criticism of themselves when a speaker lavishes praise on another.

A: I saw Jane yesterday.
B: Oh Jane. She's an absolutely delightful person, so charming and generous, a wonderful person to be with.
A: Yes. [Thinks: 'And what does that make me . . . ?']

Avoid sarcasm. A sarcastic person rejects involvement with what is being said or proposed. Take, for example, this conversation:

Wife: Shall we have the Smiths over for dinner again?
Husband: You're really bold in your choice of dinner guests, aren't you just?

The husband refuses to get involved in planning the dinner. Yet he gives no reason for his rejection – the worst kind of criticism.

Don't complain, unless you are absolutely certain that a complaint is in order. Someone who constantly complains lowers the mood of a conversation, making it difficult for others to be positive and constructive.

A: This food's cold.
B: Oh dear, shall I call the waiter?
A: No, he looks too busy anyway.
B: Mmmn.
A: I'm not very keen on the decor in here, are you?

It is difficult to maintain the necessary cooperative spirit in a conversation when one person is complaining like this. Although the complaints here are directed at the restaurant, B may get the impression that A would rather not be there at all, and, by implication, not be in B's company. Finding things to praise – no matter how difficult – is more likely to lead to enjoyable conversation.

Don't be excessively apologetic – except, of course, when you really have said or done something to offend another person. Apology is a form of self-criticism. People whose conversation is full of apologetic expressions – 'I really shouldn't say this, but . . . I hope this won't offend you . . . Please excuse me for saying this . . . Sorry . . . ' – appear ingratiating. They cannot expect others to respect what they are saying – and once again conversation will suffer as a result.

HOW TO RECEIVE CRITICISM

Avoid criticism – but learn too how to take it. Being criticised to your face can be devastating. If you are criticised, here are some points to remember.

☐ Listen and make sure that you have clearly understood exactly what the other person is saying against you.

☐ Ask other people, apart from the person making the criticism, if they think what has been said against you is valid.

☐ Be scrupulously polite. Thank the person criticising you for what he or she has said, especially if it was constructive. People have to care about you to criticise you in this way.

☐ Remember that you are free to reject the comments. If, however, you accept the criticism, be sure to do something about it!

COMPLIMENTS

In conversation, one of the best ways of encouraging another person to open up is by paying a compliment. But be sensitive how you time your compliments, and where you aim them. Some people find personal comments – even positive ones – highly intrusive, and will be embarrassed if you compliment them early in a conversation. Others, of course, will regard a compliment as a sign that you like and approve of them – they will warm to you accordingly.

Don't pay a compliment unless you really mean it. If you are worried about sounding insincere – and many people are – underplay it. State it simply, without being unnecessarily effusive. Tell your acquaintance, 'I do like that dress' – assuming that you do. It is usually best to avoid something like this: 'My dear, what an absolutely fantastic dress. It's quite gorgeous. It makes you look like a film star. And the colour – it matches your eyes perfectly.' Most British people, at least, will simply squirm under an onslaught like that.

Don't forget that the most effective compliments confirm a person's own judgment of his or her qualities and achievements. Jane, say, has worked hard for her exams. Tell her, 'Congratulations, you've done really well,' and you confirm what she already knew secretly and boost her confidence. If, however, she knows perfectly well that she has not worked hard, your congratulations will ring hollow.

EPONYMOUS WORDS – LORD SANDWICH'S SANDWICH

The *sandwich* may be a humble meal, but it takes its name from a noble lord – the 4th Earl of Sandwich (1718-1792). He preferred this simple snack to a grand dinner because he did not like to leave the gaming table. Many other words derive from the names of people in history – the *guillotine*, for example, is named after a French doctor, Joseph Ignace Guillotin (1738-1814), who in 1789 recommended its use. People (or places) whose names give rise to words in this way are known as *eponyms*; and the words derived from these names are *eponymous* words.

☐ In the following list of eponymous terms, choose the word or phrase that is closest to its meaning in the key word. Turn to pages 633-648 for the answers.

bowdlerise
A: to throw inaccurately in ball-games
B: to remove offensive passages from a book
C: to sound-proof a room
D: to protect a house from thieves

boycott
A: to decline to play for one's team
B: to refuse to have dealings with
C: to land a surprisingly large catch
D: to adopt something as one's own

chauvinism
A: exaggerated patriotism
B: excessive mistrust of women
C: absurd self-love
D: non-sexual love

Draconian
A: very large and awkward
B: lizard-like
C: extremely severe
D: sugar-coated

epicurean
A: luxurious
B: religious
C: medical
D: industrious

gerry-mander
A: to perform surgery on
B: to adjust election districts
C: to hire as an apprentice
D: to hand over power

lynch
A: to lever by means of a pulley
B: to pick someone's pockets
C: to execute without legal authority
D: to fail to appear at one's own wedding

Machia-vellian
A: evil
B: royal
C: relating to marriage
D: crafty

martinet
A: a small bird
B: a strict disciplinarian
C: a cloth puppet
D: a theatre director

mausoleum
A: a tomb
B: a gallery
C: a military court
D: a greenhouse

maverick
A: an independent individual
B: an Irish elf
C: a lone tree
D: a chess genius

mesmerism
A: enchantment
B: hypnotism
C: haughtiness
D: commercial trading

namby-pamby
A: unable to tolerate cold
B: spoilt
C: weakly sentimental
D: afraid of everything

silhouette
A: a swan
B: a ballet
C: a contrast
D: an outline

Thespian
A: a trumpeter
B: an oatmeal pudding
C: a Greek island
D: an actor or actress

Be ready also to receive compliments. Don't diminish one by dismissing it – 'Oh, it was nothing at all . . . You're exaggerating . . . This old rag, it was really cheap!' It is ungracious to dismiss compliments, and if you do so people will stop paying them to you. If you are at a loss for words, give a nice smile and respond simply with something like: 'Thank you very much for saying that.'

AVOIDING ISSUES

Don't duck embarrassing issues. Conversation can often be like treading your way across a minefield. You are deep in discussion with someone, when quite inadvertently you make a comment or reference that triggers off an unexpected explosion of, say, grief. Without realising it, you have reminded the other person of the recent loss of a husband, wife, sister, or child.

If this happens to you, don't ignore the other person's feelings. If, for example, a recently widowed woman bursts quietly into tears, don't pretend not to notice. Acknowledge her emotion – 'I'm so sorry, you must miss your husband so badly' – and allow her to give vent to it. If she then wants to change the subject, let her. If, however, she wants to talk about her husband, listen sympathetically.

If you find yourself in the embarrassing position of not knowing what has caused the outburst, be open about it: 'I'm so sorry. I seem to have upset you.'

Don't be falsely reassuring. People often try to reassure others, not to help them, but to avoid getting involved with their emotions. If a friend has done something awful, don't duck the issue – instead help him to face up to it. Suppose his careless driving caused a serious accident. Try to help him to see the incident in perspective, and point out practical actions he can take to try to mend matters.

Don't be coldly – and infuriatingly – logical. 'I've just smashed Mary's best antique china vase,' cries a friend. 'I believe it's worth hundreds of pounds.' 'You'll just have to tell her when she comes back and offer to pay for it,' you reply. You may be right, but it is not the most sympathetic advice. Better to say nothing and help your friend to clear up.

Be honest. If you find what someone is telling you very embarrassing indeed – it is too personal, perhaps – say so. Admit that you would rather talk about something else.

HAVING ALL THE ANSWERS

The know-all is another all too frequent spoiler of good conversation. A large part of someone's job may involve giving advice to others. The trouble is that many people find it hard to stop the habit outside work.

They constantly fall into the imperative mood, with almost every statement turning into a command: 'Go right back and tell him . . . Put that pen down . . . Shut the door . . . Have another sandwich . . .' without even the grace notes of a 'Please' or a 'Why don't you?' or a 'Perhaps, you might . . .'

If you want to help someone with a problem, ask questions. When forced to reply, your friend's own thinking will often clarify, and he will start discovering solutions of his own.

And avoid constant moralising. Others may feel that you consider them incapable of working out the pros and cons of things for themselves.

Pace and Pause

Learn to pace yourself in conversation. Take good deep breaths. Then, once you start to speak, you will have the breath power to sustain you for some time, and your speech will flow smoothly. If you snatch frequent breaths in your upper chest, you will have to make frequent short pauses which will fracture the flow of your speech.

On the other hand, there is no reason to be afraid of well-spaced pauses. They give someone listening to you opportunities to interject, and a confident talker does not see interjections as a threat. They show that his listener is taking in what he is saying, and are a means of getting the other person more involved in the conversation.

Reassure the listener in your pauses. In conversation, you often halt briefly to choose the right words or to correct yourself or rephrase a point. Tell your listener what you are doing: 'What I mean to say is . . .' Or 'Let me think how to put it', or 'No, I don't mean exactly that. What I want to say . . .' These self-corrections also help you not to sound glib – like a salesman who has learnt a script.

Adjust your pace according both to your environment (in cities, for example, people tend to talk more quickly than in the country, especially when involved in business dealings) and to the people you are talking to.

Remember, people from some other cultures – Americans, for instance – tend to talk more quickly than British speakers. When an American pauses in conversation, the pause is often shorter than a British person expects, and the American will have resumed talking before the British speaker can make a contribution.

If you find yourself in this situation, make a conscious effort to be quicker off the mark with your comments when the next pause comes.

If, however, you yourself are a fast speaker, don't become impatient with a slow one, expressing your irritation by interrupting or by finishing off sentences for the slow speaker.

Slow speaker:	I've been to look for that book in the library . . .
Fast speaker:	Oh yes.
Slow speaker:	. . . and they said they didn't have it, so I . . .
Fast speaker:	. . . told them I'd had it out last week.

This will only fluster or antagonise the other person, and the conversation will become steadily stickier and stickier.

Similarly, when talking to foreign people speaking English, you may want to help them as they grope for the right words. Again, restrain yourself. Their command of English may be perfectly adequate – it just takes them longer to find the words. Do them the courtesy of waiting.

Equally, with stammerers, let them come out in their own time with the word they are trying to utter – don't try to 'second-guess' them.

Using the Right Language

To make good conversation, you need to use language appropriately and effectively. Watch out for the following points:

☐ Avoid too many 'ums' and 'ers', too much use of 'I mean', 'you know', 'd'you know what I mean?', and 'actually'. All these sounds and phrases have their role, used sparingly, to let people know that you are searching for exactly the right way of expressing yourself. The trouble is that using them excessively can become an unbreakable habit that detracts from what you are saying. It indicates a lack of confidence.

☐ Watch out for jargon. It can be useful as a shorthand – but only if the other person understands it. Using words like *sheet*, *transom*, and *halyard* is fine if you are talking to a sailor. If not, your listener may end up confused. People often use jargon to impress. Usually, however, they alienate the listener.

☐ Watch your endearments. Too much use of 'darling', 'my dear', and 'love' can appear patronising or overfamiliar. Of course, there is no problem if you know the other person well, and he or she uses similar language to show affection – or if you are in a theatrical environment where traditionally such effusions are part of the common currency of conversation.

☐ Avoid offensively dogmatic expressions. Some people always preface statements of their opinions with: 'The fact is . . .', or 'The truth is . . .', or 'Definitely . . .' They seem to see their views as universal truths. It is more tactful, and honest, to say 'In my opinion . . .', or 'My view is . . .', or 'I firmly believe that . . .'

☐ Use the word *we* only when you mean 'we'. Don't be like the sole trader who responds over the phone with a 'We can help you with that'. There is a sense of collective strength behind *we*. But it is better to be honest. The Queen uses *we* as befits her rank. Others should use it only when they are referring to actions done by more than one person.

☐ Don't overuse *one* – a favourite expression with the British upper classes. It obscures meaning, and makes you sound unwilling to accept responsibility. If you say, for example, 'One goes shopping every Saturday', who are you referring to? Yourself? People in general? Say *I*.

☐ If someone uses a word you do not understand, ask for an explanation. Don't try to feign understanding. Some people deliberately use obscure words to impress. They get away with it because nobody dares to risk losing face by asking for the meaning.

- [ ] If you hear people mispronounce or misuse a word, don't humiliate them by pointing this out. The only situation where this might be acceptable would be if you knew the speaker very well and no one else was present – even then, you should do it tactfully.

- [ ] Try to improve your own vocabulary. This will help you to be more adaptable in conversation and able to talk to a wider range of people. Read more – novels, books on history and current affairs, or the quality newspapers, for example – and look words up in a dictionary when you do not understand them.

- [ ] Don't worry if you cannot find the right word in conversation. Tell your listeners what you are trying to express, and they will usually help you. Everyone forgets words from time to time, and other people enjoy supplying them.

- [ ] Avoid slang and swearing, particularly with people you do not know well. Some people use slang and swearwords to indicate their solidarity with certain social groups, or to show how direct and unpretentious they are. Others, however, will probably see this kind of language in a different light – as a sign of limited vocabulary, immaturity, and a desire to offend.

How to be a Good Listener

Listening is as important in conversation as talking. Good listening involves encouraging other people to say interesting things, understanding the things that they tell you, and being sensitive to the thoughts and feelings that underlie the things that they tell you.

Listening must be active as well as passive. It is not enough just to listen: you must show that you are listening. Body, face, eyes, and voice – all should combine to tell the other person that you are taking in what he or she is saying.

Good listening will bring out the best in your partner in conversation – even the dullest-seeming person has interesting and valuable insights to give and information to pass on. Poor listening, by contrast, will lead to misunderstanding, boredom, and ill-feeling.

THINKING AS YOU LISTEN

To listen well you need mental concentration, generosity, and self-confidence. Poor listeners are too often worrying about what they themselves are about to say next, or are distracted and lost in their own thoughts. Either way, they fail to give others sufficient attention. Conversation with them is likely to be stilted, leaping from topic to topic, with lots of interruptions.

To be a better listener, think less about yourself and more about the conversation. It is only natural to be concerned about, say, the impression you are making on another person. But don't let this obsess you. Instead, focus on the other person, and on what he or she is saying.

Respond positively to initiatives other people make in conversation. At one point, you may have to be reassuring, at another supportive, at another understanding. To give the right signals at these points requires no more than a word or two and an appropriate facial expression.

A:	Could we have a chat?	[Suggesting]
B:	Certainly	[Reassuring]
A:	I'm sorry to have been so offhand recently, only I've had an awful lot on my plate.	[Explaining]
B:	That's all right.	[Supporting]
A:	I think I've been given too much responsibility at work.	[Confiding]
B:	I see. How can I help?	[Understanding]

Notice how B responds to A's initiatives, reassuring where A suggests, supporting where A explains, sympathising where A confides. Clearly too, B sees as well as hears. He notes the worried, perhaps slightly embarrassed expression in A's eyes, the anxious pat on his arm drawing him to one side – and responds accordingly. A, meanwhile, sees and hears that B is listening, and is encouraged to continue talking. A's responsiveness has drawn out a confession that has helped B to relieve himself of what was troubling him, and has also cleared the air between the two men. Both have benefited.

Remember, conversation is almost always indirect. Often, the most important messages of a conversation are left unsaid. You must be ready to deduce them. Be alert to what lies behind another person's words. Use your eyes as well as your ears.

Take one brief exchange as an example. A colleague comes up and asks you, 'What about lunch?' He could mean simply: 'I'm going out to lunch now. I don't particularly want to eat it on my own. You're around. You're quite good company. I therefore want to have lunch with you.'

Or he might mean something much more important. For example: 'I'm sorry we had words this morning. On reflection, I suspect the fault was more mine than yours, and I want to make it up. If you say yes, I'll take it that you've accepted my apology. If you say no – unless you have an unbreakable prior engagement – I'll take it that you haven't.' It is vital, for you and for the atmosphere in your place of work, that you should hear correctly the message behind your colleague's words.

ENCOURAGING AND LISTENING

Nothing is more encouraging for a speaker than to have your undivided attention. Here are some ways of showing that you are giving it.

Maintain eye contact. A good listener looks at the speaker. If your eyes are constantly darting away, the speaker will sense that you are distracted. Don't on the other hand, overdo the eye contact. A piercing stare will seem intimidating.

Never make the mistake of feigning eye contact by looking at an area near the speaker's eyes – the forehead, say. The shift of focus is always noticed. One man always focused on the shoulder of his partner in conversation. The other person was left with the uneasy feeling that he had developed a dandruff problem!

Try a trick used by President John Kennedy. When people look and listen they tend to focus on one eye rather than both. Kennedy, however, would look from eye to eye when he listened, softening the expression in his own eyes at the same time, and so giving the impression that he cared greatly about the speaker's feelings.

If you are short-sighted, you can take off your glasses. The speaker's eyes will become a blur and you will find it easier to hold your gaze on them. But don't overdo this or you will merely discountenance the speaker.

If the problem is that you are not receiving good eye contact, try saying the other person's name to yourself every time you look at him. He may be too embarrassed, nervous, or even bored, to look you in

the eye. Whatever the reason, saying his name will help you to gauge the right pause before starting to talk when your eyes do meet, and may also help you psychologically to be more assertive in drawing his attention to you.

Make the right noises. They are vital for keeping the conversation going. This is particularly true of telephone conversations – see also page 494.

Assure the speaker that you understand what he or she is telling you by making appropriate sounds and exclamations – 'mm', 'yes', 'right', 'congratulations'. Interject the odd comment or question – 'You must feel awful about it ... Did you believe him?' Show your involvement by summarising the story so far or by repeating something – 'You passed all your exams! Well done!' Give an encouraging 'Go on ... I'm dying to hear more.'

To avoid misunderstandings, try to be precise in your vocal encouragements. If, for instance, you do not necessarily agree with everything the speaker is saying, use expressions such as 'possibly', 'perhaps', 'I'm not so sure'.

But, as with eye contact, don't overdo your interjections – or the speaker may feel overwhelmed, or mocked.

Use appropriate facial expressions. The expressions that cross your face send out signals – so make sure they are encouraging ones.

Often people assume masks that have little to do with what they are really thinking or feeling. These will not encourage the speaker. If, for example, your mask is that of tight lips and a tense jaw, with little expression, you will be giving speakers little encouragement to continue talking

The skilled conversationalist, by contrast, listens with a relaxed, responsive face and uses nods of the head, warm smiles, even twitches of the eyebrows, to give encouragement.

Adopt a relaxed stillness. Most people appreciate how rude it is to get up and walk away when someone else is talking. Yet many fail to realise how smaller gestures can indicate a similar level of distraction. Good listeners keep relatively still, only shifting position occasionally. If you are constantly fiddling or fidgeting you will appear inattentive. You will be equally unnerving as a listener if you sit or stand rigidly to attention, tapping a foot or fingers – giving the impression that you are in a hurry to hear the speaker out.

ADJUSTING YOUR LISTENING STYLE

Some people are loud fast talkers. Their faces and voices are wonderfully expressive, and they gesticulate wildly with their hands. When they listen, they do so with similar enthusiasm – nodding and shaking their heads vigorously, interposing with constant 'mmn's' and 'yes's', their faces registering every differing response to what they hear.

Others, by contrast, speak slowly and quietly, with little physical expression. They remain relatively still, say little, and feel comfortable with pauses. Their listening style is similarly underplayed.

Learn to adapt your listening style to the speaking style of the person you are in conversation with. If you are an effusive listener, you can easily overpower a less expressive speaker. Ease back.

If, however, you tend to listen in a low-key way, an energetic, expressive speaker may sense either that you are not listening at all or that you disapprove of what you are hearing. To get a response from you, the speaker will make the style and content of what he or she is saying yet more dramatic and, if there still seems to be no response, may lose the drift and trail off in mid-sentence. In this case, send out stronger signals. Make a conscious effort to nod your head. Make appropriate noises. Keep your eye contact steady.

SOCIAL SITUATIONS AND LISTENING

In some situations – large drinks parties, for example – listening becomes difficult because of background noise. Remember that everyone lip-reads to an extent, so when speaking articulate clearly. When listening, watch the speaker's facial expressions and gestures to help you to decipher what he or she is saying.

Another problem is catching people's names – and then remembering them. One tip is to forge an association between a person's name and a visual image you connect with him or her.

You are introduced, say, to Janet Newton. Think of her going to a new town, and reading a huge Janet and John book to her children in their new home. Think of the image to recall the name.

Having established a person's name, use it at suitable points in the conversation to reinforce it in your memory.

IMPROVING YOUR LISTENING SKILLS

Practice will help you to improve your listening skills. Here are two simple exercises:

☐ Take a few minutes every day to sit still in a quiet room. Then close your eyes and do nothing but listen. Listen for specific sounds and identify them. One of the problems with poor listeners is that they are more attuned to what is going on inside themselves than to what is happening in others and the outside world. This exercise will help you to forget yourself and to turn outwards.

☐ Listen to interviews on the radio and television. Pay particular attention to the people being interviewed. What are they saying? What are the thoughts, emotions, and feelings behind what they are saying? You can do the same exercise when attending lectures and talks. Regular exercise will improve your listening skills.

The Language of the Body

Good listening involves reaching into the thoughts and feelings behind a person's words. Watching someone's body language is an important way of doing this. In conversation, people's body language – the way they sit or stand, what they do with their hands – conveys a subtle but telling variety of signals. These can give you important clues to their thoughts and feelings, confirming or contradicting the words they utter.

Observe, for example, the lines of a person's body as he sits. This will tell you much about how at ease he is. In a formal situation, where someone is on his best behaviour, he will sit in a neat symmetry, legs together, arms folded in his lap, his body in a straight line. As he relaxes, however, his body begins to sprawl. He throws his legs out to one side, rests one arm in his lap, the other along the back of a chair. His body begins to assume a spreading, curved position.

Like other aspects of behaviour, body language is contagious. When a conversation is going well, people mirror each other's stance, gestures, and mannerisms. When conflict arises, body language is adjusted accordingly.

HOW TO READ BODY LANGUAGE

Don't take body language in isolation. See it as part of a larger picture, which includes tones of voice, and words spoken. And don't forget practical considerations. Your partner may be shifting in her chair because she dislikes what you are saying. Equally, however, the chair may be uncomfortable – and she is only trying to rearrange her position. Here are some signals to watch out for in people's body language.

Signs of involvement. Look for the angle of the body. If someone leans forward when you start a conversation, he is clearly suggesting that he wishes to get involved. If, later in the conversation, he angles his body away from you, with his legs crossed towards the door, his physical orientation suggests that he is less involved.

Similarly, if you enter a room to talk to your boss, and find him leaning back, hands linked behind his head, you will probably feel uneasy.

Watch people's eyes as well. If they wish to get involved in a conversation, they make eye contact. At the same time, bodies tilt towards one another, and barriers created by crossed legs, folded arms, hands over mouths are removed.

When watching other people's conversation, observe the amount of space between them. Two people standing or sitting close together while talking are clearly conversing intimately. Another conversation, where the couple are talking with some distance between them, is probably more detached and formal.

Signs of unease and insecurity. When under attack, a human being, like an animal, goes to protect his 'underbelly' – the front part of his body. A person shows that he feels the need to defend himself by folding his arms, crossing his legs, dropping his chin into his chest.

If during a conversation the person you are talking to starts to behave defensively, you may have touched upon a raw nerve. Try not to look defensive yourself, or you will appear inaccessible and unreceptive and make the situation worse.

Again, watch the eyes. An unconfident person finds it hard to maintain eye contact.

Watch out too, for grooming mannerisms, such as patting the hair, picking fluff or lint off a sleeve, hitching up the trousers. They are often signs that a

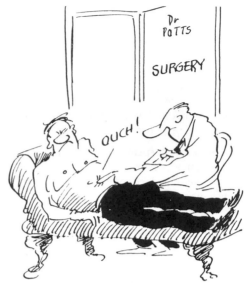

One common tell-tale sign of a person's feelings is his body language.

person is uncertain of himself, and needs reassurance. He is checking that everything is in order. He may also be channelling tension.

Actions such as folding the arms, or rubbing arms or legs, often have similar roots – as though a person were making sure that 'everything's all right'.

Notice how large or small a person makes himself seem. Body language can make someone look larger or smaller than he really is. If he stands with his feet apart, hands on his hips, head pulled back, he will seem larger than if he stands with his feet touching, arms crossed in front of his body, shoulders rounded and head tilting downwards.

Some people habitually use body language that makes them look smaller than they are and apologetic. Others establish a significant presence in most situations by using expansive body language and taking up a lot of space.

CONTROLLING YOUR BODY LANGUAGE

Adapt your body language to different people and situations. If you are not getting far with someone in a conversation, you may be sending out the wrong signals. Changing your body language could change the whole tenor of the conversation.

Remember the following points.

Don't move your head too much. In conversation, people focus mainly on the face and head of the other person. Too much head movement will distract from what you are saying, and suggest that you are desperate for approval.

As an exercise to help you to learn to control your head movements, stand with your back and head against a wall. Then try speaking while keeping your head still against the wall. Also, if you are talking to someone in a room with a mirror, watch your head movements in the mirror.

But, as always, don't overdo things. Don't keep your head rigidly still, or you will appear inflexible and reluctant to become involved in the conversation. Indicate that you are listening by tilting your head to one side – you will then seem more receptive.

Don't intrude on another person's 'territory'. Expansive speakers in particular need to beware of this. People surround themselves with an area of personal space, and if this is invaded they begin to feel insecure, even annoyed.

How large this personal space is varies from person to person, and from culture to culture. Arabs, for instance, stand much nearer to each other than Europeans do. The extent of 'territories' also varies according to the degree of intimacy between two people. Be sensitive, and watch the other person's reactions to judge if you are intruding.

Use touch. This brings warmth and friendliness to a conversation. A shake of the hands, a kiss, or a hug – according to your intimacy with the other person – will get a conversation off to a good start. The other person immediately feels your interest and affection, and barriers are broken down. As the conversation proceeds, pats, touches on the arms and back, gentle prods in the ribs – all these can express understanding, sympathy, reassurance, praise, and humour.

Again, be sensitive. Use touch only where it is appropriate. It is probably wiser not to slap, for instance, an upper-class English person of the older generation heartily on the back. And remember too that British people use touch less than continentals do, and that men generally use it less than women.

Break down physical barriers. This helps to establish good rapport. Tables and desks may give you a sense of security, but they will also make you less accessible to others.

Some people feel powerful sitting in a large chair behind a desk, with the furniture protecting them and acting as a symbol of their authority. But remember this: sitting opposite someone immediately puts you in a more confrontational position than sitting alongside that person.

With no barriers between them, people frequently feel vulnerable. But the clearer view they now get of each other's body language will build rapport.

Control your mannerisms. If you find it hard to keep your hands still, link them together to form a steeple and you will appear more confident.

How to Cope with Conflict

Conflict will inevitably arise from time to time in conversation. The only people who do not experience it are those who never express an opinion of their own. Here are some do's and don'ts for dealing with conflict:

☐ Do try to prevent conflict from arising in the first place. Keep your ears and eyes open for signs of irritation in the person you are talking to.

Try to defuse the problem before it develops any further – by, for example, adjusting your conversational style. If you tend to ask lots of questions, try backing off. The other person may be resenting your interrogation.

☐ Don't let things get out of hand, if in spite of your efforts to prevent conflict, it does develop. Make a comment on the turn the conversation has taken. For example: 'We seem to be having an argument.' Or 'Why are we getting angry about this?', or 'I've said something to upset you.'

☐ Don't suddenly raise your voice or tense your body – or the situation could get worse still. Gestures and tones of voice are more likely to spark things off than the words you use.

☐ Do be prepared to drop the subject. If the argument is simply going round and round in circles, will further discussion really increase understanding between you and the other person? Continue the discussion only if the other person clearly wants to.

☐ Do make sure you have really understood what the other person is saying, thinking, feeling. There may, for example, be more justice in his position than you had realised. Indeed, it may not be so far from your own position as in the heat of the moment you assumed.

☐ Do bear in mind that there are often things in people's backgrounds – an unfortunate experience in childhood, say – that make them take an extreme position in some particular area.

This may not justify their arguments, but it will account for their passion and apparent lack of

reason. In such circumstances, it may be wise to disengage yourself from the discussion.

☐ Don't, however, give in too easily if you choose to continue a discussion. If the other person is not taking in what you are saying, keep repeating it, without raising your voice or getting upset, until the message at last gets through.

☐ Do remember that the other person has a right to an opinion. Agree to disagree.

Talking on the Telephone

Your voice is your sole means of communicating over the telephone. Even so, watch your body language and facial expression – they affect the way you sound. If you slump, for example, you often will sound tired or breathless. To keep a bright tone in your voice, smile when talking on the phone.

Don't answer the phone in a rush. Pause a moment, take a deep breath, then breathe out slowly as you pick up the receiver. You will sound more relaxed. If you recognise the other person's voice, use his or her name in your greeting. Use it again during the conversation and when parting.

Don't judge people by what you hear immediately. Tune gradually into the nuances of their voice, their use of language, how rapidly they speak, how often and how long they pause. Some people have a very businesslike manner on the phone, and like to come straight to the point. Others like to exchange pleasantries first. Telephone styles also vary according to the situation – according to whether the call is for social or business purposes, for example.

When making a difficult call, work out beforehand exactly what you wish to say. Stand while making the call – it will help you to sound more assertive. Get fairly quickly to the point: 'The reason I'm calling is . . . ' Try to drop the pitch of your voice at the ends of sentences and phrases – it will make you sound more definite.

Even if you are speaking rapidly, take time to pause at regular intervals. If conflict develops, hear the other person out, then make your own point. If you cannot deal immediately with some point the other person raises, arrange to call back.

Always take care to speak clearly on the phone. If you are having problems in making yourself understood, or are feeling tired, articulate with more energy. Imagine that the person at the other end of the line can, in fact, see you and is trying to read your lips. Focus on a point where the other person might be sitting, and talk to him as though he were in the room with you. Use the same facial expressions and body language you would use if someone really were there.

It is sometimes difficult to get off the phone. If you know somebody is apt to talk a lot, make it clear at the start of a call that you have only a limited amount of time – that you are very busy.

There are several ways of curtailing a call: 'It's been lovely to talk to you, but I really must dash', or 'I know you're busy, so I really must go.' If all else fails, try: 'My other line is ringing', or 'I think there's someone at the front door.' If the talker made the call, try appealing to his or her parsimony by saying: 'I don't want this call to cost you any more money.'

When leaving a message on someone's answering machine, speak clearly and slowly to allow the person to take down any details as your message plays back. Many people feel uneasy with answering machines. Again, visualise the other person – and you will sound more relaxed.

When recording a message for your own answering machine, smile to make your voice sound warm and welcoming. Pace your message well so that it does not sound abrupt – or your caller may as abruptly put the receiver down. Tell callers what details to leave: name, message, and time, for example.

Public Speaking

Rhetoric is the art of ruling the minds of men.

– Plato

IT IS to their skills as orators that many great leaders owe their fame. The great speeches of Elizabeth I, Winston Churchill, and John F. Kennedy are as memorable as their achievements. Being an effective speaker is still one of the best ways of achieving prominence in public life, as well as of influencing others in your private and business life. And as with so many other things in life, success in public speaking depends on both careful preparation and careful presentation.

☐ Your preparation. Some people are so nervous about a public speaking engagement that they put off thinking about it, and end up by being inadequately prepared. Preparation is essential – to choose and organise appropriate material, to rehearse adequately, and to build up your confidence. Give yourself plenty of time – ideally a few weeks – to prepare your speech.

☐ Your presentation. Effective speakers pay as much attention to style as to content, to *how* they will speak and look, as to *what* they will say. A speaker may make the mistake of spending a great deal of time working on the content of an address, without ever rehearsing it aloud and considering the use of body and voice. Yet audiences probably respond to and remember the speaker's personality even more than his or her actual words. Aim to finish preparing the content of your speech early, to allow you to rehearse and refine it.

Preparation and Research

'The reason there are so few good talkers in public is that there are so few thinkers in private,' states an old American tome, *Woman's Home Companion*. Thinking things through before a speech will make the difference between success and failure.

KNOW WHAT IS EXPECTED

Be sure you know exactly what the organisers of an event at which you have to speak expect of you. What precisely do they want you to talk about? You may be a world-famous nuclear physicist – but do they want you to talk about nuclear physics? They may want you to speak about the life of a nuclear physicist – or even one of your hobbies.

Ask them about the audience. You cannot possibly decide what to say until you know who you will be talking to. Ask them about:

☐ the age, gender, and occupations of the audience. A young audience demands a different approach from an elderly one. A predominantly female audience may have different expectations from a mixed or all-male audience. A cross-section of working people may require a general-interest topic; whereas if most members of the audience are lawyers, say, you can focus your speech more sharply towards their likely interests and attitudes.

☐ the audience's knowledge of the subject. When your audience knows a great deal about a subject, you can make a number of assumptions; they will already understand the special language and concepts of the topic. If they know very little, on the other hand, you will have to spell out the background in more detail, and explain step by step your various arguments and the conclusions you reach.

☐ the audience's attitude towards the subject. When some members of the audience are sure to hold views strongly opposed to your own (on a political issue, perhaps), you must plan accordingly. Anticipate their most likely objections, and make sure that you deal with these in your speech. You may also have to begin your speech by establishing your credentials, pacifying likely opponents, or reacting to newspaper coverage of the issues.

Make sure that you know exactly when you are speaking, and for how long. If the audience have been assembled for a couple of hours before you make your speech, they may well be relieved if you keep it brief and to the point. You need to know if you are preceding or following other speakers, and who they are. If, for example, you are following a speaker you know to have a very different outlook from your own, you must be prepared to answer in your speech the kinds of point that speaker is likely to make in his.

If the organisers give you only vague information about timing, take things into your own hands. Tell them how long you intend to speak and whether or not you will be taking questions afterwards. If they ask for a longer speech than you want to give – and this often happens – suggest that you take the last ten to fifteen minutes for questions. Ensure too that they represent you as you would like to be represented – or the result may be a disappointed audience. If necessary, supply your own 'billing' – a brief account of your career and achievements.

Finally, ask the organisers about the size of the audience, and the room layout. Will you have to speak from behind a lectern or on a platform? Find out what technical equipment is available. As a guest speaker you may be able to have the room arranged as you want it, with any necessary technical equipment provided.

GATHERING YOUR MATERIAL

Now start gathering your material. Begin jotting down ideas and doing any necessary research immediately, even if much of what you come up with does not seem very impressive. The object at this stage is to get the ideas flowing – even a poor one may spark off something better. Later you can sort and sift your material.

If your mind remains an obstinate blank, a good trick is to write down a simple, succinct objective – this is useful even if you have plenty of ideas, as a means of keeping your researches on track. As host at an important dinner, your objective might be: 'To

A persuasive speech needs to appeal to the heart.

introduce the guest speaker, to praise her achievements, and to encourage the members of the audience to welcome her.'

Clearly, your task here is to establish the basic landmarks of the speaker's career, what makes her so remarkable, and to gather a good stock of lighter-hearted anecdotes about her. Research in libraries, the press, and *Who's Who*. If appropriate, ask friends and colleagues for information. You might telephone the speaker and ask her direct for relevant material. Most people are more than happy to supply it.

Another trick is to put yourself in the position of a member of your audience. Think of questions he or she might want to ask you – and then angle your researches accordingly. Suppose, for example, you are a member of a club committee, trying to persuade the club to reorganise. Other members might wonder:

☐ What was wrong with the old system?

☐ What are the benefits of reorganisation?

☐ How will reorganisation affect me?

☐ Will reorganisation be time-consuming?

☐ What will it cost?

Your research here will involve finding out plenty of facts and figures to help to prove your case.

Don't, though, get too bogged down in statistics and masses of information. Whatever kind of speech you are to give, try to dig out plenty of appropriate anecdotes, jokes, and quotations to lighten the load of hard fact. Even the most serious speech (an academic lecture, say) needs to entertain as well as inform – in order to keep the listeners' attention.

And a persuasive speech, such as that of the club committee member, needs to appeal to the heart as well as the intellect. In that case, canvassing the feelings of club members might produce a direct quotation from a member illustrating the general frustration felt with the club's present organisation. In other cases, flick through dictionaries of quotations, biographies, and similar sources.

Sometimes you have to talk about yourself. Perhaps you are an actor and have been asked to talk about your life in the theatre. Think of ways to make the audience identify with you. What attracted you to the theatre in the first place? Did you stumble into acting almost by accident? Or did you know from the moment your parents first took you to the pantomime that this is what you wanted to do? What has been the worst moment of your career? And what has been the most exhilarating?

Even when you are not directly talking about yourself, it is usually a good idea to establish your credentials. Your 'billing' may give these, or you may have to provide them – modestly, yet convincingly – yourself. Consider including a few brief anecdotes about your career so far. Your opinions will fall on well-prepared ground if everyone in the audience regards you as an authority.

Finally, if there is to be a question time at the end, try in the research stage to anticipate likely questions and have your answers ready. You might ask for written questions to be submitted beforehand, to give you time to prepare helpful answers.

Structuring Your Speech

Now start thinking about how you are going to structure your speech. Try to stand back from the material, and identify the few key areas you want to cover or points you want to make.

The former Conservative Prime Minister, Harold Macmillan, was as a young politician making a speech in the House of Commons. David Lloyd George, the 'Welsh Wizard' renowned for his oratory, was among the listeners. Afterwards, he offered Macmillan some advice. The younger man had made about 12 points in the course of his speech, and Lloyd George suggested that although Macmillan had spoken well, few members of the Commons would remember what he had said. Lloyd George suggested that as a junior member of the House, Macmillan should make one clear point in a speech. If he became a Cabinet Minister, he could effectively make two points. A Prime Minister could make three points effectively. In other words, the fewer points you make, the better the chance that your message will be remembered.

A proviso needs to be added. Odd numbers of points work better than even ones. As speaker, you will find it easier to remember three, five, or seven points than four, six, or eight, and your audience will more readily assimilate a structure based on odd numbers. So, contrary to Lloyd George's advice, better to make three brief points than two.

Here are some examples of ways in which you can structure a speech:

☐ Topic by topic. The speaker takes different aspects of the subject and covers them one by one. So a speaker talking about adult education might cover: evening classes; part-time courses at polytechnics, universities, and business schools; correspondence courses.

☐ Geographically. The speaker might choose to cover adult education in Britain, in America, and then in Europe. This method is particularly suitable when different countries or cultures have radically different approaches.

☐ Chronologically. This structure gives a historical perspective. Adult education could be covered thus: adult education opportunities 20 years ago; adult education opportunities now; and plans or hopes for the future.

☐ Using a problem and solution structure. Here the speaker takes a number of problem areas and proposes solutions. This is likely to produce a persuasive speech. Adult education could be dealt with like this: problems that prevent adults from getting further education; ways of overcoming these difficulties. (You would, of course, try to make an odd number of points under each heading in a speech like this.)

497

Speeches can also be a mixture of these forms. For instance, the adult education speech could be organised in this way: a history of adult education; the different sorts – evening classes, universities, polytechnics, distant learning; differences among Britain, America, and Europe; problems facing those seeking further education; finally, how to overcome them. But be careful if mixing the forms – or you may end up with an overcomplex speech.

With your structure worked out, you can then start filling it in.

THE INTRODUCTION

Seize your listeners' attention with your opening, and you are well on the way to success.

Consider the likely mood of the audience. If as an expert you are going to have a captive, silent audience, a dramatic opening may seem unnecessary. If you expect the audience to disagree with you, avoid a strongly controversial opening which will only stir up the situation further, so that the audience fail to 'hear' your reasoned case. When an audience is likely to be apathetic, on the other hand, you will need an opening that provokes interest.

Don't apologise during the opening: 'I'm afraid some of you may find this boring.' Or, 'I'm sorry, this is a horrendous experience for me . . . ' Nothing is more likely to lose your audience's attention.

Here are some tried and tested opening devices:

☐ Seize the attention of the audience, and amuse them at the same time, by saying or doing something in character with the occasion. This was the approach adopted by the well-known broadcaster Raymond Baxter, when he was asked to speak at the launch party of a book, *World At Arms*, about World War II. The guests were all assembled, drinking their cocktails, and chatting happily in small groups, when the hubbub of their conversation was silenced by a piercing parade-ground bark from Baxter: 'Parade! Par-aa-aa-aa-de, wait for it . . . SHUN!' The guests looked up to where the order had come from, and there on a balcony stood Baxter, rigidly to attention. He had his audience on his side from that moment on.

☐ Invite direct audience involvement through questions and requests. 'Good evening. How many of you have taken any formal studies after finishing full-time education? Is it something we

Find out plenty of facts and figures.

put off, thinking that "we don't have the time" or "it won't help my promotion prospects"? I'd ask you to put aside those doubts this evening, while you listen to an account of the opportunities available for adult education.'

☐ Surprise the audience and challenge its assumptions. Strong, short, controversial statements, or statements that contradict what the audience probably expected you to say (backed up by explanation later) can be effective in grabbing your listeners' attention. For example: 'I have no academic qualifications whatsoever, and yet I regard myself as an educated adult.' Or 'Adult education is a complete waste of time and money. So say the cynics . . . '

☐ Call the audience to attention, greet them, and remind them why they are gathered together: 'My lords, ladies and gentlemen, we are gathered here today to celebrate . . . ' This is appropriate for formal occasions – a mayoral banquet, say.

☐ Thank the organisers for asking you to speak, and say how pleased you are to be there. 'I'd like to thank the committee for asking me to speak and to let you all know how pleased I am to be addressing you this evening.'

Having decided on your first line, memorise it.

THE BODY OF THE SPEECH

As a public speaker you take your audience on a journey, and you need to signpost the route. Remember the old maxim, 'First I tells 'em what I'm going to tell 'em, then I tells 'em, then I tells 'em what I've tellt 'em'. This is particularly important to bear in mind when your speech is going to include a great deal of information.

At the beginning of the speech tell your listeners what areas you are going to cover, and then at various stages remind them of the points you have already established. At the beginning: 'I am going to cover adult education in Britain, America, and Europe this evening, contrasting the different approaches in each of these places . . . ' Then later: 'So much for Britain. Now what about America? Here, the picture is very different . . . '

Bear in mind the differences between the spoken and the written word. When you are speaking, you need to spell things out more clearly. While reading is active, listening is passive – and as a result listeners have poorer concentration. Most listen attentively for about ten minutes and then their attention wanders.

Plot your use of humour so that it comes at intervals throughout the speech – to revive the audience's attention. Never sabotage your jokes by saying, 'I'm going to tell you a really funny joke, now.'

Keep anecdotes pithy and to the point. Avoid sticking in tried and tested ones that have no real bearing on the subject, introducing them with: 'That reminds me of a story I once knew.' And avoid hackneyed anecdotes that the audience may well have heard several times before.

Try to surprise your audience. Direct questions do this, and if, in addition, you ask for a show of hands – 'How many people here have experience of adult education?' – you will get your audience physically involved as well. Ask for a volunteer or volunteers to help you to demonstrate something – if you are giving a talk on first aid, say, use members of the audience to demonstrate lifesaving techniques.

Get your listeners to write things down. The speech on adult education, for instance, could have a section where the speaker asks audience members to turn to their neighbours and to list all they know about available opportunities for adult education. The speaker could then get the audience to call out the opportunities they have discussed.

Visual aids and audio recordings are another way to keep your audience alert – see pages 509-512.

If you are addressing an audience of mixed ages and interests, you may be uncertain about what information to include and what to leave out. Rather than omit information that some, but not all, of your audience may already know, preface it with words such as: 'Most of you probably know . . . ' or 'Many of you are familiar with these ideas, but I think it is worth recalling them'. This way, you neither insult the intelligence of those of your audience who do know these facts, nor risk alienating the remainder through assuming that they know more than they do.

Be careful with criticism and controversy. Sharp criticism must be backed by solid argument and evidence. If you decide to be controversial, consider carefully how the audience is likely to react, and prepare your responses. Show the audience that you have considered alternatives to your own suggestions, and the drawbacks to your views. By describing these counterproposals and showing where they fall down, you show that you have reached a reasoned conclusion.

Most people like to think they are intelligent, well-informed, and generous. Appeal to them in these areas, particularly in a persuasive speech. 'I'm sure we have all been watching events in Ethiopia with deep concern, and we all long to do something to help. Here is a practical way of doing so . . . '

Appeal also to people's financial and social aspirations, or group pride – their desire to be identified with a particular group in society. For instance: 'As most of you here today are professional people . . . ' or, 'As I am talking to people who have studied the subject, I . . . '

Appeal finally to the instinct to explore new ideas. If you are trying to persuade audiences to change their habits of thinking, suggest that they are receptive to innovation – it will help your case.

THE CONCLUSION

Your conclusion needs to be memorable. After all, this is what the audience hear last. And when they leave, this will be uppermost in their minds.

Don't introduce new points into the conclusion. Reiterate in strong, memorable words and phrases the thrust of the whole speech. It is a good idea to learn your concluding, like your opening, lines.

Note as an example this extract from the ending of Martin Luther King's most famous speech:

> And He's allowed me to go up the mountain,
> And I've looked over
> And I've seen the promised land.
> I may not get there with you
> But I want you to know tonight
> That we as a people
> Will get to the promised land.
>
> So I'm happy tonight
> I'm not worried
> I'm not fearing any man
> Mine eyes have seen the glory of the coming of the Lord!

SPEAKING SPONTANEOUSLY

Sometimes, at the end of a dinner, say, you may be called upon to 'say a few words' when you are not expecting it. Quickly think of – and jot down – three questions the audience might want to have answered and make the replies your three points.

Always decide in advance what your conclusion will be; otherwise you may ramble inconclusively.

One further – very fundamental – point. Remember, if you think such an invitation likely, to limit your drinking. One or two drinks may help to clear your inhibitions, but more than that and the results could be disastrous!

Effective Delivery

To make an impact on an audience, clear structure and well-judged content need to be matched by effective delivery.

NOTES AND SCRIPTS

Apart from speaking impromptu, which is not advisable except for very accomplished speakers, there are three usual ways of delivering a speech: carrying the content and structure in your head; using notes; reading it from a script.

Audiences find the first method impressive. If you know your subject well, and feel confident that you can carry the structure in your head, then choose this method. You may still want to jot down statistics and quotations on a card.

If using notes, write them on cards the size of postcards – sheets of paper can be distracting. Write clearly and, if helpful, use different coloured inks. If using slides, note where they occur.

Some speakers write down stage directions. Before a particularly important point, you may write, for example, 'pause' or, towards the conclusion of your speech, the instruction 'louder'. Winston Churchill marked his speeches with detailed stage directions, even to the point of marking down where he would make particular gestures.

Notes should not distract you from your speech. Punch two holes at the top of your cards and tie them together to avoid muddling them. Keep your notes close to your body, and clear of your face. Try to look up at your audience most of the time.

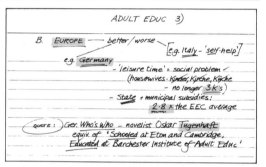

Keep refining your notes, as you prepare your speech, so that they are as economical as possible. Rather than full sentences, write down topic headings, subheadings, key phrases, statistics, and any suitable quotations.

Many people use more notes than they need. If you are familiar with your subject, but want to have notes as a safety net, keep them to one side and if necessary refer to them, informing the audience that you are checking that you have covered everything you wanted to cover. Audiences are reassured by a speaker who is obviously following a predetermined structure.

Politicians often speak from scripts. This method acts as a safeguard against slips of the tongue during speeches which will be reported in the press, or broadcast. They use professional speech writers who appreciate that the spoken word sounds very different from the written word.

Remember, though, that speaking effectively from a script requires a great deal of skill and most people

THE PLACE THAT GAVE BIRTH TO THE NAME

A place that produces some special item or idea may also produce the name for it. *Champagne* is so called because it comes from the Champagne district of France. More indirectly, *jeans* came from Genoa, the *spaniel* from Spain, and *copper* from Cyprus.

☐ In the list below, choose the word or phrase you believe is nearest in meaning to the key word. For the answers, turn to pages 633-648.

arras
A: a sheepdog
B: a salute
C: a tapestry
D: an alarm clock

artesian relating to:
A: philosophical reason
B: deep wells
C: circulation of the blood
D: fortune-telling

denim
A: a turban
B: dark blue
C: a palace
D: a strong fabric

ermine
A: a stoat
B: nonsense
C: a wooden shoe
D: tobacco

frieze
A: a wild berry
B: a decorated part of a wall
C: a crystal of sugar
D: a candle holder

hessian
A: an evergreen tree
B: sackcloth
C: a purple dye
D: pompousness

homburg
A: flattery
B: a felt hat
C: light opera
D: glue

kersey
A: a medieval headdress
B: a woollen fabric
C: a kind of pullover
D: a hawk

limousine
A: mincemeat
B: a glass bowl
C: a large car
D: a gravestone

magenta
A: a spicy sauce
B: a water lily
C: arrogance
D: deep red

majolica
A: a flower
B: a type of pottery
C: a sailing vessel
D: an underground storehouse

meander
A: to commit treason
B: to follow a twisting course
C: to feel faint
D: to refuse to forgive

milliner
A: an impersonator
B: a hat-maker
C: a hermit
D: a portrait-painter

parchment
A: an accusation
B: fruit-juice
C: paper
D: thirst

ritzy
A: shining
B: crazy
C: luxurious
D: rude

sardonic
A: mocking
B: tight-fitting
C: lazy
D: reproachful

shallot
A: a holy relic
B: a miser
C: smoothness
D: an onion

spa
A: a shopping centre
B: a mast
C: moisture
D: a health resort

Spartan
A: threatening
B: angry
C: lively
D: austere

sybaritic relating to
A: water sports
B: luxurious living
C: foxhunting
D: mental illness

turquoise
A: a rat-poison
B: politeness
C: a semi-precious stone
D: a tyrant

are better off using notes. The script can easily become a barrier between you and your audience, and the result will often be that you fail to give the audience the attention they require. If you do use this method, make a conscious effort to adopt a conversational tone and to lift your eyes up from the page as often as you can. Underline sentences, phrases, and words that you want to emphasise. Bracket off material that can be jettisoned if time is running short, or the audience unresponsive.

Some speakers learn their scripts off by heart. If they are skilled actors, the technique can be effective. Otherwise, the audience senses that the speaker is trying to remember his or her lines and the message will not seem genuine. Good speakers always communicate an element of spontaneity.

REHEARSING

When you are still considering what to include in your speech, talk various points through aloud – to yourself, if no one else is prepared to listen. This will get you used to articulating your themes. When you have got your speech structured, start rehearsing. Use a good-quality cassette or tape recorder.

A few days before you give a speech, try it out on a few friends, colleagues, or relatives. Choose people you know will give you constructive criticism. Ask them whether they could identify the main thrust of your speech, and what they thought of your delivery. Find out what impression they received from your use of voice and body language. Get them to ask you a few questions at the end. And, while you are rehearsing, check your timing too. It is always better to finish slightly before you are expected to. If you overrun, some members of the audience are likely to lose concentration.

If you are using visual aids, try to rehearse with them – see pages 509-512.

EFFECTIVE LANGUAGE AND GESTURE

Using the right language, rhetorical tricks and gestures, varying as appropriate the pace at which you give your speech – all these are important aspects of effective delivery. Here are some tips.

Short sentences and simple language. Long, convoluted sentences are difficult to follow. Shorter sentences make points precisely. When you practise giving your speech out loud, check that you are making your points crisply.

Make sure too that you are using language that your whole audience will understand. If you are speaking to an audience familiar with your subject, you may want to use technical language as a shorthand.

As a speaker addressing a mixed audience, it is better to keep to simple language that everyone will understand. That way, you will not lose any of your audience by talking over their heads.

Watch out too for words that can mean different things in different contexts – 'the marketplace', for example, means one thing to someone in advertising, another thing to the housewife. Make sure that it is clear from the context which meaning of a word you intend.

In writing you should avoid clichés – 'my face was as red as a beetroot', 'I could hardly believe my eyes'. In speaking, by contrast, these can actually be useful (so long as you do not overuse them): they give the audience time to register what you have just said. Avoid, however, the most obvious speech-formulas: 'To cut a long story short . . . '; 'Last, but not least . . . '; 'But seriously . . . '

Rhetorical tricks. Remember the effectiveness of certain rhetorical tricks for getting key points across – particularly at the beginning and end of a speech. Among the most common are repetition, contrast, and lists of three.

This extract from President John Kennedy's famous address to the people of Berlin uses all three devices to demolish views commonly held by supporters of Communism:

> There are many people in the world, who really don't understand, or say they don't understand what is the great issue between the free world and the Communist world –

> Let them come to Berlin.

> There are some who say that Communism is the way of the future –

> Let them come to Berlin.

> And there are even a few who say that it's true that Communism is an evil system but it permits us to make economic progress –

> Let them come to Berlin.

Note the repetition – 'There are . . . there are . . . there are . . . ' – and the refrain; 'Let them come to Berlin.' And the contrast: between, on the one hand, the assertions made by Communism's supporters, and, on the other, the evidence manifest in Berlin of the system's failure. Finally, observe how by listing three times what are essentially variations on the same theme, he builds up to a powerful climax.

The use of gesture. As well as his advice on the number of points to make in a speech, Lloyd George gave Macmillan some tips on the use of gesture. He suggested that a gesture should come before the point it is emphasising: in this way it stimulates the attention of the audience. Shrug your shoulders and open wide your arms in a gesture of incredulity – and then, having aroused the audience's curiosity, quote the statement that you wish to ridicule.

Lloyd George also thought that speakers should make gestures boldly from the shoulder rather than merely from the elbow; small gestures look ineffectual, whereas the speaker who uses expansive gestures will fill the space on a large platform.

SPEAKING AT SOCIAL EVENTS

Thinking of things to say for a social function – a dinner, say, or farewell party – can be particularly difficult. Here are some hints and suggestions to help you.

Making a toast. Talk about the event – how enjoyable it has proved, what it is in aid of, how much effort went into putting it on. Mention what is special about the person or persons being toasted.

Perhaps it is a golden wedding anniversary. Give succinct and entertaining anecdotes about the couple who have remained happily married for so long. Tell an amusing story about their marriage day all those years ago; draw attention to the hordes of children, children-in-law, and grandchildren happily milling around. Then ask the audience to stand and raise their glasses for the toast itself.

Replying to a toast. Thank the person who proposed the toast and comment on something about the event that has given you pleasure – the coming together, maybe, of so many relatives and friends.

Welcoming a visitor. Check beforehand how he or she would like to be introduced. Suppose it is a Rotary Club dinner, and the visitor is a successful industrialist, also known for his efforts on behalf of an international aid organisation. Ask him which of these two sets of activities he wants you to emphasise.

In the speech extend a warm welcome on your own behalf and on behalf of the audience. Let the audience know some of the visitor's achievements – how he started in business, how far he has come since then. Tell the audience why he has been invited – perhaps he recently opened a new factory in the region.

Try to find connections – perhaps amusing ones – between the present occasion and episodes from the person's past. Perhaps the visitor was wheelclamped when last visiting the town where the event is taking place. A teasing reference to some such mishap – so long as it does not still rankle in the recipient's mind – may help to break the ice.

Presenting an award. Tell the recipient (and audience) why the award or gift is being presented – perhaps for exceptionally long and faithful service to your company – and make clear the appreciation that is being expressed. Congratulate the recipient on your own behalf and on behalf of the audience.

Accepting an award. Thank the people or organisation making the presentation. Mention how much it means to you, and thank those colleagues who have given you support over the years.

Farewell speeches. Mention regret at the person's departure and show appreciation for any past achievements – those key projects he or she helped to initiate, and that have contributed so much to the success of the organisation or company.

Tell a few entertaining anecdotes about the person who is leaving. Let the audience know his or her future plans – achieving that long-held ambition to walk solo from Land's End to John O'Groats, maybe – and extend the person best wishes for the future.

In all these cases, be sure to be sincere and enthusiastic in what you are saying. Simple, heartfelt sentiments are effective. And remember also that you should keep such speeches brief and to the point.

The Skills of Good Speaking

Too many gestures, however, can distract from what you are saying. Use them economically to mark particularly significant points. And avoid irritating mannerisms, such as wagging a finger or shaking a fist, which can be off-putting for the audience, and make you seem hectoring.

Remember Hamlet's advice to the band of actors:

> ...do not saw the air too much with your hand... Suit the action to the word, the word to the action; with this special observance, that you o'erstep not the modesty of nature...

Bear also in mind that many well-known speakers, including Martin Luther King, have used stillness to great effect when speaking – to convey strength. If you are someone who does not normally gesticulate when talking, a studied stillness may be best. Adopt a relaxed but still position, letting your face and voice add expressiveness to your message. But make sure that the position is relaxed – don't stand stiffly, as if on a regimental parade ground.

You can also move around the platform to maintain an audience's interest during a long speech. If you do so, plan your movements so that they coincide with the moments at which you move from one point to the next.

Don't stand with your hands in your pockets or you may be tempted to fiddle irritatingly with loose change – and you may also find it difficult to extract your hands when you want to make a gesture. Rest your hands in a relaxed fashion on, say, the lectern. Avoid fiddling with your clothes or hair.

Clear speech. To project your speech so that the audience can hear you clearly, pay special attention to your articulation. Remember that your audience are looking at your face and that to an extent they are lip-reading. You need to form clear consonants, and to use facial expression as a visual aid.

Shortly before you make a speech, run through some of it quickly and quietly to yourself. As you do so, exaggerate the way you articulate words. This will help your muscles to warm up.

The use of pause. Pauses are a vital element in good public speaking. They can mark the end of a stage in the speech, and create expectation and suspense. A slight pause before particularly important statements, statistics, anecdotes, or quotations, will create a momentary suspense while the audience wait for what is to follow – and they will remember your point better.

Think, for example, of one of Churchill's great war speeches, given to the Canadian Houses of Parliament. He was speaking of Britain's resolve to keep on fighting, even after France had fallen to the German invaders:

> When I warned them [the French government] that Britain would fight on alone whatever they did, their Generals told their Prime Minister and his divided Cabinet: 'In three weeks England will have her neck wrung like a chicken.'

He paused – his audience wondered what was coming next. Then he simply added:

> Some chicken! Some neck!

These words – and the message of determination they implied – have never been forgotten.

Pauses also give you time to take breath, to organise your thoughts for the next point, and they give an audience time to assimilate what you have said. When making a long speech, take longer breaks. Give the audience and yourself a rest by pausing to sip some water. Change your position.

Variety of pace, pitch, and volume. The sound of your voice is especially important in keeping an audience interested. Monotonous voices soon lose the audience's attention.

Vary how fast and how loud you speak. If you want to reassure your audience at a particular point, a slower pace and a drop in volume may help. At another point where your main intention is to inspire the audience, talk louder – but don't gabble, a mistake often made by inexperienced speakers. Raise or lower the pitch of your voice when making new points.

Listen critically to yourself when you practise with a cassette or tape recorder.

Eye contact. If you do not look your audience in the eye, you cannot see how they are reacting. When speaking to a small gathering, aim to make eye contact with everyone present. Let your eyes rest on each member of the audience for a few seconds, rather than dart aimlessly around the group, which will give an impression of furtiveness.

With a large audience, pick out strategic points around the room. Rest your eyes for a few seconds on someone at each point, then sweep your eyes round to the next – that way your eye contact can appear to cover the whole audience. Steady eye contact inspires confidence.

The Equipment

Before you give your speech, check that all the equipment you need works – and how it works. Check any projectors. Make doubly sure that your slides, if you are using them, are in the right order and the right way up.

If you are going to use a microphone, check how it works. Test your voice level. Get someone to stand at the back of the room or hall to check that you can be heard clearly.

Remember, if you are using a fixed microphone, to keep your head relatively still during the speech. Clip-on radio microphones are better – if available – as they allow you far greater freedom of movement.

Microphones vary enormously in the way they pick up sound. If your voice is rather weak and breathy, the microphone will emphasise this. Don't bellow, but remember that you must speak with slightly more energy and with clearer articulation than in normal conversation.

ARRANGING THE ROOM

Beware the lectern. Many people imagine that it is safer to give an address from behind a lectern; it protects them from the audience and physical symptoms of nervousness cannot be seen. A lectern also symbolises a certain authority. But remember that, by the same token, lecterns create barriers between you and your audience, making it harder to gain their trust and warmth. If you can possibly bear to do so, try to stand beside a lectern rather than behind it, using it simply to rest your notes on.

There are similar problems with platforms. On a platform you are raised above your audience, who have, literally, to look up to you. In some cases you may be able to give your speech from in front of the platform on the same level as your audience. If you cannot, you will have to work harder at anecdotes, jokes, and similar devices in order to break down the barriers.

Amphitheatre seating, typical of many university lecture theatres, raises the opposite problem. The audience form a semicircle looking down on you, which can be daunting for the nervous speaker.

There is little you can do about this – except to remember that if you do feel overpowered it is only an effect of the seating.

Other arrangements are classroom-style seating, where you stand in front of banks of seats, and the semicircle. The latter is particularly well suited to smaller audiences. If possible, ask the organisers to arrange the seating to form a semicircle.

Before you speak, check that everyone can see you and you can see everyone. Be sure too that you are well lit. If you wear glasses, check that the light is not reflecting off the lenses and so preventing your audience from seeing your eyes. If it is, ask to have the light redirected slightly.

Make sure that the room is well ventilated, and that both you and your audience are going to be as comfortable as possible. It is difficult for listeners to maintain concentration in an atmosphere that is stuffy and claustrophobic.

Stage Fright

The very thought of speaking in public makes some people nervous. This is not necessarily a bad thing. When nervousness gets out of control – with adrenalin pumping madly in the body – it can paralyse a speaker. When controlled, on the other hand, it can lift a speaker's performance.

Nervousness can manifest itself in several ways. You may feel tense in your neck and shoulders. Your mouth may feel dry, or start to overproduce saliva. Your knees may wobble. Your chest may feel tight. Your heart may beat faster, and (to you) louder, and you may have difficulty in drawing breath.

The symptoms can be alarming. But remember this: stage fright is common, and can be helpful. Harold Macmillan, who in his later years was able to hold the House of Commons spellbound, once confessed that before making major speeches he was so nervous that he felt physically sick. The adrenalin that made him feel so ill beforehand did nothing but good when it was channelled into the delivery of his actual speech.

The great actor Laurence Olivier also suffered at times from stage fright – he managed to give memorable performances none the less.

The Skills of Good Speaking

505

And remember too the rewards when, after all, a speech does go well. The sense of satisfaction can be overwhelming, making all the previous effort worth while. Some speakers describe a sensation of soaring on the warmth and energy generated by the response of the audience.

Here, then, are some suggestions to help you to deal with stage fright.

THE RIGHT FRAME OF MIND

Above all, be prepared. Don't skimp on rehearsing. Make sure you are thoroughly comfortable with all the ideas you have to express. Remember, it is your ideas that matter rather than the words you use, and the more thought you give to them, the better.

Ask yourself: 'What is the worst thing that could possibly go wrong?' – and prepare yourself accordingly. Be prepared, if necessary, to do the speech without visual aids. If you are planning to speak without notes, or with few notes, have one card with point headings written on it, and position it where you can easily reach it in an emergency.

Spend a few moments before the speech visualising it as going well and the audience as responding to it favourably. Positive thinking like this can influence your performance.

Don't be put off by an apparent lack of response. Often this is because the audience is completely absorbed by what you are saying. Many speakers are pleasantly surprised at the end of a talk, which they feel has fallen flat, when members of the audience come up and·say how much they have enjoyed it.

Remember that many symptoms of nervousness will register only with one person – yourself. Audiences simply do not notice much of the turmoil in the mind of a nervous speaker. Remember too that the audience is usually on your side. Most will want you to succeed in your speech. Some may disagree with the content, but they will still want to hear you out. They want to be stimulated, challenged, excited by your ideas. And many of the audience will share your nervousness about public speaking. They know what it is like – and don't despise you for feeling apprehensive.

Plan in advance to do something enjoyable after your speech. This gives you something to look forward to, and prevents a sense of anticlimax when it is all over.

Learn too from experience. After a speech, consider what went well, and what did not. Jot these points down for future reference. If you had friends in the audience, ask them for constructive criticism.

CONTROLLING THE SYMPTOMS

Warm yourself up beforehand. Cold, tense muscles are more likely to succumb to nervousness than warm, relaxed ones. If you regularly swim, run, play squash, or go for long walks, try to do one of these activities a few hours before you speak. Give yourself time to relax before the speech. Sit in a chair, and work through your body from the feet upwards, tensing each part, then relaxing it completely.

Work out exactly where you tend to feel tension, and gently exercise that area to relax it. If the back of your neck gets tight, then nod the head gently to ease out bunched muscles. With shoulder tension, gently roll the shoulders back and forwards five or six times. If your arms and hands stiffen, let them get floppy and shake them out. With quivering knees or legs, give them a good shake and check that when you stand, you are not holding your ankles and knees rigidly tense.

Nervousness is not necessarily a bad thing.

Counteract facial tension by blowing your cheeks out as far as they will go and then sucking them in. Massage the cheeks and lips. Release the lips by blowing out 'brrrrrrrr'. Talk through a part of your speech in a whisper, exaggerating facial movement. Take good deep breaths from the level of the stomach. Then make a conscious effort to breathe out slowly.

Get the vocal cords warmed up by running through some of your speech, at the volume appropriate for the room – in the car, perhaps, before you arrive.

This way you will not have to clear your throat nervously at the start of your speech.

If you tend to flush at the neck when you get nervous and are self-conscious about this, wear a garment that conceals the area. If your hands perspire heavily, holding your wrists under cold running water will help to cool them down. If your mouth is very dry, you can stimulate saliva production by biting gently on the front of your tongue. If you are going to talk for a long time, check beforehand that there is water available.

Taking Questions

The question period is a time for you to amplify and build on what you have said in your speech.

At the outset of a speech, it is helpful to let the audience know that they can ask questions at the end – so that they can think of suitable questions. Sometimes, though, the question time comes, and audiences do not respond. In this case, try jump-starting them. You can say: 'Something I'm often asked is . . . ' or ask the audience their opinion of something you have commented on.

Make sure when you take a question that the rest of the audience have heard it. Repeat it loudly and clearly. This also gives you a little extra time to

Your conclusion should be memorable.

prepare your answer. Deliver your reply to the whole audience, not just to the questioner. Otherwise, the rest of the audience may feel excluded.

Occasionally, someone will ask a question that really is not a question at all, purely an expression of his or her own point of view. Quietly restate your own case, then move on to the next question.

You may be asked a question that you cannot answer. Admit that you do not know the answer, but tell the questioner that you can find it out and are willing to call him or her later. Alternatively, suggest that you need to go to sources of reference to give a full answer and, again, that you will phone.

You may also be asked a question that discretion prevents you from answering. In this case, you can stall with 'I don't know if I can answer that, but what I can say is . . . '

A question may be put in such a way that it attributes opinions to you that you do not have – either because the questioner has genuinely failed to understand what you are saying, or because he or she is seeking a confrontation. For instance: 'You've said that everyone should have adult education. But practically this just isn't possible, is it?' Make sure to correct the misunderstanding: 'That isn't exactly what I meant to express. My view is . . . '

If someone starts to challenge or heckle you, don't let your face and your body language show that you feel threatened. Keep an open posture and answer calmly. If the troublemaker keeps on challenging you, suggest that to enter into a private dialogue would be inappropriate, and that you and the challenger continue the discussion at another time. Break eye contact, turn to another part of the audience, and ask for another question.

MAKING A BEST MAN'S SPEECH

The best man's speech is the last of the speeches given at a wedding reception – after those of the bride's father, or an old friend of her family, and of the groom. The groom ends his speech by toasting the bridesmaids, and the best man replies – officially on their behalf.

In practice, however, the best man's chief task is to build up a teasing, but affectionate picture of the groom. It is quite in order for him to make the groom cringe somewhat – but overall the best man's speech should convey a likeable portrait of the person who is presumably one of his closest friends.

Traditionally, you start a best man's speech by thanking the groom for his toast to the bridesmaids, adding a few words about how attractive and charming they are. Then you turn to the main body of your speech. For this you need to have collected a fund of amusing anecdotes about the groom. When preparing the speech, dig into your own memories of him, and ask other friends and his family for further contributions – old school reports and letters home, for instance, are often a good source of amusing material. Look around too for suitable jokes and quotations – like this one from former US President Lyndon B. Johnson:

> Only two things are necessary to keep one's wife happy. One is to let her think she is having her own way, and the other, to let her have it.

Think of amusing ways to tell your audience what kind of person your friend is – his profession or line of business, his hobbies, talents, and outstanding past achievements. Take, for example, this extract from the best man's speech at the wedding of a barrister:

> To Margaret, I'd say this. You're a lucky woman – you're marrying not just one man, but several: a barrister, a wit, a sportsman, a photography buff, a gourmet . . . a nice guy. In fact, when I think of Jake, I picture him as a kind of Hindu goddess – you know, the one with six arms. In one hand, he's carrying a lawyer's brief, in another his camera, in another his tennis racket, in another a frying pan, and the last two hands

are holding the handlebars of his bike. In fact, to complete the picture, you have to imagine him, with most of his arms waving about, pedalling furiously on his bike to get to the Court of Chancery in time for a case.

Remember, of course, to be selective in what you say. Be selective of quality: avoid anything offensive or *risqué* – no references to past girlfriends or love affairs. And be selective too when it comes to quantity. Above everything else, you should aim for brevity in a best man's speech. A five-minute speech is ideal, ten minutes the maximum. As you draw towards your conclusion, the speech should take on a more serious, reflective, though never sermonising tone. Bring in more references to the bride, and how well suited she and the groom are. A brief extract from a love poem is a good device for the ending.

What we're celebrating today, in other words, is not just a marriage of two people, but what Shakespeare called 'a marriage of true minds'. There's an interesting development of this idea in a poem by T.S. Eliot. Here is the idyllic marriage as Eliot describes it:

> The breathing in unison
> Of lovers . . .
> Who think the same thoughts without need of speech
> And babble the same speech without need of meaning.
> No peevish winter wind shall chill
> No sullen tropic sun shall wither
> [TURNING TO THE BRIDE AND GROOM]
> The roses in the rose-garden which is [theirs] and [theirs] only.

Note that you might have to adapt the poem for the occasion – here, for instance, the best man has substituted the word *theirs* for the original *ours* in the last line.

One final point. Many people find the prospect of giving a best man's speech terrifying. But remember this: a best man's speech is, in fact, one of the easiest kinds of speech to give. The audience should be in jovial mood, ready to laugh even at not very funny jokes.

Using Visual Aids

An ANCIENT Chinese proverb states that 'One picture is worth a thousand words.' Pictures and other visual aids – maps, slides, films, graphs, models – certainly do make an impact, though they seldom replace words altogether. When speaking in public, they can make your point, clarify your meaning, enliven your message, and inspire your audience. Churchill's famous V-for-Victory sign in the Second World War helped almost as much as his speeches, to reinforce the nation's hope and courage.

Visual aids enable a speaker to communicate information more quickly – and listeners to absorb it more readily. As every motorist knows, road signs – whether symbols or colour codes – have an immediacy that neither the spoken nor the written word can match. A simple formula emerges:

Words + visual aids = Quick comprehension + long-lasting impressions.

Visual aids have other advantages as well. They help to keep your audience's attention: providing different visual images from time to time helps to restore slacking interest. And if you are a nervous or inexperienced speaker, visual aids are useful psychological props. They divert the listeners' attention from you, and handling them helps you to channel your own nervous energy.

HOW TO USE VISUAL AIDS

Make sure, first, to use the right visual aids. When deciding on one, consider these questions:

Will it grab the audience's attention?
Will it suit the audience and occasion?
Will it be large enough, high enough, and clear enough for people at the back of the room to read or see?
Will it really help people to understand and remember the point you are making? Or will it merely distract from your words?
Could you not convey the message better with words alone?
Will the equipment you need be available?

Here are further do's and don'ts to bear in mind when using visual aids:

☐ Do limit the number of your visual aids. You are giving a talk, not an exhibition.

☐ Don't cram too much information into any one visual aid. Overcrowding a board or screen will confuse rather than illuminate your audience

☐ Do rehearse with your visual aids. Make sure you have mastered the use of any projectors, and that they are in working order. Check that you have any extra equipment you need – extension leads, chalk, pens, dusters, pointers, and so on. And have back-ups ready. If a projector breaks down, you can then turn to your spare one, or at least to the blackboard.

☐ Do face the audience while using visual aids. It is all too tempting to face the screen or flip chart while explaining details, but this muffles your voice. For the same reason, don't try to talk and write on a board or flip chart at the same time.

☐ Don't stand in front of your visual aids. Stand to one side and use a pointer to draw attention to items on the map, chart, or illustration. And don't point across your body. This produces a cramped or closed stance – a poor use of body language that tends to push the audience away rather than draw them in.

☐ Do be specific in what you are indicating. Don't just point vaguely to parts of the picture.

Two final points. First, don't forget that visual aids are only aids. What you say and how you say it are more important. If your words are boring, or long-winded, no visual aids can hide the fact.

Secondly, remember that you yourself are your most effective visual aid. Audiences respond not only to the words you utter, but also to you. If you look alert, upright, self-assured – if your appearance inspires confidence, people will listen to your words with extra care, interest, and enthusiasm. In short, look and behave the part.

CREATING EFFECTIVE VISUAL AIDS

DISTRIBUTION CENTRES IN UK AND AREAS SERVED

1 London
2 Portsmouth
3 Gwent
4 Coventry
5 Norwich
6 Manchester
7 Newcastle
8 Edinburgh

9 Belfast
10 Dublin
11 Limerick

Map outlines can easily be traced from a good atlas. You can then fill in whatever details are relevant to your talk. You can also enlarge or reduce your map using a photocopier. Make sure to label maps, and other aids, clearly.

Clarity – not artistry – is the key to good visual aids. The audience hardly expect you to be a Leonardo, but they do want to understand what you are trying to say. Here are examples of some effective charts and diagrams, particularly suitable for use with an overhead projector. You can easily produce similar ones, using tracing and graph paper. If you know any good artists, you might get one of them to help you.

UNIVER
NUMBERS

Natural Science
Medicine
Law
English
History
Mathematics
Music

GOVERNMENT SPENDIN
DURING THE FIRST QUARTER IN AREAS B
HOSPITALS
EDUCATION
LOCA GOV
14%
7%
5%
RO
32%
13%
8%
9%
WORK
SOCIAL SERVICES
MINES

WRITING AN EFFECTIVE REPORT
Which is the writer?
Which is the reader?

EFFORTLESS

EFFORT

When appropriate, use the human face or figure in your visual aids. Here is a drawing from a seminar on report-writing. Which figure represents the writer of a report? Which the reader? A drawing like this can drive home a point very effectively. Again, no need for high artistry – even matchstick men would do.

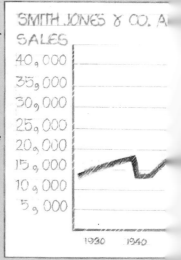

SMITH JONES & CO. A
SALES
40,000
35,000
30,000
25,000
20,000
15,000
10,000
5,000

1930   1940

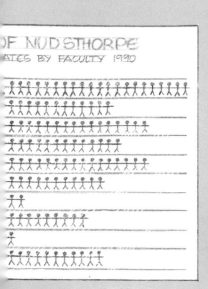

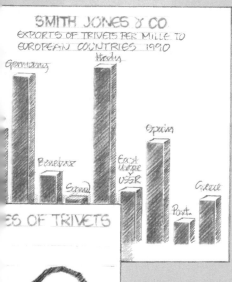

Dry statistics mean little to most people. But represent percentages in, say, a pie-chart (above left), and the eye assimilates them easily. Likewise, comparisons come across more clearly in a bar-chart (see the two examples above), and trends in a graph (left).

THE EQUIPMENT

Visual aids and the tools used to present them range from the sophistication of a video recorder to the traditional chalk and blackboard. Other visual aids are objects that you distribute to the audience, such as paper handouts or models.

PROJECTORS

Probably the most useful of all visual aids is the overhead projector, which will add a professional touch to any presentation. Slide projectors are essential if you have to show really good reproductions of, for example, paintings.

The overhead projector. The chief beauty of this is its flexibility. You can use it to project a succession of prepared maps, diagrams, graphs, and charts, or you can actually write and draw on blank sheets of acetate while you are talking. It also has the advantage that you can use it in a lighted room, and that it allows you to face your audience.

Preparing overhead projector transparencies before a presentation is a simple matter – just draw or trace your diagram onto an acetate sheet. For even smarter presentations, try the photocopied transparency. A magazine photo, say, or a typed report can be photocopied specially onto acetate – try any printer's or photocopying centre.

By laying transparencies one on top of another, you can also build up complex diagrams or pictures – use colour to make the contrasts clearer. With a sheet of card, you can mask areas of a diagram you do not want your listeners to see yet, and reveal the full picture bit by bit.

The slide projector. Slides go down well with large audiences, but they suffer from one major drawback – they have to be shown in a darkened room. Try to organise your talk so as to show all the slides in one sitting. Check before your presentation that they are in the carousel in the right order and have been fitted the right way round. It can be embarrassing if they are upside down.

Don't let the slides take over. Remember you are the speaker. Point out in each slide what it is you want to point out and then move briskly on.

The modern slide projector has a long cord attachment that allows you to bring up the next slide. Use it. It eliminates that tired old instruction: 'May we have the next slide, please.'

Film and video. These allow you to present an extended illustration of some scene or technique described in your talk.

Take care not to show too long an extract from a film or video – or it will become an alternative to your talk rather than an aid. And bear in mind that a lot of equipment and preparation are involved, particularly in the case of a film – setting up the projector, finding someone to operate it, erecting the screen, darkening the room, and so on.

The episcope and epidiascope. These enable you to project opaque materials, especially printed matter such as leaflets or magazine pictures. Unfortunately, the result on the screen is not always clear or bright enough. The preference nowadays is to have diagrams or text photocopied onto acetate, and to use an overhead projector.

BOARDS

Like overhead projectors, the various kinds of board have the advantage of flexibility. They tend to work best with smaller audiences.

The chalk board and felt-pen board. Both of these enable you to write or draw as you wish during a presentation. They allow you to show the development of an idea or process you are describing: you simply add, change, or correct images or words as you go along.

It is possible, though unusual, for the speaker to draw diagrams or charts in advance. As a rule, however, the drawing or writing takes place in the course of the presentation. To avoid slowing down the proceedings more than necessary, prepare simplified drawings that you can copy quickly onto the board. If you have the choice, go for a felt-pen board rather than a chalk board. Felt pens have a greater visual impact than chalk, and they are usually less messy.

The flip chart. This shares the advantages of chalk and felt-pen boards and has two additional ones. It encourages advance preparation; and it allows the speaker to keep diagrams hidden under a blank page until the moment arrives in his talk when he is ready to reveal them.

The magnetic board. This consists of a large sheet of steel. You attach small magnets to the backs of your visual aids and simply stick them onto the board wherever you wish. The magnetic board works well for certain kinds of presentation, especially those requiring a gradual build-up of visual detail. Suppose you want to show the expected development of a town. Using cardboard cut-outs you can build up a plan in front of your audience, adding and removing the various features as you go along.

The flannel board. This has much the same advantages as a magnetic board, and costs considerably less. It consists of a rigid sheet of plywood, fibreboard, or Masonite, covered with a piece of black flannel drawn tightly over the surface.

Organising your display is fairly time-consuming. Prepare your cut-outs on cardboard or thick paper; then paste pieces of sandpaper on the backs, using the heaviest gauge sandpaper you can find, and making sure to paste the corners down thoroughly. At the appropriate moment during your speech, press the cut-outs on to the flannel board. The sandpaper grips on to the flannel, rather like Velcro, allowing for easy removal and replacement.

OTHER AIDS

Sometimes the most effective visual aid is one that listeners can hold or examine for themselves.

Models and samples. A peep at the real thing, or a model of it, is often worth ten diagrams. Far better to let your audience see a model of a projected building, than just inspect plans on paper. Make sure, however, that any model you use is large enough for all of the audience to see, and that you can move it easily to show different aspects. Or you can hand out samples – of, say, your company's latest line in lipstick or pocket diaries.

Handouts. These can show diagrams, charts, graphs, figures, or drawings just as an overhead projector or flip chart can and have the added virtue that you can provide background notes.

Handouts have many other advantages. Your audience can keep and refer to them long after your presentation. You can prepare them well in advance, and with no equipment other than a typewriter, pen and paper, and photocopier. Very little can then go wrong – there is no projector to break down, for example.

Two notes of caution: don't hand them out until the moment that your audience actually needs to refer to them – otherwise they will probably read the handouts rather than listen to you. And always make sure you have enough handouts to go around.

Being Interviewed by the Media

THE OPPORTUNITIES for ordinary people to appear on radio and television are greater now than ever before. Broadcasting used to be the domain almost exclusively of celebrities, politicians, and professional commentators. Now, with the ever-increasing numbers of radio stations and radio phone-ins, and on television the proliferation of interview programmes, talk shows, quizzes, and game shows, more and more ordinary members of the public are making their presence felt in the different media.

Yet for many people, perhaps for most, the very idea of appearing on television or radio and answering questions is a nerve-shattering prospect. This chapter tells you how to be at your best when being interviewed on radio or television, or taking part in game shows or phone-ins, and how the experience can be enjoyable, exciting, and rewarding. It also tells you about the basic skills required to be an interviewer, how to deal with interviews with the press and one of the most testing kinds of interview – a cross-examination in court.

THE INTERVIEW

Interviews can take many forms – from the brief on-the-spot encounter when a journalist asks someone for a comment as he or she emerges from, say, a union meeting to the hour-long one-to-one probing of an in-depth interview. They can be serious, frivolous, or a mixture of both.

You might find yourself invited to take part in an interview programme:

☐ to inform and explain. If you are a doctor, say, a radio or television station might ask you to be one of a panel discussing National Health Service reforms – to give the point of view of the ordinary GP, and to explain how proposed reforms affect you and your colleagues.

☐ to entertain. You might take part in a game show or quiz – in which case your task is to enter into the spirit of the game and to provide good-natured amusement for the viewers.

☐ to argue a case, or express an opinion or point of view. You might be leading a campaign against, for instance, proposals to build a shopping precinct in your town centre. You are brought into a local radio current-affairs programme, along with a spokesman for the council, representing the opposite side, to discuss the whole issue.

☐ to probe or explore an idea or personality. A programme might be devoted to a famous actress. You knew her in her youth, and the radio or television station has invited you to give your insights into her early years.

Or you might be expected to provide a combination of all these elements. Many interview programmes and chat shows – such as the *Wogan* show on television and *Desert Island Discs* on radio – strive to maintain an even balance of information, exploration, entertainment (usually in the form of humour), and opinion.

Know what you are in for. Before you agree to be interviewed, make sure you know what you are letting yourself in for. Find out, first, what kind of interview it is to be – serious, light-hearted, in-depth, on-the-spot, rehearsed, spontaneous, and so on. Remember that if you do not feel you can do justice to yourself in a particular kind of interview, you can always refuse to go on. Find out too how long the interview is going to last. Two minutes? Thirty minutes? One hour? Or more? Usually, on-the-spot and impromptu interviews are short. The interviewer might approach you in the street to ask you for information or an opinion – what, for example, you think of a proposal to build a new remand centre in your area.

On the other hand, if you are to be interviewed on a chat show, or in-depth, the interview might go on for some time. Either way, you should know. If the interview turns out to be much shorter than you expected, the interviewer might have to cut you off before you have made your most important points. If the interview turns out to be longer than you expected, you might find it tricky to answer all the questions without repeating yourself.

Find out which areas of a subject the interviewer is planning to cover. In the case of a programme devoted to Health Service reforms, find out if the presenter will be concentrating on reforms as they affect hospitals, or GPs, or some other aspect.

Make sure you know what kind of audience the programme is aimed at. How you answer a question clearly depends on whether your audience consists of, say, children or adults.

Suppose you are a musician asked about your early days in your profession. If you are appearing on a children's programme, you will almost certainly emphasise the human side of your story – how you had to practise for hours and hours as a child, how perhaps you hated it, how you were inspired by a particular teacher.

If, by contrast, you are taking part in a Radio Three programme aimed at a sophisticated audience of music-lovers, your answers will be quite different. While not ignoring the human side, you will probably dwell much more on, for example, the technical difficulties you had as a young beginner.

Finally, be sure you know why you have been asked to appear, what your 'billing' will be. Will you be there as an expert in a particular field? As a representative member of the public? Or perhaps because you have sprung to celebrity for some special exploit – raising a record sum of money for charity, say, by swimming five times back and forth across the Channel?

Prepare yourself. Try, next, to anticipate the questions you are likely to be asked – as you might do for an exam – and work out suitable answers. Check on any recent facts and figures that have a bearing on your subject. Refresh your memory about relevant sequences of events – you do not want to be seen to fumble during the interview. If you have been invited to take part in a discussion programme, be prepared for all possible attacks from any antagonists.

Prepare yourself to make a few – say, three – points well, rather than many points skimpily. In your opposition to a proposed bypass, you may decide, for instance, to focus on these three points:

☐ that the proposed route for the new road will cut through a unique area of woodland containing many rare species of wildlife

☐ that it will divert essential business from shops in the centre of the town

☐ that it is unnecessary anyway – the new motorway being built ten miles west of the town will remove the worst of the traffic

Think too of plenty of good stories and anecdotes to enliven your interview. Very often a story will illustrate a point better than any amount of dry facts and statistics.

Rehearse your answers out loud – not just in your head. Things that people know inside-out, and do perfectly every day, can be very difficult to describe or explain verbally – simply because they are not used to explaining what they do in words. Try also writing out your answers. This will help you to get them clear, concise, exact, and relevant to the purpose of the interview. Remember the words of Francis Bacon, the Elizabethan thinker: 'Reading maketh a full man; conference a ready man; and writing an exact man.' They would make an excellent motto for anybody wishing to become a successful broadcaster, interviewee, or spokesman. Have a go too at practising your answers on a friend or relative.

Finally, remember that before the interview, you can always ask the interviewer: 'What's going to be the first question?' Then your first answer will be properly thought out and to the point. A good start is half the battle won in interviews.

Keeping on top during the interview. Keep calm during the interview. A certain feeling of 'butterflies' is good – it helps to keep you on your toes – but don't let it get out of control. For advice on how to manage stage fright and turn it around to your advantage, see pages 505-507.

Aim to get your main points or comments across as early as possible. If you delay, you might find that the interview is over before you have done so – time moves fast in interviews. To achieve this, you might have to take a question or comment aimed in one direction and turn it around to face in quite another direction – the one *you* want to go in. You are taking part in a debate on Sunday trading, say, on the side of those in favour of allowing shops to open on Sunday. The interviewer points out how this would destroy the traditional restful British Sunday. You might answer: 'Yes, I think you're making an interesting point, but surely what really matters is that nobody has the right to tell me what I can and cannot buy on a Sunday . . . ' This tactic of 'jumping the gun' is frequently used – and almost always to good effect – by politicians.

When dealing with controversial matters, avoid insults. Remember that your listeners or viewers want to hear discussion on the actual issues, not pejorative comments or slurs on people with whom you disagree. Resorting to personal comment or insult is invariably a sign that the underlying argument is weak. The public is wise to that. Remember, too, that the laws of libel apply to anything that is broadcast.

Often, in confrontational broadcasts, participants feel strongly about the issues. Emotions run high, and, up to a point, this can add excitement to the programme. But on no account lose your temper. Quiet conviction and calmly reasoned statements are stronger persuaders than much puffing and blowing. The person with an air of polite and confident composure usually wins the respect of the audience, including many of those who hold opposing views.

Keep your language straightforward. Don't shroud yourself in clichés and jargon – 'unsecured loan stock . . . scrip issues . . . yield gaps . . .' and the like. Your fellow panel-members may understand the jargon, but what about your audience? The person who can express himself simply, clearly, and interestingly – without, on the other hand, being patronising – will always have the advantage in a discussion programme.

If an interview is personal, the interviewer is bound to ask probing questions about your life and experience. Clearly, if you are prepared to reveal nothing about your private life, you should not agree to give such an interview. But even if you are happy to answer these questions, the point might come at which you want to draw the line. In this case, an honest approach is best: 'I'm sorry, but I'd rather not answer that question just now.' Even better is to provide an alternative subject to pursue in place of the embarrassing one: 'I'd rather not answer that question, but what was fascinating was a similar experience I had at the same time . . .'

Remember the interviewer. Don't forget the interviewer's point of view. Understanding his role, what he is trying to achieve in the programme, will give you confidence.

The vast majority of radio and television interviewers are helpful and sympathetic to their guests – especially to those with little or no experience of broadcasting. They will nearly always try to put you at your ease, both before and during the programme. After all, they want you to come over well. Often, they will discuss in advance the questions they are going to ask.

But don't forget that the interviewer's job is also to represent the listening or viewing public. He may therefore ask some awkward questions. His brief is nearly always to present both sides of an argument as fairly and as comprehensively as possible in the available time. He will do his best to get at the truth. And he will try to ensure that all of his guests get an equal chance to express, explain, and defend their different views.

To achieve these ends, the interviewer cannot shrink from asking challenging questions. If he asks you a provocative question, remember that he is not doing so in order to make you look foolish. He does so to meet the demands of his job. Provided your views are sound, reasonable, and based on conviction, you have nothing to fear.

In fact, many people who are regularly interviewed – politicians, for example – prefer a hard-hitting and blunt style of interview to the milder style, because it gets their adrenalin flowing. It has been said that a good interviewer is like a surgeon who cuts away the flesh to get to the seat of the disease – it is always done with the intention of causing as little pain or damage as possible.

On-site interviews. On-site interviews require a different approach from studio ones. They are by definition impromptu, held at short notice so that you have little or no advance warning, and no chance for careful preparation. Such interviews take place wherever you and the interviewer happen to be – out of doors, in the foyer of a conference centre or hotel, on the street.

Fortunately, this kind of interview is not usually very demanding – unless you are being asked for an on-the-spot expert opinion, in which case be careful not to commit yourself to a statement that you might later regret. Normally, however, the interviewer is just trying to get what is known as a *vox pop* – from the Latin *vox populi*, 'voice of the people' – a sample of public opinion on a particular issue.

In this case, you are not expected to offer carefully considered, skilfully balanced, or eloquently phrased answers to his questions. Just give the interviewer what he wants – your honest opinion of the new brand of cat food you have just bought, or

The Skills of Good Speaking

515

whatever. And remember that you have, of course, every right to make no comment at all.

If you do wish to answer or comment, apply the following rules:

☐ Listen carefully to the question asked, and make sure you understand it.

☐ Don't gabble or mumble your words.

☐ Speak as clearly and fluently as you can, without sounding unnatural or affected.

☐ Remember that your answer or comment is important to the interviewer, otherwise he would not have asked you for it. This will help to boost your confidence.

HOW TO BE AN INTERVIEWER

If your ambition is to be an interviewer – rather than an interviewee – here are some basic guidelines. Bear in mind, though, that you will also need training in the technical side of the business – camera positions, microphone technique, autocues, how to read floor manager signals, studio discipline, and so on. If you live in or near a major city, you may be able to learn these techniques in evening classes. Contact your local education authority to find out.

Preparation. Research is essential. Only a sound understanding and knowledge of the subject can prompt good questions from the interviewer, to prompt enlightening answers from the interviewee.

Words and phrasing. Both the person being interviewed and the listeners must be able to understand your questions. So your choice of words must be simple, and the phrasing unambiguous: 'What do you feel about the plans for a new bypass around Uxford?' rather than 'What in your opinion are the possible economic, social, and environmental implications – positive and negative – arising from the local council's proposal no. 5b(i) to construct a ring road to take the traffic on the A56 around rather than through Uxford?'

Patience and persistence. Remember that some guests will seize the opportunity to say what they want to say, regardless of whether it answers your question or not. You must, therefore, persist, asking the question politely but firmly a second or even a third time until you get a satisfactory answer. Don't, on the other hand, adopt the tone of an interrogation – keep your questions courteous.

Timing. Get your guest talking as soon as possible with a quick and relatively easy question – a little 'ice-breaker' – perhaps something as simple as: 'How long have you lived in Uxford?' This will help the guest to overcome any stage fright. Then move swiftly to your best or most important question. Don't leave this to the last minute of allocated time. Cutting off the reply can lead to resentment in the guest, and frustration for the viewers. Remember, the clock rules!

Listen. By all means have a list of prepared questions – but don't stick to it rigidly. Listen to the answers. Pick up any fresh points that seem interesting. Sometimes supplementary questions that arise spontaneously can lead to some extremely revealing answers.

Keep a balance. Don't shirk a challenging question. Your listeners or viewers will want to hear the answer – and, as they cannot ask the question themselves, you must put it for them. Your aim should be to present a balanced inquiry, which means asking critical and friendly questions alike.

Confidence and ease. Be hospitable and welcoming before and during the interview. Smile, exude warmth, and create a sense of security. Show that you know what you are about and are truly in command of the situation.

Enthusiasm. Ask questions because you really want to know the answers. Show keen interest in the subject, and enthusiasm.

Speech, manner, and dress. Clear speech, an attractive voice, pleasing manner, and – in the case of television – appropriate dress are essential assets for any interviewer.

Clarity of mind. The interviewer must be a clear thinker, have a quick grasp of issues, and acquire a wide general knowledge.

RADIO

Nearly all that has been said so far applies to both radio and television. But there is, of course, an obvious difference between the two media. On the radio you are totally dependent on your voice. No amount of facial expression, eye movement, gesture, or any other form of body language will help listeners to understand, enjoy, or agree with your ideas. You have to be as lucid and as *verbally* interesting and persuasive as you would be if you were talking on the phone or to a blind person.

Choose your words with particular care. As always, avoid jargon and ambiguity. Take trouble to describe briefly but vividly anything the listener needs to imagine in order to appreciate your argument. If you are campaigning, say, against the proposed development for holiday accommodation of a stretch of coastland, give the listener a word-picture of the beauty, silence, and tranquillity of the area as it now is. On television, this would be done for you with film footage of the spot.

Keeping your listener's attention also depends on how you use your voice, so aim to be *vocally* interesting as well. Because on radio – and, of course, on television – you are talking to your listeners through a microphone, you do not need to project your voice. The studio sound technicians usually make the required volume adjustments when giving you a voice test before the programme starts. They will probably advise you to talk as softly, or as loudly, during the programme as you normally do in everyday conversation.

Remember, though, that microphone technology cannot make indistinct speech sound intelligible, a monotonous voice sound lively, or a harsh tone sound mellow. For advice on how to improve the quality of your voice, see the chapter on improving your voice and speech, pages 462–480.

Dialects and foreign accents. A dialect or foreign accent is, in itself, perfectly acceptable and welcome. In fact, a range of dialects and accents adds interest, variety, and colour to broadcasting so long as your articulation is clear, your voice lively and varied, and the tone pleasing. Speak fast enough to hold your listeners' interest, and slowly enough for them to understand you with ease.

RADIO PHONE-INS

There are a great many radio phone-in programmes, and – with the possible exception of letters to the press – they are the easiest way for ordinary members of the public to make their views known on particular subjects.

General-interest phone-ins. These usually begin with the host suggesting a subject, or a number of subjects, that he or she believes will be of interest to listeners. These might be national or international political issues that are currently arousing a lot of comment, or subjects such as the care of the environment, fashion, divorce, marriage, and so on. The host then invites people to phone in with comments, views, suggestions, questions, or answers relating to the subject.

For people who are nervous of broadcasting, taking part in one of these phone-ins can be an excellent way to break the ice. You can speak on your own phone in the familiar surroundings of your home. You can decide when you wish to speak. You need only give your first name – which allows you the comfort of some degree of anonymity. And if you feel you are getting into deep water, you can simply bring your call to an end by saying a polite 'Good-bye' and ringing off.

Unless you feel your comments are particularly urgent, don't phone in at once. Listen in for a while to get some sense of the host's style – unless, of course, you are already familiar with the programme. This will help you to anticipate the sort of response the host is likely to make to your comments. Hosts have very different styles – and if you do not know what to expect, their responses can be off-putting. Some presenters have an easy-going, relaxed approach – at times bordering on the languid. Others are more aggressive – at times coming within a hair's-breadth of downright rudeness. Most, however, try to transmit a fair blend of genial politeness and forthright vigour.

Phone-ins with experts. Some phone-ins are concerned with specific topics – such as particular areas of medicine, gardening, politics, sport, crime, or legal rights – on which listeners may want advice or information. In these cases, the presenter usually has in the studio an expert on the selected topic. Listeners then phone in with their questions – or, sometimes, to argue with the expert.

Before phoning in, be sure to think your question or comment through. Make sure it is relevant to the discussion, and that it is worded as clearly, fluently, and concisely as possible. If it is a lengthy or complicated question, jot down a few reminder words on paper before making your call.

But try not to read your question out word by word. Reading aloud on the phone often sounds artificial, and most phone-in hosts discourage it – some even interrupt callers who are clearly reading their questions. Remember that you are having a conversation, not reading out a lecture.

During the call, speak directly into the mouthpiece and articulate clearly, but in a natural tone of voice. Don't interrupt – wait until the host or expert has finished before you speak. Try to imagine him sitting there in front of you as you speak – and concentrate on him. Don't rush – but, at the same time, be brief!

TELEVISION

On television you are, of course, seen as well as heard. Dress tidily, in a way that makes you feel good. It is a good idea to check beforehand with the producer of the programme what colours you should, or should not, wear. If, for example, the set is largely white, avoid wearing white – or you will simply disappear into the background. And in all cases, avoid clothes with strong, violent patterns – spots, stripes, zigzags – which often cause dazzle on television.

The studio. If you are interviewed in a television studio, don't be unnerved by the sight of cameras and microphones, monitors, platforms, lights, wires, and the often daunting appearance and

Imagine yourself talking to a friend ...

high-powered professionalism of the studio staff. Remember, they are just doing a job, which has no more mystique than dentistry or ironmongery. The studio is their workshop: the equipment, their tools.

Remember too that most broadcasters are friendly – after all, good communications are their business – and if you tell, or remind, them that you are a newcomer, they will be glad to explain things to you as far as time allows.

Facing the camera. Facing the camera can be one of the most daunting parts of a television interview. The most useful trick here is to think of the camera as a friend – have a specific and affable person in mind. Forget the audience, and imagine yourself talking to your friend. Think of the camera lens as his eye – the eye of someone who is delighted to see you and eager to hear what you have to say. This will help to relax you, boost your confidence, and reduce nervousness.

INFORMAL SHOWS

Unlike more formal interviews and discussion programmes, chat and game shows aim for a relaxed, party-like style. Learning how to fit in with this – in what is, after all, the highly artificial atmosphere of the studio – can be one of the most difficult tasks for the newcomer to television.

Chat shows. In a chat show you will probably be one of several guests, and there will usually be an audience as well. The presenter will generally invite you onto this kind of show because you have done something that makes a stir – perhaps you were caught up accidentally in a major international hostage crisis, and played a heroic role. You will meet the presenter – or a programme assistant – beforehand, and between you discuss and agree on the format of the interview.

Remember once again that the host is a friend not an enemy – he or she will want to present you in the best possible way. Aim to be at ease, as if you were with good friends. For warm-up exercises to help you to relax, see pages 506-507 in the chapter on public speaking. The presenter will start the interview by introducing you – then come the questions. Open up, be expansive. Remember that you are there to entertain – so throw in plenty of anecdotes. Behave as if you were glad to be there, not as if the programme producers were lucky to have you, and certainly not as if you were going through an ordeal.

CONJUNCTIVITIS OR PINKEYE? WORDS OFFICIAL AND UNOFFICIAL

An *aquarium* is really nothing but a *fish tank*, and the serious-sounding affliction of *acute conjunctivitis* is that common complaint called *pinkeye*. In each case, we have an everyday term, as well as its technical or 'official' synonym. Many ordinary English words have official counterparts in this way.

☐ Choose the word or phrase that is nearest in meaning to each of the following technical terms. Turn to pages 633-648 for the answers.

amnesia
A: unconsciousness
B: loss of memory
C: an official pardon
D: a speech defect

arachnid
A: a climbing plant
B: a shellfish
C: a spider
D: a geometrical figure

arboriculture
A: settlement of disputes
B: gardening
C: bee-keeping
D: cultivation of trees

archipelago
A: a group of islands
B: a small archway
C: a severe skin rash
D: an earthquake

bibliophile
A: a library
B: a card index
C: a book lover
D: a collector of ornaments

calligraphy
A: the art of handwriting
B: a fat physique
C: a temperature gauge
D: the skill of map-reading

halitosis
A: a war cry
B: a hallucination
C: bad breath
D: a glow in the night sky

kleptomania
A: an urge to steal
B: insane lust for power
C: carpet collecting
D: admiration of a pop or film star

lentigo
A: an attack of dizziness
B: a freckle
C: a poisonous fungus
D: slow musical tempo

mephitis
A: a bad smell
B: a kidney disease
C: a grammatical error
D: alcoholism

patella
A: a pressure cooker
B: the kneecap
C: rust
D: artificial jewellery

physiognomy
A: the study of fish
B: forecasting the future
C: facial features
D: gymnastics

prosthesis
A: an artificial body part
B: a total change of form
C: a figure of speech
D: a weather forecast

pyrexia
A: a wasting disease
B: the making of fireworks
C: firefighting
D: a fever

rubella
A: radioactive rock
B: German measles
C: the forehead
D: food-poisoning

somnambulist
A: an explorer
B: a stamp-collector
C: a spy
D: a sleepwalker

stenography
A: decoration using stencils
B: use of X-rays
C: tape-recording of music
D: writing in shorthand

strabismus
A: a naval battle
B: a squint
C: a tax deduction
D: a maze

Sometimes, you will not be able to see the studio audience. Don't worry. You do not have to project to them – the camera and microphones will do it for you. Be warm, friendly, approachable, and you will be transmitted favourably.

Game shows. Game shows can be the most fun – and embarrassing – shows to appear on. If it is your ambition to take part in your favourite show, telephone the television company, find out the name of the producer, and write to him or her stating simply that you are interested in taking part. What happens next will depend on the producer, but usually you will be invited to an audition. The most important thing by far in both the audition and the show – if you do eventually get invited to take part – is to *enjoy* the whole experience. Enter right into the spirit of the thing – just as you would do at a party. At the audition, aim to prove to the producer and whoever else is watching that you have the kind of bubbly, outgoing, unselfconscious personality that will make their show a success. Broadly speaking, the more you enjoy the experience, the more people will enjoy watching and listening to you.

Game shows usually revolve around a spirit of light-hearted competition. Everyone likes to win games, and walk away with prizes. So have a go! Don't worry about the mechanics of things – in the show itself you will be in the hands of an experienced presenter to guide you and, for encouragement, you will have a studio audience to cheer you on. But remember that who wins and who loses – which often depends more on luck than skill – is not very important to the viewers. Most of them watch the show to be entertained – to enjoy the fun, rather than for the competitive element. An affable, entertaining, and sporting loser can be even more popular than the lucky winner.

INTERVIEWS WITH THE PRESS

Being interviewed for a magazine or newspaper is in many ways less demanding than being interviewed on television or radio. On television, success depends on what you say, how you sound, and how you look. On radio, it depends on what you say, and how you sound. But in press interviews, you only need to concentrate on what you say. The disadvantage is that once the article or report is in print, you cannot correct, or argue with, the interviewer. What is published is published. If you feel you have been misquoted or misunderstood, various courses of action are open to you – you can, for example, write a letter to the editor pointing out the mistakes made in the article. But you have no guarantee that your letter will be published. Nor, if it is published, is there any certainty that all the readers of the original piece will see it.

Be careful, therefore, during an interview, *not* to say anything even 'off the record', that you do not want the paper to print. Similarly, be sure to mention everything that you *do* wish the resulting article to include. In the excitement of the interview, many people forget to mention some matters they want included, and let slip comments they later regret.

Remember that experienced journalists and reporters are experts in drawing out unguarded statements – for example, your true, and perhaps unflattering, opinion of some famous person you have worked with. Naturally, the interviewer is eager to print everything he believes will interest his readers – that is a major part of his job. Unfortunately, what interests his readers will not always coincide with what you want people to know.

The following guidelines will help to improve the chances that a published interview will be to your liking. And remember that, on the whole, most press articles, reports, and features are reasonably accurate – and the benefits of good publicity generally outweigh the drawbacks of minor inaccuracies or embarrassments. Here are some precautions to take before agreeing to an interview:

☐ Make sure you know which magazine or paper the interviewer represents. Knowing this should give you some idea of what kind of article to expect, what angle it is likely to take.

☐ Find out exactly which aspects of your life the interviewer is interested in. You may be known as the chairman of a dynamic young computer company, but is that the aspect of your life the interviewer is interested in? He may want to know about your hobby of growing old-fashioned roses, your favourite holiday places, or how, as well as founding your business, you became the first person to somersault right around the world. When you know what he is going to focus on, you can prepare yourself – gathering together relevant facts and stories.

☐ Ask the interviewer approximately how many words he will be writing about you. The answer will give you some idea of the amount of detail he expects you to supply.

☐ Find out if you can see the article before it goes into the magazine or newspaper, and whether any comments or objections you make will be taken into account.

Once you have obtained this information, you are in a position to decide whether to agree or refuse to be interviewed. If you agree, the essential thing is to make a note of all the points you wish to mention – rough headings will do. Keep them by you, and be sure to glance at them during the interview. Of course, the interviewer may not ask you questions on all your points – in which case you will have to steer the discussion round to them, as when being interviewed on television or radio.

Even if you do all this, you may still find that the finished article differs widely from what you expected. The writer may not have included all your answers. And even if he has, he will almost certainly have expressed them in his own way – rather than using your words – with his own interpretation. If you are lucky, however, the broad thrust of the article or report will still be more or less favourable.

If the worst happens and you are seriously unhappy with the article, a series of actions are open to you. First, write a letter of complaint to the editor. He will then decide whether or not he thinks your complaint is justified. If he decides it is, he will print a letter from you correcting the mistaken facts.

If he decides it is not justified and you still wish to pursue the matter, write – in the case of national newspapers – to the Ombudsman or Readers' Representative whose name should be printed in the paper. With local papers, or if you get no satisfactory redress from the national paper's Ombudsman, write to the Press Council, 1 Salisbury Court, London EC4Y 8AE.

Giving Evidence in Court

Cross-examination in a court of law can be one of the most gruelling forms of interview. You were a witness to a crime, say, and a suspect has been arrested and brought to trial. The prosecuting lawyers have summoned you to give evidence. Your cross-examination at the hands of their barrister should be relatively straightforward – your evidence probably favours his case. But then comes the defending lawyer. He is deliberately out to trip you up. He tries to find ambiguities in your evidence, and to suggest that you may have been mistaken. He may even be rude or aggressive in order to confuse you into contradicting yourself.

The most important rule when giving evidence, as with all other interviews, is to stay calm and keep a clear mind. Arrive at the court in good time, and ask to see the solicitor who requested your attendance. Ask him for a copy of the statement you made at the time of the crime or incident. It may all have happened many months ago, and to avoid embarrassing confusion during the examination you should refresh your mind about the details. The solicitor will also be able to inform you about the progress of the case.

You will not usually be allowed into the court until it is time to give your evidence – in case you are influenced by the other witnesses. When your turn comes, you will be shown to the witness box, where you will have to swear an oath, or give an affirmation, committing you to speak the truth. Then the lawyers will take you through your evidence, first the lawyers acting for the side that requested your attendance, followed by the representatives of the opposing side.

Take your time when answering the lawyers' questions – particularly with an aggressive, hostile lawyer. Concentrate hard on the questions, and make sure you answer them fully, clearly, and crisply. Don't let the lawyer put you off your balance. After all, if you are telling the truth, you have nothing to fear. Be prepared to spend a long time in the witness box. Lawyers go through the evidence very slowly to enable the judge to make very full notes.

After giving your evidence, don't assume that you can go home. The order to attend – known as a *subpoena* if it is a High Court case, a 'witness summons' for other courts – requires you to stay for the duration of the trial. You may be recalled later to give further evidence, or to clarify something you have said. If, however, you feel this is unlikely, you can ask to be released. If the lawyers for both sides agree that they do not need you any more, the judge will probably agree to let you go.

The Skills of Good Speaking

Job Interviews

An INTERVIEW is essentially a conversation, though with several special features: it has a specific purpose; it follows a fairly structured pattern – time, place, length, participants, and subject matter are established well in advance; and one group or participant controls the proceedings and contributes mainly questions – the other contributes mainly answers.

By its nature the interview sets up an artificial and often daunting relationship between people. The participants have to adopt roles and are not equal partners. If you take part in an interview – whether as an interviewer or interviewee – don't expect to feel completely at ease in what is after all an unnatural setting. But with practice and by adopting various strategies, you should be able to cope or even shine in the interview room.

Interviews in the workplace. Bosses or personnel managers conduct interviews: to select staff (job interviews, promotion interviews); to monitor employees' progress (appraisal interviews); and to deal with problems (disciplinary interviews).

The inequality between the participants is normally clear. The boss or interviewer is cast in the role of judge, with the power to employ, upgrade, or fire the interviewee – the person in the witness box. Both participants feel a great pressure of responsibility. The interviewee has to do him- or herself justice. The interviewer (like all judges) has to do justice, full stop. If interviewees fail to present themselves in a favourable light, they will suffer. If interviewers fail to reach the correct decision, the 'injustice' rebounds, not just on the affected individuals, but on the company as a whole.

The Interviewer

The interviewer's responsibilities extend well beyond making the right selection. Within the interview room, he or she has the basic responsibility of showing courtesy and consideration towards the candidates.

The interviewer is, after all, a host and should observe the normal formalities of social interchange. This is for the sake of the company's reputation as well as of common decency.

For most candidates, the interview supplies their first glimpse of the workings of the company or group. The impression they carry away – all the more vivid for the heightened atmosphere of the interview – is largely of the interviewer's making.

Treat the applicants fairly, and even those who are rejected will continue to think and speak highly of the company. Antagonise the applicants, and they will criticise the company whenever they have the chance. If the antagonised applicants then get jobs elsewhere, and reach positions of responsibility, their poor impressions could lead to lost business.

PREPARING AN INTERVIEW

Your task as an interviewer of job candidates begins when you prepare the advertisement for the position. Make sure to word the job description carefully (see page 307). Consider the skills, qualifications, and personal qualities you are looking for. Don't forget to look beyond the most obvious requirements.

Consider, for example, the importance of a candidate's ability to work in a team or in isolation, to lead or to follow, to be creative or to reproduce accurately someone else's pattern of work.

The more clearly you express your requirements, the fewer unsuitable candidates will apply.

The application form. The job application form offers a further opportunity for narrowing down the list of applications and selecting a short list for interview. Once again, its effectiveness depends on its wording. Think carefully about the questions it poses. And look at old application forms.

The first stage of sifting is easy enough. Some completed application forms reveal immediately a grossly inappropriate candidate – underqualified, semi-literate, or whatever. Waste no further time on these, other than to send out courtesy letters of rejection. Some application forms will indicate equally clearly a very promising candidate. To these you will respond with invitations for an interview.

The difficult applications are those from the borderline candidates. If you have worded the questions cleverly, however, you should not have too much trouble deciding which of these applicants you really feel are worth interviewing. To help you to sort out the borderline cases, you may decide to have more than one round of interviews. For the first round, you might have a short list of around twelve, say, for the second around six.

Carefully worded questions in the application form will also provide useful information for the interview. This information is of two types – background and foreground information.

Background information includes work experience, relevant skills, such as a knowledge of foreign languages, and so on. This is factual information that you as interviewer need to know. But valuable time would be wasted if you had to use the interview to discover it.

Some details of background information may come as a shock to you if disclosed only in the interview – that the applicant is deaf, for instance, or that he is the managing director's nephew. To avoid being taken unawares, try to include a catch-all question on the application form. Something to this effect:

> Mention any other personal or professional details that you feel may have some bearing on your application.

Foreground information consists of topics for exploration in the interview – typically, the candidate's attitudes, outside interests, or 'irrelevant' skills. For instance, a question about the applicant's driving licence – this might provide a lead into discussing relocation or multi-site work.

THE FORM AND STRUCTURE OF THE INTERVIEW

An interviewee is entitled to know beforehand what form the interview will take. How long will it last? How many interviewers – one, two, a panel? And who will they be with? It is a courtesy to offer this information in advance.

There are three possible forms of interview: panel interviews, interviews with two interviewers, and one-to-one interviews.

Panel interviews. These have the advantage of bringing to bear the experience of a number of people. Those who may have to work with the candidate get a chance to voice their opinions about him or her. But there are disadvantages too. Interviewees generally dislike being interviewed by a panel. It is nerve-racking enough to be questioned by one or two strangers. A whole gang of them is quite hard to handle. Of course the difficulty is averted if the interviewee sees panel members alone or in pairs – this involves the use of a scoring system, with the interviewers pooling assessments at the end. The disadvantage of this is that it takes so much time.

Two interviewers. The two-interviewer interview is often no more than a small panel interview. But sometimes it is adopted specifically to test the candidate. The interviewers may decide in advance to adopt opposing roles, the one sympathetic and the other confrontational. This method is supposed to reveal the candidate's probable reaction to pressure in the workplace.

One-to-one interviews. The one-to-one interview is the form preferred by interviewees. It more nearly resembles a conversation, rather than the third-degree of the panel interview. It has advantages for the interviewer too, for it allows one person to control the progress of the interview.

THE INTERVIEW ROOM

It pays to create a setting as comfortable as possible for both yourself and the interviewee. Redirect incoming phone calls and keep other outside interruptions to a minimum. Tidy your desk – but don't clear it. A totally clear desk is unreal and is in danger of evoking the interrogation room – thus intimidating the interviewee.

Pay careful attention to the lighting and seating. Unless you enjoy playing psychological games, you presumably will not train the light from your desk lamp directly into the interviewee's face. Remember too, that if you sit with your back to a window, the poor interviewee has to endure the glare of direct sunlight while looking at you in virtual silhouette. The applicant will have no chance of establishing eye contact, or of seeing what impression he or she is making on you.

Think twice about the usual procedure of talking across a desk or table. This often serves as a barrier rather than a channel when it comes to conveying ideas, let alone observing body language. Far more effective is to position two chairs a few feet apart at right angles to each other – comfortable office chairs, rather than armchairs. If that feels rather bleak or exposed, place a low coffee table in front of the chairs. This will prove useful if either of you has any paperwork to shuffle.

Finally, make sure that you have a clear view of a clock, on a wall or your desk – so that you do not have to keep glancing unnervingly at your watch.

THE INTERVIEWER'S BEHAVIOUR

As interviewer you have a primary duty – to be an effective listener. This involves more than just absorbing and analysing the information offered by the interviewee. You need to penetrate to the thoughts and feelings behind that information. Be watchful: you can learn a great deal from the interviewee's tone of voice, body language, and from eye contact and facial expression.

You in turn will have to use these same devices to convey to the interviewee the reassurance that you are listening carefully, and to encourage him or her to continue. Speak clearly, informally, and openly: that should ensure a corresponding speech pattern from the interviewee. Maintain eye contact, but without glaring too piercingly.

Sit in a reasonably relaxed position, but don't overdo it – hunching or slouching will only put the interviewee on his guard. Try not to be uninviting in your gestures; as by covering your mouth with your hand, frowning down your nose, and so on. Make an effort instead to show all the signs of attentiveness – nodding your head, murmuring 'mm' or 'I see' – and you will notice how freely and expansively your interviewee talks.

One common problem in interviews is that of a pause or lull in conversation. There is nothing wrong with the occasional pause: don't feel that you, as interviewer, should dart in and plug the gap. This will only panic the interviewee who was perhaps just taking thought before delivering a reply. If the pause really goes on too long and the interviewee seems about to freeze up, you can take the awkwardness out of the situation by repeating your question, rephrasing it slightly to offer the interviewee a more accessible approach.

On the whole, remember that it is the interviewee who should be doing most of the talking; your own input as interviewer should amount to no more than a fifth or sixth of the conversation.

Some interviewers use a video or tape recorder. If you are expected to do this, make sure that you are familiar with the equipment, and do reassure the candidate that this is standard procedure.

Most interviewers like to take notes, of varying detail. Take care not to let your writing distract you from what the interviewee is saying. Don't disguise what you are doing; if necessary, explain that you need to pause for a moment to jot down a few points. Then resume eye contact and continue the conversation. There is a less disruptive method, of course: take sketchy notes during the interview, and write up the details immediately afterwards.

The effective interviewer, both while conducting the interview and in passing judgment afterwards, has to deal with his or her own prejudices. Almost everyone has predispositions when it comes to strangers – anything from out-and-out sexism, to a vague distrust of beards. It is not enough to resolve to 'push to one side' such attitudes.

As interviewer you should first acknowledge any such attitudes openly to yourself, admit that they are in danger of affecting your judgment, and make special allowance for them. You should even lean over backwards, if necessary, to view favourably candidates who might be 'disadvantaged' by your predispositions.

Here are danger areas to be mindful of:

☐ You can place too much emphasis on first impressions, thereby confirming your prejudices. Look beyond the smart suit and classy voice on the one hand, or the beard and regional accent on the other.

☐ You can fail to take into account the built-in tension and artificiality of the interview setting. Don't assume that a nervous or reticent candidate would necessarily come across in the same way once employed in a familiar workplace.

☐ You can unwittingly show favouritism to interviewees whose values and interests have a lot in common with your own. You might hit it off personally in the interview, and this rapport might tempt you to overlook the candidate's inadequacies. The right person for the job is not necessarily the one you get on best with.

The Interview

An interview falls naturally into three parts: welcoming the interviewee, questioning the interviewee, and concluding the interview.

Welcoming the interviewee. Make sure to greet the interviewee in a friendly but businesslike way. You are the host and the interviewee is your guest.

Begin your encounter, as any host might, with some small talk to break the ice. A question about the interviewee's journey or the weather will do. Put the candidate at ease from the start:

☐ Tell him or her that you will treat as confidential everything said in the interview.

☐ Give an outline of the topics you want to cover.

☐ Tell the candidate how long the interview will last. If you are not sure, say so.

☐ Reassure the candidate that he or she will have a chance at the end to ask *you* questions.

Questioning the interviewee. It is your responsibility as interviewer to direct the course of the discussion. To ensure smooth progress, you should prepare a set of topics beforehand, and a list of clear questions based on these topics.

These questions are no more than a rough guide, however. Don't feel duty-bound to follow the list rigidly. If you simply reel off the questions one by one, you miss the whole point of an interview: you might as well just have added the list to the application form. The virtue of the interview is precisely its flexibility; you pick up the implications of the interviewee's responses, and adjust your questions in the light of these.

Questions can be open or closed. The skilled interviewer switches from one to the other as a way of controlling the flow of information.

Closed questions. These are questions inviting a brief answer, often just a 'yes' or 'no'. For example, 'Did you type up the answers on the application form yourself?' and 'Did you do a typing course or did you teach yourself?' Try to begin the interview with closed questions like these. And do the same when you start any new line of questioning. Closed questions give the candidate a chance to warm up. But watch your tone of voice as you change to open questions – you do not want to give the impression that you have cornered a victim for interrogation.

Open questions. These are more demanding and require more than 'yes-no' answers. They typically begin with words like *Who*, *Where*, *When*, *What*, *Why*, and *How*. You can ease the interviewee into an open question by introducing it with a closed question. You might begin by saying, for instance, 'I see you got your driver's licence soon after you left school. Do you enjoy driving?' Then follow that up with the open question, 'How do you feel about all the travelling that this job will entail?'

HOW NOT TO ASK QUESTIONS

Here are some of the common faults that interviewers commit.

☐ Asking very vague questions. It is one thing to sound relaxed and chatty while questioning a candidate. It is another to be so relaxed that you forfeit control of the interview. Seldom will you get a satisfactory response to a question as vague and undirected as 'Why don't you tell me a little about yourself?' The interviewee is likely to say either too much or too little, and will probably reflect afterwards that this was the fault of your unpreparedness.

☐ Asking double questions. For example, 'Why are you interested in this company, and where do you see yourself in five years' time?' A double question can easily fluster or confuse an interviewee. It is fairer to ask the candidate one question at a time.

☐ Asking leading questions. These suggest that you hold strong opinions, and expect certain answers – for example, 'Our main competitor markets a clearly inferior product. Do you agree?' or 'You didn't work for X for very long. They have a reputation for being an aggressive company. Didn't that suit you?' Questions like these are unfair and difficult to answer. The interviewee may feel forced to give the answer he or she thinks you want. The atmosphere of mutual trust that you have been trying to establish will certainly be jeopardised.

☐ Proceeding too quickly to the next question. If the interviewee's answer is unclear or incomplete, this is bound to leave you with a bad impression. It is only fair to give an interviewee the chance to rethink and restate a response. Try

The Skills of Good Speaking

to paraphrase the answer you do not fully understand by beginning: 'So what you are saying is . . . ', or 'In other words . . . ' This will give the interviewee the chance to correct any misunderstandings, or to clarify anything that remains vague.

☐ Putting words into a candidate's mouth. This is the opposite fault. By all means rescue an interviewee whose mind suddenly goes blank, but don't be overhelpful by feeding the answers. Your job is to guide and control the interview, not to dominate it.

COMMON DIFFICULTIES FOR THE INTERVIEWER

It takes a lot of experience to become skilful at interviewing, and there is no substitute for practice. But there are some recognised techniques for dealing with certain common difficulties.

If the interviewee is very nervous. Extend the welcoming period. Chat lightly, and make an effort to find areas of common interest with the interviewee. The answers on the application form will cue you to appropriate topics.

If the interviewee talks too much, or starts to waffle. Reduce your eye contact. Interrupt by saying, 'Can we move on to . . . ?' or 'I'd like to talk about . . . ' Ask one or more closed questions to alter the rhythm of the discussion, forcing the interviewee to give brief, pointed answers.

If the interviewee talks very little. Slow down the pace of the questions. Allow reasonable pauses and encourage the interviewee to fill these in his or her own time. Maintain eye contact, and show that you are interested in the replies. Ask open questions, and in this way force the interviewee to give more expansive answers.

If the interviewee seeks advice. If the interviewee starts pouring out personal or professional problems, you are in danger of becoming a counsellor rather than an interviewer. You must get the interview back on track directly.

Show the interviewee that you understand the problems, but remain uninvolved, and ensure that any advice you offer is general and nonpartisan. Assert yourself as soon as possible by reintroducing the topics you planned to discuss. Ask questions, especially closed ones, to which the interviewee can give positive, rational answers. This should re-establish an appropriate atmosphere.

CONCLUDING THE INTERVIEW

Once you have worked through your own questions, ask the interviewee if he or she has any questions to ask. A particularly astute question, or a particularly stupid one, can affect your assessment of the questioner. You can also turn the question back on the interviewee with a comment like this: 'That's an interesting question – what are your own views on the subject?'

As the interview draws to a close, you may want to say a few words to 'sell' the job or the company. However, be sure when you do this not to raise the interviewee's hopes unfairly. Outline the next steps in the selection process – when a decision will be taken, when the candidate will learn the results. Thank the candidate for attending. Never make anyone feel that the interview has been a waste of time. Finally, accompany the candidate to the door.

Allow yourself a break of 10 to 15 minutes to make notes about the candidate and to clear your head for the next interview. Come to a decision about the interviewee as soon after the interview as possible, while your impressions are still fresh.

Be sure you do not raise his hopes unfairly.

The Interviewee

For many people the time before an interview is a nerve-racking, adrenalin-pumping period. Try to put all that adrenalin to positive use. This means, first of all, adopting a positive attitude. The underlying strategy for success is to value yourself.

The interview does not require you to take on the role of victim. It is a dialogue, and you are an active participant. The company have to find someone to fill a post, and need the successful candidate as much as he or she needs the company. So when you walk into the interview room, remind yourself that your interviewers are under your scrutiny as much as you are under theirs.

You will, for example, be evaluating your possible future with the company. You too will be making decisions and mental notes as the interview proceeds. You too will be asking questions, either silently to yourself, or out loud to the interviewers. Does the job suit you? Is this the sort of company you want to work for? Will there be opportunities for promotion, for training, and for pay increases?

PREPARING FOR THE INTERVIEW.

You may be the best candidate for a job, but that is no guarantee that you will be offered it. Experience and qualifications are important, but you may also have to sell yourself as the best person for the post. This requires you to know as much about the position as possible.

Begin by thinking how you can make your best impression on the interviewers. Not that you should present yourself as being different from what you are, but you can present yourself in a very positive way. Consider what the interviewers' likely prejudices and dislikes may be, and take these into account when answering questions and unveiling your personality. And reflect on the personal qualities that might be necessary for the work you will be doing. These qualities will surely be looked for and perhaps even tested in the interview. If the company want an aggressive go-getter salesman, for instance, you had better not project a timid and overcautious self-image in the interview room.

Research the company. The more you know about your potential employers, the better. Investigate their products, try them if appropriate, and keep a lookout for their advertisements. Visit a library to read trade magazines, newspapers, company brochures, and reports that will bring you up to date with the latest developments in the company.

Find out what the company's priorities are. Suppose they place great emphasis on turnover and quick profit: you will then want to stress the revenue you generated in your last job, rather than the research project you supervised for five years. But if your prospective employers are deeply committed to a programme of research and development, you should play up your academic or supervisory skills.

Know your own strengths. Sit down with a pen and paper, and match your skills and experience to the job description in the advertisement. Think how the employer would benefit by choosing you, rather than another candidate.

Aside from the practical skills required, consider the less tangible qualities the employer might be searching for. Do you have potential in certain areas which could be realised if given the chance? How do you rate yourself in terms of creative thinking, leadership qualities, the ability to work under pressure? Jot down incidents in which you have displayed these characteristics.

Know your weaknesses. Good interviewers are practised at finding the weaknesses in a candidate, so don't imagine that you are certain to get away with anything. But what you cannot hide you can always explain – provided you are well-prepared. And if you think positively about yourself, you can turn those explanations to your advantage. Here are some hints on how to do this:

☐ Look objectively at your c.v. and pick out areas that may undermine the impression you want to make. Look for anything that might give a negative impression – for example, lack of promotion over a long period, frequent job changes, or long periods of unemployment.

☐ Prepare yourself to give positive answers to queries about these weak areas. Write down possible questions and answers, and rehearse these with a friend. Few people speak exactly as they write, so be prepared to make alterations to the written words. If your friend can give you constructive feedback, so much the better. Use a tape recorder to hear how you sound.

The Skills of Good Speaking

Here are examples of interviewees giving positive answers to potentially damaging questions:

Interviewer: Between 1980 and 1985 you had quite a few different jobs. Why was that?

Interviewee: At the time I was unsure about the direction I wanted my career to take. I felt the need to test my strengths and weaknesses in various kinds of employment so I could find out what I could do best. The different jobs helped a lot. They taught me a wide range of skills – word processing, selling by telephone, and small business accounting. I think these skills will always be useful, and I wouldn't have had the chance to learn them if I hadn't tried a number of different jobs.

Interviewer: What did you do between 1985 and 1987?

Interviewee: I was unemployed, but I tried to use those years constructively. I took A-level French and I learned to type. I also ran workshops at the local community centre. That gave me useful experience in organising and supervising a large group of people. During this time we also moved house. I completely renovated the new place, and learnt a number of new DIY skills.

In each case the interviewee turns an apparent failure or misfortune into an advantage. He reveals a capacity to take charge of his own destiny, to apply himself to the task in hand, and to work hard and efficiently. He seems eager to broaden his knowledge or acquire new skills.

The Interview

On the day of the interview, allow yourself plenty of time to get ready, and to travel to the venue. You also need time to relax. A last-minute rush means you will arrive flustered.

If you feel very nervous, try various relaxation exercises – see page 423. Do voice and body warm-up exercises – see page 506.

If you feel the need for support, arrange to have an encouraging friend to accompany you and chat to you beforehand. If the receptionist or secretary at the place of interview does not seem busy, strike up a conversation. This may help to relax you.

Think in advance about what you will do when the interview is over. Whether you emerge from your interview feeling high or low, you will need an activity to help you through the post-interview period. You may want to speak to a friend, go shopping, or simply go for a walk or a cup of tea – anything to keep at bay a sense of anticlimax.

Whatever you do to relax, you should also make time soon after the interview to jot down notes about how it went. Were there any questions that took you by surprise? Were there questions which you would answer more successfully given another chance? These notes will be valuable when it comes to preparing for future interviews.

Before you speak you will be seen. The style of dress you choose depends on the company and the position you are applying for. Your appearance should indicate that you have a grasp of what is acceptable dress within the company.

If the job is in an advertising agency, say, it is appropriate to dress 'creatively' and in high fashion. But it would be inappropriate to dress in that way if you were being interviewed for a job in a bank.

If you are in doubt about how to dress, phone the office secretary to ask. Or you could even go and stand outside the company building at the start or close of business, and watch the employees coming or going. Within 15 minutes you will have a good idea of the range of dress styles acceptable to management. Perhaps choose a slightly smarter version of what you would wear to work there.

Make sure that your outfit is comfortable to wear, and that it suits you. Tailored, neutral clothes are a good choice because they do not demand attention. You want to make a good impression, but you do not want to distract the interviewer with an overpowering costume.

Finally, take care not to walk into the interview room laden with all your belongings. Ask the receptionist where you can leave your coat, shopping bags, and other unnecessary paraphernalia. When you go into the interview room, take only a file or folder, or a briefcase to hold any papers you may have to refer to.

THE INTERVIEWEE'S BEHAVIOUR

First impressions are of paramount importance. The following points can help you to impress the interviewer favourably from the outset.

The greeting. Greet the interviewer by name: 'Good morning, Miss Jones.' This comes over as at once polite and assertive. Your handshake should be firm. Stand with good posture, smile, and meet the interviewer's eyes. It has been said that more jobs are lost from lack of eye contact than from lack of experience or qualifications.

Be friendly without being familiar. Don't slap the interviewer on the back. Don't clutch your heart and confide, 'I'm so nervous!' This is a business meeting. Behave accordingly.

Body language. The interviewer has probably decided in advance where you should sit. But if you have a choice, don't sit in a low soft armchair. It invites a submissive, slouching position in which you cannot easily control your body language. If the chair has arms, avoid putting your elbows on them. You risk forcing yourself into a tense, unattractive posture. You will create a better impression by sitting upright, with your back firmly supported by the chair.

Be aware of your body language. An 'open' posture, with your back straight, and arms and legs uncrossed, is better than a 'closed' posture – back hunched, arms and legs tightly crossed.

Interviewers make allowances for nervousness, but if you are feeling really jittery, focus on controlling your breathing (see page 469). If you do not know what to do with your hands, clasp them in your lap. Avoid small repetitive movements: however calm your facial expression, you will give away your nervousness and distract the interviewer if you keep waggling your foot, smoothing your hair, or nibbling your fingernails.

Make sure your body language is sufficiently receptive. Don't turn away from the interviewer, or wrap your arms around your chest in self-protection. Don't gaze out of the window, giving the interviewer the impression that you are not listening, rather than that you are thinking intently.

Establishing rapport. Interviewing is based on taking turns; the better you are at listening, the better you will know when to speak and what to say. Show the interviewer that you are listening carefully, and pause when answering to note his or her responses. Try to tune in to the interviewer, and show that you recognise who is in charge. So: wait for the interviewer to finish before you speak. And answer questions directly: don't pretend you did not hear all that the interviewer said, and don't answer a question not asked.

You might sense that you are failing to establish a rapport. Don't simply assume you have landed up with an awful interviewer. Perhaps it is you that is at fault. Consider the following points:

☐ Are you talking too much? Pause more often and shorten your answers.

☐ Are your answers so short that they sound curt? Soften your tone. Show the interviewer, by means of nods and gestures, that you are interested in the questions and comments.

☐ Respond with energy, speak clearly, and use facial expressions as a visual aid to emphasise your meaning.

TAKING QUESTIONS

You can usually predict at least a few of the broad topics that will be raised in an interview. But it is unwise to try to predict the exact questions you might be asked. The questions and answers you wrote down and practised with a friend (page 527) should be no more than a rough guide. Don't learn these answers by heart. If you do, you risk answering the wrong question.

By all means prepare your ideas, but not the exact words for conveying them.

Common questions. Although you cannot predict the interviewer's precise questions, you can at least draw up a list of likely questions:

☐ Why did you apply for this job?

☐ What makes you want to work for this company/organisation?

☐ What do you think has been your greatest achievement in your career so far?

☐ Give me an assessment of your strengths and weaknesses – as a person and in the work you have done.

The Skills of Good Speaking

- What did you like best/least about your last job?

- How do you envisage your future? Where would you like to be in ten years' time?

- How do you spend your leisure hours?

- Would you have any problems relocating if you were offered this job?

- What was your last boss like?

- Describe your ideal boss.

- Why do you think you would be good at this particular job?

DIFFICULT QUESTIONS

However much you prepare your ideas, you are bound to find yourself facing some difficult questions – those that take you by surprise, or that you hoped would never be asked. Whatever you do, don't panic. Pause, think, and take your time in answering. The interviewer is not looking for glib answers to difficult questions.

If the question is subtle or complicated, don't be ashamed to ask the interviewer to repeat it. Think about what you have been asked, and try to order your thoughts before you answer.

Don't allow yourself to be overwhelmed. Don't undersell yourself by giving up on a difficult question without first trying to answer it.

If you really are stuck and cannot answer a question, say so. Don't simply invent an answer to fill the silence. A quietly confident admission of ignorance is more impressive than bluster.

When you researched the position, you presumably gained some idea of what knowledge and experience would be expected of the successful applicant, and what would not. Remember that no applicant is expected to know everything. But he or she is expected to be educable. Far better to show that you are eager to learn, than to give the impression that you have nothing to learn.

DO'S WHEN ANSWERING QUESTIONS

- Do keep your sentences short and to the point. Once you have completed your answer, indicate to the interviewer that you have finished what you wanted to say. One way to do this is to drop the pitch of your voice on the last syllable of your final sentence.

- Do ask the interviewer to repeat a question if you did not fully understand it. Or try paraphrasing it, and ask the interviewer if you have understood the question correctly.

- Do end your answers with positive points whenever you can. For instance, if you offer some criticisms of the company that last employed you, try to end your comments with a couple of positive remarks about that company. You want to show that you are not biased, that you are able to make an even-handed assessment of your employers' pros and cons.

- Do avoid unnecessary personal disclosures. Certainly there are some matters that you are legally or morally bound to reveal – medical problems, for example, or personal problems that might affect your work. But other private matters may be best kept to yourself, particularly if they have no bearing on the job.

- Do be wary of using jargon to impress the interviewer. Technical or specialised language is fine if you are absolutely sure of its use. But if you misuse it, you will look foolish. When in doubt use plain English.

DONT'S WHEN ANSWERING QUESTIONS

- Don't launch into an answer without taking time to assemble your thoughts. The interviewer will wait for you, and will be impressed if you think things through in silence and then provide a well-constructed answer.

- Don't think that you have to keep talking until you are interrupted. Decide for yourself when you have answered the question, and stop. If the interviewer keeps interrupting, you are not answering concisely enough.

- Don't play for time. Don't make comments such as, 'That's an interesting question!', while nodding your head sagely – a head that is all too obviously empty of ideas. If you would prefer to return to a difficult question later, ask the interviewer if that would be possible. If it is not, and you cannot answer the question, say so.

- Don't talk in the abstract. This may give the impression that you cannot or will not commit yourself to a firm opinion. Don't use words such as 'one' or 'people'. Be personal, and use specific examples: 'In my experience . . . ', 'When I was at . . . ', 'I think that . . . ', and so on.

☐ Don't undersell yourself by being apologetic. For example, don't say, 'I've had only five months' experience in this kind of work.' You are inviting the interviewer to see you as underqualified. If you are not sure of your ground, say so. But avoid long, apologetic introductions such as, 'Of course it's just my opinion, and I may be wrong, but I think perhaps . . . '

☐ Don't dwell unnecessarily on failures or bad luck. If you are forced to confront something unpleasant in the past, point out the positive side of what at first glance seems negative.

☐ Don't exaggerate your current salary in the hope that this inflated figure will be matched or bettered by your prospective employer. An experienced interviewer will probably be able to estimate your income fairly accurately, and will know when you are misleading him.

CONCLUDING THE INTERVIEW

Usually you are invited at the end of an interview to ask any questions of your own. If you prepared for the interview properly, you will already have a question or two in mind. Other questions are bound to occur to you in the course of the interview. Whatever you ask, keep the form of your questions positive and constructive – for example: 'Does the company plan to expand in the near future?' 'Will there be opportunities for training?' 'What is the scope for promotion?'

This is your opportunity to show some initiative and imagination. If you are skilful in interviewing the interviewer, this will count heavily in your favour. But make sure that you do not take liberties. Although temporarily in the driver's seat, you remain essentially in the passive role. You are the person about whom a decision will be made.

If you have done your research well, you can make the most of this chance to display your knowledge and enthusiasm. You can impress the interviewer by showing that you have thought creatively about issues which have not been raised: 'Has the company considered developing X area of marketing/research?' 'I picked up such and such a detail in my reading of the company reports. Does it mean that . . . ?' And so on.

But don't overdo this. Don't take over, and don't show off. Keep your questions short, genuine, relevant, and few in number. Having weathered all that has gone before, you do not now want to bore the interviewer, or leave him or her with the impression that you are a smart aleck.

Farewell and follow-up. What should you do at the end of the interview? Smile, shake hands firmly, thank the interviewer for the time he or she has given you, and take your leave.

It is sometimes appropriate to write a follow-up letter to thank the interviewer again. You can remind the company of your interest in the job, and bring them up to date with any new developments.

Dealing with the Boss

'THE BOSS wants to see you' – these can be ominous words, and, no matter how clear your conscience, tend to produce anything from mild uneasiness to serious anxiety.

This chapter considers the difficulties that sometimes occur when dealing with the boss, and discusses ways of overcoming them – not just by reducing nervousness, but by learning to deal more creatively and more effectively with the boss, the most important person in one's working life.

Remember also the larger perspective as you read this chapter. You are, after all, employed by your boss or your company to do a job of work, not just to further your own career and general well-being. Learning to work well with your boss will benefit not only you, but your boss as well, and the organisation as a whole.

THE ORIGINS OF THE PROBLEM

Why should a meeting with the boss make you uneasy? There are many possible reasons. You can never forget that the boss has power over you and your daily life. He or she can assign you interesting and pleasant work – or the most uninteresting and unpleasant work. Directly or indirectly the boss controls your salary and your perks. Ultimately, your future lies in the boss's hands.

At one extreme, a boss may behave as little more than a senior colleague – coming round to chat constantly, asking your advice, nudging you rather than giving orders. A friend in other words, hardly a boss at all. At the other extreme, a boss may act like a distant god – keeping out of sight, yet wielding power fiercely when the occasion arises. Rumours emerge, from behind the closed door of that very private office, of fearful rows.

The chances are that your boss lies somewhere in between these two extremes – someone you have got to know quite well, and established reasonably friendly relations with, but still your boss. And at certain times he or she will bring this home to you, throwing you off balance and producing in you reactions that you have little control over.

Attitudes to the Boss

There are four basic attitudes that people can adopt towards authority: aggression, submission, and indirect aggression, which are all negative; and simple assertiveness, which is positive.

Being aggressive. Some people cover up their anxiety by adopting an aggressive, combative front. They will not listen to ideas and suggestions, they regard reasonable instructions as harsh orders, and they automatically deny responsibility if criticised. They may even reject positive encouragement, imagining it to be part of some involved plot to get the better of them. In these circumstances, all dealings with the boss become antagonistic, and all interactions are seen as battles to be won or lost.

Being submissive. Other people find that any encounter with the boss wafts them straight back to childhood, when they were dependent on the powerful people surrounding them. Everything the boss says must clearly be right, all criticism must be valid, any mistake must be of their making.

Even when the boss invites their opinion, they feel unable to give it. If they ever have an idea, they assume that it is too simple-minded to mention. So they keep quiet at meetings, keep their heads down, and avoid their boss at all costs.

Being indirectly aggressive. Some employees react inwardly rather than outwardly. They seethe with resentment or discontent, but seldom give open expression to such a feeling. They will not seek a confrontation with the boss, but neither will they avoid one if it arises. They may be clever and witty, but in a sarcastic, cynical, or bitter way.

Indirectly aggressive employees are rarely honest about their feelings and views, so their relationship with the boss might look reasonably well balanced. But it is not. They are better at criticising than proposing. They may say one thing to the boss, and another to their colleagues. Their energies disperse in negative feelings and carping comments.

The positive approach. As a subordinate, you can adopt a positive approach to authority that allows you to be yourself, to accept praise for your strengths, and to learn from mistakes. This approach is usually called assertiveness.

A word of warning: don't be put off by the word *assertive*. Assertiveness, in this context at least, is not a matter of stamping your foot and shouting. That is aggressiveness. Assertiveness means being firm but polite, determined yet flexible. The truly assertive person can be quiet, almost unnoticed – yet supremely effective in pursuing a rational course of action.

When you act assertively in this sense, you take the positive elements from aggression and submission – aggression in dealing with unnecessary obstacles, submission in accepting necessary limitations and in exercising self-control.

Assertiveness essentially means approaching situations expecting to negotiate with others as an equal; being aware of your own rights, but also being prepared to listen and respond to other people sympathetically. The result should be an easier, more productive, and less stressful life.

Ultimately, your future lies in your boss's hands.

The power of assertiveness lies above all in this – that by changing your behaviour in small ways you can change the way that people respond to you. Positive behaviour on your part makes your relations with others more positive. And this makes your feelings about yourself more positive. A cycle of benefit gets under way.

Your Rights, Choices, and Goals

Acting assertively at work involves, first of all, approaching your boss in a positive spirit. On the one hand, this means remembering that you are both part of the same team, working towards the same goal: the prosperity of your company or organisation. You will, in other words, have to work hard and efficiently at your job to play fair by the boss. On the other hand, you have to remember your own rights – and so does your boss. That is playing fair by you. You have the right to:

☐ be treated with respect

☐ express your feelings and wishes

☐ ask for what you want

☐ say No without feeling guilty

☐ make mistakes

☐ ask for information

☐ change your mind

Depending on your particular relationship with the boss, you may want to add some other important rights to the list. If you often have to work late, for example, what about your right to be given sufficient notice of when overtime is likely? Or if you feel that you are not allowed sufficient initiative, what about your right to make suggestions?

But knowing your own rights is only one element in the equation. It is just as important for you to be aware of, and to respect, the rights of others. So while you have the right to ask for what you want, your boss has an equal right to say No to you. You may feel that you deserve a pay rise or a promotion, and you may put your case assertively. But you may not get what you want, and you must accept this without bearing a grudge. Assertiveness does not mean getting your way every time.

ASSERTING YOURSELF

The assertive approach is direct, but not blunt. It is honest, open, and responsive. To take a simple example: the boss summons you at 4.30 and says 'There's a backlog of urgent work, so can you work late tonight, please?' But this is the night of your evening class, and you really should not miss it. An aggressive response would be to say 'No way!' – and then to feel angry and guilty at one and the same time. A submissive response would be to say 'Yes'.

By contrast, an assertive response would be to refuse, politely and apologetically, and then to give your reasons, and finally perhaps seeing if there is any other way to help. Something along these lines: 'It's just not possible today. It's my evening class, and if I miss this session it might mean giving up the course altogether. I could come in to work half an hour early tomorrow morning. Or if you can wait an extra day, I could work late tomorrow evening. Would that help?' This is direct, clear, honest, and helpful. You explain your wishes firmly, but you also show that you recognise the boss's problem.

LEARNING TO BE ASSERTIVE

Some people are 'naturally' assertive. But if you consider yourself either aggressive or submissive, take heart: assertiveness can be learned.

Here are some simple rules:

☐ Know what you want and justify your wanting it; in time, you will feel more confident about wanting it and more entitled to have it.

☐ Speak in a way that conveys your wants and your confidence. This often requires you to speak about yourself and how you feel. You need to say, 'I feel . . .', 'I want . . .', 'I need . . .'

☐ If you want to say No, say it, preferably as early as possible in your reply: 'No, I'm afraid I can't work late tonight.'

☐ Avoid saying things that weaken your message, such as 'when you have a moment' or 'if it's not too much trouble'.

☐ Don't undermine the effect of your words with an uncertain tone of voice or compromising body language. If you mumble and look at the floor while saying No, you betray a lack of confidence, and your refusal might be ignored.

To familiarise yourself fully with assertive behaviour, observe other people at their daily routine. Are they acting aggressively, submissively, or assertively? Ask yourself why you classify them as you do, and you will begin identifying the various techniques peculiar to each type of behaviour. Then try modelling yourself on the assertive person. Start practising your assertiveness in low-risk situations.

Suppose, for example, you are in a shop and the assistant keeps serving latecomers ahead of you. What is your normal reaction? To make a scene? To storm out of the shop? To protest in a whining voice? To shrug and sulk and wait? Instead, try a different tack this time. In a quiet but firm voice, and with a friendly smile, draw the assistant's attention with a polite 'Excuse me'. Then explain that you really do need help, and that it is your turn to be served. Insist patiently. If for some reason the assistant genuinely cannot help you, you will have to accept this graciously.

Of course, things will not always work out as you wish. Your first attempts at assertiveness may end in fiasco. But at least you can be proud of yourself for trying something new. And gradually, through practice, you will find yourself growing in confidence. Very soon you will be ready to try out a new way of handling the boss.

MAKING A BETTER IMPRESSION.

As an important first step in trying to improve relations with your boss, acknowledge to yourself that not all your encounters have proved disastrous. The really impossible boss is a very rare species. The fact is, employees tend to remember the few unpleasant encounters far more vividly than the usual humdrum exchanges. Here are a few hints on how to get on better with the boss.

Make the most of informal meetings. An old maxim among business people runs, 'More business gets done over the lunch table than over the boardroom table.' Informal meetings can benefit an employee's relationship with the boss. They include accidental get-togethers in the canteen, or in some work-based sport or leisure activity. Such occasions allow you to learn more about the boss as a person. Equally in the more relaxed atmosphere of an informal meeting, you may more easily let your boss discover who you are as a person. Sometimes, during informal meetings, you may get the praise and encouragement that you do not usually get at other times.

Don't be afraid to ask. To get a job done properly, you often ought to seek help or advice from others. You may, for example, find yourself dealing with a tricky legal problem at work, and you need time off, and the boss's backing, to consult a lawyer for specialist advice. Or you may need a more reliable word processor to help you to do your work more efficiently. Don't be afraid to ask for such things. Prepare a clear and well-balanced case, and present it assertively. You stand every chance of getting a favourable response: after all, your request indicates that you take your work seriously.

Be prepared to accept praise. Surveys show an interesting difference in perception between bosses and subordinates when it comes to the matter of praise. Bosses tend to feel that they are generous in giving praise and encouragement; subordinates tend to feel that they receive less praise and encouragement than their efforts merit. A factor behind this discrepancy may be that subordinates refuse to accept praise properly.

Suppose you have done a job well, and your boss thanks and praises you for your commitment and success. How do you respond? Do you reflect on what the boss has said, acknowledge it to yourself as your due deserts, and feel appropriately pleased? Or do you feel embarrassed, and play down the praise, as if arguing that it was undeserved? Beware of saying things such as, 'Oh, it was nothing,' or 'I was just doing my job.' This type of response may seem becomingly modest to you, but it can appear ungracious to others.

An honest, heartfelt 'thank you' for the praise, accompanied by a gratified smile would be a far more positive response – don't forget that your boss needs encouragement as well as you.

Listen to criticism. Many of the people who are deaf to praise turn out to have very acute hearing for criticism. They regard any helpful suggestion as a form of criticism, and treat any criticism as a form of personal attack.

Few people actually like to be criticised, particularly by the boss. But criticism is not necessarily destructive or demeaning; it can be a valuable form of feedback, which should help you to improve your work in future. Listen carefully to criticism, and suppress any impulse to react unthinkingly.

Remember too that people generally do not like to criticise. This partly explains why they make their criticisms so awkwardly. If your boss, in criticising you, seems to be launching a personal attack, try to make allowance for this. Separate the content of the remarks from the manner in which they are delivered. Not an easy task of course, when you are reeling from what seems like a disproportionate onslaught, but it does get easier with practice.

Treat the interview as a discussion rather than an argument. If the boss is in a blustering mood, try to calm things down by saying, in a quiet voice, a few opening words such as: 'I understand everything that you've said so far. I'd like to respond to it. Would you like to hear what I have to say?' The boss cannot very well refuse. And if your first attempt does not work, just say, again in a calm voice, something along these lines: 'This is obviously not a good time to discuss this. I'll make an appointment later, and we can talk about it then.' Then take your leave – without slamming the door behind you. Come back later in a calmer frame of mind.

If the boss does want to hear your response, take your time. Keep a cool head if you can, and go through the criticisms point by point in an assertive, adult way. Begin with those criticisms you accept as fair. Acknowledge them, accept responsibility, and if appropriate apologise. Undertake to improve things, and explain – without trying to let yourself off the hook – how you came to err or falter in the first place. Once you have made this handsome admission, the boss will be far more amenable to the next phase of your response – the part where you disagree.

When discussing the unfair criticisms, again keep a level voice: don't whine or thunder to convey your sense of injustice. Explain, in an unthreatening way.

Don't put the boss in the wrong. If the criticisms miss the mark through some factual inaccuracy, point this out in a matter-of-fact tone – don't pounce gloatingly on the error.

Even when criticism is justified, the recipients tend to react defensively. This is not only an inappropriate response – it is wasteful too. If you are busy raging inwardly, dragging up every argument in your defence, you will not take in the criticism properly, and hence will not learn the useful lessons it might contain. You may not welcome hearing that you have done a job badly or made a mistake, but at least that could teach you how to do things more effectively in future.

So don't react overdefensively to criticism, as if denying that you could ever be capable of doing anything wrong. But don't go to the other extreme either, by behaving as if you deserve more criticism than you get. If you agree with a criticism that the boss makes of you, accept your error, give your explanation, and apologise – but only once. Don't grovel and belittle yourself.

A more mature and assertive follow-up might take this form: first, if appropriate, ask what you can do to make up for your mistake and redeem yourself; and then, ask if anything else in your work performance needs improving too. This will show your boss that you are keen to learn and to do well.

The Appraisal Interview

This is a formal interview (typically held once a year) at which you and your boss discuss your job performance – past, present, and future.

Its general aim is to improve the efficiency of company staff, and hence of the company itself. From the interviewee's point of view, however, it may feel more like an ordeal, determining as it often does salary rises, suitability for promotion, further training courses, and so on.

Shortly before your appraisal interview, the boss will have spent some time thinking about you and your particular job and may have read a written report on you submitted by your immediate superior. Your boss now has to discuss with you how well you are doing, what strengths and weaknesses you have, what problems or opportunities face you, and what can be done to help you.

One way of ensuring a fair appraisal is to keep your own account of your job performance during the year. First, you need to understand clearly what is required of you, the standards that you are expected to meet and the objectives you were set. If you have any doubts about these, the sooner you clarify them the better – ask your boss, if necessary.

You can then keep an accurate record of your performance – the dates when you completed projects, tasks you did efficiently or poorly, the training that you underwent and the benefits you derived from it. These records will help you to put your case convincingly in the interview.

If you have not done as well as expected in any particular area of work, think beforehand how you can explain this in the interview. (Again, make notes to guide you.) And think too about remedies for that particular weak area – if you feel that special training will put things right, take the opportunity of the interview to ask for it.

The best preparation for the appraisal interview, however, is obviously to sustain a good regular understanding and have regular discussions with your boss during the preceding year. The appraisal interview will then seem little more than another of your occasional meetings. You will feel not only relatively relaxed, but relatively confident as well.

Remember too the importance of having the right attitude. The appraisal interview is not designed as an occasion for you to get your yearly thrashing. Like all interviews, it should be a two-way process in which both interviewer and interviewee should listen and talk frankly. If you say nothing, your boss will not thank you for it. And if you become angry or rude, you will do your cause no good either.

In particular, don't remain silent in the face of vague criticisms – ask for specific examples of your alleged shortcomings. Accept fair criticism in a positive and forward-looking spirit, and ask what you can do to improve matters. Even a stern interview can provide an opportunity for you to shine if you know how.

Suppose, in one of the worst of instances, the boss accuses you of being 'lazy and lethargic'. How do you react? You can accept the criticism submissively, or defy it aggressively. Or you can keep your head: 'Clearly, that is a serious charge you are levelling at me. In fairness to myself, I wonder if you could give me an instance of when I have been lazy and lethargic.' The boss now has to work out what gave rise to this impression. It may prove the result of one isolated incident – and, moreover, an incident the boss misinterpreted. In fact, you were suffering from a devastating migraine that day – unsurprisingly, you were not on your best form. You can explain: 'I remember that day, and yes, I'm sorry, I was not working as well as I should have been. However, I would like to explain . . . '

FREE-FLOATING NEGATIVES

Incorrect means 'not correct', and *discontented* means 'not contented'. But not all adjectives can be rewritten in this way. You cannot say an *innocent* child is *not nocent*, and it is no longer idiomatic to describe an *unkempt* boy as *not kempt* or an *unscathed* survivor as *not scathed*.

☐ In the list below choose the word or phrase you believe is *opposite in meaning* to the key word. Answers are on pages 633-648.

anodyne
A: encouraging
B: depressing
C: irritating
D: soothing

anomalous
A: strange
B: normal
C: similar
D: different

disconsolate
A: tactful
B: cheerful
C: decorative
D: despairing

disgruntled
A: comfortable
B: sad
C: hopeful
D: contented

dismantled
A: shelved
B: pleased
C: taken apart
D: put together

dissembling
A: without pretence
B: hypocritical
C: looking similar to
D: self-indulgent

ignominious
A: wise
B: stupid
C: honourable
D: shameful

impecunious
A: holy
B: sinful
C: rich
D: poor

impudent
A: polite
B: rude
C: young
D: awake

incessant
A: peaceful
B: noisy
C: occasional
D: continual

incognito
A: thirsty
B: unsatisfied
C: undisguised
D: deep-voiced

indelible
A: permanent
B: temporary
C: eatable
D: poisonous

inept
A: calm
B: skilful
C: perfect
D: pretty

inert
A: moving about
B: breathing
C: separated
D: dying

inimical
A: favourable
B: hostile
C: loyal
D: resentful

iniquitous
A: secret
B: above-board
C: virtuous
D: wicked

innocuous
A: free
B: harmful
C: protective
D: painful

inscrutable
A: easily understood
B: mysterious
C: sober
D: very drunk

insipid
A: clever
B: tasty
C: sick
D: dull

invincible
A: unrepentant
B: smartly dressed
C: easily beaten
D: unbearable

nonchalant
A: obviously worried
B: hopelessly stuck
C: able to move freely
D: apparently unconcerned

nonplussed
A: fully understanding
B: baffled
C: out of control
D: stuck

uncouth
A: cruel
B: kind
C: crude
D: sophisticated

ungainly
A: awkward
B: graceful
C: stingy
D: generous

untoward
A: favourable
B: worrying
C: friendly
D: shy

The Skills of Good Speaking

Influencing the Boss

If you want to learn to influence the boss, you have to understand how the process of influencing someone works. Note that it is a process, not a one-off accomplishment: you do not just enter your boss's office, win your point, and leave. The process has several steps, and if you miss any of these, your chances of success are reduced.

First of all, prepare a rough strategy for the presentation of your proposal – both the content and the style.

To take a simple example: your project at work is running behind schedule, and things are getting on top of you. You need an extra pair of hands in your team. You have discussed the matter briefly with one of your colleagues in charge of another project, who mentioned that he could spare one of the people working for him. The obvious course of action, then, is to transfer this person from his team to your team.

But what seems obvious to you may not be obvious to the boss. Stop to think what objections he may have. Perhaps your colleague's subordinate is a trainee, specifically assigned to his project to get experience of that kind of work. Try to anticipate such objections before approaching your boss, and think of your counterarguments.

You should also take into account the kind of person your boss is, and prepare your ground accordingly. A hard-headed, logical manager will suspect any 'hard sell', and may be put off by any sudden display of enthusiasm on your part.

A tough boss might also be unmoved by any appeal for a lighter workload for you personally. If so, you will have to tailor your presentation accordingly – pitching your proposals in a cold, systematic way, stressing how the project or company will benefit from them.

Having outlined for yourself a broad strategy, you can proceed with the opening moves.

These do not consist of rushing into the boss's office with ideas. No matter how enthusiastic you are about your proposals, never disregard the standard rules of behaviour. Exchange the usual pleasantries, and ask if it is a convenient time to meet.

When, in due course, you do have the boss's go-ahead and attention, force yourself once again to curb your impatience. Don't launch straight into your 'sales pitch' – not yet. Make soundings first on the general topic – how your boss feels about the way things are running at present, and how he might feel about any course of action that you might put forward. After all, a boss who is unaware of a problem in the first place will hardly share your enthusiasm for your proposed solution.

And remember – a simple piece of psychology, this – the boss is far likelier to see things your way if he arrives at the ideas himself rather than learning them directly from you. So ask plenty of questions – how does he view the progress of your project? And the quality of the work? Listen carefully to any criticisms. If you actually take written notes of these, this can help in two ways. First, it reassures the boss that you are taking his opinions seriously; secondly, it enables you to see more clearly what his priorities are – cost, efficiency, morale, punctuality.

Next, start to direct the interview towards your proposal. If the boss has failed, despite all your prompting, to recognise the problem you will now have to lay it out explicitly. But do so in terms that will strike a sympathetic chord. If, for example, your

You have to understand how the process of influencing someone works.

boss's main priorities seem to be efficiency and morale, explain the pressure that you and your existing team are working under and the likely mistakes, misunderstandings, and general inefficiency that this will cause sooner or later. At this point, stop to ask a few more questions, in the hope that the boss will now come up with your own idea for solving the problem. If he suggests a different – and unsuitable – solution, you should be able to argue him out of it.

Eventually you may have to spell out the solution yourself. Present it in such a way as to play up the boss's particular priority, efficiency – emphasise, for example, how the project will get back on schedule, and how, perhaps, the trainee will broaden his or her experience on your project.

You may have to argue your case quite vigorously. You may also have to make compromises, and repackage what you are proposing – perhaps work out an arrangement whereby you share the trainee. Or your boss may remember another person in the department who has time on his hands at the moment and could, in fact, serve your purposes better than the trainee. But at least, if you have made your case well, the boss is on your side.

Assuming the interview has gone well, and the boss has indicated approval of your proposals – before you leave the office, flushed with success, make sure that you pin him down. It is no help to secure an agreement 'in principle': you need to put your ideas into practice. So spell things out. Ensure that you get explicit permission for the necessary actions. You do not want any comeback later in the form of words like these: 'I didn't give permission for you to do this; we were just exploring ideas.'

To make things safer still you could follow up your meeting with a written memo, summarising your proposals once again and specifying the actions for which you received permission.

If your boss can never spare enough time for a full meeting, or has a particularly prickly or particularly indecisive character, you could divide the whole process into two stages. First, an exploratory stage, when you sound him out – how he feels about the progress of your project, and how he might take to your proposal. Ideally, this takes place at a relaxed moment, perhaps at the end of a satisfactory one-to-one meeting on another matter. After this preliminary approach, you might adjust your ideas, and come back later for the second stage.

Coping with an Unreasonable Boss

Most bosses do try to be reasonable. Sometimes, however, you may strike unlucky, and find yourself working for a compulsively unreasonable boss. Typically, this kind of boss finds fault with everything you do – mostly without justification – criticises you in public, contrasts your work sarcastically with that of a favoured colleague, and generally tries to put you down.

The rules for dealing with this very unpleasant situation are: first and foremost, never lose your temper – that would just be playing into the boss's hands. Always keep cool and listen politely. But be assertive – accept only criticism that is valid; if you shrug your shoulders at injustices, you will encourage the unreasonable boss to continue in his or her unreasonableness.

Eventually, you might feel the need to 'have it out' with the boss. Do so in a quiet, assertive way. Arrange a private meeting, and bring the problem out into the open. 'We're not getting along very well. This is no good for either of us, and I'd like to put it to rights. I feel that a lot of your criticisms are

unjustified. Please tell me what I can do – specifically – to improve things.'

Some people, in desperation, turn to yet more drastic action. They have tried all the approaches listed above – and got nowhere. So they try one of various very last resorts. They get their colleagues on their side, and issue a joint protest to the boss. Or they go over the boss's head to someone even higher in the organisation, putting this person in the picture, and requesting either intervention or a transfer to another department.

If you feel you have no option but to attempt such action, make doubly sure that your own behaviour is beyond reproach. Before turning to higher authority, seek out your boss and explain exactly what you plan to do. This interview will undoubtedly be difficult, possibly acrimonious, but it is a step you have to take if you are to be above-board and honest. In all cases remember this: playing 'politics' is a dangerous game, and you should turn to it only when all other, assertive, efforts have failed.

The Skills of Good Speaking

Dealing with Subordinates

A GOOD BOSS is like a good military commander. He is a master of strategy: he always knows what his key long-term objectives are, and how best to achieve them. He is a good tactician: he knows how to initiate actions day to day, and how to take advantage of events initiated by others. And he is a good manager of people: he gets the best out of his subordinates. He knows how to direct them most effectively, how to win their loyalty and trust, and how to stimulate their enthusiasm.

For a new manager or superior, one of the trickiest teething troubles is dealing with subordinates. If you are promoted within your company or department, you face the task of establishing new relationships with former colleagues – retaining, you hope, their friendship, but from an unfamiliar position of authority and command. And if you embark on the job as a newcomer to the company or department, you still have problems: you have to become familiar not only with a new role, but also with new people and a totally new environment.

Unless your new colleagues are exceptionally supportive, you might well feel isolated at first. You want to be a good boss but no one comes forward to talk through the problems that arise.

You could bring your subordinates into your confidence, but not if that means undermining your authority; you could approach your fellow managers for advice. But what if they are too busy or too confident to respond sympathetically to your appeals for help? Where do you start then?

LEARNING FROM EXPERIENCE

Begin by calling on your own experience of being managed – or mismanaged. Good management is essentially a question of treating others as you yourself would like to be treated. Remember the adage 'Do as you would be done by'.

Try the following exercise to get you thinking. Jot down a list of all the people who have managed or supervised you so far in your career. Then take another sheet of paper, and divide it into two columns, one labelled *Effective*, the other *Ineffective*. Now think about each of your old bosses in turn – was he or she by and large effective as a manager, or ineffective? – and write down each boss's name in the appropriate column.

Now take a third sheet of paper, divide it into the same two columns, and this time list in each column the particular aspects of your old bosses' behaviour that made you categorise them as you did. Focus on specific habits or actions, rather than on their general style of management. Pin down the things they did, or failed to do, that made you feel pleased or frustrated. Your list might end up looking something like this:

Effective	Ineffective
Anstey-Smith told me exactly what he wanted and why	Buckwell never praised my good work, but was very critical of any mistakes I made
Cowan made sure the interesting work was fairly shared	Doyle rewrote my letters, but never explained how I might do better
Fredericks really explained new tasks thoroughly	Gogarty had favourites

You will probably find that many of your old bosses were effective in some ways, but not in others. In this case, list both aspects of their behaviour in the relevant columns.

Now extract the moral. Draw up a list of good and bad managerial qualities, as you yourself experienced them. And then tailor the principles that emerge to your own needs and to those of your organisation. Suppose you admire the way a past boss used to take you aside when facing important decisions, and canvas your opinion each time. How can you do that in your position as branch manager of a bank? How can you make sure that those even in junior clerical positions are made to feel involved?

Organise Yourself

So much for your past bosses. What about yourself as boss? One of the basic rules of good management is this: to organise and manage others, you have to be able to organise and manage yourself.

If you are constantly harassed, constantly running from one place to another, never finishing tasks, never quite clear about what you are trying to achieve, you are not managing yourself well. And that sets the example for your subordinates.

So when you give them instructions or suggestions, or try to motivate and lead them, your own state of fluster and muddle contradicts what you say.

When assessing how well you organise yourself, consider two key questions:

Do you have clear objectives?
Do you manage your time as well as you should?

OBJECTIVES

When you take over a new position, try to define exactly what you want to achieve with it. What are your objectives for yourself and your section? Surprisingly few managers can state clear overall aims. Remember that your job is to lead – not simply to keep things ticking over. You cannot lead if you do not know where you are going.

For objectives to be worth while, they must be specific, measurable, and attainable.

Specific. Don't be content with open-ended aims such as 'To do better than my predecessor'. How much better? Formulate your goals precisely, and don't be afraid to be ambitious. Perhaps you have been given charge of a whole department at work. An ambitious goal might be 'To double turnover in the next two years'. Once you have worked out your goals as explicitly as this, you can start considering your strategy for achieving them.

Measurable. Break the long-term objectives or strategy into smaller, measurable units. In order to increase your department's turnover, say, you need to secure new contracts. Draw up a list of specific companies, or types of company, you need to approach. Set yourself a timetable.

By the time each deadline arrives, you will be able to measure your progress so far. You may have fallen behind – but at least you know where you are.

Attainable. Be ambitious in your objectives, yes – but don't be unrealistic. Is it really feasible to double your department's turnover in two years? Be honest with yourself. Would not three years be a more realistic target date? Striving for the impossible will produce a dangerous level of frustration for yourself – and those working under you.

When you have worked out your objectives, ask yourself these two questions to double-check them: so that? so what? You want to double turnover . . . so that? So that the company increases its profits. So what? Is this worth working towards? In this case, almost certainly yes.

MANAGING TIME

Now consider how efficiently you manage your time. Too many bosses manage their time appallingly – forever trying to do too many chores in too few hours, and looking for quick fixes and corner-cutting solutions. They spend vast amounts of time on relatively unimportant tasks, and then have to rush through tasks that are extremely important. They waste days on problems that could well be delegated to others, only to skimp on jobs that they alone are really competent to deal with.

Make sure those in junior positions feel involved.

The first step in improving the way you manage your time is to find out how exactly you are using it. Undertake a time-and-motion study of your day: keep a record of how much time you spend on your activities throughout the day's work. Make a note of the time you arrive at your workplace in the morning, when you actually settle down to the day's tasks, when you go off for lunch, and when you leave in the evening. Record too the actual time you start and finish each particular chore.

Keep this up for two or three days. Then look at the results, and try to analyse them. Do imbalances emerge? Have you spent disproportionate amounts of time on relatively minor jobs?

Now think about ways of streamlining your routine, and thereby using your time more efficiently. Remember that greater efficiency may come from doing less work – from being more selective in the range of tasks you actually perform yourself.

Here are some well-tested techniques for improving your management of time.

Work out priorities. At the beginning of each week, draw up a rough list of all the tasks you hope to achieve by the end of the week. Throw in everything. Then inspect the list, and start refining it. Identify the tasks to which you need to give priority, and those that can, if necessary, be left until later. You might work out numbered priority groups – (1) for tasks that are top priority, (2) for those that are slightly less urgent, (3) for jobs you can postpone to the next week. Then put the appropriate number by each task on your list.

Bear in mind the difference between important tasks and urgent tasks.

☐ An important task is one that will bring you closer to achieving a key objective – a task such as writing a crucial report to your own bosses, to win approval for a new business initiative.

☐ An urgent task is one that needs immediate attention even though it may not move you closer to any specific goal – a task such as checking the order book or any similar piece of humdrum administrative work.

Don't let the urgent tasks drown out the important ones. The dangers are obvious. You find at the end of a hard day, after signing a great many urgent papers, and dealing with endless urgent enquiries, that you have achieved nothing important, nothing that moves you nearer to your objectives. If this happens repeatedly, break the pattern at once.

Make time. Be quite ruthless in making time for important tasks. You could try delegating the urgent tasks to somebody else (provided that doing so does not divert him from his important tasks). You could try coming into work early on some mornings. You could try cutting out non-essential meetings, and cutting others short.

Screen out interruptions – a major time-waster. If, for example, a particularly important task arises, and you really have to remain undisturbed to concentrate on it, set up a 'meeting with yourself': to the outside world, you will be 'in a meeting' and unavailable until you emerge from it.

Limit your work load. Learn to say No, or you might as well move your bed into your office. And don't procrastinate. If you do agree to a certain task, get working on it as soon as possible.

Here finally is a checklist of questions to ask yourself when faced with new work:

Do I have to do this right now?
If I do it, what else will stop?
Do I have to do it at all?
Could someone else do it?
What is the most important thing I am trying to achieve, and will the accomplishment of this job help me to achieve it?

Organising Others

The good manager knows how to organise himself properly – to be a manager of work objectives and of timetables. But, of course, his task does not stop there. He also has to organise his subordinates – to be a manager of other people. Three key concepts govern this crucial day-to-day aspect of the business of management: communication, delegation, and motivation.

THE IMPORTANCE OF COMMUNICATION

To be a good boss, you need to know how to communicate effectively. You have a duty to set objectives for subordinates, and to follow these through. You will need to praise subordinates if they do well, encourage and direct them if they do adequately, reprimand them if they do badly.

As a boss you may have to communicate with subordinates in a variety of settings – one to one, in small groups, or in large meetings or gatherings.

Here are some key points to bear in mind:

☐ Always be clear. All too many problems between bosses and their subordinates arise out of misunderstandings. Subordinates fail to grasp their instructions properly, go away, and do the wrong thing. The boss gets angry; relations are soured. To avoid this situation, take time to spell out exactly what you want a subordinate to do, and how it fits into your overall strategy. At the end of the meeting, double check that both you and the subordinate understand exactly what you have decided.

☐ Listen. Remember that communication should run in both directions. If you do not bother to listen to your subordinates, the chances are that they will not listen properly to you. If a subordinate questions your instructions, listen especially hard. You may overrule the objections, but at least you have taken the trouble to understand them.

☐ Set clear objectives. Some bosses spell these out during annual appraisal interviews (see page 538), but that is seldom enough – people need more frequent updating. Thrash objectives out openly with both groups and individuals. Start by agreeing overall objectives, making sure to take into account any suggestions, or objections, raised by subordinates. Then break down the overall objectives into key areas – specific tasks to be accomplished. Agree on standards by which subordinates' performance can be measured. Make these yardsticks clear by stating: 'So-and-so will be performing effectively when/if . . . '

☐ Don't hide. When you do not feel fully in control of events – particularly when you have just taken up a new job – the temptation is to burrow yourself away in your office and to bombard subordinates with memos and telephone calls. This may save time, but generally speaking, try to communicate face to face with those working under you. You are more likely to solve problems when you talk them through openly.

☐ Don't pretend. If you feel any uncertainty or perplexity, don't try to disguise it under a façade of decisiveness. Far better to let your subordinates know your reservations.

You need to know how to communicate effectively.

☐ Be open about your plans and ambitions for your section. Subordinates like to know where you are leading them – and will usually work more willingly and efficiently if you let them know. With a large department this might mean regular 'communications meetings', where you tell people about the department's recent accomplishments, about the present state of affairs, and about upcoming projects and targets. In smaller departments, you can pass on this information more informally – perhaps over lunch taken with a small group of subordinates from time to time.

☐ Make communications pleasant. Observe the common social niceties. Be friendly and reasonable – 'I take your point, though I'm not sure that I altogether agree,' rather than: 'That's complete and utter rubbish, it'll never work!' Subordinates should not dread meetings with you – either because you keep reacting unpredictably or because you always reject their views without the courtesy of a fair hearing.

☐ Be accessible. Clearly subordinates should not trouble you with every minor difficulty, but they should always feel that your door is open – at least during certain hours of the day.

THE SKILLS OF DELEGATION

Delegating to subordinates can be surprisingly difficult, particularly when you are new in a job. How, for example, can you trust others – whose capabilities you are perhaps uncertain or suspicious of – with a task for which you remain ultimately responsible? If the job goes badly wrong, you will have to take the blame. And then, exactly which tasks should you delegate? The chances are that the tasks most suitable for delegation are precisely those that you yourself excel at and enjoy most. Do you really have to forgo these, now that you have become manager?

The temptation is to try to avoid delegation altogether. Unfortunately, this is not a serious option. You cannot possibly do single-handed the work of a whole section.

When you delegate, make sure, in the first place, that the task is one that you can reasonably assign to others. If you alone are really competent to do it, supervising someone else might take almost as much time as doing the job yourself.

Then, make sure that the person to whom you delegate the task is the right person – properly trained and fully prepared. To build up a substantial block of work that the subordinate can see through from beginning to end, try to supplement the task with other related tasks. This will not only give the subordinate greater satisfaction but should also ensure greater consistency.

Be specific, and realistic, about when you want the job finished: 'by 5 pm tomorrow', say, or 'by July 25' – never 'as soon as possible'.

Don't be too detailed in your briefing. Give the subordinate the chance to develop his own ideas – and skills – when working out the task. If you are nervous about his abilities, ask to see a plan of action beforehand, and then check it. And set up a system of regular checks on progress.

Remember that subordinates will not necessarily do things the way you would. You might be able to write that report more incisively yourself, or plaster that wall more smoothly. But delegated work is precisely not your work. Nothing is more depressing for a subordinate than to have work redone for no apparent reason. If the work is not good enough, point out the shortcomings, and, time permitting, let the subordinate have another go. If the work is good enough, give encouragement and praise.

Two final points. Remember, first, that delegating may not save you time in the early stages of a new job, but will almost certainly save time in the long run. Sooner or later subordinates will get used to the standards you demand, and increasingly you can leave them to their own devices.

Bear in mind, secondly, that delegation is a skill you should master early rather than late. It is easier to learn how to delegate work when you have two subordinates than when you have twenty-two. Don't make excuses by telling yourself that at the moment you can cope without delegating. Start delegating today.

MOTIVATING YOUR SUBORDINATES

To get the best out of subordinates, you need to motivate them – to fill them with enthusiasm and commitment for their work. Good communication and sensible delegation both play their part here. But there is more to the task than that.

Different people are motivated by different things in their work. For some ambitious people, it is above all the prospect of making their way to the top that excites and pushes them on. For others, money is the prime motivating factor. Others, though not indifferent to success or money, focus more on 'job satisfaction'. For them, what matters most is that their work is challenging and stimulating.

One of your crucial duties as boss is to identify these motivating energies in your work force, and then to tap them for the good of your organisation.

Here are some key points to bear in mind:

☐ Above all, know your subordinates. Be aware of what they want from their jobs, what their hopes and ambitions are – and make sure that they know they have a chance of achieving these in return for good work. One of your assistants, for example, might indicate a strong interest in working on a new market-research project. Do your best to oblige. Clearly, you cannot always meet people's wishes. You may need that assistant on another project. But you should at least explain this.

☐ Be imaginative. Try to put yourself in your subordinates' position. Many, for instance, may have young families with whom they like to spend time in the evenings. So if you ask them to do endless overtime, say, you are likely to alienate rather than motivate them.

☐ Don't forget to praise subordinates for good work. A short handwritten note expressing your appreciation for the hard work he has put in to a particular project can do wonders to spur a subordinate on to even greater efforts on the next project. And when someone's work is inadequate always be sure to explain how and why it fails to meet your standards.

☐ Watch for subordinates' reactions to your own approach. An authoritarian approach may have worked for years in your old-fashioned firm. But things change. Younger staff arrive, they have different attitudes, and do not take kindly to the old-style orders, given without explanation. You will have to consult them more, to draw them into the process of making decisions.

☐ Maintain standards. If you notice a decline in the quality of work produced by your subordinates, tackle the problem sensitively but promptly and firmly. Try to discover the cause. Perhaps the worker concerned has marriage problems, or is nearing retirement and finds it hard to work up previous enthusiasm for the job. Talk privately to the individual concerned. With some people, your showing an interest will in itself help to improve their motivation. With others, a reprimand may be necessary.

Different people are motivated by different things.

Managing Problem People

A brief private chat is usually enough to sort out a subordinate whose work falls temporarily below par. Occasionally, however, you may face a serious crisis. A particular subordinate is consistently creating problems. His work falls well below the standards you expect. He is having frequent rows with colleagues, and is disrupting the work of the whole section. Or he has a consistently poor attendance record, for no apparent reason.

Many managers try to turn a blind eye in these circumstances. They hope that matters will improve unaided, that it is all a temporary setback. And in some cases, they may be lucky – the problem may indeed solve itself. But there is no guarantee that it will – and things may get worse.

Managing problem people is one of a boss's trickiest and least enjoyable responsibilities. But as with all other duties, you had better face it boldly than ignore it. And remember one consoling factor. Almost any action – no matter how inadequate it

may seem to you at the time – is better than none. Your team will see that you know what is going on, and that you are not taking it lightly. Remember also that it is better to act early than late. A neglected problem may turn into a crisis. A neglected crisis may turn into an emergency.

How, then, do you deal with a consistently difficult member of staff – an insubordinate subordinate?

The first step is to pinpoint the problem. Define exactly what standards you expect of your subordinate, then decide where and how precisely he is failing to achieve these standards. Write it all down if this helps to clarify your thoughts.

As always, be specific. Don't simply put the problem down to 'personalities', or accuse a person of having 'the wrong attitude'. This may be true, but it gets you nowhere.

Focus instead on your subordinate's actual behaviour. What exactly is he doing that he should

545

not be doing? What is he failing to do that he should be doing? Once you start thinking in these terms, the problem will become more manageable. You have a chance of altering the subordinate's behaviour – you cannot change his personality. You might come up with something like this:

> Johnson consistently arrives late and leaves early – a total of three hours of missed work this week. He often simply refuses to do tasks set by his overseer – or argues when assigned non-routine chores, such as inspecting the transport logs. Work he does produce is usually below standard, his stock-control reports never follow the standard format. When asked to redo work, he does it grudgingly – and it's still often unsatisfactory.

Now, try to identify the circumstances that trigger off his behaviour – why he acts in the way he does, and what he gains from doing so.

In the example above, Johnson clearly resents being told what to do. Why? The answer may be that he has recently been passed over for an expected promotion. It may be more complicated – health problems, domestic anxieties, or the like. You might make discreet inquiries among his colleagues.

The next step is to think out where and how you can intervene to achieve a change. Suppose, for example, Johnson does seem to be smouldering with resentment at failure to gain promotion. Your course is clear: to have a face-to-face talk with him.

Explain in detail why the promotion went elsewhere. Explain, if appropriate, what he can do to improve his chances of promotion next time (but don't make any promises, or you will only be storing up an even greater problem for the future). Listen patiently to his views – why he feels he was treated unfairly – and answer him carefully and tactfully point by point.

IF THE WORST COMES TO THE WORST

Sometimes, things may get so bad that you feel you have no option but to sack a subordinate – or to refer the matter to a higher manager with the authority to sack him. This should only be a last resort. However tempted you might be in a moment of fury, don't even threaten dismissal, let alone order it, until you have thought through the implications. Have you tried reasoning with the unsatisfactory subordinate? Have you reprimanded him? Have you discussed the problem with your colleagues? And with him?

If you really think a parting of the ways is necessary, have an honest talk with your subordinate. Suggest that he 'would be happier elsewhere', that it would be good for both of you to 'part by mutual consent'. In other words, invite him to resign. Only if this fails, should you think of giving him the sack. And when you do, make sure you do it by the book.

The procedures for dismissing an employee are generally stated or implied in his employment contract. By law, these will provide for a minimum period of notice – from the moment when you inform your subordinate of his dismissal to the moment when it comes into effect – during which time he is entitled to receive full pay. According to some contracts, you must give him notice in writing. Be sure to study a copy of his contract.

Be careful also to avoid anything that might give your subordinate a claim for 'wrongful dismissal' or 'unfair dismissal'. Give him clear reasons for his sacking – in writing, to be on the safe side. Be sure that these reasons are clear and accurate, and that they clearly justify the action you have taken.

Some offences – embezzlement, for instance, theft at the workplace, deliberate vandalism, or violent assault on a superior – justify 'summary', on-the-spot dismissal without notice. Even in these cases, however, you should put in writing your reasons for the sacking, and include them in a follow-up letter to the sacked employee (see also page 303).

One last word: no matter what provoked the dismissal, do try to part company on civil terms. No one enjoys getting the sack, but so long as the ex-employee feels he was given a fair hearing, he represents little danger to your company. An embittered ex-employee, on the other hand, remains a constant threat – he might speak ill of your company at every turn, or even try to damage its property or products.

How to Run a Meeting

At THIS very moment thousands of meetings are taking place throughout the world. Many of these will prove highly productive; but many will be dismal failures – a waste of time and money. This chapter shows how to avoid such a destiny for any meeting you run.

To streamline the discussion, the term *chairman* is used to apply to any person running a meeting, male or female. The word *group* is used of any committee, board, team, task force, or similar body.

IS YOUR MEETING REALLY NECESSARY?

Before calling a meeting, ask yourself this simple but crucial question: 'Is the meeting really necessary?' If the answer is No, don't call one. This may seem thumpingly obvious – except that people routinely ignore it. Pointless meetings take place in obedience to the law of inertia – it has long been the custom to have such meetings, and it takes too much imagination or effort to change the pattern. Such meetings can be seriously disruptive.

Never initiate a meeting unless it looks cost-effective to have one. If any other means of communication will serve the purpose – such as a circular, notice, fax, or phone call – make use of that instead.

If you decide that a meeting really is needed, use the 'six-P guide' to help you through it:

> Purpose
> Participants
> Preparation
> Procedure
> Performance
> Post-mortem

THE PURPOSE – WHAT IS IT?

Be absolutely clear in your own mind about the purpose of the meeting. First, the broad purpose of the meeting – is it to inform, to persuade, to instruct, to decide something, to consult, or to inquire? Most meetings combine two or more of these purposes. Decide which are applicable to your meeting, then write them down, and refer to them repeatedly as a way of keeping things in focus. Next, consider the particular objectives – what exactly do you want the meeting to achieve?

To take a common example, you might formulate the broad purpose of your meeting to be: to persuade the group's members to raise money for a charity. And you might specify the particular objectives as: to encourage the members to think up and undertake methods for doing so.

If your meeting involves a strong element of persuasion, remember the acronym AIDA. This stands for 'Attention, Interest, Desire, Action'. First draw the participants' *attention* to the specific aims, next arouse their *interest* in the aims, then cultivate their *desire* to support those aims, and lastly get them to take *action*.

PARTICIPANTS

Ideally, the only people invited to a meeting should be those who will make a contribution to it. In the real world, people are often invited because of status, out of courtesy, or because they need to know what is happening. For instance, if you are convening a meeting of an established Health and Safety Committee, you must – out of courtesy – notify *all* members of the committee, even if one or two members will have little to contribute. At the same time, you might decide to invite an outside expert on, say, fire prevention.

If you are establishing a new group, on the other hand – such as a local hospital-visiting panel – you are free to include or exclude anyone you wish. But make your selection carefully. The mix of people is crucial in determining the quality of the meeting: too many ideas people and too few hands-on workers, and you have a recipe for a shouting match rather than an efficient or productive committee.

How many? Keep in mind that the larger the meeting, the less time there will be for each

Small meetings mean quicker decisions.

participant to speak. A group of no more than eight people is normally best for a meeting that intends to take decisions and get things done, but the quality of the participants is more important than the number. Decisions are usually reached more quickly at small meetings than at large ones. However, large meetings sometimes carry more weight – a recommendation unanimously agreed by twenty people might go further than one unanimously agreed by three people.

PREPARATION

When fixing a time for a meeting, start by checking the availability of key members of the group, then set a time that is likely to be convenient for the maximum number of those invited. Don't forget that meeting rooms usually have to be booked. Try to select a quiet, well-ventilated room of appropriate size, with a moderate temperature and adequate lighting. If using a slide projector, make sure the room has suitably placed power points.

Chairs and tables. Make sure that there are enough chairs for the members of the group, plus a few reserve chairs too in case of last-minute guest speakers, observers, and so on. The chairs should be comfortable but not so comfortable as to encourage those sitting on them to nod off. If possible, keep them equal in height, to avoid giving

any participant an unfair psychological advantage. Arrange them in a circle or semicircle rather than in rows: communication works best when people can see one another.

Try to position your own chair in a way that does not unduly isolate you, as chairman, from the other participants. A good chairman's authority rests in his or her conduct – not in the 'platform'.

Some meetings call for clear floor space between the chairs – for the sake of practical demonstrations of new selling techniques, for example. But for most meetings, a table is a good idea (a round table being best of all, on the King Arthur principle of equal status). Participants need something to put their papers on, and to write on. A table also helps to create a businesslike atmosphere.

Set out notepads, pencils, and rubbers on the table – and if it is going to be a long meeting, glasses and jugs of water or fruit juice, and perhaps some mints and boiled sweets.

Planning the agenda. Plan the agenda with care. Don't try to cover too many items – better to cover a few well, than several skimpily. When this is not possible, and the meeting is unavoidably long, arrange a ten-minute break about halfway through.

No single meeting should last more than 90 minutes without a break. Decide also what time you intend your meeting to finish. (For more detailed advice on agendas, see pages 324-327.)

Leave nothing to chance. A secretary, if there is one, can look after the administrative tasks such as booking and arranging the room and fixing the time, sending out the 'notices of meeting', informing those invited of the time and place, preparing and circulating the agenda, and later writing up the minutes (see pages 327-330). But the ultimate responsibility for the success or failure of the meeting rests with the chairman. So you must check every detail and leave nothing to chance.

Don't forget to inform participants of any last-minute change of venue. Many meetings get off to a bad start because participants have the chore of rushing from room to room in search of the meeting place. They arrive late, feeling justifiably angry.

Carry out one last inspection shortly before the meeting, to check that everything has been provided and arranged as planned. Use a checklist, and tick off all the items one by one. If anything has been forgotten or overlooked, act fast to put it right.

PROCEDURE

All meetings, ranging from the most formal and highly structured to the most informal and relaxed, have rules of procedure. The chairman is responsible for enforcing them. The basic procedural rules for formal meetings are covered below. If you have to chair such a meeting, make sure that you are thoroughly familiar with them, and with any variations detailed in your group's constitution and 'standing orders' – its agreed rules of debate.

But bear in mind that many business meetings nowadays are conducted on a relatively informal basis. The chairman simply steers the meeting through the points on the agenda, making sure that an appropriate amount of time is spent on each, that a consensus is reached or decision taken by majority vote on all key issues. In this case, observe the rules in the next section, *Performance*.

Motions. By convention, discussion at formal meetings revolves around a series of motions – proposals put forward by individual participants.

One member proposes a motion, another seconds it, discussion proceeds. The motion – known as the 'substantive motion', whether in its original form or in an amended version – is later put to the vote. If passed, it becomes a 'resolution'.

Unless a proposed motion is very short and simple, it should be written out and circulated. This serves to make clear the exact issues under discussion.

Bear in mind that procedural rules vary from group to group. Some standing orders allow the proposer to present his or her arguments before a seconder comes forward; others forbid debate unless a seconder comes forward right away. Here is an everyday example of procedure in operation.

The Springfield Sports Club executive committee is holding an emergency meeting. About halfway through, it is the turn of Mr Kealey, a long-serving member of the committee, to present his motion:

> Mr Chairman, I move 'That £5000 be allocated to the renovation of the clubhouse, and that the work begin in July this year'.

The chairman would be entitled, at this point, to rule the motion out of order, if it violated club rules. And other participants might raise various objections to it right away (see below). But since it is a legitimate and reasonable motion, the chairman asks Mr Kealey to give his reasons for proposing it.

Mr Kealey explains, briefly, and the chairman then calls for a seconder. Ms White volunteers, announcing formally, 'Mr Chairman, I second the motion.' The chairman then invites her to give her reasons in turn, but she says that she prefers to reserve this right (as the committee's rules allow her to do) until later in the meeting.

The chairman then opens the debate to the meeting, inviting speeches alternately from those supporting the motion and those opposing it.

The discussion does not always run smoothly, of course. In the case of the Springfield committee debate, there are several hiccups along the way, but eventually all opinions get an airing.

With one exception, each participant at a meeting may speak only once on each motion or amendment. The exception is the proposer, who is always allowed the last word. As the debate draws to an end, the chairman accordingly calls on Mr Kealey to answer his opponents and to sum up. Then, as soon as Mr Kealey has finished speaking, that particular debate is closed.

The chairman now puts the motion to the vote: usually he reads the motion out loud, and then asks all those in favour to raise their hand

Finally, he announces the figures, and formally declares the result. Mr Kealey has won the day in this instance, so the chairman says, 'I therefore declare the motion carried.' It now becomes a resolution, is recorded as such in the minutes, and becomes official club policy.

Amending the motion. As it happens, the motion voted on was not quite the original motion put forward by Mr Kealey.

A motion can be amended at any time after it has been proposed and before it has been voted on. A speaker may wish to add to or subtract from the wording of the motion, or change it in some other way. Suppose, for example, another member of the Springfield Sports Club, Dr Frost, had jumped in at an early stage, and said: 'Mr Chairman, I move that the words "and that the work begin in July this year" be deleted from the motion.'

Those present at the meeting would now have watched events unwind in the following way: the chairman duly turns to Mr Kealey, the proposer of the motion, and asks him if he accepts Dr Frost's amendment. If he agrees to it, the new shorter motion will replace the original version as the substantive motion, and become the subject of the debate. But Mr Kealey, in the event, objects to the amendment. A subdebate now gets under way, to decide the merits of Dr Frost's motion. First Dr Frost explains his reasons:

> Mr Chairman, we can't decide here and now the starting date for the renovations. We just haven't enough information. It's a separate question – the works committee should look into it first.

A seconder volunteers; Mr Kealey puts forward his arguments against the amendment; debate rages to and fro. Finally, it is the vote that decides matters – a majority vote in favour of the amendment. The chairman announces:

> The motion before the committee now reads: 'That £5000 be allocated to the renovation of the clubhouse.'

And the debate continues.

Adjournment and procedural motions. These are designed primarily to ensure the orderly running of the meeting, but are often also used as tactical weapons in debate, particularly as a means of disposing of a particular motion.

There are five main ways of bringing a debate to a halt; each involves a member of the meeting proposing, and another seconding, a special kind of motion. First, the two adjournment motions – 'That the debate be adjourned' and 'That the meeting be adjourned'. Either motion, if passed, has the effect of suspending, not cancelling, debate on the substantive motion – discussion should resume at a later session. The break may well prove very useful, however, in cooling tempers or even resolving a deadlock. Informal negotiations over a cup of tea sometimes result in compromises that seemed impossible within the meeting room itself.

More definite in their intention are the three procedural motions – 'closure', 'the next business', and 'the previous question'.

The closure motion. This occurs when some impatient member of the group proposes, 'That the question be now put'. This says in effect, 'Enough talk – let's stop this debate now and vote on the motion.' A member of the Springfield executive, for example, feels that the debate on the renovation proposal has continued long enough. She butts in, 'Mr Chairman, I move that the question be now put.' Another member says, 'Mr Chairman, I second the motion.' The closure motion is immediately put to

the meeting to vote on. Many members remain unclear about the renovations, however, and accordingly vote against the closure motion. Debate on the renovations motion then resumes.

If the closure motion had been passed, the debate would have been short-circuited. The chairman would call on the proposer, Mr Kealey, to deliver his closing reply, then put the motion to the vote.

The next business motion. This occurs when an exasperated member of the group proposes, 'That the meeting proceed to the next business'. If seconded and passed, this would get rid of the substantive motion altogether – no summing-up, no vote, just an immediate advance to the next item on the agenda. If the next business motion is not seconded or not passed, however, the substantive motion returns.

The previous question motion. This occurs when an anxious member of the group proposes, 'That the question be not now put'. Its purpose is to delay a decision, but not the debate.

Another member of the Springfield executive, for example, wants to discuss the whole question of renovations at this meeting, but feels equally strongly that no decision should yet be taken.

He wants the debate to go on, but the vote to be postponed – pending further estimates, say, for the cost of the project. In the event, his proposal strikes the rest of the committee as needlessly timid, and he fails to find a seconder. The renovations debate therefore continues.

If the previous question motion had secured a seconder, the effect would be rather more complex than with the other procedural motions. The previous question motion would not be voted on immediately. The meeting would continue to discuss the renovations, but at the same time it would discuss the wisdom of delaying a decision.

When the debate draws to a close, the previous question motion is first put to the vote. If passed, the renovations motion is set aside, possibly to be discussed at a later date. If it is defeated, the mover of the original renovations motion, Mr Kealey, exercises as normal his right of reply, and the substantive motion is put to the vote.

Points of order. At times the chairman of a meeting needs to be reminded of the rules, or corrected if he breaches them. Members of the group see to this by raising 'points of order'.

Perhaps the proposer of a motion is going beyond an agreed time limit, or being abusive, or making irrelevant points. If another participant suspects the breach of a rule, he or she calls out 'Point of order, Mr Chairman'. Debate is suspended immediately, and the chairman asks the objector to explain the point of order – to identify the rule that is allegedly being infringed.

The chairman then either upholds the point of order or overrules it, and the debate continues.

The power and the duties of the chairman. As chairman your ruling on any matter of procedure is final. But it had better be wise as well.

If you make illogical or biased rulings, the meeting will lose confidence in your chairmanship, sometimes to the point of taking a vote of 'no confidence' in you and casting you out of office.

Your primary duty is to ensure the orderly and economical running of the meeting. At formal meetings, participants must address all comments to or through you as chairman. If they do not, you should call them to order.

This rule, like so many of the formal debating procedures of meetings, may seem fussy, but it does help the meeting to run smoothly, and stops debate from getting out of hand.

Insist too that only one person speaks at a time. If any members of the group start a private conversation in the middle of a debate, you should bring them to order swiftly and thereby minimise the disruption. But try to do so in a genial and businesslike way rather than aggressively. Say something like, 'Can we have just one meeting at a time, please.'

As chairman you must be absolutely fair and impartial when interpreting and enforcing procedural rules. This does not prohibit you from expressing your personal views on the matter under discussion (though it is wise to keep these brief). What it does prohibit you from doing is, for instance, allowing Dr Frost to speak at length simply because you share his views, and cutting Mr Kealey short just because you disagree with him.

According to the standing rules of most organisations, the chairman also has the right to a 'casting vote'. This is used when the votes for and against a motion are equal in number. You, as chairman, are then allowed a second, or casting, vote in order to break the deadlock.

PERFORMANCE

Careful preparation and planning will go a long way to ensure that your meeting is a success. But success also depends on the quality of your performance as chairman at the meeting.

Opening the meeting. Make sure to arrive early enough to greet participants, especially newcomers. Remember, you are the host. Offer people refreshments if available. A friendly rapport established before the meeting can smooth things along during the meeting.

Start the meeting on time. Don't wait more than a few minutes for latecomers. A prompt start will show that you mean business.

Opening moves. Before turning to your agenda, welcome all who are present and introduce newcomers. But keep these preliminaries brief – try to limit your remarks to two minutes.

Keep close at hand a list of names of all present. In the meeting it is all too easy to forget names you normally remember without trouble.

Now get launched into the agenda. Normally, the first three items are: 'Apologies for absence', 'Minutes of the last meeting', and 'Matters arising from the minutes' (see pages 324-330).

Work your way briskly through these. As a rule, the minutes will have been circulated already, and can be 'taken as read'. It is the section that follows that is the heart of the meeting – when the important matters, or 'special business', are discussed.

During the meeting. As you guide the meeting through the agenda, remember you as chairman are the person who: sets the tone and pace; steers the meeting in the right direction; upholds correct procedure; strives for agreement; and minimises conflict between participants.

Be alert throughout the meeting. Watch out for participants raising their hands, or in other ways trying to catch your eye, to indicate that they wish to speak. Take them on a 'first come, first served' basis, though if several participants have an equal claim, you should consider giving priority to those who speak less often.

Never lose your temper – or the meeting will probably collapse.

Be a keen listener. The chairman must hear everything if he is to direct the course of the meeting effectively. Encourage shy or inexperienced people to express their thoughts, but never coerce or embarrass them into doing so. Be firm with participants who talk too much. Bring them to order swiftly but courteously. A well-timed 'thank you' will often do the trick.

If a garrulous member tries to butt in repeatedly cut him off with a comment such as: 'We know that you have strong views on the matter, but I was wondering what the others feel about it.'

Be patient with poor speakers. They may well have excellent ideas to contribute. Steer them along tactfully, gently suggesting an appropriate word or phrase to sum up their thoughts.

Speak clearly, purposefully, and fluently. Don't gabble, mumble, or boom out your words.

Make frequent, though brief, summaries during the meeting. These will serve as progress indicators and help to consolidate positions reached.

Clarify constantly, or demand clarification. Ensure that what is said by one participant is understood by all. You can do this by:

☐ asking questions about aspects that might have been missed – 'There is one question we haven't asked: What time should the show start? Bill, what do you think?'

☐ extracting details – 'The one point we haven't covered is the cost of advertising. How does this affect the plan?'

☐ defining words that could be ambiguous – 'Elaine, when you say that his idea is "critical" to the plan, do you mean that the plan wouldn't work without it?'

☐ asking speakers to elaborate – 'Jim, would you say a little more on that point?'

Don't be long-winded or high-falutin. Take a lesson from the proverbial chairman who sent his entire committee to sleep with speeches such as this:

May I venture to suggest, with your permission, that having discussed this matter at considerable length, and in view of the time, which – I am sure you all agree – marches on so relentlessly, we ought at this juncture of a most stimulating meeting to consider the matter of turning our attention to the next item on the agenda.

All he really meant to say could be summed up in seven words: 'We must now move to item 4.'

Use humour to reduce tension. It can be a wonderful antidote to rising tempers. But use it sparingly. Don't launch into a string of jokes: a serious meeting is hardly the place for a comic turn. To adapt a well-known saying: 'If at first you *do* succeed, *do not* try again,' at least not for a while! Tolerant quick fire wit is best. Take care, however, not to be flippant about serious matters.

Never ignore or conceal a problem. Recognise conflicting ideas and point them out to the group. Bring things out into the open where they can be examined in intelligent discussion. Ask the conflicting participants: 'Where exactly do you stand?' and then: 'What do you suggest we do?' In this way you can defuse the tension and encourage fresh thinking on a difficult question.

Keep the meeting moving. As soon as an argument starts to go round in circles, draw it to a conclusion, preferably by a consensus agreement, or if you fail to reach that, by a majority vote.

Winding up the meeting. Once all the items on the agenda have been worked through, you should then – under the heading of 'Any other business' – invite participants to raise other matters of interest or concern. This will give you all an opportunity to exchange information, announce events, and comment briefly on matters relevant to the group.

If, however, a participant raises an important or complicated matter calling for lengthy discussion, point out that there is not enough time to do the issue justice. Suggest including the matter on the agenda of a future meeting or, if the matter is really urgent, arrange a special meeting for the near future in order to discuss the issue at greater leisure.

After that, sum up the decisions taken, then announce the date, time, and place of the next scheduled meeting. Finally, thank the participants for attending and declare the meeting 'concluded'.

POST-MORTEM

After the next meeting you run, ask yourself the following five questions:

Did I start the meeting on time?
Did the meeting cover every item on the agenda adequately?
Did we reach constructive decisions?
Was the meeting held in a spirit of co-operation?
Did I keep to the timetable?

If your answer is Yes to all five of the questions, congratulate yourself. You performed very much better than average as a chairman.

If your answer is No to one or more of the questions, try to pinpoint exactly what went wrong, and why, so that you can get everything right next time.

If your answer is No to all five questions, congratulate yourself on being so honest and reread this entire chapter carefully.

INFORMAL MEETINGS

For some meetings, such as a 'brainstorming', rules are best kept to a minimum. Brainstorming is an intensive discussion in which participants are encouraged to offer suggestions as possible solutions to a problem. The task might be, for example, to think up a catchy name for a new brand of soap, or to suggest ways of reducing traffic congestion.

This is an essentially creative process that could be greatly hampered by formal restrictions. The leader must, therefore, tread a fine line between rigour and anarchy – taking care to maintain reasonable discipline, but without stifling creativity. To run this sort of meeting successfully takes as much discretion and dexterity as the running of formal meetings. The golden rule at a brainstorming is that nobody should criticise an idea. A brainstorming is a time for creativity, and the quantity of ideas is what matters. Judging quality comes later.

A FINAL WORD

The most valuable asset of all that you can have at any meeting – whether as chairman or participant – is a clear mind. Try to get a good sleep the night before your meeting. Avoid eating a heavy meal shortly before the meeting. A light snack and a short brisk walk will prepare you better for the fray.

GLOSSARY: MEETINGS AND THEIR TERMINOLOGY

abstention	voting neither for nor against a motion
addendum (pl. **addenda**)	a word or set of words added to a motion
ad hoc	for a specific purpose; especially, referring to a committee set up temporarily for a special reason (Latin, literally, 'towards this')
adjournment	the suspension of a meeting or its postponement
agenda	the programme of business to be dealt with at a meeting, usually in the form of a numbered list of items
casting vote	a vote, cast by the chairman, when the members' votes are tied, to produce a definite decision
amendment	an alteration to a motion
minutes	the official record of the proceedings and decisions of a meeting
nem. con.	with no one opposing – in other words, without any votes against the resolution, though possibly with one or more abstentions (abbreviation of Latin *nemine contradicente*, that is, 'with no one contradicting')
quorum	the minimum number of members who must be present before a meeting can start or continue officially
resolution	a motion in its final form when passed by the meeting
standing orders	the rules or bye-laws governing or guiding a group in the running of its business and meetings
substantive motion	a motion for debate, often in an amended form, dealing with actual policy matters rather than just with the running of the meeting itself

The Skills of Good Speaking

Negotiating and Selling

THE ABILITY to negotiate is something that everybody ought to acquire. Everyone – from the world statesman negotiating treaties that affect the lives of millions, to the company employee asking for a pay rise or the young person applying for his or her first mortgage – needs constantly to reach agreements with other people. This calls for a mastery of the skills of persuasion, compromise, diplomacy, clear speaking, and attentive listening.

'The shortest and best way to make your fortune is to let people see clearly that it is in their interests to promote yours,' commented, somewhat cynically, the 17th-century French satirist Jean de la Bruyère. It is certainly true that one of the basic secrets of persuasion is to convince other people that what is good for you is also good for them. The skilful negotiator is the one whose opponents too come out of the talks feeling well-satisfied with the outcome. Your boss is happy to give you an eight per cent pay rise in order to keep your services and goodwill – and you are happy too, having banked on no more than seven per cent.

Selling and negotiating have much in common. In one you are selling products, in the other ideas. Both usually come down to money.

And both involve selling yourself. Once others view you as dependable, you are on the way to success.

THE LONG-TERM VIEW

Always take the long-term view in negotiations. See them as a campaign, not as a one-off battle. It is possible to lose individual battles and win the campaign. It is equally possible to win individual battles and lose the campaign.

Take an extreme example. Suppose it is a pay rise you want. You are an almost indispensable member of a team in your company. Only you really understand the finer workings of the computer system that has recently been installed. Knowing that you are in a position of strength, you go to your boss and demand a 20 per cent rise, even though inflation stands at only 9.5 per cent and you have a fairly ample salary anyway. The boss objects that this is unreasonable but you insist, perhaps threatening to resign. You may – just – get away with it. The office is under great pressure at the moment, and to have someone else trained to do your job would make that pressure intolerable. Reluctantly, the boss will give way.

You have won the battle, but how have you fared in the longer term? The boss will not forget behaviour that amounts almost to blackmail, and will try to make sure he never again finds himself in a similar position. The chances are that he will immediately set about training other people to learn your job. And the next time you try to pull that trick, he will call your bluff. You have lost the campaign.

Now take a constrasting case. You really are badly paid compared with other people in your company who have similar responsibilities – you have facts and figures to prove it. You go to your boss and ask for a relatively modest ten per cent rise. The boss demurs. Times are difficult. Recession has brought a downturn in business. The extra money is simply not available. You accept this – and get perhaps a disappointing six per cent rise. This is hardly what you hoped for – it does not even cover inflation – but you take it all with good grace.

You have lost the battle, but you may have won the campaign. The boss will know that you have had a bad deal. Your gracious acceptance will have won his goodwill – and an element of guilt may come into play as well. In the next pay round, all these factors may come together to produce an unexpectedly generous pay rise.

Not, of course, that you should be supine, always taking No for an answer. Another key to successful negotiating is persistence – quiet but forceful persistence. This is particularly true of selling. Suppose you have just set up a small business baking and selling cakes. You approach food shops in your local area, and get little response. Don't give up. Keep trying new shops until you do win some sales.

Then, after a decent interval, try the first shops again. If your product is good, they will begin to take you seriously and start to buy your cakes.

So much for the overview. Now for the particulars. Again, remember that negotiations make up a campaign – and, as in all campaigns, success depends on careful planning. You have to identify the right person or people to approach, set up a meeting, prepare your case, and finally face the people you are going to negotiate with.

SETTING UP THE MEETING

Usually, it will be fairly clear whom you should approach. If you are after a pay rise, your boss is the obvious person. If it is a bank loan, then your bank manager is the person you need. If you are selling a product, approach the owners or managers of appropriate smaller shops, or the buyers of larger stores. When you are marketing a service or idea, you need to target suitable companies or organisations, and to find the name of the person with the authority to deal with you.

To set up a meeting with someone within your own company or organisation, all you need to do is to ask that person – on the phone, in person, or by memo. If you are going to deal with someone outside your company, a telephone call to ask for an appointment is usually the best initial approach.

Phone quite early in the day, before people are too bound up in their daily tasks. Keep a note of all names and extension numbers, and on future occasions ask for people by name.

There is no need to feel embarrassed about asking for an interview. It is, after all, the job of buyers, shopkeepers, bank managers, and the rest to have dealings with people like you, and if you sound businesslike they have no reason to keep you away.

If you have a product or idea to sell, you should give the other person a brief idea of what it is. But don't try to sell it over the phone – no one will buy without seeing you first, and buyers will resent having their time wasted. Leave the selling until the interview. Something like this is enough:

Hello. Is that Brian Simms, deliveries manager? My name is Elaine Brierly. How do you do? Mrs Carl suggested that I speak to you about courier services. I represent Express Deliveries. We're a new company based in the area, specialising in moving small consignments around the country

No need to feel embarrassed . . .

at short notice. We reckon that we are very competitive in this field. I wonder whether it would be possible to see you and describe our services in more detail.

If Mr Simms says that he is satisfied with his present couriers, you might just briefly mention one or two of your special services to see if that will tip the balance – perhaps you alone among the local courier companies deliver anywhere in the UK within 24 hours. But don't push – you will only irritate the other person. If he still shows no interest, call off politely and try another company.

PREPARE YOUR CASE

Never walk cold into a meeting. Half, at least, of the battle is won before the face-to-face meeting. First of all, you must know your subject.

The strongest weapon in your armoury of persuasion is detailed comparison. Collect and set out all facts and figures neatly in tables or, where helpful, in charts and graphs. If you are selling something, you should know what rival products other companies are selling and how your product compares for price, reliability, and service. If you are negotiating, for example, a pay rise, collect plenty of data about company profits and expenditure, inflation, and pay in other comparable industries and in your own company.

All this takes time and effort – a lot of ploughing through dry documents and extracting what is important. But without evidence you will not convince anyone of anything.

Know the other person's subject too. Put yourself in his or her position. Imagine the counterarguments you might face, and have your replies ready. Practise out loud the answers you will give.

Find reasons why agreeing with you is in the other person's interests. What, precisely, can your product or idea do for him or his company? During the meeting, be direct about this. Don't waste time, as some inexperienced negotiators do, by going over your early struggles or other irrelevant details. Get to the point, and stay there.

Decide on and jot down the order in which you intend to present your arguments – but be prepared to be flexible. In the meeting you may have to change your order, as one tack seems unfruitful and another more promising.

Be absolutely clear about what exactly you hope to get out of the meeting, and what, realistically, you think you are likely to get. Write down beforehand a list in three sections:

> Your minimum demands
> Your actual demands
> Your most optimistic hopes

Your minimum demands. Work out the line below which you are not prepared to do a deal. You will not settle for fewer than, say, 24 tins of your corned beef as a sample, a ten per cent pay rise in line with inflation, a moratorium on repayments of your loan until September when new funds arrive. Don't pitch these sticking points too high.

In the meeting, try to keep your minimum demands to yourself for as long as possible. They are what you fall back on when the going gets tough. If you ever need to mention them, try to do so in passing, as if they were so self-evident that they hardly need to be mentioned: 'Two dozen tins of the corned beef might do as a sample, but more would be better to give the product a fair try'; 'Apart from the ten per cent to cover inflation, we'd like to look at the question of parity with head office'; 'I could perhaps start repayments in November – there's no real chance before September.'

Your actual demands. These are what you hope realistically to get from the meeting. Make sure they really are within the realms of realism.

All your arguments should be mustered in support of the items on this predecided list – all your data and comparisons should go into showing that they are feasible and reasonable. Pencil in on an order sheet precise numbers of what you expect to sell; have full details of the costs to the company of awarding eight per cent to you – and perhaps others – and the reason why you deserve it; produce your projected cash-flow statement in such a way that there is obviously no point in pressing for early repayment.

Your most optimistic hopes. Again, make sure these are reasonable. You will just be laughed at if you suggest that the shop you are negotiating with can take several dozen of a completely new and unadvertised product. Or if you start off asking for a 25 per cent pay rise. Or if you seem to expect the bank to waive the interest while you cannot pay.

But do be fairly optimistic – these 'demands' are there to be shot down. You suggest that the shop should stock three dozen of your imported rugs. The owner reckons he cannot shift more than 30. You are more than happy with that; two dozen was what you had reckoned on.

Remember this key point: very seldom do both sides get absolutely everything they want from negotiations. So it is useful to have a claim that you are prepared to give way on, to show that you are reasonable and willing to compromise.

INSPIRING CONFIDENCE

However nervous you feel underneath, display a quiet confidence as you enter the meeting room. Introduce yourself to everyone there, proffer your hand for a firm handshake, look people straight in the eye, and smile as you say 'How do you do?' Get all names sorted out at once, and use them often during the meeting. If you do not quite catch somebody's name, don't be embarrassed to ask him to repeat it. Good, straightforward, and unaffected manners will give you an air of confidence.

Pay attention to your appearance – that is obvious. But remember: as a rule, clothing in itself is surprisingly unimportant, so long as you dress in a way which suggests that you take a professional attitude, and in a way appropriate to the job you have to do. If you are selling insurance, for example, you would be unwise to wear a boiler suit. If you are demonstrating a hydraulic pump, you will look silly in a £500 pinstripe suit.

SELLING POINTS

Before you can sell a product or service, you must have its 'selling points' clearly worked out in your mind – the 'special' qualities that will make it attractive to the buyer. Consider these questions:

What exactly are you offering the buyer? What will your product or service be able to do for him?
How will it benefit or enhance his life? What makes it stand out from other similar products or services?

Jot down your answers to the questions.

To sharpen your selling skills, you might try this game. Pick an item – for example, a vase, video recorder, or tin-opener – in your home or in a shop window, and make a list of all its good qualities and benefits. Then note what you would say in its favour if you were going to sell it. Try putting a price on it.

Better still, get a friend to play the game with you. Ask your friend to play the role of buyer or customer. Get him or her to list all the negative qualities of an item, and to raise objections to your selling points.

Then choose another item and swap roles. Let your friend play the salesman while you play the customer. The more you practise the game, the better you will become at it, and the better equipped to sell your own products.

More important is personal tidiness and cleanliness – hair, shoes, fingernails, and make-up. And so is your personal organisation.

Lay out your papers neatly on the table, so that they are there to hand – nothing looks less impressive than a desperate scramble through a briefcase and a muttered 'I know it's here somewhere.' Keep your pen ready to take notes (and don't be afraid to ask for time to take notes when necessary). Being organised will allow you to keep your mind firmly fixed on the real matter in hand – persuasion.

What further qualities should you display during the meeting?

Enthusiasm and a positive approach. If you are selling, you must believe in your product or idea. Dwell on its practical benefits, how it meets the other person's needs. Don't, however, make derogatory comments about the competition. Better to acknowledge the qualities of your rivals, and then to show how your product or scheme is superior.

If you are negotiating for pay, don't dwell on the injustice of others' being better paid. Show that you, or those you represent, have made a special contribution that deserves financial recognition.

Flattery is a good weapon, but don't make it obvious. Remarks about a shop's 'good location' and 'excellent range' will go down well with its owner or manager (and can be used to show that he or she should therefore stock your product). You think your company should raise your wages – let your boss know how happy you are working for it, and how well it treats its staff (and hence, why it should be treating you just that little bit better).

Honesty and reliability. Avoid all unfounded claims. People will not just take your word for it that your product is the one for them, or that you deserve a pay rise. You have to prove it. If your product or scheme does have drawbacks, don't leave it to the other person to bring them up. Pre-empt objections by mentioning them yourself, and then show how the advantages outweigh the drawbacks.

Competence. Present your case in a way that attests to your efficiency. Raise your points one at a time in the order you have decided. Build up your case gradually. Make sure that the other people fully understand both the general thrust of your argument and each item of it.

Inevitably, the other people will have questions to ask. How you handle these depends on how many people you are dealing with. If you are presenting your case to just one person or a few people, it is usually best to answer the questions as they come.

With a larger group, you should probably agree beforehand to make your presentation first, then take questions.

Flexibility. Keep your wits about you. Be ready to compromise, especially on less important issues. If you see that one approach is getting you nowhere, withdraw gracefully and move on to something else. You can always return to the stumbling block.

Even when you meet with a firm No, don't let the experience go to waste. Use it to improve your skills for next time. After the meeting, analyse the responses you received, and try to work out why some approaches worked better than others.

The Skills of Good Speaking

SPEAK SIMPLY

The best, and easiest, way to speak is naturally. It will inspire confidence. Cut out jargon, and you will sound more intelligent and reliable – and so be more convincing

Speak fairly slowly and speak out. Be sure the other person can hear what you are saying. Cut down the *um*'s and *er*'s. Use short sentences. If someone throws a nonsensical comment at you, say: 'Sorry, I didn't understand that. Can you explain?'

Don't be afraid to ask direct questions: 'What exactly would that mean in cash?' 'Can you tell me the names of the people this would apply to?' Asking Yes/No questions helps to elicit direct answers: 'Would you be able to take delivery next week?' 'Wouldn't that be one way out?' 'Surely our company can match X for wages?'

KEEP COOL

Never give the impression of being pushy. If people feel pressured, they are unlikely to come to a favourable decision. If there is a lull in the conversation, don't rush in to fill it. Silence can sometimes be your best argument – especially the silence that shows you have listened carefully to what the other side has said and you are thinking things over seriously.

Don't interrupt. If the other person is getting into a tangle, don't help him out. Use the time to work out your next move. If the other person keeps interrupting you, fix your eyes on him and say politely, 'Excuse me, could I just make a point or two.' If you both start speaking at once, let the other person go first: 'Sorry, after you.' Even in the heat of the moment, don't lose your composure. And don't jump in the moment the other person has had his say with 'Yes, but . . . ' Let him finish, and then pause and consider before replying.

GOOD RELATIONS

The meeting should take place in an atmosphere of politeness and goodwill. Let the person you are speaking to know that you appreciate his position and problems. You both have the task of representing some interest as well as you can, only from different sides.

A little humour often helps, so long as it is not at the expense of others and is not overdone.

Keep your eyes on the person you are dealing with. Watch for favourable responses and exploit them. Search for areas of agreement and build on them. Be ready with helpful advice.

There will usually be disagreements. Raise your objections tactfully – 'I'm sorry, I don't quite understand your point', 'I'm afraid I can't agree with you there', 'Are you quite sure about that?' – and then prove your point with relevant facts and figures.

Be gracious in victory: 'Thank you for your help'; 'Well, we've dealt with that pretty thoroughly'. Even more important, be gracious in defeat and learn how to back down when necessary: 'I understand your difficulty'; 'I have to admit you're right on this point, but what about . . . ?'

THE END OF THE MEETING

A good negotiator knows when to call it a day. As the negotiations proceed, you should sense whether you are going to win. Don't loiter.

If things drag on, don't be afraid to ask directly for a final answer. Be ready with emergency alternatives and special offers (your minimum demands, or some adaptation of the product or scheme to meet the other person's needs). If you are selling something, take out a pen and an order sheet and say simply, 'Are you interested in ordering?' The buyer can always say No.

Don't show irritation or impatience if your efforts have failed. Make it clear that you appreciate the other person's problems, and leave the door open for the future: 'Would you be interested in placing an order later this year?'

And if your efforts have met with success? Before the meeting closes, go back over the points you have raised. Give an item by item summary of what you have agreed on. List what still has to be done and who has to do it – supplying further information, placing an order, and the like. As you leave, thank the other person for his or her time. Shake hands. And make it clear that there will be a next time: 'I'll phone back in about six months.'

Whatever the outcome, it is good long-term policy to write within a couple of days to thank the other person for seeing you. It gives you an opportunity to confirm in writing the points agreed on at the meeting and to supply any further details – and, when appropriate, to mention that you look forward to meeting the other person again.

Ready-Reference Word Guide

What is the difference between *prescribing* something and
proscribing it? *Occurred*? Are there really two *c*'s and two *r*'s?
Where does the stress come in the word *pejorative*?
Here is a directory of the most common problems and dangers in
English grammar, spelling, pronunciation, and use of words.

a, an 1. The indefinite article is *a* before consonant sounds, including /h/, /w/, and /y/ (*a tree, a union*), and *an* before vowel sounds (*an apple, an old car*). Some words beginning with *h-* clearly begin with a consonant sound (*horse, holiday, haircut*); others clearly begin with a vowel (*hour, honour*). These words follow the usual rule. It is therefore incorrect to say, or write, ✗*an hostel,* ✗*an horrible day,* ✗*an heavy load.*

Slightly trickier is a word such as *hotel*, whose opening *h*-sound is very weak because its syllable is unstressed. In rapid speech the /h/ is often lost, so the word invites an *an*: *an hotel, an habitual liar, an whodunit.* However, to write *an* in such places, rather than just to say it, is considered an affectation nowadays.

The consonant/vowel rule applies also to abbreviations. In speech there is no problem: when *M.P.* is pronounced /em-pee/, you use *an* before it when speaking; in writing, however, you could use *a* instead, as before the words 'Member of Parliament'.

2. In British English the pronunciation /ay/ for *a* is considered either primly overcorrect or vulgar – ✗/ay boy/ – except when the word is stressed, usually through being contrasted with a plural or with the definite article: *You said /ay/ friend, not seven; He may be /ay/ Peter Shilton, but he's not /thee/ Peter Shilton.*

3. A single *a* or *an* can be used for all the individual items in a list: *We need a knife, saw, or axe; I'm an actress, singer, and mother of three.* Note that in each example the actual form, *a* or *an*, is governed by the word immediately following, even though later items would normally require the other form. It is pedantic to insist on *We need a knife, a saw, or an axe.*

However, you should repeat the indefinite article if the items in the list are considered separately: *A conservative and a socialist will view things differently; Objects were scattered around – a cup, a plate, a large frying pan, and a kettle.*

And do repeat the article before each appropriate item when it would be inappropriate before some of the other items in the list: *You'll need a pen, a pencil, an empty jam jar, some crayons, a pair of scissors, and glue.*

4. At times *a* or *an* is optional; for instance:

☐ before idiomatic pairs or lists – *All I want is (a) needle and thread.*

☐ after *as* – *He's better known as (a) singer than (an) actor.*

☐ when its noun is in apposition to a personal name – *Capt. Singleton, (a) well-known pirate; (A) Birmingham housewife, Elaine Mac-Williams, will be...* The last example would be informal other than in journalism.

☐ before the name of a book, play, film, or the like which is preceded by an adjective, possessive phrase, or the like: *Have you seen Kubrick's* CLOCKWORK ORANGE? *I saw a wretched* MIDSUMMER NIGHT'S DREAM *recently.*

aberration Note the spelling: one *b* and two *r*'s.

abjure, adjure Take care not to confuse these two formal verbs. The prefix *ab-* means 'away from' – so the verb *to abjure* means 'to renounce or abstain *from*, as if by formal oath': *I urge you to abjure alcohol.* By contrast, *to adjure* means 'to command or entreat, as if by formal oath': *He adjured me to give up alcohol.* Both words are stressed on the second syllable.

about 1. Avoid *about* when the sentence already suggests approximateness, as when a range of possibilities is given: **?** *I noticed a nervous man of about 30 to 35;* **?** *The crowd was estimated at about 20,000.*

2. The following three uses of *about* are common in American English. They are not, however, fully accepted in British English.

☐ *About*, 'aiming at, intended to achieve', as in **?** *Our strike is all about political equality.* This use of the word invites confusion with the normal sense of 'concerning, dealing with'.

☐ *What it's all about*, as in this expression: **?** *Money – that's what it's all about.* The expression is both slangy and clichéd. Try instead something like *Money – everything turns on it.*

☐ *Not about to,* 'unwilling to; unlikely to', as in **?** *I've broken my leg once while mountaineering, and I'm not about to do that again.* Here the risk of confusion is with the standard sense of 'not soon going to do something'.

above The *above* in the sense of 'what has been said just before' is common in legal, business, official, and technical writing, but it sounds stilted in other contexts: **?** *Covert advertising, as in the above, is dishonest.* You might try *of this kind* instead, or *like those just mentioned*, or *like that mentioned above.*

As adjectives with related meanings, both *above* and *below* are unobjectionable; but do use them sparingly: *The above passage illustrates her style; The example below is from the Elizabethan poet Edmund Spenser.*

abscess Note the spelling: *-sc-*, unlike *recess* or *absence.*

accommodate Note the double *c* and double *m* in the spelling.

acoustic Note the spelling: only one *c* immediately following the *a*, unlike *accuse* or *account.*

acquirement, acquisition An *acquirement* is '(the act or power of gaining) a skill or quality': *Typing is a useful acquirement in business; my acquirement of knowledge.*

An *acquisition* is '(the act or power of gaining) a new physical object': *My latest acquisition is this telescope; the acquisition of wealth.*

act Standard British English uses an adverb rather than an adjective after *to act*: *acted strangely*; **??***acted strange*.

AD, BC The abbreviations are fully acceptable either without or with full stops. But they should not be italicised or separated by spaces.

AD stands for *Anno Domini*, /**an**no **dom**mi-nī/, 'in the year of the Lord'. It is normally placed before the year number, though when used with centuries or millennia it is best placed after: *took place in AD 1325*; *in the second century AD*.

BC stands for 'before Christ', and always comes after the date: *55 BC*; *the third millennium BC*.

Some non-Christians prefer to use the forms *BCE* ('before the common era') and *CE* ('in the common era'). In each case the abbreviation comes after the date: *55 BCE, 1325 CE*.

See also CENTURIES.

address Note the spelling – two *d*'s, two *s*'s – and the pronunciation: /ə-**dress**/ in British English; the noun can be /**ad**dress/ in American English.

adieu The pronunciation has been Anglicised to /ə-**dew**/.

adjure see ABJURE.

admission, admittance The verb *to admit* means either 'to acknowledge or confess' or 'to allow to enter'. The noun corresponding to the first of these senses is always *admission*: *an admission of guilt*. The noun *admission* also corresponds to the second verb use – *Admission is free; admission charges* – though *admittance* is also sometimes possible, especially in formal and legal contexts: *No admittance after 11 p.m.*; *admittance to a school*.

See also ADMIT.

admit 1. *To admit of* typically has an abstract subject and can mean only 'to allow the possibility of; to leave room for': *The measurements admit of a certain margin of error*. Don't use it in place of *to admit*: **X** *I admit of the justice of your claim*. And don't use it with personal subjects to mean 'to allow (for)': **X** *I admit of a margin of error in my measurements*; **X** *We admit of no further discussion*.

2. *To admit to* should be used only in the sense 'to lead into': *The door admits to the main hall*. Don't use it where the simple *to admit* is appropriate: **??***I admitted to the justice of*

the claim/the error of my ways*; **??***She admits to juggling the figures*.

See also ADMISSION, ADMITTANCE.

adversary The stress falls on the first syllable in British English – /**ad**vər-səri, -sri/ – unlike *adversity*.

adverse See AVERSE.

advice, advise *Advice* is the noun: *She gave me good advice*. *Advise* is the verb: *Can you advise me?* The different pronunciations should help you to remember the spellings.

The use of *to advise* in commercial jargon to mean 'to tell, notify, inform' is both hackneyed and unnecessary: **?***Kindly advise us of your prices*. It can also lead to ambiguity: does **?** *We would advise that the shares are bought* mean 'We inform you that someone has bought the shares' or 'We counsel you to buy the shares'?

Similarly, the sense of 'to consult, take counsel', common in American political jargon, is not accepted in standard British usage: **?** *The President is advising with his aides*.

aegis The pronunciation is /**ee**jis/, not **X**/ī-jis/.

aesthetic The noun *aesthetics* is used, in the singular, to mean 'the study or perception of beauty': *Aesthetics interests me*. The rarer and rather formal and technical noun *aesthetic* means 'a principle or 'theory of beauty': *the aesthetic of surrealism*. An *aesthete* is a person whose dominant interest is in the beauty of things.

The adjective *aesthetic* relates to the study and appreciation of beauty, especially in art: *Modern jazz offends my aesthetic sensibilities*. Hence, a person with refined tastes may be called *aesthetic*, though some purists dislike this use.

Less acceptably, *aesthetic* is used to mean 'guided by good taste' or simply 'beautiful': **??** *an aesthetic living room*. Describe it instead as *aesthetically pleasing* or better still, as *beautiful*.

In British English the usual pronunciation is /eess-**thet**ik/, though the first syllable can also be /ess-/ or /iss-/. *Aesthete* is always pronounced /**eess**-theet/. American spelling allows *esthetic* and *esthete*, but not British.

affect, effect The pronunciation difference is a slight one: *affect* is /ə-**fekt**/ and *effect* is /i-**fekt**/. A better

guide to distinguishing the two words, where their meanings are similar, is the grammatical difference: *to affect* is a verb, meaning 'to influence'; *an effect* is a noun, meaning 'the result of an influence': *This book affected me profoundly*; *This book had a profound effect on me*.

The verb *to affect* has other related meanings: 'to touch, to move emotionally': *I find the death of Little Nell deeply affecting*; 'to have a harmful effect upon': *The smoke is affecting my eyes*; and 'to put on, pretend, feign': *affecting indifference*; *affected a posh accent*. From the last of these come the noun *affectation*, 'artificiality, pretentiousness', and the adjective *affected*, 'insincere and conceited': *an affected, snobbish little man*.

Effect can also serve as a verb, meaning 'to bring about, bring into existence': *The police effected an arrest*. So if you *effect a reform*, you introduce it; if you *affect it*, you simply influence it.

There is also a rare noun *affect*, pronounced /**aff**ekt/, restricted to psychology, meaning 'an emotion'. Slightly commoner is the related adjective *affective*, meaning 'relating to emotion rather than thought': *affective disorders*. Since it is stressed on the second syllable, take care not to confuse it with *effective*.

See also EFFECTIVE.

afflict See INFLICT.

again The pronunciation /ə-**gen**/ is slightly more common in British English than /ə-**gayn**/; both are fully acceptable. Similarly with *against*.

aged The adjective is normally pronounced /**ay**jid/, but it can also be /ayjd/, as in *aged brandy*, or *a man aged 30*.

ageing, aging Both spellings are acceptable; *ageing* is preferable.

aggravate This verb originally meant only 'to make heavier or more serious': *The chafing aggravated the injury*; *The attitude of management aggravated the dispute*. By extension, it took on the secondary meaning of 'to irritate, annoy, exasperate': **?***Stop aggravating me*. Similarly the noun *aggravation*: **?** *He's an aggravation to his party*. Some purists still object to this secondary meaning; there are plenty of alternatives if you wish to avoid it.

aggressive The use of this adjective to mean 'forceful, assertive' is at once voguish and hackneyed, and possibly misleading as well: an *aggressive marketing campaign* sounds like a protection racket.

Note the spelling: two *g*'s as well as two *s*'s.

agree The prepositions used after *to agree* often cause problems. The main accepted constructions are:

☐ *to agree with*. 'to regard favourably': *I agree with your ideas*; 'to share an opinion with': *I agree with you on this matter*; 'to accord with': *Their accounts agree with each other*; *Verbs agree with nouns*; and, usually in negative sentences, 'not to have a bad effect on the health of': *Cider doesn't agree with me*.

☐ *to agree to*. 'to accept, endorse, or consent to': *I can't agree to all your demands*; *I agree to your proposal, though I don't agree with it*.

☐ *to agree on* (or *upon* or *about*). 'to reach a common decision about': *They can't agree on terms*. British English can here, at a pinch, drop the preposition: *They can't agree terms*.

Informally, the *to* in *agree to* is often dropped: **?** *I can't agree all your demands*. More careful usage here prefers *approve, accept, ratify, permit*, or, of course, *agree to*.

ain't This verb form is no longer standard unless used for literary or jocular effect – *Einstein he ain't*; *Things ain't what they used to be*.

The blanket condemnation is a great pity, since it means that no acceptable contraction for *am not* exists. Standard grammar would far prefer **?** *Ain't I invited?* to **?** *Aren't I invited?* (which corresponds to the glaringly incorrect **✗** *Are I invited?*), yet usage regards *Aren't I?* as just informal, and **?** *Ain't I?* as slangy or downright 'wrong'.

algae The best pronunciation here is /al-jee/.

alibi In legal terminology, and hence in ordinary language, an *alibi* is a defence (or the evidence supporting it) presented by an accused person claiming to have been somewhere else at the time that the offence was committed: *Her alibi is that she was at the cinema*. By extension, *alibi* has also come to refer, especially in North America, to the person corroborating the story: **?** *My mother is my alibi – I had lunch with her on Sunday*. This usage is still not considered standard in British English.

Even less acceptable is the use of *alibi* in the sense simply of 'an excuse or justification': **??** *Late again – what's your alibi this time?* Slightly less objectionable, though still nonstandard, is the verb use, with the sense 'to provide with an alibi': **?** *I won't alibi you if it means perjuring myself*.

The pronunciation is /al-i-bī/. The plural is *alibis*.

all 1. The *of* is often optional after *all*: *All (of) human life was there*; *All (of) my friends have left me*. British speakers tend to drop the *of* more readily than North Americans do.

2. Take care not to use *all* when it is superfluous: **?** *All visitors should report to reception*.

3. Think twice about placing *all* before a negative. While *All is not lost* is accepted by idiom, sentences such as **?** *All the runners didn't finish* are clumsy and ambiguous. Does it mean 'Not all the runners finished'? Or 'None of the runners finished'? Use either of these wordings in preference.

See NOT 1.

4. As a pronoun referring to all things or people, *all* is rather old-fashioned: *All is as it was*; *All who knew her respected her*. Modern idiom prefers *everything* and *everyone*.

5. *All* applies to three or more items or people; if there are only two, use *both*. **✗** *All/Both of the protesters were arrested*. In some contexts, however, notably sports, the use of *all* for two is fully idiomatic: *fifteen all*; *Crewe and Tranmere drew two all*.

See also BOTH; EACH; EVERYBODY.

all right Despite *altogether, always*, and the like, the spelling **✗** *alright* is not accepted as standard. Write it as two words: *all right*.

allude, allusion If you *allude* to something, you refer to it in a roundabout way: *He is alluding to the boss whenever he says 'A little bird told me'*.

If you use the boss's name, or say *our boss*, or the like, you are not *alluding* to him, but simply *mentioning* him: **✗** *He alluded to the Prime Minister six times by name*.

Don't confuse the words *allude, allusion*, and *allusive* with similar-sounding words such as *elude, illusion*, and *elusive*. The verb *to elude* means 'to avoid capture or understanding': *The winger eluded the tackle*; *Your meaning eludes me*. Something *elusive* is 'slippery' or hard to

define. Literary style would be *elusive* if its effects or methods are hard to pin down, but *allusive* if it is full of oblique references. The two adjectives often go together, and so demand extra care.

See DELUSION.

already, all ready 1. In the sense of 'before, previously', *already* requires a perfect tense: *I have/had already washed it*. With simple tenses it remains nonstandard: **✗** *I already washed it*. But when it means 'by a specified or implied time', simple tenses are acceptable: *By then I already knew I'd be late*.

North American English, perhaps through German influence, often uses this second meaning before *in* and *at*: **??** *Already in the 3rd century Saxon raids were beginning to upset the Roman settlements*. Normal English idiom would require something like *as early as, as long ago as, even*, or sometimes *by*.

2. Don't write *already* when you mean *all ready*. If the *all* can be dropped, then write two words: *Your lunch is all ready in the oven* (that is, 'completely prepared').

3. The Jewish-American use of *already* to express impatience or surprise is not British idiom: **✗** *That's enough complaining already!* Compare the slang use of *yet* (see YET 6).

alright See ALL RIGHT.

also 1. *Also* is an adverb, in contrast to the conjunctions *and* and *but* and the preposition *as well as*. So it is technically wrong to write **?** *I speak French and German, also I read Spanish*. Use either *and* or *and also*, or perhaps a semicolon or dash before *also* to indicate a sentence break.

2. Like *only, also* needs careful placing in a sentence: (I'm a trained electrician but) *I've also studied Greek*; (I've studied Latin but) *I've studied Greek also*; (You're a classicist and) *I also have studied Greek*. (In the last example, *I too have studied Greek* would be more normal). See ONLY 1.

altar, alter Don't confuse the spellings. Churches contain *altars*. If you change something, you *alter* it.

alternate, alternative 1. As an adjective, *alternate* /awl-**ter**-nət/ means 'by turns, one after the other': *alternate showers and sun*. As a verb *alternate*, /**awl**-tər-nayt/, means 'to go to and fro, to take turns': *He alternates between joy and despair*; *alternating current*.

Alternative means 'offering or requiring a choice between possibilities; other, different': *Can you suggest an alternative plan?* Similarly, *alternatively*: *I can come on Tuesday or, alternatively, on Thursday. Alternative* can also be a noun: *no alternative.*

Avoid the current tendency, chiefly American, to use *alternate* for *alternative*: ✗ *an alternate plan/spelling.* Avoid too the opposite mistake ✗*alternative light and shade.*

2. Pedants have argued from the Latin origins of the word that *alternative* should not be used when more than two possibilities exist. But English usage seems to reject any such restriction, treating sentences such as *We must consider all the alternatives* as fully idiomatic. The word does sound better, however, when the number of possibilities is limited: compare *a few alternatives* and ❓*lots of alternatives.* Here *choices* or *options* would be more likely.

Note the danger of ambiguity when numbers are used before *alternative.* Does *There are three alternatives* mean three possibilities altogether, or four? It is therefore safer to say *There are three (other) choices/options/ possible courses of action.*

3. Avoid *(an)other* and similar redundant words before *alternative.* ✗*There was no other alternative than to pay* should be *There was no alternative but to pay* or *There was no other possibility than to pay.*

4. As an adjective, *alternative* is often used as a pretentious alternative for simpler words, such as *other, new,* or *revised*: ❓*an alternative date* ('other'); ❓*an alternative restaurant* ('different'); ❓ *After scrapping the old system, management have come up with an alternative plan* ('new, revised').

Recently, *alternative* has also taken on the meaning of 'untraditional; anti-establishment': *alternative medicine; alternative comedy.* The new meaning is in danger of overuse – ❓ *alternative agriculture* – and can lead to ambiguity. Does ❓ *He changed jobs and went to work in an alternative school* mean 'in a different school' or 'in an unconventional school'?

although, though 1. The spellings ❓*altho'* and ❓*tho'* (often without the apostrophes) occur in informal writing, but are inappropriate for formal contexts.

2. Wherever *although* is possible, so is *though.* The reverse is not true. *Though* alone is used:

a. in compounds such as *even though* and *as though*;

b. where the conjunction is moved from the beginning of its clause: *I kept going, tired though I was*;

c. as an adverb meaning 'however': ❓*He's 45 – he doesn't look it, though.*

3. Note that some purists object to this last use, though it is now very widespread and widely accepted.

4. Even where *though* and *although* are both possible, one or other tends to be preferable according to the context. *Although* is considered more formal and more emphatic, and is preferred at the beginning of a sentence when introducing a factual clause containing a verb: *Although he apologised, I remained unsatisfied. Though* is preferred before verbless clauses: *Though nervous, I answered boldly.* And *though* is considerably commoner than *although* when the meaning is *but*: *I think you're right, though I'll have to check; He's a pilot, though you'd never think so.*

5. Note that some purists also object to this last use. It is used mainly in informal contexts and should perhaps be avoided in very formal writing.

6. The use of the present subjunctive after *though* or *although* in hypothetical clauses is now archaic or biblical: *Though his life be gravely sinful, God will have mercy.* Modern English would prefer *(Even) though his life may be gravely sinful* or *Even if/though his life were/was/* ❓ *is gravely sinful.*

See also BUT **3, 4.**

ambiguous, ambivalent These adjectives are not synonymous: roughly, *ambiguous* refers to meanings, *ambivalent* refers to feelings or attitudes.

Ambiguous means primarily 'having more than one possible meaning or interpretation'; hence 'obscure, difficult to understand': *an ambiguous line of verse; ambiguous behaviour.*

Ambivalent means 'feeling different or contradictory emotions, having two opposing attitudes to someone or something': *He is/feels ambivalent towards his mother – admiring her but also resenting her interference.*

America, American Take care that your meaning is clear when you use these terms. They can refer either to the United States of America, or to 'the Americas' – that is, North, South, and Central America (and perhaps the Caribbean islands too).

The greatest danger, in most contexts, is ambiguity over the inclusion of Canada. If necessary, use such wordings as *U.S. factories, North American English,* or *U.S. and Canadian forests* to make your meaning clear.

amiable, amicable These two adjectives are close in meaning, but have slightly different uses. *Amiable* means 'friendly, congenial, agreeable', and commonly applies to people, conversation, social environments, pieces of writing, or the like: *an amiable chap; an amiable grin; an amiable crowd/ atmosphere.*

Amicable tends to refer to relationships, joint enterprises, or decisions in the sense of 'characterised by goodwill or friendliness': *an amicable settlement/divorce.*

among, amongst In modern idiom, *amongst* is far less common than *among.* Some speakers and writers still prefer *amongst* in figurative contexts, especially at the beginning of a sentence: *Amongst all the animals, none is so cruel as man.*

Even here, however, *among* is equally suitable, and it is clearly preferable in literal contexts, especially in the middle of a sentence: *He walked about fearlessly among all the animals.*

See BETWEEN.

amoral See IMMORAL.

an See A, AN.

analogous It is spelt *-ogous,* not ✗ *-agous.* And the pronunciation /ə-*nall*əgəs/ is clearly preferable to ❓ /ə-*nall*əjəs/.

analyse, analysis 1. These have become vogue words, overused in contexts far removed from their proper technical areas of chemistry, philosophy, psychology, and the like: ❓❓ *Let's analyse the possibilities – we can hire a car, go by train, or take the bus.* Use *consider, examine, look at, discuss,* or the like, if that is all you mean.

Strictly, *to analyse* and *an analysis* involve the breaking down and classification of a complex whole into parts, in order to investigate and understand more easily.

2. Avoid too the pretentious phrase *in the last/final/ultimate analysis,* unless you are talking about a real analysis.

3. The traditional British spelling is *analyse.* The American *analyze* is, however, becoming fairly common.

Ready-Reference Word Guide

The usual plural of *analysis* is *analyses*.

and 1. Don't feel awkward about beginning sentences with *and* (and *but* and *or*), if style calls for it. The schoolroom prohibition has no basis in usage or logic.

An opening *And* serves, for example, to produce a dramatic effect: *They brought the four kids and their granny. And even the dog.* And it helps to break up long sentences. Between short clauses or phrases, however, it is best to keep the *and* within the middle of a single sentence. To begin a very short sentence with *and* tends to produce an awkward staccato effect: **?** *I got three months. And the ringleader got two years.* Similarly, **??** *I like chicken. And my husband pork.*

2. Two nouns joined by *and* do not necessarily make a plural, even when one is itself plural. Sometimes they 'fuse' into a single concept, to be treated as singular: *You son and heir is here; Fish and chips is my favourite dish;* **?** *Love and marriage remains the norm even today.*

Modern usage tends to accept this kind of 'notional singular'. However, when it is clearly two things that are being talked about, a singular verb is obviously incorrect: **X** *His love for her and his later marriage were the highlight of his life.* When the verb comes before a plural or double subject, informal usage often allows a singular verb: **?** *There's a lot of things to do;* **??** *Never before has Britain, and Europe in general, suffered such a spell of cold weather.*

The opposite inconsistency is also common, and less tolerated: **X** *The inclusion of Williams at right back and Meadows to strengthen the midfield have improved the balance of the team.* The subject is in fact *inclusion*, which is singular and requires the singular verb *has improved*.

For further details, see pages 173, 175.

3. Take care with any pronoun after *and*. The rule is that the pronoun should be in the same case as it would if it stood alone: **X** *You should have invited George and I.*

Omit part of the *and*-phrase, and the mistake immediately becomes apparent: **X** *You should have invited I.* So the correct version is: *You should have invited George and me.*

For further details, see page 183.

4. The pattern *A, B, C, and D* in lists applies only when all the items are of the same grammatical status. A very

common mistake is to leave out an *and* because of another one later in the sentence: **X** *She has been a secretary, waitress, singer, and has even worked as a dancer.* Here there should be an *and* before *singer*, since *and has even ...* is not part of the same list. For further details, see page 198.

5. In lists, the comma before the final *and* is optional. This book uses it for the sake of extra clarity, though it is less common in British than in American usage: *She has worked as a secretary, waitress(,) and journalist.*

In simple sentences, there is usually no comma before *and*, especially where the second verb is omitted: *He comes from Glasgow(,) and works in Preston; She stays in London during the week and with her parents at weekends.* But do use a comma if it helps to make the meaning of the sentence clear. To omit the comma in the following sentence, for example, would suggest that I sued a couple called Bill and Mary Vincent: *I sued Bill, and Mary Vincent.*

6. Among the other dubious uses of *and* are these:

☐ using *and* in place of *to* after *try*, *be sure*, and the like: **?** *Try and get here on time;* **??** *You must be sure and get enough sleep.* (See TRY AND.)

☐ using *and* to yoke artificially together two or more ideas that do not have enough in common to form a single idea: **??** *The school has 450 pupils and was founded in 1924.* The two ideas here would be better expressed in two separate sentences.

☐ using *and* before words that already contain the idea of *and*, such as *moreover*, *nor*, and *as well*.

and/or In legal, technical, business, and informal usage, *and/or* serves neatly to indicate that there are three possibilities – *A* or *B* or *both*: *punishable by a fine and/or a term of imprisonment.* Outside such contexts, it tends to sound either lazy or pseudo-technical (or both), and is best avoided. And it should never be used when either *and* or *or* is enough: **??** *It can be used in the home and/or the car.*

ante-, anti- In British English both these prefixes are pronounced /**an**ti/. Americans tend to pronounce *anti-* /**an**tī/.

Ante- means 'in front of' as in *anteroom*, or 'before, pre-' as in *antenatal*. It is virtually never hyphenated.

Anti- means 'against' as in *antiseptic and antifreeze*, or 'opposite to/of' as in *anticlockwise and anticlimax*. It can also be used as a preposition – *I'm anti the new law* – and as a noun: *On the matter of hunting, I'm an anti.* (In each case, the opposite is *pro*.) It tends to be hyphenated before any elements that begin with a capital (*anti-American*) or, sometimes, with a vowel, especially *i-* (*anti-industrial*).

antenna Note the plurals: *antennae* when referring to the sensory equipment on the head of an insect; *antennas* when referring to aerials.

anticipate *To anticipate* is often used as a rather pompous synonym of *to expect*: **?** *Everyone is anticipating a change of government.* Traditionally, the word suggests not just the idea of foreseeing something, but also the idea of preventing or preceding something: *The boxer ducked, anticipating the punch; Before she could complain, he anticipated her and explained the problem; In his imagery, Hopkins anticipates the Modernist movement.* The second and third of these perhaps sound rather formal nowadays.

See also EXPECT.

Antigua The name of this Caribbean island is pronounced /an-**tee**gə/.

anxious Some purists object to *anxious* when used with any meaning other than 'worried': *anxious about one's health.* It is now widely used in the sense of 'eager', more acceptably when retaining an element of worry – *I'm anxious to get the results of my exam* – than when discarding all suggestion of worry: **?** *Everyone was anxious to help.* Modern idiom also now generally accepts the sense 'worrying': *an anxious moment for the goalkeeper.*

any *Any* can be used with either a singular or plural verb: *Is any of the men ill?* (implying 'any one'); *Are any of the men ill?* (implying 'some').

The constructions **?** *best of any* and **?** *better than any* are not quite logical or acceptable: **??** *the best recording of any that she has made;* **?** *a better recording than any that she has made.* These should preferably read: *the best recording of all that she has made; a better recording than any other that she has made.*

anyone, any one *Anyone* means exactly the same as *anybody*, and is used in exactly the same way. *Any one* can be used of both people and things, as in: *Of these prizes, you can choose any one you like; I'm better than any one of you lot.*

Similarly with *everyone/every one* and *someone/some one*: *I hate every one of you; Have you eaten every one?* But the preferred spelling is *no one*, regardless of meaning: *I saw no one; There's no one newspaper that I read regularly.*

See also EVERYBODY; HE; and pages 90 and 176.

Apennines Note the spelling: only one *p*, and a double *n* in the middle.

apostasy Note the spelling: *-asy*, not **X** *-acy* as in *democracy*.

apparatus Note the spelling: a double *p*, unlike *apartment*. Two plurals are permissible: *apparatus* and *apparatuses*, but not **X** *apparati*.

appendix The plural varies according to the sense used. A surgeon might remove two *appendixes* in a day. A book might have two *appendices*, /ə-**pen**di-seez/, at the back.

appraise, apprise Take care not to confuse these two verbs. *To appraise* means 'to evaluate, estimate the worth of': *The valuer appraised the painting; It was difficult to appraise their contribution.* Note the derived nouns: *the valuer's appraisement/appraisal of the painting; an annual appraisal of your work performance.*

Appraisal (as in *an appraisal of commercial prospects*) and especially *reappraisal* (often meaning no more than 'a second look') have become vogue words in business and politics, and should be used sparingly.

To apprise is a formal verb meaning little more than 'to tell, to notify'. It often occurs in the passive and is almost always followed by *of: We were apprised of the facts behind the dispute.* It has a rather pompous ring to it.

appreciate This verb is closely linked to the idea of value: *Your capital will appreciate; Only those present could appreciate her contribution.* From this comes the slightly pompous use of *to appreciate* in the sense 'to be grateful for': *I should appreciate it if you helped a bit.*

Less acceptable is the sense 'to realise or understand', common in business jargon: **?** *You will appreciate my concern;* **?** *It is appreciated that delays may occur.* The objections fade, however, when the 'realising' involves a

degree of careful evaluation: *She appreciates that there will have to be changes.*

apprise See APPRAISE.

aqueduct Note the spelling: *aque-*, not **X** *aqua-* as in *aquatic*.

archaeology, archeology Both spellings are acceptable in British English now, though the traditional *archaeology* remains the preferred form among purists. American usage, by contrast, favours *archeology*. The old spelling with the digraph, *archæology*, has fallen into disuse.

Arctic Don't neglect to sound the first hard *c* when pronouncing the word.

aren't I? See AIN'T.

arise See RISE.

aristocrat British English favours placing the main stress on the first syllable; American English usually stresses the second syllable.

Arkansas The correct pronunciation is /**ar**kən-saw/.

around, round 1. British English nowadays favours *round* slightly (whereas American English still favours *around*): *spinning round and round; looked round expectantly.* Sometimes the rhythm seems to demand *around* in preference, however: *He gets around; famous for miles around.* In most such cases, *about* is also possible.

2. In some uses, British English favours *about* where American uses *around: just sitting about/around idly.* In the sense 'roughly, approximately', *about* is still strongly preferred by British purists: *about a hundred onlookers; at about half-past eight.*

See also ABOUT; CENTRE AROUND.

artist, artiste An *artiste* is not the same thing as a female *artist*. An *artiste* is a singer, dancer, or other professional entertainer, whether male or female. The word sounds rather affected nowadays, and seems to have dropped out of fashion.

as 1. When do you say *as I* and when *as me*? Simply add the missing verb mentally to the sentence, and the answer should become clear: *She loves you just as much as I (love you); She loves you just as much as (she loves) me.* A common mistake is to use *as me* instead of *as I* in the first of the

examples. To make sure of being correctly understood, you can always add the missing verb explicitly: *She loves you just as much as I love you* (or *as I do*).

For further details, see page 185.

2. Don't insert *as* needlessly into a sentence. In the following examples, the *as* is superfluous or simply wrong: **?** *As from tomorrow, roll-call will be at 8.30;* **??** *He was named as Most Promising Graduate;* **X** *We consider you as unworthy to continue here.*

3. Don't confuse *as* and *that*: *That's the same man as I saw yesterday* (not *that*); *I could murder the man that/who dented my car door* (not *as*).

4. As a complex preposition, the phrase *as to* sometimes has a role to play: *The discovery provides a hint as to the origins of life.* But it is often inserted needlessly into a sentence: **??** *the question as to whether he should appeal or give up* (leave out the *as to*, or change it to *of*); **??** *I have my doubts as to these figures* (use *about* instead of *as to*).

Use it sparingly, always testing whether it can be omitted or replaced.

5. Take care not to use such sentences as **X** *A is as good or better than B.* This common form of wording is an ungrammatical fusion of two constructions: *A is as good as B; A is better than B.* The correct combination is *A is as good as or better than B.*

If you find this correct form to be unacceptably jerky, you could adjust the phrasing somewhat to read *A is as good as B, or better* or simply *A is as good or better.*

Note that a similar careless omission can affect other combinations too: **X** *ideas that are similar though not the same as yours* (add *to* after *similar*); **X** *profits that are equal if not higher than last year's* (add *to* after *equal*).

See also EQUAL; LIKE[1] **1**, THAN.

as far as . . . is concerned Awkward though this construction often is, don't try to streamline it by leaving out the second element: **X** *As far as the motives behind the crime, we are following up some reports from our informers.* Add the words *are concerned* after *crime.* Or, better still, use a different preposition altogether if possible: *as for, regarding*, or the like.

as such Make sure that this phrase really has a task to perform before you allow it into your speech or writing. Some of its legitimate uses are illustrated in the following sentences: *She is a highly-strung woman, and as such is given to sudden attacks of anxiety* (= 'accordingly'); *Profit as such is not our purpose* (= 'merely in itself').

Some of its more recent uses have attracted some criticism, however: **?** *He didn't disobey me as such...* (= 'exactly, really'); **?** *I have no objection to the plan as such, but...* (= 'in principle').

Sometimes the phrase seems to have no meaning at all, and is inserted into a sentence only for its supposedly impressive sound: **??** *I cannot accept the view that politics as such is simply about power.*

as well as See AS **1**, and also page 174.

Asian, Asiatic *Asiatic*, whether noun or adjective, is nowadays considered discourteous or insulting, except in certain fixed phrases such as *Asiatic cholera*. Use *Asian* instead. In British English, *Asian* is now widely used to refer to people from the Indian subcontinent or Sri Lanka living elsewhere: *the Asian Community of Bradford*; *an Asian newspaper*. If you use *Asian* to refer to any other peoples from Asia, such as Thais or Chinese, take care not to be misunderstood.

In pronunciation, *Asian* is best kept to two syllables: British English prefers /**ay**sh'n/ slightly; American English favours /**ay**zh'n/.

See also INDIAN.

asinine Note the spelling: no double letters, despite the association with the word *ass*.

asphalt Note the spelling: *asph-* as in *asphyxiate*; not **X** *ash-*, or **X** *-felt*.

assume, presume Difficulties arise only with the one sense shared by these two verbs: 'to suppose or take for granted'. They are usually interchangeable nowadays, but you might for precision's sake try to preserve a few traditional distinctions.

First, *to assume* is perhaps slightly more timid and tentative; *to presume* is more confident and positive.

Then, *to assume* tends to be used of completed conditions, past actions, and so on; *to presume* of the present or future: *I assume you attended the funeral*; *I presume you will attend the funeral*.

Then, *to assume* introduces a theory; *to presume* introduces an opinion. Hence the adverbs: *assumedly*, 'in

keeping with the theory', and *presumably*, 'on the basis of the evidence'. And the nouns have corresponding senses: an *assumption* is a provisional hypothesis; a *presumption* is a common or established theory, often a near-certainty: *The presumption is that he died at sea*.

Finally, each verb has overtones derived from its other meanings: *to assume a pose*; *an assumed name*; *Assuming the plan fails...* And *to presume upon my good nature*; *She presumed to argue with me*. Hence the politeness of Stanley's greeting: *Doctor Livingstone, I presume*. He was in effect saying: 'I know I am taking a liberty – being *presumptuous*, having great *presumption* – in saying your name without being certain.'

assure, ensure, insure Though they are sometimes interchangeable, these three verbs are usually distinct in meaning.

To assure commonly means 'to attempt to convince': *I assured her that I would return*. The past participle *assured* has become an independent adjective: *a very assured actor* ('self-confident'); *an assured success* ('guaranteed, certain'). In British English *to assure oneself* is to make financial provision for certain misfortunes, notably death. Hence *life assurance*.

By contrast, *to insure oneself* is traditionally to make financial provision for *possible* misfortunes, such as theft or illness. But *to insure* and *insurance* now usually range more broadly, and cover *assurance* as well, especially in American English. In still wider contexts, *to insure* means 'to protect against harm' generally: *steps to insure the country against famine*.

To ensure, finally, means 'to make certain, guarantee': *steps to ensure that the country would escape famine*; *Please ensure that your car is locked*. Unfortunately, American English often favours the spelling *insure* for this sense.

asthma Note the spelling: the *-th-* follows the *s*. To incorporate it into the pronunciation is optional.

ate In British English, both /ayt/ and the more usual /et/ are fully acceptable; in American English, only /ayt/ is really standard.

aural, oral *Aural* means 'to do with the ear, or hearing': *an aural examination* or simply *an aural* – as conducted, for example, by a doctor or by a music teacher.

Oral usually means either 'to do with the mouth or speech' or 'spoken rather than written'. Hence *an oral examination* – as conducted either by the dentist or by the French teacher, for example. The spoken exam can also be *an oral* or *orals*.

The adjective *verbal* is a common but inadequate substitute for *oral*, especially in the old phrase **?** *a verbal agreement*. Strictly, *verbal* means 'in words' – whether written or spoken. To be on the safe side, use *an oral agreement* or *a spoken agreement* instead.

The pronunciation of both *oral* and *aural* is /**aw**-r'l/. Some speakers use different pronunciations, perhaps deliberately to distinguish the two words: **?** /**ow**-r'l/ for *aural*; **?** /**orr**'l/ or **?** /**o**-r'l/ for *oral*. None of these alternatives is acceptable in formal speech, unfortunately.

authoritative When pronouncing or writing the word, make sure not to leave out the *-it-* or *-at-* in the middle.

avenge See REVENGE.

averse, adverse *Averse*, like *averted*, means 'turned away', though in a metaphorical sense: 'reluctant, opposed'. It occurs most often in the phrase *not averse to*: *I am certainly not averse to the idea of a merger*.

Adverse also means 'opposed or hostile', but in a slightly different way and in different constructions: *The play failed because of adverse reviews*; *high waves adverse to/for windsurfing*. Similarly *adverse winds*; *adverse conditions*.

Averse is always stressed on the second syllable; *adverse* can be stressed either on the first or the second.

The noun from *averse* is *aversion*: *a particular aversion to cheap perfume*.

The noun from *adverse* is *adverseness* rather than *adversity*, which refers instead to hardship or calamity: *in the face of adversity*; *plagued by many adversities*.

await See WAIT.

awake See WAKE.

away See WAY.

awfully The sense of *awe* has long since been driven out of this word by misuse and overuse. Formerly meaning 'awesomely or majestically', it declined first (in step with *awful*) into a synonym of *badly* or *sloppily* – *She dances/dresses awfully* – and then into a mere synonym of *very* or *extremely*: *She tries awfully hard*; *That's awfully kind of you*.

So too with *dreadfully*, *terribly*, *frightfully*, and so on. And you cannot hope to restore their original meanings without risk of being misunderstood. But do at least use them sparingly in their new weakened senses, and avoid them altogether in formal contexts.

Doubly informal is the regional or slangy American use of *awful* for *awfully*, as in **??** *Poor Mary, she tries awful hard*.

bail, bale The different words pronounced /bayl/ are spelt as follows:

bail: the system of providing a cash security for the release of a prisoner; the security itself; the person providing it; the release itself; (as a verb, usually with *out*) to provide the security for this purpose, or to save from any tricky situation: *to go/stand bail for the prisoner*; *The company is bankrupt, and they now expect me to bail them out*.

bail: the crosspiece of a wicket in cricket; a small bar, as on a typewriter or in a stable.

bail (or *bale*): (often with *out*) to remove water from a boat; a bucket used for this purpose.

bail (or *bale*): a hooplike handle on a bucket or kettle; any of the hoops supporting the canopy of a covered wagon.

bale: a large bundle (of hay, paper, or the like); to pile or wrap into such a bundle; to jump from an aircraft in an emergency (sometimes spelt *bail* in North America); (informal) to abandon a project because of problems: *We're losing a lot of money – it's time for us to bale out*.

baleful, baneful *Baleful* means 'having an evil influence' and 'foreboding evil, threatening'. In this second sense, it sometimes describes facial expressions: *a baleful stare*. It was formerly used to mean 'sad, doleful': *the spaniel's baleful eyes*.

Baneful is related to *bane*, as in *That child is the bane of my life*. *Bane* originally meant 'a killer or cause of death', and so *baneful* meant 'poisonous, deadly'. It now means 'harmful, destructive'.

The two words obviously have a lot in common and can often be used in the same context: *the baleful/baneful effect of television on a child's reading*.

balk See BAULK.

banal The French pronunciation /bə-**naal**/ remains more common and slightly more acceptable than the Anglicised /**bayn**'l/.

baneful See BALEFUL.

basically This has become a buzz word, used as an unnecessary introduction to comments and answers to questions: **??** *Basically, I enjoyed the film*; **??** *Basically, we're going to play tennis this evening*. Worse still, the information in the sentence is often anything but basic; compare *Basically, we lost because they were better than us* and **??** *Basically, we lost because their tactic of playing defenders wide down the flanks pulled our mid-field out of position*.

Try to restrict the word to its literal sense, usually immediately in front of adjectives: *The panels are basically O.K., but they need some work done on them*. Think twice before using *basically* at the beginning of sentences.

Consider some alternatives – *at heart*, *fundamentally*, *more or less*, *in short*, *in effect*, *in fact*; or do without such a word or phrase altogether.

basis The plural of this word is *bases* not **X** *basises*, and is pronounced /**bay**-seez/. But *bases* as the plural of *base* is pronounced /**bay**siz/.

bated, baited *Bated* is a variant of *abated*: *with bated breath*. *Baited* comes from the noun *bait* (meaning 'enticement'), or the verb *to bait* (meaning 'to torment'): *He baited the trap*; *They baited the bear with dogs*.

bath, bathe In British English (and sometimes in American English), to *bathe* means 'to swim in the sea' or 'to apply liquid in order to soothe'; in American usage it can also mean 'to take a bath'.

In British English, but not American English, to *bath* is used to mean 'to give a bath to': *to bath the baby*.

Both verbs give the forms *bathing* and *bathed*, but pronunciation differentiates the meaning – *bath* produces /**baa**thing/ and /baatht/; *bathe* produces /**bay**thing/ and /baythd/.

bathos, bathetic See PATHETIC.

battalion Note the spelling: double *t* as in *battle*, single *l*, unlike *stallion*.

baulk, balk *Baulk* is the more common spelling of this word in British English, but *balk* is also acceptable, and is the standard American spelling. The standard pronunciation is /bawk/, but /bawlk/ is also acceptable.

BC See AD.

be *Be* is correct, though old-fashioned, as a subjunctive (see pages 169 and 195): *However good that racehorse be, it shouldn't cost that much*. Normal practice these days is to write *may be* or *is* instead: *However good that racehorse may be/is . . .*

The phrase *been and*, to express surprise, is colloquial and informal: **?** *He's been and wrecked the car*. So too is the phrase *being as* or *being that*, in the sense of 'because or since': **?** *Being as you're the oldest, you should go first*.

Beaulieu Note the pronunciation: usually /**bew**li/ in English.

beg the question The metaphorical expression *to beg the question* traditionally means 'to assume that the issue under discussion is already proved; to presuppose the conclusion in one's argument': *Your proof that the Earth is flat begs the question*. It has also come to mean, very dubiously, 'to evade the issue; to equivocate': **??** *I'm afraid your answer begs the question of responsibility for giving the fatal order*. Say *evades the question* instead.

Worse still, *to beg the question* is now used to mean 'to prompt or raise the question': **X** *All the evidence so far revealed begs the question: Who gave the fatal order?* Say *raises the question* instead.

Behalf *On behalf of X* means either 'as a representative of X' or 'in the interest of X': *He negotiated peace on behalf of his government*; *They protested on behalf of fair play*. The latter usage is slightly awkward. The phrase *in behalf of* scarcely exists any more in British English; in North America, it is a common variant for both senses.

Take care not to use *on behalf of* when you mean 'on the part of, by' **X** *The war started because of aggression on behalf of the Greeks*.

behove, behoove. This is a somewhat old-fashioned and very formal verb; it means 'to be proper for'. British usage favours the form *behove*; the North American standard form is *behoove*. It is used only in impersonal constructions – that is, the verb takes *it* (or *which* or the like) as its subject: *It* *behoves us to treat the vanquished honourably; She spoke with great dignity, as (it) behoved a woman of her station.*

The related noun *behoof*, meaning 'benefit, advantage', is now very old-fashioned and is best avoided.

being as See BE.

below See ABOVE.

benefit The verb forms are *benefited* and *benefiting* – only one *t*, since the syllable *-fit-* is unstressed. Contrast *commit*.

benevolent, beneficial, benign, beneficent These adjectives all suggest good intentions or results.

Benevolent means 'wanting to do good': *Their policies, though benevolent, sometimes end in disaster.* Its related noun is *benevolence*; the opposites are *malevolent* (adjective) and *malevolence* (noun).

Beneficial means 'doing good'. It applies to things or abstractions rather than to people: *Vitamin pills are beneficial to one's health.* Its exact opposite is the rare word *malefic*, though *detrimental* would usually be more appropriate. Its related nouns are *benefit* and the very uncommon *beneficialness*.

Beneficent, pronounced /bi-**neffi**-sənt/, means 'doing good': *Mother Theresa is a beneficent woman.* Its opposite is *maleficent*. Its related noun is *beneficence*.

Benign, pronounced /bi-**nīn**/, means 'well-disposed, kindly': *Under Father García's benign influence, my people renounced cannibalism.* Its related noun is *benignity*, pronounced /bi-**nig**-niti/; the opposites are *malign* and *malignity*. In medicine, a cancerous tumour is *malignant*, whereas a non-cancerous one is *benign*.

Compare MALICIOUS.

berserk Note the *r* before the *s* in the spelling.

beside, besides The preposition *beside* means 'next to' or 'in comparison with': *standing beside his daughter; This year's profits look puny beside last year's.*

Besides, as preposition or adverb, means 'as well as; moreover; other than': *Besides being an explorer he was a fine writer; I would drive, but I don't know the way – besides, I've been drinking; Any left-handers here besides me?*

Take care not to confuse the one with the other: **X** *This year's profits look puny besides last year's.*

best To be strictly correct, use *best* only when comparing three or more people or things. A comparison between two things requires *better*, except in a few long-established idioms such as *May the best team/man win*.

between, among 1. According to formal rules, *between* relates two elements, whereas *among* relates three or more: *The bond between the two sisters was very strong; The rivalry among the various officers was very intense.*

But the rule does not account for all the uses of *between*. The important factor is really the nature of the relationships, rather than the number of participants. If all the relationships referred to are two-way, *between* remains appropriate: *Even after the feud was settled, there was always hostility between Diego, Pablo, and Manuel.*

So too when a cooperative group activity is under discussion: *After passing the hat round, they collected £250 between them; Just between ourselves, the boss will announce cuts next week.*

2. The word that goes with *between* is *and*, not *or*, *in contrast to*, or the like: **X** *The choice between death or cowardice didn't trouble Falstaff for long.* If each element itself contains an *and*, the temptation to use *or* increases further: **X** *To choose between sin and damnation or virtue and salvation sounds easier than it is.*

The *or* has to change to an *and*; to reduce possible confusion, you could add the phrases *on the one hand* and *one the other* after *damnation* and *salvation* respectively.

3. Unlike many other prepositions, *between* cannot be repeated before each element. The danger is at its most acute when the two elements are long and complex: **X** *The difference between Sam, who was reeling around blind drunk convinced that he could drive home, and between Richard, who was reeling around looking for a taxi, was more one of wealth than sense.* Delete the second *between*.

4. *Between each* and *between every* are illogical constructions. Avoid them: **X** *The interval between each contraction was now thirteen seconds.*

See also AMONG; BETWEEN YOU AND I.

between you and I This common phrase is grammatically incorrect. The correct form is *between you and me*. *Between* is a preposition, and should take the object-form of pronouns; this is obvious if you reverse the pronouns: **X** *between I and you*.

Though the phrase has been defended in various ways, it is best avoided. See also page 183.

biased, biasing These are the preferred spellings, though a double *s* is also possible.

biennial, biannual The prefix *bi-* can suggest either 'double' or 'half'. *Bimonthly* is genuinely ambiguous, meaning either 'twice a month' or 'once every two months'. *Biweekly* is similarly ambiguous. The distinction between *biennial* and *biannual* prevents ambiguity: *biennial* means 'every two years'; *biannual* means 'twice a year': *a biennial plant; a biannual meeting*.

One way of remembering the meaning of *biennial* is through its related noun *biennium*, which means 'a two-year period' in the same way as *millenium* means 'a thousand-year period'. You can avoid confusion by using the simpler terms *two-yearly* for *biennial*, and *twice-yearly* for *biannual*.

billion 1. Traditionally, the British *billion* was a million million. To North Americans, this is a *trillion*; their *billion* is a thousand million – as it widely is in British English too now (it used to be called a *milliard*). If any danger of ambiguity arises, however, avoid the term altogether – use *thousand million* (or *million million*) instead, or write the figure out in numbers. Similarly with *trillion*, *quadrillion*, and so on.

2. In specific plurals, *billion* (like *million*) retains its singular form and does not take *of*: *a research programme costing three billion dollars*.

If you omit the noun (*dollars*), the plural form *billions* is correct: *costing several billions*.

For an indefinite quantity, *billions of* is correct: *The Andromeda galaxy lies billions of miles away*.

bizarre Note the single *z*, double *r* in the spelling.

black *Black* is the preferred term, both noun and adjective, for people from the dark-skinned ethnic groups, especially those groups that are of ultimately African origin.

Not all those whose ultimate ethnic origin is the Indian sub-continent welcome the label *black*. The normal British English term for these people is *Asian*. (See ASIAN.)

The word *coloured*, particularly when used as a noun (plural *coloureds*), is nowadays considered offensive when used to refer indiscriminately to non-Caucasians. In South Africa, it is a term for people of mixed race.

Negro and *Negress* are now usually also offensive terms except in certain technical contexts.

blame Traditionally, one *blames* someone *for* something: *He blamed the government for the border dispute*. It has now become idiomatic to *blame* something *on* someone/something: **?** *Don't blame it on me!* **?** *He blamed the border dispute on the government*. This construction still jars with some purists, but is safe to use in all but the most formal contexts.

blanch, blench, bleach These verbs all mean 'to turn white or pale'. They can all be used both transitively and intransitively, and although they are effectively synonymous, idiom restricts them to different contexts.

To blanch is usually to steep vegetables or almonds briefly in boiling water, prior to freezing or peeling – a process which turns them pale: *blanched almonds*. It can also be used of people, though *blench* is preferable: *He blanched/blenched as the policeman approached*.

However, there is a different word *blench*, meaning 'to recoil, flinch, cower', that often causes ambiguity, as in the above example.

To bleach is usually to remove the colouring from something, as by chemicals – *bleached her hair* – though it too can be used of people, in a metaphorical way: *a miserly man, bleached of human compassion*.

blatant, flagrant Both adjectives suggest behaviour that is conspicuous and offensive, *blatant* relating more to the former quality, *flagrant* to the latter.

Blatant refers to things, people, or acts that intrude glaringly or objectionably on the observer's awareness: *a blatant cheat/error/flirtation*.

Flagrant applies to abstract things and actions, but rarely to people. It signifies that something is conspicuous because it is offensive: *a flagrant injustice*.

The distinction between the two words is a subtle one, perhaps best expressed by the following short definitions: *blatant* means 'offensively conspicuous'. *Flagrant* means 'conspicuously offensive'.

bleach, blench see BLANCH.

boatswain Note the pronunciation: /bō-s'n/; hence the variant spellings *bo's'n* and *bosun*.

bona fide, bona fides Both terms refer to good faith; they are pronounced /bōnə fīdi, fīdeez/ respectively. You no longer need to underline either of these terms or put it in italics.

Bona fide is, strictly, an adverb, meaning 'with good faith': *We agreed to the ceasefire bona fide*. It serves more commonly nowadays as an adjective (sometimes hyphenated), meaning 'sincere' or, more loosely, 'authentic, genuine': *a promise that seemed bona fide; a bona-fide Stradivarius*.

Don't use *bona fide* as a noun. The noun form is *bona fides*, meaning 'good faith, honest intention'; it takes a singular verb: *The enemy general's bona fides was accepted*.

Since there is really no plural form, you should, strictly, seek an alternative or extended wording when referring to the *bona fides* of several people: *the declarations of bona fides by both generals*.

both 1. *Both* applies only to two elements, though either or both of them (preferably only the second) may be in the plural: *We visited both the mainland and the islands*. Don't use *both* of more than two elements: **X** *We visited both the coast, the mountains, and the lakes*.

2. *Both* is appropriate when considering two elements together; *each* is appropriate when considering them separately: *Both girls shouted at the dog* but *Each girl shouted at the other*. See EACH; EITHER.

3. The following three constructions before plural nouns are equally correct: *Both cars were damaged; Both the cars were damaged; Both of the cars were damaged*.

British English used to avoid the third pattern, but now uses it quite freely.

4. The following constructions are nonstandard:

a. The phrase *the both*, as in **?** *He's invited the both of you*. Either replace *both* with *two*, or delete *the*.

b. Nouns or pronouns + *both*, as in **?** *He's invited you and him both*. *Both* should come before its elements in standard British English, except in certain rare idiomatic usages: *We're in the same boat, you and me both*.

5. When using the construction *both X and Y*, ensure that *X* and *Y* are of parallel structure. So, you may write: *I caught a glimpse of both the mother and the children*, or *I caught a glimpse both of the mother and of the children*, but not **X** *I caught a glimpse both of the mother and the children*. For further details, see pages 198-199.

6. Look out for redundancy. Avoid using *both* together with *also*, *as well as*, *same*, *agree*, *jointly*, *alike*, or *equally*: **X** *They both go to the same school*; **X** *That shop sells both clothing as well as linen*.

7. Look out for ambiguity. It can take several forms, in view of the versatility of *both*: **??** *We visited both the islands and the mainland*; **?** *My brother and I have both lived in luxury and been on the dole*; **??** *Alex and Ben both won a prize*; **?** *Both of your essays need revising*.

In the first example, you might reverse the two elements. In the second, you might transfer *both* to the start of the sentence, or omit it altogether, according to the sense intended. In the third, you might change *both* to *each* or to *jointly*, according to the sense intended. The fourth might change to *Your essays both need revising* or *Both of you need to revise your essays*.

bottleneck In the sense of an obstruction or a restricted flow of something, the noun *bottleneck* has become a vogue word. Use it sparingly. If possible, substitute other, more precise terms like *backlog*, *congestion*, or *hold-up*.

Bottleneck is difficult to intensify: **?** *a big bottleneck* could suggest an easy flow rather than a very slow flow, whereas **?** *a narrow bottleneck* hardly sounds impressive.

Adjectives such as *bad* or *troublesome* might be more useful intensifiers.

bouquet Note the pronunciations: /boō-**kay**/ is preferable, but /bō-/ is possible.

bourgeois Note the spelling, particularly the *e* after the *g*.

bravura, bravado *Bravura* is an adjective or noun referring to a dazzling and showy performance. Originally, it applied only to music, but it can now apply more widely: *a bravura violin solo; He acts with great bravura but no subtlety*.

Bravado is a noun meaning 'a swaggering and conspicuous show of courage': *He showed a lot of swashbuckling bravado during the battle, but to be truly brave you need to appreciate the risks*.

breach, breech, broach These are three quite different words. Take care not to confuse them.

1. *Breach*, with an *a*, is related to *break*. As a noun it means 'an opening, a gap broken through something', and by extension, 'a rift in relations' and 'the breaking of a bond': *Once more unto the breach, dear friends, once more!; a breach between the two nations*.

The verb *to breach* means 'to make or cause a breach in': *He struggled to breach the champion's defences*.

2. *Breech* is a noun meaning 'the back or lower part of something'. It refers usually to the rear end of a gun barrel, the lower part of a human trunk, or the buttocks. A *breech birth* is accordingly a birth in which the baby is born feet or buttocks first.

Breeches, pronounced /**brich**iz/, means 'trousers, especially knee-length ones'. Like *trousers*, it takes a plural verb.

3. *To broach* is a verb meaning 'to pierce', and by extension, 'to open, initiate, or embark upon': *He broached the wine cask; He broached the dangerous subject fearlessly*. Don't misspell it as *brooch*, which refers to an item of jewellery.

Britain, Great Britain, the British Isles, the United Kingdom, England. *Britain* is an unofficial and loose substitute for the various other names listed above, especially *Great Britain*.

Great Britain is the name of the island that contains England, Scotland, and Wales. It usually covers the small islands belonging to them (but excludes the Isle of Man and the Channel Islands, and the province of Northern Ireland), and also refers to the political union of the three regions.

The *United Kingdom*, strictly the *United Kingdom of Great Britain and Northern Ireland*, refers to the political rather than the geographical unit. The Isle of Man and the Channel Islands, although they are 'possessions' of the Crown, are not strictly part of the United Kingdom.

The *British Isles* is an unofficial name, referring to the United Kingdom, the Republic of Ireland, the Isle of Man, and the Channel Islands. Irish people may dislike the association of the Republic of Ireland with the *British Isles*, so always make it clear that you are using the term as a geographical rather than political name.

England refers simply to one division of the United Kingdom. Foreigners (and some English people) often use it to refer loosely to Great Britain or even the United Kingdom. This obviously tends to offend the Scots, the Welsh, and the Irish.

There is unfortunately no simple, elegant word meaning 'a citizen of the United Kingdom'. *Briton* comes closest (better than *Brit* or *Britisher*), but even that sounds rather haughty and is probably inappropriate for someone from Northern Ireland.

Northern Ireland comprises six counties – Antrim, Armagh, Down, Fermanagh, Derry or Londonderry, and Tyrone. It is often loosely called *Ulster*, but strictly speaking, Ulster also contains the counties Cavan, Donegal, and Monaghan, which are now in the Republic of Ireland.

broach, brooch See BREACH.

buffet The pronunciation is /**boo**f-fay/ when it refers to refreshments, /**buff**it/ for the verb meaning 'to strike' or the noun meaning 'a blow'.

buoy Note the spelling: the *u* comes before the *o* – not **X** *bouy*.

bureaucracy Note the spelling: the first part of the word as in *bureau*. Don't use the faulty model of words such as *democracy*.

burn The past tense and past participle of *burn* can be either *burnt* or *burned*. British English favours *burnt* to indicate an action that is completed, and *burned* to indicate a continuing or repeated process: *The toast was burnt to a crisp; The fires burned all night; while being burned at the stake*.

bus The preferred spelling of the plural is *buses*; the verb forms are usually *buses*, *busing*, and *bused*, though a double *s* is fairly common too, and equally acceptable.

but 1. There is little sensible basis, in logic or grammar or history, for the schoolroom rule outlawing the use of *but* at the start of a sentence. The possible alternatives – *yet, still, however* – will not always suffice.

For linking very long clauses, or for creating a deliberate staccato effect, *but* not only can but should begin a fresh sentence. But don't overdo it.

See HOWEVER.

2. The punctuation mark usually preceding *but* is the comma. Between very short clauses you may omit it. *She said she'd reply but she didn't*. And sometimes you *should* omit it: *She said she'd reply but didn't*. Don't omit the ·comma, however, in sentences where it might tempt the reader briefly into a misunderstanding: *The woman who replied wasn't Wanda, but Mary gave her the information anyway*. Without that comma as guide, the reader might begin to misread the sentence as meaning that the woman who replied was Mary.

3. *But* often accompanies various other words or phrases in a way that seems redundant: **?** *but nevertheless*, **?** *but despite that*, and so on. Some of these, especially *but still*, are now almost fully accepted as idioms. But do think twice before using any of them, in particular **??** *but however*, which continues to provoke strong objections: **??** *So he said – but we decided to ignore his advice once again, however*.

4. Take care too not to use *but* where the two linked ideas are not really in opposition. You can say *She cheated us glaringly, but we never noticed*, but not really **??** *She cheated us cunningly, but we never noticed*, since here the two ideas are in harmony rather than in conflict.

5. When *but* means 'except', the problem of pronouns arises: *nobody but me* or *nobody but I*? The former is usually preferable – see page 185.

6. The phrase *but that* (or *but* alone) is slightly questionable where *that* alone would suffice: *I shouldn't wonder that your letter has arrived*; **?** *I shouldn't wonder but that your letter has arrived*.

The combination of *shouldn't* + *but* in such sentences suggests a double negative, and sounds rather pompous in any case.

See also NO QUESTION.

7. The phrase *but what* is a silly and archaic substitute for *but that, that . . . not*, or *without* + *-ing*: **?** *I don't doubt but what your letter has arrived*; **?** *I can't taste aniseed but what I think back to my childhood*.

See also CAN BUT; NOT ONLY...BUT ALSO; NOT SO MUCH...AS.

by, bye Take care with the spelling: *by* is a preposition or adverb meaning 'near' or 'beside', while *bye* is a noun meaning 'a side issue'. Note the following phrases: *by the bye* (the variant *by the by* is now also acceptable); *by and by*; *a leg bye*.

In most compound words, the prefix *by-* is standard (though *bye-* is sometimes accepted now): *bylaw* (though this *by-* has a different origin), *by-election*, *bygone*, *bypass*, and so on.

Don't confuse the prefix *by-* with the combining form *bi-*, which means 'twice' or 'doubly', as in *bilingual*.

byword The construction *a byword for* can introduce either a favourable or an unfavourable idea: *That restaurant is a byword for excellent/appalling food*. The sense here is 'a perfect representative or proverbial example of'.

When used independently, *byword* always has unfavourable associations: *That restaurant is a byword among knowing diners*. The sense here is 'an object of scorn or notoriety'.

cactus Two plurals are possible, *cactuses* and *cacti*.

caddie, caddy A tea *caddy* is a small container for tea. It is always spelt with a *y*.

A *caddie* is an attendant who carries a golfer's clubs around the course. The verb *to caddie* means 'to act as a caddie'. Both noun and verb are usually spelt *-ie*, but can also be spelt *caddy*.

café The acute accent in *café* is slowly disappearing in informal written English. The correct pronunciation is /**kaf**fay/, but /**kaf**fi/ is widely used as well; **?**/kaf/ and **?**/kayf/ are British mispronunciations based on the accentless spelling of the word. In American English, the stress falls on the second syllable: /kaf**fay**/.

callipers Note the spelling: double *l* in Britain; single *l* in America; only one *p*.

callous, callus *Callous* is an adjective meaning 'hard-hearted, insensitive'; it is related to the noun *callus*, 'a hardened patch of skin'.

Callous can also mean 'covered in calluses', though *callused* is the more common form for this sense.

camaraderie Note the spelling of the word: *-mara-*, unlike *camera*.

camel, dromedary There are two main kinds of camel:

The *Bactrian camel*, which has two humps, and is found in central and southwest Asia; the *Arabian camel*, which has one hump, and is found in North Africa and southwest Asia (and now Australia).

The *dromedary* is simply an Arabian camel that has been specially bred for riding and racing.

camellia Note the spelling: single *m*, double *l* unlike *Amelia*.

can, may Traditionally, *can* expresses capability, and *may* expresses permission: *May I open the window? Can you open the window? – it's very stiff*.

In current idiom, however, *can* is frequently used for expressing permission, and is often less ambiguous than *may*: **?** *I may not go to the party*; **?** *I cannot go to the party*. Both sentences are ambiguous. The first can mean 'I have been forbidden to go', or 'I shall perhaps not go'; the second can mean 'I have been forbidden to go', or 'I am unable to go'. But the ambiguity in the second sentence is less extreme: either way, the speaker will definitely not be at the party.

In the past tense, *could* is more common and less ambiguous than *might*; and in negative sentences *can not*, *cannot*, and *can't* are preferable to the more strictly formal-sounding *may not*, *mayn't*.

See also pages 192-193.

can but, cannot but, cannot help but If you must use any of these old-fashioned expressions, use either of the first two: *You can but win*; *You cannot but win*. The third, as in **??** *You cannot help but win*, contains a triple negative, inconsistent with the positive sense. See page 204.

candelabra Strictly speaking, this is the plural form, the singular being *candelabrum*, 'a large, decorative, many-branched candlestick or light fitting'. However, *candelabra* has come to be used as a singular noun, and is widely accepted as such. Three plural forms now compete. They are, in order of preference, *candelabra*, *candelabrums*, *candelabras*. Note the spelling in the middle, *-del-*, in contrast to *candle*.

canon, cannon Watch out for the spelling of these words. *Canon*, with

one *n*, is the spelling of two separate though related words. It refers to:

a. church law (*canon law*), and hence the official list of books in the Bible, a part of the Mass, and the calendar of Saints. It also refers to ordinary law, and by extension to a standard or criterion for judgment (*canons of taste*); also an authoritative list, as of a writer's works or a cultural tradition (*the literary canon*).

b. a person living under a rule; specifically, a priest in a cathedral chapter or collegiate church, or a member of certain close-knit religious communities.

Cannon, with two *n*'s, has several meanings. It most commonly refers to a big gun; then, the loop at the top of a bell, a horse's bit or leg bone, and a shot in billiards (the last is called a *carom* in American English). *Cannon* is also a verb meaning 'to bombard', 'to fire cannon', 'to collide', and 'to make a cannon shot in billiards'.

canvas, canvass Take care with the spelling of these words. *Canvas* refers to the coarse cloth, used for making tents, sails, rucksacks, and so on; since *canvas* is also the material upon which artists paint, the word has come to mean 'a painting done on canvas'.

To canvass is a verb meaning 'to survey people's opinions', 'to scrutinise', and 'to enlist support or solicit votes': *The committee resolved to canvass opposition to the toll road*.

carcase, carcass Both spellings are acceptable in British English; only *carcass* is standard in American usage.

Caribbean Note the spelling: one *r*, double *b*. The pronunciation is /**karri**bee**-**ən/ in British English, but /kə**rib**bi-ən/ in the West Indies.

case 1. There is nothing wrong with using *case* in phrases such as *in that case*, *in your case*, and *which isn't the case*. But take care not to overuse it: **?** *Smoking is permitted in most rooms, but in the case of the laboratory, it is forbidden*. This would read much more sharply and effectively when phrased simply as: *Smoking is permitted in most rooms, but not in the laboratory*.

2. In British English, *in case* means 'to provide for the possibility that': *Do leave the ash-trays there, in case Dylan brings his pipe; Do leave the ash-trays there, just in case*. Note that the

Ready-Reference Word Guide

second, shorter version is slightly informal.

North Americans can use *in case* to mean 'if' or 'in the event that': *In case you see Sophia, can you say Hi to her for me?* This is nonstandard in British English, though it is increasingly common.

caster, castor Some senses of these words allow both spellings, but others allow only one.

The finely ground white sugar is always *caster sugar*, while the purgative oil is always *castor oil*. And *castor* alone is the fixative used in perfumes.

Both spellings can be used for the small swivelling wheels sometimes fitted under furniture (though *castor* is preferred); also for any 'person or thing that casts' (though *caster* is preferred): hence, *sugar caster/castor*.

catarrh Note the spelling: *-rrh*, as in *haemorrhage*.

caviar, caviare Both spellings are acceptable.

censor, censure Be careful not to confuse these two verbs. *To censor*, /**sen**-sər/, means 'to impose censorship on' something or someone. It implies 'inspecting, changing, and deleting material', as in newspapers or films or soldiers' letters, to make it conform to official policy: *censored the film/the violence in the film/the dissident film-maker*.

To censure, /**sen**-shər/, means 'to disapprove of', or 'to criticise strongly', often by official decision: *censured the film's bias/the government's censorship policy*.

Note the nouns and adjectives related to these verbs. The nouns from *to censor* are *a censor* (not to be confused with *censer*, 'a vessel in which incense is burned') and *censorship*; those from *to censure* are *a censurer* and *censure*. The adjective from *to censor* is *censorial*; that from *to censure* is *censorious*.

centre around Purists object to the phrase **??** *to centre around* (or *round* or *about*), as in **??** *The discussions all centred around compensation payments*. Logically, things are found around centres; centres cannot be around things. The idiom is perhaps a mix of two other phrases: *to centre on* (or *upon*) and *to revolve around*. For safety's sake, use either of these in preference to **??** *to centre around*.

Similarly, use *to focus on* instead of the illogical **??** *to focus around*.

centrifugal, centripetal The stress is best put on the second syllable in each case: /sen-**trif**ewg'l/, /sen-**trip**-pit'l/; also acceptable, and increasingly common, are stresses on both first and third syllables in each case.

centuries The world will probably celebrate the start of the 21st century on 1 January 2000. But the new century will actually begin one year later, on 1 January 2001. The reason is this: there was no year 0. The first century ran from AD 1 to the end of AD 100 (rather than from 0 to AD 99). The second century therefore began at the start of AD 101. So the 20th century began on 1 January 1901 and will end on 31 December 2000.

It is sometimes less confusing to talk in terms of hundreds: *the 1900s* is the period of 1 January 1900 to 31 December 1999.

See also AD.

ceremonial, ceremonious These words both relate to the noun *ceremony*, but in different ways.

Ceremonial is usually an adjective relating to traditional or ritual customs, procedures, or behaviour: *in ceremonial dress; the ceremonial opening of Parliament*.

Ceremonious is an adjective relating to pomp and formality: *an extravagantly ceremonious bow*.

Unceremonious and *unceremoniously*, once simply the opposites of *ceremonious* and *ceremoniously*, now usually mean 'brusque, or rudely, roughly': *The gunman bundled me unceremoniously into the car*.

Ceremonial can also be a noun (usually plural) meaning 'a set of ritual ceremonies, or the observance of them': *The May Day ceremonials were marred by the death of the President*.

cervical The pronunciation /ser-**vik**'l/ is considered slightly preferable to /**ser**-vik'l/.

chairman, chairwoman, chairperson, chair The word *chairman* has been a major debating-point in feminist discussions of sexism in the English language. Several alternatives have been proposed.

Feminine forms: *lady chairman*, *woman chairman*, *chairwoman*, and the form of address *Madam Chairman*. However, many women object to

terms which include the *-man* element, and *chairwoman* is problematic if the sex of the presiding officer is unknown or irrelevant.

Neutral forms: *chairperson*, *chair*. But *chairperson* can sound artificial and over-earnest, and is not very versatile: to address someone as **??** *Mister/ Madam Chairperson* is hardly practical. And though *chair* is quite commonly used, it can sound absurd, as if a person were a piece of furniture: **?** *What does the chair think?*

As for *chairman* itself, it can be used in a 'unisex' way, and is clearly the least distracting of all these terms. But since feminists find it objectionable, and traditionalists object to *chairperson*, you face a tricky decision. The best strategy is to judge your audience carefully, and choose whichever term or terms will cause least offence.

See also pages 89-90.

chamois Note the pronunciations: the antelope is a /**sham**-waa/, plural /**sham**-waaz/ (spelling unchanged); the leather is /**sham**mi/.

changeable Note the spelling: an *e* follows the *g*.

character See NATURE.

charade British usage still prefers the pronunciation /shə-**raad**/ to the Anglicised /shə-**rayd**/ that is used in North America.

charisma Traditionally, *charisma*, /kə-**riz**mə/, was a theological term referring to God-granted powers, such as healing. This sense has the plural *charismata*, and has the variant form *charism*.

Nowadays, *charisma* and its adjective *charismatic*, /**kar**riz-**mat**tik/, are used to refer to magnetic personal or public appeal. This extension of meaning is acceptable, since it fills a gap in the English vocabulary. What is less defensible is to use *charisma* as a synonym for mere *charm*.

chauffeur The Anglicised pronunciation /**shō**-fər/ is now slightly preferable to /shō-**fur**/.

chauvinist, chauvinism These words derive from the fanatical patriotic zeal displayed by Nicolas Chauvin, one of Napoleon's followers. In the 1960s, the feminist movement coined the term *male chauvinist* (shortened to *chauvinist*) to refer to a man with an unreasonable bias against women.

Chauvinist, chauvinistic, and *chauvinism* have come to refer to any prejudiced belief in the superiority of one's field or group: *chauvinistic philosophy lecturers who always sneer at the speculations of laymen.*

To avoid confusion or ambiguity, you may sometimes have to refer to a fanatical patriot as a *jingoist,* and to a misogynist as a *sexist* or a *male chauvinist.*

check, cheque, checker, chequer *Cheque* is the British word referring to the money order, as in *cheque book* and *traveller's cheques.* In all its other uses the word is spelt *check.* (In North America, *check* is the only spelling, even when the sense is 'money order'.)

North Americans have several meanings for *check* that the British do not share. *To check* can mean 'to deposit or receive into safekeeping': *I'm going to check my bag.* It can also mean 'to tick'. A *check* can mean 'a tick' or 'an invoice' – what speakers of British English call a *bill.* (To add to the confusion, Americans use *bill* to mean 'a note' when referring to money: *a dollar bill.)*

To check out is an Americanism – meaning 'to survey, inspect, try out'. It is becoming increasingly popular in British English, but is still considered nonstandard. The phrases *to check up* and *to check up on,* however, are perfectly acceptable.

In British English, the alternative name for *draughts* is either *chequers* or *checkers.* Only *checkers* is acceptable in American English. The same is true of the pieces: *chequer/checker* in British English, only *checker* in American English.

Cheers As an interjection, this word is used as a toast, as an informal farewell greeting in place of 'Goodbye', and as an informal alternative to 'Thank you'.

All of these uses, in ascending order of intensity, provoke annoyance among many sensitive and careful users of English. If you are uncertain of your audience, avoid the term.

Cherwell The name of this Oxford river is pronounced /**char**wəl/.

chilblain Note the spelling: no double *l* as in *chill.*

chilli, chili Both spellings are correct for the word for hot pepper. British usage favours *chilli;* American *chili,* or the rare form *chile.* The South American country is *Chile.*

Chiswick The pronunciation of this London place name is /**chizz**ik/.

Cholmondeley The pronunciation of this surname is usually /**chum**li/.

chord The combination of notes in music is a *chord;* within the larynx are the *vocal cords.* Mind the *h.*

Christian name, first name, forename, given name *Christian name* (sometimes with a small *c*) refers properly to the baptismal name of a Christian. In times past, when most English speakers were Christians, the term was suitable for referring to a person's first name.

The situation is now more complex. *Christian name* is an obviously inappropriate term for Muslims, Jews, Buddhists, and even atheists. The usual solution is to say or write *first name/s* instead, as is standard in American practice.

In official documents, the terms *forename* or *given name* are commonly used; they are both rather too formal for general purposes, perhaps.

First name remains the most suitable term, unless you are referring specifically to Christians; in more formal situations, *forename* and *given name* are appropriate; use *given name* when referring to people from cultures that put surnames first, such as Chinese or Hungarian.

chronic *Chronic* is an adjective meaning 'lasting for a long time' or 'constantly recurring'; when referring to a disease, it can also mean 'slow in developing'.

As the word is associated with unpleasant things such as diseases, shortages, and unemployment, it has developed the slang meaning of 'terrible, dreadful' in British English: *That party was absolutely chronic!* Avoid using the word in this sense in formal contexts.

claim The verb *to claim* has come to be used very loosely. Strictly speaking, *to claim* something is 'to make a forceful demand' – as when laying claim to something, or insisting upon some unlikely or defiant boast or belief: *This stranger claims to be my son!*

Purists dislike the modern tendency to dilute the word by using it in contexts where the verbs *contend, insist, allege,* or *say* would be appropriate: **?** *The police claim that I was double-parked.*

The phrase **?** *to claim responsibility for* is dubious when used of terrorist atrocities. When *claim* precedes a noun, it typically announces some goal or desirable achievement: *to claim victory/credit.* To report that a criminal group **?** *has claimed responsibility for yesterday's car bombing* could sound as though the responsibility were desirable and worth claiming. Better to use the verb *to admit* or *to declare* instead: *has admitted responsibility for yesterday's car bombing.*

classic, classical The adjective *classic* essentially means 'typical or outstanding of its class': *a classic case of the heebie-jeebies; the classic encounter between McEnroe and Borg.* It can also refer to tradition: *a classic fairy-tale.* As a noun, *classic* has the same range of reference: *'Blue Suede Shoes' is a rock'n'roll classic; 'Shooting an Elephant' is a classic of the essay genre.*

If *classic* corresponds to *class,* then *classical* corresponds to the *classics* – the study of Latin and Greek language and culture (and sometimes those of other ancient and authoritative civilisations).

Classical can refer to people or things from those times themselves – *Homer, Virgil, and other classical poets* – or to things that are made in imitation of them: *the classical drama of seventeenth-century France.*

Since classical Greek and Roman art was typically characterised by clarity, proportion, notions of ideal beauty, graceful lines, and modest self-control, *classical* often refers to artistic styles that stress formal elegance rather than emotional display; hence the traditional opposition of *Classical* versus *Romantic.*

In music, *classical* can mean three different things. Often, it refers to music which is held to be 'serious', as distinct from 'popular' music such as folk, rock, or jazz. More particularly, it can refer to such music of about 1600-1800, the *Classical* era as opposed to the later, more passionate *Romantic* era. Within that period, it can refer specifically to post-Baroque music, of roughly 1750-1800, of the type composed by Haydn and Mozart.

Finally, *classical* can refer to a superseded, formalised system in science, such as Newtonian physics or Euclidian geometry.

climacteric The rare word *climacteric* as both noun and adjective, relates to a critical period or turning point: *The bombing of Pearl Harbor was climacteric* (or *a climacteric event*) *in the progress of the war.*

As a noun, *climacteric* also refers to the menopause, male or female – the physical and psychological changes that set in during middle age.

Take care not to confuse *climacteric* with *climax* and its adjective *climactic*, or *climate* and its adjective *climatic*.

Climacteric is pronounced either /klī-**mak**tərik/ or /**klī**mak-**ter**rik/.

Cockburn The pronunciation of this surname is often /**kō**-bərn/.

coherent, cohesive, cogent The adjectives *coherent* and *cohesive* both stem from the verb *to cohere*, but they have different meanings. *Coherent* means 'orderly and well-organised, in such a way as to aid understanding or recognition': *a coherent plan for reviving the company.*

Cohesive means 'showing or producing fusion or attachment, especially between the parts of a whole'. It can apply literally to things with glue-like properties, or by extension it can apply to humans: *the cohesive power of superglue; a cohesive family unit.* The nouns for *coherent* and *cohesive* are *coherence* and *cohesion* respectively. *Coherent* is also sometimes confused with the adjective *cogent* (noun *cogency*). *Cogent* typically applies to arguments or reasoning, and means 'convincing in a forceful way, persuasive': So: *The argument was coherent enough, but insufficiently cogent to convince the panel.*

See also ADHERENCE.

colonnade Note the spelling: a single *l* as in *column*; and a double *n*.

colossal Note the spelling: single *l* in the middle, double *s*.

Colosseum, Coliseum The Roman amphitheatre is usually spelt *Colosseum*, and a modern theatre *Coliseum*, though the reverse is possible in each case.

coloured See BLACK.

Colquhoun The pronunciation of this name is usually /kə-**hoōn**/.

comic, comical The usual distinction between these two adjectives is this: something that is generally *comic* is intended to make people laugh (whether or not it succeeds), whereas something *comical* actually does make people laugh (whether or not it was intended to). So: a joke is a *comic* story, while a very fat man's squeezing into a very small car could be considered a *comical* event. *Comical* things are often odd, incongruous, or unintentional.

commit The verb forms are *committed* and *committing* – double *t*, since the syllable *-mit-* takes the stress. Contrast *benefit*.

committee Note the spelling: double *m*, double *t*, double *e*.

Committee can take a singular or plural verb, often according to context: *The committee was disbanded; The committee were divided.* See page 175.

common See MUTUAL.

common sense, commonsense The noun should be written as two words; the one-word form should be reserved for adjectival use: *a commonsense solution.*

comparable The standard pronunciation is /**kom**pərəb'l/ – stressed on the first syllable.

comparatively See RELATIVELY.

compare with, compare to The traditional distinction between these two forms is fairly subtle but very useful.

To compare to is used when considering one thing, and observing surprising similarities between it and another otherwise very dissimilar thing: *Trollope compared Signora Neroni to a summer storm.*

To compare with is used when considering two similar things and observing the dissimilarities (or occasionally the similarities) between them. It combines the emphases of *to compare to* and *to contrast with*: *comparing French wines with German wines; My first flight was awful, but compared with my second it no longer seems so bad.*

When *to compare* is used in the sense of 'to bear comparison', it always takes the preposition *with*: *The new film of the novel can't compare with the old.*

Similarly, the phrases *in/by comparison* and *as compared* almost always take *with*. The adjectival form *comparable* ought to do so as well, though *comparable to* is now far more common than *comparable with*, and seems to be accepted as standard idiom.

complacent, complaisant, compliant *Complacent*, /kəm-**play**ss'nt/, is sometimes confused with *complaisant*, /kəm-**play**z'nt/. Both adjectives derive from the same Latin word (meaning 'pleasing'), but their meanings are quite different.

Complacent can mean simply 'easy to please, or contented'; or, more negatively, 'smug, self-satisfied', or 'unjustifiably contented, ignoring possible danger': *His complacent belief in his own expertise was the cause of his downfall.*

Complaisant, now very formal or rather old-fashioned, means 'eager to please, cheerfully obliging': *a complaisant waiter who quickly responded to my complaints.* The word is not always positive, however: it can suggest an excessive wish to please, to the point of self-humiliation: *a complaisant wife who never complains of her husband's cruelty.*

Complaisant is also sometimes confused with *compliant*, because of their similarity of sense. Note the differences, however: *compliant*, /kəm-**plī**ənt/, means 'obliging or yielding', as through automatic obedience or docile submissiveness rather than through eagerness to please: *The boss surrounded himself with compliant subordinates and yes-men.*

Finally, the nouns related to *complacent* are *complacency* and *complacence*. *Complaisant* has the noun *complaisance*; and *compliant* has *compliance* and, rather more rarely, *compliancy*.

complement, supplement These words differ very subtly in meaning. *To complement* means 'to add something to something else to complete a whole'. *To supplement* means 'to add something extra to something almost complete'. So, bread might *supplement* chicken soup, but it would *complement* chicken in a sandwich.

As a helpful reminder, note that *to complement* is related to *to complete*, and *to supplement* to *to supply*.

So too with the two nouns: the *complement* of a ship, for instance, is its full crew; the *supplement* of a newspaper is an extra section.

A corresponding distinction applies to the adjectives *complementary* and *supplementary*.

See also COMPLIMENT.

complete Since *complete* is usually an absolute term, you should not, strictly, use words such as *more* and *most* to qualify it. When the word refers to comparisons of scope or thoroughness, however, it can take *more* and *most*: *Her knowledge of computers is more complete than mine.*

See also UNIQUE; VERY; and page 202.

compliant see COMPLACENT.

complicated, complex Both of these adjectives apply to single things or ideas made of many parts or strands. *Complicated* stresses the difficulty of analysing or disentangling these elements; *complex* stresses the abundance or intricate interweaving of them. So a *complex problem* might be fairly easy to solve, though it would involve a great many steps; a *complicated problem* would be difficult to solve, no matter how few or how many steps were involved.

A second slight difference lies in the tone. *Complicated* tends to be more negative: *complicated language* or *a complicated woman* would often convey unfavourable or unsympathetic feelings; *complex language* or a *complex woman* could suggest interesting depths.

The noun forms raise a difficulty. *Complexity* can apply to either *complex* or *complicated*. So a phrase such as *the complexity of a problem* leaves the nuance unclear: *complicatedness* or ? *complexness*.

The noun *complication* has a different sense – 'a problematic addition': when a patient develops *a complication*, the illness has taken a worsening turn.

The noun *complex* means broadly 'a whole consisting of closely related parts' – such as a group of buildings. In psychology, *complex* is a technical term referring to a set of unconscious or repressed ideas, or the abnormal mental state produced by them.

Don't use *complex*, in formal contexts anyway, to refer to any obsession, fear, or other emotional problem.

compliment, complement Take care not to confuse or misspell these two words.

A compliment, to compliment, and *complimentary* all relate to praise: *I complimented my mother on her hat.* The adjective *complimentary* also applies to something acquired free: *complimentary seats at the opera.*

A complement, to complement and *complementary* all relate to the com-

pleting of a whole by means of adding a part: *My mother's hat complemented her outfit.*

See also COMPLEMENT, SUPPLEMENT.

compose, comprise, constitute To *compose*, when applying to the parts of a *composite* whole, almost always appears in the passive: *The crew is composed of scoundrels and ruffians.*

To constitute, when used in the corresponding sense, is usually active and plural. Its subject is the parts not the whole: *Scoundrels and ruffians constitute the crew.* (*To constitute* can also mean 'to amount to', and here it can be singular: *A poached kipper constitutes a glorious feast.*)

To comprise always has the whole as its subject, never the parts: *The crew comprises scoundrels and ruffians.* Don't use it in the passive: **X** *The crew is comprised of scoundrels and ruffians.* Use *consists of* or *is composed of* instead of **X** *is comprised of* here.

See also CONSIST OF.

confidant, confident The noun is spelt *confidant* (or the feminine *confidante*) – 'someone confided in'. *Confident* can also be used in this way, but should really be kept as an adjective. Note the pronunciations of *confidant*: /**kon**fi-**dant**/ and /**kon**fi-**doN**/ are usual; /**kon**fi-**daant**/ is a possible American variant.

conjugal The standard pronunciation is /**kon**jŏŏg'l/, with the stress on the first syllable.

conjurer, conjuror Both spellings are correct.

Connecticut The pronunciation is /kə-**net**ti-kət/, with a silent middle *c*.

connoisseur Note the spelling: double *n*, double *s*, separated by the double vowel *oi*.

connote, denote To *denote* means 'to indicate directly' or 'to mean literally'. The word *home* might denote a house or flat, a special hospital, or the like. *To connote* means 'to reveal indirectly, to suggest, to convey secondary feelings or ideas'. The word *home* might connote security or welcome, for instance.

The noun *connotation*, 'an implication or association', has become something of a vogue word: ? *What are the connotations of this announcement?* This means no more than *What does this new announcement mean/imply?*

consensus Avoid using the phrases ?? *general consensus* and ?? *consensus of opinion*. They are tautological – *consensus* means 'generally held opinion': *The consensus of legal experts is that the judge erred.*

Note the spelling: *consensus*, not **X** *concensus*. A useful reminder: the word is related to *consent*.

consequent, consequential, subsequent *Consequent* applies to the results or logical conclusion of something; *subsequent* applies to the events immediately following, whether connected or not: *the car crash and consequent hospital bills; the car crash and subsequent rainstorm.*

When not directly attached to their nouns, the two adjectives take different prepositions: *Her hospital bills were consequent upon/on the car crash; The rainstorm was subsequent to the car crash.*

Consequential is very rare nowadays, and its main sense is now 'pompous' rather than 'consequent': *My uncle was a smug consequential man.* The opposite *inconsequential*, 'unimportant', is far more common.

conservative A *conservative estimate* is 'restrained, cautious, moderate' – as if made by a prudent or conservative person. It is usually, therefore, a low estimate – hence the dubious use of *conservative* to apply to small or modest amounts: ? *asked a very conservative price for the house.*

consider To *consider*, in the sense 'to regard as, to deem', can occur in various patterns, but not ordinarily followed directly by the preposition *as*. So: *We consider the man a fool/foolish; We consider him to be a fool/foolish*, but not **X** *We consider him as a fool/foolish.*

considerable To use the adjective *considerable* to mean 'quite a lot of' is really just to disguise vagueness: ? *considerable support for the strike.* If you do use it, limit it to abstract nouns, at least in British English: *a woman of considerable experience; I've eaten a considerable amount of spaghetti*, but not ? *I've eaten considerable spaghetti.* However, in various other senses – 'large', 'important', 'severe' – *considerable* can qualify concrete nouns: *That's a considerable cake; She's a considerable musician; a considerable blow to my pride.*

consist of, consist in To *consist of* means 'to be made up of, to compose'.

It usually introduces a set of ingredients, in the form of concrete nouns: *The kit consists of three brackets, six screws, and a long plank*.

To consist in means 'to have as the essential part, to amount to'.

It typically occurs in definitions, and introduces verbal or abstract nouns: *True love consists in accepting the other fully and in total tolerance*.

See also COMPOSE.

constitute See COMPOSE.

contact Two senses of *contact* attract criticism: *to contact* in the sense of 'to get in touch with'; and *a contact* in the sense of 'a useful acquaintance': *Contact me when you know where the party is; Don't worry about your summons – I have a contact in the CID*.

Both senses are very useful and well established now. Valid objections could still be made, however, to the overuse of *contact*, and to its imprecise use – to saying **?** *Please contact me* when you mean *Please phone me*.

contemporary, contemporaneous 1. *Contemporary* means primarily 'belonging wholly or partly to the same period or era': *Wordsworth was contemporary with Coleridge*. It can also be a noun: *Wordsworth and Coleridge were contemporaries*.

By extension, *contemporary* has come to mean 'contemporary with the present day, modern, current': *Contemporary rock music tends to reject the double-bass in favour of the bass guitar*. This is perfectly acceptable (as is its noun form), though the sense 'very modern, up-to-date' is still suspect: **?** *This novel is too contemporary for my tastes*.

(*Contemporary* also has various technical uses, referring to a 50s style of decoration or furniture, for instance.)

Beware of redundancy: **X** *Wordsworth and Coleridge were contemporaries of each other*. Omit the phrase *of each other*.

2. *Contemporaneous* means much the same as *contemporary* in its first sense does. It is the less common of the two adjectives when relating to human subjects, and probably more common when relating to nonhuman subjects. And of the adverb forms, *contemporaneously* is more common than *contemporarily*. Hence: *Wordsworth wrote contemporaneously with Coleridge; Wordsworth's poetry was contemporaneous with Coleridge's*.

continual, continuous Both words can refer to continuity through time, though in slightly different ways. *Continual* means 'repeated at regular intervals'; and *continuous* means 'unbroken, going on without any pauses': *The continual bursts of gunfire through the night; the continuous hum of machinery*.

Only *continuous* can refer to continuity through space: *The road was a continuous, winding ribbon of tarmac*.

These distinctions also apply to the adverb forms – *continually* and *continuously*.

contribute The stress traditionally falls on the second syllable. Purists dislike the modern tendency to stress the first syllable instead.

controversy Should you say *con*troversy or con*trov*ersy? Traditionally, **con**troversy is correct, though both are now standard in British English. The reason for the shift seems to be a British aversion to runs of three unstressed syllables: despite such familiar words as **dif***fi*culty and **pres***i*dency, the preference remains for a more balanced stress pattern, as in a**pol***o*gy and rhi**noc***e*ros.

The shift to this pattern is noticeable in many words other than con*trov*ersy – for example, *formidable* and *ignominy*. In each case, traditionalists resist the trend, and still place the stress on the first syllable.

And speakers of American English seem not to share the British preference. They still consistently put the main stress on the first syllable of controversy – and also on *laboratory* and *metallurgy*.

No simple answer is available. If you are concerned about your listeners' response, adjust your pronunciation to suit their likely preference – **con**troversy for the traditionalists and purists; con**trov**ersy for the under-50s and progressives.

cooperate, coopt, coordinate These are all now usually written as single words, though they can be hyphenated, as in *co-opt*. American English uses a dieresis over the second *o*, as in *coöpt*.

Copenhagen The correct English pronunciation of the Danish capital is /kōpən-**hay**gən/. Don't attempt to make it sound more foreign by saying **?** /kōpən-**haa**gən/: the Danes themselves spell and pronounce the name quite differently.

corps, corpse, corpus All these nouns relate to the word *body*, but in different ways.

A *corps* is a body of people – usually an army unit or the group of non-soloists in a ballet troupe. When singular, it is spelt *corps* and pronounced /kor/; when plural, it is spelt *corps* and pronounced /korz/.

A *corpse* is a dead body, specifically a human body. (A dead animal body is generally a *carcase* or *carcass*.) The plural of *corpse* is standard – *corpses*.

A *corpus* is usually a body of works, especially written works: *Shakespeare's complete corpus of plays and poems*. The plural is technically *corpora*, but many people use *corpuses* – to the dismay of the purists.

could See CAN, MAY.

council, counsel A *council* is a committee, assembly, or meeting. So a member of a *council* is a *councillor*. In Britain, *council* often refers to the elected representative body of local government and its belongings or responsibilities – hence, *all council property, a council house*.

Counsel is a noun meaning 'advice or consultation' or a verb meaning 'to advise'. A person who offers *counsel* is a *counsellor* – or, in special legal contexts, *Counsel* (capital C, no *a* or *the*): *Counsel for the defence will approach the bar*. The plural of *Counsel* is also *Counsel*, though the plural of QC (*Queen's Counsel*) is QCs.

couple Strictly, *a couple of* means 'two, a pair'. Informally, *a couple of* can mean 'a few' – *I had to pick up a couple of things from home*. Best avoid the phrase if it causes ambiguity.

According to context or level of formality, *couple* might take a singular or a plural verb: *The happy couple don't look very happy in the wedding photos; A couple of tower blocks now obscures the view; A couple of problems remain unsolved*. See also page 175.

The phrase **??** *a couple or three* is both slangy and clichéd.

covert The pronunciation /**kuv**vərt/ is traditionally correct, though **?** /kō-vert/ has become common on the model of *overt*.

cowardly The adjective *cowardly* means 'lacking in courage'. By association, a sense of 'secretive and evasive' has developed – much favoured by journalists: **?** *a cowardly mugging;*

? *cowardly terrorist outrages.* Think twice before using the word in this dubious way: muggers and terrorists are not necessarily lacking in courage.

coxswain The standard naval pronunciation is /**kok**-s'n/, though /**kok**-swayn/ is just acceptable too.

crescendo *Crescendo*, pronounced /kri-**shen**-do/, is primarily a music term, referring to a smooth increase in volume or to a passage containing such an increase. It is often represented by the symbol <.

It can refer to sound in general, and by extension to other types of development: *His anger rose in a crescendo until it pushed out prudence.*

Since *crescendo* implies a growing process or an increase, it strictly should not be used to mean 'a climax': **X** *His anger reached a crescendo of fury;* **X** *His anger grew to a crescendo.* Beware, too, of redundancy: **X** *an increasing crescendo.*

The plural is either *crescendos* or – in technical contexts – *crescendi*; the verb forms are *to crescendo, crescendoes, crescendoing, crescendoed.*

crisis Traditionally, *crisis* suggests a dramatic turning point, a major switch in the course of events: *a mid-life crisis; The fall of Constantinople provoked a crisis of European history.*

Its recent extended sense – 'any emergency, or any serious state of affairs' – is slightly dubious: **?** *Two goals down after 20 minutes, Arsenal has a crisis on its hands.*

The plural of *crisis* is *crises*, pronounced /**kri**-seez/.

See also CLIMACTERIC. And compare CRUCIAL.

criterion, criteria *Criterion* is the singular; *criteria* the plural. Don't use *criteria* as the singular, and don't use **??** *criterions*, or **X** *criterias* as the plural.

Compare DATA; MEDIA; PHENOMENON.

crucial *Crucial* is related to *crux*, 'the essential feature'. It suggests more than merely 'important' – it means 'decisive, of vital importance, affecting the outcome': *Holding on to the Falklands was crucial to Galtieri – failure spelt political doom.*

Compare CRISIS.

cul-de-sac The Anglicised pronunciation /**kul**-də-sak/ is now slightly preferable to the French form /koŏl-də-**sak**/. And the plural *cul-de-sacs* is preferable to *culs-de-sac*.

curb, kerb For most senses, the spelling is *curb* – 'a fender', 'a chain for restraining a horse', 'to control or restrain'. In American English *curb* also refers to the edge of a pavement; but in Britain, the spelling for that sense is *kerb*, as is the verb sense 'to supply with a kerb'.

currant, current The fruit – dried grapes and *redcurrants* alike – are spelt with an *a*, as are the plants bearing them. For all other senses, the spelling is *current* – 'present, now in progress', 'a flow, as of air or water', and so on.

curriculum Note the spelling: double *r*, single *c*'s. The plural can be either *curriculums* or – preferably – *curricula*. The plural of *curriculum vitae* is *curricula vitae*.

cygnet, signet The young swan is a *cygnet*; a *signet* is a seal (as in *signet ring*) of the type used with sealing wax.

czar See TSAR.

dais Note the spelling: -*ai*-, not **X** -*ia*- as in *bias*. The pronunciation /**day**-iss/ is standard.

Dalyell This surname is usually pronounced /dee-**el**/.

dare The verb *dare* has two different grammatical functions, as in *if Tom dares to jump* and *if Tom dare jump*. Take care not to confuse the two patterns: **X** *if Tom dare to jump*.

See page 193 for further details.

data The standard pronunciation is /**day**-tə/, though Americans often say /**daa**-tə/ or /**datt**ə/.

The word is a plural noun; the singular is *datum*, though a phrase such as *one of the data* is often used instead.

Many people, especially in North America, treat *data* as an uncountable noun, and give it a singular verb. But purists still object: **??** *The data proves my conclusions;* **??** *There is no data to support your views.*

When talking about quantity of data, you may say *a large amount/quantity of data; three of the data*. It sounds slightly odd to say **?** *three data* and **?** *There are many data*. And purists object to **?** *a lot of data* and **?** *much data*. You may sometimes find it safest to drop *data* altogether in favour of *facts, evidence, statistics*, and the like.

Compare CRITERION; MEDIA; and PHENOMENON.

day See YEAR.

decimate Pedants insist that *to decimate* means 'to kill ten per cent of'. Certainly it originally had this meaning: in Latin, *decimare* meant 'to kill every tenth soldier' in a mutinous or cowardly Roman battalion.

But English writers have, since the 17th century, been using *decimate* to mean 'to kill a great deal of, to devastate': *The Black Death decimated the population of Europe.*

This sense seems firmly rooted now, though you might want to avoid the word altogether if you suspect that it will either raise hackles or arouse puzzlement. And looser uses of *decimate* – 'to destroy', 'to get rid of', 'to defeat decisively', and so on – can be dubious and provocative, and are best avoided: **??** *Television has decimated the book trade;* **??** *The West Indies pace bowlers decimated the English batsmen yesterday.*

decrepit Note the final *t* in the spelling; not -*d* as in *intrepid*.

deduction, induction Each of these nouns corresponds to two verbs: *deduction* to *to deduct* and *to deduce*; and *induction* to *to induct* and *to induce*. Take care not to confuse the members of each pair.

To deduct means 'to subtract': *You deducted £2.50 from my pay. To induct* usually means 'to install in office': *The new president was inducted at midday.*

To deduce means 'to reach a conclusion by reasoning from general principles': *As liberty is a fundamental human right, we may deduce that slavery is immoral. To induce* can mean 'to persuade': *induced us to cooperate;* 'to stimulate the occurrence of': *induce a fever/childbirth/electric current;* or 'to reach a general conclusion from particular statements or observations': *From his red cheeks, I induce that Tom must be extremely healthy.* This last sense is very rare, however; *infer* would be more usual in such a sentence.

Deduction and *induction* accordingly, are different modes of reasoning: *deduction* proceeds from general principles to particular conclusions, as in logic; *induction* from particular statements or observations to general conclusions or rules, as in science.

defective, deficient These adjectives are seldom interchangeable, and are not really synonymous. *Defective* relates to *defect*, 'a fault', and so means 'faulty'; *deficient* relates to *deficiency*, 'a lack', and so usually means 'lacking some important quality or part'.

Accordingly, *defective* is far likelier to refer to artificial things than *deficient* is: *defective machinery*. And *deficient* is far likelier to add details – it usually makes the deficiency explicit: *This meter is deficient in power*.

When referring to mentally retarded people, the traditional term *defective*, as noun or adjective, is nowadays liable to cause offence. The phrases *mental deficiency* or *mentally deficient* seem to be free from objections.

Note, finally, that *deficient* does not mean quite the same as *insufficient*: *Our provisions were deficient in fruit; Our provisions were insufficient – after two days we ran out of food*.

defence, defensive Note the spelling: *c* in the noun, *s* in the adjective. In North America, *s* tends to occur in both.

definite, definitive These adjectives have similar meanings, but are not identical.

Definite means 'unambiguous, precise': *She never offered a definite opinion about anything*.

Take care not to use *definite* or its adverb *definitely* as a vague intensifier: **?** *definitely a messy piece of work*; **?** *a definite foul-up*.

Definitive has two meanings: 'final, complete, authoritative' or 'defining precisely': *I regard this as the definitive biography of Churchill; an anecdotal rather than definitive look at Relevance Theory*.

Don't use *definitive* simply as a stronger word for *definite*: **X** *no definitive opinion about the likely winner*.

deity The pronunciation /**dee**-əti/ is older than /**day**-əti/, though both are correct.

delusion, illusion Both of these nouns refer to mistaken impressions, but in different ways. An *illusion* is a false appearance, or the misleading impression produced by it. It is often easy to disperse or remedy.

A *delusion* tends to be more powerful and disturbing: it is harder to eradicate, and it influences behaviour.

Various idioms favour one noun or the other: *optical illusions, conjuror's illusions, delusions of grandeur; suffering from delusions, labouring under an illusion*.

Both nouns are related to various other common words: the verb *to delude* and the adjectives *delusive* and *delusory*; and the adjectives *illusive* (rare) and *illusory*.

Don't confuse these words with the similar-sounding words *allusion, allusive*, and *elusive*. See ALLUDE.

demonstrable Traditionally, the stress falls on the first syllable; second-syllable stress is now widespread, however, and generally considered acceptable.

denote See CONNOTE.

depend The verb *depend* should, strictly, always take the preposition *on* or *upon*, even when a full clause follows: *It depends on what price they are asking*. Don't drop the preposition except in informal contexts.

Similarly, the full sentence **?** *It (all) depends*, though common and useful, is best avoided in formal contexts.

dependent, dependant Note the spellings: the adjective ends in *-ent*; the noun, meaning 'one who depends', ends in *-ant*. In North American usage, the noun is often spelt *-ent*, and the adjective occasionally *-ant*.

Derby, derby Note the pronunciations: the English town, horse race, and cheese are all /**dar**bi/; the American horse race and hat are /**der**bi/.

description See NATURE.

descriptive, prescriptive See PRESCRIBE.

desert, dessert Only the word meaning 'pudding' is spelt with a double *s*. For all other senses, the word is *desert*.

desperate Note the spelling: *-per-*, not **X** *-par-* as in *separate*.

despicable Traditionally, the stress falls on the first syllable; second-syllable stress is now widespread, however, and generally considered acceptable.

despite, in spite of Both these expressions are shortenings of the old phrase *in despite of*. For some reason, *despite*

has a reputation for being more affected than *in spite of*. But it has the advantage of being more concise, which more than restores the balance.

What is affected, and needlessly cumbersome, is the expression **??** *despite/in spite of the fact that*. Use *although* or *even though* instead.

Note that *in spite of* is three words: don't reduce the phrase to **X** *inspite of*.

deteriorate Don't forget the *-or-* syllable when writing or speaking.

diagnosis The plural is *diagnoses*, not **X** *diagnosises*.

diagram Note the spelling: never **X** *-gramme* as in *programme*.

diarrhoea Note the spelling: *-rrh-* as in *haemorrhage*; and don't omit the *o*, unless in North America.

dichotomy Originally a technical term in scientific or philosophical contexts, *dichotomy* today applies more widely to a clear-cut division or schism: *an absolute dichotomy between the Liberals and the Republicans*. It can also mean 'a discrepancy', or a lack of correspondence': *a dichotomy between what they preach and what they practise*.

It has become something of a vogue word. Use it sparingly – it tends to sound quite affected even when used once.

different 1. *Different from, different to*, or *different than?* Traditionally, *different from* is the only acceptable form, even if it makes the sentence clumsy: *My tastes are different from yours;* **?** *I bought my dress from a different shop from the one you bought yours from*. This second example would sound better if *different from* changed to *different to*, a form widely used in Britain (though not in North America): *I bought my dress from a different shop to the one you bought yours from*.

Different than is common (though not completely standard) in North America. In Britain it is unacceptable as a simple substitute for *different from* when introducing a simple noun, pronoun, or short noun phrase: **??** *My tastes are different than yours*. But it is very convenient when introducing an adverb or full clause, and is therefore not so unacceptable in such sentences: **?** *Her rendering of the third movement is very different than (it was) when I last heard her play it*.

This wording is less of a mouthful than the traditional ... *very different from the way it was when I last heard her play it*. Similarly, **?** *She's playing a different version than before* is more economical than *She's playing a different version from the one she played before*.

Nevertheless, if you are writing for fastidious readers, you had better keep to the safe, traditional form *different from*.

2. Watch out for the redundant use of *different*: **??** *She speaks six different languages*; **??** *He travelled to eleven different countries*. If you do want to intensify the number in each of these examples, you could try using *separate* or *distinct* instead, though these seem just as tautological. The best procedure, as always, is to rethink the sentence somewhat: *He travelled to no fewer than eleven countries*.

3. In formal contexts, avoid using *different* to mean 'several', 'various', or 'unusual': **??** *Different universities have tried to solve the problem* (use *various* or *several*); **?** *a new and different shampoo* (use *unusual* or *special* or *distinctive*.)

4. Avoid too using *different* in place of *differently*: **X** *They do things different there*.

differential Don't use *differential* simply as an impressive-sounding synonym of *difference*. Outside its various technical senses, *differential* usually refers to a gap or factor based on a difference, or producing a difference. So a *pay differential* is a difference in rates of pay based upon a difference in skills or conditions.

dilapidated Note the spelling: *di-*, not **X** *de-* as in *deteriorated*.

dilemma A *dilemma* is more than a mere problem or difficulty.

Strictly, it is a predicament in which one has to choose between two equal – and unattractive – options: *She found herself in a difficult dilemma: pay double for a first-class seat, or wait an extra day for the next flight*.

Deviations from these defining requirements vary in acceptability:

☐ If the choices number three or more, *dilemma* is still fairly acceptable.

☐ If the options are attractive rather than unattractive, *dilemma* is really not the appropriate word: **??** *in a dilemma: whether to go by Concorde or on the QEII*.

☐ If there is no choice at all, but only a problem, *dilemma* is quite wrong: **X** *Here's the dilemma: how to get to New York by midday without taking the night flight*.

diphtheria The first syllable is spelt *diph-*, not **X** *dip-*; and it is best pronounced /dif-/, though /dip-/ is also acceptable.

direct, directly 1. *Direct* can be an adverb, just as *directly* is: *The boat sails direct to Lerwick*. Note that *direct* here means 'straight, or uninterruptedly'; by contrast, *directly* means 'immediately, quickly': *Hurry – the boat is leaving directly*. Some contexts allow either *direct* or *directly*, though the meaning differs: *Get in touch with David direct/directly*.

2. The colloquial British use of *directly* as a conjunction is inappropriate for formal contexts: **?** *I tried to phone directly I got there*. Either replace *directly* with *as soon as*, or change the construction: *I tried to phone directly on getting there*.

disc, disk *Disc* is usually standard in Britain; *disk* in North America. But when referring to computer equipment, *disk* is acceptable in British English alongside *disc*.

Compare PROGRAMME.

disciplinary Traditionally, the stress falls on the first syllable only; an added stress on the third syllable is now very common, and widely accepted.

discomfit *Discomfit* sounds just like *discomfort*, and overlaps with it in meaning, but the two words are not synonymous. *To discomfit* means 'to foil or to embarrass': *Why must you always discomfit me in front of my friends?* The verb is very rare and formal nowadays.

The noun form is *discomfiture*.

discreet, discrete Watch out for the spelling. The adjective meaning 'prudent, reserved, modest, or unobtrusive' is spelt *-eet*; the adjective meaning 'separate, distinct' is spelt *-ete*: *a discreet silence; attempting to fuse several discrete arguments*.

disingenuous See INGENIOUS.

disinterested, uninterested Beware of blurring the distinction between these two adjectives. *Disinterested* has come to mean 'impartial, unprejudiced, fair'; and *uninterested* to mean 'not interested, bored'. So a *disinter-*

ested spectator cheers both sides; an *uninterested* spectator falls asleep.

Try to avoid using *disinterested* to mean 'uninterested': it will only attract censure from purists. The noun *disinterest* is more problematic: it suggests either a lack of self-interest (corresponding to *disinterested*) or a lack of all interest (corresponding to *uninterested*). Take care, when using the word, to make clear which meaning you intend.

disorient, disorientate See ORIENT.

dispatch, despatch Both spellings are correct; *dispatch* is more usual.

dispute Strictly, the stress falls on the second syllable for both noun and verb. A first-syllable stress is now often used for the noun, but it is not recommended.

dissatisfied, unsatisfied *Dissatisfied* means 'discontented, particularly about a lack of something'; *unsatisfied* refers only to an absence of satisfaction in general: *a dissatisfied and frustrated child; an unsatisfied desire for fame*.

dissect Note the spelling: double *s*, unlike *bisect*.

distil Note the spelling: single *l*, unlike *distillery*; in American English, the word has a double *l*.

distinct, distinctive Both of these adjectives relate to the verb *to distinguish*. *Distinct* means 'easy to distinguish, unmistakable, definite, different': *The blur slowly became distinct*.

Distinctive means 'serving to distinguish, characteristic': *Renoir's distinctive brushwork; the distinctive smell of ammonia*.

Don't confuse the two words: keep them distinct, since they have their own distinctive meanings.

distribute The stress traditionally falls on the second syllable. An increasing tendency to stress the first syllable instead is opposed by purists.

dived, dove The normal past tense of *to dive* is *dived*. In some regions, *dove* exists as an alternative: *We dove for cover*. The form *dove* is fairly widely accepted in North America except in very formal contexts, but in Britain it remains a local dialect term. The past participle always remains *dived*: *We had dived for cover*.

do 1. To avoid repetition, *to do* or *to do so* often stands in for a verb phrase: *I asked him to help us, and he did so*.

Be careful not to take this convenient usage beyond its acceptable limits. The test is to replace the *do*-form with the main verb, and check that it really is working as it should.

✗ *That dreadful wound is something only a tiger could do*. (One cannot **✗** *do a wound*; change *do* to *cause* or *inflict*.)

✗ *He is in favour of tax reform only when doing so reduces his own tax bill.* (Replace *doing so* by *being so*; or else replace *is in favour of* by *favours*.)

✗ *She has no money, or at least no more than I do.* (Purists would use *have* rather than *do* here: a traditional rule forbids *to do* in place of *to have*.)

2. The colloquial or slangy form **✗** *I already done it* or **✗** *Who done the washing-up?* is obviously nonstandard, and quite unacceptable in formal contexts. Insert a *have* or *has* as necessary: *I've already done it*.

Similarly, the form **✗** *He don't like me* or **✗** *It don't hurt a bit* is very informal. The correct form here is *doesn't*.

do's and don'ts The positioning of the apostrophes in this common phrase is a vexed question. The version here probably strikes the best balance.

doge The pronunciation is /doj/, with a *j*-sound as in *dodge*, not **✗** /do<u>zh</u>/, with a *g* as in *mirage*.

dogma Two plurals are possible: *dogmas* and *dogmata*.

dominate, domineer *To dominate* means 'to exercise power or influence over' or 'to overlook from a high position': *Becker dominated his opponent in the first set; Marxism dominates his thinking; The volcano dominated the tiny village*. The verb does not imply tyranny.

To domineer has a distinctly unfavourable tone. It means 'to exercise a bullying or tyrannical influence'. It is usually followed by *over*: *My brother-in-law domineers over my sister*. More common is the adjective form *domineering*: *Her domineering manner only strengthens my opposition*.

done See DO 2.

don't See DO 2.

dote, doat Both spellings are correct; *dote* is more usual.

dour Note the pronunciation: /door/ to rhyme with *moor*; in American English, /dowr/, rhyming with *power*.

douse, dowse Both of these verbs relate to water. Take care not to confuse them.

To dowse means 'to search for and/or find water or minerals by means of a divining rod or pendulum', and by extension, 'to discover by means of supernatural powers'. It is pronounced /dowz/ usually, though /dowss/ is acceptable.

Various distantly related verbs are spelt *douse*. One means 'to soak, drench, plunge into water'. Another means 'to extinguish (a light or fire)'. The first is very occasionally spelt *dowse*; both are pronounced /dowss/.

dove See DIVED.

draconian *Draconian* strictly means 'excessively and unnecessarily severe'. It qualifies nouns such as *laws* and *punishments*: *draconian measures to put down the rebellion*.

The word comes from *Draco* (not *dragon*), the name of an ancient Greek lawgiver who prescribed capital punishment for relatively minor crimes. Although applicable today to harsh penalties other than capital punishment, it remains a powerful adjective. Don't weaken it by using it of any over-severe regulation or punishment: **??** *a draconian fine of £400 for fare-dodging*.

draft, draught British English assigns various senses to each spelling; in American English, the only recognised spelling is *draft*.

Draft refers to a preliminary version: *the draft of a treaty, a draft treaty, to draft a treaty*. A money order is a *draft*; so too is a special assignment of soldiers (in North America, *the draft* refers to military call-up): one *drafts* soldiers and *drafts in* helpers when necessary.

A man who drafts a legal document might be called a *draftsman*, but one who draws plans for machines or buildings is a *draughtsman*.

An indoor wind is a *draught*; *draught* horses pull *draughts* or loads; when thirsty you might take a long *draught* of *draught* beer. The board-game of *draughts* (which takes a singular verb) is called *checkers* in North America.

drawing Avoid the pronunciation /draw-ring/, with its intrusive *r*.

dreadfully See AWFULLY.

dream Both *dreamt* and *dreamed* are acceptable past forms of *to dream*. *Dreamt* is usual in Britain; *dreamed* in North America.

drunken The standard past tense of *to drink* is *drank*, and the past participle is *drunk*: *I drank it; I've drunk it*.

The choice is tricky when it comes to adjectives. The useful standard distinction does not really hold good – *drunk* for a temporary state, *drunken* for a chronic habit: *a drunk guest; her drunken husband*. True enough, *drunk driving* seems to be ousting *drunken driving*, but the phrases *drunken singing* and *a drunken stupor* remain unchallenged.

due to, owing to When used adjectivally (following the verb *to be*, for instance), both *due to* and *owing to* are acceptable: *Her limp is due to/owing to a riding accident*.

But only *owing to* is strictly appropriate for use as a preposition (relating directly to a noun, pronoun, or noun phrase following it): *Owing to a riding accident, Mary Partridge now walks with a limp*.

Purists object to the use of *due to* in such sentences. In fact, it is very seldom formally correct to use *due to* to begin a sentence.

Roughly, *owing to* has the wide-ranging sense 'because of', and *due to* has the narrower sense 'caused by' or 'resulting from'. One further test: if you are inclined to use *due to*, ask yourself the question: *'What is due?'* If you cannot provide an answer from the words within the sentence, you should use *owing to* instead.

duffelcoat Note the spelling: *-el*, not **✗** *-le*.

dyke, dike Both spellings are correct for all senses of this word; but *dyke* is more usual in British English, and *dike* is standard in American English.

dynast, dynasty In British English, the first syllable is best pronounced like *din* rather than *dine*.

each 1. *Each*, whether pronoun or adjective, is singular and must take a singular verb, possessive pronoun, or the like, however much you may be tempted to use plural forms instead: **??** *Each of my parents are about to change their job.*

The *are* should be *is*; but to change the *their* to *his* would produce this sexist and ridiculous sentence: **??** *Each of my parents is about to change his job.* In such cases, avoid *each* altogether, and recast the statement: *Both of my parents are about to change their jobs.*

In a sentence such as *Jane and Neil each follow their own career*, however, the plural verb is now correct because *each* is grammatically subordinate to the plural subject *Jane and Neil*.

2. There is a traditional objection to the use of *each* immediately following a plural pronoun: **?** *He brought us each a present;* **?** *We each knelt and kissed the ground.* The unobjectionably correct forms are: *He brought each of us a present; Each of us knelt and kissed the ground.*

See also BETWEEN; EACH AND EVERY; EVERY; EVERYBODY; and page 176.

each and every Avoid this phrase. It is a cliché, and a tautologous one as well: **?** *My thanks to each and every one of you.* Either *each* or *every* on its own is quite enough.

each other, one another 1. The purists' rule is that *each other* is used of two elements, and *one another* of more than two: *a pair of overgrown children constantly taunting each other; the noise of her fourteen dogs barking at one another.*

Logically and historically, this rule has very little foundation, though it does create a distinction that might – very occasionally – prevent confusion. If you are dealing with traditionalists, at any rate, you had better respect the rule.

2. *One another* has a vagueness and flexibility that gives it an advantage over the more specific and focused *each other* in some contexts. It is possible to say *We fought blindly, slaughtering one another* (which allows for survivors), but not really **??** *We fought blindly, slaughtering each other.*

Even so, avoid this use of *one another* where it conjures up absurd images: *We all stood upon one another's shoulders.*

3. Don't use *each other* or *one another* as a grammatical subject: **X** *They were unaware of what each other were/was doing. Each other* and *one another* can only be objects of verbs or prepositions; so the sentence should read either *They were each unaware of what the other was doing* or *Each was unaware of what the other was doing.*

eatable, edible *Eatable* and *edible* are often interchangeable: *The food in that restaurant is only just eatable/edible.* *Edible* sounds more formal, however, and differs slightly in emphasis.

Eatable tends to refer to the tastiness of prepared food; it means 'reasonably tasty; acceptable': *This rice really needs to boil for a few more minutes before it's eatable.*

Edible tends to refer to different types of food, regardless of their state of preparation; it also distinguishes food from substances that are harmful, or that cannot be swallowed or digested: *edible berries; edible coins – made of chocolate.*

The opposites are *uneatable* and *inedible*; they too are sometimes interchangeable and sometimes distinct in meaning.

For liquids, the adjectives corresponding to *eatable* and *edible* are *drinkable* and *potable.* But *potable* is now rare, and *drinkable* tends to cover both senses.

economic, economical *Economic* is the adjective from *economics* and *the economy*: *a well-read economic theorist; a policy for economic renewal.*

Economical is the adjective from the noun *economy* in the sense of 'thrift'. It can apply to people or organisations (in the sense 'thrifty, or careful in managing resources'), or to things (in the sense 'good value for money, not wasteful'): *hardly the most economical of housewives.*

To complicate matters, *economic* can sometimes be used to suggest thrift too: *It's more economic/economical to buy a whole sheep.*

The two adjectives tend to have different emphases in such contexts, however: *economic* suggests the point of view of the producer, seller, or lessor; *economical* the point of view of the consumer, buyer, or lessee.

So *economic rents* are those that give the landlord a small profit; *economical rents* are those that give the tenant good value.

The two adjectives share a single adverb, *economically*, which is quite wide-ranging accordingly. The verb *to economise* relates to *economical* rather than to *economic.*

See also -ICS.

edible See EATABLE.

effect See AFFECT.

effective, effectual, efficient, efficacious These adjectives do overlap somewhat in meaning, but need to be distinguished.

1. The main sense of *effective* is 'producing the desired effect': *an effective way of keeping your licence.* It can also mean 'impressive', and 'in effect, in operation': *an effective public speaker; The curfew is effective between dusk and dawn.*

Effective can also be used to mean 'in practice, though not in theory'; the adverb *effectively* is perhaps more common in this sense: *Though we were still at war, fighting had effectively ceased.*

2. *Efficient* also suggests the producing of desired results, particularly in a continuing, effortless, and economical process: *a surprisingly efficient military operation.*

3. *Effectual* shares the primary sense of *effective* – 'producing satisfactory results, achieving the intended purpose': *The bombing raid was effective/effectual in closing the railway.*

Effectual can also mean 'capable of achieving results', and here it is preferable to *effective*; its negative is *ineffectual*: *not a very effectual teacher; a mousy, ineffectual little man.*

4. *Efficacious* is rarely used of people; it most commonly refers to remedies or treatments, and means 'potentially effective, capable of producing the desired effect': *an efficacious cure for stress.*

All four adjectives have opposites beginning with *in-*, and adverbs ending in *-ly*.

See also DEFECTIVE.

effeminate, effete The adjective *effeminate* is applied almost exclusively to men. Not to be confused with *feminine* ('womanly'), it means 'unmanly, or womanish': *his effeminate voice.*

Don't confuse it with *effete* either. This adjective originally meant 'exhausted by childbearing', and today properly means 'exhausted, drained of vitality'. Under the influence of *effeminate*, however, it now often has unfavourable tones, and conveys the idea of 'soft, decadent, over-refined, lacking energy or vigour': *an aristocracy grown effete through too much leisure.*

e.g., i.e. 1. Don't confuse these two abbreviations: *e.g.* stands for *exempli gratia*, and means 'for example'; *i.e.* stands for *id est*, and means 'that is, in other words'. So *e.g.* introduces examples, while *i.e.* restates more fully what has preceded: *Grammatical jargon, e.g. 'aspect' or 'medio-passive', is often unhelpful. The Home Office – i.e. the ministry responsible for internal affairs – is the province of the Home Secretary*.

2. The use of either of these abbreviations often indicates laziness on the part of the writer, or at least a rather casual approach. Restrict them to writing that is either very informal on the one hand or very official or technical on the other. Elsewhere use full English phrases, such as *that is (to say), for example, for instance*. Don't, in ordinary usage, expand the abbreviations into full Latin words.

3. If you start a list with *e.g.*, don't end it with *etc*. Each implies that the list is incomplete, so one will be redundant.

4. It is no longer necessary to italicise these abbreviations in running texts; streamlined texts also tend to omit the full stops between the letters – if you do dispense with full stops, try at least to insert a half-space between the two letters each time.

Avoid beginning a sentence with *i.e.* or *e.g.*; the required capital letter would look very strange: **X** *I.e.*, **X** *E.g.*

Some kind of punctuation mark is necessary before these abbreviations – usually a comma, dash, semi-colon, or bracket. But don't use a comma immediately afterwards.

See also VIZ.

egoist, egotist Both of these nouns refer to people who are self-centred, though in different ways. An *egoist* is self-seeking, selfish, and usually ambitious or even ruthless in pursuit of his own interests. An *egotist* is self-important, boastful, and pompous. The *egotist* will relate everything to himself, and so tends to be at worst tiresome and silly. The *egoist* will ensure that everything works to his advantage, and so can be two-faced and dangerous. The *egotist* tends to talk about himself constantly, using the word *I* a great deal. The *egoist* may well, out of devious self-interest, avoid talking about himself altogether.

Related to *egoist* and *egotist* are the nouns *egoism* and *egotism*, and the adjectives *egoistic/al* and *egotistic/al*. In British English, the first syllable of all these words is pronounced like *egg*, though their root word *ego* can also be pronounced with a long *e*: /**ee**goh/. In American English, the long *e* is standard pronunciation for all these words.

egregious The rather impressive ring of this word is perhaps what misleads some people into taking it to mean 'outstanding, excellent'. In fact, in modern English it always has an extremely unfavourable sense, 'outstandingly bad, outrageous': *an egregious lie/liar*. The word is rather high-falutin, and hardly appropriate for everyday speech. If you do happen to say it, make sure to pronounce it correctly. The first *g* is hard, the second soft: /i-**gree**-jəss/.

eighth Note the spelling: two *h*'s, only one *t*.

either 1. *Either* (and *neither*) should be used when referring to two elements only; if there are more than two, use *any* instead: *Of the two, either could win; Of the three, any could win*.

2. *Either* is grammatically singular, so related verbs, pronouns, or possessive adjectives must also be singular: *I don't think either of my children cares about his education*.

The temptation to use plural forms is obviously strong – both because of the plural sense of the sentence and because of the sexist slant of *his*. Hence: **??** *I don't think either of my children care about their education*.

For further details about this and related complications, see pages 176-177.

3. A similar choice of verb will confront you in *either . . . or* constructions that contain pronouns. Again, the verb should agree with the subject closer to it: *Either John or you are going to China; Either I or he is going to China*; **?** *Either he or I am going to China*.

And again, you can avoid the awkwardness of such constructions by rewording the sentence, or by choosing an invariable verb: *Either he is going to China, or I am; Either he or I must go to China*.

4. Although the usual sense of *either* is 'one of two'; it can also mean 'each of two; both' when referring to natural pairs: *There are houses on either side of the road; We have shops at either end of our lane*. This is in fact the oldest sense of *either*, yet some pedants object strongly to it. You can avoid a dispute by using *each* or *both* instead of *either*: *at each end of our lane*, or *at both ends of our lane*.

5. Since *either* strictly applies to two elements only, there is much criticism of the pattern **?** *either . . . or . . . or*: **?** *Either John or James or Mary will help you*. This pattern is very common,

even among good writers of English, and is sometimes disguised by having only one *or*: **?** *Either John, James, or Mary will help you*. It is best to avoid both forms.

6. Ensure that the construction introduced by *either* is of the same pattern as that introduced by *or*, so that a grammatical balance exists in the sentence. The following sentence, for example, is asymmetrical: **X** *The restaurant is either empty or it is full*. You can restore its grammatical balance in several ways: *The restaurant is either empty or full; Either the restaurant is empty or it is full*.

7. Note that both /**ī**thər/ and /**ee**thər/ are acceptable pronunciations. The former is more common in British English, and the latter in American English.

See also NEITHER; NOR; OR; WHETHER.

elder, eldest, older, oldest *Elder* and *eldest* have a narrower range of application than *older* and *oldest*. *Elder/eldest* can refer only to people (usually in family relationships), whereas *older/oldest* can refer to people, things, practices, and so on. And *elder/eldest* is appropriate for fewer grammatical constructions.

Both *elder/eldest* and *older/oldest* can be used as adjectives – *John is the elder/older brother* – and as nouns: *Jane is the eldest/oldest of my three children*. But only *older/oldest* can be used as adjectives detached from their nouns: *Is Jane older than John? Yes, but the child who is oldest is James*.

If *elder* and *eldest* are detached from their nouns, they are no longer adjectives but nouns, preceded by *the, my, an*, and so on: *Jane is the elder; James is the eldest of my children. Older* and *oldest* would be equally appropriate in these sentences, but less appropriate when the immediately preceding word is *an* or *my*: *As an elder daughter she has a lot of responsibilities; James is my eldest*.

Note that only *older* can be followed by *than*, never *elder*.

Outside the context of family relationships, *elder* can be used as an adjective or noun to refer to a longer-serving, older, or senior person: *Of the two, Mr Mills is the elder partner; He is your elder by two years; elders and betters*. And the terms *village elders* and *church elders* have special senses of their own.

elicit, illicit Both words are pronounced /i-**liss**it/, but are otherwise totally unconnected. *Elicit* is a verb meaning 'to draw out, evoke': *I tried to elicit some enthusiasm for his scheme*. *Illicit* is an adjective meaning 'illegal; not allowed by custom or law': *a dealer in illicit drugs*.

See ILLEGAL.

elixir The standard pronunciation is /i-**liks**ər/.

elude, elusive See ALLUDE.

embarrass Note the spelling: double *r*, double *s*.

emigrate, immigrate *To emigrate* means 'to leave one's native country to settle abroad'; *to immigrate* means 'to enter and settle in a new country'. To fix the difference in your mind, think of an *emigrant* as someone who makes an *exit*, and an *immigrant* as someone who comes *in*. A person who *emigrates* is an *emigrant*; one who *immigrates* is an *immigrant*. Note the spellings: *emigrate* and its derivatives have only one *m*; *immigrate* and its derivatives have two.

In Britain, *immigrant* is sometimes used, as noun or adjective, for referring to people who are not white: *the immigrant communities of Bradford*. This may be considered offensive, and is clearly demeaning when applied to people born in the UK. (See also BLACK.)

Finally, don't confuse *to migrate*, meaning 'to move regularly from place to place', with *to emigrate* and *to immigrate* (though *migrant* is sometimes used to mean 'an immigrant'). People *migrate*, but so do birds, animals, and fish.

Note the related noun *migration*, and the common adjective *migrant*: *migrant birds; migrant workers*.

eminent, imminent, immanent These three adjectives are similar in sound, but are quite unrelated in meaning.

Eminent means 'important, prominent, outstanding': *Lord Acton was an eminent historian*.

Imminent means 'about to happen; threatening': *her imminent departure for York*.

Immanent is a rarer word, meaning 'inherent, existing within': *She was blessed with immanent grace*. In philosophical contexts, it means 'occurring only in the mind', and in theological contexts it relates to God's presence throughout the universe.

All three adjectives have related nouns ending in *-ence*.

empathy See SYMPATHY.

encyclopaedia, encyclopedia Both spellings are standard, though *-pedia* is more common in North America, and increasingly common in Britain. The old form *-pædia* is now very rare.

The adjective *encyclopaedic/-pedic* occurs often today in the sense 'comprehensive, covering many subjects': *an encyclopaedic knowledge*.

enervate The verb *to enervate* is sometimes incorrectly used to mean **X** 'to energise' or **X** 'to irritate'. In fact, it means 'to devitalise; to deprive of strength or energy', and occurs most often in its present- or past-participle forms: *the enervating heat; I feel enervated by the heat*.

enjoy The verb *to enjoy* should take a direct object when used in the active voice: *Enjoy the trip! Did you enjoy the show?* Think twice before using the fashionable intransitive exclamation **??** *Enjoy!*, which started its vogue in the U.S. Include a simple object: *Enjoy yourself! Enjoy it/the party!*

ennui The pronunciation is /**oN**-nwee/; the word has not yet lost its French sound.

enormity To careful users of English, the noun *enormity* has strong moral overtones. It means 'extreme wickedness' – *the enormity of the crime* – or 'a monstrous or evil act': *the enormities of the Roman circus*.

Avoid the (increasingly common) use of *enormity* as a morally neutral word meaning 'enormousness, immensity': **X** *the enormity of the mountain*; **X** *with an enormity of effort*.

enquiry, inquiry Some careful users of British English distinguish the two forms. For them, *enquiry* refers to a request for information, and is often in the plural: *I'll make some enquiries about prices*; whereas *inquiry* refers to an investigation, and is often singular: *a court of inquiry*.

Note that North American speakers often stress the first syllable rather than the second: /**ing**-kwəri/.

The related verbs *to enquire* (about) and *to inquire* (into) have developed corresponding senses, though these are less widely observed: British English tends to prefer *enquire* and American *inquire* for both senses.

enrol Note the spelling: single *l* in British English, double *l* in American English.

ensure See ASSURE.

enthral Note the spelling: single *l* in British English, unlike *thrall*; but double *l* in American English.

entomology See ETYMOLOGY.

envelope The pronunciation /**en**-və-lōp/ is standard; the variants /**on**-və-lōp, **oN**-və-lōp/ are acceptable but unnecessary attempts to approach the original French.

The related verb is pronounced /en-**vel**əp/ and spelt *envelop* – no *e* at the end; compare *develop*.

equal, equally As a rule, *equal* cannot be used with the adverbs *more* and *most*: if two things are equal, one cannot be more equal than another. However, *more/most equal* is perhaps permissible if intended to mean 'more/most just or equable' or 'more/most nearly equal': *a more equal share of the estate; the most equal allocation we can achieve*.

Avoid using *equally* with the conjunction *as*: **X** *His wife is equally as accomplished*. This should be either *His wife is as accomplished*, or *His wife is equally accomplished*. And when comparing two things, use only *as*: *His wife is as accomplished as he is*.

Only when *as* is a preposition can it appear with *equally*: *She is equally accomplished as a writer and as a surgeon*.

Note, finally, that when two elements are compared after *equally*, they should be joined by *and*, not *or*: *This is equally offensive to men and women*.

errata Note the correct forms of the word: *erratum* is singular, *errata* is plural – even when *errata* is a collective noun meaning 'a list of mistakes': *The errata appear on page xiv*.

especially See SPECIALLY.

et al. 1. This abbreviation (usually of the Latin *et alii*, 'and others') is useful in formal legal documents or technical reports (but should be avoided in everyday speech and writing): *The editors are Murray, Bradley, et al.*

Note that *et al.* means 'and others' or 'and other people', not 'and all'. And it tends to refer to people, rather than to things or places, for which you should use *etc.* instead. As with *etc.*, try to include at least two named items before writing *et al.*

2. Use *et al.* only if what it refers to is clear. Don't use it out of laziness or ignorance.

Since *et* means 'and', never write *and et al.*

Furthermore, don't use *et al.* at the end of a list that begins with *e.g.*, *such as*, or *for example*. To do so would be tautologous.

See also ET CETERA.

et cetera, etc. 1. The abbreviation *etc.* is best avoided in formal writing, except perhaps in business letters and technical documents. And even the full form *et cetera* (or *etcetera*) sometimes causes censure. It might give the impression of laziness on the part of the writer, an unwillingness to finish the list. Or it might sound pretentious, when good English phrases such as *and so on* or *and the like* are available.

2. Note that *etc.* is usually followed by a full stop, and is best preceded by a comma: *oxygen, hydrogen, helium, etc.*

3. Do make a point of naming at least two items on the list before using *etc.*

And make sure that no uncertainty is possible over what *etc.* refers to: **??** *Many animals – dolphins etc. – can understand commands.* Here the *etc.* merely gives an impression of clumsiness, laziness, or ignorance on the part of the writer.

4. Since the *et* of *et cetera* means 'and', the formula **X** *and etc.* is clearly tautologous. So too is the use of *etc.* at the end of a list that begins *e.g.*, *for example*, or *such as*. These expressions already indicate a list that is incomplete.

5. Although in Latin *et cetera* means 'and the remaining things', in English it is also used to mean 'and/or other things': *You may be offered pâté, asparagus, shrimps, etc.* It can also mean 'and other people', though here the expression *et al.* remains preferable. (See ET AL.)

6. Use *et cetera* even more sparingly when speaking than when writing. If you ever do say the word out loud, make sure to pronounce it something like /et-**set**trə/, not /ek-**set**trə/ as so many people do.

ethical, moral Although these adjectives both have to do with the distinction between right and wrong, they differ in emphasis: *ethical* suggests a theory or system for judging right

from wrong, whereas *moral* tends to refer to concrete choices or actions.

So a dishonest lawyer acts in an *unethical* way, violating his profession's code of *ethics*; and theft is an *immoral*, criminal act, or a violation of *morality*.

The context too plays a part in the choice of word: abortion and contraception tend to be *moral* problems for ordinary people, but *ethical* problems for doctors or scientists. A work of art that champions good against evil is said to be a *moral* work, not an *ethical* one. A medicine that is sold only on prescription is known as an *ethical* drug.

etymology, entomology Be careful not to confuse these two similar-sounding nouns. *Etymology*, means 'the study of the history or origin of words' or simply 'the history of a word'. *Entomology*, refers to the scientific study of insects. Think of the *ent-* in *entomology* as resembling *ant*, and you should remember the distinction easily enough.

even Note how the position of the adverb *even* can alter the meaning of a sentence: *Even I couldn't eat that food* (so no one else could either); *I couldn't even eat that food* (let alone enjoy it); *I couldn't eat even that food* (and it's their *best* food apparently).

The logical position of *even*, then, is as close as possible to the word or phrase it relates to. In idiomatic usage, however, the *even* tends to float about somewhat. So long as there is no danger of ambiguity, the 'neutral' position is acceptable in informal English: *She couldn't even run two miles.* But if ambiguity does threaten, and in formal writing at all times, position the *even* logically rather than idiomatically: *She couldn't run even two miles.*

See also ONLY.

ever 1. In informal questions, the adverb *ever* stands as a separate word when it intensifies *when*, *what*, *how*, or the like: *When ever are you going to finish?* When expressing a collective or general notion in other types of clause, the *-ever* is fused with the preceding word: *Whenever I finish a project, I celebrate.*

2. Take care to position *ever* as close as possible to the element it relates to.

Note the difference in meaning between the following sentences: *Do you ever think you will go home? Do*

you think you will ever go home? The first question assumes that you will go home, and asks whether you think about doing so. The second question seeks only to establish whether you will go home or not.

See also ONLY.

every Note that *every*, like *each*, is grammatically singular, so that all nouns, pronouns, verbs, and possessive adjectives relating to it must be singular too: *Every one of the soldiers present was obliged to swear his allegiance.*

If this seems unduly formal, make the entire sentence plural: *All the soldiers present were obliged to swear their allegiance.*

See also EACH; EACH AND EVERY; EVERY-BODY; and page 176.

everybody, anybody, nobody, somebody Strictly speaking, *everybody*, *nobody*, and so on require singular verbs and pronouns. The same applies to *everyone* and *everything*, *neither*, *either*, *each*, *a person*, *a teacher*, and the like: *Not everyone who applies is certain of a place*; *Anybody who knows should raise his hand*. In colloquial use, or to avoid the alleged sexism of *he*, *him*, and *his*, people often use plural forms: **??** *Does everyone have their passport ready for inspection?* **??** *It's not easy living with an elderly relative when they are not able to look after themselves.*

For ways of avoiding both possible sexism and dubious grammar, see HE, and pages 90 and 176.

See also ANYONE.

exaggerate Note the spelling, one *x*, double *g*.

exalt, exult Don't confuse these two verbs. To *exalt*, /ig-**zawlt**/, means 'to raise (someone) in rank or dignity' or 'to praise highly, glorify, honour': *The dancers ceremonially exalted the king.*

Its related noun is *exaltation*, meaning 'elevation', or 'praise', or 'spiritual delight' – *Sing in exaltation of the Lord!* – and its related adjective is *exalted*, meaning 'raised in rank' or 'lofty, sublime, noble': *the exalted achievements of science.*

To *exult*, /ig-**zult**/, means 'to rejoice greatly' (usually in triumph or victory). Unlike *exalt*, it does not take a direct object: *They exulted at/over the defeat of their enemies.* Its related adjective is *exultant*, and its related noun is *exultation* (not **X** *exultance*).

execrable The stress falls on the first syllable, as in *execute*; second-syllable stress is nonstandard.

exhilarating When writing the word, don't forget the *h*, as in *hilarity*.

exhort Note the spelling: don't omit the *h* even though it is not sounded in the pronunciation.

expatriate This is the correct spelling for the noun, verb, and adjective; **✗** *expatriot* is a common mistake.

expect The verb *to expect* has long been used in the sense of 'to suppose', and is now well established: *Why did he run away? – I expect you frightened him*. Some purists continue to object to this usage, insisting that *expect* should apply only to the anticipation of future events. To be on the safe side, you could use any of the various synonyms instead: *suppose, assume, believe, consider likely*, and so on.

See also ANTICIPATE.

exquisite The stress tends to fall on the second syllable nowadays; the traditional first-syllable stress sounds rather old-fashioned or affected.

extenuate 1. The verb *to extenuate* means 'to make or attempt to make (something) less blameworthy or apparently less serious': *Poverty doesn't extenuate burglary or murder; Don't try to extenuate your guilt.*

Note that *to extenuate* takes as its object an abstract noun with an unfavourable sense; avoid using it with a human object: **✗** *An unhappy childhood does not extenuate him.*

And avoid the common mistake of using *to extenuate* as a synonym for *to justify* or *to excuse*; *to extenuate* an offence or a fault is not to grant a pardon or remove all blame, merely to reduce the blame.

Consider the technical legal phrase *extenuating circumstances* (sometimes called *mitigating circumstances*). In criminal law, these are circumstances – such as drunkenness or provocation – that existed at the time of a crime, and that effectively reduce an offender's legal (though not moral) blameworthiness. *Extenuating circumstances* do not alter a conviction; they merely reduce the offender's punishment.

2. Note also that *to extenuate* is not identical in meaning to *to mitigate*, which means 'to moderate, make less harsh, soften'. Outside its technical senses, *to mitigate* might occur alongside *to extenuate* in criminal law contexts, but not synonymously with it: *The judge accepted the extenuating circumstances, and mitigated his punishment accordingly.*

See also MILITATE.

extraordinary The pronunciation can be either identical to *extra ordinary*, or – slightly preferably – slurred somewhat and stressed on the second syllable: /ik-**strord**'n-ri/.

exult See EXALT.

fabulous The adjective *fabulous* strictly means 'based on or occurring in fable or legend': *The unicorn is a fabulous beast*. By extension, it also means 'astonishing, incredible': *a woman of fabulous wealth.*

Fabulous (or the British contraction *fab*) has now come to be used as a vague term of approval meaning 'splendid, excellent, enjoyable, or the like': **?** *Win a fabulous holiday!* **?** *We had a fabulous day at the beach.*

Avoid such expressions in formal contexts, and avoid overusing them in informal contexts.

Compare FANTASTIC.

facility, faculty Among their many meanings, both these nouns can, in formal settings, refer to a person's power or ability to do something.

Specifically, *facility* means 'an acquired effortless aptitude for doing something, particularly as a result of practice': *a facility in/with/for chess; Living in Paris has given her a facility with French argot.*

By contrast, *faculty* refers to an innate or inherent ability to do something: *is endowed with a faculty for imitating birdsong.*

Note that *faculty* can also refer to any of the innate powers of the body or mind: *the faculty of speech; His faculties are acute, despite his age.*

fact 1. In both speech and writing, be sparing in your use of idioms containing the word *fact: in fact, as a matter of fact, in point of fact, That's a fact, Is that a fact?* and so on. The overuse of such expressions quickly develops into an irritating mannerism.

2. Avoid the ugly and pretentious phrase *the fact that:* **?** *because/due to/in view of the fact that;* **?** *despite/notwithstanding the fact that.* Use *because, although, even though,* or simply *that* instead.

3. Avoid tautologous phrases such as **?** *the true/actual/real facts* and **?** *in actual fact.* A fact is by definition true.

factitious, factious See FICTIONAL.

factor Among its various senses, *factor* quite acceptably means 'an active element or cause that contributes to a process or result': *Increasingly, poverty is a factor in the rising crime rate.*

Factor is also widely used rather more loosely to mean 'a point, feature, possibility, or the like' – without any sense of active contribution: **?** *Everyone has different factors in his childhood.* Think twice before using *factor* in this more generalised sense.

Avoid also the unfortunate practice of combining *factor* with a perfectly good noun to create an unnecessary abstraction: **??** *Don't forget to take the weather factor into account.*

Compare SITUATION.

fahrenheit Note the spelling – not **✗** *-height.*

falter Note the spelling: no *u*; contrast *fault.*

fantastic The adjective *fantastic* originally applied to fantasy: *a fantastic story of elves and goblins*. Nowadays, the word is more commonly used in the vague sense of 'excellent' or 'enjoyable': *We had a fantastic day at the beach.*

Keep this weak use of *fantastic* to a minimum by using more accurate and descriptive adjectives instead. And since the original meaning has been heavily eroded, you may now – when referring to fantasy – have to use *fantastical, imaginative, fanciful,* or the like to avoid ambiguity.

Compare FABULOUS.

Farquhar This surname is usually pronounced /**far**kər/.

farther See FURTHER.

fatal, fateful The basic meaning of *fatal* is 'causing death', as in *a fatal accident*. By extension, it also means 'causing destruction' or 'disastrous': *a fatal error of judgment; Your appearance is fatal to your chances of landing the job*. Popularly, *fatal* has been weakened by overuse to mean simply 'unfortunate' or 'serious': **?** *It's fatal going out without an umbrella.*

Fateful is closer to the idea of *fate*. It means 'affecting one's future destiny',

Ready-Reference Word Guide

and so 'having momentous conse-quences': *All these changes followed on from her fateful decision.* The consequences are usually – though not necessarily – bad. So the word can mean 'ominous' or 'worrying': *the fateful sound of approaching feet.* There is often a strong sense of something preordained, as in *the fateful day that I met him.*

faun, fawn A *faun* is a mythological deity, half man, half goat; a *fawn* is a young deer; *fawn* is a brownish colour; a different word, *to fawn*, means 'to show affection or flatter'.

feasible Strictly, *feasible* means 'prac-ticable, possible to do or accomplish': *Your plan isn't feasible.* Loosely it is used to mean 'plausible', as in **?** *a feasible outcome*, and even 'possible' in almost any sense: **??** *Rain is feasible today.* This usage is pretentious and unnecessary where *possible* or *likely* is available instead.

Compare PRACTICAL.

Featherstonehaugh This surname is often pronounced /**fan**-shaw/.

feature *Feature* tends to be overused. Careful speakers restrict the verb to usages such as *a film featuring Sean Connery*, and avoid it where it means little more than 'to have' or 'to display': **?** *The garden features a pagoda*, or 'to play a part in': **?** *Bad luck featured prominently in his life.* Use a more precise term where possible, such as *exhibit*, *affect*, or *loom*.

As a noun, *feature* is often used thoughtlessly and sloppily, as in *A parade will be one feature of the celebrations.* Why not *highlight of?*

February When pronouncing the word, try to sound the first *r*, even though it is now considered accept-able to neglect it.

feel *To feel* can be followed by either an adjective or an adverb. *I feel certain* or *I feel strong* describes what I think or feel. *I feel differently/strongly about it* describes how I think or feel.

I feel bad can have either emphasis – 'I feel unwell' or 'I'm sorry'. Don't say **??** *I feel badly about losing your hat.*

female See WOMAN

ferment See FOMENT

fervent, fervid Both of these adjec-tives mean 'intensely enthusiastic, passionate, ardent'. However, *fervid*

(and even more so *perfervid*) will usually have a negative tone of excess or fanaticism. So, you might give *fervent support* to the government, but your stupid neighbour lends *fervid support* to the opposition. For this reason, one would be unlikely to say **??** *I fervidly hope he wins.*

Fervid seldom applies directly to people; typically, it describes what they do, say or think: *a fervid speech*, but probably not **?** *a fervid speaker.* *Fervent* has no such limitations.

fewer, less The basic rule is: use *fewer* before plural nouns (*fewer women*, *fewer cars*) and *less* before singular ones (*less money*, *less trouble*). Avoid using *less* before plurals: **X** *a lot less people now than before*; **X** *less than five people.* The same applies to *fewest* and *least* (but *more* and *most* can each take a singular or a plural noun).

For some qualifications to this rule, see page 177.

See also LESS.

fictional, fictitious, factitious, fac-tious, fractious The two adjectives *fictional* and *fictitious* are sometimes interchangeable though usually dis-tinct. *A fictional character* is one, like Sherlock Holmes, who exists in *fiction* – obviously invented story-telling or perhaps a child's imagin-ation. *A fictitious name and address* might be given to the police as *a fiction*, a deliberate attempt to mislead by lying.

Factitious shares with *fictitious* an element of 'bogusness'. It means 'affected, artificially contrived, dis-honestly produced for a special pur-pose', as in *a factitious smile* or *a factitious overvaluation of shares bol-stered by speculation.*

Factious derives from *a faction*, a disapproving term for a small, active group within a political party or movement. So you might speak of *factious in-fighting* or *factious debate.*

Fractious is quite unrelated, meaning 'unruly, troublesome, quarrelsome' – *in a fractious mood* – or 'irritable, peevish': *a fractious infant.*

fiery Note the spelling, reversing the last two letters of *fire.*

fifth When pronouncing the word, don't neglect to sound the second *f.*

finalise This verb smacks of business jargon and is best avoided in other contexts. Try replacing it with a

simple, elegant synonym such as *finish*, *conclude*, *complete*, or *put into final form.*

first 1. Some purists still insist that you should enumerate items in lists *first, secondly, thirdly . . . last.* There is no logic to the rule, though to ignore it may brand you as a philistine in the eyes of some of your audience.

2. Take care not to use *first* tautolo-gously, as in **??** *It was first discovered in 1922* (delete *first*) and **??** *when we had first met* (use *just* or some equivalent term).

See also LAST.

flaccid Purists favour the pronun-ciation /**flak**-sid/, but /**flas**-sid/ is perfectly acceptable.

flagrant See BLATANT.

flammable See INFLAMMABLE.

flaunt, flout If you *flout* authority, the law, and the like, you deliberately disobey it, usually in an open and contemptuous way. If you *flaunt* your wealth, your sex appeal, or the like, you display it ostentatiously or provo-catively, as is clear from the slogan *If you've got it, flaunt it.* A common and ludicrous mistake is to use *flaunt* in place of *flout*: **X** *She flaunts all the written and unwritten regulations.*

floors In Britain you enter buildings on the *ground floor* and go up to the *first floor*, *second floor*, and so on. North Americans tend to start on the *first floor* (sometimes the *ground floor*), the next one up being the *second floor.* Most Latin American countries follow the American system, but the rest of the world tends to share the British system.

See also STOREY.

flotsam, jetsam Cargo or wreckage floating on the surface of the sea is *flotsam.* (Think of *flotsam* as *floating.*) *Jetsam* is either cargo thrown over-board or material that the sea has thrown up on the shore. (Think of *jetsam* as *jettisoned.*)

flounder, founder Take care to keep these two verbs distinct in your speech or writing. Ships *founder* (or *are foundered*) when they sink. Buildings or horses can *founder* when they collapse or stumble. If a company or plan *founders*, it fails.

You might *flounder around* or *about* in the dark or in thick undergrowth; that is, you move clumsily or struggle to keep your balance. You might also *flounder on* through an examination if you struggle on in hopeless confusion. At least if you *flounder* through, you do manage – just – to get through, whereas if you *founder* you probably fail to get through.

flout See FLAUNT.

flu, flue Although *flu* is a contraction of *influenza*, it is now a standard spelling and needs no apostrophe either before or after. A *flue* is the inside of a chimney or similar duct.

focus around See CENTRE AROUND.

focused, focusing These are the preferred spellings in British usage, though a double *s* is also possible.

foment, ferment The verb *to ferment* means literally 'to (cause to) brew or bubble'. Beer *ferments*, or you might *ferment* grape juice. Figuratively, it also means 'to stir up in a dangerous way' or 'to be turbulent'. So you might *ferment* trouble in a crowd (though you can hardly *ferment* the crowd itself), or trouble might *ferment* among the crowd.

Don't confuse it with *to foment*, which also usually means 'to stir up', but in the sense of 'to instigate or excite' – especially trouble or conflict in a subversive manner: *The agitator fomented strife and hatred among the people.* The verb is transitive, and its object is always the resulting trouble; you cannot say **X** *Trouble fomented among the onlookers.*

Sometimes either verb is possible: *Her speech fomented/***?** *fermented a riot.* Worse, both verbs are normally pronounced identically, /fə-**ment**/; when necessary you can use the 'spelling pronunciations' /fō-**ment**/ and /fer-**ment**/ to distinguish them.

forbear, forebear The noun *forebear* means literally 'one who has been before'; that is, 'an ancestor, progenitor, or *forefather*'. It is stressed on the first syllable: /**for**-bair/.

The verb meaning 'to refrain from, to hold back from' is nowadays always spelt *forbear*. It has a past tense *forbore* and a (rare) past participle *forborne*: *I forbore to comment.* Note that it is stressed on the second syllable: /fawr-**bair**, fər-/.

forbid The following patterns are correct: *I forbid you to go; I forbid your going*; and *I forbid your departure*.

The construction **??** *I forbid you from going* is probably modelled on *to prohibit*. Though not standard English, it is now so common that it may soon become fully acceptable. The past tense of *forbid* is spelt *forbade* but usually pronounced /fər-**bad**/, rather than /-**bayd**/.

forecastle The best pronunciation is /**fōk**-s'l/; hence the occasional variant spelling *fo'c'sle*.

forehead The traditional pronunciation is /**for**rid/, like *torrid*, but /**for**-hed/ is acceptable and increasingly common, especially in North America.

forensic The adjective *forensic* means 'relating to or used in law cases or courts'. A *forensic scientist* works, usually for the police, at analysing clues and evidence; and *forensic medicine* (or *medical jurisprudence*) is the application of medical science to legal problems.

So it is tautologous to speak of *presenting forensic evidence to a court* – all court evidence is *forensic*. Use *technical*, *scientific*, or *medical* instead, as applicable.

forever, for ever Careful writers maintain a distinction between *forever*, meaning 'constantly, or incessantly', and *for ever*, meaning 'for all time, eternally'. So you might write *He is forever complaining about them*, but *I'll love you for ever* and *Liverpool for ever!*

foreword This is the correct spelling for the word referring to the preface of a book. Think of it as the *words* that appear be*fore* the main body of the text, and you should then avoid the common mistake of spelling it *forward* or **X** *forword*.

forgo, forego The *foregoing* comments are ones that have gone before. A *foregone conclusion* is one that is utterly predictable. But if you *forgo* (past tense *forwent*) an opportunity, you give it up or do without it.

Compare FORBEAR.

former, latter 1. These are useful words sometimes, helping to avoid ambiguity or long-winded repetition: *Professor Heinrich von Hügel and the Marquis de Charenton were there – the former tall and elegant, the latter short and scruffy.*

But don't use them if they complicate rather than simplify matters, or if you

just intend to sound 'impressive': **??** *Mr and Mrs Jones were there – the former tall and elegant, the latter short and scruffy.* Here the simple *he* and *she* would be more appropriate. And when used in long sentences, *former* and *latter* tend to force the reader to look back to find out what is being referred to. In such cases it is usually better to repeat the noun or name.

2. There must be two and only two similar items:

X *Jones, Smith, and Brown were there – the former tall and elegant as ever.* In such cases, use *the first* or *the last*, or repeat the name. **X** *The manager congratulated me and handed me my bonus – the latter came to £250.* Use *it* or *which* instead.

And make sure it is clear which is *the former* and which *the latter*: **??** *P.C. Blake stopped Watts because he was laughing at him: the latter then allegedly started swearing.* Who swore, Blake or Watts?

See also RESPECTIVE.

formidable Traditionally, the stress falls on the first syllable; second-syllable stress is now widespread, however, and generally considered acceptable.

formula The plural *formulae* is slightly preferable in all scientific contexts – *chemical/mathematical formulae* – and *formulas* elsewhere: *political formulas*.

forte Strictly speaking, the correct pronunciation is /fort/: the word was adopted from French rather than Italian, and /fort/ seems to be the favoured pronunciation in North America. But in British English, /**for**-tay/ and /**for**-ti/ are more common, and are widely accepted.

fortuitous This adjective does not mean the same as *fortunate*. Though both are related to *fortune*, *fortuitous* has a neutral rather than favourable tone. It means simply 'accidental, unplanned, by chance': *a fortuitous meeting, a fortuitous discovery*. Don't say: **X** *I found the lost key through a fortuitous coincidence* if you really mean *a fortunate coincidence* (or *happy* or *felicitous coincidence*). In any event, all coincidences are fortuitous, so the sentence is tautologous.

founder See FLOUNDER.

fount, font The forms *fount* and *font* are both used to refer to a complete set of printing type. Traditionally, both are pronounced /font/, with *fount* the British spelling and *font* the American.

The spelling *font* is becoming more common in British English too, and some of those who still use *fount* tend to mispronounce it /fownt/.

fraction A *fraction* can just as well be nine-tenths as one-tenth, so the use of *only a fraction* to mean 'only a very small proportion' would seem to be very risky. It is now so widespread, however, that it probably qualifies as a standard idiom.

See also PER CENT; PROPORTION.

fractious See FICTIONAL.

Frankenstein In Mary Shelley's novel and the films based on it, *Frankenstein* is the scientist who creates the monster, not the monster itself. So to say that **X** *Stalin created a Frankenstein in his secret police* is wrong. Stalin was the Frankenstein; the secret police was a Frankenstein's monster.

frightfully See AWFULLY.

-ful The modern plurals are *two spoonfuls*, *three cupfuls*, and the like.

fulfil Note the spelling: in British English, a single *l* in each syllable; hence *fulfilment* (though usually *fulfill* and *fulfillment* in North America).

But the second *l* is doubled in *fulfilled* and *fulfilling*.

fulsome In modern English the adjective *fulsome* does not mean 'full, lavish'. It usually occurs in expressions such as *fulsome praise* or *fulsome enthusiasm*, and means 'overabundant, excessive' and so 'extravagant and insincere'.

The current standard pronunciation is /fool-səm/, with the first syllable sounding like *full*; /fulsəm/, with the first syllable rhyming with *hull*, is now out of date.

function Both as a noun and as a verb, function has become a vogue word or buzz word, inviting excessive or pretentious use, as in all the following examples: *my function within the company* ('my role'); *I don't function well in the mornings* ('I'm not much good'); *an official function* ('party, lunch, event'); *Increased costs are a function of high wages* ('High wages cause increased costs').

Use *function* sparingly. For the verb, consider such alternatives as *to work*, *to perform*, *to serve*, *to operate*, *to depend on*. For the noun, try *use*, *job*, *role*, *duty*, and the like.

fungus, fungous The noun is *fungus*, and the adjective *fungous* (pronounced identically) or *fungal*.

The plural of *fungus* is *fungi*, pronounced /fung-gi/ or /fun-ji/. *Funguses* is also now acceptable.

furore The pronunciation /fewr-**raw**-ri/ is preferable to **?**/fewr-or/, unless it is spelt *furor*, as in American English.

further, farther Both as adjectives and adverbs these forms are usually interchangeable. *Further* is commoner in colloquial British English, especially when the use is figurative: *further from the truth*. When speaking of literal distances, many people prefer *farther*: *a little farther to your right*. (These comments apply equally to *furthest* and *farthest*.)

Sometimes only *further* is possible: *one further suggestion*; *I further suggest...*; *Further to my letter of...*; *Further, I object to your attitude*.

Furthermore, only *further* acts as a verb, as in *His sole concern seems to be to further his own aims*.

gala The miner's festival is still a /**gay**lə/, but the swimming competition is usually a /**gaa**-lə/ nowadays.

gallant The pronunciation /**gal**-ənt/ is standard for all uses, but /gə-**lant**/ is also used in the senses 'a woman's lover' or 'attentive to women, chivalrous'; **?**/gə-**laant**/ is a regional or affected usage.

gaol See JAIL.

garage The pronunciation can be /**garr**-aazh/ or – slightly preferably – /**garr**ij/ in British English; in American English the stress shifts to the second syllable: /gə-**raazh**, -**raaj**/.

gas The preferred spelling of the plural is *gases*, but the verb forms are usually *gasses*, *gassing*, and *gassed*.

gauge Note the spelling: -au-, not **X** *guage*; the form *gage* occurs sometimes in North American English and in seamen's usage.

gay It is now very difficult to use the adjective *gay* unselfconsciously with the sense 'brightly-coloured' or 'cheerful, fun-loving, in high spirits, chirpy'. Everyone realises that the commonest current meaning is 'homosexual', and people only sound reactionary by insisting on using it as if it were not. Note, however, that this sense does not extend to derived words, such as *gaiety* and *gaily/gayly*.

In its modern sense, the word remains slightly informal: in technical or formal contexts, *homosexual* would be more appropriate. As an adjective it applies to men or women equally: *gay London*; *a gay disco*. But as a noun it generally refers only to male homosexuals: *a disco for gays and lesbians*.

genealogy Note the spelling and pronunciation: *-alogy* not **X** *-ology*; hence /**jee**ni-**all**ə-ji/.

genius For the sense 'a brilliantly talented person', the plural is *geniuses*. For the senses 'a guardian spirit' and 'a demon in Muslim folklore', the plural is *genii*.

geometry Note the pronunciation – there are four syllables: /jee-**om**-ətri/, **X** /**jom**-ətri/.

get, got, gotten 1. Being the most grammatically versatile verb in English, *get* is often criticised for being overused. But you cannot always avoid it, even if you wanted to: *I got up late*; *They got engaged/started*; *Get lost! Get well soon!*

The level of formality of *get* varies. Some usages, such as *I get on well with him* and *They got married*, are fully acceptable in all except the most formal contexts. Others, such as **?** *That work will get itself done in no time* and **?** *It's time you got doing something useful*, are very informal.

Don't go out of your way to weed out all the *get*'s in normal speaking or writing. *I got a book* serves adequately for 'received' or 'obtained'; *I got to work* for 'arrived'; *I got impatient* for 'became'; *I got the flu* for 'caught' or 'suffered from', and so on.

Over-formality is as much an error of style as 'over-informality'.

2. The same is true of *have got* in the sense of 'to own, have', and *have got to* in the sense of 'must'. Stylistically these forms are seldom used in formal written English, but are normal for everyday speech: *Have you got a light? Have you got to leave?* The alternatives – *Do you have a light?* **?** *Have you a light? Do you have to leave?* **??** *Have you to leave* – sound either American or old-fashioned. See HAVE **2, 3**.

When using *have got* constructions, don't drop the *have*: **X** *I got three* *sisters*. **✗** *How many you got?* **✗** *Sorry, I got to go now.*

3. British and American usage differs in some respect. American English prefers *Do you have any ideas?* where British English prefers *Have you got any ideas?* Whereas the past participle *gotten* has faded from British English except in the phrase *ill-gotten gains*, American English retains it in 'active' senses of *get*. So Americans can distinguish between *I've got a new book* (= I have a new book) and *I've gotten a new book* (= I've acquired/ bought a new book); between *I've got to go to the party* (= I must go to the party) and *I've gotten to go to the party* (= I've managed to obtain an invitation to the party).

girl See WOMAN.

glacier The pronunciation can be either /**glas**-i-ər/ or /**glay**si-ər/; in North American English, the word is sometimes pronounced /**glay**-shər/ and even /**glay**-zhər/. The adjective *glacial* is best pronounced /**glay**-sh'l/, rhyming with *racial*.

glower The correct pronunciation is: /**glow**-ər, glowr/, to rhyme with *power*; never **✗** /**glō**-wər/.

got, gotten See GET.

gourmand, gourmet A *gourmand* is someone who enjoys eating heartily – almost a glutton. Its traditional English pronunciation is /**goor**mənd/ but the Frenchified /goor-**moN**/ has taken over. The verb *to gormandise* – note the spelling – means 'to stuff oneself, gorge'. Another noun, *gourmandise*, /goormən-**deez**/, has a more favourable sense, as though related to *gourmet*. It means 'a refined appreciation of good food'.

A *gourmet* is a person with refined tastes in food. The word is often used as an adjective, as in *a gourmet dinner*. In such constructions, it is often little more than an affected way of saying 'fine and fancy'. As a fairly recent borrowing, *gourmet* maintains its more or less French pronunciation of /**goor**-may/ or even /goor-**may**/.

government When pronouncing the word, try to sound the first *n*, even though it is now considered acceptable to neglect it.

graffiti Note the spelling: double *f*, single *t*.

Graffiti is widely used as an 'uncountable' noun, and treated as singular: *All*

that graffiti upsets me. Some purists insist that it is really plural – *All those graffiti upset me* – and for the singular form would use something like *an item of graffiti* or even **?** *a graffito*.

granddad The double *d* in the spelling is preferable to **?** *grandad*.

Great Britain See BRITAIN.

Greek, Grecian Should you speak of a *Greek urn* or a *Grecian urn?*

Greek is the general adjective used for Greece, ancient or modern, its people, language, customs, and church. So a *Greek urn* is perfectly correct.

The poet Keats, however, wrote an ode on the subject of a *Grecian urn*. Although the urn was presumably from Greece, *Grecian* usually has the less restricted sense 'in or of a Greek style'. Buildings in London have *Grecian columns*; a *Grecian nose* is long and straight, forming an unbroken line down from the forehead.

Greenwich Note the pronunciation: /**grinn**-ij , **grenn**-, -ich/.

Grenada Note the spelling and pronunciation for this Caribbean island: /grə-**nay**də/, much like *grenade*. Contrast the Spanish city of Granada, /grə-**naa**də/.

grey Note the spelling. But the American spelling is *gray* – except in *greyhound*. Be careful with names: Zane *Grey* the novelist, but Thomas *Gray* the poet; Lady Jane *Grey* but *Gray's* Inn, London.

grisly, gristly, grizzly Note the spellings: *a grisly murder, gristly meat, a grizzly bear.*

guerrilla, guerilla Both spellings are acceptable, but double *r* is preferable, being closer to the Spanish original, the diminutive of *guerra*, 'war'. Don't omit the *u*.

The pronunciation is identical to that of *gorilla*; it sounds affected to pronounce the first syllable in a more foreign-sounding way.

gunwale The pronunciation of this common nautical term is /**gun**-n'l/, rhyming with *tunnel*; hence the alternative spelling *gunnel*.

Gypsy, Gipsy Both spellings are correct, though the former is slightly preferable, since the word derives from *Egyptian*. Either form can be spelt with a small *g*.

haemorrhage, haemorrhoid Note the spellings: -*rrh*-, as in *catarrh* and *diarrhoea*. The first element is *haemo*- in British English, but generally *hemo*- in American English.

hallo See HELLO.

hangar, hanger A *hangar* is the garage for aircraft; *hanger* as in *coathanger* is a different word entirely.

hanged See HUNG.

harass, harassment Note the spelling: single *r*, double *s*. In pronunciation, the stress traditionally falls on the first syllable: /**har**rəss/; a second-syllable stress has now become fairly common – **?** /hə-**rass**, **?** /hə-**rass**mənt/ – to the dismay of purists.

hardly 1. The adverb from *hard* is *hard*, not *hardly*: *to work hard for one's exams; to hit hard.*

2. The words *hardly, barely*, and *scarcely* are 'semi-negatives' and should not be used with other negatives: **✗** *I couldn't hardly believe my eyes.*

3. *Hardly* and *scarcely* are not comparative forms. So **✗** *Hardly had I arrived than the fire started* is incorrect; it should read *Hardly had I arrived when the fire started.*

have 1. Some writers look back to a supposed old distinction between *I haven't (got) any money* (= at present) and *I don't have any money* (= usually, generally). Whether or not such a distinction ever was consistently observed, it is very rarely made in modern English.

2. North American English favours the constructions *Do you have any children?* and *I don't have any children.* British English tend to prefer *Have you got any children?* and *I haven't got any children.* But neither variety is consistent in its usage. And for the past tense, both varieties favour the forms *Did you have any children?* and *I didn't have any children.*

Have you any children? and *I haven't any children* are slightly old-fashioned and formal. *I have no children*, however, is less so.

For positive statements, American English tends towards *I have two children.* This is common in British English also, alongside *I've got two children.*

3. Similar variations occur with *have to* and *have got to*, meaning 'must'.

American English tends towards *I have to go now* and British English towards *I've got to go now*, though both forms are fully acceptable in both varieties. For the negative form, British English allows both *I haven't got to go* and *I don't have to go*; American English admits only the latter.

4. In ordinary speech, both *have* and *of* are often reduced to the sound /əv/: *I could* /əv/ *done it*; *a couple* /əv/ *eggs*. The danger arises, then, of saying (or writing) *of* instead of *have* when expanding this sound to its full form: **✗** *I could of done it*; **✗** *I most certainly could of*.

5. A traditional rule frowns on sentences such as **?** *I have dark hair, just as my father did*, preferring to repeat the *have*: *I have dark hair, just as my father had*. But both forms are acceptable nowadays.

6. The verb *have* is sometimes inserted or repeated needlessly in a sentence: **??** *Even if I'd have known, I wouldn't have gone*. This should read *Even if I'd known, ...*

For further details, see pages 188-189.

Hawaii Note the spelling; accordingly, the word *Hawaiian* has four vowels in a row.

hazelnut Note the spelling: *-el-*, not **✗** *-le*.

he, him, his Traditionally, these forms can refer to any human being, male or female, when the sex is unknown or irrelevant. But the suggestion of sexism has recently put such usages under a cloud: *Everyone can solve his own problems if he tries*; *When a child hears a riddle, it riles him*, and so on.

Various alternatives are available, often unsatisfactory; for example:

Everyone can solve his or her own problems if he or she tries. This non-sexist version does unfortunately sometimes sound pedantic, especially if overused.

? *Everyone can solve their own problems if they try*. The grammatical conflict between the singular *everyone* and the plural *them* or *their* makes this version unacceptable in formal contexts. In less formal speech or writing, it is now very common.

The two best strategies, if suitable, are to use *you*, *your*, *yours*; and to couch everything in the plural: *You can solve your own problems if you try*; *When children hear a riddle, it intrigues them*.

See also ONE; YOU; MAN; and pages 90 and 176.

hegemony Two pronunciations, /hi-**gem**məni/ and /**heji**-məni/, are standard; /hi-**jem**məni/ is common in North American speech.

heinous The best pronunciation is /**hay**nəss/, rhyming with *Janus*; a form rhyming with *Venus* is also possible; but pronunciation like that of *highness* is nonstandard.

hello, hallo, hullo All three spellings are correct; as listed, they are probably in order of current frequency.

help 1. The common construction *cannot help but*, as in **?** *I couldn't help but admire her*, is time-honoured in colloquial English. But if you analyse it, its logical structure suggests the very opposite of what it is intended to mean. Accordingly, it is best to avoid it in more formal contexts. It comes from a blend of the somewhat formal *I could not but admire her* and *I couldn't help admiring her*.

2. The common expressions *more than I can help* and *as little as I can help* also suffer from a lack of logic, and provoke objections accordingly: **?** *I won't work any harder than I can help*; **?** *I made as little noise as I could help*. To be on the safe side, use *more than I have to*, *as little as I could*, or the like.

3. Sentences such as **?** *I helped Bob wash up* are very widespread nowadays. But many careful writers still insist on retaining the traditional *to*: *I helped Bob to wash up*. All the more so when the subject is a thing: *These pills will help you to relax*.

hence, hither These words are archaic or extremely old-fashioned when they refer to place: **?** *He went hence/came hither yesterday*. In their other senses they tend to be rather formal or jocular.

Hither is now restricted to certain fixed idioms: *hither and thither* ('all over the place'); *a come-hither look* ('alluring').

Hence has two main meanings in current English: 'from now', as in *five months hence*; and 'therefore, consequently', as in *I was not there, and hence do not know*. Don't use **??** *from hence* in either construction.

hero The plural is *heroes*, not **?** *heros*.

hiccup, hiccough The original and preferable form is *hiccup*. *Hiccough*,

with the same pronunciation, is a later (incorrect) attempt to explain the origin of the word. Both forms are acceptable in both literal and figurative senses (*a hiccup in our plans*), though *hiccup* is far commoner. Note the spelling of *hiccupping* and *hiccupped* – each with a double *p*.

him, his See HE.

hire, rent, let, lease In British English, if you pay for the temporary use of something you *hire* or *rent* it. Typically, you *hire* vehicles and clothes, or a room or building for a short period: *They hired a hall for the exhibition*; the owner *hires* them *out* to you. You can *rent* a television and land, or a room or building for a longer term, or a car (though you would *charter* a bus, ship, or aircraft); the owner *lets* or *rents* them to you. A landlord or tenant *leases* land or a building by contract for a stated, usually long, period.

Usage in American English is more fluid, with *rent* being used more widely. Both the owner and the payer can *rent* a room or suit for a single evening.

See also LOAN.

historic, historical Something *historic* is so important that it is deserving of a place in history; something *historical* is not necessarily important: it is simply something that happened in the past. So you can talk on the one hand of *historical research*; *historical novels*; *historical events* (events that actually happened, as opposed to fictional ones); and on the other hand *tomorrow's historic meeting between the superpowers*.

The word *historic* is overused and should be avoided if the events are less than truly important: **?** *a historic victory for Welsh weightlifting*.

See also A, AN.

hither See HENCE.

hoard, horde These verbs both suggest large numbers but they usually need careful distinguishing.

A *hoard* is a secret store or accumulation, of food, gold, ideas or the like. The word is used informally in the plural to mean 'a very large amount': *hoards of time*. As a verb it has a negative tone of miserliness or selfishness: *to hoard jewels*; *hoarded food*. A *horde* is a large, and usually unruly or threatening group of people or animals: *barbarian hordes*; *a horde of football hooligans*; *a horde of stamped-*

ing buffalo. Loosely, *hordes* can be used disapprovingly of any large group of people: *We're expecting hordes of relatives*.

Holborn This London place-name is usually pronounced /**hō**bən/.

honorary Note the spelling: like *honorarium*, and unlike *honourable*, it contains no *u*.

When pronouncing *honorary*, try to retain the second and third syllables: /**on**nə-rəri/, rather than **??** /**on**-ri/.

hopefully Nobody objects to the use of *hopefully* as an adverb of manner: *Rover looked up hopefully as I opened the tin*. But traditionalists shudder when it is used to mean 'I hope, it is to be hoped': *Hopefully she'll be back soon*. They consider it a corrupt and unnecessary Americanism, and a source of ambiguity.

But in its new sense, *hopefully* functions in a very similar way to that of other, uncontroversial, sentence adverbs, as in: *Regrettably I can't come* and *Frankly I'm disgusted*. The possibility of ambiguity is as slight as it is with, say, *sadly*: *Sadly, I can't come*; *He looked at her sadly*.

It is not always easy to replace *hopefully* by *I hope, it is to be hoped, with luck*, or the like. Consider the difference in tone between the following two sentences: *I hope Sunderland get promoted*; *Hopefully Sunderland will get promoted*. The first suggests a personal wish; the second sounds more like a disinterested judgment on what is best for everyone. Similarly, note the difference between *Hopefully the jury will acquit him* and *With luck the jury will acquit him*.

Similar objections and counterarguments apply to *mercifully* – *Mercifully, it's stopped raining* – and, with more justice, to *regretfully*: **?** *Regretfully, it's stopped raining*. Here the use of *Regrettably* is surely preferable.

As so often, those who object to the new use of *hopefully* are fighting against the inevitable. The usage is now firmly entrenched in modern English idiom. The only reason to avoid it is a wish not to sound illiterate in the ears of traditionalists.

horde See HOARD.

horrid, horrible These words originally referred to 'horror' or 'bristling with fear', and had distinct meanings. *Horrid* meant 'shaggy, bristling', *horrible* 'creating horror'.

As with many other words having unfavourable suggestions – *dreadful, terrible, frightful*, and so on – these and related adjectives and adverbs have been weakened in informal language, and now often suggest merely a general disapproval: **?** *a horrid/ horrible day*.

Use such words sparingly – try *disagreeable, outrageous, nasty*, and the like. And make clear what you are doing if you do use one of them in its original meaning: *truly horrible pictures of the famine*.

See also AWFULLY.

hospitable Traditionally, the stress falls on the first syllable; second-syllable stress is more common now, however, and generally considered acceptable.

however 1. Don't confuse *however* and *how ever*, as in *How ever did you do it?* See EVER **1** for more on when to use one word and when two.

2. *However* usually has the same meaning as 'nevertheless, but'; but unlike *but*, it can appear elsewhere than at the start of a clause. When *but* and *however* mean the same, don't use both: **X** *But I should add, however, that there are problems*. In other senses of *however*, this does not apply: *But however you do it, do it well*.

3. Though *however* in the sense of 'but' certainly may open sentences, it often sounds better if positioned after an opening phrase or clause. In very correct speech, it should be used directly after the word or phrase that is being held up for contrast. Compare: *I, however, do not agree* (= Most people agree but I don't) with *I do not, however, agree* (= Despite the arguments, I still don't agree).

4. In Standard English *however* is often 'bracketed' by commas. In line with the modern tendency to reduce unnecessary punctuation however, the commas are often omitted, especially the first one. Do use commas, however, if omitting them might lead your readers down the wrong track. Compare: *However she decided to do it, she always made sure she did it well* with *However, she decided to do it and did it well*.

hullo See HELLO.

humorous Note how the second *u* of *humour* is dropped in the spelling.

hung, hanged Traditionally, pictures are *hung* and condemned men are

hanged. Careful speakers still observe this distinction. *Hanged*, then, is the past tense and past participle of the transitive verb *to hang* when it means 'to kill by hanging': *Judas went and hanged himself*.

hypo-, hyper- These word elements are usually opposites, *hypo-* meaning 'under, insufficiently', and *hyper-* meaning 'over, excessively'. So *hyperthermia* means 'excessively high body temperature'. *Hypothermia*, the far commoner word, means 'excessively low body temperature'.

And don't confuse the adjectives *hypercritical*, /**hī**pər-**krit**ik'l/, 'excessively critical, nitpicking', and *hypocritical*, /**hip**pə-**krit**tik'l/, 'insincere, two-faced'. Note how the associated nouns are spelt: a *hypocrite* is a person who is guilty of *hypocrisy*.

I See ME.

-ic, -ical See CLASSIC; COMIC; ECONOMIC; HISTORIC.

-ics *Politics is* or *politics are*? Nouns ending in *-ics* take a singular verb when they refer to the subject, study, or science: *Gymnastics is fun*. They take a plural verb when they refer to a set of practices, operations, or qualities: *His mental gymnastics are beyond me*; *The acoustics were poor*; *My politics are none of your business*.

A hint to help: when the word is preceded by *the*, *my*, *your*, or the like, the verb is likely to be plural: *Your statistics are misleading*. When the word is preceded by *a* or by no such word at all, the verb is likely to be singular: *Statistics is a dull subject*; *He favoured a politics of hatred*.

idiosyncrasy Note the spelling: two *i*'s, and two *y*'s; *-syn-*, not **X** *-sin-*; ends in *-asy*, as in *ecstasy*, not **X** *-acy*, as in *democracy*.

i.e. See E.G.

if Compare *She will come if you invite her* with *She would come if you invited her*. The first poses an open or likely condition, and so takes ordinary indicative verb forms; the second poses a remote or hypothetical (or impossible) condition, and therefore takes subjunctive verb forms.

Similarly, *If I am ill, I shall not go* and *If I were you, I should not go*.

Note that *should* is now commonly added to modernise the subjunctive form. Instead of the old-fashioned

If I be killed . . ., modern idiom favours *If I should be killed . . .*

See also WHETHER, and page 195.

if and when Other than in legal formulas, this phrase is usually unnecessary and verbose: **??** *If and when he comes, I'll be ready. If* includes *when*. Say *When he comes, I'll be ready* if he is certain to come. Say *If he comes, I'll be ready* if there is any doubt.

Think twice too before using the similar phrases *as and when* and *unless and until*.

ilk This word, originally meaning 'the same, identical', was for centuries restricted to Scottish personal names, such as *Ruthven of that ilk*.

The modern extensions of this usage can sound pretentious (or jocular). *Of that ilk*, in the sense 'of that type' – as in *I can't stand people/films of that ilk* is generally acceptable in modern English idiom, though best avoided in very formal contexts. Closely related constructions such as **?** *I can't stand people of his ilk* and **?** *I can't stand him and his ilk* are less acceptable. There are plenty of alternatives: *people like him, him and his like/sort/lot, the likes of him*, and so on.

Using *ilk* with *same* is not acceptable: **X** *I can't stand him and people of the same ilk*.

illegal, illegitimate, illicit, unlawful These four adjectives overlap but tend to be used in different contexts.

Something *illegal* is against the law of the land – *illegal drugs* – or some other fixed code of regulations: *an illegal shot in snooker*. *Unlawful* means much the same, but it is rather old-fashioned and usually restricted to set legal phrases – *unlawful wounding* – or religious contexts: *Eating pork is unlawful in Judaism and Islam*.

Illegitimate is used most often of children born out of wedlock; it means literally 'not recognised by law'. It also has a wider sense of 'not according to the laws of justice, propriety, reason, or logic': *an illegitimate deduction from the data*.

Illicit is close to 'unlicensed'. You can speak of *illicit stills* and *illicit gambling* – what is forbidden here is not the things themselves but the way in which they are performed.

Of the opposites, *legal, lawful*, and *legitimate* are in common use, but *licit* is very rare.

See also ELICIT; LEGAL.

immigrate, immigrant See EMIGRATE.

imminent, immanent See EMINENT.

immoral, amoral An *immoral* act or person is one that goes against normal moral standards, and so means 'wicked, corrupt'. An *amoral* act or person is one that makes no reference to moral standards: *amoral business practices*.

imperial, imperious, imperative These three adjectives share shades of meaning but should be kept distinct.

The chief meanings of *imperial* are 'relating to an empire or emperor': *the imperial crown*; 'commanding, or majestic': *an imperial bearing*; and 'of the traditional system of weights and measures': *the imperial pint*.

The second of these meanings is also found in *imperious*, but here there is always a negative tone of 'overbearing, haughty; domineering': *an imperious demand/leader brooking no refusal*.

Something that is *imperative* expresses a command or plea. In grammar the *imperative* is the verb form used in commands: *Shut up! Gentlemen, raise your glasses*.

It can also mean 'peremptory, abrupt' – *an imperative tone of voice* – but nowadays occurs most often in a looser sense of 'essential, obligatory': *It's imperative to leave at once*.

Imperative can also be a noun, meaning 'an order'. The noun from *imperious* is *imperiousness*.

Note the pronunciations: *imperative* has a short *e*: /im-**per**rətiv/; the others have a long /ee/ sound: /im-**peer**-i-əl/ and /im-**peer**-i-əss/.

impious The pronunciation is /**im**pi-əss/. Contrast *pious*.

imply, infer In modern English these verbs are quite distinct.

To imply means 'to suggest, or to indicate': *Are you implying that I'm stupid*. Don't use *infer* here: **X** *Are you inferring that I'm stupid*. This is a very common error.

The other chief meaning of *to imply* is 'to have as an inevitable consequence': *Poverty need not imply squalor*.

To infer means 'to conclude from the given information': *I infer from this that you disagree*. It is the speaker who *implies* something and the listener who *infers* it.

Curiously, 'to infer' did mean 'to imply' in past centuries (and vice versa), but careful speakers today keep strictly to the modern distinction.

Note the spelling and stress patterns: *infer, inferred*, and *inferring* have the emphasis on the second syllable; *inference* has it on the first.

See also DEDUCTION.

impotent The correct pronunciation is /**im**pətənt/. Contrast *potent*.

impractical, impracticable See PRAC-TICABLE.

in so far as This is often written as two words – **?** *insofar as*. Purists prefer it as four: *in so far as*.

in spite of See DESPITE.

inasmuch as 1. Unlike **?** *insofar as*, both *inasmuch as* and *in as much as* are fully acceptable. The variant **X** *in as much that* is incorrect. The forms *insomuch as* and *in so much as* are rather old-fashioned.

2. The phrase *inasmuch as* raises various problems; think twice before using it at all.

In its modern sense it is merely a pompous way of saying 'since' or 'because': **?** *I cannot be blamed, inasmuch as I was absent that day*.

In this example a colon or dash would be quite sufficient.

It is also ambiguous. In the sentence *My day was spoiled inasmuch as I had to watch the children*, does *inasmuch as* mean 'because' or 'to the extent that'?

inches The correct abbreviation is *in*. rather than **?** *ins*.

inconceivable See UNTHINKABLE.

index Note the plural forms. Alphabetic lists of contents are *indexes*. Use *indices* only when referring to formulas in mathematics, economics, and the like.

Indian Take care when using this word. Its precise meaning varies according to context. Is *an Indian drum* from India or Canada? Would it be proper to call a Punjabi a *West Indian*? If there is any doubt, spell out your intended meaning more fully.

The chief meanings are:

☐ A citizen or inhabitant of the Republic of India.

☐ In references before 1947, an indigenous inhabitant of the entire subcontinent, including Pakistan, Bangladesh, and perhaps Sri Lanka, and sometimes other areas such as Malaya, which was part of the 'East Indies'.

☐ A descendant of someone from these regions living in Britain, Africa, the West Indies, or elsewhere. In Britain the term *Asian* is now more common in this sense. (See ASIAN.)

☐ An indigenous inhabitant of the Americas (except for an Inuit – that is, an Eskimo). The expression *Red Indian* is now considered offensive. Increasingly the ambiguity is avoided by terms such as *American Indian*, *Amerindian*, *Aboriginal American*, or *Native American*. Best of all is to specify the group: *Amazon Indian*, *Hopi Indian*.

See also BLACK.

indigenous Note the spelling: the -*gen*- stem is shared by *genetics*, *progenitor*, and so on.

individual As nouns, *individual* and *individuals* mean little more than simply 'a person' and 'people': **?** *I arrested a number of individuals for abusive language*. Such uses tend to sound irritatingly pompous or quaint, unless intended for humorous effect: *What a scruffy individual!*

Where the noun is fully justifiable is in emphasising the difference between the *individual* and the group: *the rights of the individual*.

induction See DEDUCTION.

inequity, iniquity The noun *inequity* is the opposite of *equity* and means 'unfairness, injustice': *the inequity of their inherited shares*. Its adjective is *inequitable*, 'unjust'.

Iniquity means 'wickedness, or immorality' – *a den of iniquity* – or 'an immoral act, a sin'. The adjective is *iniquitous*, 'wicked'.

infer See IMPLY.

infinite, infinitely Something *infinite* is 'endless', whether in distance, number, quality, or whatever. Inevitably the word has been debased to mean merely 'very great', as in **?** *infinite harm* or **?** *an infinitely better chance*. Do think twice before using it in this loose way. Try alternatives such as *incalculable*, *vast*, or *considerably*.

infinitesimal Don't be misled by the impressive ring of this adjective and its kinship with *infinite* into thinking it means something like 'vast' or 'magnificent'. In fact it means 'infinitely or immeasurably small': *an infinitesimal particle/wink*.

The main stress falls on the fourth syllable: /**in**-fini-**tess**i-m'l/.

inflammable, inflammatory, flammable Both *inflammable* and *flammable* mean 'tending to catch fire easily'. Purists prefer *inflammable*, but *flammable* is now encouraged by safety officers because the *in-* of *inflammable* might suggest the opposite of the true meaning. The true opposite is *nonflammable*.

In figurative use, *inflammable* remains the correct choice, meaning 'easily moved to strong emotion, passionate' – *an inflammable temper* – or 'likely to erupt into violence or disorder, volatile': *an inflammable situation*. The adjective *inflammatory* has the complementary sense of 'arousing strong emotions, provocative': *an inflammatory speech*.

ingenious, ingenuous, disingenuous The adjective *ingenious* has gone downhill. It originally corresponded to the noun *genius* – that is, it meant 'brilliantly clever' – but it now means little more than 'cleverly inventive, cunning': *an ingenious contraption/excuse*. The corresponding noun is *ingenuity*.

The same is true of *ingenuous*. Once meaning 'noble, honest', it now has the sense 'innocent; unsophisticated, naive': *an ingenuous smile; ingenuous trust*. The corresponding abstract noun is *ingenuousness*.

Note too the noun *ingenue* or *ingénue*, /**aN**-zhay-noo/, taken from French, meaning 'an inexperienced or ingenuous young woman'.

Disingenuous is the reverse of *ingenuous*, and means 'underhand, devious, crafty, dishonest – putting on the appearance of ingenuousness': *a disingenuous answer, disingenuous advertising*.

iniquity See INEQUITY.

innocuous Note the spelling: double *n* and single *c*, like *innocent*.

inoculate Note the spelling: single *n* as well as single *c*, unlike *innocent* and *innocuous*.

inquiry See ENQUIRY.

insidious, invidious Something that is *insidious* spreads or works harmfully in a subtle or stealthy way: *an insidious cancer*. It is often used of utterances that are treacherous or intended to trap by guile: *an insidious rumour; insidious propaganda*. The adverb form is especially common: *insidiously*, 'by stealth'.

Invidious means 'likely to cause ill will or malice, offensive', as through a real or imagined insult or injustice. *An invidious comparison* is typically an unfairly selective one that is likely to hurt one of the people compared.

instantly, instantaneously *Instantly* means 'at once, immediately'. And *instantaneously* means 'done in an instant, taking no time to happen'.

In some contexts the adverbs are more or less interchangeable: *I decided instantly/instantaneously*. More often the meanings are distinct: *They arrived instantly* (immediately); *They both arrived instantaneously* (virtually at the same moment).

insure See ASSURE.

intensive *Intensive* does not mean the same as *intense* ('extreme'): **X** *intensive pain*, **X** *intensive efforts*. It means 'concentrated in a small area' and suggests quality where *extensive* suggests depth and quantity: *intensive TV coverage of the World Cup*, *intensive farming*, *labour-intensive* ('using much labour rather than machinery').

interface Both as noun and as verb, *interface* is best left to its technical contexts: *the interface between two surfaces, interfacing programs on a computer*.

In other contexts, it has become a vogue word and tends to sound pretentious: **?** *the East-West interface*, **?** *Government policy must interface with the needs of the public*. If possible, use alternatives such as *relationship*, *meeting-place*, and *interaction*.

internecine The commonest uses of the adjective *internecine* are fairly modern and not fully accepted by purists. It tends to occur in contexts of quarrelling or in-fighting within a group: **?** *internecine squabbling within the Republican Party*; **??** *an internecine household*. *Internal* would do in the first example, *quarrelsome* in the second. Even the stronger sense of 'mutually destructive' is still frowned on: **?** *the internecine conflict in Beirut*. The *inter-* element encourages all of these senses, but is in fact misleading.

The original meaning of the word, and the only one fully accepted as standard, is merely 'extremely destructive, characterised by slaughter': *the internecine battles of the Great War*. Even here you have many simpler alternatives at your disposal, such as *bloody*, *costly*, and *disastrously destructive*.

The standard modern pronunciation is /intər-**nee**-sīn/. In North America it can also be /intər-**ness**-een/ or /in-**ter**nə-seen/.

into, in to 1. *Into* is a single preposition and should not be used where the two parts have separate functions. You pour water *into* a kettle, but you might be invited *in to* sit down, or be taken *in to* a meeting. In the last two examples, *in* is an adverb.

Compare ONTO.

2. The modern use of *into* to mean 'interested or involved in' is very informal: **??** *She's into cricket*. This usage is more acceptable when referring to starting an interest or involvement: **?** *I want to get into marketing*.

invaluable The *in-* in *invaluable* is not a negative prefix but an intensifying one. So *an invaluable comment* is one that is extremely valuable or even indispensable.

inveigh, inveigle When you *inveigh against* something, you protest vehemently or rail at it: *inveigh against bureaucratic incompetence*. The related noun is *invective*: *(an) invective directed at the local council*.

Inveigle conveys the idea of deceptive flattery. You can *inveigle* someone into doing something ('entice'), or *inveigle* your way into a party, or *inveigle* money out of someone ('obtain by cajolery'). The noun is *inveiglement*.

Note the spellings, both with *-ei-*, and the pronunciations: /in-**vay**/ and /in-**vayg**'l/ or, less commonly, /in-**veeg**'l/.

inventory The pronunciation is /**in**vəntri/, with the stress on the first syllable, unlike *invention*.

invidious See INSIDIOUS.

involve As commonly used, *to involve* tends to be uninformative. If you speak of being *involved* in, say, a decision, you are not even telling your listener whether you have some part in making it or are simply affected by it. Try to substitute something more precise: for **?** *everyone involved in the event*, say *taking part*; for **?** *I don't want to get involved in this dispute*, say

drawn into; for **?** *deceit was involved*, say *used*; for **?** *charges involving fraud* say *of*.

Save the word for occasions when the sense of 'enwrap' is sharper; that is, where there is a clear idea of close interconnection, logical implication, entanglement, or deep concentration: *heavily involved in the scandal*; *involved in one's studies*. Other fully accepted senses include 'intricate and (over)complicated' and 'romantically attached'.

In the south of England, many speakers give the word a long *o* sound, as in *roll* rather than as in *doll*. This pronunciation is not fully accepted as standard, however.

ironic, sarcastic *Irony* implies a 'double view' of something – contrasting what someone says and what he actually means, perhaps, or what happened at one time and what happened later. Used gently, it tends to convey amused mockery or satire: *They are secretly engaged – only half the village knows about it*.

Situations, as well as utterances, can be ironic: *It's ironic how many vitamin-C addicts keep getting colds*. Many critics dislike this looser sense of *ironic* and *irony*. It should be used sparingly. If the situation is merely odd, remarkable, incongruous, or a strange coincidence, these are better words to use.

The adjective *ironical* is usually applied to people given to using irony: *an ironical writer*. Comments, writings, situations, and the like are usually *ironic*.

Sarcasm is the use of taunting words intended to hurt or belittle. It typically makes use of irony – biting rather than gentle irony this time: *Sure you take good care of me! – the way a cat takes good care of a mouse*. You can speak of *a sarcastic person* and *a sarcastic remark*, but you cannot speak of *a sarcastic situation*.

irregardless See REGARD 3.

irreparable The stress falls on the second syllable, not on the first and the third.

it 1. Beware of ambiguity. Make sure, when using *it* or any other pronoun, that people will know what you are referring to: **?** *A year after we planted grass in the garden, it looked very nice*. What looked nice, the grass or the garden? For other examples of ambiguity with *it*, see page 34.

2. Try also to avoid the trap of using a pronoun early in a sentence and keeping your readers or listeners waiting for its 'referent', the noun it refers to. If they have to wait too long, they are likely to lose the thread: **?** *Once it has been checked by the invoice clerks, the order form is passed on to Accounts*.

The usual remedy is to transpose the *it* and the noun: *Once the order form has been checked . . . , it is passed . . .*

Alternatively, reverse the order of the clauses: *The order form is passed on to Accounts once it has been checked by the invoice clerks*.

See also ITS, IT'S; and pages 51-52 and 183-184.

itinerary Don't neglect the *-er-* or *-ar-* syllable in the spelling. And include both of them when pronouncing the word: two distinct *r*-sounds.

its, it's One of the commonest errors in writing is to slip an apostrophe into *its*: **X** *That parcel will have to wait it's turn*. The problem arises because *its* is possessive, and the possessive usually takes *'s*. If you write *the dog's collar*, why not also **X** *it's collar*?

Think of *its* as closely related to *his*, and you should then remember to leave out the apostrophe.

With the apostrophe, *it's* is the contraction of either 'it is' or 'it has', and is used in informal contexts: *It's much better since it's been treated*.

jail, gaol Both spellings are fully acceptable in British English. This is true also of derivatives such as *jailer/gaoler* and *jailbird/gaolbird*.

Jail is by far the commoner, and the only form recognised in North American English. Whichever you decide to use, be consistent.

jetsam See FLOTSAM.

jewellery Note the pronunciation: /**joo**-əl-ri/ is standard; **?** **jool**-ri/ and **?** /**jool**əri/ are best avoided. The North American spelling is *jewelry*.

judgment, judgement Both spellings are correct, though *judgment* is now slightly favoured; some British publishers still prefer *judgement* for the legal sense.

judicial, judicious These adjectives are both related to the word *judge*.

Judicial is related to it in the legal sense, referring to courts, judgments, and the like: *a judicial review, judicial chambers*. *Judicious* is related to *judge* in the psychological sense, and means 'having sound judgment; prudent, wise': *a judicious choice*. It sometimes has an ironic tone: *trying to hide his age through the judicious application of hair dye*.

So *a judicial summing-up* is, strictly speaking, the judge's summing-up (or a judge-like summing-up), and *a judicious summing-up* is a thoughtful and prudent one.

just 1. The adverb *just* has several distinct meanings. When it means 'very recently', it demands a perfect form of the verb – using *has, have*, or *had*: *She has just arrived*. The use of the simple past here is nonstandard in both British and American English: **?** *She just arrived*.

When *just* means 'only' or 'almost not', the simple past may be used: *She just arrived ten minutes ago*; *She just got here on time*.

2. As with *only*, take care where you place *just* in a sentence – especially in writing, which lacks intonation to help you to avoid ambiguity.

Compare *They are just making a ten per cent profit* with *They are making just a ten per cent profit*. In the first sentence, *just* modifies *making*, and means 'barely managing, almost failing'. In the second sentence, it qualifies *ten per cent*, and means 'only, no more than'. A common mistake is to use the first word order for the second meaning. (See ONLY for more details.)

3. Don't combine *just* and *exactly*: **??** *Just what exactly are you up to?* **??** *She weighs just exactly 8 stone*.

just now 1. **?** *ICI ordinary shares cost 635 pence just now*. Does this mean 'at this very moment', or 'a short while ago'? To complicate matters even further, *just now* in Indian and South African English means 'in the very near future'? If there is any real risk of misunderstanding, choose another expression.

2. The choice of verb tense appears to depend on the position of *just now* in the sentence: *She arrived home just now*; *She has just now arrived home*. In the first example, *just now* means 'only a moment ago'; in the second, it seems to mean little more than 'just, barely'.

kerb See CURB.

kilometre See METER.

kind of See SORT OF; and also pages 175-176.

Kirkudbright This Scottish place-name is pronounced /kir-**kōō**bri/.

lacquer Note the spelling: it ends *-er*, not **X** *-eur* as in *liqueur*; and don't forget the *c* before the *qu*.

laden See LOADED.

lady See WOMAN.

laid, lain See LIE.

lama, llama The one-*l lama* is the Tibetan or Mongolian Buddhist monk. When used as part of a title, it takes a capital *L*: *the Dalai Lama*. The two-*l llama* is the South American animal. Both words are pronounced /**laa**mə/.

lamentable Traditionally, the stress falls on the first syllable; second-syllable stress is now widespread, however, and generally considered acceptable.

last 1. Those who dislike starting a list with *firstly* rather than *first* sometimes also object to ending it with *lastly* rather than *last*. But this 'rule' is now widely disregarded. (See FIRST.)

2. *The last two chapters* of a book are the penultimate and final chapters of one book. *The two last chapters* would be the final chapters of two different books.

3. Where *last* is ambiguous, try to reword. For instance, **?** *In the last chapter* could be 'in the preceding chapter' or 'in the final chapter'; **?** *the last time she came here* might be 'the time she was last here' or 'on her final visit'.

4. There is a traditional objection to expressions such as **?** *second last*, **?** *third worst*, and **?** *fourth farthest*. The objection applies only to the 'lower' end of a scale, not the top end: *second best*, for instance, is never queried. Some purists prefer *last but one* or *next to (the) last, worst but two*, and so on: *She finished last but one*. There are also the words *penultimate* and *antepenultimate*, but they are rather formal and they cannot be used adverbially: **X** *She finished penultimately in the 500m*.

last but not least Avoid this thoughtless cliché, and its variants *last not least* and *last but by no means least*. At best it is unnecessary; at worst, it is patronising to the person or thing listed last – rather as if you had expected people to assume 'last and least'.

latter See FORMER.

law and order This phrase has become something of a clichéd slogan. Use it sparingly. And when you say it, don't pronounce it as if it were the name *Laura Norder*, with that intrusive *r* in the middle.

lawful See LEGAL.

lay See LIE.

lb This is the correct abbreviation for *pounds* (weight) – not **?** *lbs*. It comes from the Latin *libra*, and should not take the English plural ending of *-s*. A full stop after *lb* is optional – the modern streamlining tendency is to do without it.

lead, led Pronounced /leed/, *lead* is a verb or noun: *Lead the way; a dog's lead*. The past of the verb is *led*, /led/: *He led a dog's life*. Don't confuse this word with the metal *lead*: **X** *He lead a dog's life*.

leading question A *leading question* is one, usually in court or in police examination, that directs or 'leads' the person asked towards a particular answer. A barrister might legitimately ask *What were you doing on Sunday?* Asking *Is it not true that you stayed at home on Sunday?* is asking an unfair and leading question.

Don't use *leading question* to refer to a question that is simply unwelcome, embarrassing, or tricky to answer: **??** *You asked me what my holiday plans are – that's a leading question*.

lean In British English the past tense and past participle can be either *leant*, /lent/, or, less commonly, *leaned*, /leend/. American English usually favours *leaned*.

leap In British English the past tense and past participle can be written either *leapt* or, less commonly, *leaped*, and is pronounced either /lept/ or /leept/. Note that *leaped* is by far the commoner spelling outside Britain.

learn In British English the past tense and past participle can be written either *learnt* or *learned*, both normally pronounced /lernt/. If you prefer to say /lernd/, you should use the spelling *learned*. This is the commoner spelling outside Britain, especially in North America; but it has the disadvantage of possible confusion with the adjective /**ler**nid/, as in *a learned professor.*

Don't use *to learn* to mean 'to teach': **X** *My teachers didn't learn me anything.* Though fairly common in regional speech, it is a glaring error elsewhere unless used for humorous effect.

legal, lawful, legitimate The basic meaning of 'authorised by or conforming with the law or rules' is shared by all three of these adjectives: *a legal/lawful/legitimate tackle in rugby.* But each has its own special uses.

Lawful is rather old-fashioned other than in set phrases, such as *his lawful wife, going about her lawful business,* and *on all lawful occasions.* It is also used with reference to moral or divine law: *our lawful duty to pray each day.* The related noun is *lawfulness.*

Legal is the word to use in the general sense of 'relating to lawyers and the law': *the legal profession, legal documents.* The noun *legality* refers to the legal status of something: *of dubious legality.* Another adjective, *legalistic,* suggests a nitpicking adherence to the letter rather than spirit of the law: *Don't try to blind me with your legalistic arguments.*

Legitimate has various specific senses of its own, as in *a legitimate child* ('born within wedlock'); *a legitimate conclusion* ('conforming to logic'); *legitimate grounds for complaint* ('justified').

You can also speak of the *legitimacy* of a child, conclusion, or complaint.

The related verbs are *legalise, legitimate,* and *legitimise. To legalise* means simply 'to make legal': *moves to legalise Sunday trading. To legitimate* means 'to justify, establish as legitimate': *The generals tried to legitimate the coup by holding local elections. To legitimise* is also used in this way, and in the sense of making a child legitimate: *He legitimised his children by marrying his mistress.*

Note the pronunciation of *legitimate.* The adjective is /li-**jit**ti-mət/, the verb /li-**jit**ti-mayt/.

See also ILLEGAL.

less, lesser, lessor *Less* is the comparative form of *little* or *a little* and, like them, is used both as an adverb – *I like him less now; a less important task* – and as an adjective with singular uncountable nouns: *less money; The pay is less than I thought.*

With plural nouns or verbs use *fewer: so fewer people,* not **X** *less people.*

(See FEWER, and also page 177.) With singular countable nouns, use *smaller, lower, lesser,* or some equivalent: *a smaller sum of money,* not **X** *a less sum of money.*

Lesser is more restricted than *less.* As noted, it is used before countable nouns, both singular and plural – *lesser sculptors than Bernini* – and is a sort of double comparative meaning 'less serious or impressive than the others': *a lesser responsibility.* It occurs in set phrases – *the lesser of two evils, lesser brethren, the Lesser Antilles* – and in combinations such as *lesser-known.* It is best not to use it to mean 'less numerous, less big, or the like': **?** *a lesser sum of money.* Use *smaller* or some equivalent instead.

The person who *lets out* a property – that is, the landlord – is the *lessor.*

let See HIRE.

let's In *Let us* or *let's* constructions, you may sometimes want to specify who the *us* is. The pattern **?** *Let's you and me try again, shall we?* is informal, and **?** *Let you and me try again, shall we?* is dubious and awkward. The only solution is something like *Let's try again, you and me, shall we?*

The usual negative form of *let's* is *let's not: Let's not get angry. Don't let's* is also acceptable in British English. **X** *Let's don't* occurs in North America, but is considered nonstandard.

liaison Note the spelling: *-iai-.* Don't neglect the second *i.*

library When pronouncing the word, try to sound the *-ra-* syllable in the middle, even though it is now considered acceptable to neglect it.

licence, license *Licence* is the noun; *to license* is the verb: *a dog licence, to license a gun.* Think of *advice* (noun) and *advise* (verb).

In American English, however, *license* is used for both.

lichen Two pronunciations of the word are acceptable – one sounding the same as *liken,* the other rhyming with *kitchen.*

lie, lay Note the tenses and forms of these verbs, and take care not to confuse them.

I lie in bed every morning
I lay in bed yesterday morning
I have lain in bed all morning

I lay the tarot cards out every morning
I laid the tarot cards out yesterday morning
I have laid the tarot cards out many times

For full details, see page 188.

The nouns follow the verbs – a golf ball has a bad *lie* but hens go into *lay.* North Americans often speak of **??** *the lay of the land,* but in standard English it is *the lie of the land.* Some derived words may appear to break the rules but are fully established by idiom: *a lay-by, a layabout.*

The unrelated verb *to lie* meaning 'to tell an untruth' has the regular forms *lie, lies, lying, lied, lied.*

light Both *lighted* and *lit* are fully acceptable as the past tense and past participle of *to light: I lighted/lit the touchpaper.* When the verb means 'to provide illumination', *lighted* is the commoner: *I was lighted by the moon on my way. Lighted* is also the commoner before nouns – *a lighted match* – though when there is a qualifying adverb *lit* is just as likely – *a well-lighted/well-lit room.*

lightning, lightening Without an *e, lightning* refers to the electric flashes in the sky. Hence the adjectival use in *a lightning strike* or *a lightning move.*

With an *e, lightening* comes from the verb *to lighten: the lightening of her load/cares; lightening one's hair with peroxide.*

like[1] **1.** A traditional rule forbids the use of *like* as a conjunction (that is, introducing a clause with a full verb): **??** *The boss treats his secretary like a sultan treats a slave.* Strictly, *like* should be changed here to *in the same way as* or simply *as.* Similarly, **??** *She carried on typing like nothing had happened;* here *like* should strictly be *as if* or *as though.* Sometimes a fairly drastic rewording is necessary to get rid of the *like.*

Idiom has more or less established the use of *like* in **?** *It looks like he will resign* and **?** *Like I said, he will resign,* though in very formal contexts you would have to use *as if* and *as* instead.

By contrast, *like* is usually fully acceptable when used as a preposition (that is, introducing a noun or noun equivalent rather than a clause): *The boss treats his secretary like a slave; She carried on typing like a maniac; It looks like a skull.*

2. Some purists object to the use of *like* to introduce examples: **?** *Good wines,* *like claret, cost more*. The objection is that if claret is *like* ('resembling') a good wine, it cannot in fact be one. If *like* is intended to mean 'such as', use *such as* instead, to be on the safe side.

The objection does not apply to *unlike*: *Poor wines, unlike claret, cost little*.

3. Avoid, other than for ironic effect or special emphasis, the use of *like* as a space filler, similar to *you know*: **??** *I'm like still thinking about it*. It has a slangy American or hippie feel to it.

4. Don't use *like* in formal contexts when you mean *likely* or *as likely*: **??** *I'm like to scream if you don't be quiet*; **??** *Like as not it'll rain*.

5. The use of *like* as a noun is nonstandard in the following patterns: **??** *Have you ever heard the like of it?* ('Have you ever heard anything like it?'); **??** *Don't speak to the likes of him* ('Don't speak to people like him').

But the phrase *and/or the like* is fully acceptable: *celery, cress, and the like*. (See ET CETERA.) And of course, *like* can be a noun in the sense of 'a wish, pleasure': *among my likes and dislikes*.

See also LIKE[2]; SUCHLIKE.

like[2] 1. Don't use *for* after *to like* in sentences such as **??** *I'd like for you to help me*. The *for* is unnecessary. After *what* clauses, however, the *for* is acceptable: *What I'd like is for you to help me*.

Note that in very correct British English the full form of *I'd like* is *I should like* rather than **✗** *I would like*.

See SHOULD.

2. After *would/should have liked*, don't use the perfect infinitive (*to have done*): **??** *I'd have liked you to have spoken*. The simple infinitive is enough: *I'd have liked you to speak*.

For further details, see page 188.

likely When used as an adverb, *likely* needs to be preceded by a qualifying adverb in standard southern British English. The sentence **?** *He'll likely come late* is perfectly correct in Scottish, Irish, and American English and some other varieties. But in standard British English it would have to be *He'll very likely come late*. Other adverbs commonly appearing before *likely* include *quite, extremely, most*, and *more*. Alternatively, you could substitute *probably* for *likely*, or else rephrase: *He's likely to come late*.

liquefy Note the spelling: an *e* after the *qu*, though *liquify* on the model of

liquid, has become an acceptable variant.

liqueur Note the spelling – *-ueur* – and the pronunciation: an Anglicised /li-**kewr**/ is preferable to the Frenchified /li-**ker**/.

liquor Note the spelling: no *c* before the *q*, and ends *-uor* unlike *lacquer*.

litany, liturgy A *litany* is a form of Christian prayer in which the clergyman leads the congregation in a series of requests and responses, asking forgiveness for sins. From this come two extended uses: 'a repetitive series of questions and answers', as in a *litany of interrogation by journalists*; and 'a long and repetitive list of errors or problems', as in a *litany of vengeful violence*.

Liturgy is the ritual side of worship in any religion. In Anglicanism, it refers to the service prescribed in the 1629 *Book of Common Prayer*.

literally Don't abuse language, and common sense, by using *literally* where it does not belong. It might be true to say *He was literally speechless with rage*; it cannot be true that **✗** *He literally exploded with rage*. If something happens *literally*, it really happens; the events correspond to the words at their face value. If this is not the case, the words are being used *figuratively* or *metaphorically* – the very opposite of *literally*.

As a general intensifier, *literally* is not only misleading but usually unnecessary. To say **✗** *Those buskers literally rake in the money* probably conveys your feelings less effectively – through hectoring the reader or listener and through being over-emphatic – than the simpler *Those buskers rake in the money*.

If you really do mean *literally* and are worried that it will be ignored or misunderstood as a general intensifier, you can always use an alternative such as *strictly speaking* or *in the literal sense*. Or you can shift the *literally* to the beginning or end of the sentence: the statement *Cider literally makes me sick* would be in less danger of being misunderstood if reordered to read *Cider makes me sick, literally*.

liturgy See LITANY.

loaded, laden *Loaded* is the past tense and past participle of *to load*: *I loaded the furniture into the lorry; a loaded gun; loaded with money*. *Laden* is an old past participle of the same

verb. It is slightly literary, and is used only in the sense 'heavily weighted down': *The table was laden with food; laden with cares*.

loan *Loan* is almost always a noun in English: *a loan of £10*. The corresponding verb is *to lend*. The use of *to loan* for *to lend* is probably standard in American English, but not in British English: **??** *Can you loan me your car?* In British English the verb is proper only in the sense 'to put on loan; to transfer (something valuable) formally, especially to an institution': *She refused to loan her collection of antique silver to the museum*.

loath, loth Both spellings are acceptable for the adjective meaning 'reluctant'. The verb meaning 'to detest' is spelt *loathe*.

loch, lough A Scottish lake is a *loch*; an Irish lake is a *lough*. Both are best pronounced /lo<u>kh</u>/.

lot, lots These words are both singular and plural: *There is lots of money*; *There are a lot/lots of people*. They have a slightly informal ring, and in very formal contexts should be replaced by *a great deal of, a great many*, or the like: **?** *We the undersigned object to lots of the government's policies*. A bare *much* or *many*, however, is often an inadequate alternative, producing a rather stiff and unidiomatic wording: **?** *I know many people here*; **??** *She has much money*. See MANY.

loud As adverbs, *loud* and *loudly* are usually interchangeable: *Don't talk so loud/loudly*. In formal contexts *loudly* is preferable; so too in sentences where the idea is not simply one of volume but one of insistent noise: *The voters protested loudly*.

See also page 200.

lower, lour Either spelling is acceptable for the verb 'to scowl or look dark or sullen', and for the noun 'a menacing appearance'. Both forms are pronounced to rhyme with *power*. Not to be confused with the comparative of *low*, which rhymes with *slower*.

lunch, luncheon 1. The usual word for the midday meal is now *lunch*. *Luncheon* sounds affected, except when referring to a formal function – *the guest of honour at the annual luncheon* – or in set phrases such as *luncheon voucher* and *luncheon meat*.

2. As a verb, *to lunch* is now widely used and accepted, especially when intransitive (without a direct object): *We are lunching together on Tuesday.* When transitive in the sense 'to provide lunch for', *to lunch* still has a rather slangy feel about it perhaps: **?** *I'm lunching our two new clients at the Savoy tomorrow.*

luxury, luxurious, luxuriant The adjective *luxurious* relates to *luxury*: *a luxurious hotel.* It can take on a tone of indulgence and excess: *luxurious idleness.* From *luxurious* comes the noun *luxuriousness.* Note that *luxury* too is now widely used as an adjective: *a luxury hotel.*

Don't use *luxuriant* when you mean *luxurious. Luxuriant* means 'growing abundantly, profuse' or 'producing abundantly, very fertile': *luxuriant vegetation/hair; luxuriant soil.* It can also be used figuratively to mean 'florid, exuberant': *a luxuriant imagination; a luxuriant style of writing.* The related noun is *luxuriance.*

The verb *to luxuriate* corresponds to both *luxuriant* and *luxurious.* So you may speak of *ferns luxuriating in the jungle,* though the word more often has the meaning 'to indulge oneself, bask, revel': *luxuriating in a hot bath.*

All the words mentioned except *luxury* are stressed on their second syllables. *Luxury* usually has a *sh*-sound in the middle, /**luk**-shəri/, but with the others, the preferred pronunciation involves a z- or zh-sound, such as /lug-**zewr**-i-əss/ for *luxurious.*

machinations Though closely related in origin, the words *machine* and *machinations* (pronounced /**mac**ki-**nay**shˈnz/, or sometimes /**mash**i-**nay**shnˈz/) now have very different meanings.

Machinations, almost always in the plural, means 'a hostile conspiracy' or 'devious manoeuvrings': *The machinations of the traitors infuriated the king.*

There is a related verb, *to machinate,* very rare or formal, meaning 'to plot or conspire'.

machismo, macho Note the pronunciations: *macho* is always /**mach**o/, though *machismo* can be /-**chiz**-/ or /-**kiz**-/ in the middle.

madam, madame As terms of address, these words often cause difficulties.

Madam is the polite term for addressing a woman in speech or writing, particularly if she is married or elderly. You can also use it for addressing any woman whose name you do not know, though it does sound rather formal and old-fashioned nowadays. This is a pity, since English has no adequate substitute. *Lady, Mrs,* and *Miss* are too informal – though *Miss* is acceptable for addressing a young woman or a child in American usage, and fairly acceptable for any woman.

Madam is also used in business correspondence as the female equivalent of *Sir: Dear Sir or Madam* . . . And in formal contexts *Madam* is used as the equivalent of *Mr* before a woman's official designation: *Madam Chairman; Madam President.*

The plural of *Madam* is *Mesdames* (pronounced /**may**-dam/ or /may-**daam**/), but this form is very rarely used today.

Madame retains the French spelling – in French, it means literally 'my lady', but is used as the equivalent of *Mrs* and *Madam.* It is pronounced /mə-**daam**/, and its plural is again *Mesdames.* In English, *Madame* is used as a courtesy title for important foreign women, particularly diplomatic and artistic VIPs: *The Swedish Ambassador and Madame Eriksson; Madame Sevelius will give a rendition of Schumann's Arabesque.*

In other contexts, *Madam* can be used flatteringly in the third person, as in a restaurant: *Is Madame ready to order?* And *Madame* is also used instead of *Mrs* by women who wish to give themselves an appearance of being foreign: *Madame Emile & Co., purveyors of fine cosmetics.*

Madam and *madame* also function as self-standing nouns. Both are used to refer to a woman who owns a brothel, though strictly only *madam* is correct in this sense. In informal British speech, *madam* also means 'a bossy or cheeky girl or young woman', especially in the phrase 'a little madam'. The plural *madams* is acceptable for both these senses.

See also MISS; WOMAN.

Magdalen, Magdalene The pronunciation of *Magdalen* College, Oxford and *Magdalene* College, Cambridge is /**mawd**lin/ in each case.

majority, minority 1. Each of these nouns has a number of subtly different meanings. Depending on the sense intended, they can take plural or singular verbs: *The majority of our* members are officers; The government's majority was an overwhelming 160; Most of the council support the motion, but a minority is/are likely to abstain.* In this third example, *is* would be used if the abstainers were a unified group, and *are* if they were acting as individuals.

2. Be careful of using *greater/greatest* in combination with *majority.* It is clearly quite all right in the following example: *The previous government has the greatest majority in the history of Parliament.* But the combination usually produces an unacceptable tautology: **X** *The greater majority of our members never come to meetings.*

3. Beware of ambiguity. A phrase such as **?** *a small minority* could refer to a very small opposition group or to a very large one. And the phrase **?** *a majority of ten* could mean either that the majority group has ten members, or that it has ten more members than the minority group.

4. *Majority* is also ambiguous when applied to elections or opinion polls. It can mean either 'the number of votes separating the winner from the runner-up' or 'the number of votes separating the winner from all the other candidates combined'. American English avoids this ambiguity by using *plurality* for the first of these senses.

Similarly, when referring to the winning group in a poll or election: American English limits *majority* to a group winning over 50 per cent of the poll, using *plurality* for a winning group whose share is less than 50 per cent of the total vote. But in British English, *majority* is used for both types, and is therefore ambiguous.

5. Use *majority* and *minority* only when referring to several elements: *The majority of restaurants are empty on Mondays.*

Don't use *majority* or *minority* when only a single element is under discussion: **X** *The majority of the restaurant was dimly lit;* **X** *The minority of the magazine consists of pictures.*

In these last two examples, replace *majority* and *minority* with expressions such as *more/less than half, the greater/lesser part,* or *a large/small amount.*

malicious, malignant, malevolent *Malicious* means 'wishing to cause harm', and 'produced by or resulting from a wish to harm': *the malicious gossip that circulates in the office.* In legal terminology, *malicious* can refer to any unjust scheme, usually criminal, that will cause harm to others. The usual phrase is *malicious intent*. The noun *malice* also occurs in the legal phrases *malice aforethought* and *malice prepense*.

Malevolent, like *malicious*, means 'wishing to do harm; having ill-will': *an arrogant and malevolent smile*.

Malignant is a stronger term; like the closely related *malign*, /mə-**lın**/, it suggests far greater ill-will, and means 'actively evil in nature' or 'extremely harmful or dangerous': *malignant persecution; the malign obstinacy of the authorities*.

In medical terminology, *malignant* (though not *malign*) is used to refer to conditions or growths that are threatening to life, resistant to treatment, or likely to spread rapidly: *malignant tumours*.

Malign is also a verb meaning 'to slander, defame; to speak evil of': *society hostesses blithely maligning their rivals*.

The rare adjective *maleficent* (or *malefic*), means 'evil in nature' and 'capable of causing evil'; it is largely confined to literary contexts.

Only the noun *malice* is stressed on its first syllable. All the above adjectives, together with the verb *malign*, are stressed on their second syllables.

Note too that the *g* is silent in *malign*, but is sounded in *malignant* and the related nouns *malignance, malignancy*, and *malignity*. Other related nouns are *maliciousness, malevolence*, and *maleficence*.

See also BENEVOLENT.

mall In most uses the pronunciation is /mawl/; but it is /mal/ in the game *pall-mall* and in the London streets *The Mall* and *Pall Mall*.

man Although *man* is still used in the neutral sense of 'a human being', as in *Man is ruining the planet* or *man-made*, its sexist implications lead many careful speakers and writers to use truly neutral terms instead, such as *human, person*, and *people*. This policy is particularly advisable in contexts where the use of *man* might appear to belittle or dismiss the role of women: **?** *man's many technological achievements in the 20th century*.

However, *man* in its neutral sense remains very useful when human beings are being compared, implicitly or explicitly, with animals: *Man is both affectionate and aggressive by nature*.

And there are many traditional formulaic expressions that are not easily changed: *mankind; man-hours; one man, one vote; the man in the street*.

See also CHAIRMAN; and pages 89-90.

mandatory Traditionally, the stress falls on the first syllable; second-syllable stress is now widespread, however, and generally considered acceptable.

Manila Note the spelling of this Philippine city: no double *l* as in *vanilla*; but the colour, paper, cigar, or hemp fibre (usually with a small *m*) can take a double *l*.

manoeuvre Note the spelling: *-oeu-* in the middle and *-re* at the end; the American spelling is *maneuver*.

many, much These words tend to sound unnecessarily formal in simple positive statements: *I have made many friends; I have much money*. You can reduce the stiffness by adding a *great* before *many – I have a great many friends –* or by substituting *a lot of: I have a lot of friends/money*.

The effect of *much* and *many* seems slightly less formal in questions, negative statements, and so on: *Have you made many friends?; I don't have many hours to spare*.

Marylebone The pronunciation of this London street name is /**marri**-ləbən/, or /**mar**li-bən/.

masterly, masterful These two adjectives correspond to the two chief senses of the noun *master*: 'the man in charge' – *the master of the house* – and 'a person (of either sex) who is expert or very skilled': *She is a master of the backhand volley*.

The abstract noun *mastery*, the adjective *master*, and the verb *to master* can all be used in ways corresponding to both senses.

But the adjective *masterful* nowadays relates mainly to the first sense, and *masterly* to the second.

Masterly means 'very skilful or expert, showing the skill of a master': *Olivier was a masterly actor; a masterly debate between the two philosophers*.

Masterful can mean simply 'powerful, having command' – *the conductor's masterful influence* – or, more unfavourably, 'domineering, imperious': *a masterful employer*.

Occasionally, *masterful* too is used in this sense, but usually some subtle

emphasis distinguishes the two adjectives. A *masterly/masterful performance* is a skilful performance, but there is an added suggestion in *masterful* of a complete command of stagecraft. As a rule, *masterly* is the safer choice in such contexts.

One factor working against the distinction is this: *masterly* has no straightforward adverb form. Since **??** *masterlily* is impossibly awkward, and *in a masterly way* a bit long-winded at times, writers or speakers often opt for *masterfully* instead: **?** *He played the sonata masterfully*. You can avoid the problem by restructuring the sentence to omit the adverb altogether: *His performance of the sonata was masterly*.

materialise Strictly speaking, the verb *to materialise* means 'to make real, to invest with material form' – *He materialised his dream by building his own boat* – or 'to assume material form, to become real': *The apparition materialised in a corner of the room*.

It is now also widely used to mean 'to happen' or 'to turn up', a sense still criticised by some purists: *The eclipse of the Sun never materialised; The customs officers waited patiently but the smugglers never materialised*. Such expressions are unnecessarily long-winded, but the idiom is now firmly established in all but the most formal contexts.

Compare TRANSPIRE.

mathematics See -ICS.

mattress Note the spelling: double *t* as well as double *s*.

mawkish, maudlin These adjectives both mean 'sentimental', though in slightly different ways.

Mawkish today means primarily 'excessively or falsely sentimental, especially in a sickly, weak way': *mawkish poems of childhood*.

Maudlin means 'tearfully sentimental' (the word derives from the name of *Mary Magdalene*, who was often shown weeping with penitence in early paintings) and can also mean 'foolishly and tearfully sentimental when drunk': *a maudlin farewell scene; Maudlin from the wine, I brooded on my sad past*.

Both these adjectives have a disapproving tone.

In some contexts, either adjective will fit, though the emphasis would differ slightly: *a maudlin/mawkish love song*.

may, might In requests for permission, the form *May I...?*, *Might I...?*, and *Can I...?* are all possible, according to the context. See CAN, and pages 192-193.

When referring to possible states of affairs, *may* and *might* are often equally appropriate. But sometimes only *might* is possible, as when the main verb is in the past – *I began to worry that the boat might capsize* – and when the possibility no longer exists: *I might have succeeded, if only I'd had more time*. See page 192 for fuller details.

maybe In British English, *maybe* (stressed on its first syllable) is a rather informal word: *Maybe I'll go to town today*. (Less so when placed at the end of a clause or sentence and stressed on the second syllable: *The markets may crash tomorrow may**be**, but he will not sell*.)

Fully formal contexts allow *may be*, as two words, often followed by *that*: *It may be that she will repent; That may be so, but my decision stands*.

me, my 1. Very strictly speaking, the correct answer to the question *Who is there?* should be *It is I*, but *It's me* usually sounds more natural – and just as acceptable. See pages 183-184 for details.

2. Where *than* or *as* appears in a comparison, formal writing demands the subject form of pronouns – *She is taller than I* – while informal contexts favour the object form: *She is taller than me*. However, if the construction continues, the subject form is always standard: *Jane is taller than I am*. See THAN, and page 185.

3. Before an *-ing* form of a verb, a pronoun traditionally takes the possessive form (*my, your, his, her*, and so on): *I remember your saying so*. But in most contexts, modern idiom now allows the object form instead: *I remember you saying so*. See page 186 for details.

mean There are three possible constructions for the verb *mean*, in the sense 'to intend': you can mean *to do* something – *I meant to go shopping* – or you can mean *someone to do* something – *I meant you to go shopping*. More formally, you can mean *that* someone *should* do something: *I meant that you should go shopping*.

Note that the construction using *for* is nonstandard in both British and American English: **??** *I meant for you to go shopping*.

meaningful In its extended sense of 'valuable or important', *meaningful* has become a mindless vogue word – **?** *a meaningful conference*; **??** *a meaningful relationship* (often meaning simply 'a love affair').

If possible use a less clichéd adjective to express the importance of something – *serious*, or *promising*, or *far-reaching*, or simply *important*.

See also SIGNIFICANT.

means Does this noun call for a singular or a plural verb? In the sense 'financial resources or income', *means* takes a plural verb: *My means are just adequate*. In the sense 'a method or way', *means* takes a singular verb when preceded by *a, any, each*, and other singular markers, and a plural verb when preceded by *all, several, many, such*, and so on: *Either means is valid; Such means aren't yet acceptable*. Used with *the, means* can take a singular or a plural verb, depending on whether you are referring to a single method or more than one.

media *Media* is a plural noun – the Latin form of the plural of *medium*, as in *a culture medium for bacteria* or *the medium of radio*. (But for the human *medium* who conducts spiritual seances, the plural is *mediums*.)

Since the various mass media are often discussed collectively, the term *the media* tends to be treated as grammatically singular: **?** *The media has again shown its seamy side*. Change *has* to *have*, and *its* to *their*.

Similarly, avoid using *media* to refer to a single medium – **✗** *The media of television is very influential* – and avoid the form **✗** *medias* as the supposed plural.

Compare CRITERION; PHENOMENON; DATA.

medieval Three pronunciations are possible: they are, in order of preference, /**med**di-eev'l, med-, **mee**di-/.

The spelling *mediaeval* is also acceptable, though it has an old-fashioned look to it, and now occurs infrequently in British English, and very seldom in American English.

Mediterranean You can remember the spelling by thinking of the elements: *medi*, 'middle' + *terra*, 'earth'; one *d*, one *t*, double *r*, and ending in *-ean*, not **✗** *-ian*.

meet Take care with the phrases *to meet with* and *to meet up (with)*. In some contexts they are fully acceptable: *His scheme met with general approval; The project met with disaster*. In others, they amount to no more than ungainly substitutes for *to meet*: **??** *At which pub are we meeting with Tony and Louise?* **??** *What time should we meet up tonight?*

memento Note the spelling: the word begins *mem-* as in *memory*; don't use the model of *moment*. The plural is *mementos* or possibly *mementoes*.

mendacious, mendicant These two words have very different meanings. As an adjective, *mendicant* /**men**di-kənt/, means 'begging': *a mendicant friar*. As a noun, it means either 'a member of a mendicant religious order (of friars)', or, more rarely, 'a beggar': *As a youth I lived the life of a mendicant*.

By contrast, the formal adjective *mendacious*, /men-**day**shəss/, means 'lying, deceitful, or untrue': *You are a mendacious coward; You have uttered a mendacious slander*.

The nouns *mendacity* and *mendicity* also look dangerously alike. *Mendicity* (more commonly, *mendicancy*) refers to the state of being a beggar, or the habit of begging, or the existence of beggars: *Mendicity is rife in the slums*.

Mendacity (or *mendaciousness*) can mean 'lying', especially 'habitual lying', or it can simply be a long-winded synonym for a *lie*: *Your mendacity makes you untrustworthy; Mendacities such as yours are despicable*.

Menzies The pronunciation of this surname in Scotland is often /**ming**-iss/ or /**meng**-iz/.

mercifully See HOPEFULLY.

meretricious Don't confuse this adjective with *meritorious*, 'praiseworthy, deserving merit'. The two words are almost opposites.

Meretricious (note that the second vowel is an *e*, not an *i*) derives from Latin *meretrix*, 'a prostitute', and originally meant 'of, like, or relating to a prostitute'. Today it usually means 'insincere' – *a meretricious argument* – or 'superficially or vulgarly attractive': *meretricious decorations*.

meter, metre In American English, *meter* is always the correct spelling. Not so in British English: a *meter* is a measuring instrument, or one that regulates or records time, distance, speed, and so on: *a parking meter, a gas meter*. So, the verb *to meter* means 'to measure, record, or regulate with a metering device'.

A *metre* is a unit of length in the metric system, as well as a measure of the rhythmic patterns of poetry. (To complicate matters, the specific measures of poetic rhythm – *pentameter, hexameter*, and so on – are spelt *-er*.)

Don't confuse the two adjectives *metric* and *metrical*. *Metric* relates to a *metre* as a unit of length: *the metric system, a metric ton*. And *metrical* means either 'relating to verse metre' – *metrical complexity* – or 'relating to measurement in general': *a metrical impossibility*.

Pronunciation can be tricky. Compounds with *-meter* tend to be stressed on the syllable immediately preceding *-meter*, causing the first *e* of meter to change sound: /thər-**mom**mitər/, /pen-**tam**mitər/.

Compounds with *-metre* tend to be stressed on their first syllables: /**milli**-meetər/. Strictly, *kilometre* should be pronounced /**killə**-meetər/, but it is often stressed on its second syllable: **?** /ki-**lom**mitər/, perhaps following the mistaken model of *thermometer* or *barometer*.

meticulous Many careful speakers still resist the use of this adjective as a substitute for *scrupulous* or *conscientious* – **?** *He is meticulous about his appearance* – arguing that its real meaning is 'excessively precise, painstakingly careful about details, even trivial ones'. *Meticulous* derived from Latin *metus*, 'fear', and suggests a nitpicking or very fussy overconscientiousness that arises from fear of failure or criticism.

You can help to preserve this dying distinction by using *conscientious* and *scrupulous* in neutral or favourable contexts, and reserving *meticulous* (and *fastidious*) for contexts where you intend criticism: *His meticulous attention to detail means that he never finishes on time*.

metre See METER.

might See MAY.

migraine The pronunciations /**mee**-grayn, **mī**-/ are both acceptable, though the former is more favoured in British English.

migrate, migrant See EMIGRATE.

militate, mitigate Avoid the expression **X** *to mitigate against*; the correct expression here is *to militate against*.

The verb *to mitigate* means 'to soften', or 'reduce the severity of': *The new evidence caused the judge to mitigate his harsh views; A breeze mitigated the fierce desert heat*.

To militate means 'to have powerful influence or effect', or 'to serve as strong evidence'. Related to *military*, it conveys a sense of fighting for or against something; it is used with a preposition, usually *for, against*, or *towards*: *The new evidence militated against the possibility of acquittal*.

See also EXTENUATE.

million See BILLION.

mineralogy Note the spelling and pronunciation: *-alogy* (from *mineral*), not **X** *-ology*.

miniature Note the spelling: don't forget the *a* in the middle.

minority See MAJORITY.

minuscule Note the spelling: *minus-*, not **X** *mini-* as in *minimum*.

minutiae Note the pronunciation: /mɪ-**new**-shi-ee, mi-/.

mischievous Note the spelling and pronunciation: ends in *-ous* not **X** *-ious*; hence only three syllables when pronounced: /**miss**-chivəss/ not **X** /mis-**chee**vi-əss/.

Miss, Mrs, Ms Only in the 19th century were *Miss* and *Mrs* clearly distinguished as referring to unmarried and married women respectively. In recent times, feminists have raised objections to the terms – the male equivalent, *Mr*, indicates nothing about the man's marital status – and adopted the alternative title *Ms* (pronounced /miz/).

Use it with discretion. Some women object to it. But if you do not know and cannot find out the marital status of a woman, then *Ms* is at least less risky than either *Miss* or *Mrs*. You can also use *Ms* fairly safely in addressing a married woman who has retained her maiden name; and perhaps an unmarried woman aged between 20 and 65.

For a very young unmarried woman and for a very elderly unmarried woman, *Miss* is still the best choice. And for a married woman who has adopted her husband's surname, *Mrs* is still best. (But avoid the old-fashioned practice, except in formal invitations perhaps, of using her husband's first name instead of her own.

Write to *Mrs Mary Johnstone*, not **X** *Mrs Paul Johnstone*.)

Note finally that *Mrs* and *Ms* nowadays lack full stops more often than not in British English, whereas American English still prefers to retain them.

See also WOMAN, and pages 89-90.

misspell Note the spelling: double *s*, no hyphen, double *l*.

mitigate See EXTENUATE; MILITATE.

moat See MOTE.

moment The phrase *the moment of truth* referred originally to the matador's final thrust of the sword during a bullfight. By extension it has come to refer to a critical point in an experiment, personal challenge, or the like, in which the true quality or ability of the person or thing is revealed.

It has become something of a cliché now, with a slightly different and weakened sense, referring to any moment of testing or checking something – taking a cake out of the oven, unveiling a statue, starting up a cold car engine, or the like. Do use the phrase sparingly and accurately.

The phrase *at this moment in time* is both clichéd and long-winded. It almost always can be replaced by a simple *now*.

momentous, momentary, momentarily, momently These words are all related to the noun *moment*, whose many meanings include: 'a short period of time': *I'll be there in a moment*; 'the present time': *I'm busy at the moment*; 'an important time or event': *It was a great moment when our son was born*; 'importance in general': *The battle was of no great moment*.

The adjective *momentous* relates to the third and fourth of the above senses, and means 'of great significance; having serious implications or consequences': *a momentous election victory that would change the course of history*.

The adjective *momentary* relates to the first and second of the above senses. Its primary sense is 'temporary, lasting only a short time': *a momentary loss of nerve*. It also, though rarely now, means 'at very short notice' – *a momentary decision* – and 'present or occurring at every moment': *in momentary fear of being discovered*.

Don't confuse *a momentary decision* with *a momentous decision*.

The adverb *momentarily* also has three senses, corresponding to the above three senses of *momentary*. However, only one of these senses is strictly acceptable: 'for an instant, temporarily; very briefly': *I lost my nerve momentarily.*

Momentarily is also used to mean 'from moment to moment; at every moment', but such senses can produce ambiguity – **?** *I was momentarily afraid of being discovered* – so purists would prefer *momently* for this sense: *I was momently afraid of being discovered.*

The third sense of *momentarily* is chiefly confined to informal American usage: 'very soon; in a moment' – **?** *I'll be there momentarily.*

Note the pronunciations: *momentous* is stressed on its second syllable, all the others on their first.

mongoose The plural is *mongooses*, not **X** *mongeese*.

month See YEAR.

moral See ETHICAL.

more 1. When forming the comparative degree of an adverb or adjective, you can either place *more* in front of the word, or add *-er* to the end of it. But not both – **X** *a more sadder person you never saw*. Similarly, look out for redundant expressions such as **X** *more superior*, and **X** *more major*.

2. Limit *more* to longer words: *more dangerous*. For words of one syllable, and many of two syllables, use *-er*: *kinder*. Exceptions occur in unusual constructions: *David is more kind than stingy; Henry's no more kind than Attila the Hun.*

Some words, such as *unkind*, can take either *more* or *-er*, and so can many compound adjectives: *an unkinder man, a more unkind man; a kinder-hearted man, a more kind-hearted man.*

3. Remember that *more* and *-er* are appropriate only in comparisons of two elements. Three or more elements require *most* and *-est*: *Which great city do you find most appealing?*

Think twice before using the increasingly popular construction *One of the/our more* . . . : **?** *one of the more important novels of this century.* Usually, *one of the most* . . . is more appropriate.

4. *More* and *-er*, as well as *most* and *-est*, are generally inappropriate in combination with adjectives that suggest completeness or perfection: **X** *a more complete picture*; **X** *a most perfect answer*; **??** *a more cloudless day than yesterday.* A construction such as *a more nearly complete picture* expresses the idea rather more logically.

5. Take care with the phrase *more than one*. Though plural in meaning, it is singular in form, and therefore takes a singular verb and pronouns: *More than one pilot owes his life to his parachute.* Everything becomes plural, however, if a plural noun is placed between *more than* and *one*: *More pilots than one owe their lives to their parachutes.*

mortgage Note the spelling: don't leave out the *t*, which is silent in standard pronunciation: /**mor**gij /. A common but nonstandard regional pronunciation, as in Scotland, is /**mort**-gayj/.

Moslem See MUSLIM.

most 1. Don't use *most* in conjunction with the superlative form of an adjective or adverb, as in **X** *most unkindest*. The combination creates redundancy.

2. To form the superlative degree of adverbs and adjectives, add *-est* to words of one syllable (and sometimes those with two or even three syllables) *kindest, tenderest* – and *most* to more unwieldy words: *most dangerous.*

Some words can take either form – *the unkindest man, the most unkind man, the most kind-hearted man, the kindest-hearted man.*

3. Remember that *more* is used of two elements, and *most* of three or more: *Which of the twins is the more intelligent?; Which of the triplets is the most intelligent?*

4. Avoid using *most* with adjectives or adverbs that already convey a sense of perfection or completeness: **X** *the most cloudless day so far*; **X** *the most unique experience possible.* (See VERY.)

5. Nowadays, *most* sounds unnecessarily formal when it is used as an intensifier before simple adjectives or adverbs: **?** *James is a most careful speaker*; **?** *I am most grateful for your help.* Replace *most* with *very* to avoid such stiffness.

6. Don't confuse *most* and *mostly. Most* can be an adverb of degree meaning 'to the greatest extent': *Those most affected by the strike were the strikers.* Avoid *mostly* in such contexts, and confine it to the senses 'almost entirely' and 'usually': *My ice cream had mostly melted in the sun; I mostly avoid town on a Saturday.*

mote, moat Don't confuse these two nouns. A *mote* is a tiny speck, particularly a speck of dust: *a mote in my eye.* A *moat* is a ditch, usually wide and filled with water, surrounding a castle, football field, or the like.

Mrs, Ms See MISS.

much See MANY; VERY.

Munich The standard pronunciation of the name of this German city is /**mew**nik/. Don't attempt a more foreign-sounding version, since the Germans themselves use a different name, *München*.

Muslim, Moslem The form *Muslim* (as adjective or noun) rather than *Moslem* is now preferred by scholars and by most Muslims themselves.

Avoid the now old-fashioned (and often offensive) terms *Mohammedan* and *Musselman*.

The related adjective *Islamic* is also widely used, though never of people: *Islamic art, Islamic culture.*

Muslim is pronounced /**mŏŏss**-lim, **mŏŏz**-lim, **muz**-lim/, and *Moslem* is pronounced /**moz**-ləm/.

must 1. As a verb, *must* has two main uses: it expresses certainty or conviction (on the part of the speaker); and it expresses necessity, compulsion, or obligation.

Certainty or conviction is found in a sentence such as *You must be tired if you slept badly last night; You must be joking!* (In North American English, *must* is often replaced by *have (got) to: You've got to be joking!*)

In standard British English, the opposite idea would be expressed by *cannot* or *can't* – *You can't be tired if you slept all day.*

Necessity, compulsion, or obligation is found in a sentence such as *You must leave early, or you'll miss the train.* This sense has two opposites: the action is either unnecessary – *You needn't leave early; You don't have to leave early* – or it is forbidden: *You mustn't/mayn't leave early.*

Must has a number of forms in the past tense, depending on the sense and construction employed: *If you slept badly the night before, you must have been tired on your journey; You had to be joking; You couldn't have been tired if you'd slept all day; You had to leave then, or you would have missed the train; You needn't have left early; You couldn't have left early.*

2. *Must* is also used as a noun: *Frayed jeans are a must.* This is an informal and rather voguish term, which is best used sparingly if at all. Even more informal is the North American use of *must* as an adjective: **?** *a must production of Hamlet.*

mutual, reciprocal 1. *Mutual* and *mutually* apply to a relationship in which both parties involved (or sometimes more than two) act or feel towards each other in exactly the same way: *mutual suspicion; The two boxers were mutually contemptuous.*

It is possible that *three boxers are mutually contemptuous* in the sense that they are all contemptuous of one another. But don't introduce a third party who is not an equal partner in the relationship, as in **X** *The two boxers were mutually contemptuous of the referee.* This sentence should read either *The two boxers were equally/ both/jointly contemptuous of the referee* or, if the referee returns the contempt: *The two boxers and the referee were mutually contemptuous.*

Other common expressions that introduce an unequal third party are **?** *a mutual rival*; **X** *a decision mutually taken*; **?** *our mutual enemy/friend*, and so on. The correct forms are *a common rival/enemy; a decision jointly taken, a decision taken together; our shared/common friend.*

The phrase **?** *our mutual friend* is now virtually idiomatic (thanks to Dickens's novel), but it is problematic for another reason: *mutual* should govern only an abstract or nonhuman noun, and never a human noun. So, *our mutual friendship/hatred*, but not **?** *our mutual admirer.*

2. Beware of redundancy when using *mutual* and *mutually.* These words already imply a two-way relationship, and so should not be combined with other words that convey the same idea: **X** *Her two suitors are mutually jealous of each other.*

Similarly, *mutual* is redundant in phrases such as **X** *their mutual rivalry*, **X** *a mutual exchange of prisoners*, and **X** *shared mutual distrust.*

3. The adjective *reciprocal* is rather more flexible than *mutual*, it can almost always replace *mutual*, but not the other way round. Like *mutual*, *reciprocal* can refer to a two-way

relationship considered from both sides, though with a slightly different emphasis: *our mutual/reciprocal distrust.* Here *reciprocal* considers the two sides separately or alternatively, while *mutually* considers them jointly.

Unlike *mutual*, *reciprocal* can also refer to a two-way relationship from only one side: *I know she doesn't trust me – my reciprocal distrust of her makes us even.* But not **X** *my mutual distrust of her.*

my See ME.

myself Avoid using *myself* as a simple substitute for *I* or *me*, especially in formal contexts: **X** *James and myself are going skating*; **?** *The manager will choose between Alice and myself for Captain.*

For other uses – acceptable and dubious – of *myself* (and also *himself*, *themselves*, and so on), see page 183.

naive, naivety These are now standard spellings in British English. In American English, the French forms are still used: *naïve/naïf* for the adjective, and *naïveté* for the noun. In British English too, the adjective or noun *faux-naïf* retains the French spelling, as does the rare noun *naïf* (feminine: *naïve*), meaning 'a person who is naive'.

name See CHRISTIAN NAME.

naturally See OF COURSE.

nature This word is often used by speakers or writers in an attempt to sound impressive: **?** *Her reputation is of a dubious nature*; **?** *a concerto of a technically advanced nature.* The words *description* and *character* are sometimes used in such constructions: **?** *a concerto of a technically advanced description.*

The effect tends to be pompous rather than impressive. If an abstract noun is really needed, use *kind*, *sort*, *type*, or *variety* instead. But better still, relate the adjective directly to its appropriate noun: *Her reputation is dubious* or *She has a dubious reputation; a technically advanced concerto.*

nauseous Purists limit *nauseous* to the sense 'sickening, nauseating, causing nausea', or 'offensive, repulsive, or disgusting': *the nauseous mixture of flavours.* The word is now commonly used in the sense 'nauseated, suffering from nausea': *The car journey made me terribly nauseous.* This usage is virtually standard now. If any possible

ambiguity arises (as in **?** *a nauseous travelling companion*), you can use *nauseated* (or *ill*, *bilious*, *sick*) or *nauseating* (or *sickening*) instead.

nautical, naval *Nautical* is a wide-ranging adjective; it means 'relating to, or involving seamen, ships, shipping or navigation': *nautical miles; nautical traffic; nautical charts.* *Naval* is more restricted: it means 'relating to, or characteristic of a navy – its equipment, personnel, customs, and so on': *naval warfare; naval manoeuvres.* It can also mean 'having a navy': *a great naval power.*

Take care how you spell *naval* – with an *a*. *Navel*, with an *e*, refers to one's 'belly button'.

necessarily A double stress is permissible – /**ness**ə-**serr**əli/ – though the single-stressed /**ness**ə-sərəli/ remains preferable in British English.

need The verb *need* can be used in two different ways in standard English: as a full verb, or as an auxiliary verb. You can say either *No one needs to fear them* or *No one need fear them*, but don't mix the two constructions: **X** *No one needs fear them.* See also page 193.

When referring to past actions, the full and auxiliary verbs can convey slightly different meanings. *I didn't need to go* (full verb) can be used whether you went or not; but *I needn't have gone* (auxiliary) implies that you did go.

Negro See BLACK.

neither 1. Whether pronoun or adjective, *neither* (like *either*) should refer to two subjects, no more and no less: *Neither of the twins will cooperate; Neither Tom nor Gideon will cooperate.* Where there are more than two elements, use *none*, *no*, or *not*: *None of the three brothers will cooperate.* The pattern **X** *Neither Tom nor Gideon nor Howard will cooperate*, though very common nowadays, is not strictly standard.

2. *Neither* is usually interpreted as *not either*, and because *either* is grammatically singular, so too is *neither.* Consequently, all related verbs, pronouns, and so on should also be singular: *Neither of my children is happy at his school.* Yet the grammatically incorrect form – **X** *Neither of my children are happy at their school* – is very inviting, since it both emphasises the plurality and avoids the sexism of the word *his.* For a discussion of the problem, see pages 89-90.

Where a plural verb is grammatically correct is in a *neither . . . nor* construction having either or both subjects in the plural: *Neither my parents nor my brother approve of the plan*.

3. Even if both subjects in a *neither . . . nor* construction are singular, you may still face a decision over the verb form – specifically, when the subjects include a pronoun. The rule is to give priority to the subject that is closer to the verb: *Neither you nor Jane has a chance; Neither Jane nor you have a chance*. For the sake of elegance, you may want to recast such sentences at times: *Jane has no chance, and neither have you*.

4. A *neither . . . nor* sentence requires symmetry: instead of the unbalanced ✗ *He is neither convinced by us nor them*, you could rephrase in various ways: *He is convinced by neither us nor them; He is convinced neither by us nor by them; He is neither convinced by us nor convinced by them*. See pages 198-199, 205.

5. Two obvious mistakes to avoid. First, using *or* rather than *nor* in a *neither . . . nor* construction: ✗ *Neither the judge or the jury believed her alibi*. Secondly, using *neither* rather than *either* in a sentence that already contains a negative: ✗ *It wasn't hot, and it wasn't cold neither*.

6. Both pronunciations of *neither* are acceptable: /**nī**thər/ and /**nee**thər/. The former is more common in British English, and the latter in North American usage.

See also EITHER; NOR; WHETHER.

neurosis The plural is *neuroses*, not ✗ *neurosises*.

never In standard English, *never* is used of a *period* of time: *This area has never suffered such floods; I'd never heard the rumour until yesterday*.

It should not be used to refer to a specific occasion: ✗ *I asked you to turn off the stove, but you never did*. This should read: *. . . but you didn't*.

See also NOT.

nice The adjective *nice* has changed considerably in meaning over the years. Deriving from Latin *nescius*, 'ignorant', it originally meant 'silly, foolish, or ignorant' in English. It later came to mean 'shy, modest', and 'wanton, or naughty'. Later still, 'demanding or fussy', and hence 'subtle, delicate, or discriminating': *a nice logical distinction; a nice appreciation of modern art*.

Some purists would like to restrict *nice* to the last of the above senses in modern usage. But the other modern senses are obviously widely established: 'kind, or friendly, or well-mannered': *a nice gesture/salesman*; 'pleasant or commendable': *a nice day*; 'precise; skilful': *a nice fit*. The problem is the 'lazy' or over-frequent use of *nice* as a term of mild approval: *What a nice dress; Let's have a nice chat over a nice cup of tea*. Do try to use adjectives that express your thoughts more accurately or expressively. A dress can be *elegant* or *colourful*; a chat can be *friendly* or *agreeable*, and so on.

Watch out too for the casual expressions *coming along nicely, doing very nicely for himself, nice and warm*, and so on. They are not acceptable in formal contexts, however widespread they may be in everyday speech.

nicety Don't confuse the noun *nicety* with *niceness* in the sense of 'pleasantness or kindness'. *Nicety* means 'refinement, subtlety, precision, or fastidiousness': *She tiptoed with ladylike nicety; conducted with the nicety of diplomatic protocol*. Hence the phrase *to a nicety*, 'exactly, with precision': *His volleys are all timed to a nicety*.

Nowadays *nicety* probably occurs more often in the specific sense of 'a subtle point, detail, or distinction; a refinement': *a nicety of etiquette*.

The plural form is perhaps more common: *diplomatic niceties; the niceties of formal grammar*.

In informal speech, *niceties* is also used to mean 'polite formalities': *Forget the niceties – we haven't got much time*.

niche The Anglicised pronunciation /nich/ is slightly preferable to the French form /neesh/.

nickel Note the spelling: the word ends in *-el*, not ✗ *-le* as in *fickle*.

no 1. It is still acceptable, though rather old-fashioned, to use the phrase *or no* instead of *or not*: *It will happen whether you like it or no*.

2. The idiom *to say no* (or *yes*) requires neither a capital letter nor quotation marks for the words *no* or *yes*: *I've asked three times, but he still says no*. Similarly, *The answer's still no; I won't take no for an answer*.

3. Take care when using *no* (and other negative words such as *none, not*, and *neither . . . nor*) in compound or complex sentences. If the subject is introduced by *no*, the negative sense may

carry over into later clauses. If you forget this, you may produce a faulty construction such as: ✗ *No prisoners will be exempt, but will have to appear on parade as usual*. What this sentence actually says is: *No prisoners . . . will have to appear on parade as usual*. To give the second clause its intended positive sense you would have to insert the word *all* after *but*.

no one See ANYONE.

no question Beware of the possible ambiguity lurking in the phrase *no question*: **?** *There can be no question that he's a thief*; **?** *There's no question of my returning tomorrow*. If in doubt, use alternative wording such as *no doubt* and *no possibility*. For more on *no question*, see page 204.

noisome This formal and rather literary adjective is unrelated to the words *noise* or *noisy*. *Noisome* is related to *annoy*; it usually means 'offensive, disgusting', especially in reference to smells: *a noisome rubbish dump*. Another sense, far less common, is 'harmful or dangerous': *a noisome chemical*.

Note the spelling – one *e*, which comes at the end – and the pronunciation: /**noy**-səm/, not ✗ /**noy**-zəm/.

non- 1. Should *non-* words have a hyphen? Sometimes you can choose freely: *non-flammable; nonflammable*. It is advisable to retain the hyphen in the following cases: when the base word begins with an *n* (*non-nuclear*) or a capital letter (*non-Chinese*) or a vowel (*non-event*) – though there are certain long-established exceptions, such as *nonentity*.

2. Many words take the negative prefixes *non-, un-*, or *in-* to form their opposites. Note that *non-* often produces a 'neutral' opposite, whereas *un-* or *in-* tends to produce unfavourable overtones. Compare: *unprofessional, nonprofessional; inhuman, nonhuman; unscientific, nonscientific*.

This distinction is a useful one. But be mindful of the fashionable trend to overuse the prefix *non-* – either to form an additional opposite when the original is already quite neutral (*nonessential* for *inessential*) or to form a new opposite when none is needed (*nontransparent* for *opaque*).

nonchalant The pronunciation is now a thoroughly Anglicised /**non**-shələnt/. To try anything closer to the French pronunciation would simply sound affected.

none The pronoun *none* can be variously understood as the equivalent of the following distinct phrases: *not one, no one, no people, not any*.

When it is understood as *not one, none* is singular and takes a singular verb: *The earthquake had destroyed every building – none was left standing*. Similarly when *none* is understood as *no one: None but he deserves our thanks*.

By contrast, *none* can legitimately take a plural verb when it is understood as *no people: There are none so blind as those who will not see*. Similarly, when *none* is understood as *not any: I searched everywhere for tomatoes, but there were none in the shop*. You could treat *none* as singular here (in the sense 'not one') but this might make the sentence sound stiff: **?** *but there was none in the shop*.

At other times, *none* could be understood equally well as *not one* or *not any: Twenty runners set out, but so far none has/have returned*.

none the less The expression *none the less* is traditionally written as three words, unlike *nevertheless*.

Although the fused form **?** *nonetheless* is increasingly common, particularly in American English, it is best avoided in formal writing.

nor, or 1. In *neither . . . nor* constructions, don't use *or* in place of *nor*: **✗** *He is neither involved or interested*.

2. Be careful of using *nor* when the first phrase is introduced by *not, never, no*, and so on. Here *or* or *and not* is usually more appropriate than *nor: He is not involved or even interested; They will never win a battle, and certainly not the war*. To use *nor* in such sentences would add a dubious second negative: **?** *He is not involved nor even interested*.

Note, however, that when the two negative alternatives are expressed in quite separate clauses, *nor* is appropriate, since the negative form of the first clause does not carry over to the second verb: *I am not involved, nor am I even interested*.

3. The phrases *and nor* and *but nor* are often found in informal British English: **?** *I didn't do it, and nor did my sister*. This usage is considered unsuitable for formal contexts (though curiously, no such objection applies to *and neither* or *but neither*).

4. Despite old schoolroom rules, *nor* can quite legitimately begin a sentence – and often very effectively. *The enemy's defences were simply too strong for us. Nor should it be forgotten that our soldiers were weakened by malaria*.

See also NEITHER.

nostalgia, nostalgic Originally meaning 'homesickness', *nostalgia* has developed a looser sense, and now refers to any yearning or sentimental longing for past circumstances or events: *She felt great nostalgia for her years as an undergraduate*.

The adjective *nostalgic* has undergone a similar development, and gone further still – or perhaps too far – in referring to any desire, memory, or attraction, whether painful or not.

Even less acceptably, *nostalgic* is sometimes applied to things (that cause nostalgia) rather than to people (who suffer it): **?** *a nostalgic smell*; **?** *a nostalgic little pub*. Use some other adjective instead: *touching, heart-rending, old-fashioned*, or the like.

not 1. Where to place *not* in a sentence is a common problem. Where *not* relates to the whole sentence, the 'natural' position is quite appropriate: *You will not go today*. But where *not* applies to only one part of the sentence, the natural position is dubious: **?** *You will not go today but tomorrow*. Such a sentence is neither symmetrical nor logical: for symmetry and logic, the *not* should appear as close as possible to the one element it relates to, so as to contrast it with the other element: *You will go not today but tomorrow*. If this sounds too stiff for the context, you could reword the sentence as follows: *You will not go today, but you will go tomorrow*.

In some idiomatic expressions, the 'illogical' positioning of *not* is enshrined by convention, and no misunderstanding is likely: **?** *All is not lost*; **?** *All that glistens is not gold*.

Sometimes, however, the positioning of *not* gives rise to real confusion or ambiguity, especially in sentences containing *because*: **?** *The rescuers did not stay behind because of the approaching storm*. Did the rescuers stay behind or not? If they did, a safer wording would be: *The rescuers stayed behind, though not because of the approaching storm*. If not, the safer wording would be: *Because of the approaching storm, the rescuers did not stay behind*.

2. Various other common errors and ambiguities afflict *not*:

☐ faulty range: **??** *If you do not shut up and keep pestering me, you will regret it*. Grammatically, this reads: *If you do not . . . keep pestering me, you will regret it* – hardly the intended meaning.

☐ faulty 'double negatives': **✗** *I didn't see nothing*; **✗** *I'm not listening to no more lies*.

☐ faulty 'multiple negatives': **??** *I shouldn't be surprised if David doesn't finish early*; **✗** *Even a bus strike could not prevent Robyn's thousands of fans from missing her match against Martina*. When the reader does eventually unravel such sentences, he or she will find that they probably express the opposite of the sense intended.

For a further discussion, see pages 203-205. See also NOT UN-.

not about to See ABOUT.

not only . . . but also When introducing parallel constructions, *not (only)* and *but (also)* must each be followed by the same kind of item: *I not only saw a trout, but also caught one* (two verbs); *I saw not only a trout but also a salmon* (two objects). To use non-parallel items would be to destroy the symmetry: **✗** *I not only saw a trout but also a salmon* (one verb, one noun). See pages 198-199.

not so much . . . as 1. Take care to retain the *as* in idiomatic constructions such as: *It was not so much a humiliating setback as a sobering one*. A common mistake is to replace *as* with *but* or *more*.

2. Such sentences need to be symmetrical – the two elements *not so much* and *as* should introduce parallel phrases or clauses. The following sentence unacceptably mixes the two patterns, using a verb (*felt*) in the *not so much* element, but omitting a verb in the *as* element: **✗** *Her view is not so much that she felt humiliated by the setback as sobered by it*. See pages 198-199.

not un- Handle with care the construction *not un-* (or *not im-, not dis-*, and so on), as in a *not unfair result* or a *not displeasing score*. Its critics (notably George Orwell) accuse it of being weak and euphemistic, and of creating unnecessary ambiguity. A positive adjective, they argue, would convey a clearer and bolder meaning. Compare: *This is a welcome message* and *This is a not unwelcome message*.

Yet in some ways the *not un-* construction enriches rather than impoverishes the English language, allowing a

605

useful degree of qualification: *I'm not unhappy with your work* is clearly different from *I'm happy with your work*. So the warning is not so much against using the construction as against overusing it. It is highly conspicuous, and should be reserved for special effects.

nubile Originally *nubile* meant 'ready or suitable for marriage, of marriageable age' and could be used of any young woman, attractive or not.

Nowadays, however, *nubile* is usually applied to adolescent girls or young women in the sense 'physically or sexually attractive', often with a somewhat leering tone: *a vision of nubile bodies on a tropical beach*. A number of purists still object to this looser use of the word, but it is now firmly established.

number When preceded by *the*, *number* takes a singular verb: *The number of students who fail is falling*. When preceded by *a* or *any*, *number* usually takes a plural verb: *A large number of students have failed; Any number of cancellations are possible*.

O, oh *O* is rare nowadays, and confined to literary contexts in which it introduces a direct appeal or imperative: *O Captain, my Captain; Hear, O Israel; O ye of little faith*. It is always written as a capital, and is usually not followed by a comma.

Oh is used quite differently. It introduces exclamations or calls (*Oh Mary, there's a letter for you*), or expresses an emotion or a reflective pause. It takes a capital *o* only at the beginning of a sentence. And the punctuation following it varies according to context: *Oh dear; Oh for the wings of a dove; Oh, must we go?; Oh! Help! Stop him!*

oasis Note the plural. It is *oases*, not ✗ *oasises*.

objective, subjective 1. The adjectives *objective* and *subjective* both have technical meanings in grammar, medicine, and philosophy. In philosophical settings, *objective* means essentially 'existing independently of an observer', and *subjective* 'relating to the mind of a perceiver'. In ordinary language, several looser senses have developed from these philosophical meanings, with the general effect of distinguishing external, material, observable reality from internal mental processes and impressions: *Her fear of an invasion is totally subjective – there's simply no objec-*

tive reason for it at all. Such uses are now wholly acceptable.

Also acceptable, just, is the use of *objective* to mean 'unbiased; free from prejudice or personal interest; not influenced by emotion', and the use of *subjective* to mean 'biased; subject to personal prejudice, emotion or speculation': *Let's put aside our rivalry and approach this problem in an objective way*.

Take care, however, not to overuse *objective* and *subjective* as pompous or pretentious synonyms for *fair*, *honest*, or *accurate* on the one hand, and *distorted*, *dubious*, or *personal* on the other: ❓ *Give me an objective opinion/valuation*; ❓ *Her comments on the firm are full of subjective whims*. Use a simpler and more accurate adjective in such cases.

2. As a noun, *objective* has technical meanings in philosophy, grammar, and optics. It also has the sense of 'a goal, specifically of a military operation' – *The bridge was our next objective* – though nowadays it can refer to any goal, aim, or intention: *The company's objective is (to establish) a larger share of the market*. Some purists dislike the loose and widespread use of *objective*, particularly when followed by verbal constructions, preferring unpretentious nouns such as *object*, *goal*, *aim*, or intention.

occurred Note the spelling: double *c* and double *r*.

octopus Two plurals are correct: *octopuses* and *octopi*.

oculist, optician, optometrist An *oculist*, now more commonly known as an *ophthalmologist* or *ophthalmic surgeon*, is a specialist medical doctor.

Note the spelling of *oculist*: only one *c*, unlike *occult*; and note the spelling *ophth-* in *ophthalmologist*, and the pronunciation /ofth-/.

An *optician* specialises in lenses, glasses, or other optical instruments. A *dispensing optician* makes and sells glasses according to the prescription of an oculist or optometrist.

An *optometrist*, also known as an *ophthalmic optician*, is trained and qualified to test eyes and prescribe corrective lenses.

of 1. In spoken English, *have* is often contracted to the sound /əv/, as in *could've*. Some speakers, particularly children, confuse this sound with the word *of*: ✗ *I could of hit him*.

2. In certain dialects, *of* is still used instead of *on* in sentences such as: *He's always late of a Friday evening*. In standard English this should be... *on a Friday evening* or... *on Friday evenings*.

3. Remember that *of* is necessary in certain simple constructions: *a couple of eggs, a pair of socks* and so on. Don't omit it. On the other hand, don't insert it in constructions that do not call for it: ✗ *What colour of car would you like?*

4. In longer and more complicated sentences, the temptation to omit or insert *of* inappropriately is even greater: ✗ *I can't tell the difference between a pearl cultured in a pearl farm and of one found in a 'wild' oyster*. The *of* apparently marks off the second element, but has no grammatical justification.

On the other hand: ✗ *We spoke in Greek, the rudiments of which we both had some grasp*. This should be *the rudiments of which we both had some grasp of*.

5. Do try, however, to limit the frequency of *of* in a sentence – it does tend to over-abound. Standard simplifying techniques are shown in these examples: *the theories of Newton – Newton's theories; the theories of relativity – relativity theories; theories of the cosmos – cosmic theories*. But don't use such simplifications without thinking: you cannot safely reduce *theories of the universe* to ❓ *universal theories*, since it causes ambiguity; and you cannot really reduce *the movement of luggage* to ❓ *luggage movement*.

of course Many speakers use the phrase *of course* unthinkingly as a nervous, but irritating, conversational tic, much like *you know* or *actually*. But it does have its uses – the phrase can be subtle, devious, or mischievous, as by implying that something is obvious when the opposite is true: ❓❓ *Cardinal Mezzofanti could of course read 164 languages, so he understood the text perfectly*.

Among its many other uses, *of course* is good for coaxing: ❓ *Of course we understand your problem, but try to see it from our point of view*; for flattering: ❓ *My daughter has seen all your films of course, and would love your autograph*; even for deception: ❓ *I believe in free speech, of course, but this is going too far*.

To argue that *of course* is illogical or redundant is not necessarily to disqualify it: language is not a completely logical system, and often benefits from the leavening within such words or phrases as *of course, clearly, needless to say*, and *as you know*. But whatever your justification for using it, do at least use it sparingly.

off of The complex preposition *off of* is common in American English speech, and in some British dialects: **✗** *Get off of my chair!* This is non-standard: use *off* on its own. And don't use *off of*, or even *off*, in place of *from*: **✗** *I borrowed it off (of) my friend.*

often The *t* is now sounded quite frequently, but the older pronunciation /**off**'n/ is still more common and is perhaps slightly preferable; **?** /**awf**'n/ sounds very old-fashioned, however.

The forms *oftener* and *oftenest* are acceptable alongside *more often* and *most often*.

Oh See O, OH.

O.K., okay *O.K.* has failed to shake off its feel of American informality, and remains unacceptable in formal contexts.

O.K. is usually written with full stops, but the form *OK*, without full stops, is now fairly widespread too – whether as an adjective, adverb, noun, or interjection. When used as a verb, the expanded form *okay* is preferable than *O.K.* – *Has the boss okayed our long leave?* – though *O.K.'d* and *OK'd* are also acceptable.

older, oldest See ELDER.

omelette Note the spelling: an *e* before the *l*, and ending -*ette*. The spelling *omelet* is American.

on behalf of See BEHALF.

on to, onto 1. The one-word form *onto* still meets resistance from many careful speakers of British English. Yet when used as a preposition meaning 'to a position on', *onto* is no more objectionable than *into*: *jumped onto a chair; jumped into the pool.*

The two-word *on to* clearly is necessary, however, when *on* expresses continuity, or when *to* is part of the infinitive (or both): *Move right on to the end, please; She stayed on to complete her degree.*

2. In informal usage, *onto* is also used to mean 'in contact with, in communication with' – **?** *Get onto headquar-*

ters *for clarification* – and 'on the trail of' or 'aware of': **?** *I think I'm onto something*; **?** *The boss is onto your little tricks.* Such uses are not appropriate in formal contexts.

one 1. The indefinite personal pronoun *one*, 'a person, anyone', needs careful handling. It can sound pretentious if overused: **?** *When one sets out in life, one may not anticipate all the obstacles that one may have to face.*

Use any of the elegant alternatives available: *When someone/a person sets out...he may not...; When people set out...they may not; When you set out...you may not...* See EVERYBODY; HE; YOU; and also pages 186-187.

If you do begin a sentence with *one*, don't switch to another pronoun in mid-sentence: **✗** *One cannot know what life has in store for you.*

2. When *one* is used instead of *I* or *we*, it can sound even more pompous: **?** *One enjoyed one's schooldays, but how one looked forward to college.* Use first-person pronouns and adjectives: *I, me, my*, and so on.

3. Note that the construction *one of those who* or *one of the Xs that* should be followed by a plural verb: the *who* or *that* refers not to *one*, but to *those* or *the Xs: She is one of those rare people who inspire deep trust; He is one of the few boxers that have retired unhurt.* See page 173.

4. Should a singular or a plural verb follow the construction *one in two/three/four...* (or *one out of two...*)?

The plural often sounds more natural and more logical: **?** *One in twenty children are underfed.* But strictly, the subject is *one*, and so the verb should be singular: *Only one out of three students is male.*

5. Avoid faulty constructions of this pattern: **✗** *He is one of the finest, if not the finest, pianists to perform here.* The correct phrasing is: *He is one of the finest pianists, if not the finest (pianist), to perform here.*

See also ANYONE; EACH OTHER.

one another See EACH OTHER.

only 1. When it comes to the positioning of *only* in a sentence, logic conflicts with idiom. Logic favours placing *only* as close as possible to the word or phrase it relates to: *He drinks only wine; I can give you only five pounds/give you five pounds only.* Idiom usually favours placing *only*

between the subject and the verb: *He only drinks wine; I can only give you five pounds.* See page 201.

In general, the idiomatic positioning is adequate for speech and most informal writing. Avoid it if ambiguity threatens, however, and try to avoid it always in formal writing. If the logical positioning sounds stiff and unnatural, however, try a different wording altogether: *All I can give you is five pounds.* And note that some idiomatic constructions will not allow a 'logical' rephrasing: *She only sighed more deeply; in what can only be described as an atrocity.*

These considerations apply also to *merely, even*, and *just*, and sometimes to *solely*. However, few people object to positioning *just* before a verb: *I just want 50p.*

2. In colloquial English, *only* is also used as a conjunction meaning 'but' or 'however': *I'd love to go, only I can't.* This usage is suitable for informal contexts only. Avoid it in formal writing.

3. Take care how you use the combination *only too*. Used properly, it suggests excess or disproportion: *They are only too likely to resume hostilities; It's only too true.* Think of *only too* as appropriate when it can be replaced by *all too*.

In its looser sense, near to 'extremely', *only too* is best avoided in formal contexts: **?** *I'll be only too glad to help.* Understood literally, this sentence is more insulting than reassuring.

optician See OCULIST.

optimism, optimistic, pessimism, pessimistic The nouns *optimism* and *pessimism* refer primarily to states of mind or dispositions – the tendency to see the best/worst in everything and expect the best/worst to happen.

The related adjectives *optimistic* and *pessimistic* convey similar meanings, chiefly: 'expecting a favourable/unfavourable outcome'; having a hopeful/hopeless outlook'.

All four words have acquired extended senses – criticised by some purists – and are often used as little more than impressive-sounding substitutes for cheerfulness/gloominess, hopeful/hopeless, encouraging/discouraging, and the like. Certainly they can be more appropriate at times: *a pessimistic medical report*, for example, is preferable to *a gloomy medical report*. But more often than not they have a pretentious ring if simply replacing a plain traditional term: **?** *We are optimistic about an early reply; no cause for pessimism.*

optometrist See OCULIST.

or 1. When *or* joins two or more singular nouns as the subject of a clause, the subject remains singular and requires a singular verb: *Not even a howling wind or a banging door is enough to wake me.* (If *and* joins singular nouns, they become jointly a plural subject requiring a plural verb.) If all the nouns joined by *or* are plural, a plural verb is needed. If some are singular, and some plural, the verb should match whichever noun is closest to it.

2. Similarly, when *or* connects pronouns, the form of the verb is determined by the pronoun closest to it: **?** *Am I or you going to do it?* **?** *You or she is going to pay for this.* But these are hardly elegant constructions, and are best reworded: *Am I going to do it, or are you? One of you is going to pay for this.*

3. When listing several alternatives, you may write *A,B,C, or D* (the last comma is optional), or *A or B or C or D*, or even *A, B, C, D* – provided that *A, B, C,* and *D* have the same status in grammar.

If any of the elements differs in status, it needs to be clearly separated: **X** *You can shout, scream, throw a fit, or you can cooperate and start talking.* Another *or* is necessary after *scream*: it would serve to distinguish the three grammatically equivalent elements *shout, scream* and *throw a fit* from one another; the second *or* would then distinguish this group from the grammatically (and practically) different element *you can cooperate and start talking.*

4. In *neither...nor* sentences, *or* cannot replace *nor*: **X** *I want neither to go or to stay.*

In certain other negative constructions, *or* can replace *nor* – *I don't want to go nor/or to stay* – so long as the negative force of the first part of the sentence is properly transferred to the second part. The following sentence lacks the necessary grammatical parallels between the two elements, so *or* is inadequate to relay the negative sense onto the second element: **X** *He could see no end to the road or keep walking any longer...* Use *nor* instead of *or*, or else restructure the first clause to produce a symmetrical sentence: *He couldn't see an end to the road or/nor keep walking any longer.*

5. Whatever the schoolroom rule may be, feel free to use *or* at the start of a sentence: *Or so it seems.*

oral See AURAL.

ordinance, ordnance, ordonnance An *ordinance* is a regulation, statute, or decree. It can also be a long-established custom, and a religious rite, especially Holy Communion.

Ordnance is military weaponry, munitions, and supplies.

Ordonnance is an old variant of *ordinance*, and is still used of ordinances in French law. Nowadays it also refers to the systematic arrangement of the elements of a building or of a literary or artistic composition.

oregano The pronunciation /**orri**-**gaa**no/ is standard; /aw-**regg**ənō/ is American.

orient, orientate As a verb, *to orient* originally meant 'to position (a church) facing east', but has come to mean 'to align in a particular direction': *oriented our beds north to south.* Hence such extended meanings as 'to familiarise (someone/oneself) with new surroundings', or 'to get one's bearings': *He was soon oriented to their strange ways; I oriented myself by means of the mountain peak.*

The past participle form, *oriented*, is often used to mean 'interested in; inclined towards': **?** *a law-oriented Arts degree.* This lazy usage is inappropriate for formal contexts, which would favour a paraphrase such as *specialising in* or *concentrating on*.

The noun for *to orient* is *orientation*, and from it derives the British variant verb *to orientate*. This form is often used without a direct object – *Eastern Europe is orientating strongly towards the West* – and as a past participle: *more fun- than work-orientated.*

other See EACH OTHER.

ought In standard English, *ought* is typically followed by *to* and another verb: *You ought not/oughtn't to help him; Ought/Oughtn't you to help him?*

In American English, *should* and *shouldn't* are used in questions and negative constructions in preference to *ought.* Though not wrong, it loses the stronger moral force of *ought.*

Don't omit the *to* when *ought* introduces another verb – **??** *You ought help him.* In questions and negative sentences, omitting *to* is more common, though still not standard in formal usage: **?** *You oughtn't help him;* **?** *Ought you help him?* You may, however, omit the *to* when *ought* appears at the end of a sentence: *Must we go? We really ought (to).*

over In much modern writing, especially journalism, *over* is used rather unthinkingly and sloppily in place of other words or phrases: *a strike over (for) better conditions; a strike over (provoked by) an unfair dismissal; worried over (about) the delay; a reduction over (on/from) last year's costs.* Think twice before using *over* as a catch-all preposition.

overly In American and Scottish English, *overly* is widely used in the sense 'excessively': *His mistakes have been overly criticised.* In British English, the word is catching on in negative sentences – *I'm not overly anxious* – but is not yet acceptable in formal speech or writing. Use the prefix *over-* instead, or an alternative adverb such as *excessively, unduly,* or *inordinately.*

owing to See DUE TO.

pace The Latin preposition *pace*, /**pay**-si/ or /**paa**-chay/, means literally 'with peace to ...' In English, it is used to mean roughly 'despite the view of...', and is placed before a person's name when his or her opinion is being respectfully rejected: *A little knowledge,* PACE *Alexander Pope, is not really a dangerous thing.*

Note that *pace* does not mean 'according to' or 'despite the example of'; and it cannot precede a noun that refers to a thing rather than a person: **X** *A little knowledge,* PACE *Pope's opinion, is not really a dangerous thing;* **X** *A little knowledge,* PACE *Alexander Pope, is a dangerous thing.*

paean, paeon, peon A *paean* (sometimes *pean* in American English) is a song of praise; a *paeon* is a metrical unit in Greek verse; and a *peon* is a pauper or a peasant in Latin America.

pair The noun *pair* can take either a singular or a plural verb. Use a singular verb when the two items are considered a unit – *This pair of loudspeakers is now on sale* – and a plural verb when two items are considered separate individuals: *The pair of them get on better than ever before.* See also page 175.

The plural *pairs* is sometimes reduced to *pair* in regional or informal speech:

? *two pair of boots*. This is obviously unsuitable for formal contexts.

Pandora's box In Greek mythology, the gods sent Pandora and her box to punish man. Disobeying their orders, she opened the box out of curiosity, and thereby released all the evils that have since plagued the world. All that remained in the box was hope.

In ordinary use, the phrase now refers to any source of great suffering or troubles, especially one that may originally have seemed relatively harmless: *Those conducting the appeasement policy were opening a Pandora's box*.

The term does not mean 'a treasure chest': **X** *We aren't a Pandora's box, so keep your pay demands within limits*.

paradigm Outside its technical meanings in philosophy, psychology, and grammar, the noun *paradigm*, /**par**rə-dīm/, tends to be used as a grandiose term for '(a perfect) model', 'a standard', '(an excellent) example', or the like: *His actions are a paradigm for other world leaders*. In common with most vogue words, it is not so much wrong as pretentious.

Note that *paradigm* cannot apply directly to people, only to things or attributes. A person who is 'a perfect model' or 'an excellent example' is described as a *paragon*. Compare: *She is a paragon of virtue; Her virtue is a paradigm worthy of imitation*.

The adjective of *paradigm* is *paradigmatic* – it is pronounced /**par**rə-dig-**mat**tik/.

parallel Note the spelling: single *r*, double *l*, then single *l*.

parameter From its original role as a technical term in mathematics, *parameter/s* has become a vogue word, meaning roughly the same as *constraint*, *boundary*, or *limit* – **??** *budgetary parameters*; **??** *some parameters of social acceptability* – and also as *characteristic feature*: **??** *parameters of democracy*.

In such general contexts, the word is usually grandiose and imprecise, a poor alternative to an established synonym such as *restraint*, *border*, *scope*, *outline*, or *range*.

paranoia, paranoid, paranoiac *Paranoia* is a serious mental disorder characterised by delusions of grandeur or persecution. The derived forms *paranoid* and *paranoiac* are both acceptable, both as nouns and

adjectives (though some psychiatrists favour one over the other).

But in formal contexts, don't use either term as a loose synonym for *anxious*, *suspicious*, or *touchy* – and don't use *paranoia* itself to refer to mere anxiety or suspiciousness.

participle The standard pronunciation is /**par**ti-sipp'l/; the common pronunciation using second-syllable stress, **?** /paar-**tis**sip'l/ is still frowned on slightly.

particularly This adverb needs careful positioning, as the following two examples show: *He doesn't particularly want to go; He particularly doesn't want to go*.

Don't neglect the -*lar*- syllable when pronouncing the word.

partly, partially These two adverbs are sometimes interchangeable, but usually have slightly different meanings. Here are some guidelines for deciding which to use.

Use *partly* when discussing a physical object and emphasising the part as opposed to the whole: *a house partly of brick*; also in the sense 'to some extent': *partly to blame; partly due to human error*.

Use *partially* when discussing a condition (rather than an object), and emphasising the whole rather than a part. It means roughly 'to a limited degree; not fully': *He is partially sighted; The judge partially upheld the lower court's decision*.

The distinction can be very fine, the difference between 'in parts' (*partly*) and 'in part' (*partially*). So perhaps the difference between *a partly built house* and *a partially built house* is the difference between a house that is complete in some parts but incomplete in others (*partly*), and a house that is well under way generally but as yet not complete in any part (*partially*).

passed, past *Passed* is the form of the past tense and past participle of to *pass*: *She passed by; The winter has passed, and spring has come*.

The form of the related adjective, adverb, preposition, and noun is *past*: *the past ten years; She hurried past; He ran past me; Think of the past*.

Beware of confusing the adjective and the past participle: *The danger was past; The danger has passed*.

patent British English favours different pronunciations for different

senses: /**patt**'nt/ for legal and official uses (*letters patent; inventor's patent*) and /**payt**'nt/ for general, non-technical uses (*a patent of respectability; patent honesty*).

pathetic The traditional meaning of *pathetic* – still current – is 'arousing or expressing sympathy or sadness': *a pathetic cry of grief*.

In informal or slangy usage, the word can mean 'feeble, inadequate' – *such a pathetic fire* – or 'uninteresting, worthless': *a pathetic crowd at the party*. Avoid these unfavourable senses in formal contexts. And beware of ambiguity in all contexts: **?** *Mathilda Sorenson gave a pathetic performance as Lady Macbeth*.

Don't confuse *pathetic* (and the noun *pathos*) with *bathetic* (and *bathos*), which refers to anticlimax: *a bathetic end to an otherwise powerful play*.

patriot The pronunciations /**pay**tri-ət/ and /**patt**ri-ət/ are both acceptable.

pavilion Note the spelling: no double letters as in *million*.

Pearl Harbor This was an American base, and should therefore keep the American spelling. Resist the temptation to give it the British form of **?** *Pearl Harbour*.

pedagogical The second g is preferably soft, /**pedd**ə-**goj**ik'l/, though a hard g is also acceptable: /-**gogg**ik'l/.

pejorative Note the spelling: *pej*-, not **X** *perj*-. In pronunciation, a second-syllable stress is now standard, though the traditional first-syllable stress remains acceptable.

penchant The Frenchified pronunciation /**poN**-shoN/ is perhaps still slightly preferable to the Anglicised /**pen**chənt/.

penicillin Note the spelling: the only double letter is the *l*; think of *pencilling*.

penny Since the change to decimal currency in the United Kingdom in 1971, *penny* has largely died out as a term for referring to currency. The informal abbreviation *p*, /pee/, or the word *pence* is used instead: *a five-p coin; fifty pence, please*.

In the United States, *penny* is still used to refer to a one-cent coin. And in British English, the word survives in various forms: *I haven't a penny to my name; turns up like a bad penny; gone to spend a penny*.

per Certain formulas and ratios are always expressed with the preposition *per*: *miles per gallon; miles per hour; metres per second per second; three billion dollars per annum.*

But in informal or unofficial contexts, *per* is now usually unnecessary and affected: **?** *I sleep eight hours per night;* **?** *Take one pill three times per day.* The preposition *a* is preferable here: *I sleep eight hours a night.*

Avoid also using *per* (and *via*) as a grandiose substitute for *by*: **✗** *Will you travel per air or sea;* **✗** *It has been sent per express delivery.* And avoid too, in ordinary usage, the jargon phrase **?** *as per instructions* and the jocular phrase **??** *as per usual.* The appropriate standard forms are *according to instructions* and *as usual.*

per cent, percentage 1. In North America, *per cent* is often written as one word, *percent.* This spelling is still considered unacceptable in formal British English.

2. In American English, *percent* is often used as a noun. In British English, the noun form of *per cent* is *percentage*: *What percentage of your income do you save?*

3. Avoid using *percentage* in the sense 'a small percentage/number': **✗** *Only a percentage of workers supported the strike.* (See also FRACTION; PROPORTION.)

4. Use *percentages* sparingly in ordinary discussions. Simple fractions are often preferable: say or write *a third* rather than $33\frac{1}{3}\%$, and refer to *(a) half* rather than *50%.*

5. Percentages usually take a plural verb when the related noun (stated or implied) is plural: *Ten per cent of the trees are dying; One per cent of cars are untaxed.*

When the related noun is singular, use a singular verb: *Ten per cent of the orchard is lost; Ten per cent is a very low mark.*

6. *Percentage* is sometimes used to mean 'advantage; a slight gain or benefit' – *There's no percentage in working overtime* – and, adjectivally, 'relying on small, safe gains, rather than profitable risks': *played a percentage game.* These senses are fully accepted in sports journalism, but should otherwise be restricted to informal contexts.

perfect Since *perfect* strictly means 'flawless, complete in all respects', it does not really allow qualifying words

such as *more, most,* or *very*: **??** *a most perfect gemstone.* You may, however, speak of one thing as being *more nearly perfect* than another. (See VERY, and page 202.)

When used more loosely to mean 'excellent', *perfect* can take qualifying words before: *a most perfect day; The weather couldn't be more perfect.*

-person See CHAIRMAN.

personal, personally These words are useful in their proper places, as when confirming that a person acted or suffered directly rather than indirectly – *The chef makes a personal inspection of each dish; The chef inspects each dish personally* – or highlighting a contrast: *You may disagree, but personally I think we can't lose.*

But *personal* and *personally* are now used more loosely, and often quite superfluously, to give a vague emphasis to a sentence: **??** *I'll tell you what I personally think;* **??** *He makes a point of shaking hands personally with the staff;* **??** *She's a personal friend of mine;* **??** *He paid me a personal visit.*

Think twice before allowing *personal* and *personally* in such contexts.

perspicacious, perspicuous Don't confuse these two adjectives.

Perspicacious means 'acutely perceptive, or understanding; shrewdly discerning', and is usually applied to people or their faculties: *a perspicacious mind/critic.*

Similar in meaning are the two adjectives *perceptive* and *percipient.*

Perspicuous means 'lucid or clearly expressed; easy to understand', and is usually applied to speech or writing: *a perspicuous lecture.* More rarely, it means 'expressing clearly': *a perspicuous lecturer.*

The corresponding nouns are *perspicacity* (or *perspicaciousness*) and *perspicuity.*

pessimism See OPTIMISM.

pharaoh Note the spelling: it ends in *-aoh.*

phenomenon, phenomena, phenomenal 1. From its original technical sense in philosophy, *phenomenon* has come to refer to any extraordinary or remarkable person, event, or thing: *He is a phenomenon of agility; Space flight is no longer the phenomenon it*

once was. *Phenomenon* can also mean, even more loosely, 'something slightly peculiar or unusual': *the phenomenon of a sandless beach.*

Similarly, *phenomenal* is now most often used in the sense 'extraordinary, outstanding, remarkable': *a phenomenal achievement/success; a man of phenomenal strength.*

Use these and all other voguish intensifiers sparingly. If everything noteworthy is a *phenomenon* or *phenomenal*, these words will rapidly lose all impact.

2. Note that *phenomenon* is singular, and *phenomena* (very rarely *phenomenons*) is plural. Don't use *phenomena* as a singular, and avoid the false plural **✗** *phenomenas.* Compare CRITERION; DATA; MEDIA.

Philippines Note the spelling: single *l,* then double *p.*

phoney, phony The spelling *phoney* is favoured in British English, *phony* in American English.

piracy The pronunciation is /pīr-əsi/, not **?** /pirrəsi/ as in *conspiracy.*

plain, plane To distinguish these easily confused words, remember that *plain* has many senses as an adjective – 'clear', 'pure', 'straightforward', 'ordinary', 'unattractive', and so on – but only one nontechnical sense as a noun: 'a flat, treeless stretch of land' – *the Salisbury Plain.*

Conversely, *plane* has many noun senses – 'a geometrical surface', 'an aeroplane', 'a level or grade', and so on – but only one nontechnical sense as an adjective: 'flat', as in *a plane surface. Plane* can also be a verb: *to plane* is 'to smooth with a carpenter's plane'. The *plane* in *plane tree* is a quite unconnected word.

plenty 1. Children and some dialect speakers often omit the *of* from the construction *plenty of X/Xs*: **?** *There's plenty wine in the cellar;* **?** *We've plenty eggs.* This is nonstandard, and unacceptable in formal contexts.

2. *Plenty* is often used informally, especially in American English, to mean 'very' or 'sufficiently, quite': **??** *He's plenty rich;* **??** *Your letter is plenty long enough.* Avoid such constructions in formal speech or writing.

3. Unless you intend some joky or archaic effect, avoid the forms *plenteous, aplenty,* and *in plenty.* They sound affected, even in formal contexts: **?** *We had champagne aplenty/in* plenty; **?** *a plenteous supply of champagne and caviar.*

plus When used as a preposition meaning 'with, in addition to', *plus* does not create a compound subject in the way that *and* does. So the verb should agree with the noun that precedes *plus*: *A good job plus a new car is very desirable; Savings plus interest amount to just over £5000.*

In informal contexts, *plus* is also used as a conjunction, meaning 'and' – **?** *I've a good job, plus I'm rich* – and as a noun, meaning 'something positive; an advantage or gain': *The company car is a plus.* Restrict such uses to informal speech or writing.

pogrom Note the pronunciation: /pə-**grom**/ is the traditional standard, being closest to the Russian original, but /**pog**-rəm/ or /**pog**-rom/ is now also acceptable.

point In informal usage, the noun *point* is often followed directly by the *-ing* form of the verb: **?** *There's no point waiting.* More formal usage requires the insertion of the preposition *in*: *There's no point in waiting.*

point of view The phrase *point of view* refers to a general mental attitude, or to a standpoint or position from which things are observed: *The novel is written from the point of view of a Gestapo officer.*

The phrase is therefore not synonymous with *view/s* or *opinion/s*, especially when these are specific: **X** *My tutor gave me a low mark because he disagrees with my point of view;* **X** *My point of view is that this stalemate cannot last.* Avoid using *point of view* in this way.

And avoid using the phrase to create needlessly complex prepositions: **??** *Our staff are expert from the point of view of providing financial advice* (or even worse; **??** *Our staff are expert from a financial advice point of view*). It is far simpler and more elegant to say *Our staff are expert at providing financial advice.*

police The standard pronunciation is /pə-**leess**/ – two distinct syllables; don't slur it into the single-syllabled **??** /pleess/.

politics See -ICS.

pommel Note the pronunciation: /**pum**m'l/ is traditionally preferred, but /**pom**m'l/ is also acceptable.

Portuguese Note the spelling: don't neglect the second *u*.

practicable This adjective means primarily 'feasible, workable, capable of being done': *It's just not practicable to move the sofa through such a narrow doorway.* People often use *practical* – rather dubiously – in such sentences.

Practicable can also mean 'usable, reasonably suitable and efficient': *This vehicle is practicable for dirt roads.* In such contexts, *practical* is quite appropriate too, though the emphases differ somewhat: *practicable* is more qualified, as though conveying the unstated comment 'though hardly ideal'; *practical* is more positive, suggesting considerable efficiency.

The difference between *practical* and *practicable* is most apparent in their opposites. Something that is *not practicable* (that is, *impracticable*) is impossible, and cannot be carried out. Something that is *not practical* (that is, *impractical* or sometimes *unpractical*) may be both theoretically and physically possible, but is too inefficient or wasteful to be worth carrying out.

Note finally that *practicable* cannot ordinarily apply directly to people, whereas *practical* obviously can: *a practical woman, who can tell a practicable project from an impossible dream.*

practice, practise Don't confuse the noun *practice* with the verb *to practise*. Compare *licence* and *to license*. As an aid to memory, think of *advice* (noun) and *advise* (verb), where the difference in pronunciation provides a clear guide to the spelling. And don't be confused by American English, in which *practice* (like *license*) serves for both noun and verb.

Take care when using these words as adjectives: *a practice session; a well-practised athlete.*

practitioner Note the spelling: *-tition-* in the middle, as in *petitioner.* Don't model it on *practice* or *practise.*

precedence, precedent Both of these words are related to the verb *to precede*, 'to go before'. A *precedent* is an event (or, specifically, a judicial decision) that serves as a model or example for later cases: *This wage formula sets/creates a dangerous precedent; no precedent for doing that.*

Precedent can also be an adjective, meaning 'preceding' – a very old-fashioned usage: *My claim was pre-*

cedent to yours; Hers is the precedent claim. The derived form *unprecedented* – 'unheard of, unique' – is fairly common: *an unprecedented show of public dissatisfaction.*

The noun *precedence* (sometimes *precedency*) suggests priority in importance or status rather than in time: *Eventually, political realism takes precedence over revolutionary idealism.* More specifically, *precedence* refers to the ceremonial order of social or other rank, especially on formal occasions: *A general has precedence over/of a brigadier, and a major gives precedence to a colonel.*

As nouns, both *precedence* and *precedent* can be pronounced /**preess**-/, though /**press**-/ is preferable. As an adjective, *precedent* moves the stress to its second syllable: /pri-**seed**'nt/.

precipitate, precipitous Don't confuse these adjectives. The primary sense of *precipitate*, /pri-**sip**i-tət/, is 'rushing ahead, or headlong': *a precipitate retreat.* It can also mean 'sudden, abrupt' – *a precipitate end to the trial* – and 'done rashly, over-hasty': *a precipitate decision.*

By contrast, *precipitous* refers primarily to terrain, and means 'like a precipice', 'having many precipices', or simply 'very steep': *the castle's huge precipitous walls; a precipitous region, unfit for cattle; the road's precipitous descent.* Figuratively, *precipitous* and its adverb *precipitously* are used of dramatic, often disastrous, declines: *a precipitous fall in the company's fortunes; profits declining precipitously.*

The use of *precipitous* for *precipitate* in the sense 'rash or over-hasty' – as in **?** *a precipitous decision* – is now fairly common, and perhaps approaching acceptability. Careful writers, however, still keep these adjectives and their related adverbs distinct.

prefer, preferable 1. Don't use *more* or *most* to qualify the adjective *preferable* and the verb *to prefer*. That would be redundant: **X** *Choose whichever you find the more/most preferable.*

2. When both elements of a preference are mentioned, the correct pattern is *to prefer X to Y*: *I prefer wine to beer.* Most other constructions indicating preference also use the preposition *to*: *I find wine preferable to beer; I drink wine in preference to beer.* But: *I have a preference for wine over water.*

Don't confuse these constructions, and don't use the prepositions *over, above, before, instead of,* or *than* when

Ready-Reference Word Guide

to is required: **✗** *I find wine preferable than water*.

3. Note that *preference* and *preferable* are both stressed on the first syllable, and that neither has a double *r*.

To prefer, however, does double its final *r* in the forms *preferred* and *preferring*.

premise, premiss *Premise* is the standard spelling of noun and verb, but *premiss* can also be used in the sense of 'a proposition in logic'.

prescribe, proscribe These two verbs, though almost exactly opposite in meaning, are easily confused.

To prescribe, /pri-**scrīb**/, means primarily 'to lay down as a rule, to order, or advise': *Monasticism prescribes abstinence*. In medical terminology, it also means 'to recommend or order the use of (a drug or treatment)': *She prescribed antibiotics*.

To proscribe, /pro-**skrīb**/, means 'to condemn or prohibit, especially by law; to outlaw, banish': *The General proscribed all trade unions*.

So *a prescribed book* is one recommended for study, while *a proscribed book* is one banned by censors.

The related adjectives are *prescriptive* and *proscriptive*. *Prescriptive* is often contrasted with *descriptive*: *Should a grammar book be prescriptive or descriptive of current usage?*

present Using the adjective *present* before a noun tends to create an over-formal or pompous effect: *the present writer; at the present time; Present circumstances will not permit it*. Reword such constructions: *I/me; now; We cannot do it/It is not possible*.

presently This adverb once meant 'immediately' or 'currently'. Its chief meaning, now, though rather old-fashioned, is 'soon; in a short while': *He opened his eyes, and presently rose from his bed*.

In American and Scottish English, the old sense of 'currently, now, at the moment' is fairly common: **?** *I'm presently unemployed*. It is undergoing a revival in England too, though remains nonstandard. Use *currently* or *at present* instead in formal speech or writing.

prestigious Though originally associated with conjuring or trickery, *prestigious* now means 'conferring high status or prestige' – *a prestigious prize* – and 'having or enjoying prestige, renowned': *a prestigious actor*. Both these senses, and particularly the latter, still infuriate some purists, though they are firmly established. If you want to avoid any chance of controversy, you can always choose a synonym: *esteemed, renowned, admired, influential, highly valued*, and so on. You can also use *prestige* itself adjectivally before a noun: *a prestige appointment*.

presume See ASSUME.

presumptuous Note the spelling – three *u*'s. By contrast, *presumption* has only one.

prevaricate, procrastinate Both of these verbs suggest irresponsible evasion – but of different things.

To prevaricate is to evade the truth: 'to speak or act falsely in order to deceive'. If you *prevaricate* you are effectively lying, though the verbs *to equivocate, quibble*, and *temporise* are perhaps closer in tone.

To procrastinate, however, means simply 'to delay; to put off doing something': *If you procrastinate any more, you'll miss the train*. If you make the common mistake of using *to prevaricate* instead of *to procrastinate*, you could be making an undeserved and serious allegation: **✗** *The Presidential aide prevaricated in dealing with the complaint sent to him last year*.

prevent, preventive, preventative 1. The correct pattern for using the verb *to prevent* ('to stop, hinder') in formal contexts is *to prevent X's doing* (note the use of the possessive): *Cramp prevented Mary's winning; They prevented my/his/our leaving*.

Less formally, the pattern *to prevent X from doing* is now also acceptable: *Cramp prevented Mary from winning; They prevented me/him/us from leaving*. However, what is not yet fully acceptable is the omission of both the possessive form and *from*: **?** *Cramp prevented Mary winning*; **?** *They prevented me/him/us leaving*.

2. The adjectives *preventive* and *preventative* are simply two forms of the same word: *preventive/preventative measures for fire control*. Both forms are acceptable, though perhaps *preventive* is the favoured form in the medical sense, 'averting illness or damage': *preventive medicine*.

Each form can also be used as a noun, though *preventive* is again generally preferable. But *preventative* seems to be more commonly used in the sense of 'a contraceptive'.

primarily In standard British pronunciation, the stress falls on the first syllable; second-syllable stress is standard in North American speech only.

primeval This spelling is now favoured in British as well as North American usage. The form *primaeval* is slightly old-fashioned.

principal, principle Beware of confusing these two words. As an adjective, *principal* means 'first in importance, rank, or value; primary, chief: *the country's principal export; my principal objection*. *Principal* can also be a noun with several different senses: 'the head of a school or college', 'the lead actor or musician', 'capital or property', and so on.

The noun *principle* refers to any basic rule, law, policy, moral standard, process, or the like: *without moral principles; the principles of modern science; It's not the money – it's the principle*.

pristine The adjective *pristine*, /**priss**-teen/, properly means 'in its primitive or original state'; hence 'uncorrupted; undamaged; in a state of original purity'. The word has definite suggestions of antiquity: *an ancient statue in pristine condition*.

More loosely, *pristine* has come to mean 'absolutely pure, clean, or fresh', a sense that most purists find unacceptable: **?** *I've tidied my room to pristine condition*. Avoid using *pristine* in this way in formal contexts.

privacy The British pronunciation is /**priv**vəsi/, though it allows as a variant the standard North American form /**prī**-vəsi/.

privilege Note the spelling: two *i*'s, and ends in *-ege*, not **✗** *-edge*.

probably Don't omit the middle syllable when pronouncing the word: **??** /**prob**-li/ sounds sloppy and is nonstandard.

procrastinate See PREVARICATE.

prodigy, protégé These nouns are not connected in either origin or meaning. A *prodigy* is a marvel – a person (especially a child) of exceptional talents, or anything so extraordinary that it inspires wonder in people: *a child prodigy; a prodigy of* *nature*. The word can also mean 'a monster; something abnormal' and 'an omen', though both these senses are rare today.

The word *protégé* is French in origin, and means literally '(one who is) protected'. Accordingly, a *protégé* (feminine: *protégée*) is a person (usually young) who is under the protection, guidance, instruction, or patronage of another, more influential person: *He was the protégé of a court musician, but soon surpassed his patron in fame*.

Note the pronunciation: /**prott**ə-zhay/ for both masculine and feminine forms of the word.

professor Note the spelling: single *f*, double *s*; and ending in *-or* like *confessor*, not **✗** *-er*.

programme, program The usual British spelling is *programme: a radio programme; the government's economic programme*. The usual American spelling is *program*. British English has adopted this spelling for computer terminology: *that word-processing program*.

Compare DISC.

prohibit Note the two standard patterns: you can *prohibit* something, or you can *prohibit* someone *from* doing something: *The law prohibits drugs/ the sale of drugs/your selling drugs; The law prohibits you from selling/ importing drugs*.

Don't use other constructions, specifically those for the verbs *to forbid* and *to stop*. You can *forbid* someone *to do* something, and you can *stop* someone *doing* something: *I forbid you to go tonight; The law stops you selling drugs*. By using these models wrongly, you might produce such faulty sentences as **✗** *I prohibit you to go tonight*; **✗** *The law prohibits you selling drugs*.

promenade Note the pronunciation: /**promm**ə-**naad**, -naad/ is standard for all senses; /**promm**ə-**nayd**/ can also be used to refer to a square dance or country dance.

prone, supine These adjectives both mean 'lying down', but *prone* means 'lying face down' and *supine* means 'lying on one's back'. Think of *supine* as containing the word *spine*, and you should remember which is which. A further adjective, *prostrate*, means 'lying down in either position (face down or face up), as through submission, exhaustion, or helplessness'.

Prone can also mean 'having an inclination to do something': *She's prone to weep/weeping*, or 'liable to suffer something': *accident-prone; prone to illness*.

Supine can also mean, figuratively, 'lethargic, passive, having no interest, or being reluctant to act': *the government's supine response to the challenge of inflation*.

See also PROSTRATE.

pronunciation Oddly enough, many people mispronounce this word. The second syllable is /**nun**/ rather than **✗** /**nown**/ as in *pronounce*. Note the different spelling of that syllable in the two words. So too with *announce/ annunciation, renounce/renunciation*.

propeller Note the spelling: the word ends in *-er*, not **✗** *-or*, though in American English the *-or* spelling is an accepted variant.

prophecy, prophesy The noun is *prophecy* – 'a prediction or revelation'; it is spelt with a *c* (sometimes with an *s* in North America), and is pronounced /**proff**ə-sī/. The verb is *prophesy* – 'to predict, or speak as a prophet'; it is spelt with an *s*, and is pronounced /**proff**i-sī/.

proportion Try to reserve the word *proportion/s* for contexts in which there is a strong feeling of ratio – of a part viewed in relation to other parts or to the whole: *The proportion of drivers convicted of drunkenness has fallen*.

Don't use *a large proportion* simply as an impressive-sounding alternative to *a large part, many, much,* or *most*: **?** *A large proportion of drivers regularly exceed the speed limit*. And avoid using *proportions* simply as a grandiose synonym for *size* or *extent*: **?** *an explosion of vast proportions*; **?** *someone of your proportions*.

See also FRACTION; PER CENT.

proportional, proportionate The primary meaning of these adjectives is precisely the same: 'being in proper proportion, forming a relationship with other parts or quantities'. But the two words tend to be used in different constructions: *proportional* usually appears directly in front of a noun – *a proportional amount* – and *proportionate* usually after a noun or verb, or in front of the preposition *to: is proportionate to one's ability to pay*.

In their secondary senses, the words diverge. *Proportional* can mean

'relating to proportions' – as in the phrase *proportional representation* – and *proportionate* can mean 'of similar intensity, comparable': *a punishment that is proportionate to the crime*.

As an adjective and noun, *proportional* has technical senses in mathematics. And *proportionate* can be used as a verb, meaning 'to make proportionate'.

As for the opposites, *disproportionate/ly* is far more common than *disproportional/ly*. Note that it often conveys a negative sense of undeserved intensity or severity, or of overreaction: *a disproportionate fine; a disproportionate outburst; I've suffered disproportionately*. So if the *disproportion* goes in a positive direction, do spell it out: *Your punishment was disproportionately lenient*.

proscribe See PRESCRIBE.

prostrate, prostate The noun *prostate*, with a single *r* refers to the gland in male mammals that lies next to the bladder and secretes seminal fluid.

Prostrate, with two *r*'s, is unrelated. As an adjective, stressed on the first syllable, it means 'lying down' – *the prostrate forms of the slain* – and 'physically or emotionally exhausted; incapacitated; helpless': *the prostrate condition of a once-mighty ruler*. As a verb, stressed on the second syllable, *prostrate* means 'to lay (oneself) face down, in reverence, pleading, or the like': *prostrated himself before the tyrant*.

See also PRONE.

protagonist The noun *protagonist* derives from *protagonistes*, a technical term in ancient Greek drama meaning, literally, 'the first actor' to appear on stage. The original and proper sense of *protagonist* in English is duly 'the leading character, as in a play or story': *Her latest novel has a loathsome protagonist*.

Avoid adding tautological adjectives, as in **✗** *chief protagonist* or **✗** *leading protagonist*. And be aware that some purists object to the plural *protagonists* in reference to a single work. They would insist that there can be only one protagonist, by definition.

Protagonist has developed two further senses. First, quite legitimately, 'a leading or principal figure', especially 'the originator of a cause, political party, or philosophical doctrine': *She was the protagonist of the suffragette movement*; secondly, but not so acceptably, 'any supporter, campaigner, proponent, or champion': **??** *She is one of the most fiery protagonists of our movement*; **??** *The protagonists of the strike defend the violence*. But *protagonist* is not the opposite of *antagonist* (its prefix is *proto-* not *pro-*). Best avoid this usage in formal contexts.

protégé See PRODIGY.

protest, protestation Don't use *protestation* as a supposedly impressive synonym for the noun *protest*. The two words differ in meaning, being related to different senses of the verb *to protest*:

☐ 'to express strong objection or disagreement'; hence the noun *protest*, 'a declaration of disapproval or dissent; an objection': *They staged a protest*.

☐ 'to state or affirm formally or solemnly (especially something that is in doubt)', as in *I protested my innocence*; hence the noun *protestation*, 'a formal or emphatic statement or declaration': *a protestation of innocence*.

Note that the verb *to protest* is typically followed by *against* (or *about* or *at*) in British English: *They protested at/against the delay in compensation*. North American English also allows the simple transitive use – *They protested the delay in compensation* – but this remains nonstandard in British English.

proved, proven In British English, the preferred past-participle form of the verb *to prove* is *proved*, the same as the past tense: *I proved my point; The prediction has proved true*. The alternative form *proven* – pronounced /ˈpro͞ov'n/ or /ˈprōv'n/ – is restricted mainly to formal, literary, or legal contexts, as in the verdict *not proven* in Scottish law.

North American English, by contrast, now slightly prefers *proven* as the past participle: *I was proven right*.

Note, however, that *proven*, 'tried, tested', is the correct adjectival form before the noun in both British and American English: *a proven record; a warrior of proven courage*.

Punjab The name of this Indian state is best pronounced /ˈpun-jaab, jaab/; the variants /ˈpo͝on-/ and **?** /-jab/ are less favoured.

purposefully, purposely Both of these adverbs imply having a purpose in mind, but *purposefully* stresses the determination with which that purpose is carried out. It means 'in a determined way, as if influenced by a strong purpose': *The king strode purposefully away*.

Purposely means simply 'on purpose, intentionally; for a particular purpose': *purposely drew the enemy's fire*.

putrefy Note the spelling: the word ends in *-efy* as in *liquefy*, not **X** *-ify*, despite the *i* in the adjective *putrid*.

pyramidal The traditional pronunciation of this word, /pi-**ram**mid'l/, remains the best.

qua This very formal preposition, pronounced /kway/ or sometimes /kwaa/, means 'in the role or capacity of', 'considered as', or 'by virtue of being': *society's duties towards me qua war veteran*. (Note that *qua* is never followed by *a* or *the*.)

Since *qua* implies seeing the subject from a particular point of view, it cannot always simply replace the preposition *as*: **X** *She is succeeding in her career qua lawyer*.

And it does not mean 'about, regarding': **X** *the new Minister's statements qua industry*.

Finally, although *qua* cannot always replace *as*, *as* can usually replace *qua* for a less formal tone: *society's duties towards me as war veteran*.

question See NO QUESTION.

questionnaire Note the double *n* in the spelling, unlike *questioner* or *millionaire*. The French-style pronunciation /kest-/ now sounds very old-fashioned; it is standard nowadays to pronounce the first two syllables as *question*.

quick In informal contexts, *quick* is commonly used as an adverb, especially in commands and certain set phrases: *Come quick! boils quicker with a lid; to get rich quick*.

In very formal contexts, the form *quickly* is preferred, though the adverb *quick* is still acceptable in certain compound expressions: *quick-setting cement; quick-frozen foods*.

Compare SLOW.

quite 1. The adverb *quite* has two virtually opposing senses: 'partially, somewhat, fairly' and 'totally, completely, absolutely'. The first sense tends to occur with adjectives, verbs, or adverbs that can be modified by words such as *more*, *less*, and *very*: *a quite pleasant afternoon; I quite like it*. In the sense 'completely', *quite* usually occurs with adjectives, verbs, or adverbs that cannot be modified – *a quite impossible request* – or that at least suggest extremes: *a quite exquisite dress; She quite excelled herself*.

In some sentences, ambiguity is a distinct possibility: **?** *The bottle is quite full*. If intonation or context does not make clear which meaning you intend, replace *quite* with *fairly* or *absolutely*, for instance.

2. A related ambiguity affects the phrase **?** *quite good*, which written in British English can mean either 'very good' or 'fair'. (In American English, it would usually mean 'very good'.) In spoken British English, the stress pattern would make clear the intended meaning: stressing the *good* produces the sense 'very good'; stressing the *quite* produces the sense 'fair'.

3. Constructions using *quite a* to indicate a large quantity – *quite a few; quite a while; quite a number* – are slightly informal in tone. They are best avoided in very formal contexts.

All the more so with constructions using *quite a* (or *quite some*) to indicate some remarkable quality: *That was quite an event; Quite some gal!* Such expressions are distinctly informal.

4. When *quite* precedes both an adjective and a noun, it can take either of two constructions, provided that *quite* means 'fairly': *It was a quite interesting evening; It was quite an interesting evening*. But when *quite* means 'absolutely', only one pattern is fully acceptable: *That was a quite unnecessary display*; not **??** *That was quite an unnecessary display*.

racket, racquet In British English, tennis is played with the traditional *racket* or with the Frenchified *racquet*. In North America, only *racket* is used.

A quite different word, spelt only *racket*, refers to 'a noisy commotion', 'a shoddy or illegal business', or, informally, 'any business or occupation': *What's your racket?*

rarely, seldom The two expressions **X** *rarely ever* and **X** *seldom ever*, though common in casual speech, are not strictly correct: the *ever* is redundant.

The following combinations are perfectly acceptable – *rarely/seldom if ever; rarely/seldom or never: I rarely if ever travel by bus*.

raspberry When writing the word, don't forget to include the silent *p*. The first syllable can be pronounced either /**raaz**-/ or /**raass**-/.

rather 1. British speakers often use the adverb *rather* to moderate verbs, adverbs, and adjectives into very controlled expressions of feeling: *I rather admire her; Don't you think this is rather good?*

Unless you are striving for some quaint or jocular effect, don't use *rather* to moderate any words that refer to extreme conditions: **?** *It's rather freezing tonight*; **?** *That was a rather wonderful evening*.

2. The contraction *I'd rather* could be expanded as either *I had rather* or *I should/would rather*. According to a traditional distinction, now all but dead, *had rather* expresses a real preference – *I had rather not go* – whereas *should/would rather* expresses a hypothetical preference: *I should rather be a hammer than a nail.*

In fact, *had rather* now sounds very old-fashioned, and is likely to be used only when a full clause follows the *rather: I had rather you went at once.*

At the beginning of a question, only *should/would rather* is possible: *Would you rather go now? Should I rather pay in cash?*

3. When the phrase *rather than* contrasts two pronouns, these should always agree grammatically, in formal usage: *He, rather than she, is my best friend* (subject forms: *he, she*) – not **?** *He, rather than her . . . .*

Similarly, the pronoun before *rather than* determines the form of the verb: *You, rather than she, are my best friend* – not **X** *is my best friend.* See also THAN.

4. Since *rather than* has two slightly different senses – 'in preference to' and 'instead of' – ambiguity might arise: **?** *I'll meet you for lunch rather than dinner.* When the sense is 'in preference to', try to keep the verb following *rather than* in its simple infinitive form: *She resigned rather than accept his authority.* When the sense is 'instead of', the verb can take the *-s, -ed*, or *-ing* form: *She rejected rather than accepted his authority.*

5. Avoid using *rather than* in place of *than* after comparative words such as *more, slower*, and *better*: **X** *It's easier to walk rather than to drive.*

6. Take care how you position *rather* when using it in the sense of 'somewhat'. When *rather* relates to a noun, the formula is *rather a/an X: Richard's rather a charmer.* But don't keep this construction if you add an adjective: **??** *He's rather a shallow charmer.* The correct form is: *He's a rather shallow charmer.*

re The preposition *re* is an abbreviated form of the Latin *in re*, 'in the matter of', not of the English *referring to* or *regarding*. It should be used only in very formal writing, such as official or legal documents, or possibly the opening words of a stiff business letter – *re: Your invoice of 25 Sept 90* – or in very informal writing, such as a chatty postcard: *Have you found anyone re your flat.*

In other writings, and in speech, use *about, on, regarding*, or *concerning*.

real, really 1. *Real* has become something of a vogue word, frequently substituted for *important, considerable, threatening*, or the like: **?** *It will cause real harm*; **?** *a very real problem*. Avoid this usage in formal contexts.

Beware too of combining *real* with such terms as *very, more*, and *most*. *Real* is properly an 'absolute' adjective – something is either real or not real – and so cannot be qualified. (See also UNIQUE; VERY).

2. Don't use *real* before nouns that cannot properly be qualified or intensified, as in **??** *the real facts of the matter*. What other kinds of fact are there?

3. Don't overuse *really* as a casual intensifier: **??** *She really laid into me, so I got really angry.* And avoid using *really* as an intensifier in metaphorical contexts: **??** *You can really get your teeth into this book.* The literal meaning of *really* tends to intrude, producing a comical image in the mind of the reader or listener. Compare LITERALLY.

4. Beware of using *unreal* as a catch-all extreme adjective: **??** *This weather is unreal* (= amazing); **??** *That party was unreal* (= very good/bad). Outside very informal contexts, such uses sound very silly or sloppy.

realism, realistic, unrealistic The noun *realism* has several specialised senses in philosophy, psychology, and the arts, usually suggesting fidelity to everyday experience and reality, as opposed to the abstract or the idealistic. Its related adjective is *realistic*, the negative of which in these contexts is *nonrealistic*.

In more general usage, *realistic* and *unrealistic* have become rather debased vogue words, often meaning little more than *good, sensible, practical, possible*, or the like, and *bad, imprudent, unworkable, impractical, stupid*, or the like: **?** *The totally unrealistic policies of the government.* Take care not to use these words unthinkingly in this way. Choose a more descriptive word whenever you can: for example, *possible* for *realistic, risky* for *unrealistic*, and *common sense* for *realism*.

reason 1. The correct construction is *The reason is that . . .*, not **X** *The reason is because/owing to*, or the like: **X** *The reason for the slump in share prices is because of uncertainty in the market.*

The word *reason* already contains the idea of 'because, owing to', so it is tautologous to use these words.

2. Many purists also object to the construction **?** *the reason why*, even though it is an idiomatic usage of long standing. If you want to avoid all chance of controversy, use *for* or *that* instead of *why: The reason that we lost is . . .*

rebound, redound, resound To *rebound* means either 'to bounce back' – *The ball rebounded off the wall* – or 'to recoil or misfire, and harm the perpetrator': *Unfortunately, their plan rebounded.*

To *resound*, means 'to reverberate or echo with sound' – *The hall/organ resounded* – or, by extension, 'to be celebrated or extolled as famous': *Her achievements resounded through the country.*

To *redound*, when followed by the preposition *to*, means 'to have an effect or consequence (good or bad)': *Your bravery will redound to your advantage.* When followed by *on* or *upon, redound* can also mean 'to recoil or return harmfully', a sense very close to that of *rebound: The new tax will rebound/redound on the government.*

reciprocal See MUTUAL.

recognise Note the pronunciation: though the g-sound is commonly left out in British English today, it should properly be sounded.

recommend You can remember the spelling by thinking of the elements: *re-* + *commend*: single *c*, double *m*.

Two controversial idiomatic usages are now fairly widespread, especially in North American English: **?** *They* *recommended us to read a good book* and **??** *They recommended us a good book.*

Avoid them in formal contexts. The first example reads better if *advised* replaces *recommended*, or if it reads *They recommended that we read a good book.*

The second example should read *They recommended a good book to us.*

reconnaissance Note the spelling: double *n* in the middle, unlike *renaissance.*

reconnoitre Note the spelling: single *c*, double *n*; contrast its slang derivative *recce.*

recount, re-count The verb *to recount*, /ri-**kownt**/, means 'to narrate, to tell (a story)': *I'll recount my adventure over dinner.* This is quite different from *re-count*, /**ree-kownt**/, which as a verb means 'to count again', and as a noun 'a further count': *to re-count the votes.*

recourse See RESOURCE.

redound See REBOUND.

refer Note the doubling of the second *r* in *referred, referring,* and *referral*; contrast *reference* and *referee.*

Although widely used, the expression *to refer back*, in the sense 'to direct to a source of information', is tautologous and therefore best avoided: **X** *I then referred him back to my recent book.* The *re-* of *refer* already contains the sense 'back'.

However, *back* is appropriate when a second act of referring is involved – *I referred him back to the passage we had discussed earlier* – or when *refer* is used in the sense of returning a document or question to its source for further consideration: *We referred the matter back to the committee.*

refute The correct meaning of *to refute* is 'to disprove (a statement, allegation, or argument); to prove wrong': *He refuted their figures/the chairman with a more sophisticated statistical analysis.*

Unfortunately, *to refute* is also used in the weaker sense of 'to deny, oppose, reject, dispute' and the like: **?** *The Minister hotly refutes the slur on his character.* Avoid this widespread but unacceptable usage.

regard 1. Certain idioms use the plural form *regards*, such as *as regards* or *kind regards.* Take care not to use the *-s* ending in idioms that take the singular form *regard*, such as *with regard to* and *to have regard for.*

2. Note further that the expressions *in/with regard to, as regards,* and *regarding* are often slightly affected. Use them sparingly. Simple, forthright prepositions such as *about* (or sometimes *concerning*), *on, to,* and *in* are usually preferable. They would read far less pompously in the following sentence: **?** *He seemed indifferent in regard to my problem, and had no thoughts regarding a solution.* (See also RE.)

3. Avoid the common faulty formation **X** *irregardless.* The correct word is either *regardless* or *irrespective.*

4. *To regard* and *to consider* take different constructions: *I regard him as a genius; I consider him a genius* (or *I consider him to be a genius*).

Don't be tempted to omit the *as* after *regard* in such sentences, or to replace it with *to be.*

The temptation is particularly strong in two special cases: one, when *regard as* comes at the end of a clause: **X** *No matter how deserving she may regard herself, she'll never win the prize*; two, when *regard as* should come immediately before another *as*: **X** *I regard this book as authoritative as Empson's.*

You could hardly add the missing *as* to this last sentence, however, without risking severe awkwardness. You would have to restructure the sentence, or else substitute *consider* for *regard as.*

See also CONSIDER.

regretfully See HOPEFULLY.

relation, relative, relationship Our parents, brothers, cousins, and so on are our *relations* or *relatives.* In some contexts, idiom favours one form over the other. We speak of *poor relations* but *elderly relatives.*

A *relationship* (other than a family relationship) is often referred to as *relations* when the connection is specified – *business relations, the relations between landlord and tenant* – and as *relation* in abstract or non-human contexts: *the relation between alcoholism and wife-beating.*

In view of the varying senses of *relation* or *relative*, be on the alert for ambiguity: **?** *We have no banking relations* could refer to financial dealings or to wealthy uncles.

relatively, comparatively These adverbs are often used, imprecisely or questionably, as substitutes for *fairly, somewhat, rather,* and the like: **?** *arrived relatively recently*; **?** *a comparatively successful performance.*

Relatively and *comparatively*, together with the corresponding adjectives *relative* and *comparative*, ought to suggest some comparison, even if it is only implicit: *He is relatively thin for a Sumo wrestler; She is a comparatively young professor.*

remembrance Note the spelling: the last *e* of *remember* is dropped.

renaissance, renascence These spellings are both correct: *renaissance* is the older version, from French; *renascence*, although the Anglicised version, seems slightly more affected.

Note that there are no double *n*'s in either form. The English pronunciation of either spelling is usually /ri-**nayss**'nss/, though *renascence* can be /ri-**nass**-'nss/. *Renaissance* can also be pronounced the French way: /**ren**nay-soNss/ or /rennə-**soNss**/.

With a small *r*, the word can indicate any revival or rebirth, especially of culture or learning: *a renaissance/ renascence of classical composition.* With a capital *R*, *Renaissance* usually refers to the flowering of European culture that began in Italy in the 14th century.

rent See HIRE.

repetitious, repetitive Both these adjectives mean essentially 'characterised by repetition'. But whereas *repetitive* is usually neutral in tone, *repetitious* is almost always distinctly unfavourable or critical, suggesting that the repetition is unnecessary or tedious: *the repetitive rhythms of the music; a frustratingly repetitious essay.*

replace See SUBSTITUTE.

resound See REBOUND.

respective, respectively These two words are useful in clarifying the meaning of a sentence that refers to several people or things considered individually and in the order mentioned: *Accommodation for men and women is on the north and south sides respectively* (= accommodation for men is on the north side; for women, on the south side).

Take care, however, not to use these words as unnecessary ornaments, where clarification is not really necessary: **??** *The Ministers of defence, education, and agriculture have all excelled themselves in their respective departments.* (In which other departments would they excel themselves? Omit *respective* or substitute *various* if you want an adjective here.)

Beware too of using *respective/ly* in sentences that are worded in the singular; it will be wholly redundant: **✗** *Each of the chefs submitted his respective creation.*

Finally, don't use *respective* or *respectively* as a substitute for *both* or *each other's:* **✗** *She won prizes for playing the violin and the piano respectively;* **✗** *The two chess players were hoping to capture their respective queens.*

Reserve *respective* and *respectively* for contexts where they genuinely serve to disentangle the meaning to save a sentence from ambiguity.

See also FORMER.

respite The word is stressed on its first syllable – /**ress**pit/ or perhaps /**ress**pīt/ – rather than on its second, as *despite* is.

restaurant The Anglicised pronunciation /**rest**ə-rant, -rənt/ and the Frenchified /**rest**ə-roN/ are equally acceptable.

restaurateur Note the spelling: no *n* or *n*-sound as in *restaurant*.

restive Don't confuse *restive* with *restful*, as in **✗** *a restive and invigorating holiday. Restive* is in fact much closer to *restless*, and traditionally means 'unruly, disobedient; resistant to control or discipline': *a restive child who ignores all authority.*

Nowadays, *restive* is widely used as a synonym for *restless* (or *nervous, impatient,* or *uneasy*), though many purists still object to this extension of meaning: **?** *She was restive and bored:* **?** *He paced the room with growing restiveness.* Though well established, this sense is not yet fully acceptable in the most formal contexts.

result A *result*, unless specifically indicated, can surely be either good or bad.

In recent British usage, however, *result/s* often appears to mean 'a good, successful, or decisive result': **?** *I want results from you;* **?** *I expected a result, but the teams drew.* Restrict such uses to informal contexts.

resurrect Note the double *r* and the *u* in the spelling – doubly different from *erect.*

revenge, vengeance These nouns differ slightly in tone. *Vengeance* suggests a justified and often large-scale retribution for a serious and unjust injury: *Only vengeance would soothe the pain in her bereaved heart.*

Revenge has a strong sense of malice, and sometimes suggests a petty retaliation, for a trivial and even imaginary injury: *She took her revenge on the critics by lampooning them in her next novel.*

The related verbs *to avenge* and *to revenge* (*oneself*) differ slightly too: *to avenge* suggests a just motive and an objective righting of wrongs; *to revenge* (*oneself*) a vindictive motive and the dubious settling of scores. Note the different grammatical patterns: *to avenge a murder/one's murdered uncle; to revenge oneself on one's critics.* These verbs are fairly rare. More common are the phrases *to be avenged, to take revenge, to wreak vengeance,* and so on.

Finally, the related adjectives *vengeful* and *revengeful*: the distinction is now extremely slight, though perhaps *revengeful* – the far less common word – still conveys a greater sense of vindictiveness.

reverent, reverential, reverend
1. The adjectives *reverent* and *reverential* both mean 'showing or resulting from reverence': *an attitude of reverent/reverential piety. Reverent* can also mean 'feeling or characterised by reverence' – *a reverent pilgrim* – while *reverential* can imply mere respectfulness: *bowed his head with reverential attentiveness.*

By contrast, *reverend* means 'deserving reverence' – *a reverend and saintly person* – or 'relating to or characteristic of the clergy or a clergyman': *the reverend gentleman.*

2. As a title for clergymen below the rank of dean, *Reverend* (abbreviated to *Rev.* or *Revd.*) should be used with *Mr* or *Dr,* or with a first name or initial: *(The) Rev. P./Peter Jones; (The) Rev. Dr/Mr Jones.* In some Protestant churches, particularly in North America, people speak simply of *Reverend Jones,* but this is unacceptable in the English Anglican church.

Reverend is also a useful way of addressing a clergyman whose name you do not know; but avoid referring to a known clergyman as **?** *the Reverend.*

review, revue The noun *review* refers to an inspection or (re-)examination of something – troops, a legal verdict, a book, play, film, or the like. (A *review* can also be the journal in which such assessments appear.)

There is also the verb *to review* – *to review a film* – and the adjective: *a review article.*

The noun *revue* refers to a form of light entertainment, consisting of dances, songs, and sketches, often satirical. *Revue* can be spelled *review,* but this may cause confusion and is best avoided.

rhododendron Note the spelling: *rh-* at the start, *-dod-* in the middle, and *-on,* not **✗** *-um* at the end.

rhythm Don't forget the first *h* when writing the word; note the spelling – similar to that of *rhyme.*

rigour, rigor Note the spellings: *rigour,* meaning 'harshness', ends *-our* (*-or* in American English); but this *u* is dropped in the adjective *rigorous.* In medical senses, the Latin spelling *rigor* is used, as in *rigor mortis;* it can be pronounced /**rī**-gər/ as well as /**rig**gər/.

rise, arise, raise, rouse, arouse The general rule is that *to rise* and *to arise* are intransitive verbs (they do not take a direct object and cannot be used in the passive), while *to raise, to rouse,* and *to arouse* are transitive.

Moreover, *to rise, to raise,* and *to rouse* are generally used in a literal way of people and animals, while *to arise* and *to arouse* are used, more figuratively, of things.

More specifically, *to arise* nowadays usually means 'to come into existence; become apparent; result': *A mood of optimism arose among the people; Opportunities will arise;* and (more literally) *A hot wind arose.*

To arouse now means chiefly 'to bring into existence, or to provoke or excite' – *The film arouses fear/ controversy* – or, with a personal object, 'to awaken sexual feelings in': *That dancer intended to arouse her audience.*

Note the following, more literal, uses of *to rise, to raise,* and *to rouse: I rise at dawn; The temperature/feelings rose; I raised my hat; Hopes were raised; My clock rouses me at 8am; Your opinions roused me to action.*

round See AROUND; CENTRE AROUND.

rural, rustic These adjectives both mean essentially 'relating to or characteristic of the country, country life, or farming', but they have rather different overtones.

The more general and neutral word is *rural: the fragility of the rural environment*. By contrast, *rustic* can be anything from affectionate – by implying unspoilt simplicity or quaintness – to disdainful, by implying crudeness or uncouthness: *the area's rustic charm; the rustic pleasure of brawling on the village green*.

Rustic also has technical meanings when applied to furniture or architecture. As a noun, it means 'a rural person', or, more specifically, 'a country bumpkin'.

Ruthven This Scottish surname is pronounced /**rivv**'n/.

saccharin, saccharine Note the spelling: *-cch-* in the middle; the noun ends *-in*; the adjective *-ine*.

sacrilegious Note the spelling: *-rile-*, not **X** *-reli-* as in *religious*.

same When *same* is joined to a following word, phrase, or clause, the preposition *as* is used to form the link: *Your eyes are the same colour as mine; We are going to see the same film as you saw yesterday*. In informal English, *as* is often omitted, or replaced by *that* or *which*, when there is a following clause: **?** *We are going to see the same film (that) you saw yesterday*. Avoid this formation in formal contexts.

Same or *the same* is still sometimes used as a pronoun in business and legal contexts in the sense 'the persons or things just mentioned' (so too *said* and *such*): *We enclose payment for books – please deliver same next week*. Outside these special contexts, this usage is unacceptable, except perhaps as a joke or for particular stylistic effect.

Same serves as an adverb in informal contexts: **?** *He travels by bus, same as you do*. This use is not suitable for formal speech and writing.

sarcastic See IRONIC.

scarcely See HARDLY.

scarify Don't confuse the verb *to scarify*, pronounced /**skarr**i-fī/ or sometimes /**skair**i-fī/, with the completely unrelated verb *to scare*. To *scarify* is a medical term meaning 'to make small incisions or punctures in the skin, as for inoculation', or a farming term meaning 'to loosen the topsoil' or 'to scratch the surface of seeds (to promote faster germination)'.

It has also acquired a more figurative meaning, 'to wound with very harsh criticism': *a long-suffering poet scarified by foolish critics*.

schedule Note the pronunciation: /**shed**dewl/ in British English; but /**skej**-əl, **shej**-, -ool/ in North American English.

schism The pronunciations /**siz**'m/ and /**skiz**'m/ are now both standard, though the former is preferred.

scone The pronunciation /skon/ is slightly preferable to /skōn/, which tends to sound rather non-U (or 'genteel', in the bad sense). *Scone*, the village in Scotland, is pronounced /skōon/, as is the stone in the coronation chair.

Scots, Scotch, Scottish A person from Scotland usually likes to be referred to as a *Scot*. The terms *Scotsman/Scotswoman* are rather more formal, and *Scotchman/Scotchwoman* are unacceptable, even offensive, to the Scots.

Scots is again the correct term for the people of Scotland collectively; *the Scottish* is possible, but *the Scotch* is no longer acceptable. (In North America, the term *Scotch-Irish* refers to Protestant immigrants from Ulster, and their descendants.)

Note the corresponding adjectives: *Scots* and *Scottish* are used of the people: *a Scots/Scottish architect*. For things or institutions located in Scotland, *Scottish* is the usual term – *Scottish universities/newspapers* – though some institutions require *Scots: Scots law; the Scots guards*.

The controversial adjective *Scotch* is generally reserved for products originating in or associated with Scotland: so, *Scotch whisky/broth/wool*. (Scots themselves speak simply of *whisky*, rather than *Scotch* or *Scotch whisky*).

Finally, the type of English spoken in Scotland is called *Scottish English* if it is reasonably similar to standard widely understood English. Marked regional dialects, however, are called *Scots*, and so is the quite different language Scottish Gaelic.

seasonal, seasonable Take care not to confuse these adjectives. The first, *seasonal*, means 'relating to the season or seasons', or 'dependent on, varying with, or occurring during different seasons': *seasonal labourers picking the seasonal fruits; the seasonal adjustment of the unemployment statistics*.

By contrast, *seasonable* means 'suitable for the season' – *seasonable weather; These rains are seasonable, though unpleasant* – or 'happening at an opportune time': *saved by a seasonable bank overdraft*.

Note that there is no opposite for *seasonal*, but *seasonable* has the opposite *unseasonable: the unseasonable snows of last summer*.

secretary When pronouncing the word, don't neglect the first *r*.

sedentary The stress falls on the first syllable, not the second.

seize The normal spelling rule does not apply: here *e* comes before *i*, not **X** *-ie-*.

seldom See RARELY.

self, -self Avoid using the word *self* as a synonym for *me*, except jokingly or in strictly commercial jargon: *Item: £10 taken from petty cash for self*.

See also MYSELF, and page 183.

self-deprecation See DEPRECATE.

sensual, sensuous Both of these adjectives can mean simply 'sensory; relating to the senses', but both also refer to enjoyment of physical sensations – though in slightly different ways.

The primary meaning of *sensuous* nowadays is 'pleasing to one's (refined) senses' – *all the sensuous pleasures of music and poetry; the sensuous delights of fine cuisine/a noble wine/an expensive cigar*.

By contrast, *sensual* suggests self-indulgence; it means 'strongly or excessively inclined to gratify one's (coarse) senses or physical desires' – *a sensual man who persistently eats himself sick* – and 'tending to arouse the bodily appetites': *the sensual images of an erotic poem*. In fact, *sensual* is now most often associated with sexual pleasure or indulgence: *the sensual feel of silk sheets*.

separate Note the spelling: *-par-*, not **X** *-per-* as in *desperate*.

sewage, sewerage *Sewage* refers to industrial or domestic waste material that is carried away in sewers or drains: *a sewage farm; tons of sewage pumped straight into the sea*. Although *sewerage* is also sometimes used in this sense, it usually means 'the system or method of removing water or sewage', or 'the network of sewers and drains': *improved sewerage for the city*. Since *sewerage* implies a system, the expression **?** *a sewerage system* is really tautologous; speak of *a sewage system* instead.

Finally, note that the preferred pronunciation for both words is /**sew**-/, rather than /**soo**-/.

shall, will The traditional rules for choosing between *shall* and *will* are rather more complicated than the schoolroom version that most people remember. They are outlined on pages 190-191 – alongside all the exceptions to them!

For most speakers, intuition is usually the best guide, both in questions and statements. The one case that needs conscious attention (at least for those in England) is the use, in formal writing, of *shall* after *I* and *we* in ordinary unemphatic statements about the future: *I shall meet you at Euston at 7pm, and we shall dine at my club.*

should, would 1. The traditional rules are outlined on page 191. In practice, your ear or natural sense of idiom will usually guide you correctly. The one case to keep consciously in mind is the use, in formal writing, of *should* rather than *would* after *I* or *we* in ordinary statements (so long as no ambiguity arises): *We should be grateful for an early reply.*

2. Two warnings about contractions: *would've* should expand as *would have* not **✗** *would of* as in **✗** *She would of liked to discuss her plans*. And *'d better* usually expands as *had better* rather than *should better*: *You had better admit it.*

See also HAVE; RATHER; SHALL.

shrink The verb *to shrink* has two past-tense forms: *shrank* and *shrunk*. In the sense 'to withdraw, recoil, or flinch from', the preferred form is *shrank* – *She shrank from his touch* – while *shrunk* is generally used of fabrics that have contracted: *Your shirt shrunk in the wash.*

The past participle is now always *shrunk: I'm afraid your shirt has shrunk*. The form *shrunken* (previously a past participle) is now restricted to adjectival use: *a shrunken head; the shrunken figure of the mummy.*

sibyl The prophetess is a *sibyl*; but the woman's name is usually *Sybil*.

sic This Latin word, meaning 'thus' or 'so', typically occurs (in italics usually, and inside brackets) within or after a quotation. In official or academic writing, *sic* serves to reassure a reader that the word or words are in fact correctly quoted; this is particularly useful when a strange or unexpected form of a word or expression has been quoted: *John Donne was described as 'a great visiter (sic) of ladies'.*

Sic is also used, in a rather mean or superior way, to show up and ridicule the spelling, grammatical, or typographical errors of authors or their printers. One giveaway is the inclusion of an exclamation mark: (*sic!*).

Use *sic* sparingly, and only as a precaution to dissociate yourself from some oddity in a quotation that you have used.

Siena, sienna The Italian town has a single *n*; the colour has a double *n*.

significant The primary senses of this adjective are 'having or expressing a meaning' – *a significant but undeciphered set of marks* – and 'having a hidden meaning; suggestive': *a significant glance.*

Significant has also developed the sense of 'notable, momentous'; it then attracts much criticism for being just a fashionable substitute for such words as *serious, valuable, important*: **?** *a significant new play by one of today's most significant young playwrights*; **?** *a significant exhibition of art treasures*; **?** *the most significant gem in the collection*. If possible, avoid using *significant* unless there is some reference to the conveying of meaning.

Curiously, *insignificant*, in the sense 'unimportant, trivial', has not aroused similar criticism. It is quite acceptable to speak of *an insignificant novelist/contribution/obstacle.*

silicon, silicone Don't confuse these two nouns. *Silicon*, /**sill**i-kən, -kon/, is one of the chemical elements. It is hard and non-metallic, and forms the main ingredient of sand. *Silicon* is used in transistors and computer chips. Hence the terms *silicon chip* and *Silicon Valley* (in California, where such chips are made).

The second noun, *silicone*, /**sill**i-kōn/, refers to a compound made up of carbon, oxygen, and silicon. It is a plastic used in breast implants, for coating non-stick cookware, and for a

number of other industrial and surgical purposes.

simplistic Don't use *simplistic* as just a fancy form of *simple* or *very simple*. Applied to people or their ideas, *simplistic* means 'characterised by extreme simplicity; naive'; it also means 'oversimplified' or 'oversimplifying; making unrealistically simple judgments or analyses': *a simplistic documentary on a complex issue; a simplistic acceptance of military propaganda.*

Simplistic is clearly unfavourable in tone, whereas *simple* is usually either neutral or admiring: *a simple system that works well; She leads a simple life of work and prayer.*

Note too that the expression *too simplistic* is tautologous: *simplistic* already implies an excessive simplicity or an oversimplification. Use *too simple*, or just *simplistic.*

sink The verb *to sink* has two past-tense forms: *sank*, which is more common, and *sunk*, which is slightly informal: *She sank/* **?** *sunk on to the couch; The submarine sank/* **?** *sunk an enemy ship.*

The past participle is now always *sunk: The lifeboat has sunk*. The form *sunken* is now restricted to adjectival use: *a sunken treasure ship.*

situation In several of its senses, *situation* is a very useful word – 'location or position': *the situation of the stream beside the road*; 'a job': *a situation suitable for my interests*; 'a state of affairs': *a hypothetical situation.*

In the last of the above senses *situation* is often carelessly overused. It has become a vogue word, often merely padding out some simple concrete idea into a bloated and pretentious abstract phrase: **?** *a no-win situation*; **?** *in the classroom situation*; **?** *a learning situation*; **?** *the weather situation*; **?** *the ongoing situation*; **?** *my financial situation*. All these expressions can be profitably replaced by a simple word or phrase that conveys the intended meaning more sharply and less affectedly: so, *in the classroom, the weather*, and so on.

ski The other forms of the verb are spelt *skis, skied*, and *skiing.*

skilful Note the spelling: single *l*'s in British English, though American English favours *skillful.*

skimpy See SCANT.

sleight of hand Although the pronunciation is the same as that of *slight*, the spelling has an added *e*.

slough Note the pronunciations: /slow/ (rhyming with *cow*) for the ditch, as in 'the Slough of Despond', but /sloo/ in this sense in North America; the word for a snake's shed skin and the verb meaning 'to shed' are both pronounced /sluf/.

slow In formal speech and writing, the usual adverbial form is *slowly*. In informal contexts, however, *slow* too is used as an adverb: *Go slow/slowly; Speak slower/more slowly*. Note also that *slow* is standard in the road sign *Dead Slow*; as well as in certain fixed phrases – *a go-slow; the trains are running slow* (that is, 'running late', not necessarily 'moving slowly') – and some compound expressions: *slow-moving traffic; a slow-acting drug*.

Compare QUICK.

smell In British English, the past-tense and past-participle forms of *to smell* are *smelt*, and, slightly less commonly, *smelled*. In North America *smelled* is the preferred form.

Note the different emphases in the following constructions: *It smells strong* (neutral); *It smells strongly* (negative); *It smells strongly of sawdust* (neutral and specific).

so 1. When *so* begins a sentence, it is not usually followed by a comma – *So we all came home* – unless it introduces some parenthetical wording: *So, as you know, we all came home*.

A clause introduced by *so* or *so that* expresses either purpose – *I bought a car so that I could travel* – or result: *The car was ready, so I set off*.

Note the comma that precedes *so* in a clause of result. Note also the slight preference for *so that* to indicate purpose, and for *so* to indicate result.

In purpose clauses, *so that* can be replaced by *in order that* but not simply by *so as*: **??** *I bought a car so as I could travel*. What *so as* takes is the infinitive, not a clause: *I bought a car so as to travel*. (Some purists object even to *so as to travel*, on the ground that *so as* is redundant.)

2. The phrase *doing so* or *to do so* is useful if you want to avoid repeating a verb phrase: *You can stay here tonight, but if you do so you will have to share a room*.

Take care to observe the following guidelines. First, the original verb has to be in the active voice, not the passive: **??** *You can be accommodated here tonight, but if you do so you will have to share a room*.

Secondly, keep the verb forms parallel, especially if the first verb is in the *-ing* form: **??** *Staying tonight will be possible, but if you do so you will have to share a room*. Change the phrase *if you do so* to *doing so means that*.

Thirdly, take particular care when using these expressions that they accurately convey the sense you want: **✗** *You've eaten nothing, and I'm not going until you do so*. Unravelled, this means 'until you eat nothing'!

3. In informal conversation, *so* is often used as a simple intensifier meaning 'very': *I am feeling so angry*. In formal contexts, it is safer to use *very* or *extremely* instead.

Note, however, that the following usage is perfectly acceptable: *I have never felt so angry* (before). It is based on a different construction: *I have never felt so/as angry as this* (before).

4. In the following construction, *so* is acceptable, though not essential: *You can stay with us if you so wish/desire*. But *so* is nonstandard in the following sentence, and should be omitted: **??** *You can have as much as you so wish/desire/want*.

See also AS; SUCH; VERY.

sober Note the spelling – *-er* at the end, not **✗** *-re* as in *sombre*.

social, sociable These adjectives relate to different senses of the noun *society*. The first, *social*, relates to *society* in its general senses involving human (or animal) groups or relationships. Hence: *social classes, social studies, man as a social animal*.

Don't use *social* to mean 'friendly, companionable': **✗** *She wants me to be more social*. The correct word here is *sociable*, which relates to a rather old-fashioned sense of *society* – 'companionship, the company of other people'. Hence: *a very standoffish crowd, not in the least sociable*.

Sociable can also apply to an occasion or location: *a sociable evening/club*. Contrast *a social evening/club*, which may or may not prove to be welcoming or *sociable*.

The opposite of *sociable* is *unsociable*, meaning 'reserved, not companiable' or 'unwelcoming, cold': *an unsociable colleague/atmosphere*.

The opposite of *social* is not really *unsocial* (which means 'not compatible with or not conducive to a full social life': *the unsocial hours of the night shift*), but rather *antisocial*, meaning 'opposed to or interfering with the general welfare of society, or contravening its customs': *antisocial lager louts; Smoking is an antisocial habit*. Beware of using *antisocial* as a voguish synonym for *unsociable* or *unfriendly*: **??** *Such intense questions are very antisocial at dinner*.

Sofia The pronunciation of the name of the Bulgarian capital used to be /sə-**fi**-ə/, but is now commonly /**sō**fi-ə/ or /**sō**fee-ə/.

sojourn The stress falls on the first syllable in British English – /**soj**-ərn/ is the best pronunciation – though North American speech allows second-syllable stress.

solder The pronunciation /**sōl**dər/ is preferred to /**sōl**dər/; the American variants /**sod**dər/ and /**saw**-dər/ are considered regional or old-fashioned in British speech.

soliloquy The plural is *soliloquies*, not **✗** *soliloquys*.

some *Some* occurs in various exclamations, either admiring – *It took (quite) some guts to contradict the boss! That was some meal!* – or scornful: *Some chef! – he couldn't even fry an egg*. Useful though such expressions are, they remain slightly slangy, and are not really appropriate for formal contexts.

someone See ANYONE.

sometime, some time, some times 1. As an adjective, *sometime* means 'one-time; former': *Abe Beame, the sometime mayor of New York*. Avoid using the word in the very dubious sense of 'occasional': **??** *My sometime drinking binges worry my wife greatly*. Use *occasional* instead.

As an adverb, *sometime* means 'at some unspecified point of time': *Come and visit me sometime; I cleaned my room sometime last month*. Some purists object to this sense, arguing that the expression is an abbreviated form of *at some time*, and should at least be written as two words. However, the form *sometime* is generally acceptable in all but the most formal contexts.

2. In other senses, *some time* obviously has to be two words: *Name some time that will suit you; It all happened some time ago*. Take care similarly to distinguish *sometimes* from *some* times: *Sometimes I wish it was all over; There are some times when I wish it was all over*.

soporific The adjective *soporific* properly means 'sleep-inducing': *a soporific drink; a soporific lecture*. As a noun, *soporific* means specifically 'a sleep-inducing drug or agent': *In the navy, rum served as a soporific and anaesthetic*.

Nowadays, the adjective *soporific* is also used to mean 'drowsy, sleepy', as in **?** *a soporific yawn*. Though fairly well established, this extended sense still offends many careful speakers. To be on the safe side, avoid it in formal contexts. It tends to sound rather pompous in any case, as if *drowsy* or *sleepy* were not good enough.

sort of 1. The phrases *(a) sort of, type of, kind of*, and so on are normally followed by a simple singular noun: *What sort of car (do you drive)?* Usually it is incorrect to insert *a* or *an* in front of the noun, but it is permissible when discussing the quality rather than the classification of the object. Compare *What sort of car is it? – It's a Ford* with *What sort of a car is it? – It's a very reliable car*.

2. The construction *this sort of thing* is often cast in the plural – needlessly: **?** *I like these sorts of car*. (The same is true for *that kind of, this type of, that breed of*, and so on.) Far preferable to say simply *I like this sort of car* or *I like cars of this sort*, unless you are talking specifically about more than one *type* of car: *I can't decide between the VW Golf and the Peugeot 205 – I like both these sorts of car*.

Note that *car* here is singular: *these sorts of car*. This form is preferable to the constructions *these sorts of cars* and **?** *these/this sort of cars*.

3. The phrases *sort of* and *kind of* are often used adverbially in the sense 'in a way, to some extent'. Although distinctly informal, they can be very useful in conveying an ironic tone – *The rebel MP apologised, sort of, to the House* – or in indicating an unavoidable inaccuracy: *It's sort of peppery in flavour*. But avoid using these phrases simply out of laziness or as meaningless verbal tics or conversational tags: **?** *I have a sort of a pain in my arm*; **X** *I was sort of walking down the path when I saw this sort of huge spider*.

4. The phrase *all sorts of* is acceptable in informal contexts: *She has all sorts of problems*. So too is *all kinds of*, but the equally common **?** *all kind of* is

nowadays considered nonstandard. Curiously, however, the similar phrase *all manner of* remains fully acceptable.

Southwark The pronunciation of this London place name is /ˈsuthək/.

spare, sparse See SCANT.

speciality, specialty For most senses, British English favours the form *speciality: the speciality of the house is roast duck; The new lecturer's speciality is Greek tragedy*.

American English prefers *specialty*, which in British English is limited to a technical legal sense.

specially, especially These two adverbs are not really interchangeable, though *specially* is often incorrectly used in place of *especially*.

Specially means 'in a special way' or 'in this particular way, or for this particular purpose; specifically': *specially trained dogs; made an effort specially for the occasion*. Note that *specially* tends to modify verbs rather than adjectives or adverbs.

Especially can apply to adverbs, adjectives, verbs, and perhaps even nouns.

It means 'extremely, to a great extent', or 'in particular, above all': *She sang especially shrilly; He is an especially talented player; They especially like almonds; He dislikes intellectuals, especially professors*.

In some contexts, either adverb may be appropriate – *She sang specially for me; She sang especially for me* – though even here the meanings do differ somewhat. Usually, the word order determines the choice: *She sang especially shrilly to annoy me; She sang shrilly specially to annoy me*.

A corresponding distinction used to apply to *special* and *especial*, but *special* now commonly – and acceptably – does service for both: *special circumstances; a special/especial dislike of shrill voices*.

species Note the pronunciation: /ˈspee-sheez/; the sound in the middle should be /-sh-/ rather than **?**/-s-/.

specious, spurious These adjectives overlap slightly in meaning, but have clearly individual emphases. *Specious*, /ˈspee-shəss/, means 'seemingly attractive, genuine, or persuasive, but not really so; deceptive': *a specious excuse/argument; specious flattery*.

Spurious means 'invalid, or not of genuine origin, fake': *a spurious claim*

to the inheritance; *spurious charges of assault*.

Even in shared combinations – *such as a specious/spurious similarity*; or *specious/spurious reasoning* – a slight difference persists. *Specious* has a more disapproving tone: it hints at deliberate deception, and emphasises a falsely attractive appearance. *Spurious* emphasises the notion of a bogus origin.

spill In British English, the past tense and past participle of the verb *to spill* can be *spilt*, or less commonly, *spilled*. American English favours the form *spilled*.

In both varieties, however, *spilled* is preferable when the verb has no direct object and means 'overflowed': *It spilled onto the floor*.

And both varieties prefer *spilt* as the adjectival form directly in front of a noun: *crying over spilt milk*.

spirt, spurt Whether verb or noun, the usual spelling is *spurt*. You may use *spirt* as an alternative when writing about a fast flow or squirt – *a spurt/ spirt of water/emotion; It spurted/ spirted onto my new suit* – but not when writing about a sudden burst of effort: *a spurt of energy; spurted across the finishing line*.

spoil In British English, the past tense and past participle of the verb *to spoil* can be *spoilt* or, less commonly, *spoiled*. American English favours the form *spoiled*.

The correct adjectival form in British English (and also for many North Americans) is *spoilt: a spoilt brat*.

spoonful See -FUL.

spurious See SPECIOUS.

squalor Note the spelling: the word ends in *-or*, not **X** *-our* as in *valour*.

stalactite, stalagmite A *stalactite* grows downwards, and hangs like an icicle, a *stalagmite* grows upwards, and resembles a half-burnt candle. Here is just one memory-aid: *c* from the *ceiling; g* from the *ground*.

In British English, each of the words is stressed on the first syllable. North Americans usually stress each of them on the second syllable.

stationary, stationery Take care with the spelling: *stationary* is the adjective meaning 'standing still, motionless'; *stationery* is the noun referring to pens, paper, pencils, and so on. Remember that *stationery* is sold by a *stationer* – which, like *butcher* or *grocer*, is spelt -*er*.

stigma This noun has two plurals: *stigmata* and *stigmas*. For the marks or sores corresponding to the crucifixion wounds of Jesus, the word is *stigmata*. For the parts of a flower that receive pollen, the word is *stigmas*. Either form is appropriate as the plural of the various other senses of *stigma*, such as 'a mark or token of shame': *old-fashioned enough to suffer the twin stigmas/stigmata of being unemployed and being divorced*.

Stigmata can be stressed on the second syllable – /stig-**maa**tə/ – but a first-syllable stress remains preferable: /**stig**-mətə/.

stile See STYLE.

stiletto Note the spelling: single *l*, then double *t*. The plural *stilettos* is best, though *stilettoes* is also acceptable.

stop, stoppage In British English, the usual pattern is *to stop something happening*: *The police stopped the riot/riot's spreading beyond the square*. In American English, the usual pattern is *to stop something from happening*.

The use of *to stop* in the sense 'to stay, to reside briefly' is informal or regional: **?** *They stopped at a friend's for a few nights on the way back*. In formal contexts, use *to stay* instead. In the sense 'to visit briefly', however, *to stop* is full acceptable: *They stopped at a friend's for tea on the way back*.

The noun *stoppage*, though useful in its place, tends often to be used needlessly as a fancier-sounding version of *stop*: **?** *a temporary stoppage in deliveries from the suppliers*.

storey, story In British English, the noun *storey* (plural *storeys*) refers to a floor or level of a building; and *story* means 'a tale'. In American English, *story* (plural *stories*) is commonly used for both words (though *storey* does sometimes occur).

As adjectival forms, both *three-storeyed* and *three-storey* are acceptable, though -*storey* is more common for buildings other than private houses: *a 100-storey skyscraper*.

Note that in both Britain and North America, the street-level floor is included when you calculate the number of storeys. So the top floor of a ten-storey building in Britain would usually be the ninth floor (but in North America, the tenth floor). See FLOOR.

stratum The correct plural of the noun *stratum* is *strata*: *All strata of society were affected*. Avoid the forms **??** *stratums* and **✗** *stratas*. And avoid using *strata* as a singular noun: **✗** *a single strata of society*.

stricture The meaning of *stricture* is quite different from that of *strictness*. *Stricture* is a formal noun meaning primarily 'a severe criticism, censure, or adverse remark': *a successful play despite the reviewers' strictures*.

Another sense is 'something that restricts or restrains', or specifically, in medicine, 'an abnormal narrowing of a passage': *a stricture of the bowel*.

stupefy Note the *e* in the spelling: contrast *stupid* and *terrify*.

sty, stye A pigpen is a *sty*; the eye infection can be spelt *sty* or *stye*.

style, stile Take care with the spelling. *Style* is the familiar noun referring to the appearance or form of something – *a new style of swimsuit* – or to the way in which something is written, performed, or the like: *a beautifully lucid prose style*.

There are two nouns spelt *stile*. The first means 'a set of steps for getting over a fence or wall' or 'a turnstile'. The second *stile* refers to an upright support in a panel, frame, ladder, window, or the like.

subjective See OBJECTIVE.

subsequent See CONSEQUENT.

subsidence Two pronunciations are acceptable, the stress falling either on the first syllable or on the second.

substitute, replace 1. *To substitute* means 'to put in the place of', whereas *to replace* means 'to take the place of'. Each verb has its distinctive pattern: *to substitute A for B*; and *to replace A by/with B*; or *A replaces B*. So *The Captain substituted Hendley for McAlister as opening bowler; Cotton has been replaced by/with synthetic fibres in most shirts*. Don't confuse these patterns: **✗** *Goats should substitute sheep where grazing is poor*.

2. Beware of potential ambiguity in the verb *to replace*. The statement **?** *I must replace this cup* could mean 'I must put it back on the shelf', or 'I must buy another, as I've broken it', or 'I must exchange it, as it's faulty'. Use another verb if there is any risk of being misunderstood.

such 1. The traditional rule is that *such* should not replace *so* as an intensifier. Since the basic form is *The complaint is so trivial*, the related construction should be *It is so trivial a complaint* rather than *It is such a trivial complaint*. But this use of *such* is now so well established that only the most pedantic person would still object to it.

2. Another traditional rule is that pronouns following *such as* should be in the subject form: *A man such as he should be locked up*.

This sounds extremely formal today, and in most contexts the object form of a pronoun is acceptable: *A man such as him* ... (In informal English, *like* would probably replace *such as*. See AS; LIKE.)

3. The correct relative pronoun to partner *such* when forming a correlative pair is *as*: *The ruling applies only to such items as have passed the test*.

Avoid the common mistake of using *that*, *which*, *who*, or *where*, instead of *as*: **✗** *She speaks in such a way that makes her sound less stupid than she really is*.

4. The prepositional phrase *such as* should be followed by a noun or by the -*ing* form of the verb, not by a preposition: **??** *The hill can be captured in various ways, such as by an assault, or simply by waiting*. Omit the two *by*'s.

5. Note also that the negative form of *such an X* is *no such X*, and not **✗** *no such an X*: **✗** *There is no such a thing as a ghost*. Omit the first *a* here.

6. Avoid substituting *such* for the pronouns *this*, *it*, *them*, *those*, and so on (unless for deliberately jocular effect): **??** *Anyone finding treasure must leave such treasure alone, and must report such to the police*.

See also AS SUCH; LIKE; SUCHLIKE.

suffrage Note the spelling: no *e* in the middle as *suffering* has. The two words are unrelated.

supersede Note the spelling of the last syllable. Don't be misled by the false models of *succeed* and *precede*.

supine See PRONE.

supplement See COMPLEMENT.

susceptible When *susceptible* means 'easily affected by, having little resistance to', it is followed by *to: susceptible to flattery; susceptible to chest infections*. It is followed by *of* (or occasionally *to*) in its more formal sense of 'capable of undergoing' or 'yielding readily to': *a novel susceptible of several interpretations; not susceptible to discipline*.

Avoid using *susceptible* to mean 'frequently displaying' or 'prone to, liable to', especially in formal contexts: **??** *She is susceptible to fits of rage;* **??** *He is susceptible to bouts of heavy drinking*. Use *prone* or *liable* instead.

Note the spelling: *-ible*, not **X** *-able*.

suspect, suspicious These adjectives can both mean 'giving rise to suspicion': *suspicious/suspect actions*. Since *suspicious* also often means 'feeling suspicion, distrustful', ambiguity may arise: **?** *the suspicious detective* could be one who suspects others, or one who is himself suspected by others.

Suspect too has a second meaning that might cause ambiguity – 'of doubtful quality or appropriateness': *a suspect wheel bearing; suspect meat*. So this time, **?** *the suspect detective* could be either unreliable or under suspicion. If there is any real risk of being misunderstood, reword the phrase or expand the context.

Finally, note that as an adjective and as a noun *suspect* is stressed on its first syllable; as a verb it is stressed on its second syllable.

swap, swop The usual spelling of the word, whether noun or verb, is *swap*. But the form *swop* is now a perfectly acceptable variant.

swat, swot The form *swat*, whether noun or verb, refers to a sharp slap or blow. The form *swot* is restricted to British English. As a verb *swot* means 'to study hard'. As a noun, it means 'a period of hard study', or 'a subject requiring hard study', or, somewhat disapprovingly, 'a person who studies hard'.

Both words are slightly informal in tone, except in the phrase *to swat flies*.

swell The usual past participle of the verb *to swell* is *swollen: The river is swollen; The problem has swollen out of all proportion*.

The form *swelled* is sometimes used to express an increase in size or amount: *Our ranks were swelled by enthusiastic volunteers*. By contrast with the neutral *swelled*, *swollen* can suggest an undesirable or harmful increase:

Our ranks were swollen by misfits eager for a brawl.

Swollen is also the usual adjectival form before a noun: *swollen ankles, a swollen head*. However, *swelled* does occur in the idiom *a swelled head*, especially in American English.

symbiosis See SYNTHESIS.

sympathy, empathy *Empathy* is not simply a synonym for *sympathy*. *Empathy* and the verb *to empathise* refer to one's ability to enter imaginatively into the emotions of someone or something else – to 'identify with' a fellow human being, to 'share the feelings of' an animal, to 'get into the spirit of a work of art', and so on: *The twins displayed an uncanny empathy with each other*.

Empathy can also refer to the attribution of feelings or thoughts to an inanimate object, as in the phrases *brooding clouds, an angry sky*, and *cheerful daffodils*.

Empathy is accordingly more specific and restricted than *sympathy*, which has the general sense of 'sharing someone's feelings or views', or 'pity, compassion, or emotional understanding': *sympathy for the underdog; Our views are in sympathy; There is extremely little sympathy between warders and prisoners*.

syndrome The noun *syndrome* is a technical medical term meaning 'any combination of signs or symptoms that occur together and indicate a particular disease or disorder'. It often forms part of the name of a specific disorder: *Down's syndrome*.

In more general usage, *syndrome* has come to refer to any set of actions, characteristics, or the like that indicate a problem and occur together in a more or less predictable pattern: *mid-life syndrome; the jilted-lover syndrome*. This modern sense is an acceptable extension, though *syndrome* has become something of a vogue word, used much too often and too loosely.

Avoid using *syndrome* where there is no real pattern of symptoms – **?** *the businesswoman syndrome* – or as a grandiose substitute for *symptom, pattern, obsession*, or similar words: **X** *You're showing the syndromes of exhaustion;* **X** *You've got a syndrome about physical fitness*.

synthesis, symbiosis The noun *synthesis* is a technical term in science, linguistics, and philosophy. Avoid

using it liberally as a modish and supposedly impressive synonym for *combination, fusion, union*, or the like: **?** *a unique synthesis of flavours;* **?** *a subtle synthesis of different styles*.

The noun *symbiosis* is a technical term referring to the close association of animals or plants that are dependent on each other. In more general contexts, *symbiosis* tends to sound rather pretentious: **?** *the symbiosis of buyer and seller*.

Tangier The official name of this Moroccan city is now *Tanger*; the variant *Tangier* is preferable to the old form **?** *Tangiers*.

target 1. The noun *target* has developed the metaphorical sense of 'an objective, a goal, a desired end or quota': *an ambitious target of £1 million for charity*.

Take care not to use this extended sense of the word in expressions that jar with its literal sense: **?** *exceeding/increasing the target;* **??** *circling/chasing the target;* **?** *being on course for the target*. It is quite appropriate, by contrast, to speak of *aiming at, missing, hitting*, or *just falling short of a target*.

2. The verb *to target* now acceptably means 'to have as a target' or 'to make a target of': *We have targeted Camden for our new campaign*. Avoid using it in the extended and voguish sense of 'to strive for, to intend, to work towards': **?** *The government has targeted a zero rate of inflation by January*.

3. Note the spellings *targeted* and *targeting* – no double *t* in either form.

tariff Note the spelling: single *r*, and double *f*.

tassel Note the spelling: the word ends in *-el*, not **X** *-le* as in *hassle*.

taxi The other forms of the verb are usually spelt *taxied, taxiing*, and *taxis* or *taxies*.

temerity Don't confuse *temerity* with *timidity* or *timorousness*. In fact, it has virtually the opposite meaning, 'foolish or reckless disregard of danger; impetuous boldness; rashness': *She had the temerity to argue with the duke*.

temporary, temporarily Don't omit the syllable *-or-* when writing the word, even though it is often omitted – slightly unwisely – in the pronunciation. In British English, the stress in *temporarily* traditionally and preferably falls on the first syllable only, though an added third-syllable stress is now fairly common.

terminal, terminus These nouns both mean 'a station at the end (and beginning) of a route', but they tend to occur in different settings. *Terminal* usually refers to an airline building, whether at an airport or in a city. And *terminus* usually refers to a bus or railway station. (In American English, *terminal* is preferred in all cases.)

Note that the plural of *terminus* can be *terminuses* or *termini* (pronounced /**ter**minī/).

terrible, terrific In general usage, neither of these adjectives retains any sense of 'causing terror'. *Terrible* is often simply a term of general disapproval – *The play was terrible* – while *terrific*, paradoxically, has become a term of approval: *What a terrific day!*

The two words converge, however, in the meaning 'very great': *I have a terrible/terrific amount of work to do*. So too with their adverbial forms, which can apply to both favourable and unfavourable contexts: *What a terribly/terrifically boring party! That was a terribly/terrifically interesting lecture on Keats*.

Use both words sparingly. The above examples are all distinctly informal, and perhaps have a rather childish ring to them as well.

than 1. *Than* usually serves as a conjunction, introducing a clause – that is, a verb or implied verb follows it closely: *Mary works faster than Joe (does)*. *Than* can also be a preposition, with no verb or implied verb following: *It costs less than £5; The thief was none other than Henry*.

Which pronouns to use immediately after *than*? After the preposition *than*, the pronoun will take the object form (*me, him/her, us, them*): *The thief was none other than him*. After the conjunction *than*, it takes either the object form or the subject form (*I, he/she, we, they*) according to the dictates of the implied verb: *The crash afflicted her more than him* (= *than it afflicted him*); *Mary works faster than he* (= *than he works*).

Since this last example sounds rather stiff, informal usage would phrase it **?** *Mary works faster than him* instead. The way to avoid both stiffness and dubious grammar is to supply the missing verb: *Mary works faster than he does*. This strategy is particularly advisable where ambiguity threatens:

? *She treats me worse than you* should read either *She treats me worse than you do* or *She treats me worse than she treats you*.

2.a. Take care not to use *than* mistakenly in place of *as* (or vice versa): *Their rules allow for twice as many defaults as ours; Their rules allow for more defaults than ours*.

b. Avoid using *than* mistakenly in place of *when*, especially after *hardly, barely*, or *scarcely*: **✗** *I had hardly woken up than the alarm rang*. Change *than* to *when* here. This common confusion is probably due to the model of the construction *No sooner had I woken up than the alarm rang*.

c. And avoid using *than* in place of *to* after *superior, inferior, senior*, and *junior*: **✗** *It is superior in quality than earlier models*. Change *than* to *to* here.

See also AS; DIFFERENT; RATHER; WHAT **2**.

thankfully See HOPEFULLY.

that 1. *that* vs *which* in relative clauses. Consider these two sentences: *The guitar which/that I play is a Fender; The guitar, which is the national instrument of Spain, has six strings*. The first contains a 'restrictive' (or 'defining') relative clause, which can usually be introduced by either *which* or *that*; the second contains a 'non-restrictive' clause, which is introduced by *which* only, not by *that*. For fuller details, see page 173.

2. *that* vs *who*. *That* can be used for people in restrictive relative clauses, especially when it is not the subject of the clause: *The girl (that/whom/***?***who) you met yesterday is my sister*. In very formal contexts, however, it is safest to use *whom*.

3. Note that in such sentences, the relative pronoun *that* (or *which/who/whom*) can be omitted unless it is the subject of the relative clause. And as a conjunction, *that* can almost always be omitted: *I knew/said (that) he would be there*. But occasionally it is best to retain it, as in very complex sentences, or after certain verbs – *She implored that he be released* – or to avoid ambiguity: *I heard yesterday that he was ill* vs *I heard that yesterday he was ill*.

4. The use of *that* to mean 'so, to the extent that' or 'to such an extent' is not fully standard: **??** *I'm that tired I could drop*; **?** *I wouldn't buy a car that old*. In more formal contexts, use *so* instead, or rephrase along the lines of *I wouldn't buy a car as old as that*.

Similarly, the negative forms *not that* and *not all that* are often criticised: **?** *I'm not (all) that keen to go*. In more formal contexts use *not very* or *not especially* or the like. When strongly stressed, the *that* constructions are more acceptable: *I may be stupid, but I'm not* THAT *stupid*.

See also BUT **6**; THIS **4**; WHATEVER; WHICH; WHO.

the 1. The traditional rule for pronouncing *the* is this: if the following word begins with a vowel-sound, *the* is pronounced /thee/; before consonants and the 'glides' or 'weak' consonants (*h, w, y*), *the* is pronounced /thə/.

Note that the stronger /thee/ is tolerable before an *h* when the *h*-syllable is unstressed: *the habitual liar*. And /thee/ is acceptable before consonants when some special emphasis is needed: *You're not* THE *David Owen, are you?*

But avoid the common tendency to use only /thee/. This tends to sound needlessly stiff, or even pretentious.

See also A, AN **2**.

2. A single *the* can refer to several items listed together: *The captain, bo's'n, and first mate were drowned*. Additional *the*'s are optional in such sentences, but note that if one extra *the* is inserted, then every item in the list will then need its own *the*.

A single *the* is mandatory when the items are part of a single concept: *The Oxford and Cambridge boat race has been postponed*. Conversely, separate *the*'s are essential when the items on the list need to be considered separately: *The B.A.s and the M.A.s will graduate in the morning and the afternoon respectively*.

3. The names or titles of newspapers, periodicals, ships, literary or musical works, and the like may or may not start with a *The* (sometimes *A*): *The Sunday Times; A Portrait of a Lady; New Scientist; Messiah* by Handel (never **✗** *The Messiah*).

It is often perfectly acceptable to drop the *The*, or to reduce it to a subordinate position: *Have you read this morning's 'Guardian'?*

4. *The* is often omitted from established pairs or lists of nouns: *Lawyer and client are entitled to private discussions* – or when the noun is in apposition to a person's name: *Ruth Rendell, author of many crime novels, agrees*. (But think twice before you adopt the American and journalistic habit of omitting *the* when the elements are reversed: **?** *Author Ruth Rendell agrees.*) You may also omit *the* before nouns naming 'unique' offices – *He became Professor of English at 32; as Captain of the rugby team* – and, less acceptably, before *Synod, Conference,* and similar nouns referring to major meetings, organisations, or the like: *a vital question for Conference to consider, yesterday in Synod.* Omitting *the* here marks you as an insider. To say *the Conference* could place you on the outside.

See also YE.

then Some careful users of English object to the use of *then* as an adjective meaning 'existing or working at that time': *the then Prime Minister.*

The construction is usefully succinct, and now well established, but it does sometimes smack of laziness. For a more elegant wording, try something like *the Prime Minister at the time.*

there is 1. The singular form *there is/was* should not normally introduce a plural noun, noun phrase, or pronoun: **??** *There's four of us at home.*

The exceptions are:

☐ if the noun is thought of as a single unit: *There is £40 in your account*;

☐ if the first noun in a string of nouns is singular: *There was dust, heat, flies.* Compare: *There were flies, heat, dust.*

The same considerations apply also to *here is/was* and *where is/was.*

2. Use the phrase *there is* sparingly. Useful though it is for indicating the existence or location of something, or for introducing a topic for discussion, it usually sounds rather weak and impersonal. Instead of *There's cake for tea,* try the vividness of a more active verb: *I've bought a cake for tea.* (See also pages 51-52.)

thesaurus The stress falls on the second syllable of the word, not the first: the standard pronunciation is /thi-**saw**rəss/.

The plural can be either *thesauruses* or *thesauri,* pronounced /thi-**saw**-rī/.

they, them, their 1. For the use of *they/them/their* to refer to singular nouns of indeterminate gender, as in **??** *Everyone must have their papers ready,* see HE, and pages 90 and 176.

2. For sentences like *It's them again,* see ME. For fuller details, see pages 183-184.

3. The use of *them* or *them there* for *those* is nonstandard: **??** *Them's lousy sausages*; **??** *Give me some more of them peas*; **??** *What are them there people up to?* Such constructions are commoner in North American than in British English. In neither type are they considered appropriate except in regional speech or extremely informal use, or for jocular effect.

this 1. Purists dislike the use of *this* as an adverb meaning 'to this extent': **?** *I didn't expect it to be this crowded*; **?** *If you shout this loud you'll wake the children once again.* In formal contexts, use *so* or *as this* instead. Compare THAT **4**.

2. As a pronoun, *this* is often an unsatisfactory replacement for *it, they, them,* and so on: **?** *I enjoy reading Yeats's poetry, for this is both well-crafted and profound.* Good usage favours *it* or *this poetry* over the detached *this.*

3. In formal speech or writing, avoid using *this* without any previous mention of what it might refer to: **?** *I've discovered this wonderful little restaurant in Barnes.*

4. Finally, note that many purists object to *this* in responses: **?** *Our team simply doesn't train hard enough. This is true.* Use *that* instead.

And avoid especially the phrase *This is it* as an expression of agreement. Use *Exactly, I quite agree,* or *That's (just) it* instead.

those The determiner *those* is redundant in the following sentence: **?** *All those constables who were on duty will be questioned.* Strictly, this should read either *All (the) constables who were on duty . . . ,* or *All those who were on duty . . . .* The construction is now so widespread, however, that you can get away with it in all except the most formal contexts. And *those constables* would be a perfectly acceptable combination in other, appropriate sentences: *Those constables agree, but these do not.*

though See ALTHOUGH.

threshold Note the spelling: there is no double *h* in the middle, unlike *withhold.* In pronouncing the word, you may choose between sounding the middle *h* or leaving it silent.

Take care when using the constructions *a low/high threshold of pain/ boredom.* Think of it this way: since the basic meaning of *threshold* is 'a doorsill, the plank or stone at the foot

of a door', things happen only *above* (or *beyond*) the threshold. So *a low threshold of boredom* means that serious boredom begins fairly soon – in other words, 'a low tolerance to dullness'.

through 1. In American English, *thru-way* is an official term for a motorway. In all other cases, the spellings *thro'* and *thru'* (sometimes without the apostrophe) should be restricted to very informal writing.

2. Several modern senses of *through* are more or less widely used, but are still not fully acceptable in formal British English. They are 'finished', 'ruined', 'having no further dealings with' – **?** *Are you through with the phone*; **?** *My business is through financially*; **?** *I'm through with that creep!* – and 'up to and including': *The course runs from April through October* (this useful construction is standard only in North American English).

thus 1. Many purists dislike the use of *thus* as the first word of a sentence; they prefer *therefore, accordingly,* and *so,* or *consequently.* But *thus* can in fact provide an effective means of capturing attention before stating an important conclusion: *We are all soldiers. Thus, though we cannot win, we will fight on.* Let your ear be the judge.

2. So too with inverted word order introduced by *thus.* Does its dramatic effectiveness outweigh its rather old-fashioned ring? – *Thus did the enemy violate the peace.*

3. Since *thus* is an adverb, the form **??** *thusly* is an unnecessary – and incorrect – elaboration. Use it only in jocular contexts.

till See UNTIL.

timbre The pronunciations /**tam**bər/ and /**taN**bər/ are standard, and preferable to the Anglicised **?**/**tim**-bər/.

titillate, titivate The verb *to titillate* means literally 'to tickle', and more figuratively 'to arouse, tease, or excite pleasurably (often sexually)': *It titillates my sense of humour; The nudity in the film titillates the audience, without giving offence.*

To titillate and its related noun *titillation* suggest superficiality and self-indulgence or immediate pleasure at the expense of good sense or morality.

The verb *to titivate* (very occasionally spelt *tittivate*) is quite distinct. It means to 'smarten up, tidy, preen';

it often occurs in the pattern *to titivate oneself*, and tends to be used in a rather arch, self-conscious way: *titivating herself in front of the mirror; They've titivated the restaurant since we were last there.*

to 1. The single word *to* is so useful that it can easily clutter a text: **?** *If it happens to come to your attention that we need to move to new premises . . .*

Try to keep your *to*'s under control, but take care not to omit an essential *to* for fear of overcrowding a sentence: **X** *Try to put your mind to what the author could be referring here;* **X** *We're quite unsure as to whom it is addressed.* These should read *be referring to here*, and *is addressed to*. See also page 208.

2. The 'split infinitive', as in **?** *to boldly go*, still raises the hackles of purists.

Where possible, try to keep the *to* adjacent to the verb form, as in *boldly to go* or *to go boldly*. For a fuller discussion, see page 194.

See also DIFFERENT; TRY AND.

together with See WITH.

tomato The plural is *tomatoes*, not **X** *tomatos*.

too 1. The use of *too* in the sense 'very, so' sounds affected, and is best avoided in writing and formal speech: **?** *That's really too nice of you.*

Rather less affected, but still suitable only in informal contexts, is *not too* in the sense 'not very, not entirely': **?** *His joke was not too successful.* Note the danger of ambiguity: does the *too* in **?** *I'm not too interested in sports* mean 'very' or 'excessively'?

The phrase *not too* meaning 'not very' is often used in understatements: *She's not too bright.* This, like *not exactly*, is rather colloquial; the formal equivalent is *none too bright*.

2. Some adjectives, adverbs, and past participles are 'absolute'; that is, they cannot really take *too, very,* or the like: **??** *too perfect;* **??** *too unique to be possible;* **??** *too maligned.* See VERY, and page 202.

3. In negative sentences, *too* is often redundant, or at least obvious, and is therefore avoided by careful speakers: **?** *Don't take it too much to heart;* **?** *I don't want too many chips.*

4. When used as a sentence adverb meaning 'in addition', *too* should not be the first word in its sentence or clause: **??** *Costs are rising; too, sales are falling.* Move the *too* further along (*sales are falling too*), or add a neutral word such as *then* or *and* before *too*, or use a synonym such as *moreover, furthermore,* or *in addition*.

topsail The pronunciation /**top**-sayl/ is acceptable, but the nautical pronunciation is /**tops**'l/.

tortoise The pronunciation /**tor**-təss/ is standard; /**tor**-toyz/ is regional.

tortuous, torturous The primary meaning of *tortuous* is 'twisted, winding': *a tortuous road.* It also means, more figuratively, 'intricate, complex' – *a tortuous plot* – as well as 'devious, cunning': *a tortuous mind.*

The adjective *torturous* is quite unconnected: it means 'resembling or causing torture, agonising': *torturous self-doubt; a torturous death from lung cancer.*

trade union The standard form of this noun is *trade union* (plural *trade unions*), though *trades union* (plural *trades unions*) is also common and acceptable. The British TUC is in fact the *Trades Union Congress.*

trait Note the pronunciations: the *t* is traditionally silent – /tray/; but /trayt/ is increasingly common, and is approaching acceptability.

transpire The verb *to transpire* originally meant 'to perspire', and it is still used in this sense in botany.

In general usage, it means 'to come to light, become known': *It transpired that he was a double agent.*

More loosely, it is also used in the sense 'to happen, occur': **?** *It transpired that the weather was too bad for our journey.* Purists object to this usage, which can sound rather affected. Use *turned out* or *happened*.

Compare MATERIALISE.

transport, transportation In British English, *transport* is the usual word for the system of conveying people or goods: *public transport; They used elephants as a means of transport.*

American English often uses *transportation* in this sense. British English is doing so increasingly as well now, though traditionally its use of *transportation* is to refer to the conveying of convicts to a penal colony.

British and American English alike allow the terms *a troop transport* and *transports of joy.*

trauma *Trauma* refers primarily to a bodily injury or wound: *the trauma of a broken leg; the trauma clinic.*

By extension it refers to any serious psychological shock or deeply distressing experience, especially if it has long-lasting effects: *the trauma suffered by survivors of the Titanic.*

Unfortunately *trauma* has become a weakened vogue word for any experience that is merely annoying or mildly unpleasant: **?** *the trauma of missing the bus;* **?** *the trauma of arguing with the boss.* So too with the adjective *traumatic* and the verb *to traumatise.* Use these words sparingly, and only to refer to serious wounds, either psychological or physical.

The pronunciation of *trauma* is now usually /**traw**mə/, though /**trow**mə/ is still possible.

trilogy This term for a group of three linked plays, novels, or the like is spelt with only one *o*. Don't model it on *biology* and spell it as **X** *triology*, and don't pronounce it as if it were spelt that way. The pronunciation is simply /**trill**əji/.

triumphal, triumphant These two adjectives are not usually interchangeable.

Triumphant means 'successful, victorious' – *the triumphant team* – as well as 'exulting in success or victory': *a triumphant return home.*

Triumphal is more restricted in meaning – 'celebrating a triumph or victory': *a triumphal arch/procession.*

trooper, trouper A soldier is a *trooper*, belonging to the *troops*; an actor is a *trouper*, belonging to a *troupe*. An *old trouper* (not **X** *old trooper*) is a person of experience, an old friend, or good sport.

truism A *truism* is not simply something that happens to be true. Don't use the word as a fancy substitute for *fact* or *truth*: **X** *the truism that crime rates rise in the summer.*

Strictly speaking, a *truism* refers to a tautology, or the statement of a self-evident truth, such as *Criminals are law-breakers.* It can also be a platitude or statement of an absurdly obvious truth such as *Some crimes are increasing in frequency.*

try and The construction *try to* often becomes *try and* in informal usage, particularly after *to* – *He decided to try and cheer her up* – and in expressions of defiance: *Just you try and make me do it!* In formal contexts, however, such constructions are not fully acceptable, and are best avoided.

tsar, tzar, czar Of these variant spellings, British English favours *tsar*. The pronunciation can be either /tsar/ or /zar/.

turbulent, turbid, turgid, tumid The adjectives *tumid* and *turgid*, /**tur**-jid/, both mean literally 'enlarged, swollen, distended': *He ate until his stomach was turgid/tumid*. *Turgid* can also be used metaphorically to mean 'overtight, rigid': *the turgid rulebooks*.

And both *turgid* and *tumid* have the extended sense of 'inflated' or 'high-flown, ornate, pompous' when referring to speech or writing: *turgid/tumid prose; his turgid/tumid style*.

Confusingly similar is the extended meaning of *turbid* – 'confused, or unclear': *a turbid argument*. More literally, *turbid* means 'muddy, or cloudy' – *turbid waters* – or 'dense, thick': *turbid smog*. It can also mean 'muddled, in confusion or turmoil': *the turbid streets of the casbah*.

In this last sense, *turbid* comes quite close to *turbulent*: 'in a state of disorder or agitation'. Note, however, that *turbulent waters* are not quite the same as *turbid waters*. More metaphorically, *turbulent* also means 'restless, chaotic' – *a turbulent period of history* – and 'insubordinate, unruly, disorderly': *a turbulent writer*.

turquoise Several pronunciations are permissible: the most common, in order of preference, are /**tur**-kwoyz, **tur**-koyz, **tur**-kwaaz/.

twelfth When pronouncing the word, don't neglect to sound the *f*.

type of See SORT OF.

tyre, tire In British English, *tyre* is now the only acceptable spelling of the word meaning 'the covering of a wheel'. In American English, the same word is spelt *tire*.

In both British and American English, *to tire* is the verb meaning 'to weary' or 'to become fatigued'.

umbrella Don't add an extra syllable in the middle when pronouncing the word: **X** /umbər-**el**-lə/.

unceremonious See CEREMONIAL.

under way, underway See WAY.

uneatable See EATABLE.

uninterested See DISINTERESTED.

unique Logically, something is either unique or not unique – it cannot be *more or less unique, very unique*, or *rather unique*. Yet such phrases are very common nowadays, suggesting a weakened meaning such as 'remarkable or unusual' or 'impressive; of high quality': **?** *a rather unique discovery*; **?** *This wine is so unique*. Use such expressions sparingly if at all, and only in informal contexts.

Note, however, that there are degrees of closeness to being *unique*. So it is quite acceptable to refer to something as being *more nearly unique* or *far from unique*.

And, in informal usage at least, you can feel free to intensify the adjective in such expressions as *utterly /quite/ absolutely unique*.

See also VERY, and page 202.

United Kingdom See BRITAIN.

unlawful See ILLEGAL.

unreal See REAL.

unrealistic See REALISM.

unsatisfied See DISSATISFIED.

unthinkable The adjective *unthinkable* used to be a word kept in reserve for times when a dramatic effect was required. Like *inconceivable* and *unimaginable*, it was useful for referring to things very painful to contemplate or very difficult to believe: *It is unthinkable/inconceivable that our troops could commit such atrocities; a scene of unimaginable devastation*.

Nowadays, however, all of these terms tend to be used unthinkingly as vogue words meaning little more than *impractical, undesirable, unacceptable*, or *unlikely*: **??** *The union's new demands are quite unthinkable at the moment*. Similarly the adverbial form: **??** *the new government's unthinkably short-sighted policy*.

Avoid using these words unless you clearly are describing something 'extremely difficult to imagine' or 'too horrible to contemplate'.

until, till 1. As prepositions and conjunctions, *till* and *until* are virtually interchangeable. Perhaps *until* is slightly more formal, and is preferable in very formal contexts (except in the archaic phrases *till death us do part*

and *true till death*) or at the start of a sentence: *Until I hear otherwise, I shall continue trading*.

Until is also preferable when referring to cause and effect in the sense of 'to the point or extent that': *He droned on and on until I could bear no more*.

2. Avoid the redundant phrase *up till* or *up until*, which appears to be a thoughtless variant of *up to*: **??** *The weather was cold up until yesterday*. Omit the *up*, or use *up to* instead.

3. Also redundant are the popular phrase *until such time as* – **?** *You will be grounded until such time as you apologise* – and the legal formula *unless and until*: **?** *Let us keep that arrangement unless and until either of us objects*. In both cases, *until* is perfectly adequate on its own.

us See ME; WE.

used to 1. Don't use the pattern **X** *I am/became used to walk to work*. It is an unacceptable mix of *I am/became used to walking to work* (*used to* meaning 'accustomed to') and *I used to walk to work* (*used to* meaning 'did habitually').

2. This latter sense of *used to* raises problems in negative, interrogative, and emphatic sentences. British English regards the reduction of *used to* use as not fully acceptable in formal contexts: **?** *He didn't use to walk to work*; **?** *He did use to walk to work*; **?** *Did/didn't he use to walk to work?* Yet the 'correct' interrogative form sounds very old-fashioned: *Used/Usedn't he to walk to work?* To avoid the tricky choice, try rephrasing the sentence each time: *Is it true that he used to walk to work?* or simply *Did he walk to work?*

utilise The verb *to utilise* is now often simply treated as a grandiose synonym of *to use*, especially in business and official jargon: **??** *Permission has been granted for you to utilise the company's kitchen facilities*. Avoid this pretentious and voguish usage.

The correct sense of *to utilise* is narrower than that of *to use*; it means 'to make productive use of, to exploit profitably': *We must utilise all available resources to the full*.

vaccinate Note the spelling: double *c*, single *n*; contrast *vacillate*.

vagary The noun *vagary*, nowadays pronounced /**vay**gəri/, is not a synonym of *vagueness*. A *vagary* is a whim, an erratic or eccentric notion or action. It occurs most often in the plural: *the vagaries of the weather; He can afford such vagaries*.

valet The Anglicised pronunciation /**val**lit/ is slightly preferable to the French form /**val**lay/.

Van Gogh The favoured pronunciation in British speech is /**van gokh**/; /van-/ and /-**gof**/ are also acceptable; /van-**go**/ is American; the correct Dutch pronunciation is more like /**fun khokh**/.

vase In British speech /vaaz/ is now the standard pronunciation; /vawz/ is old-fashioned; /vayz/ and /vayss/ are mainly American.

venal, venial Take care not to confuse these unrelated adjectives. The main meanings of *venal* are 'mercenary, easily bribed or corrupted' – *a venal customs officer* – or 'characterised by corruption and bribery': *venal conduct; a venal decade*.

Venial applies to sins, offences, or errors, and means 'not grave; easily excused or forgiven': *venial sins vs mortal sins; a venial misspelling*.

The related nouns are *venality* and *veniality* (or *venialness*).

vengeance See REVENGE.

venison The pronunciation was traditionally /**venz**'n/, but /**ven**ni-z'n/ and /**ven**ni-s'n/ are now more common, and considered acceptable.

verbal See AURAL.

vertebra The preferred plural in technical contexts is *vertebrae* (pronounced /-bree/ at the end); elsewhere, *vertebras* is generally considered an acceptable alternative.

very, much 1. Not all adjectives and adverbs can be intensified with *very*: **??** *very certain*, **??** *very unique*. These adjectives have 'absolute' meanings that do not allow for qualification. Similarly *complete, dead, essential, worthless, perfect*, and their corresponding adverbs.

Slightly more acceptable are **?** *more certain* and **?** *less perfect*, perhaps as a shorthand for the fully acceptable *more nearly certain* and *less near to perfect*. And *absolutely certain* and *totally worthless* make good sense, though they are tautologous. Usually it is only for special effect that absolute adjectives and adverbs can become gradable: *By the time I've finished with*

him he'll be very dead indeed. See also PERFECT; UNIQUE; and page 202.

2. Past participles that serve as full adjectives can take *very*: *very pleased, very interested, very worried*, and so on. But past participles that still feel like verbs rather than full adjectives cannot take *very*: **?** *very displeased* is dubious; **X** *very criticised* is impossible. Such verbal adjectives require adverbs that can intensify verbs, such as *much, severely*, or *greatly*: *much/severely criticised, greatly displeased*. Other examples include *discussed, used, admired*, and *improved*.

veterinary Don't forget the *-er-* syllable when writing or pronouncing the word. And note that the next syllable is *-in*, not **X** *-an* as in *veteran*.

via This preposition means 'by way of; in transit through': *We are flying to Athens via Cairo*. Avoid using it as a grandiose synonym of *by* or *by means of*: **??** *sent it via the post*...; **??** *travelling via Concorde*; **??** *achieved via underhand methods*. The correct pronunciation is /**vī**-ə/ – far preferable to **?** /**vee**-ə/.

Compare PER.

viable This adjective has become a fashionable but clichéd substitute for words such as *possible, valid*, and *feasible*: **?** *a viable solution/alternative; economically viable*; **?** *a viable future*; **?** *poses no viable threat*.

The older sense of the word is 'capable of living, especially on its own, or in favourable circumstances': *a viable foetus; viable seeds/eggs*.

By extension, *a viable settlement* is one that is capable of developing into a town; and *a viable scheme* is one that is capable of being realised, or of becoming self-sustaining. The noun *viability* is used correspondingly: *Check on the viability of the new company before investing in it*.

Think twice before using *viable* and *viability* in contexts other than those in which the continued or potential existence of something is in question.

victuals, victualler The *c* is silent: so, /**vitt**'lz/ and /**vitt**'l-ər/.

visitation Except in jocular contexts, don't use *visitation* as a substitute for the simpler *visit*.

A *visitation* refers to a formal visit of inspection, made by an official, or by a bishop to his diocese. It can also refer to the arrival of punishment or reward

from heaven, or of any disaster or catastrophe: *the visitation of a plague*. And it can also refer to the appearance of a supernatural being; *a visitation by a ghost/a host of angels*.

In informal or jocular usage, *a visitation* may be an unduly prolonged social call: *Aunt Elaine's weekly visitation*. And in American English, *visitation* refers to a divorced or separated parent's right of access to his or her children.

viz The word *viz* is an abbreviation of the Latin adverb *videlicet*, meaning literally 'it is permitted to see'. When read out loud, it is often rendered as *namely*, though informally it might be /viz/ and very formally /vi-**dee**li-set/ or /vī-**day**li-ket/.

Typically, *viz* is used when listing items just mentioned or hinted at: *The three offenders – viz Brown, Jones, and Bailey – died*. It is similar to *i.e.*, except that *i.e.*, tends to explain rather than simply to list.

Note that *viz* does not need to be italicised, or followed by a full stop or a comma.

See also E.G., I.E..

voluntarily In formal British speech, the stress falls on the first syllable alone. Purists dislike an added third-syllable stress, as in North American usage.

vulnerable Try not to neglect the first *l* when pronouncing the word: /**vul**-nərəb'l/ is preferable to **?** /**vun**-rəb'l/.

waistcoat The two pronunciations /**wayss**-kōt, **wayst**-/ are standard; /**wess**-kət, -kit/ were standard, but now sound old-fashioned.

wait, await The verb *to wait* occasionally takes a direct object, as in the phrase *to wait one's turn*. Generally, however, *to wait* is used intransitively (without a direct object), often with the preposition *for*: *I'll wait; It will have to wait; We are still waiting for your reply*.

To await, on the other hand, is always used transitively (with a direct object, or in the passive): *We are awaiting the final results; The outcome was eagerly awaited*.

Note that *await* can sound extremely formal when referring to people or physical objects: *I shall await her in the hall; We are awaiting the train*. Here, *waiting for* is far preferable.

Nevertheless, *await* can comfortably take a human object in the sense 'to be in store for': *A surprise awaits her at home*. And *await* is only slightly more formal than *wait* when applied to intangible things or abstract notions: *We're awaiting the announcement/outcome*.

waive, wave, waiver, waver The verb *to waive* means 'to give up or defer (a right or claim) voluntarily': *to waive diplomatic immunity; She waived her right to appeal*.

Don't confuse *to waive* with *to wave aside*, meaning 'to dismiss from consideration, as by a flick of the hand': *She waved aside all our warnings*.

And don't confuse the noun *waiver* with the verb *to waver*. *Waiver* is related to the verb *to waive*; it means 'the relinquishing of a right' and also 'a formal document certifying such a relinquishment'.

To waver is 'to hesitate or falter, fail in courage or decisiveness': *He wavered at the sight of the monster*.

wake, awake, awaken, waken The most common of these verbs is *to wake*, with the past form *woke* and past participle *woken*: *I woke (up) at midnight; I was woken at midnight*. (The form *waked* is also possible in both examples, but sounds rather old-fashioned in British English.)

To wake can also mean 'to be awake, to remain awake', though now only in the idioms *waking or sleeping* and *waking hours*.

To awake and *to awaken* are now old-fashioned when used in the literal sense of 'to wake up'. But they still occur fairly often in metaphorical contexts; here *awaken* is transitive, and *awake* intransitive: *It awakened their suspicions; Our fears awoke at once; a rude awakening*.

The form *awoken* used to be non-standard – *woken* or *awaked* being preferred – but it is generally accepted today: *Our doubts were immediately awoken*.

To waken, usually occurring in the passive, is now a rather old-fashioned alternative to *to wake* in both literal and metaphorical contexts: *I was wakened by a noise; They were wakened from their complacency*.

In both of these examples, *woken* would sound more in keeping with current idiom.

wander, wonder Take care with the spellings and pronunciations of these two words. Remember that *wander*, 'to roam or digress', has an *a* as in *meander*, yet rhymes with *yonder*. And *wonder*, 'to marvel or doubt' has an *o* as in *ponder*, but rhymes with *thunder*.

want 1. The two main meanings of the verb *to want* might very occasionally cause ambiguity. **?** *These children want some discipline at home*. The probable sense of *want* here is 'lack or need', though it could possibly be 'desire'.

2. In regional British English, *to want*, in the sense 'to desire', often occurs in unconventional patterns: **?** *Do you want it wrapping?* **?** *The car wants mended*. These are unsuitable for formal speech and writing.

3. The phrase *to want for*, meaning 'to lack', survives chiefly in such idioms as *She wants for nothing; He didn't want for anything*.

In the sense 'to wish', a simple *to want* is better than the redundant *to want for*: **?** *They want for us to visit them*. But the *for* is acceptable when separated from the *want*: *They want very much for us to visit them; What they want is for us to visit them*.

4. The expression *to want in/out*, meaning *to want to be included/released*, is now widespread in informal English, both British and American: *to want into a deal; to want out of a contract*. It remains inappropriate for formal speech and writing.

was See WERE.

wastage Don't use *wastage* simply as an impressive-sounding variant of *waste*. *Wastage* refers to loss by natural processes, such as decay, leakage, death, or retirement: *wastage from the reservoir owing to evaporation; reducing the workforce by natural wastage*.

Unlike *waste* in the sense 'squandering', *wastage* seldom implies moral censure.

way 1. In phrases such as *way over budget, way above my head, way over there* and the like, *way* is a shortened form of *away*, functioning as an adverb, and is still slightly informal.

2. Note that a ship, project, or the like gets *under way*, never **X** *under weigh*. However, *weigh* is correct in the expressions *to weigh anchor* and *Anchors aweigh!* – never **X** *Anchors away!*

The phrase *under way* is properly two words, though the one-word form is widespread and now approaching acceptability: **?** *It was well underway when disaster struck*.

-ways See -WISE.

we, us, our 1. The 'royal' *we* has become the 'editorial' *we*, frequently used in newspaper editorials to preserve a collective anonymity. In most other contexts, it is now used mostly for jocular effect, occasionally with the odd reflexive form *ourself*: *We shall now take ourself to bed*.

2. In colloquial usage, *us* sometimes appears instead of *we* as the subject of a sentence when joined to a plural noun: **X** *Only us Burke kids saw the murderer*. To avoid this error, some people go to the opposite extreme, and use *we* when *us* is needed: **X** *It was beyond the grasp of we novices*.

3. Note the spelling of *ours* – there is no apostrophe.

4. For the choice between *us* and *we* in *as fast as us/we* and *faster than us/we*, see AS; THAN.

See also ME; MYSELF; SELF.

Wednesday Sounding the first *d* is not obligatory when pronouncing the word, though purists prefer it.

week See YEAR.

were The subjunctive form *were* often occurs after the conjunctions *if, as if*, and *as though*; it takes the place of the usual forms *am, is, was* in suppositions that are clearly imaginary or untrue: *If I were you . . .; If I were rich . . .; She stared at me as if I were mad*.

If the supposition is factual or possible, then the indicative form *am, is*, or *was* would be appropriate: *If she is there now, she is in trouble*.

When the *if* is followed by *not*, *were* is preferable to *was*: *If it were not for his family, he would resign*. And only *were* is acceptable as the first word of a conditional sentence: *Were it not for his family, he would resign*.

Conversely, only *was* is acceptable when the *if* can be replaced by *whether*: *I asked her if/whether she was happy*.

wet, whet The verb *to whet* means 'to sharpen (a knife or tool)', usually on a *whetstone*. Figuratively, it means 'to stimulate or heighten (curiosity, appetite, interest, or the like)': *The war merely whetted his appetite for violence*. Take care not to misspell *whet* as *wet*.

what 1. *What* cannot be used in standard English as a simple relative pronoun like *that*, *which*, and *who*: **X** *That's the dog what bit me.* It should mean something like *that which* or *the thing which* instead: *What I like about him is his humour; I've done what I can.*

2. *What* is also often wrongly used after *as* and *than*. The rule in such cases is this – if you can leave *what* out, you should leave it out: **X** *Do it the same as what I do;* **X** *She's smaller than what he is;* **??** *The damage was less than what I'd expected;* **?** *Is that book the same as what you were reading yesterday morning?*

The last example is more or less acceptable, since *what* can stand for *the thing which*. Even so, it would sound better to omit the *what*.

3. Some *what*-clauses raise the problem of whether to take a singular or plural verb. Here are some possibilities, in descending order: *What worries him is the rumours;* **??** *What worry him are the rumours;* **??** *What worries him are the rumours.* In formal contexts, base your sentences on the first example.

See also BUT 7; WHICH 4.

whatever, what ever The phrase *what ever* introduces questions; the *ever* simply makes the *what* more emphatic: *What ever are you up to?* To spell it as a single word is common but still nonstandard. See EVER 1.

The one-word form *whatever* has several senses, the most common of them illustrated by the following sentences: *I'll do whatever you say; Whatever you do, tell the truth; I can see no point whatever in continuing; Use a pencil or crayon or whatever.*

This last usage still has a slightly informal ring to it, and is best avoided in formal contexts.

Take care not to insert a needless *that*, as in **X** *He keeps calm in whatever difficulties that he encounters.*

whenever, when ever See EVER 1.

wherefore The archaic word *wherefore* does not mean 'where', as headline writers sometimes seem to think. It means 'why'. When Juliet, in *Romeo and Juliet*, asks rhetorically *Wherefore art thou Romeo?*, she is really asking 'Why do you have to be Romeo?' – that is, someone she is unable to marry because of the family feud.

wherever, where ever See EVER 1.

whether, if 1. An indirect question can be introduced either by *if* or, more formally, by *whether*: *I asked whether/ if she would agree.*

Whether is preferable when two or more conditions are fully expressed: *I asked whether she was going to the theatre or staying for dinner.* And *whether* is essential when a preposition precedes: *It depends on whether he is sober.*

2. A succinct construction such as *We debated whether to drop the matter* is perfectly adequate. There is no need to add the phrase *or not* or an explicit alternative – such as *or to take it further* – unless it is considered equally important.

3. However, in the sense 'regardless of the circumstance that', *whether* must be explicitly followed by all the options: *Whether she wins or loses, this is her last race.*

Note that in formal writing, the subjunctive form of the verb may still be found here: *Whether she win or lose . . .* But the phrase *whether or no* now sounds extremely old-fashioned: **?** *I'm off to the pub, whether you like it or no.*

4. Finally, make sure that an option stated after *whether* is stated only once, not twice: **X** *Whether or not she wins or loses, she plans to retire.* Omit either *or not* or *or loses.*

See also IF, and page 195.

which 1. *that* vs *which* in relative clauses. See THAT 1. For further information on relative clauses, see also pages 173, 209, 211.

2. *whose* vs *of which.* See WHO 1.

3. *Which* usually refers to a preceding noun, such as *journeys* in *She took several journeys, which were very interesting.* But sometimes *which* refers to the whole preceding clause or sentence: *She told us about her journeys, which was very interesting.* Here it is the whole of 'She told us about her journeys' which was interesting.

Sometimes there is a danger of ambiguity: **?** *She told us about her journey, which was very interesting.* Was it the 'telling' or the 'journey' that was interesting? If the former, change *which* to *and that*, and the meaning becomes clear.

4. *which* vs *what.* In questions, *which* and *what* are often interchangeable, whether as pronouns (*Which/What did you buy?*) or as determiners (*Which/What book did you buy?*). The difference is that *which* (like *each*)

suggests a limited set of options, and *what* (like *every*) suggests a large or limitless set, and therefore assumes no knowledge of the possible answers.

while, whilst 1. Some purists object to the use of *while* in the sense 'whereas', though it is now fully established: *John is a pessimist, while I am an optimist; While she enjoys opera, her husband detests it.* But since *while* carries the notion of simultaneous time, it can lead to ludicrous images – **??** *While William the Conqueror came from Normandy, William of Orange came from Holland* – or to comic ambiguity: **?** *While I use the shower, my wife likes to bath.* In such cases, use *whereas* instead of *while.*

2. *While* is also used, rather more loosely, as a synonym for *and, but, what is more,* and the like: **?** *Inflation has risen considerably, while lending rates have gone up too;* **?** *I have an appointment at 10 o'clock, while Paul is expecting me at 10.15.* Such uses sound affected and often cause ambiguity. Use *and* or *but* instead.

3. In theory, *whilst* covers all senses of *while.* Some users draw a distinction: *while* for 'during the time that'; *whilst* for 'although' or 'whereas'.

This is an artificial distinction, and in any case, *whilst* tends to sound markedly old-fashioned or affected these days. Think twice before using it in any context.

4. The verb *to while* is sometimes, just acceptably, spelt *wile*: *We whiled/ wiled away the morning by playing cards.*

The noun *while* ('a period of time') is quite distinct from the noun *wile* ('trickery, or a deception'): *Stay for a while; Don't fall for his wiles.*

5. Finally, note the adverb *awhile*, meaning 'for a short time': *to stay/ linger awhile.* It is equally acceptable to say *to stay (for) a while*, but not **X** *to stay for awhile.*

whisky The spirit distilled in Scotland and Canada is called *whisky;* that produced in Ireland and the United States is *whiskey.*

whither, wither If you need to remember which word contains an extra *h*, consider that the archaic *whither* – meaning 'where to' or 'to which' – begins with *wh-* as in *where.*

The verb *to wither*, meaning 'to dry up or shrivel', has only one *h*. So too the noun *withers*, referring to the point between a horse's shoulder blades.

who, whom, whose 1. *who* vs *which* vs *that*. As a general rule, *who* and *whom* are used of people; *which* of things; and *that* of either (see THAT **2**).

The main exceptions: babies and very young children are sometimes referred to by *which* – *the baby, which was born on Tuesday . . .* – and 'human-like' nouns sometimes take *who*: *Our pet dog, who is called Eric, . . . ; The committee who were looking into the matter have reached their decision*.

Unlike *who*, the possessive *whose* is now widely and acceptably applied to nonhuman objects in many types of sentence. Compare the old-fashioned form using *of which* – **?** *The Titanic, the very name of which became synonymous with disaster, sank in 1912* – with the streamlined modern form using *whose*: *The Titanic, whose very name became synonymous with disaster, sank in 1912.* This use of *whose* for things is particularly helpful in prepositional phrases; compare *The tree, in the upper branches of which we used to play, fell down* with *The tree, in whose upper branches we used to play, fell down.*

2. *who* vs *whom*. Traditionally, in both questions and relative clauses, *who* is used for subjects, and *whom* for objects of verbs or prepositions: *Who did that?* – *That woman who was here before; Whom did you meet?* – *The man whom you told me about.* So too with *whoever* and *whomever*.

In modern usage, especially in questions, *whom* is very formal, and often sounds rather fussy, particularly when emphasised. Colloquial usage prefers *who*, regardless of case: *Who did you meet?* – *The man (who) you told me about.* The exception is directly after prepositions, where *whom* is obligatory: *With whom did she come?* – *The man with whom she lives.* (But see **3.** below.) In less formal contexts these sentences would be rearranged so that *who/whom* no longer followed the preposition; and then *who* would again become possible: *Who(m) did she come with? The man who(m) she lives with.*

Another reason for the decline of *whom* is that, except after prepositions, it can always be omitted from relative clauses: *That's the fellow (whom/who/that) you told me about.*

But note that subject *who* cannot be omitted in this way – **✗** *That's the man worked with me* – other than in certain colloquial usages: **?** *There's a man here says he knows you.*

For further details, see page 184.

3. Problems with *who* and *whom*. When you do use *whom*, at least make sure that you use it correctly. Consider the following two examples: **✗** *Richards, whom the papers say will soon be signing for Chester, was unavailable for comment* (the underlying statement here is 'The papers say he will soon be signing', so *who* not *whom* is correct); *Richards, whom the papers report to be about to sign for Chester, was unavailable for comment* (here *whom* is indeed the object of *report*, as in 'The papers report *him* to be about to sign'). For a fuller discussion, see page 184.

One or two fixed idioms have *who* where you might expect *whom*: *He's always going on about you know who.*

4. *commas*. Sometimes the *who*-phrase has commas around it, and sometimes not; with a 'restrictive' (or 'defining') phrase, not: *The governor whom you know will be there*; with a 'nonrestrictive' clause, yes: *The governor, whom you know, will be there.* For fuller details, see page 173.

5. *and who, but who*. Make sure not to omit, include, or misuse *who*, *whom*, and *whose* if the grammar of the sentence would be obscured.

To take just one example: **✗** *Representatives whose children live abroad and who go to fee-paying schools should apply for extra funds.* Here the *who* should be omitted: it suggests that it is the representatives rather than their children who are going to school.

6. *whose, who's. Who's* means *who is* or *who has; whose* is a possessive form. So the following are correct: *Whose (handbag) is that? Who's that? The woman whose handbag was stolen has got compensation; The woman who's complained about the theft has got compensation.*

7. In formal usage, the verb after *who* takes its form from the noun or pronoun that the *who* refers to: *I, who am 64, still enjoy pop music; You, who are 64, still enjoy pop music; He argued with me, who am an acknowledged expert on the subject.*

In informal usage, this is true only of nonrestrictive relative clauses, as in the first three examples. In restrictive relative clauses, as in the fourth example, the verb can also be in the third person: *It's you who's wrong.*

See also ONE; THAT; WHICH.

whoever See WHO **2**; EVER **1**; WHATEVER; and page 185.

wile See WHILE.

will See SHALL.

-wise, -ways 1. These forms are added to nouns to produce adverbs or adjectives. Often either form is appropriate – *lengthways/lengthwise* – though sometimes only one form is acceptable: *sideways, clockwise.*

New formations tend to take *-wise* only: *We slithered snakewise through the grass.*

2. A note of caution: don't follow the American habit of inventing ugly adverbs with *-wise*: **?** *It's really our worst month weatherwise*; **?** *Strategywise, our options are limited.*

But adjectival combinations with *-wise* in its sense of 'having wisdom' are usually quite unobjectionable: *the accurate forecasts of the weatherwise farmer; streetwise kids.*

with When *with* links a singular subject to a following noun or its equivalent, the verb should remain singular, even if the following noun is plural: *The mayor, with his daughters, is due at 8pm.*

The same rule applies to the expressions *together with, as with, along with, as well as, in addition to, like,* and *plus.* See page 174.

wither See WHITHER.

withhold Note the spelling: two *h*'s in the middle, unlike *threshold.*

Wodehouse The pronunciation of this name is usually /**wŏŏd**-howss/.

woman, lady, girl, female The associations, ranges of application, and acceptability of all these terms are changing constantly.

In most contexts, *lady* is still the most polite term available. It is essential in official or formal settings: *Show the lady to her seat; Has one of the ladies of your party lost a glove?*

Many modern women object to the genteel associations of *lady*, however, preferring the more forthright *woman.*

And in the context of professions, *woman* (used adjectivally) is definitely preferred: *women teachers; a woman doctor.* (Curiously, in humbler occupations, the noun *lady* still occurs commonly: *a cleaning lady; the tea lady.*) In many contexts, the two nouns may sound equally natural: *the ladies'/women's final; a young lady/woman.*

Girl has fallen out of favour as a term for adult women in general, and specifically female domestic servants and office assistants. Women sometimes refer to themselves collectively as *girls*, but for a man to do so might be objectionable.

Female often serves as a safe compromise, especially as an adjective: *three female spies*. But it is a distinctly inelegant noun outside biological contexts: **?** *What this party needs is a female or two*.

See also CHAIRMAN; and pages 89-90.

wonder See WANDER.

Xmas This shortened form of *Christmas* is clearly informal. Avoid using it in formal writing, and avoid particularly the pronunciation /**ekss**-məss/, which many Christians find offensive.

ye In supposedly old-fashioned signs, such as *Ye Olde Inne*, *ye* simply represents the article *the*, and should, strictly speaking, be pronounced as such. The *y* in this *ye* is a corrupted version of a now obsolete letter, called a *thorn*, which represented the sounds /th/ and /<u>th</u>/ in Old and Middle English. The modern use of *ye* to mean 'the' is a bogus, and often irritating, attempt to look or sound quaintly antique.

year, month, week, day Note the forms of the following constructions: *a two-year expedition; a three-month stay; a one-day match; a three months' stay; one day's grace; a month's visit; a month-long visit*. Use either the hyphen or – rather more formally – the apostrophe, but not both.

yes See NO.

yet 1. In modern idiom, *yet* as conjunction comes directly before the subject of a sentence or clause: *I received little encouragement, yet I persevered*. Unless for special effect, avoid the archaic inversion that places the verb before the subject: **?** *... yet did I persevere*.

2. Note that *yet*, in the sense 'up to a particular time', is used with the present perfect or past perfect tense: *Have they finished it yet? They had not yet finished it*. Avoid the informal American use of the simple past tense: **?** *Did they finish it yet?* See JUST **1**.

3. *Yet* is redundant in the presence of a synonym such as *but, however, nevertheless*, or *still*: **?** *Yet I still managed to free myself, however*. See also BUT **3**.

4. The Jewish-American use of *yet* at the end of a phrase or exclamation – *not just a car: a sports car yet!* – is distinctly slangy, and usually self-consciously jocular, obviously inappropriate for formal contexts.

yolk, yoke When you are referring to the yellow of an egg, remember that *yolk* has an *l*, as in *yellow*. In other settings, *yoke* is the word: *the yoke for the oxen, the yoke of marriage, the yoke of slavery*, and so on.

you and I See BETWEEN YOU AND I.

you, your, yours 1. These words are all used more widely nowadays than they used to be.

a. *You* occurs more commonly than the impersonal *one*: *You can't expect brutality to civilise a man!* This is acceptable even in fairly formal contexts, provided that *you* and *one* are not mixed: **X** *One can't expect gratitude if you are never generous*.

b. Writers (or speakers) often use *you* instead of *I* or *one* in order to draw the reader (or listener) more closely into their own experiences: *When you finally stand on the peak of Everest, you feel a unique thrill*.

c. Even in official documentation, *you/your/yours* now often occurs in place of the cumbersome third person of former times. A major advantage is that *you* is of indefinite number and gender: *If you win but are under 18, you must return your prize*. This avoids each of the possible objections to the third-person construction – sexist, ungainly, or ungrammatical wording:

> **?** *If the winner is under 18, he must return his prize*.
> **?** *If the winner is under 18, he or she must return his or her prize*.
> **X** *If the winner is under 18, they must return their prize*.

(See HE, and also pages 90 and 176.)

2. Don't confuse *your* and *you're*, which many speakers pronounce identically: *You're to check that your laces are tied*.

And note the spelling of *yours*: no apostrophe.

you know Take care not to overuse *you know* when talking, and especially not to allow it to become a nervous conversational tic: **X** *And all the time, she was, you know, looking at me and sort of – you know – leering*.

So too the irritating use of *You know what I mean?* or *Know what I mean?*

yourself In casual speech, *yourself* is often used as a substitute for *you*: **?** *I'd like to visit John and yourself*; **?** *Yourself and John must come for drinks*. This is not acceptable in formal contexts. Use *you* instead.

Quiz Answers

The following pages give the answers to the various tests of word-power, style, and usage scattered around the book. You might find it useful to keep the marker ribbon here, among the answers, as you move from quiz to quiz.

THE NURSERY RHYMES

The answers to the various quizzes on nursery rhymes appear on the following pages arranged in their proper sequence.

First, however, here are the ungarbled texts of all the rhymes or fragments used, in the quizzes and the discussions alike, in the *Style and Structure* section at the beginning of this book.

(In some cases, the wording might differ slightly from your own remembered version. Anonymous songs and verses are part of the folk tradition, and seldom go back to a single definitive printed source. The variations from one version to another, however, are usually only very slight.)

Three blind mice

Three blind mice,
three blind mice.
See how they run!
See how they run!
They all ran after
the farmer's wife,
Who cut off their tails . . .

Twinkle, twinkle, little star

Twinkle, twinkle, little star,
How I wonder what you are . . .

There was an old woman who lived in a shoe

There was an old woman
who lived in a shoe.
She had so many children
she didn't know what to do.
She gave them some broth
without any bread,
Then whipped them all soundly
and sent them to bed.

Deedle deedle dumpling, my son John

Deedle deedle dumpling,
my son John
Went to bed
with his stockings on,
One shoe off, and one shoe on,
Deedle deedle dumpling,
my son John.

Bye, baby bunting

Bye, baby bunting,
Daddy's gone a-hunting,
Mummy's gone a-milking,
Sister's gone a-silking,
Brother's gone to buy a skin
To wrap the baby bunting in.

There was a crooked man

There was a crooked man,
and he walked a crooked mile;
He found a crooked sixpence
upon a crooked stile;
He bought a crooked cat,
which caught a crooked mouse,
And they all lived together
in a crooked little house.

Little Bo-peep

Little Bo-peep has lost her sheep,
And doesn't know where
to find them.
Leave them alone,
and they will come home,
Dragging their tails behind them.

Little Bo-peep fell fast asleep,
And dreamt she heard
them bleating.
But when she awoke,
she found it a joke,
For they were still a-fleeting.

Then up she took her little crook,
Determined for to find them.
She found them indeed,
but it made her heart bleed,
For they'd left their tails
behind them.

Goosey goosey gander

Goosey goosey gander,
Whither shall I wander?
Upstairs and downstairs
And in my lady's chamber.
There I met an old man
Who wouldn't say his prayers,
So I took him by the left leg
And threw him down the stairs.

Cross patch, draw the latch

Cross patch,
Draw the latch,
Sit by the fire and spin.
Take a cup,
And drink it up;
Then call the neighbours in.

I had a little pony

I had a little pony –
His name was Dapple Grey.
I sent him to a lady
To ride a mile away.

She whipped him,
she slashed him,
She rode him through the mire:
I would not lend my pony now
For any lady's hire.

Georgie Porgie

Georgie Porgie, pudding and pie,
Kissed the girls
and made them cry.
When the boys came out to play,
Georgie Porgie ran away.

Humpty Dumpty

Humpty Dumpty sat on a wall;
Humpty Dumpty had a great fall:
All the king's horses
and all the king's men
Couldn't put Humpty
together again.

Jack Sprat could eat no fat

Jack Sprat could eat no fat;
His wife could eat no lean.
And so betwixt the two of them
They licked the platter clean.

Old Mother Hubbard

Old Mother Hubbard
Went to the cupboard
To get her poor dog a bone;
But when she got there,
The cupboard was bare,
So the poor little doggie
had none.

Pussy cat, pussy cat

Pussy cat, pussy cat,
where have you been?
I've been up to London
to visit the queen.
Pussy cat, pussy cat,
what did you there?
I frightened a little mouse
under the chair.

I had a little nut-tree

I had a little nut-tree:
nothing would it bear
But a silver nutmeg
and a golden pear.
The king of Spain's daughter
came to visit me,
And all for the sake
of my little nut-tree.

Hey diddle diddle

Hey diddle diddle!
The cat and the fiddle,
The cow jumped over the Moon:
The little dog laughed
To see such fun,
And the dish ran away
with the spoon.

Ride a cock horse

Ride a cock horse
to Banbury Cross
To see a fine lady
upon a white horse.
With rings on her fingers
and bells on her toes,
She shall have music
wherever she goes.

Sing a song of sixpence

> Sing a song of sixpence,
> A pocketful of rye –
> Four-and-twenty blackbirds
> Baked in a pie.
>
> When the pie was opened,
> The birds began to sing:
> Wasn't that a dainty dish
> To set before the king?

RECOGNISE THE RHYMES?
(page 26)

The high-falutin passages represent the opening lines of the following three nursery rhymes:

> *Three blind mice*
> *Twinkle, twinkle, little star*
> *There was an old woman who lived in a shoe*

(For the correct versions of the texts, see pages 633 and 634.)

THE 'UNPUNCTUAL' SENTENCE
(page 47)

Note that these are, of course, only suggested answers. Your own solutions, though different, may be perfectly acceptable.

1. The first of the 'unpunctual' sentences needs a simple reordering: the list of items should come after the main verb rather than before it. A few minor adjustments, and the sense now unfolds far more easily:

> Owing to a lack of communication between departments, the corporation is failing to address several key management issues: utilisation, the matching of property to service needs, the reduction of running costs, and indirectly owned property.

2. The second of the unpunctual sentences needs to be turned on its head. The main idea, contained in the words *caused controversy*, should occur near the beginning of the long sentence rather than at the end. Here is one simple rewrite:

> Two recent developments have caused controversy: the Prime Minister's decision to refuse funding for a survey of sexual behaviour to further research about the spread of Aids, and a new way of counting people in the poorest category of the population which reduced the number by one million.

3. The last of the three sample sentences requires more radical surgery. Here is one possible version:

> How did it get out, the secret of Andrew Young's July 26 meeting with Zehdi Labib Terzi, the leader of the permanent UN observer mission of the PLO? This is itself still a secret.

PASSIVE OR IMPERATIVE
(page 50)

Here is a list of the clauses containing passive verbs. (Those in brackets are quite unobjectionable: they are common idioms, and you cannot really convert them into active form without twisting the meaning.)

> Care should be taken . . .

> A suitable publisher should be chosen . . .

> all too often this is done.

> A preliminary letter is appreciated by most publishers . . .

> (whether the publisher would be prepared to read it . . .)

> (writers have been known to send out such letters . . .)

> (an approach [that is] not calculated to stimulate . . .)

> it must be understood that . . .

> although every reasonable care is taken of material . . .

> responsibility cannot be accepted . . .

> Authors are strongly advised not to pay . . .

> attention is called to the paragraphs . . .

Here now is a snappier version of the passage. Don't think of it as *the* correct version: a great many other versions are possible. But do compare your own version against this one.

SUBMITTING MANUSCRIPTS

Take care when submitting manuscripts to book publishers. First choose a suitable publisher – make sure that he is suitable by studying his list of publications or examining in the bookshops the type of book he specialises in. It is a waste of time and money sending the typescript of a novel to a publisher who publishes no fiction, or poetry to one who publishes no verse (though

writers all too often do just that!). Most publishers appreciate a preliminary letter. It is a good idea to send one: use it to explain briefly what the typescript is about and how long it is, and to ask whether the publisher is prepared to read it. (Do make sure that the letter you send is an original and personalised version. Sending a carbon copy or rote-letter, for instance – as some writers tend to do – is hardly calculated to fire a publisher's enthusiasm.)

Enclose a s.a.e. or stamps with your typescript to ensure its safe return. But bear in mind that the publisher cannot accept responsibility for any loss of or damage to the typescript, even though he should take every reasonable care of it while it is in his possession.

We urge all authors not to pay anybody to publish their work. If a MS. deserves publishing, a reputable publisher will publish it at his own expense. (Academic books are a special case.) For more details, read the paragraphs on *Self-publishing* and *Vanity Publishing* at the end of this section.

TO BE OR – SOME OTHER VERB
(page 51)

The sentences below will probably correspond only once or twice to your own versions. No matter, so long as yours also omit the verb *to be* in all cases, and retain the sense of the originals with reasonable accuracy.

Remember to keep exercises such as this in perspective. They serve to hone your skills and provide practice in various useful techniques. They are not meant to get you to apply these techniques unthinkingly in all possible cases. Take your cue from the context always: if the rhythm or emphasis of the paragraph favours a phrase such as *It should be clear by now that* or *It is a truth universally acknowledged that*, don't go and change it.

Here now are the sample revised versions:

> Make absolutely sure that you bring the documents with you.

> The agenda contains far too many items.

Ideas abound.

Please help us by withdrawing your objection.

Why carry on taking those pills?

Diners order Menu C more often than any other.

A hybrid word combines word-elements from two or more languages.

Pedants used to ridicule hybrid words.

Hybrid words vary.

Punishing a child disproportionately will simply cause resentment rather than cooperation.

Life remains hard for the ethnic Germans, who still number about two million within Soviet borders.

OUT OF COURT AT WIMBLEDON
(page 52)

Here are the stylistic faults in clause (i) of the off-form ticket:

In the event of – officialese

In the event of . . . it is regretted . . . – non-sequitur: the second part of the sentence follows from the first part syntactically, but it does not really follow logically

curtailment or abandonment – high-falutin abstract nouns

due to any cause whatsoever – tautology

it is regretted that no refund can be made – passive voice twice over

hereof – officialese

And here is a courteous and clear version of the full text, no less legally binding than the original:

NOTE TO TICKET-HOLDERS

The AELTC has to impose certain conditions of sale for this ticket, and does so to ensure the safe and smooth running of the tournament.

(i) Unfortunately we cannot make any refund. Do bear in mind that bad weather, or various other problems, can interrupt the day's play or even prevent it altogether; we regret that it is just not possible to reimburse ticket-holders affected in this way.

(ii) The ticket is valid only for the day printed on its face, and we are not able to accept it on a different day.

(iii) We regret we cannot exchange tickets either.

(iv) We reserve the right to refuse admission to a ticket-holder, as for disruptive or dangerous behaviour.

(v) Flashlight photography disrupts the players' game, and we have had to forbid it formally. Please make sure that your flashlight does not go off when you take a photograph.

JIGSAW PARAGRAPH PUZZLE
(page 55)

The correct sequence of the sentences is: 5, 3, 6, 4, 1, 7, 2. In other words:

> There are also differences between British and American English in stress and intonation. In general, southeastern English uses more violent stress contrasts and a wider range of pitch than American does. Where the Englishman gives a word one heavy stress and several very weak ones, the American often gives it a secondary stress on one of the weak syllables. This is the case, for example, with words ending in *-ary*, like *military* and *temporary*, where the American has a secondary stress on the third syllable. As a result, southeastern English on the whole moves faster than American English, since there are fewer stresses . . . And it tends to have more reduced vowels than American English (as in the third syllable of *military*). Northern English speech, however, is closer to American in movement than southeastern English is.
> – C.L. Barber,
> *The Story of Language*

If you chose a different sequence, compare the two versions and decide if you can still justify yours. Does the sense unfold as methodically as in the author's own version? Do the 'signpost' terms – *In general . . . , As a result*, and so on – still do the same efficient work?

The likeliest disagreement is over the positioning of sentence 7. It is something of a rogue, true enough, and could perhaps justifiably appear in position three or five rather than position six. But if you compare the possibilities critically, you will probably come round eventually to the view that position six is, after all, the best.

ABSTRACTION AND DULLNESS
(page 77)

The four nursery rhymes hidden within the bloated abstract versions cited are these:

> *Georgie Porgie*
> *Humpty Dumpty*
> *There was an old woman who lived in a shoe*
> *Jack Sprat could eat no fat*

(For the correct texts, see pages 633 and 634.)

Now for the rewriting exercise. Your own rewrites of the bland abstract sentences are certain to differ from the suggested versions below. No matter – so long as yours show a similar amount of detail and personal or visual interest.

1. The monthly premium of £290 on a typical £30,000 mortgage will rise to about £315 now that the Chancellor has again raised the base rate by 1.5 per cent. This latest development will have a significant impact on price stability.

2. Where is the saddle-bag? Where is the derailleur adjustment key? Where are the spoke reflectors? Where are the spare brake pads? These are not optional extras: your mail-order catalogue, page 56, specified all of these as part of the quick-reply bonus. Several of the promised features are missing.

3. According to Report 212 of the Market Research department, published yesterday, the Teach-Yourself-Macramé kit should generate sales of £240,000 over the next two years, producing a net profit of £78,000. This contrasts with Report 187, published six months ago, which estimated profits of only £54,500. Market research suggests a more favourable outlook for the product's long-term profitability than previous assessments had indicated.

4. The AA consumer reports on January 1990, as well as Stecker's own advertisements, claim that the TJ143 Automatic does 0-60 in 8 seconds, and manages 42 m.p.g. in town driving. The model I bought from you on 16 Oct 1990 (invoice no. 83711) takes 28 seconds to do 0-60, and I find I am averaging no more than 22 m.p.g. Do you still think I am 'complaining about nothing'? The vehicle's performance is quite unsatisfactory.

5. You really must computerise stock-control in your Radley warehouse. You should begin by speaking to Mrs Dorothy Kingsway, supervisor of the Abingdon warehouse, and Ms Patricia Stott, computer operations manager at Head Office. But at some point – January 1991 by the latest – you will need to call in a specialist computer firm, such as CompuTem, to compile programs and install the system. A different approach is advisable, drawing on outside expertise as well as internal management experience.

TECHNICAL RHYMES
(page 83)

The five nursery rhymes obscured by the jargon of the 'technical' versions are as follows (for the correct texts, see pages 633 and 634):

> *Old Mother Hubbard*
> *Goosey Goosey Gander*
> *Pussy cat, pussy cat*
> *I had a little nut-tree*
> *Hey diddle diddle*

CLICHÉS AND CLASSICS
(page 85)

The two nursery rhymes cloaked in clichés are:

> *Ride a cock horse*
> *Cross patch, draw the latch*

(For the full versions, see pages 633 and 634.)

EXERCISE IN REWRITING
(page 100)

Here is a fairly simple rewrite of the ornate and complex extract. Study its style and structure, and consider how it stands up against your own version, and how both of these fare against the original.

> When top business managers encounter an unusual problem, they tend to call to their aid an 'Expert Consultant' from a specialist firm. They would do far better to call in a 'Visiting Fellow' – a very *non*-expert fellow manager from a similar organisation to their own.

The Expert Consultant's traditional virtues are in many ways serious disadvantages – his special expertise, for example, and his back-up resources at headquarters. He will diagnose the client's problem and recommend treatment (sometimes with the costly help of a colleague or of a superspecialist) in keeping either with his own preconceptions and past prescriptions or with those of his clients

He will soon withdraw his services – perhaps because the client company can no longer afford them – leaving the clients to implement a fairly rigid course of action. They may go about this with enthusiasm enough, but they will not have any real understanding or control.

The thinking behind such an approach is all wrong. It takes the diagnosis and the choice of treatment out of the hands of the business's managers, whereas in fact it is the managers alone who can make a proper diagnosis and direct an appropriate treatment.

And, by imposing a passive role on the managers, it fails to teach them any really important lesson – true learning comes from doing, and vice versa – and so leaves them unprepared for meeting future challenges.

With a Visiting Fellow, however, things are quite different. His apparent weakness – his ignorance – is in fact his major strength. The effect of it is to spur the managers into engaging and solving their own problems, and taking full responsibility, rather than subduing them into dependency as the Expert Consultant does.

Contrast the Visiting Fellow's role and attitudes with those of the Expert Consultant. The Visiting Fellow, being a manager himself from a comparable organisation, is an equal: he studies the problem from the same viewing position as the internal managers do, and like them hopes to learn something from the process. The Expert Consultant on the other hand is a (supposed) superior, and studies the problem from a lofty or expert viewing position.

The Visiting Fellow can afford to give brutally honest advice – he has nothing to lose by it, whereas the Expert Consultant stands to lose his clients' goodwill and readiness to pay, and the possibility of an attractive job-offer from them.

The Visiting Fellow wrestles with a problem from the inside, challenging his host managers to think up new strategies, and in that way drawing out solutions exactly appropriate to their needs and capabilities.

The Expert Consultant, by contrast, can always go back to his headquarters for support – possibly of a kind quite disproportionate to his client's resources.

And the Visiting Fellow is no respecter of persons – including his own. He gladly admits his ignorance and his eagerness to learn; he has no preconceived solutions. And he listens to everybody with equal attention, no matter what their rank, and examines all data with equal seriousness, in the effort to arrive at objective findings and recommendations. The Expert Consultant by contrast, although interested in everybody's ideas (and happy enough to claim them as his own if convenient), cannot be truly open to them. After all, it is *he* who is the expert – it is *he* who tells *them* what is best. Moreover, his lordly advice is often far from objective and even-handed: he tends to overvalue the opinions of the top manager, and often bases his recommendations on them – expedient perhaps, but hardly in the best interests of the client firm as a whole.

If you were managing director of a troubled company, and needed some outside advice, which approach would you prefer?

THE LURE OF THE EAST
(page 121)

Here are the meanings of the words from the Orient, with an account in each case of how the word arrived in the English language.

alcove (**al**-kōv) – B: a recessed area in a wall or room. From Arabic *al-qubbah*, literally, the vault.

antimacassar (**an**ti-mə-**kas**sər) – C: a cloth covering on a chair, especially to protect against dirt. *Anti-* (protection against) + *macassar* (a hair-oil), after *Makassar*, today called Ujung Pandang, a city in Indonesia which exported the ingredients for hair-oil.

arsenal (**ars**s'n'l) – C: a stock of weapons; also, a place where they are stored, made, or repaired. From Arabic *dar-as-sina'ah*, literally, a house of manufacture.

attar (**at**tər) – B: a perfume made from petals, as in *attar of roses*. Persian *attar*, perfumed.

azure (**azh**-ər, **az**zewr) – A: sky-blue. From Arabic *al-lazaward*, the gemstone lapis lazuli.

calico (**kal**-i-kō) – A: a cotton cloth – plain and white in Britain, coarse and dyed in the United States. After *Calicut*, today Kozhikode, a seaport in southwestern India, where it was produced and shipped

cipher (**sī**fər) – B: a numeral; also, the numeral zero; an insignificant person; a system of secret writing, and so on. From Arabic *sifr*, zero; related to *decipher*.

drub (drub) – A: to beat with a stick. Arabic *daraba*, to beat.

garble (**garb**'l) – D: to confuse. To garble a message or report is to confuse it so badly that it becomes incomprehensible. From Arabic *ghirbal*, a sieve.

gingham (**ging**-əm) – D: a cotton fabric, woven from coloured yarns in stripes, checks, or plaids. From Malay *ginggang*, striped cloth.

hookah (**hoo**kə) – A: an Eastern smoking pipe, with a tube for passing the smoke through water to cool it. From Arabic *huqqah*, a small box.

kedgeree (**kej**ə-ree) – C: in England, a hot dish of fish, rice, and eggs; in India, a dish of lentils, rice, eggs, and onions. Hindi *khichri*.

kowtow (**kow**-**tow**) – C: to be over-respectful, to behave in a slavishly submissive way, as in *kowtowed to her in all her unreasonable demands*. Originally, a Chinese greeting involving a deep bow until one's forehead touches the ground. Mandarin Chinese, *ke*, to bump + *tou*, the head.

nabob (**nay**-bob) – A: a wealthy and important man; originally, a ruler in India in the days of the Mogul Empire. Portuguese *nababo*, from Urdu *nawwab*, a ruler.

pagoda (pə-**gō**də) – C: a temple or tower, usually ornate and many-storeyed, in the Far East. Probably from Persian *butkada*: *but*, an idol + *kada*, a temple.

pariah (pə-**rī**-ə) – B: an outcast; originally, a member of a low caste of drummers in South India. Tamil *paraiyan*, a drummer.

pundit (**pun**-dit) – C: an expert or authority in a particular field; originally, a Hindu scholar. Hindi *pandit*, a learned man.

purdah (**pur**-daa) – C: the seclusion of women; originally, a curtain used in the East to conceal women from men, particularly in India. Hindi *pardah*, a screen, from Persian.

shanghai (**shang**-**hī** – B: to kidnap a man, often by drugging him, to serve on shipboard; press-gang. After *Shanghai*, the great Chinese seaport: sailing ships heading there were often crewed by such kidnap-victims.

SHORT WORDS, TRICKY MEANINGS
(page 135)

Here is the meaning of each of the words, with a brief account of its history.

ague (**ay**gew) – A: an attack of fever, especially malaria. From Medieval Latin *(febris) acuta*, literally, a sharp (fever).

aver (ə-**ver**) – A: to state or declare positively, affirm. From Latin *ad*, to + *verus*, true; related to *verity*, *verify*, *very*.

awl (awl) – A: a small tool consisting of a thin spike attached to a handle, and used for piercing holes. Old English *ael*, probably from Germanic.

bock (bok) – C: a strong, dark beer. From German *Bockbier*, from *Eimbockbier*, literally, beer from the town of Einbeck.

brig (brig) – A: a two-masted sailing ship. Short for *brigantine*, from Italian *brigantino*, a pirate ship, from *brigante*, a fighter or pirate.

cleg (kleg) – C: a horsefly. Old Norse *kleggi*.

coy (koy) – C: shy and modest. From Latin *quietus*, at rest, still, silent; related to *quiet*.

guy (gī) – B: to ridicule, make fun of. After *Guy* Fawkes, and the old custom of carrying an effigy of him about the streets on the anniversary of the gunpowder plot.

hie (hī) – B: to hurry or speed onwards (a poetic word). Old English *higian*, to strive or be eager.

holt (hōlt) – A: a wood, grove, or copse; also a wooded hill. Old English.

ire (īr) – A: anger, wrath. From Latin *ira*, anger; related to *irate*, *irascible*.

jape (jayp) – A: a joke or prank. Old French *japper*, to yap.

keen (keen) – B: to wail over the dead. From Old Irish *coinim*, to wail.

laud (lawd) – D: to praise, express devotion to, glorify. Latin *laudare*, to praise.

lea (lee) – B: a meadow or pasture (a poetic word). Old English *leah*.

limn (lim) – A: to depict by drawing or painting; to describe in words. From Old French *luminer*, to illuminate (a manuscript), from Latin *lumen*, light.

maw (maw) – C: the jaws, mouth, gullet, or stomach, especially of a mammal or fish. Old English *maga*, stomach.

ogle (**ō**g'l) – C: to stare at, often in a sexually suggestive way. From Low German *oegen*, to eye.

rife (rīf) – C: common, widespread, abundant, or numerous, as in *Rumours were rife*. Probably from Old Norse, *rifr*, acceptable.

rill (ril) – D: a small stream, a brook. Low German *rille*.

roué (**roo**-ay) – a sexually immoral man, an overindulgent womaniser, as Rhett Butler was thought to be in *Gone with the Wind*. French, literally, broken on the wheel (a dreadful punishment) – first used of the members of the notoriously immoral circle of Philippe, Duke of Orleans (1674-1723), and Regent of France, with the implication that this was the fate they deserved.

sot (sot) – D: a habitual drunkard. Medieval Latin *sottus*, a fool.

wan (won) – D: unusually pale, suggesting ill health or unhappiness. Old English *wann*, dark or gloomy.

OPPOSITES AND SYNONYMS
(page 140)

Did you sort out the confusibles? Here is what you should have come up with.

A. 1. perspicuous
    2. complacent
    3. complaisant
    4. perspicacious

B. 1. complacent
    2. perspicuous
    3. perspicacious
    4. complaisant

THE SYNONYM GAME
(page 145)

The adjectives listed move in descending order each time, from fairly positive or mild or complimentary to negative or intense or hostile.

These answers are only suggestions. You may have other items for the list, or perhaps disagree with the positioning of various items. Remember, the exact meaning of any word you use depends on the context and tone of voice, not just on the dictionary definition.

1. slim, slender, svelte, sylph-like; thin, lean, slight, spare; skinny, bony, meagre, spindly, scrawny, wizened; gaunt; pinched, emaciated, anorexic, cadaverous, skeletal.

2. poorly off, hard up, a bit pressed, strapped, short, out of pocket; skint, broke, needy, bankrupt, insolvent; impecunious, poverty-stricken, penniless, impoverished, pauperised, destitute, beggared, penurious, indigent.

3. slow, unintelligent, unperceptive, dull, vacant, gormless; stupid, dense, obtuse, not much up top; half-witted, thick, bovine, dim-witted; imbecilic, hare-brained, moronic, cretinous, witless, brainless.

4. careful, thoughtful, thorough, attentive, heedful, conscientious, mindful, vigilant; cautious, wary, chary, prudent, painstaking, methodical, particular, scrupulous; finicky, fussy, choosy, fastidious, punctilious, meticulous.

5. penny-wise, careful, thrifty, economical, prudent, canny, frugal, sparing; parsimonious, mean, money-conscious, close, illiberal; scrimping, penny-pinching, cheese-paring, tight-fisted, miserly, stingy, niggardly.

6. modest, demure, retiring, reserved, undemonstrative, unassuming, humble, unobtrusive, self-effacing; self-conscious, diffident, bashful, coy; shrinking, embarrassed, timorous, sheepish, shamefaced, tremulous.

7. friendly, affable, amiable, outgoing, gregarious, neighbourly, genial, cordial, agreeable, well-disposed, accessible, obliging; extraverted, chummy, hail-fellow-well-met, hearty, effusive, demonstrative, buddy-buddy; doting, complaisant, overwhelming, oppressive, smothering, stifling, ingratiating, saccharin, unctuous, fawning, sycophantic.

8. polite, courteous, mannerly, respectful, civil, well-bred, gallant, genteel, decorous; deferential, gracious, refined, courtly, suave, acquiescent, complaisant; toadyish, ingratiating, sycophantic, fawning, unctuous, saccharin.

DIMINUTIVES IN DISGUISE
(page 163)

Here are the hidden diminutives. How many did you recognise?

1. granules (**gran**newlz) – small, solid particles of a substance. From Late Latin *granum*, grain; related to *grain*.

2. rosettes (rō-**zets**) – ornamental badges made of ribbons gathered into the shape of a rose. French, literally, small roses, from Latin *rosa*, a rose.

3. manikin, mannikin (**man**ni-kin) – a model of the human body, used for study in art and medical schools. Middle Dutch *mannekin*, diminutive of *man*, a man; related to *mannequin* (originally a French form), a tailor's dummy or model for clothes.

4. baronet (**bar**rə-net) – a British hereditary knight, ranking next below a baron, not entitled to a seat in the House of Lords. From Old French, diminutive of *baron*.

5. reticule (**ret**ti-kewl) – an old-fashioned handbag, typically made of netted fabric and closed with a drawstring. French, from Latin *reticulum*, diminutive of *rete*, a net.

6. bumpkins (**bump**-kinz) – country dwellers, viewed by others as being unsophisticated. Probably from Middle Dutch *boomken*, a squat person, diminutive of *boom*, a tree.

7. underling (**un**dərling) – a subordinate treated as unimportant. Middle English *under* + suffix *-ling*, small or inferior.

8. bracelets (**brayss**-ləts) – an ornamental band or chain encircling the wrist. Old French, diminutive of *bracel*, literally, a little arm, hence an armband or bracelet.

9. pullet (**poo**llit) – a young hen, usually less than one year old. From Old French *poulet*, *pollet*, diminutive of *poul* or *poule*, a chicken, from Latin *pullus*, the young of an animal.

10. corpuscles (**kor**-puss'lz, kawr-**puss**'lz) – cells capable of free movement rather than fixed in tissue, especially blood cells. Latin *corpusculum*, diminutive of *corpus*, a body.

GRAMMAR – PRELIMINARY QUIZ
(page 166)

For confirmation or explanation of the answers, refer to the chapter on grammar, pages 165-211.

1. fewer
2. remain
3. which
4. cares
5. are
6. has
7. have
8. All those
9. was
10. is
11. me
12. me
13. whom
14. me
15. Who
16. Whom
17. whoever
18. my
19. us
20. as
21. hanged
22. laid
23. shrank
24. dare
25. will
26. would
27. were
28. might
29. was
30. probably
31. solid
32. unusual
33. direct
34. Regrettably

PLURALS – A QUIZ
(page 180)

For confirmation or explanation of the preferred answers in each case, refer to the sections on plurals, pages 173-182.

1. Mollys
2. soliloquies
3. embryos
4. storeys (in British English; American English usually, though not always, prefers *stories*)
5. trout
6. appendixes
7. censuses
8. stigmas
9. fungi
10. criteria
11. diagnoses
12. sopranos
13. cherubs
14. stone
15. have
16. have
17. is
18. is
19. is
20. have
21. pays
22. is

SPEAK FREE, SPEAK FREELY
(page 200)

Here are the adverbs you should have chosen.

1.	a. clean	b. cleanly
2.	a. closely	b. close
3.	a. direct	b. directly
4.	a. evenly	b. even
5.	a. freely	b. free
6.	a. hard	b. hardly
7.	a. highly	b. high
8.	a. justly	b. just
9.	a. lately	b. late
10.	a. near	b. nearly
11.	a. pretty	b. prettily

GRAMMAR QUIZ
(page 210)

Some of the answers provide two or more versions – when the original sentence suffered from ambiguity, for instance, or where rival corrections seem equally appropriate. Even then, these answers do not exhaust the possibilities: your own version may well be quite correct too.

For confirmation or explanation of the suggested answers below, refer to the text of the chapter on grammar, pages 165-211.

1. A knight's armour could weigh as much as or more than the knight himself.

2. I'd hurry up if I were you.

3. The smell of lemons and limes wafts me back to childhood.

4. She is one of those women who never let bureaucracy stand in their way.

5. That book contains fewer anecdotes than its companion volume.

6. The minister as well as his advisors is shown emerging from the meeting.

7. Everybody should provide his or her own transport/All participants should provide their own transport/All of you should provide your own transport.

8. There are so many things I have to remember.

9. I find these sorts of comment most unhelpful.

10. Congress have reassembled after their break for the public holiday/Congress has reassembled after its break for the public holiday.

11. If anyone phones, tell him or her I'll be back at six o'clock/If anyone phones, say I'll be back at six o'clock.

12. Neither of them was prepared to help the old woman cross the street.

13. The media were unsparing in their criticism

14. Either Sam or his wife is going to babysit for us.

15. All the available data suggest that acid rain is the culprit.

16. The standard criterion is a high IQ.

17. That book has two indexes – an author index and a general index.

18. My younger son, just between you and me, has been shortlisted for a scholarship to Cambridge.

19. Who do you think is most likely to succeed?

20. The onlookers suddenly vanished as if they had evaporated.

21. Please allow my husband and me to offer our condolences.

22. What a challenge that would be for us women to face.

23. Joel complained to the governors, who he suspected were misusing the school funds.

24. The assistant murdered his boss and later attempted to murder the boss's wife/The assistant murdered his boss and later attempted to murder his own wife.

25. Please bear in mind that the argument is between the vicar and me, and concerns nobody else.

26. However seldom you have dreams, you should write them down.

27. I can't stand his humming like that the whole time.

28. One can always try herbal remedies, can't one?

29. It's the same poem as I recited last week.

30. Your new proposal seems hardly different at all from the one I've just rejected.

31. As a lifelong music buff, I know of nothing more delightful than the Salzburg Festival/For me as a lifelong music buff, there is nothing more delightful than the Salzburg Festival.

32. Entering the gallery, I at once noticed the large sculpture in the corner/As I entered the gallery, my attention was at once drawn to the large sculpture in the corner.

33. You should have tried to let me know at once.

34. The day-trippers promenaded in a leisurely fashion along the broadwalk.

35. She would have agreed readily if only you had asked her.

36. An attempt will be made to storm the fortress at dawn.

37. If they'd heard about the auction in time, they'd have probably put in a bid for the statue.

38. It is hoped that all former pupils will be invited to the reunion/All former pupils are expected to be invited to the reunion.

39. I'll be very surprised if she dares to tell him/I'll be very surprised if she dare tell him.

40. Whatever you may feel about it, I will press ahead.

41. How can you expect to understand my anxieties fully?

42. The cat seems to like me more than you do/The cat seems to like me more than it likes you.

43. He was stark naked except for the shoes and blue socks on his feet/He was stark naked except for the blue socks and blue shoes on his feet.

44. Just before he went on holiday, Jack had a row with his father/Jack had a row with his father just before his father went on holiday.

45. The commission reported on the trade imbalance of 1989/The commission reported in 1989 on the trade imbalance.

46. The victim might have recovered if a blood transfusion had arrived in time.

47. She ran about as if she were possessed by a demon.

48. If the verdict be guilty and he go to prison, the public will rejoice/If the verdict is guilty and he goes to prison, the public will rejoice.

49. He laid the rug along the flagstones.

50. Even the best-laid plans sometimes go wrong.

51. The argument can be settled only between the two leaders themselves.

52. I feel even more tired today than I did yesterday.

53. The Reading train nowadays goes direct to Oxford.

54. A backwater provides almost ideal conditions for pollination/A backwater provides the best conditions for pollination.

55. With luck, his reign of terror is now over for ever/Let's hope his reign of terror is now over for ever/I hope his reign of terror is now over for ever.

56. No new applicants will be considered – all will have to reapply for the post in January next year.

57. Regrettably, profits fell by 20 per cent last year.

NEW WORDS FROM OLD BOOKS
(page 238)

Here are the correct meanings of each word in this quiz, with brief accounts of each word's mythological or biblical origins.

aeolian (ee-**ō**li-ən) – B: produced by the wind or relating to the wind, as in *aeolian erosion*. An *aeolian harp* – or 'wind harp' – is a sound box with strings that produce musical sounds when the wind passes over them. After *Aeolus*, the Greek god of the winds.

bacchanalian (**bac**kə-**nay**li-ən) – A: given to drunken revelry, riotously drunken. Also a drunken reveller. After *Bacchus*, the Roman god of grape-growing, wine, and pleasure.

chimerical (kī-**mer**rik'l) – D: imaginary, unreal, wildly fanciful. After *Khimaira*, literally, she-goat, a fire-eating monster in Greek mythology, usually with a lion's head, a goat's body, and a serpent's tail.

gorgon (**gor**gən) – A: a frighteningly ugly woman. After any of three monstrous sisters in Greek mythology who had live snakes for hair, and turned anyone who looked at them to stone.

iridescent (**irri-dess**'nt) – C: producing a shimmering, rainbow-like array of colours. After *Iris*, Greek goddess of the rainbow.

Janus-faced (**jay**nəss-fayst) – D: hypocritical, two-faced. After *Janus*, the Roman god of gates and doorways, usually represented with two faces looking in opposite directions.

jeremiad (jerri-**mī**-əd) – A: a prolonged and mournful complaint, lament, warning, or criticism. After *Jeremiah*, the Old Testament prophet, and reputed author of lamentations on the moral and spiritual decline of the kingdom of Judah and its approaching downfall at the hands of the Babylonians.

jeroboam (**jer**re-**bō**-əm) – A: a very large wine-bottle or goblet, in Britain usually containing the equivalent of six normal bottles. After *Jeroboam I*, the Old Testament king of Israel, and a mighty man of valour.

jovial (**jō**v-yəl) – D: merry, jolly, convivial; originally, born under the influence of the planet Jupiter, considered by astrologers to be the source of happiness. From Latin *jovialis*, of or relating to Jupiter.

Junoesque (**joo**-nō-esk) – A: having a stately bearing and imposing beauty. After *Juno* the principal Roman goddess, patroness of marriage.

martial (**mar**sh'l) – C: of, relating to, or characteristic of war or the military life. After *Mars*, the Roman god of war.

matutinal (**mat**tew-**fī**n'l, mə-**tew**tin'l) – C: relating to the morning, early. After *Matuta*, the Roman goddess of dawn.

mentor (**men**-tawr) – A: a wise adviser, a faithful teacher or guide. Ultimately after *Mentor*, Odysseus's faithful friend and counsellor in Homer's *Odyssey*, who became the teacher and guardian of Odysseus's son Telemachus; probably the direct source of the word is a later version of the same character, in the moral romance *Télémaque* (1699) by the French philosopher François Fénelon.

mercurial (mər-**kewr**-i-əl) – A: volatile, changeable in character, as in *a mercurial temperament*; sprightly, lively, shrewd. After *Mercury*, the Roman god of commerce, travel, and thievery, and also the messenger of the other gods.

narcissism (naar-**siss**-iz'm) – C: self-love and admiration. After *Narcissus*, in Ovid's *Metamorphoses*, who fell in love with his own reflection in a spring.

nemesis (**nem**mi-siss) – C: a person or thing that inflicts revenge or retribution, an avenger; also, the execution or workings of retributive justice. Greek, literally, retribution; also the goddess of retribution; from *nemein*, to distribute what is due.

odyssey (**od**di-si) – A: a long, adventurous, and wandering journey. After the ancient Greek epic poem the *Odyssey* by Homer, describing the ten years' wanderings of Odysseus on his way home to Ithaca after the fall of Troy.

paean (**pee**-ən) – B: a song or passionate expression of praise or thanksgiving. From Greek *paian*, a song or chant addressed to Apollo, from his title *Paian* as physician to the gods.

palladium (pə-**lay**di-əm) – B: a safeguard; anything believed to ensure the safety of a nation, institution, or the like, as in *trial by jury*, *the palladium of Britain's liberties*. From Greek *Palladion*, the statue of the goddess *Pallas* Athena in Troy, on which the safety of the city was held to depend.

Philistine (**fill**iss-tīn) – B: a coarse, boorish person, lacking in culture and often actively hostile towards it. After the *Philistines*, the people of ancient Philistia in Old Testament times, for long the chief enemies and oppressors of the Israelites; adapted from German *Philister*, a Philistine, a name once applied by German university students to townspeople who were not members of their university.

saturnine (**satt**ər-nīn) – D: having a taciturn, gloomy character; showing the characteristics of one born under the astrological sign Saturn. After *Saturn*, the Roman god of sowing or seed.

LONG WORDS ARE EASY
(page 253)

How accurate were your calculations – or your guesses? Here are the meanings of the words, as well as of their component parts.

1. geochronology (**jee**-ō-krə-**noll**əji) – the study of the age of rocks:

geo-, the Earth; compare *geology*, *geothermal*

-chrono-, -chron-, time; compare *chronometer*, *chronic*

-ology, -logy, the study or science of; compare *biology*, *musicology*

2. heliocentric (**heeli**-ō-**sen**trik) – with the Sun at the centre (of the universe):

helio-, the Sun; compare *helium*, *heliotrope*, *heliograph*

-centric, in the centre; compare *egocentric*, *centrifugal*

3. megalopolis (**megg**ə-**lopp**ə-liss) – an immense city, an urban complex made up of several closely linked cities and their surrounding areas; usually larger than a *conurbation*:

megalo-, very large or too large; compare *megalomania*

-polis, a city; compare *metropolis*

4. anthropophagi (**anthr**ə-**poff**ə-jī, -gī) – eaters of human flesh, cannibals; singular *-gus* (-gəss):

anthropo-, a human being; compare *anthropology*, *philanthropic*

-phago-, eating, feeding on; compare *phyllophagous* (feeding on leaves), *bacteriophage*

5. ichthyolatry (**ikthi**-**oll**ətri) – the worship of fish:

ichthy-, fish; compare *ichthyosaur* (a marine dinosaur), *ichthyology*

-olatry, -latry, worship; compare *idolatry*

6. zoomorphic (**zō**-ə-**morf**ik) – using shapes based on animals:

zoo- an animal; compare *zoological*

-morph-, shape; compare *amorphous* (without a shape), *endomorphic* (having a fat or flabby body)

7. androphobe (**andr**ə-fōb) – a person with a morbid fear or hatred of men or boys:

andro-, andr-, a man, male; compare *androgen* (a 'male' hormone); *polyandry* (the custom of having more than one husband at a time)

-phobe, a person with a morbid fear or hatred of something; compare *claustrophobe*, *Francophobe*, *xenophobe*

8. palaeolithic (**palli**-ə-**lith**ik, **payli**-) – relating to the Old Stone Age, from about 3,000,000 years ago to about 12,000 years ago:

palaeo-, ancient; compare *palaeography* (the study of ancient texts), *palaeontology* (the study of fossils and ancient life-forms)

-lith-, stone; compare *megalith* (a massive standing stone, as at Stonehenge), *lithography*, *lithosphere* (the solid outer layer of the Earth)

9. holograph (**holl**-ə-graaf, -graf) – a document wholly in the handwriting of the person who composed or signed it:

holo-, hol-, whole, entirely, genuine; compare *holocaust*, *holism* (a philosophic approach that favours treating systems as wholes rather than as an assembly of parts)

-graph, writing, depiction; compare *photograph*, *cardiograph*

10. endogamy (en-**dogg**əmi) – marriage restricted to one's own group, or tribe; the opposite is *exogamy*:

endo-, within, inside; compare *endocrine* (referring to glands secreting internally into the body), *endoscope*

-gamy, marriage; compare *monogamy*, *bigamy*

11. heptarchy (**hep**-taarki) – government by seven; a state divided into seven self-governing parts; specifically the Heptarchy of Anglo-Saxon England during the period when it consisted of the seven separate kingdoms of Wessex, Sussex, Kent, Essex, East Anglia, Mercia, and Northumbria:

hept-, seven; compare *heptateuch* (the first seven books of the Old Testament), *heptameter*

-archy, a system of government; compare *monarchy* (literally, government by a single individual), *patriarchy*

12. haemostatic (**heem**ə-**statt**ik) – acting to stop the flow of blood or bleeding:

haemo-, haem-, blood; compare *haemorrhage*, *haemophilia*, *haematology*

-stat-, stationary or regulating; compare *thermostat*

13. idiolect (**iddi**-ə-lekt) – the unique speech pattern of an individual person:

idio-, individuality; compare *idiosyncrasy*

-lect, speech; compare *dialect*

14. anaerobic (**an**-ə-**rō**bik, -air-) – not requiring air or oxygen to survive:

an-, without; compare *anaesthetic* (literally, without feeling)

aero-, aer-, air, gas; compare *aeroplane*, *aerosol*

bio-, -b-, bi-, life; compare *biology*, *microbe*

15. iconoclastic (ī-**konn**ə-**klast**ik) – destroying sacred images; destroying or attacking accepted values and traditions:

icono-, icon-, likeness, image; compare *icon*, *iconography*

-clast, breaker, destroyer; compare *osteoclast* (a surgical instrument for the fracturing of bones)

16. pseudopod (**sew**-də-pod) –
a temporary extension from a single-celled organism such as the amoeba, allowing movement and the taking in of food:

pseudo-, pseud-, false; compare *pseudoscientific, pseudonym*

-pod, foot; compare *podium, tripod*

17. hypocaust (**hī**-pə-kawst) –
the under-floor hot-air heating system used in Roman houses:

hypo-, below, beneath; compare *hypodermic, hypothermia*

-caust, burning; compare *holocaust* (originally total destruction by fire), *caustic*

18. theocracy (thi-**ock**rə-si) –
government by, or a state governed by, priests representing a supreme spirit or god:

theo-, a god; compare *theology*

-cracy, form of government; compare *aristocracy, democracy*

19. synchronic (sing-**kron**nik) –
dealing with events and conditions at a single point in time, rather than with their historical development; the opposite is *diachronic*:

syn-, together; compare *syndicate, synonym*

-chron-, time; compare *chronometer, chronic*

20. mammogram (**mamm**ə-gram) –
an X-ray photograph of the breast, especially to detect signs of cancerous growths:

mammo-, mamm-, a breast; compare *mammal* (an animal that suckles its young), *mammary*

-gram, a drawing or writing; compare *diagram, telegram*

21. necropolis (ne-**krop**pə-liss) –
a cemetery, especially a large and elaborate one belonging to an ancient city:

necro-, dead, a corpse; compare *necrophagous* (feeding on carrion), *necromancy* (calling up the spirits of the dead)

-polis, a city; compare *metropolis*

22. mesocephalic (**mess**-ō-**seff**l-ik, **meess**-) – referring to a person or people having a head shape intermediate between broad and long; compare *brachycephalic* (having a short, wide, round head); *dolichocephalic* (having a long, narrow head)

meso-, the centre, intermediate; compare *mesomorphic* (having a powerfully built body, neither fat nor weak), *mesolithic* (of or from the Middle Stone Age)

-cephal-, a head or brain; compare *cephalic* (relating to the head), *hydrocephalus* ('water on the brain'), *electroencephalograph* (a medical machine for plotting nerve impulses in the brain)

MASTERING ROMAN NUMERALS
(page 257)

Here are the Roman numerals with their equivalents in Arabic numerals.

DCLXXVIII	678
IC	99
MLXVI	1066
MCMXXXIX	1939
DCCCLXXXVIII	888

Note that there is some disagreement among experts about how numbers such as 99 and 999 should be rendered in Roman numerals. Should they be IC (as above) or XCIX, IM or XMXCIX? In practice, the forms IC and IM are simplest, and therefore probably best. But whichever form you choose, you will find one group of scholars to support you!

GIFTS FROM LITERATURE
(page 286)

Here are the correct meanings of each word, with a brief account in each case of the character-name or place-name that the word is derived from.

diddle (**did**d'l) – C: cheat or swindle. Probably after Jeremy *Diddler*, a swindler in James Kennedy's play *Raising The Wind* (1803).

euphuism (**yoo**few-iz'm) – B: an affectedly high-flown style of writing or speaking. After *Euphues*, a character in two works by John Lyly, a contemporary of Shakespeare's, who popularised an elaborate and high-falutin style of writing; the name derives in turn from Greek *euphues*, shapely, well-grown.

Falstaffian (Fawl-**staaf**i-ən) – A: fat, jolly, loose-living, and boastful. After Sir John *Falstaff*, the lazy and immoral but fun-loving knight who appears in Shakespeare's *Henry IV* plays and *The Merry Wives of Windsor*.

gamp (gamp) – A: a large, shabby umbrella (a very old-fashioned word). After Mrs Sarah *Gamp*, a character in Dickens's novel *Martin Chuzzlewit* (1844), who owns a large, baggy umbrella.

gargantuan (gaar-**gan**tew-ən) – D: enormous, gigantic, huge. After King *Gargantua*, the huge and energetic hero of satirical books by the 16th-century French humorist, François Rabelais.

Grundyism (**grun**di-iz'm) – B: prudish or narrow-minded moral criticism of books, behaviour, or the like. After Mrs *Grundy*, a stern old-fashioned character in Thomas Morton's play *Speed the Plough* (1798).

Lilliputian (**lilli**-pewsh'n) – C: a very small person or being; also, tiny or puny. After the tiny inhabitants of *Lilliput*, an imaginary island in Jonathan Swift's satire *Gulliver's Travels* (1726).

lotus-eater (**lō**təss-eetər) – B: a person who neglects work and lives only for pleasure. After a North African people in Homer's *Odyssey* who lived on the fruit of the lotus in a state of drugged indolence.

malapropism (**mal**-ə-prop-iz'm) – D: a misapplication of a word by confusing it with one that sounds similar, as in 'He is the very *pineapple* of politeness' (instead of *pinnacle*). After Mrs *Malaprop*, a character in Richard Brinsley Sheridan's comic play *The Rivals* (1775), who habitually makes such mistakes; the name derives in turn from the French *mal à propos*, literally, not to the purpose.

Pecksniffian (pek-**sniff**iən) – B: constantly talking, often hypocritically, about kindness and other such virtues. After the self-righteous Seth *Pecksniff* in Dickens's novel *Martin Chuzzlewit* (1844).

quixotic (kwik-**sott**ik) – C: romantically idealistic, ignoring practical realities; caught up in the romance of noble ideals and deeds. After Don *Quixote*, the hero of satirical romances by the Spanish writer Miguel de Cervantes (1547-1616).

serendipity (**ser**rən-**dip**pəti) – B: the faculty of making lucky discoveries by chance. After the lucky heroes of the *Three Princes of Serendip*, a traditional fairy tale set in Sri Lanka (at one time known as Serendip); the term was coined in 1754 by the writer Horace Walpole.

utopian (yōō-**tō**pi-ən) – D: very worthy but impractical or unrealistic, as in *a utopian proposal for reform*. After *Utopia*, the imaginary island representing a perfect society, described in Sir Thomas More's book of the same name (1516).

yahoo (yaa-**hōō**) – A: a coarse or brutish person. After the ape-like *Yahoos*, representing humanity at its most brutish in Swift's *Gulliver's Travels* (1726).

THE GREEK WORD FOR 'WORD'
(page 323)

Here are the *-logy* words with their meanings and in each case the more common 'subject' words they should go with.

cardiology (**kar**di-**ol**ləji) – 1.h. the medical study of the heart, especially of its functioning and diseases. Greek *kardia*, the heart; related to *cardiac*.

conchology (kong-**kol**ləji) – 2.d. the study of shells and molluscs. Greek *konkhe*, a shell.

cosmology (koz-**mol**ləji) – 3.r. the study of the universe, its origin, structure, and so on. Greek *kosmos*, order, the universe; related to *cosmic*.

dermatology (**der**mə-**tol**ləji) – 4.z. the medical study of the skin, including the treatment of skin diseases. Greek *derma*, the skin.

entomology (**ent**ə-**mol**ləji) – 5.a. the scientific study of insects. Greek *entomon*, an insect, literally, a thing having a body cut up into segments.

epistemology (e-**pist**i-**mol**ləji) – 6.e. the philosophical study of knowledge, its nature, and its origins. Greek *episteme*, knowledge or understanding, from *epi-*, upon + *histanai*, to stand.

eschatology (**esk**ə-**tol**ləji) – 7.w. the theological study of the afterlife, specifically of death, judgment, heaven, and hell. Greek *eskhatos*, final, last.

ethology (ee-**thol**ləji) – 8.u. the scientific study of animal behaviour. Greek *ethos*, a characteristic or custom.

etymology (**etti**-**mol**ləji) – 9.j. the study of word origins and development. From Greek, *etumos*, true or real.

graphology (gra-**fol**ləji) – 10.v. the study of handwriting, especially as a guide to the writer's personality. Greek, *graphein*, to write; related to *graph*, *graphic*, *geography*, and so on.

haematology (**heem**ə-**tol**ləji) – 11.g. the scientific or medical study of blood, including its disorders and treatment, structure, and functioning. Greek *haima*, blood; related to *haemorrhage*, *haemophilia*.

histology (hi-**stol**ləji) – 12.p. the scientific or medical study of plant and animal tissue. From Greek *histos*, a web.

horology (ho-**rol**ləji) – 13.m. the study of clocks and watches, and the science of measuring time. From Greek, *hora*, time, a season; related to *hour*.

ichthyology (**ikthi**-**ol**ləji) – 14.l. the scientific study of fishes. From Greek *ikhthus*, a fish.

meteorology (**meet**i-ə-**rol**ləji) – 15.s. the scientific study of the weather and atmospheric conditions. From Greek *meteoros*, high in the air; related to *meteor*.

neurology (newr-**ol**ləji) – 16.t. the medical study of the nervous system, including its functioning and disorders. From Greek *neuron*, a tendon or nerve; related to *neurotic*, *neurosis*, and so on.

oenology (ee-**nol**ləji) – 17.f. the study of wine. Greek *oinos*, wine.

oncology (ong-**kol**ləji) – 18.c. the scientific or medical study of tumours, including the treatment of cancer. Greek *onkos*, a mass.

ophthalmology (**of**-thal-**mol**ləji) – 19.i. the medical study of the eye, including its structure, disorders, and treatment. Greek *ophthalmos*, an eye.

ornithology (**orni**-**thol**ləji) – 20.k. the scientific study of birds. Greek *ornis*, a bird.

osteology (**osti**-**ol**ləji) – 21.n. the scientific study of bones, especially the bones of living humans. Greek *osteon*, a bone.

palaeontology (**pal**-i-on-**tol**ləji) – 22.q. the scientific study of fossils and extinct plants and animals. Greek *palaios*, ancient + *on*, being.

pharmacology (**farm**ə-**kol**ləji) – 23.x. the scientific study of medical drugs. Greek *pharmakon*, a medicine or poison.

psephology (si-**fol**ləji) – 24.b. the study of elections, including voting trends and systems. Greek *psephos*, a pebble, hence a vote (since pebbles were used to cast votes in ancient Greece).

seismology (sīz-**mol**ləji). – 25.o. the scientific study of earthquakes and other conditions of the Earth's crust and interior. Greek *seismos*, an earthquake, from *seien*, to shake.

sinology (sī-**nol**ləji). – 26.y. the study of China, including its language, literature, and history. From Greek *Sinai*, from Mandarin *Qin*, dynastic name for China.

INDEPENDENT ADJECTIVES
(page 349)

Here is a list of the adjectives, followed in each case by the noun that the adjective refers to. The Latin, Greek, or in one case Hebrew root word for the adjective is also given.

adipose (**ad**di-**pōss**) : fat. From Latin *adeps*, fat.

arboreal (aar-**baw**ri-əl) : tree. Latin *arbor*, a tree.

avian (**ay**v-yən) : bird. Latin *avis*, a bird.

avuncular (ə-**vung**kewlər) : uncle. Latin *avunculus*, one's maternal uncle.

bovine (**bō**-vīn) : ox or cow. From Latin *bos*, an ox or cow.

caprine (**kapp**rīn) : goat. Latin, *caper*, a he-goat.

cardiac (**kard**i-ak) : heart. From Greek *kardia*, the heart.

cranial (**kray**ni-əl) : skull. From Greek *kranion*, a skull.

crepuscular (kri-**pus**kewlər) : twilight. Latin *crepusculum*, twilight.

diurnal (dī-**urn**'l) : day. Latin *diurnus*, daily.

episcopal (i-**pisk**əp'l) : bishop. From Latin *episcopus*, a bishop, from Greek, *epi-*, over + *skopos*, a watcher or seer; related to *telescope*, *microscope*, and so on.

epistolary (i-**pist**ə-ləri) : letter. From Latin *epistola*, a letter.

equine (**ek**-wīn) : horse. Latin, *equus*, a horse.

farinaceous (**farri-nay**shəss) : flour. From Latin *farina*, ground corn.

feline (**fee**-līn) : cat. Latin, *feles*, a cat.

ferric (**fer**rik) : iron. Latin *ferrum*, iron.

fraternal (frə-**ter**n'l) : brother. From Latin *frater*, a brother.

gastric (**gass**-trik) : stomach. From Greek *gaster*, the belly or womb.

haemal (**heem**'l) : blood. Greek *haima*, blood.

Hellenic (hi-**lee**nik, hi-**len**nik) : Greece. From Greek *Hellas*, Greece.

hepatic (hi-**pat**tik) : liver. From Greek *hepar*, the liver.

Hibernian (hī-**ber**ni-ən) : Ireland. Latin *Hibernia*, Ireland.

labial (**lay**bi-əl) : lips. Latin, *labium*, a lip.

lupine (**loo**-pīn) : wolf. Latin, *lupus*, a wolf.

ocular (**ock**ewlər) : eye. From Latin *oculus*, an eye.

olfactory (ol-**fak**tri) : sense of smell. Latin, *olfacere*, to smell.

paschal (**paa**sk'l, **pas**k'l) : Passover or Easter. From Hebrew *Pesach*, Passover.

pulmonary (**pul**-mənri) : lungs. Latin, *pulmo*, a lung.

renal (**reen**'l) : kidneys. From Latin *renes*, the kidneys.

sartorial (saar-**taw**ri-əl) : clothes. Latin *sartor*, a tailor.

simian (**sim**mi-ən) : monkey. Latin *simia*, an ape.

solar (**sō**lər) : the Sun. Latin, *sol*, the Sun.

stellar (**stel**lər) : star. Latin, *stella*, a star.

ursine (**ur**-sīn) : bear. Latin, *ursus*, a bear.

vermicular (ver-**mic**kewlər) : worm. Latin, *vermis*, a worm.

vulpine (**vul**-pīn) : fox. Latin, *vulpes*, a fox.

A GAME FOR ALL THE FAMILY
(page 381)

Here are the 'family' words you should have chosen, with a brief history of each word.

1. fraternal (frə-**tern**'l) – C: brotherly. From Latin *frater*, a brother.

2. patrimony (**patt**ri-məni) – D: an inheritance from a father or other ancestor; a legacy or heritage. From Latin *pater*, a father.

3. hussy (**huss**i, **huz**zi) – B: a cheeky or frivolous girl, or a vulgar or promiscuous woman. From Old English *huswif*, from *house* + *wife*; the same as Modern English *housewife*.

4. sorority (sə-**rorr**əti) – D: a social club for female students at a U.S. college or university; literally, a sisterhood. From Latin *soror*, a sister.

5. compere (**kom**-pair) – B: a master of ceremonies or link-man. Old French, a godfather. From Latin *pater*, a father.

6. paternalism (pə-**tern**'l-iz'm) – C: a policy of governing people in a fatherly manner, especially by providing for their needs without giving them responsibility. From Latin *pater*, a father.

7. virago (vi-**raa**-gō, -**ray**-) – D: a noisy, bossy, domineering woman. Latin, from *vir*, a man + *ago* (feminine suffix).

8. triumvirate (trī-**um**vər-ət) – D: a group of three men governing jointly. From Latin *trium vir*, literally, one man of three.

9. fraternise (**frat**tər-nīz) – C: to associate with in a friendly way, especially with enemy occupiers in times of war. From Latin *frater*, a brother.

10. effeminate (i-**fem**mi-nət) – B: being like a woman, unmanly (used only of a man). From Latin *effeminare*, literally, to make a woman out of; *ex-*, out of + *femina*, a woman.

11. uxorious (uk-**saw**-ri-əss) – D: excessively devoted to one's wife; typical of a man devoted to his wife. From Latin, *uxor*, a wife.

12. nepotism (**nepp**ə-tiz'm) – B: favouritism shown or patronage given by people in positions of power to their own relatives. Italian *nepotismo*, 'favouring of nephews' (by 16th-century prelates), from Latin *nepos*, a nephew.

13. puerile (**pewr**-īl) – C: childish, childishly simple or uninformed. From Latin *puer*, a boy, child.

14. patriotic (**payt**ri-ottik, **patt**ri-) – D: motivated by love for or duty to one's homeland. From Latin *patria*, one's native country, from *pater*, a father.

NAMING NAMES – A 'SCROOGE' AND AN 'EINSTEIN'
(page 419)

Here are the meanings that each of the names has come to acquire in general speech.

Adonis (ə-**dō**niss) – C: a beautiful youth. After the young man in Greek mythology adored by Aphrodite, the goddess of love and beauty.

Caliban (**kal**-i-ban) – A: a brutish person, typically deformed both in appearance and in personality. After the character in Shakespeare's *The Tempest*.

Casanova (**kass**ə-**nō**və) – D: a playboy noted for his amorous adventures, a ladykiller. After the Italian adventurer and womaniser, Giovanni Giacomo *Casanova* (1725-1798).

Cassandra (kə-**san**drə) – B: a prophet of doom, particularly one whose warnings are unheeded. After the Trojan princess in Greek mythology, who was endowed with the gift of prophecy but destined never to be believed.

Galahad (**gal**-ə-had) – D: a chivalrous and gallant man. After the knight of King Arthur's Round Table, celebrated for his pure and noble character.

Jezebel (**jezz**ə-bel) – A: a shamelessly immoral or scheming woman. After *Jezebel*, wife of Ahab, the Old Testament king of Israel; she promoted idolatry and the murder of prophets.

Martha (**mar**thə) – A: a worrier, a person constantly preoccupied with everyday chores and cares, often at the expense of things of higher significance. After the sister of Lazarus and Mary, who busied herself with household tasks while Mary listened to Jesus (Luke 10).

Mata Hari (**maat**ə **haar**i) – C: a female spy, typically very beautiful or glamorous. After the Dutch spy, Margaretha Geertruida Zelle (1876-1917), who worked as a dancer in Paris under the stage name *Mata Hari* and spied for both France and Germany in the First World War. She was finally executed by the French.

Micawber (mi-**kaw**bər) – A: an incurable optimist, a poor person who remains doggedly hopeful despite all his misfortunes. After Wilkins *Micawber* in Dickens's novel *David Copperfield* (1850), who keeps insisting that 'something will turn up'.

Midas (**mī**-dəss) – C: a person with the gift of making money. Hence *the Midas touch*: the gift of making money. After the legendary king of Phrygia to whom the god Dionysus gave the power of turning to gold all he touched.

Baron Münchhausen (**barr**ən **münkh**-howz'n) – B: a person who tells tall stories. After the fictionalised hero of a book of fantastic adventures, published in 1785, by the German traveller Rudolph Raspe.

quisling (**kwiz**-ling) – A: a traitor, specifically a person collaborating with enemy occupiers. After Vidkun *Quisling* (1887-1945), the fascist leader in Norway who was installed as 'minister president' by the Nazis in 1942.

Rasputin (rass-**pew**-tin) – B: a faith healer, particularly one who gains a sinister hold over those who fall under his influence. After the monk Grigori *Rasputin* (1872-1916), who treated the haemophiliac son of the last Russian Tsar, and exerted an extraordinary influence over the Russian Imperial Family as a whole.

Robespierre (**rōbz**-pyair) – D: a person fanatically and cold-bloodedly dedicated to a cause. After the French revolutionary leader Maximilien *Robespierre* (1758-94), chief architect of the Reign of Terror and famous for his austere and incorruptible character.

Svengali (sveng-**gaal**i) – A: a person with mysterious powers to make others do his will. After the villainous musician in George Du Maurier's novel *Trilby* (1894), who powerfully influences and manipulates Trilby, the heroine.

Tartuffe (taar-**toof**) – B: a religious hypocrite. After the title character of Molière's comic play *Tartuffe*.

Walter Mitty (**wawl**-tər **mit**ti) – B: an impractical daydreamer, a person who escapes his humdrum life by indulging in vivid daydreams of romantic adventures and personal triumphs. After the central character in James Thurber's story, 'The Secret Life of Walter Mitty' (1939).

DESCRIBING PEOPLE
(page 457)

Here are the adjectives to describe Alex, Ben, Charlie, and the rest.

1. Alex is **gullible** (**gull**ə-b'l). Probably from dialectal *gull*, a young bird.

2. Ben is **lugubrious** (loo-**goo**bri-əss). From Latin *lugere*, to mourn.

3. Charlie is **sycophantic** (sĭckə-**fan**tik, **sī**kə-). From Greek *sukon*, a fig + *phanein*, to show; in ancient times, a flatterer was often an informer and would denounce criminals by making a 'fig' gesture with his hand.

4. Deidre is **supercilious** (soo-pə-**silli**-əss). From Latin *supercilium*, an eyebrow, hence haughtiness.

5. Eric is **querulous** (**kwerr**ew-ləss). From Latin *queri*, to complain.

6. Fred is **malleable** (**mal**-i-ə-b'l). Extended sense of *malleable*, shapable, as iron is; from Medieval Latin *malleare*, to hammer.

7. Gary is **sagacious** (sə-**gay**shəss). Latin *sagax*, wise.

8. Harry is **irascible** (i-**rass**ə-b'l). From Latin *ira*, anger.

9. Ian is **quixotic** (kwik-**sott**ik). After *Don Quixote*, the hopelessly idealistic and chivalric adventurer in Cervantes' romance.

10. Joan is **laconic** (lə-**kon**nik). From Greek *Lakonikos*, relating to the Spartans (who were noted for their terseness).

11. Kate is **contrite** (**kon**-trīt, kən-**trīt**). From Medieval Latin *contritus*, literally, broken (in spirit), hence repentant, from Latin *conterere*, to grind or bruise severely.

12. Larry is **truculent** (**truc**kew-lənt). From Latin *trux*, fierce.

13. Molly is **magnanimous** (mag-**nann**iməss). From Latin *magnus*, large + *animus*, one's soul or spirit.

14. Nell is **callow** (**kal**-ō). Originally meaning bald, hence unfeathered as a baby bird is; from Old English *calu*, probably from Latin *calvus*, bald.

15. Oscar is **taciturn** (**tass**i-turn). From Latin *tacitus*, silent.

16. Pauline is **effervescent** (**eff**ər-**vess**n't). Extended sense of *effervescent*, emitting small bubbles, as fizzy drinks do; from Latin *fervere*, to boil.

17. Quentin is **enigmatic** (**enn**ig-**matt**ik). From Greek *ainissesthai*, to speak in riddles, hint.

18. Ruth is **recalcitrant** (ri-**kalsi**-trənt). From Latin *recalcitrare*, to kick back, from *calx*, a heel.

19. Sally is **ostentatious** (**oss**-ten-**tay**shəss). From Latin *ostendere*, to show.

20. Terry is **affable** (**aff**əb'l). From Latin *affabilis*, from *affari*, to speak to: *ad-*, to + *fari*, to speak.

21. Ulric is **fastidious** (fə-**stidd**i-əss, fa-). Latin *fastidium*, a loathing.

22. Veronica is **redoubtable** (ri-**dowt**əb'l). Old French *redouter*, to dread: *re-* (intensive) + *douter*, to fear, doubt.

23. Wilfred is **gregarious** (gri-**gair**i-əss). Latin *gregarius*, belonging to a flock, from *grex*, a herd, flock.

24. Xanthea is **complacent** (kəm-**play**ss'nt). Originally, pleasing, from Latin *placere*, to please.

FALSE FRIENDS – DECEIVING FAMILIARITY
(page 467)

Here are the true meanings of all the false friends, with brief histories of the words.

disinterested (diss-**in**trəstid) – B: unbiased, lacking all self-interest or advance preference, as judges are supposed to be. The word *interest* within *disinterested* refers to self-interest, advantage, or partiality, rather than to the more usual sense of fascination or curiosity. From Latin *dis*, not + *interesse*, to matter, be of concern, from *inter-*, between + *esse*, to be.

enervate (**enn**ər-vayt) – A: to exhaust or weaken seriously, drain the energy or strength from. Latin *enervare*, literally, to remove the sinews from, from *ex-*, out of + *nervus*, a nerve or sinew; related to *nerve*.

enormity (i-**nor**məti) – B: great wickedness or outrageousness; an outrage or act of great wickedness. Latin *ex-*, out of + *norma*, a pattern or rule; related to *enormous, normal*.

friable (**frī**-əb'l) – B: easily crumbled, as in *friable soil*. From Latin *friare*, to crumble.

ingenious (in-**jee**ni-əss) – B: clever, displaying skill, cunning, or imagination. From Latin *ingenium*, natural talent, skill; related to *engine, engineer*.

insufferable (in-**suff**rə-b'l) –
C: intolerable, unbearable, as in *an insufferable bore*. The sense of *suffer* involved here is the less usual one of tolerating or putting up with something objectionable, as in *He doesn't suffer fools gladly*. From Latin *in*, not + *sufferre*, to sustain, from *sub*, up from under + *ferre*, to bear.

libertine (**lib**bər-teen) – A: an immoral person, especially in sexual matters. From Latin *libertus*, set free, from *liber*, free; related to *liberty*, *liberate*.

limpid (**lim**pid) – C: transparently clear, as a mountain stream or a literary style might be. From Latin *limpidus*, clear.

lurid (**lewr**-id) – B: shocking or causing horror; unnaturally bright. Originally, pale in complexion. Latin *luridus*, pale, yellowish, ghastly.

munificent (mew-**niff**i-sənt) – B: very generous, bountiful. Latin, *munificus*, literally, giving presents.

noisome (**noy**-səm) – D: disgusting, foul, offensive, as in *a noisome smell*. Middle English, *anoien*, to annoy.

officious (ə-**fish**əss) – A: overinsistent in offering advice or help, meddlesome. Latin, *officium*, duty, service; related to *office*, *official*.

protestation (**prott**-ess-**taysh**'n) – D: a firm announcement or statement, as in *protestations of undying love*. From Latin *pro-*, publicly + *testari*, to make a will, to assert, to be a witness; related to *protest*, *testimony*, *testament*.

remonstrate (**rem**mən-strayt) – D: to protest, object, or argue, as in *The manager remonstrated with the picketers*. From Latin *re-*, completely + *monstrare*, to show; related to *demonstrate*.

solicitous (sə-**liss**itəss) – C: attentive, caring, or concerned; anxious or nervous; eager. From Latin *sollicitus*, moved, agitated; related to *solicit*, *solicitor*.

stricture (**strik**-chər) – D: a criticism, critical remark, or misgiving; also, anything that restricts, such as a narrowing in a vein. Latin *strictus*, tight or narrow; related to *strict*, *restrict*.

temerity (ti-**merr**əti) – A: recklessness, foolhardy ignoring of dangers. Latin *temere*, rashly, thoughtlessly.

tortuous (**tor**tew-əss) – C: twisting, winding, as a road or argument might be. From Latin *tortus*, a twist; related to *torture*, *tort*.

unsparingly (un-**spair**-ing-li) – B: abundantly, lavishly, generously; also severely, harshly. The sense of *spare* involved here is the less usual one of withholding or refraining, as in *Spare the rod and spoil the child*. Old English *un-*, not + *sparian*, to leave unharmed, show mercy.

unstudied (**un-studd**id) – C: natural, uncontrived, not put on for effect, as in *She moved with unstudied grace*. The sense of *study* involved here is the old-fashioned one of consciously attempting something or deliberately having as one's purpose, as in *She studied to appear indifferent to his attentions*. *Un-*, not + Latin *studere*, to be eager, study.

vicarious (vi-**kair**-i-əss, vī-) – A: done or undergone by a substitute, as in *vicarious punishment*; undergone through imaginative participation in another person's experiences, as in *vicarious enjoyment*. Latin *vicarius*, substituting, from *vicis*, a change, taking turns; related to *vicar*, *vice-admiral*, *vice-chairman*, and so on.

EPONYMOUS WORDS – LORD SANDWICH'S SANDWICH
(page 486)

Here are the meanings for each of the eponymous words.

An account is given of the person who gave rise to the word.

bowdlerise (**bowd**-lərīz) – B: to leave out or remove words or passages considered indecent from a book, play, or other literary work. After Dr Thomas *Bowdler* (1754-1825), who published in 1818 an edition of Shakespeare shorn of all words and passages 'which cannot with propriety be read aloud in a family'.

boycott (**boy**-kot) – B: to shun or refuse to have dealings with, as a means of protest or to force change. After Captain Charles *Boycott*, a 19th-century Irish land agent who was snubbed and shunned by local tenants for refusing to lower their rents.

chauvinism (**shō**vin-iz'm) – A: exaggerated and usually warlike patriotism. After Nicolas *Chauvin*, a veteran French soldier from the time of the French Revolution and Napoleon, whose fervent patriotism was first celebrated and then ridiculed by his fellow-countrymen.

Draconian (drə-**kō**ni-ən) – C: rigorous, harsh, or cruel. After *Draco*, chief magistrate of Athens, who introduced a harsh penal code in 621 BC.

epicurean (**ep**pi-kewr-**ee**-ən) – A: devoted to pleasure, luxury, good food, and ease. After *Epicurus* (341-270 BC), a Greek philosopher, whose moral code – not really epicurean in the modern sense – was based on the avoidance of pain rather than the pursuit of pleasure.

gerrymander (**jerri-man**dər) – B: to set the boundaries of voting districts in such a way that one political party will have an unfair advantage in elections. After Elbridge *Gerry*, U.S. politician + *(sala)mander*, from the salamander-like shape of an electoral district formed in 1812 while Gerry was governor of Massachusetts.

lynch (linch) – C: to execute summarily, usually by hanging, without a proper trial. Probably after Captain William *Lynch*, an 18th-century Virginian planter and Justice of the Peace.

Machiavellian (**mack**i-ə-**vell**i-ən) – D: cunning, crafty, seizing opportunities. After Niccolò *Machiavelli* (1469-1527), a Florentine statesman; in his book *The Prince*, he described how a determined ruler could gain and keep political power regardless of morality.

martinet (**mar**ti-**net**) – B: a strict disciplinarian, especially in the army. After Jean *Martinet*, a French general in the reign of Louis XIV who played a key role in transforming the French army into the best-trained fighting force of the day.

mausoleum (**maw**zə-**lee**-əm) – A: a stately and magnificent tomb. From Greek *Mausoleion*, the tomb of *Mausolus*, King of Caria, one of the seven wonders of the world.

maverick (**mav**vərik) – A: a person with independent or unusual views; originally, a calf or other animal found without an owner's brand. After Samuel *Maverick* (1803-1870), a Texan rancher who habitually neglected to brand his calves.

mesmerism (**mez**mə-riz'm) – B: the process or practice of inducing a hypnotic state; or the state itself. After Dr Franz Anton *Mesmer* (1734-1815), a German physician who popularised the practice.

namby-pamby (**nam**bi-**pam**bi) – C: weakly sentimental or childishly simple. From '*Namby-Pamby*', a poem of about 1715, written by Henry Carey to satirise the sentimental verses of his fellow-poet *Ambrose* Philips: *Namby* is a baby-talk nickname for *Ambrose*.

silhouette (**sill**oo-**et**) – D: a portrait made by tracing the outline of a profile, head, or figure, and filling it in with black. After Etienne de *Silhouette* (1709-1767), a French author and politician, possibly because he decorated his residence with outline portraits.

Thespian (**thes**pi-ən) – D: an actor or actress; also, relating to drama or the theatre. After *Thespis*, a poet of the 6th century BC, traditionally regarded as the father of Greek tragedy.

THE PLACE THAT GAVE BIRTH TO THE NAME
(page 501)

Here are the words, with their meanings, and the places that gave birth to the names.

arras (**arr**əss) – C: a tapestry, usually hanging on a wall. French (*drap de*) *Arras*, cloth of *Arras*, a city in northern France.

artesian (aar-**teez**-yən) – B: relating to deep wells, from which water flows under pressure. French (*puit*) *artésien*, well of *Artois*, a region in northern France where such wells were first drilled.

denim (**den**nim) – D: a tough cotton cloth, often dyed blue, as used for jeans and overalls. French (*serge*) de *Nîmes*, serge cloth from *Nîmes*, a city in southern France.

ermine (**er**min) – A: a stoat whose coat turns white in winter; also, its valuable white fur. From Medieval Latin (*mus*) *Armenius*, mouse of *Armenia*.

frieze (freez) – B: a decorated panel running horizontally along a wall, often just below the ceiling; also, the decorated band at the top of a classical column. From Latin (*opus*) *Phrygium*, work of *Phrygia* (today part of Turkey), famous for its gold embroidery.

hessian (**hes**si-ən) – B: a coarse fabric like sacking, made of jute; as in *bales packed in hessian*. After *Hesse*, now a state in Germany, where it was originally produced.

homburg (**hom**-burg) – B: a man's felt hat, with an upturned brim and a dented crown. After *Homburg*, a small town in Germany, where it was first manufactured.

kersey (**ker**zi) – B: a woollen fabric, woven with diagonal lines or ribs, often used for coats. Probably after the Suffolk village of *Kersey*.

limousine (**lim**mə-zeen) – C: a large motor car, often having three rows of seats. French *limousine*, originally meaning a cloak, worn by shepherds in *Limousin*, a region in west central France: the name was then applied to early motor cars because the projecting roof on some of them apparently resembled a cloak in shape.

magenta (mə-**jen**tə) – D: a deep red colour; also, a red dye. After *Magenta*, a town in northern Italy: the blood shed in a famous battle there, in 1859, gave rise to the name of the newly discovered red dye.

majolica (mə-**yoll**i-kə) – B: a type of decorated and enamelled pottery, glazed in rich colours, widely made in 16th-century Italy, and imitated in the 19th century. Also known as *maiolica*. From *Majolica*, a medieval name for the Balearic island of Mallorca (or Majorca), where the style originated.

meander (mee-**an**dər) – B: to follow a winding route, as a river might; also, to wander about aimlessly. After the winding river *Maiandros* or *Maeander* in Phrygia – today the river Menderes in Turkey.

milliner (**mill**i-nər) – B: a maker or seller of women's hats. Earlier *Milaner*, a seller of fine clothing and other goods from *Milan*.

parchment (**parch**-mənt) – C: a kind of stiff paper, formerly made of goatskin or sheepskin. Partly after *Pergamum*, an ancient Greek city in Asia Minor, where animal skins were treated – today Bergama in Turkey.

ritzy (**rit**si) – C: luxurious; very fancy or fashionable (a slang word). After the elegant *Ritz* hotels, especially the *Ritz-Carlton* hotel in New York.

sardonic (saar-**don**nik) – A: mocking; scornful; as in *She declined the offer with a sardonic smile*. Partly after Latin (*herba*) *Sardonica*, herb of *Sardinia*, a poisonous plant so bitter that one tends to pull a face on tasting it.

shallot (shə-**lot**) – D: an edible bulb similar to the onion. From Latin *Ascalonia* (*caepa*), onion of *Ascalon*, a seaport in ancient Palestine – today Ashkelon in Israel.

spa (spaa) – D: a health resort having mineral waters; also, a mineral spring. After *Spa*, a resort in Belgium noted for its mineral waters.

Spartan (**spart**'n) – D: austere; rigorous; as in *a spartan childhood at boarding school*. After *Sparta*, an ancient Greek city-state famous for its harsh military discipline and cultural rigidity.

sybaritic (**sibb**ə-**ritt**ik) – B: relating to luxurious living; as in *indulging in sybaritic vices*. After *Sybaris*, a very wealthy and notoriously loose-living ancient Greek colony in southern Italy.

turquoise (**tur**-kwoyz, **tur**-kwaaz) – C: an opaque blue-green gemstone; also, a blue-green colour. From Old French (*pierre*) *turqueise*, stone of *Turkey* or *Turkestan*, where it was first mined.

CONJUNCTIVITIS OR PINKEYE? WORDS OFFICIAL AND UNOFFICIAL
(page 519)

This list gives you the meanings of the words, together with their Greek and Latin roots.

amnesia (am-**nee**zi-ə) – B: loss of memory. From Greek *a-*, not + *mnasthai*, to remember.

arachnid (ə-**rak**-nid) – C: a spider, tick, scorpion, or related creature. From Greek *arakhne*, a spider.

aboriculture (**ar**bəri-kulchər) – D: cultivation of trees. Latin *arbor*, a tree + *cultura*, cultivation.

archipelago (**ar**ki-**pell**əgo) – A: a group of islands; also, a sea dotted with many islands, such as the Aegean Sea. From Greek *Aigaion pelagos*, the Aegean Sea, misinterpreted in Italian as the Chief Sea or *Arch-sea*.

bibliophile (**bib**bli-ə-fil) – C: a book lover. From Greek *biblion*, a book (related to *Bible*) + *philos*, beloved or loving.

calligraphy (kə-**lig**grəfi) – A: handwriting, or the art of fine handwriting. From Greek *kallos*, beauty + *graphein*, to write.

halitosis (**hal**-i-**tō**-siss) – C: bad breath. Latin *halare*, to breathe (related to *inhale*) + Greek *-osis*, a condition or process.

kleptomania (**klep**tə-**may**ni-ə) – A: an obsessive urge to steal. From Greek *kleptein*, to steal + *mania*, madness.

lentigo (len-**tīgō**) – B: a freckle. Latin *lentigo*, freckles, from *lens*, a lentil.

mephitis (me-**fīt**iss) – A: a bad or poisonous smell. Latin *mefitis*, a bad smell.

patella (pə-**tell**ə) – B: the kneecap. Latin, a small plate.

physiognomy (fizzi-**on**nə-mi) – C: facial features; strictly, the study of facial features as a guide to personality. From Greek, *phusis*, nature + *gnomon*, a judge or interpreter.

prosthesis (pross-**thee**siss) – A: an artificial limb, tooth, or other body part. From Greek, *pros-*, extra + *tithenai*, to put.

pyrexia (pīr-**reks**i-ə) – D: fever. From Greek *purexis*, fever, from *pur*, fire.

rubella (roo-**bell**ə) – B: German measles. Latin *rubellus*, reddish.

somnambulist (som-**nam**bew-list) – D: a sleepwalker. Latin *somnus*, sleep + *ambulare*, to walk.

stenography (stə-**nog**grəfi) – D: writing in shorthand. From Greek *stenos*, narrow + *graphein*, to write.

strabismus (strə-**biz**məss) – B: a squint. From Greek, *strabos*, squinting.

FREE-FLOATING NEGATIVES
(page 537)

Here are the negative words together with the word or phrase you should have chosen.

Don't forget that the letter refers to the answer that is *opposite* in meaning to the headword. The definition, however, applies to the headword.

anodyne (**ann**ə-dīn) – C: soothing, relieving pain; also bland, feebly inoffensive, as in *an anodyne sermon*. From Greek *an-*, not or without + *odune*, pain.

anomalous (ə-**nom**mələss) – B: abnormal, irregular, departing from the usual order. From Greek *an-*, not + *homos*, same.

disconsolate (diss-**kon**sə-lət) – B: hopelessly sad, beyond consoling. Latin *dis-*, not + *consolari*, to comfort; related to *console*, *inconsolable*.

disgruntled (diss-**grunt**'ld) – D: discontented, in a bad mood. Latin *dis-*, not + English dialect *gruntle*, to grumble; probably related to *grunt*.

dismantled (diss-**mant**'ld) – D: taken apart or demolished. Old French *desmanteler*, literally, to remove a cloak from, from Latin *dis-*, not, apart + *mantellum*, a little cloak.

dissembling (di-**semb**'ling) – A: disguising the real nature of; concealing one's real motives, nature, or feelings. Old French *des-*, from Latin *dis-* (reversal) + *sembler*, to be like, appear, seem.

ignominious (**ig**-nə-**min**ni-əss) – C: dishonourable, shameful, disgraceful, despicable. Latin *in-*, not + *nomen*, a name or reputation.

impecunious (**im**pi-**kew**ni-əss) – C: penniless, completely without money. Latin *in-*, not + *pecunia* money; related to *pecuniary*.

impudent (**im**pewdənt) – A: disrespectful, rude. Latin *in-*, not + *pudere*, to be ashamed.

incessant (in-**sess**n't) – C: unceasing, continual, going on without interruption. Latin *in-*, not + *cessare*, to stop or delay; related to *cease*.

incognito (**in**-kog-nee-**tō**) – C: in disguise or under a false name, hiding one's true identity, as in *to travel incognito*. From Latin, *in-*, not + *cognitus*, known; related to *recognise*, *cognisance*.

indelible (in-**dell**ə-b'l) – B: permanent, enduring, as in *made an indelible impression on her mind*; impossible to erase or wash away, as in *indelible ink*. Latin *in-*, not + *delere*, to wipe out; related to *delete*.

inept (in-**ept**) – B: clumsy, or inappropriate. Latin *in-*, not + *aptus*, fit, suited; related to *apt*, *aptitude*, *adaptable*.

inert (in-**ert**) – A: motionless, unable to move, act, or resist; also sluggish, passive. Latin *in-*, not + *ars*, skill; related to *art*.

inimical (i-**nim**mik'l) – A: harmful, adverse, as in *Smoking is inimical to healthy lungs*; also, unfriendly, hostile. Latin *in-*, not + *amicus*, a friend; related to *amicable*, *amiable*, *enemy*.

iniquitous (i-**nik**witəss) – C: wicked, sinful. From Latin *in-*, not + *aequus*, just, even, level; related to *equitable*, *equal*.

innocuous (i-**nock**ew-əss) – B: harmless or inoffensive. Latin *in-*, not + *nocere*, to harm; related to *innocent*.

inscrutable (in-**skroot**ə-b'l) – A: mysterious, impossible to understand, as in *an inscrutable smile*. Latin *in-*, not + *scrutari*, to search or inspect, literally, to search through a rubbish heap; related to *scrutiny*, *scrutinise*.

insipid (in-**sip**pid) – B: dull, unexciting, as in *an insipid play*; or bland, almost tasteless, as in *insipid food*. Latin *in-*, not + *sapere*, to taste; related to *savour*.

invincible (in-**vin**səb'l) – C: unbeatable, unconquerable. Latin *in-*, not + *vincere*, to conquer; related to *vanquish*.

nonchalant (**non**shələnt) – A: apparently unconcerned, indifferent. Old French *non-*, not + *chaloir*, to be interested or concerned, from Latin *calere*, to be warm.

nonplussed (**non**-**plusst**) – A: baffled, perplexed. Latin *non plus*, literally no more (can be said), *non*, not + *plus*, more.

uncouth (un-**kooth**) – D: crude, badly behaved, or unrefined. Originally, *uncouth* meant foreign or unknown; from Old English *un-*, not + *cuth*, known.

ungainly (un-**gayn**li) – B: clumsy, moving ungracefully. Old English *un-*, not + (possibly) Middle English *geinli*, graceful or suitable.

untoward (**un**tə-**wawrd**) – A: unfavourable or unfortunate, as in *untoward circumstances*; or inappropriate, as in *untoward behaviour*. Old English *un-*, not + *toweard*, forthcoming, favourable, future.

Index

Note: Page numbers in *italics* refer to boxes and panel features.

A

abbreviations 215, 229, 230, 239, 251-254
    in dictionaries 262
    plurals 252
    see also acronyms
absolutes 196
abstract, writing 99, 321, 452
abstraction 33, *50*, 64, 75-78, *76*, *77*, 81
    see also nouns, abstract/concrete
academic writing 37, *53*, *54*, 452-460
accents, spoken 462, 478, 484, 517
accuracy 346-347
acronyms 122, 252-254
address, forms of,
    academics 421-422
    armed forces 418
    clergy 407-409
    government and Parliament 415-416
    governors and diplomats 416
    the Law 416-417
    local government 420
    organisations 404-405
    peerage and other titles 405, 410-412
    police 421
    professional 420-421
    royalty 406
    Scottish and Irish 413
    untitled people 414
    women 89, 405, 407, 410-411, 412, 413, 414
addresses, writing 219, 350-352
adjectives 169-170, 199-201, *349*
    absolute 202
    compound 220, 221
    gradable (comparative) 170, 201-202
    and infinitives 211
    -ly 199
    proper 244
    proper superlative 201-202
    ungradable 218
    unnecessary 32-33, 84, 104
admission cards 401
adverbs 170, 199-201, *200*, *202*
    adverbial phrases 167
    comparative 202
    and infinitives 194
    -ly 201, *202*
    and prepositions 171
    'sentence' 201
    superlative 202
    unnecessary 32-33, 84, 104

advertising 53, 54, 251, 289, *376*
    for staff 307
affixes *160*
African English 134
Afrikaans, influence on English *119*, 133
age 256
agendas *182*, 324-327, 548, *553*
agreement,
    failure of *18*
    notional 175
alliteration 29, *30*, 65, 67, 69
allusions 84, 232
'although' 20
ambiguity 23, *24*, 28, 34, 35, *36-37*, 104
    and grammar 185-186, 194, 197-199, *198*, 205, 207
    and punctuation *36*, 205, *214*, 218, 221-222, 248, 251
anacoluthon *18*
'and' *36*, 39-40, 55, 176
Anglo-Saxon 25, 112, 113-114, 115
announcements,
    birth 396-397
    death 395-396
    engagement and wedding 386-388, 389-391
answering machine, using 494
antithesis 65
aphesis 229
apocope 229
apology, letters of 284, 289, 361
apostrophe,
    in abbreviations 230, 252
    in contractions 229, 245, 252
    in plurals 229, *230*, 256
    possessive 178, 212, 221, 228-229
apostrophe (figure of speech) 65
applications, job 331-343
    forms 522-523,
    see also business letters, covering letter; c.v.; references, employment
apposition 217
    false 196
appropriateness, in written style *16-17*, 17, 209
Arabic *464*
    influence on English 117, *119*
argument, circular 22
Arnold, Matthew 59
articles 171, 246, 248
articulation 474-477, 491, 494, 504, 505
Ascham, Roger 118
assonance 65, 67
asyndeton 66
At Home cards 393, 400
audience 495-496, 498-499, 506, 509, 514
    see also reader
Australian English 129-132, 175

B

back-formation 32
Bacon, Francis 444, 514
Balzac, Honoré de *106*
bank, writing to 279-281
Basic English 138
'because' 39
begging the question 21-22
Belloc, Hilaire 71
bereavement 395-396
Bible 249, 359
bibliographies 456, *455*, 548
    see also references, bibliographical
birth 396-397
boards, as visual aids 512
body language 15, 491-493, 494, 502, 509, 524, 529, 534
book review writing 450-451
boss,
    and appraisal interview *300-301*, 536
    attitudes to 532-533
    influencing 95-97, 538-539, 554
    and self-assertion 533-536
    and subordinates 540-546
    unreasonable 539
brackets 218, 239-240
    punctuation with 239-240
    square 232, 240-241
    within brackets 241
brainstorming *553*
breathing,
    exercises 469-470, 471, 529
    and stress 469, 507
    and voice 468-469, 487, *494*
brevity 15, 60, 347, 383-384, *508*
    thoughtless *36-37*
Browne, Sir Thomas 118
Browning, Robert 245
business letters 220, 226, 270-313
    acceptance/confirmation 279
    apology 284, 289, 361
    circular 294
    closing 272-273, 276, 292-293
    covering letters 277, 294-295, 331, 332, 339-341, 342
    customer enquiries 278-279
    drafting 271-273
    enclosures *275*, 352
    estimates/quotations/tenders 277-278
    fax/telex/telegram 276
    financial matters 279-283, *281*
    follow-up 297
    from home 364-375
    giving notice 303-304
    handing notice *305*
    handling complaints 283-285
    invoices and price increases 278
    layout 273-276, *274-275*, 290
    legal implications 287-288
    making complaints 285-287
    pay rise 270, 298, *299*
    planning 271
    presentation 273-276, *274-275*, 290
    redundancy 304

of reprimand 299-302
and sales 278, 289-297
to staff 270, 298-304
taking on staff 289, 306-313
vocabulary 25
see also applications, job
business writing 25, *46*, 63, 75-77, 270
see also business letters; report
'but' 20, *55*, 185, 216, 224
Butler, Samuel 449
buzz words *140*
buzz-phrase generator *81*

C

c.v. (*curriculum vitae*) 331, 338
capsule 332, 335-337
for first job *338*
job description 333-335, *334*, 342
skills profile 335, *336*
campaigning 380
Canadian English 126, 129, 229
capitals 243-249
for first word 244-245
for organisations 246
for personal names 245-246
for place-names 246-247
for proper names 244
Carroll, Lewis 201
case 170, 183-185
Celtic language 113, 124, 125
chairing a meeting 90, 549-551
change in language 122-123, 126, 165, 258
Chaucer, Geoffrey 116
Chesterton, G.K. 71, 89, 444
Children and language *464*
Churchill, Winston 52, 55, 65, 75, 127, *319*, 495, 500, 504, 509
clarity,
of speech 465
in writing 15, 95, 272, 347-348
clauses *46*, 171-172
adverbial *172*
conditional 195
punctuation 215-216
relative *172*, *173*, 209
restrictive *173*
as subjects 174-175
verbless *172*, 197
clichés 32, 61, 69, 76, 78, 83-84, *85*, 104, *140*, 145, 272, 502, 515
mixed *70-71*
Cobbett, William 165
Coleridge, S.T. 94
collection, letters of 281-283
collocations 144-145, 263
colloquialisms 89, 184-185, 188, 205
see also slang
colon 39-40, 224, 225-226, 232, 233, 245
and dash (:-) 225, 228
in headings and references 226
in lists 225
in parallels and contrasts 225
in quotations and salutations 225-226

combining forms 159-163, *160-163*, 259
comma *36*, 212-213, 215-220, *234*, 235
in lists 218-219
in long sentence 40, 41-42
in names and addresses 219-220
in numbers 219, 256
as parentheses 217-218
splice 40, *216*
commercialese 25, 82
'compare with/to' 208
comparison 170, 185, 195, 201-202, 208
complements 167, 175, 183-184, 200
compliments 485-487
concentration 17, 20
conciseness 60-61
concreteness 33, 50, 64, 77-78, 104
conjunctions 31, 66, 171, *172*, 185, 215-216, 224, 246
correlative *19*, 171, 198-199
connotations 143-144
Conrad, Joseph *106*
consistency 62-63, 101, 103, *128*, 175, *192*, 244, 248
consonants, articulation 475-477, 504
constructions, parallel 206-207
contents, table of 99, 103, 321
context, and meaning 142-143
contraction *174*, 191, 229, 252
contracts of employment *310-312*
contrast, false 20
conversation,
coping with conflict 482, 493-494
and language 488-489
listening 489-491
maintaining 483-487
pace and pause 487-488, 524, 526
starting 481-483
on telephone 490, 494
see also body language
correspondence card 401-402, *403*
councillors, writing to 377
court, giving evidence in 521
creoles 134-136
cummings, e.e. 245

D

'dare' 193
dashes 218, 222, 226-228, 232, 242, 243
and colon (:-) 225, 228
en-dash 222, 228
in omissions 228
and parenthesis 41
in summaries, explanations, and interruptions 227-228
dates 62, 220, 226, 243, 255, 276, 351
debt,
chasing 281-283
deferring *281*
Defoe, Daniel 451
determiners 167, 170-171
Dewey decimal system *454*
dialects 123, 124-135, 187, 517
dialogue 233, 251, 256
Dickens, Charles 67, 228, *313*

dictionaries 27, 103, 118, 141-144
choosing 23-24, 258-260
definitions 145, *261*, 263-264
encyclopaedic 258
reverse 23, 268
synonym 264-265, 266
using 260-264, *261*
'different from/to' 208
diminutives *163*
diphthongs 475
discussion 105-107
dismissal notices 303-304
dots, three, *see* ellipsis
drafts 94, 95, 103, 109-110, 318-320, 331, 446-448, *446-447*
of letters 271-273
Dryden, John 209
Dumas, Alexandre *106*
Dutch, influence on English 117, *119*, 126

E

'each, every' 176
editing 60-61, 103-104, 110, 273, 448
'either/neither' 176-177
Eliot, George *106*
Eliot, T.S. *508*
elision 229
ellipsis 216-217, 228
faulty *19*, 205-207
in quotations 242
rhetorical 242
three-dots 66, 67, 101, 222, 232, 241-242
emphasis 30, *31*, 32-33, 183, 215
punctuation for 218, *233*, 240, 250-251
in speech 473
endnotes 290, 321-322, 548
engagements, announcement 389-391
English,
origins 112-118, *119*
recent history 120-123
varieties 123-138
as world language *130-131*, 137-138, 259
environment, working 109
eponyms 244
Esq. 414
essay writing 425-428, 444-448, *460*
etymology 123, 146-164, *147-151*, *155-157*, *160-162*, 260, *261*, 264
euphemisms 21, 66, 78, 81, 88-89, *88*, 104, 123, 359
euphuism 118, *286*
'everyone' 176
evidence, giving 521
examples, giving 73-75, 77, 104, 428, 446
exams,
essay questions 110, 424-428
general strategies 423-424
multiple-choice questions 429-432
planning a study timetable *433*, 442-443

exclamation mark 232, 235-236, 237-239
exclamations *46*, 211, 237
expression, facial 15
eye contact 483, 490, 492, 504, 507, 523-524, 526, 529

F

'fewer' 177
fiction,
    punctuation 213
    showing/telling 73-74
figures of speech 65-73, *70-71*
film and video, as visual aids 512
'firstly' 201
Flaubert, Gustave *106*
Fleming, Ian *75*
footnotes 290, 321-322, 456-458, *459*
Ford, Ford Madox 15
foreign words 250
formality,
    in speech 15, 186, 191, 405
    in writing 17, 89, 103, 319-320, 388-390, 402-403
forms, filling in 368-369, *370*
Fowler, H.W. 26
fractions 222, 243, 256
Franklin, Benjamin 71
Frederick II, Holy Roman Emperor *464*
French,
    influence on English 25, 115-117, *119*, 124, 126, *147*, 152-153, *164*
    plurals 180-181
full stops 39-40, 42-43, 213-215, 232, *234*
    in abbreviations 215, 251-254, *255*

G

Gaelic *119*, 124, 125
generalisation 73-74, 77-78, 122-123
    blanket 22
gerund *168*, 186
gesture 15, 500, 503-504, 524
Gibbon, Edward 118, 209
gloss 234, 250
Godden, Rumer 215
Gowers, Sir Ernest *209*
grammar 165-211, *166*, 263
    basics 167-173
    errors *18-19*, 20, 103
    omission of words 205-207
    quizzes *166*, *210-211*
    singulars and plurals 173-182
    symmetry 195-199
    and using new words 144
    see also adjectives; adverbs; conjunctions; interjections; nouns; phrases; prepositions; pronouns; sentences; verbs

Greek *464*
    influence of 25, 117, 118, 120, 145, *147-151*, 152, *155-157*, 159-163, *160-162*, *164*, *323*
    plurals 180-181, *182*

H

half-rhyme 29, 65, 73
Hall, Angus *75*
handwriting 348-349, 350, 353, 359, 369, 388, 398, 426
'have/of' 188-189
Hazlitt, William 59
headings 63, 99-101, *102*, 103, 330
    in letters 226, 271, 318, 352-353, 355
    numbering 322-323
Hebrew *464*
    plurals 182
Hemingway, Ernest *106*
Herrick, Robert 118
homographs 262
homonyms 261
'hopefully' 201
house styles 62, 213, 322
'however' 20, 224
humour *16-17*, 358, 379, 499
hyperbole 66, 67-68
hypercorrection 183, 185, 195
hyphens 220-223, 244, 248
    in compounds 220-222
    as link 222
    in numbers 222, 256-257
    omitted *214*
    in word breaks 222-223, *223*

I

idiom 62
    mixed *70-71*, 71, 104
    overused 83-84
'if' 194-195
imagery, *see* metaphors
impediments, speech 477, 478
imperative *46*, *50*, 63, 237
indexes 323
indicatives 195
Indo-European languages 112-113
infinitives *168-169*
    perfect 189
    split 194
inflection,
    grammatical 114
    voice 472-473
informality,
    in speech 127, 191, 201, 215
    in writing 17, 89, 123, *128*, 191, 398, 402-403
innuendo 66
insertions 241
intensifiers 158
interjections 171, 215, 237
International Phonetic Alphabet (IPA) 262

interrabang/interrobang 237
interviews,
    appraisal *300-301*, 536
    job,
        interviewee 527-531
        interviewer 522-526
    media,
        interviewee 513-521
        interviewer 516
intonation 471-473
introductions, social 482-483
inversion 65, 231
invitations,
    imaginative 398-399
    informal 401-402
    to official functions 400-401, 403
    refusing 386-387, 403
    replying to 348, 386, 388-389, 402-403
    sending 351, 387-392, 396, 397-402
    withdrawal 395
Irish English 125, 190-191, 199
irony 66, 104, 191, 233, *233*, 237
-*ise*/-*ize* verbs 32, 62, 103, 232
Italian,
    influence on English 117
    plurals 181
italics,
    for authorial disclaimer 233
    for emphasis 250-251
    for titles 234-235, 249, 250
    for words and phrases 250, 458

J

James, Henry *16*
jargon 78-82, *83*, 84, 85, 104, 530
    avoiding 15, 82, 272, 426, 488, 515, 558
    elitist 79
    for manipulation 80
    obscure 80-82
jingles 28-29, *30*, 76, 448
job descriptions 306-307, 333-335, *334*, 337, 342, 522
Johnson, Lyndon B. *508*
Johnson, Samuel 59, 92, *106*, 118, *366*
joke, structure *91*
journalism 53, 54, *81*, 84, *87*, *88*, 213, 251, 520-521

K

Kafka, Franz *106*
Kennedy, John F. 490, 495, 502
'kind of/sort of' 175-176
King, Martin Luther 500, 504
Kipling, Rudyard 445

L

Lamb, Charles 444, *460*
Latin *464*
    influence 25, 114, 115-117, 118, 120, 145-159, *147-151*, *155-157*, *160-162*, *163*, *164*
    influence on grammar 188
    plurals 180-181, *182*
layout 63, 99-101, *102*, 103, 458-460
    invitations 388-389
    letters 273-276, *274-275*, 290, 346, 348, 350-355, 378, 383
    reports 317, 322-323
legalese *52*, 80
'less' 177
letters,
    of apology or anger 284, 289, 361-362
    'begging' 364
    of commiseration 360-361
    of complaint 89, 285-287, 370-375, 385, 521
    of condolence 105, 349, 350, 351, 359-361, 395-396
    of congratulation 63, 348-349, 358-359, 385, 391, 397
    to creditors 375
    of enquiry 365-368
    of introduction 363-364
    length 347
    love letters 362-363
    to the media 382-385
    official 352-355, 375-380
    personal 56, 251, 344-364
    planning 346
    reader 15, 289-290, 293, 332, 347, 355, 362
    replying 348, 368-370
    of thanks 355-358, 394
    see also business letters; layout; salutations
library, using 454-455
'lie/lay' *188*
listener, awareness of 15
    see also audience
listening 489-491, 524, 529
lists 99, 207, 218, 224, 225, 240
litotes 66
Lloyd George, David 497, 503
logic, in writing 15, 17-22, 54
Lyly, John 118

M

Macmillan, Harold 497, 503, 505
malapropism 26, 27, 70, *286*, 426
malentendu 27
Mansfield, Katherine 228
'many' 177
Márquez, Gabriel García *106*
Maugham, Somerset *31*, 59, 69
'may/can' 192-193
'may/might' 192

meaning,
    changed 122, 126
    and context 142-143
    and punctuation 212-213, *214*, 219
media,
    interviews 513-521
    letters to 382-385
meetings,
    agendas 324-327
    glossary *553*
    informal 553
    minutes 327-330, *328-329*, *553*
    notices of 324, *325*
    participants 547-548
    performance 551-552
    post-mortem 552-553
    preparation 548, 555-556
    procedure 549-551
    purpose 547
Melville, Herman 222
metaphors 66, 67-69, *70*, 84, *87*, 89
    dubious *70*
    inappropriate *70*
    mixed 68-69, *70-71*, 104
metonymy 66
Middle English 116
minutes, writing 327-330, *328-329*, 553
mnemonics 440-441
modifiers 196, 202
money 255
Monsarrat, Nicholas *106*
mood, *see* verbs, subjunctive/ indicative moods
Moravia, Alberto *106*
'more than' 177
morph 145
morpheme 23, 145
MPs, writing to 377-380, 415
Munro, H.H., *see* Saki
Murdoch, Iris *106*

N

names 219, 389, 392, *419*
    proper 167, 179, 229, 244, 245-246, 247
    remembering 491
narrative writing *46*, 56, 60, *61*, 73
'need' 193
negatives *36*, 203-205
    double 203, 204
    near 193, 203
    triple 204
negotiating 554-558
'neither/nor' *19*, 171, 204-205, 216
nervousness 505-507
New Zealand English 132
nicknames 84
Nicolson, Adam 243
'no question' 204
non sequiturs 43
'none' 177
Normans 115-116
Norse 113, 114-115, 124, 125
North American English 124, 126-129, 171, 190-191, *192*, 199, 202, 229

'not ... because' 205
'not ... but' 205
note-taking 316, 435-436, *438-439*, 455-456, *455*, 557
notice, giving 303-304, 546
notices *102*
nouns 167-168
    abstract/concrete 33, *50*, 76-78, 104, 117, 167
    as adjectives (attributive) 33-34, 168
    collective 175
    compound 218, 221
    countable/uncountable 167-168, 177, 178-179, 180-181, *182*
    group *19*
    proper 167, 179, 230, 244, 245-246, 247
    singular and plural 167, 173-177, 178-182, *182*, 262
numbers,
    in figures 225, 254, 257
    plurals 229, 256
    punctuation 215, 219, 222, 256
    Roman 257, *257*
    in words 254-257

O

object 167, 218
    omitted 32, 167
officialese 80-82, 104
Old English 113-114, 115, 145, *147*, *156-157*, *162*, *164*
    plurals 179
'one' 186-187
'only' 201
onomatopoeia 66, 89
opening,
    in public speech 498
    striking 41, 44, 73, 75, 77-78, *460*
opposites *140*
Orwell, George 75, 76
outlines 94-95, 318-319, 426
overstatements *87*
oxymoron 66

P

p.p. 274-275
paradox 66, 69
paragraphs 52-58, 103-104, 251
    length 52-54, *53*
    in letters 272, 353
    link words 55-56, *55*
    in quotations 231
paralysis, writer's 109-110
parentheses 215, 217-218, 226-227, 239-241
parenthesis 40-41
participle,
    misrelated *18-19*, 72, 195-197
    past 117, *168-169*, 187-188, *192*
    present 117, *168*

Partridge, Eric *219*
Pascal, Blaise 61, 347
passives, *see* verbs, passive
pathetic fallacy 66
personification 66
phrases 172
    adverbial 167, 172, 199
    foreign 84
    high-falutin 25, *26*, 76, *87*, 264
    linked 207
    noun 42, 47, 76, 172, 206, 221
    prepositional 171, 197
    verbal 205-206
phrasing, variety of 64-65, 104
pidgins 133, 134-136, *137*
pitch 15, 463, 471-473, 504
place-names 230, 246-247
planning, for essays 425-426, *427*,
    446-448, *446-447*
Plato 495
pleonasm 61-62
plurals 167, 178-182, *180*, 229, *230*, 252
    foreign words 179-182
    without -*s* 179
poetry 60, 245, 249
polysyndeton 66
Pope, Alexander 60
portmanteau words 122
Portuguese, influence on English 118,
    119, 133
possessives 167, 178-179, 186, 228-229
postcards, holiday 363
posture, and speaking 465-468, *470*, 507
précis writing 449-450
precision 23-24
predicates 213
prefixes 122, 152-159, *155-157*, *160*, 220,
    244, 245, 259
prepositions 31, 171, 185, 207-209
    added 32
    and adverbs 171
    compound 171
    to end a sentence 118, 165,
    209-211, *209*
    omitted 32
presentation 273-276, *274-275*, 318, 332,
    383, 424, 448, 458-460
press, interviews 520-521
press releases 295-297
projection, voice 479-480
projectors 511-512
pronouns 28, 34, 57, 170, 182-187,
    247-248
    and case 183-185
    demonstrative 170
    emphatic 183
    indefinite 170
    interrogative 184-185
    personal 49, 170, 183-184, 186, 229
    possessive 229, *230*
    reflexive *169*, 170, 183
    relative 40, 170, *172*, 173, 184
pronunciation 116, 134, 262, 478
Proust, Marcel *106*
psychobabble *81*, 82
punctuation 39-40, 212-257
    heavy/light 213

puns *24*, 69, 71-73
    unintended *70*, 72, 73
put-downs *366*

Q

question *46*, 209-211
    indirect 215, 236
    rhetorical 66
    tag 138, 216, 236
question mark 215, 232, 235-237, 241
    to express doubt 237
questionnaires 316-317
Quirk, Sir Randolph *37*
quotation marks 62, 225, 230-235, *234*
    as authorial disclaimer 233
    in glosses and titles 234
quotations 84, 103, 225-226, 231-233,
    241, 242, 256

R

radio,
    interviews 516-517
    phone-ins 517-518
range, uncertain *36*
reader,
    awareness of 14-17, 44, 88, 99,
    103-104
    see also letters; report
reading 437-440, 450
    and vocabulary learning 142
reasoning, false 21-22
Received Pronunciation 478
redundancy of style 61-62
references,
    bibliographical 226, 321-322, 337,
    456-458, *459*
    in business and official letters 99,
    276, 277, 352, 372
    employment 308-309, *309*, 344
reflection 105
register 143
repetition,
    bad 26, 28-29, 34, 285
    effective 29-31, *30*, *31*, 136, 502
report 49-51, *53*, 54, 56, 63, 99, 314-323
    appraisal *300-301*
    drafting 318-320
    opening and closing *75*, 320-323
    planning 94, 95-97, *98*
    reader 15, 314-315, 452
    research 315-318
    science 451-452
    terms of reference 314, 315, 321
reprimands 299-302
requests 236, 367
research,
    academic *53*, 452-460
    for public speaking 496-497
    for report 107
resignation letters *305*
resonance 463, 473-474
rewriting *100-101*

rhoticity 125
rhymes 29, *30*, 69, 73, 103
rhythm,
    speech 471
    in writing *30*, 34, 68, 103
Roget, Peter Mark 265
royalty,
    addressing 406
    invitations from 403
    referring to 400
rules 118, 165, 194, 209, 386
    see also grammar

S

Saki (H.H. Munro) *16*
salutations 226, 276, 320, 351, 352
Scott, Sir Walter *106*
Scottish English 124, 190-191, 199
'-self' 183
selling 554-555, 557-558, *557*
semicolon 213, 216, 223-224, 225, 232
    with adverbs 224
    alternatives to 224
    in lists 224
sentences 35-52, 171-172
    complex *46*, 64, 172, 203
    compound *46*, 64, 172, 215-216
    compound-complex *46*
    declarative 213-215
    length 35-43, *38*, *43*, 64, 104,
    272, 502, 558
    loose/periodic *46*, 64
    main point 44-47
    order 54, 55
    overloaded 35, 41-44, *43*
    simple *46*, 64, 172, 176
    topic 56
    unpunctual 44-47, *47*
    verbless 45
    see also exclamations; imperative
    (command); questions; statement
sexist language 89-90, 104, 120, 176, 243
Shakespeare, William 27, 84, *85*, 118,
    123, *137*, 176, *214*, 225, 233, 462
'shall/will' 190-191, 193
Shaw, George Bernard 59, 230
Sheridan, Richard Brinsley 15, 27
'should/would' 191
sic 240-241
Sidney, Sir Philip 355
signature 353-354
signposts,
    grammatical 55-56, 57, 104
    structural 92-93, *93*, 99-102,
    100-101, *102*, 103, 499
Simenon, Georges *106*
simile 66, 67, 68-69, *70*, 84, 104
singulars 167, 173-177
skills profile 333, 335, *336*
slang 78, 79, 89, 104, 123, 127, 489
    Australian 130
slash 240, 243
slogans 84, 101, *102*
small talk 481-482, 525
Smith, Logan Pearsall 69

Smith, Sydney 60
sociologese *81*, 82
solidus, *see* slash
South African English 124, 133
South Asian English 133-134
space, personal 493
Spanish, influence on English 117-118, *119*
Spark, Muriel *106*
speaking,
    effect on listener 15, 462
    emphasis 473
    habits 465, 478
    impediments 477, 478
    pace and pause 15, 470-471, 504
    spontaneous 500
    see also pronunciation; voice
speaking in public,
    best man's speech *508*
    delivery 500-504
    equipment 496, 499, 505, 509, 511-512
    preparation 495-497
    stage fright 505-507
    structure 497-500
    taking questions 496, 497, 507
    visual aids 509-512, *510-511*
spelling 62, 103, 127, 129, 262-263
Spenser, Edmund 118
Standard American English 126-127, *128*, *130-131*, 175, 187
Standard British English 116, 126, 133, 134, 174, 182, 187, *188*
statement *46*
stationery 273, 290, 349-350, 352
Steinbeck, John *75*
Stendhal *106*
stroke, *see* slash
structure 91-102, *93*, 103, 165, *198*, 448, 460
    planning 94-98, 109
    of public speech 497-500
    signposting 92-93, *93*, 99-102, *100-101*, *102*, 103, 499
    symmetrical 198-199
study techniques,
    general strategies 434-435
    memorising 440-441
    note-taking 435-436, *438-439*
    reading 437-440
    swotting 441-443
    see also essay writing; exams; précis writing; research
style 59-90, 200-201
    brightness 63-78, 104, 445
    conversational 482, 483-484, 493
    listening 491
    plain 59-60
    public speaking 495
    and punctuation 213
    telephone 494
    written 15-17, 37-39, 103, 272, 426
subject of sentence *18*, 48, 167, 173, 200
    double *175*
    multiple 174, 177
subjunctives 195
subordinates, dealing with 540-546

suffixes 122, 152, *160*, 163, *163*, *164*, 220, 249
summary 99, 103, 321, 448, 452
superlatives 170, *173*, 201-202
syllepsis 66, 67
symmetry,
    false *19*
    grammatical 205, 206, *216*
syncope 229
synecdoche 66
synonyms 23-25, *140*, 143-144, *145*
    dictionary 264-265, 266
    slangy 87

T

tautology *18*, 32, 61-62, 202
Taylor, A.J.P. *106*
telephone conversations 494
television,
    interviews 518
    shows 518-520
telling and showing 73-74
tense 188-189
    double perfect 189
    past 187, *192*
    past perfect (pluperfect) *169*
    perfect *169*, 187
    perfect infinitive 189
    present perfect *169*
    progressive *168-169*
'that'/'which' 173
thesaurus 23-24, 264-268
thinking, and word power 140
Thurber, James 142
time 255
titles 234-235, 248, 249, 451
    personal 246, 389, 392-393
    for reports 320-321
'to' *36*
'to be' 31-32, 51-52, *51*, 104, 136, 183-184
tone,
    of voice 15, 201, 463, 471, 493, 524, 536
    in writing 17, 26, 27, 103, 371, 426
topic,
    and paragraph 52-54, 56
    in public speech 497
touch 493
trade names 122
transferred epithet 66
transitions 56-58, *57*
tree diagram *92*, 94, 97
triphthongs 475
Trollope, Anthony 59, 94, *106-107*
Twain, Mark 69
typewriter 239, 240, 348-349, 350
typography 58, 63, 99-101

U

'used to' 193-194

V

variation, elegant 26-28, *28*, 64
variety,
    in phrasing 25, 64-65
    in word use 23, 24-25
verbs 168, *168-169*
    active 47-51, *168*
    auxiliary 168
    compound 221
    converted 32
    defective 188
    double passive 189-190
    finite/non-finite 168
    impersonal *168*
    irregular 187, *192*
    -ise/-ize 32, 62, 103, 232
    modal 193
    passive 31, 47-51, *50*, 81, 104, *168*, 206, 211, 272, 330
    phrasal 138, *169*
    reflexive 32, *169*
    singular/plural 173-177, 178-179
    strong/weak *169*
    subjunctive/indicative moods *169*, 330
    transitive/intransitive 32, 49, *169*, *188*
    see also tenses
Vikings 114-115, 125
visual aids 509-512, *510-511*
visualisation 440-441
vocabulary,
    borrowed *119*, 124, 127
    British/American 126-127, *128*, *130-131*
    high-falutin 24-26, *26*, 76, 87, 104, 264, 448
    improving 139-164, 489
    learning 139-145, *467*
    passive/active 139, 141
    see also words
vogue words 81, *81*, 85-86, *86-87*, 104
voice,
    articulation 474-477, 491, 494, 504, 505
    and breathing 468-470
    care of 480
    exercises 472, 473-474, 475-477, 479, 528
    improving 462, 465
    inflection 472-473
    pitch 15, 463, 471-473, 504
    and posture 465-468, 470, 507
    projecting 479-480
    qualities 463-465
    resonance 463, 473-474
    volume 463-465, 504
    see also pronunciation; speaking
volume, voice 463-465, 504
vowels, articulation 475
vulgarisms 89, 123

W

warnings 303
Waugh, Evelyn 142
Webster, Noam 127
wedding,
    best man's speech *508*
    invitations 386-389, 391-395
Welsh English 125
West Indian English 136-137
Wharton, Edith *16*
'who/whom' 184-185
Wilde, Oscar 69, 126
'will/shall' 190-191, 193
Wilson, A.N. *106*
Wodehouse, P.G. 34, 67-68, *71*, 142
Woolf, Virginia *460*
word order 35, 65, 170, 197, *198*, 201

word processor,
    and job applications 308, 332
    for letter-writing 289, 348, 350
    for report writing 316, 322, 458
wordplay *30*, 63, 69-73
    accidental 73
words 23-34, 104
    breaks 222-223, *223*
    changed meanings 122-123, 126
    with combining forms 159-163,
    160-162
    elements 145-164
    learning 140-145
    new 86, *119*, 120-122, 126-127, *238*
    omitting 205-207, 216-217
    positioning 35
    roots 146-154, *147-151*, *155*, 159
    see also vocabulary; vogue words

work avoidance 108-109
'would/should' 191
'writer's block' 105, 108-110
writing,
    for communication 14-17, 444
    methods 105-110, *106-107*
    and speaking *30*, 110

Z

zeugma 66

ACKNOWLEDGMENTS

The publishers would like to thank the following for their special assistance:

Maggie Brough; Meg Davies; Peter Fairfoul; Janet Goss; Helen Harris; Tim Healey; John Hutchinson; Carl Meek; John Meek; Robert Sackville West

The publishers are indebted to:

Cambridge University Press, for permission to reproduce a page from *Reason in Ethics* by Stephen Toulmin (1964)

Oxford University Press, for permission to reproduce a page from *Ethics Since 1900* by Mary Warnock (1966)

The publishers also acknowledge their indebtedness to the following books, which were consulted for reference:

Debrett's *Correct Form*
Debrett's *Etiquette and Modern Manners*
The Cambridge Encyclopedia of Language, ed. David Crystal (Cambridge University Press)
Readymade Business Letters, Jim Dening (Kogan Page)
The Secrets of Successful Business Letters and Reports, Clive Goodworth (Heinemann Professional Publishing)
Janner's Complete Letterwriter, Greville Janner (Hutchinson Business)
Whitaker's Almanack

Page make-up and origination by Elite Typesetting
Techniques, Southampton
Paper: Papeis Inapa S.A. Portugal
Printing and Binding: BPC Hazell Books Ltd, Aylesbury   40/248/3